HARPER COLLINS
DICCIONARIO
ESPAÑOL
ESPAÑOL · INGLÉS
INGLÉS · ESPAÑOL

HarperResource
An Imprint of HarperCollins *Publishers*

ISBN 0-06-103160-7

The HarperCollins website address is
www.harpercollins.com

The HarperCollins UK website address is
www.fireandwater.com

Harper*Resource*   A Division of HarperCollins*Publishers*
10 East 53rd Street, New York, N.Y. 10022

first published 1990
second edition 2000

© William Collins Sons & Co. Ltd. 1990
© HarperCollins Publishers 2000

First Harper*Resource* printing: 2000

Typeset by Morton Word Processing Ltd, Scarborough
Printed in the United States of America

Harper*Resource* and colophons are trademarks of
HarperCollins*Publishers*

ÍNDICE		CONTENTS

Marcas Registradas

Note on trademarks

INTRODUCCIÓN

Estamos muy satisfechos de que hayas decidido comprar el Diccionario de Inglés Collins y esperamos que lo disfrutes y que te sirva de gran ayuda ya sea en el colegio, en el trabajo, en tus vacaciones o en casa.

Esta introducción pretende darte algunas indicaciones para ayudarte a sacar el mayor provecho de este diccionario; no sólo de su extenso vocabulario, sino de toda la información que te proporciona cada entrada. Esta te ayudará a leer y comprender — y también a comunicarte y a expresarte — en inglés moderno.

El Diccionario de Inglés Collins comienza con una lista de abreviaturas utilizadas en el texto y con una ilustración de los sonidos representados por los símbolos fonéticos. Al final del diccionario encontrarás una tabla de los verbos irregulares del inglés, y para terminar, una sección sobre el uso de los números y de las expresiones de tiempo.

EL MANEJO DE TU DICCIONARIO COLLINS

La amplia información que te ofrece este diccionario aparece presentada en distintas tipografías, con caracteres de diversos tamaños y con distintos símbolos, abreviaturas y paréntesis. Los apartados siguientes explican las reglas y símbolos utilizados.

Entradas

Las palabras que consultas en el diccionario — las "entradas" — aparecen ordenadas alfabéticamente y en **caracteres gruesos** para una identificación más rápida. Las dos palabras que ocupan el margen superior de cada página indican la primera y la última entrada de la página en cuestión.

La información sobre el uso o la forma de determinadas entradas aparece entre paréntesis, detrás de la transcripción fonética, y generalmente en forma abreviada y en cursiva (p.ej.: (*fam*), (*COM*)).

En algunos casos se ha considerado oportuno agrupar palabras de una misma familia (**nación, nacionalismo; accept, acceptance**) bajo una misma entrada, en caracteres gruesos de tamaño algo más pequeño que los de la entrada principal.
Las expresiones de uso corriente en las que aparece una entrada se dan en negrita (p.ej.: **to be in a hurry**).

Símbolos fonéticos

La transcripción fonética de cada entrada (que indica su pronunciación) aparece entre corchetes, inmediatamente después de la entrada (p.ej.: **knead** [ni:d]). En la página xiii encontrarás una lista de los símbolos fonéticos utilizados en este diccionario.

Traducciones

Las traducciones de las entradas aparecen en caracteres normales, y en los casos en los que existen significados o usos diferentes, éstos aparecen separados mediante un punto y coma. A menudo encontrarás también otras palabras en cursiva y entre paréntesis antes de las traducciones. Estas sugieren contextos en los que la entrada podría aparecer (p.ej.: **rough** (*voice*) o (*weather*)) o proporcionan sinónimos (p.ej.: **rough** (*violent*)).

Palabras clave

Particular relevancia reciben ciertas palabras inglesas y españolas que han sido consideradas palabras "clave" en cada lengua. Estas pueden, por ejemplo, ser de utilización muy corriente o tener distintos usos (**de, haber; get, that**). La combinación de rombos ◆ y números te permitirá distinguir las diferentes categorías gramaticales y los diferentes significados. Las indicaciones en cursiva y entre paréntesis proporcionan además importante información adicional.

Información gramatical

Las categorías gramaticales aparecen en forma abreviada y en cursiva después de la transcripción fonética de cada entrada (*vt, adv, conj*).

También se indican la forma femenina y los plurales irregulares de los sustantivos del ingels (**child, ~ren**).

INTRODUCTION

We are delighted you have decided to buy the Collins Spanish Dictionary and hope you will enjoy and benefit from using it at school, at home, on holiday or at work.

This introduction gives you a few tips on how to get the most out of your dictionary — not simply from its comprehensive wordlist but also from the information provided in each entry. This will help you to read and understand modern Spanish, as well as communicate and express yourself in the language.

The Collins Spanish Dictionary begins by listing the abbreviations used in the text and illustrating the sounds shown by the phonetic symbols. You will find Spanish verb tables at the back, followed by a final section on numbers and time expressions.

USING YOUR COLLINS DICTIONARY

A wealth of information is presented in the dictionary, using various type-faces, sizes of type, symbols, abbreviations and brackets. The conventions and symbols used are explained in the following sections.

Headwords

The words you look up in a dictionary — "headwords" — are listed alpha-betically. They are printed in **bold type** for rapid identification. The two headwords appearing at the top of each page indicate the first and last word dealt with on the page in question.

Information about the usage or form of certain headwords is given in brackets after the phonetic spelling. This usually appears in abbreviated form and in italics (e.g. *(fam)*, *(COMM)*).

Where appropriate, words related to headwords are grouped in the same entry (**nación, nacionalismo; accept, acceptance**) in a slightly smaller bold type than the headword.

Common expressions in which the headword appears are shown in a different bold roman type (e.g. **hacer calor**).

Phonetic spellings

The phonetic spelling of each headword (indicating its pronunciation) is given in square brackets immediately after the headword (e.g. **dónde** ['donde]). A list of these symbols is given on page xiii.

Translations

Headword translations are given in ordinary type and, where more than one meaning or usage exists, these are separated by a semi-colon. You will often find other words in italics in brackets before the translations. These offer suggested contexts in which the headword might appear (e.g.

grande (*de tamaño*) or provide synonyms (e.g. **grande** (*alto*) *o* (*distinguido*)).

"Key" words

Special status is given to certain Spanish and English words which are considered as "key" words in each language. They may, for example, occur very frequently or have several types of usage (e.g. **de, haber**). A combination of lozenges ♦ and numbers helps you to distinguish different parts of speech and different meanings. Further helpful information is provided in brackets and in italics.

Grammatical information

Parts of speech are given in abbreviated form in italics after the phonetic spellings of headwords (e.g. *vt, adv, conj*).

Genders of Spanish nouns are indicated as follows: *nm* for a masculine and *nf* for a feminine noun. Feminine and irregular plural forms of nouns are also shown (**irlandés, esa; luz**, (*pl* **luces**)).

ABREVIATURAS

ABBREVIATIONS

abreviatura	ab(b)r	abbreviation
adjetivo, locución adjetiva	adj	adjective, adjectival phrase
administración	ADMIN	administration
adverbio, locución adverbial	adv	adverb, adverbial phrase
agricultura	AGR	agriculture
América Latina	AM	Latin America
anatomía	ANAT	anatomy
arquitectura	ARQ, ARCH	architecture
el automóvil	AUT(O)	the motor car and motoring
aviación, viajes aéreos	AVIAT	flying, air travel
biología	BIO(L)	biology
botánica, flores	BOT	botany
inglés británico	BRIT	British English
química	CHEM	chemistry
comercio, finanzas, banca	COM(M)	commerce, finance, banking
informática	COMPUT	computers
conjunción	conj	conjunction
construcción	CONSTR	building
compuesto	cpd	compound element
cocina	CULIN	cookery
economía	ECON	economics
electricidad, electrónica	ELEC	electricity, electronics
enseñanza, sistema escolar y universitario	ESCOL	schooling, schools and universities
España	Esp	Spain
especialmente	esp	especially
exclamación, interjección	excl	exclamation, interjection
femenino	f	feminine
lengua familiar (! vulgar)	fam (!)	colloquial usage (! particularly offensive)
ferrocarril	FERRO	railways
uso figurado	fig	figurative use
fotografía	FOTO	photography
(verbo inglés) del cual la partícula es inseparable	fus	(phrasal verb) where the particle is inseparable
generalmente	gen	generally
geografía, geología	GEO	geography, geology
geometría	GEOM	geometry
uso familiar (! vulgar)	inf (!)	colloquial usage (! particularly offensive)
infinitivo	infin	infinitive
informática	INFORM	computers
invariable	inv	invariable
irregular	irreg	irregular
lo jurídico	JUR	law
América Latina	LAM	Latin America
gramática, lingüística	LING	grammar, linguistics
masculino	m	masculine

ABREVIATURAS

ABBREVIATIONS

matemáticas	MATH	mathematics
masculino/femenino	m/f	masculine/feminine
medicina	MED	medicine
lo militar, ejército	MIL	military matters
música	MUS	music
sustantivo, nombre	n	noun
navegación, náutica	NAUT	sailing, navigation
sustantivo numérico	num	numeral noun
complemento	obj	(grammatical) object
	o.s.	oneself
peyorativo	pey, pej	derogatory, pejorative
fotografía	PHOT	photography
fisiología	PHYSIOL	physiology
plural	pl	plural
política	POL	politics
participio de pasado	pp	past participle
preposición	prep	preposition
pronombre	pron	pronoun
psicología, psiquiatría	PSICO, PSYCH	psychology, psychiatry
tiempo pasado	pt	past tense
química	QUÍM	chemistry
ferrocarril	RAIL	railways
religión	REL	religion
	sb	somebody
enseñanza, sistema escolar y universitario	SCH	schooling, schools and universities
singular	sg	singular
España	SP	Spain
	sth	something
sujeto	su(b)j	(grammatical) subject
subjuntivo	subjun	subjunctive
tauromaquia	TAUR	bullfighting
también	tb	also
técnica, tecnología	TEC(H)	technical term, technology
telecomunicaciones	TELEC, TEL	telecommunications
imprenta, tipografía	TIP, TYP	typography, printing
televisión	TV	television
universidad	UNIV	university
inglés norteamericano	US	American English
verbo	vb	verb
verbo intransitivo	vi	intransitive verb
verbo pronominal	vr	reflexive verb
verbo transitivo	vt	transitive verb
zoología	ZOOL	zoology
marca registrada	®	registered trademark
indica un equivalente cultural	≈	introduces a cultural equivalent

SPANISH PRONUNCIATION

Consonants

c	[k]	caja	c before a, o or u is pronounced as in cat
ce, ci	[θe, θi]	cero cielo	c before e or i is pronounced as in thin
ch	[tʃ]	chiste	ch is pronounced as ch in chair
d	[d, ð]	danés ciudad	at the beginning of a phrase or after l or n, d is pronounced as in English. In any other position it is pronounced like th in the
g	[g, ɤ]	gafas paga	g before a, o or u is pronounced as in gap, if at the beginning of a phrase or after n. In other positions the sound is softened
ge, gi	[xe, xi]	gente girar	g before e or i is pronounced similar to ch in Scottish loch
h		haber	h is always silent in Spanish
j	[x]	jugar	j is pronounced similar to ch in Scottish loch
ll	[ʎ]	talle	ll is pronounced like the lli in million
ñ	[ɲ]	niño	ñ is pronounced like the ni in onion
q	[k]	que	q is pronounced as k in king
r, rr	[r, rr]	quitar garra	r is always pronounced in Spanish, unlike the silent r in dancer. rr is trilled, like a Scottish r
s	[s]	quizás isla	s is usually pronounced as in pass, but before b, d, g, l, m or n it is pronounced as in rose
v	[b, ß]	vía dividir	v is pronounced something like b. At the beginning of a phrase or after m or n it is pronounced as b in boy. In any other position the sound is softened
z	[θ]	tenaz	z is pronounced as th in thin

b, f, k, l, m, n, p, t and x are pronounced as in English.

Vowels

a	[a]	p*a*ta	not as long as *a* in f*a*r. When followed by a consonant in the same syllable (i.e. in a closed syllable), as in am*a*nte, the *a* is short, as in b*a*t
e	[e]	m*e*	like *e* in th*ey*. In a closed syllable, as in g*e*nte, the *e* is short as in p*e*t
i	[i]	p*i*no	as in m*ea*n or mach*i*ne
o	[o]	l*o*	as in l*o*cal. In a closed syllable, as in c*o*ntrol, the *o* is short as in c*o*t
u	[u]	l*u*nes	as in r*u*le. It is silent after *q*, and in *gue, gui*, unless marked *güe, güi* e.g. antig*ü*edad

Diphthongs

ai, ay	[ai]	b*ai*le	as *i* in r*i*de
au	[au]	*au*to	as *ou* in sh*ou*t
ei, ey	[ei]	bu*ey*	as *ey* in gr*ey*
eu	[eu]	d*eu*da	both elements pronounced independently |e|/|u|
oi, oy	[oi]	h*oy*	as *oy* in t*oy*

Stress

The rules of stress in Spanish are as follows:
(a)   when a word ends in a vowel or in *n* or *s*, the second last syllable is stressed: pat*a*ta, pat*a*tas, c*o*me, c*o*men
(b)   when a word ends in a consonant other than *n* or *s*, the stress falls on the last syllable: par*e*d, habl*a*r
(c)   when the rules set out in a and b are not applied, an acute accent appears over the stressed vowel: com*ú*n, geograf*í*a, ingl*é*s

In the phonetic transcription, the symbol |'| precedes the syllable on which the stress falls.

PRONUNCIACIÓN INGLESA

Vocales y diptongos

	Ejemplo inglés	*Ejemplo español/explicación*
ɑː	f**a**ther	Entre *a* de p**a**dre y *o* de n**o**che
ʌ	b**u**t, c**o**me	*a* muy breve
æ	m**a**n, c**a**t	Se mantienen los labios en la posición de *e* en p**e**na y luego se pronuncia el sonido *a*
ə	fath**er**, **a**go	Sonido indistinto parecido a una *e* u *o* casi mudas
əː	b**ir**d, h**ear**d	Entre *e* abierta, y *o* cerrada, sonido alargado
ɛ	g**e**t, b**e**d	como en p**e**rro
ɪ	**i**t, b**i**g	Más breve que en s**i**
iː	t**ea**, s**ee**	Como en f**i**no
ɔ	h**o**t, w**a**sh	Como en t**o**rre
ɔː	s**aw**, **a**ll	Como en p**o**r
u	p**u**t, b**oo**k	Sonido breve, más cerrado que en b**u**rro
uː	t**oo**, y**ou**	Sonido largo, como en **u**no
aɪ	fl**y**, h**igh**	Como en fr**ai**le
au	h**ow**, h**ou**se	Como en p**au**sa
ɛə	th**ere**, b**ear**	Casi como en v**ea**, pero el sonido *a* se mezcla con el indistinto [ə]
eɪ	d**ay**, ob**ey**	*e* cerrada seguida por una *i* débil
ɪə	h**ere**, h**ear**	Como en man**ía**, mezclándose el sonido *a* con el indistinto [ə]
əu	g**o**, n**o**te	[ə] seguido por una breve *u*
ɔɪ	b**oy**, **oi**l	Como en v**oy**
uə	p**oor**, s**ure**	*u* bastante larga más el sonido indistinto [ə]

Consonantes

	Ejemplo inglés	Ejemplo español/explicación
d	men*d*ed	Como en con*d*e, an*d*ar
g	*g*o, *g*et, bi*g*	Como en *g*rande, *g*ol
dʒ	*g*in, ju*dg*e	Como en la *ll* andaluza y en *G*eneralitat (catalán)
ŋ	si*ng*	Como en ví*n*culo
h	*h*ouse, *h*e	Como la jota hispanoamericana
j	*y*oung, *y*es	Como en *y*a
k	*c*ome, mo*ck*	Como en *c*aña, Es*c*ocia
r	*r*ed, t*r*ead	Se pronuncia con la punta de la lengua hacia atrás y sin hacerla vibrar
s	*s*and, ye*s*	Como en *c*asa, *s*esión
z	ro*s*e, *z*ebra	Como en de*s*de, mi*s*mo
ʃ	*sh*e, ma*ch*ine	Como en *ch*ambre (francés), ro*x*o (portugués)
tʃ	*ch*in, ri*ch*	Como en *ch*ocolate
v	*v*alley	Como en f, pero se retiran los dientes superiores vibrándolos contra el labio inferior
w	*w*ater, *wh*ich	Como en la *u* de h*u*evo, p*u*ede
ʒ	vi*s*ion	Como en *j*ournal (francés)
θ	*th*ink, my*th*	Como en re*c*eta, *z*apato
ð	*th*is, *th*e	Como en la *d* de habla*d*o, verda*d*

b, p, f, m, n, l, t iguales que en español.

El signo * indica que la r final escrita apenas se pronuncia en inglés británico cuando la palabra siguiente empieza con vocal.

El signo ['] indica la sílaba acentuada.

A, a

PALABRA CLAVE
---

a [a] (a + el = al) prep **1** (dirección): to; **fueron ~ Madrid/Grecia** they went to Madrid/Greece; **me voy ~ casa** I'm going home
2 (distancia): **está ~ 15 km de aquí** it's 15 km from here
3 (posición): **estar ~ la mesa** to be at table; **al lado de** next to, beside; ver tb **puerta**
4 (tiempo): **~ las 10/~ medianoche** at 10/ midnight; **~ la mañana siguiente** the following morning; **~ los pocos días** after a few days; **estamos ~ 9 de julio** it's the ninth of July; **~ los 24 años** at the age of 24; **al año/~ la semana** (AM) a year/week later
5 (manera): **~ la francesa** the French way; **~ caballo** on horseback; **~ oscuras** in the dark
6 (medio, instrumento): **~ lápiz** in pencil; **~ mano** by hand; **cocina ~ gas** gas stove
7 (razón): **~ 30 ptas el kilo** at 30 pesetas a kilo; **~ más de 50 km/h** at more than 50 km per hour
8 (dativo): **se lo di ~ él** I gave it to him; **vi al policía** I saw the policeman; **se lo compré ~ él** I bought it from him
9 (tras ciertos verbos): **voy ~ verle** I'm going to see him; **empezó ~ trabajar** he started working o to work
10 (+ infin): **al verle, le reconocí inmediatamente** when I saw him I recognized him at once; **el camino ~ recorrer** the distance we (etc) have to travel; **¡~ callar!** keep quiet!; **¡~ comer!** let's eat!

abad, esa [a'ßaö, 'öesa] nm/f abbot/abbess; **~ía** nf abbey
abajo [a'ßaxo] adv (situación) (down) below, underneath; (en edificio) downstairs; (dirección) down, downwards; **el piso de ~** the downstairs flat; **la parte de ~** the lower part; **¡~ el gobierno!** down with the government!; **cuesta/río ~** downhill/ downstream; **de arriba ~** from top to bottom; **el ~ firmante** the undersigned; **más ~** lower o further down
abalanzarse [aßalan'θarse] vr: **~ sobre** o **contra** to throw o.s. at
abandonado, a [aßando'naöo, a] adj derelict; (desatendido) abandoned; (desierto) deserted; (descuidado) neglected

abandonar [aßando'nar] vt to leave; (persona) to abandon, desert; (cosa) to abandon, leave behind; (descuidar) to neglect; (renunciar a) to give up; (INFORM) to quit; **~se** vr: **~se a** to abandon o.s. to;
abandono nm (acto) desertion, abandonment; (estado) abandon, neglect; (renuncia) withdrawal, retirement; **ganar por abandono** to win by default
abanicar [aßani'kar] vt to fan; **abanico** nm fan; (NAUT) derrick
abaratar [aßara'tar] vt to lower the price of; **~se** vr to go o come down in price
abarcar [aßar'kar] vt to include, embrace; (AM) to monopolize
abarrotado, a [aßarro'taöo, a] adj packed
abarrotar [aßarro'tar] vt (local, estadio, teatro) to fill, pack
abarrotero, a [aßarro'tero, a] (AM) nm/f grocer; **abarrotes** nmpl (AM) groceries, provisions
abastecer [aßaste'θer] vt: **~ (de)** to supply (with); **abastecimiento** nm supply
abasto [a'ßasto] nm supply; **no dar ~ a** to be unable to cope with
abatido, a [aßa'tiöo, a] adj dejected, downcast
abatimiento [aßati'mjento] nm (depresión) dejection, depression
abatir [aßa'tir] vt (muro) to demolish; (pájaro) to shoot o bring down; (fig) to depress; **~se** vr to get depressed; **~se sobre** to swoop o pounce on
abdicación [aßöika'θjon] nf abdication
abdicar [aßöi'kar] vi to abdicate
abdomen [aß'öomen] nm abdomen; **abdominales** nmpl (tb: ejercicios abdominales) sit-ups
abecedario [aßeθe'öarjo] nm alphabet
abedul [aße'öul] nm birch
abeja [a'ßexa] nf bee
abejorro [aße'xorro] nm bumblebee
abertura [aßer'tura] nf = **apertura**
abeto [a'ßeto] nm fir
abierto, a [a'ßjerto, a] pp de **abrir** ♦ adj open; (AM) generous
abigarrado, a [aßiɣa'rraöo, a] adj multi-coloured
abismal [aßis'mal] adj (fig) vast, enormous
abismar [aßis'mar] vt to humble, cast down;

~se vr to sink; **~se en** (fig) to be plunged into

abismo [a'βismo] nm abyss

abjurar [aβxu'rar] vi: **~ de** to abjure, forswear

ablandar [aβlan'dar] vt to soften; **~se** vr to get softer

abnegación [aβneɣa'θjon] nf self-denial

abnegado, a [aβne'ɣaðo, a] adj self-sacrificing

abocado, a [aβo'kaðo, a] adj: **verse ~ al desastre** to be heading for disaster

abochornar [aβotʃor'nar] vt to embarrass

abofetear [aβofete'ar] vt to slap (in the face)

abogado, a [aβo'ɣaðo, a] nm/f lawyer; (notario) solicitor; (en tribunal) barrister (BRIT), attorney (US); **~ defensor** defence lawyer o attorney (US)

abogar [aβo'ɣar] vi: **~ por** to plead for; (fig) to advocate

abolengo [aβo'lengo] nm ancestry, lineage

abolición [aβoli'θjon] nf abolition

abolir [aβo'lir] vt to abolish; (cancelar) to cancel

abolladura [aβoʎa'ðura] nf dent

abollar [aβo'ʎar] vt to dent

abominable [aβomi'naβle] adj abominable

abonado, a [aβo'naðo, a] adj (deuda) paid(-up) ♦ nm/f subscriber

abonar [aβo'nar] vt (deuda) to settle; (terreno) to fertilize; (idea) to endorse; **~se** vr to subscribe; **abono** nm payment; fertilizer; subscription

abordar [aβor'ðar] vt (barco) to board; (asunto) to broach

aborigen [aβo'rixen] nm/f aborigine

aborrecer [aβorre'θer] vt to hate, loathe

abortar [aβor'tar] vi (malparir) to have a miscarriage; (deliberadamente) to have an abortion; **aborto** nm miscarriage; abortion

abotonar [aβoto'nar] vt to button (up), do up

abovedado, a [aβoβe'ðaðo, a] adj vaulted, domed

abrasar [aβra'sar] vt to burn (up); (AGR) to dry up, parch

abrazar [aβra'θar] vt to embrace, hug

abrazo [a'βraθo] nm embrace, hug; **un ~** (en carta) with best wishes

abrebotellas [aβreβo'teʎas] nm inv bottle opener

abrecartas [aβre'kartas] nm inv letter opener

abrelatas [aβre'latas] nm inv tin (BRIT) o can opener

abreviar [aβre'βjar] vt to abbreviate; (texto) to abridge; (plazo) to reduce; **abreviatura** nf abbreviation

abridor [aβri'ðor] nm bottle opener; (de latas) tin (BRIT) o can opener

abrigar [aβri'ɣar] vt (proteger) to shelter; (suj: ropa) to keep warm; (fig) to cherish

abrigo [a'βriɣo] nm (prenda) coat, overcoat; (lugar protegido) shelter

abril [a'βril] nm April

abrillantar [aβriʎan'tar] vt to polish

abrir [a'βrir] vt to open (up) ♦ vi to open; **~se** vr to open (up); (extenderse) to open out; (cielo) to clear; **~se paso** to find o force a way through

abrochar [aβro'tʃar] vt (con botones) to button (up); (zapato, con broche) to do up

abrumar [aβru'mar] vt to overwhelm; (sobrecargar) to weigh down

abrupto, a [a'βrupto, a] adj abrupt; (empinado) steep

absceso [aβs'θeso] nm abscess

absentismo [aβsen'tismo] nm absenteeism

absolución [aβsolu'θjon] nf (REL) absolution; (JUR) acquittal

absoluto, a [aβso'luto, a] adj absolute; **en ~** adv not at all

absolver [aβsol'βer] vt to absolve; (JUR) to pardon; (: acusado) to acquit

absorbente [aβsor'βente] adj absorbent; (interesante) absorbing

absorber [aβsor'βer] vt to absorb; (embeber) to soak up

absorción [aβsor'θjon] nf absorption; (COM) takeover

absorto, a [aβ'sorto, a] pp de **absorber** ♦ adj absorbed, engrossed

abstemio, a [aβs'temjo, a] adj teetotal

abstención [aβsten'θjon] nf abstention

abstenerse [aβste'nerse] vr: **~ (de)** to abstain o refrain (from)

abstinencia [aβsti'nenθja] nf abstinence; (ayuno) fasting

abstracción [aβstrak'θjon] nf abstraction

abstracto, a [aβ'strakto, a] adj abstract

abstraer [aβstra'er] vt to abstract; **~se** vr to be o become absorbed

abstraído, a [aβstra'iðo, a] adj absent-minded

absuelto [aβ'swelto] pp de **absolver**

absurdo, a [aβ'surðo, a] adj absurd

abuchear [aβutʃe'ar] vt to boo

abuelo, a [a'βwelo, a] nm/f grandfather/mother; **~s** nmpl grandparents

abulia [a'βulja] nf apathy

abultado, a [aβul'taðo, a] adj bulky

abultar [aβul'tar] vi to be bulky

abundancia [aβun'danθja] nf: **una ~ de** plenty of; **abundante** adj abundant, plentiful

abundar [aβun'dar] vi to abound, be plentiful

aburguesarse [aβurɣe'sarse] vr to become middle-class

aburrido, a [aβu'rriðo, a] adj (hastiado) bored; (que aburre) boring; **aburrimiento**

nm boredom, tedium
aburrir [aβu'rrir] *vt* to bore; **~se** *vr* to be bored, get bored
abusar [aβu'sar] *vi* to go too far; **~ de** to abuse
abusivo, a [aβu'siβo, a] *adj* (*precio*) exorbitant
abuso [a'βuso] *nm* abuse
abyecto, a [aβ'jekto, a] *adj* wretched, abject
acá [a'ka] *adv* (*lugar*) here; ¿**de cuándo ~?** since when?
acabado, a [aka'βaðo, a] *adj* finished, complete; (*perfecto*) perfect; (*agotado*) worn out; (*fig*) masterly ♦ *nm* finish
acabar [aka'βar] *vt* (*llevar a su fin*) to finish, complete; (*consumir*) to use up; (*rematar*) to finish off ♦ *vi* to finish, end; **~se** *vr* to finish, stop; (*terminarse*) to be over; (*agotarse*) to run out; **~ con** to put an end to; **~ de llegar** to have just arrived; **~ por hacer** to end (up) by doing; **¡se acabó!** it's all over!; (*¡basta!*) that's enough!
acábose [a'kaβose] *nm*: **esto es el ~** this is the last straw
academia [aka'ðemja] *nf* academy; **académico, a** *adj* academic
acaecer [akae'θer] *vi* to happen, occur
acallar [aka'ʎar] *vt* (*persona*) to silence; (*protestas, rumores*) to suppress
acalorado, a [akalo'raðo, a] *adj* (*discusión*) heated
acalorarse [akalo'rarse] *vr* (*fig*) to get heated
acampar [akam'par] *vi* to camp
acantilado [akanti'laðo] *nm* cliff
acaparar [akapa'rar] *vt* to monopolize; (*acumular*) to hoard
acariciar [akari'θjar] *vt* to caress; (*esperanza*) to cherish
acarrear [akarre'ar] *vt* to transport; (*fig*) to cause, result in
acaso [a'kaso] *adv* perhaps, maybe; (**por**) **si ~** (just) in case
acatamiento [akata'mjento] *nm* respect; (*ley*) observance
acatar [aka'tar] *vt* to respect; (*ley*) obey
acatarrarse [akata'rrarse] *vr* to catch a cold
acaudalado, a [akauða'laðo, a] *adj* well-off
acaudillar [akauði'ʎar] *vt* to lead, command
acceder [akθe'ðer] *vi*: **~ a** (*petición etc*) to agree to; (*tener acceso a*) to have access to; (*INFORM*) to access
accesible [akθe'siβle] *adj* accessible
acceso [ak'θeso] *nm* access, entry; (*camino*) access, approach; (*MED*) attack, fit
accesorio, a [akθe'sorjo, a] *adj, nm* accessory
accidentado, a [akθiðen'taðo, a] *adj* uneven; (*montañoso*) hilly; (*azaroso*) eventful

♦ *nm/f* accident victim
accidental [akθiðen'tal] *adj* accidental; **accidentarse** *vr* to have an accident
accidente [akθi'ðente] *nm* accident; **~s** *nmpl* (*de terreno*) unevenness *sg*
acción [ak'θjon] *nf* action; (*acto*) action, act; (*COM*) share; (*JUR*) action, lawsuit; **accionar** *vt* to work, operate; (*INFORM*) to drive
accionista [akθjo'nista] *nm/f* shareholder, stockholder
acebo [a'θeβo] *nm* holly; (*árbol*) holly tree
acechar [aθe'tʃar] *vt* to spy on; (*aguardar*) to lie in wait for; **acecho** *nm*: **estar al acecho (de)** to lie in wait (for)
aceitar [aθei'tar] *vt* to oil, lubricate
aceite [a'θeite] *nm* oil; (*de oliva*) olive oil; **~ra** *nf* oilcan; **aceitoso, a** *adj* oily
aceituna [aθei'tuna] *nf* olive
acelerador [aθelera'ðor] *nm* accelerator
acelerar [aθele'rar] *vt* to accelerate
acelga [a'θelʁa] *nf* chard, beet
acento [a'θento] *nm* accent; (*acentuación*) stress
acentuar [aθen'twar] *vt* to accent; to stress; (*fig*) to accentuate
acepción [aθep'θjon] *nf* meaning
aceptable [aθep'taβle] *adj* acceptable
aceptación [aθepta'θjon] *nf* acceptance; (*aprobación*) approval
aceptar [aθep'tar] *vt* to accept; (*aprobar*) to approve
acequia [a'θekja] *nf* irrigation ditch
acera [a'θera] *nf* pavement (*BRIT*), sidewalk (*US*)
acerca [a'θerka]: **~ de** *prep* about, concerning
acercar [aθer'kar] *vt* to bring o move nearer; **~se** *vr* to approach, come near
acerico [aθe'riko] *nm* pincushion
acero [a'θero] *nm* steel
acérrimo, a [a'θerrimo, a] *adj* (*partidario*) staunch; (*enemigo*) bitter
acertado, a [aθer'taðo, a] *adj* correct; (*apropiado*) apt; (*sensato*) sensible
acertar [aθer'tar] *vt* (*blanco*) to hit; (*solución*) to get right; (*adivinar*) to guess ♦ *vi* to get it right, be right; **~ a** to manage to; **~ con** to happen o hit on
acertijo [aθer'tixo] *nm* riddle, puzzle
achacar [atʃa'kar] *vt* to attribute
achacoso, a [atʃa'koso, a] *adj* sickly
achantar [atʃan'tar] (*fam*) *vt* to scare, frighten; **~se** *vr* to back down
achaque *etc* [a'tʃake] *vb ver* **achacar** ♦ *nm* ailment
achicar [atʃi'kar] *vt* to reduce; (*NAUT*) to bale out
achicharrar [atʃitʃa'rrar] *vt* to scorch, burn
achicoria [atʃi'korja] *nf* chicory
aciago, a [a'θjaβo, a] *adj* ill-fated, fateful

acicalar [aθika'lar] vt to polish; (*persona*) to dress up; **~se** vr to get dressed up

acicate [aθi'kate] nm spur

acidez [aθi'ðeθ] nf acidity

ácido, a ['aθiðo, a] adj sour, acid ♦ nm acid

acierto etc [a'θjerto] vb ver **acertar** ♦ nm success; (*buen paso*) wise move; (*solución*) solution; (*habilidad*) skill, ability

aclamación [aklama'θjon] nf acclamation; (*aplausos*) applause

aclamar [akla'mar] vt to acclaim; (*aplaudir*) to applaud

aclaración [aklara'θjon] nf clarification, explanation

aclarar [akla'rar] vt to clarify, explain; (*ropa*) to rinse ♦ vi to clear up; **~se** vr (*explicarse*) to understand; **~se la garganta** to clear one's throat

aclaratorio, a [aklara'torjo, a] adj explanatory

aclimatación [aklimata'θjon] nf acclimatization

aclimatar [aklima'tar] vt to acclimatize; **~se** vr to become acclimatized

acné [ak'ne] nm acne

acobardar [akoßar'ðar] vt to intimidate

acodarse [ako'ðarse] vr: **~ en** to lean on

acogedor, a [akoxe'ðor, a] adj welcoming; (*hospitalario*) hospitable

acoger [ako'xer] vt to welcome; (*abrigar*) to shelter; **~se** vr to take refuge

acogida [ako'xiða] nf reception; refuge

acometer [akome'ter] vt to attack; (*emprender*) to undertake; **acometida** nf attack, assault

acomodado, a [akomo'ðaðo, a] adj (*persona*) well-to-do

acomodador, a [akomoða'ðor, a] nm/f usher(ette)

acomodar [akomo'ðar] vt to adjust; (*alojar*) to accommodate; **~se** vr to conform; (*instalarse*) to install o.s.; (*adaptarse*): **~se (a)** to adapt (to)

acompañar [akompa'ɲar] vt to accompany; (*documentos*) to enclose

acondicionar [akondiθjo'nar] vt to arrange, prepare; (*pelo*) to condition

acongojar [akongo'xar] vt to distress, grieve

aconsejar [akonse'xar] vt to advise, counsel; **~se** vr: **~se con** to consult

acontecer [akonte'θer] vi to happen, occur; **acontecimiento** nm event

acopio [a'kopjo] nm store, stock

acoplamiento [akopla'mjento] nm coupling, joint; **acoplar** vt to fit; (*ELEC*) to connect; (*vagones*) to couple

acorazado, a [akora'θaðo, a] adj armour-plated, armoured ♦ nm battleship

acordar [akor'ðar] vt (*resolver*) to agree, resolve; (*recordar*) to remind; **~se** vr to agree; **~se (de algo)** to remember (sth); **acorde** adj (*MUS*) harmonious; **acorde con** (*medidas etc*) in keeping with ♦ nm chord

acordeón [akorðe'on] nm accordion

acordonado, a [akorðo'naðo, a] adj (*calle*) cordoned-off

acorralar [akorra'lar] vt to round up, corral

acortar [akor'tar] vt to shorten; (*duración*) to cut short; (*cantidad*) to reduce; **~se** vr to become shorter

acosar [ako'sar] vt to pursue relentlessly; (*fig*) to hound, pester; **acoso** nm harassment; **acoso sexual** sexual harassment

acostar [akos'tar] vt (*en cama*) to put to bed; (*en suelo*) to lay down; **~se** vr to go to bed; to lie down; **~se con uno** to sleep with sb

acostumbrado, a [akostum'braðo, a] adj usual; **~ a** used to

acostumbrar [akostum'brar] vt: **~ a uno a algo** to get sb used to sth ♦ vi: **~ (a) hacer** to be in the habit of doing; **~se** vr: **~se a** to get used to

acotación [akota'θjon] nf marginal note; (*GEO*) elevation mark; (*de límite*) boundary mark; (*TEATRO*) stage direction

ácrata ['akrata] adj, nm/f anarchist

acre ['akre] adj (*olor*) acrid; (*fig*) biting ♦ nm acre

acrecentar [akreθen'tar] vt to increase, augment

acreditar [akreði'tar] vt (*garantizar*) to vouch for, guarantee; (*autorizar*) to authorize; (*dar prueba de*) to prove; (*COM: abonar*) to credit; (*embajador*) to accredit; **~se** vr to become famous

acreedor, a [akree'ðor, a] adj: **~ de** worthy of ♦ nm/f creditor

acribillar [akriβi'ʎar] vt: **~ a balazos** to riddle with bullets

acróbata [a'kroßata] nm/f acrobat

acta ['akta] nf certificate; (*de comisión*) minutes pl, record; **~ de nacimiento/de matrimonio** birth/marriage certificate; **~ notarial** affidavit

actitud [akti'tuð] nf attitude; (*postura*) posture

activar [akti'ßar] vt to activate; (*acelerar*) to speed up

actividad [aktißi'ðað] nf activity

activo, a [ak'tißo, a] adj active; (*vivo*) lively ♦ nm (*COM*) assets pl

acto ['akto] nm act, action; (*ceremonia*) ceremony; (*TEATRO*) act; **en el ~** immediately

actor [ak'tor] nm actor; (*JUR*) plaintiff ♦ adj: **parte ~a** prosecution

actriz [ak'triθ] nf actress

actuación [aktwa'θjon] nf action; (*comportamiento*) conduct, behaviour; (*JUR*) proceedings *pl*; (*desempeño*) performance

actual [ak'twal] *adj* present(-day), current; **~idad** *nf* present; **~idades** *nfpl* (*noticias*) news *sg*; **en la ~idad** at present; (*hoy día*) nowadays

actualizar [aktwali'θar] *vt* to update, modernize

actualmente [aktwal'mente] *adv* at present; (*hoy día*) nowadays

actuar [ak'twar] *vi* (*obrar*) to work, operate; (*actor*) to act, perform ♦ *vt* to work, operate; **~ de** to act as

acuarela [akwa'rela] *nf* watercolour

acuario [a'kwarjo] *nm* aquarium; (*ASTROLOGÍA*): **A~** Aquarius

acuartelar [akwarte'lar] *vt* (*MIL*) to confine to barracks

acuático, a [a'kwatiko, a] *adj* aquatic

acuchillar [akutʃi'ʎar] *vt* (*TEC*) to plane (down), smooth

acuciante [aku'θjante] *adj* urgent

acuciar [aku'θjar] *vt* to urge on

acudir [aku'ðir] *vi* (*asistir*) to attend; (*ir*) to go; **~ a** (*fig*) to turn to; **~ en ayuda de** to go to the aid of

acuerdo *etc* [a'kwerðo] *vb ver* **acordar** ♦ *nm* agreement; **¡de ~!** agreed!; **de ~ con** (*persona*) in agreement with; (*acción, documento*) in accordance with; **estar de ~** to be agreed, agree

acumular [akumu'lar] *vt* to accumulate, collect

acuñar [aku'ɲar] *vt* (*moneda*) to mint; (*frase*) to coin

acupuntura [akupun'tura] *nf* acupuncture

acurrucarse [akurru'karse] *vr* to crouch; (*ovillarse*) to curl up

acusación [akusa'θjon] *nf* accusation

acusar [aku'sar] *vt* to accuse; (*revelar*) to reveal; (*denunciar*) to denounce

acuse [a'kuse] *nm*: **~ de recibo** acknowledgement of receipt

acústica, a [a'kustika] *nf* acoustics *pl*

acústico, a [a'kustiko, a] *adj* acoustic

adaptación [aðapta'θjon] *nf* adaptation

adaptador [aðapta'ðor] *nm* (*ELEC*) adapter

adaptar [aðap'tar] *vt* to adapt; (*acomodar*) to fit

adecuado, a [aðe'kwaðo, a] *adj* (*apto*) suitable; (*oportuno*) appropriate

adecuar [aðe'kwar] *vt* to adapt; to make suitable

a. de J.C. *abr* (= *antes de Jesucristo*) B.C.

adelantado, a [aðelan'taðo, a] *adj* advanced; (*reloj*) fast; **pagar por ~** to pay in advance

adelantamiento [aðelanta'mjento] *nm* (*AUTO*) overtaking

adelantar [aðelan'tar] *vt* to move forward;

(*avanzar*) to advance; (*acelerar*) to speed up; (*AUTO*) to overtake ♦ *vi* to go forward, advance; **~se** *vr* to go forward, advance

adelante [aðe'lante] *adv* forward(s), ahead ♦ *excl* come in!; **de hoy en ~** from now on; **más ~** later on; (*más allá*) further on

adelanto [aðe'lanto] *nm* advance; (*mejora*) improvement; (*progreso*) progress

adelgazar [aðelɣa'θar] *vt* to thin (down) ♦ *vi* to get thin; (*con régimen*) to slim down, lose weight

ademán [aðe'man] *nm* gesture; **ademanes** *nmpl* manners; **en ~ de** as if to

además [aðe'mas] *adv* besides; (*por otra parte*) moreover; (*también*) also; **~ de** besides, in addition to

adentrarse [aðen'trarse] *vr*: **~ en** to go into, get inside; (*penetrar*) to penetrate (into)

adentro [a'ðentro] *adv* inside, in; **mar ~** out at sea; **tierra ~** inland

adepto, a [a'ðepto, a] *nm/f* supporter

aderezar [aðere'θar] *vt* (*ensalada*) to dress; (*comida*) to season; **aderezo** *nm* dressing; seasoning

adeudar [aðeu'ðar] *vt* to owe; **~se** *vr* to run into debt

adherirse [aðe'rirse] *vr*: **~ a** to adhere to; (*partido*) to join

adhesión [aðe'sjon] *nf* adhesion; (*fig*) adherence

adicción [aðik'θjon] *nf* addiction

adición [aði'θjon] *nf* addition

adicto, a [a'ðikto, a] *adj*: **~ a** addicted to; (*dedicado*) devoted to ♦ *nm/f* supporter, follower; (*toxicómano etc*) addict

adiestrar [aðjes'trar] *vt* to train, teach; (*conducir*) to guide, lead; **~se** *vr* to practise; (*enseñarse*) to train o.s.

adinerado, a [aðine'raðo, a] *adj* wealthy

adiós [a'ðjos] *excl* (*para despedirse*) goodbye!, cheerio!; (*al pasar*) hello!

aditivo [aði'tißo] *nm* additive

adivinanza [aðißi'nanθa] *nf* riddle

adivinar [aðißi'nar] *vt* to prophesy; (*conjeturar*) to guess; **adivino, a** *nm/f* fortune-teller

adj *abr* (= *adjunto*) encl.

adjetivo [aðxe'tißo] *nm* adjective

adjudicación [aðxuðika'θjon] *nf* award; adjudication

adjudicar [aðxuði'kar] *vt* to award; **~se** *vr*: **~se algo** to appropriate sth

adjuntar [aðxun'tar] *vt* to attach, enclose; **adjunto, a** *adj* attached, enclosed ♦ *nm/f* assistant

administración [aðministra'θjon] *nf* administration; (*dirección*) management; **administrador, a** *nm/f* administrator; manager(ess)

administrar [aðminis'trar] *vt* to administer;
  administrativo, a *adj* administrative
admirable [aðmi'raßle] *adj* admirable
admiración [aðmira'θjon] *nf* admiration;
  (*asombro*) wonder; (*LING*) exclamation mark
admirar [aðmi'rar] *vt* to admire; (*extrañar*) to
  surprise; **~se** *vr* to be surprised
admisible [aðmi'sißle] *adj* admissible
admisión [aðmi'sjon] *nf* admission;
  (*reconocimiento*) acceptance
admitir [aðmi'tir] *vt* to admit; (*aceptar*) to
  accept
admonición [aðmoni'θjon] *nf* warning
adobar [aðo'ßar] *vt* (*CULIN*) to season
adobe [a'ðoße] *nm* adobe, sun-dried brick
adoctrinar [aðoktri'nar] *vt*: **~ en** to
  indoctrinate with
adolecer [aðole'θer] *vi*: **~ de** to suffer from
adolescente [aðoles'θente] *nm/f* adolescent,
  teenager
adonde [a'ðonðe] *conj* (to) where
adónde [a'ðonðe] *adv* = **dónde**
adopción [aðop'θjon] *nf* adoption
adoptar [aðop'tar] *vt* to adopt
adoptivo, a [aðop'tißo, a] *adj* (*padres*)
  adoptive; (*hijo*) adopted
adoquín [aðo'kin] *nm* paving stone
adorar [aðo'rar] *vt* to adore
adormecer [aðorme'θer] *vt* to put to sleep;
  ~se *vr* to become sleepy; (*dormirse*) to fall
  asleep
adornar [aðor'nar] *vt* to adorn
adorno [a'ðorno] *nm* ornament; (*decoración*)
  decoration
adosado, a [aðo'saðo, a] *adj*: **casa adosada**
  semi-detached house
adquiero *etc vb ver* **adquirir**
adquirir [aðki'rir] *vt* to acquire, obtain
adquisición [aðkisi'θjon] *nf* acquisition
adrede [a'ðreðe] *adv* on purpose
adscribir [aðskri'ßir] *vt* to appoint
adscrito *pp de* **adscribir**
aduana [a'ðwana] *nf* customs *pl*
aduanero, a [a'ðwa'nero, a] *adj* customs *cpd*
  ♦ *nm/f* customs officer
aducir [aðu'θir] *vt* to adduce; (*dar como
  prueba*) to offer as proof
adueñarse [aðwe'ɲarse] *vr*: **~ de** to take
  possession of
adulación [aðula'θjon] *nf* flattery
adular [aðu'lar] *vt* to flatter
adulterar [aðulte'rar] *vt* to adulterate
adulterio [aðul'terjo] *nm* adultery
adúltero, a [a'ðultero, a] *adj* adulterous
  ♦ *nm/f* adulterer/adulteress
adulto, a [a'ðulto, a] *adj, nm/f* adult
adusto, a [a'ðusto, a] *adj* stern; (*austero*)
  austere
advenedizo, a [aðßene'ðiθo, a] *nm/f*
  upstart
advenimiento [aðßeni'mjento] *nm* arrival;
  (*al trono*) accession
adverbio [að'ßerßjo] *nm* adverb
adversario, a [aðßer'sarjo, a] *nm/f* adversary
adversidad [aðßersi'ðað] *nf* adversity;
  (*contratiempo*) setback
adverso, a [að'ßerso, a] *adj* adverse
advertencia [aðßer'tenθja] *nf* warning;
  (*prefacio*) preface, foreword
advertir [aðßer'tir] *vt* to notice; (*avisar*): **~ a
  uno de** to warn sb about o of
Adviento [að'ßjento] *nm* Advent
advierto *etc vb ver* **advertir**
adyacente [aðja'θente] *adj* adjacent
aéreo, a [a'ereo, a] *adj* aerial
aerobic [ae'roßik] *nm* aerobics *sg*
aerodeslizador [aeroðesliθa'ðor] *nm*
  hovercraft
aeromozo, a [aero'moθo, a] (*AM*) *nm/f* air
  steward(ess)
aeronáutica [aero'nautika] *nf* aeronautics *sg*
aeronave [aero'naße] *nm* spaceship
aeroplano [aero'plano] *nm* aeroplane
aeropuerto [aero'pwerto] *nm* airport
aerosol [aero'sol] *nm* aerosol
afabilidad [afaßili'ðað] *nf* friendliness;
  afable *adj* affable
afamado, a [afa'maðo, a] *adj* famous
afán [a'fan] *nm* hard work; (*deseo*) desire
afanar [afa'nar] *vt* to harass; (*fam*) to pinch;
  ~se *vr*: **~se por hacer** to strive to do
afear [afe'ar] *vt* to disfigure
afección [afek'θjon] *nf* (*MED*) disease
afectación [afekta'θjon] *nf* affectation;
  afectado, a *adj* affected
afectar [afek'tar] *vt* to affect
afectísimo, a [afek'tisimo, a] *adj*
  affectionate; **suyo ~** yours truly
afectivo, a [afek'tißo, a] *adj* (*problema etc*)
  emotional
afecto [a'fekto] *nm* affection; **tenerle ~ a uno**
  to be fond of sb
afectuoso, a [afek'twoso, a] *adj* affectionate
afeitar [afei'tar] *vt* to shave; **~se** *vr* to shave
afeminado, a [afemi'naðo, a] *adj* effeminate
Afganistán [afxanis'tan] *nm* Afghanistan
afianzamiento [afjanθa'mjento] *nm*
  strengthening; security
afianzar [afjan'θar] *vt* to strengthen; to
  secure; **~se** *vr* to become established
afiche [a'fitʃe] (*AM*) *nm* poster
afición [afi'θjon] *nf* fondness, liking; **la ~** the
  fans *pl*; **pinto por ~** I paint as a hobby;
  aficionado, a *adj* keen, enthusiastic; (*no
  profesional*) amateur ♦ *nm/f* enthusiast, fan;
  amateur; **ser aficionado a algo** to be very
  keen on o fond of sth
aficionar [afiθjo'nar] *vt*: **~ a uno a algo** to

make sb like sth; **~se** *vr*: **~se a algo** to grow fond of sth

afilado, a [afi'laðo, a] *adj* sharp

afilar [afi'lar] *vt* to sharpen

afiliarse [afi'ljarse] *vr* to affiliate

afín [a'fin] *adj* (*parecido*) similar; (*conexo*) related

afinar [afi'nar] *vt* (*TEC*) to refine; (*MUS*) to tune ♦ *vi* (*tocar*) to play in tune; (*cantar*) to sing in tune

afincarse [afin'karse] *vr* to settle

afinidad [afini'ðað] *nf* affinity; (*parentesco*) relationship; **por ~** by marriage

afirmación [afirma'θjon] *nf* affirmation

afirmar [afir'mar] *vt* to affirm, state; **afirmativo, a** *adj* affirmative

aflicción [aflik'θjon] *nf* affliction; (*dolor*) grief

afligir [afli'xir] *vt* to afflict; (*apenar*) to distress; **~se** *vr* to grieve

aflojar [aflo'xar] *vt* to slacken; (*desatar*) to loosen, undo; (*relajar*) to relax ♦ *vi* to drop; (*bajar*) to go down; **~se** *vr* to relax

aflorar [aflo'rar] *vi* to come to the surface, emerge

afluente [aflu'ente] *adj* flowing ♦ *nm* tributary

afluir [aflu'ir] *vi* to flow

afmo, a *abr* (= *afectísimo(a) suyo(a)*) Yours

afónico, a [a'foniko, a] *adj*: **estar ~** to have a sore throat; to have lost one's voice

aforo [a'foro] *nm* (*de teatro etc*) capacity

afortunado, a [afortu'naðo, a] *adj* fortunate, lucky

afrancesado, a [afranθe'saðo, a] *adj* francophile; (*pey*) Frenchified

afrenta [a'frenta] *nf* affront, insult; (*deshonra*) dishonour, shame

África ['afrika] *nf* Africa; **africano, a** *adj, nm/f* African

afrontar [afron'tar] *vt* to confront; (*poner cara a cara*) to bring face to face

afuera [a'fwera] *adv* out, outside; **~s** *nfpl* outskirts

agachar [aɣa'tʃar] *vt* to bend, bow; **~se** *vr* to stoop, bend

agalla [a'ɣaʎa] *nf* (*ZOOL*) gill; **tener ~s** (*fam*) to have guts

agarradera [aɣarra'ðera] (*esp AM*) *nf* handle

agarrado, a [aɣa'rraðo, a] *adj* mean, stingy

agarrar [aɣa'rrar] *vt* to grasp, grab; (*AM*) to take, catch; (*recoger*) to pick up ♦ *vi* (*planta*) to take root; **~se** *vr* to hold on (tightly)

agarrotar [aɣarro'tar] *vt* (*persona*) to squeeze tightly; (*reo*) to garrotte; **~se** *vr* (*motor*) to seize up; (*MED*) to stiffen

agasajar [aɣasa'xar] *vt* to treat well, fête

agazaparse [aɣaθa'parse] *vr* to crouch down

agencia [a'xenθja] *nf* agency; **~ inmobiliaria** estate (*BRIT*) o real estate (*US*) agent's

(*office*); **~ de viajes** travel agency

agenciarse [axen'θjarse] *vr* to obtain, procure

agenda [a'xenda] *nf* diary

agente [a'xente] *nm/f* agent; (*de policía*) policeman/policewoman; **~ inmobiliario** estate agent (*BRIT*), realtor (*US*); **~ de seguros** insurance agent

ágil ['axil] *adj* agile, nimble; **agilidad** *nf* agility, nimbleness

agilizar [axili'θar] *vt* (*trámites*) to speed up

agitación [axita'θjon] *nf* (*de mano etc*) shaking, waving; (*de líquido etc*) stirring; (*fig*) agitation

agitado, a [axi'taðo, a] *adj* hectic; (*viaje*) bumpy

agitar [axi'tar] *vt* to wave, shake; (*líquido*) to stir; (*fig*) to stir up, excite; **~se** *vr* to get excited; (*inquietarse*) to get worried o upset

aglomeración [aɣlomera'θjon] *nf*: **~ de tráfico/gente** traffic jam/mass of people

aglomerar [aɣlome'rar] *vt* to crowd together; **~se** *vr* to crowd together

agnóstico, a [aɣ'nostiko, a] *adj, nm/f* agnostic

agobiar [aɣo'βjar] *vt* to weigh down; (*oprimir*) to oppress; (*cargar*) to burden

agolparse [aɣol'parse] *vr* to crowd together

agonía [aɣo'nia] *nf* death throes *pl*; (*fig*) agony, anguish

agonizante [aɣoni'θante] *adj* dying

agonizar [aɣoni'θar] *vi* to be dying

agosto [a'ɣosto] *nm* August

agotado, a [aɣo'taðo, a] *adj* (*persona*) exhausted; (*libros*) out of print; (*acabado*) finished; (*COM*) sold out

agotador, a [aɣota'ðor, a] *adj* exhausting

agotamiento [aɣota'mjento] *nm* exhaustion

agotar [aɣo'tar] *vt* to exhaust; (*consumir*) to drain; (*recursos*) to use up, deplete; **~se** *vr* to be exhausted; (*acabarse*) to run out; (*libro*) to go out of print

agraciado, a [aɣra'θjaðo, a] *adj* (*atractivo*) attractive; (*en sorteo etc*) lucky

agradable [aɣra'ðaβle] *adj* pleasant, nice

agradar [aɣra'ðar] *vt*: **él me agrada** I like him

agradecer [aɣraðe'θer] *vt* to thank; (*favor etc*) to be grateful for; **agradecido, a** *adj* grateful; **¡muy agradecido!** thanks a lot!; **agradecimiento** *nm* thanks *pl*; gratitude

agradezco *etc vb ver* **agradecer**

agrado [a'ɣraðo] *nm*: **ser de tu etc ~** to be to your *etc* liking

agrandar [aɣran'dar] *vt* to enlarge; (*fig*) to exaggerate; **~se** *vr* to get bigger

agrario, a [a'ɣrarjo, a] *adj* agrarian, land *cpd*; (*política*) agricultural, farming

agravante [aɣra'βante] *adj* aggravating ♦ *nm*: **con el ~ de que ...** with the further difficulty that ...

agravar [aɣra'ßar] vt (pesar sobre) to make heavier; (irritar) to aggravate; **~se** vr to worsen, get worse

agraviar [aɣra'ßjar] vt to offend; (ser injusto con) to wrong; **~se** vr to take offence; **agravio** nm offence; wrong; (JUR) grievance

agredir [aɣre'ðir] vt to attack

agregado, a [aɣre'ɣaðo, a] nm/f: **A~** ≈ teacher (who is not head of department) ♦ nm aggregate; (persona) attaché

agregar [aɣre'ɣar] vt to gather; (añadir) to add; (persona) to appoint

agresión [aɣre'sjon] nf aggression

agresivo, a [aɣre'sißo, a] adj aggressive

agriar [a'ɣrjar] vt to (turn) sour; **~se** vr to turn sour

agrícola [a'ɣrikola] adj farming cpd, agricultural

agricultor, a [aɣrikul'tor, a] nm/f farmer

agricultura [aɣrikul'tura] nf agriculture, farming

agridulce [aɣri'ðulθe] adj bittersweet; (CULIN) sweet and sour

agrietarse [aɣrje'tarse] vr to crack; (piel) to chap

agrimensor, a [aɣrimen'sor, a] nm/f surveyor

agrio, a [a'ɣrjo, a] adj bitter

agrupación [aɣrupa'θjon] nf group; (acto) grouping

agrupar [aɣru'par] vt to group

agua ['aɣwa] nf water; (NAUT) wake; (ARQ) slope of a roof; **~s** nfpl (de piedra) water sg, sparkle sg; (MED) water sg, urine sg; (NAUT) waters; **~s abajo/arriba** downstream/ upstream; **~ bendita/destilada/potable** holy/ distilled/drinking water; **~ caliente** hot water; **~ corriente** running water; **~ de colonia** eau de cologne; **~ mineral (con/sin gas)** (carbonated/uncarbonated) mineral water; **~ oxigenada** hydrogen peroxide; **~s jurisdiccionales** territorial waters

aguacate [aɣwa'kate] nm avocado (pear)

aguacero [aɣwa'θero] nm (heavy) shower, downpour

aguado, a [a'ɣwaðo, a] adj watery, watered down

aguafiestas [aɣwa'fjestas] nm/f inv spoilsport, killjoy

aguanieve [aɣwa'njeße] nf sleet

aguantar [aɣwan'tar] vt to bear, put up with; (sostener) to hold up ♦ vi to last; **~se** vr to restrain o.s.; **aguante** nm (paciencia) patience; (resistencia) endurance

aguar [a'ɣwar] vt to water down

aguardar [aɣwar'ðar] vt to wait for

aguardiente [aɣwar'ðjente] nm brandy, liquor

aguarrás [aɣwa'rras] nm turpentine

agudeza [aɣu'ðeθa] nf sharpness; (ingenio) wit

agudizar [aɣuði'θar] vt (crisis) to make worse; **~se** vr to get worse

agudo, a [a'ɣuðo, a] adj sharp; (voz) high-pitched, piercing; (dolor, enfermedad) acute

agüero [a'ɣwero] nm: **buen/mal ~** good/bad omen

aguijón [aɣi'xon] nm sting; (fig) spur

águila ['aɣila] nf eagle; (fig) genius

aguileño, a [aɣi'leɲo, a] adj (nariz) aquiline; (rostro) sharp-featured

aguinaldo [aɣi'naldo] nm Christmas box

aguja [a'ɣuxa] nf needle; (de reloj) hand; (ARQ) spire; (TEC) firing-pin; **~s** nfpl (ZOOL) ribs; (FERRO) points

agujerear [aɣuxere'ar] vt to make holes in

agujero [aɣu'xero] nm hole

agujetas [aɣu'xetas] nfpl stitch sg; (rigidez) stiffness sg

aguzar [aɣu'θar] vt to sharpen; (fig) to incite

ahí [a'i] adv there; **de ~ que** so that, with the result that; **~ llega** here he comes; **por ~** that way; (allá) over there; **200 o por ~** 200 or so

ahijado, a [ai'xaðo, a] nm/f godson/daughter

ahínco [a'inko] nm earnestness

ahogar [ao'ɣar] vt to drown; (asfixiar) to suffocate, smother; (fuego) to put out; **~se** vr (en el agua) to drown; (por asfixia) to suffocate

ahogo [a'oɣo] nm breathlessness; (fig) financial difficulty

ahondar [aon'dar] vt to deepen, make deeper; (fig) to study thoroughly ♦ vi: **~ en** to study thoroughly

ahora [a'ora] adv now; (hace poco) a moment ago, just now; (dentro de poco) in a moment; **~ voy** I'm coming; **~ mismo** right now; **~ bien** now then; **por ~** for the present

ahorcar [aor'kar] vt to hang

ahorita [ao'rita] (fam: esp AM) adv right now

ahorrar [ao'rrar] vt (dinero) to save; (esfuerzos) to save, avoid; **ahorro** nm (acto) saving; **ahorros** nmpl (dinero) savings

ahuecar [awe'kar] vt to hollow (out); (voz) to deepen; **~se** vr to give o.s. airs

ahumar [au'mar] vt to smoke, cure; (llenar de humo) to fill with smoke ♦ vi to smoke; **~se** vr to fill with smoke

ahuyentar [aujen'tar] vt to drive off, frighten off; (fig) to dispel

airado, a [ai'raðo, a] adj angry

airar [ai'rar] vt to anger; **~se** vr to get angry

aire ['aire] nm air; (viento) wind; (corriente) draught; (MUS) tune; **~s** nmpl: **darse ~s** to give o.s. airs; **al ~ libre** in the open air; **~ acondicionado** air conditioning; **airearse** (persona) to go out for a breath of fresh air;

airoso, a adj windy; draughty; (fig) graceful

aislado, a [ais'laðo, a] adj isolated; (incomunicado) cut-off; (ELEC) insulated

aislar [ais'lar] vt to isolate; (ELEC) to insulate

ajardinado, a [axarði'naðo, a] adj landscaped

ajedrez |axe'ðreθ| nm chess

ajeno, a [a'xeno, a] adj (que pertenece a otro) somebody else's; ~ a foreign to

ajetreado, a [axetre'aðo, a] adj busy

ajetreo [axe'treo] nm bustle

ají [a'xi] (AM) nm chil(l)i, red pepper; (salsa) chil(l)i sauce

ajillo [a'xiʎo] nm: **gambas al ~** garlic prawns

ajo ['axo] nm garlic

ajuar [a'xwar] nm household furnishings pl; (de novia) trousseau; (de niño) layette

ajustado, a [axus'taðo, a] adj (tornillo) tight; (cálculo) right; (ropa) tight(-fitting); (resultado) close

ajustar |axus'tar| vt (adaptar) to adjust; (encajar) to fit; (TEC) to engage; (IMPRENTA) to make up; (apretar) to tighten; (concertar) to agree (on); (reconciliar) to reconcile; (cuentas, deudas) to settle ♦ vi to fit; ~se vr: **~se a** (precio etc) to be in keeping with, fit in with; **~ las cuentas a uno** to get even with sb

ajuste |a'xuste| nm adjustment; (COSTURA) fitting; (acuerdo) compromise; (de cuenta) settlement

al |al| (= a + el) ver a

ala ['ala] nf wing; (de sombrero) brim; (futbolista) winger; **~ delta** nf hang-glider

alabanza [ala'ßanθa] nf praise

alabar |ala'ßar| vt to praise

alacena |ala'θena| nf kitchen cupboard (BRIT), kitchen closet (US)

alacrán |ala'kran| nm scorpion

alambique [alam'bike] nm still

alambrada [alam'braða] nf wire fence; (red) wire netting

alambrado [alam'braðo] nm = alambrada

alambre |a'lambre| nm wire; **~ de púas** barbed wire

alameda [ala'meða] nf (plantío) poplar grove; (lugar de paseo) avenue, boulevard

álamo ['alamo] nm poplar; **~ temblón** aspen

alarde |a'larðe| nm show, display; **hacer ~ de** to boast of

alargador [alarxa'ðor] nm (ELEC) extension lead

alargar |alar'xar| vt to lengthen, extend; (paso) to hasten; (brazo) to stretch out; (cuerda) to pay out; (conversación) to spin out; **~se** vr to get longer

alarido |ala'riðo| nm shriek

alarma |a'larma| nf alarm

alarmar vt to alarm; **~se** to get alarmed; **alarmante** |alar'mante| adj alarming

alba ['alßa] nf dawn

albacea [alßa'θea] nm/f executor/executrix

albahaca [al'ßaka] nf basil

Albania [al'ßanja] nf Albania

albañil [alßa'ɲil] nm bricklayer; (cantero) mason

albarán [alßa'ran] nm (COM) delivery note, invoice

albaricoque [alßari'koke] nm apricot

albedrío [alße'ðrio] nm: **libre ~** free will

alberca [al'ßerka] nf reservoir; (AM) swimming pool

albergar [alßer'var] vt to shelter

albergue etc [al'ßerve] vb ver **albergar** ♦ nm shelter, refuge; **~ juvenil** youth hostel

albóndiga [al'ßondixa] nf meatball

albornoz [alßor'noθ] nm (de los árabes) burnous; (para el baño) bathrobe

alborotar [alßoro'tar] vi to make a row ♦ vt to agitate, stir up; **~se** vr to get excited; (mar) to get rough; **alboroto** nm row, uproar

alborozar [alßoro'θar] vt to gladden; **~se** vr to rejoice

alborozo [alßo'roθo] nm joy

álbum [al'ßum] (pl **~s**, **~es**) nm album; **~ de recortes** scrapbook

alcachofa [alka'tʃofa] nf artichoke

alcalde, esa [al'kalde, esa] nm/f mayor(ess)

alcaldía [alkal'dia] nf mayoralty; (lugar) mayor's office

alcance etc [al'ßerve] vb ver **alcanzar** ♦ nm reach; (COM) adverse balance

alcantarilla [alkanta'riʎa] nf (de aguas cloacales) sewer; (en la calle) gutter

alcanzar [alkan'θar] vt (algo: con la mano, el pie) to reach; (alguien: en el camino etc) to catch up with; (autobús) to catch; (suj: bala) to hit, strike ♦ vi (ser suficiente) to be enough; **~ a hacer** to manage to do

alcaparra [alka'parra] nf caper

alcayata [alka'jata] nf hook

alcázar [al'kaθar] nm fortress; (NAUT) quarter-deck

alcoba [al'koßa] nf bedroom

alcohol [al'kol] nm alcohol; **~ metílico** methylated spirits pl (BRIT), wood alcohol (US); **alcohólico, a** adj, nm/f alcoholic

alcoholímetro [alko'limetro] nm Breathalyser ® (BRIT), drunkometer (US)

alcoholismo [alko'lismo] nm alcoholism

alcornoque [alkor'noke] nm cork tree; (fam) idiot

alcurnia [al'kurnja] nf lineage

aldaba [al'daßa] nf (door) knocker

aldea [al'dea] nf village; **~no, a** adj village cpd ♦ nm/f villager

aleación [alea'θjon] nf alloy

aleatorio, a [alea'torjo, a] adj random

aleccionar [alekθjo'nar] vt to instruct; (adiestrar) to train

alegación [aleɣa'θjon] nf allegation

alegar [ale'ɣar] vt to claim; (JUR) to plead ♦ vi (AM) to argue

alegato [ale'ɣato] nm (JUR) allegation; (AM) argument

alegoría [aleɣo'ria] nf allegory

alegrar [ale'ɣrar] vt (causar alegría) to cheer (up); (fuego) to poke; (fiesta) to liven up; ~se vr (fam) to get merry o tight; ~se de to be glad about

alegre [a'leɣre] adj happy, cheerful; (fam) merry, tight; (chiste) risqué, blue; **alegría** nf happiness; merriment

alejamiento [alexa'mjento] nm removal; (distancia) remoteness

alejar [ale'xar] vt to remove; (fig) to estrange; ~se vr to move away

alemán, ana [ale'man, ana] adj, nm/f German ♦ nm (LING) German

Alemania [ale'manja] nf: ~ Occidental/ Oriental West/East Germany

alentador, a [alenta'ðor, a] adj encouraging

alentar [alen'tar] vt to encourage

alergia [a'lerxja] nf allergy

alero [a'lero] nm (de tejado) eaves pl; (de carruaje) mudguard

alerta [a'lerta] adj, nm alert

aleta [a'leta] nf (de pez) fin; (de ave) wing; (de foca, DEPORTE) flipper; (AUTO) mudguard

aletargar [aletar'ɣar] vt to make drowsy; (entumecer) to make numb; ~se vr to grow drowsy; to become numb

aletear [alete'ar] vi to flutter

alevín [ale'ßin] nm fry, young fish

alevosía [aleßo'sia] nf treachery

alfabeto [alfa'ßeto] nm alphabet

alfalfa [al'falfa] nf alfalfa, lucerne

alfarería [alfare'ria] nf pottery; (tienda) pottery shop; **alfarero, a** nm/f potter

alféizar [al'feiθar] nm window-sill

alférez [al'fereθ] nm (MIL) second lieutenant; (NAUT) ensign

alfil [al'fil] nm (AJEDREZ) bishop

alfiler [alfi'ler] nm pin; (broche) clip; **alfiletero** nm needlecase

alfombra [al'fombra] nf carpet; (más pequeña) rug; **alfombrar** vt to carpet; **alfombrilla** nf rug, mat; (INFORM) mouse mat o pad

alforja [al'forxa] nf saddlebag

algarabía [alɣara'ßia] (fam) nf gibberish; (griterío) hullabaloo

algas ['alɣas] nfpl seaweed

álgebra ['alxeßra] nf algebra

álgido, a ['alxiðo, a] adj (momento etc) crucial, decisive

algo ['alɣo] pron something; anything ♦ adv somewhat, rather; ¿~ más? anything else?; (en tienda) is that all?; por ~ será there must be some reason for it

algodón [alɣo'ðon] nm cotton; (planta) cotton plant; ~ de azúcar candy floss (BRIT), cotton candy (US); ~ hidrófilo cotton wool (BRIT), absorbent cotton (US)

algodonero, a [alɣoðo'nero, a] adj cotton cpd ♦ nm/f cotton grower ♦ nm cotton plant

alguacil [alɣwa'θil] nm bailiff; (TAUR) mounted official

alguien ['alɣjen] pron someone, somebody; (en frases interrogativas) anyone, anybody

alguno, a [al'ɣuno, a] adj (delante de nm: algún) some; (después de n): no tiene talento ~ he has no talent, he doesn't have any talent ♦ pron (alguien) someone, somebody; algún que otro libro some book or other; algún día iré I'll go one o some day; sin interés ~ without the slightest interest; ~ que otro occasional one; ~s piensan some (people) think

alhaja [a'laxa] nf jewel; (tesoro) precious object, treasure

alhelí [ale'li] nm wallflower, stock

aliado, a [a'ljaðo, a] adj allied

alianza [a'ljanθa] nf alliance; (anillo) wedding ring

aliar [a'ljar] vt to ally; ~se vr to form an alliance

alias ['aljas] adv alias

alicates [ali'kates] nmpl pliers; ~ de uñas nail clippers

aliciente [ali'θjente] nm incentive; (atracción) attraction

alienación [aljena'θjon] nf alienation

aliento [a'ljento] nm breath; (respiración) breathing; sin ~ breathless

aligerar [alixe'rar] vt to lighten; (reducir) to shorten; (aliviar) to alleviate; (mitigar) to ease; (paso) to quicken

alijo [a'lixo] nm consignment

alimaña [ali'maɲa] nf pest

alimentación [alimenta'θjon] nf (comida) food; (acción) feeding; (tienda) grocer's (shop); **alimentador** nm: alimentador de papel sheet-feeder

alimentar [alimen'tar] vt to feed; (nutrir) to nourish; ~se vr to feed

alimenticio, a [alimen'tiθjo, a] adj food cpd; (nutritivo) nourishing, nutritious

alimento [ali'mento] nm food; (nutrición) nourishment

alineación [alinea'θjon] nf alignment; (DEPORTE) line-up

alinear [aline'ar] vt to align; ~se vr (DEPORTE) to line up; ~se en to fall in with

aliñar [ali'ɲar] vt (CULIN) to season; **aliño** nm (CULIN) dressing

alioli [ali'oli] *nm* garlic mayonnaise

alisar [ali'sar] *vt* to smooth

aliso [a'liso] *nm* alder

alistarse [alis'tarse] *vr* to enlist; (*inscribirse*) to enrol

aliviar [ali'βjar] *vt* (*carga*) to lighten; (*persona*) to relieve; (*dolor*) to relieve, alleviate

alivio [a'lißjo] *nm* alleviation, relief

aljibe [al'xiße] *nm* cistern

allá [a'ʎa] *adv* (*lugar*) there; (*por ahí*) over there; (*tiempo*) then; ~ **abajo** down there; **más** ~ further on; **más** ~ **de** beyond; **¡~ tú!** that's your problem!

allanamiento [aʎana'mjento] *nm*: ~ **de morada** burglary

allanar [aʎa'nar] *vt* to flatten, level (out); (*igualar*) to smooth (out); (*fig*) to subdue; (*JUR*) to burgle, break into

allegado, a [aʎe'ɣaðo, a] *adj* near, close ♦ *nm/f* relation

allí [a'ʎi] *adv* there; ~ **mismo** right there; **por** ~ over there; (*por ese camino*) that way

alma ['alma] *nf* soul; (*persona*) person

almacén [alma'θen] *nm* (*depósito*) warehouse, store; (*MIL*) magazine; (*AM*) shop; (**grandes**) **almacenes** *nmpl* department store *sg*; **almacenaje** *nm* storage

almacenar [almaθe'nar] *vt* to store, put in storage; (*proveerse*) to stock up with; **almacenero** *nm* (*AM*) shopkeeper

almanaque [alma'nake] *nm* almanac

almeja [al'mexa] *nf* clam

almendra [al'mendra] *nf* almond; **almendro** *nm* almond tree

almíbar [al'mißar] *nm* syrup

almidón [almi'ðon] *nm* starch; **almidonar** *vt* to starch

almirante [almi'rante] *nm* admiral

almirez [almi'reθ] *nm* mortar

almizcle [al'miθkle] *nm* musk

almohada [almo'aða] *nf* pillow; (*funda*) pillowcase; **almohadilla** *nf* cushion; (*TEC*) pad; (*AM*) pincushion

almohadón [almoa'ðon] *nm* large pillow; bolster

almorranas [almo'rranas] *nfpl* piles, haemorrhoids

almorzar [almor'θar] *vt*: ~ **una tortilla** to have an omelette for lunch ♦ *vi* to (have) lunch

almuerzo *etc* [al'mwerθo] *vb ver* **almorzar** ♦ *nm* lunch

alocado, a [alo'kaðo, a] *adj* crazy

alojamiento [aloxa'mjento] *nm* lodging(s) (*pl*); (*viviendas*) housing

alojar [alo'xar] *vt* to lodge; ~**se** *vr* to lodge, stay

alondra [a'londra] *nf* lark, skylark

alpargata [alpar'ɣata] *nf* rope-soled sandal, espadrille

Alpes ['alpes] *nmpl*: **los** ~ the Alps

alpinismo [alpi'nismo] *nm* mountaineering, climbing; **alpinista** *nm/f* mountaineer, climber

alpiste [al'piste] *nm* birdseed

alquilar [alki'lar] *vt* (*suj: propietario: inmuebles*) to let, rent (out); (: *coche*) to hire out; (: *TV*) to rent (out); (*suj: alquilador: inmuebles, TV*) to rent; (: *coche*) to hire; "**se alquila casa**" "house to let (*BRIT*) o for rent (*US*)"

alquiler [alki'ler] *nm* renting; letting; hiring; (*arriendo*) rent; hire charge; ~ **de automóviles** car hire; **de** ~ for hire

alquimia [al'kimja] *nf* alchemy

alquitrán [alki'tran] *nm* tar

alrededor [alreðe'ðor] *adv* around, about; ~ **de** around, about; **mirar a su** ~ to look (round) about one; ~**es** *nmpl* surroundings

alta ['alta] *nf* (certificate of) discharge; **dar de** ~ to discharge

altanería [altane'ria] *nf* haughtiness, arrogance; **altanero, a** *adj* arrogant, haughty

altar [al'tar] *nm* altar

altavoz [alta'ßoθ] *nm* loudspeaker; (*amplificador*) amplifier

alteración [altera'θjon] *nf* alteration; (*alboroto*) disturbance

alterar [alte'rar] *vt* to alter; to disturb; ~**se** *vr* (*persona*) to get upset

altercado [alter'kaðo] *nm* argument

alternar [alter'nar] *vt* to alternate ♦ *vi* to alternate; (*turnar*) to take turns; ~**se** *vr* to alternate; to take turns; ~ **con** to mix with; **alternativa** *nf* alternative; (*elección*) choice; **alternativo, a** *adj* alternative; (*alterno*) alternating; **alterno, a** *adj* alternate; (*ELEC*) alternating

Alteza [al'teθa] *nf* (*tratamiento*) Highness

altibajos [alti'ßaxos] *nmpl* ups and downs

altiplanicie [altipla'niθje] *nf* high plateau

altiplano [alti'plano] *nm* = **altiplanicie**

altisonante [altiso'nante] *adj* high-flown, high-sounding

altitud [alti'tuð] *nf* height; (*AVIAT, GEO*) altitude

altivez [alti'ßeθ] *nf* haughtiness, arrogance; **altivo, a** *adj* haughty, arrogant

alto, a ['alto, a] *adj* high; (*persona*) tall; (*sonido*) high, sharp; (*noble*) high, lofty ♦ *nm* halt; (*MUS*) alto; (*GEO*) hill; (*AM*) pile ♦ *adv* (*de sitio*) high; (*de sonido*) loud, loudly ♦ *excl* halt!; **la pared tiene 2 metros de** ~ the wall is 2 metres high; **en alta mar** on the high seas; **en voz alta** in a loud voice; **las altas horas de la noche** the small o wee hours; **en lo** ~ **de** at

the top of; **pasar por ~** to overlook
altoparlante [altopar'lante] (AM) nm
loudspeaker
altruismo [altru'ismo] nm altruism
altura [al'tura] nf height; (NAUT) depth; (GEO)
latitude; **la pared tiene 1.80 de ~** the wall is 1
metre 80cm high; **a estas ~s** at this stage; **a
estas ~s del año** at this time of the year
alubia [a'luβja] nf bean
alucinación [aluθina'θjon] nf hallucination
alucinar [aluθi'nar] vi to hallucinate ♦ vt to
deceive; (fascinar) to fascinate
alud [a'luð] nm avalanche; (fig) flood
aludir [alu'ðir] vi: **~ a** to allude to; **darse por
aludido** to take the hint
alumbrado [alum'braðo] nm lighting;
alumbramiento nm lighting; (MED)
childbirth, delivery
alumbrar [alum'brar] vt to light (up) ♦ vi
(MED) to give birth
aluminio [alu'minjo] nm aluminium (BRIT),
aluminum (US)
alumno, a [a'lumno, a] nm/f pupil, student
alunizar [aluni'θar] vi to land on the moon
alusión [alu'sjon] nf allusion
alusivo, a [alu'siβo, a] adj allusive
aluvión [aluβ'jon] nm alluvium; (fig) flood
alverja [al'ßerxa] (AM) nf pea
alza ['alθa] nf rise; (MIL) sight
alzada [al'θaða] nf (de caballos) height; (JUR)
appeal
alzamiento [alθa'mjento] nm (rebelión)
rising
alzar [al'θar] vt to lift (up); (precio, muro) to
raise; (cuello de abrigo) to turn up; (AGR) to
gather in; (IMPRENTA) to gather; **~se** vr to get
up, rise; (rebelarse) to revolt; (COM) to go
fraudulently bankrupt; (JUR) to appeal
ama ['ama] nf lady of the house; (dueña)
owner; (institutriz) governess; (madre
adoptiva) foster mother; **~ de casa** housewife;
~ de llaves housekeeper
amabilidad [amaßili'ðað] nf kindness;
(simpatía) niceness; **amable** adj kind; nice;
es usted muy amable that's very kind of you
amaestrado, a [amaes'traðo, a] adj
(animal: en circo etc) performing
amaestrar [amaes'trar] vt to train
amago [a'mayo] nm threat; (gesto)
threatening gesture; (MED) symptom
amainar [amai'nar] vi (viento) to die down
amalgama [amal'yama] nf amalgam;
amalgamar vt to amalgamate; (combinar)
to combine, mix
amamantar [amaman'tar] vt to suckle,
nurse
amanecer [amane'θer] vi to dawn ♦ nm
dawn; **~ afiebrado** to wake up with a fever
amanerado, a [amane'raðo, a] adj affected

amansar [aman'sar] vt to tame; (persona) to
subdue; **~se** vr (persona) to calm down
amante [a'mante] adj: **~ de** fond of ♦ nm/f
lover
amapola [ama'pola] nf poppy
amar [a'mar] vt to love
amargado, a [amar'yaðo, a] adj bitter
amargar [amar'yar] vt to make bitter; (fig) to
embitter; **~se** vr to become embittered
amargo, a [a'maro, a] adj bitter;
amargura nf bitterness
amarillento, a [amari'ʎento, a] adj
yellowish; (tez) sallow; **amarillo, a** adj, nm
yellow
amarrar [ama'rrar] vt to moor; (sujetar) to
tie up
amarras [a'marras] nfpl: **soltar ~** to set sail
amasar [ama'sar] vt (masa) to knead;
(mezclar) to mix, prepare; (confeccionar) to
concoct; **amasijo** nm kneading; mixing;
(fig) hotchpotch
amateur ['amatur] nm/f amateur
amazona [ama'θona] nf horsewoman; **A~s**
nm: **el A~s** the Amazon
ambages [am'baxes] nmpl: **sin ~** in plain
language
ámbar ['ambar] nm amber
ambición [ambi'θjon] nf ambition;
ambicionar vt to aspire to; **ambicioso, a**
adj ambitious
ambidextro, a [ambi'ðekstro, a] adj
ambidextrous
ambientación [ambjenta'θjon] nf (CINE,
TEATRO etc) setting; (RADIO) sound effects
ambiente [am'bjente] nm (tb fig)
atmosphere; (medio) environment
ambigüedad [ambiɣwe'ðað] nf ambiguity;
ambiguo, a adj ambiguous
ámbito ['ambito] nm (campo) field; (fig)
scope
ambos, as ['ambos, as] adj pl, pron pl both
ambulancia [ambu'lanθja] nf ambulance
ambulante [ambu'lante] adj travelling cpd,
itinerant
ambulatorio [ambula'torio] nm state
health-service clinic
amedrentar [ameðren'tar] vt to scare
amén [a'men] excl amen; **~ de** besides
amenaza [ame'naθa] nf threat
amenazar [amena'θar] vt to threaten ♦ vi:
~ con hacer to threaten to do
amenidad [ameni'ðað] nf pleasantness
ameno, a [a'meno, a] adj pleasant
América [a'merika] nf America; **~ del Norte/
del Sur** North/South America; **~ Central/
Latina** Central/Latin America; **americana** nf
coat, jacket; ver tb **americano**; **americano, a**
adj, nm/f American
amerizar [ameri'θar] vi (avión) to land (on

the sea)

ametralladora [ametraʎaˈðora] nf machine gun

amianto [aˈmjanto] nm asbestos

amigable [amiˈɣaßle] adj friendly

amígdala [aˈmiɣðala] nf tonsil; **amigdalitis** nf tonsillitis

amigo, a [aˈmiɣo, a] adj friendly ♦ nm/f friend; (amante) lover; **ser ~ de algo** to be fond of sth; **ser muy ~s** to be close friends

amilanar [amilaˈnar] vt to scare; **~se** vr to get scared

aminorar [aminoˈrar] vt to diminish; (reducir) to reduce; **~ la marcha** to slow down

amistad [amisˈtað] nf friendship; **~es** nfpl (amigos) friends; **amistoso, a** adj friendly

amnesia [amˈnesja] nf amnesia

amnistía [amnisˈtia] nf amnesty

amo [ˈamo] nm owner; (jefe) boss

amodorrarse [amoðoˈrrarse] vr to get sleepy

amoldar [amolˈdar] vt to mould; (adaptar) to adapt

amonestación [amonestaˈθjon] nf warning; **amonestaciones** nfpl (REL) marriage banns

amonestar [amonesˈtar] vt to warn; (REL) to publish the banns of

amontonar [amontoˈnar] vt to collect, pile up; **~se** vr to crowd together; (acumularse) to pile up

amor [aˈmor] nm love; (amante) lover; **hacer el ~** to make love; **~ propio** self-respect

amoratado, a [amoraˈtaðo, a] adj purple

amordazar [amorðaˈθar] vt to muzzle; (fig) to gag

amorfo, a [aˈmorfo, a] adj amorphous, shapeless

amoroso, a [amoˈroso, a] adj affectionate, loving

amortajar [amortaˈxar] vt to shroud

amortiguador [amortiɣwaˈðor] nm shock absorber; (parachoques) bumper; **~es** nmpl (AUTO) suspension sg

amortiguar [amortiˈɣwar] vt to deaden; (ruido) to muffle; (color) to soften

amortización [amortiθaˈθjon] nf (de deuda) repayment; (de bono) redemption

amotinar [amotiˈnar] vt to stir up, incite (to riot); **~se** vr to mutiny

amparar [ampaˈrar] vt to protect; **~se** vr to seek protection; (de la lluvia etc) to shelter; **amparo** nm help, protection; **al amparo de** under the protection of

amperio [amˈperjo] nm ampère, amp

ampliación [ampljaˈθjon] nf enlargement; (extensión) extension

ampliar [amˈpljar] vt to enlarge; to extend

amplificación [amplifikaˈθjon] nf enlargement; **amplificador** nm amplifier

amplificar [amplifiˈkar] vt to amplify

amplio, a [ˈampljo, a] adj spacious; (de falda etc) full; (extenso) extensive; (ancho) wide; **amplitud** nf spaciousness; extent; (fig) amplitude

ampolla [amˈpoʎa] nf blister; (MED) ampoule

ampuloso, a [ampuˈloso, a] adj bombastic, pompous

amputar [ampuˈtar] vt to cut off, amputate

amueblar [amweˈßlar] vt to furnish

amurallar [amuraˈʎar] vt to wall up o in

anacronismo [anakroˈnismo] nm anachronism

anales [aˈnales] nmpl annals

analfabetismo [analfaßeˈtismo] nm illiteracy; **analfabeto, a** adj, nm/f illiterate

analgésico [analˈxesiko] nm painkiller, analgesic

análisis [aˈnalisis] nm inv analysis

analista [anaˈlista] nm/f (gen) analyst

analizar [analiˈθar] vt to analyse

analogía [analoˈxia] nf analogy

analógico, a [anaˈloxiko, a] adj (INFORM) analog; (reloj) analogue (BRIT), analog (US)

análogo, a [aˈnaloɣo, a] adj analogous, similar

ananá(s) [anaˈna(s)] (AM) nm pineapple

anaquel [anaˈkel] nm shelf

anarquía [anarˈkia] nf anarchy; **anarquismo** nm anarchism; **anarquista** nm/f anarchist

anatomía [anatoˈmia] nf anatomy

anca [ˈanka] nf rump, haunch; **~s** nfpl (fam) behind sg

ancho, a [ˈantʃo, a] adj wide; (falda) full; (fig) liberal ♦ nm width; (FERRO) gauge; **ponerse ~** to get conceited; **estar a sus anchas** to be at one's ease

anchoa [anˈtʃoa] nf anchovy

anchura [anˈtʃura] nf width; (extensión) wideness

anciano, a [anˈθjano, a] adj old, aged ♦ nm/f old man/woman; elder

ancla [ˈankla] nf anchor; **~dero** nm anchorage; **anclar** vi to (drop) anchor

andadura [andaˈðura] nf gait; (de caballo) pace

Andalucía [andaluˈθia] nf Andalusia; **andaluz, a** adj, nm/f Andalusian

andamiaje [andaˈmjaxe] nm = **andamio**

andamio [anˈdamjo] nm scaffold(ing)

andar [anˈdar] vt to go, cover, travel ♦ vi to go, walk, travel; (funcionar) to go, work; (estar) to be ♦ nm walk, gait, pace; **~se** vr to go away; **~ a pie/a caballo/en bicicleta** to go on foot/on horseback/by bicycle; **~ haciendo algo** to be doing sth; **¡anda!** (sorpresa) come on!; **anda por o en los 40** he's about 40

andén [anˈden] nm (FERRO) platform; (NAUT) quayside; (AM: de la calle) pavement (BRIT),

1

sidewalk (US)

Andes ['andes] nmpl: **los ~** the Andes

Andorra [an'dorra] nf Andorra

andrajo [an'draxo] nm rag; **~so, a** adj ragged

anduve etc [an'duße] vb ver **andar**

anécdota [a'nekðota] nf anecdote, story

anegar [ane'xar] vt to flood; (ahogar) to drown; **~se** vr to drown; (hundirse) to sink

anejo, a [a'nexo, a] adj, nm = **anexo**

anemia [a'nemja] nf anaemia

anestesia [anes'tesja] nf (sustancia) anaesthetic; (proceso) anaesthesia

anexar [anek'sar] vt to annex; (documento) to attach; **anexión** nf annexation; **anexionamiento** nm annexation; **anexo, a** adj attached ♦ nm annexe

anfibio, a [an'fißjo, a] adj amphibious ♦ nm amphibian

anfiteatro [anfite'atro] nm amphitheatre; (TEATRO) dress circle

anfitrión, ona [anfi'trjon, ona] nm/f host(ess)

ángel ['anxel] nm angel; **~ de la guarda** guardian angel; **tener ~** to be charming; **angelical** adj, **angélico, a** adj angelic(al)

angina [an'xina] nf (MED) inflammation of the throat; **~ de pecho** angina; **tener ~s** to have tonsillitis

anglicano, a [angli'kano, a] adj, nm/f Anglican

anglosajón, ona [anglosa'xon, ona] adj Anglo-Saxon

angosto, a [an'gosto, a] adj narrow

anguila [an'gila] nf eel

angula [an'gula] nf elver, baby eel

ángulo ['angulo] nm angle; (esquina) corner; (curva) bend

angustia [an'gustja] nf anguish; **angustiar** vt to distress, grieve

anhelar [ane'lar] vt to be eager for; (desear) to long for, desire ♦ vi to pant, gasp; **anhelo** nm eagerness; desire

anidar [ani'ðar] vi to nest

anillo [a'niʎo] nm ring; **~ de boda** wedding ring

animación [anima'θjon] nf liveliness; (vitalidad) life; (actividad) activity; bustle

animado, a [ani'maðo, a] adj lively; (vivaz) animated; **animador, a** nm/f (TV) host(ess), compère; (DEPORTE) cheerleader

animadversión [animaðßer'sjon] nf ill-will, antagonism

animal [ani'mal] adj animal; (fig) stupid ♦ nm animal; (fig) fool; (bestia) brute

animar [ani'mar] vt (BIO) to animate, give life to; (fig) to liven up, brighten up, cheer up; (estimular) to stimulate; **~se** vr to cheer up; to feel encouraged; (decidirse) to make up

one's mind

ánimo ['animo] nm (alma) soul; (mente) mind; (valentía) courage ♦ excl cheer up!

animoso, a [ani'moso, a] adj brave; (vivo) lively

aniquilar [aniki'lar] vt to annihilate, destroy

anís [a'nis] nm aniseed; (licor) anisette

aniversario [anißer'sarjo] nm anniversary

anoche [a'notʃe] adv last night; **antes de ~** the night before last

anochecer [anotʃe'θer] vi to get dark ♦ nm nightfall, dark; **al ~** at nightfall

anodino, a [ano'ðino, a] adj dull, anodyne

anomalía [anoma'lia] nf anomaly

anonadado, a [anona'ðaðo, a] adj: **estar/quedar/sentirse ~** to be overwhelmed o amazed

anonimato [anoni'mato] nm anonymity

anónimo, a [a'nonimo, a] adj anonymous; (COM) limited ♦ nm (carta) anonymous letter; (: maliciosa) poison-pen letter

anormal [anor'mal] adj abnormal

anotación [anota'θjon] nf note; annotation

anotar [ano'tar] vt to note down; (comentar) to annotate

anquilosamiento [ankilosa'mjento] nm (fig) paralysis; stagnation

anquilosarse [ankilo'sarse] vr (fig: persona) to get out of touch; (método, costumbres) to go out of date

ansia ['ansja] nf anxiety; (añoranza) yearning; **ansiar** vt to long for

ansiedad [ansje'ðað] nf anxiety

ansioso, a [an'sjoso, a] adj anxious; (anhelante) eager; **~ de** o **por algo** greedy for sth

antagónico, a [anta'yoniko, a] adj antagonistic; (opuesto) contrasting; **antagonista** nm/f antagonist

antaño [an'tano] adv long ago, formerly

Antártico [an'tartiko] nm: **el ~** the Antarctic

ante ['ante] prep before, in the presence of; (problema etc) faced with ♦ nm (piel) suede; **~ todo** above all

anteanoche [antea'notʃe] adv the night before last

anteayer [antea'jer] adv the day before yesterday

antebrazo [ante'ßraθo] nm forearm

antecedente [anteθe'ðente] adj previous ♦ nm antecedent; **~s** nmpl (JUR): **~s penales** criminal record; (procedencia) background

anteceder [anteθe'ðer] vt to precede, go before

antecesor, a [anteθe'sor, a] nm/f predecessor

antedicho, a [ante'ðitʃo, a] adj aforementioned

antelación [antela'θjon] nf: **con ~** in

advance

antemano [ante'mano]: **de ~** adv beforehand, in advance

antena [an'tena] nf antenna; (de televisión etc) aerial; **~ parabólica** satellite dish

anteojo [ante'oxo] nm eyeglass; **~s** nmpl (AM) glasses, spectacles

antepasados [antepa'saðos] nmpl ancestors

anteponer [antepo'ner] vt to place in front; (fig) to prefer

anteproyecto [antepro'jekto] nm preliminary sketch; (fig) blueprint

anterior [ante'rjor] adj preceding, previous; **~idad** nf: **con ~idad a** prior to, before

antes ['antes] adv (con prioridad) before ♦ prep: **~ de** before ♦ conj: **~ de ir/de que te vayas** before going/before you go; **~ bien** (but) rather; **dos días ~** two days before o previously; **no quiso venir ~** she didn't want to come any earlier; **tomo el avión ~ que el barco** I take the plane rather than the boat; **~ que yo** before me; **lo ~ posible** as soon as possible; **cuanto ~ mejor** the sooner the better

antiaéreo, a [antia'ereo, a] adj anti-aircraft

antibalas [anti'ßalas] adj inv: **chaleco ~** bullet-proof jacket

antibiótico [anti'ßjotiko] nm antibiotic

anticiclón [antiθi'klon] nm anticyclone

anticipación [antiθipa'θjon] nf anticipation; **con 10 minutos de ~** 10 minutes early

anticipado, a [antiθi'paðo, a] adj (pago) advance; **por ~** in advance

anticipar [antiθi'par] vt to anticipate; (adelantar) to bring forward; (COM) to advance; **~se** vr: **~se a su época** to be ahead of one's time

anticipo [anti'θipo] nm (COM) advance

anticonceptivo, a [antikonθep'tißo, a] adj, nm contraceptive

anticongelante [antikonxe'lante] nm antifreeze

anticuado, a [anti'kwaðo, a] adj out-of-date, old-fashioned; (desusado) obsolete

anticuario [anti'kwarjo] nm antique dealer

anticuerpo [anti'kwerpo] nm (MED) antibody

antidepresivo [antiðepre'sißo] nm antidepressant

antídoto [an'tiðoto] nm antidote

antiestético, a [anties'tetiko, a] adj unsightly

antifaz [anti'faθ] nm mask; (velo) veil

antigualla [anti'ɣwaʎa] nf antique; (reliquia) relic

antiguamente [antiɣwa'mente] adv formerly; (hace mucho tiempo) long ago

antigüedad [antiɣwe'ðað] nf antiquity; (artículo) antique; (rango) seniority

antiguo, a [an'tiɣwo, a] adj old, ancient; (que fue) former

Antillas [an'tiʎas] nfpl: **las ~** the West Indies

antílope [an'tilope] nm antelope

antinatural [antinatu'ral] adj unnatural

antipatía [antipa'tia] nf antipathy, dislike; **antipático, a** adj disagreeable, unpleasant

antirrobo [anti'rroßo] adj inv (alarma etc) anti-theft

antisemita [antise'mita] adj anti-Semitic ♦ nm/f anti-Semite

antiséptico, a [anti'septiko, a] adj antiseptic ♦ nm antiseptic

antítesis [an'titesis] nf inv antithesis

antojadizo, a [antoxa'ðiθo, a] adj capricious

antojarse [anto'xarse] vr (desear): **se me antoja comprarlo** I have a mind to buy it; (pensar): **se me antoja que** I have a feeling that

antojo [an'toxo] nm caprice, whim; (rosa) birthmark; (lunar) mole

antología [antolo'xia] nf anthology

antorcha [an'tortʃa] nf torch

antro ['antro] nm cavern

antropófago, a [antro'pofaxo, a] adj, nm/f cannibal

antropología [antropolo'xia] nf anthropology

anual [a'nwal] adj annual

anuario [a'nwarjo] nm yearbook

anudar [anu'ðar] vt to knot, tie; (unir) to join; **~se** vr to get tied up

anulación [anula'θjon] nf annulment; (cancelación) cancellation

anular [anu'lar] vt (contrato) to annul, cancel; (ley) to revoke, repeal; (suscripción) to cancel ♦ nm ring finger

Anunciación [anunθja'θjon] nf (REL) Annunciation

anunciante [anun'θjante] nm/f (COM) advertiser

anunciar [anun'θjar] vt to announce; (proclamar) to proclaim; (COM) to advertise

anuncio [a'nunθjo] nm announcement; (señal) sign; (COM) advertisement; (cartel) poster

anzuelo [an'θwelo] nm hook; (para pescar) fish hook

añadidura [aɲaði'ðura] nf addition, extra; **por ~** besides, in addition

añadir [aɲa'ðir] vt to add

añejo, a [a'ɲexo, a] adj old; (vino) mellow

añicos [a'ɲikos] nmpl: **hacer ~** to smash, shatter

añil [a'ɲil] nm (BOT, color) indigo

año ['aɲo] nm year; **¡Feliz A~ Nuevo!** Happy New Year!; **tener 15 ~s** to be 15 (years old); **los ~s 90** the nineties; **~ bisiesto/escolar** leap/school year; **el ~ que viene** next year

añoranza [aɲoˈranθa] nf nostalgia; (*anhelo*) longing

apabullar [apaβuˈʎar] vt (*tb fig*) to crush, squash

apacentar [apaθenˈtar] vt to pasture, graze

apacible [apaˈθiβle] adj gentle, mild

apaciguar [apaθiˈɣwar] vt to pacify, calm (down)

apadrinar [apaðriˈnar] vt to sponsor, support; (*REL*) to be godfather to

apagado, a [apaˈɣaðo, a] adj (*volcán*) extinct; (*color*) dull; (*voz*) quiet; (*sonido*) muted, muffled; (*persona: apático*) listless; estar ~ (*fuego, luz*) to be out; (*RADIO, TV etc*) to be off

apagar [apaˈɣar] vt to put out; (*ELEC, RADIO, TV*) to turn off; (*sonido*) to silence, muffle; (*sed*) to quench

apagón [apaˈɣon] nm blackout; power cut

apalabrar [apalaˈβrar] vt to agree to; (*contratar*) to engage

apalear [apaleˈar] vt to beat, thrash

apañar [apaˈnar] vt to pick up; (*asir*) to take hold of, grasp; (*reparar*) to mend, patch up; ~se vr to manage, get along

aparador [aparaˈðor] nm sideboard; (*AM: escaparate*) shop window

aparato [apaˈrato] nm apparatus; (*máquina*) machine; (*doméstico*) appliance; (*boato*) ostentation; ~ de facsímil facsimile (machine), fax; ~ digestivo (*ANAT*) digestive system; ~so, a adj showy, ostentatious

aparcamiento [aparkaˈmjento] nm car park (*BRIT*), parking lot (*US*)

aparcar [aparˈkar] vt, vi to park

aparear [apareˈar] vt (*objetos*) to pair, match; (*animales*) to mate; ~se vr to make a pair; to mate

aparecer [apareˈθer] vi to appear; ~se vr to appear

aparejado, a [apareˈxaðo, a] adj fit, suitable; llevar o traer ~ to involve; **aparejador, a** nm/f (*ARQ*) master builder

aparejo [apaˈrexo] nm harness; rigging; (*de poleas*) block and tackle

aparentar [aparenˈtar] vt (*edad*) to look; (*fingir*): ~ tristeza to pretend to be sad

aparente [apaˈrente] adj apparent; (*adecuado*) suitable

aparezco etc vb ver **aparecer**

aparición [apariˈθjon] nf appearance; (*de libro*) publication; (*espectro*) apparition

apariencia [apaˈrjenθja] nf (*outward*) appearance; en ~ outwardly, seemingly

apartado, a [aparˈtaðo, a] adj separate; (*lejano*) remote ♦ nm (*tipográfico*) paragraph; ~ (**de correos**) post office box

apartamento [apartaˈmento] nm apartment, flat (*BRIT*)

apartamiento [apartaˈmjento] nm separation; (*aislamiento*) remoteness, isolation; (*AM*) apartment, flat (*BRIT*)

apartar [aparˈtar] vt to separate; (*quitar*) to remove; ~se vr to separate, part; (*irse*) to move away; to keep away

aparte [aˈparte] adv (*separadamente*) separately; (*además*) besides ♦ nm aside; (*tipográfico*) new paragraph

aparthotel [apartoˈtel] nm serviced apartments

apasionado, a [apasjoˈnaðo, a] adj passionate

apasionar [apasjoˈnar] vt to excite; **le apasiona el fútbol** she's crazy about football; ~se vr to get excited

apatía [apaˈtia] nf apathy

apático, a [aˈpatiko, a] adj apathetic

Apdo. abr (= *Apartado (de Correos)*) PO Box

apeadero [apeaˈðero] nm halt, stop, stopping place

apearse [apeˈarse] vr (*jinete*) to dismount; (*bajarse*) to get down o out; (*AUTO, FERRO*) to get off o out

apechugar [apetʃuˈɣar] vr: ~ con algo to face up to sth

apedrear [apeðreˈar] vt to stone

apegarse [apeˈɣarse] vr: ~ a to become attached to; **apego** nm attachment, devotion

apelación [apelaˈθjon] nf appeal

apelar [apeˈlar] vi to appeal; ~ a (*fig*) to resort to

apellidar [apeʎiˈðar] vt to call, name; ~se vr: **se apellida Pérez** her (sur)name's Pérez

apellido [apeˈʎiðo] nm surname

apelmazarse [apelmaˈθarse] vr (*masa, arroz*) to go hard; (*prenda de lana*) to shrink

apenar [apeˈnar] vt to grieve, trouble; (*AM: avergonzar*) to embarrass; ~se vr to grieve; (*AM*) to be embarrassed

apenas [aˈpenas] adv scarcely, hardly ♦ conj as soon as, no sooner

apéndice [aˈpendiθe] nm appendix; **apendicitis** nf appendicitis

aperitivo [aperiˈtiβo] nm (*bebida*) aperitif; (*comida*) appetizer

apero [aˈpero] nm (*AGR*) implement; ~s nmpl farm equipment sg

apertura [aperˈtura] nf opening; (*POL*) liberalization

apesadumbrar [apesaðumˈbrar] vt to grieve, sadden; ~se vr to distress o.s.

apestar [apesˈtar] vt to infect ♦ vi: ~ (a) to stink (of)

apetecer [apeteˈθer] vt: ¿te apetece un café? do you fancy a (cup of) coffee?; **apetecible** adj desirable; (*comida*) appetizing

apetito [apeˈtito] nm appetite; ~so, a adj

appetizing; (*fig*) tempting

apiadarse [apja'ðarse] *vr*: ~ **de** to take pity on

ápice ['apiθe] *nm* whit, iota

apilar [api'lar] *vt* to pile o heap up; **~se** *vr* to pile up

apiñarse [api'ɲarse] *vr* to crowd o press together

apio ['apjo] *nm* celery

apisonadora [apisona'ðora] *nf* steamroller

aplacar [apla'kar] *vt* to placate; **~se** *vr* to calm down

aplanar [apla'nar] *vt* to smooth, level; (*allanar*) to roll flat, flatten

aplastante [aplas'tante] *adj* overwhelming; (*lógica*) compelling

aplastar [aplas'tar] *vt* to squash (flat); (*fig*) to crush

aplatanarse [aplata'narse] *vr* to get lethargic

aplaudir [aplau'ðir] *vt* to applaud

aplauso [a'plauso] *nm* applause; (*fig*) approval, acclaim

aplazamiento [aplaθa'mjento] *nm* postponement

aplazar [apla'θar] *vt* to postpone, defer

aplicación [aplika'θjon] *nf* application; (*esfuerzo*) effort

aplicado, a [apli'kaðo, a] *adj* diligent, hard-working

aplicar [apli'kar] *vt* (*ejecutar*) to apply; **~se** *vr* to apply o.s.

aplique *etc* [a'plike] *vb ver* **aplicar** ♦ *nm* wall light

aplomo [a'plomo] *nm* aplomb, self-assurance

apocado, a [apo'kaðo, a] *adj* timid

apodar [apo'ðar] *vt* to nickname

apoderado [apoðe'raðo] *nm* agent, representative

apoderarse [apoðe'rarse] *vr*: ~ **de** to take possession of

apodo [a'poðo] *nm* nickname

apogeo [apo'xeo] *nm* peak, summit

apolillarse [apoli'ʎarse] *vr* to get moth-eaten

apología [apolo'xia] *nf* eulogy; (*defensa*) defence

apoltronarse [apoltro'narse] *vr* to get lazy

apoplejía [aople'xia] *nf* apoplexy, stroke

apoquinar [apoki'nar] (*fam*) *vt* to fork out, cough up

aporrear [aporre'ar] *vt* to beat (up)

aportar [apor'tar] *vt* to contribute ♦ *vi* to reach port; **~se** *vr* (*AM*: *llegar*) to arrive, come

aposento [apo'sento] *nm* lodging; (*habitación*) room

aposta [a'posta] *adv* deliberately, on purpose

apostar [apos'tar] *vt* to bet, stake; (*tropas etc*) to station, post ♦ *vi* to bet

apóstol [a'postol] *nm* apostle

apóstrofo [a'postrofo] *nm* apostrophe

apoyar [apo'jar] *vt* to lean, rest; (*fig*) to support, back; **~se** *vr*: **~se en** to lean on; **apoyo** *nm* (*gen*) support; backing, help

apreciable [apre'θjaβle] *adj* considerable; (*fig*) esteemed

apreciar [apre'θjar] *vt* to evaluate, assess; (*COM*) to appreciate, value; (*persona*) to respect; (*tamaño*) to gauge, assess; (*detalles*) to notice

aprecio [a'preθjo] *nm* valuation, estimate; (*fig*) appreciation

aprehender [apreen'der] *vt* to apprehend, detain

apremiante [apre'mjante] *adj* urgent, pressing

apremiar [apre'mjar] *vt* to compel, force ♦ *vi* to be urgent, press; **apremio** *nm* urgency

aprender [apren'der] *vt*, *vi* to learn

aprendiz, a [apren'diθ, a] *nm/f* apprentice; (*principiante*) learner; ~ **de conductor** learner driver; **~aje** *nm* apprenticeship

aprensión [apren'sjon] *nm* apprehension, fear; **aprensivo, a** *adj* apprehensive

apresar [apre'sar] *vt* to seize; (*capturar*) to capture

aprestar [apres'tar] *vt* to prepare, get ready; (*TEC*) to prime, size; **~se** *vr* to get ready

apresurado, a [apresu'raðo, a] *adj* hurried, hasty; **apresuramiento** *nm* hurry, haste

apresurar [apresu'rar] *vt* to hurry, accelerate; **~se** *vr* to hurry, make haste

apretado, a [apre'taðo, a] *adj* tight; (*escritura*) cramped

apretar [apre'tar] *vt* to squeeze; (*TEC*) to tighten; (*presionar*) to press together, pack ♦ *vi* to be too tight

apretón [apre'ton] *nm* squeeze; ~ **de manos** handshake

aprieto [a'prjeto] *nm* squeeze; (*dificultad*) difficulty; **estar en un** ~ to be in a fix

aprisa [a'prisa] *adv* quickly, hurriedly

aprisionar [aprisjo'nar] *vt* to imprison

aprobación [aproβa'θjon] *nf* approval

aprobar [apro'βar] *vt* to approve (of); (*examen, materia*) to pass ♦ *vi* to pass

apropiación [apropja'θjon] *nf* appropriation

apropiado, a [apro'pjaðo, a] *adj* appropriate

apropiarse [apro'pjarse] *vr*: ~ **de** to appropriate

aprovechado, a [aproβe'tʃaðo, a] *adj* industrious, hard-working; (*económico*) thrifty; (*pey*) unscrupulous; **aprovechamiento** *nm* use; exploitation

aprovechar [aproβe'tʃar] *vt* to use; (*explotar*) to exploit; (*experiencia*) to profit from; (*oferta, oportunidad*) to take advantage of ♦ *vi* to progress, improve; **~se** *vr*: **~se de** to make use of; to take advantage of; ¡**que aproveche**! enjoy your meal!

aproximación [aproksima'θjon] nf
approximation; (de lotería) consolation prize;
aproximado, a adj approximate

aproximar [aproksi'mar] vt to bring nearer;
~se vr to come near, approach

apruebo etc vb ver **aprobar**

aptitud [apti'tuð] nf aptitude

apto, a ['apto, a] adj suitable

apuesta [a'pwesta] nf bet, wager

apuesto, a [a'pwesto, a] adj neat, elegant

apuntador [apunta'ðor] nm prompter

apuntalar [apunta'lar] vt to prop up

apuntar [apun'tar] vt (con arma) to aim at;
(con dedo) to point at o to; (anotar) to note
(down); (TEATRO) to prompt; **~se** vr (DEPORTE:
tanto, victoria) to score; (ESCOL) to enrol

apunte [a'punte] nm note

apuñalar [apuɲa'lar] vt to stab

apurado, a [apu'raðo, a] adj needy; (difícil)
difficult; (peligroso) dangerous; (AM) hurried,
rushed

apurar [apu'rar] vt (agotar) to drain;
(recursos) to use up; (molestar) to annoy; **~se**
vr (preocuparse) to worry; (darse prisa) to
hurry

apuro [a'puro] nm (aprieto) fix, jam; (escasez)
want, hardship; (vergüenza) embarrassment;
(AM) haste, urgency

aquejado, a [ake'xaðo, a] adj: **~ de** (MED)
afflicted by

aquél, aquélla [a'kel, a'keʎa] (pl **aquéllos,
as**) pron that (one); (pl) those (ones)

aquel, aquella [a'kel, a'keʎa] (pl **aquellos,
as**) adj that; (pl) those

aquello [a'keʎo] pron that, that business

aquí [a'ki] adv (lugar) here; (tiempo) now;
~ arriba up here; **~ mismo** right here; **~ yace**
here lies; **de ~ a siete días** a week from now

aquietar [akje'tar] vt to quieten (down),
calm (down)

ara ['ara] nf: **en ~s de** for the sake of

árabe ['araße] adj, nm/f Arab ♦ nm (LING)
Arabic

Arabia [a'raßja] nf: **~ Saudí** o **Saudita** Saudi
Arabia

arado [a'raðo] nm plough

Aragón [ara'yon] nm Aragon; **aragonés,
esa** adj, nm/f Aragonese

arancel [aran'θel] nm tariff, duty; **~ de
aduanas** customs (duty)

arandela [aran'dela] nf (TEC) washer

araña [a'raɲa] nf (ZOOL) spider; (lámpara)
chandelier

arañar [ara'ɲar] vt to scratch

arañazo [ara'ɲaθo] nm scratch

arar [a'rar] vt to plough, till

arbitraje [arßi'traxe] nm arbitration

arbitrar [arßi'trar] vt to arbitrate in; (DEPORTE)
to referee ♦ vi to arbitrate

arbitrariedad [arßitrarje'ðað] nf
arbitrariness; (acto) arbitrary act; **arbitrario,
a** adj arbitrary

arbitrio [ar'ßitrjo] nm free will; (JUR)
adjudication, decision

árbitro ['arßitro] nm arbitrator; (DEPORTE)
referee; (TENIS) umpire

árbol ['arßol] nm (BOT) tree; (NAUT) mast;
(TEC) axle, shaft; **arbolado, a** adj wooded;
(camino etc) tree-lined ♦ nm woodland

arboleda [arßo'leða] nf grove, plantation

arbusto [ar'ßusto] nm bush, shrub

arca ['arka] nf chest, box

arcada [ar'kaða] nf arcade; (de puente) arch,
span; **~s** nfpl (náuseas) retching sg

arcaico, a [ar'kaiko, a] adj archaic

arce ['arθe] nm maple tree

arcén [ar'θen] nm (de autopista) hard
shoulder; (de carretera) verge

archipiélago [artʃi'pjelaxo] nm archipelago

archivador [artʃißa'ðor] nm filing cabinet

archivar [artʃi'ßar] vt to file (away); **archivo**
nm file, archive(s) (pl)

arcilla [ar'θiʎa] nf clay

arco ['arko] nm arch; (MAT) arc; (MIL, MUS)
bow; **~ iris** rainbow

arder [ar'ðer] vi to burn; **estar que arde**
(persona) to fume

ardid [ar'ðið] nm ploy, trick

ardiente [ar'ðjente] adj burning, ardent

ardilla [ar'ðiʎa] nf squirrel

ardor [ar'ðor] nm (calor) heat; (fig) ardour;
~ de estómago heartburn

arduo, a ['arðwo, a] adj arduous

área ['area] nf area; (DEPORTE) penalty area

arena [a'rena] nf sand; (de una lucha) arena;
~ movedizas quicksand sg

arenal [are'nal] nm (arena movediza)
quicksand

arengar [aren'gar] vt to harangue

arenisca [are'niska] nf sandstone; (cascajo)
grit

arenoso, a [are'noso, a] adj sandy

arenque [a'renke] nm herring

argamasa [arɣa'masa] nf mortar, plaster

Argel [ar'xel] n Algiers; **Argelia** nf Algeria;
argelino, a adj, nm/f Algerian

Argentina [arxen'tina] nf: **(la) ~** Argentina

argentino, a [arxen'tino, a] adj Argentinian;
(de plata) silvery ♦ nm/f Argentinian

argolla [ar'ɣoʎa] nf (large) ring

argot [ar'ɣol] (pl **~s**) nm slang

argucia [ar'ɣuθja] nf subtlety, sophistry

argüir [ar'ɣwir] vt to deduce; (discutir) to
argue; (indicar) to indicate, imply; (censurar)
to reproach ♦ vi to argue

argumentación [arɣumenta'θjon] nf (line
of) argument

argumentar [arɣumen'tar] vt, vi to argue

argumento [arɣu'mento] *nm* argument; (*razonamiento*) reasoning; (*de novela etc*) plot; (*CINE, TV*) storyline

aria ['arja] *nf* aria

aridez [ari'ðeθ] *nf* aridity, dryness

árido, a ['ariðo, a] *adj* arid, dry; ~s *nmpl* (*COM*) dry goods

Aries ['arjes] *nm* Aries

ario, a ['arjo, a] *adj* Aryan

arisco, a [a'risko, a] *adj* surly; (*insociable*) unsociable

aristócrata [aris'tokrata] *nm/f* aristocrat

aritmética [arit'metika] *nf* arithmetic

arma ['arma] *nf* arm; ~s *nfpl* arms; ~ blanca blade, knife; (*espada*) sword; ~ de fuego firearm; ~s cortas small arms

armada [ar'maða] *nf* armada; (*flota*) fleet

armadillo [arma'ðiʎo] *nm* armadillo

armado, a [ar'maðo, a] *adj* armed; (*TEC*) reinforced

armador [arma'ðor] *nm* (*NAUT*) shipowner

armadura [arma'ðura] *nf* (*MIL*) armour; (*TEC*) framework; (*ZOOL*) skeleton; (*FÍSICA*) armature

armamento [arma'mento] *nm* armament; (*NAUT*) fitting-out

armar [ar'mar] *vt* (*soldado*) to arm; (*máquina*) to assemble; (*navío*) to fit out; ~la, ~ un lío to start a row, kick up a fuss

armario [ar'marjo] *nm* wardrobe; (*de cocina, baño*) cupboard

armatoste [arma'toste] *nm* (*mueble*) monstrosity; (*máquina*) contraption

armazón [arma'θon] *nf o m* body, chassis; (*de mueble etc*) frame; (*ARQ*) skeleton

armería [arme'ria] *nf* gunsmith's

armiño [ar'miɲo] *nm* stoat; (*piel*) ermine

armisticio [armis'tiθjo] *nm* armistice

armonía [armo'nia] *nf* harmony

armónica [ar'monika] *nf* harmonica

armonioso, a [armo'njoso, a] *adj* harmonious

armonizar [armoni'θar] *vt* to harmonize; (*diferencias*) to reconcile ♦ *vi*: ~ con (*fig*) to be in keeping with; (*colores*) to tone in with, blend

arnés [ar'nes] *nm* armour; **arneses** *nmpl* (*de caballo etc*) harness *sg*

aro ['aro] *nm* ring; (*tejo*) quoit; (*AM: pendiente*) earring

aroma [a'roma] *nm* aroma, scent

aromático, a [aro'matiko, a] *adj* aromatic

arpa ['arpa] *nf* harp

arpía [ar'pia] *nf* shrew

arpillera [arpi'ʎera] *nf* sacking, sackcloth

arpón [ar'pon] *nm* harpoon

arquear [arke'ar] *vt* to arch, bend; ~se *vr* to arch, bend

arqueología [arkeolo'xia] *nf* archaeology; **arqueólogo, a** *nm/f* archaeologist

arquero [ar'kero] *nm* archer, bowman

arquetipo [arke'tipo] *nm* archetype

arquitecto [arki'tekto] *nm* architect; **arquitectura** *nf* architecture

arrabal [arra'ßal] *nm* suburb; (*AM*) slum; ~es *nmpl* (*afueras*) outskirts

arraigado, a [arrai'ɣaðo, a] *adj* deep-rooted; (*fig*) established

arraigar [arrai'ɣar] *vt* to establish ♦ *vi* to take root; ~se *vr* to take root; (*persona*) to settle

arrancar [arran'kar] *vt* (*sacar*) to extract, pull out; (*arrebatar*) to snatch (away); (*INFORM*) to boot; (*fig*) to extract ♦ *vi* (*AUTO, máquina*) to start; (*ponerse en marcha*) to get going; ~ de to stem from

arranque *etc* [a'rranke] *vb ver* **arrancar** ♦ *nm* sudden start; (*AUTO*) start; (*fig*) fit, outburst

arrasar [arra'sar] *vt* (*aplanar*) to level, flatten; (*destruir*) to demolish

arrastrado, a [arras'traðo, a] *adj* poor, wretched; (*AM*) servile

arrastrar [arras'trar] *vt* to drag (along); (*fig*) to drag down, degrade; (*suj: agua, viento*) to carry away ♦ *vi* to drag, trail on the ground; ~se *vr* to crawl; (*fig*) to grovel; **llevar algo arrastrado** to drag sth along

arrastre [a'rrastre] *nm* drag, dragging

arre ['arre] *excl* gee up!

arrear [arre'ar] *vt* to drive on, urge on ♦ *vi* to hurry along

arrebatado, a [arreßa'taðo, a] *adj* rash, impetuous; (*repentino*) sudden, hasty

arrebatar [arreßa'tar] *vt* to snatch (away), seize; (*fig*) to captivate; ~se *vr* to get carried away, get excited

arrebato [arre'ßato] *nm* fit of rage, fury; (*éxtasis*) rapture

arrecife [arre'θife] *nm* (*tb*: ~ de coral) reef

arredrarse [arre'ðrarse] *vr*: ~ (ante algo) to be intimidated (by sth)

arreglado, a [arre'ɣlaðo, a] *adj* (*ordenado*) neat, orderly; (*moderado*) moderate, reasonable

arreglar [arre'ɣlar] *vt* (*poner orden*) to tidy up; (*algo roto*) to fix, repair; (*problema*) to solve; ~se *vr* to reach an understanding; **arreglárselas** (*fam*) to get by, manage

arreglo [a'rreɣlo] *nm* settlement; (*orden*) order; (*acuerdo*) agreement; (*MUS*) arrangement, setting

arrellanarse [arreʎa'narse] *vr*: ~ en to sit back in/on

arremangar [arreman'gar] *vt* to roll up, turn up; ~se *vr* to roll up one's sleeves

arremeter [arreme'ter] *vi*: ~ contra to attack, rush at

arrendamiento [arrenda'mjento] *nm* letting; (*alquilar*) hiring; (*contrato*) lease; (*alquiler*) rent; **arrendar** *vt* to let, lease; to rent; **arrendatario, a** nm/f tenant

arreos [a'rreos] nmpl (de caballo) harness sg, trappings

arrepentimiento [arrepenti'mjento] nm regret, repentance

arrepentirse [arrepen'tirse] vr to repent; ~ **de** to regret

arrestar [arres'tar] vt to arrest; (encarcelar) to imprison; **arresto** nm arrest; (MIL) detention; (audacia) boldness, daring; **arresto domiciliario** house arrest

arriar [a'rrjar] vt (velas) to haul down; (bandera) to lower, strike; (cable) to pay out

---

PALABRA CLAVE

arriba [a'rriβa] adv **1** (posición) above; **desde** ~ from above; ~ **de todo** at the very top, right on top; **Juan está** ~ Juan is upstairs; **lo** ~ **mencionado** the aforementioned

2 (dirección): **calle** ~ up the street

3: de ~ **abajo** from top to bottom; **mirar a uno de** ~ **abajo** to look sb up and down

4: para ~: **de 5000 pesetas para** ~ from 5000 pesetas up(wards)

♦ adj: **de** ~: **el piso de** ~ the upstairs flat (BRIT) o apartment; **la parte de** ~ the top o upper part

♦ prep: ~ **de** (AM) above; ~ **de 200 dólares** more than 200 dollars

♦ excl: ¡~! up!; ¡**manos** ~! hands up!; ¡~ **España!** long live Spain!

---

arribar [arri'βar] vi to put into port; (llegar) to arrive

arribista [arri'βista] nm/f parvenu(e), upstart

arriendo etc [a'rrjendo] vb ver **arrendar** ♦ nm = **arrendamiento**

arriero [a'rrjero] nm muleteer

arriesgado, a [arrjes'xaðo, a] adj (peligroso) risky; (audaz) bold, daring

arriesgar [arrjes'xar] vt to risk; (poner en peligro) to endanger; ~**se** vr to take a risk

arrimar [arri'mar] vt (acercar) to bring close; (poner de lado) to set aside; ~**se** vr to come close o closer; ~**se a** to lean on

arrinconar [arrinko'nar] vt (colocar) to put in a corner; (enemigo) to corner; (fig) to put on one side; (abandonar) to push aside

arrodillarse [arroði'ʎarse] vr to kneel (down)

arrogancia [arro'xanθja] nf arrogance; **arrogante** adj arrogant

arrojar [arro'xar] vt to throw, hurl; (humo) to emit, give out; (COM) to yield, produce; ~**se** vr to throw o hurl o.s.

arrojo [a'rroxo] nm daring

arrollador, a [arroʎa'ðor, a] adj overwhelming

arrollar [arro'ʎar] vt (AUTO etc) to run over,

knock down; (DEPORTE) to crush

arropar [arro'par] vt to cover, wrap up; ~**se** vr to wrap o.s. up

arroyo [a'rrojo] nm stream; (de la calle) gutter

arroz [a'rroθ] nm rice; ~ **con leche** rice pudding

arruga [a'rruxa] nf (de cara) wrinkle; (de vestido) crease

arrugar [arru'xar] vt to wrinkle; to crease; ~**se** vr to get creased

arruinar [arrwi'nar] vt to ruin, wreck; ~**se** vr to be ruined, go bankrupt

arrullar [arru'ʎar] vi to coo ♦ vt to lull to sleep

arsenal [arse'nal] nm naval dockyard; (MIL) arsenal

arsénico [ar'seniko] nm arsenic

arte [ˈarte] (gen m en sg y siempre f en pl) nm art; (maña) skill, guile; ~**s** nfpl (bellas ~s) arts

artefacto [arte'fakto] nm appliance

arteria [ar'terja] nf artery

artesanía [artesa'nia] nf craftsmanship; (artículos) handicrafts pl; **artesano, a** nm/f artisan, craftsman/woman

ártico, a [ˈartiko, a] adj Arctic ♦ nm: **el Á~** the Arctic

articulación [artikula'θjon] nf articulation; (MED, TEC) joint; **articulado, a** adj articulated; jointed

articular [artiku'lar] vt to articulate; to join together

artículo [ar'tikulo] nm article; (cosa) thing, article; ~**s** nmpl (COM) goods

artífice [ar'tifiθe] nm/f (fig) architect

artificial [artifi'θjal] adj artificial

artificio [arti'fiθjo] nm art, skill; (astucia) cunning

artillería [artiʎe'ria] nf artillery

artillero [arti'ʎero] nm artilleryman, gunner

artilugio [arti'luxjo] nm gadget

artimaña [arti'maɲa] nf trap, snare; (astucia) cunning

artista [ar'tista] nm/f (pintor) artist, painter; (TEATRO) artist, artiste; ~ **de cine** film actor/actress; **artístico, a** adj artistic

artritis [ar'tritis] nf arthritis

arveja [ar'βexa] (AM) nf pea

arzobispo [arθo'βispo] nm archbishop

as [as] nm ace

asa [ˈasa] nf handle; (fig) lever

asado [a'saðo] nm roast (meat); (AM: barbacoa) barbecue

asador [asa'ðor] nm spit

asadura [asa'ðura] nf entrails pl, offal

asalariado, a [asala'rjaðo, a] adj paid, salaried ♦ nm/f wage earner

asaltante [asal'tante] nm/f attacker

asaltar [asal'tar] vt to attack, assault; (fig) to

assail; **asalto** *nm* attack, assault; (*DEPORTE*) round

asamblea [asam'blea] *nf* assembly; (*reunión*) meeting

asar [a'sar] *vt* to roast

asbesto [as'ßesto] *nm* asbestos

ascendencia [asθen'denθja] *nf* ancestry; (*AM*) ascendancy; **de ~ francesa** of French origin

ascender [asθen'der] *vi* (*subir*) to ascend, rise; (*ser promovido*) to gain promotion ♦ *vt* to promote; **~ a** to amount to; **ascendiente** *nm* influence ♦ *nm/f* ancestor

ascensión [asθen'sjon] *nf* ascent; (*REL*): **la A~** the Ascension

ascenso [as'θenso] *nm* ascent; (*promoción*) promotion

ascensor [asθen'sor] *nm* lift (*BRIT*), elevator (*US*)

ascético, a [as'θetiko, a] *adj* ascetic

asco ['asko] *nm*: **¡qué ~!** how revolting o disgusting!; **el ajo me da ~** I hate o loathe garlic; **estar hecho un ~** to be filthy

ascua ['askwa] *nf* ember; **estar en ~s** to be on tenterhooks

aseado, a [ase'aðo, a] *adj* clean; (*arreglado*) tidy; (*pulcro*) smart

asear [ase'ar] *vt* to clean, wash; to tidy (up)

asediar [ase'ðjar] *vt* (*MIL*) to besiege, lay siege to; (*fig*) to chase, pester; **asedio** *nm* siege; (*COM*) run

asegurado, a [aseɣu'raðo, a] *adj* insured

asegurador, a *nm/f* insurer

asegurar [aseɣu'rar] *vt* (*consolidar*) to secure, fasten; (*dar garantía de*) to guarantee; (*preservar*) to safeguard; (*afirmar, dar por cierto*) to assure, affirm; (*tranquilizar*) to reassure; (*tomar un seguro*) to insure; **~se** *vr* to assure o.s., make sure

asemejarse [aseme'xarse] *vr* to be alike; **~ a** to be like, resemble

asentado, a [asen'taðo, a] *adj* established, settled

asentar [asen'tar] *vt* (*sentar*) to seat, sit down; (*poner*) to place, establish; (*alisar*) to level, smooth down o out; (*anotar*) to note down ♦ *vi* to be suitable, suit

aseo [a'seo] *nm* cleanliness; **~s** *nmpl* (*servicios*) toilet *sg* (*BRIT*), cloakroom *sg* (*BRIT*), restroom *sg* (*US*)

aséptico, a [a'septiko, a] *adj* germ-free, free from infection

asequible [ase'kißle] *adj* (*precio*) reasonable; (*meta*) attainable; (*persona*) approachable

aserradero [aserra'ðero] *nm* sawmill; **aserrar** *vt* to saw

asesinar [asesi'nar] *vt* to murder; (*POL*) to

assassinate; **asesinato** *nm* murder; assassination

asesino, a [ase'sino, a] *nm/f* murderer, killer; (*POL*) assassin

asesor, a [ase'sor, a] *nm/f* adviser, consultant

asesorar [aseso'rar] *vt* (*JUR*) to advise, give legal advice to; (*COM*) to act as consultant to; **~se** *vr*: **~se con** o **de** to take advice from, consult; **asesoría** *nf* (*cargo*) consultancy; (*oficina*) consultant's office

asestar [ases'tar] *vt* (*golpe*) to deal, strike

asfalto [as'falto] *nm* asphalt

asfixia [as'fiksja] *nf* asphyxia, suffocation

asfixiar [asfik'sjar] *vt* to asphyxiate, suffocate; **~se** *vr* to be asphyxiated, suffocate

asgo *etc vb ver* **asir**

así [a'si] *adv* (*de esta manera*) in this way, like this, thus; (*aunque*) although; (*tan pronto como*) as soon as; **~ que** so; **~ como** as well as; **~ y todo** even so; **¿no es ~?** isn't it?, didn't you? *etc*; **~ de grande** this big

Asia ['asja] *nf* Asia; **asiático, a** *adj, nm/f* Asian, Asiatic

asidero [asi'ðero] *nm* handle

asiduidad [asiðwi'ðað] *nf* assiduousness; **asiduo, a** *adj* assiduous; (*frecuente*) frequent ♦ *nm/f* regular (customer)

asiento [a'sjento] *nm* (*mueble*) seat, chair; (*de coche, en tribunal etc*) seat; (*localidad*) seat, place; (*fundamento*) site; **~ delantero/trasero** front/back seat

asignación [asiɣna'θjon] *nf* (*atribución*) assignment; (*reparto*) allocation; (*sueldo*) salary; **~ (semanal)** pocket money

asignar [asiɣ'nar] *vt* to assign, allocate

asignatura [asiɣna'tura] *nf* subject; course

asilado, a [asi'laðo, a] *nm/f* inmate; (*POL*) refugee

asilo [a'silo] *nm* (*refugio*) asylum, refuge; (*establecimiento*) home, institution; **~ político** political asylum

asimilación [asimila'θjon] *nf* assimilation

asimilar [asimi'lar] *vt* to assimilate

asimismo [asi'mismo] *adv* in the same way, likewise

asir [a'sir] *vt* to seize, grasp

asistencia [asis'tenθja] *nf* audience; (*MED*) attendance; (*ayuda*) assistance; **asistente** *nm/f* assistant; **los asistentes** those present; **asistente social** social worker

asistido, a [asis'tiðo, a] *adj*: **~ por ordenador** computer-assisted

asistir [asis'tir] *vt* to assist, help ♦ *vi*: **~ a** to attend, be present at

asma ['asma] *nf* asthma

asno ['asno] *nm* donkey; (*fig*) ass

asociación [asoθja'θjon] *nf* association; (*COM*) partnership; **asociado, a** *adj* associate ♦ *nm/f* associate; (*COM*) partner

asociar [aso'θjar] vt to associate

asolar [aso'lar] vt to destroy

asomar [aso'mar] vt to show, stick out ♦ vi to appear; **~se** vr to appear, show up; **~ la cabeza por la ventana** to put one's head out of the window

asombrar [asom'brar] vt to amaze, astonish; **~se** vr (*sorprenderse*) to be amazed; (*asustarse*) to get a fright; **asombro** nm amazement, astonishment; (*susto*) fright; **asombroso, a** adj astonishing, amazing

asomo [a'somo] nm hint, sign

aspa ['aspa] nf (*cruz*) cross; (*de molino*) sail; **en ~** X-shaped

aspaviento [aspa'βjento] nm exaggerated display of feeling; (*fam*) fuss

aspecto [as'pekto] nm (*apariencia*) look, appearance; (*fig*) aspect

aspereza [aspe'reθa] nf roughness; (*agrura*) sourness; (*de carácter*) surliness; **áspero, a** adj rough; bitter, sour; harsh

aspersión [asper'sjon] nf sprinkling

aspiración [aspira'θjon] nf breath, inhalation; (*MUS*) short pause; **aspiraciones** nfpl (*ambiciones*) aspirations

aspirador [aspira'ðor] nm = **aspiradora**

aspiradora [aspira'ðora] nf vacuum cleaner, Hoover ®

aspirante [aspi'rante] nm/f (*candidato*) candidate; (*DEPORTE*) contender

aspirar [aspi'rar] vt to breathe in ♦ vi: **~ a** to aspire to

aspirina [aspi'rina] nf aspirin

asquear [aske'ar] vt to sicken ♦ vi to be sickening; **~se** vr to feel disgusted; **asqueroso, a** adj disgusting, sickening

asta ['asta] nf lance; (*arpón*) spear; (*mango*) shaft, handle; (*ZOOL*) horn; **a media ~** at half mast

asterisco [aste'risko] nm asterisk

astilla [as'tiʎa] nf splinter; (*pedacito*) chip; **~s** nfpl (*leña*) firewood sg

astillero [asti'ʎero] nm shipyard

astringente [astrin'xente] adj, nm astringent

astro ['astro] nm star

astrología [astrolo'xia] nf astrology; **astrólogo, a** nm/f astrologer

astronauta [astro'nauta] nm/f astronaut

astronave [astro'naβe] nm spaceship

astronomía [astrono'mia] nf astronomy; **astrónomo, a** nm/f astronomer

astucia [as'tuθja] nf astuteness; (*ardid*) clever trick

asturiano, a [astu'rjano, a] adj, nm/f Asturian

astuto, a [as'tuto, a] adj astute; (*taimado*) cunning

asumir [asu'mir] vt to assume

asunción [asun'θjon] nf assumption; (*REL*): **A~** Assumption

asunto [a'sunto] nm (*tema*) matter, subject; (*negocio*) business

asustar [asus'tar] vt to frighten; **~se** vr to be (*o become*) frightened

atacar [ata'kar] vt to attack

atadura [ata'ðura] nf bond, tie

atajar [ata'xar] vt (*enfermedad, mal*) to stop ♦ vi (*persona*) to take a short cut

atajo [a'taxo] nm short cut

atañer [ata'ɲer] vi: **~ a** to concern

ataque etc [a'take] vb ver **atacar** ♦ nm attack; **~ cardíaco** heart attack

atar [a'tar] vt to tie, tie up

atardecer [atarðe'θer] vi to get dark ♦ nm evening; (*crepúsculo*) dusk

atareado, a [atare'aðo, a] adj busy

atascar [atas'kar] vt to clog up; (*obstruir*) to jam; (*fig*) to hinder; **~se** vr to stall; (*cañería*) to get blocked up; **atasco** nm obstruction; (*AUTO*) traffic jam

ataúd [ata'uð] nm coffin

ataviar [ata'βjar] vt to deck, array; **~se** vr to dress up

atavío [ata'βio] nm attire, dress; **~s** nmpl finery sg

atemorizar [atemori'θar] vt to frighten, scare; **~se** vr to get scared

Atenas [a'tenas] n Athens

atención [aten'θjon] nf attention; (*bondad*) kindness ♦ excl (be) careful!, look out!

atender [aten'der] vt to attend to, look after ♦ vi to pay attention

atenerse [ate'nerse] vr: **~ a** to abide by, adhere to

atentado [aten'taðo] nm crime, illegal act; (*asalto*) assault; **~ contra la vida de uno** attempt on sb's life

atentamente [atenta'mente] adv: **Le saluda ~** Yours faithfully

atentar [aten'tar] vi: **~ a o contra** to commit an outrage against

atento, a [a'tento, a] adj attentive, observant; (*cortés*) polite, thoughtful

atenuante [ate'nwante] adj extenuating

atenuar [ate'nwar] vt (*disminuir*) to lessen, minimize

ateo, a [a'teo, a] adj atheistic ♦ nm/f atheist

aterciopelado, a [aterθjope'laðo, a] adj velvety

aterido, a [ate'riðo, a] adj: **~ de frío** frozen stiff

aterrador, a [aterra'ðor, a] adj frightening

aterrar [ate'rrar] vt to frighten; to terrify

aterrizaje [aterri'θaxe] nm landing

aterrizar [aterri'θar] vi to land

aterrorizar [aterrori'θar] vt to terrify

atesorar [ateso'rar] vt to hoard

atestado, a [ates'taðo, a] adj packed ♦ nm

(*JUR*) affidavit

atestar [ates'tar] *vt* to pack, stuff; (*JUR*) to attest, testify to

atestiguar [atesti'ɣwar] *vt* to testify to, bear witness to

atiborrar [atiβo'rrar] *vt* to fill, stuff; **~se** *vr* to stuff o.s.

ático ['atiko] *nm* attic; **~ de lujo** penthouse (flat (*BRIT*) o apartment)

atinado, a [ati'naðo, a] *adj* (*sensato*) wise; (*correcto*) right, correct

atinar [ati'nar] *vi* (*al disparar*): **~ al blanco** to hit the target; (*fig*) to be right

atisbar [atis'βar] *vt* to spy on; (*echar una ojeada*) to peep at

atizar [ati'θar] *vt* to poke; (*horno etc*) to stoke; (*fig*) to stir up, rouse

atlántico, a [at'lantiko, a] *adj* Atlantic ♦ *nm*: **el (océano) A~** the Atlantic (Ocean)

atlas ['atlas] *nm* atlas

atleta [at'leta] *nm* athlete; **atlético, a** *adj* athletic; **atletismo** *nm* athletics *sg*

atmósfera [at'mosfera] *nf* atmosphere

atolladero [atoʎa'ðero] *nm* (*fig*) jam, fix

atolondramiento [atolondra'mjento] *nm* bewilderment; (*insensatez*) silliness

atómico, a [a'tomiko, a] *adj* atomic

atomizador [atomiθa'ðor] *nm* atomizer; (*de perfume*) spray

átomo ['atomo] *nm* atom

atónito, a [a'tonito, a] *adj* astonished, amazed

atontado, a [aton'taðo, a] *adj* stunned; (*bobo*) silly, daft

atontar [aton'tar] *vt* to stun; **~se** *vr* to become confused

atormentar [atormen'tar] *vt* to torture; (*molestar*) to torment; (*acosar*) to plague, harass

atornillar [atorni'ʎar] *vt* to screw on o down

atosigar [atosi'ɣar] *vt* to harass, pester

atracador, a [atraka'ðor, a] *nm/f* robber

atracar [atra'kar] *vt* (*NAUT*) to moor; (*robar*) to hold up, rob ♦ *vi* to moor; **~se** *vr*: **~se (de)** to stuff o.s. (with)

atracción [atrak'θjon] *nf* attraction

atraco [a'trako] *nm* holdup, robbery

atracón [atra'kon] *nm*: **darse o pegarse un ~ (de)** (*fam*) to stuff o.s. (with)

atractivo, a [atrak'tiβo, a] *adj* attractive ♦ *nm* appeal

atraer [atra'er] *vt* to attract

atragantarse [atraɣan'tarse] *vr*: **~ (con)** to choke (on); **se me ha atragantado el chico** I can't stand the boy

atrancar [atran'kar] *vt* (*puerta*) to bar, bolt

atrapar [atra'par] *vt* to trap; (*resfriado etc*) to catch

atrás [a'tras] *adv* (*movimiento*) back(wards);

(*lugar*) behind; (*tiempo*) previously; **ir hacia ~** to go back(wards); to go to the rear; **estar ~** to be behind o at the back

atrasado, a [atra'saðo, a] *adj* slow; (*pago*) overdue, late; (*país*) backward

atrasar [atra'sar] *vi* to be slow; **~se** *vr* to remain behind; (*tren*) to be o run late; **atraso** *nm* slowness; lateness, delay; (*de país*) backwardness; **atrasos** *nmpl* (*COM*) arrears

atravesar [atraβe'sar] *vt* (*cruzar*) to cross (over); (*traspasar*) to pierce; to go through; (*poner al través*) to lay o put across; **~se** *vr* to come in between; (*intervenir*) to interfere

atravieso *etc vb ver* **atravesar**

atrayente [atra'jente] *adj* attractive

atreverse [atre'βerse] *vr* to dare; (*insolentarse*) to be insolent; **atrevido, a** *adj* daring; insolent; **atrevimiento** *nm* daring; insolence

atribución [atriβu'θjon] *nf*: **atribuciones** (*POL*) powers; (*ADMIN*) responsibilities

atribuir [atriβu'ir] *vt* to attribute; (*funciones*) to confer

atribular [atriβu'lar] *vt* to afflict, distress

atributo [atri'βuto] *nm* attribute

atril [a'tril] *nm* (*para libro*) lectern; (*MUS*) music stand

atrocidad [atroθi'ðað] *nf* atrocity, outrage

atropellar [atrope'ʎar] *vt* (*derribar*) to knock over o down; (*empujar*) to push (aside); (*AUTO*) to run over, run down; (*agraviar*) to insult; **~se** *vr* to act hastily; **atropello** *nm* (*AUTO*) accident; (*empujón*) push; (*agravio*) wrong; (*atrocidad*) outrage

atroz [a'troθ] *adj* atrocious, awful

ATS *nmf abr* (= *Ayudante Técnico Sanitario*) nurse

atto, a *abr* = **atento**

atuendo [a'twendo] *nm* attire

atún [a'tun] *nm* tuna

aturdir [atur'ðir] *vt* to stun; (*de ruido*) to deafen; (*fig*) to dumbfound, bewilder

atusar [atu'sar] *vt* to smooth (down)

audacia [au'ðaθja] *nf* boldness, audacity; **audaz** *adj* bold, audacious

audible [au'ðiβle] *adj* audible

audición [auði'θjon] *nf* hearing; (*TEATRO*) audition

audiencia [au'ðjenθja] *nf* audience; **A~** (*JUR*) High Court

audífono [au'ðifono] *nm* (*para sordos*) hearing aid

auditor [auði'tor] *nm* (*JUR*) judge advocate; (*COM*) auditor

auditorio [auði'torjo] *nm* audience; (*sala*) auditorium

auge ['auxe] *nm* boom; (*clímax*) climax

augurar [auɣu'rar] *vt* to predict; (*presagiar*)

to portend
augurio [au'xurjo] nm omen
aula ['aula] nf classroom; (en universidad etc) lecture room
aullar [au'ʎar] vi to howl, yell
aullido [au'ʎiðo] nm howl, yell
aumentar [aumen'tar] vt to increase; (precios) to put up; (producción) to step up; (con microscopio, anteojos) to magnify ♦ vi to increase, be on the increase; **~se** vr to increase, be on the increase; **aumento** nm increase; rise
aun [a'un] adv even; **~ así** even so; **~ más** even o yet more
aún [a'un] adv: **~ está aquí** he's still here; **~ no lo sabemos** we don't know yet; **¿no ha venido ~?** hasn't she come yet?
aunque [a'unke] conj though, although, even though
aúpa [a'upa] excl come on!
aureola [aure'ola] nf halo
auricular [auriku'lar] nm (TEL) earpiece, receiver; **~es** nmpl (para escuchar música etc) headphones
aurora [au'rora] nf dawn
auscultar [auskul'tar] vt (MED: pecho) to listen to, sound
ausencia [au'senθja] nf absence
ausentarse [ausen'tarse] vr to go away; (por poco tiempo) to go out
ausente [au'sente] adj absent
auspicios [aus'piθjos] nmpl auspices
austeridad [austeri'ðað] nf austerity; **austero, a** adj austere
austral [aus'tral] adj southern ♦ nm monetary unit of Argentina
Australia [aus'tralja] nf Australia; **australiano, a** adj, nm/f Australian
Austria ['austrja] nf Austria; **austríaco, a** adj, nm/f Austrian
auténtico, a [au'tentiko, a] adj authentic
auto ['auto] nm (JUR) edict, decree; (: orden) writ, (AUTO) car; **~s** nmpl (JUR) proceedings; (: acta) court record sg
autoadhesivo [autoaðe'sißo] adj self-adhesive; (sobre) self-sealing
autobiografía [autoßjoɣra'fia] nf autobiography
autobronceador [autoßronθea'ðor] adj self-tanning
autobús [auto'ßus] nm bus
autocar [auto'kar] nm coach (BRIT), (passenger) bus (US)
autóctono, a [au'toktono, a] adj native, indigenous
autodefensa [autoðe'fensa] nf self-defence
autodeterminación [autoðetermina'θjon] nf self-determination
autodidacta [autoði'ðakta] adj self-taught

autoescuela [autoes'kwela] nf driving school
autógrafo [au'toɣrafo] nm autograph
autómata [au'tomata] nm automaton
automático, a [auto'matiko, a] adj automatic ♦ nm press stud
automotor, triz [automo'tor, 'triθ] adj self-propelled ♦ nm diesel train
automóvil [auto'moßil] nm (motor) car (BRIT), automobile (US); **automovilismo** nm (actividad) motoring; (DEPORTE) motor racing; **automovilista** nm/f motorist, driver; **automovilístico, a** adj (industria) motor cpd
autonomía [autono'mia] nf autonomy; **autónomo, a** (ESP), **autonómico, a** (ESP) adj (POL) autonomous
autopista [auto'pista] nf motorway (BRIT), freeway (US); **~ de peaje** toll road (BRIT), turnpike road (US)
autopsia [au'topsja] nf autopsy, postmortem
autor, a [au'tor, a] nm/f author
autoridad [autori'ðað] nf authority; **autoritario, a** adj authoritarian
autorización [autoriθa'θjon] nf authorization; **autorizado, a** adj authorized; (aprobado) approved
autorizar [autori'θar] vt to authorize; (aprobar) to approve
autorretrato [autorre'trato] nm self-portrait
autoservicio [autoser'ßiθjo] nm (tienda) self-service shop (BRIT) o store (US); (restaurante) self-service restaurant
autostop [auto'stop] nm hitch-hiking; **hacer ~** to hitch-hike; **~ista** nm/f hitch-hiker
autosuficiencia [autosufi'θjenθja] nf self-sufficiency
autovía [auto'ßia] nf ≈ A-road (BRIT), dual carriageway (BRIT), ≈ state highway (US)
auxiliar [auksi'ljar] vt to help ♦ nm/f assistant; **auxilio** nm assistance, help; **primeros auxilios** first aid sg
Av abr (= Avenida) Av(e).
aval [a'ßal] nm guarantee; (persona) guarantor
avalancha [aßa'lantʃa] nf avalanche
avance [a'ßanθe] nm advance; (pago) advance payment; (CINE) trailer
avanzar [aßan'θar] vt, vi to advance
avaricia [aßa'riθja] nf avarice, greed; **avaricioso, a** adj avaricious, greedy
avaro, a [a'ßaro, a] adj miserly, mean ♦ nm/f miser
avasallar [aßasa'ʎar] vt to subdue, subjugate
Avda abr (= Avenida) Av(e).
AVE ['aße] nm abr (= Alta Velocidad Española) ≈ bullet train
ave ['aße] nf bird; **~ de rapiña** bird of prey
avecinarse [aßeθi'narse] vr (tormenta, fig)

to be on the way

avellana [aβe'ʎana] nf hazelnut; **avellano** nm hazel tree

avemaría [aβema'ria] nm Hail Mary, Ave Maria

avena [a'βena] nf oats pl

avenida [aβe'niða] nf (calle) avenue

avenir [aβe'nir] vt to reconcile; **~se** vr to come to an agreement, reach a compromise

aventajado, a [aβenta'xaðo, a] adj outstanding

aventajar [aβenta'xar] vt (sobrepasar) to surpass, outstrip

aventura [aβen'tura] nf adventure; **aventurado, a** adj risky; **aventurero, a** adj adventurous

avergonzar [aβerɣon'θar] vt to shame; (desconcertar) to embarrass; **~se** vr to be ashamed; to be embarrassed

avería [aβe'ria] nf (TEC) breakdown, fault

averiado, a [aβe'rjaðo, a] adj broken down; "**~**" "out of order"

averiguación [aβeriɣwa'θjon] nf investigation; (descubrimiento) ascertainment

averiguar [aβeri'ɣwar] vt to investigate; (descubrir) to find out, ascertain

aversión [aβer'sjon] nf aversion, dislike

avestruz [aβes'truθ] nm ostrich

aviación [aβja'θjon] nf aviation; (fuerzas aéreas) air force

aviador, a [aβja'ðor, a] nm/f aviator, airman/woman

avicultura [aβikul'tura] nf poultry farming

avidez [aβi'ðeθ] nf avidity, eagerness; **ávido, a** adj avid, eager

avinagrado, a [aβina'ɣraðo, a] adj sour, acid

avión [a'βjon] nm aeroplane; (ave) martin; **~ de reacción** jet (plane)

avioneta [aβjo'neta] nf light aircraft

avisar [aβi'sar] vt (advertir) to warn, notify; (informar) to tell; (aconsejar) to advise, counsel; **aviso** nm warning; (noticia) notice

avispa [a'βispa] nf wasp

avispado, a [aβis'paðo, a] adj sharp, clever

avispero [aβis'pero] nm wasp's nest

avispón [aβis'pon] nm hornet

avistar [aβis'tar] vt to sight, spot

avituallar [aβitwa'ʎar] vt to supply with food

avivar [aβi'βar] vt to strengthen, intensify; **~se** vr to revive, acquire new life

axila [ak'sila] nf armpit

axioma [ak'sjoma] nm axiom

ay [ai] excl (dolor) ow!, ouch!; (aflicción) oh!, oh dear!; ¡**~ de mí!** poor me!

aya ['aja] nf governess; (niñera) nanny

ayer [a'jer] adv, nm yesterday; **antes de ~** the day before yesterday

ayote [a'jote] (AM) nm pumpkin

ayuda [a'juða] nf help, assistance ♦ nm page; **ayudante, a** nm/f assistant, helper; (ESCOL) assistant; (MIL) adjutant

ayudar [aju'ðar] vt to help, assist

ayunar [aju'nar] vi to fast; **ayunas** nfpl: **estar en ayunas** to be fasting; **ayuno** nm fast; fasting

ayuntamiento [ajunta'mjento] nm (consejo) town (o city) council; (edificio) town (o city) hall

azabache [aθa'βatʃe] nm jet

azada [a'θaða] nf hoe

azafata [aθa'fata] nf air stewardess

azafrán [aθa'fran] nm saffron

azahar [aθa'ar] nm orange/lemon blossom

azar [a'θar] nm (casualidad) chance, fate; (desgracia) misfortune, accident; **por ~** by chance; **al ~** at random

azoramiento [aθora'mjento] nm alarm; (confusión) confusion

azorar [aθo'rar] vt to alarm; **~se** vr to get alarmed

Azores [a'θores] nfpl: **las ~** the Azores

azotar [aθo'tar] vt to whip, beat; (pegar) to spank; **azote** nm (látigo) whip; (latigazo) lash, stroke; (en las nalgas) spank; (calamidad) calamity

azotea [aθo'tea] nf (flat) roof

azteca [aθ'teka] adj, nm/f Aztec

azúcar [a'θukar] nm sugar; **azucarado, a** adj sugary, sweet

azucarero, a [aθuka'rero, a] adj sugar cpd ♦ nm sugar bowl

azucena [aθu'θena] nf white lily

azufre [a'θufre] nm sulphur

azul [a'θul] adj, nm blue; **~ marino** navy blue

azulejo [aθu'lexo] nm tile

azuzar [aθu'θar] vt to incite, egg on

B, b

B.A. abr (= Buenos Aires) B.A.

baba ['baβa] nf spittle, saliva; **babear** vi to drool, slaver

babero [ba'βero] nm bib

babor [ba'βor] nm port (side)

baboso, a [ba'βoso, a] (AM: fam) adj silly

baca ['baka] nf (AUTO) luggage o roof rack

bacalao [baka'lao] nm cod(fish)

bache ['batʃe] nm pothole, rut; (fig) bad patch

bachillerato [batʃiʎe'rato] nm higher secondary school course

bacteria [bak'terja] nf bacterium, germ

báculo ['bakulo] nm stick, staff

bagaje [ba'xaxe] nm baggage, luggage

Bahama [ba'ama]: **las (Islas) ~** nfpl the Bahamas

bahía [ba'ia] *nf* bay

bailar [bai'lar] *vt*, *vi* to dance; **~ín, ina** *nm/f* (ballet) dancer; **baile** *nm* dance; (*formal*) ball

baja ['baxa] *nf* drop, fall; (*MIL*) casualty; **dar de ~** (*soldado*) to discharge; (*empleado*) to dismiss

bajada [ba'xaða] *nf* descent; (*camino*) slope; (*de aguas*) ebb

bajar [ba'xar] *vi* to go down, come down; (*temperatura, precios*) to drop, fall ♦ *vt* (*cabeza*) to bow; (*escalera*) to go down, come down; (*precio, voz*) to lower; (*llevar abajo*) to take down; **~se** *vr* (*de coche*) to get out; (*de autobús, tren*) to get off; **~ de** (*coche*) to get out of; (*autobús, tren*) to get off

bajeza [ba'xeθa] *nf* baseness *no pl*; (*una ~*) vile deed

bajío [ba'xio] *nm* (*AM*) lowlands *pl*

bajo, a ['baxo, a] *adj* (*mueble, número, precio*) low; (*piso*) ground; (*de estatura*) small, short; (*color*) pale; (*sonido*) faint, soft, low; (*voz: en tono*) deep; (*metal*) base; (*humilde*) low, humble ♦ *adv* (*hablar*) softly, quietly; (*volar*) low ♦ *prep* under, below, underneath ♦ *nm* (*MUS*) bass; **~ la lluvia** in the rain

bajón [ba'xon] *nm* fall, drop

bakalao [baka'lao] (*fam*) *nm* rave (music)

bala ['bala] *nf* bullet

balance [ba'lanθe] *nm* (*COM*) balance; (*: libro*) balance sheet; (*: cuenta general*) stocktaking

balancear [balanθe'ar] *vt* to balance ♦ *vi* to swing (to and fro); (*vacilar*) to hesitate; **~se** *vr* to swing (to and fro); to hesitate; **balanceo** *nm* swinging

balanza [ba'lanθa] *nf* scales *pl*, balance; (*ASTROLOGÍA*): **B~** Libra; **~ comercial** balance of trade; **~ de pagos** balance of payments

balar [ba'lar] *vi* to bleat

balaustrada [balaus'traða] *nf* balustrade; (*pasamanos*) banisters *pl*

balazo [ba'laθo] *nm* (*golpe*) shot; (*herida*) bullet wound

balbucear [balβuθe'ar] *vi*, *vt* to stammer, stutter; **balbuceo** *nm* stammering, stuttering

balbucir [balβu'θir] *vi*, *vt* to stammer, stutter

balcón [bal'kon] *nm* balcony

balde ['balde] *nm* bucket, pail; **de ~** (for) free, for nothing; **en ~** in vain

baldío, a [bal'dio, a] *adj* uncultivated; (*terreno*) waste ♦ *nm* waste land

baldosa [bal'dosa] *nf* (*azulejo*) floor tile; (*grande*) flagstone; **baldosín** *nm* (small) tile

Baleares [bale'ares] *nfpl*: **las (Islas) ~** the Balearic Islands

balido [ba'liðo] *nm* bleat, bleating

baliza [ba'liθa] *nf* (*AVIAT*) beacon; (*NAUT*) buoy

ballena [ba'ʎena] *nf* whale

ballesta [ba'ʎesta] *nf* crossbow; (*AUTO*) spring

ballet [ba'le] (*pl* **~s**) *nm* ballet

balneario, a [balne'arjo, a] *adj*: **estación balnearia** (*AM*) (bathing) resort ♦ *nm* spa, health resort

balón [ba'lon] *nm* ball

baloncesto [balon'θesto] *nm* basketball

balonmano [balon'mano] *nm* handball

balonvolea [balombo'lea] *nm* volleyball

balsa ['balsa] *nf* raft; (*BOT*) balsa wood

bálsamo ['balsamo] *nm* balsam, balm

baluarte [ba'lwarte] *nm* bastion, bulwark

bambolear [bambole'ar] *vi* to swing, sway; (*silla*) to wobble; **~se** *vr* to swing, sway; to wobble; **bamboleo** *nm* swinging, swaying, wobbling

bambú [bam'bu] *nm* bamboo

banana [ba'nana] (*AM*) *nf* banana; **banano** (*AM*) *nm* banana tree

banca ['banka] *nf* (*COM*) banking

bancario, a [ban'karjo, a] *adj* banking *cpd*, bank *cpd*

bancarrota [banka'rrota] *nf* bankruptcy; **hacer ~** to go bankrupt

banco ['banko] *nm* bench; (*ESCOL*) desk; (*COM*) bank; (*GEO*) stratum; **~ de crédito/de ahorros** credit/savings bank; **~ de arena** sandbank; **~ de datos** databank

banda ['banda] *nf* band; (*pandilla*) gang; (*NAUT*) side, edge; **la B~ Oriental** Uruguay; **~ sonora** soundtrack

bandada [ban'daða] *nf* (*de pájaros*) flock; (*de peces*) shoal

bandazo [ban'daθo] *nm*: **dar ~s** to sway from side to side

bandeja [ban'dexa] *nf* tray

bandera [ban'dera] *nf* flag

banderilla [bande'riʎa] *nf* banderilla

banderín [bande'rin] *nm* pennant, small flag

bandido [ban'diðo] *nm* bandit

bando ['bando] *nm* (*edicto*) edict, proclamation; (*facción*) faction; **los ~s** (*REL*) the banns

bandolera [bando'lera] *nf*: **llevar en ~** to wear across one's chest

bandolero [bando'lero] *nm* bandit, brigand

banquero [ban'kero] *nm* banker

banqueta [ban'keta] *nf* stool; (*AM: en la calle*) pavement (*BRIT*), sidewalk (*US*)

banquete [ban'kete] *nm* banquet; (*para convidados*) formal dinner

banquillo [ban'kiʎo] *nm* (*JUR*) dock, prisoner's bench; (*banco*) bench; (*para los pies*) footstool

bañador [baɲa'ðor] *nm* swimming costume (*BRIT*), bathing suit (*US*)

bañar [ba'ɲar] *vt* to bath, bathe; (*objeto*) to

dip; (*de barniz*) to coat; **~se** *vr* (*en el mar*) to bathe, swim; (*en la bañera*) to have a bath

bañera [ba'ɲera] *nf* bath(tub)

bañero, a [ba'ɲero, a] (*AM*) *nm/f* lifeguard

bañista [ba'ɲista] *nm/f* bather

baño ['baɲo] *nm* (*en bañera*) bath; (*en río*) dip, swim; (*cuarto*) bathroom; (*bañera*) bath(tub); (*capa*) coating

baqueta [ba'keta] *nf* (*MUS*) drumstick

bar [bar] *nm* bar

barahúnda [bara'unda] *nf* uproar, hubbub

baraja [ba'raxa] *nf* pack (of cards); **barajar** *vt* (*naipes*) to shuffle; (*fig*) to jumble up

baranda [ba'randa] *nf* = **barandilla**

barandilla [baran'diʎa] *nf* rail, railing

baratija [bara'tixa] *nf* trinket

baratillo [bara'tiʎo] *nm* (*tienda*) junkshop; (*subasta*) bargain sale; (*conjunto de cosas*) secondhand goods *pl*

barato, a [ba'rato, a] *adj* cheap ♦ *adv* cheap, cheaply

baraúnda [bara'unda] *nf* = **barahúnda**

barba ['barßa] *nf* (*mentón*) chin; (*pelo*) beard

barbacoa [barßa'koa] *nf* (*parrilla*) barbecue; (*carne*) barbecued meat

barbaridad [barßari'ðað] *nf* barbarity; (*acto*) barbarism; (*atrocidad*) outrage; **una ~** (*fam*) loads; **¡qué ~!** (*fam*) how awful!

barbarie [bar'ßarje] *nf* barbarism, savagery; (*crueldad*) barbarity

barbarismo [barßa'rismo] *nm* = **barbarie**

bárbaro, a [bar'ßaro, a] *adj* barbarous, cruel; (*grosero*) rough, uncouth ♦ *nm/f* barbarian ♦ *adv*: **lo pasamos ~** (*fam*) we had a great time; **¡qué ~!** (*fam*) how marvellous!; **un éxito ~** (*fam*) a terrific success; **es un tipo ~** (*fam*) he's a great bloke

barbecho [bar'ßetʃo] *nm* fallow land

barbero [bar'ßero] *nm* barber, hairdresser

barbilla [bar'ßiʎa] *nf* chin, tip of the chin

barbo ['barßo] *nm* barbel; **~ de mar** red mullet

barbotear [barßote'ar] *vt, vi* to mutter, mumble

barbudo, a [bar'ßuðo, a] *adj* bearded

barca ['barka] *nf* (*small*) boat; **~ pesquera** fishing boat; **~ de pasaje** ferry; **~za** *nf* barge; **~za de desembarco** landing craft

Barcelona [barθe'lona] *n* Barcelona

barcelonés, esa [barθelo'nes, esa] *adj* of o from Barcelona

barco ['barko] *nm* boat; (*grande*) ship; **~ de carga** cargo boat; **~ de vela** sailing ship

baremo [ba'remo] *nm* (*MAT, fig*) scale

barítono [ba'ritono] *nm* baritone

barman ['barman] *nm* barman

Barna *n* = **Barcelona**

barniz [bar'niθ] *nm* varnish; (*en la loza*) glaze; (*fig*) veneer; **~ar** *vt* to varnish; (*loza*)

to glaze

barómetro [ba'rometro] *nm* barometer

barquero [bar'kero] *nm* boatman

barquillo [bar'kiʎo] *nm* cone, cornet

barra ['barra] *nf* bar, rod; (*de un bar, café*) bar; (*de pan*) French stick; (*palanca*) lever; **~ de carmín** o **de labios** lipstick; **~ libre** free bar

barraca [ba'rraka] *nf* hut, cabin

barranco [ba'rranko] *nm* ravine; (*fig*) difficulty

barrena [ba'rrena] *nf* drill; **barrenar** *vt* to drill (through), bore; **barreno** *nm* large drill

barrer [ba'rrer] *vt* to sweep; (*quitar*) to sweep away

barrera [ba'rrera] *nf* barrier

barriada [ba'rrjaða] *nf* quarter, district

barricada [barri'kaða] *nf* barricade

barrida [ba'rriða] *nf* sweep, sweeping

barrido [ba'rriðo] *nm* = **barrida**

barriga [ba'rriɣa] *nf* belly; (*panza*) paunch; **barrigón, ona** *adj* potbellied; **barrigudo, a** *adj* potbellied

barril [ba'rril] *nm* barrel, cask

barrio ['barrjo] *nm* (*vecindad*) area, neighborhood (*US*); (*en las afueras*) suburb; **~ chino** red-light district

barro ['barro] *nm* (*lodo*) mud; (*objetos*) earthenware; (*MED*) pimple

barroco, a [ba'rroko, a] *adj, nm* baroque

barrote [ba'rrote] *nm* (*de ventana*) bar

barruntar [barrun'tar] *vt* (*conjeturar*) to guess; (*presentir*) to suspect; **barrunto** *nm* guess; suspicion

bartola [bar'tola] *nf*: **a la ~** *adv*: **tirarse a la ~** to take it easy, be lazy

bártulos ['bartulos] *nmpl* things, belongings

barullo [ba'ruʎo] *nm* row, uproar

basar [ba'sar] *vt* to base; **~se** *vr*: **~se en** to be based on

báscula ['baskula] *nf* (*platform*) scales

base ['base] *nf* base; **a ~ de** on the basis of; (*mediante*) by means of; **~ de datos** (*INFORM*) database

básico, a ['basiko, a] *adj* basic

basílica [ba'silika] *nf* basilica

PALABRA CLAVE
---

bastante [bas'tante] *adj* **1** (*suficiente*) enough; **~ dinero** enough o sufficient money; **~s libros** enough books

2 (*valor intensivo*): **~ gente** quite a lot of people; **tener ~ calor** to be rather hot

♦ *adv*: **~ bueno/malo** quite good/rather bad; **~ rico** pretty rich; **(lo) ~ inteligente (como) para hacer algo** clever enough o sufficiently clever to do sth

bastar [bas'tar] *vi* to be enough o sufficient;

~se *vr* to be self-sufficient; **~ para** to be enough to; **¡basta!** (that's) enough!
bastardilla [bastar'ðiʎa] *nf* italics
bastardo, a [bas'tarðo, a] *adj, nm/f* bastard
bastidor [basti'ðor] *nm* frame; (*de coche*) chassis; (*TEATRO*) wing; **entre ~es** (*fig*) behind the scenes
basto, a ['basto, a] *adj* coarse, rough; **~s** *nmpl* (*NAIPES*) ≈ clubs
bastón [bas'ton] *nm* stick, staff; (*para pasear*) walking stick
bastoncillo [baston'θiʎo] *nm* cotton bud
basura [ba'sura] *nf* rubbish (*BRIT*), garbage (*US*)
basurero [basu'rero] *nm* (*hombre*) dustman (*BRIT*), garbage man (*US*); (*lugar*) dump; (*cubo*) (rubbish) bin (*BRIT*), trash can (*US*)
bata ['bata] *nf* (*gen*) dressing gown; (*cubretodo*) smock, overall; (*MED, TEC etc*) lab(oratory) coat
batalla [ba'taʎa] *nf* battle; **de ~** (*fig*) for everyday use
batallar [bata'ʎar] *vi* to fight
batallón [bata'ʎon] *nm* battalion
batata [ba'tata] *nf* sweet potato
batería [bate'ria] *nf* battery; (*MUS*) drums; **~ de cocina** kitchen utensils
batido, a [ba'tiðo, a] *adj* (*camino*) beaten, well-trodden ♦ *nm* (*CULIN*): **~ (de leche)** milk shake
batidora [bati'ðora] *nf* beater, mixer; **~ eléctrica** food mixer, blender
batir [ba'tir] *vt* to beat, strike; (*vencer*) to beat, defeat; (*revolver*) to beat, mix; **~se** *vr* to fight; **~ palmas** to clap, applaud
batuta [ba'tuta] *nf* baton; **llevar la ~** (*fig*) to be the boss, be in charge
baúl [ba'ul] *nm* trunk; (*AUTO*) boot (*BRIT*), trunk (*US*)
bautismo [bau'tismo] *nm* baptism, christening
bautizar [bauti'θar] *vt* to baptize, christen; (*fam: diluir*) to water down; **bautizo** *nm* baptism, christening
baya ['baja] *nf* berry
bayeta [ba'jeta] *nf* floorcloth
bayoneta [bajo'neta] *nf* bayonet
baza ['baθa] *nf* trick; **meter ~** to butt in
bazar [ba'θar] *nm* bazaar
bazofia [ba'θofja] *nf* trash
BCE *nm abr* (= *Banco Central Europeo*) ECB
beato, a [be'ato, a] *adj* blessed; (*piadoso*) pious
bebé [be'βe] (*pl* **~s**) *nm* baby
bebedor, a [beβe'ðor, a] *adj* hard-drinking
beber [be'βer] *vt, vi* to drink
bebida [be'βiða] *nf* drink; **bebido, a** *adj* drunk
beca ['beka] *nf* grant, scholarship

becario, a [be'karjo, a] *nm/f* scholarship holder, grant holder
bedel [be'ðel] *nm* (*ESCOL*) janitor; (*UNIV*) porter
béisbol ['beisβol] *nm* (*DEPORTE*) baseball
belén [be'len] *nm* (*de navidad*) nativity scene, crib; **B~** Bethlehem
belga ['belxa] *adj, nm/f* Belgian
Bélgica [be'ʎexika] *nf* Belgium
bélico, a ['beliko, a] *adj* (*actitud*) warlike; **belicoso, a** *adj* (*guerrero*) warlike; (*agresivo*) aggressive, bellicose
beligerante [belixe'rante] *adj* belligerent
belleza [be'ʎeθa] *nf* beauty
bello, a ['beʎo, a] *adj* beautiful, lovely; **Bellas Artes** Fine Art
bellota [be'ʎota] *nf* acorn
bemol [be'mol] *nm* (*MUS*) flat; **esto tiene ~es** (*fam*) this is a tough one
bencina [ben'θina] (*AM*) *nf* (*gasolina*) petrol (*BRIT*), gasoline (*US*)
bendecir [bende'θir] *vt* to bless
bendición [bendi'θjon] *nf* blessing
bendito, a [ben'dito, a] *pp de* **bendecir** ♦ *adj* holy; (*afortunado*) lucky; (*feliz*) happy; (*sencillo*) simple ♦ *nm/f* simple soul
beneficencia [benefi'θenθja] *nf* charity
beneficiar [benefi'θjar] *vt* to benefit, be of benefit to; **~se** *vr* to benefit, profit; **~io, a** *nm/f* beneficiary
beneficio [bene'fiθjo] *nm* (*bien*) benefit, advantage; (*ganancia*) profit, gain; **~so, a** *adj* beneficial
benéfico, a [be'nefiko, a] *adj* charitable
beneplácito [bene'plaθito] *nm* approval, consent
benevolencia [beneβo'lenθja] *nf* benevolence, kindness; **benévolo, a** *adj* benevolent, kind
benigno, a [be'niɣno, a] *adj* kind; (*suave*) mild; (*MED: tumor*) benign, non-malignant
berberecho [berβe'retʃo] *nm* (*ZOOL, CULIN*) cockle
berenjena [beren'xena] *nf* aubergine (*BRIT*), eggplant (*US*)
Berlín [ber'lin] *n* Berlin; **berlinés, esa** *adj* of o from Berlin ♦ *nm/f* Berliner
bermudas [ber'muðas] *nfpl* Bermuda shorts
berrear [berre'ar] *vi* to bellow, low
berrido [be'rriðo] *nm* bellow(ing)
berrinche [be'rrintʃe] (*fam*) *nm* temper, tantrum
berro ['berro] *nm* watercress
berza ['berθa] *nf* cabbage
besamel [besa'mel] *nf* (*CULIN*) white sauce, bechamel sauce
besar [be'sar] *vt* to kiss; (*fig: tocar*) to graze; **~se** *vr* to kiss (one another); **beso** *nm* kiss
bestia ['bestja] *nf* beast, animal; (*fig*) idiot;

~ de carga beast of burden

bestial [bes'tjal] *adj* bestial; (*fam*) terrific; **~idad** *nf* bestiality; (*fam*) stupidity

besugo [be'suɣo] *nm* sea bream; (*fam*) idiot

besuquear [besuke'ar] *vt* to cover with kisses; **~se** *vr* to kiss and cuddle

betún [be'tun] *nm* shoe polish; (*QUÍM*) bitumen

biberón [biße'ron] *nm* feeding bottle

Biblia ['bißlja] *nf* Bible

bibliografía [bißljoʏra'fia] *nf* bibliography

biblioteca [bißljo'teka] *nf* library; (*mueble*) bookshelves; **~ de consulta** reference library; **~rio, a** *nm/f* librarian

bicarbonato [bikarßo'nato] *nm* bicarbonate

bicho ['bitʃo] *nm* (*animal*) small animal; (*sabandija*) bug, insect; (*TAUR*) bull

bici ['biθi] (*fam*) *nf* bike

bicicleta [biθi'kleta] *nf* bicycle, cycle; **ir en ~** to cycle

bidé [bi'ðe] (*pl* **~s**) *nm* bidet

bidón [bi'ðon] *nm* (*de aceite*) drum; (*de gasolina*) can

PALABRA CLAVE
---

bien [bjen] *nm* 1 (*bienestar*) good; **te lo digo por tu ~** I'm telling you for your own good; **el ~ y el mal** good and evil

2 (*posesión*): **~es** goods; **~es de consumo** consumer goods; **~es inmuebles** o **raíces/~es muebles** real estate *sg*/personal property *sg*

♦ *adv* 1 (*de manera satisfactoria, correcta etc*) well; **trabaja/come ~** she works/eats well; **contestó ~** he answered correctly; **me siento ~** I feel fine; **no me siento ~** I don't feel very well; **se está ~ aquí** it's nice here

2 (*frases*): **hiciste ~ en llamarme** you were right to call me

3 (*valor intensivo*) very; **un cuarto ~ caliente** a nice warm room; **~ se ve que ...** it's quite clear that ...

4: **estar ~**: **estoy muy ~ aquí** I feel very happy here; **está ~ que vengan** it's all right for them to come; **¡está ~! lo haré** oh all right, I'll do it

5 (*de buena gana*): **yo ~ que iría pero ...** I'd gladly go but ...

♦ *excl*: **¡~!** (*aprobación*) O.K.!; **¡muy ~!** well done!

♦ *adj inv* (*matiz despectivo*): **niño ~** rich kid; **gente ~** posh people

♦ *conj* 1: **~ ... ~:** **~ en coche ~ en tren** either by car or by train

2: **no ~** (*esp AM*): **no ~ llegue te llamaré** as soon as I arrive I'll call you

3: **si ~** even though; *ver tb* **más**

bienal [bje'nal] *adj* biennial

bienaventurado, a [bjenaßentu'raðo, a] *adj* (*feliz*) happy, fortunate

bienestar [bjenes'tar] *nm* well-being, welfare

bienhechor, a [bjene'tʃor, a] *adj* beneficent ♦ *nm/f* benefactor/benefactress

bienvenida [bjembe'niða] *nf* welcome; **dar la ~ a uno** to welcome sb

bienvenido [bjembe'niðo] *excl* welcome!

bife ['bife] (*AM*) *nm* steak

bifurcación [bifurka'θjon] *nf* fork

bifurcarse [bifur'karse] *vr* (*camino, carretera, río*) to fork

bigamia [bi'ɣamja] *nf* bigamy; **bígamo, a** *adj* bigamous ♦ *nm/f* bigamist

bigote [bi'ɣote] *nm* moustache; **bigotudo, a** *adj* with a big moustache

bikini [bi'kini] *nm* bikini; (*CULIN*) toasted ham and cheese sandwich

bilbaíno, a [bilßa'ino, a] *adj* from o of Bilbao

bilingüe [bi'lingwe] *adj* bilingual

billar [bi'ʎar] *nm* billiards *sg*; (*lugar*) billiard hall; (*mini-casino*) amusement arcade; **~ americano** pool

billete [bi'ʎete] *nm* ticket; (*de banco*) (bank)note (*BRIT*), bill (*US*); (*carta*) note; **~ sencillo, ~ de ida solamente** single (*BRIT*) o one-way (*US*) ticket; **~ de ida y vuelta** return (*BRIT*) o round-trip (*US*) ticket; **~ de 20 libras** £20 note

billetera [biʎe'tera] *nf* wallet

billetero [biʎe'tero] *nm* = billetera

billón [bi'ʎon] *nm* billion

bimensual [bimen'swal] *adj* twice monthly

bimotor [bimo'tor] *adj* twin-engined ♦ *nm* twin-engined plane

bingo [biŋgo] *nm* bingo

biodegradable [bioðeʏra'ðaßle] *adj* biodegradable

biografía [bjoʏra'fia] *nf* biography; **biógrafo, a** *nm/f* biographer

biología [bjolo'xia] *nf* biology; **biológico, a** *adj* biological; (*cultivo, producto*) organic; **biólogo, a** *nm/f* biologist

biombo ['bjombo] *nm* (folding) screen

biopsia [bi'opsja] *nf* biopsy

biquini [bi'kini] *nm* bikini

birlar [bir'lar] (*fam*) *vt* to pinch

Birmania [bir'manja] *nf* Burma

birria ['birrja] *nf*: **ser una ~** (*película, libro*) to be rubbish

bis [bis] *excl* encore! ♦ *adv*: **viven en el 27 ~** they live at 27a

bisabuelo, a [bisa'ßwelo, a] *nm/f* great-grandfather/mother

bisagra [bi'saʏra] *nf* hinge

bisiesto [bi'sjesto] *adj*: **año ~** leap year

bisnieto, a [bis'njeto, a] *nm/f* great-grandson/daughter

bisonte [bi'sonte] *nm* bison

bisté [bis'te] *nm* = bistec

bistec [bis'tek] *nm* steak

bisturí [bistu'ri] nm scalpel

bisutería [bisute'ria] nf imitation o costume jewellery

bit [bit] nm (INFORM) bit

bizco, a ['biθko, a] adj cross-eyed

bizcocho [biθ'kotʃo] nm (CULIN) sponge cake

bizquear [biθke'ar] vi to squint

blanca ['blanka] nf (MUS) minim; **estar sin ~** to be broke; ver tb blanco

blanco, a ['blanko, a] adj white ♦ nm/f white man/woman, white ♦ nm (color) white; (en texto) blank; (MIL, fig) target; **en ~** blank; **noche en ~** sleepless night

blancura [blan'kura] nf whiteness

blandir [blan'dir] vt to brandish

blando, a ['blando, a] adj soft; (tierno) tender, gentle; (carácter) mild; (fam) cowardly; **blandura** nf softness; tenderness; mildness

blanquear [blanke'ar] vt to whiten; (fachada) to whitewash; (paño) to bleach ♦ vi to turn white; **blanquecino, a** adj whitish

blasfemar [blasfe'mar] vi to blaspheme, curse; **blasfemia** nf blasphemy

blasón [bla'son] nm coat of arms

bledo ['bleðo] nm: **me importa un ~** I couldn't care less

blindado, a [blin'daðo, a] adj (MIL) armour-plated; (antibala) bullet-proof; **coche** (ESP) o **carro** (AM) **~** armoured car

blindaje [blin'daxe] nm armour, armour-plating

bloc [blok] (pl **~s**) nm writing pad

bloque ['bloke] nm block; (POL) bloc; **~ de cilindros** cylinder block

bloquear [bloke'ar] vt to blockade; **bloqueo** nm blockade; (COM) freezing, blocking

blusa ['blusa] nf blouse

boato [bo'ato] nm show, ostentation

bobada [bo'βaða] nf foolish action; foolish statement; **decir ~s** to talk nonsense

bobería [boβe'ria] nf = **bobada**

bobina [bo'βina] nf (TEC) bobbin; (FOTO) spool; (ELEC) coil

bobo, a ['boβo, a] adj (tonto) daft, silly; (cándido) naïve ♦ nm/f fool, idiot ♦ nm (TEATRO) clown, funny man

boca ['boka] nf mouth; (de crustáceo) pincer; (de cañón) muzzle; (entrada) mouth, entrance; **~s** nfpl (de río) mouth sg; **~ abajo/ arriba** face down/up; **se me hace agua la ~** my mouth is watering

bocacalle [boka'kaʎe] nf (entrance to a) street; **la primera ~** the first turning o street

bocadillo [boka'ðiʎo] nm sandwich

bocado [bo'kaðo] nm mouthful, bite; (de caballo) bridle; **~ de Adán** Adam's apple

bocajarro [boka'xarro]: **a ~** adv (disparar, preguntar) point-blank

bocanada [boka'naða] nf (de vino) mouthful, swallow; (de aire) gust, puff

bocata [bo'kata] (fam) nm sandwich

bocazas [bo'kaθas] (fam) nm inv bigmouth

boceto [bo'θeto] nm sketch, outline

bochorno [bo'tʃorno] nm (vergüenza) embarrassment; (color): **hace ~** it's very muggy; **~so, a** adj muggy; embarrassing

bocina [bo'θina] nf (MUS) trumpet; (AUTO) horn; (para hablar) megaphone

boda ['boða] nf (tb: **~s**) wedding, marriage; (fiesta) wedding reception; **~s de plata/de oro** silver/golden wedding

bodega [bo'ðeɣa] nf (de vino) (wine) cellar; (depósito) storeroom; (de barco) hold

bodegón [boðe'ɣon] nm (ARTE) still life

bofe ['bofe] nm (tb: **~s**: de res) lights

bofetada [bofe'taða] nf slap (in the face)

bofetón [bofe'ton] nm = **bofetada**

boga ['boɣa] nf: **en ~** (fig) in vogue

bogar [bo'ɣar] vi (remar) to row; (navegar) to sail

bogavante [boɣa'ßante] nm lobster

Bogotá [boɣo'ta] n Bogotá

bohemio, a [bo'emjo, a] adj, nm/f Bohemian

boicot [boi'kot] (pl **~s**) nm boycott; **~ear** vt to boycott; **~eo** nm boycott

boina ['boina] nf beret

bola ['bola] nf ball; (canica) marble; (NAIPES) (grand) slam; (betún) shoe polish; (mentira) tale, story; **~s** (AM) nfpl bolas sg; **~ de billar** billiard ball; **~ de nieve** snowball

bolchevique [boltʃe'ßike] adj, nm/f Bolshevik

boleadoras [bolea'ðoras] (AM) nfpl bolas sg

bolera [bo'lera] nf skittle o bowling alley

boleta [bo'leta] (AM) nf (billete) ticket; (permiso) pass, permit

boletería [bolete'ria] (AM) nf ticket office

boletín [bole'tin] nm bulletin; (periódico) journal, review; **~ de noticias** news bulletin

boleto [bo'leto] nm ticket

boli ['boli] (fam) nm Biro ®, pen

bolígrafo [bo'liɣrafo] nm ball-point pen, Biro ®

bolívar [bo'lißar] nm monetary unit of Venezuela

Bolivia [bo'lißja] nf Bolivia; **boliviano, a** adj, nm/f Bolivian

bollería [boʎe'ria] nf cakes pl and pastries pl

bollo ['boʎo] nm (pan) roll; (bulto) bump, lump; (abolladura) dent

bolo ['bolo] nm skittle; (píldora) (large) pill; (juego de) **~s** nmpl skittles sg

bolsa ['bolsa] nf bag; (AM) pocket; (ANAT) cavity, sac; (COM) stock exchange; (MINERÍA) pocket; **de ~** pocket cpd; **~ de agua caliente** hot water bottle; **~ de aire** air pocket; **~ de**

papel paper bag; **~ de plástico** plastic bag
bolsillo [bol'siʎo] *nm* pocket; (*cartera*) purse; **de ~** pocket(-size)
bolsista [bol'sista] *nm/f* stockbroker
bolso ['bolso] *nm* (*bolsa*) bag; (*de mujer*) handbag
bomba ['bomba] *nf* (*MIL*) bomb; (*TEC*) pump ♦ (*fam*) *adj*: **noticia ~** bombshell ♦ (*fam*) *adv*: **pasarlo ~** to have a great time; **~ atómica/de humo/de efecto retardado** atomic/smoke/time bomb
bombardear [bombarðe'ar] *vt* to bombard; (*MIL*) to bomb; **bombardeo** *nm* bombardment; bombing
bombardero [bombar'ðero] *nm* bomber
bombear [bombe'ar] *vt* (*agua*) to pump (out o up); **~se** *vr* to warp
bombero [bom'bero] *nm* fireman
bombilla [bom'biʎa] (*ESP*) *nf* (light) bulb
bombín [bom'bin] *nm* bowler hat
bombo ['bombo] *nm* (*MUS*) bass drum; (*TEC*) drum
bombón [bom'bon] *nm* chocolate
bombona [bom'bona] *nf* (*de butano, oxígeno*) cylinder
bonachón, ona [bona'tʃon, ona] *adj* good-natured, easy-going
bonanza [bo'nanθa] *nf* (*NAUT*) fair weather; (*fig*) bonanza; (*MINERÍA*) rich pocket o vein
bondad [bon'dað] *nf* goodness, kindness; **tenga la ~ de** (please) be good enough to; **~oso, a** *adj* good, kind
bonificación [bonifika'θjon] *nf* bonus
bonito, a [bo'nito, a] *adj* pretty; (*agradable*) nice ♦ *nm* (*atún*) tuna (fish)
bono ['bono] *nm* voucher; (*FIN*) bond
bonobús [bono'βus] (*ESP*) *nm* bus pass
bonoloto [bono'loto] *nf* state-run weekly lottery
boquerón [boke'ron] *nm* (*pez*) (kind of) anchovy; (*agujero*) large hole
boquete [bo'kete] *nm* gap, hole
boquiabierto, a [bokia'βjerto, a] *adj*: **quedar ~** to be amazed o flabbergasted
boquilla [bo'kiʎa] *nf* (*para riego*) nozzle; (*para cigarro*) cigarette holder; (*MUS*) mouthpiece
borbotón [borβo'ton] *nm*: **salir a borbotones** to gush out
borda ['borða] *nf* (*NAUT*) (ship's) rail; **tirar algo/caerse por la ~** to throw sth/fall overboard
bordado [bor'ðaðo] *nm* embroidery
bordar [bor'ðar] *vt* to embroider
borde ['borðe] *nm* edge, border; (*de camino etc*) side; (*en la costura*) hem; **al ~ de** (*fig*) on the verge o brink of; **ser ~** (*ESP: fam*) to be rude; **~ar** *vt* to border
bordillo [bor'ðiʎo] *nm* kerb (*BRIT*), curb (*US*)

bordo ['borðo] *nm* (*NAUT*) side; **a ~** on board
borinqueño, a [borin'kenjo, a] *adj, nm/f* Puerto Rican
borla ['borla] *nf* (*adorno*) tassel
borrachera [borra'tʃera] *nf* (*ebriedad*) drunkenness; (*orgía*) spree, binge
borracho, a [bo'rratʃo, a] *adj* drunk ♦ *nm/f* (*habitual*) drunkard, drunk; (*temporal*) drunk, drunk man/woman
borrador [borra'ðor] *nm* (*escritura*) first draft, rough sketch; (*goma*) rubber (*BRIT*), eraser
borrar [bo'rrar] *vt* to erase, rub out
borrasca [bo'rraska] *nf* storm
borrico, a [bo'rriko, a] *nm/f* donkey/she-donkey; (*fig*) stupid man/woman
borrón [bo'rron] *nm* (*mancha*) stain
borroso, a [bo'rroso, a] *adj* vague, unclear; (*escritura*) illegible
bosque ['boske] *nm* wood; (*grande*) forest
bosquejar [boske'xar] *vt* to sketch; **bosquejo** *nm* sketch
bostezar [boste'θar] *vi* to yawn; **bostezo** *nm* yawn
bota ['bota] *nf* (*calzado*) boot; (*para vino*) leather wine bottle; **~s de agua, ~s de goma** Wellingtons
botánica [bo'tanika] *nf* (*ciencia*) botany; *ver tb* **botánico**
botánico, a [bo'taniko, a] *adj* botanical ♦ *nm/f* botanist
botar [bo'tar] *vt* to throw, hurl; (*NAUT*) to launch; (*AM*) to throw out ♦ *vi* to bounce
bote ['bote] *nm* (*salto*) bounce; (*golpe*) thrust; (*vasija*) tin, can; (*embarcación*) boat; **de ~ en ~** packed, jammed full; **~ de la basura** (*AM*) dustbin (*BRIT*), trashcan (*US*); **~ salvavidas** lifeboat
botella [bo'teʎa] *nf* bottle; **botellín** *nm* small bottle
botica [bo'tika] *nf* chemist's (shop) (*BRIT*), pharmacy; **~rio, a** *nm/f* chemist (*BRIT*), pharmacist
botijo [bo'tixo] *nm* (earthenware) jug
botín [bo'tin] *nm* (*calzado*) half boot; (*polaina*) spat; (*MIL*) booty
botiquín [boti'kin] *nm* (*armario*) medicine cabinet; (*portátil*) first-aid kit
botón [bo'ton] *nm* button; (*BOT*) bud; **~ de oro** buttercup
botones [bo'tones] *nm inv* bellboy (*BRIT*), bellhop (*US*)
bóveda ['boβeða] *nf* (*ARQ*) vault
boxeador [boksea'ðor] *nm* boxer
boxear [bokse'ar] *vi* to box
boxeo [bok'seo] *nm* boxing
boya ['boja] *nf* (*NAUT*) buoy; (*de caña*) float
boyante [bo'jante] *adj* prosperous
bozal [bo'θal] *nm* (*de caballo*) halter; (*de perro*) muzzle

bracear [braθe'ar] vi (agitar los brazos) to wave one's arms

bracero [bra'θero] nm labourer; (en el campo) farmhand

bragas ['braɣas] nfpl (de mujer) panties, knickers (BRIT)

bragueta [bra'ɣeta] nf fly, flies pl

braille [breil] nm braille

bramar [bra'mar] vi to bellow, roar; **bramido** nm bellow, roar

brasa ['brasa] nf live o hot coal

brasero [bra'sero] nm brazier

Brasil [bra'sil] nm: (el) ~ Brazil; **brasileño, a** adj, nm/f Brazilian

bravata [bra'βata] nf boast

braveza [bra'βeθa] nf (valor) bravery; (ferocidad) ferocity

bravío, a [bra'βio, a] adj wild; (feroz) fierce

bravo, a ['braβo, a] adj (valiente) brave; (feroz) ferocious; (salvaje) wild; (mar etc) rough, stormy ♦ excl bravo!; **bravura** nf bravery; ferocity

braza ['braθa] nf fathom; **nadar a la ~** to swim (the) breast-stroke

brazada [bra'θaða] nf stroke

brazado [bra'θaðo] nm armful

brazalete [braθa'lete] nm (pulsera) bracelet; (banda) armband

brazo ['braθo] nm arm; (ZOOL) foreleg; (BOT) limb, branch; **luchar a ~ partido** to fight hand-to-hand; **ir cogidos del ~** to walk arm in arm

brea ['brea] nf pitch, tar

brebaje [bre'βaxe] nm potion

brecha ['bretʃa] nf (hoyo, vacío) gap, opening; (MIL, fig) breach

brega ['breɣa] nf (lucha) struggle; (trabajo) hard work

breva ['breβa] nf early fig

breve ['breβe] adj short, brief ♦ nf (MUS) breve; **~dad** nf brevity, shortness

brezo ['breθo] nm heather

bribón, ona [bri'βon, ona] adj idle, lazy ♦ nm/f (pícaro) rascal, rogue

bricolaje [briko'laxe] nm do-it-yourself, DIY

brida ['briða] nf bridle, rein; (TEC) clamp; **a toda ~** at top speed

bridge [britʃ] nm bridge

brigada [bri'ɣaða] nf (unidad) brigade; (trabajadores) squad, gang ♦ nm ≈ staff-sergeant, sergeant-major

brillante [bri'ʎante] adj brilliant ♦ nm diamond

brillar [bri'ʎar] vi (tb fig) to shine; (joyas) to sparkle

brillo ['briʎo] nm shine; (brillantez) brilliance; (fig) splendour; **sacar ~ a** to polish

brincar [brin'kar] vi to skip about, hop about, jump about; **está que brinca** he's hopping mad

brinco ['brinko] nm jump, leap

brindar [brin'dar] vi: ~ **a** o **por** to drink (a toast) to ♦ vt to offer, present

brindis ['brindis] nm inv toast

brío ['brio] nm spirit, dash; **brioso, a** adj spirited, dashing

brisa ['brisa] nf breeze

británico, a [bri'taniko, a] adj British ♦ nm/f Briton, British person

brizna ['briθna] nf (de hierba, paja) blade; (de tabaco) leaf

broca ['broka] nf (TEC) drill, bit

brocal [bro'kal] nm rim

brocha ['brotʃa] nf (large) paintbrush; ~ **de afeitar** shaving brush

broche ['brotʃe] nm brooch

broma ['broma] nf joke; **en ~** in fun, as a joke; ~ **pesada** practical joke; **bromear** vi to joke

bromista [bro'mista] adj fond of joking ♦ nm/f joker, wag

bronca ['bronka] nf row; **echar una ~ a uno** to tick sb off

bronce ['bronθe] nm bronze; ~**ado, a** adj bronze; (por el sol) tanned ♦ nm (sun)tan; (TEC) bronzing

bronceador [bronθea'ðor] nm suntan lotion

broncearse [bronθe'arse] vr to get a suntan

bronco, a ['bronko, a] adj (manera) rude, surly; (voz) harsh

bronquio ['bronkjo] nm (ANAT) bronchial tube

bronquitis [bron'kitis] nf inv bronchitis

brotar [bro'tar] vi (BOT) to sprout; (aguas) to gush (forth); (MED) to break out

brote ['brote] nm (BOT) shoot; (MED, fig) outbreak

bruces ['bruθes]: **de ~** adv: **caer** o **dar de ~** to fall headlong, fall flat

bruja ['bruxa] nf witch; **brujería** nf witchcraft

brujo ['bruxo] nm wizard, magician

brújula ['bruxula] nf compass

bruma ['bruma] nf mist; **brumoso, a** adj misty

bruñir [bru'ɲir] vt to polish

brusco, a ['brusko, a] adj (súbito) sudden; (áspero) brusque

Bruselas [bru'selas] n Brussels

brutal [bru'tal] adj brutal

brutalidad [brutali'ðað] nf brutality

bruto, a ['bruto, a] adj (idiota) stupid; (bestial) brutish; (peso) gross; **en ~** raw, unworked

Bs.As. abr (= Buenos Aires) B.A.

bucal [bu'kal] adj oral; **por vía ~** orally

bucear [buθe'ar] vi to dive ♦ vt to explore; **buceo** nm diving

bucle ['bukle] nm curl

budismo [bu'ðismo] *nm* Buddhism
buen [bwen] *adj m ver* **bueno**
buenamente [bwena'mente] *adv* (*fácilmente*) easily; (*voluntariamente*) willingly
buenaventura [bwenaßen'tura] *nf* (*suerte*) good luck; (*adivinación*) fortune

PALABRA CLAVE

bueno, a ['bweno, a] *adj* (*antes de nmsg*: **buen**) **1** (*excelente etc*) good; **es un libro ~, es un buen libro** it's a good book; **hace ~, hace buen tiempo** the weather is fine, it is fine; **el ~ de Paco** good old Paco; **fue muy ~ conmigo** he was very nice o kind to me
2 (*apropiado*): **ser ~ para** to be good for; **creo que vamos por buen camino** I think we're on the right track
3 (*irónico*): **le di un buen rapapolvo** I gave him a good o real ticking off; **¡buen conductor estás hecho!** some o fine driver you are!; **¡estaría ~ que ...!** a fine thing it would be if ...!
4 (*atractivo, sabroso*): **está ~ este bizcocho** this sponge is delicious; **Carmen está muy buena** Carmen is gorgeous
5 (*saludos*): **¡buen día!, ¡~s días!** (good) morning!; **¡buenas (tardes)!** (good) afternoon!; (*más tarde*) (good) evening!; **¡buenas noches!** good night!
6 (*otras locuciones*): **estar de buenas** to be in a good mood; **por las buenas o por las malas** by hook or by crook; **de buenas a primeras** all of a sudden
♦ *excl*: **¡~!** all right!; **~, ¿y qué?** well, so what?

Buenos Aires *nm* Buenos Aires
buey [bwei] *nm* ox
búfalo ['bufalo] *nm* buffalo
bufanda [bu'fanda] *nf* scarf
bufar [bu'far] *vi* to snort
bufete [bu'fete] *nm* (*despacho de abogado*) lawyer's office
buffer ['bufer] *nm* (*INFORM*) buffer
bufón [bu'fon] *nm* clown
buhardilla [buar'ðiʎa] *nf* attic
búho ['buo] *nm* owl; (*fig*) hermit, recluse
buhonero [buo'nero] *nm* pedlar
buitre ['bwitre] *nm* vulture
bujía [bu'xia] *nf* (*vela*) candle; (*ELEC*) candle (power); (*AUTO*) spark plug
bula ['bula] *nf* (*papal*) bull
bulbo ['bulßo] *nm* bulb
bulevar [bule'ßar] *nm* boulevard
Bulgaria [bul'ɣarja] *nf* Bulgaria; **búlgaro, a** *adj*, *nm/f* Bulgarian
bulla ['buʎa] *nf* (*ruido*) uproar; (*de gente*) crowd
bullicio [bu'ʎiθjo] *nm* (*ruido*) uproar; (*movimiento*) bustle

bullir [bu'ʎir] *vi* (*hervir*) to boil; (*burbujear*) to bubble
bulto ['bulto] *nm* (*paquete*) package; (*fardo*) bundle; (*tamaño*) size, bulkiness; (*MED*) swelling, lump; (*silueta*) vague shape
buñuelo [bu'ɲwelo] *nm* ≈ doughnut (*BRIT*), ≈ donut (*US*); (*fruta de sartén*) fritter
BUP [bup] *nm abr* (*ESP*: = *Bachillerato Unificado Polivalente*) secondary education and leaving certificate for 14–17 age group
buque ['buke] *nm* ship, vessel
burbuja [bur'ßuxa] *nf* bubble; **burbujear** *vi* to bubble
burdel [bur'ðel] *nm* brothel
burdo, a ['burðo, a] *adj* coarse, rough
burgués, esa [bur'ɣes, esa] *adj* middle-class, bourgeois; **burguesía** *nf* middle class, bourgeoisie
burla ['burla] *nf* (*mofa*) gibe; (*broma*) joke; (*engaño*) trick
burladero [burla'ðero] *nm* (bullfighter's) refuge
burlar [bur'lar] *vt* (*engañar*) to deceive ♦ *vi* to joke; **~se** *vr* to joke; **~se de** to make fun of
burlesco, a [bur'lesko, a] *adj* burlesque
burlón, ona [bur'lon, ona] *adj* mocking
burocracia [buro'kraθja] *nf* civil service
burócrata [bu'rokrata] *nm/f* civil servant
burrada [bu'rraða] *nf*: **decir/soltar ~s** to talk nonsense; **hacer ~s** to act stupid; **una ~ (mucho)** a (hell of a) lot
burro, a ['burro, a] *nm/f* donkey/she-donkey; (*fig*) ass, idiot
bursátil [bur'satil] *adj* stock-exchange *cpd*
bus [bus] *nm* bus
busca ['buska] *nf* search, hunt ♦ *nm* (*TEL*) bleeper; **en ~ de** in search of
buscar [bus'kar] *vt* to look for, search for, seek ♦ *vi* to look, search, seek; **se busca secretaria** secretary wanted
busque *etc vb ver* **buscar**
búsqueda ['buskeða] *nf* = **busca** *nf*
busto ['busto] *nm* (*ANAT*, *ARTE*) bust
butaca [bu'taka] *nf* armchair; (*de cine, teatro*) stall, seat
butano [bu'tano] *nm* butane (gas)
buzo ['buθo] *nm* diver
buzón [bu'θon] *nm* (*en puerta*) letter box; (*en la calle*) pillar box

C, c

C. *abr* (= *centígrado*) C; (= *compañía*) Co.
c. *abr* (= *capítulo*) ch.
C/ *abr* (= *calle*) St
c.a. *abr* (= *corriente alterna*) AC
cabal [ka'ßal] *adj* (*exacto*) exact; (*correcto*) right, proper; (*acabado*) finished, complete;

~es *nmpl*: **estar en sus ~es** to be in one's right mind

cábalas ['kaßalas] *nfpl*: **hacer ~** to guess

cabalgar [kaßal'ɣar] *vt, vi* to ride

cabalgata [kaßal'ɣata] *nf* procession

caballa [ka'ßaʎa] *nf* mackerel

caballeresco, a [kaßaʎe'resko, a] *adj* noble, chivalrous

caballería [kaßaʎe'ria] *nf* mount; (*MIL*) cavalry

caballeriza [kaßaʎe'riθa] *nf* stable; **caballerizo** *nm* groom, stableman

caballero [kaßa'ʎero] *nm* gentleman; (*de la orden de caballería*) knight; (*trato directo*) sir

caballerosidad [kaßaʎerosi'ðað] *nf* chivalry

caballete [kaßa'ʎete] *nm* (*ARTE*) easel; (*TEC*) trestle

caballito [kaßa'ʎito] *nm* (*caballo pequeño*) small horse, pony; **~s** *nmpl* (*en verbena*) roundabout, merry-go-round

caballo [ka'ßaʎo] *nm* horse; (*AJEDREZ*) knight; (*NAIPES*) queen; **ir en ~** to ride; **~ de vapor** o **de fuerza** horsepower; **~ de carreras** racehorse

cabaña [ka'ßaɲa] *nf* (*casita*) hut, cabin

cabaré [kaßa're] (*pl* **~s**) *nm* cabaret

cabaret [kaßa're] (*pl* **~s**) *nm* cabaret

cabecear [kaßeθe'ar] *vt, vi* to nod

cabecera [kaße'θera] *nf* head; (*IMPRENTA*) headline

cabecilla [kaße'θiʎa] *nm* ringleader

cabellera [kaße'ʎera] *nf* (head of) hair; (*de cometa*) tail

cabello [ka'ßeʎo] *nm* (*tb*: **~s**) hair

caber [ka'ßer] *vi* (*entrar*) to fit, go; **caben 3 más** there's room for 3 more

cabestrillo [kaßes'triʎo] *nm* sling

cabestro [ka'ßestro] *nm* halter

cabeza [ka'ßeθa] *nf* head; (*POL*) chief, leader; **~ rapada** skinhead; **~da** *nf* (*golpe*) butt; **dar ~das** to nod off; **cabezón, ona** *adj* (*vino*) heady; (*fam: persona*) pig-headed

cabida [ka'ßiða] *nf* space

cabildo [ka'ßildo] *nm* (*de iglesia*) chapter; (*POL*) town council

cabina [ka'ßina] *nf* cabin; (*de camión*) cab; **~ telefónica** telephone box (*BRIT*) o booth

cabizbajo, a [kaßiθ'ßaxo, a] *adj* crestfallen, dejected

cable ['kaßle] *nm* cable

cabo ['kaßo] *nm* (*de objeto*) end, extremity; (*MIL*) corporal; (*NAUT*) rope, cable; (*GEO*) cape; **al ~ de 3 días** after 3 days

cabra ['kaßra] *nf* goat

cabré *etc vb ver* **caber**

cabrear [kaßre'ar] (*fam*) *vt* to bug; **~se** *vr* (*enfadarse*) to fly off the handle

cabrío, a [ka'ßrio, a] *adj* goatish; **macho ~** (he-)goat, billy goat

cabriola [ka'ßrjola] *nf* caper

cabritilla [kaßri'tiʎa] *nf* kid, kidskin

cabrito [ka'ßrito] *nm* kid

cabrón [ka'ßron] *nm* cuckold; (*fam!*) bastard (*!*)

caca ['kaka] (*fam*) *nf* pooh

cacahuete [kaka'wete] (*ESP*) *nm* peanut

cacao [ka'kao] *nm* cocoa; (*BOT*) cacao

cacarear [kakare'ar] *vi* (*persona*) to boast; (*gallina*) to crow

cacería [kaθe'ria] *nf* hunt

cacerola [kaθe'rola] *nf* pan, saucepan

cachalote [katʃa'lote] *nm* (*ZOOL*) sperm whale

cacharro [ka'tʃarro] *nm* earthenware pot; **~s** *nmpl* pots and pans

cachear [katʃe'ar] *vt* to search, frisk

cachemir [katʃe'mir] *nm* cashmere

cacheo [ka'tʃeo] *nm* searching, frisking

cachete [ka'tʃete] *nm* (*ANAT*) cheek; (*bofetada*) slap (in the face)

cachiporra [katʃi'porra] *nf* truncheon

cachivache [katʃi'ßatʃe] *nm* (*trasto*) piece of junk; **~s** *nmpl* junk *sg*

cacho ['katʃo] *nm* (small) bit; (*AM: cuerno*) horn

cachondeo [katʃon'deo] (*fam*) *nm* farce, joke

cachondo, a [ka'tʃondo, a] *adj* (*ZOOL*) on heat; (*fam: sexualmente*) randy; (*: gracioso*) funny

cachorro, a [ka'tʃorro, a] *nm/f* (*perro*) pup, puppy; (*león*) cub

cacique [ka'θike] *nm* chief, local ruler; (*POL*) local party boss; **caciquismo** *nm* system of control by the local boss

caco ['kako] *nm* pickpocket

cacto ['kakto] *nm* cactus

cactus ['kaktus] *nm inv* cactus

cada ['kaða] *adj inv* every; (*antes de número*) every; **~ día** each day, every day; **~ dos días** every other day; **~ uno/a** each one, every one; **~ vez más/menos** more and more/less and less; **uno de ~ diez** one out of every ten

cadalso [ka'ðalso] *nm* scaffold

cadáver [ka'ðaßer] *nm* (dead) body, corpse

cadena [ka'ðena] *nf* chain; (*TV*) channel; **trabajo en ~** assembly line work; **~ perpetua** (*JUR*) life imprisonment

cadencia [ka'ðenθja] *nf* rhythm

cadera [ka'ðera] *nf* hip

cadete [ka'ðete] *nm* cadet

caducar [kaðu'kar] *vi* to expire; **caduco, a** *adj* expired; (*persona*) very old

caer [ka'er] *vi* to fall (down); **~se** *vr* to fall (down); **me cae bien/mal** I get on well with him/I can't stand him; **~ en la cuenta** to realize; **su cumpleaños cae en viernes** her birthday falls on a Friday

café [ka'fe] (*pl* **~s**) *nm* (*bebida, planta*) coffee;

(*lugar*) café ♦ *adj* (*color*) brown; **~ con leche** white coffee; **~ solo** black coffee

cafetera [kafe'tera] *nf* coffee pot

cafetería [kafete'ria] *nf* (*gen*) café

cafetero, a [kafe'tero, a] *adj* coffee *cpd*; **ser muy ~** to be a coffee addict

cagar [ka'var] (*fam!*) *vt* to bungle, mess up ♦ *vi* to have a shit (*!*)

caída [ka'iða] *nf* fall; (*declive*) slope; (*disminución*) fall, drop

caído, a [ka'iðo, a] *adj* drooping

caiga *etc vb ver* **caer**

caimán [kai'man] *nm* alligator

caja ['kaxa] *nf* box; (*para reloj*) case; (*de ascensor*) shaft; (*COM*) cashbox; (*donde se hacen los pagos*) cashdesk; (: *en super-mercado*) checkout, till; **~ de ahorros** savings bank; **~ de cambios** gearbox; **~ fuerte, ~ de caudales** safe, strongbox

cajero, a [ka'xero, a] *nm/f* cashier; **~ automático** cash dispenser

cajetilla [kaxe'tiʎa] *nf* (*de cigarrillos*) packet

cajón [ka'xon] *nm* big box; (*de mueble*) drawer

cal [kal] *nf* lime

cala ['kala] *nf* (*GEO*) cove, inlet; (*de barco*) hold

calabacín [kalaßa'θin] *nm* (*BOT*) baby marrow; (: *más pequeño*) courgette (*BRIT*), zucchini (*US*)

calabaza [kala'ßaθa] *nf* (*BOT*) pumpkin

calabozo [kala'ßoθo] *nm* (*cárcel*) prison; (*celda*) cell

calada [ka'laða] *nf* (*de cigarrillo*) puff

calado, a [ka'laðo, a] *adj* (*prenda*) lace *cpd* ♦ *nm* (*NAUT*) draught

calamar [kala'mar] *nm* squid *no pl*

calambre [ka'lambre] *nm* (*tb*: **~s**) cramp

calamidad [kalami'ðað] *nf* calamity, disaster

calar [ka'lar] *vt* to soak, drench; (*penetrar*) to pierce, penetrate; (*comprender*) to see through; (*vela*) to lower; **~se** *vr* (*AUTO*) to stall; **~se las gafas** to stick one's glasses on

calavera [kala'ßera] *nf* skull

calcar [kal'kar] *vt* (*reproducir*) to trace; (*imitar*) to copy

calcetín [kalθe'tin] *nm* sock

calcinar [kalθi'nar] *vt* to burn, blacken

calcio ['kalθjo] *nm* calcium

calcomanía [kalkoma'nia] *nf* transfer

calculador, a [kalkula'ðor, a] *adj* (*persona*) calculating

calculadora [kalkula'ðora] *nf* calculator

calcular [kalku'lar] *vt* (*MAT*) to calculate, compute; **~ que ...** to reckon that ...; **cálculo** *nm* calculation

caldear [kalde'ar] *vt* to warm (up), heat (up)

caldera [kal'dera] *nf* boiler

calderilla [kalde'riʎa] *nf* (*moneda*) small

change

caldero [kal'dero] *nm* small boiler

caldo ['kaldo] *nm* stock; (*consomé*) consommé

calefacción [kalefak'θjon] *nf* heating; **~ central** central heating

calendario [kalen'darjo] *nm* calendar

calentador [kalenta'ðor] *nm* heater

calentamiento [kalenta'mjento] *nm* (*DEPORTE*) warm-up

calentar [kalen'tar] *vt* to heat (up); **~se** *vr* to heat up, warm up; (*fig: discusión etc*) to get heated

calentura [kalen'tura] *nf* (*MED*) fever, (high) temperature

calibrar [kali'ßrar] *vt* to gauge, measure; **calibre** *nm* (*de cañón*) calibre, bore; (*diámetro*) diameter; (*fig*) calibre

calidad [kali'ðað] *nf* quality; **de ~** quality *cpd*; **en ~ de** in the capacity of, as

cálido, a ['kaliðo, a] *adj* hot; (*fig*) warm

caliente *etc* [ka'ljente] *vb ver* **calentar** ♦ *adj* hot; (*fig*) fiery; (*disputa*) heated; (*fam: cachondo*) randy

calificación [kalifika'θjon] *nf* qualification; (*de alumno*) grade, mark

calificar [kalifi'kar] *vt* to qualify; (*alumno*) to grade, mark; **~ de** to describe as

calima [ka'lima] *nf* (*cerca del mar*) mist

cáliz ['kaliθ] *nm* chalice

caliza [ka'liθa] *nf* limestone

calizo, a [ka'liθo, a] *adj* lime *cpd*

callado, a [ka'ʎaðo, a] *adj* quiet

callar [ka'ʎar] *vt* (*asunto delicado*) to keep quiet about, say nothing about; (*persona, opinión*) to silence ♦ *vi* to keep quiet, be silent; **~se** *vr* to keep quiet, be silent; **¡cállate! be quiet!, shut up!**

calle ['kaʎe] *nf* street; (*DEPORTE*) lane; **~ arriba/abajo** up/down the street; **~ de un solo sentido** one-way street

calleja [ka'ʎexa] *nf* alley, narrow street; **callejear** *vi* to wander (about) the streets; **callejero, a** *adj* street *cpd* ♦ *nm* street map; **callejón** *nm* alley, passage; **callejón sin salida** cul-de-sac; **callejuela** *nf* side-street, alley

callista [ka'ʎista] *nm/f* chiropodist

callo ['kaʎo] *nm* callus; (*en el pie*) corn; **~s** *nmpl* (*CULIN*) tripe *sg*

calma ['kalma] *nf* calm

calmante [kal'mante] *nm* sedative, tranquillizer

calmar [kal'mar] *vt* to calm, calm down ♦ *vi* (*tempestad*) to abate; (*mente etc*) to become calm

calmoso, a [kal'moso, a] *adj* calm, quiet

calor [ka'lor] *nm* heat; (*agradable*) warmth; **hace ~** it's hot; **tener ~** to be hot

caloría [kalo'ria] *nf* calorie

calumnia [ka'lumnja] nf calumny, slander; **calumnioso, a** adj slanderous

caluroso, a [kalu'roso, a] adj hot; (sin exceso) warm; (fig) enthusiastic

calva ['kalβa] nf bald patch; (en bosque) clearing

calvario [kal'βarjo] nm stations pl of the cross

calvicie [kal'βiθje] nf baldness

calvo, a ['kalβo, a] adj bald; (terreno) bare, barren; (tejido) threadbare

calza ['kalθa] nf wedge, chock

calzada [kal'θaða] nf roadway, highway

calzado, a [kal'θaðo, a] adj shod ♦ nm footwear

calzador [kalθa'ðor] nm shoehorn

calzar [kal'θar] vt (zapatos etc) to wear; (un mueble) to put a wedge under; **~se** vr: **~se los zapatos** to put on one's shoes; **¿qué (número) calza?** what size do you take?

calzón [kal'θon] nm (tb: calzones nmpl) shorts; (AM: de hombre) (under)pants; (: de mujer) panties

calzoncillos [kalθon'θiʎos] nmpl underpants

cama ['kama] nf bed; **~ individual/de matrimonio** single/double bed

camafeo [kama'feo] nm cameo

camaleón [kamale'on] nm chameleon

cámara ['kamara] nf chamber; (habitación) room; (sala) hall; (CINE) cine camera; (fotográfica) camera; **~ de aire** inner tube; **~ de comercio** chamber of commerce; **~ frigorífica** cold-storage room

camarada [kama'raða] nm comrade, companion

camarera [kama'rera] nf (en restaurante) waitress; (en casa, hotel) maid

camarero [kama'rero] nm waiter

camarilla [kama'riʎa] nf clique

camarón [kama'ron] nm shrimp

camarote [kama'rote] nm cabin

cambiable [kam'bjaβle] adj (variable) changeable, variable; (intercambiable) interchangeable

cambiante [kam'bjante] adj variable

cambiar [kam'bjar] vt to change; (dinero) to exchange ♦ vi to change; **~se** vr (mudarse) to move; (de ropa) to change; **~ de idea** to change one's mind; **~ de ropa** to change (one's clothes)

cambio ['kambjo] nm change; (trueque) exchange; (COM) rate of exchange; (oficina) bureau de change; (dinero menudo) small change; **en ~** on the other hand; (en lugar de) instead; **~ de divisas** foreign exchange; **~ de velocidades** gear lever

camelar [kame'lar] vt to sweet-talk

camello [ka'meʎo] nm camel; (fam: traficante) pusher

camerino [kame'rino] nm dressing room

camilla [ka'miʎa] nf (MED) stretcher

caminante [kami'nante] nm/f traveller

caminar [kami'nar] vi (marchar) to walk, go ♦ vt (recorrer) to cover, travel

caminata [kami'nata] nf long walk; (por el campo) hike

camino [ka'mino] nm way, road; (sendero) track; **a medio ~** halfway (there); **en el ~** on the way, en route; **~ de** on the way to; **~ particular** private road

camión [ka'mjon] nm lorry (BRIT), truck (US); **~ cisterna** tanker; **camionero, a** nm/f lorry o truck driver

camioneta [kamjo'neta] nf van, light truck

camisa [ka'misa] nf shirt; (BOT) skin; **~ de fuerza** straitjacket; **camisería** nf outfitter's (shop)

camiseta [kami'seta] nf (prenda) tee-shirt; (: ropa interior) vest; (de deportista) top

camisón [kami'son] nm nightdress, nightgown

camorra [ka'morra] nf: **buscar ~** to look for trouble

campamento [kampa'mento] nm camp

campana [kam'pana] nf bell; **~ de cristal** bell jar; **~da** nf peal; **~rio** nm belfry

campanilla [kampa'niʎa] nf small bell

campaña [kam'paɲa] nf (MIL, POL) campaign

campechano, a [kampe'tʃano, a] adj (franco) open

campeón, ona [kampe'on, ona] nm/f champion; **campeonato** nm championship

campesino, a [kampe'sino, a] adj country cpd, rural; (gente) peasant cpd ♦ nm/f countryman/woman; (agricultor) farmer

campestre [kam'pestre] adj country cpd, rural

camping ['kampin] (pl ~s) nm camping; (lugar) campsite; **ir de o hacer ~** to go camping

campo ['kampo] nm (fuera de la ciudad) country, countryside; (AGR, ELEC) field; (de fútbol) pitch; (de golf) course; (MIL) camp; **~ de batalla** battlefield; **~ de deportes** sports ground, playing field

camposanto [kampo'santo] nm cemetery

camuflaje [kamu'flaxe] nm camouflage

cana ['kana] nf white o grey hair; **tener ~s** to be going grey

Canadá [kana'ða] nm Canada; **canadiense** adj, nm/f Canadian ♦ nf fur-lined jacket

canal [ka'nal] nm canal; (GEO) channel, strait; (de televisión) channel; (de tejado) gutter; **~ de Panamá** Panama Canal; **~izar** vt to channel

canalla [ka'naʎa] nf rabble, mob ♦ nm swine

canalón [kana'lon] nm (conducto vertical) drainpipe; (del tejado) gutter

canapé [kana'pe] (pl ~s) nm sofa, settee;

(*CULIN*) canapé

Canarias [ka'narjas] *nfpl*: (**las Islas**) ~ the Canary Islands, the Canaries

canario, a [ka'narjo, a] *adj, nm/f* (native) of the Canary Isles ♦ *nm* (*ZOOL*) canary

canasta [ka'nasta] *nf* (round) basket; **canastilla** *nf* small basket; (*de niño*) layette

canasto [ka'nasto] *nm* large basket

cancela [kan'θela] *nf* gate

cancelación [kanθela'θjon] *nf* cancellation

cancelar [kanθe'lar] *vt* to cancel; (*una deuda*) to write off

cáncer ['kanθer] *nm* (*MED*) cancer; (*ASTROLOGÍA*): **C~** Cancer

cancha ['kantʃa] *nf* (*de baloncesto, tenis etc*) court; (*AM: de fútbol*) pitch

canciller [kanθi'ʎer] *nm* chancellor

canción [kan'θjon] *nf* song; ~ **de cuna** lullaby; **cancionero** *nm* song book

candado [kan'daðo] *nm* padlock

candente [kan'dente] *adj* red-hot; (*fig: tema*) burning

candidato, a [kandi'ðato, a] *nm/f* candidate

candidez [kandi'ðeθ] *nf* (*sencillez*) simplicity; (*simpleza*) naiveté; **cándido, a** *adj* simple; naive

candil [kan'dil] *nm* oil lamp; ~**ejas** *nfpl* (*TEATRO*) footlights

candor [kan'dor] *nm* (*sinceridad*) frankness; (*inocencia*) innocence

canela [ka'nela] *nf* cinnamon

canelones [kane'lones] *nmpl* cannelloni

cangrejo [kan'grexo] *nm* crab

canguro [kan'guro] *nm* kangaroo; **hacer de ~** to babysit

caníbal [ka'niβal] *adj, nm/f* cannibal

canica [ka'nika] *nf* marble

canijo, a [ka'nixo, a] *adj* frail, sickly

canino, a [ka'nino, a] *adj* canine ♦ *nm* canine (tooth)

canjear [kanxe'ar] *vt* to exchange

cano, a [ka'no, a] *adj* grey-haired, white-haired

canoa [ka'noa] *nf* canoe

canon ['kanon] *nm* canon; (*pensión*) rent; (*COM*) tax

canónigo [ka'noniɣo] *nm* canon

canonizar [kanoni'θar] *vt* to canonize

canoso, a [ka'noso, a] *adj* grey-haired

cansado, a [kan'saðo, a] *adj* tired, weary; (*tedioso*) tedious, boring

cansancio [kan'sanθjo] *nm* tiredness, fatigue

cansar [kan'sar] *vt* (*fatigar*) to tire, tire out; (*aburrir*) to bore; (*fastidiar*) to bother; ~**se** *vr* to tire, get tired; (*aburrirse*) to get bored

cantábrico, a [kan'taβriko, a] *adj* Cantabrian; **mar C~** Bay of Biscay

cantante [kan'tante] *adj* singing ♦ *nm/f* singer

cantar [kan'tar] *vt* to sing ♦ *vi* to sing; (*insecto*) to chirp ♦ *nm* (*acción*) singing; (*canción*) song; (*poema*) poem

cántara ['kantara] *nf* large pitcher

cántaro ['kantaro] *nm* pitcher, jug; **llover a ~s** to rain cats and dogs

cante ['kante] *nm*: ~ **jondo** flamenco singing

cantera [kan'tera] *nf* quarry

cantidad [kanti'ðað] *nf* quantity, amount

cantimplora [kantim'plora] *nf* (*frasco*) water bottle, canteen

cantina [kan'tina] *nf* canteen; (*de estación*) buffet

canto ['kanto] *nm* singing; (*canción*) song; (*borde*) edge, rim; (*de un cuchillo*) back; ~ **rodado** boulder

cantor, a [kan'tor, a] *nm/f* singer

canturrear [kanturre'ar] *vi* to sing softly

canuto [ka'nuto] *nm* (*tubo*) small tube; (*fam: droga*) joint

caña ['kaɲa] *nf* (*BOT: tallo*) stem, stalk; (*carrizo*) reed; (*vaso*) tumbler; (*de cerveza*) glass of beer; (*ANAT*) shinbone; ~ **de azúcar** sugar cane; ~ **de pescar** fishing rod

cañada [ka'ɲaða] *nf* (*entre dos montañas*) gully, ravine; (*camino*) cattle track

cáñamo ['kaɲamo] *nm* hemp

cañería [kaɲe'ria] *nf* (*tubo*) pipe

caño ['kaɲo] *nm* (*tubo*) tube, pipe; (*de albañal*) sewer; (*MUS*) pipe; (*de fuente*) jet

cañón [ka'ɲon] *nm* (*MIL*) cannon; (*de fusil*) barrel; (*GEO*) canyon, gorge

caoba [ka'oβa] *nf* mahogany

caos ['kaos] *nm* chaos

cap. *abr* (= *capítulo*) ch.

capa ['kapa] *nf* cloak, cape; (*GEO*) layer, stratum; **so ~ de** under the pretext of; ~ **de ozono** ozone layer

capacidad [kapaθi'ðað] *nf* (*medida*) capacity; (*aptitud*) capacity, ability

capacitar [kapaθi'tar] *vt*: ~ **a algn para (hacer)** to enable sb to (do)

capar [ka'par] *vt* to castrate, geld

caparazón [kapara'θon] *nm* shell

capataz [kapa'taθ] *nm* foreman

capaz [ka'paθ] *adj* able, capable; (*amplio*) capacious, roomy

capcioso, a [kap'θjoso, a] *adj* wily, deceitful

capellán [kape'ʎan] *nm* chaplain; (*sacerdote*) priest

caperuza [kape'ruθa] *nf* hood

capicúa [kapi'kua] *adj inv* (*número, fecha*) reversible

capilla [ka'piʎa] *nf* chapel

capital [kapi'tal] *adj* capital ♦ *nm* (*COM*) capital ♦ *nf* (*ciudad*) capital; ~ **social** share o authorized capital

capitalismo [kapita'lismo] *nm* capitalism; **capitalista** *adj, nm/f* capitalist

capitán [kapi'tan] nm captain

capitanear [kapitane'ar] vt to captain

capitulación [kapitula'θjon] nf (rendición) capitulation, surrender; (acuerdo) agreement, pact; **capitulaciones (matrimoniales)** nfpl marriage contract sg

capitular [kapitu'lar] vi to make an agreement

capítulo [ka'pitulo] nm chapter

capó [ka'po] nm (AUTO) bonnet

capón [ka'pon] nm (gallo) capon

capota [ka'pota] nf (de mujer) bonnet; (AUTO) hood (BRIT), top (US)

capote [ka'pote] nm (abrigo: de militar) greatcoat; (: de torero) cloak

capricho [ka'pritʃo] nm whim, caprice; **~so, a** adj capricious

Capricornio [kapri'kornjo] nm Capricorn

cápsula ['kapsula] nf capsule

captar [kap'tar] vt (comprender) to understand; (RADIO) to pick up; (atención, apoyo) to attract

captura [kap'tura] nf capture; (JUR) arrest; **capturar** vt to capture; to arrest

capucha [ka'putʃa] nf hood, cowl

capullo [ka'puʎo] nm (BOT) bud; (ZOOL) cocoon; (fam) idiot

caqui ['kaki] nm khaki

cara ['kara] nf (ANAT, de moneda) face; (de disco) side; (descaro) boldness; **~ a** facing; **de ~** opposite, facing; **dar la ~** to face the consequences; **¿~ o cruz?** heads or tails?; **¡qué ~ (más dura)!** what a nerve!

carabina [kara'ßina] nf carbine, rifle; (persona) chaperone

Caracas [ka'rakas] n Caracas

caracol [kara'kol] nm (ZOOL) snail; (concha) (sea) shell

carácter [ka'rakter] (pl caracteres) nm character; **tener buen/mal ~** to be good natured/bad tempered

característica [karakte'ristika] nf characteristic

característico, a [karakte'ristiko, a] adj characteristic

caracterizar [karakteri'θar] vt to characterize, typify

caradura [kara'ðura] nm/f: **es un ~** he's got a nerve

carajillo [kara'xiʎo] nm coffee with a dash of brandy

carajo [ka'raxo] (fam!) nm: **¡~!** shit! (!)

caramba [ka'ramba] excl good gracious!

carámbano [ka'rambano] nm icicle

caramelo [kara'melo] nm (dulce) sweet; (azúcar fundida) caramel

caravana [kara'ßana] nf caravan; (fig) group; (AUTO) tailback

carbón [kar'ßon] nm coal; **papel ~** carbon

paper; **carboncillo** nm (ARTE) charcoal; **carbonero, a** nm/f coal merchant; **carbonilla** [-'niʎa] nf coal dust

carbonizar [karßoni'θar] vt to carbonize; (quemar) to char

carbono [kar'ßono] nm carbon

carburador [karßura'ðor] nm carburettor

carburante [karßu'rante] nm (para motor) fuel

carcajada [karka'xaða] nf (loud) laugh, guffaw

cárcel [kar'θel] nf prison, jail; (TEC) clamp; **carcelero, a** adj prison cpd ♦ nm/f warder

carcoma [kar'koma] nf woodworm

carcomer [karko'mer] vt to bore into, eat into; (fig) to undermine; **~se** vr to become worm-eaten; (fig) to decay

cardar [kar'ðar] vt (pelo) to backcomb

cardenal [karðe'nal] nm (REL) cardinal; (MED) bruise

cardíaco, a [kar'ðiako, a] adj cardiac, heart cpd

cardinal [karði'nal] adj cardinal

cardo ['karðo] nm thistle

carearse [kare'arse] vr to come face to face

carecer [kare'θer] vi: **~ de** to lack, be in need of

carencia [ka'renθja] nf lack; (escasez) shortage; (MED) deficiency

carente [ka'rente] adj: **~ de** lacking in, devoid of

carestía [kares'tia] nf (escasez) scarcity, shortage; (COM) high cost

careta [ka'reta] nf mask

carga ['karɣa] nf (peso, ELEC) load; (de barco) cargo, freight; (MIL) charge; (responsabilidad) duty, obligation

cargado, a [kar'ɣaðo, a] adj loaded; (ELEC) live; (café, té) strong; (cielo) overcast

cargamento [karɣa'mento] nm (acción) loading; (mercancías) load, cargo

cargar [kar'ɣar] vt (barco, arma) to load; (ELEC) to charge; (COM: algo en cuenta) to charge; (INFORM) to load ♦ vi (MIL) to charge; (AUTO) to load (up); **~ con** to pick up, carry away; (peso, fig) to shoulder, bear; **~se** (fam) vr (estropear) to break; (matar) to bump off

cargo ['karɣo] nm (puesto) post, office; (responsabilidad) duty, obligation; (JUR) charge; **hacerse ~ de** to take charge of o responsibility for

carguero [kar'ɣero] nm freighter, cargo boat; (avión) freight plane

Caribe [ka'riße] nm: **el ~** the Caribbean; **del ~** Caribbean

caribeño, a [kari'ßeɲo, a] adj Caribbean

caricatura [karika'tura] nf caricature

caricia [ka'riθja] nf caress

caridad [kari'ðað] nf charity

caries ['karjes] nf inv tooth decay

cariño [ka'riɲo] nm affection, love; (caricia) caress; (en carta) love ...; **tener ~ a** to be fond of; **~so, a** adj affectionate

carisma [ka'risma] nm charisma

caritativo, a [karita'tiβo, a] adj charitable

cariz [ka'riθ] nm: **tener o tomar buen/mal ~** to look good/bad

carmesí [karme'si] adj, nm crimson

carmín [kar'min] nm lipstick

carnal [kar'nal] adj carnal; **primo ~** first cousin

carnaval [karna'βal] nm carnival

carne ['karne] nf flesh; (CULIN) meat; **~ de cerdo/cordero/ternera/vaca** pork/lamb/veal/beef; **~ de gallina** (fig): **se me pone la ~ de gallina sólo verlo** I get the creeps just seeing it

carné [kar'ne] (pl **~s**) nm: **~ de conducir** driving licence (BRIT), driver's license (US); **~ de identidad** identity card

carnero [kar'nero] nm sheep, ram; (carne) mutton

carnet [kar'ne] (pl **~s**) nm = **carné**

carnicería [karniθe'ria] nf butcher's (shop); (fig: matanza) carnage, slaughter

carnicero, a [karni'θero, a] adj carnivorous ♦ nm/f (tb fig) butcher; (carnívoro) carnivore

carnívoro, a [kar'niβoro, a] adj carnivorous

carnoso, a [kar'noso, a] adj beefy, fat

caro, a ['karo, a] adj dear; (COM) dear, expensive ♦ adv dear, dearly

carpa ['karpa] nf (pez) carp; (de circo) big top; (AM: de camping) tent

carpeta [kar'peta] nf folder, file

carpintería [karpinte'ria] nf carpentry, joinery; **carpintero** nm carpenter

carraspear [karraspe'ar] vi to clear one's throat

carraspera [karras'pera] nf hoarseness

carrera [ka'rrera] nf (acción) run(ning); (espacio recorrido) run; (competición) race; (trayecto) course; (profesión) career; (ESCOL) course

carreta [ka'rreta] nf wagon, cart

carrete [ka'rrete] nm reel, spool; (TEC) coil

carretera [karre'tera] nf (main) road, highway; **~ de circunvalación** ring road; **~ nacional** ≈ A road (BRIT), ≈ state highway (US)

carretilla [karre'tiʎa] nf trolley; (AGR) (wheel)barrow

carril [ka'rril] nm furrow; (de autopista) lane; (FERRO) rail

carrillo [ka'rriʎo] nm (ANAT) cheek; (TEC) pulley

carrito [ka'rrito] nm trolley

carro ['karro] nm cart, wagon; (MIL) tank; (AM: coche) car

carrocería [karroθe'ria] nf bodywork,

coachwork

carroña [ka'rroɲa] nf carrion no pl

carroza [ka'rroθa] nf (carruaje) coach

carrusel [karru'sel] nm merry-go-round, roundabout

carta ['karta] nf letter; (CULIN) menu; (naipe) card; (mapa) map; (JUR) document; **~ de ajuste** (TV) test card; **~ de crédito** credit card; **~ certificada** registered letter; **~ marítima** chart; **~ verde** (AUTO) green card

cartabón [karta'βon] nm set square

cartel [kar'tel] nm (anuncio) poster, placard; (ESCOL) wall chart; (COM) cartel; **~era** nf hoarding, billboard; (en periódico etc) entertainments guide; **"en ~era"** "showing"

cartera [kar'tera] nf (de bolsillo) wallet; (de colegial, cobrador) satchel; (de señora) handbag; (para documentos) briefcase; (COM) portfolio; **ocupa la ~ de Agricultura** she is Minister of Agriculture

carterista [karte'rista] nm/f pickpocket

cartero [kar'tero] nm postman

cartilla [kar'tiʎa] nf primer, first reading book; **~ de ahorros** savings book

cartón [kar'ton] nm cardboard; **~ piedra** papier-mâché

cartucho [kar'tutʃo] nm (MIL) cartridge

cartulina [kartu'lina] nf card

casa ['kasa] nf house; (hogar) home; (COM) firm, company; **en ~** at home; **~ consistorial** town hall; **~ de huéspedes** boarding house; **~ de socorro** first aid post

casado, a [ka'saðo, a] adj married ♦ nm/f married man/woman

casamiento [kasa'mjento] nm marriage, wedding

casar [ka'sar] vt to marry; (JUR) to quash, annul; **~se** vr to marry, get married

cascabel [kaska'βel] nm (small) bell

cascada [kas'kaða] nf waterfall

cascanueces [kaska'nweθes] nm inv nutcrackers pl

cascar [kas'kar] vt to crack, split, break (open); **~se** vr to crack, split, break (open)

cáscara ['kaskara] nf (de huevo, fruta seca) shell; (de fruta) skin; (de limón) peel

casco ['kasko] nm (de bombero, soldado) helmet; (NAUT: de barco) hull; (ZOOL: de caballo) hoof; (botella) empty bottle; (de ciudad): **el ~ antiguo** the old part; **el ~ urbano** the town centre; **los ~s azules** the UN peace-keeping force, the blue berets

cascote [kas'kote] nm rubble

caserío [kase'rio] nm hamlet; (casa) country house

casero, a [ka'sero, a] adj (pan etc) home-made ♦ nm/f (propietario) landlord/lady; **ser muy ~** to be home-loving; **"comida casera"** "home cooking"

caseta [ka'seta] nf hut; (para bañista) cubicle; (de feria) stall

casete [ka'sete] nm o f cassette

casi ['kasi] adv almost, nearly; ~ **nada** hardly anything; ~ **nunca** hardly ever, almost never; ~ **te caes** you almost fell

casilla [ka'siʎa] nf (casita) hut, cabin; (AJEDREZ) square; (para cartas) pigeonhole; **casillero** nm (para cartas) pigeonholes pl

casino [ka'sino] nm club; (de juego) casino

caso ['kaso] nm case; **en ~ de** ... in case of ...; **en ~ de que** ... in case ...; **el ~ es que** the fact is that; **en ese** ~ in that case; **hacer ~ a** to pay attention to; **hacer o venir al ~** to be relevant

caspa ['kaspa] nf dandruff

cassette [ka'sete] nm o f = **casete**

casta ['kasta] nf caste; (raza) breed; (linaje) lineage

castaña [kas'taɲa] nf chestnut

castañetear [kastaɲete'ar] vi (dientes) to chatter

castaño, a [kas'taɲo, a] adj chestnut (-coloured), brown ♦ nm chestnut tree

castañuelas [kasta'ɲwelas] nfpl castanets

castellano, a [kaste'ʎano, a] adj, nm/f Castilian ♦ nm (LING) Castilian, Spanish

castidad [kasti'ðað] nf chastity, purity

castigar [kasti'ɣar] vt to punish; (DEPORTE) to penalize; **castigo** nm punishment; (DEPORTE) penalty

Castilla [kas'tiʎa] nf Castile

castillo [kas'tiʎo] nm castle

castizo, a [kas'tiθo, a] adj (LING) pure

casto, a ['kasto, a] adj chaste, pure

castor [kas'tor] nm beaver

castrar [kas'trar] vt to castrate

castrense [kas'trense] adj (disciplina, vida) military

casual [ka'swal] adj chance, accidental; ~**idad** nf chance, accident; (combinación de circunstancias) coincidence; **¡qué ~idad!** what a coincidence!

cataclismo [kata'klismo] nm cataclysm

catador, a [kata'ðor, a] nm/f wine taster

catalán, ana [kata'lan, ana] adj, nm/f Catalan ♦ nm (LING) Catalan

catalizador [kataliθa'ðor] nm catalyst; (AUT) catalytic convertor

catalogar [katalo'ɣar] vt to catalogue; ~ **a algn (de)** (fig) to categorize sb (as)

catálogo [ka'taloɣo] nm catalogue

Cataluña [kata'luɲa] nf Catalonia

catar [ka'tar] vt to taste, sample

catarata [kata'rata] nf (GEO) waterfall; (MED) cataract

catarro [ka'tarro] nm catarrh; (constipado) cold

catástrofe [ka'tastrofe] nf catastrophe

catear [kate'ar] (fam) vt (examen, alumno) to fail

cátedra ['kateðra] nf (UNIV) chair, professorship

catedral [kate'ðral] nf cathedral

catedrático, a [kate'ðratiko, a] nm/f professor

categoría [kateɣo'ria] nf category; (rango) rank, standing; (calidad) quality; **de ~** (hotel) top-class

categórico, a [kate'ɣoriko, a] adj categorical

cateto, a ['kateto, a] (pey) nm/f peasant

catolicismo [katoli'θismo] nm Catholicism

católico, a [ka'toliko, a] adj, nm/f Catholic

catorce [ka'torθe] num fourteen

cauce ['kauθe] nm (de río) riverbed; (fig) channel

caucho ['kautʃo] nm rubber; (AM: llanta) tyre

caución [kau'θjon] nf bail; **caucionar** vt (JUR) to bail, go bail for

caudal [kau'ðal] nm (de río) volume, flow; (fortuna) wealth; (abundancia) abundance; ~**oso, a** adj (río) large

caudillo [kau'ðiʎo] nm leader, chief

causa ['kausa] nf cause; (razón) reason; (JUR) lawsuit, case; **a ~ de** because of

causar [kau'sar] vt to cause

cautela [kau'tela] nf caution, cautiousness; **cauteloso, a** adj cautious, wary

cautivar [kauti'ßar] vt to capture; (atraer) to captivate

cautiverio [kauti'ßerjo] nm captivity

cautividad [kautißi'ðað] nf = **cautiverio**

cautivo, a [kau'tißo, a] adj, nm/f captive

cauto, a ['kauto, a] adj cautious, careful

cava ['kaßa] nm champagne-type wine

cavar [ka'ßar] vt to dig

caverna [ka'ßerna] nf cave, cavern

cavidad [kaßi'ðað] nf cavity

cavilar [kaßi'lar] vt to ponder

cayado [ka'jaðo] nm (de pastor) crook; (de obispo) crozier

cayendo etc vb ver **caer**

caza ['kaθa] nf (acción: gen) hunting; (: con fusil) shooting; (una ~) hunt, chase; (animales) game ♦ nm (AVIAT) fighter

cazador, a [kaθa'ðor, a] nm/f hunter; **cazadora** nf jacket

cazar [ka'θar] vt to hunt; (perseguir) to chase; (prender) to catch

cazo ['kaθo] nm saucepan

cazuela [ka'θwela] nf (vasija) pan; (guisado) casserole

CD abbr (= compact disc) CD

CD-ROM abbr m CD-ROM

CE nf abr (= Comunidad Europea) EC

cebada [θe'ßaða] nf barley

cebar [θe'ßar] vt (animal) to fatten (up); (anzuelo) to bait; (MIL, TEC) to prime

cebo ['θeßo] nm (para animales) feed, food;

(*para peces*, *fig*) bait; (*de arma*) charge
cebolla [θe'βoʎa] *nf* onion; **cebolleta** *nf*
spring onion; **cebollín** *nm* spring onion
cebra ['θeβra] *nf* zebra
cecear [θeθe'ar] *vi* to lisp; **ceceo** *nm* lisp
ceder [θe'ðer] *vt* to hand over, give up, part
with ♦ *vi* (*renunciar*) to give in, yield;
(*disminuir*) to diminish, decline; (*romperse*) to
give way
cedro ['θeðro] *nm* cedar
cédula ['θeðula] *nf* certificate, document
cegar [θe'xar] *vt* to blind; (*tubería etc*) to
block up, stop up ♦ *vi* to go blind; **~se** *vr*:
~se (de) to be blinded (by)
ceguera [θe'xera] *nf* blindness
CEI *abbr* (= *Confederación de Estados
Independientes*) CIS
ceja ['θexa] *nf* eyebrow
cejar [θe'xar] *vi* (*fig*) to back down
celador, a [θela'ðor, a] *nm/f* (*de edificio*)
watchman; (*de museo etc*) attendant
celda ['θelda] *nf* cell
celebración [θeleβra'θjon] *nf* celebration
celebrar [θele'βrar] *vt* to celebrate; (*alabar*)
to praise ♦ *vi* to be glad; **~se** *vr* to occur, take
place
célebre ['θelebre] *adj* famous
celebridad [θeleβri'ðað] *nf* fame; (*persona*)
celebrity
celeste [θe'leste] *adj* (*azul*) sky-blue
celestial [θeles'tjal] *adj* celestial, heavenly
celibato [θeli'βato] *nm* celibacy
célibe ['θeliβe] *adj, nm/f* celibate
celo[1] ['θelo] *nm* zeal; (*REL*) fervour; (*ZOOL*): **en
~** on heat; **~s** *nmpl* jealousy *sg*; **tener ~s** to be
jealous
celo[2] ® ['θelo] *nm* Sellotape ®
celofán [θelo'fan] *nm* cellophane
celoso, a [θe'loso, a] *adj* jealous; (*trabajador*)
zealous
celta ['θelta] *adj* Celtic ♦ *nm/f* Celt
célula ['θelula] *nf* cell; **~ solar** solar cell
celulitis [θelu'litis] *nf* cellulite
celuloide [θelu'loiðe] *nm* celluloid
cementerio [θemen'terjo] *nm* cemetery,
graveyard
cemento [θe'mento] *nm* cement; (*hormigón*)
concrete; (*AM*: *cola*) glue
cena ['θena] *nf* evening meal, dinner
cenagal [θena'xal] *nm* bog, quagmire
cenar [θe'nar] *vt* to have for dinner ♦ *vi* to
have dinner
cenicero [θeni'θero] *nm* ashtray
cenit [θe'nit] *nm* zenith
ceniza [θe'niθa] *nf* ash, ashes *pl*
censo ['θenso] *nm* census; **~ electoral**
electoral roll
censura [θen'sura] *nf* (*POL*) censorship
censurar [θensu'rar] *vt* (*idea*) to censure;

(*cortar*: *película*) to censor
centella [θen'teʎa] *nf* spark
centellear [θenteʎe'ar] *vi* (*metal*) to gleam;
(*estrella*) to twinkle; (*fig*) to sparkle
centenar [θente'nar] *nm* hundred
centenario, a [θente'narjo, a] *adj*
centenary; hundred-year-old ♦ *nm* centenary
centeno [θen'teno] *nm* (*BOT*) rye
centésimo, a [θen'tesimo, a] *adj* hundredth
centígrado [θen'tiɣraðo] *adj* centigrade
centímetro [θen'timetro] *nm* centimetre
(*BRIT*), centimeter (*US*)
céntimo ['θentimo] *nm* cent
centinela [θenti'nela] *nm* sentry, guard
centollo [θen'toʎo] *nm* spider crab
central [θen'tral] *adj* central ♦ *nf* head office;
(*TEC*) plant; (*TEL*) exchange; **~ eléctrica** power
station; **~ nuclear** nuclear power station;
~ telefónica telephone exchange
centralita [θentra'lita] *nf* switchboard
centralizar [θentrali'θar] *vt* to centralize
centrar [θen'trar] *vt* to centre
céntrico, a ['θentriko, a] *adj* central
centrifugar [θentrifu'xar] *vt* to spin-dry
centrista [θen'trista] *adj* centre *cpd*
centro ['θentro] *nm* centre; **~ comercial**
shopping centre; **~ juvenil** youth club; **~ de
llamadas** call centre
centroamericano, a [θentroameri'kano,
a] *adj, nm/f* Central American
ceñido, a [θe'ɲiðo, a] *adj* (*chaqueta,
pantalón*) tight(-fitting)
ceñir [θe'ɲir] *vt* (*rodear*) to encircle, surround;
(*ajustar*) to fit (tightly)
ceño ['θeɲo] *nm* frown, scowl; **fruncir el ~** to
frown, knit one's brow
CEOE *nf abr* (*ESP*: = *Confederación Española de
Organizaciones Empresariales*) ≈ CBI (*BRIT*),
employers' organization
cepillar [θepi'ʎar] *vt* to brush; (*madera*) to
plane (down)
cepillo [θe'piʎo] *nm* brush; (*para madera*)
plane; **~ de dientes** toothbrush
cera ['θera] *nf* wax
cerámica [θe'ramika] *nf* pottery; (*arte*)
ceramics
cerca ['θerka] *nf* fence ♦ *adv* near, nearby,
close; **~ de** near,.close to
cercanías [θerka'nias] *nfpl* (*afueras*) outskirts,
suburbs
cercano, a [θer'kano, a] *adj* close, near
cercar [θer'kar] *vt* to fence in; (*rodear*) to
surround
cerciorar [θerθjo'rar] *vt* (*asegurar*) to assure;
~se *vr* (*asegurarse*) to make sure
cerco ['θerko] *nm* (*AGR*) enclosure; (*AM*)
fence; (*MIL*) siege
cerdo, a ['θerðo, a] *nm/f* pig/sow
cereal [θere'al] *nm* cereal; **~es** *nmpl* cereals,

grain sg

cerebro [θe'reβro] nm brain; (fig) brains pl

ceremonia [θere'monja] nf ceremony; **ceremonial** adj, nm ceremonial; **ceremonioso, a** adj ceremonious

cereza [θe'reθa] nf cherry

cerilla [θe'riʎa] nf (fósforo) match

cernerse [θer'nerse] vr to hover

cero ['θero] nm nothing, zero

cerrado, a [θe'rraðo, a] adj closed, shut; (con llave) locked; (tiempo) cloudy, overcast; (curva) sharp; (acento) thick, broad

cerradura [θerra'ðura] nf (acción) closing; (mecanismo) lock

cerrajero [θerra'xero] nm locksmith

cerrar [θe'rrar] vt to close, shut; (paso, carretera) to close; (grifo) to turn off; (cuenta, negocio) to close ♦ vi to close, shut; (la noche) to come down; ~se vr to close, shut; ~ con llave to lock; ~ un trato to strike a bargain

cerro ['θerro] nm hill

cerrojo [θe'rroxo] nm (herramienta) bolt; (de puerta) latch

certamen [θer'tamen] nm competition, contest

certero, a [θer'tero, a] adj (gen) accurate

certeza [θer'teθa] nf certainty

certidumbre [θerti'ðumßre] nf = **certeza**

certificado [θertifi'kaðo] nm certificate

certificar [θertifi'kar] vt (asegurar, atestar) to certify

cervatillo [θerβa'tiʎo] nm fawn

cervecería [θerßeθe'ria] nf (fábrica) brewery; (bar) public house, pub

cerveza [θer'ßeθa] nf beer

cesante [θe'sante] adj redundant

cesar [θe'sar] vi to cease, stop ♦ vt (funcionario) to remove from office

cesárea [θe'sarea] nf (MED) Caesarean operation o section

cese ['θese] nm (de trabajo) dismissal; (de pago) suspension

césped ['θespeð] nm grass, lawn

cesta ['θesta] nf basket

cesto ['θesto] nm (large) basket, hamper

cetro ['θetro] nm sceptre

cfr abr (= confróntese) cf.

chabacano, a [tʃaßa'kano, a] adj vulgar, coarse

chabola [tʃa'ßola] nf shack; **barrio de ~s** shanty town sg

chacal [tʃa'kal] nm jackal

chacha [tʃatʃa] (fam) nf maid

cháchara ['tʃatʃara] nf chatter; **estar de ~** to chatter away

chacra ['tʃakra] (AM) nf smallholding

chafar [tʃa'far] vt (aplastar) to crush; (plan etc) to ruin

chal [tʃal] nm shawl

chalado, a [tʃa'lado, a] (fam) adj crazy

chalé [tʃa'le] (pl ~s) nm villa; ≈ detached house

chaleco [tʃa'leko] nm waistcoat, vest (US); ~ **salvavidas** life jacket

chalet [tʃa'le] (pl ~s) nm = **chalé**

champán [tʃam'pan] nm champagne

champaña [tʃam'paɲa] nm = **champán**

champiñón [tʃampi'ɲon] nm mushroom

champú [tʃam'pu] (pl **champúes, champús**) nm shampoo

chamuscar [tʃamus'kar] vt to scorch, sear, singe

chance ['tʃanθe] (AM) nm chance

chancho, a ['tʃantʃo, a] (AM) nm/f pig

chanchullo [tʃan'tʃuʎo] (fam) nm fiddle

chandal [tʃan'dal] nm tracksuit

chantaje [tʃan'taxe] nm blackmail

chapa ['tʃapa] nf (de metal) plate, sheet; (de madera) board, panel; (AM: AUTO) number (BRIT) o license (US) plate; ~**do, a** adj: ~**do en oro** gold-plated

chaparrón [tʃapa'rron] nm downpour, cloudburst

chapotear [tʃapote'ar] vi to splash about

chapurrear [tʃapurre'ar] vt (idioma) to speak badly

chapuza [tʃa'puθa] nf botched job

chapuzón [tʃapu'θon] nm: **darse un ~** to go for a dip

chaqueta [tʃa'keta] nf jacket

chaquetón [tʃake'ton] nm long jacket

charca ['tʃarka] nf pond, pool

charco ['tʃarko] nm pool, puddle

charcutería [tʃarkute'ria] nf (tienda) shop selling chiefly pork meat products; (productos) cooked pork meats pl

charla ['tʃarla] nf talk, chat; (conferencia) lecture

charlar [tʃar'lar] vi to talk, chat

charlatán, ana [tʃarla'tan, ana] nm/f (hablador) chatterbox; (estafador) trickster

charol [tʃa'rol] nm varnish; (cuero) patent leather

chascarrillo [tʃaska'rriʎo] (fam) nm funny story

chasco ['tʃasko] nm (desengaño) disappointment

chasis ['tʃasis] nm inv chassis

chasquear [tʃaske'ar] vt (látigo) to crack; (lengua) to click; **chasquido** nm crack; click

chatarra [tʃa'tarra] nf scrap (metal)

chato, a ['tʃato, a] adj flat; (nariz) snub

chaval, a [tʃa'ßal, a] nm/f kid, lad/lass

checo, a ['tʃeko, a] adj, nm/f Czech ♦ nm (LING) Czech

checo(e)slovaco, a [tʃeko(e)slo'ßako, a] adj, nm/f Czech, Czechoslovak

Checo(e)slovaquia [tʃeko(e)slo'ßakja] nf Czechoslovakia .

cheque ['tʃeke] nm cheque (BRIT), check (US); **~ de viajero** traveller's cheque (BRIT), traveler's check (US)

chequeo [tʃe'keo] nm (MED) check-up; (AUTO) service

chequera [tʃe'kera] (AM) nf chequebook (BRIT), checkbook (US)

chicano, a [tʃi'kano, a] adj, nm/f chicano

chícharo ['tʃitʃaro] (AM) nm pea

chichón [tʃi'tʃon] nm bump, lump

chicle ['tʃikle] nm chewing gum

chico, a ['tʃiko, a] adj small, little ♦ nm/f (niño) child; (muchacho) boy/girl

chiflado, a [tʃi'flaðo, a] adj crazy

chiflar [tʃi'flar] vt to hiss, boo

Chile ['tʃile] nm Chile; **chileno, a** adj, nm/f Chilean

chile ['tʃile] nm chilli pepper

chillar [tʃi'ʎar] vi (persona) to yell, scream; (animal salvaje) to howl; (cerdo) to squeal

chillido [tʃi'ʎiðo] nm (de persona) yell, scream; (de animal) howl

chillón, ona [tʃi'ʎon, ona] adj (niño) noisy; (color) loud, gaudy

chimenea [tʃime'nea] nf chimney; (hogar) fireplace

China ['tʃina] nf: **(la) ~** China

chinche ['tʃintʃe] nf (insecto) (bed)bug; (TEC) drawing pin (BRIT), thumbtack (US) ♦ nm/f nuisance, pest

chincheta [tʃin'tʃeta] nf drawing pin (BRIT), thumbtack (US)

chino, a ['tʃino, a] adj, nm/f Chinese ♦ nm (LING) Chinese

chipirón [tʃipi'ron] nm (ZOOL, CULIN) squid

Chipre ['tʃipre] nf Cyprus; **chipriota** adj, nm/f Cypriot

chiquillo, a [tʃi'kiʎo, a] nm/f (fam) kid

chirimoya [tʃiri'moja] nf custard apple

chiringuito [tʃirin'ʃito] nm small open-air bar

chiripa [tʃi'ripa] nf fluke

chirriar [tʃi'rrjar] vi to creak, squeak

chirrido [tʃi'rriðo] nm creak(ing), squeak(ing)

chis [tʃis] excl sh!

chisme ['tʃisme] nm (habladurías) piece of gossip; (fam: objeto) thingummyjig

chismoso, a [tʃis'moso, a] adj gossiping ♦ nm/f gossip

chispa ['tʃispa] nf spark; (fig) sparkle; (ingenio) wit; (fam) drunkenness

chispear [tʃispe'ar] vi (lloviznar) to drizzle

chisporrotear [tʃisporrote'ar] vi (fuego) to throw out sparks; (leña) to crackle; (aceite) to hiss, splutter

chiste ['tʃiste] nm joke, funny story

chistoso, a [tʃis'toso, a] adj funny, amusing

chivo, a ['tʃiβo, a] nm/f (billy-/nanny-) goat; **~ expiatorio** scapegoat

chocante [tʃo'kante] adj startling; (extraño) odd; (ofensivo) shocking

chocar [tʃo'kar] vi (coches etc) to collide, crash ♦ vt to shock; (sorprender) to startle; **~ con** to collide with; (fig) to run into, run up against; **¡chócala!** (fam) put it there!

chochear [tʃotʃe'ar] vi to dodder, be senile

chocho, a ['tʃotʃo, a] adj doddering, senile; (fig) soft, doting

chocolate [tʃoko'late] adj, nm chocolate; **chocolatina** nf chocolate

chofer [tʃo'fer] nm = **chófer**

chófer ['tʃofer] nm driver

chollo ['tʃoʎo] (fam) nm bargain, snip

choque etc ['tʃoke] vb ver **chocar** ♦ nm (impacto) impact; (golpe) jolt; (AUTO) crash; (fig) conflict; **~ frontal** head-on collision

chorizo [tʃo'riθo] nm hard pork sausage, (type of) salami

chorrada [tʃo'rraða] (fam) nf: **¡es una ~!** that's crap! (!); **decir ~s** to talk crap (!)

chorrear [tʃorre'ar] vi to gush (out), spout (out); (gotear) to drip, trickle

chorro ['tʃorro] nm jet; (fig) stream

choza ['tʃoθa] nf hut, shack

chubasco [tʃu'ßasko] nm squall

chubasquero [tʃußas'kero] nm lightweight raincoat

chuchería [tʃutʃe'ria] nf trinket

chuleta [tʃu'leta] nf chop, cutlet

chulo ['tʃulo] nm (de prostituta) pimp

chupar [tʃu'par] vt to suck; (absorber) to absorb; **~se** vr to grow thin

chupete [tʃu'pete] nm dummy (BRIT), pacifier (US)

chupito [tʃu'pito] (fam) nm shot

churro ['tʃurro] nm (type of) fritter

chusma ['tʃusma] nf rabble, mob

chutar [tʃu'tar] vi to shoot (at goal)

Cía abr (= compañía) Co.

cianuro [θja'nuro] nm cyanide

cibercafé [θißerka'fe] nf cybercafé

cicatriz [θika'triθ] nf scar; **~arse** vr to heal (up), form a scar

ciclismo [θi'klismo] nm cycling

ciclista [θi'klista] adj cycle cpd ♦ nm/f cyclist

ciclo ['θiklo] nm cycle; **~turismo** nm: **hacer ~turismo** to go on a cycling holiday

ciclón [θi'klon] nm cyclone

ciego, a ['θjeɣo, a] adj blind ♦ nm/f blind man/woman

cielo ['θjelo] nm sky; (REL) heaven; **¡~s!** good heavens!

ciempiés [θjem'pjes] nm inv centipede

cien [θjen] num ver **ciento**

ciénaga ['θjenaɣa] nf marsh, swamp

ciencia [ˈθjenθja] nf science; **~s** nfpl (ESCOL)
    science sg; **~-ficción** nf science fiction
cieno [ˈθjeno] nm mud, mire
científico, a [θjenˈtifiko, a] adj scientific
    ♦ nm/f scientist
ciento [ˈθjento] (tb: cien) num hundred;
    pagar al 10 por ~ to pay at 10 per cent
cierre etc [ˈθjerre] vb ver cerrar ♦ nm closing,
    shutting; (con llave) locking; **~ de cremallera**
    zip (fastener)
cierro etc vb ver cerrar
cierto, a [ˈθjerto, a] adj sure, certain; (un tal)
    a certain; (correcto) right, correct; **~ hombre**
    a certain man; **ciertas personas** certain o
    some people; **sí, es ~** yes, that's correct
ciervo [ˈθjerβo] nm deer; (macho) stag
cierzo [ˈθjerθo] nm north wind
cifra [ˈθifra] nf number; (secreta) code
cifrar [θiˈfrar] vt to code, write in code
cigala [θiˈɣala] nf Norway lobster
cigarra [θiˈɣarra] nf cicada
cigarrillo [θiɣaˈrriʎo] nm cigarette
cigarro [θiˈɣarro] nm cigarette; (puro) cigar
cigüeña [θiˈɣweɲa] nf stork
cilíndrico, a [θiˈlindriko, a] adj cylindrical
cilindro [θiˈlindro] nm cylinder
cima [ˈθima] nf (de montaña) top, peak; (de
    árbol) top; (fig) height
cimbrearse [θimbreˈarse] vr to sway
cimentar [θimenˈtar] vt to lay the
    foundations of; (fig: fundar) to found
cimiento [θiˈmjento] nm foundation
cinc [θink] nm zinc
cincel [θinˈθel] nm chisel; **~ar** vt to chisel
cinco [ˈθinko] num five
cincuenta [θinˈkwenta] num fifty
cine [ˈθine] nm cinema
cineasta [θineˈasta] nm/f film director
cinematográfico, a [θinematoˈɣrafiko, a]
    adj cine-, film cpd
cínico, a [ˈθiniko, a] adj cynical ♦ nm/f cynic
cinismo [θiˈnismo] nm cynicism
cinta [ˈθinta] nf band, strip; (de tela) ribbon;
    (película) reel; (de máquina de escribir)
    ribbon; **~ adhesiva** sticky tape; **~ de vídeo**
    videotape; **~ magnetofónica** tape; **~ métrica**
    tape measure
cintura [θinˈtura] nf waist
cinturón [θintuˈron] nm belt; **~ de seguridad**
    safety belt
ciprés [θiˈpres] nm cypress (tree)
circo [ˈθirko] nm circus
circuito [θirˈkwito] nm circuit
circulación [θirkulaˈθjon] nf circulation;
    (AUTO) traffic
circular [θirkuˈlar] adj, nf circular ♦ vi, vt to
    circulate ♦ vi (AUTO) to drive; **"circule por la
    derecha"** "keep (to the) right"
círculo [ˈθirkulo] nm circle; **~ vicioso** vicious

circle
circuncidar [θirkunθiˈdar] vt to circumcise
circundar [θirkunˈdar] vt to surround
circunferencia [θirkunfeˈrenθja] nf
    circumference
circunscribir [θirkunskriˈβir] vt to
    circumscribe; **~se** vr to be limited
circunscripción [θirkunskripˈθjon] nf (POL)
    constituency
circunspecto, a [θirkunsˈpekto, a] adj
    circumspect, cautious
circunstancia [θirkunsˈtanθja] nf
    circumstance
cirio [ˈθirjo] nm (wax) candle
ciruela [θiˈrwela] nf plum; **~ pasa** prune
cirugía [θiruˈxia] nf surgery; **~ estética** o
    plástica plastic surgery
cirujano [θiruˈxano] nm surgeon
cisne [ˈθisne] nm swan
cisterna [θisˈterna] nf cistern, tank
cita [ˈθita] nf appointment, meeting; (de
    novios) date; (referencia) quotation
citación [θitaˈθjon] nf (JUR) summons sg
citar [θiˈtar] vt (gen) to make an appointment
    with; (JUR) to summons; (un autor, texto) to
    quote; **~se** vr: **se citaron en el cine** they
    arranged to meet at the cinema
cítricos [ˈθitrikos] nmpl citrus fruit(s)
ciudad [θjuˈðað] nf town; (más grande) city;
    ~anía nf citizenship; **~ano, a** nm/f citizen
cívico, a [ˈθiβiko, a] adj civic
civil [θiˈβil] adj civil ♦ nm (guardia) policeman
civilización [θiβiliθaˈθjon] nf civilization
civilizar [θiβiliˈθar] vt to civilize
civismo [θiˈβismo] nm public spirit
cizaña [θiˈθaɲa] nf (fig) discord
cl. abr (= centilitro) cl.
clamar [klaˈmar] vt to clamour for, cry out for
    ♦ vi to cry out, clamour
clamor [klaˈmor] nm clamour, protest
clandestino, a [klandesˈtino, a] adj
    clandestine; (POL) underground
clara [ˈklara] nf (de huevo) egg white
claraboya [klaraˈβoja] nf skylight
clarear [klareˈar] vi (el día) to dawn; (el cielo)
    to clear up, brighten up; **~se** vr to be
    transparent
clarete [klaˈrete] nm rosé (wine)
claridad [klariˈðað] nf (del día) brightness;
    (de estilo) clarity
clarificar [klarifiˈkar] vt to clarify
clarinete [klariˈnete] nm clarinet
clarividencia [klariβiˈðenθja] nf
    clairvoyance; (fig) far-sightedness
claro, a [ˈklaro, a] adj clear; (luminoso)
    bright; (color) light; (evidente) clear, evident;
    (poco espeso) thin ♦ nm (en bosque) clearing
    ♦ adv clearly ♦ excl (tb: **~ que sí**) of course!
clase [ˈklase] nf class; **~ alta/media/obrera**

upper/middle/working class; **~s particulares** private lessons, private tuition *sg*

clásico, a |'klasiko, a| *adj* classical

clasificación |klasifika'θjon| *nf* classification; (*DEPORTE*) league (table)

clasificar |klasifi'kar| *vt* to classify

claudicar |klauði'kar| *vi* to give in

claustro |'klaustro| *nm* cloister

cláusula |'klausula| *nf* clause

clausura |klau'sura| *nf* closing, closure; **clausurar** *vt* (*congreso etc*) to bring to a close

clavar |kla'ßar| *vt* (*clavo*) to hammer in; (*cuchillo*) to stick, thrust

clave |'klaße| *nf* key; (*MUS*) clef

clavel |kla'ßel| *nm* carnation

clavícula |kla'ßikula| *nf* collar bone

clavija |kla'ßixa| *nf* peg, dowel, pin; (*ELEC*) plug

clavo |'klaßo| *nm* (*de metal*) nail; (*BOT*) clove

claxon |'klakson| (*pl* **~s**) *nm* horn

clemencia |kle'menθja| *nf* mercy, clemency

cleptómano, a |klep'tomano, a| *nm/f* kleptomaniac

clérigo |'kleriɣo| *nm* priest

clero |'klero| *nm* clergy

cliché |kli'tʃe| *nm* cliché; (*FOTO*) negative

cliente, a |'kljente, a| *nm/f* client, customer

clientela |kljen'tela| *nf* clientele, customers *pl*

clima |'klima| *nm* climate

climatizado, a |klimati'θaðo, a| *adj* air-conditioned

clímax |'klimaks| *nm inv* climax

clínica |'klinika| *nf* clinic; (*particular*) private hospital

clip |klip| (*pl* **~s**) *nm* paper clip

clítoris |'klitoris| *nm inv* (*ANAT*) clitoris

cloaca |klo'aka| *nf* sewer

cloro |'kloro| *nm* chlorine

club |klub| (*pl* **~s** o **~es**) *nm* club; **~ de jóvenes** youth club

cm *abr* (= *centímetro, centímetros*) cm

C.N.T. (*ESP*) *abr* = *Confederación Nacional de Trabajo*

coacción |koak'θjon| *nf* coercion, compulsion; **coaccionar** *vt* to coerce

coagular |koaɣu'lar| *vt* (*leche, sangre*) to clot; **~se** *vr* to clot; **coágulo** *nm* clot

coalición |koali'θjon| *nf* coalition

coartada |koar'taða| *nf* alibi

coartar |koar'tar| *vt* to limit, restrict

coba |'koßa| *nf*: **dar ~ a uno** to soft-soap sb

cobarde |ko'ßarðe| *adj* cowardly ♦ *nm* coward; **cobardía** *nf* cowardice

cobaya |ko'ßaja| *nf* guinea pig

cobertizo |koßer'tiθo| *nm* shelter

cobertura |koßer'tura| *nf* cover

cobija |ko'ßixa| (*AM*) *nf* blanket

cobijar |koßi'xar| *vt* (*cubrir*) to cover;

(*proteger*) to shelter; **cobijo** *nm* shelter

cobra |'koßra| *nf* cobra

cobrador, a |koßra'ðor, a| *nm/f* (*de autobús*) conductor/conductress; (*de impuestos, gas*) collector

cobrar |ko'ßrar| *vt* (*cheque*) to cash; (*sueldo*) to collect, draw; (*objeto*) to recover; (*precio*) to charge; (*deuda*) to collect ♦ *vi* to be paid; **cóbrese al entregar** cash on delivery

cobre |'koßre| *nm* copper; **~s** *nmpl* (*MUS*) brass instruments

cobro |'koßro| *nm* (*de cheque*) cashing; **presentar al ~** to cash

cocaína |koka'ina| *nf* cocaine

cocción |kok'θjon| *nf* (*CULIN*) cooking; (*en agua*) boiling

cocear |koθe'ar| *vi* to kick

cocer |ko'θer| *vt, vi* to cook; (*en agua*) to boil; (*en horno*) to bake

coche |'kotʃe| *nm* (*AUTO*) car (*BRIT*), automobile (*US*); (*de tren, de caballos*) coach, carriage; (*para niños*) pram (*BRIT*), baby carriage (*US*); **ir en ~** to drive; **~ celular** Black Maria, prison van; **~ de bomberos** fire engine; **~ fúnebre** hearse; **coche-cama** (*pl* **coches-cama**) *nm* (*FERRO*) sleeping car, sleeper

cochera |ko'tʃera| *nf* garage; (*de autobuses, trenes*) depot

coche restaurante (*pl* **coches restaurante**) *nm* (*FERRO*) dining car, diner

cochinillo |kotʃi'niʎo| *nm* (*CULIN*) suckling pig, sucking pig

cochino, a |ko'tʃino, a| *adj* filthy, dirty ♦ *nm/f* pig

cocido |ko'θiðo| *nm* stew

cocina |ko'θina| *nf* kitchen; (*aparato*) cooker, stove; (*acto*) cookery; **~ eléctrica/de gas** electric/gas cooker; **~ francesa** French cuisine; **cocinar** *vt, vi* to cook

cocinero, a |koθi'nero, a| *nm/f* cook

coco |'koko| *nm* coconut

cocodrilo |koko'ðrilo| *nm* crocodile

cocotero |koko'tero| *nm* coconut palm

cóctel |'koktel| *nm* cocktail

codazo |ko'ðaθo| *nm*: **dar un ~ a uno** to nudge sb

codicia |ko'ðiθja| *nf* greed; **codiciar** *vt* to covet; **codicioso, a** *adj* covetous

código |'koðiɣo| *nm* code; **~ de barras** bar code; **~ civil** common law; **~ de (la) circulación** highway code; **~ postal** postcode

codillo |ko'ðiʎo| *nm* (*ZOOL*) knee; (*TEC*) elbow (joint)

codo |'koðo| *nm* (*ANAT, de tubo*) elbow; (*ZOOL*) knee

codorniz |koðor'niθ| *nf* quail

coerción |koer'θjon| *nf* coercion

coetáneo, a |koe'taneo, a| *adj, nm/f* contemporary

coexistir |koe(k)sis'tir| vi to coexist

cofradía |kofra'ðia| nf brotherhood, fraternity

cofre |'kofre| nm (de joyas) case; (de dinero) chest

coger |ko'xer| (ESP) vt to take (hold of); (objeto caído) to pick up; (frutas) to pick, harvest; (resfriado, ladrón, pelota) to catch ♦ vi: ~ por el buen camino to take the right road; ~se vr (el dedo) to catch; ~se a algo to get hold of sth

cogollo |ko'xoλo| nm (de lechuga) heart

cogote |ko'xote| nm back o nape of the neck

cohabitar |koaßi'tar| vi to live together, cohabit

cohecho |ko'etʃo| nm (acción) bribery; (soborno) bribe

coherente |koe'rente| adj coherent

cohesión |koe'sjon| nm cohesion

cohete |ko'ete| nm rocket

cohibido, a |koi'ßiðo, a| adj (PSICO) inhibited; (tímido) shy

cohibir |koi'ßir| vt to restrain, restrict

coincidencia |koinθi'ðenθja| nf coincidence

coincidir |koinθi'ðir| vi (en idea) to coincide, agree; (en lugar) to coincide

coito |'koito| nm intercourse, coitus

coja etc vb ver **coger**

cojear |koxe'ar| vi (persona) to limp, hobble; (mueble) to wobble, rock

cojera |ko'xera| nf limp

cojín |ko'xin| nm cushion; **cojinete** nm (TEC) ball bearing

cojo, a etc |'koxo, a| vb ver **coger** ♦ adj (que no puede andar) lame, crippled; (mueble) wobbly ♦ nm/f lame person, cripple

cojón |ko'xon| (fam) nm: ¡cojones! shit! (!); **cojonudo, a** (fam) adj great, fantastic

col |kol| nf cabbage; ~es de Bruselas Brussels sprouts

cola |'kola| nf tail; (de gente) queue; (lugar) end, last place; (para pegar) glue, gum; **hacer ~** to queue (up)

colaborador, a |kolaßora'ðor, a| nm/f collaborator

colaborar |kolaßo'rar| vi to collaborate

colada |ko'laða| nf: **hacer la ~** to do the washing

colador |kola'ðor| nm (de líquidos) strainer; (para verduras etc) colander

colapso |ko'lapso| nm collapse; ~ nervioso nervous breakdown

colar |ko'lar| vt (líquido) to strain off; (metal) to cast ♦ vi to ooze, seep (through); ~se vr to jump the queue; ~se en to get into without paying; (fiesta) to gatecrash

colcha |'koltʃa| nf bedspread

colchón |kol'tʃon| nm mattress; ~ inflable o neumático air bed, air mattress

colchoneta |koltʃo'neta| nf (en gimnasio)

mat; (de playa) air bed

colección |kolek'θjon| nf collection; **coleccionar** vt to collect; **coleccionista** nm/f collector

colecta |ko'lekta| nf collection

colectivo, a |kolek'tißo, a| adj collective, joint ♦ nm (AM) (small) bus

colega |ko'leɣa| nm/f colleague

colegial, a |kole'xjal, a| nm/f schoolboy/girl

colegio |ko'lexjo| nm college; (escuela) school; (de abogados etc) association; ~ electoral polling station; ~ mayor hall of residence

colegir |kole'xir| vt to infer, conclude

cólera |'kolera| nf (ira) anger; (MED) cholera; **colérico, a** |ko'leriko, a| adj irascible, bad-tempered

colesterol |koleste'rol| nm cholesterol

coleta |ko'leta| nf pigtail

colgante |kol'ɣante| adj hanging ♦ nm (joya) pendant

colgar |kol'ɣar| vt to hang (up); (ropa) to hang out ♦ vi to hang; (TELEC) to hang up

cólico |'koliko| nm colic

coliflor |koli'flor| nf cauliflower

colilla |ko'liλa| nf cigarette end, butt

colina |ko'lina| nf hill

colisión |koli'sjon| nf collision; ~ de frente head-on crash

collar |ko'λar| nm necklace; (de perro) collar

colmar |kol'mar| vt to fill to the brim; (fig) to fulfil, realize

colmena |kol'mena| nf beehive

colmillo |kol'miλo| nm (diente) eye tooth; (de elefante) tusk; (de perro) fang

colmo |'kolmo| nm: ¡es el ~! it's the limit!

colocación |koloka'θjon| nf (acto) placing; (empleo) job, position

colocar |kolo'kar| vt to place, put, position; (dinero) to invest; (poner en empleo) to find a job for; ~se vr to get a job

Colombia |ko'lombja| nf Colombia; **colombiano, a** adj, nm/f Colombian

colonia |ko'lonja| nf colony; (de casas) housing estate; (agua de ~) cologne

colonización |koloniθa'θjon| nf colonization; **colonizador, a** |koloniθa'ðor, a| adj colonizing ♦ nm/f colonist, settler

colonizar |koloni'θar| vt to colonize

coloquio |ko'lokjo| nm conversation; (congreso) conference

color |ko'lor| nm colour

colorado, a |kolo'raðo, a| adj (rojo) red; (LAM: chiste) rude

colorante |kolo'rante| nm colouring

colorear |kolore'ar| vt to colour

colorete |kolo'rete| nm blusher

colorido |kolo'riðo| nm colouring

columna |ko'lumna| nf column; (pilar) pillar;

(*apoyo*) support

columpiar [kolum'pjar] *vt* to swing; **~se** *vr* to swing; **columpio** *nm* swing

coma ['koma] *nf* comma ♦ *nm* (MED) coma

comadre [ko'maðre] *nf* (*madrina*) godmother; (*chismosa*) gossip; **comadrona** *nf* midwife

comandancia [koman'danθja] *nf* command

comandante [koman'dante] *nm* commandant

comarca [ko'marka] *nf* region

comba ['komba] *nf* (*curva*) curve; (*cuerda*) skipping rope; **saltar a la ~** to skip

combar [kom'bar] *vt* to bend, curve

combate [kom'bate] *nm* fight; **combatiente** *nm* combatant

combatir [komba'tir] *vt* to fight, combat

combinación [kombina'θjon] *nf* combination; (QUÍM) compound; (*prenda*) slip

combinar [kombi'nar] *vt* to combine

combustible [kombus'tiβle] *nm* fuel

combustión [kombus'tjon] *nf* combustion

comedia [ko'meðja] *nf* comedy; (TEATRO) play, drama

comediante [kome'ðjante] *nm/f* (comic) actor/actress

comedido, a [kome'ðiðo, a] *adj* moderate

comedor, a [kome'ðor, a] *nm* (*habitación*) dining room; (*cantina*) canteen

comensal [komen'sal] *nm/f* fellow guest (o diner)

comentar [komen'tar] *vt* to comment on

comentario [komen'tarjo] *nm* comment, remark; (*literario*) commentary; **~s** *nmpl* (*chismes*) gossip *sg*

comentarista [komenta'rista] *nm/f* commentator

comenzar [komen'θar] *vt*, *vi* to begin, start; **~ a hacer algo** to begin o start doing sth

comer [ko'mer] *vt* to eat; (DAMAS, AJEDREZ) to take, capture ♦ *vi* to eat; (*almorzar*) to have lunch; **~se** *vr* to eat up

comercial [komer'θjal] *adj* commercial; (*relativo al negocio*) business *cpd*; **comercializar** *vt* (*producto*) to market; (*pey*) to commercialize

comerciante [komer'θjante] *nm/f* trader, merchant

comerciar [komer'θjar] *vi* to trade, do business

comercio [ko'merθjo] *nm* commerce, trade; (*negocio*) business; (*fig*) dealings *pl*; **~ electrónico** e-commerce

comestible [komes'tiβle] *adj* eatable, edible; **~s** *nmpl* food *sg*, foodstuffs

cometa [ko'meta] *nm* comet ♦ *nf* kite

cometer [kome'ter] *vt* to commit

cometido [kome'tiðo] *nm* task, assignment

comezón [kome'θon] *nf* itch, itching

cómic ['komik] *nm* comic

comicios [ko'miθjos] *nmpl* elections

cómico, a ['komiko, a] *adj* comic(al) ♦ *nm/f* comedian

comida [ko'miða] *nf* (*alimento*) food; (*almuerzo, cena*) meal; (*de mediodía*) lunch

comidilla [komi'ðiʎa] *nf*: **ser la ~ de la ciudad** to be the talk of the town

comienzo *etc* [ko'mjenθo] *vb ver* **comenzar** ♦ *nm* beginning, start

comillas [ko'miʎas] *nfpl* quotation marks

comilona [komi'lona] (*fam*) *nf* blow-out

comino [ko'mino] *nm*: **(no) me importa un ~** I don't give a damn

comisaría [komisa'ria] *nf* (*de policía*) police station; (MIL) commissariat

comisario [komi'sarjo] *nm* (MIL *etc*) commissary; (POL) commissar

comisión [komi'sjon] *nf* commission

comité [komi'te] (*pl* **~s**) *nm* committee

comitiva [komi'tiβa] *nf* retinue

como ['komo] *adv* as; (*tal* **~**) like; (*aproximadamente*) about, approximately ♦ *conj* (*ya que, puesto que*) as, since; **¡~ no!** of course!; **~ no lo haga hoy** unless he does it today; **~ si** as if; **es tan alto ~ ancho** it is as high as it is wide

cómo ['komo] *adv* how?, why? ♦ *excl* what?, I beg your pardon? ♦ *nm*: **el ~ y el porqué** the whys and wherefores

cómoda ['komoða] *nf* chest of drawers

comodidad [komoði'ðað] *nf* comfort; **venga a su ~** come at your convenience

comodín [komo'ðin] *nm* joker

cómodo, a ['komoðo, a] *adj* comfortable; (*práctico, de fácil uso*) convenient

compact disc *nm* compact disk player

compacto, a [kom'pakto, a] *adj* compact

compadecer [kompaðe'θer] *vt* to pity, be sorry for; **~se** *vr*: **~se de** to pity, be o feel sorry for

compadre [kom'paðre] *nm* (*padrino*) godfather; (*amigo*) friend, pal

compañero, a [kompa'ɲero, a] *nm/f* companion; (*novio*) boy/girlfriend; **~ de clase** classmate

compañía [kompa'ɲia] *nf* company

comparación [kompara'θjon] *nf* comparison; **en ~ con** in comparison with

comparar [kompa'rar] *vt* to compare

comparecer [kompare'θer] *vi* to appear (in court)

comparsa [kom'parsa] *nm/f* (TEATRO) extra

compartimiento [komparti'mjento] *nm* (FERRO) compartment

compartir [kompar'tir] *vt* to share; (*dinero, comida etc*) to divide (up), share (out)

compás [kom'pas] *nm* (MUS) beat, rhythm;

(MAT) compasses pl; (NAUT etc) compass

compasión [kompa'sjon] nf compassion, pity

compasivo, a [kompa'sißo, a] adj compassionate

compatibilidad [kompatißili'ðað] nf compatibility

compatible [kompa'tißle] adj compatible

compatriota [kompa'trjota] nm/f compatriot, fellow countryman/woman

compendiar [kompen'djar] vt to summarize; **compendio** nm summary

compenetrarse [kompene'trarse] vr to be in tune

compensación [kompensa'θjon] nf compensation

compensar [kompen'sar] vt to compensate

competencia [kompe'tenθja] nf (incumbencia) domain, field; (JUR, habilidad) competence; (rivalidad) competition

competente [kompe'tente] adj competent

competición [kompeti'θjon] nf competition

competir [kompe'tir] vi to compete

compilar [kompi'lar] vt to compile

complacencia [kompla'θenθja] nf (placer) pleasure; (tolerancia excesiva) complacency

complacer [kompla'θer] vt to please; **~se** vr to be pleased

complaciente [kompla'θjente] adj kind, obliging, helpful

complejo, a [kom'plexo, a] adj, nm complex

complementario, a [komplemen'tarjo, a] adj complementary

completar [komple'tar] vt to complete

completo, a [kom'pleto, a] adj complete; (perfecto) perfect; (lleno) full ♦ nm full complement

complicado, a [kompli'kaðo, a] adj complicated; **estar ~ en** to be mixed up in

cómplice ['kompliθe] nm/f accomplice

complot [kom'plo(t)] (pl ~s) nm plot

componer [kompo'ner] vt (MUS, LITERATURA, IMPRENTA) to compose; (algo roto) to mend, repair; (arreglar) to arrange; **~se** vr: **~se de** to consist of; **componérselas para hacer algo** to manage to do sth

comportamiento [komporta'mjento] nm behaviour, conduct

comportarse [kompor'tarse] vr to behave

composición [komposi'θjon] nf composition

compositor, a [komposi'tor, a] nm/f composer

compostura [kompos'tura] nf (actitud) composure

compra ['kompra] nf purchase; **ir de ~s** to go shopping; **comprador, a** nm/f buyer, purchaser

comprar [kom'prar] vt to buy, purchase

comprender [kompren'der] vt to understand; (incluir) to comprise, include

comprensión [kompren'sjon] nf understanding; **comprensivo, a** adj (actitud) understanding

compresa [kom'presa] nf: **~ higiénica** sanitary towel (BRIT) o napkin (US)

comprimido, a [kompri'miðo, a] adj compressed ♦ nm (MED) pill, tablet

comprimir [kompri'mir] vt to compress

comprobante [kompro'ßante] nm proof; (COM) voucher; **~ de recibo** receipt

comprobar [kompro'ßar] vt to check; (probar) to prove; (TEC) to check, test

comprometer [komprome'ter] vt to compromise; (poner en peligro) to endanger; **~se** vr (involucrarse) to get involved

compromiso [kompro'miso] nm (obligación) obligation; (cometido) commitment; (convenio) agreement; (apuro) awkward situation

compuesto, a [kom'pwesto, a] adj: **~ de** composed of, made up of ♦ nm compound

computador [komputa'ðor] nm computer; **~ central** mainframe computer; **~ personal** personal computer

computadora [komputa'ðora] nf = **computador**

cómputo ['komputo] nm calculation

comulgar [komul'var] vi to receive communion

común [ko'mun] adj common ♦ nm: **el ~** the community

comunicación [komunika'θjon] nf communication; (informe) report

comunicado [komuni'kaðo] nm announcement; **~ de prensa** press release

comunicar [komuni'kar] vt, vi to communicate; **~se** vr to communicate; **está comunicando** (TEL) the line's engaged (BRIT) o busy (US); **comunicativo, a** adj communicative

comunidad [komuni'ðað] nf community; **~ autónoma** (POL) autonomous region; **C~ Económica Europea** European Economic Community

comunión [komu'njon] nf communion

comunismo [komu'nismo] nm communism; **comunista** adj, nm/f communist

PALABRA CLAVE

con [kon] prep **1** (medio, compañía) with; **comer ~ cuchara** to eat with a spoon; **pasear ~ uno** to go for a walk with sb

2 (a pesar de): **~ todo, merece nuestros respetos** all the same, he deserves our respect

3 (para ~): **es muy bueno para ~ los niños** he's very good with (the) children

4 (+ _infin_): ~ **llegar tan tarde se quedó sin comer** by arriving so late he missed out on eating
♦ _conj_: ~ **que: será suficiente ~ que le escribas** it will be sufficient if you write to her

---

conato [ko'nato] _nm_ attempt; ~ **de robo** attempted robbery

concebir [konθe'βir] _vt_, _vi_ to conceive

conceder [konθe'ðer] _vt_ to concede

concejal, a [konθe'xal, a] _nm/f_ town councillor

concentración [konθentra'θjon] _nf_ concentration

concentrar [konθen'trar] _vt_ to concentrate; ~**se** _vr_ to concentrate

concepción [konθep'θjon] _nf_ conception

concepto [kon'θepto] _nm_ concept

concernir [konθer'nir] _vi_ to concern; **en lo que concierne a ...** as far as ... is concerned; **en lo que a mí concierne** as far as I'm concerned

concertar [konθer'tar] _vt_ (MUS) to harmonize; (_acordar: precio_) to agree; (: _tratado_) to conclude; (_trato_) to arrange, fix up; (_combinar: esfuerzos_) to coordinate ♦ _vi_ to harmonize, be in tune

concesión [konθe'sjon] _nf_ concession

concesionario [konθesjo'narjo] _nm_ (licensed) dealer, agent

concha ['kontʃa] _nf_ shell

conciencia [kon'θjenθja] _nf_ conscience; **tener/tomar ~ de** to be/become aware of; **tener la ~ limpia/tranquila** to have a clear conscience

concienciar [konθjen'θjar] _vt_ to make aware; ~**se** _vr_ to become aware

concienzudo, a [konθjen'θuðo, a] _adj_ conscientious

concierto etc [kon'θjerto] _vb ver_ **concertar** ♦ _nm_ concert; (_obra_) concerto

conciliar [konθi'ljar] _vt_ to reconcile

concilio [kon'θiljo] _nm_ council

conciso, a [kon'θiso, a] _adj_ concise

concluir [konklu'ir] _vt_, _vi_ to conclude; ~**se** _vr_ to conclude

conclusión [konklu'sjon] _nf_ conclusion

concluyente [konklu'jente] _adj_ (_prueba, información_) conclusive

concordar [konkor'ðar] _vt_ to reconcile ♦ _vi_ to agree, tally

concordia [kon'korðja] _nf_ harmony

concretar [konkre'tar] _vt_ to make concrete, make more specific; ~**se** _vr_ to become more definite

concreto, a [kon'kreto, a] _adj_, _nm_ (AM) concrete; **en ~** (_en resumen_) to sum up; (_especificamente_) specifically; **no hay nada en ~** there's nothing definite

concurrencia [konku'rrenθja] _nf_ turnout

concurrido, a [konku'rriðo, a] _adj_ (_calle_) busy; (_local, reunión_) crowded

concurrir [konku'rrir] _vi_ (_juntarse: ríos_) to meet, come together; (: _personas_) to gather, meet

concursante [konkur'sante] _nm/f_ competitor

concurso [kon'kurso] _nm_ (_de público_) crowd; (ESCOL, DEPORTE, _competencia_) competition; (_ayuda_) help, cooperation

condal [kon'dal] _adj_: **la Ciudad C~** Barcelona

conde ['konde] _nm_ count

condecoración [kondekora'θjon] _nf_ (MIL) medal

condecorar [kondeko'rar] _vt_ (MIL) to decorate

condena [kon'dena] _nf_ sentence

condenación [kondena'θjon] _nf_ condemnation; (REL) damnation

condenar [konde'nar] _vt_ to condemn; (JUR) to convict; ~**se** _vr_ (REL) to be damned

condensar [konden'sar] _vt_ to condense

condesa [kon'desa] _nf_ countess

condición [kondi'θjon] _nf_ condition; **condicional** _adj_ conditional

condicionar [kondiθjo'nar] _vt_ (_acondicionar_) to condition; ~ **algo a** to make sth conditional on

condimento [kondi'mento] _nm_ seasoning

condolerse [kondo'lerse] _vr_ to sympathize

condón [kon'don] _nm_ condom

conducir [kondu'θir] _vt_ to take, convey; (AUTO) to drive ♦ _vi_ to drive; (_fig_) to lead; ~**se** _vr_ to behave

conducta [kon'dukta] _nf_ conduct, behaviour

conducto [kon'dukto] _nm_ pipe, tube; (_fig_) channel

conductor, a [konduk'tor, a] _adj_ leading, guiding ♦ _nm_ (FÍSICA) conductor; (_de vehículo_) driver

conduje etc _vb ver_ **conducir**

conduzco etc _vb ver_ **conducir**

conectado, a [konek'taðo, a] _adj_ (INFORM) on-line

conectar [konek'tar] _vt_ to connect (up); (_enchufar_) plug in

conejillo [kone'xiʎo] _nm_: ~ **de Indias** (ZOOL) guinea pig

conejo [ko'nexo] _nm_ rabbit

conexión [konek'sjon] _nf_ connection

confección [konfe(k)'θjon] _nf_ preparation; (_industria_) clothing industry

confeccionar [konfekθjo'nar] _vt_ to make (up)

confederación [konfeðera'θjon] _nf_ confederation

conferencia [konfe'renθja] _nf_ conference; (_lección_) lecture; (TEL) call

conferir [konfe'rir] vt to award

confesar [konfe'sar] vt to confess, admit

confesión [konfe'sjon] nf confession

confesionario [konfesjo'narjo] nm confessional

confeti [kon'feti] nm confetti

confiado, a [kon'fjaðo, a] adj (crédulo) trusting; (seguro) confident

confianza [kon'fjanθa] nf trust; (seguridad) confidence; (familiaridad) intimacy, familiarity

confiar [kon'fjar] vt to entrust ♦ vi to trust

confidencia [konfi'ðenθja] nf confidence

confidencial [konfiðen'θjal] adj confidential

confidente [konfi'ðente] nm/f confidant/e; (policial) informer

configurar [konfiɣu'rar] vt to shape, form

confín [kon'fin] nm limit; **confines** nmpl confines, limits

confinar [konfi'nar] vi to confine; (desterrar) to banish

confirmar [konfir'mar] vt to confirm

confiscar [konfis'kar] vt to confiscate

confite [kon'fite] nm sweet (BRIT), candy (US)

confitería [konfite'ria] nf (tienda) confectioner's (shop)

confitura [konfi'tura] nf jam

conflictivo, a [konflik'tiβo, a] adj (asunto, propuesta) controversial; (país, situación) troubled

conflicto [kon'flikto] nm conflict; (fig) clash

confluir [kon'flwir] vi (ríos) to meet; (gente) to gather

conformar [konfor'mar] vt to shape, fashion ♦ vi to agree; **~se** vr to conform; (resignarse) to resign o.s.

conforme [kon'forme] adj (correspondiente): ~ con in line with; (de acuerdo): estar ~s (con algo) to be in agreement (with sth) ♦ adv as ♦ excl agreed! ♦ prep: ~ a in accordance with; quedarse ~ (con algo) to be satisfied (with sth)

conformidad [konformi'ðað] nf (semejanza) similarity; (acuerdo) agreement; **conformista** adj, nm/f conformist

confortable [konfor'taβle] adj comfortable

confortar [konfor'tar] vt to comfort

confrontar [konfron'tar] vt to confront; (dos personas) to bring face to face; (cotejar) to compare

confundir [konfun'dir] vt (equivocar) to mistake, confuse; (turbar) to confuse; **~se** vr (turbarse) to get confused; (equivocarse) to make a mistake; (mezclarse) to mix

confusión [konfu'sjon] nf confusion

confuso, a [kon'fuso, a] adj confused

congelado, a [konxe'laðo, a] adj frozen; **~s** nmpl frozen food(s); **congelador** nm (aparato) freezer, deep freeze

congelar [konxe'lar] vt to freeze; **~se** vr (sangre, grasa) to congeal

congeniar [konxe'njar] vi to get on (BRIT) o along (US) well

congestión [konxes'tjon] nf congestion

congestionar [konxestjo'nar] vt to congest

congoja [kon'goxa] nf distress, grief

congraciarse [kongra'θjarse] vr to ingratiate o.s.

congratular [kongratu'lar] vt to congratulate

congregación [kongreɣa'θjon] nf congregation

congregar [kongre'ɣar] vt to gather together; **~se** vr to gather together

congresista [kongre'sista] nm/f delegate, congressman/woman

congreso [kon'greso] nm congress

congrio ['kongrjo] nm conger eel

conjetura [konxe'tura] nf guess; **conjeturar** vt to guess

conjugar [konxu'ɣar] vt to combine, fit together; (LING) to conjugate

conjunción [konxun'θjon] nf conjunction

conjunto, a [kon'xunto, a] adj joint, united ♦ nm whole; (MUS) band; en ~ as a whole

conjurar [konxu'rar] vt (REL) to exorcise; (fig) to ward off ♦ vi to plot

conmemoración [konmemora'θjon] nf commemoration

conmemorar [konmemo'rar] vt to commemorate

conmigo [kon'miɣo] pron with me

conmoción [konmo'θjon] nf shock; (fig) upheaval; ~ **cerebral** (MED) concussion

conmovedor, a [konmoβe'ðor, a] adj touching, moving; (emocionante) exciting

conmover [konmo'βer] vt to shake, disturb; (fig) to move

conmutador [konmuta'ðor] nm switch; (AM: TEL: centralita) switchboard; (: central) telephone exchange

cono ['kono] nm cone

conocedor, a [konoθe'ðor, a] adj expert, knowledgeable ♦ nm/f expert

conocer [kono'θer] vt to know; (por primera vez) to meet, get to know; (entender) to know about; (reconocer) to recognize; **~se** vr (una persona) to know o.s.; (dos personas) to (get to) know each other

conocido, a [kono'θiðo, a] adj (well-) known ♦ nm/f acquaintance

conocimiento [konoθi'mjento] nm knowledge; (MED) consciousness; **~s** nmpl (saber) knowledge sg

conozco etc vb ver **conocer**

conque ['konke] conj and so, so then

conquista [kon'kista] nf conquest; **conquistador, a** adj conquering ♦ nm conqueror

conquistar [konkis'tar] vt to conquer

consagrar [konsa'ɣrar] vt (REL) to consecrate; (fig) to devote

consciente [kons'θjente] adj conscious

consecución [konseku'θjon] nf acquisition; (de fin) attainment

consecuencia [konse'kwenθja] nf consequence, outcome; (coherencia) consistency

consecuente [konse'kwente] adj consistent

consecutivo, a [konseku'tißo, a] adj consecutive

conseguir [konse'ɣir] vt to get, obtain; (objetivo) to attain

consejero, a [konse'xero, a] nm/f adviser, consultant; (POL) councillor

consejo [kon'sexo] nm advice; (POL) council; ~ **de administración** (COM) board of directors; ~ **de guerra** court martial; ~ **de ministros** cabinet meeting

consenso [kon'senso] nm consensus

consentimiento [konsenti'mjento] nm consent

consentir [konsen'tir] vt (permitir, tolerar) to consent to; (mimar) to pamper, spoil; (aguantar) to put up with ♦ vi to agree, consent; ~ **que uno haga algo** to allow sb to do sth

conserje [kon'serxe] nm caretaker; (portero) porter

conservación [konserßa'θjon] nf conservation; (de alimentos, vida) preservation

conservador, a [konserßa'ðor, a] adj (POL) conservative ♦ nm/f conservative

conservante [konser'ßante] nm preservative

conservar [konser'ßar] vt to conserve, keep; (alimentos, vida) to preserve; ~**se** vr to survive

conservas [kon'serßas] nfpl canned food(s) (pl)

conservatorio [konserßa'torjo] nm (MUS) conservatoire, conservatory

considerable [konsiðe'raßle] adj considerable

consideración [konsiðera'θjon] nf consideration; (estimación) respect

considerado, a [konsiðe'raðo, a] adj (atento) considerate; (respetado) respected

considerar [konsiðe'rar] vt to consider

consigna [kon'sixna] nf (orden) order, instruction; (para equipajes) left-luggage office

consigo etc [kon'sixo] vb ver **conseguir** ♦ pron (m) with him; (f) with her; (Vd) with you; (reflexivo) with o.s.

consiguiendo etc vb ver **conseguir**

consiguiente [konsi'xjente] adj consequent; **por** ~ and so, therefore, consequently

consistente [konsis'tente] adj consistent; (sólido) solid, firm; (válido) sound

consistir [konsis'tir] vi: ~ **en** (componerse de) to consist of

consola [kon'sola] nf (mueble) console table; (de videojuegos) console

consolación [konsola'θjon] nf consolation

consolar [konso'lar] vt to console

consolidar [konsoli'ðar] vt to consolidate

consomé [konso'me] (pl ~**s**) nm consommé, clear soup

consonante [konso'nante] adj consonant, harmonious ♦ nf consonant

consorcio [kon'sorθjo] nm consortium

conspiración [konspira'θjon] nf conspiracy

conspirador, a [konspira'ðor, a] nm/f conspirator

conspirar [konspi'rar] vi to conspire

constancia [kon'stanθja] nf constancy; **dejar** ~ **de** to put on record

constante [kons'tante] adj, nf constant

constar [kons'tar] vi (evidenciarse) to be clear o evident; ~ **de** to consist of

constatar [konsta'tar] vt to verify

consternación [konsterna'θjon] nf consternation

constipado, a [konsti'paðo, a] adj: **estar** ~ to have a cold ♦ nm cold

constitución [konstitu'θjon] nf constitution; **constitucional** adj constitutional

constituir [konstitu'ir] vt (formar, componer) to constitute, make up; (fundar, erigir, ordenar) to constitute, establish

constituyente [konstitu'jente] adj constituent

constreñir [konstre'ɲir] vt (restringir) to restrict

construcción [konstruk'θjon] nf construction, building

constructor, a [konstruk'tor, a] nm/f builder

construir [konstru'ir] vt to build, construct

construyendo etc vb ver **construir**

consuelo [kon'swelo] nm consolation, solace

cónsul ['konsul] nm consul; **consulado** nm consulate

consulta [kon'sulta] nf consultation; (MED): **horas de** ~ surgery hours

consultar [konsul'tar] vt to consult

consultorio [konsul'torjo] nm (MED) surgery

consumar [konsu'mar] vt to complete, carry out; (crimen) to commit; (sentencia) to carry out

consumición [konsumi'θjon] nf consumption; (bebida) drink; (comida) food; ~ **mínima** cover charge

consumidor, a [konsumi'ðor, a] nm/f consumer

consumir [konsu'mir] vt to consume; ~**se** vr

to be consumed; (*persona*) to waste away

consumismo [konsu'mismo] *nm*
consumerism

consumo [kon'sumo] *nm* consumption

contabilidad [kontaβili'ðað] *nf* accounting,
book-keeping; (*profesión*) accountancy;
contable *nm/f* accountant

contacto [kon'takto] *nm* contact; (*AUTO*)
ignition

contado, a [kon'taðo, a] *adj*: **~s** (*escasos*)
numbered, scarce, few ♦ *nm*: **pagar al ~** to
pay (in) cash

contador [konta'ðor] *nm* (*aparato*) meter;
(*AM: contante*) accountant

contagiar [konta'xjar] *vt* (*enfermedad*) to
pass on, transmit; (*persona*) to infect; **~se** *vr*
to become infected

contagio [kon'taxjo] *nm* infection;
contagioso, a *adj* infectious; (*fig*) catching

contaminación [kontamina'θjon] *nf*
contamination; (*polución*) pollution

contaminar [kontami'nar] *vt* to
contaminate; (*aire, agua*) to pollute

contante [kon'tante] *adj*: **dinero ~ (y
sonante)** cash

contar [kon'tar] *vt* (*páginas, dinero*) to count;
(*anécdota, chiste etc*) to tell ♦ *vi* to count;
~ con to rely on, count on

contemplación [kontempla'θjon] *nf*
contemplation

contemplar [kontem'plar] *vt* to
contemplate; (*mirar*) to look at

contemporáneo, a [kontempo'raneo, a]
adj, nm/f contemporary

contendiente [konten'djente] *nm/f*
contestant

contenedor [kontene'ðor] *nm* container

contener [konte'ner] *vt* to contain, hold;
(*retener*) to hold back, contain; **~se** *vr* to
control o restrain o.s.

contenido, a [konte'niðo, a] *adj* (*moderado*)
restrained; (*risa etc*) suppressed ♦ *nm*
contents *pl*, content

contentar [konten'tar] *vt* (*satisfacer*) to
satisfy; (*complacer*) to please; **~se** *vr* to be
satisfied

contento, a [kon'tento, a] *adj* (*alegre*)
pleased; (*feliz*) happy

contestación [kontesta'θjon] *nf* answer,
reply

contestador [kontesta'ðor] *nm*:
~ automático answering machine

contestar [kontes'tar] *vt* to answer, reply;
(*JUR*) to corroborate, confirm

contexto [kon'te(k)sto] *nm* context

contienda [kon'tjenda] *nf* contest

contigo [kon'tiɣo] *pron* with you

contiguo, a [kon'tiɣwo, a] *adj* adjacent,
adjoining

continente [konti'nente] *adj, nm* continent

contingencia [kontin'xenθja] *nf*
contingency; (*riesgo*) risk; **contingente** *adj*,
nm contingent

continuación [kontinwa'θjon] *nf*
continuation; **a ~** then, next

continuar [konti'nwar] *vt* to continue, go on
with ♦ *vi* to continue, go on; **~ hablando** to
continue talking o to talk

continuidad [kontinwi'ðað] *nf* continuity

continuo, a [kon'tinwo, a] *adj* (*sin
interrupción*) continuous; (*acción perseverante*)
continual

contorno [kon'torno] *nm* outline; (*GEO*)
contour; **~s** *nmpl* neighbourhood *sg*,
surrounding area *sg*

contorsión [kontor'sjon] *nf* contortion

contra ['kontra] *prep, ad* against ♦ *nm inv*
con ♦ *nf*: **la C~** (*de Nicaragua*) the Contras *pl*

contraataque [kontraa'take] *nm* counter-
attack

contrabajo [kontra'βaxo] *nm* double bass

contrabandista [kontraβan'dista] *nm/f*
smuggler

contrabando [kontra'βando] *nm* (*acción*)
smuggling; (*mercancías*) contraband

contracción [kontrak'θjon] *nf* contraction

contracorriente [kontrako'rrjente]: **(a) ~**
adv against the current

contradecir [kontraðe'θir] *vt* to contradict

contradicción [kontraðik'θjon] *nf*
contradiction

contradictorio, a [kontraðik'torjo, a] *adj*
contradictory

contraer [kontra'er] *vt* to contract; (*limitar*)
to restrict; **~se** *vr* to contract; (*limitarse*) to
limit o.s.

contraluz [kontra'luθ] *nf*: **a ~** against the
light

contrapartida [kontrapar'tiða] *nf*: **como
~ (de)** in return (for)

contrapelo [kontra'pelo]: **a ~** *adv* the wrong
way

contrapesar [kontrape'sar] *vt* to
counterbalance; (*fig*) to offset; **contrapeso**
nm counterweight

contraportada [kontrapor'taða] *nf* (*de
revista*) back cover

contraproducente [kontraproðu'θente]
adj counterproductive

contrariar [kontra'rjar] *vt* (*oponerse*) to
oppose; (*poner obstáculo*) to impede;
(*enfadar*) to vex

contrariedad [kontrarje'ðað] *nf* (*obstáculo*)
obstacle, setback; (*disgusto*) vexation,
annoyance

contrario, a [kon'trarjo, a] *adj* contrary;
(*persona*) opposed; (*sentido, lado*) opposite
♦ *nm/f* enemy, adversary; (*DEPORTE*)

opponent; **al/por el ~** on the contrary; **de lo ~**
otherwise

contrarreloj [kontrarre'loχ] *nf* (*tb: prueba ~*)
time trial

contrarrestar [kontrarres'tar] *vt* to
counteract

contrasentido [kontrasen'tiðo] *nm*: **es un
~ que él ...** it doesn't make sense for him to ...

contraseña [kontra'seɲa] *nf* (*INFORM*)
password

contrastar [kontras'tar] *vt, vi* to contrast

contraste [kon'traste] *nm* contrast

contratar [kontra'tar] *vt* (*firmar un acuerdo
para*) to contract for; (*empleados, obreros*) to
hire, engage; **~se** *vr* to sign on

contratiempo [kontra'tjempo] *nm* setback

contratista [kontra'tista] *nm/f* contractor

contrato [kon'trato] *nm* contract

contravenir [kontraβe'nir] *vi*: **~ a** to
contravene, violate

contraventana [kontraβen'tana] *nf* shutter

contribución [kontriβu'θjon] *nf* (*municipal
etc*) tax; (*ayuda*) contribution

contribuir [kontriβu'ir] *vt, vi* to contribute;
(*COM*) to pay (in taxes)

contribuyente [kontriβu'jente] *nm/f* (*COM*)
taxpayer; (*que ayuda*) contributor

contrincante [kontrin'kante] *nm* opponent

control [kon'trol] *nm* control; (*inspección*)
inspection, check; **~ador, a** *nm/f* controller;
~ador aéreo air-traffic controller

controlar [kontro'lar] *vt* to control;
(*inspeccionar*) to inspect, check

controversia [kontro'βersja] *nf* controversy

contundente [kontun'dente] *adj*
(*instrumento*) blunt; (*argumento, derrota*)
overwhelming

contusión [kontu'sjon] *nf* bruise

convalecencia [kombale'θenθja] *nf*
convalescence

convalecer [kombale'θer] *vi* to convalesce,
get better

convaleciente [kombale'θjente] *adj, nm/f*
convalescent

convalidar [kombali'ðar] *vt* (*título*) to
recognize

convencer [komben'θer] *vt* to convince

convencimiento [kombenθi'mjento] *nm*
(*certidumbre*) conviction

convención [komben'θjon] *nf* convention

conveniencia [kombe'njenθja] *nf* suitability;
(*conformidad*) agreement; (*utilidad, provecho*)
usefulness; **~s** *nfpl* (*convenciones*)
conventions; (*COM*) property *sg*

conveniente [kombe'njente] *adj* suitable;
(*útil*) useful

convenio [kom'benjo] *nm* agreement, treaty

convenir [kombe'nir] *vi* (*estar de acuerdo*) to
agree; (*venir bien*) to suit, be suitable

convento [kom'bento] *nm* convent

convenza *etc vb ver* **convencer**

converger [komber'χer] *vi* to converge

convergir [komber'χir] *vi* = **converger**

conversación [kombersa'θjon] *nf*
conversation

conversar [komber'sar] *vi* to talk, converse

conversión [komber'sjon] *nf* conversion

convertir [komber'tir] *vt* to convert

convicción [kombik'θjon] *nf* conviction

convicto, a [kom'bikto, a] *adj* convicted

convidado, a [kombi'ðaðo, a] *nm/f* guest

convidar [kombi'ðar] *vt* to invite

convincente [kombin'θente] *adj* convincing

convite [kom'bite] *nm* invitation; (*banquete*)
banquet

convivencia [kombi'βenθja] *nf* coexistence,
living together

convivir [kombi'βir] *vi* to live together

convocar [kombo'kar] *vt* to summon, call
(together)

convocatoria [komboka'torja] *nf* (*de
oposiciones, elecciones*) notice; (*de huelga*) call

convulsión [kombul'sjon] *nf* convulsion

conyugal [konχu'βal] *adj* conjugal; **cónyuge**
['konχuxe] *nm/f* spouse

coñac [ko'ɲa(k)] (*pl* **~s**) *nm* cognac, brandy

coño ['koɲo] (*fam!*) *excl* (*enfado*) shit! (*!*);
(*sorpresa*) bloody hell! (*!*)

cooperación [koopera'θjon] *nf* cooperation

cooperar [koope'rar] *vi* to cooperate

cooperativa [koopera'tiβa] *nf* cooperative

coordinadora [koorðina'ðora] *nf* (*comité*)
coordinating committee

coordinar [koorði'nar] *vt* to coordinate

copa ['kopa] *nf* cup; (*vaso*) glass; (*bebida*):
(**tomar una**) **~** (to have a) drink; (*de árbol*)
top; (*de sombrero*) crown; **~s** *nfpl* (*NAIPES*) ≈
hearts

copia ['kopja] *nf* copy; **~ de respaldo** *o*
seguridad (*INFORM*) back-up copy; **copiar** *vt*
to copy

copioso, a [ko'pjoso, a] *adj* copious, plentiful

copla ['kopla] *nf* verse; (*canción*) (popular)
song

copo ['kopo] *nm*: **~ de nieve** snowflake; **~s de
maíz** cornflakes

coqueta [ko'keta] *adj* flirtatious, coquettish;
coquetear *vi* to flirt

coraje [ko'raxe] *nm* courage; (*ánimo*) spirit;
(*ira*) anger

coral [ko'ral] *adj* choral ♦ *nf* (*MUS*) choir ♦ *nm*
(*ZOOL*) coral

coraza [ko'raθa] *nf* (*armadura*) armour;
(*blindaje*) armour-plating

corazón [kora'θon] *nm* heart

corazonada [koraθo'naða] *nf* impulse;
(*presentimiento*) hunch

corbata [kor'βata] *nf* tie

corchete [kor'tʃete] nm catch, clasp

corcho ['kortʃo] nm cork; (PESCA) float

cordel [kor'ðel] nm cord, line

cordero [kor'ðero] nm lamb

cordial [kor'ðjal] adj cordial; **~idad** nf warmth, cordiality

cordillera [korði'ʎera] nf range (of mountains)

Córdoba ['korðoßa] n Cordova

cordón [kor'ðon] nm (cuerda) cord, string; (de zapatos) lace; (MIL etc) cordon

cordura [kor'ðura] nf: **con ~** (obrar, hablar) sensibly

corneta [kor'neta] nf bugle

cornisa [kor'nisa] nf (ARQ) cornice

coro ['koro] nm chorus; (conjunto de cantores) choir

corona [ko'rona] nf crown; (de flores) garland; **coronación** nf coronation; **coronar** vt to crown

coronel [koro'nel] nm colonel

coronilla [koro'niʎa] nf (ANAT) crown (of the head)

corporación [korpora'θjon] nf corporation

corporal [korpo'ral] adj corporal, bodily

corpulento, a [korpu'lento a] adj (persona) heavily-built

corral [ko'rral] nm farmyard

correa [ko'rrea] nf strap; (cinturón) belt; (de perro) lead, leash

corrección [korrek'θjon] nf correction; (reprensión) rebuke; **correccional** nm reformatory

correcto, a [ko'rrekto, a] adj correct; (persona) well-mannered

corredizo, a [korre'ðiθo, a] adj (puerta etc) sliding

corredor, a [korre'ðor, a] nm (pasillo) corridor; (balcón corrido) gallery; (COM) agent, broker ♦ nm/f (DEPORTE) runner

corregir [korre'xir] vt (error) to correct; **~se** vr to reform

correo [ko'rreo] nm post, mail; (persona) courier; **C~s** nmpl Post Office sg; **~ aéreo** airmail; **~ electrónico** electronic mail, e-mail

correr [ko'rrer] vt to run; (cortinas) to draw; (cerrojo) to shoot ♦ vi to run; (líquido) to run, flow; **~se** vr to slide, move; (colores) to run

correspondencia [korrespon'denθja] nf correspondence; (FERRO) connection

corresponder [korrespon'der] vi to correspond; (convenir) to be suitable; (pertenecer) to belong; (concernir) to concern; **~se** vr (por escrito) to correspond; (amarse) to love one another

correspondiente [korrespon'djente] adj corresponding

corresponsal [korrespon'sal] nm/f correspondent

corrida [ko'rriða] nf (de toros) bullfight

corrido, a [ko'rriðo, a] adj (avergonzado) abashed; **3 noches corridas** 3 nights running; **un kilo ~** a good kilo

corriente [ko'rrjente] adj (agua) running; (dinero etc) current; (común) ordinary, normal ♦ nf current ♦ nm current month; **~ eléctrica** electric current

corrija etc vb ver **corregir**

corrillo [ko'rriʎo] nm ring, circle (of people); (fig) clique

corro ['korro] nm ring, circle (of people)

corroborar [korroßo'rar] vt to corroborate

corroer [korro'er] vt to corrode; (GEO) to erode

corromper [korrom'per] vt (madera) to rot; (fig) to corrupt

corrosivo, a [korro'sißo, a] adj corrosive

corrupción [korrup'θjon] nf rot, decay; (fig) corruption

corsé [kor'se] nm corset

cortacésped [korta'θespeð] nm lawn mower

cortado, a [kor'taðo, a] adj (gen) cut; (leche) sour; (tímido) shy; (avergonzado) embarrassed ♦ nm coffee (with a little milk)

cortar [kor'tar] vt to cut; (suministro) to cut off; (un pasaje) to cut out ♦ vi to cut; **~se** vr (avergonzarse) to become embarrassed; (leche) to turn, curdle; **~se el pelo** to have one's hair cut

cortauñas [korta'uɲas] nm inv nail clippers pl

corte ['korte] nm cut, cutting; (de tela) piece, length ♦ nf: **las C~s** the Spanish Parliament; **~ y confección** dressmaking; **~ de luz** power cut

cortejar [korte'xar] vt to court

cortejo [kor'texo] nm entourage; **~ fúnebre** funeral procession

cortés [kor'tes] adj courteous, polite

cortesía [korte'sia] nf courtesy

corteza [kor'teθa] nf (de árbol) bark; (de pan) crust

cortijo [kor'tixo] nm farm, farmhouse

cortina [kor'tina] nf curtain

corto, a ['korto, a] adj (breve) short; (tímido) bashful; **~ de luces** not very bright; **~ de vista** short-sighted; **estar ~ de fondos** to be short of funds; **~circuito** nm short circuit; **~metraje** nm (CINE) short

cosa ['kosa] nf thing; **~ de** about; **eso es ~ mía** that's my business

coscorrón [kosko'rron] nm bump on the head

cosecha [ko'setʃa] nf (AGR) harvest; (de vino) vintage

cosechar [kose'tʃar] vt to harvest, gather (in)

coser [ko'ser] vt to sew

cosmético, a [kos'metiko, a] adj, nm cosmetic

cosquillas [kos'kiʎas] *nfpl:* **hacer ~** to tickle; **tener ~** to be ticklish

costa ['kosta] *nf* (*GEO*) coast; **C~ Brava** Costa Brava; **C~ Cantábrica** Cantabrian Coast; **C~ del Sol** Costa del Sol; **a toda ~** at all costs

costado [kos'taðo] *nm* side

costar [kos'tar] *vt* (*valer*) to cost; **me cuesta hablarle** I find it hard to talk to him

Costa Rica *nf* Costa Rica; **costarricense** *adj, nm/f* Costa Rican; **costarriqueño, a** *adj, nm/f* Costa Rican

coste ['koste] *nm* = **costo**

costear [koste'ar] *vt* to pay for

costero, a [kos'tero, a] *adj* (*pueblecito, camino*) coastal

costilla [kos'tiʎa] *nf* rib; (*CULIN*) cutlet

costo ['kosto] *nm* cost, price; **~ de la vida** cost of living; **~so, a** *adj* costly, expensive

costra ['kostra] *nf* (*corteza*) crust; (*MED*) scab

costumbre [kos'tumbre] *nf* custom, habit

costura [kos'tura] *nf* sewing, needlework; (*zurcido*) seam

costurera [kostu'rera] *nf* dressmaker

costurero [kostu'rero] *nm* sewing box *o* case

cotejar [kote'xar] *vt* to compare

cotidiano, a [koti'ðjano, a] *adj* daily, day to day

cotilla [ko'tiʎa] *nm/f* (*fam*) gossip; **cotillear** *vi* to gossip; **cotilleo** *nm* gossip(ing)

cotización [kotiθa'θjon] *nf* (*COM*) quotation, price; (*de club*) dues *pl*

cotizar [koti'θar] *vt* (*COM*) to quote, price; **~se** *vr:* **~se a** to sell at, fetch; (*BOLSA*) to stand at, be quoted at

coto ['koto] *nm* (*terreno cercado*) enclosure; (*de caza*) reserve

cotorra [ko'torra] *nf* parrot

COU [kou] (*ESP*) *nm abr* (= *Curso de Orientación Universitaria*) 1 year course leading to final school-leaving certificate and university entrance examinations

coyote [ko'jote] *nm* coyote, prairie wolf

coyuntura [kojun'tura] *nf* juncture, occasion

coz [koθ] *nf* kick

crack *nm* (*droga*) crack

cráneo ['kraneo] *nm* skull, cranium

cráter ['krater] *nm* crater

creación [krea'θjon] *nf* creation

creador, a [krea'ðor, a] *adj* creative ♦ *nm/f* creator

crear [kre'ar] *vt* to create, make

crecer [kre'θer] *vi* to grow; (*precio*) to rise

creces ['kreθes]: **con ~** *adv* amply, fully

crecido, a [kre'θiðo, a] *adj* (*persona, planta*) full-grown; (*cantidad*) large

creciente [kre'θjente] *adj* growing; (*cantidad*) increasing; (*luna*) crescent ♦ *nm* crescent

crecimiento [kreθi'mjento] *nm* growth;

(*aumento*) increase

credenciales [kreðen'θjales] *nfpl* credentials

crédito ['kreðito] *nm* credit

credo ['kreðo] *nm* creed

crédulo, a ['kreðulo, a] *adj* credulous

creencia [kre'enθja] *nf* belief

creer [kre'er] *vt, vi* to think, believe; **~se** *vr* to believe o.s. (to be); **~ en** to believe in; **¡ya lo creo!** I should think so!

creíble [kre'iβle] *adj* credible, believable

creído, a [kre'iðo, a] *adj* (*engreído*) conceited

crema ['krema] *nf* cream; **~ pastelera** (confectioner's) custard

cremallera [krema'ʎera] *nf* zip (fastener)

crematorio [krema'torjo] *nm* (*tb:* **horno ~**) crematorium

crepitar [krepi'tar] *vi* to crackle

crepúsculo [kre'puskulo] *nm* twilight, dusk

cresta ['kresta] *nf* (*GEO, ZOOL*) crest

creyendo *vb ver* **creer**

creyente [kre'jente] *nm/f* believer

creyó *etc vb ver* **creer**

crezco *etc vb ver* **crecer**

cría *etc* ['kria] *vb ver* **criar** ♦ *nf* (*de animales*) rearing, breeding; (*animal*) young; *ver tb* **crío**

criadero [kria'ðero] *nm* (*ZOOL*) breeding place

criado, a [kri'aðo, a] *nm* servant ♦ *nf* servant, maid

criador [kria'ðor] *nm* breeder

crianza [kri'anθa] *nf* rearing, breeding; (*fig*) breeding

criar [kri'ar] *vt* (*educar*) to bring up; (*producir*) to grow, produce; (*animales*) to breed

criatura [kria'tura] *nf* creature; (*niño*) baby, (*small*) child

criba ['kriβa] *nf* sieve; **cribar** *vt* to sieve

crimen ['krimen] *nm* crime

criminal [krimi'nal] *adj, nm/f* criminal

crin [krin] *nf* (*tb:* **~es** *nfpl*) mane

crío, a ['krio, a] (*fam*) *nm/f* (*niño*) kid

crisis ['krisis] *nf inv* crisis; **~ nerviosa** nervous breakdown

crispar [kris'par] *vt* (*nervios*) to set on edge

cristal [kris'tal] *nm* crystal; (*de ventana*) glass, pane; (*lente*) lens; **~ino, a** *adj* crystalline; (*fig*) clear ♦ *nm* lens (of the eye); **~izar** *vt, vi* to crystallize

cristiandad [kristjan'daθ] *nf* Christendom

cristianismo [kristja'nismo] *nm* Christianity

cristiano, a [kris'tjano, a] *adj, nm/f* Christian

Cristo ['kristo] *nm* Christ; (*crucifijo*) crucifix

criterio [kri'terjo] *nm* criterion; (*juicio*) judgement

crítica ['kritika] *nf* criticism; *ver tb* **crítico**

criticar [kriti'kar] *vt* to criticize

crítico, a ['kritiko, a] *adj* critical ♦ *nm/f* critic

Croacia *nf* Croatia

croar [kro'ar] *vi* to croak

cromo ['kromo] *nm* chrome

crónica ['kronika] *nf* chronicle, account

crónico, a ['kroniko, a] *adj* chronic

cronómetro [kro'nometro] *nm* stopwatch

croqueta [kro'keta] *nf* croquette

cruce *etc* ['kruθe] *vb ver* **cruzar** ♦ *nm* crossing; (*de carreteras*) crossroads

crucificar [kruθifi'kar] *vt* to crucify

crucifijo [kruθi'fixo] *nm* crucifix

crucigrama [kruθi'ɣrama] *nm* crossword (puzzle)

crudo, a ['kruðo, a] *adj* raw; (*no maduro*) unripe; (*petróleo*) crude; (*rudo, cruel*) cruel ♦ *nm* crude (oil)

cruel [krwel] *adj* cruel; **~dad** *nf* cruelty

crujido [kru'xiðo] *nm* (*de madera etc*) creak

crujiente [kru'xjente] *adj* (*galleta etc*) crunchy

crujir [kru'xir] *vi* (*madera etc*) to creak; (*dedos*) to crack; (*dientes*) to grind; (*nieve, arena*) to crunch

cruz [kruθ] *nf* cross; (*de moneda*) tails *sg*; **~ gamada** swastika

cruzada [kru'θaða] *nf* crusade

cruzado, a [kru'θaðo, a] *adj* crossed ♦ *nm* crusader

cruzar [kru'θar] *vt* to cross; **~se** *vr* (*líneas etc*) to cross; (*personas*) to pass each other

Cruz Roja *nf* Red Cross

cuaderno [kwa'ðerno] *nm* notebook; (*de escuela*) exercise book; (*NAUT*) logbook

cuadra ['kwaðra] *nf* (*caballeriza*) stable; (*AM*) block

cuadrado, a [kwa'ðraðo, a] *adj* square ♦ *nm* (*MAT*) square

cuadrar [kwa'ðrar] *vt* to square ♦ *vi*: **~ con** to square with, tally with; **~se** *vr* (*soldado*) to stand to attention

cuadrilátero [kwaðri'latero] *nm* (*DEPORTE*) boxing ring; (*GEOM*) quadrilateral

cuadrilla [kwa'ðriʎa] *nf* party, group

cuadro ['kwaðro] *nm* square; (*ARTE*) painting; (*TEATRO*) scene; (*diagrama*) chart; (*DEPORTE, MED*) team; **tela a ~s** checked (*BRIT*) o chequered (*US*) material

cuádruple ['kwaðruple] *adj* quadruple

cuajar [kwa'xar] *vt* (*leche*) to curdle; (*sangre*) to congeal; (*CULIN*) to set; **~se** *vr* to curdle; to congeal; to set; (*llenarse*) to fill up

cuajo ['kwaxo] *nm*: **de ~** (*arrancar*) by the roots; (*cortar*) completely

cual [kwal] *adv* like, as ♦ *pron*: **el ~** *etc* which; (*persona: sujeto*) who; (: *objeto*) whom ♦ *adj* such as; **cada ~** each one; **déjalo tal ~** leave it just as it is

cuál [kwal] *pron interr* which (one)

cualesquier(a) [kwales'kjer(a)] *pl de* **cualquier(a)**

cualidad [kwali'ðað] *nf* quality

cualquier [kwal'kjer] *adj ver* **cualquiera**

cualquiera [kwal'kjera] (*pl* **cualesquiera**) *adj* (*delante de nm y f*: **cualquier**) any ♦ *pron* anybody; **un coche ~ servirá** any car will do; **no es un hombre ~** he isn't just anybody; **cualquier día/libro** any day/book; **eso ~ lo sabe hacer** anybody can do that; **es un ~** he's a nobody

cuando ['kwando] *adv* when; (*aún si*) if, even if ♦ *conj* (*puesto que*) since ♦ *prep*: **yo, ~ niño ...** when I was a child ...; **~ no sea así** even if it is not so; **~ más** at (the) most; **~ menos** at least; **~ no** if not, otherwise; **de ~ en ~** from time to time

cuándo ['kwando] *adv* when; **¿desde ~?, ¿de ~ acá?** since when?

cuantía [kwan'tia] *nf* (*importe: de pérdidas, deuda, daños*) extent

cuantioso, a [kwan'tjoso, a] *adj* substantial

PALABRA CLAVE

cuanto, a ['kwanto, a] *adj* **1** (*todo*): **tiene todo ~ desea** he's got everything he wants; **le daremos ~s ejemplares necesite** we'll give him as many copies as o all the copies he needs; **~s hombres la ven** all the men who see her
2: **unos ~s**: **había unos ~s periodistas** there were a few journalists
3 (+ *más*): **~ más vino bebes peor te sentirás** the more wine you drink the worse you'll feel ♦ *pron*: **tiene ~ desea** he has everything he wants; **tome ~/~s quiera** take as much/many as you want
♦ *adv*: **en ~: en ~ profesor** as a teacher; **en ~ a mí** as for me; *ver tb* **antes**
♦ *conj* **1**: **~ más gana menos gasta** the more he earns the less he spends; **~ más joven más confiado** the younger you are the more trusting you are
2: **en ~: en ~ llegue/llegué** as soon as I arrive/arrived

cuánto, a ['kwanto, a] *adj* (*exclamación*) what a lot of; (*interr: sg*) how much?; (: *pl*) how many? ♦ *pron, adv* how; (*interr: sg*) how much?; (: *pl*) how many?; **¡cuánta gente!** what a lot of people!; **¿~ cuesta?** how much does it cost?; **¿a ~s estamos?** what's the date?; **Señor no sé ~s** Mr. So-and-So

cuarenta [kwa'renta] *num* forty

cuarentena [kwaren'tena] *nf* quarantine

cuaresma [kwa'resma] *nf* Lent

cuarta ['kwarta] *nf* (*MAT*) quarter, fourth; (*palmo*) span

cuartel [kwar'tel] *nm* (*MIL*) barracks *pl*; **~ general** headquarters *pl*

cuarteto [kwar'teto] *nm* quartet

cuarto, a ['kwarto, a] *adj* fourth ♦ *nm* (*MAT*) quarter, fourth; (*habitación*) room; **~ de baño**

bathroom; ~ **de estar** living room; ~ **de hora** quarter (of an) hour; ~ **de kilo** quarter kilo

cuatro ['kwatro] *num* four

Cuba ['kuβa] *nf* Cuba; **cubano, a** *adj, nm/f* Cuban

cuba ['kuβa] *nf* cask, barrel

cubata [ku'βata] *nm* (*fam*) large drink (*of rum and coke etc*)

cúbico, a ['kuβiko, a] *adj* cubic

cubierta [ku'βjerta] *nf* cover, covering; (*neumático*) tyre; (*NAUT*) deck

cubierto, a [ku'βjerto, a] *pp de* **cubrir** ♦ *adj* covered ♦ *nm* cover; (*lugar en la mesa*) place; ~s *nmpl* cutlery *sg*; **a ~** under cover

cubil [ku'βil] *nm* den; **~ete** *nm* (*en juegos*) cup

cubito [ku'βito] *nm*: ~ **de hielo** ice-cube

cubo ['kuβo] *nm* (*MATH*) cube; (*balde*) bucket, tub; (*TEC*) drum

cubrecama [kuβre'kama] *nm* bedspread

cubrir [ku'βrir] *vt* to cover; **~se** *vr* (*cielo*) to become overcast

cucaracha [kuka'ratʃa] *nf* cockroach

cuchara [ku'tʃara] *nf* spoon; (*TEC*) scoop; **~da** *nf* spoonful; **~dita** *nf* teaspoonful

cucharilla [kutʃa'riʎa] *nf* teaspoon

cucharón [kutʃa'ron] *nm* ladle

cuchichear [kutʃitʃe'ar] *vi* to whisper

cuchilla [ku'tʃiʎa] *nf* (*large*) knife; (*de arma blanca*) blade; ~ **de afeitar** razor blade

cuchillo [ku'tʃiʎo] *nm* knife

cuchitril [kutʃi'tril] *nm* hovel

cuclillas [ku'kliʎas] *nfpl*: **en ~** squatting

cuco, a ['kuko, a] *adj* pretty; (*astuto*) sharp ♦ *nm* cuckoo

cucurucho [kuku'rutʃo] *nm* cornet

cuello ['kweʎo] *nm* (*ANAT*) neck; (*de vestido, camisa*) collar

cuenca ['kwenka] *nf* (*ANAT*) eye socket; (*GEO*) bowl, deep valley

cuenco ['kwenko] *nm* bowl

cuenta *etc* ['kwenta] *vb ver* **contar** ♦ *nf* (*cálculo*) count, counting; (*en café, restaurante*) bill (*BRIT*), check (*US*); (*COM*) account; (*de collar*) bead; **a fin de ~s** in the end; **caer en la ~** to catch on; **darse ~ de** to realize; **tener en ~** to bear in mind; **echar ~s** to take stock; ~ **corriente/de ahorros** current/savings account; ~ **atrás** countdown; **~kilómetros** *nm inv* ≈ milometer; (*de velocidad*) speedometer

cuento *etc* ['kwento] *vb ver* **contar** ♦ *nm* story

cuerda ['kwerða] *nf* rope; (*fina*) string; (*de reloj*) spring; **dar ~ a un reloj** to wind up a clock; ~ **floja** tightrope

cuerdo, a ['kwerðo, a] *adj* sane; (*prudente*) wise, sensible

cuerno ['kwerno] *nm* horn

cuero ['kwero] *nm* leather; **en ~s** stark naked; ~ **cabelludo** scalp

cuerpo ['kwerpo] *nm* body

cuervo ['kwerβo] *nm* crow

cuesta *etc* ['kwesta] *vb ver* **costar** ♦ *nf* slope; (*en camino etc*) hill; ~ **arriba/abajo** uphill/downhill; **a ~s** on one's back

cueste *etc vb ver* **costar**

cuestión [kwes'tjon] *nf* matter, question, issue

cueva ['kweβa] *nf* cave

cuidado [kwi'ðaðo] *nm* care, carefulness; (*preocupación*) care, worry ♦ *excl* careful!, look out!

cuidadoso, a [kwiða'ðoso, a] *adj* careful; (*preocupado*) anxious

cuidar [kwi'ðar] *vt* (*MED*) to care for; (*ocuparse de*) to take care of, look after ♦ *vi*: ~ **de** to take care of, look after; **~se** *vr* to look after o.s.; **~se de hacer algo** to take care to do sth

culata [ku'lata] *nf* (*de fusil*) butt

culebra [ku'leβra] *nf* snake

culebrón [kule'βron] (*fam*) *nm* (*TV*) soap(-opera)

culinario, a [kuli'narjo, a] *adj* culinary, cooking *cpd*

culminación [kulmina'θjon] *nf* culmination

culo ['kulo] *nm* bottom, backside; (*de vaso, botella*) bottom

culpa ['kulpa] *nf* fault; (*JUR*) guilt; **por ~ de** because of; **tener la ~ (de)** to be to blame (for); **~bilidad** *nf* guilt; **~ble** *adj* guilty ♦ *nm/f* culprit

culpar [kul'par] *vt* to blame; (*acusar*) to accuse

cultivar [kulti'βar] *vt* to cultivate

cultivo [kul'tiβo] *nm* (*acto*) cultivation; (*plantas*) crop

culto, a ['kulto, a] *adj* (*que tiene cultura*) cultured, educated ♦ *nm* (*homenaje*) worship; (*religión*) cult

cultura [kul'tura] *nf* culture

culturismo [kultu'rismo] *nm* body-building

cumbre ['kumbre] *nf* summit, top

cumpleaños [kumple'aɲos] *nm inv* birthday

cumplido, a [kum'pliðo, a] *adj* (*abundante*) plentiful; (*cortés*) courteous ♦ *nm* compliment; **visita de ~** courtesy call

cumplidor, a [kumpli'ðor, a] *adj* reliable

cumplimentar [kumplimen'tar] *vt* to congratulate

cumplimiento [kumpli'mjento] *nm* (*de un deber*) fulfilment; (*acabamiento*) completion

cumplir [kum'plir] *vt* to carry out, obey; (*promesa*) to carry out, fulfil; (*condena*) to serve ♦ *vi*: ~ **con** (*deberes*) to carry out, fulfil; **~se** *vr* (*plazo*) to expire; **hoy cumple dieciocho años** he is eighteen today

cúmulo ['kumulo] *nm* heap

cuna ['kuna] nf cradle, cot

cundir [kun'dir] vi (noticia, rumor, pánico) to spread; (rendir) to go a long way

cuneta [ku'neta] nf ditch

cuña ['kuɲa] nf wedge

cuñado, a [ku'ɲaðo, a] nm/f brother-/sister-in-law

cuota ['kwota] nf (parte proporcional) share; (cotización) fee, dues pl

cupe etc vb ver caber

cupiera etc vb ver caber

cupo ['kupo] vb ver caber ♦ nm quota

cupón [ku'pon] nm coupon

cúpula ['kupula] nf dome

cura ['kura] nf (curación) cure; (método curativo) treatment ♦ nm priest

curación [kura'θjon] nf cure; (acción) curing

curandero, a [kuran'dero, a] nm/f quack

curar [ku'rar] vt (MED: herida) to treat, dress; (: enfermo) to cure; (CULIN) to cure, salt; (cuero) to tan; ~se vr to get well, recover

curiosear [kurjose'ar] vt to glance at, look over ♦ vi to look round, wander round; (explorar) to poke about

curiosidad [kurjosi'ðað] nf curiosity

curioso, a [ku'rjoso, a] adj curious ♦ nm/f bystander, onlooker

currante [ku'rrante] (fam) nm/f worker

currar [ku'rrar] (fam) vi to work

currículo [ku'rrikulo] = curriculum

curriculum [ku'rrikulum] nm curriculum vitae

cursi ['kursi] (fam) adj affected

cursillo [kur'siʎo] nm short course

cursiva [kur'siβa] nf italics pl

curso ['kurso] nm course; en ~ (año) current; (proceso) going on, under way

cursor [kur'sor] nm (INFORM) cursor

curtido, a [kur'tiðo, a] adj (cara etc) weather-beaten; (fig: persona) experienced

curtir [kur'tir] vt (cuero etc) to tan

curva ['kurβa] nf curve, bend

cúspide ['kuspiðe] nf (GEO) peak; (fig) top

custodia [kus'toðja] nf safekeeping; custody; custodiar vt (conservar) to take care of; (vigilar) to guard

cutis ['kutis] nm inv skin, complexion

cutre ['kutre] (fam) adj (lugar) grotty

cuyo, a ['kujo, a] pron (de quien) whose; (de que) whose, of which; en ~ caso in which case

C.V. abr (= caballos de vapor) H.P.

D, d

D. abr (= Don) Esq.

Da. abr = Doña

dádiva ['daðiβa] nf (donación) donation;

(regalo) gift; dadivoso, a adj generous

dado, a ['daðo, a] pp de dar ♦ nm die; ~s nmpl dice; ~ que given that

daltónico, a [dal'toniko, a] adj colour-blind

dama ['dama] nf (gen) lady; (AJEDREZ) queen; ~s nfpl (juego) draughts sg

damnificar [damnifi'kar] vt to harm; (persona) to injure

danés, esa [da'nes, esa] adj Danish ♦ nm/f Dane

danzar [dan'θar] vt, vi to dance

dañar [da'ɲar] vt (objeto) to damage; (persona) to hurt; ~se vr (objeto) to get damaged

dañino, a [da'ɲino, a] adj harmful

daño ['daɲo] nm (a un objeto) damage; (a una persona) harm, injury; ~s y perjuicios (JUR) damages; hacer ~ a to damage; (persona) to hurt, injure; hacerse ~ to hurt o.s.

PALABRA CLAVE

dar [dar] vt 1 (gen) to give; (obra de teatro) to put on; (film) to show; (fiesta) to hold; ~ algo a uno to give sb sth o sth to sb; ~ de beber a uno to give sb a drink

2 (producir: intereses) to yield; (fruta) to produce

3 (locuciones + n): da gusto escucharle it's a pleasure to listen to him; ver tb paseo y otros sustantivos

4 (+ n: = perífrasis de verbo): me da asco it sickens me

5 (considerar): ~ algo por descontado/entendido to take sth for granted/as read; ~ algo por concluido to consider sth finished

6 (hora): el reloj dio las 6 the clock struck 6 (o'clock)

7: me da lo mismo it's all the same to me; ver tb igual, más

♦ vi 1: ~ con: dimos con él dos horas más tarde we came across him two hours later; al final di con la solución I eventually came up with the answer

2: ~ en (blanco, suelo) to hit; el sol me da en la cara the sun is shining (right) on my face

3: ~ de sí (zapatos etc) to stretch, give

♦ ~se vr 1: ~se por vencido to give up

2 (ocurrir): se han dado muchos casos there have been a lot of cases

3: ~se a: se ha dado a la bebida he's taken to drinking

4: se me dan bien/mal las ciencias I'm good/bad at science

5: dárselas de: se las da de experto he fancies himself o poses as an expert

---

dardo ['darðo] nm dart

datar [da'tar] vi: ~ de to date from

dátil ['datil] nm date

dato ['dato] nm fact, piece of information; **~s personales** personal details

DC abbr m (= disco compacto) CD

dcha. abr (= derecha) r.h.

d. de J.C. abr (= después de Jesucristo) A.D.

PALABRA CLAVE
---

de [de] prep (de + el = del) **1** (posesión) of; **la casa ~ Isabel/mis padres** Isabel's/my parents' house; **es ~ ellos** it's theirs

2 (origen, distancia, con números) from; **soy ~ Gijón** I'm from Gijón; **~ 8 a 20** from 8 to 20; **salir del cine** to go out o leave the cinema; **~ 2 en 2** 2 by 2, 2 at a time

3 (valor descriptivo): **una copa ~ vino** a glass of wine; **la mesa ~ la cocina** the kitchen table; **un billete ~ 1000 pesetas** a 1000 peseta note; **un niño ~ tres años** a three-year-old (child); **una máquina ~ coser** a sewing machine; **ir vestido ~ gris** to be dressed in grey; **la niña del vestido azul** the girl in the blue dress; **trabaja ~ profesora** she works as a teacher; **~ lado** sideways; **~ atrás/delante** rear/front

4 (hora, tiempo): **a las 8 ~ la mañana** at 8 o'clock in the morning; **~ día/noche** by day/ night; **~ hoy en ocho días** a week from now; **~ niño era gordo** as a child he was fat

5 (comparaciones): **más/menos ~ cien personas** more/less than a hundred people; **el más caro ~ la tienda** the most expensive in the shop; **menos/más ~ lo pensado** less/more than expected

6 (causa): **del calor** from the heat; **~ puro tonto** out of sheer stupidity

7 (tema) about; **clases ~ inglés** English classes; **¿sabes algo ~ él?** do you know anything about him?; **un libro ~ física** a physics book

8 (adj + de + infin): **fácil ~ entender** easy to understand

9 (oraciones pasivas): **fue respetado ~ todos** he was loved by all

10 (condicional + infin) if; **~ ser posible** if possible; **~ no terminarlo hoy** if I etc don't finish it today

dé vb ver **dar**

deambular [deambu'lar] vi to wander

debajo [de'ßaxo] adv underneath; **~ de** below, under; **por ~ de** beneath

debate [de'ßate] nm debate; **debatir** vt to debate

deber [de'ßer] nm duty ♦ vt to owe ♦ vi: **debe (de)** it must, it should; **~es** nmpl (ESCOL) homework; **debo hacerlo** I must do it; **debe de ir** he should go; **~se** vr: **~se a** to be owing o due to

debido, a [de'ßiðo, a] adj proper, just; **~ a** due to, because of

débil ['deßil] adj (persona, carácter) weak; (luz) dim; **debilidad** nf weakness; dimness

debilitar [deßili'tar] vt to weaken; **~se** vr to grow weak

debutar [deßu'tar] vi to make one's debut

década ['dekaða] nf decade

decadencia [deka'ðenθja] nf (estado) decadence; (proceso) decline, decay

decaer [deka'er] vi (declinar) to decline; (debilitarse) to weaken

decaído, a [deka'iðo, a] adj: **estar ~** (abatido) to be down

decaimiento [dekai'mjento] nm (declinación) decline; (desaliento) discouragement; (MED: estado débil) weakness

decano, a [de'kano, a] nm/f (de universidad etc) dean

decapitar [dekapi'tar] vt to behead

decena [de'θena] nf: **una ~** ten (or so)

decencia [de'θenθja] nf decency

decente [de'θente] adj decent

decepción [deθep'θjon] nf disappointment

decepcionar [deθepθjo'nar] vt to disappoint

decidir [deθi'ðir] vt, vi to decide; **~se** vr: **~se a** to make up one's mind to

décimo, a ['deθimo, a] adj tenth ♦ nm tenth

decir [de'θir] vt to say; (contar) to tell; (hablar) to speak ♦ nm saying; **~se** vr: **se dice que** it is said that; **~ para o entre sí** to say to o.s.; **querer ~** to mean; **¡dígame!** (TEL) hello!; (en tienda) can I help you?

decisión [deθi'sjon] nf (resolución) decision; (firmeza) decisiveness

decisivo, a [deθi'sißo, a] adj decisive

declaración [deklara'θjon] nf (manifestación) statement; (de amor) declaration; **~ de ingresos** o **de la renta** o **fiscal** income-tax return

declarar [dekla'rar] vt to declare ♦ vi to declare; (JUR) to testify; **~se** vr to propose

declinar [dekli'nar] vt (gen) to decline; (JUR) to reject ♦ vi (el día) to draw to a close

declive [de'kliße] nm (cuesta) slope; (fig) decline

decodificador [dekoðifika'ðor] nm decoder

decolorarse [dekolo'rarse] vr to become discoloured

decoración [dekora'θjon] nf decoration

decorado [deko'raðo] nm (CINE, TEATRO) scenery, set

decorar [deko'rar] vt to decorate; **decorativo, a** adj ornamental, decorative

decoro [de'koro] nm (respeto) respect; (dignidad) decency; (recato) propriety; **~so, a** adj (decente) decent; (modesto) modest; (digno) proper

decrecer [dekre'θer] vi to decrease, diminish

decrépito, a |de'krepito, a| adj decrepit

decretar [dekre'tar] vt to decree; **decreto** nm decree

dedal [de'ðal] nm thimble

dedicación [deðika'θjon] nf dedication

dedicar [deði'kar] vt (libro) to dedicate; (tiempo, dinero) to devote; (palabras: decir, consagrar) to dedicate, devote; **dedicatoria** nf (de libro) dedication

dedo ['deðo] nm finger; ~ (del pie) toe; ~ **pulgar** thumb; ~ **índice** index finger; ~ **corazón** middle finger; ~ **meñique** little finger; **hacer** ~ (fam) to hitch (a lift)

deducción [deðuk'θjon] nf deduction

deducir [deðu'θir] vt (concluir) to deduce, infer; (COM) to deduct

defecto [de'fekto] nm defect, flaw; **defectuoso, a** adj defective, faulty

defender [defen'der] vt to defend

defensa [de'fensa] nf defence ♦ nm (DEPORTE) defender, back; **defensivo, a** adj defensive; **a la defensiva** on the defensive

defensor, a [defen'sor, a] adj defending ♦ nm/f (abogado ~) defending counsel; (protector) protector

deficiencia [defi'θjenθja] nf deficiency

deficiente [defi'θjente] adj (defectuoso) defective; ~ **en** lacking o deficient in; **ser un** ~ **mental** to be mentally handicapped

déficit ['defiθit] (pl ~s) nm deficit

definición [defini'θjon] nf definition

definir [defi'nir] vt (determinar) to determine, establish; (decidir) to define; (aclarar) to clarify; **definitivo, a** adj definitive; **en definitiva** definitively; (en resumen) in short

deformación [deforma'θjon] nf (alteración) deformation; (RADIO etc) distortion

deformar [defor'mar] vt (gen) to deform; ~**se** vr to become deformed; **deforme** adj (informe) deformed; (feo) ugly; (malhecho) misshapen

defraudar [defrau'ðar] vt (decepcionar) to disappoint; (estafar) to defraud

defunción [defun'θjon] nf death, demise

degeneración [dexenera'θjon] nf (de las células) degeneration; (moral) degeneracy

degenerar [dexene'rar] vi to degenerate

degollar [dexo'ʎar] vt to behead; (fig) to slaughter

degradar [dexra'ðar] vt to debase, degrade; ~**se** vr to demean o.s.

degustación [dexusta'θjon] nf sampling, tasting

deificar [deifi'kar] vt to deify

dejadez [dexa'ðeθ] nf (negligencia) neglect; (descuido) untidiness, carelessness

dejar [de'xar] vt to leave; (permitir) to allow, let; (abandonar) to abandon, forsake;

(beneficios) to produce, yield ♦ vi: ~ **de** (parar) to stop; (no hacer) to fail to; **no dejes de comprar un billete** make sure you buy a ticket; ~ **a un lado** to leave o set aside

dejo ['dexo] nm (LING) accent

del [del] (= **de+** el) ver **de**

delantal [delan'tal] nm apron

delante [de'lante] adv in front, (enfrente) opposite; (adelante) ahead; ~ **de** in front of, before

delantera [delan'tera] nf (de vestido, casa etc) front part; (DEPORTE) forward line; **llevar la** ~ **(a uno)** to be ahead (of sb)

delantero, a |delan'tero, a| adj front ♦ nm (DEPORTE) forward, striker

delatar [dela'tar] vt to inform on o against, betray; **delator, a** nm/f informer

delegación [delexa'θjon] nf (acción, delegados) delegation; (COM: oficina) office, branch; ~ **de policía** police station

delegado, a [dele'xaðo, a] nm/f delegate; (COM) agent

delegar [dele'xar] vt to delegate

deletrear [deletre'ar] vt to spell (out)

deleznable [deleθ'naβle] adj brittle; (excusa, idea) feeble

delfín [del'fin] nm dolphin

delgadez [delxa'ðeθ] nf thinness, slimness

delgado, a [del'xaðo, a] adj thin; (persona) slim, thin; (tela etc) light, delicate

deliberación [deliβera'θjon] nf deliberation

deliberar [deliβe'rar] vt to debate, discuss

delicadeza [delika'ðeθa] nf (gen) delicacy; (refinamiento, sutileza) refinement

delicado, a [deli'kaðo, a] adj (gen) delicate; (sensible) sensitive; (quisquilloso) touchy

delicia [de'liθja] nf delight

delicioso, a [deli'θjoso, a] adj (gracioso) delightful; (exquisito) delicious

delimitar [delimi'tar] vt (funciones, responsabilidades) to define

delincuencia [delin'kwenθja] nf delinquency; **delincuente** nm/f delinquent; (criminal) criminal

delineante [deline'ante] nm/f draughtsman/woman

delinear [deline'ar] vt (dibujo) to draw; (fig, contornos) to outline

delinquir [delin'kir] vi to commit an offence

delirante [deli'rante] adj delirious

delirar [deli'rar] vi to be delirious, rave

delirio [de'lirjo] nm (MED) delirium; (palabras insensatas) ravings pl

delito [de'lito] nm (gen) crime; (infracción) offence

delta ['delta] nm delta

demacrado, a [dema'kraðo, a] adj: **estar** ~ to look pale and drawn, be wasted away

demagogo, a |dema'xoxo, a| nm/f

demagogue

demanda [de'manda] *nf* (*pedido*, COM) demand; (*petición*) request; (*JUR*) action, lawsuit

demandante [deman'dante] *nm/f* claimant

demandar [deman'dar] *vt* (*gen*) to demand; (*JUR*) to sue, file a lawsuit against

demarcación [demarka'θjon] *nf* (*de terreno*) demarcation

demás [de'mas] *adj*: **los ~ niños** the other children, the remaining children ♦ *pron*: **los/las ~** the others, the rest (of them); **lo ~** the rest (of it)

demasía [dema'sia] *nf* (*exceso*) excess, surplus; **comer en ~** to eat to excess

demasiado, a [dema'sjaðo, a] *adj*: **~ vino** too much wine ♦ *adv* (*antes de adj*, *adv*) too; **~s libros** too many books; **¡esto es ~!** that's the limit!; **hace ~ calor** it's too hot; **~ despacio** too slowly; **~s** too many

demencia [de'menθja] *nf* (*locura*) madness; **demente** *nm/f* lunatic ♦ *adj* mad, insane

democracia [demo'kraθja] *nf* democracy

demócrata [de'mokrata] *nm/f* democrat; **democrático, a** *adj* democratic

demoler [demo'ler] *vt* to demolish; **demolición** *nf* demolition

demonio [de'monjo] *nm* devil, demon; **¡~s!** hell!, damn!; **¿cómo ~s?** how the hell?

demora [de'mora] *nf* delay; **demorar** *vt* (*retardar*) to delay, hold back; (*detener*) to hold up ♦ *vi* to linger, stay on; **~se** *vr* to be delayed

demos *vb ver* **dar**

demostración [demostra'θjon] *nf* (MAT) proof; (*de afecto*) show, display

demostrar [demos'trar] *vt* (*probar*) to prove; (*mostrar*) to show; (*manifestar*) to demonstrate

demudado, a [demu'ðaðo, a] *adj* (*rostro*) pale

den *vb ver* **dar**

denegar [dene'var] *vt* (*rechazar*) to refuse; (*JUR*) to reject

denigrar [deni'vrar] *vt* (*desacreditar*, *infamar*) to denigrate; (*injuriar*) to insult

denotar [deno'tar] *vt* to denote

densidad [densi'ðað] *nf* density; (*fig*) thickness

denso, a ['denso, a] *adj* dense; (*espeso*, *pastoso*) thick; (*fig*) heavy

dentadura [denta'ðura] *nf* (*set of*) teeth *pl*; **~ postiza** false teeth *pl*

dentera [den'tera] *nf* (*sensación desagradable*) the shivers *pl*

dentífrico, a [den'tifriko, a] *adj* dental ♦ *nm* toothpaste

dentista [den'tista] *nm/f* dentist

dentro ['dentro] *adv* inside ♦ *prep*: **~ de** in,

inside, within; **por ~** (on the) inside; **mirar por ~** to look inside; **~ de tres meses** within three months

denuncia [de'nunθja] *nf* (*delación*) denunciation; (*acusación*) accusation; (*de accidente*) report; **denunciar** *vt* to report; (*delatar*) to inform on o against

departamento [departa'mento] *nm* (*sección administrativa*) department, section; (*AM*: *apartamento*) flat (*BRIT*), apartment

dependencia [depen'denθja] *nf* dependence; (*POL*) dependency; (*COM*) office, section

depender [depen'der] *vi*: **~ de** to depend on

dependienta [depen'djenta] *nf* saleswoman, shop assistant

dependiente [depen'djente] *adj* dependent ♦ *nm* salesman, shop assistant

depilar [depi'lar] *vt* (*con cera*) to wax; (*cejas*) to pluck; **depilatorio** *nm* hair remover

deplorable [deplo'raßle] *adj* deplorable

deplorar [deplo'rar] *vt* to deplore

deponer [depo'ner] *vt* to lay down ♦ *vi* (*JUR*) to give evidence; (*declarar*) to make a statement

deportar [depor'tar] *vt* to deport

deporte [de'porte] *nm* sport; **hacer ~** to play sports; **deportista** *adj* sports *cpd* ♦ *nm/f* sportsman/woman; **deportivo, a** *adj* (*club*, *periódico*) sports *cpd* ♦ *nm* sports car

depositar [deposi'tar] *vt* (*dinero*) to deposit; (*mercancías*) to put away, store; **~se** *vr* to settle; **~io, a** *nm/f* trustee

depósito [de'posito] *nm* (*gen*) deposit; (*almacén*) warehouse, store; (*de agua*, *gasolina etc*) tank; **~ de cadáveres** mortuary

depreciar [depre'θjar] *vt* to depreciate, reduce the value of; **~se** *vr* to depreciate, lose value

depredador, a [depreða'ðor, a] *adj* predatory ♦ *nm* predator

depresión [depre'sjon] *nf* depression

deprimido, a [depri'miðo, a] *adj* depressed

deprimir [depri'mir] *vt* to depress; **~se** *vr* (*persona*) to become depressed

deprisa [de'prisa] *adv* quickly, hurriedly

depuración [depura'θjon] *nf* purification; (*POL*) purge

depurar [depu'rar] *vt* to purify; (*purgar*) to purge

derecha [de'retfa] *nf* right(-hand) side; (*POL*) right; **a la ~** (*estar*) on the right; (*torcer etc*) (to the) right

derecho, a [de'retfo, a] *adj* right, right-hand ♦ *nm* (*privilegio*) right; (*lado*) right(-hand) side; (*leyes*) law ♦ *adv* straight, directly; **~s** *nmpl* (*de aduana*) duty *sg*; (*de autor*) royalties; **tener ~ a** to have a right to

deriva [de'rißa] *nf*: **ir o estar a la ~** to drift, be adrift

derivado [deri'ßaðo] nm (COM) by-product

derivar [deri'ßar] vt to derive; (desviar) to direct ♦ vi to derive, be derived; (NAUT) to drift; ~se vr to derive, be derived; to drift

derramamiento [derrama'mjento] nm (dispersión) spilling; ~ **de sangre** bloodshed

derramar [derra'mar] vt to spill; (verter) to pour out; (esparcir) to scatter; ~se vr to pour out; ~ **lágrimas** to weep

derrame [de'rrame] nm (de líquido) spilling; (de sangre) shedding; (de tubo etc) overflow; (pérdida) leakage; (MED) discharge

derredor [derre'ðor] adv: **al** o **en** ~ **de** around, about

derretido, a [derre'tiðo, a] adj melted; (metal) molten

derretir [derre'tir] vt (gen) to melt; (nieve) to thaw; ~se vr to melt

derribar [derri'ßar] vt to knock down; (construcción) to demolish; (persona, gobierno, político) to bring down

derrocar [derro'kar] vt (gobierno) to bring down, overthrow

derrochar [derro'tʃar] vt to squander; **derroche** nm (despilfarro) waste, squandering

derrota [de'rrota] nf (NAUT) course; (MIL, DEPORTE etc) defeat, rout; **derrotar** vt (gen) to defeat; **derrotero** nm (rumbo) course

derruir [derru'ir] vt (edificio) to demolish

derrumbar [derrum'bar] vt (edificio) to knock down; ~se vr to collapse

derruyendo etc vb ver **derruir**

des vb ver **dar**

desabotonar [desaßoto'nar] vt to unbutton, undo; ~se vr to come undone

desabrido, a [desa'ßriðo, a] adj (comida) insipid, tasteless; (persona) rude, surly; (respuesta) sharp; (tiempo) unpleasant

desabrochar [desaßro'tʃar] vt (botones, broches) to undo, unfasten; ~se vr (ropa etc) to come undone

desacato [desa'kato] nm (falta de respeto) disrespect; (JUR) contempt

desacertado, a [desaθer'taðo, a] adj (equivocado) mistaken; (inoportuno) unwise

desacuerdo [desa'ðjerto] nm mistake, error

desaconsejado, a [desakonse'xaðo, a] adj ill-advised

desaconsejar [desakonse'xar] vt to advise against

desacreditar [desakreði'tar] vt (desprestigiar) to discredit, bring into disrepute; (denigrar) to run down

desacuerdo [desa'kwerðo] nm disagreement, discord

desafiar [desa'fjar] vt (retar) to challenge; (enfrentarse a) to defy

desafilado, a [desafi'laðo, a] adj blunt

desafinado, a [desafi'naðo, a] adj: **estar** ~ to be out of tune

desafinar [desafi'nar] vi (al cantar) to be o go out of tune

desafío etc [desa'fio] vb ver **desafiar** ♦ nm (reto) challenge; (combate) duel; (resistencia) defiance

desaforado, a [desafo'raðo, a] adj (grito) ear-splitting; (comportamiento) outrageous

desafortunadamente [desafortunaða'mente] adv unfortunately

desafortunado, a [desafortu'naðo, a] adj (desgraciado) unfortunate, unlucky

desagradable [desaɣra'ðaßle] adj (fastidioso, enojoso) unpleasant; (irritante) disagreeable

desagradar [desaɣra'ðar] vi (disgustar) to displease; (molestar) to bother

desagradecido, a [desaɣraðe'θiðo, a] adj ungrateful

desagrado [desa'ɣraðo] nm (disgusto) displeasure; (contrariedad) dissatisfaction

desagraviar [desaɣra'ßjar] vt to make amends to

desagüe [des'aɣwe] nm (de un líquido) drainage; (cañería) drainpipe; (salida) outlet, drain

desaguisado [desaɣi'saðo] nm outrage

desahogado, a [desao'xaðo, a] adj (holgado) comfortable; (espacioso) roomy, large

desahogar [desao'xar] vt (aliviar) to ease, relieve; (ira) to vent; ~se vr (relajarse) to relax; (desfogarse) to let off steam

desahogo [desa'oxo] nm (alivio) relief; (comodidad) comfort, ease

desahuciar [desau'θjar] vt (enfermo) to give up hope for; (inquilino) to evict; **desahucio** nm eviction

desairar [desai'rar] vt (menospreciar) to slight, snub

desaire [des'aire] nm (menosprecio) slight; (falta de garbo) unattractiveness

desajustar [desaxus'tar] vt (desarreglar) to disarrange; (desconcertar) to throw off balance; ~se vr to get out of order; (aflojarse) to loosen

desajuste [desa'xuste] nm (de máquina) disorder; (situación) imbalance

desalentador, a [desalenta'ðor, a] adj discouraging

desalentar [desalen'tar] vt (desanimar) to discourage

desaliento etc [desa'ljento] vb ver **desalentar** ♦ nm discouragement

desaliño [desa'liɲo] nm slovenliness

desalmado, a [desal'maðo, a] adj (cruel) cruel, heartless

desalojar [desalo'xar] vt (*expulsar, echar*) to eject; (*abandonar*) to move out of ♦ vi to move out

desamor [desa'mor] nm (*frialdad*) indifference; (*odio*) dislike

desamparado, a [desampa'raðo, a] adj (*persona*) helpless; (*lugar: expuesto*) exposed; (*desierto*) deserted

desamparar [desampa'rar] vt (*abandonar*) to desert, abandon; (*JUR*) to leave defenceless; (*barco*) to abandon

desandar [desan'dar] vt: ~ **lo andado** o **el camino** to retrace one's steps

desangrar [desan'grar] vt to bleed; (*fig: persona*) to bleed dry; ~**se** vr to lose a lot of blood

desanimado, a [desani'maðo, a] adj (*persona*) downhearted; (*espectáculo, fiesta*) dull

desanimar [desani'mar] vt (*desalentar*) to discourage; (*deprimir*) to depress; ~**se** vr to lose heart

desapacible [desapa'θiβle] adj (*gen*) unpleasant

desaparecer [desapare'θer] vi (*gen*) to disappear; (*el sol, la luz*) to vanish; **desaparecido, a** adj missing; **desaparición** nf disappearance

desapasionado, a [desapasjo'naðo, a] adj dispassionate, impartial

desapego [desa'peɣo] nm (*frialdad*) coolness; (*distancia*) detachment

desapercibido, a [desaperθi'βiðo, a] adj (*desprevenido*) unprepared; **pasar ~** to go unnoticed

desaprensivo, a [desapren'siβo, a] adj unscrupulous

desaprobar [desapro'βar] vt (*reprobar*) to disapprove of; (*condenar*) to condemn; (*no consentir*) to reject

desaprovechado, a [desaproβe'tʃaðo, a] adj (*oportunidad, tiempo*) wasted; (*estudiante*) slack

desaprovechar [desaproβe'tʃar] vt to waste

desarmar [desar'mar] vt (*MIL, fig*) to disarm; (*TEC*) to take apart, dismantle; **desarme** nm disarmament

desarraigar [desarrai'xar] vt to uproot; **desarraigo** nm uprooting

desarreglar [desarre'ɣlar] vt (*desordenar*) to disarrange; (*trastocar*) to upset, disturb

desarreglo [desa'rreɣlo] nm (*de casa, persona*) untidiness; (*desorden*) disorder

desarrollar [desarro'ʎar] vt (*gen*) to develop; ~**se** vr to develop; (*ocurrir*) to take place; (*FOTO*) to develop; **desarrollo** nm development

desarticular [desartiku'lar] vt (*hueso*) to dislocate; (*objeto*) to take apart; (*fig*) to break up

desasir [desa'sir] vt to loosen

desasosegar [desasose'ɣar] vt (*inquietar*) to disturb, make uneasy; ~**se** vr to become uneasy

desasosiego etc [desaso'sjeɣo] vb ver **desasosegar** ♦ nm (*intranquilidad*) uneasiness, restlessness; (*ansiedad*) anxiety

desastrado, a [desas'traðo, a] adj (*desaliñado*) shabby; (*sucio*) dirty

desastre [de'sastre] nm disaster; **desastroso, a** adj disastrous

desatado, a [desa'taðo, a] adj (*desligado*) untied; (*violento*) violent, wild

desatar [desa'tar] vt (*nudo*) to untie; (*paquete*) to undo; (*separar*) to detach; ~**se** vr (*zapatos*) to come untied; (*tormenta*) to break

desatascar [desatas'kar] vt (*cañería*) to unblock, clear

desatender [desaten'der] vt (*no prestar atención a*) to disregard; (*abandonar*) to neglect

desatento, a [desa'tento, a] adj (*distraído*) inattentive; (*descortés*) discourteous

desatinado, a [desati'naðo, a] adj foolish, silly; **desatino** nm (*idiotez*) foolishness, folly; (*error*) blunder

desatornillar [desatorni'ʎar] vt to unscrew

desatrancar [desatran'kar] vt (*puerta*) to unbolt; (*cañería*) to clear, unblock

desautorizado, a [desautori'θaðo, a] adj unauthorized

desautorizar [desautori'θar] vt (*oficial*) to deprive of authority; (*informe*) to deny

desavenencia [desaβe'nenθja] nf (*desacuerdo*) disagreement; (*discrepancia*) quarrel

desayunar [desaju'nar] vi to have breakfast ♦ vt to have for breakfast; **desayuno** nm breakfast

desazón [desa'θon] nf anxiety

desazonarse [desaθo'narse] vr to worry, be anxious

desbandarse [desβan'darse] vr (*MIL*) to disband; (*fig*) to flee in disorder

desbarajuste [desβara'xuste] nm confusion, disorder

desbaratar [desβara'tar] vt (*deshacer, destruir*) to ruin

desbloquear [desβloke'ar] vt (*negociaciones, tráfico*) to get going again; (*COM: cuenta*) to unfreeze

desbocado, a [desβo'kaðo, a] adj (*caballo*) runaway

desbordar [desβor'ðar] vt (*sobrepasar*) to go beyond; (*exceder*) to exceed; ~**se** vr (*río*) to overflow; (*entusiasmo*) to erupt

descabalgar [deskaβal'xar] vi to dismount

descabellado, a |deskaβeʼʎaðo, a| *adj*
(*disparatado*) wild, crazy

descafeinado, a [deskafeiʼnaðo, a] *adj*
decaffeinated ♦ *nm* decaffeinated coffee

descalabro |deskaʼlaβro| *nm* blow;
(*desgracia*) misfortune

descalificar [deskalifiʼkar] *vt* to disqualify;
(*desacreditar*) to discredit

descalzar |deskalʼθar| *vt* (*zapato*) to take off;
descalzo, a *adj* barefoot(ed)

descambiar [deskamʼbjar] *vt* to exchange

descaminado, a [deskamiʼnaðo, a] *adj*
(*equivocado*) on the wrong road; (*fig*)
misguided

descampado [deskamʼpaðo] *nm* open space

descansado, a [deskanʼsaðo, a] *adj* (*gen*)
rested; (*que tranquiliza*) restful

descansar [deskanʼsar] *vt* (*gen*) to rest ♦ *vi*
to rest, have a rest; (*echarse*) to lie down

descansillo [deskanʼsiʎo] *nm* (*de escalera*)
landing

descanso [desʼkanso] *nm* (*reposo*) rest;
(*alivio*) relief; (*pausa*) break; (*DEPORTE*)
interval, half time

descapotable [deskapoʼtaβle] *nm* (*tb: coche*
~) convertible

descarado, a |deskaʼraðo, a| *adj* shameless;
(*insolente*) cheeky

descarga |desʼkarγa| *nf* (*ARQ, ELEC, MIL*)
discharge; (*NAUT*) unloading

descargar |deskarʼγar| *vt* to unload; (*golpe*)
to let fly; ~se *vr* to unburden o.s.; **descargo**
nm (*COM*) receipt; (*JUR*) evidence

descaro |desʼkaro| *nm* nerve

descarriar |deskaʼrrjar| *vt* (*descaminar*) to
misdirect; (*fig*) to lead astray; ~se *vr*
(*perderse*) to lose one's way; (*separarse*) to
stray; (*pervertirse*) to err, go astray

descarrilamiento [deskarrilaʼmjento] *nm*
(*de tren*) derailment

descarrilar [deskarriʼlar] *vi* to be derailed

descartar [deskarʼtar] *vt* (*rechazar*) to reject;
(*eliminar*) to rule out; ~se *vr* (*NAIPES*) to
discard; ~se de to shirk

descascarillado, a [deskaskariʼʎaðo, a] *adj*
(*paredes*) peeling

descendencia [desθenʼdenθja] *nf* (*origen*)
origin, descent; (*hijos*) offspring

descender |desθenʼder| *vt* (*bajar: escalera*)
to go down ♦ *vi* to descend; (*temperatura,
nivel*) to fall, drop; ~ **de** to be descended
from

descendiente [desθenʼdjente] *nm/f*
descendant

descenso |desʼθenso| *nm* descent; (*de
temperatura*) drop

descifrar [desθiʼfrar] *vt* to decipher;
(*mensaje*) to decode

descolgar [deskolʼγar] *vt* (*bajar*) to take

down; (*teléfono*) to pick up; ~se *vr* to let o.s.
down

descolorido, a [deskoloʼriðo, a] *adj* faded;
(*pálido*) pale

descompasado, a [deskompaʼsaðo, a] *adj*
(*sin proporción*) out of all proportion;
(*excesivo*) excessive

descomponer [deskompoʼner] *vt*
(*desordenar*) to disarrange, disturb; (*TEC*) to
put out of order; (*dividir*) to break down
(into parts); (*fig*) to provoke; ~se *vr*
(*corromperse*) to rot, decompose; (*TEC*) to
break down

descomposición [deskomposiʼθjon] *nf* (*de
un objeto*) breakdown; (*de fruta etc*)
decomposition; ~ **de vientre** stomach upset,
diarrhoea

descompuesto, a [deskomʼpwesto, a] *adj*
(*corrompido*) decomposed; (*roto*) broken

descomunal [deskomuʼnal] *adj* (*enorme*)
huge

desconcertado, a |deskonθerʼtaðo, a| *adj*
disconcerted, bewildered

desconcertar |deskonθerʼtar| *vt* (*confundir*)
to baffle; (*incomodar*) to upset, put out; ~se
vr (*turbarse*) to be upset

desconchado, a [deskonʼtʃaðo, a] *adj*
(*pintura*) peeling

desconcierto *etc* [deskonʼθjerto] *vb ver*
desconcertar ♦ *nm* (*confusión*) disorder;
(*desorientación*) uncertainty; (*inquietud*)
uneasiness

desconectar [deskonekʼtar] *vt* to disconnect

desconfianza [deskonʼfjanθa] *nf* distrust

desconfiar [deskonʼfjar] *vi* to be distrustful;
~ **de** to distrust, suspect

descongelar [deskonxeʼlar] *vt* to defrost;
(*COM, POL*) to unfreeze

descongestionar [deskonxestjoʼnar] *vt*
(*cabeza, tráfico*) to clear

desconocer |deskonoʼθer| *vt* (*ignorar*) not
to know, be ignorant of

desconocido, a |deskonoʼθiðo, a| *adj*
unknown ♦ *nm/f* stranger

desconocimiento |deskonoθiʼmjento| *nm*
(*falta de conocimientos*) ignorance

desconsiderado, a |deskonsiðeʼraðo, a|
adj inconsiderate; (*insensible*) thoughtless

desconsolar [deskonsoʼlar] *vt* to distress;
~se *vr* to despair

desconsuelo *etc* [deskonʼswelo] *vb ver*
desconsolar ♦ *nm* (*tristeza*) distress;
(*desesperación*) despair

descontado, a [deskonʼtaðo, a] *adj*: **dar por**
~ (**que**) to take (it) for granted (that)

descontar [deskonʼtar] *vt* (*deducir*) to take
away, deduct; (*rebajar*) to discount

descontento, a [deskonʼtento, a] *adj*
dissatisfied ♦ *nm* dissatisfaction, discontent

descorazonar |deskoraθo'nar| vt to discourage, dishearten

descorchar |deskor'tʃar| vt to uncork

descorrer |desko'rrer| vt (cortinas, cerrojo) to draw back

descortés |deskor'tes| adj (mal educado) discourteous; (grosero) rude

descoser |desko'ser| vt to unstitch; **~se** vr to come apart (at the seams)

descosido, a |desko'siðo, a| adj (COSTURA) unstitched

descrédito |des'kreðito| nm discredit

descreído, a |deskre'iðo, a| adj (incrédulo) incredulous; (falto de fe) unbelieving

descremado, a |deskre'maðo, a| adj skimmed

describir |deskri'βir| vt to describe; **descripción** |deskrip'θjon| nf description

descrito |des'krito| pp de describir

descuartizar |deskwarti'θar| vt (animal) to cut up

descubierto, a |desku'βjerto, a| pp de descubrir ♦ adj uncovered, bare; (persona) bareheaded ♦ nm (bancario) overdraft; **al ~ in** the open

descubrimiento |deskuβri'mjento| nm (hallazgo) discovery; (revelación) revelation

descubrir |desku'βrir| vt to discover, find; (inaugurar) to unveil; (vislumbrar) to detect; (revelar) to reveal, show; (destapar) to uncover; **~se** vr to reveal o.s.; (quitarse sombrero) to take off one's hat; (confesar) to confess

descuento etc |des'kwento| vb ver descontar ♦ nm discount

descuidado, a |deskwi'ðaðo, a| adj (sin cuidado) careless; (desordenado) untidy; (olvidadizo) forgetful; (dejado) neglected; (desprevenido) unprepared

descuidar |deskwi'ðar| vt (dejar) to neglect; (olvidar) to overlook; **~se** vr (distraerse) to be careless; (abandonarse) to let o.s. go; (desprevenirse) to drop one's guard; **¡descuida!** don't worry!; **descuido** nm (dejadez) carelessness; (olvido) negligence

---

desde |'desðe| prep **1** (lugar) from; **~ Burgos hasta mi casa hay 30 km** it's 30 kms from Burgos to my house

2 (posición): **hablaba ~ el balcón** she was speaking from the balcony

3 (tiempo: + ad, n): **~ ahora** from now on; **~ la boda** since the wedding; **~ niño** since I etc was a child; **~ 3 años atrás** since 3 years ago

4 (tiempo: + vb, fecha) since; for; **nos conocemos ~ 1992/ ~ hace 20 años** we've known each other since 1992/for 20 years;

no le veo ~ 1997/~ hace 5 años I haven't seen him since 1997/for 5 years

5 (gama): **~ los más lujosos hasta los más económicos** from the most luxurious to the most reasonably priced

6: **~ luego (que no)** of course (not)

♦ conj: **~ que**: **~ que recuerdo** for as long as I can remember; **~ que llegó no ha salido** he hasn't been out since he arrived

---

desdecirse |desðe'θirse| vr to retract; **~ de** to go back on

desdén |des'ðen| nm scorn

desdeñar |desðe'ɲar| vt (despreciar) to scorn

desdicha |des'ðitʃa| nf (desgracia) misfortune; (infelicidad) unhappiness; **desdichado, a** adj (sin suerte) unlucky; (infeliz) unhappy

desdoblar |desðo'βlar| vt (extender) to spread out; (desplegar) to unfold

desear |dese'ar| vt to want, desire, wish for

desecar |dese'kar| vt to dry up; **~se** vr to dry up

desechar |dese'tʃar| vt (basura) to throw out o away; (ideas) to reject, discard; **desechos** nmpl rubbish sg, waste sg

desembalar |desemba'lar| vt to unpack

desembarazar |desembara'θar| vt (desocupar) to clear; (desenredar) to free; **~se** vr: **~se de** to free o.s. of, get rid of

desembarcar |desembar'kar| vt (mercancías etc) to unload ♦ vi to disembark; **~se** vr to disembark

desembocadura |desemboka'ðura| nf (de río) mouth; (de calle) opening

desembocar |desembo'kar| vi (río) to flow into; (fig) to result in

desembolso |desem'bolso| nm payment

desembragar |desembra'xar| vi to declutch

desembrollar |desembro'ʎar| vt (madeja) to unravel; (asunto, malentendido) to sort out

desemejanza |deseme'xanθa| nf dissimilarity

desempaquetar |desempake'tar| vt (regalo) to unwrap; (mercancía) to unpack

desempatar |desempa'tar| vi to replay, hold a play-off; **desempate** nm (FÚTBOL) replay, play-off; (TENIS) tie-break(er)

desempeñar |desempe'ɲar| vt (cargo) to hold; (papel) to perform; (lo empeñado) to redeem; **~ un papel** (fig) to play (a role)

desempeño |desem'peɲo| nm redeeming; (de cargo) occupation

desempleado, a |desemple'aðo, a| nm/f unemployed person; **desempleo** nm unemployment

desempolvar |desempol'βar| vt (muebles etc) to dust; (lo olvidado) to revive

desencadenar |desenkaðe'nar| vt to

unchain; (*ira*) to unleash; **~se** *vr* to break loose; (*tormenta*) to burst; (*guerra*) to break out

desencajar [desenka'xar] *vt* (*hueso*) to dislocate; (*mecanismo, pieza*) to disconnect, disengage

desencanto [desen'kanto] *nm* disillusionment

desenchufar [desentʃu'far] *vt* to unplug

desenfadado, a [desenfa'ðaðo, a] *adj* (*desenvuelto*) uninhibited; (*descarado*) forward; **desenfado** *nm* (*libertad*) freedom; (*comportamiento*) free and easy manner; (*descaro*) forwardness

desenfocado, a [desenfo'kaðo, a] *adj* (*FOTO*) out of focus

desenfrenado, a [desenfre'naðo, a] *adj* (*descontrolado*) uncontrolled; (*inmoderado*) unbridled; **desenfreno** *nm* wildness; (*de las pasiones*) lack of self-control

desenganchar [desengan'tʃar] *vt* (*gen*) to unhook; (*FERRO*) to uncouple

desengañar [desenga'ɲar] *vt* to disillusion; **~se** *vr* to become disillusioned; **desengaño** *nm* disillusionment; (*decepción*) disappointment

desenlace [desen'laθe] *nm* outcome

desenmarañar [desenmara'ɲar] *vt* (*fig*) to unravel

desenmascarar [desenmaska'rar] *vt* to unmask

desenredar [desenre'ðar] *vt* (*pelo*) to untangle; (*problema*) to sort out

desenroscar [desenros'kar] *vt* to unscrew

desentenderse [desenten'derse] *vr*: **~ de** to pretend not to know about; (*apartarse*) to have nothing to do with

desenterrar [desente'rrar] *vt* to exhume; (*tesoro, fig*) to unearth, dig up

desentonar [desento'nar] *vi* (*MUS*) to sing (*o play*) out of tune; (*color*) to clash

desentrañar [desentra'ɲar] *vt* (*misterio*) to unravel

desentumecer [desentume'θer] *vt* (*pierna etc*) to stretch

desenvoltura [desenβol'tura] *nf* ease

desenvolver [desenβol'ßer] *vt* (*paquete*) to unwrap; (*fig*) to develop; **~se** *vr* (*desarrollarse*) to unfold, develop; (*arreglárselas*) to cope

deseo [de'seo] *nm* desire, wish; **~so, a** *adj*: **estar ~so de** to be anxious to

desequilibrado, a [desekili'ßraðo, a] *adj* unbalanced

desertar [deser'tar] *vi* to desert

desértico, a [de'sertiko, a] *adj* desert *cpd*

desesperación [desespera'θjon] *nf* (*impaciencia*) desperation, despair; (*irritación*) fury

desesperar [desespe'rar] *vt* to drive to despair; (*exasperar*) to drive to distraction ♦ *vi*: **~ de** to despair of; **~se** *vr* to despair, lose hope

desestabilizar [desestaßili'θar] *vt* to destabilize

desestimar [desesti'mar] *vt* (*menospreciar*) to have a low opinion of; (*rechazar*) to reject

desfachatez [desfatʃa'teθ] *nf* (*insolencia*) impudence; (*descaro*) rudeness

desfalco [des'falko] *nm* embezzlement

desfallecer [desfaʎe'θer] *vi* (*perder las fuerzas*) to become weak; (*desvanecerse*) to faint

desfasado, a [desfa'saðo, a] *adj* (*anticuado*) old-fashioned; **desfase** *nm* (*diferencia*) gap

desfavorable [desfaßo'raßle] *adj* unfavourable

desfigurar [desfixu'rar] *vt* (*cara*) to disfigure; (*cuerpo*) to deform

desfiladero [desfila'ðero] *nm* gorge

desfilar [desfi'lar] *vi* to parade; **desfile** *nm* procession

desfogarse [desfo'xarse] *vr* (*fig*) to let off steam

desgajar [desxa'xar] *vt* (*arrancar*) to tear off; (*romper*) to break off; **~se** *vr* to come off

desgana [des'xana] *nf* (*falta de apetito*) loss of appetite; (*apatía*) unwillingness; **~do, a** *adj*: **estar ~do** (*sin apetito*) to have no appetite; (*sin entusiasmo*) to have lost interest

desgarrador, a [desxarra'ðor, a] *adj* (*fig*) heartrending

desgarrar [desxa'rrar] *vt* to tear (up); (*fig*) to shatter; **desgarro** *nm* (*en tela*) tear; (*aflicción*) grief

desgastar [desxas'tar] *vt* (*deteriorar*) to wear away *o* down; (*estropear*) to spoil; **~se** *vr* to get worn out; **desgaste** *nm* wear (and tear)

desglosar [desxlo'sar] *vt* (*factura*) to break down

desgracia [des'xraθja] *nf* misfortune; (*accidente*) accident; (*vergüenza*) disgrace; (*contratiempo*) setback; **por ~** unfortunately

desgraciado, a [desxra'θjaðo, a] *adj* (*sin suerte*) unlucky, unfortunate; (*miserable*) wretched; (*infeliz*) miserable

desgravación [desxraßa'θjon] *nf* (*COM*): **~ fiscal** tax relief

desgravar [desxra'ßar] *vt* (*impuestos*) to reduce the tax *o* duty on

deshabitado, a [desaßi'taðo, a] *adj* uninhabited

deshacer [desa'θer] *vt* (*casa*) to break up; (*TEC*) to take apart; (*enemigo*) to defeat; (*diluir*) to melt; (*contrato*) to break; (*intriga*) to solve; **~se** *vr* (*disolverse*) to melt; (*despedazarse*) to come apart *o* undone; **~se de** to get rid of; **~se en lágrimas** to burst into tears

desharrapado, a [desarra'paðo, a] *adj*
(*persona*) shabby

deshecho, a [des'etʃo, a] *adj* undone; (*roto*)
smashed; (*persona*): **estar ~** to be shattered

desheredar [desere'ðar] *vt* to disinherit

deshidratar [desiðra'tar] *vt* to dehydrate

deshielo [des'jelo] *nm* thaw

deshonesto, a [deso'nesto, a] *adj* indecent

deshonra [des'onra] *nf* (*deshonor*) dishonour; (*vergüenza*) shame

deshora [des'ora]: **a ~** *adv* at the wrong time

deshuesar [deswe'sar] *vt* (*carne*) to bone;
(*fruta*) to stone

desierto, a [des'sjerto, a] *adj* (*casa, calle,
negocio*) deserted ♦ *nm* desert

designar [desiɣ'nar] *vt* (*nombrar*) to
designate; (*indicar*) to fix

designio [de'siɣnjo] *nm* plan

desigual [desi'ɣwal] *adj* (*terreno*) uneven;
(*lucha etc*) unequal

desilusión [desilu'sjon] *nf* disillusionment;
(*decepción*) disappointment; **desilusionar** *vt*
to disillusion; to disappoint; **desilusionarse** *vr*
to become disillusioned

desinfectar [desinfek'tar] *vt* to disinfect

desinflar [desin'flar] *vt* to deflate

desintegración [desinteɣra'θjon] *nf*
disintegration

desinterés [desinte'res] *nm* (*desgand*) lack
of interest; (*altruismo*) unselfishness

desintoxicarse [desintoksi'karse] *vr*
(*drogadicto*) to undergo detoxification

desistir [desis'tir] *vi* (*renunciar*) to stop, desist

desleal [desle'al] *adj* (*infiel*) disloyal; (*COM:
competencia*) unfair; **~tad** *nf* disloyalty

desleír [desle'ir] *vt* (*líquido*) to dilute; (*sólido*)
to dissolve

deslenguado, a [deslen'gwaðo, a] *adj*
(*grosero*) foul-mouthed

desligar [desli'ɣar] *vt* (*desatar*) to untie,
undo; (*separar*) to separate; **~se** *vr* (*de un
compromiso*) to extricate o.s.

desliz [des'liθ] *nm* (*fig*) lapse; **~ar** *vt* to slip,
slide

deslucido, a [deslu'θiðo, a] *adj* dull; (*torpe*)
awkward, graceless; (*deslustrado*) tarnished

deslumbrar [deslum'brar] *vt* to dazzle

desmadrarse [desma'ðrarse] (*fam*) *vr*
(*descontrolarse*) to run wild; (*divertirse*) to let
one's hair down; **desmadre** (*fam*) *nm*
(*desorganización*) chaos; (*jaleo*) commotion

desmán [des'man] *nm* (*exceso*) outrage;
(*abuso de poder*) abuse

desmandarse [desman'darse] *vr* (*portarse
mal*) to behave badly; (*excederse*) to get out
of hand; (*caballo*) to bolt

desmantelar [desmante'lar] *vt* (*deshacer*) to
dismantle; (*casa*) to strip

desmaquillador [desmakiʎa'ðor] *nm*
make-up remover

desmayar [desma'jar] *vi* to lose heart; **~se** *vr*
(*MED*) to faint; **desmayo** *nm* (*MED: acto*)
faint; (: *estado*) unconsciousness

desmedido, a [desme'ðiðo, a] *adj* excessive

desmejorar [desmexo'rar] *vt* (*dañar*) to
impair, spoil; (*MED*) to weaken

desmembrar [desmem'brar] *vt* (*MED*) to
dismember; (*fig*) to separate

desmemoriado, a [desmemo'rjaðo, a] *adj*
forgetful

desmentir [desmen'tir] *vt* (*contradecir*) to
contradict; (*refutar*) to deny

desmenuzar [desmenu'θar] *vt* (*deshacer*) to
crumble; (*carne*) to chop; (*examinar*) to
examine closely

desmerecer [desmere'θer] *vt* to be
unworthy of ♦ *vi* (*deteriorarse*) to deteriorate

desmesurado, a [desmesu'raðo, a] *adj*
disproportionate

desmontable [desmon'taßle] *adj* (*que se
quita: pieza*) detachable; (*que se puede plegar
etc*) collapsible, folding

desmontar [desmon'tar] *vt* (*deshacer*) to
dismantle; (*tierra*) to level ♦ *vi* to dismount

desmoralizar [desmorali'θar] *vt* to
demoralize

desmoronar [desmoro'nar] *vt* to wear
away, erode; **~se** *vr* (*edificio, dique*) to
collapse; (*economía*) to decline

desnatado, a [desna'taðo, a] *adj* skimmed

desnivel [desni'ßel] *nm* (*de terreno*)
unevenness

desnudar [desnu'ðar] *vt* (*desvestir*) to
undress; (*despojar*) to strip; **~se** *vr*
(*desvestirse*) to get undressed; **desnudo, a**
adj naked ♦ *nm/f* nude; **desnudo de** devoid o
bereft of

desnutrición [desnutri'θjon] *nf*
malnutrition; **desnutrido, a** *adj*
undernourished

desobedecer [desoßeðe'θer] *vt, vi* to
disobey; **desobediencia** *nf* disobedience

desocupado, a [desoku'paðo, a] *adj* at
leisure; (*desempleado*) unemployed;
(*deshabitado*) empty, vacant

desocupar [desoku'par] *vt* to vacate

desodorante [desoðo'rante] *nm* deodorant

desolación [desola'θjon] *nf* (*de lugar*)
desolation; (*fig*) grief

desolar [deso'lar] *vt* to ruin, lay waste

desorbitado, a [desorßi'taðo, a] *adj*
(*excesivo: ambición*) boundless; (*deseos*)
excessive; (: *precio*) exorbitant

desorden [des'orðen] *nm* confusion;
(*político*) disorder, unrest

desorganizar [desorɣani'θar] *vt*
(*desordenar*) to disorganize;

desorganización nf (de persona) disorganization; (en empresa, oficina) disorder, chaos

desorientar [desorjen'tar] vt (extraviar) to mislead; (confundir, desconcertar) to confuse; ~se vr (perderse) to lose one's way

despabilado, a [despaßi'laðo, a] adj (despierto) wide-awake; (fig) alert, sharp

despabilar [despaßi'lar] vt (el ingenio) to sharpen ♦ vi to wake up; (fig) to get a move on; ~se vr to wake up; to get a move on

despachar [despa't∫ar] vt (negocio) to do, complete; (enviar) to send, dispatch; (vender) to sell, deal in; (billete) to issue; (mandar ir) to send away

despacho [des'pat∫o] nm (oficina) office; (de paquetes) dispatch; (venta) sale; (comunicación) message

despacio [des'paθjo] adv slowly

desparpajo [despar'paxo] nm self-confidence; (pey) nerve

desparramar [desparra'mar] vt (esparcir) to scatter; (líquido) to spill

despavorido, a [despaßo'riðo, a] adj terrified

despecho [des'pet∫o] nm spite; a ~ de in spite of

despectivo, a [despek'tißo, a] adj (despreciativo) derogatory; (LING) pejorative

despedazar [despeða'θar] vt to tear to pieces

despedida [despe'ðiða] nf (adiós) farewell; (de obrero) sacking

despedir [despe'ðir] vt (visita) to see off, show out; (empleado) to dismiss; (inquilino) to evict; (objeto) to hurl; (olor etc) to give out o off; ~se vr: ~se de to say goodbye to

despegar [despe'var] vt to unstick ♦ vi (avión) to take off; ~se vr to come loose, come unstuck; **despego** nm detachment

despegue etc [des'peve] vb ver **despegar** ♦ nm takeoff

despeinado, a [despei'naðo, a] adj dishevelled, unkempt

despejado, a [despe'xaðo, a] adj (lugar) clear, free; (cielo) clear; (persona) wide-awake, bright

despejar [despe'xar] vt (gen) to clear; (misterio) to clear up ♦ vi (el tiempo) to clear; ~se vr (tiempo, cielo) to clear (up); (misterio) to become clearer; (cabeza) to clear

despellejar [despeλe'xar] vt (animal) to skin

despensa [des'pensa] nf larder

despeñadero [despeɲa'ðero] nm (GEO) cliff, precipice

despeñarse [despe'ɲarse] vr to hurl o.s. down; (coche) to tumble over

desperdicio [desper'ðiθjo] nm (despilfarro) squandering; ~s nmpl (basura) rubbish sg

(BRIT), garbage sg (US); (residuos) waste sg

desperdigarse [desperði'varse] vr (rebaño, familia) to scatter, spread out; (granos de arroz, semillas) to scatter

desperezarse [despere'θarse] vr to stretch

desperfecto [desper'fekto] nm (deterioro) slight damage; (defecto) flaw, imperfection

despertador [desperta'ðor] nm alarm clock

despertar [desper'tar] nm awakening ♦ vt (persona) to wake up; (recuerdos) to revive; (sentimiento) to arouse ♦ vi to awaken, wake up; ~se vr to awaken, wake up

despiadado, a [despja'ðaðo, a] adj (ataque) merciless; (persona) heartless

despido etc [des'piðo] vb ver **despedir** ♦ nm dismissal, sacking

despierto, a etc [des'pjerto, a] vb ver **despertar** ♦ adj awake; (fig) sharp, alert

despilfarro [despil'farro] nm (derroche) squandering; (lujo desmedido) extravagance

despistar [despis'tar] vt to throw off the track o scent; (confundir) to mislead, confuse; ~se vr to take the wrong road; (confundirse) to become confused

despiste [des'piste] nm absent-mindedness; un ~ a mistake, slip

desplazamiento [desplaθa'mjento] nm displacement

desplazar [despla'θar] vt to move; (NAUT) to displace; (INFORM) to scroll; (fig) to oust; ~se vr (persona) to travel

desplegar [desple'var] vt (tela, papel) to unfold, open out; (bandera) to unfurl; **despliegue** etc [des'pleve] vb ver **desplegar** ♦ nm display

desplomarse [desplo'marse] vr (edificio, gobierno, persona) to collapse

desplumar [desplu'mar] vt (ave) to pluck; (fam: estafar) to fleece

despoblado, a [despo'ßlaðo, a] adj (sin habitantes) uninhabited

despojar [despo'xar] vt (alguien: de sus bienes) to divest, deprive of; (casa) to strip, leave bare; (alguien: de su cargo) to strip of

despojo [des'poxo] nm (acto) plundering; (objetos) plunder, loot; ~s nmpl (de ave, res) offal sg

desposado, a [despo'saðo, a] adj, nm/f newly-wed

desposar [despo'sar] vt to marry; ~se vr to get married

desposeer [despose'er] vt: ~ a uno de (puesto, autoridad) to strip sb of

déspota ['despota] nm/f despot

despreciar [despre'θjar] vt (desdeñar) to despise, scorn; (afrentar) to slight; **desprecio** nm scorn, contempt; slight

desprender [despren'der] vt (broche) to

unfasten; (*olor*) to give off; **~se** *vr* (*botón: caerse*) to fall off; (*broche*) to come unfastened; (*olor, perfume*) to be given off; **~se de algo que** ... to draw from sth that ...

desprendimiento [desprendi'mjento] *nm* (*gen*) loosening; (*generosidad*) disinterestedness; (*de tierra, rocas*) landslide

despreocupado, a [despreoku'paðo, a] *adj* (*sin preocupación*) unworried, nonchalant; (*negligente*) careless

despreocuparse [despreoku'parse] *vr* not to worry; **~ de** to have no interest in

desprestigiar [despresti'xjar] *vt* (*criticar*) to run down; (*desacreditar*) to discredit

desprevenido, a [despreβe'niðo, a] *adj* (*no preparado*) unprepared, unready

desproporcionado, a [desproporθjo'naðo, a] *adj* disproportionate, out of proportion

desprovisto, a [despro'βisto, a] *adj*: **~ de** devoid of

después [des'pwes] *adv* afterwards, later; (*próximo paso*) next; **~ de comer** after lunch; **un año ~** a year later; **~ se debatió el tema** next the matter was discussed; **~ de corregido el texto** after the text had been corrected; **~ de todo** after all

desquiciado, a [deski'θjaðo, a] *adj* deranged

desquite [des'kite] *nm* (*satisfacción*) satisfaction; (*venganza*) revenge

destacar [desta'kar] *vt* to emphasize, point up; (*MIL*) to detach, detail ♦ *vi* (*resaltarse*) to stand out; (*persona*) to be outstanding o exceptional; **~se** *vr* to stand out; to be outstanding o exceptional

destajo [des'taxo] *nm*: **trabajar a ~** to do piecework

destapar [desta'par] *vt* (*botella*) to open; (*cacerola*) to take the lid off; (*descubrir*) to uncover; **~se** *vr* (*revelarse*) to reveal one's true character

destartalado, a [destarta'laðo, a] *adj* (*desordenado*) untidy; (*ruinoso*) tumbledown

destello [des'teʎo] *nm* (*de estrella*) twinkle; (*de faro*) signal light

destemplado, a [destem'plaðo, a] *adj* (*MUS*) out of tune; (*voz*) harsh; (*MED*) out of sorts; (*tiempo*) unpleasant, nasty

desteñir [deste'ɲir] *vt* to fade ♦ *vi* to fade; **~se** *vr* to fade; **esta tela no destiñe** this fabric will not run

desternillarse [desterni'ʎarse] *vr*: **~ de risa** to split one's sides laughing

desterrar [deste'rrar] *vt* (*exilar*) to exile; (*fig*) to banish, dismiss

destiempo [des'tjempo]: **a ~** *adv* out of turn

destierro *etc* [des'tjerro] *vb ver* **desterrar** ♦ *nm* exile

destilar [desti'lar] *vt* to distil; **destilería** *nf* distillery

destinar [desti'nar] *vt* (*funcionario*) to appoint, assign; (*fondos*): **~ (a)** to set aside (for)

destinatario, a [destina'tarjo, a] *nm/f* addressee

destino [des'tino] *nm* (*suerte*) destiny; (*de avión, viajero*) destination

destituir [destitu'ir] *vt* to dismiss

destornillador [destorniʎa'ðor] *nm* screwdriver

destornillar [destorni'ʎar] *vt* (*tornillo*) to unscrew; **~se** *vr* to unscrew

destreza [des'treθa] *nf* (*habilidad*) skill; (*maña*) dexterity

destrozar [destro'θar] *vt* (*romper*) to smash, break (up); (*estropear*) to ruin; (*nervios*) to shatter

destrozo [des'troθo] *nm* (*acción*) destruction; (*desastre*) smashing; **~s** *nmpl* (*pedazos*) pieces; (*daños*) havoc *sg*

destrucción [destruk'θjon] *nf* destruction

destruir [destru'ir] *vt* to destroy

desuso [des'uso] *nm* disuse; **caer en ~** to become obsolete

desvalido, a [desβa'liðo, a] *adj* (*desprotegido*) destitute; (*sin fuerzas*) helpless

desvalijar [desβali'xar] *vt* (*persona*) to rob; (*casa, tienda*) to burgle; (*coche*) to break into

desván [des'βan] *nm* attic

desvanecer [desβane'θer] *vt* (*disipar*) to dispel; (*borrar*) to blur; **~se** *vr* (*humo etc*) to vanish, disappear; (*color*) to fade; (*recuerdo, sonido*) to fade away; (*MED*) to pass out; (*duda*) to be dispelled

desvanecimiento [desβaneθi'mjento] *nm* (*desaparición*) disappearance; (*de colores*) fading; (*evaporación*) evaporation; (*MED*) fainting fit

desvariar [desβa'rjar] *vi* (*enfermo*) to be delirious; **desvarío** *nm* delirium

desvelar [desβe'lar] *vt* to keep awake; **~se** *vr* (*no poder dormir*) to stay awake; (*preocuparse*) to be vigilant o watchful

desvelos [des'βelos] *nmpl* worrying *sg*

desvencijado, a [desβenθi'xaðo, a] *adj* (*silla*) rickety; (*máquina*) broken-down

desventaja [desβen'taxa] *nf* disadvantage

desventura [desβen'tura] *nf* misfortune

desvergonzado, a [desβerɣon'θaðo, a] *adj* shameless

desvergüenza [desβer'ɣwenθa] *nf* (*descaro*) shamelessness; (*insolencia*) impudence; (*mala conducta*) effrontery

desvestir [desβes'tir] *vt* to undress; **~se** *vr* to undress

desviación [desβja'θjon] *nf* deviation; (*AUTO*) diversion, detour

desviar [des'ßjar] *vt* to turn aside; (*río*) to alter the course of; (*navío*) to divert, re-route; (*conversación*) to sidetrack; **~se** *vr* (*apartarse del camino*) to turn aside; (: *barco*) to go off course

desvío *etc* [des'ßio] *vb ver* **desviar ♦** *nm* (*desviación*) detour, diversion; (*fig*) indifference

desvirtuar [desßir'twar] *vt* to distort

desvivirse [desßi'ßirse] *vr*: **~ por** (*anhelar*) to long for, crave for; (*hacer lo posible por*) to do one's utmost for

detallar [deta'ʎar] *vt* to detail

detalle [de'taʎe] *nm* detail; (*gesto*) gesture, token; **al ~** in detail; (*COM*) retail

detallista [deta'ʎista] *nm/f* (*COM*) retailer

detective [detek'tiße] *nm/f* detective

detener [dete'ner] *vt* (*gen*) to stop; (*JUR*) to arrest; (*objeto*) to keep; **~se** *vr* to stop; (*demorarse*): **~se en** to delay over, linger over

detenidamente [deteniða'mente] *adv* (*minuciosamente*) carefully; (*extensamente*) at great length

detenido, a [dete'niðo, a] *adj* (*arrestado*) under arrest **♦** *nm/f* person under arrest, prisoner

detenimiento [deteni'mjento] *nm*: **con ~** thoroughly; (*observar, considerar*) carefully

detergente [deter'xente] *nm* detergent

deteriorar [deterjo'rar] *vt* to spoil, damage; **~se** *vr* to deteriorate; **deterioro** *nm* deterioration

determinación [determina'θjon] *nf* (*empeño*) determination; (*decisión*) decision; **determinado, a** *adj* specific

determinar [determi'nar] *vt* (*plazo*) to fix; (*precio*) to settle; **~se** *vr* to decide

detestar [detes'tar] *vt* to detest

detractor, a [detrak'tor, a] *nm/f* slanderer, libeller

detrás [de'tras] *adv* behind; (*atrás*) at the back; **~ de** behind

detrimento [detri'mento] *nm*: **en ~ de** to the detriment of

deuda ['deuða] *nf* debt

devaluación [deßalwa'θjon] *nf* devaluation

devastar [deßas'tar] *vt* (*destruir*) to devastate

devoción [deßo'θjon] *nf* devotion

devolución [deßolu'θjon] *nf* (*reenvío*) return, sending back; (*reembolso*) repayment; (*JUR*) devolution

devolver [deßol'ßer] *vt* to return; (*lo extraviado, lo prestado*) to give back; (*carta al correo*) to send back; (*COM*) to repay, refund **♦** *vi* (*vomitar*) to be sick

devorar [deßo'rar] *vt* to devour

devoto, a [de'ßoto, a] *adj* devout **♦** *nm/f* admirer

devuelto *pp de* **devolver**

devuelva *etc vb ver* **devolver**

di *vb ver* **dar; decir**

día ['dia] *nm* day; **¿qué ~ es?** what's the date?; **estar/poner al ~** to be/keep up to date; **el ~ de hoy/de mañana** today/tomorrow; **al ~ siguiente** (on) the following day; **vivir al ~** to live from hand to mouth; **de ~** by day, in daylight; **en pleno ~** in full daylight; **D~ de Reyes** Epiphany; **~ festivo** (*ESP*) o **feriado** (*AM*) holiday; **~ libre** day off

diabetes [dja'ßetes] *nf* diabetes

diablo ['djaßlo] *nm* devil; **diablura** *nf* prank

diadema [dja'ðema] *nf* tiara

diafragma [dja'fraxma] *nm* diaphragm

diagnosis [djax'nosis] *nf inv* diagnosis

diagnóstico [djax'nostiko] *nm* = **diagnosis**

diagonal [djaxo'nal] *adj* diagonal

diagrama [dja'xrama] *nm* diagram; **~ de flujo** flowchart

dial [djal] *nm* dial

dialecto [dja'lekto] *nm* dialect

dialogar [djalo'xar] *vi*: **~ con** (*POL*) to hold talks with

diálogo ['djaloxo] *nm* dialogue

diamante [dja'mante] *nm* diamond

diana ['djana] *nf* (*MIL*) reveille; (*de blanco*) centre, bull's-eye

diapositiva [djaposi'tißa] *nf* (*FOTO*) slide, transparency

diario, a ['djarjo, a] *adj* daily **♦** *nm* newspaper; **a ~** daily; **de ~** everyday

diarrea [dja'rrea] *nf* diarrhoea

dibujar [dißu'xar] *vt* to draw, sketch; **dibujo** *nm* drawing; **dibujos animados** cartoons

diccionario [dikθjo'narjo] *nm* dictionary

dice *etc vb ver* **decir**

dicho, a ['ditʃo, a] *pp de* **decir ♦** *adj*: **en ~s países** in the aforementioned countries **♦** *nm* saying

dichoso, a [di'tʃoso, a] *adj* happy

diciembre [di'θjembre] *nm* December

dictado [dik'taðo] *nm* dictation

dictador [dikta'ðor] *nm* dictator; **dictadura** *nf* dictatorship

dictamen [dik'tamen] *nm* (*opinión*) opinion; (*juicio*) judgment; (*informe*) report

dictar [dik'tar] *vt* (*carta*) to dictate; (*JUR*: *sentencia*) to pronounce; (*decreto*) to issue; (*AM*: *clase*) to give

didáctico, a [di'ðaktiko, a] *adj* educational

diecinueve [djeθi'nweße] *num* nineteen

dieciocho [djeθi'otʃo] *num* eighteen

dieciséis [djeθi'seis] *num* sixteen

diecisiete [djeθi'sjete] *num* seventeen

diente ['djente] *nm* (*ANAT, TEC*) tooth; (*ZOOL*) fang; (: *de elefante*) tusk; (*de ajo*) clove; **hablar entre ~s** to mutter, mumble

diera *etc vb ver* **dar**

diesel ['disel] *adj*: **motor ~** diesel engine

diestro, a ['djestro, a] *adj* (*derecho*) right; (*hábil*) skilful

dieta ['djeta] *nf* diet; **dietética** *nf*: **tienda de dietética** health food shop; **dietético, a** *adj* diet (*atr*), dietary

diez [djeθ] *num* ten

diezmar [djeθ'mar] *vt* (*población*) to decimate

difamar [difa'mar] *vt* (*JUR*: *hablando*) to slander; (: *por escrito*) to libel

diferencia [dife'renθja] *nf* difference; **diferenciar** *vt* to differentiate between ♦ *vi* to differ; **diferenciarse** *vr* to differ, be different; (*distinguirse*) to distinguish o.s.

diferente [dife'rente] *adj* different

diferido [dife'riðo] *nm*: **en ~** (*TV etc*) recorded

difícil [di'fiθil] *adj* difficult

dificultad [difikul'taθ] *nf* difficulty; (*problema*) trouble

dificultar [difikul'tar] *vt* (*complicar*) to complicate, make difficult; (*estorbar*) to obstruct

difteria [dif'terja] *nf* diphtheria

difundir [difun'dir] *vt* (*calor, luz*) to diffuse; (*RADIO, TV*) to broadcast; **~ una noticia** to spread a piece of news; **~se** *vr* to spread (out)

difunto, a [di'funto, a] *adj* dead, deceased ♦ *nm/f* deceased (person)

difusión [difu'sjon] *nf* (*RADIO, TV*) broadcasting

diga *etc vb ver* **decir**

digerir [dixe'rir] *vt* to digest; (*fig*) to absorb; **digestión** *nf* digestion; **digestivo, a** *adj* digestive

digital [dixi'tal] *adj* digital

dignarse [diɣ'narse] *vr* to deign to

dignatario, a [diɣna'tarjo, a] *nm/f* dignitary

dignidad [diɣni'ðað] *nf* dignity

digno, a ['diɣno, a] *adj* worthy

digo *etc vb ver* **decir**

dije *etc vb ver* **decir**

dilapidar [dilapi'ðar] *vt* (*dinero, herencia*) to squander, waste

dilatar [dila'tar] *vt* (*cuerpo*) to dilate; (*prolongar*) to prolong

dilema [di'lema] *nm* dilemma

diligencia [dili'xenθja] *nf* diligence; (*ocupación*) errand, job; **~s** *nfpl* (*JUR*) formalities; **diligente** *adj* diligent

diluir [dilu'ir] *vt* to dilute

diluvio [di'lußjo] *nm* deluge, flood

dimensión [dimen'sjon] *nf* dimension

diminuto, a [dimi'nuto, a] *adj* tiny, diminutive

dimitir [dimi'tir] *vi* to resign

dimos *vb ver* **dar**

Dinamarca [dina'marka] *nf* Denmark

dinámico, a [di'namiko, a] *adj* dynamic

dinamita [dina'mita] *nf* dynamite

dínamo ['dinamo] *nf* dynamo

dineral [dine'ral] *nm* large sum of money, fortune

dinero [di'nero] *nm* money; **~ contante, ~ efectivo** (ready) cash; **~ suelto** (loose) change

dio *vb ver* **dar**

dios [djos] *nm* god; **¡D~ mío!** (oh,) my God!

diosa ['djosa] *nf* goddess

diploma [di'ploma] *nm* diploma

diplomacia [diplo'maθja] *nf* diplomacy; (*fig*) tact

diplomado, a [diplo'maðo, a] *adj* qualified

diplomático, a [diplo'matiko, a] *adj* diplomatic ♦ *nm/f* diplomat

diputación [diputa'θjon] *nf* (*tb*: **~ provincial**) ≈ county council

diputado, a [dipu'taðo, a] *nm/f* delegate; (*POL*) ≈ member of parliament (*BRIT*), ≈ representative (*US*)

dique ['dike] *nm* dyke

diré *etc vb ver* **decir**

dirección [direk'θjon] *nf* direction; (*señas*) address; (*AUTO*) steering; (*gerencia*) management; (*POL*) leadership; **~ única/ prohibida** one-way street/no entry

directa [di'rekta] *nf* (*AUT*) top gear

directiva [direk'tißa] *nf* (*DEP, tb*: **junta ~**) board of directors

directo, a [di'rekto, a] *adj* direct; (*RADIO, TV*) live; **transmitir en ~** to broadcast live

director, a [direk'tor, a] *adj* leading ♦ *nm/f* director; (*ESCOL*) head(teacher) (*BRIT*), principal (*US*); (*gerente*) manager(ess); (*PRENSA*) editor; **~ de cine** film director; **~ general** managing director

dirigente [diri'xente] *nm/f* (*POL*) leader

dirigir [diri'xir] *vt* to direct; (*carta*) to address; (*obra de teatro, film*) to direct; (*MUS*) to conduct; (*negocio*) to manage; **~se** *vr*: **~se a** to go towards; make one's way towards; (*hablar con*) to speak to

dirija *etc vb ver* **dirigir**

discernir [disθer'nir] *vt* to discern

disciplina [disθi'plina] *nf* discipline

discípulo, a [dis'θipulo, a] *nm/f* disciple

disco ['disko] *nm* disc; (*DEPORTE*) discus; (*TEL*) dial; (*AUTO*: *semáforo*) light; (*MUS*) record; (*INFORM*): **~ flexible/rígido** floppy/hard disk; **~ compacto/de larga duración** compact disc/ long-playing record; **~ de freno** brake disc

disconforme [diskon'forme] *adj* differing; **estar ~ (con)** to be in disagreement (with)

discordia [dis'korðja] *nf* discord

discoteca [disko'teka] *nf* disco(theque)

discreción [diskre'θjon] *nf* discretion; (*reserva*) prudence; **comer a ~** to eat as much as one wishes; **discrecional** *adj* (*facultativo*) discretionary

discrepancia [diskre'panθja] nf (*diferencia*) discrepancy; (*desacuerdo*) disagreement

discreto, a [dis'kreto, a] adj discreet

discriminación [diskrimina'θjon] nf discrimination

disculpa [dis'kulpa] nf excuse; (*pedir perdón*) apology; **pedir ~s a/por** to apologize to/for; **disculpar** vt to excuse, pardon; **disculparse** vr to excuse o.s.; to apologize

discurrir [disku'rrir] vi (*pensar, reflexionar*) to think, meditate; (*el tiempo*) to pass, go by

discurso [dis'kurso] nm speech

discusión [disku'sjon] nf (*diálogo*) discussion; (*riña*) argument

discutir [disku'tir] vt (*debatir*) to discuss; (*pelear*) to argue about; (*contradecir*) to argue against ♦ vi (*debatir*) to discuss; (*pelearse*) to argue

disecar [dise'kar] vt (*conservar: animal*) to stuff; (: *planta*) to dry

diseminar [disemi'nar] vt to disseminate, spread

diseñar [dise'ɲar] vt, vi to design

diseño [di'seɲo] nm design

disfraz [dis'fraθ] nm (*máscara*) disguise; (*excusa*) pretext; **~ar** vt to disguise; **~arse** vr: **~arse de** to disguise o.s. as

disfrutar [disfru'tar] vt to enjoy ♦ vi to enjoy o.s.; **~ de** to enjoy, possess

disgregarse [disɣre'ɣarse] vr (*muchedumbre*) to disperse

disgustar [disɣus'tar] vt (*no gustar*) to displease; (*contrariar, enojar*) to annoy, upset; **~se** vr (*enfadarse*) to get upset; (*dos personas*) to fall out

disgusto [dis'ɣusto] nm (*contrariedad*) annoyance; (*tristeza*) grief; (*riña*) quarrel

disidente [disi'ðente] nm dissident

disimular [disimu'lar] vt (*ocultar*) to hide, conceal ♦ vi to dissemble

disipar [disi'par] vt to dispel; (*fortuna*) to squander; **~se** vr (*nubes*) to vanish; (*indisciplinarse*) to dissipate

dislocarse [dislo'karse] vr (*articulación*) to sprain, dislocate

disminución [disminu'θjon] nf decrease, reduction

disminuido, a [disminu'iðo, a] nm/f: **~ mental/físico** mentally/physically handicapped person

disminuir [disminu'ir] vt to decrease, diminish

disociarse [diso'θjarse] vr: **~ (de)** to dissociate o.s. (from)

disolver [disol'ßer] vt (*gen*) to dissolve; **~se** vr to dissolve; (*COM*) to go into liquidation

dispar [dis'par] adj different

disparar [dispa'rar] vt, vi to shoot, fire

disparate [dispa'rate] nm (*tontería*) foolish remark; (*error*) blunder; **decir ~s** to talk nonsense

disparo [dis'paro] nm shot

dispensar [dispen'sar] vt to dispense; (*disculpar*) to excuse

dispersar [disper'sar] vt to disperse; **~se** vr to scatter

disponer [dispo'ner] vt (*arreglar*) to arrange; (*ordenar*) to put in order; (*preparar*) to prepare, get ready ♦ vi: **~ de** to have, own; **~se** vr: **~se a o para hacer** to prepare to do

disponible [dispo'nißle] adj available

disposición [disposi'θjon] nf arrangement, disposition; (*INFORM*) layout; **a la ~ de** at the disposal of; **~ de animo** state of mind

dispositivo [disposi'tißo] nm device, mechanism

dispuesto, a [dis'pwesto, a] pp de **disponer** ♦ adj (*arreglado*) arranged; (*preparado*) disposed

disputar [dispu'tar] vt (*carrera*) to compete in

disquete [dis'kete] nm floppy disk, diskette

distancia [dis'tanθja] nf distance

distanciar [distan'θjar] vt to space out; **~se** vr to become estranged

distante [dis'tante] adj distant

distar [dis'tar] vi: **dista 5km de aquí** it is 5km from here

diste vb ver **dar**

disteis ['disteis] vb ver **dar**

distension [disten'sjon] nf (*en las relaciones*) relaxation; (*POL*) détente; (*muscular*) strain

distinción [distin'θjon] nf distinction; (*elegancia*) elegance; (*honor*) honour

distinguido, a [distin'ɡiðo, a] adj distinguished

distinguir [distin'ɡir] vt to distinguish; (*escoger*) to single out; **~se** vr to be distinguished

distintivo [distin'tißo] nm badge; (*fig*) characteristic

distinto, a [dis'tinto, a] adj different; (*claro*) clear

distracción [distrak'θjon] nf distraction; (*pasatiempo*) hobby, pastime; (*olvido*) absent-mindedness, distraction

distraer [distra'er] vt (*atención*) to distract; (*divertir*) to amuse; (*fondos*) to embezzle; **~se** vr (*entretenerse*) to amuse o.s.; (*perder la concentración*) to allow one's attention to wander

distraído, a [distra'iðo, a] adj (*gen*) absent-minded; (*entretenido*) amusing

distribuidor, a [distrißui'ðor, a] nm/f distributor; **distribuidora** nf (*COM*) dealer, agent; (*CINE*) distributor

distribuir [distrißu'ir] vt to distribute

distrito [dis'trito] nm (sector, territorio) region; (barrio) district

disturbio [dis'turβjo] nm disturbance; (desorden) riot

disuadir [diswa'ðir] vt to dissuade

disuelto [di'swelto] pp de **disolver**

disyuntiva [disjun'tiβa] nf dilemma

DIU nm abr (= dispositivo intrauterino) IUD

diurno, a ['djurno, a] adj day cpd

divagar [diβa'ɣar] vi (desviarse) to digress

diván [di'βan] nm divan

divergencia [diβer'xenθja] nf divergence

diversidad [diβersi'ðað] nf diversity, variety

diversificar [diβersifi'kar] vt to diversify

diversión [diβer'sjon] nf (gen) entertainment; (actividad) hobby, pastime

diverso, a [di'βerso, a] adj diverse; ~s libros several books; ~s nmpl sundries

divertido, a [diβer'tiðo, a] adj (chiste) amusing; (fiesta etc) enjoyable

divertir [diβer'tir] vt (entretener, recrear) to amuse; ~se vr (pasarlo bien) to have a good time; (distraerse) to amuse o.s.

dividendos [diβi'ðendos] nmpl (COM) dividends

dividir [diβi'ðir] vt (gen) to divide; (distribuir) to distribute, share out

divierta etc vb ver **divertir**

divino, a [di'βino, a] adj divine

divirtiendo etc vb ver **divertir**

divisa [di'βisa] nf (emblema) emblem, badge; ~s nfpl foreign exchange sg

divisar [diβi'sar] vt to make out, distinguish

división [diβi'sjon] nf (gen) division; (de partido) split; (de país) partition

divorciar [diβor'θjar] vt to divorce; ~se vr to get divorced; **divorcio** nm divorce

divulgar [diβul'ɣar] vt (ideas) to spread; (secreto) to divulge

DNI (ESP) nm abr (= Documento Nacional de Identidad) national identity card

Dña. abr (= doña) Mrs

do [do] nm (MUS) do, C

dobladillo [doβla'ðiʎo] nm (de vestido) hem; (de pantalón: vuelta) turn-up (BRIT), cuff (US)

doblar [do'βlar] vt to double; to fold; (caño) to bend; (la esquina) to turn, go round; (film) to dub ♦ vi to turn; (campana) to toll; ~se vr (plegarse) to fold (up), crease; (encorvarse) to bend

doble ['doβle] adj double; (de dos aspectos) dual; (fig) two-faced ♦ nm double ♦ nm/f (TEATRO) double, stand-in; ~s nmpl (DEPORTE) doubles sg; **con sentido ~** with a double meaning

doblegar [doβle'ɣar] vt to fold, crease; ~se vr to yield

doblez [do'βleθ] nm fold, hem ♦ nf insincerity, duplicity

doce ['doθe] num twelve; ~na nf dozen

docente [do'θente] adj: **centro/personal ~** teaching establishment/staff

dócil ['doθil] adj (pasivo) docile; (obediente) obedient

docto, a ['dokto, a] adj: ~ **en** instructed in

doctor, a [dok'tor, a] nm/f doctor

doctorado [dokto'raðo] nm doctorate

doctrina [dok'trina] nf doctrine, teaching

documentación [dokumenta'θjon] nf documentation, papers pl

documental [dokumen'tal] adj, nm documentary

documento [doku'mento] nm (certificado) document; ~ **national de identidad** identity card

dólar ['dolar] nm dollar

doler [do'ler] vt, vi to hurt; (fig) to grieve; ~se vr (de su situación) to grieve, feel sorry; (de las desgracias ajenas) to sympathize; **me duele el brazo** my arm hurts

dolor [do'lor] nm pain; (fig) grief, sorrow; ~ **de cabeza** headache; ~ **de estómago** stomachache

domar [do'mar] vt to tame

domesticar [domesti'kar] vt = **domar**

doméstico, a [do'mestiko, a] adj (vida, servicio) home; (tareas) household; (animal) tame, pet

domiciliación [domiθilia'θjon] nf: ~ **de pagos** (COM) standing order

domicilio [domi'θiljo] nm home; ~ **particular** private residence; ~ **social** (COM) head office; **sin ~ fijo** of no fixed abode

dominante [domi'nante] adj dominant; (persona) domineering

dominar [domi'nar] vt (gen) to dominate; (idiomas) to be fluent in ♦ vi to dominate, prevail; ~se vr to control o.s.

domingo [do'mingo] nm Sunday

dominio [do'minjo] nm (tierras) domain; (autoridad) power, authority; (de las pasiones) grip, hold; (de idiomas) command

don [don] nm (talento) gift; ~ **Juan Gómez** Mr Juan Gómez, Juan Gómez Esq (BRIT)

donaire [do'naire] nm charm

donar [do'nar] vt to donate

donativo [dona'tiβo] nm donation

doncella [don'θeʎa] nf (criada) maid

donde ['donde] adv where ♦ prep: **el coche está allí ~ el farol** the car is over there by the lamppost o where the lamppost is; **en ~** where, in which

dónde ['donde] adv interrogativo where?; ¿a ~ **vas?** where are you going (to)?; ¿de ~ **vienes?** where have you been?; ¿por ~? where?, whereabouts?

dondequiera [donde'kjera] adv anywhere; **por ~** everywhere, all over the place ♦ conj:

~ que wherever

doña ['dona] *nf*: **~ Alicia** Alicia; **~ Victoria Benito** Mrs Victoria Benito

dorado, a [do'raðo, a] *adj* (*color*) golden; (*TEC*) gilt

dormir [dor'mir] *vt*: **~ la siesta** to have an afternoon nap ♦ *vi* to sleep; **~se** *vr* to fall asleep

dormitar [dormi'tar] *vi* to doze

dormitorio [dormi'torjo] *nm* bedroom; **~ común** dormitory

dorsal [dor'sal] *nm* (*DEPORTE*) number

dorso ['dorso] *nm* (*de mano*) back; (*de hoja*) other side

dos [dos] *num* two

dosis ['dosis] *nf inv* dose, dosage

dotado, a [do'taðo, a] *adj* gifted; **~ de** endowed with

dotar [do'tar] *vt* to endow; **dote** *nf* dowry; **dotes** *nfpl* (*talentos*) gifts

doy *vb ver* **dar**

dragar [dra'xar] *vt* (*río*) to dredge; (*minas*) to sweep

drama ['drama] *nm* drama

dramaturgo [drama'turxo] *nm* dramatist, playwright

drástico, a ['drastiko, a] *adj* drastic

drenaje [dre'naxe] *nm* drainage

droga ['droxa] *nf* drug

drogadicto, a [droxa'ðikto, a] *nm/f* drug addict

droguería [droxe'ria] *nf* hardware shop (*BRIT*) o store (*US*)

ducha ['dutʃa] *nf* (*baño*) shower; (*MED*) douche; **ducharse** *vr* to take a shower

duda ['duða] *nf* doubt; **dudar** *vt, vi* to doubt; **dudoso, a** [du'ðoso, a] *adj* (*incierto*) hesitant; (*sospechoso*) doubtful

duela *etc vb ver* **doler**

duelo ['dwelo] *vb ver* **doler** ♦ *nm* (*combate*) duel; (*luto*) mourning

duende ['dwende] *nm* imp, goblin

dueño, a ['dweno, a] *nm/f* (*propietario*) owner; (*de pensión, taberna*) landlord/lady; (*empresario*) employer

duermo *etc vb ver* **dormir**

dulce ['dulθe] *adj* sweet ♦ *adv* gently, softly ♦ *nm* sweet

dulzura [dul'θura] *nf* sweetness; (*ternura*) gentleness

duna ['duna] *nf* (*GEO*) dune

dúo ['duo] *nm* duet

duplicar [dupli'kar] *vt* (*hacer el doble de*) to duplicate; **~se** *vr* to double

duque ['duke] *nm* duke; **~sa** *nf* duchess

duración [dura'θjon] *nf* (*de película, disco etc*) length; (*de pila etc*) life; (*curso: de acontecimientos etc*) duration

duradero, a [dura'ðero, a] *adj* (*tela etc*)

hard-wearing; (*fe, paz*) lasting

durante [du'rante] *prep* during

durar [du'rar] *vi* to last; (*recuerdo*) to remain

durazno [du'raθno] *(AM) nm* (*fruta*) peach; (*árbol*) peach tree

durex ['dureks] *(AM) nm* (*tira adhesiva*) Sellotape ® (*BRIT*), Scotch tape ® (*US*)

dureza [du'reθa] *nf* (*calidad*) hardness

duro, a ['duro, a] *adj* hard; (*carácter*) tough ♦ *adv* hard ♦ *nm* (*moneda*) five peseta coin o piece

DVD *nm abr* (= *disco de vídeo digital*) DVD

E, e

E *abr* (= *este*) E

e [e] *conj* and

ebanista [eßa'nista] *nm/f* cabinetmaker

ébano ['eßano] *nm* ebony

ebrio, a ['eßrjo, a] *adj* drunk

ebullición [eßuʎi'θjon] *nf* boiling

eccema [ek'θema] *nf* (*MED*) eczema

echar [e'tʃar] *vt* to throw; (*agua, vino*) to pour (out); (*empleado: despedir*) to fire, sack; (*hojas*) to sprout; (*cartas*) to post; (*humo*) to emit, give out ♦ *vi*: **~ a correr/llorar** to run off/burst into tears; **~se** *vr* to lie down; **~ llave a** to lock (up); **~ abajo** (*gobierno*) to overthrow; (*edificio*) to demolish; **~ mano a** to lay hands on; **~ una mano a uno** (*ayudar*) to give sb a hand; **~ de menos** to miss

eclesiástico, a [ekle'sjastiko, a] *adj* ecclesiastical

eclipse [e'klipse] *nm* eclipse

eco ['eko] *nm* echo; **tener ~** to catch on

ecología [ekolo'xia] *nf* ecology; **ecológico, a** *adj* (*producto, método*) environmentally-friendly; (*agricultura*) organic; **ecologista** *adj* ecological, environmental ♦ *nm/f* environmentalist

economato [ekono'mato] *nm* cooperative store

economía [ekono'mia] *nf* (*sistema*) economy; (*carrera*) economics

económico, a [eko'nomiko, a] *adj* (*barato*) cheap, economical; (*ahorrativo*) thrifty; (*COM: año etc*) financial; (: *situación*) economic

economista [ekono'mista] *nm/f* economist

ECU [eku] *nm* ECU

ecuador [ekwa'ðor] *nm* equator; **(el) E~** Ecuador

ecuánime [e'kwanime] *adj* (*carácter*) level-headed; (*estado*) calm

ecuatoriano, a [ekwato'rjano, a] *adj, nm/f* Ecuadorian

ecuestre [e'kwestre] *adj* equestrian

eczema [ek'θema] *nm* = **eccema**

edad [e'ðað] *nf* age; **¿qué ~ tienes?** how old

are you?; **tiene ocho años de ~** he is eight
(years old); **de ~ mediana/avanzada** middle-
aged/advanced in years; **la E~ Media** the
Middle Ages

edición [eði'θjon] *nf* (*acto*) publication;
(*ejemplar*) edition

edificar [edifi'kar] *vt, vi* to build

edificio [eði'fiθjo] *nm* building; (*fig*) edifice,
structure

Edimburgo [eðim'burxo] *nm* Edinburgh

editar [eði'tar] *vt* (*publicar*) to publish;
(*preparar textos*) to edit

editor, a [eði'tor, a] *nm/f* (*que publica*)
publisher; (*redactor*) editor ♦ *adj*: **casa ~a**
publishing house, publisher; **~ial** *adj* editorial
♦ *nm* leading article, editorial; **casa ~ial**
publishing house, publisher

edredón [eðre'ðon] *nm* eiderdown

educación [eðuka'θjon] *nf* education;
(*crianza*) upbringing; (*modales*) (good)
manners *pl*

educado, a [eðu'kaðo, a] *adj*: **bien/mal ~**
well/badly behaved

educar [eðu'kar] *vt* to educate; (*criar*) to
bring up; (*voz*) to train

EE. UU. *nmpl abr* (= *Estados Unidos*) US(A)

efectista [efek'tista] *adj* sensationalist

efectivamente [efektiβa'mente] *adv* (*como
respuesta*) exactly, precisely; (*verdaderamente*)
really; (*de hecho*) in fact

efectivo, a [efek'tiβo, a] *adj* effective; (*real*)
actual, real ♦ *nm*: **pagar en ~ to** pay (in)
cash; **hacer ~ un cheque** to cash a cheque

efecto [e'fekto] *nm* effect, result; **~s** *nmpl* (*~s
personales*) effects; (*bienes*) goods, (*COM*)
assets; **en ~** in fact; (*respuesta*) exactly,
indeed; **~ 2000** millennium bug;
~ invernadero greenhouse effect

efectuar [efek'twar] *vt* to carry out; (*viaje*) to
make

eficacia [efi'kaθja] *nf* (*de persona*) efficiency;
(*de medicamento etc*) effectiveness

eficaz [efi'kaθ] *adj* (*persona*) efficient;
(*acción*) effective

eficiente [efi'θjente] *adj* efficient

efusivo, a [efu'siβo, a] *adj* effusive; **mis más
efusivas gracias** my warmest thanks

EGB (*ESP*) *nf abr* (*ESCOL*) = *Educación General
Básica*

egipcio, a [e'xipθjo, a] *adj, nm/f* Egyptian

Egipto [e'xipto] *nm* Egypt

egoísmo [eɣo'ismo] *nm* egoism

egoísta [eɣo'ista] *adj* egoistical, selfish ♦ *nm/f*
egoist

egregio, a [e'xrexjo, a] *adj* eminent,
distinguished

Eire ['eire] *nm* Eire

ej. *abr* (= *ejemplo*) eg

eje ['exe] *nm* (*GEO, MAT*) axis; (*de rueda*) axle;

(*de máquina*) shaft, spindle

ejecución [exeku'θjon] *nf* execution;
(*cumplimiento*) fulfilment; (*MUS*)
performance; (*JUR: embargo de deudor*)
attachment

ejecutar [exeku'tar] *vt* to execute, carry out;
(*matar*) to execute; (*cumplir*) to fulfil; (*MUS*)
to perform; (*JUR: embargar*) to attach, distrain
(on)

ejecutivo, a [exeku'tiβo, a] *adj* executive; **el
(poder) ~** the executive (power)

ejemplar [exem'plar] *adj* exemplary ♦ *nm*
example; (*ZOOL*) specimen; (*de libro*) copy;
(*de periódico*) number, issue

ejemplo [e'xemplo] *nm* example; **por ~** for
example

ejercer [exer'θer] *vt* to exercise; (*influencia*)
to exert; (*un oficio*) to practise ♦ *vi*
(*practicar*): **~ (de)** to practise (as)

ejercicio [exer'θiθjo] *nm* exercise; (*período*)
tenure; **~ comercial** financial year

ejército [e'xerθito] *nm* army; **entrar en el ~** to
join the army, join up

ejote [e'xote] (*AM*) *nm* green bean

PALABRA CLAVE

el [el] (*f* **la,** *pl* **los, las,** *neutro* **lo**) *art def* **1** the;
el libro/la mesa/los estudiantes the book/
table/students

2 (*con n abstracto: no se traduce*): **el amor/la
juventud** love/youth

3 (*posesión: se traduce a menudo por adj
posesivo*): **romperse el brazo** to break one's
arm; **levantó la mano** he put his hand up; **se
puso el sombrero** she put her hat on

4 (*valor descriptivo*): **tener la boca grande/los
ojos azules** to have a big mouth/blue eyes

5 (*con días*) on; **me iré el viernes** I'll leave on
Friday; **los domingos suelo ir a nadar** on
Sundays I generally go swimming

6 (*lo + adj*): **lo difícil/caro** what is difficult/
expensive; (= *cuán*): **no se da cuenta de lo
pesado que es** he doesn't realise how boring
he is

♦ *pron demos* **1**: **mi libro y el de usted** my
book and yours; **las de Pepe son mejores**
Pepe's are better; **no la(s) blanca(s) sino la(s)
gris(es)** not the white one(s) but the grey
one(s)

2: **lo de: lo de ayer** what happened
yesterday; **lo de las facturas** that business
about the invoices

♦ *pron relativo*: **el que** etc **1** (*indef*): **el (los)
que quiera(n) que se vaya(n)** anyone who
wants to can leave; **llévese el que más le
guste** take the one you like best

2 (*def*): **el que compré ayer** the one I bought
yesterday; **los que se van** those who leave

3: **lo que: lo que pienso yo/más me gusta**

what I think/like most

♦ *conj*: **el que**: **el que lo diga** the fact that he says so; **el que sea tan vago me molesta** his being so lazy bothers me

♦ *excl*: **¡el susto que me diste!** what a fright you gave me!

♦ *pron personal* **1** (*persona: m*) him; (: *f*) her; (: *pl*) them; **lo/las veo** I can see him/them **2** (*animal, cosa: sg*) it; (: *pl*) them; **lo** (**o la**) **veo** I can see it; **los** (**o las**) **veo** I can see them

3: **lo** (*como sustituto de frase*): **no lo sabía** I didn't know; **ya lo entiendo** I understand now

él [el] *pron* (*persona*) he; (*cosa*) it; (*después de prep: persona*) him; (: *cosa*) it; **de ~** his

elaborar [elaβo'rar] *vt* (*producto*) to make, manufacture; (*preparar*) to prepare; (*madera, metal etc*) to work; (*proyecto etc*) to work on o out

elasticidad [elastiθi'ðað] *nf* elasticity

elástico, a [e'lastiko, a] *adj* elastic; (*flexible*) flexible ♦ *nm* elastic; (*un ~*) elastic band

elección [elek'θjon] *nf* election; (*selección*) choice, selection

electorado [elekto'raðo] *nm* electorate, voters *pl*

electricidad [elektriθi'ðað] *nf* electricity

electricista [elektri'θista] *nm/f* electrician

eléctrico, a [e'lektriko, a] *adj* electric

electro... [elektro] *prefijo* electro...; **~cardiograma** *nm* electrocardiogram; **~cutar** *vt* to electrocute; **~do** *nm* electrode; **~domésticos** *nmpl* (*electrical*) household appliances; **~magnético, a** *adj* electromagnetic

electrónica [elek'tronika] *nf* electronics *sg*

electrónico, a [elek'troniko, a] *adj* electronic

elefante [ele'fante] *nm* elephant

elegancia [ele'xanθja] *nf* elegance, grace; (*estilo*) stylishness

elegante [ele'xante] *adj* elegant, graceful; (*estiloso*) stylish, fashionable

elegir [ele'xir] *vt* (*escoger*) to choose, select; (*optar*) to opt for; (*presidente*) to elect

elemental [elemen'tal] *adj* (*claro, obvio*) elementary; (*fundamental*) elemental, fundamental

elemento [ele'mento] *nm* element; (*fig*) ingredient; **~s** *nmpl* elements, rudiments

elepé [ele'pe] (*pl*: **elepés**) *nm* L.P.

elevación [eleβa'θjon] *nf* elevation; (*acto*) raising, lifting; (*de precios*) rise; (*GEO etc*) height, altitude

elevar [ele'βar] *vt* to raise, lift (up); (*precio*) to put up; **~se** *vr* (*edificio*) to rise; (*precios*) to go up

eligiendo *etc vb ver* **elegir**

elija *etc vb ver* **elegir**

eliminar [elimi'nar] *vt* to eliminate, remove

eliminatoria [elimina'torja] *nf* heat, preliminary (round)

elite [e'lite] *nf* elite

ella ['eʎa] *pron* (*persona*) she; (*cosa*) it; (*después de prep: persona*) her; (: *cosa*) it; **de ~ theirs**

ellas ['eʎas] *pron* (*personas y cosas*) they; (*después de prep*) them; **de ~ theirs**

ello ['eʎo] *pron* it

ellos ['eʎos] *pron* they; (*después de prep*) them; **de ~ theirs**

elocuencia [elo'kwenθja] *nf* eloquence

elogiar [elo'xjar] *vt* to praise; **elogio** *nm* praise

elote [e'lote] (*AM*) *nm* corn on the cob

eludir [elu'ðir] *vt* to avoid

emanar [ema'nar] *vi*: **~ de** to emanate from, come from; (*derivar de*) to originate in

emancipar [emanθi'par] *vt* to emancipate; **~se** *vr* to become emancipated, free o.s.

embadurnar [embaður'nar] *vt* to smear

embajada [emba'xaða] *nf* embassy

embajador, a [embaxa'ðor, a] *nm/f* ambassador/ambassadress

embalaje [emba'laxe] *nm* packing

embalar [emba'lar] *vt* to parcel, wrap (up); **~se** *vr* to go fast

embalsamar [embalsa'mar] *vt* to embalm

embalse [em'balse] *nm* (*presa*) dam; (*lago*) reservoir

embarazada [embara'θaða] *adj* pregnant ♦ *nf* pregnant woman

embarazo [emba'raθo] *nm* (*de mujer*) pregnancy; (*impedimento*) obstacle, obstruction; (*timidez*) embarrassment; **embarazoso, a** *adj* awkward, embarrassing

embarcación [embarka'θjon] *nf* (*barco*) boat, craft; (*acto*) embarkation, boarding

embarcadero [embarka'ðero] *nm* pier, landing stage

embarcar [embar'kar] *vt* (*cargamento*) to ship, stow; (*persona*) to embark, put on board; **~se** *vr* to embark, go on board

embargar [embar'xar] *vt* (*JUR*) to seize, impound

embargo [em'barxo] *nm* (*JUR*) seizure; (*COM, POL*) embargo

embargue [em'barxe] *etc vb ver* **embargar**

embarque *etc* [em'barke] *vb ver* **embarcar** ♦ *nm* shipment, loading

embaucar [embau'kar] *vt* to trick, fool

embeber [embe'βer] *vt* (*absorber*) to absorb, soak up; (*empapar*) to saturate ♦ *vi* to shrink; **~se** *vr*: **~se en un libro** to be engrossed o absorbed in a book

embellecer [embeʎe'θer] *vt* to embellish, beautify

embestida [embes'tiða] *nf* attack, onslaught; (*carga*) charge

embestir [embes'tir] *vt* to attack, assault; to charge, attack ♦ *vi* to attack

emblema [em'blema] *nm* emblem

embobado, a [embo'ßaðo, a] *adj* (*atontado*) stunned, bewildered

embolia [em'bolja] *nf* (*MED*) clot

émbolo ['embolo] *nm* (*AUTO*) piston

embolsar [embol'sar] *vt* to pocket, put in one's pocket

emborrachar [emborra't∫ar] *vt* to make drunk, intoxicate; **~se** *vr* to get drunk

emboscada [embos'kaða] *nf* ambush

embotar [embo'tar] *vt* to blunt, dull; **~se** *vr* (*adormecerse*) to go numb

embotellamiento [emboteʎa'mjento] *nm* (*AUTO*) traffic jam

embotellar [embote'ʎar] *vt* to bottle

embrague [em'braɣe] *nm* (*tb: pedal de ~*) clutch

embriagar [embrja'ɣar] *vt* (*emborrachar*) to make drunk; **~se** *vr* (*emborracharse*) to get drunk

embrión [em'brjon] *nm* embryo

embrollar [embro'ʎar] *vt* (*el asunto*) to confuse, complicate; (*implicar*) to involve, embroil; **~se** *vr* (*confundirse*) to get into a muddle o mess

embrollo [em'broʎo] *nm* (*enredo*) muddle, confusion; (*aprieto*) fix, jam

embrujado, a [embru'xaðo, a] *adj* bewitched; **casa embrujada** haunted house

embrutecer [embrute'θer] *vt* (*atontar*) to stupefy; **~se** *vr* to be stupefied

embudo [em'buðo] *nm* funnel

embuste [em'buste] *nm* (*mentira*) lie; **~ro, a** *adj* lying, deceitful ♦ *nm/f* (*mentiroso*) liar

embutido [embu'tiðo] *nm* (*CULIN*) sausage; (*TEC*) inlay

emergencia [emer'xenθja] *nf* emergency; (*surgimiento*) emergence

emerger [emer'xer] *vi* to emerge, appear

emigración [emiɣra'θjon] *nf* emigration; (*de pájaros*) migration

emigrar [emi'ɣrar] *vi* (*personas*) to emigrate; (*pájaros*) to migrate

eminencia [emi'nenθja] *nf* eminence; **eminente** *adj* eminent, distinguished; (*elevado*) high

emisario [emi'sarjo] *nm* emissary

emisión [emi'sjon] *nf* (*acto*) emission; (*COM etc*) issue; (*RADIO, TV: acto*) broadcasting; (*: programa*) broadcast, programme (*BRIT*), program (*US*)

emisora [emi'sora] *nf* radio o broadcasting station

emitir [emi'tir] *vt* (*olor etc*) to emit, give off; (*moneda etc*) to issue; (*opinión*) to express; (*RADIO*) to broadcast

emoción [emo'θjon] *nf* emotion; (*excitación*) excitement; (*sentimiento*) feeling

emocionante [emoθjo'nante] *adj* (*excitante*) exciting, thrilling

emocionar [emoθjo'nar] *vt* (*excitar*) to excite, thrill; (*conmover*) to move, touch; (*impresionar*) to impress

emotivo, a [emo'tiβo, a] *adj* emotional

empacar [empa'kar] *vt* (*gen*) to pack; (*en caja*) to bale, crate

empacho [em'pat∫o] *nm* (*MED*) indigestion; (*fig*) embarrassment

empadronarse [empaðro'narse] *vr* (*POL: como elector*) to register

empalagoso, a [empala'ɣoso, a] *adj* cloying; (*fig*) tiresome

empalmar [empal'mar] *vt* to join, connect ♦ *vi* (*dos caminos*) to meet, join; **empalme** *nm* joint, connection; junction; (*de trenes*) connection

empanada [empa'naða] *nf* pie, pasty

empantanarse [empanta'narse] *vr* to get swamped; (*fig*) to get bogged down

empañarse [empa'narse] *vr* (*cristales etc*) to steam up

empapar [empa'par] *vt* (*mojar*) to soak, saturate; (*absorber*) to soak up, absorb; **~se** *vr*: **~se de** to soak up

empapelar [empape'lar] *vt* (*paredes*) to paper

empaquetar [empake'tar] *vt* to pack, parcel up

empastar [empas'tar] *vt* (*embadurnar*) to paste; (*diente*) to fill

empaste [em'paste] *nm* (*de diente*) filling

empatar [empa'tar] *vi* to draw, tie; **empate** *nm* draw, tie

empecé *etc vb ver* **empezar**

empedernido, a [empeðer'niðo, a] *adj* hard, heartless; (*fumador*) inveterate

empedrado, a [empe'ðraðo, a] *adj* paved ♦ *nm* paving

empeine [em'peine] *nm* (*de pie, zapato*) instep

empellón [empe'ʎon] *nm* push, shove

empeñado, a [empe'naðo, a] *adj* (*persona*) determined; (*objeto*) pawned

empeñar [empe'nar] *vt* (*objeto*) to pawn, pledge; (*persona*) to compel; **~se** *vr* (*endeudarse*) to get into debt; **~se en** to be set on, be determined to

empeño [em'peno] *nm* (*determinación, insistencia*) determination, insistence; **casa de ~s** pawnshop

empeorar [empeo'rar] *vt* to make worse, worsen ♦ *vi* to get worse, deteriorate

empequeñecer [empekene'θer] *vt* to dwarf; (*minusvalorar*) to belittle

emperador [empera'ðor] *nm* emperor; **emperatriz** *nf* empress

empezar [empe'θar] *vt, vi* to begin, start

empiece *etc vb ver* **empezar**

empiezo *etc vb ver* **empezar**

empinar [empi'nar] *vt* to raise; **~se** *vr* (*persona*) to stand on tiptoe; (*animal*) to rear up; (*camino*) to climb steeply

empírico, a [em'piriko, a] *adj* empirical

emplasto [em'plasto] *nm* (*MED*) plaster

emplazamiento [emplaθa'mjento] *nm* site, location; (*JUR*) summons *sg*

emplazar [empla'θar] *vt* (*ubicar*) to site, place, locate; (*JUR*) to summons; (*convocar*) to summon

empleado, a [emple'aðo, a] *nm/f* (*gen*) employee; (*de banco etc*) clerk

emplear [emple'ar] *vt* (*usar*) to use, employ; (*dar trabajo a*) to employ; **~se** *vr* (*conseguir trabajo*) to be employed; (*ocuparse*) to occupy o.s.

empleo [em'pleo] *nm* (*puesto*) job; (*puestos: colectivamente*) employment; (*uso*) use, employment

empobrecer [empoβre'θer] *vt* to impoverish; **~se** *vr* to become poor *o* impoverished

empollar [empo'ʎar] (*fam*) *vt, vi* to swot (up); **empollón, ona** (*fam*) *nm/f* swot

emporio [em'porjo] *nm* (*AM: gran almacén*) department store

empotrado, a [empo'traðo, a] *adj* (*armario etc*) built-in

emprender [empren'der] *vt* (*empezar*) to begin, embark on; (*acometer*) to tackle, take on

empresa [em'presa] *nf* (*de espíritu etc*) enterprise; (*COM*) company, firm; **~rio, a** *nm/f* (*COM*) businessman/woman

empréstito [em'prestito] *nm* (public) loan

empujar [empu'xar] *vt* to push, shove

empujón [empu'xon] *nm* push, shove

empuñar [empu'ɲar] *vt* (*asir*) to grasp, take (firm) hold of

emular [emu'lar] *vt* to emulate; (*rivalizar*) to rival

PALABRA CLAVE

en [en] *prep* **1** (*posición*) in; (: *sobre*) on; **está ~ el cajón** it's in the drawer; **~ Argentina/La Paz** in Argentina/La Paz; **~ la oficina/el colegio** at the office/school; **está ~ el suelo/quinto piso** it's on the floor/the fifth floor

2 (*dirección*) into; **entró ~ el aula** she went into the classroom; **meter algo ~ el bolso** to put sth into one's bag

3 (*tiempo*) in; on; **~ 1605/3 semanas/invierno** in 1605/3 weeks/winter; **~ (el mes de) enero** in (the month of) January; **~ aquella**

ocasión/época on that occasion/at that time

4 (*precio*) for; **lo vendió ~ 20 dólares** he sold it for 20 dollars

5 (*diferencia*) by; **reducir/aumentar ~ una tercera parte/un 20 por ciento** to reduce/increase by a third/20 per cent

6 (*manera*): **~ avión/autobús** by plane/bus; **escrito ~ inglés** written in English

7 (*después de vb que indica gastar etc*) on; **han cobrado demasiado ~ dietas** they've charged too much to expenses; **se le va la mitad del sueldo ~ comida** he spends half his salary on food

8 (*tema, ocupación*): **experto ~ la materia** expert on the subject; **trabaja ~ la construcción** he works in the building industry

9 (*adj* + **en** + *infin*): **lento ~ reaccionar** slow to react

---

enaguas [e'naɣwas] *nfpl* petticoat *sg*, underskirt *sg*

enajenación [enaxena'θjon] *nf*: **~ mental** mental derangement

enajenar [enaxe'nar] *vt* (*volver loco*) to drive mad

enamorado, a [enamo'raðo, a] *adj* in love ♦ *nm/f* lover

enamorar [enamo'rar] *vt* to win the love of; **~se** *vr*: **~se de alguien** to fall in love with sb

enano, a [e'nano, a] *adj* tiny ♦ *nm/f* dwarf

enardecer [enarðe'θer] *vt* (*pasiones*) to fire, inflame; (*persona*) to fill with enthusiasm; **~se** *vr*: **~se por** to get excited about; (*entusiasmarse*) to get enthusiastic about

encabezamiento [enkaβeθa'mjento] *nm* (*de carta*) heading; (*de periódico*) headline

encabezar [enkaβe'θar] *vt* (*movimiento, revolución*) to lead, head; (*lista*) to head, be at the top of; (*carta*) to put a heading to

encadenar [enkaðe'nar] *vt* to chain (together); (*poner grilletes a*) to shackle

encajar [enka'xar] *vt* (*ajustar*): **~ (en)** to fit (into); (*fam: golpe*) to take ♦ *vi* to fit (well); (*fig: corresponder a*) to match; **~se** *vr*: **~se en un sillón** to squeeze into a chair

encaje [en'kaxe] *nm* (*labor*) lace

encalar [enka'lar] *vt* (*pared*) to whitewash

encallar [enka'ʎar] *vi* (*NAUT*) to run aground

encaminar [enkami'nar] *vt* to direct, send; **~se** *vr*: **~se a** to set out for

encantado, a [enkan'taðo, a] *adj* (*hechizado*) bewitched; (*muy contento*) delighted; **¡~!** how do you do, pleased to meet you

encantador, a [enkanta'ðor, a] *adj* charming, lovely ♦ *nm/f* magician, enchanter/enchantress

encantar [enkan'tar] *vt* (*agradar*) to charm,

delight; (*hechizar*) to bewitch, cast a spell on; **me encanta eso** I love that; **encanto** *nm* (*hechizo*) spell, charm; (*fig*) charm, delight

encarcelar [enkarθe'lar] *vt* to imprison, jail

encarecer [enkare'θer] *vt* to put up the price of; **~se** *vr* to get dearer

encarecimiento [enkareθi'mjento] *nm* price increase

encargado, a [enkar'vaðo, a] *adj* in charge ♦ *nm/f* agent, representative; (*responsable*) person in charge

encargar [enkar'var] *vt* to entrust; (*recomendar*) to urge, recommend; **~se** *vr*: **~se de** to look after, take charge of

encargo [en'karvo] *nm* (*tarea*) assignment, job; (*responsabilidad*) responsibility; (*COM*) order

encariñarse [enkari'narse] *vr*: **~ con** to grow fond of, get attached to

encarnación [enkarna'θjon] *nf* incarnation, embodiment

encarnizado, a [enkarni'θaðo, a] *adj* (*lucha*) bloody, fierce

encarrilar [enkarri'lar] *vt* (*tren*) to put back on the rails; (*fig*) to correct, put on the right track

encasillar [enkasi'ʎar] *vt* (*tb fig*) to pigeonhole; (*actor*) to typecast

encauzar [enkau'θar] *vt* to channel

encendedor [enθende'ðor] *nm* lighter

encender [enθen'der] *vt* (*con fuego*) to light; (*luz, radio*) to put on, switch on; (*avivar: pasiones*) to inflame; **~se** *vr* to catch fire; (*excitarse*) to get excited; (*de cólera*) to flare up; (*el rostro*) to blush

encendido [enθen'diðo] *nm* (*AUTO*) ignition

encerado [enθe'raðo] *nm* (*ESCOL*) blackboard

encerar [enθe'rar] *vt* (*suelo*) to wax, polish

encerrar [enθe'rrar] *vt* (*confinar*) to shut in, shut up; (*comprender, incluir*) to include, contain

encharcado, a [entʃar'kaðo, a] *adj* (*terreno*) flooded

encharcarse [entʃar'karse] *vr* to get flooded

enchufado, a [entʃu'faðo, a] *nm/f* well-connected person

enchufar [entʃu'far] *vt* (*ELEC*) to plug in; (*TEC*) to connect, fit together; **enchufe** *nm* (*ELEC: clavija*) plug; (: *toma*) socket; (*de dos tubos*) joint, connection; (*fam: influencia*) contact, connection; (: *puesto*) cushy job

encía [en'θia] *nf* gum

encienda *etc vb ver* **encender**

encierro *etc* [en'θjerro] *vb ver* **encerrar** ♦ *nm* shutting in, shutting up; (*calabozo*) prison

encima [en'θima] *adv* (*sobre*) above, over; (*además*) besides; **~ de** (*en*) on, on top of; (*sobre*) above, over; (*además de*) besides, on top of; **por ~ de** over; **¿llevas dinero ~?** have

you (got) any money on you?; **se me vino ~** it took me by surprise

encina [en'θina] *nf* holm oak

encinta [en'θinta] *adj* pregnant

enclenque [en'klenke] *adj* weak, sickly

encoger [enko'xer] *vt* to shrink, contract; **~se** *vr* to shrink, contract; (*fig*) to cringe; **~se de hombros** to shrug one's shoulders

encolar [enko'lar] *vt* (*engomar*) to glue, paste; (*pegar*) to stick down

encolerizar [enkoleri'θar] *vt* to anger, provoke; **~se** *vr* to get angry

encomendar [enkomen'dar] *vt* to entrust, commend; **~se** *vr*: **~se a** to put one's trust in

encomiar [enko'mjar] *vt* to praise, pay tribute to

encomienda *etc* [enko'mjenda] *vb ver* **encomendar** ♦ *nf* (*encargo*) charge, commission; (*elogio*) tribute; **~ postal** (*AM*) parcel post

encontrado, a [enkon'traðo, a] *adj* (*contrario*) contrary, conflicting

encontrar [enkon'trar] *vt* (*hallar*) to find; (*inesperadamente*) to meet, run into; **~se** *vr* to meet (each other); (*situarse*) to be (situated); **~se con** to meet; **~se bien (de salud)** to feel well

encrespar [enkres'par] *vt* (*cabellos*) to curl; (*fig*) to anger, irritate; **~se** *vr* (*el mar*) to get rough; (*fig*) to get cross, get irritated

encrucijada [enkruθi'xaða] *nf* crossroads *sg*

encuadernación [enkwaðerna'θjon] *nf* binding

encuadernador, a [enkwaðerna'ðor, a] *nm/f* bookbinder

encuadrar [enkwa'ðrar] *vt* (*retrato*) to frame; (*ajustar*) to fit, insert; (*contener*) to contain

encubrir [enku'ßrir] *vt* (*ocultar*) to hide, conceal; (*criminal*) to harbour, shelter

encuentro *etc* [en'kwentro] *vb ver* **encontrar** ♦ *nm* (*de personas*) meeting; (*AUTO etc*) collision, crash; (*DEPORTE*) match, game; (*MIL*) encounter

encuesta [en'kwesta] *nf* inquiry, investigation; (*sondeo*) (public) opinion poll; **~ judicial** post mortem

encumbrar [enkum'brar] *vt* (*persona*) to exalt

endeble [en'deßle] *adj* (*argumento, excusa, persona*) weak

endémico, a [en'demiko, a] *adj* (*MED*) endemic; (*fig*) rife, chronic

endemoniado, a [endemo'njaðo, a] *adj* possessed (of the devil); (*travieso*) devilish

enderezar [endere'θar] *vt* (*poner derecho*) to straighten (out); (: *verticalmente*) to set upright; (*situación*) to straighten o sort out; (*dirigir*) to direct; **~se** *vr* (*persona sentada*) to straighten up

endeudarse [endeu'ðarse] *vr* to get into debt

endiablado, a [endja'ßlaðo, a] *adj* devilish, diabolical; (*travieso*) mischievous

endilgar [endil'var] (*fam*) *vt*: **~le algo a uno** to lumber sb with sth; **~le un sermón a uno** to lecture sb

endiñar [endi'ɲar] (*fam*) *vt* (*bofetón*) to land, belt

endosar [endo'sar] *vt* (*cheque etc*) to endorse

endulzar [endul'θar] *vt* to sweeten; (*suavizar*) to soften

endurecer [endure'θer] *vt* to harden; **~se** *vr* to harden, grow hard

enema [e'nema] *nm* (*MED*) enema

enemigo, a [ene'miɣo, a] *adj* enemy, hostile ♦ *nm/f* enemy

enemistad [enemis'tað] *nf* enmity

enemistar [enemis'tar] *vt* to make enemies of, cause a rift between; **~se** *vr* to become enemies; (*amigos*) to fall out

energía [ener'xia] *nf* (*vigor*) energy, drive; (*empuje*) push; (*TEC, ELEC*) energy, power; **~ eólica** wind power; **~ solar** solar energy/power

enérgico, a [e'nerxiko, a] *adj* (*gen*) energetic; (*voz, modales*) forceful

energúmeno, a [ener'vumeno, a] (*fam*) *nm/f* (*fig*) madman/woman

enero [e'nero] *nm* January

enfadado, a [enfa'ðaðo, a] *adj* angry, annoyed

enfadar [enfa'ðar] *vt* to anger, annoy; **~se** *vr* to get angry o annoyed

enfado [en'faðo] *nm* (*enojo*) anger, annoyance; (*disgusto*) trouble, bother

énfasis ['enfasis] *nm* emphasis, stress

enfático, a [en'fatiko, a] *adj* emphatic

enfermar [enfer'mar] *vt* to make ill ♦ *vi* to fall ill, be taken ill

enfermedad [enferme'ðað] *nf* illness; **~ venérea** venereal disease

enfermera [enfer'mera] *nf* nurse

enfermería [enferme'ria] *nf* infirmary; (*de colegio etc*) sick bay

enfermero [enfer'mero] *nm* (male) nurse

enfermizo, a [enfer'miθo, a] *adj* (*persona*) sickly, unhealthy; (*fig*) unhealthy

enfermo, a [en'fermo, a] *adj* ill, sick ♦ *nm/f* invalid, sick person; (*en hospital*) patient

enflaquecer [enflake'θer] *vt* (*adelgazar*) to make thin; (*debilitar*) to weaken

enfocar [enfo'kar] *vt* (*foto etc*) to focus; (*problema etc*) to approach

enfoque *etc* [en'foke] *vb ver* **enfocar** ♦ *nm* focus.

enfrascarse [enfras'karse] *vr*: **~ en algo** to bury o.s. in sth

enfrentar [enfren'tar] *vt* (*peligro*) to face (up to), confront; (*oponer*) to bring face to face; **~se** *vr* (*dos personas*) to face o confront each other; (*DEPORTE: dos equipos*) to meet; **~se a** o **con** to face up to, confront

enfrente [en'frente] *adv* opposite; **la casa de ~** the house opposite, the house across the street; **~ de** opposite, facing

enfriamiento [enfria'mjento] *nm* chilling, refrigeration; (*MED*) cold, chill

enfriar [enfri'ar] *vt* (*alimentos*) to cool, chill; (*algo caliente*) to cool down; **~se** *vr* to cool down; (*MED*) to catch a chill; (*amistad*) to cool

enfurecer [enfure'θer] *vt* to enrage, madden; **~se** *vr* to become furious, fly into a rage; (*mar*) to get rough

engalanar [engala'nar] *vt* (*adornar*) to adorn; (*ciudad*) to decorate; **~se** *vr* to get dressed up

enganchar [engan'tʃar] *vt* to hook; (*dos vagones*) to hitch up; (*TEC*) to couple, connect; (*MIL*) to recruit; **~se** *vr* (*MIL*) to enlist, join up

enganche [en'gantʃe] *nm* hook; (*TEC*) coupling, connection; (*acto*) hooking (up); (*MIL*) recruitment, enlistment; (*AM: depósito*) deposit

engañar [enga'ɲar] *vt* to deceive; (*estafar*) to cheat, swindle; **~se** *vr* (*equivocarse*) to be wrong; (*disimular la verdad*) to deceive o.s.

engaño [en'gaɲo] *nm* deceit; (*estafa*) trick, swindle; (*error*) mistake, misunderstanding; (*ilusión*) delusion; **~so, a** *adj* (*tramposo*) crooked; (*mentiroso*) dishonest, deceitful; (*aspecto*) deceptive; (*consejo*) misleading

engarzar [engar'θar] *vt* (*joya*) to set, mount; (*fig*) to link, connect

engatusar [engatu'sar] (*fam*) *vt* to coax

engendrar [enxen'drar] *vt* to breed; (*procrear*) to beget; (*causar*) to cause, produce; **engendro** *nm* (*BIO*) foetus; (*fig*) monstrosity

englobar [englo'ßar] *vt* to include, comprise

engordar [engor'ðar] *vt* to fatten ♦ *vi* to get fat, put on weight

engorroso, a [engo'rroso, a] *adj* bothersome, trying

engranaje [engra'naxe] *nm* (*AUTO*) gear

engrandecer [engrande'θer] *vt* to enlarge, magnify; (*alabar*) to praise, speak highly of; (*exagerar*) to exaggerate

engrasar [engra'sar] *vt* (*TEC: poner grasa*) to grease; (*: lubricar*) to lubricate, oil; (*manchar*) to make greasy

engreído, a [engre'iðo, a] *adj* vain, conceited

engrosar [engro'sar] *vt* (*ensanchar*) to enlarge; (*aumentar*) to increase; (*hinchar*) to swell

enhebrar [ene'ßrar] vt to thread

enhorabuena [enora'ßwena] excl: ¡~!
congratulations! ♦ nf: dar la ~ a to
congratulate

enigma [e'niɣma] nm enigma; (problema)
puzzle; (misterio) mystery

enjabonar [enxaßo'nar] vt to soap; (fam:
adular) to soft-soap

enjambre [en'xambre] nm swarm

enjaular [enxau'lar] vt to (put in a) cage;
(fam) to jail, lock up

enjuagar [enxwa'ɣar] vt (ropa) to rinse (out)

enjuague etc [en'xwaɣe] vb ver **enjuagar**
♦ nm (MED) mouthwash; (de ropa) rinse,
rinsing

enjugar [enxu'ɣar] vt to wipe (off);
(lágrimas) to dry; (déficit) to wipe out

enjuiciar [enxwi'θjar] vt (JUR: procesar) to
prosecute, try; (fig) to judge

enjuto, a [en'xuto, a] adj (flaco) lean, skinny

enlace [en'laθe] nm link, connection;
(relación) relationship; (tb: ~ matrimonial)
marriage; (de carretera, trenes) connection;
~ **sindical** shop steward

enlatado, a [enla'tado, a] adj (comida,
productos) tinned, canned

enlazar [enla'θar] vt (unir con lazos) to bind
together; (atar) to tie; (conectar) to link,
connect; (AM) to lasso

enlodar [enlo'ðar] vt to cover in mud; (fig:
manchar) to stain; (: rebajar) to debase

enloquecer [enloke'θer] vt to drive mad
♦ vi to go mad; **~se** vr to go mad

enlutado, a [enlu'tado, a] adj (persona) in
mourning

enmarañar [enmara'ɲar] vt (enredar) to
tangle (up), entangle; (complicar) to
complicate; (confundir) to confuse; **~se** vr
(enredarse) to become entangled;
(confundirse) to get confused

enmarcar [enmar'kar] vt (cuadro) to frame

enmascarar [enmaska'rar] vt to mask; **~se**
vr to put on a mask

enmendar [enmen'dar] vt to emend,
correct; (constitución etc) to amend;
(comportamiento) to reform; **~se** vr to reform,
mend one's ways; **enmienda** nf correction;
amendment; reform

enmohecerse [enmoe'θerse] vr (metal) to
rust, go rusty; (muro, plantas) to get mouldy

enmudecer [enmuðe'θer] vi (perder el
habla) to fall silent; (guardar silencio) to
remain silent

ennegrecer [ennexre'θer] vt (poner negro)
to blacken; (oscurecer) to darken; **~se** vr to
turn black; (oscurecerse) to get dark, darken

ennoblecer [ennoßle'θer] vt to ennoble

enojar [eno'xar] vt (encolerizar) to anger;
(disgustar) to annoy, upset; **~se** vr to get
angry; to get annoyed

enojo [e'noxo] nm (cólera) anger; (irritación)
annoyance; **~so, a** adj annoying

enorgullecerse [enoryuʎe'θerse] vr to be
proud; ~ **de** to pride o.s. on, be proud of

enorme [e'norme] adj enormous, huge; (fig)
monstrous; **enormidad** nf hugeness,
immensity

enrarecido, a [enrare'θiðo, a] adj
(atmósfera, aire) rarefied

enredadera [enreða'ðera] nf (BOT) creeper,
climbing plant

enredar [enre'ðar] vt (cables, hilos etc) to
tangle (up), entangle; (situación) to
complicate, confuse; (meter cizaña) to sow
discord among o between; (implicar) to
embroil, implicate; **~se** vr to get entangled,
get tangled (up); (situación) to get
complicated; (persona) to get embroiled;
(AM: fam) to meddle

enredo [en'reðo] nm (maraña) tangle;
(confusión) mix-up, confusion; (intriga)
intrigue

enrejado [enre'xaðo] nm fence, railings pl

enrevesado, a [enreße'saðo, a] adj (asunto)
complicated, involved

enriquecer [enrike'θer] vt to make rich,
enrich; **~se** vr to get rich

enrojecer [enroxe'θer] vt to redden ♦ vi
(persona) to blush; **~se** vr to blush

enrolar [enro'lar] vt (MIL) to enlist; (reclutar)
to recruit; **~se** vr (MIL) to join up; (afiliarse) to
enrol

enrollar [enro'ʎar] vt to roll (up), wind (up)

enroscar [enros'kar] vt (torcer, doblar) to coil
(round), wind; (tornillo, rosca) to screw in;
~se vr to coil, wind

ensalada [ensa'laða] nf salad; **ensaladilla
(rusa)** nf Russian salad

ensalzar [ensal'θar] vt (alabar) to praise,
extol; (exaltar) to exalt

ensamblaje [ensam'blaxe] nm assembly;
(TEC) joint

ensanchar [ensan'tʃar] vt (hacer más ancho)
to widen; (agrandar) to enlarge, expand;
(COSTURA) to let out; **~se** vr to get wider,
expand; **ensanche** nm (de calle) widening

ensangrentar [ensangren'tar] vt to stain
with blood

ensañar [ensa'ɲar] vt to enrage; **~se** vr: **~se
con** to treat brutally

ensartar [ensar'tar] vt (cuentas, perlas etc) to
string (together)

ensayar [ensa'jar] vt to test, try (out);
(TEATRO) to rehearse

ensayo [en'sajo] nm test, trial; (QUÍM)
experiment; (TEATRO) rehearsal; (DEPORTE) try;
(ESCOL, LITERATURA) essay

enseguida [ense'ɣiða] adv at once, right away

ensenada [ense'naða] nf inlet, cove

enseñanza [ense'nanθa] nf (educación) education; (acción) teaching; (doctrina) teaching, doctrine

enseñar [ense'nar] vt (educar) to teach; (mostrar, señalar) to show

enseres [en'seres] nmpl belongings

ensillar [ensi'ʎar] vt to saddle (up)

ensimismarse [ensimis'marse] vr (abstraerse) to become lost in thought; (AM) to become conceited

ensombrecer [ensombre'θer] vt to darken, cast a shadow over; (fig) to overshadow, put in the shade

ensordecer [ensorðe'θer] vt to deafen ♦ vi to go deaf

ensortijado, a [ensorti'xaðo, a] adj (pelo) curly

ensuciar [ensu'θjar] vt (manchar) to dirty, soil; (fig) to defile; ~se vr to get dirty; (niño) to wet o.s.

ensueño [en'sweno] nm (sueño) dream, fantasy; (ilusión) illusion; (soñando despierto) daydream

entablar [enta'βlar] vt (recubrir) to board (up); (AJEDREZ, DAMAS) to set up; (conversación) to strike up; (JUR) to file ♦ vi to draw

entablillar [entaβli'ʎar] vt (MED) to (put in a) splint

entallar [enta'ʎar] vt (traje) to tailor ♦ vi: **el traje entalla bien** the suit fits well

ente ['ente] nm (organización) body, organization; (fam: persona) odd character

entender [enten'der] vt (comprender) to understand; (darse cuenta) to realize ♦ vi to understand; (creer) to think, believe; ~se vr (comprenderse) to be understood; (2 personas) to get on together; (ponerse de acuerdo) to agree, reach an agreement; ~ **de** to know all about; ~ **algo de** to know a little about; ~ **en** to deal with, have to do with; ~se **mal** (2 personas) to get on badly

entendido, a [enten'diðo, a] adj (comprendido) understood; (hábil) skilled; (inteligente) knowledgeable ♦ nm/f (experto) expert ♦ excl agreed!; **entendimiento** nm (comprensión) understanding; (inteligencia) mind, intellect; (juicio) judgement

enterado, a [ente'raðo, a] adj well-informed; **estar** ~ **de** to know about, be aware of

enteramente [entera'mente] adv entirely, completely

enterar [ente'rar] vt (informar) to inform, tell; ~se vr to find out, get to know

entereza [ente'reθa] nf (totalidad) entirety; (fig: carácter) strength of mind; (: honradez) integrity

enternecer [enterne'θer] vt (ablandar) to soften; (apiadar) to touch, move; ~se vr to be touched, be moved

entero, a [en'tero, a] adj (total) whole, entire; (fig: honesto) honest; (: firme) firm, resolute ♦ nm (COM: punto) point; (AM: pago) payment

enterrador [enterra'ðor] nm gravedigger

enterrar [ente'rrar] vt to bury

entibiar [enti'βjar] vt (enfriar) to cool; (calentar) to warm; ~se vr (fig) to cool

entidad [enti'ðað] nf (empresa) firm, company; (organismo) body; (sociedad) society; (FILOSOFÍA) entity

entiendo etc vb ver **entender**

entierro [en'tjerro] nm (acción) burial; (funeral) funeral

entonación [entona'θjon] nf (LING) intonation

entonar [ento'nar] vt (canción) to intone; (colores) to tone; (MED) to tone up ♦ vi to be in tune

entonces [en'tonθes] adv then, at that time; **desde** ~ since then; **en aquel** ~ at that time; (**pues**) ~ and so

entornar [entor'nar] vt (puerta, ventana) to half close, leave ajar; (los ojos) to screw up

entorpecer [entorpe'θer] vt (entendimiento) to dull; (impedir) to obstruct, hinder; (: tránsito) to slow down, delay

entrada [en'traða] nf (acción) entry, access; (sitio) entrance, way in; (INFORM) input; (COM) receipts pl, takings pl; (CULIN) starter; (DEPORTE) innings sg; (TEATRO) house, audience; (billete) ticket; (COM): ~s **y salidas** income and expenditure; (TEC): ~ **de aire** air intake ♦ inlet; **de** ~ from the outset

entrado, a [en'traðo, a] adj: ~ **en años** elderly; **una vez** ~ **el verano** in the summer(time), when summer comes

entramparse [entram'parse] vr to get into debt

entrante [en'trante] adj next, coming; **mes/año** ~ next month/year; ~s nmpl starters

entraña [en'trana] nf (fig: centro) heart, core; (raíz) root; ~s nfpl (ANAT) entrails; (fig) heart sg; **sin** ~s (fig) heartless; **entrañable** adj close, intimate; **entrañar** vt to entail

entrar [en'trar] vt (introducir) to bring in; (INFORM) to input ♦ vi (meterse) to go in, come in, enter; (comenzar): ~ **diciendo** to begin by saying; **hacer** ~ to show in; **no me entra** I can't get the hang of it

entre |'entre] prep (dos) between; (más de dos) among(st)

entreabrir [entrea'βrir] vt to half-open, open halfway

entrecejo [entre'θexo] nm: **fruncir el** ~ to

frown

entrecortado, a [entrekor'taðo, a] *adj*
(*respiración*) difficult; (*habla*) faltering

entredicho [entre'ðitʃo] *nm* (*JUR*) injunction;
poner en ~ to cast doubt on; **estar en ~** to be
in doubt

entrega [en'treɣa] *nf* (*de mercancías*)
delivery; (*de novela etc*) instalment

entregar [entre'ɣar] *vt* (*dar*) to hand (over),
deliver; **~se** *vr* (*rendirse*) to surrender, give in,
submit; (*dedicarse*) to devote o.s.

entrelazar [entrela'θar] *vt* to entwine

entremeses [entre'meses] *nmpl* hors
d'œuvres

entremeter [entreme'ter] *vt* to insert, put
in; **~se** *vr* to meddle, interfere;
entremetido, a *adj* meddling, interfering

entremezclar [entremeθ'klar] *vt* to
intermingle; **~se** *vr* to intermingle

entrenador, a [entrena'ðor, a] *nm/f* trainer,
coach

entrenarse [entre'narse] *vr* to train

entrepierna [entre'pjerna] *nf* crotch

entresacar [entresa'kar] *vt* to pick out, select

entresuelo [entre'swelo] *nm* mezzanine

entretanto [entre'tanto] *adv* meanwhile,
meantime

entretejer [entrete'xer] *vt* to interweave

entretener [entrete'ner] *vt* (*divertir*) to
entertain, amuse; (*detener*) to hold up, delay;
~se *vr* (*divertirse*) to amuse o.s.; (*retrasarse*)
to delay, linger; **entretenido, a** *adj*
entertaining, amusing; **entretenimiento** *nm*
entertainment, amusement

entrever [entre'βer] *vt* to glimpse, catch a
glimpse of

entrevista [entre'βista] *nf* interview;
entrevistar *vt* to interview; **entrevistarse** *vr*
to have an interview

entristecer [entriste'θer] *vt* to sadden,
grieve; **~se** *vr* to grow sad

entrometerse [entrome'terse] *vr*: **~ (en)** to
interfere (in o with)

entroncar [entron'kar] *vi* to be connected o
related

entumecer [entume'θer] *vt* to numb,
benumb; **~se** *vr* (*por el frío*) to go o become
numb; **entumecido, a** *adj* numb, stiff

enturbiar [entur'βjar] *vt* (*el agua*) to make
cloudy; (*fig*) to confuse; **~se** *vr* (*oscurecerse*)
to become cloudy; (*fig*) to get confused,
become obscure

entusiasmar [entusjas'mar] *vt* to excite, fill
with enthusiasm; (*gustar mucho*) to delight;
~se *vr*: **~se con** o **por** to get enthusiastic o
excited about

entusiasmo [entu'sjasmo] *nm* enthusiasm;
(*excitación*) excitement

entusiasta [entu'sjasta] *adj* enthusiastic

♦ *nm/f* enthusiast

enumerar [enume'rar] *vt* to enumerate

enunciación [enunθja'θjon] *nf* enunciation

enunciado [enun'θjaðo] *nm* enunciation

envainar [embai'nar] *vt* to sheathe

envalentonar [embalento'nar] *vt* to give
courage to; **~se** *vr* (*pey: jactarse*) to boast,
brag

envanecer [embane'θer] *vt* to make
conceited; **~se** *vr* to grow conceited

envasar [emba'sar] *vt* (*empaquetar*) to pack,
wrap; (*enfrascar*) to bottle; (*enlatar*) to can;
(*embolsar*) to pocket

envase [em'base] *nm* (*en paquete*) packing,
wrapping; (*en botella*) bottling; (*en lata*)
canning; (*recipiente*) container; (*paquete*)
package; (*botella*) bottle; (*lata*) tin (*BRIT*), can

envejecer [embexe'θer] *vt* to make old, age
♦ *vi* (*volverse viejo*) to grow old; (*parecer
viejo*) to age; **~se** *vr* to grow old; to age

envenenar [embene'nar] *vt* to poison; (*fig*)
to embitter

envergadura [emberɣa'ðura] *nf* (*fig*) scope,
compass

envés [em'bes] *nm* (*de tela*) back, wrong side

enviar [em'bjar] *vt* to send

enviciarse [embi'θjarse] *vr*: **~ (con)** to get
addicted (to)

envidia [em'biðja] *nf* envy; **tener ~ a** to envy,
be jealous of; **envidiar** *vt* to envy

envío [em'bio] *nm* (*acción*) sending; (*de
mercancías*) consignment; (*de dinero*)
remittance

enviudar [embju'ðar] *vi* to be widowed

envoltura [embol'tura] *nf* (*cobertura*) cover;
(*embalaje*) wrapper, wrapping; **envoltorio**
nm package

envolver [embol'βer] *vt* to wrap (up);
(*cubrir*) to cover; (*enemigo*) to surround;
(*implicar*) to involve, implicate

envuelto [em'bwelto] *pp de* **envolver**

enyesar [enje'sar] *vt* (*pared*) to plaster;
(*MED*) to put in plaster

enzarzarse [enθar'θarse] *vr*: **~ en** (*pelea*) to
get mixed up in; (*disputa*) to get involved in

épica ['epika] *nf* epic

épico, a ['epiko, a] *adj* epic

epidemia [epi'ðemja] *nf* epidemic

epilepsia [epi'lepsja] *nf* epilepsy

epílogo [e'piloɣo] *nm* epilogue

episodio [epi'soðjo] *nm* episode

epístola [e'pistola] *nf* epistle

época ['epoka] *nf* period, time; (*HISTORIA*)
age, epoch; **hacer ~** to be epoch-making

equilibrar [ekili'βrar] *vt* to balance;
equilibrio *nm* balance, equilibrium;
equilibrista *nm/f* (*funámbulo*) tightrope
walker; (*acróbata*) acrobat

equipaje [eki'paxe] *nm* luggage; (*avíos*):

~ de mano hand luggage

equipar [eki'par] vt (proveer) to equip

equipararse [ekipa'rarse] vr: **~ con** to be on a level with

equipo [e'kipo] nm (conjunto de cosas) equipment; (DEPORTE) team; (de obreros) shift

equis ['ekis] nf inv (the letter) X

equitación [ekita'θjon] nf horse riding

equitativo, a [ekita'tiβo, a] adj equitable, fair

equivalente [ekiβa'lente] adj, nm equivalent

equivaler [ekiβa'ler] vi to be equivalent o equal

equivocación [ekiβoka'θjon] nf mistake, error

equivocado, a [ekiβo'kaðo, a] adj wrong, mistaken

equivocarse [ekiβo'karse] vr to be wrong, make a mistake; **~ de camino** to take the wrong road

equívoco, a [e'kiβoko, a] adj (dudoso) suspect; (ambiguo) ambiguous ♦ nm ambiguity; (malentendido) misunderstanding

era ['era] vb ver **ser** ♦ nf era, age

erais vb ver **ser**

éramos vb ver **ser**

eran vb ver **ser**

erario [e'rarjo] nm exchequer (BRIT), treasury

eras vb ver **ser**

erección [erek'θjon] nf erection

eres vb ver **ser**

erguir [er'xir] vt to raise, lift; (poner derecho) to straighten; **~se** vr to straighten up

erigir [eri'xir] vt to erect, build; **~se** vr: **~se en** to set o.s. up as

erizarse [eri'θarse] vr (pelo: de perro) to bristle; (: de persona) to stand on end

erizo [e'riθo] nm (ZOOL) hedgehog; **~ de mar** sea-urchin

ermita [er'mita] nf hermitage

ermitaño, a [ermi'taɲo, a] nm/f hermit

erosión [ero'sjon] nf erosion

erosionar [erosjo'nar] vt to erode

erótico, a [e'rotiko, a] adj erotic; **erotismo** nm eroticism

erradicar [erraði'kar] vt to eradicate

errante [e'rrante] adj wandering, errant

errar [e'rrar] vi (vagar) to wander, roam; (equivocarse) to be mistaken ♦ vt: **~ el camino** to take the wrong road; **~ el tiro** to miss

erróneo, a [e'rroneo, a] adj (equivocado) wrong, mistaken

error [e'rror] nm error, mistake; (INFORM) bug; **~ de imprenta** misprint

eructar [eruk'tar] vt to belch, burp

erudito, a [eru'ðito, a] adj erudite, learned

erupción [erup'θjon] nf eruption; (MED) rash

es vb ver **ser**

esa ['esa] (pl **esas**) adj demos ver **ese**

ésa ['esa] (pl **ésas**) pron ver **ése**

esbelto, a [es'βelto, a] adj slim, slender

esbozo [es'βoθo] nm sketch, outline

escabeche [eska'βetʃe] nm brine; (de aceitunas etc) pickle; **en ~** pickled

escabroso, a [eska'βroso, a] adj (accidentado) rough, uneven; (fig) tough, difficult; (: atrevido) risqué

escabullirse [eskaβu'Airse] vr to slip away, to clear out

escafandra [eska'fandra] nf (buzo) diving suit; (~ espacial) space suit

escala [es'kala] nf (proporción, MUS) scale; (de mano) ladder; (AVIAT) stopover; **hacer ~ en** to stop o call in at

escalafón [eskala'fon] nm (escala de salarios) salary scale, wage scale

escalar [eska'lar] vt to climb, scale

escalera [eska'lera] nf stairs pl, staircase; (escala) ladder; (NAIPES) run; **~ mecánica** escalator; **~ de caracol** spiral staircase

escalfar [eskal'far] vt (huevos) to poach

escalinata [eskali'nata] nf staircase

escalofriante [eskalo'frjante] adj chilling

escalofrío [eskalo'frio] nm (MED) chill; **~s** nmpl (fig) shivers

escalón [eska'lon] nm step, stair; (de escalera) rung

escalope [eska'lope] nm (CULIN) escalope

escama [eska'ma] nf (de pez, serpiente) scale; (de jabón) flake; (fig) resentment

escamar [eska'mar] vt (fig) to make wary o suspicious

escamotear [eskamote'ar] vt (robar) to lift, swipe; (hacer desaparecer) to make disappear

escampar [eskam'par] vb impers to stop raining

escandalizar [eskandali'θar] vt to scandalize, shock; **~se** vr to be shocked; (ofenderse) to be offended

escándalo [es'kandalo] nm scandal; (alboroto, tumulto) row, uproar; **escandaloso, a** adj scandalous, shocking

escandinavo, a [eskandi'naβo, a] adj, nm/f Scandinavian

escaño [es'kaɲo] nm bench; (POL) seat

escapar [eska'par] vi (gen) to escape, run away; (DEPORTE) to break away; **~se** vr to escape, get away; (agua, gas) to leak (out)

escaparate [eskapa'rate] nm shop window

escape [es'kape] nm (de agua, gas) leak; (de motor) exhaust

escarabajo [eskara'βaxo] nm beetle

escaramuza [eskara'muθa] nf skirmish

escarbar [eskar'βar] vt (tierra) to scratch

escarceos [eskar'θeos] nmpl (fig): **en mis ~ con la política** ... in my dealings with politics ...; **~ amorosos** love affairs

escarcha [es'kartʃa] nf frost

escarchado, a [eskar'tʃaðo, a] adj (CULIN: fruta) crystallized

escarlata [eskar'lata] adj inv scarlet; **escarlatina** nf scarlet fever

escarmentar [eskarmen'tar] vt to punish severely ♦ vi to learn one's lesson

escarmiento etc [eskar'mjento] vb ver **escarmentar** ♦ nm (ejemplo) lesson; (castigo) punishment

escarnio [es'karnjo] nm mockery; (injuria) insult

escarola [eska'rola] nf endive

escarpado, a [eskar'paðo, a] adj (pendiente) sheer, steep; (rocas) craggy

escasear [eskase'ar] vi to be scarce

escasez [eska'seθ] nf (falta) shortage, scarcity; (pobreza) poverty

escaso, a [es'kaso, a] adj (poco) scarce; (raro) rare; (ralo) thin, sparse; (limitado) limited

escatimar [eskati'mar] vt to skimp (on), be sparing with

escayola [eska'jola] nf plaster

escena [es'θena] nf scene

escenario [esθe'narjo] nm (TEATRO) stage; (CINE) set; (fig) scene; **escenografía** nf set design

escepticismo [esθepti'θismo] nm scepticism; **escéptico, a** adj sceptical ♦ nm/f sceptic

escisión [esθi'sjon] nf (de partido, secta) split

esclarecer [esklare'θer] vt (misterio, problema) to shed light on

esclavitud [esklaβi'tuð] nf slavery

esclavizar [esklaβi'θar] vt to enslave

esclavo, a [es'klaβo, a] nm/f slave

esclusa [es'klusa] nf (de canal) lock; (compuerta) floodgate

escoba [es'koβa] nf broom; **escobilla** nf brush

escocer [esko'θer] vi to burn, sting; **~se** vr to chafe, get chafed

escocés, esa [esko'θes, esa] adj Scottish ♦ nm/f Scotsman/woman, Scot

Escocia [es'koθja] nf Scotland

escoger [esko'xer] vt to choose, pick, select; **escogido, a** adj chosen, selected

escolar [esko'lar] adj school cpd ♦ nm/f schoolboy/girl, pupil

escollo [es'koʎo] nm (obstáculo) pitfall

escolta [es'kolta] nf escort; **escoltar** vt to escort

escombros [es'kombros] nmpl (basura) rubbish sg; (restos) debris sg

esconder [eskon'der] vt to hide, conceal; **~se** vr to hide; **escondidas** (AM) nfpl: a **escondidas** secretly; **escondite** nm hiding place; (juego) hide-and-seek; **escondrijo** nm hiding place, hideout

escopeta [esko'peta] nf shotgun

escoria [es'korja] nf (de alto horno) slag; (fig) scum, dregs pl

Escorpio [es'korpjo] nm Scorpio

escorpión [eskor'pjon] nm scorpion

escotado, a [esko'taðo, a] adj low-cut

escote [es'kote] nm (de vestido) low neck; **pagar a ~** to share the expenses

escotilla [esko'tiʎa] nf (NAUT) hatch(way)

escozor [esko'θor] nm (dolor) sting(ing)

escribir [eskri'βir] vt, vi to write; **~ a máquina** to type; **¿cómo se escribe?** how do you spell it?

escrito, a [es'krito, a] pp de **escribir** ♦ nm (documento) document; (manuscrito) text, manuscript; **por ~** in writing

escritor, a [eskri'tor, a] nm/f writer

escritorio [eskri'torjo] nm desk

escritura [eskri'tura] nf (acción) writing; (caligrafía) (hand)writing; (JUR: documento) deed

escrúpulo [es'krupulo] nm scruple; (minuciosidad) scrupulousness; **escrupuloso, a** adj scrupulous

escrutar [eskru'tar] vt to scrutinize, examine; (votos) to count

escrutinio [eskru'tinjo] nm (examen atento) scrutiny; (POL: recuento de votos) count(ing)

escuadra [es'kwaðra] nf (MIL etc) squad; (NAUT) squadron; (de coches etc) fleet; **escuadrilla** nf (de aviones) squadron; (AM: de obreros) gang

escuadrón [eskwa'ðron] nm squadron

escuálido, a [es'kwaliðo, a] adj skinny, scraggy; (sucio) squalid

escuchar [esku'tʃar] vt to listen to ♦ vi to listen

escudilla [esku'ðiʎa] nf bowl, basin

escudo [es'kuðo] nm shield

escudriñar [eskuðri'nar] vt (examinar) to investigate, scrutinize; (mirar de lejos) to scan

escuela [es'kwela] nf school; **~ de artes y oficios** (ESP) ≈ technical college; **~ normal** teacher training college

escueto, a [es'kweto, a] adj plain; (estilo) simple

escuincle [es'kwinkle] (AM: fam) nm/f kid

esculpir [eskul'pir] vt to sculpt; (grabar) to engrave; (tallar) to carve; **escultor, a** nm/f sculptor/tress; **escultura** nf sculpture

escupidera [eskupi'ðera] nf spittoon

escupir [esku'pir] vt, vi to spit (out)

escurreplatos [eskurre'platos] nm inv plate rack

escurridizo, a [eskurri'ðiθo, a] adj slippery

escurridor [eskurri'ðor] nm colander

escurrir [esku'rrir] vt (ropa) to wring out; (verduras, platos) to drain ♦ vi (líquidos) to drip; **~se** *vr* (*secarse*) to drain; (*resbalarse*) to slip, slide; (*escaparse*) to slip away

ese ['ese] (*f* **esa**, *pl* **esos, esas**) *adj demos* (*sg*) that; (*pl*) those

ése ['ese] (*f* **ésa**, *pl* **ésos, ésas**) *pron* (*sg*) that (one); (*pl*) those (ones); **~ ... éste ...** the former ... the latter ...; **no me vengas con ésas** don't give me any more of that nonsense

esencia [e'senθja] *nf* essence; **esencial** *adj* essential

esfera [es'fera] *nf* sphere; (*de reloj*) face; **esférico, a** *adj* spherical

esforzarse [esfor'θarse] *vr* to exert o.s., make an effort

esfuerzo *etc* [es'fwerθo] *vb ver* **esforzar** ♦ *nm* effort

esfumarse [esfu'marse] *vr* (*apoyo, esperanzas*) to fade away

esgrima [es'ɣrima] *nf* fencing

esgrimir [esɣri'mir] *vt* (*arma*) to brandish; (*argumento*) to use

esguince [es'ɣinθe] *nm* (*MED*) sprain

eslabón [esla'ßon] *nm* link

eslip [ez'lip] *nm* pants *pl* (*BRIT*), briefs *pl*

eslovaco, a [eslo'ßako, a] *adj, nm/f* Slovak, Slovakian ♦ *nm* (*LING*) Slovak, Slovakian

Eslovaquia [eslo'ßakja] *nf* Slovakia

esmaltar [esmal'tar] *vt* to enamel; **esmalte** *nm* enamel; **esmalte de uñas** nail varnish o polish

esmerado, a [esme'raðo, a] *adj* careful, neat

esmeralda [esme'ralda] *nf* emerald

esmerarse [esme'rarse] *vr* (*aplicarse*) to take great pains, exercise great care; (*afanarse*) to work hard

esmero [es'mero] *nm* (great) care

esnob [es'nob] (*pl* **~s**) *adj* (*persona*) snobbish ♦ *nm/f* snob; **~ismo** *nm* snobbery

eso ['eso] *pron* that, that thing o matter; **~ de su coche** that business about his car; **~ de ir al cine** all that about going to the cinema; **~ de las cinco** at about five o'clock; **en ~** thereupon, at that point; **~ es** that's it; **¡~ sí que es vida!** now that is really living!; **por ~ te lo dije** that's why I told you; **y ~ que llovía** in spite of the fact it was raining

esos ['esos] *adj demos ver* **ese**

ésos ['esos] *pron ver* **ése**

espabilar *etc* [espaßi'lar] = **despabilar** *etc*

espacial [espa'θjal] *adj* (*del espacio*) space *cpd*

espaciar [espa'θjar] *vt* to space (out)

espacio [es'paθjo] *nm* space; (*MUS*) interval; (*RADIO, TV*) programme (*BRIT*), program (*US*); **el ~** space; **~so, a** *adj* spacious, roomy

espada [es'paða] *nf* sword; **~s** *nfpl* (*NAIPES*) spades

espaguetis [espa'ɣetis] *nmpl* spaghetti *sg*

espalda [es'palda] *nf* (*gen*) back; **~s** *nfpl* (*hombros*) shoulders; **a ~s de uno** behind sb's back; **tenderse de ~s** to lie (down) on one's back; **volver la ~ a alguien** to cold-shoulder sb

espantajo [espan'taxo] *nm* = **espantapájaros**

espantapájaros [espanta'paxaros] *nm inv* scarecrow

espantar [espan'tar] *vt* (*asustar*) to frighten, scare; (*ahuyentar*) to frighten off; (*asombrar*) to horrify, appal; **~se** *vr* to get frightened o scared; to be appalled

espanto [es'panto] *nm* (*susto*) fright; (*terror*) terror; (*asombro*) astonishment; **~so, a** *adj* frightening; terrifying; astonishing

España [es'paɲa] *nf* Spain; **español, a** *adj* Spanish ♦ *nm/f* Spaniard ♦ *nm* (*LING*) Spanish

esparadrapo [espara'ðrapo] *nm* (sticking) plaster (*BRIT*), adhesive tape (*US*)

esparcimiento [esparθi'mjento] *nm* (*dispersión*) spreading; (*diseminación*) scattering; (*fig*) cheerfulness

esparcir [espar'θir] *vt* to spread; (*diseminar*) to scatter; **~se** *vr* to spread (out); to scatter; (*divertirse*) to enjoy o.s.

espárrago [es'parraɣo] *nm* asparagus

esparto [es'parto] *nm* esparto (grass)

espasmo [es'pasmo] *nm* spasm

espátula [es'patula] *nf* spatula

especia [es'peθja] *nf* spice

especial [espe'θjal] *adj* special; **~idad** *nf* speciality (*BRIT*), specialty (*US*)

especie [es'peθje] *nf* (*BIO*) species; (*clase*) kind, sort; **en ~** in kind

especificar [espeθifi'kar] *vt* to specify; **específico, a** *adj* specific

espécimen [es'peθimen] (*pl* **especímenes**) *nm* specimen

espectáculo [espek'takulo] *nm* (*gen*) spectacle; (*TEATRO etc*) show

espectador, a [espekta'ðor, a] *nm/f* spectator

espectro [es'pektro] *nm* ghost; (*fig*) spectre

especular [espeku'lar] *vt, vi* to speculate

espejismo [espe'xismo] *nm* mirage

espejo [es'pexo] *nm* mirror; **~ retrovisor** rear-view mirror

espeluznante [espeluθ'nante] *adj* horrifying, hair-raising

espera [es'pera] *nf* (*pausa, intervalo*) wait; (*JUR: plazo*) respite; **en ~ de** waiting for; (*con expectativa*) expecting

esperanza [espe'ranθa] *nf* (*confianza*) hope; (*expectativa*) expectation; **hay pocas ~s de que venga** there is little prospect of his coming

esperar [espe'rar] *vt* (*aguardar*) to wait for; (*tener expectativa de*) to expect; (*desear*) to hope for ♦ *vi* to wait; to expect; to hope

esperma [es'perma] *nf* sperm

espesar [espe'sar] vt to thicken; **~se** vr to thicken, get thicker

espeso, a [es'peso, a] adj thick; **espesor** nm thickness

espía [es'pia] nm/f spy; **espiar** vt (observar) to spy on

espiga [es'piɣa] nf (BOT: de trigo etc) ear

espigón [espi'ɣon] nm (BOT) ear; (NAUT) breakwater

espina [es'pina] nf thorn; (de pez) bone; **~ dorsal** (ANAT) spine

espinaca [espi'naka] nf spinach

espinazo [espi'naθo] nm spine, backbone

espinilla [espi'niʎa] nf (ANAT: tibia) shin(bone); (grano) blackhead

espinoso, a [espi'noso, a] adj (planta) thorny, prickly; (asunto) difficult

espionaje [espjo'naxe] nm spying, espionage

espiral [espi'ral] adj, nf spiral

espirar [espi'rar] vt to breathe out, exhale

espiritista [espiri'tista] adj, nm/f spiritualist

espíritu [es'piritu] nm spirit; **espiritual** adj spiritual

espita [es'pita] nf tap

espléndido, a [es'plendiðo, a] adj (magnífico) magnificent, splendid; (generoso) generous

esplendor [esplen'dor] nm splendour

espolear [espole'ar] vt to spur on

espoleta [espo'leta] nf (de bomba) fuse

espolón [espo'lon] nm sea wall

espolvorear [espolßore'ar] vt to dust, sprinkle

esponja [es'ponxa] nf sponge; (fig) sponger; **esponjoso, a** adj spongy

espontaneidad [espontanei'ðað] nf spontaneity; **espontáneo, a** adj spontaneous

esposa [es'posa] nf wife; **~s** nfpl handcuffs; **esposar** vt to handcuff

esposo [es'poso] nm husband

espray [es'prai] nm spray

espuela [es'pwela] nf spur

espuma [es'puma] nf foam; (de cerveza) froth, head; (de jabón) lather; **espumadera** nf (utensilio) skimmer; **espumoso, a** adj frothy, foamy; (vino) sparkling

esqueleto [eske'leto] nm skeleton

esquema [es'kema] nm (diagrama) diagram; (dibujo) plan; (FILOSOFÍA) schema

esquí [es'ki] (pl **~s**) nm (objeto) ski; (DEPORTE) skiing; **~ acuático** water-skiing; **esquiar** vi to ski

esquilar [eski'lar] vt to shear

esquimal [eski'mal] adj, nm/f Eskimo

esquina [es'kina] nf corner

esquinazo [eski'naθo] nm: **dar ~ a algn** to give sb the slip

esquirol [eski'rol] nm blackleg

esquivar [eski'ßar] vt to avoid

esquivo, a [es'kißo, a] adj evasive; (tímido) reserved; (huraño) unsociable

esta ['esta] adj ver **este²**

está vb ver **estar**

ésta ['esta] pron ver **éste**

estabilidad [estaßili'ðað] nf stability; **estable** adj stable

establecer [estaßle'θer] vt to establish; **~se** vr to establish o.s.; (echar raíces) to settle (down); **establecimiento** nm establishment

establo [es'taßlo] nm (AGR) stable

estaca [es'taka] nf stake, post; (de tienda de campaña) peg

estacada [esta'kaða] nf (cerca) fence, fencing; (palenque) stockade

estación [esta'θjon] nf station; (del año) season; **~ de autobuses** bus station; **~ balnearia** seaside resort; **~ de servicio** service station

estacionamiento [estaθjona'mjento] nm (AUTO) parking; (MIL) stationing

estacionar [estaθjo'nar] vt (AUTO) to park; (MIL) to station; **~io, a** adj stationary; (COM: mercado) slack

estadio [es'taðjo] nm (fase) stage, phase; (DEPORTE) stadium

estadista [esta'ðista] nm (POL) statesman; (ESTADÍSTICA) statistician

estadística [esta'ðistika] nf figure, statistic; (ciencia) statistics sg

estado [es'taðo] nm (POL: condición) state; **~ de ánimo** state of mind; **~ de cuenta** bank statement; **~ de sitio** state of siege; **~ civil** marital status; **~ mayor** staff; **estar en ~** to be pregnant; **(los) E~s Unidos** nmpl the United States (of America) sg

estadounidense [estaðouni'ðense] adj United States cpd, American ♦ nm/f American

estafa [es'tafa] nf swindle, trick; **estafar** vt to swindle, defraud

estafeta [esta'feta] nf (oficina de correos) post office; **~ diplomática** diplomatic bag

estáis vb ver **estar**

estallar [esta'ʎar] vi to burst; (bomba) to explode, go off; (epidemia, guerra, rebelión) to break out; **~ en llanto** to burst into tears; **estallido** nm explosion; (fig) outbreak

estampa [es'tampa] nf print, engraving

estampado, a [estam'paðo, a] adj printed ♦ nm (impresión: acción) printing; (: efecto) print; (marca) stamping

estampar [estam'par] vt (imprimir) to print; (marcar) to stamp; (metal) to engrave; (poner sello en) to stamp; (fig) to stamp, imprint

estampida [estam'piða] nf stampede

estampido [estam'piðo] nm bang, report

están vb ver **estar**

estancado, a [estanˈkaðo, a] *adj* stagnant

estancar [estanˈkar] *vt* (*aguas*) to hold up, hold back; (*COM*) to monopolize; (*fig*) to block, hold up; **~se** *vr* to stagnate

estancia [estanˈθja] *nf* (*permanencia*) stay; (*sala*) room; (*AM*) farm, ranch; **estanciero** (*AM*) *nm* farmer, rancher

estanco, a [esˈtanko, a] *adj* watertight ♦ *nm* tobacconist's (shop), cigar store (*US*)

estándar [esˈtandar] *adj, nm* standard; **estandarizar** *vt* to standardize

estandarte [estanˈdarte] *nm* banner, standard

estanque [esˈtanke] *nm* (*lago*) pool, pond; (*AGR*) reservoir

estanquero, a [estanˈkero, a] *nm/f* tobacconist

estante [esˈtante] *nm* (*armario*) rack, stand; (*biblioteca*) bookcase; (*anaquel*) shelf; (*AM*) prop; **estantería** *nf* shelving, shelves *pl*

estaño [esˈtaɲo] *nm* tin

PALABRA CLAVE
---

estar [esˈtar] *vi* **1** (*posición*) to be; **está en la plaza** it's in the square; **¿está Juan?** is Juan in?; **estamos a 30 km de Junín** we're 30 kms from Junín

2 (+ *adj: estado*) to be; **~ enfermo** to be ill; **está muy elegante** he's looking very smart; **¿cómo estás?** how are you keeping?

3 (+ *gerundio*) to be; **estoy leyendo** I'm reading

4 (*uso pasivo*): **está condenado a muerte** he's been condemned to death; **está envasado en** ... it's packed in ...

5 (*con fechas*): **¿a cuántos estamos?** what's the date today?; **estamos a 5 de mayo** it's the 5th of May

6 (*locuciones*): **¿estamos?** (*¿de acuerdo?*) okay?; (*¿listo?*) ready?; **¡ya está bien!** that's enough!

7: **~ de**: **~ de vacaciones/viaje** to be on holiday/away o on a trip; **está de camarero** he's working as a waiter

8: **~ para**: **está para salir** he's about to leave; **no estoy para bromas** I'm not in the mood for jokes

9: **~ por** (*propuesta etc*) to be in favour of; (*persona etc*) to support, side with; **está por limpiar** it still has to be cleaned

10: **~ sin**: **~ sin dinero** to have no money; **está sin terminar** it isn't finished yet

♦ **~se** *vr*: **se estuvo en la cama toda la tarde** he stayed in bed all afternoon

estas [ˈestas] *adj demos ver* **este²**

éstas [ˈestas] *pron ver* **éste**

estatal [estaˈtal] *adj* state *cpd*

estático, a [esˈtatiko, a] *adj* static

estatua [esˈtatwa] *nf* statue

estatura [estaˈtura] *nf* stature, height

estatuto [estaˈtuto] *nm* (*JUR*) statute; (*de ciudad*) bye-law; (*de comité*) rule

este¹ [ˈeste] *nm* east

este² [ˈeste] (*f* **esta**, *pl* **estos, estas**) *adj demos* (*sg*) this; (*pl*) these

esté *etc vb ver* **estar**

éste [ˈeste] (*f* **ésta**, *pl* **éstos, éstas**) *pron* (*sg*) this (one); (*pl*) these (ones); **ése ... ~ ...** the former ... the latter ....

estelar [esteˈlar] *adj* (*ASTRO*) stellar; (*actuación, reparto*) star (*atr*)

estén *etc vb ver* **estar**

estepa [esˈtepa] *nf* (*GEO*) steppe

estera [esˈtera] *nf* mat(ting)

estéreo [esˈtereo] *adj inv, nm* stereo; **estereotipo** *nm* stereotype

estéril [esˈteril] *adj* sterile, barren; (*fig*) vain, futile; **esterilizar** *vt* to sterilize

esterlina [esterˈlina] *adj*: **libra ~** pound sterling

estés *etc vb ver* **estar**

estética [esˈtetika] *nf* aesthetics *sg*

estético, a [esˈtetiko, a] *adj* aesthetic

estibador [estiβaˈðor] *nm* stevedore, docker

estiércol [esˈtjerkol] *nm* dung, manure

estigma [esˈtiɣma] *nm* stigma

estilarse [estiˈlarse] *vr* to be in fashion

estilo [esˈtilo] *nm* style; (*TEC*) stylus; (*NATACIÓN*) stroke; **algo por el ~** something along those lines

estima [esˈtima] *nf* esteem, respect

estimación [estimaˈθjon] *nf* (*evaluación*) estimation; (*aprecio, afecto*) esteem, regard

estimar [estiˈmar] *vt* (*evaluar*) to estimate; (*valorar*) to value; (*apreciar*) to esteem, respect; (*pensar, considerar*) to think, reckon

estimulante [estimuˈlante] *adj* stimulating ♦ *nm* stimulant

estimular [estimuˈlar] *vt* to stimulate; (*excitar*) to excite

estímulo [esˈtimulo] *nm* stimulus; (*ánimo*) encouragement

estipulación [estipulaˈθjon] *nf* stipulation, condition

estipular [estipuˈlar] *vt* to stipulate

estirado, a [estiˈraðo, a] *adj* (*tenso*) (stretched o drawn) tight; (*fig: persona*) stiff, pompous

estirar [estiˈrar] *vt* to stretch; (*dinero, suma etc*) to stretch out; **~se** *vr* to stretch

estirón [estiˈron] *nm* pull, tug; (*crecimiento*) spurt, sudden growth; **dar un ~** (*niño*) to shoot up

estirpe [esˈtirpe] *nf* stock, lineage

estival [estiˈβal] *adj* summer *cpd*

esto [ˈesto] *pron* this, this thing o matter; **~ de la boda** this business about the wedding

Estocolmo [esto'kolmo] *nm* Stockholm

estofado [esto'faðo] *nm* stew

estofar [esto'far] *vt* to stew

estómago [es'tomaɣo] *nm* stomach; **tener ~** to be thick-skinned

estorbar [estor'βar] *vt* to hinder, obstruct; (*molestar*) to bother, disturb ♦ *vi* to be in the way; **estorbo** *nm* (*molestia*) bother, nuisance; (*obstáculo*) hindrance, obstacle

estornudar [estornu'ðar] *vi* to sneeze

estos ['estos] *adj demos ver* **este²**

éstos ['estos] *pron ver* **éste**

estoy *vb ver* **estar**

estrado [es'traðo] *nm* platform

estrafalario, a [estrafa'larjo, a] *adj* odd, eccentric

estrago [es'traɣo] *nm* ruin, destruction; **hacer ~s en** to wreak havoc among

estragón [estra'ɣon] *nm* tarragon

estrambótico, a [estram'botiko, a] *adj* (*persona*) eccentric; (*peinado, ropa*) outlandish

estrangulador, a [estrangula'ðor, a] *nm/f* strangler ♦ *nm* (*TEC*) throttle; (*AUTO*) choke

estrangular [estrangu'lar] *vt* (*persona*) to strangle; (*MED*) to strangulate

estratagema [estrata'xema] *nf* (*MIL*) stratagem; (*astucia*) cunning

estrategia [estra'texja] *nf* strategy; **estratégico, a** *adj* strategic

estrato [es'trato] *nm* stratum, layer

estrechamente [es'tretʃamente] *adv* (*íntimamente*) closely, intimately; (*pobremente: vivir*) poorly

estrechar [estre'tʃar] *vt* (*reducir*) to narrow; (*COSTURA*) to take in; (*abrazar*) to hug, embrace; **~se** *vr* (*reducirse*) to narrow, grow narrow; (*abrazarse*) to embrace; **~ la mano** to shake hands

estrechez [estre'tʃeθ] *nf* narrowness; (*de ropa*) tightness; **estrecheces** *nfpl* (*dificultades económicas*) financial difficulties

estrecho, a [es'tretʃo, a] *adj* narrow; (*apretado*) tight; (*íntimo*) close, intimate; (*miserable*) mean ♦ *nm* strait; **~ de miras** narrow-minded

estrella [es'treʎa] *nf* star; **~ de mar** (*ZOOL*) starfish; **~ fugaz** shooting star; **estrellado, a** *adj* (*forma*) star-shaped; (*cielo*) starry

estrellar [estre'ʎar] *vt* (*hacer añicos*) to smash (to pieces); (*huevos*) to fry; **~se** *vr* to smash; (*chocarse*) to crash; (*fracasar*) to fail

estremecer [estreme'θer] *vt* to shake; **~se** *vr* to shake, tremble; **estremecimiento** *nm* (*temblor*) trembling, shaking

estrenar [estre'nar] *vt* (*vestido*) to wear for the first time; (*casa*) to move into; (*película, obra de teatro*) to première; **~se** *vr* (*persona*) to make one's début; **estreno** *nm* (*CINE etc*) première

estreñido, a [estre'ɲiðo, a] *adj* constipated

estreñimiento [estreɲi'mjento] *nm* constipation

estrépito [es'trepito] *nm* noise, racket; (*fig*) fuss; **estrepitoso, a** *adj* noisy; (*fiesta*) rowdy

estría [es'tria] *nf* groove

estribación [estriβa'θjon] *nf* (*GEO*) spur, foothill

estribar [estri'βar] *vi*: **~ en** to lie on

estribillo [estri'βiʎo] *nm* (*LITERATURA*) refrain; (*MUS*) chorus

estribo [es'triβo] *nm* (*de jinete*) stirrup; (*de coche, tren*) step; (*de puente*) support; (*GEO*) spur; **perder los ~s** to fly off the handle

estribor [estri'βor] *nm* (*NAUT*) starboard

estricto, a [es'trikto, a] *adj* (*riguroso*) strict; (*severo*) severe

estridente [estri'ðente] *adj* (*color*) loud; (*voz*) raucous

estropajo [estro'paxo] *nm* scourer

estropear [estrope'ar] *vt* to spoil; (*dañar*) to damage; **~se** *vr* (*objeto*) to get damaged; (*persona: la piel etc*) to be ruined

estructura [estruk'tura] *nf* structure

estruendo [es'trwendo] *nm* (*ruido*) racket, din; (*fig: alboroto*) uproar, turmoil

estrujar [estru'xar] *vt* (*apretar*) to squeeze; (*aplastar*) to crush; (*fig*) to drain, bleed

estuario [es'twarjo] *nm* estuary

estuche [es'tutʃe] *nm* box, case

estudiante [estu'ðjante] *nm/f* student; **estudiantil** *adj* student *cpd*

estudiar [estu'ðjar] *vt* to study

estudio [es'tuðjo] *nm* study; (*CINE, ARTE, RADIO*) studio; **~s** *nmpl* studies; (*erudición*) learning *sg*; **~so, a** *adj* studious

estufa [es'tufa] *nf* heater, fire

estupefaciente [estupefa'θjente] *nm* drug, narcotic

estupefacto, a [estupe'fakto, a] *adj* speechless, thunderstruck

estupendo, a [estu'pendo, a] *adj* wonderful, terrific; (*fam*) great; **~!** that's great!, fantastic!

estupidez [estupi'ðeθ] *nf* (*torpeza*) stupidity; (*acto*) stupid thing (to do)

estúpido, a [es'tupiðo, a] *adj* stupid, silly

estupor [estu'por] *nm* stupor; (*fig*) astonishment, amazement

estuve *etc vb ver* **estar**

esvástica [es'βastika] *nf* swastika

ETA ['eta] (*ESP*) *nf abr* (= *Euskadi ta Askatasuna*) ETA

etapa [e'tapa] *nf* (*de viaje*) stage; (*DEPORTE*) leg; (*parada*) stopping place; (*fase*) stage, phase

etarra [e'tarra] *nm/f* member of ETA

etc. *abr* (= *etcétera*) etc

etcétera [et'θetera] *adv* etcetera

eternidad [eterni'ðað] *nf* eternity; **eterno, a** *adj* eternal, everlasting

ética ['etika] *nf* ethics *pl*

ético, a ['etiko, a] *adj* ethical

etiqueta [eti'keta] *nf* (*modales*) etiquette; (*rótulo*) label, tag

Eucaristía [eukaris'tia] *nf* Eucharist

eufemismo [eufe'mismo] *nm* euphemism

euforia [eu'forja] *nf* euphoria

euro ['euro] *sm* (*moneda*) euro

eurodiputado, a [eurodipu'taðo, a] *nm/f* Euro MP, MEP

Europa [eu'ropa] *nf* Europe; **europeo, a** *adj, nm/f* European

Euskadi [eus'kaði] *nm* the Basque Country o Provinces *pl*

euskera [eus'kera] *nm* (*LING*) Basque

evacuación [eßakwa'θjon] *nf* evacuation

evacuar [eßa'kwar] *vt* to evacuate

evadir [eßa'ðir] *vt* to evade, avoid; **~se** *vr* to escape

evaluar [eßa'lwar] *vt* to evaluate

evangelio [eßan'xeljo] *nm* gospel

evaporar [eßapo'rar] *vt* to evaporate; **~se** *vr* to vanish

evasión [eßa'sjon] *nf* escape, flight; (*fig*) evasion; **~ de capitales** flight of capital

evasiva [eßa'sißa] *nf* (*pretexto*) excuse

evasivo, a [eßa'sißo, a] *adj* evasive, non-committal

evento [e'ßento] *nm* event

eventual [eßen'twal] *adj* possible, conditional (upon circumstances); (*trabajador*) casual, temporary

evidencia [eßi'ðenθja] *nf* evidence, proof; **evidenciar** *vt* (*hacer patente*) to make evident; (*probar*) to prove, show; **evidenciarse** *vr* to be evident

evidente [eßi'ðente] *adj* obvious, clear, evident

evitar [eßi'tar] *vt* (*evadir*) to avoid; (*impedir*) to prevent

evocar [eßo'kar] *vt* to evoke, call forth

evolución [eßolu'θjon] *nf* (*desarrollo*) evolution, development; (*cambio*) change; (*MIL*) manoeuvre; **evolucionar** *vi* to evolve; to manoeuvre

ex [eks] *adj* ex-; **el ~ ministro** the former minister, the ex-minister

exacerbar [eksaθer'ßar] *vt* to irritate, annoy

exactamente [eksakta'mente] *adv* exactly

exactitud [eksakti'tuð] *nf* exactness; (*precisión*) accuracy; (*puntualidad*) punctuality; **exacto, a** *adj* exact; accurate; punctual; **¡exacto!** exactly!

exageración [eksaxera'θjon] *nf* exaggeration

exagerar [eksaxe'rar] *vt, vi* to exaggerate

exaltado, a [eksal'taðo, a] *adj* (*apasionado*) over-excited, worked-up; (*POL*) extreme

exaltar [eksal'tar] *vt* to exalt, glorify; **~se** *vr* (*excitarse*) to get excited o worked-up

examen [ek'samen] *nm* examination

examinar [eksami'nar] *vt* to examine; **~se** *vr* to be examined, take an examination

exasperar [eksaspe'rar] *vt* to exasperate; **~se** *vr* to get exasperated, lose patience

Exca. *abr* = **Excelencia**

excavadora [ekskaßa'ðora] *nf* excavator

excavar [ekska'ßar] *vt* to excavate

excedencia [eksθe'ðenθja] *nf*: **estar en ~** to be on leave; **pedir o solicitar la ~** to ask for leave

excedente [eksθe'ðente] *adj, nm* excess, surplus

exceder [eksθe'ðer] *vt* to exceed, surpass; **~se** *vr* (*extralimitarse*) to go too far

excelencia [eksθe'lenθja] *nf* excellence; **E~** Excellency; **excelente** *adj* excellent

excentricidad [eksθentriθi'ðað] *nf* eccentricity; **excéntrico, a** *adj, nm/f* eccentric

excepción [eksθep'θjon] *nf* exception; **excepcional** *adj* exceptional

excepto [eks'θepto] *adv* excepting, except (for)

exceptuar [eksθep'twar] *vt* to except, exclude

excesivo, a [eksθe'sißo, a] *adj* excessive

exceso [eks'θeso] *nm* (*gen*) excess; (*COM*) surplus; **~ de equipaje/peso** excess luggage/weight

excitación [eksθita'θjon] *nf* (*sensación*) excitement; (*acción*) excitation

excitado, a [eksθi'taðo, a] *adj* excited; (*emociones*) aroused

excitar [eksθi'tar] *vt* to excite; (*incitar*) to urge; **~se** *vr* to get excited

exclamación [eksklama'θjon] *nf* exclamation

exclamar [ekskla'mar] *vi* to exclaim

excluir [eksklu'ir] *vt* to exclude; (*dejar fuera*) to shut out; (*descartar*) to reject; **exclusión** *nf* exclusion

exclusiva [eksklu'sißa] *nf* (*PRENSA*) exclusive, scoop; (*COM*) sole right

exclusivo, a [eksklu'sißo, a] *adj* exclusive; **derecho ~** sole o exclusive right

Excmo. *abr* = **excelentísimo**

excomulgar [ekskomul'xar] *vt* (*REL*) to excommunicate

excomunión [ekskomu'njon] *nf* excommunication

excursión [ekskur'sjon] *nf* excursion, outing; **excursionista** *nm/f* (*turista*) sightseer

excusa [eks'kusa] *nf* excuse; (*disculpa*) apology

excusar [eksku'sar] *vt* to excuse; **~se** *vr*
(*disculparse*) to apologize

exhalar [eksa'lar] *vt* to exhale, breathe out;
(*olor etc*) to give off; (*suspiro*) to breathe,
heave

exhaustivo, a [eksaus'tiβo, a] *adj* (*análisis*)
thorough; (*estudio*) exhaustive

exhausto, a [ek'sausto, a] *adj* exhausted

exhibición [eksiβi'θjon] *nf* exhibition,
display, show

exhibir [eksi'βir] *vt* to exhibit, display, show

exhortar [eksor'tar] *vt*: **~ a** to exhort to

exigencia [eksi'xenθja] *nf* demand,
requirement; **exigente** *adj* demanding

exigir [eksi'xir] *vt* (*gen*) to demand, require;
~ el pago to demand payment

exiliado, a [eksi'ljaðo, a] *adj* exiled ♦ *nm/f*
exile

exilio [ek'siljo] *nm* exile

eximir [eksi'mir] *vt* to exempt

existencia [eksis'tenθja] *nf* existence; **~s** *nfpl*
stock(s) (*pl*)

existir [eksis'tir] *vi* to exist, be

éxito ['eksito] *nm* (*triunfo*) success; (*MUS etc*)
hit; **tener ~** to be successful

exonerar [eksone'rar] *vt* to exonerate; **~ de
una obligación** to free from an obligation

exorbitante [eksorβi'tante] *adj* (*precio*)
exorbitant; (*cantidad*) excessive

exorcizar [eksorθi'θar] *vt* to exorcize

exótico, a [ek'sotiko, a] *adj* exotic

expandir [ekspan'dir] *vt* to expand

expansión [ekspan'sjon] *nf* expansion

expansivo, a [ekspan'siβo, a] *adj*: **onda ~a**
shock wave

expatriarse [ekspa'trjarse] *vr* to emigrate;
(*POL*) to go into exile

expectativa [ekspekta'tiβa] *nf* (*espera*)
expectation; (*perspectiva*) prospect

expedición [ekspeði'θjon] *nf* (*excursión*)
expedition

expediente [ekspe'ðjente] *nm* expedient;
(*JUR: procedimento*) action, proceedings *pl*;
(: *papeles*) dossier, file, record

expedir [ekspe'ðir] *vt* (*despachar*) to send,
forward; (*pasaporte*) to issue

expendedor, a [ekspende'ðor, a] *nm/f*
(*vendedor*) dealer

expensas [eks'pensas] *nfpl*: **a ~ de** at the
expense of

experiencia [ekspe'rjenθja] *nf* experience

experimentado, a [eksperimen'taðo, a]
adj experienced

experimentar [eksperimen'tar] *vt* (*en
laboratorio*) to experiment with; (*probar*) to
test, try out; (*notar, observar*) to experience;
(*deterioro, pérdida*) to suffer; **experimento**
nm experiment

experto, a [eks'perto, a] *adj* expert, skilled

♦ *nm/f* expert

expiar [ekspi'ar] *vt* to atone for

expirar [ekspi'rar] *vi* to expire

explanada [ekspla'naða] *nf* (*llano*) plain

explayarse [ekspla'jarse] *vr* (*en discurso*) to
speak at length; **~ con uno** to confide in sb

explicación [eksplika'θjon] *nf* explanation

explicar [ekspli'kar] *vt* to explain; **~se** *vr* to
explain (o.s.)

explícito, a [eks'pliθito, a] *adj* explicit

explique *etc vb ver* **explicar**

explorador, a [eksplora'ðor, a] *nm/f*
(*pionero*) explorer; (*MIL*) scout ♦ *nm* (*MED*)
probe; (*TEC*) (*radar*) scanner

explorar [eksplo'rar] *vt* to explore; (*MED*) to
probe; (*radar*) to scan

explosión [eksplo'sjon] *nf* explosion;
explosivo, a *adj* explosive

explotación [eksplota'θjon] *nf* exploitation;
(*de planta etc*) running

explotar [eksplo'tar] *vt* to exploit; to run,
operate ♦ *vi* to explode

exponer [ekspo'ner] *vt* to expose; (*cuadro*)
to display; (*vida*) to risk; (*idea*) to explain;
~se *vr*: **~se a (hacer) algo** to run the risk of
(doing) sth

exportación [eksporta'θjon] *nf* (*acción*)
export; (*mercancías*) exports *pl*

exportar [ekspor'tar] *vt* to export

exposición [eksposi'θjon] *nf* (*gen*)
exposure; (*de arte*) show, exhibition;
(*explicación*) explanation; (*declaración*)
account, statement

expresamente [ekspresa'mente] *adv* (*decir*)
clearly; (*a propósito*) expressly

expresar [ekspre'sar] *vt* to express;
expresión *nf* expression

expresivo, a [ekspre'siβo, a] *adj* (*persona,
gesto, palabras*) expressive; (*cariñoso*)
affectionate

expreso, a [eks'preso, a] *pp de* **expresar**
♦ *adj* (*explícito*) express; (*claro*) specific,
clear; (*tren*) fast ♦ *adv*: **mandar ~** to send by
express (delivery)

express [eks'pres] (*AM*) *adv*: **enviar algo ~** to
send sth special delivery

exprimidor [eksprimi'ðor] *nm* squeezer

exprimir [ekspri'mir] *vt* (*fruta*) to squeeze;
(*zumo*) to squeeze out

expropiar [ekspro'pjar] *vt* to expropriate

expuesto, a [eks'pwesto, a] *pp de* **exponer**
♦ *adj* exposed; (*cuadro etc*) on show, on
display

expulsar [ekspul'sar] *vt* (*echar*) to eject,
throw out; (*alumno*) to expel; (*despedir*) to
sack, fire; (*DEPORTE*) to send off; **expulsión**
nf expulsion; sending-off

exquisito, a [ekski'sito, a] *adj* exquisite;
(*comida*) delicious

éxtasis ['ekstasis] nm ecstasy

extender [eksten'der] vt to extend; (los brazos) to stretch out, hold out; (mapa, tela) to spread (out), open (out); (mantequilla) to spread; (certificado) to issue; (cheque, recibo) to make out; (documento) to draw up; **~se** vr (gen) to extend; (persona: en el suelo) to stretch out; (epidemia) to spread;
extendido, a adj (abierto) spread out, open; (brazos) outstretched; (costumbre) widespread

extensión [eksten'sjon] nf (de terreno, mar) expanse, stretch; (de tiempo) length, duration; (TEL) extension; **en toda la ~ de la palabra** in every sense of the word

extenso, a [eks'tenso, a] adj extensive

extenuar [ekste'nwar] vt (debilitar) to weaken

exterior [ekste'rjor] adj (de fuera) external; (afuera) outside, exterior; (apariencia) outward; (deuda, relaciones) foreign ♦ nm (gen) exterior, outside; (aspecto) outward appearance; (DEPORTE) wing(er); (países extranjeros) abroad; **en el ~** abroad; **al ~** outwardly, on the surface

exterminar [ekstermi'nar] vt to exterminate; **exterminio** nm extermination

externo, a [eks'terno, a] adj (exterior) external, outside; (superficial) outward ♦ nm/f day pupil

extinguir [ekstin'gir] vt (fuego) to extinguish, put out; (raza, población) to wipe out; **~se** vr (fuego) to go out; (BIO) to die out, become extinct

extinto, a [eks'tinto, a] adj extinct

extintor [ekstin'tor] nm (fire) extinguisher

extirpar [ekstir'par] vt (MED) to remove (surgically)

extorsión [ekstor'sjon] nf extortion

extra ['ekstra] adj inv (tiempo) extra; (chocolate, vino) good-quality ♦ nm/f extra ♦ nm extra; (bono) bonus

extracción [ekstrak'θjon] nf extraction; (en lotería) draw

extracto [eks'trakto] nm extract

extradición [ekstraði'θjon] nf extradition

extraer [ekstra'er] vt to extract, take out

extraescolar [ekstraesko'lar] adj: **actividad ~** extracurricular activity

extralimitarse [ekstralimi'tarse] vr to go too far

extranjero, a [ekstran'xero, a] adj foreign ♦ nm/f foreigner ♦ nm foreign countries pl; **en el ~** abroad

extrañar [ekstra'nar] vt (sorprender) to find strange o odd; (echar de menos) to miss; **~se** vr (sorprenderse) to be amazed, be surprised

extrañeza [ekstra'neθa] nf (rareza) strangeness, oddness; (asombro) amazement,

surprise

extraño, a [eks'traɲo, a] adj (extranjero) foreign; (raro, sorprendente) strange, odd

extraordinario, a [ekstraorði'narjo, a] adj extraordinary; (edición, número) special ♦ nm (de periódico) special edition; **horas extraordinarias** overtime sg

extrarradio [ekstra'rraðjo] nm suburbs

extravagancia [ekstraßa'vanθja] nf oddness; outlandishness; **extravagante** adj (excéntrico) eccentric; (estrafalario) outlandish

extraviado, a [ekstra'ßjaðo, a] adj lost, missing

extraviar [ekstra'ßjar] vt (persona: desorientar) to mislead, misdirect; (perder) to lose, misplace; **~se** vr to lose one's way, get lost; **extravío** nm loss; (fig) deviation

extremar [ekstre'mar] vt to carry to extremes; **~se** vr to do one's utmost, make every effort

extremaunción [ekstremaun'θjon] nf extreme unction

extremidad [ekstremi'ðað] nf (punta) extremity; **~es** nfpl (ANAT) extremities

extremo, a [eks'tremo, a] adj extreme; (último) last ♦ nm end; (límite, grado sumo) extreme; **en último ~** as a last resort

extrovertido, a [ekstroßer'tiðo, a] adj, nm/f extrovert

exuberancia [eksuße'ranθja] nf exuberance; **exuberante** adj exuberant; (fig) luxuriant, lush

eyacular [ejaku'lar] vt, vi to ejaculate

F, f

f.a.b. abr (= franco a bordo) f.o.b.

fabada [fa'ßaða] nf bean and sausage stew

fábrica ['faßrika] nf factory; **marca de ~** trademark; **precio de ~** factory price

fabricación [faßrika'θjon] nf (manufactura) manufacture; (producción) production; **de ~ casera** home-made; **~ en serie** mass production

fabricante [faßri'kante] nm/f manufacturer

fabricar [faßri'kar] vt (manufacturar) to manufacture, make; (construir) to build; (cuento) to fabricate, devise

fábula ['faßula] nf (cuento) fable; (chisme) rumour; (mentira) fib

fabuloso, a [faßu'loso, a] adj (oportunidad, tiempo) fabulous, great

facción [fak'θjon] nf (POL) faction; **facciones** nfpl (del rostro) features

faceta [fa'θeta] nf facet

facha ['fatʃa] nf (fam) (aspecto) look; (cara) look

fachada [fa'tʃaða] nf (ARQ) façade, front

fácil ['faθil] *adj* (*simple*) easy; (*probable*) likely

facilidad [faθili'ðað] *nf* (*capacidad*) ease; (*sencillez*) simplicity; (*de palabra*) fluency; **~es** *nfpl* facilities

facilitar [faθili'tar] *vt* (*hacer fácil*) to make easy; (*proporcionar*) to provide

fácilmente |faθil'mente| *adv* easily

facsímil [fak'simil] *nm* facsimile, fax

factible [fak'tiβle] *adj* feasible

factor [fak'tor] *nm* factor

factura [fak'tura] *nf* (*cuenta*) bill; **facturación** *nf* (*de equipaje*) check-in; **facturar** *vt* (*COM*) to invoice, charge for; (*equipaje*) to check in

facultad [fakul'tað] *nf* (*aptitud, ESCOL etc*) faculty; (*poder*) power

faena [fa'ena] *nf* (*trabajo*) work; (*quehacer*) task, job

faisán [fai'san] *nm* pheasant

faja ['faxa] *nf* (*para la cintura*) sash; (*de mujer*) corset; (*de tierra*) strip

fajo ['faxo] *nm* (*de papeles*) bundle; (*de billetes*) wad

falacia [fa'laθja] *nf* fallacy

falda ['falda] *nf* (*prenda de vestir*) skirt

falla ['faʎa] *nf* (*defecto*) fault, flaw

fallar [fa'ʎar] *vt* (*JUR*) to pronounce sentence on ♦ *vi* (*memoria*) to fail; (*motor*) to miss

fallecer [faʎe'θer] *vi* to pass away, die; **fallecimiento** *nm* decease, demise

fallido, a [fa'ʎiðo, a] *adj* (*gen*) frustrated, unsuccessful

fallo ['faʎo] *nm* (*JUR*) verdict, ruling; (*fracaso*) failure; **~ cardíaco** heart failure

falsedad [false'ðað] *nf* falseness; (*hipocresía*) hypocrisy; (*mentira*) falsehood

falsificar [falsifi'kar] *vt* (*firma etc*) to forge; (*moneda*) to counterfeit

falso, a ['falso, a] *adj* false; (*documento, moneda etc*) fake; **en ~** falsely

falta ['falta] *nf* (*defecto*) fault, flaw; (*privación*) lack, want; (*ausencia*) absence; (*carencia*) shortage; (*equivocación*) mistake; (*DEPORTE*) foul; **echar en ~** to miss; **hacer ~** hacer algo to be necessary to do sth; **me hace ~ una pluma** I need a pen; **~ de educación** bad manners *pl*

faltar [fal'tar] *vi* (*escasear*) to be lacking, be wanting; (*ausentarse*) to be absent, be missing; **faltan 2 horas para llegar** there are 2 hours to go till arrival; **~ al respeto a uno** to be disrespectful to sb; **¡no faltaba más!** (*no hay de qué*) don't mention it

fama ['fama] *nf* (*renombre*) fame; (*reputación*) reputation

famélico, a |fa'meliko, a| *adj* starving

familia [fa'milja] *nf* family; **~ política** in-laws *pl*

familiar [fami'ljar] *adj* (*relativo a la familia*) family *cpd*; (*conocido, informal*) familiar ♦ *nm* relative, relation; **~idad** *nf* (*gen*) familiarity; (*informalidad*) homeliness; **~izarse** *vr:* **~izarse con** to familiarize o.s. with

famoso, a [fa'moso, a] *adj* (*renombrado*) famous

fanático, a [fa'natiko, a] *adj* fanatical ♦ *nm/f* fanatic; (*CINE, DEPORTE*) fan; **fanatismo** *nm* fanaticism

fanfarrón, ona [fanfa'rron, ona] *adj* boastful

fango ['fango] *nm* mud; **~so, a** *adj* muddy

fantasía [fanta'sia] *nf* fantasy, imagination; **joyas de ~** imitation jewellery *sg*

fantasma [fan'tasma] *nm* (*espectro*) ghost, apparition; (*fanfarrón*) show-off

fantástico, a [fan'tastiko, a] *adj* fantastic

farmacéutico, a [farma'θeutiko, a] *adj* pharmaceutical ♦ *nm/f* chemist (*BRIT*), pharmacist

farmacia [far'maθja] *nf* chemist's (shop) (*BRIT*), pharmacy; **~ de turno** duty chemist; **~ de guardia** all-night chemist

fármaco ['farmako] *nm* drug

faro ['faro] *nm* (*NAUT: torre*) lighthouse; (*AUTO*) headlamp; **~s antiniebla** fog lamps; **~s delanteros/traseros** headlights/rear lights

farol [fa'rol] *nm* lantern, lamp

farola [fa'rola] *nf* street lamp (*BRIT*) o light (*US*)

farsa ['farsa] *nf* (*gen*) farce

farsante [far'sante] *nm/f* fraud, fake

fascículo [fas'θikulo] *nm* (*de revista*) part, instalment

fascinar [fasθi'nar] *vt* (*gen*) to fascinate

fascismo [fas'θismo] *nm* fascism; **fascista** *adj, nm/f* fascist

fase ['fase] *nf* phase

fastidiar [fasti'ðjar] *vt* (*molestar*) to annoy, bother; (*estropear*) to spoil; **~se** *vr:* **¡que se fastidie!** (*fam*) he'll just have to put up with it!

fastidio [fas'tiðjo] *nm* (*molestia*) annoyance; **~so, a** *adj* (*molesto*) annoying

fastuoso, a |fas'twoso, a| *adj* (*banquete, boda*) lavish; (*acto*) pompous

fatal |fa'tal| *adj* (*gen*) fatal; (*desgraciado*) ill-fated; (*fam: malo, pésimo*) awful; **~idad** *nf* (*destino*) fate; (*mala suerte*) misfortune

fatiga [fa'tiɣa] *nf* (*cansancio*) fatigue, weariness

fatigar [fati'ɣar] *vt* to tire, weary; **~se** *vr* to get tired

fatigoso, a [fati'ɣoso, a] *adj* (*cansador*) tiring

fatuo, a ['fatwo, a] *adj* (*vano*) fatuous; (*presuntuoso*) conceited

favor [fa'ßor] *nm* favour; **estar a ~ de** to be in favour of; **haga el ~ de...** would you be so good as to..., kindly...; **por ~** please; **~able** *adj* favourable

favorecer [faβore'θer] vt to favour; (*vestido etc*) to become, flatter; **este peinado le favorece** this hairstyle suits him

favorito, a [faβo'rito, a] adj, nm/f favourite

fax [faks] nm inv fax; **mandar por ~ to** fax

faz [faθ] nf face; **la ~ de la tierra** the face of the earth

fe [fe] nf (*REL*) faith; (*documento*) certificate; **prestar ~ a** to believe, credit; **actuar con buena/mala ~** to act in good/bad faith; **dar ~ de** to bear witness to

fealdad [feal'daδ] nf ugliness

febrero [fe'ßrero] nm February

febril [fe'ßril] adj (*fig: actividad*) hectic; (*mente, mirada*) feverish

fecha ['fetʃa] nf date; **~ de caducidad** (*de producto alimenticio*) sell-by date; (*de contrato etc*) expiry date; **con ~ adelantada** postdated; **en ~ próxima** soon; **hasta la ~** to date, so far; **poner ~** to date; **fechar** vt to date

fecundar [fekun'dar] vt (*generar*) to fertilize, make fertile; **fecundo, a** adj (*fértil*) fertile; (*fig*) prolific; (*productivo*) productive

federación [feδera'θjon] nf federation

felicidad [feliθi'δaδ] nf happiness; **~es** nfpl (*felicitaciones*) best wishes, congratulations

felicitación [feliθita'θjon] nf: **¡felicitaciones!** congratulations!

felicitar [feliθi'tar] vt to congratulate

feligrés, esa [feli'xres, esa] nm/f parishioner

feliz [fe'liθ] adj happy

felpudo [fel'puδo] nm doormat

femenino, a [feme'nino, a] adj, nm feminine

feminista [femi'nista] adj, nm/f feminist

fenómeno [fe'nomeno] nm phenomenon; (*fig*) freak, accident ♦ adj great ♦ excl great!, marvellous!; **fenomenal** adj = **fenómeno**

feo, a ['feo, a] adj (*gen*) ugly; (*desagradable*) bad, nasty

féretro ['feretro] nm (*ataúd*) coffin; (*sarcófago*) bier

feria ['ferja] nf (*gen*) fair; (*descanso*) holiday, rest day; (*AM: mercado*) village market; (: *cambio*) loose o small change

fermentar [fermen'tar] vi to ferment

ferocidad [feroθi'δaδ] nf fierceness, ferocity

feroz [fe'roθ] adj (*cruel*) cruel; (*salvaje*) fierce

férreo, a ['ferreo, a] adj iron

ferretería [ferrete'ria] nf (*tienda*) ironmonger's (shop) (*BRIT*), hardware store

ferrocarril [ferroka'rril] nm railway

ferroviario, a [ferro'ßjarjo, a] adj rail cpd

fértil ['fertil] adj (*productivo*) fertile; (*rico*) rich; **fertilidad** nf (*gen*) fertility; (*productividad*) fruitfulness

ferviente [fer'ßjente] adj fervent

fervor [fer'ßor] nm fervour; **~oso, a** adj fervent

festejar [feste'xar] vt (*celebrar*) to celebrate

festejo [fes'texo] nm celebration; **festejos** nmpl (*fiestas*) festivals

festín [fes'tin] nm feast, banquet

festival [festi'ßal] nm festival

festividad [festißi'δaδ] nf festivity

festivo, a [fes'tißo, a] adj (*de fiesta*) festive; (*CINE, LITERATURA*) humorous; **día ~** holiday

fétido, a ['fetiδo, a] adj foul-smelling

feto ['feto] nm foetus

fiable ['fjaßle] adj (*persona*) trustworthy; (*máquina*) reliable

fiador, a [fia'δor, a] nm/f (*JUR*) surety, guarantor; (*COM*) backer; **salir ~ por uno** to stand bail for sb

fiambre ['fjambre] nm cold meat

fianza ['fjanθa] nf surety; (*JUR*): **libertad bajo ~** release on bail

fiar [fi'ar] vt (*salir garante de*) to guarantee; (*vender a crédito*) to sell on credit; (*secreto*) **~ a** to confide (to) ♦ vi to trust; **~se** vr to trust (in), rely on; **~se de uno** to rely on sb

fibra ['fißra] nf fibre; **~ óptica** optical fibre

ficción [fik'θjon] nf fiction

ficha ['fitʃa] nf (*TEL*) token; (*en juegos*) counter, marker; (*tarjeta*) (index) card; **fichar** vt (*archivar*) to file, index; (*DEPORTE*) to sign; **estar fichado** to have a record; **fichero** nm box file; (*INFORM*) file

ficticio, a [fik'tiθjo, a] adj (*imaginario*) fictitious; (*falso*) fabricated

fidelidad [fiδeli'δaδ] nf (*lealtad*) fidelity, loyalty; **alta ~** high fidelity, hi-fi

fideos [fi'δeos] nmpl noodles

fiebre ['fjeßre] nf (*MED*) fever; (*fig*) fever, excitement; **~ amarilla/del heno** yellow/hay fever; **~ palúdica** malaria; **tener ~** to have a temperature

fiel [fjel] adj (*leal*) faithful, loyal; (*fiable*) reliable; (*exacto*) accurate, faithful ♦ nm: **los ~es** the faithful

fieltro [fjeltro] nm felt

fiera ['fjera] nf (*animal feroz*) wild animal o beast; (*fig*) dragon; *ver tb* **fiero**

fiero, a ['fjero, a] adj (*cruel*) cruel; (*feroz*) fierce; (*duro*) harsh

fiesta ['fjesta] nf party; (*de pueblo*) festival; (*vacaciones, tb: ~s*) holiday sg; (*REL*): **~ de guardar** day of obligation

figura [fi'ɣura] nf (*gen*) figure; (*forma, imagen*) shape, form; (*NAIPES*) face card

figurar [fiɣu'rar] vt (*representar*) to represent; (*fingir*) to figure ♦ vi to figure; **~se** vr (*imaginarse*) to imagine; (*suponer*) to suppose

fijador [fixa'δor] nm (*FOTO etc*) fixative; (*de pelo*) gel

fijar [fi'xar] vt (*gen*) to fix; (*estampilla*) to affix, stick (on); **~se** vr: **~se en** to notice

fijo, a ['fixo, a] adj (*gen*) fixed; (*firme*) firm;

(*permanente*) permanent ♦ *adv*: **mirar ~ to stare**

fila ['fila] *nf* row; (*MIL*) rank; **ponerse en ~ to line up, get into line**

filántropo, a [fi'lantropo, a] *nm/f* philanthropist

filatelia [fila'telja] *nf* philately, stamp collecting

filete [fi'lete] *nm* (*carne*) fillet steak; (*pescado*) fillet

filiación [filja'θjon] *nf* (*POL*) affiliation

filial [fi'ljal] *adj* filial ♦ *nf* subsidiary

Filipinas [fili'pinas] *nfpl*: **las ~ the Philippines; filipino, a** *adj, nm/f* Philippine

filmar [fil'mar] *vt* to film, shoot

filo ['filo] *nm* (*gen*) edge; **sacar ~ a to sharpen; al ~ del mediodía at about midday; de doble ~** double-edged

filón [fi'lon] *nm* (*MINERÍA*) vein, lode; (*fig*) goldmine

filosofía [filoso'fia] *nf* philosophy; **filósofo, a** *nm/f* philosopher

filtrar [fil'trar] *vt, vi* to filter, strain; **~se** *vr* to filter; **filtro** *nm* (*TEC, utensilio*) filter

fin [fin] *nm* end; (*objetivo*) aim, purpose; **al ~ y al cabo** when all's said and done; **a ~ de** in order to; **por ~** finally; **en ~** in short; **~ de semana** weekend

final [fi'nal] *adj* final ♦ *nm* end, conclusion ♦ *nf* final; **~idad** *nf* (*propósito*) purpose, intention; **~ista** *nm/f* finalist; **~izar** *vt* to end, finish; (*INFORM*) to log out o off ♦ *vi* to end, come to an end

financiar [finan'θjar] *vt* to finance; **financiero, a** [finan'θjero, a] *adj* financial ♦ *nm/f* financier

finca ['finka] *nf* (*bien inmueble*) property, land; (*casa de campo*) country house; (*AM*) farm

fingir [fin'xir] *vt* (*simular*) to simulate, feign ♦ *vi* (*aparentar*) to pretend

finlandés, esa [finlan'des, esa] *adj* Finnish ♦ *nm/f* Finn ♦ *nm* (*LING*) Finnish

Finlandia [fin'landja] *nf* Finland

fino, a ['fino, a] *adj* fine; (*delgado*) slender; (*de buenas maneras*) polite, refined; (*jerez*) fino, dry

firma ['firma] *nf* signature; (*COM*) firm, company

firmamento [firma'mento] *nm* firmament

firmar [fir'mar] *vt* to sign

firme ['firme] *adj* firm; (*estable*) stable; (*sólido*) solid; (*constante*) steady; (*decidido*) resolute ♦ *nm* road (surface); **~mente** *adv* firmly; **~za** *nf* firmness; (*constancia*) steadiness; (*solidez*) solidity

fiscal [fis'kal] *adj* fiscal ♦ *nm/f* public prosecutor; **año ~** tax o fiscal year

fisco ['fisko] *nm* (*hacienda*) treasury, exchequer (*BRIT*)

fisgar [fis'var] *vt* to pry into

fisgonear [fisvone'ar] *vt* to poke one's nose into ♦ *vi* to pry, spy

física ['fisika] *nf* physics *sg; ver tb* **físico**

físico, a ['fisiko, a] *adj* physical ♦ *nm* physique ♦ *nm/f* physicist

fisura [fi'sura] *nf* crack; (*MED*) fracture

flác(c)ido, a [‖'fla(k)θido, a] *adj* flabby

flaco, a ['flako, a] *adj* (*muy delgado*) skinny, thin; (*débil*) weak, feeble

flagrante [fla'vrante] *adj* flagrant

flamante [fla'mante] (*fam*) *adj* brilliant; (*nuevo*) brand-new

flamenco, a [fla'menko, a] *adj* (*de Flandes*) Flemish; (*baile, música*) flamenco ♦ *nm* (*baile, música*) flamenco

flan [flan] *nm* creme caramel

flaqueza [fla'keθa] *nf* (*delgadez*) thinness, leanness; (*fig*) weakness

flash [flaʃ] (*pl* **~s** o **~es**) *nm* (*FOTO*) flash

flauta ['flauta] *nf* (*MUS*) flute

flecha ['fletʃa] *nf* arrow

flechazo [fle'tʃaθo] *nm* love at first sight

fleco ['fleko] *nm* fringe

flema ['flema] *nm* phlegm

flequillo [fle'kiʎo] *nm* (*pelo*) fringe

flexible [flek'sißle] *adj* flexible

flexión [flek'sjon] *nf* press-up

flexo ['flekso] *nm* adjustable table-lamp

flojera [flo'xera] (*AM: fam*) *nf*: **me da ~ I** can't be bothered

flojo, a ['floxo, a] *adj* (*gen*) loose; (*sin fuerzas*) limp; (*débil*) weak

flor [flor] *nf* flower; **a ~ de on the surface of; ~ecer** *vi* (*BOT*) to flower, bloom; (*fig*) to flourish; **~eciente** *adj* (*BOT*) in flower, flowering; (*fig*) thriving; **~ero** *nm* vase; **~istería** *nf* florist's (shop)

flota ['flota] *nf* fleet

flotador [flota'ðor] *nm* (*gen*) float; (*para nadar*) rubber ring

flotar [flo'tar] *vi* (*gen*) to float; **flote** *nm*: **a flote** afloat; **salir a flote** (*fig*) to get back on one's feet

fluctuar [fluk'twar] *vi* (*oscilar*) to fluctuate

fluidez [flui'ðeθ] *nf* fluidity; (*fig*) fluency

flúido, a ['fluiðo, a] *adj, nm* fluid

fluir [flu'ir] *vi* to flow

flujo ['fluxo] *nm* flow; **~ y reflujo** ebb and flow

flúor ['fluor] *nm* fluoride

fluvial [flußi'al] *adj* (*navegación, cuenca*) fluvial, river *cpd*

foca ['foka] *nf* seal

foco ['foko] *nm* focus; (*ELEC*) floodlight; (*AM*) (light) bulb

fofo, a [‖'fofo, a] *adj* soft, spongy; (*carnes*) flabby

fogata [fo'vata] *nf* bonfire

fogón [fo'ɣon] nm (de cocina) ring, burner

fogoso, a [fo'ɣoso, a] adj spirited

folio ['foljo] nm folio, page

follaje [fo'ʎaxe] nm foliage

folletín [foʎe'tin] nm newspaper serial

folleto [fo'ʎeto] nm (POL) pamphlet

follón [fo'ʎon] (fam) nm (lío) mess; (conmoción) fuss; **armar un ~** to kick up a row

fomentar [fomen'tar] vt (MED) to foment; **fomento** nm (promoción) promotion

fonda ['fonda] nf inn

fondo ['fondo] nm (de mar) bottom; (de coche, sala) back; (ARTE etc) background; (reserva) fund; **~s** nmpl (COM) funds, resources; **una investigación a ~** a thorough investigation; **en el ~** at bottom, deep down

fonobuzón [fonoßu'θon] nm voice mail

fontanería [fontane'ria] nf plumbing; **fontanero, a** nm/f plumber

footing ['futin] nm jogging; **hacer ~** to jog, go jogging

forastero, a [foras'tero, a] nm/f stranger

forcejear [forθexe'ar] vi (luchar) to struggle

forense [fo'rense] nm/f pathologist

forjar [for'xar] vt to forge

forma ['forma] nf (figura) form, shape; (MED) fitness; (método) way, means; **las ~s** the conventions; **estar en ~** to be fit

formación [forma'θjon] nf (gen) formation; (educación) education; **~ profesional** vocational training

formal [for'mal] adj (gen) formal; (fig: serio) serious; (: de fiar) reliable; **~idad** nf formality; seriousness; **~izar** vt (JUR) to formalize; (situación) to put in order, regularize; **~izarse** vr (situación) to be put in order, be regularized

formar [for'mar] vt (componer) to form, shape; (constituir) to make up, constitute; (ESCOL) to train, educate; **~se** vr (ESCOL) to be trained, educated; (cobrar forma) to form, take form; (desarrollarse) to develop

formatear [formate'ar] vt to format

formativo, a [forma'tiβo, a] adj (lecturas, años) formative

formato [for'mato] nm format

formidable [formi'ðaßle] adj (temible) formidable; (estupendo) tremendous

fórmula ['formula] nf formula

formular [formu'lar] vt (queja) to make, lodge; (petición) to draw up; (pregunta) to pose

formulario [formu'larjo] nm form

fornido, a [for'niðo, a] adj well-built

forrar [fo'rrar] vt (abrigo) to line; (libro) to cover; **forro** nm (de cuaderno) cover; (COSTURA) lining; (de sillón) upholstery

fortalecer [fortale'θer] vt to strengthen

fortaleza [forta'leθa] nf (MIL) fortress,

stronghold; (fuerza) strength; (determinación) resolution

fortuito, a [for'twito, a] adj accidental

fortuna [for'tuna] nf (suerte) fortune, (good) luck; (riqueza) fortune, wealth

forzar [for'θar] vt (puerta) to force (open); (compeler) to compel

forzoso, a [for'θoso, a] adj necessary

fosa ['fosa] nf (sepultura) grave; (en tierra) pit; **~s nasales** nostrils

fósforo ['fosforo] nm (QUÍM) phosphorus; (cerilla) match

foso ['foso] nm ditch; (TEATRO) pit; (AUTO): **~ de reconocimiento** inspection pit

foto ['foto] nf photo, snap(shot); **sacar una ~** to take a photo o picture

fotocopia [foto'kopja] nf photocopy; **fotocopiadora** nf photocopier; **fotocopiar** vt to photocopy

fotografía [fotoɣra'fia] nf (ARTE) photography; (una ~) photograph; **fotografiar** vt to photograph

fotógrafo, a [fo'toɣrafo, a] nm/f photographer

fracasar [fraka'sar] vi (gen) to fail

fracaso [fra'kaso] nm failure

fracción [frak'θjon] nf fraction; **fraccionamiento** nm (AM) housing estate

fractura [frak'tura] nf fracture, break

fragancia [fra'ɣanθja] nf (olor) fragrance, perfume

frágil ['fraxil] adj (débil) fragile; (COM) breakable

fragmento [fraɣ'mento] nm (pedazo) fragment

fragua ['fraɣwa] nf forge; **fraguar** vt to forge; (fig) to concoct ♦ vi to harden

fraile ['fraile] nm (REL) friar; (: monje) monk

frambuesa [fram'bwesa] nf raspberry

francamente adv (hablar, decir) frankly; (realmente) really

francés, esa [fran'θes, esa] adj French ♦ nm/f Frenchman/woman ♦ nm (LING) French

Francia ['franθja] nf France

franco, a ['franko, a] adj (cándido) frank, open; (COM: exento) free ♦ nm (moneda) franc

francotirador, a [frankotira'ðor, a] nm/f sniper

franela [fra'nela] nf flannel

franja ['franxa] nf fringe

franquear [franke'ar] vt (camino) to clear; (carta, paquete postal) to frank, stamp; (obstáculo) to overcome

franqueo [fran'keo] nm postage

franqueza [fran'keθa] nf (candor) frankness

frasco ['frasko] nm bottle, flask; **~ al vacío** (vacuum) flask

frase ['frase] nf sentence; ~ **hecha** set phrase; (pey) stock phrase

fraterno, a [fra'terno, a] adj brotherly, fraternal

fraude ['frauðe] nm (cualidad) dishonesty; (acto) fraud; **fraudulento, a** adj fraudulent

frazada [fra'saða] (AM) nf blanket

frecuencia [fre'kwenθja] nf frequency; **con ~** frequently, often

frecuentar [frekwen'tar] vt to frequent

fregadero [freɣa'ðero] nm (kitchen) sink

fregar [fre'ɣar] vt (frotar) to scrub; (platos) to wash (up); (AM) to annoy

fregona [fre'ɣona] nf mop

freír [fre'ir] vt to fry

frenar [fre'nar] vt to brake; (fig) to check

frenazo [fre'naθo] nm: **dar un ~** to brake sharply

frenesí [frene'si] nm frenzy; **frenético, a** adj frantic

freno ['freno] nm (TEC, AUTO) brake; (de cabalgadura) bit; (fig) check

frente ['frente] nm (ARQ, POL) front; (de objeto) front part ♦ nf forehead, brow; ~ **a** in front of; (en situación opuesta de) opposite; **al ~ de** (fig) at the head of; **chocar de ~** to crash head-on; **hacer ~ a** to face up to

fresa ['fresa] (ESP) nf strawberry

fresco, a ['fresko, a] adj (nuevo) fresh; (frío) cool; (descarado) cheeky ♦ nm (aire) fresh air; (ARTE) fresco; (AM: jugo) fruit drink ♦ nm/f (fam): **ser un ~** to have a nerve; **tomar el ~** to get some fresh air; **frescura** nf freshness; (descaro) cheek, nerve

frialdad [frial'dað] nf (gen) coldness; (indiferencia) indifference

fricción [frik'θjon] nf (gen) friction; (acto) rub(bing); (MED) massage

frigidez [frixi'ðeθ] nf frigidity

frigorífico [friɣo'rifiko] nm refrigerator

frijol [fri'xol] nm kidney bean

frío, a etc ['frio, a] vb ver **freír** ♦ adj cold; (indiferente) indifferent ♦ nm cold; indifference; **hace ~** it's cold; **tener ~** to be cold

frito, a ['frito, a] adj fried; **me trae ~ ese hombre** I'm sick and tired of that man; **fritos** nmpl fried food

frívolo, a ['friβolo, a] adj frivolous

frontal [fron'tal] adj frontal; **choque ~** head-on collision

frontera [fron'tera] nf frontier; **fronterizo, a** adj frontier cpd; (contiguo) bordering

frontón [fron'ton] nm (DEPORTE: cancha) pelota court; (: juego) pelota

frotar [fro'tar] vt to rub; **~se** vr: **~se las manos** to rub one's hands

fructífero, a [fruk'tifero, a] adj fruitful

fruncir [frun'θir] vt to pucker; (COSTURA) to

pleat; ~ **el ceño** to knit one's brow

frustrar [frus'trar] vt to frustrate

fruta ['fruta] nf fruit; **frutería** nf fruit shop; **frutero, a** adj fruit cpd ♦ nm/f fruiterer ♦ nm fruit bowl

frutilla [fru'tiʎa] (AM) nf strawberry

fruto ['fruto] nm fruit; (fig: resultado) result; (: beneficio) benefit; **~s secos** nuts; (pasas etc) dried fruit sg

fue vb ver **ser**; **ir**

fuego ['fweɣo] nm (gen) fire; **a ~ lento** on a low heat; **¿tienes ~?** have you (got) a light?; **~s artificiales** o **de artificio** fireworks

fuente ['fwente] nf fountain; (manantial, fig) spring; (origen) source; (plato) large dish

fuera ['fwera] vb ver **ser**, **ir** ♦ adv out(side); (en otra parte) away; (excepto, salvo) except, save ♦ prep: ~ **de** outside; (fig) besides; ~ **de sí** beside o.s.; **por ~** (on the) outside

fuera-borda [fwera'ßorða] nm speedboat

fuerte ['fwerte] adj strong; (golpe) hard; (ruido) loud; (comida) rich; (lluvia) heavy; (dolor) intense ♦ adv strongly; hard; loud(ly)

fuerza etc ['fwerθa] vb ver **forzar** ♦ nf (fortaleza) strength; (TEC, ELEC) power; (coacción) force; (MIL: tb: ~s) forces pl; **a ~ de** by dint of; **cobrar ~s** to recover one's strength; **tener ~s para** to have the strength to; **a la ~** forcibly, by force; **por ~** of necessity; ~ **de voluntad** willpower

fuga ['fuɣa] nf (huida) flight, escape; (de gas etc) leak

fugarse [fu'ɣarse] vr to flee, escape

fugaz [fu'ɣaθ] adj fleeting

fugitivo, a [fuxi'tiβo, a] adj, nm/f fugitive

fui vb ver **ser**; **ir**

fulano, a [fu'lano, a] nm/f so-and-so, what's-his-name/what's-her-name

fulminante [fulmi'nante] adj (fig: mirada) fierce; (MED: enfermedad, ataque) sudden; (fam: éxito, golpe) sudden

fumador, a [fuma'ðor, a] nm/f smoker

fumar [fu'mar] vt, vi to smoke; ~ **en pipa** to smoke a pipe

función [fun'θjon] nf function; (en trabajo) duties pl; (espectáculo) show; **entrar en funciones** to take up one's duties

funcionar [funθjo'nar] vi (gen) to function; (máquina) to work; **"no funciona"** "out of order"

funcionario, a [funθjo'narjo, a] nm/f civil servant

funda ['funda] nf (gen) cover; (de almohada) pillowcase

fundación [funda'θjon] nf foundation

fundamental [fundamen'tal] adj fundamental, basic

fundamentar [fundamen'tar] vt (poner

base) to lay the foundations of; (*establecer*) to found; (*fig*) to base; **fundamento** *nm* (*base*) foundation

fundar [fun'dar] *vt* to found; **~se** *vr*: **~se en** to be founded on

fundición [fundi'θjon] *nf* fusing; (*fábrica*) foundry

fundir [fun'dir] *vt* (*gen*) to fuse; (*metal*) to smelt, melt down; (*nieve etc*) to melt; (*COM*) to merge; (*estatua*) to cast; **~se** *vr* (*colores etc*) to merge, blend; (*unirse*) to fuse together; (*ELEC: fusible, lámpara etc*) to fuse, blow; (*nieve etc*) to melt

fúnebre ['funeβre] *adj* funeral *cpd*, funereal

funeral [fune'ral] *nm* funeral; **funeraria** *nf* undertaker's

funesto, a [fu'nesto, a] *adj* (*día*) ill-fated; (*decisión*) fatal

furgón [fur'γon] *nm* wagon; **furgoneta** *nf* (*AUTO, COM*) (transit) van (*BRIT*), pick-up (truck) (*US*)

furia ['furja] *nf* (*ira*) fury; (*violencia*) violence; **furibundo, a** *adj* furious; **furioso, a** *adj* (*iracundo*) furious; (*violento*) violent; **furor** *nm* (*cólera*) rage

furtivo, a [fur'tiβo, a] *adj* furtive ♦ *nm* poacher

fusible [fu'siβle] *nm* fuse

fusil [fu'sil] *nm* rifle; **~ar** *vt* to shoot

fusión [fu'sjon] *nf* (*gen*) melting; (*unión*) fusion; (*COM*) merger

fútbol ['futβol] *nm* football; **futbolín** *nm* table football; **futbolista** *nm* footballer

futuro, a [fu'turo, a] *adj, nm* future

G, g

gabardina [gaβar'ðina] *nf* raincoat, gabardine

gabinete [gaβi'nete] *nm* (*POL*) cabinet; (*estudio*) study; (*de abogados etc*) office

gaceta [ga'θeta] *nf* gazette

gachas ['gatʃas] *nfpl* porridge *sg*

gafas ['gafas] *nfpl* glasses; **~ de sol** sunglasses

gafe ['gafe] *nm* jinx

gaita ['gaita] *nf* bagpipes *pl*

gajes ['gaxes] *nmpl*: **los ~ del oficio** occupational hazards

gajo ['gaxo] *nm* (*de naranja*) segment

gala ['gala] *nf* (*traje de etiqueta*) full dress; **~s** *nfpl* (*ropa*) finery *sg*; **estar de ~** to be in one's best clothes; **hacer ~ de** to display

galante [ga'lante] *adj* gallant; **galantería** *nf* (*caballerosidad*) gallantry; (*cumplido*) politeness; (*comentario*) compliment

galápago [ga'lapaxo] *nm* (*ZOOL*) turtle

galardón [galar'ðon] *nm* award, prize

galaxia [ga'laksja] *nf* galaxy

galera [ga'lera] *nf* (*nave*) galley; (*carro*) wagon; (*IMPRENTA*) galley

galería [gale'ria] *nf* (*gen*) gallery; (*balcón*) veranda(h); (*pasillo*) corridor

Gales ['gales] *nm* (*tb: País de ~*) Wales; **galés, esa** *adj* Welsh ♦ *nm/f* Welshman/woman ♦ *nm* (*LING*) Welsh

galgo, a ['galxo, a] *nm/f* greyhound

galimatías [galima'tias] *nmpl* (*lenguaje*) gibberish *sg*, nonsense *sg*

gallardía [gaʎar'ðia] *nf* (*valor*) bravery

gallego, a [ga'ʎexo, a] *adj, nm/f* Galician

galleta [ga'ʎeta] *nf* biscuit (*BRIT*), cookie (*US*)

gallina [ga'ʎina] *nf* hen ♦ *nm/f* (*fam: cobarde*) chicken; **gallinero** *nm* henhouse; (*TEATRO*) top gallery

gallo ['gaʎo] *nm* cock, rooster

galón [ga'lon] *nm* (*MIL*) stripe; (*COSTURA*) braid; (*medida*) gallon

galopar [galo'par] *vi* to gallop

gama ['gama] *nf* (*fig*) range

gamba ['gamba] *nf* prawn (*BRIT*), shrimp (*US*)

gamberro, a [gam'berro, a] *nm/f* hooligan, lout

gamuza [ga'muθa] *nf* chamois

gana ['gana] *nf* (*deseo*) desire, wish; (*apetito*) appetite; (*voluntad*) will; (*añoranza*) longing; **de buena ~** willingly; **de mala ~** reluctantly; **me da ~s de** I feel like, I want to; **no me da la ~** I don't feel like it; **tener ~s de** to feel like

ganadería [ganaðe'ria] *nf* (*ganado*) livestock; (*ganado vacuno*) cattle *pl*; (*cría, comercio*) cattle raising

ganado [ga'naðo] *nm* livestock; **~ lanar** sheep *pl*; **~ mayor** cattle *pl*; **~ porcino** pigs *pl*

ganador, a [gana'ðor, a] *adj* winning ♦ *nm/f* winner

ganancia [ga'nanθja] *nf* (*lo ganado*) gain; (*aumento*) increase; (*beneficio*) profit; **~s** *nfpl* (*ingresos*) earnings; (*beneficios*) profit *sg*, winnings

ganar [ga'nar] *vt* (*obtener*) to get, obtain; (*sacar ventaja*) to gain; (*salario etc*) to earn; (*DEPORTE, premio*) to win; (*derrotar a*) to beat; (*alcanzar*) to reach ♦ *vi* (*DEPORTE*) to win; **~se** *vr*: **~se la vida** to earn one's living

ganchillo [gan'tʃiʎo] *nm* crochet

gancho ['gantʃo] *nm* (*gen*) hook; (*colgador*) hanger

gandul, a [gan'dul, a] *adj, nm/f* good-for-nothing, layabout

ganga ['ganga] *nf* bargain

gangrena [gan'grena] *nf* gangrene

ganso, a ['ganso, a] *nm/f* (*ZOOL*) goose; (*fam*) idiot

ganzúa [gan'θua] *nf* skeleton key

garabatear [garaβate'ar] *vi, vt* (*al escribir*) to scribble, scrawl

garabato [gara'βato] *nm* (*escritura*) scrawl,

scribble

garaje [ga'raxe] *nm* garage

garante [ga'rante] *adj* responsible ♦ *nm/f* guarantor

garantía [garan'tia] *nf* guarantee

garantizar [garanti'θar] *vt* to guarantee

garbanzo [gar'ßanθo] *nm* chickpea (*BRIT*), garbanzo (*US*)

garbo ['garßo] *nm* grace, elegance

garfio ['garfjo] *nm* grappling iron

garganta [gar'xanta] *nf* (*ANAT*) throat; (*de botella*) neck; **gargantilla** *nf* necklace

gárgaras ['garxaras] *nfpl*: **hacer ~** to gargle

garita [ga'rita] *nf* cabin, hut; (*MIL*) sentry box

garra ['garra] *nf* (*de gato, TEC*) claw; (*de ave*) talon; (*fam: mano*) hand, paw

garrafa [ga'rrafa] *nf* carafe, decanter

garrapata [garra'pata] *nf* tick

garrote [ga'rrote] *nm* (*palo*) stick; (*porra*) cudgel; (*suplicio*) garrotte

garza ['garθa] *nf* heron

gas [gas] *nm* gas

gasa ['gasa] *nf* gauze

gaseosa [gase'osa] *nf* lemonade

gaseoso, a [gase'oso, a] *adj* gassy, fizzy

gasoil [ga'soil] *nm* diesel (oil)

gasóleo [ga'soleo] *nm* = **gasoil**

gasolina [gaso'lina] *nf* petrol, gas(oline) (*US*); **gasolinera** *nf* petrol (*BRIT*) o gas (*US*) station

gastado, a [gas'taðo, a] *adj* (*dinero*) spent; (*ropa*) worn out; (*usado: frase etc*) trite

gastar [gas'tar] *vt* (*dinero, tiempo*) to spend; (*fuerzas*) to use up; (*desperdiciar*) to waste; (*llevar*) to wear; **~se** *vr* to wear out; (*estropearse*) to waste; **~ en** to spend on; **~ bromas** to crack jokes; **¿qué número gastas?** what size (shoe) do you take?

gasto ['gasto] *nm* (*desembolso*) expenditure, spending; (*consumo, uso*) use; **~s** *nmpl* (*desembolsos*) expenses; (*cargos*) charges, costs

gastronomía [gastrono'mia] *nf* gastronomy

gatear [gate'ar] *vi* (*andar a gatas*) to go on all fours

gatillo [ga'tiʎo] *nm* (*de arma de fuego*) trigger; (*de dentista*) forceps

gato, a ['gato, a] *nm/f* cat ♦ *nm* (*TEC*) jack; **andar a gatas** to go on all fours

gaviota [ga'ßjota] *nf* seagull

gay [ge] *adj inv, nm* gay, homosexual

gazpacho [gaθ'patʃo] *nm* gazpacho

gel [xel] *nm* (*tb*: **~ de baño/ducha**) gel

gelatina [xela'tina] *nf* jelly; (*polvos etc*) gelatine

gema ['xema] *nf* gem

gemelo, a [xe'melo, a] *adj, nm/f* twin; **~s** *nmpl* (*de camisa*) cufflinks; (*prismáticos*) field glasses, binoculars

gemido [xe'miðo] *nm* (*quejido*) moan, groan; (*aullido*) howl

Géminis ['xeminis] *nm* Gemini

gemir [xe'mir] *vi* (*quejarse*) to moan, groan; (*aullar*) to howl

generación [xenera'θjon] *nf* generation

general [xene'ral] *adj* general ♦ *nm* general; **por lo o en ~** in general; **G~itat** *nf* Catalan parliament; **~izar** *vt* to generalize; **~izarse** *vr* to become generalized, spread; **~mente** *adv* generally

generar [xene'rar] *vt* to generate

género ['xenero] *nm* (*clase*) kind, sort; (*tipo*) type; (*BIO*) genus; (*LING*) gender; (*COM*) material; **~ humano** human race

generosidad [xenerosi'ðað] *nf* generosity; **generoso, a** *adj* generous

genial [xe'njal] *adj* inspired; (*idea*) brilliant; (*afable*) genial

genio ['xenjo] *nm* (*carácter*) nature, disposition; (*humor*) temper; (*facultad creadora*) genius; **de mal ~** bad-tempered

genital [xeni'tal] *adj* genital; **genitales** *nmpl* genitals

gente ['xente] *nf* (*personas*) people *pl*; (*parientes*) relatives *pl*

gentil [xen'til] *adj* (*elegante*) graceful; (*encantador*) charming; **~eza** *nf* grace; charm; (*cortesía*) courtesy

gentío [xen'tio] *nm* crowd, throng

genuino, a [xe'nwino, a] *adj* genuine

geografía [xeoxra'fia] *nf* geography

geología [xeolo'xia] *nf* geology

geometría [xeome'tria] *nf* geometry

gerencia [xe'renθja] *nf* management; **gerente** *nm/f* (*supervisor*) manager; (*jefe*) director

geriatría [xeria'tria] *nf* (*MED*) geriatrics *sg*

germen ['xermen] *nm* germ

germinar [xermi'nar] *vi* to germinate

gesticular [xestiku'lar] *vi* to gesticulate; (*hacer muecas*) to grimace; **gesticulación** *nf* gesticulation; (*mueca*) grimace

gestión [xes'tjon] *nf* management; (*diligencia, acción*) negotiation; **gestionar** *vt* (*lograr*) to try to arrange; (*dirigir*) to manage

gesto ['xesto] *nm* (*mueca*) grimace; (*ademán*) gesture

Gibraltar [xißral'tar] *nm* Gibraltar; **gibraltareño, a** *adj, nm/f* Gibraltarian

gigante [xi'xante] *adj, nm/f* giant; **gigantesco, a** *adj* gigantic

gilipollas [xili'poʎas] (*fam*) *adj inv* daft ♦ *nm/f inv* wally

gimnasia [xim'nasja] *nf* gymnastics *pl*; **gimnasio** *nm* gymnasium; **gimnasta** *nm/f* gymnast

gimotear [ximote'ar] *vi* to whine, whimper

ginebra [xi'neßra] *nf* gin

ginecólogo, a [xine'koloɣo, a] nm/f gynaecologist

gira ['xira] nf tour, trip

girar [xi'rar] vt (dar la vuelta) to turn (around); (: rápidamente) to spin; (COM: giro postal) to draw; (: letra de cambio) to issue ♦ vi to turn (round); (rápido) to spin

girasol [xira'sol] nm sunflower

giratorio, a [xira'torjo, a] adj revolving

giro ['xiro] nm (movimiento) turn, revolution; (LING) expression; (COM) draft; ~ **bancario/postal** bank giro/postal order

gis [xis] (AM) nm chalk

gitano, a [xi'tano, a] adj, nm/f gypsy

glacial [gla'θjal] adj icy, freezing

glaciar [gla'θjar] nm glacier

glándula ['glandula] nf gland

global [glo'βal] adj global

globo ['gloβo] nm (esfera) globe, sphere; (aerostato, juguete) balloon

glóbulo ['gloβulo] nm globule; (ANAT) corpuscle

gloria ['glorja] nf glory

glorieta [glo'rjeta] nf (de jardín) bower, arbour; (plazoleta) roundabout (BRIT), traffic circle (US)

glorificar [glorifi'kar] vt (enaltecer) to glorify, praise

glorioso, a [glo'rjoso, a] adj glorious

glotón, ona [glo'ton, ona] adj gluttonous, greedy ♦ nm/f glutton

glucosa [glu'kosa] nf glucose

gobernador, a [goβerna'ðor, a] adj governing ♦ nm/f governor; **gobernante** adj governing

gobernar [goβer'nar] vt (dirigir) to guide, direct; (POL) to rule, govern ♦ vi to govern; (NAUT) to steer

gobierno etc [go'βjerno] vb ver **gobernar** ♦ nm (POL) government; (dirección) guidance, direction; (NAUT) steering

goce etc ['goθe] vb ver **gozar** ♦ nm enjoyment

gol [gol] nm goal

golf [golf] nm golf

golfa ['golfa] (fam!) nf (mujer) slut, whore

golfo ['golfo, a] nm (GEO) gulf ♦ nm/f (fam: niño) urchin; (gamberro) lout

golondrina [golon'drina] nf swallow

golosina [golo'sina] nf (dulce) sweet; **goloso, a** adj sweet-toothed

golpe ['golpe] nm blow; (de puño) punch; (de mano) smack; (de remo) stroke; (fig: choque) clash; **no dar** ~ to be bone idle; **de un** ~ with one blow; **de** ~ suddenly; ~ **(de estado)** coup (d'état); **golpear** vt, vi to strike, knock; (asestar) to beat; (de puño) to punch; (golpetear) to tap

goma ['goma] nf (caucho) rubber; (elástico) elastic; (una ~) elastic band; ~ **espuma** foam

rubber; ~ **de pegar** gum, glue; ~ **de borrar** eraser, rubber (BRIT)

gomina [go'mina] nf hair gel

gordo, a ['gorðo, a] adj (gen) fat; (fam) enormous; **el (premio)** ~ (en lotería) first prize; **gordura** nf fat; (corpulencia) fatness, stoutness

gorila [go'rila] nm gorilla

gorjear [gorxe'ar] vi to twitter, chirp

gorra ['gorra] nf cap; (de niño) bonnet; (militar) bearskin; **entrar de** ~ (fam) to gatecrash; **ir de** ~ to sponge

gorrión [go'rrjon] nm sparrow

gorro ['gorro] nm (gen) cap; (de niño, mujer) bonnet

gorrón, ona [go'rron, ona] nm/f scrounger; **gorronear** (fam) vi to scrounge

gota ['gota] nf (gen) drop; (de sudor) bead; (MED) gout; **gotear** vi to drip; (lloviznar) to drizzle; **gotera** nf leak

gozar [go'θar] vi to enjoy o.s.; ~ **de** (disfrutar) to enjoy; (poseer) to possess

gozne ['goθne] nm hinge

gozo ['goθo] nm (alegría) joy; (placer) pleasure

gr. abr (= gramo, gramos) g

grabación [graβa'θjon] nf recording

grabado [gra'βaðo] nm print, engraving

grabadora [graβa'ðora] nf tape-recorder

grabar [gra'βar] vt to engrave; (discos, cintas) to record

gracia ['graθja] nf (encanto) grace, gracefulness; (humor) humour, wit; **¡(muchas) ~s!** thanks (very much)!; ~**s a** thanks to; **tener** ~ (chiste etc) to be funny; **no me hace** ~ I am not keen; **gracioso, a** adj (divertido) funny, amusing; (cómico) comical ♦ nm/f (TEATRO) comic character

grada ['graða] nf (de escalera) step; (de anfiteatro) tier, row; ~**s** nfpl (DEPORTE: de estadio) terraces

gradería [graðe'ria] nf (gradas) (flight of) steps pl; (de anfiteatro) tiers pl, rows pl; (DEPORTE: de estadio) terraces pl; ~ **cubierta** covered stand

grado ['graðo] nm degree; (de aceite, vino) grade; (grada) step; (MIL) rank; **de buen** ~ willingly

graduación [graðwa'θjon] nf (del alcohol) proof, strength; (ESCOL) graduation; (MIL) rank

gradual [gra'ðwal] adj gradual

graduar [gra'ðwar] vt (gen) to graduate; (MIL) to commission; ~**se** vr to graduate; ~**se la vista** to have one's eyes tested

gráfica ['grafika] nf graph

gráfico, a ['grafiko, a] adj graphic ♦ nm diagram; ~**s** nmpl (INFORM) graphics

grajo ['graxo] nm rook

Gral *abr* (= *General*) Gen.

gramática [graˈmatika] *nf* grammar

gramo [ˈgramo] *nm* gramme (*BRIT*), gram (*US*)

gran [gran] *adj ver* **grande**

grana [ˈgrana] *nf* (*color, tela*) scarlet

granada [graˈnaða] *nf* pomegranate; (*MIL*) grenade

granate [graˈnate] *adj* deep red

Gran Bretaña [-breˈtaɲa] *nf* Great Britain

grande [ˈgrande] (*antes de nmsg*: **gran**) *adj* (*de tamaño*) big, large; (*alto*) tall; (*distinguido*) great; (*impresionante*) grand ♦ *nm* grandee; **grandeza** *nf* greatness

grandioso, a [granˈdjoso, a] *adj* magnificent, grand

granel [graˈnel]: **a ~** *adv* (*COM*) in bulk

granero [graˈnero] *nm* granary, barn

granito [graˈnito] *nm* (*AGR*) small grain; (*roca*) granite

granizado [graniˈθaðo] *nm* iced drink

granizar [graniˈθar] *vi* to hail; **granizo** *nm* hail

granja [ˈgranxa] *nf* (*gen*) farm; **granjear** *vt* to win, gain; **granjearse** *vr* to win, gain; **granjero, a** *nm/f* farmer

grano [ˈgrano] *nm* grain; (*semilla*) seed; (*de café*) bean; (*MED*) pimple, spot

granuja [graˈnuxa] *nm/f* rogue; (*golfillo*) urchin

grapa [ˈgrapa] *nf* staple; (*TEC*) clamp; **grapadora** *nf* stapler

grasa [ˈgrasa] *nf* (*gen*) grease; (*de cocinar*) fat, lard; (*sebo*) suet; (*mugre*) filth; **grasiento, a** *adj* greasy; (*de aceite*) oily; **graso, a** *adj* (*leche, queso, carne*) fatty; (*pelo, piel*) greasy

gratificación [gratifikaˈθjon] *nf* (*bono*) bonus; (*recompensa*) reward

gratificar [gratifiˈkar] *vt* to reward

gratinar [gratiˈnar] *vt* to cook au gratin

gratis [ˈgratis] *adv* free

gratitud [gratiˈtuð] *nf* gratitude

grato, a [ˈgrato, a] *adj* (*agradable*) pleasant, agreeable

gratuito, a [graˈtwito, a] *adj* (*gratis*) free; (*sin razón*) gratuitous

gravamen [graˈβamen] *nm* (*impuesto*) tax

gravar [graˈβar] *vt* to tax

grave [ˈgraβe] *adj* heavy; (*serio*) grave, serious; **~dad** *nf* gravity

gravilla [graˈβiʎa] *nf* gravel

gravitar [graβiˈtar] *vi* to gravitate; **~ sobre** to rest on

graznar [graθˈnar] *vi* (*cuervo*) to squawk; (*pato*) to quack; (*hablar ronco*) to croak

Grecia [ˈgreθja] *nf* Greece

gremio [ˈgremjo] *nm* trade, industry

greña [ˈgreɲa] *nf* (*cabellos*) shock of hair

gresca [ˈgreska] *nf* uproar

griego, a [ˈgrjeɣo, a] *adj, nm/f* Greek

grieta [ˈgrjeta] *nf* crack

grifo [ˈgrifo] *nm* tap; (*AM: AUTO*) petrol (*BRIT*) o gas (*US*) station

grilletes [griˈʎetes] *nmpl* fetters

grillo [ˈgriʎo] *nm* (*ZOOL*) cricket

gripe [ˈgripe] *nf* flu, influenza

gris [gris] *adj* (*color*) grey

gritar [griˈtar] *vt, vi* to shout, yell; **grito** *nm* shout, yell; (*de horror*) scream

grosella [groˈseʎa] *nf* (red)currant; **~ negra** blackcurrant

grosería [groseˈria] *nf* (*actitud*) rudeness; (*comentario*) vulgar comment; **grosero, a** *adj* (*poco cortés*) rude, bad-mannered; (*ordinario*) vulgar, crude

grosor [groˈsor] *nm* thickness

grotesco, a [groˈtesko, a] *adj* grotesque

grúa [ˈgrua] *nf* (*TEC*) crane; (*de petróleo*) derrick

grueso, a [ˈgrweso, a] *adj* thick; (*persona*) stout ♦ *nm* bulk; **el ~ de** the bulk of

grulla [ˈgruʎa] *nf* crane

grumo [ˈgrumo] *nm* clot, lump

gruñido [gruˈɲiðo] *nm* grunt; (*de persona*) grumble

gruñir [gruˈɲir] *vi* (*animal*) to growl; (*persona*) to grumble

grupa [ˈgrupa] *nf* (*ZOOL*) rump

grupo [ˈgrupo] *nm* group; (*TEC*) unit, set

gruta [ˈgruta] *nf* grotto

guadaña [gwaˈðaɲa] *nf* scythe

guagua [ˈgwaɣwa] (*AM*) *nf* (*niño*) baby; (*bus*) bus

guante [ˈgwante] *nm* glove; **~ra** *nf* glove compartment

guapo, a [ˈgwapo, a] *adj* good-looking, attractive; (*elegante*) smart

guarda [ˈgwarða] *nm/f* (*persona*) guard, keeper ♦ *nf* (*acto*) guarding; (*custodia*) custody; **~bosques** *nm inv* gamekeeper; **~costas** *nm inv* coastguard vessel ♦ *nm/f* guardian, protector; **~espaldas** *nm/f inv* bodyguard; **~meta** *nm/f* goalkeeper; **guardar** *vt* (*gen*) to keep; (*vigilar*) to guard, watch over; (*dinero: ahorrar*) to save; **guardarse** *vr* (*preservarse*) to protect o.s.; (*evitar*) to avoid; **guardar cama** to stay in bed; **~rropa** *nm* (*armario*) wardrobe; (*en establecimiento público*) cloakroom

guardería [gwarðeˈria] *nf* nursery

guardia [ˈgwarðja] *nf* (*MIL*) guard; (*cuidado*) care, custody ♦ *nm/f* guard; (*policía*) policeman/woman; **estar de ~** to be on guard; **montar ~** to mount guard; **G~ Civil** Civil Guard; **G~ Nacional** National Guard

guardián, ana [gwarˈðjan, ana] *nm/f* (*gen*) guardian, keeper

guarecer [gwareˈθer] *vt* (*proteger*) to protect;

(*abrigar*) to shelter; **~se** *vr* to take refuge

guarida [gwa'riða] *nf* (*de animal*) den, lair; (*refugio*) refuge

guarnecer [gwarne'θer] *vt* (*equipar*) to provide; (*adornar*) to adorn; (*TEC*) to reinforce; **guarnición** *nf* (*de vestimenta*) trimming; (*de piedra*) mount; (*CULIN*) garnish; (*arneses*) harness; (*MIL*) garrison

guarro, a ['gwarro, a] *nm/f* pig

guasa ['gwasa] *nf* joke; **guasón, ona** *adj* (*bromista*) joking ♦ *nm/f* wit; joker

Guatemala [gwate'mala] *nf* Guatemala

guay [gwai] (*fam*) *adj* super, great

gubernativo, a [guβerna'tiβo, a] *adj* governmental

guerra ['gerra] *nf* war; **~ civil** civil war; **~ fría** cold war; **dar ~** to annoy; **guerrear** *vi* to wage war; **guerrero, a** *adj* fighting; (*carácter*) warlike ♦ *nm/f* warrior

guerrilla [ge'rriʎa] *nf* guerrilla warfare; (*tropas*) guerrilla band *o* group

guía *etc* ['gia] *vb ver* **guiar** ♦ *nf* (*libro*) guidebook; **~ de ferrocarriles** railway timetable; **~ telefónica** telephone directory

guiar [gi'ar] *vt* to guide, direct; (*AUTO*) to steer; **~se** *vr*: **~se por** to be guided by

guijarro [gi'xarro] *nm* pebble

guillotina [giʎo'tina] *nf* guillotine

guinda ['ginda] *nf* morello cherry

guindilla [gin'diʎa] *nf* chilli pepper

guiñapo [gi'ɲapo] *nm* (*harapo*) rag; (*persona*) reprobate, rogue

guiñar [gi'ɲar] *vt* to wink

guión [gi'on] *nm* (*LING*) hyphen, dash; (*CINE*) script; **guionista** *nm/f* scriptwriter

guiri ['giri] (*fam: pey*) *nm/f* foreigner

guirnalda [gir'nalda] *nf* garland

guisado [gi'saðo] *nm* stew

guisante [gi'sante] *nm* pea

guisar [gi'sar] *vt, vi* to cook; **guiso** *nm* cooked dish

guitarra [gi'tarra] *nf* guitar

gula ['gula] *nf* gluttony, greed

gusano [gu'sano] *nm* worm; (*lombriz*) earthworm

gustar [gus'tar] *vt* to taste, sample ♦ *vi* to please, be pleasing; **~ de algo** to like *o* enjoy sth; **me gustan las uvas** I like grapes; **le gusta nadar** she likes *o* enjoys swimming

gusto ['gusto] *nm* (*sentido, sabor*) taste; (*placer*) pleasure; **tiene ~ a menta** it tastes of mint; **tener buen ~** to have good taste; **sentirse a ~** to feel at ease; **mucho ~ (en conocerle)** pleased to meet you; **el ~ es mío** the pleasure is mine; **con ~** willingly, gladly; **~so, a** *adj* (*sabroso*) tasty; (*agradable*) pleasant

H, h

ha *vb ver* **haber**

haba ['aβa] *nf* bean

Habana [a'βana] *nf*: **la ~** Havana

habano [a'βano] *nm* Havana cigar

habéis *vb ver* **haber**

PALABRA CLAVE
---

haber [a'βer] *vb aux* **1** (*tiempos compuestos*) to have; **había comido** I had eaten; **antes/después de ~lo visto** before seeing/after seeing *o* having seen it

2: **¡~lo dicho antes!** you should have said so before!

3: **~ de: he de hacerlo** I have to do it; **ha de llegar mañana** it should arrive tomorrow

♦ *vb impers* **1** (*existencia: sg*) there is; (*: pl*) there are; **hay un hermano/dos hermanos** there is one brother/there are two brothers; **¿cuánto hay de aquí a Sucre?** how far is it from here to Sucre?

2 (*obligación*): **hay que hacer algo** something must be done; **hay que apuntarlo para acordarse** you have to write it down to remember

3: **¡hay que ver!** well I never!

4: **¡no hay de o por (AM) qué!** don't mention it!, not at all!

5: **¿qué hay?** (*¿qué pasa?*) what's up?, what's the matter?; (*¿qué tal?*) how's it going?

♦ **~se** *vr*: **habérselas con uno** to have it out with sb

♦ *vt*: **he aquí unas sugerencias** here are some suggestions; **no hay cintas blancas pero sí las hay rojas** there aren't any white ribbons but there are some red ones

♦ *nm* (*en cuenta*) credit side; **~es** *nmpl* assets; **¿cuánto tengo en el ~?** how much do I have in my account?; **tiene varias novelas en su ~** he has several novels to his credit

---

habichuela [aβi'tʃwela] *nf* kidney bean

hábil ['aβil] *adj* (*listo*) clever, smart; (*capaz*) fit, capable; (*experto*) expert; **día ~** working day; **habilidad** *nf* skill, ability

habilitar [aβili'tar] *vt* (*capacitar*) to enable; (*dar instrumentos*) to equip; (*financiar*) to finance

hábilmente [aβil'mente] *adv* skilfully, expertly

habitación [aβita'θjon] *nf* (*cuarto*) room; (*BIO: morada*) habitat; **~ sencilla** *o* **individual** single room; **~ doble** *o* **de matrimonio** double room

habitante [aβi'tante] *nm/f* inhabitant

habitar [aβi'tar] *vt* (*residir en*) to inhabit;

(*ocupar*) to occupy ♦ *vi* to live

hábito [ˈaβito] *nm* habit

habitual [aβiˈtwal] *adj* usual

habituar [aβiˈtwar] *vt* to accustom; **~se** *vr*: **~se a** to get used to

habla [ˈaβla] *nf* (*capacidad de hablar*) speech; (*idioma*) language; (*dialecto*) dialect; **perder el ~** to become speechless; **de ~ francesa** French-speaking; **estar al ~** to be in contact; (*TEL*) to be on the line; **¡González al ~!** (*TEL*) González speaking!

hablador, a [aβlaˈðor, a] *adj* talkative ♦ *nm/f* chatterbox

habladuría [aβlaðuˈria] *nf* rumour; **~s** *nfpl* gossip *sg*

hablante [aˈβlante] *adj* speaking ♦ *nm/f* speaker

hablar [aˈβlar] *vt* to speak, talk ♦ *vi* to speak; **~se** *vr* to speak to each other; **~ con** to speak to; **~ de** to speak of o about; **"se habla inglés"** "English spoken here"; **¡ni ~!** it's out of the question!

habré *etc vb ver* **haber**

hacendoso, a [aθenˈdoso, a] *adj* industrious

hacer [aˈθer] *vt* **1** (*fabricar, producir*) to make; (*construir*) to build; **~ una película/un ruido** to make a film/noise; **el guisado lo hice yo** I made o cooked the stew

2 (*ejecutar: trabajo etc*) to do; **~ la colada** to do the washing; **~ la comida** to do the cooking; **¿qué haces?** what are you doing?; **~ el malo** o **el papel del malo** (*TEATRO*) to play the villain

3 (*estudios, algunos deportes*) to do; **~ español/económicas** to do o study Spanish/economics; **~ yoga/gimnasia** to do yoga/go to gym

4 (*transformar, incidir en*): **esto lo hará más difícil** this will make it more difficult; **salir te hará sentir mejor** going out will make you feel better

5 (*cálculo*): **2 y 2 hacen 4** 2 and 2 make 4; **éste hace 100** this one makes 100

6 (*+ sub*): **esto hará que ganemos** this will make us win; **harás que no quiera venir** you'll stop him wanting to come

7 (*como sustituto de vb*) to do; **él bebió y yo hice lo mismo** he drank and I did likewise

8: **no hace más que criticar** all he does is criticize

♦ *vb semi-aux*: **hacer + infin 1** (*directo*): **les hice venir** I made o had them come;

~ trabajar a los demás to get others to work

2 (*por intermedio de otros*): **~ reparar algo** to get sth repaired

♦ *vi* **1**: **haz como que no lo sabes** act as if you don't know

2 (*ser apropiado*): **si os hace** if it's alright with you

3: **~ de**: **~ de madre para uno** to be like a mother to sb; (*TEATRO*): **~ de Otelo** to play Othello

♦ *vb impers* **1**: **hace calor/frío** it's hot/cold; *ver tb* **bueno; sol; tiempo**

2 (*tiempo*): **hace 3 años** 3 years ago; **hace un mes que voy/no voy** I've been going/I haven't been for a month

3: **¿cómo has hecho para llegar tan rápido?** how did you manage to get here so quickly?

♦ **~se** *vr* **1** (*volverse*) to become; **se hicieron amigos** they became friends

2 (*acostumbrarse*): **~se a** to get used to

3: **se hace con huevos y leche** it's made out of eggs and milk; **eso no se hace** that's not done

4 (*obtener*): **~se de** o **con algo** to get hold of sth

5 (*fingirse*): **~se el sueco** to turn a deaf ear

hacha [ˈatʃa] *nf* axe; (*antorcha*) torch

hachís [aˈtʃis] *nm* hashish

hacia [ˈaθja] *prep* (*en dirección de*) towards; (*cerca de*) near; (*actitud*) towards; **~ arriba/abajo** up(wards)/down(wards); **~ mediodía** about noon

hacienda [aˈθjenda] *nf* (*propiedad*) property; (*finca*) farm; (*AM*) ranch; **~ pública** public finance; **(Ministerio de) H~** Exchequer (*BRIT*), Treasury Department (*US*)

hada [ˈaða] *nf* fairy

hago *etc vb ver* **hacer**

Haití [aiˈti] *nm* Haiti

halagar [alaˈɣar] *vt* to flatter

halago [aˈlaɣo] *nm* flattery; **halagüeño, a** *adj* flattering

halcón [alˈkon] *nm* falcon, hawk

hallar [aˈʎar] *vt* (*gen*) to find; (*descubrir*) to discover; (*toparse con*) to run into; **~se** *vr* to be (situated); **hallazgo** *nm* discovery; (*cosa*) find

halterofilia [alteroˈfilja] *nf* weightlifting

hamaca [aˈmaka] *nf* hammock

hambre [ˈambre] *nf* hunger; (*plaga*) famine; (*deseo*) longing; **tener ~** to be hungry; **hambriento, a** *adj* hungry, starving

hamburguesa [amburˈɣesa] *nf* hamburger; **hamburguesería** *nf* burger bar

han *vb ver* **haber**

harapiento, a [araˈpjento, a] *adj* tattered, in rags

harapos [aˈrapos] *nmpl* rags

haré *etc vb ver* **hacer**

harina [aˈrina] *nf* flour

hartar [arˈtar] *vt* to satiate, glut; (*fig*) to tire, sicken; **~se** *vr* (*de comida*) to fill o.s., gorge o.s.; (*cansarse*) to get fed up (*de* with);

hartazgo *nm* surfeit, glut; **harto, a** *adj* (*lleno*) full; (*cansado*) fed up ♦ *adv* (*bastante*) enough; (*muy*) very; **estar harto de** to be fed up with

has *vb ver* **haber**

hasta ['asta] *adv* even ♦ *prep* (*alcanzando a*) as far as; up to; down to; (*de tiempo: a tal hora*) till, until; (*antes de*) before ♦ *conj*: **~ que** until; **~ luego/el sábado** see you soon/ on Saturday

hastiar [as'tjar] *vt* (*gen*) to weary; (*aburrir*) to bore; **~se** *vr*: **~se de** to get fed up with; **hastío** *nm* weariness; boredom

hatillo [a'tiʎo] *nm* belongings *pl*, kit; (*montón*) bundle, heap

hay *vb ver* **haber**

Haya ['aja] *nf*: **la ~** The Hague

haya *etc* ['aja] *vb ver* **haber** ♦ *nf* beech tree

haz [aθ] *vb ver* **hacer** ♦ *nm* (*de luz*) beam

hazaña [a'θaɲa] *nf* feat, exploit

hazmerreír [aθmerre'ir] *nm inv* laughing stock

he *vb ver* **haber**

hebilla [e'βiʎa] *nf* buckle, clasp

hebra ['eβra] *nf* thread; (*BOT: fibra*) fibre, grain

hebreo, a [e'βreo, a] *adj, nm/f* Hebrew ♦ *nm* (*LING*) Hebrew

hechizar [etʃi'θar] *vt* to cast a spell on, bewitch

hechizo [e'tʃiθo] *nm* witchcraft, magic; (*acto de magia*) spell, charm

hecho, a ['etʃo, a] *pp de* **hacer** ♦ *adj* (*carne*) done; (*COSTURA*) ready-to-wear ♦ *nm* deed, act; (*dato*) fact; (*cuestión*) matter; (*suceso*) event ♦ *excl* agreed!, done!; **¡bien ~!** well done!; **de ~** in fact, as a matter of fact

hechura [e'tʃura] *nf* (*forma*) form, shape; (*de persona*) build

hectárea [ek'tarea] *nf* hectare

heder [e'ðer] *vi* to stink, smell

hediondo, a [e'ðjondo, a] *adj* stinking

hedor [e'ðor] *nm* stench

helada [e'laða] *nf* frost

heladera [ela'ðera] (*AM*) *nf* (*refrigerador*) refrigerator

helado, a [e'laðo, a] *adj* frozen; (*glacial*) icy; (*fig*) chilly, cold ♦ *nm* ice cream

helar [e'lar] *vt* to freeze, ice (up); (*dejar atónito*) to amaze; (*desalentar*) to discourage ♦ *vi* to freeze; **~se** *vr* to freeze

helecho [e'letʃo] *nm* fern

hélice ['eliθe] *nf* (*TEC*) propeller

helicóptero [eli'koptero] *nm* helicopter

hembra ['embra] *nf* (*BOT, ZOOL*) female; (*mujer*) woman; (*TEC*) nut

hemorragia [emo'rraxja] *nf* haemorrhage

hemorroides [emo'rroiðes] *nfpl* haemorrhoids, piles

hemos *vb ver* **haber**

hendidura [endi'ðura] *nf* crack, split

heno ['eno] *nm* hay

herbicida [erβi'θiða] *nm* weedkiller

heredad [ere'ðað] *nf* landed property; (*granja*) farm

heredar [ere'ðar] *vt* to inherit; **heredero, a** *nm/f* heir(ess)

hereje [e'rexe] *nm/f* heretic

herencia [e'renθja] *nf* inheritance

herida [e'riða] *nf* wound, injury; *ver tb* **herido**

herido, a [e'riðo, a] *adj* injured, wounded ♦ *nm/f* casualty

herir [e'rir] *vt* to wound, injure; (*fig*) to offend

hermanastro, a [erma'nastro, a] *nm/f* stepbrother/sister

hermandad [erman'dað] *nf* brotherhood

hermano, a [er'mano, a] *nm/f* brother/sister; **~ gemelo** twin brother; **hermana gemela** twin sister; **~ político** brother-in-law; **hermana política** sister-in-law

hermético, a [er'metiko, a] *adj* hermetic; (*fig*) watertight

hermoso, a [er'moso, a] *adj* beautiful, lovely; (*estupendo*) splendid; (*guapo*) handsome; **hermosura** *nf* beauty

hernia ['ernja] *nf* hernia

héroe ['eroe] *nm* hero

heroína [ero'ina] *nf* (*mujer*) heroine; (*droga*) heroin

heroísmo [ero'ismo] *nm* heroism

herradura [erra'ðura] *nf* horseshoe

herramienta [erra'mjenta] *nf* tool

herrero [e'rrero] *nm* blacksmith

herrumbre [e'rrumbre] *nf* rust

hervidero [erβi'ðero] *nm* (*fig*) swarm; (*POL etc*) hotbed

hervir [er'βir] *vi* to boil; (*burbujear*) to bubble; (*fig*): **~ de** to teem with; **~ a fuego lento** to simmer; **hervor** *nm* boiling; (*fig*) ardour, fervour

heterosexual [eterosek'swal] *adj* heterosexual

hice *etc vb ver* **hacer**

hidratante [iðra'tante] *adj*: **crema ~** moisturizing cream, moisturizer; **hidratar** *vt* (*piel*) to moisturize; **hidrato** *nm*: **hidratos de carbono** carbohydrates

hidráulica [i'ðraulika] *nf* hydraulics *sg*

hidráulico, a [i'ðrauliko, a] *adj* hydraulic

hidro... [iðro] *prefijo* hydro..., water-...; **~eléctrico, a** *adj* hydroelectric; **~fobia** *nf* hydrophobia, rabies; **~hidrógeno** *nm* hydrogen

hiedra ['jeðra] *nf* ivy

hiel [jel] *nf* gall, bile; (*fig*) bitterness

hiela *etc vb ver* **helar**

hielo ['jelo] *nm* (*gen*) ice; (*escarcha*) frost; (*fig*) coldness, reserve

hiena ['jena] nf hyena

hierba ['jerßa] nf (pasto) grass; (CULIN, MED: planta) herb; **mala ~** weed; (fig) evil influence; **~buena** nf mint

hierro ['jerro] nm (metal) iron; (objeto) iron object

hígado ['iɣaðo] nm liver

higiene [i'xjene] nf hygiene; **higiénico, a** adj hygienic

higo ['iɣo] nm fig; **higuera** nf fig tree

hijastro, a [i'xastro, a] nm/f stepson/daughter

hijo, a ['ixo, a] nm/f son/daughter, child; **~s** nmpl children, sons and daughters; **~ de papá/mamá** daddy's/mummy's boy; **~ de puta** (fam!) bastard (!), son of a bitch (!)

hilar [i'lar] vt to spin; **~ fino** to split hairs

hilera [i'lera] nf row, file

hilo ['ilo] nm thread; (BOT) fibre; (metal) wire; (de agua) trickle, thin stream

hilvanar [ilßa'nar] vt (COSTURA) to tack (BRIT), baste (US); (fig) to do hurriedly

himno ['imno] nm hymn; **~ nacional** national anthem

hincapié [inka'pje] nm: **hacer ~ en** to emphasize

hincar [in'kar] vt to drive (in), thrust (in); **~se** vr: **~se de rodillas** to kneel down

hincha ['intʃa] (fam) nm/f fan

hinchado, a [in'tʃaðo, a] adj (gen) swollen; (persona) pompous

hinchar [in'tʃar] vt (gen) to swell; (inflar) to blow up, inflate; (fig) to exaggerate; **~se** vr (inflarse) to swell up; (fam: de comer) to stuff o.s.; **hinchazón** nf (MED) swelling; (altivez) arrogance

hinojo [i'noxo] nm fennel

hipermercado [ipermer'kaðo] nm hypermarket, superstore

hípico, a ['ipiko, a] adj horse cpd

hipnotismo [ipno'tismo] nm hypnotism; **hipnotizar** vt to hypnotize

hipo ['ipo] nm hiccups pl

hipocresía [ipokre'sia] nf hypocrisy; **hipócrita** adj hypocritical ♦ nm/f hypocrite

hipódromo [i'poðromo] nm racetrack

hipopótamo [ipo'potamo] nm hippopotamus

hipoteca [ipo'teka] nf mortgage

hipótesis [i'potesis] nf inv hypothesis

hiriente [i'rjente] adj offensive, wounding

hispánico, a [is'paniko, a] adj Hispanic

hispano, a [is'pano, a] adj Hispanic, Spanish, Hispano- ♦ nm/f Spaniard; **H~américa** nf Latin America; **~americano, a** adj, nm/f Latin American

histeria [is'terja] nf hysteria

historia [is'torja] nf history; (cuento) story, tale; **~s** nfpl (chismes) gossip sg; **dejarse de ~s**

to come to the point; **pasar a la ~** to go down in history; **~dor, a** nm/f historian;

historial nm (profesional) curriculum vitae, C.V.; (MED) case history; **histórico, a** adj historical; (memorable) historic

historieta [isto'rjeta] nf tale, anecdote; (dibujos) comic strip

hito ['ito] nm (fig) landmark

hizo vb ver **hacer**

Hnos abr (= Hermanos) Bros.

hocico [o'θiko] nm snout

hockey ['xoki] nm hockey; **~ sobre hielo** ice hockey

hogar [o'ɣar] nm fireplace, hearth; (casa) home; (vida familiar) home life; **~eño, a** adj home cpd; (persona) home-loving

hoguera [o'ɣera] nf (gen) bonfire

hoja ['oxa] nf (gen) leaf; (de flor) petal; (de papel) sheet; (página) page; **~ de afeitar** razor blade

hojalata [oxa'lata] nf tin(plate)

hojaldre [o'xaldre] nm (CULIN) puff pastry

hojear [oxe'ar] vt to leaf through, turn the pages of

hola ['ola] excl hello!

Holanda [o'landa] nf Holland; **holandés, esa** adj Dutch ♦ nm/f Dutchman/woman ♦ nm (LING) Dutch

holgado, a [ol'ɣaðo, a] adj (ropa) loose, baggy; (rico) comfortable

holgar [ol'ɣar] vi (descansar) to rest; (sobrar) to be superfluous; **huelga decir que** it goes without saying that

holgazán, ana [olɣa'θan, ana] adj idle, lazy ♦ nm/f loafer

holgura [ol'ɣura] nf looseness, bagginess; (TEC) play, free movement; (vida) comfortable living

hollín [o'ʎin] nm soot

hombre ['ombre] nm (gen) man; (raza humana): **el ~** man(kind) ♦ excl: **¡sí ~!** (claro) of course!; (para énfasis) man, old boy; **~ de negocios** businessman; **~ de pro** honest man; **~-rana** frogman

hombrera [om'brera] nf shoulder strap

hombro ['ombro] nm shoulder

hombruno, a [om'bruno, a] adj mannish

homenaje [ome'naxe] nm (gen) homage; (tributo) tribute

homicida [omi'θiða] adj homicidal ♦ nm/f murderer; **homicidio** nm murder, homicide

homologar [omolo'ɣar] vt (COM: productos, tamaños) to standardize; **homólogo, a** nm/f: **su** etc **homólogo** his etc counterpart o opposite number

homosexual [omosek'swal] adj, nm/f homosexual

hondo, a ['ondo, a] adj deep; **lo ~** the depth(s) (pl), the bottom; **~nada** nf hollow, depression; (*cañón*) ravine

Honduras [on'duras] *nf* Honduras

hondureño, a [ondu'reɲo, a] *adj, nm/f* Honduran

honestidad [onesti'ðað] *nf* purity, chastity; (*decencia*) decency; **honesto, a** *adj* chaste; decent, honest; (*justo*) just

hongo ['ongo] *nm* (*BOT: gen*) fungus; (*: comestible*) mushroom; (*: venenoso*) toadstool

honor [o'nor] *nm* (*gen*) honour; **en ~ a la verdad** to be fair; **~able** *adj* honourable

honorario, a [ono'rarjo, a] *adj* honorary; **~s** *nmpl* fees

honra ['onra] *nf* (*gen*) honour; (*renombre*) good name; **~dez** *nf* honesty; (*de persona*) integrity; **~do, a** *adj* honest, upright

honrar [on'rar] *vt* to honour; **~se** *vr*: **~se con algo/de hacer algo** to be honoured by sth/to do sth

honroso, a [on'roso, a] *adj* (*honrado*) honourable; (*respetado*) respectable

hora ['ora] *nf* (*una ~*) hour; (*tiempo*) time; **¿qué ~ es?** what time is it?; **¿a qué ~?** at what time?; **media ~** half an hour; **a la ~ de recreo** at playtime; **a primera ~** first thing (in the morning); **a última ~** at the last moment; **a altas ~s** in the small hours; **¡a buena ~!** about time, too!; **dar la ~** to strike the hour; **~s de oficina/de trabajo** office/working hours; **~s de visita** visiting times; **~s extras** *o* **extraordinarias** overtime *sg*; **~s punta** rush hours

horadar [ora'ðar] *vt* to drill, bore

horario, a [o'rarjo, a] *adj* hourly, hour *cpd* ♦ *nm* timetable; **~ comercial** business hours *pl*

horca ['orka] *nf* gallows *sg*

horcajadas [orka'xaðas] **: a ~** *adv* astride

horchata [or'tʃata] *nf* cold drink made from tiger nuts and water, tiger nut milk

horizontal [oriθon'tal] *adj* horizontal

horizonte [ori'θonte] *nm* horizon

horma ['orma] *nf* mould

hormiga [or'miɣa] *nf* ant; **~s** *nfpl* (*MED*) pins and needles

hormigón [ormi'ɣon] *nm* concrete; **~ armado/pretensado** reinforced/prestressed concrete

hormigueo [ormi'ɣeo] *nm* (*comezón*) itch

hormona [or'mona] *nf* hormone

hornada [or'naða] *nf* batch (of loaves *etc*)

hornillo [or'niʎo] *nm* (*cocina*) portable stove

horno ['orno] *nm* (*CULIN*) oven; (*TEC*) furnace; **alto ~** blast furnace

horóscopo [o'roskopo] *nm* horoscope

horquilla [or'kiʎa] *nf* hairpin; (*AGR*) pitchfork

horrendo, a [o'rrendo, a] *adj* horrendous, frightful

horrible [o'rriβle] *adj* horrible, dreadful

horripilante [orripi'lante] *adj* hair-raising,

horrifying

horror [o'rror] *nm* horror, dread; (*atrocidad*) atrocity; **¡qué ~!** (*fam*) how awful!; **~izar** *vt* to horrify, frighten; **~izarse** *vr* to be horrified; **~oso, a** *adj* horrifying, ghastly

hortaliza [orta'liθa] *nf* vegetable

hortelano, a [orte'lano, a] *nm/f* (market) gardener

hortera [or'tera] (*fam*) *adj* tacky

hosco, a ['osko, a] *adj* sullen, gloomy

hospedar [ospe'ðar] *vt* to put up; **~se** *vr* to stay, lodge

hospital [ospi'tal] *nm* hospital

hospitalario, a [ospita'larjo, a] *adj* (*acogedor*) hospitable; **hospitalidad** *nf* hospitality

hostal [os'tal] *nm* small hotel

hostelería [ostele'ria] *nf* hotel business *o* trade

hostia ['ostja] *nf* (*REL*) host, consecrated wafer; (*fam!: golpe*) whack, punch ♦ *excl* (*fam!*): **¡~(s)!** damn!

hostigar [osti'ɣar] *vt* to whip; (*fig*) to harass, pester

hostil [os'til] *adj* hostile; **~idad** *nf* hostility

hotel [o'tel] *nm* hotel; **~ero, a** *adj* hotel *cpd* ♦ *nm/f* hotelier

hoy [oi] *adv* (*este día*) today; (*la actualidad*) now(adays) ♦ *nm* present time; **~ (en) día** now(adays)

hoyo ['ojo] *nm* hole, pit; **hoyuelo** *nm* dimple

hoz [oθ] *nf* sickle

hube *etc vb ver* **haber**

hucha ['utʃa] *nf* money box

hueco, a ['weko, a] *adj* (*vacío*) hollow, empty; (*resonante*) booming ♦ *nm* hollow, cavity

huelga *etc* ['welɣa] *vb ver* **holgar** ♦ *nf* strike; **declararse en ~** to go on strike, come out on strike; **~ de hambre** hunger strike

huelguista [wel'ɣista] *nm/f* striker

huella ['weʎa] *nf* (*pisada*) tread; (*marca del paso*) footprint, footstep; (*: de animal, máquina*) track; **~ digital** fingerprint

huelo *etc vb ver* **oler**

huérfano, a ['werfano, a] *adj* orphan(ed) ♦ *nm/f* orphan

huerta ['werta] *nf* market garden; (*en Murcia y Valencia*) irrigated region

huerto ['werto] *nm* kitchen garden; (*de árboles frutales*) orchard

hueso ['weso] *nm* (*ANAT*) bone; (*de fruta*) stone

huésped, a ['wespeð, a] *nm/f* guest

huesudo, a [we'suðo, a] *adj* bony, big-boned

hueva ['weβa] *nf* roe

huevera [we'βera] *nf* eggcup

huevo ['weβo] *nm* egg; **~ duro/escalfado/frito/**

(*ESP*) o **estrellado** (*AM*)/**pasado por agua** hard-boiled/poached/fried/soft-boiled egg; **~s revueltos** scrambled eggs

huida [u'iða] *nf* escape, flight

huidizo, a [ui'ðiθo, a] *adj* shy

huir [u'ir] *vi* (*escapar*) to flee, escape; (*evitar*) to avoid; **~se** *vr* (*escaparse*) to escape

hule ['ule] *nm* oilskin

humanidad [umani'ðað] *nf* (*género humano*) man(kind); (*cualidad*) humanity

humanitario, a [umani'tarjo, a] *adj* humanitarian

humano, a [u'mano, a] *adj* (*gen*) human; (*humanitario*) humane ♦ *nm* human; **ser ~** human being

humareda [uma'reða] *nf* cloud of smoke

humedad [ume'ðað] *nf* (*del clima*) humidity; (*de pared etc*) dampness; **a prueba de ~** damp-proof; **humedecer** *vt* to moisten, wet; **humedecerse** *vr* to get wet

húmedo, a ['umeðo, a] *adj* (*mojado*) damp, wet; (*tiempo etc*) humid

humildad [umil'dað] *nf* humility, humbleness; **humilde** *adj* humble, modest

humillación [umiʎa'θjon] *nf* humiliation; **humillante** *adj* humiliating

humillar [umi'ʎar] *vt* to humiliate; **~se** *vr* to humble o.s., grovel

humo ['umo] *nm* (*de fuego*) smoke; (*gas nocivo*) fumes *pl*; (*vapor*) steam, vapour; **~s** *nmpl* (*fig*) conceit *sg*

humor [u'mor] *nm* (*disposición*) mood, temper; (*lo que divierte*) humour; **de buen/mal ~** in a good/bad mood; **~ista** *nm/f* comic; **~ístico, a** *adj* funny, humorous

hundimiento [undi'mjento] *nm* (*gen*) sinking; (*colapso*) collapse

hundir [un'dir] *vt* to sink; (*edificio, plan*) to ruin, destroy; **~se** *vr* to sink, collapse

húngaro, a ['ungaro, a] *adj, nm/f* Hungarian

Hungría [un'gria] *nf* Hungary

huracán [ura'kan] *nm* hurricane

huraño, a [u'raɲo, a] *adj* (*antisocial*) unsociable

hurgar [ur'xar] *vt* to poke, jab; (*remover*) to stir (up); **~se** *vr*: **~se (las narices)** to pick one's nose

hurón, ona [u'ron, ona] *nm* (*ZOOL*) ferret

hurtadillas [urta'ðiʎas]: **a ~** *adv* stealthily, on the sly

hurtar [ur'tar] *vt* to steal; **hurto** *nm* theft, stealing

husmear [usme'ar] *vt* (*oler*) to sniff out, scent; (*fam*) to pry into

huyo *etc vb ver* **huir**

I, i

iba *etc vb ver* **ir**

ibérico, a [i'ßeriko, a] *adj* Iberian

iberoamericano, a [ißeroameri'kano, a] *adj, nm/f* Latin American

Ibiza [i'ßiθa] *nf* Ibiza

iceberg [iθe'ßer] *nm* iceberg

icono [i'kono] *nm* ikon, icon

iconoclasta [ikono'klasta] *adj* iconoclastic ♦ *nm/f* iconoclast

ictericia [ikte'riθja] *nf* jaundice

I + D *abr* (= *Investigación y Desarrollo*) R & D

ida ['iða] *nf* going, departure; **~ y vuelta** round trip, return

idea [i'ðea] *nf* idea; **no tengo la menor ~** I haven't a clue

ideal [iðe'al] *adj, nm* ideal; **~ista** *nm/f* idealist; **~izar** *vt* to idealize

idear [iðe'ar] *vt* to think up; (*aparato*) to invent; (*viaje*) to plan

ídem ['iðem] *pron* ditto

idéntico, a [i'ðentiko, a] *adj* identical

identidad [iðenti'ðað] *nf* identity

identificación [iðentifika'θjon] *nf* identification

identificar [iðentifi'kar] *vt* to identify; **~se** *vr*: **~se con** to identify with

ideología [iðeolo'xia] *nf* ideology

idilio [i'ðiljo] *nm* love-affair

idioma [i'ðjoma] *nm* (*gen*) language

idiota [i'ðjota] *adj* idiotic ♦ *nm/f* idiot; **idiotez** *nf* idiocy

ídolo ['iðolo] *nm* (*tb: fig*) idol

idóneo, a [i'ðoneo, a] *adj* suitable

iglesia [i'ɣlesja] *nf* church

ignorancia [iɣno'ranθja] *nf* ignorance; **ignorante** *adj* ignorant, uninformed ♦ *nm/f* ignoramus

ignorar [iɣno'rar] *vt* not to know, be ignorant of; (*no hacer caso a*) to ignore

igual [i'ɣwal] *adj* (*gen*) equal; (*similar*) like, similar; (*mismo*) (the) same; (*constante*) constant; (*temperatura*) even ♦ *nm/f* equal; **~ que** like, the same as; **me da o es ~** I don't care; **son ~es** they're the same; **al ~ que** *prep, conj* like, just like

igualada [iɣwa'laða] *nf* equaliser

igualar [iɣwa'lar] *vt* (*gen*) to equalize, make equal; (*allanar, nivelar*) to level (off), even (out); **~se** *vr* (*platos de balanza*) to balance out

igualdad [iɣwal'dað] *nf* equality; (*similaridad*) sameness; (*uniformidad*) uniformity

igualmente [iɣwal'mente] *adv* equally; (*también*) also, likewise ♦ *excl* the same to you!

ikurriña [iku'rriɲa] nf Basque flag

ilegal [ile'val] adj illegal

ilegítimo, a [ile'xitimo, a] adj illegitimate

ileso, a [i'leso, a] adj unhurt

ilícito, a [i'liθito] adj illicit

ilimitado, a [ilimi'taðo, a] adj unlimited

ilógico, a [i'loxiko, a] adj illogical

iluminación [ilumina'θjon] nf illumination; (alumbrado) lighting

iluminar [ilumi'nar] vt to illuminate, light (up); (fig) to enlighten

ilusión [ilu'sjon] nf illusion; (quimera) delusion; (esperanza) hope; **hacerse ilusiones** to build up one's hopes; **ilusionado, a** adj excited; **ilusionar** vt: **le ilusiona ir de vacaciones** he's looking forward to going on holiday; **ilusionarse** vr: **ilusionarse (con)** to get excited (about)

ilusionista [ilusjo'nista] nm/f conjurer

iluso, a [i'luso, a] adj easily deceived ♦ nm/f dreamer

ilusorio, a [ilu'sorjo, a] adj (de ilusión) illusory, deceptive; (esperanza) vain

ilustración [ilustra'θjon] nf illustration; (saber) learning, erudition; **la l~** the Enlightenment; **ilustrado, a** adj illustrated; learned

ilustrar [ilus'trar] vt to illustrate; (instruir) to instruct; (explicar) to explain, make clear; **~se** vr to acquire knowledge

ilustre [i'lustre] adj famous, illustrious

imagen [i'maxen] nf (gen) image; (dibujo) picture

imaginación [imaxina'θjon] nf imagination

imaginar [imaxi'nar] vt (gen) to imagine; (idear) to think up; (suponer) to suppose; **~se** vr to imagine; **~io, a** adj imaginary; **imaginativo, a** adj imaginative

imán [i'man] nm magnet

imbécil [im'beθil] nm/f imbecile, idiot

imitación [imita'θjon] nf imitation

imitar [imi'tar] vt to imitate; (parodiar, remedar) to mimic, ape

impaciencia [impa'θjenθja] nf impatience; **impaciente** adj impatient; (nervioso) anxious

impacto [im'pakto] nm impact

impar [im'par] adj odd

imparcial [impar'θjal] adj impartial, fair

impartir [impar'tir] vt to impart, give

impasible [impa'siβle] adj impassive

impecable [impe'kaβle] adj impeccable

impedimento [impeði'mento] nm impediment, obstacle

impedir [impe'ðir] vt (obstruir) to impede, obstruct; (estorbar) to prevent

impenetrable [impene'traβle] adj impenetrable; (fig) incomprehensible

imperar [impe'rar] vi (reinar) to rule, reign; (fig) to prevail, reign; (precio) to be current

imperativo, a [impera'tiβo, a] adj (urgente, LING) imperative

imperceptible [imperθep'tiβle] adj imperceptible

imperdible [imper'ðiβle] nm safety pin

imperdonable [imperðo'naβle] adj unforgivable, inexcusable

imperfección [imperfek'θjon] nf imperfection

imperfecto, a [imper'fekto, a] adj imperfect

imperial [impe'rjal] adj imperial; **~ismo** nm imperialism

imperio [im'perjo] nm empire; (autoridad) rule, authority; (fig) pride, haughtiness; **~so, a** adj imperious; (urgente) urgent; (imperativo) imperative

impermeable [imperme'aβle] adj waterproof ♦ nm raincoat, mac (BRIT)

impersonal [imperso'nal] adj impersonal

impertinencia [imperti'nenθja] nf impertinence; **impertinente** adj impertinent

imperturbable [impertur'ßaβle] adj imperturbable

ímpetu ['impetu] nm (impulso) impetus, impulse; (impetuosidad) impetuosity; (violencia) violence

impetuoso, a [impe'twoso, a] adj impetuous; (río) rushing; (acto) hasty

impío, a [im'pio, a] adj impious, ungodly

implacable [impla'kaβle] adj implacable

implantar [implan'tar] vt to introduce

implicar [impli'kar] vt to involve; (entrañar) to imply

implícito, a [im'pliθito, a] adj (tácito) implicit; (sobreentendido) implied

implorar [implo'rar] vt to beg, implore

imponente [impo'nente] adj (impresionante) impressive, imposing; (solemne) grand

imponer [impo'ner] vt (gen) to impose; (exigir) to exact; **~se** vr to assert o.s.; (prevalecer) to prevail; **imponible** adj (COM) taxable

impopular [impopu'lar] adj unpopular

importación [importa'θjon] nf (acto) importing; (mercancías) imports pl

importancia [impor'tanθja] nf importance; (valor) value, significance; (extensión) size, magnitude; **importante** adj important; valuable, significant

importar [impor'tar] vt (del extranjero) to import; (costar) to amount to ♦ vi to be important, matter; **me importa un rábano** I couldn't care less; **no importa** it doesn't matter; **¿le importa que fume?** do you mind if I smoke?

importe [im'porte] nm (total) amount; (valor) value

importunar [importu'nar] *vt* to bother, pester

imposibilidad [imposiβili'ðað] *nf* impossibility; **imposibilitar** *vt* to make impossible, prevent

imposible [impo'siβle] *adj* (*gen*) impossible; (*insoportable*) unbearable, intolerable

imposición [imposi'θjon] *nf* imposition; (*COM: impuesto*) tax; (: *inversión*) deposit

impostor, a [impos'tor, a] *nm/f* impostor

impotencia [impo'tenθja] *nf* impotence; **impotente** *adj* impotent

impracticable [imprakti'kaβle] *adj* (*irrealizable*) impracticable; (*intransitable*) impassable

impreciso, a [impre'θiso, a] *adj* imprecise, vague

impregnar [imprev'nar] *vt* to impregnate; **~se** *vr* to become impregnated

imprenta [im'prenta] *nf* (*acto*) printing; (*aparato*) press; (*casa*) printer's; (*letra*) print

imprescindible [impresθin'diβle] *adj* essential, vital

impresión [impre'sjon] *nf* (*gen*) impression; (*IMPRENTA*) printing; (*edición*) edition; (*FOTO*) print; (*marca*) imprint; **~ digital** fingerprint

impresionable [impresjo'naβle] *adj* (*sensible*) impressionable

impresionante [impresjo'nante] *adj* impressive; (*tremendo*) tremendous; (*maravilloso*) great, marvellous

impresionar [impresjo'nar] *vt* (*conmover*) to move; (*afectar*) to impress, strike; (*película fotográfica*) to expose; **~se** *vr* to be impressed; (*conmoverse*) to be moved

impreso, a [im'preso, a] *pp de* **imprimir** ♦ *adj* printed; **~s** *nmpl* printed matter; **impresora** *nf* printer

imprevisto, a [impre'βisto, a] *adj* (*gen*) unforeseen; (*inesperado*) unexpected

imprimir [impri'mir] *vt* to imprint, impress, stamp; (*textos*) to print; (*INFORM*) to output, print out

improbable [impro'βaβle] *adj* improbable; (*inverosímil*) unlikely

improcedente [improθe'ðente] *adj* inappropriate

improductivo, a [improðuk'tiβo, a] *adj* unproductive

improperio [impro'perjo] *nm* insult

impropio, a [im'propjo, a] *adj* improper

improvisado, a [improβi'saðo, a] *adj* improvised

improvisar [improβi'sar] *vt* to improvise

improviso, a [impro'βiso, a] *adj*: **de ~** unexpectedly, suddenly

imprudencia [impru'ðenθja] *nf* imprudence; (*indiscreción*) indiscretion; (*descuido*) carelessness; **imprudente** *adj*
unwise, imprudent; (*indiscreto*) indiscreet

impúdico, a [im'puðiko, a] *adj* shameless; (*lujurioso*) lecherous

impuesto, a [im'pwesto, a] *adj* imposed ♦ *nm* tax; **~ sobre el valor añadido** value added tax

impugnar [impuv'nar] *vt* to oppose, contest; (*refutar*) to refute, impugn

impulsar [impul'sar] *vt* to drive; (*promover*) to promote, stimulate

impulsivo, a [impul'siβo, a] *adj* impulsive; **impulso** *nm* impulse; (*fuerza, empuje*) thrust, drive; (*fig: sentimiento*) urge, impulse

impune [im'pune] *adj* unpunished

impureza [impu'reθa] *nf* impurity; **impuro, a** *adj* impure

imputar [impu'tar] *vt* to attribute

inacabable [inaka'βaβle] *adj* (*infinito*) endless; (*interminable*) interminable

inaccesible [inakθe'siβle] *adj* inaccessible

inacción [inak'θjon] *nf* inactivity

inaceptable [inaθep'taβle] *adj* unacceptable

inactividad [inaktiβi'ðað] *nf* inactivity; (*COM*) dullness; **inactivo, a** *adj* inactive

inadecuado, a [inaðe'kwaðo, a] *adj* (*insuficiente*) inadequate; (*inapto*) unsuitable

inadmisible [inaðmi'siβle] *adj* inadmissible

inadvertido, a [inaðβer'tiðo, a] *adj* (*no visto*) unnoticed

inagotable [inavo'taβle] *adj* inexhaustible

inaguantable [inavwan'taβle] *adj* unbearable

inalterable [inalte'raβle] *adj* immutable, unchangeable

inanición [inani'θjon] *nf* starvation

inanimado, a [inani'maðo, a] *adj* inanimate

inapreciable [inapre'θjaβle] *adj* (*cantidad, diferencia*) imperceptible; (*ayuda, servicio*) invaluable

inaudito, a [inau'ðito, a] *adj* unheard-of

inauguración [inauvura'θjon] *nf* inauguration; opening

inaugurar [inauvu'rar] *vt* to inaugurate; (*exposición*) to open

inca ['inka] *nm/f* Inca

incalculable [inkalku'laβle] *adj* incalculable

incandescente [inkandes'θente] *adj* incandescent

incansable [inkan'saβle] *adj* tireless, untiring

incapacidad [inkapaθi'ðað] *nf* incapacity; (*incompetencia*) incompetence; **~ física/ mental** physical/mental disability

incapacitar [inkapaθi'tar] *vt* (*inhabilitar*) to incapacitate, render unfit; (*descalificar*) to disqualify

incapaz [inka'paθ] *adj* incapable

incautación [inkauta'θjon] *nf* confiscation

incautarse [inkau'tarse] *vr*: **~ de** to seize, confiscate

incauto, a [in'kauto, a] adj (*imprudente*) incautious, unwary

incendiar [inθen'djar] vt to set fire to; (*fig*) to inflame; **~se** vr to catch fire; **~io, a** adj incendiary

incendio [in'θendjo] nm fire

incentivo [inθen'tiβo] nm incentive

incertidumbre [inθerti'ðumbre] nf (*inseguridad*) uncertainty; (*duda*) doubt

incesante [inθe'sante] adj incessant

incesto [in'θesto] nm incest

incidencia [inθi'ðenθja] nf (MAT) incidence

incidente [inθi'ðente] nm incident

incidir [inθi'ðir] vi (*influir*) to influence; (*afectar*) to affect; **~ en un error** to fall into error

incienso [in'θjenso] nm incense

incierto, a [in'θjerto, a] adj uncertain

incineración [inθinera'θjon] nf incineration; (*de cadáveres*) cremation

incinerar [inθine'rar] vt to burn; (*cadáveres*) to cremate

incipiente [inθi'pjente] adj incipient

incisión [inθi'sjon] nf incision

incisivo, a [inθi'siβo, a] adj sharp, cutting; (*fig*) incisive

incitar [inθi'tar] vt to incite, rouse

inclemencia [inkle'menθja] nf (*severidad*) harshness, severity; (*del tiempo*) inclemency

inclinación [inklina'θjon] nf (*gen*) inclination; (*de tierras*) slope, incline; (*de cabeza*) nod, bow; (*fig*) leaning, bent

inclinar [inkli'nar] vt to incline; (*cabeza*) to nod, bow ♦ vi to lean, slope; **~se** vr to bow; (*encorvarse*) to stoop; **~se a** (*parecerse a*) to take after, resemble; **~se ante** to bow down to; **me inclino a pensar que** I'm inclined to think that

incluir [inklu'ir] vt to include; (*incorporar*) to incorporate; (*meter*) to enclose

inclusive [inklu'siβe] adv inclusive ♦ prep including

incluso [in'kluso] adv even

incógnita [in'koɣnita] nf (MAT) unknown quantity

incógnito [in'koɣnito] nm: **de ~** incognito

incoherente [inkoe'rente] adj incoherent

incoloro, a [inko'loro, a] adj colourless

incólume [in'kolume] adj unhurt, unharmed

incomodar [inkomo'ðar] vt to inconvenience; (*molestar*) to bother, trouble; (*fastidiar*) to annoy; **~se** vr to put o.s. out; (*fastidiarse*) to get annoyed

incomodidad [inkomoði'ðað] nf inconvenience; (*fastidio, enojo*) annoyance; (*de vivienda*) discomfort

incómodo, a [in'komoðo, a] adj (*inconfortable*) uncomfortable; (*molesto*) annoying; (*inconveniente*) inconvenient

incomparable [inkompa'raβle] adj incomparable

incompatible [inkompa'tiβle] adj incompatible

incompetencia [inkompe'tenθja] nf incompetence; **incompetente** adj incompetent

incompleto, a [inkom'pleto, a] adj incomplete, unfinished

incomprensible [inkompren'siβle] adj incomprehensible

incomunicado, a [inkomuni'kaðo, a] adj (*aislado*) cut off, isolated; (*confinado*) in solitary confinement

inconcebible [inkonθe'βiβle] adj inconceivable

incondicional [inkondiθjo'nal] adj unconditional; (*apoyo*) wholehearted; (*partidario*) staunch

inconexo, a [inko'nekso, a] adj (*gen*) unconnected; (*desunido*) disconnected

inconfundible [inkonfun'diβle] adj unmistakable

incongruente [inkon'grwente] adj incongruous

inconsciencia [inkons'θjenθja] nf unconsciousness; (*fig*) thoughtlessness; **inconsciente** adj unconscious; thoughtless

inconsecuente [inkonse'kwente] adj inconsistent

inconsiderado, a [inkonsiðe'raðo, a] adj inconsiderate

inconsistente [inkonsis'tente] adj weak; (*tela*) flimsy

inconstancia [inkon'stanθja] nf inconstancy; (*inestabilidad*) unsteadiness; **inconstante** adj inconstant

incontable [inkon'taβle] adj countless, innumerable

incontestable [ínkontes'taβle] adj unanswerable; (*innegable*) undeniable

incontinencia [inkonti'nenθja] nf incontinence

inconveniencia [inkombe'njenθja] nf unsuitability, inappropriateness; (*descortesía*) impoliteness; **inconveniente** adj unsuitable; impolite ♦ nm obstacle; (*desventaja*) disadvantage; **el inconveniente es que ...** the trouble is that ...

incordiar [inkor'ðjar] (*fam*) vt to bug, annoy

incorporación [inkorpora'θjon] nf incorporation

incorporar [inkorpo'rar] vt to incorporate; **~se** vr to sit up

incorrección [inkorrek'θjon] nf (*gen*) incorrectness, inaccuracy; (*descortesía*) bad-mannered behaviour; **incorrecto, a** adj (*gen*) incorrect, wrong; (*comportamiento*) bad-mannered

incorregible [inkorre'xiβle] *adj* incorrigible

incredulidad [inkreδuli'δaδ] *nf* incredulity; (*escepticismo*) scepticism; **incrédulo, a** *adj* incredulous, unbelieving; sceptical

increíble [inkre'iβle] *adj* incredible

incremento [inkre'mento] *nm* increment; (*aumento*) rise, increase

increpar [inkre'par] *vt* to reprimand

incruento, a [in'krwento, a] *adj* bloodless

incrustar [inkrus'tar] *vt* to incrust; (*piedras: en joya*) to inlay

incubar [inku'βar] *vt* to incubate

inculcar [inkul'kar] *vt* to inculcate

inculpar [inkul'par] *vt* (*acusar*) to accuse; (*achacar, atribuir*) to charge, blame

inculto, a [in'kulto, a] *adj* (*persona*) uneducated; (*grosero*) uncouth ♦ *nm/f* ignoramus

incumplimiento [inkumpli'mjento] *nm* non-fulfilment; ~ **de contrato** breach of contract

incurrir [inku'rrir] *vi*: ~ **en** to incur; (*crimen*) to commit; ~ **en un error** to make a mistake

indagación [indaxa'θjon] *nf* investigation; (*búsqueda*) search; (*JUR*) inquest

indagar [inda'var] *vt* to investigate; to search; (*averiguar*) to ascertain

indecente [inde'θente] *adj* indecent, improper; (*lascivo*) obscene

indecible [inde'θiβle] *adj* unspeakable; (*indescriptible*) indescribable

indeciso, a [inde'θiso, a] *adj* (*por decidir*) undecided; (*vacilante*) hesitant

indefenso, a [inde'fenso, a] *adj* defenceless

indefinido, a [indefi'niδo, a] *adj* indefinite; (*vago*) vague, undefined

indeleble [inde'leβle] *adj* indelible

indemne [in'demne] *adj* (*objeto*) undamaged; (*persona*) unharmed, unhurt

indemnizar [indemni'θar] *vt* to indemnify; (*compensar*) to compensate

independencia [indepen'denθja] *nf* independence

independiente [indepen'djente] *adj* (*libre*) independent; (*autónomo*) self-sufficient

indeterminado, a [indetermi'naδo, a] *adj* indefinite; (*desconocido*) indeterminate

India ['indja] *nf*: **la ~** India

indicación [indika'θjon] *nf* indication; (*señal*) sign; (*sugerencia*) suggestion, hint

indicado, a [indi'kaδo, a] *adj* (*momento, método*) right; (*tratamiento*) appropriate; (*solución*) likely

indicador [indika'δor] *nm* indicator; (*TEC*) gauge, meter

indicar [indi'kar] *vt* (*mostrar*) to indicate, show; (*termómetro etc*) to read, register; (*señalar*) to point to

índice ['indiθe] *nm* index; (*catálogo*) catalogue; (*ANAT*) index finger, forefinger

indicio [in'diθjo] *nm* indication, sign; (*en pesquisa etc*) clue

indiferencia [indife'renθja] *nf* indifference; (*apatía*) apathy; **indiferente** *adj* indifferent

indígena [in'dixena] *adj* indigenous, native ♦ *nm/f* native

indigencia [indi'xenθja] *nf* poverty, need

indigestión [indixes'tjon] *nf* indigestion

indigesto, a [indi'xesto, a] *adj* (*alimento*) indigestible; (*fig*) turgid

indignación [indixna'θjon] *nf* indignation

indignar [indix'nar] *vt* to anger, make indignant; ~**se** *vr*: ~**se por** to get indignant about

indigno, a [in'divno, a] *adj* (*despreciable*) low, contemptible; (*inmerecido*) unworthy

indio, a ['indjo, a] *adj, nm/f* Indian

indirecta [indi'rekta] *nf* insinuation, innuendo; (*sugerencia*) hint

indirecto, a [indi'rekto, a] *adj* indirect

indiscreción [indiskre'θjon] *nf* (*imprudencia*) indiscretion; (*irreflexión*) tactlessness; (*acto*) gaffe, faux pas

indiscreto, a [indis'kreto, a] *adj* indiscreet

indiscriminado, a [indiskrimi'naδo, a] *adj* indiscriminate

indiscutible [indisku'tiβle] *adj* indisputable, unquestionable

indispensable [indispen'saβle] *adj* indispensable, essential

indisponer [indispo'ner] *vt* to spoil, upset; (*salud*) to make ill; ~**se** *vr* to fall ill; ~**se con uno** to fall out with sb

indisposición [indisposi'θjon] *nf* indisposition

indispuesto, a [indis'pwesto, a] *adj* (*enfermo*) unwell, indisposed

indistinto, a [indis'tinto, a] *adj* indistinct; (*vago*) vague

individual [indiβi'δwal] *adj* individual; (*habitación*) single ♦ *nm* (*DEPORTE*) singles *sg*

individuo, a [indi'βiδwo, a] *adj, nm* individual

índole ['indole] *nf* (*naturaleza*) nature; (*clase*) sort, kind

indómito, a [in'domito, a] *adj* indomitable

inducir [indu'θir] *vt* to induce; (*inferir*) to infer; (*persuadir*) to persuade

indudable [indu'δaβle] *adj* undoubted; (*incuestionable*) unquestionable

indulgencia [indul'xenθja] *nf* indulgence

indultar [indul'tar] *vt* (*perdonar*) to pardon, reprieve; (*librar de pago*) to exempt; **indulto** *nm* pardon; exemption

industria [in'dustrja] *nf* industry; (*habilidad*) skill; **industrial** *adj* industrial ♦ *nm* industrialist

inédito, a [in'eδito, a] *adj* (*texto*)

unpublished; (*nuevo*) new
inefable [ine'faßle] *adj* ineffable,
indescribable
ineficaz [inefi'kaθ] *adj* (*inútil*) ineffective;
(*ineficiente*) inefficient
ineludible [inelu'ðißle] *adj* inescapable,
unavoidable
ineptitud [inepti'tuð] *nf* ineptitude,
incompetence; **inepto, a** *adj* inept,
incompetent
inequívoco, a [ine'kißoko, a] *adj*
unequivocal; (*inconfundible*) unmistakable
inercia [in'erθja] *nf* inertia; (*pasividad*)
passivity
inerme [in'erme] *adj* (*sin armas*) unarmed;
(*indefenso*) defenceless
inerte [in'erte] *adj* inert; (*inmóvil*) motionless
inesperado, a [inespe'raðo, a] *adj*
unexpected, unforeseen
inestable [ines'taßle] *adj* unstable
inevitable [neßi'taßle] *adj* inevitable
inexactitud [ineksakti'tuð] *nf* inaccuracy;
inexacto, a *adj* inaccurate; (*falso*) untrue
inexperto, a [inek'sperto, a] *adj* (*novato*)
inexperienced
infalible [infa'lißle] *adj* infallible; (*plan*)
foolproof
infame [in'fame] *adj* infamous; (*horrible*)
dreadful; **infamia** *nf* infamy; (*deshonra*)
disgrace
infancia [in'fanθja] *nf* infancy, childhood
infantería [infante'ria] *nf* infantry
infantil [infan'til] *adj* (*pueril, aniñado*)
infantile; (*cándido*) childlike; (*literatura, ropa
etc*) children's
infarto [in'farto] *nm* (*tb: ~ de miocardio*)
heart attack
infatigable [infati'yaßle] *adj* tireless, untiring
infección [infek'θjon] *nf* infection;
infeccioso, a *adj* infectious
infectar [infek'tar] *vt* to infect; **~se** *vr* to
become infected
infeliz [infe'liθ] *adj* unhappy, wretched
♦ *nm/f* wretch
inferior [infe'rjor] *adj* inferior; (*situación*)
lower ♦ *nm/f* inferior, subordinate
inferir [infe'rir] *vt* (*deducir*) to infer, deduce;
(*causar*) to cause
infestar [infes'tar] *vt* to infest
infidelidad [infiðeli'ðað] *nf* (*gen*) infidelity,
unfaithfulness
infiel [in'fjel] *adj* unfaithful, disloyal; (*erróneo*)
inaccurate ♦ *nm/f* infidel, unbeliever
infierno [in'fjerno] *nm* hell
infiltrarse [infil'trarse] *vr:* **~ en** to infiltrate
in(to); (*persona*) to work one's way in(to)
ínfimo, a [ˈinfimo, a] *adj* (*más bajo*) lowest;
(*despreciable*) vile, mean
infinidad [infini'ðað] *nf* infinity;

(*abundancia*) great quantity
infinito, a [infi'nito, a] *adj, nm* infinite
inflación [infla'θjon] *nf* (*hinchazón*) swelling;
(*monetaria*) inflation; (*fig*) conceit;
inflacionario, a *adj* inflationary
inflamar [infla'mar] *vt* (*MED, fig*) to inflame;
~se *vr* to catch fire; to become inflamed
inflar [in'flar] *vt* (*hinchar*) to inflate, blow up;
(*fig*) to exaggerate; **~se** *vr* to swell (up); (*fig*)
to get conceited
inflexible [inflek'sißle] *adj* inflexible; (*fig*)
unbending
infligir [infli'xir] *vt* to inflict
influencia [influ'enθja] *nf* influence;
influenciar *vt* to influence
influir [influ'ir] *vt* to influence
influjo [in'fluxo] *nm* influence
influya *etc vb ver* **influir**
influyente [influ'jente] *adj* influential
información [informa'θjon] *nf* information;
(*noticias*) news *sg*; (*JUR*) inquiry; **I~** (*oficina*)
Information Office; (*mostrador*) Information
Desk; (*TEL*) Directory Enquiries
informal [infor'mal] *adj* (*gen*) informal
informar [infor'mar] *vt* (*gen*) to inform;
(*revelar*) to reveal, make known ♦ *vi* (*JUR*) to
plead; (*denunciar*) to inform; (*dar cuenta de*)
to report on; **~se** *vr* to find out; **~se de** to
inquire into
informática [infor'matika] *nf* computer
science, information technology
informe [in'forme] *adj* shapeless ♦ *nm* report
infortunio [infor'tunjo] *nm* misfortune
infracción [infrak'θjon] *nf* infraction,
infringement
infranqueable [infranke'aßle] *adj*
impassable; (*fig*) insurmountable
infravalorar [infrabalo'rar] *vt* to undervalue,
underestimate
infringir [infrin'xir] *vt* to infringe, contravene
infructuoso, a [infruk'twoso, a] *adj*
fruitless, unsuccessful
infundado, a [infun'daðo, a] *adj*
groundless, unfounded
infundir [infun'dir] *vt* to infuse, instil
infusión [infu'sjon] *nf* infusion; **~ de
manzanilla** camomile tea
ingeniar [inxe'njar] *vt* to think up, devise;
~se *vr:* **~se para** to manage to
ingeniería [inxenje'ria] *nf* engineering;
~ genética genetic engineering; **ingeniero, a**
nm/f engineer; **ingeniero de caminos/de
sonido** civil engineer/sound engineer
ingenio [in'xenjo] *nm* (*talento*) talent;
(*agudeza*) wit; (*habilidad*) ingenuity,
inventiveness; **~ azucarero** (*AM*) sugar refinery
ingenioso, a [inxe'njoso, a] *adj* ingenious,
clever; (*divertido*) witty
ingenuidad [inxenwi'ðað] *nf* ingenuousness;

(*sencillez*) simplicity; **ingenuo, a** *adj* ingenuous

ingerir [inxe'rir] *vt* to ingest; (*tragar*) to swallow; (*consumir*) to consume

Inglaterra [ingla'terra] *nf* England

ingle ['ingle] *nf* groin

inglés, esa [in'gles, esa] *adj* English ♦ *nm/f* Englishman/woman ♦ *nm* (*LING*) English

ingratitud [ingrati'tuð] *nf* ingratitude; **ingrato, a** *adj* (*gen*) ungrateful

ingrediente [ingre'ðjente] *nm* ingredient

ingresar [ingre'sar] *vt* (*dinero*) to deposit ♦ *vi* to come in; ~ **en un club** to join a club; ~ **en el hospital** to go into hospital

ingreso [in'greso] *nm* (*entrada*) entry; (: *en hospital etc*) admission; **~s** *nmpl* (*dinero*) income *sg*; (: *COM*) takings *pl*

inhabitable [inaβi'taβle] *adj* uninhabitable

inhalar [ina'lar] *vt* to inhale

inherente [ine'rente] *adj* inherent

inhibir [ini'βir] *vt* to inhibit

inhóspito, a [i'nospito, a] *adj* (*región, paisaje*) inhospitable

inhumano, a [inu'mano, a] *adj* inhuman

inicial [ini'θjal] *adj, nf* initial

iniciar [ini'θjar] *vt* (*persona*) to initiate; (*empezar*) to begin, commence; (*conversación*) to start up

iniciativa [iniθja'tiβa] *nf* initiative; **la ~ privada** private enterprise

ininterrumpido, a [ininterrum'piðo, a] *adj* uninterrupted

injerencia [inxe'renθja] *nf* interference

injertar [inxer'tar] *vt* to graft; **injerto** *nm* graft

injuria [in'xurja] *nf* (*agravio, ofensa*) offence; (*insulto*) insult; **injuriar** *vt* to insult; **injurioso, a** *adj* offensive; insulting

injusticia [inxus'tiθja] *nf* injustice

injusto, a [in'xusto, a] *adj* unjust, unfair

inmadurez [inmaðu'reθ] *nf* immaturity

inmediaciones [inmeðja'θjones] *nfpl* neighbourhood *sg*, environs

inmediato, a [inme'ðjato, a] *adj* immediate; (*contiguo*) adjoining; (*rápido*) prompt; (*próximo*) neighbouring, next; **de ~** immediately

inmejorable [inmexo'raβle] *adj* unsurpassable; (*precio*) unbeatable

inmenso, a [in'menso, a] *adj* immense, huge

inmerecido, a [inmere'θiðo, a] *adj* undeserved

inmigración [inmixra'θjon] *nf* immigration

inmiscuirse [inmisku'irse] *vr* to interfere, meddle

inmobiliaria [inmoβi'ljarja] *nf* estate agency

inmobiliario, a [inmoβi'ljarjo, a] *adj* real-estate *cpd*, property *cpd*

inmolar [inmo'lar] *vt* to immolate, sacrifice

inmoral [inmo'ral] *adj* immoral

inmortal [inmor'tal] *adj* immortal; **~izar** *vt* to immortalize

inmóvil [in'moβil] *adj* immobile

inmueble [in'mweβle] *adj*: **bienes ~s** real estate, landed property ♦ *nm* property

inmundicia [inmun'diθja] *nf* filth; **inmundo, a** *adj* filthy

inmune [in'mune] *adj*: ~ **(a)** (*MED*) immune (to)

inmunidad [inmuni'ðað] *nf* immunity

inmutarse [inmu'tarse] *vr* to turn pale; **no se inmutó** he didn't turn a hair

innato, a [in'nato, a] *adj* innate

innecesario, a [inneθe'sarjo, a] *adj* unnecessary

innoble [in'noβle] *adj* ignoble

innovación [innoβa'θjon] *nf* innovation

innovar [inno'βar] *vt* to introduce

inocencia [ino'θenθja] *nf* innocence

inocentada [inoθen'taða] *nf* practical joke

inocente [ino'θente] *adj* (*ingenuo*) naive, innocent; (*inculpable*) innocent; (*sin malicia*) harmless ♦ *nm/f* simpleton

inodoro [ino'ðoro] *nm* toilet, lavatory (*BRIT*)

inofensivo, a [inofen'siβo, a] *adj* inoffensive, harmless

inolvidable [inolβi'ðaβle] *adj* unforgettable

inopinado, a [inopi'naðo, a] *adj* unexpected

inoportuno, a [inopor'tuno, a] *adj* untimely; (*molesto*) inconvenient

inoxidable [inoksi'ðaβle] *adj*: **acero ~** stainless steel

inquebrantable [inkeβran'taβle] *adj* unbreakable

inquietar [inkje'tar] *vt* to worry, trouble; **~se** *vr* to worry, get upset; **inquieto, a** *adj* anxious, worried; **inquietud** *nf* anxiety, worry

inquilino, a [inki'lino, a] *nm/f* tenant

inquirir [inki'rir] *vt* to enquire into, investigate

insaciable [insa'θjaβle] *adj* insatiable

insalubre [insa'luβre] *adj* unhealthy

inscribir [inskri'βir] *vt* to inscribe; ~ **a uno en** (*lista*) to put sb on; (*censo*) to register sb on; **inscripción** [inskrip'θjon] *nf* inscription; (*ESCOL etc*) enrolment; (*censo*) registration

insecticida [insekti'θiða] *nm* insecticide

insecto [in'sekto] *nm* insect

inseguridad [inseɣuri'ðað] *nf* insecurity

inseguro, a [inse'ɣuro, a] *adj* insecure; (*inconstante*) unsteady; (*incierto*) uncertain

insensato, a [insen'sato, a] *adj* foolish, stupid

insensibilidad [insensiβili'ðað] *nf* (*gen*) insensitivity; (*dureza de corazón*) callousness

insensible [insen'sißle] *adj* (*gen*) insensitive; (*movimiento*) imperceptible; (*sin sentido*) numb

insertar [inser'tar] *vt* to insert

inservible [inser'ßißle] *adj* useless

insidioso, a [insi'ðjoso, a] *adj* insidious

insignia [in'siɣnja] *nf* (*señal distintiva*) badge; (*estandarte*) flag

insignificante [insiɣnifi'kante] *adj* insignificant

insinuar [insi'nwar] *vt* to insinuate, imply

insípido, a [in'sipiðo, a] *adj* insipid

insistencia [insis'tenθja] *nf* insistence

insistir [insis'tir] *vi* to insist; ~ **en algo** to insist on sth; (*enfatizar*) to stress sth

insolación [insola'θjon] *nf* (*MED*) sunstroke

insolencia [inso'lenθja] *nf* insolence; **insolente** *adj* insolent

insólito, a [in'solito, a] *adj* unusual

insoluble [inso'lußle] *adj* insoluble

insolvencia [insol'ßenθja] *nf* insolvency

insomnio [in'somnjo] *nm* insomnia

insondable [inson'daßle] *adj* bottomless; (*fig*) impenetrable

insonorizado, a [insonori'θaðo, a] *adj* (*cuarto etc*) soundproof

insoportable [insopor'taßle] *adj* unbearable

insospechado, a [insospe'tʃaðo, a] *adj* (*inesperado*) unexpected

inspección [inspek'θjon] *nf* inspection, check; **inspeccionar** *vt* (*examinar*) to inspect, examine; (*controlar*) to check

inspector, a [inspek'tor, a] *nm/f* inspector

inspiración [inspira'θjon] *nf* inspiration

inspirar [inspi'rar] *vt* to inspire; (*MED*) to inhale; ~**se** *vr*: ~**se en** to be inspired by

instalación [instala'θjon] *nf* (*equipo*) fittings *pl*, equipment; ~ **eléctrica** wiring

instalar [insta'lar] *vt* (*establecer*) to instal; (*erguir*) to set up, erect; ~**se** *vr* to establish o.s.; (*en una vivienda*) to move into

instancia [ins'tanθja] *nf* (*JUR*) petition; (*ruego*) request; **en última ~** as a last resort

instantánea [instan'tanea] *nf* snap(shot)

instantáneo, a [instan'taneo, a] *adj* instantaneous; **café ~** instant coffee

instante [ins'tante] *nm* instant, moment

instar [ins'tar] *vt* to press, urge

instaurar [instau'rar] *vt* (*costumbre*) to establish; (*normas, sistema*) to bring in, introduce; (*gobierno*) to instal

instigar [insti'ɣar] *vt* to instigate

instinto [ins'tinto] *nm* instinct; **por ~** instinctively

institución [institu'θjon] *nf* institution, establishment

instituir [institu'ir] *vt* to establish; (*fundar*) to found; **instituto** *nm* (*gen*) institute; (*ESP: ESCOL*) ≈ comprehensive (*BRIT*) o high (*US*) school

institutriz [institu'triθ] *nf* governess

instrucción [instruk'θjon] *nf* instruction

instructivo, a [instruk'tißo, a] *adj* instructive

instruir [instru'ir] *vt* (*gen*) to instruct; (*enseñar*) to teach, educate

instrumento [instru'mento] *nm* (*gen*) instrument; (*herramienta*) tool, implement

insubordinarse [insußorði'narse] *vr* to rebel

insuficiencia [insufi'θjenθja] *nf* (*carencia*) lack; (*inadecuación*) inadequacy; **insuficiente** *adj* (*gen*) insufficient; (*ESCOL: calificación*) unsatisfactory

insufrible [insu'frißle] *adj* insufferable

insular [insu'lar] *adj* insular

insultar [insul'tar] *vt* to insult; **insulto** *nm* insult

insumiso, a [insu'miso, a] *nm/f* (*POL*) person who refuses to do military service or its substitute, community service

insuperable [insupe'raßle] *adj* (*excelente*) unsurpassable; (*problema etc*) insurmountable

insurgente [insur'xente] *adj, nm/f* insurgent

insurrección [insurrek'θjon] *nf* insurrection, rebellion

intachable [inta'tʃaßle] *adj* irreproachable

intacto, a [in'takto, a] *adj* intact

integral [inte'ɣral] *adj* integral; (*completo*) complete; **pan ~** wholemeal (*US*) bread

integrar [inte'ɣrar] *vt* to make up, compose; (*MAT, fig*) to integrate

integridad [inteɣri'ðað] *nf* wholeness; (*carácter*) integrity; **íntegro, a** *adj* whole, entire; (*honrado*) honest

intelectual [intelek'twal] *adj, nm/f* intellectual

inteligencia [inteli'xenθja] *nf* intelligence; (*ingenio*) ability; **inteligente** *adj* intelligent

inteligible [inteli'xißle] *adj* intelligible

intemperie [intem'perje] *nf*: **a la ~** out in the open, exposed to the elements

intempestivo, a [intempes'tißo, a] *adj* untimely

intención [inten'θjon] *nf* (*gen*) intention, purpose; **con segundas intenciones** maliciously; **con ~** deliberately

intencionado, a [intenθjo'naðo, a] *adj* deliberate; **bien ~** well-meaning; **mal ~** ill-disposed, hostile

intensidad [intensi'ðað] *nf* (*gen*) intensity; (*ELEC, TEC*) strength; **llover con ~** to rain hard

intenso, a [in'tenso, a] *adj* intense; (*sentimiento*) profound, deep

intentar [inten'tar] *vt* (*tratar*) to try, attempt; **intento** *nm* attempt

interactivo, a [interak'tißo, a] *adj* (*INFORM*)

interactive

intercalar [interka'lar] *vt* to insert

intercambio [inter'kambjo] *nm* exchange, swap

interceder [interθe'ðer] *vi* to intercede

interceptar [interθep'tar] *vt* to intercept

intercesión [interθe'sjon] *nf* intercession

interés [inte'res] *nm* (*gen*) interest; (*parte*) share, part; (*pey*) self-interest; **intereses creados** vested interests

interesado, a [intere'saðo, a] *adj* interested; (*prejuiciado*) prejudiced; (*pey*) mercenary, self-seeking

interesante [intere'sante] *adj* interesting

interesar [intere'sar] *vt, vi* to interest, be of interest to; **~se** *vr*: **~se en** o **por** to take an interest in

interferir [interfe'rir] *vt* to interfere with; (*TEL*) to jam ♦ *vi* to interfere

interfono [inter'fono] *nm* intercom

interino, a [inte'rino, a] *adj* temporary ♦ *nm/f* temporary holder of a post; (*MED*) locum; (*ESCOL*) supply teacher

interior [inte'rjor] *adj* inner, inside; (*COM*) domestic, internal ♦ *nm* interior, inside; (*fig*) soul, mind; **Ministerio del I~** ≈ Home Office (*BRIT*), ≈ Department of the Interior (*US*)

interjección [interxek'θjon] *nf* interjection

interlocutor, a [interloku'tor, a] *nm/f* speaker

intermediario, a [interme'ðjarjo, a] *nm/f* intermediary

intermedio, a [inter'meðjo, a] *adj* intermediate ♦ *nm* interval

interminable [intermi'naßle] *adj* endless

intermitente [intermi'tente] *adj* intermittent ♦ *nm* (*AUTO*) indicator

internacional [internaθjo'nal] *adj* international

internado [inter'naðo] *nm* boarding school

internar [inter'nar] *vt* to intern; (*en un manicomio*) to commit; **~se** *vr* (*penetrar*) to penetrate

Internet [inter'net] *nm* o *nf* Internet

interno, a [in'terno, a] *adj* internal, interior; (*POL etc*) domestic ♦ *nm/f* (*alumno*) boarder

interponer [interpo'ner] *vt* to interpose, put in; **~se** *vr* to intervene

interpretación [interpreta'θjon] *nf* interpretation

interpretar [interpre'tar] *vt* to interpret; (*TEATRO, MUS*) to perform, play; **intérprete** *nm/f* (*LING*) interpreter, translator; (*MUS, TEATRO*) performer, artist(e)

interrogación [interroxa'θjon] *nf* interrogation; (*LING: tb: signo de ~*) question mark

interrogar [interro'var] *vt* to interrogate, question

interrumpir [interrum'pir] *vt* to interrupt

interrupción [interrup'θjon] *nf* interruption

interruptor [interrup'tor] *nm* (*ELEC*) switch

intersección [intersek'θjon] *nf* intersection

interurbano, a [interur'ßano, a] *adj*: **llamada interurbana** long-distance call

intervalo [inter'ßalo] *nm* interval; (*descanso*) break; **a ~s** at intervals, every now and then

intervenir [interße'nir] *vt* (*controlar*) to control, supervise; (*MED*) to operate on ♦ *vi* (*participar*) to take part, participate; (*mediar*) to intervene

interventor, a [interßen'tor, a] *nm/f* inspector; (*COM*) auditor

intestino [intes'tino] *nm* intestine

intimar [inti'mar] *vi* to become friendly

intimidad [intimi'ðað] *nf* intimacy; (*familiaridad*) familiarity; (*vida privada*) private life; (*JUR*) privacy

íntimo, a ['intimo, a] *adj* intimate

intolerable [intole'raßle] *adj* intolerable, unbearable

intoxicación [intoksika'θjon] *nf* poisoning

intranet [intra'net] *nf* intranet

intranquilizarse [intrankili'θarse] *vr* to get worried o anxious; **intranquilo, a** *adj* worried

intransigente [intransi'xente] *adj* intransigent

intransitable [intransi'taßle] *adj* impassable

intrépido, a [in'trepiðo, a] *adj* intrepid

intriga [in'triva] *nf* intrigue; (*plan*) plot; **intrigar** *vt, vi* to intrigue

intrincado, a [intrin'kaðo, a] *adj* intricate

intrínseco, a [in'trinseko, a] *adj* intrinsic

introducción [introðuk'θjon] *nf* introduction

introducir [introðu'θir] *vt* (*gen*) to introduce; (*moneda etc*) to insert; (*INFORM*) to input, enter

intromisión [intromi'sjon] *nf* interference, meddling

introvertido, a [introßer'tiðo, a] *adj, nm/f* introvert

intruso, a [in'truso, a] *adj* intrusive ♦ *nm/f* intruder

intuición [intwi'θjon] *nf* intuition

inundación [inunda'θjon] *nf* flood(ing); **inundar** *vt* to flood; (*fig*) to swamp, inundate

inusitado, a [inusi'taðo, a] *adj* unusual, rare

inútil [in'util] *adj* useless; (*esfuerzo*) vain, fruitless; **inutilidad** *nf* uselessness

inutilizar [inutili'θar] *vt* to make o render useless; **~se** *vr* to become useless

invadir [imba'ðir] *vt* to invade

inválido, a [im'baliðo, a] *adj* invalid ♦ *nm/f* invalid

invariable [imba'rjaßle] *adj* invariable

invasión [imba'sjon] *nf* invasion

invasor, a [imba'sor, a] *adj* invading ♦ *nm/f* invader

invención [imben'θjon] *nf* invention

inventar [imben'tar] *vt* to invent

inventario [imben'tarjo] *nm* inventory

inventiva [imben'tiβa] *nf* inventiveness

invento [im'bento] *nm* invention

inventor, a [imben'tor, a] *nm/f* inventor

invernadero [imberna'ðero] *nm* greenhouse

inverosímil [imbero'simil] *adj* implausible

inversión [imber'sjon] *nf* (COM) investment

inverso, a [im'berso, a] *adj* inverse, opposite; **en el orden ~** in reverse order; **a la inversa** inversely, the other way round

inversor, a [imber'sor, a] *nm/f* (COM) investor

invertir [imber'tir] *vt* (COM) to invest; (*volcar*) to turn upside down; (*tiempo etc*) to spend

investigación [imbestiɣa'θjon] *nf* investigation; (ESCOL) research; **~ de mercado** market research

investigar [imbesti'ɣar] *vt* to investigate; (ESCOL) to do research into

invierno [im'bjerno] *nm* winter

invisible [imbi'siβle] *adj* invisible

invitado, a [imbi'taðo, a] *nm/f* guest

invitar [imbi'tar] *vt* to invite; (*incitar*) to entice; (*pagar*) to buy, pay for

invocar [imbo'kar] *vt* to invoke, call on

involucrar [imbolu'krar] *vt*: **~ en** to involve in; **~se** *vr* (*persona*): **~ en** to get mixed up in

involuntario, a [imbolun'tarjo, a] *adj* (*movimiento, gesto*) involuntary; (*error*) unintentional

inyección [injek'θjon] *nf* injection

inyectar [injek'tar] *vt* to inject

PALABRA CLAVE

ir [ir] *vi* **1** to go; (*a pie*) to walk; (*viajar*) to travel; **~ caminando** to walk; **fui en tren** I went *o* travelled by train; **¡(ahora) voy!** (I'm just) coming!

2: **~ (a) por**: **~ (a) por el médico** to fetch the doctor

3 (*progresar: persona, cosa*) to go; **el trabajo va muy bien** work is going very well; **¿cómo te va?** how are things going?; **me va muy bien** I'm getting on very well; **le fue fatal** it went awfully badly for him

4 (*funcionar*): **el coche no va muy bien** the car isn't running very well

5: **te va estupendamente ese color** that colour suits you fantastically well

6 (*locuciones*): **¿vino? – ¡que va!** did he come? – of course not!; **vamos, no llores** come on, don't cry; **¡vaya coche!** what a car!, that's some car!

7: **no vaya a ser: tienes que correr, no vaya a ser que pierdas el tren** you'll have to run so as not to miss the train

8 (+ *pp*): **iba vestido muy bien** he was very well dressed

9: **no me** *etc* **va ni me viene** I *etc* don't care ♦ *vb aux* **1**: **~ a: voy/iba a hacerlo hoy** I am/ was going to do it today

2 (+ *gerundio*): **iba anocheciendo** it was getting dark; **todo se me iba aclarando** everything was gradually becoming clearer to me

3 (+ *pp = pasivo*): **van vendidos 300 ejemplares** 300 copies have been sold so far ♦ **~se** *vr* **1**: **¿por dónde se va al zoológico?** which is the way to the zoo?

2 (*marcharse*) to leave; **ya se habrán ido** they must already have left *o* gone

---

ira ['ira] *nf* anger, rage

Irak [i'rak] *nm* = **Iraq**

Irán [i'ran] *nm* Iran; **iraní** *adj*, *nm/f* Iranian

Iraq [i'rak] *nm* Iraq; **iraquí** *adj*, *nm/f* Iraqui

iris ['iris] *nm inv* (*tb*: **arco ~**) rainbow; (ANAT) iris

Irlanda [ir'landa] *nf* Ireland; **irlandés, esa** *adj* Irish ♦ *nm/f* Irishman/woman; **los irlandeses** the Irish

ironía [iro'nia] *nf* irony; **irónico, a** *adj* ironic(al)

IRPF ['i 'erre 'pe 'efe] *n abr* (=*Impuesto sobre la Renta de las Personas Físicas*) (personal) income tax

irreal [irre'al] *adj* unreal

irrecuperable [irrekupe'raβle] *adj* irrecoverable, irretrievable

irreflexión [irreflek'sjon] *nf* thoughtlessness

irregular [irreɣu'lar] *adj* (*gen*) irregular; (*situación*) abnormal

irremediable [irreme'ðjaβle] *adj* irremediable; (*vicio*) incurable

irreparable [irrepa'raβle] *adj* (*daños*) irreparable; (*pérdida*) irrecoverable

irresoluto, a [irreso'luto, a] *adj* irresolute, hesitant

irrespetuoso, a [irrespe'twoso, a] *adj* disrespectful

irresponsable [irrespon'saβle] *adj* irresponsible

irreversible [irreßer'sible] *adj* irreversible

irrigar [irri'ɣar] *vt* to irrigate

irrisorio, a [irri'sorjo, a] *adj* derisory, ridiculous

irritar [irri'tar] *vt* to irritate, annoy

irrupción [irrup'θjon] *nf* irruption; (*invasión*) invasion

isla ['isla] *nf* island

islandés, esa [islan'des, esa] *adj* Icelandic ♦ *nm/f* Icelander

Islandia [is'landja] nf Iceland
isleño, a [is'leɲo, a] adj island cpd ♦ nm/f islander
Israel [isra'el] nm Israel; **israelí** adj, nm/f Israeli
istmo ['istmo] nm isthmus
Italia [i'talja] nf Italy; **italiano, a** adj, nm/f Italian
itinerario [itine'rarjo] nm itinerary, route
IVA ['iβa] nm abr (= impuesto sobre el valor añadido) VAT
izar [i'θar] vt to hoist
izdo, a abr (= izquierdo, a) l.
izquierda [iθ'kjerda] nf left; (POL) left (wing); **a la ~** (estar) on the left; (torcer etc) (to the) left
izquierdista [iθkjer'δista] nm/f left-winger, leftist
izquierdo, a [iθ'kjerðo, a] adj left

J, j

jabalí [xaβa'li] nm wild boar
jabalina [xaβa'lina] nf javelin
jabón [xa'βon] nm soap; **jabonar** vt to soap
jaca ['xaka] nf pony
jacinto [xa'θinto] nm hyacinth
jactarse [xak'tarse] vr to boast, brag
jadear [xaðe'ar] vi to pant, gasp for breath; **jadeo** nm panting, gasping
jaguar [xa'ɣwar] nm jaguar
jalea [xa'lea] nf jelly
jaleo [xa'leo] nm racket, uproar; **armar un ~** to kick up a racket
jalón [xa'lon] (AM) nm tug
jamás [xa'mas] adv never
jamón [xa'mon] nm ham; **~ dulce, ~ de York** cooked ham; **~ serrano** cured ham
Japón [xa'pon] nm: **el ~** Japan; **japonés, esa** adj, nm/f Japanese ♦ nm (LING) Japanese
jaque ['xake] nm: **~ mate** checkmate
jaqueca [xa'keka] nf (very bad) headache, migraine
jarabe [xa'raβe] nm syrup
jarcia ['xarθja] nf (NAUT) ropes pl, rigging
jardín [xar'ðin] nm garden; **~ de infancia** (ESP) o **de niños** (AM) nursery (school); **jardinería** nf gardening; **jardinero, a** nm/f gardener
jarra ['xarra] nf jar; (jarro) jug
jarro ['xarro] nm jug
jarrón [xa'rron] nm vase
jaula ['xaula] nf cage
jauría [xau'ria] nf pack of hounds
jazmín [xaθ'min] nm jasmine
J. C. abr (= Jesucristo) J.C.
jefa ['xefa] nf ver **jefe**
jefatura [xefa'tura] nf: **~ de policía** police headquarters sg

jefe, a ['xefe, a] nm/f (gen) chief, head; (patrón) boss; **~ de cocina** chef; **~ de estación** stationmaster; **~ de estado** head of state
jengibre [xen'xiβre] nm ginger
jeque ['xeke] nm sheik
jerarquía [xerar'kia] nf (orden) hierarchy; (rango) rank; **jerárquico, a** adj hierarchic(al)
jerez [xe'reθ] nm sherry
jerga ['xerɣa] nf jargon
jeringa [xe'ringa] nf syringe; (AM) annoyance, bother; **~ de engrase** grease gun; **jeringar** vt (fam) to annoy, bother; **jeringuilla** nf syringe
jeroglífico [xero'ɣlifiko] nm hieroglyphic
jersey [xer'sei] (pl **~s**) nm jersey, pullover, jumper
Jerusalén [xerusa'len] n Jerusalem
Jesucristo [xesu'kristo] nm Jesus Christ
jesuita [xe'swita] adj, nm Jesuit
Jesús [xe'sus] nm Jesus; **¡~!** good heavens!; (al estornudar) bless you!
jinete, a [xi'nete, a] nm/f horseman/woman, rider
jipijapa [xipi'xapa] (AM) nm straw hat
jirafa [xi'rafa] nf giraffe
jirón [xi'ron] nm rag, shred
jocoso, a [xo'koso, a] adj humorous, jocular
joder [xo'ðer] (fam!) vt, vi to fuck(!)
jofaina [xo'faina] nf washbasin
jornada [xor'naða] nf (viaje de un día) day's journey; (camino o viaje entero) journey; (día de trabajo) working day
jornal [xor'nal] nm (day's) wage; **~ero** nm (day) labourer
joroba [xo'roβa] nf hump, hunched back; **~do, a** adj hunchbacked ♦ nm/f hunchback
jota ['xota] nf (the letter) J; (danza) Aragonese dance; **no saber ni ~** to have no idea
joven ['xoβen] (pl **jóvenes**) adj young ♦ nm young man, youth ♦ nf young woman, girl
jovial [xo'βjal] adj cheerful, jolly
joya ['xoja] nf jewel, gem; (fig: persona) gem; **joyería** nf (joyas) jewellery; (tienda) jeweller's (shop); **joyero** nm (persona) jeweller; (caja) jewel case
juanete [xwa'nete] nm (del pie) bunion
jubilación [xuβila'θjon] nf (retiro) retirement
jubilado, a [xuβi'laðo, a] adj retired ♦ nm/f pensioner (BRIT), senior citizen
jubilar [xuβi'lar] vt to pension off, retire; (fam) to discard; **~se** vr to retire
júbilo ['xuβilo] nm joy, rejoicing; **jubiloso, a** adj jubilant
judía [xu'ðia] nf (CULIN) bean; **~ verde** French bean; ver tb **judío**
judicial [xuði'θjal] adj judicial
judío, a [xu'ðio, a] adj Jewish ♦ nm/f Jew(ess)
judo ['xuðo] nm judo

juego *etc* ['xweɣo] *vb ver* **jugar ♦** *nm* (*gen*) play; (*pasatiempo, partido*) game; (*en casino*) gambling; (*conjunto*) set; **fuera de ~** (*DEPORTE: persona*) offside; (: *pelota*) out of play; **J~s Olímpicos** Olympic Games

juerga ['xwerɣa] *nf* binge; (*fiesta*) party; **ir de ~** to go out on a binge

jueves ['xweβes] *nm inv* Thursday

juez [xweθ] *nm/f* judge; **~ de línea** linesman; **~ de salida** starter

jugada [xu'ɣaða] *nf* play; **buena ~** good move/shot/stroke *etc*

jugador, a [xuɣa'ðor, a] *nm/f* player; (*en casino*) gambler

jugar [xu'ɣar] *vt, vi* to play; (*en casino*) to gamble; (*apostar*) to bet; **~ al fútbol** to play football

juglar [xu'ɣlar] *nm* minstrel

jugo ['xuɣo] *nm* (*BOT*) juice; (*fig*) essence, substance; **~ de fruta** (*AM*) fruit juice; **~so, a** *adj* juicy; (*fig*) substantial, important

juguete [xu'ɣete] *nm* toy; **~ar** *vi* to play; **~ría** *nf* toyshop

juguetón, ona [xuɣe'ton, ona] *adj* playful

juicio ['xwiθjo] *nm* judgement; (*razón*) sanity, reason; (*opinión*) opinion; **~so, a** *adj* wise, sensible

julio ['xuljo] *nm* July

junco ['xunko] *nm* rush, reed

jungla ['xungla] *nf* jungle

junio ['xunjo] *nm* June

junta ['xunta] *nf* (*asamblea*) meeting, assembly; (*comité, consejo*) board, council, committee; (*TEC*) joint

juntar [xun'tar] *vt* to join, unite; (*maquinaria*) to assemble, put together; (*dinero*) to collect; **~se** *vr* to join, meet; (*reunirse: personas*) to meet, assemble; (*arrimarse*) to approach, draw closer; **~se con uno** to join sb

junto, a ['xunto, a] *adj* joined; (*unido*) united; (*anexo*) near, close; (*contiguo, próximo*) next, adjacent **♦** *adv*: **todo ~** all at once; **~s** together; **~ a** near (to), next to

jurado [xu'raðo] *nm* (*JUR: individuo*) juror; (: *grupo*) jury; (*de concurso: grupo*) panel (of judges); (: *individuo*) member of a panel

juramento [xura'mento] *nm* oath; (*maldición*) oath, curse; **prestar ~** to take the oath; **tomar ~ a** to swear in, administer the oath to

jurar [xu'rar] *vt, vi* to swear; **~ en falso** to commit perjury; **jurárselas a uno** to have it in for sb

jurídico, a [xu'riðiko, a] *adj* legal

jurisdicción [xurisðik'θjon] *nf* (*poder, autoridad*) jurisdiction; (*territorio*) district

jurisprudencia [xurispru'ðenθja] *nf* jurisprudence

jurista [xu'rista] *nm/f* jurist

justamente [xusta'mente] *adv* justly, fairly; (*precisamente*) just, exactly

justicia [xus'tiθja] *nf* justice; (*equidad*) fairness, justice; **justiciero, a** *adj* just, righteous

justificación [xustifika'θjon] *nf* justification; **justificar** *vt* to justify

justo, a ['xusto, a] *adj* (*equitativo*) just, fair, right; (*preciso*) exact, correct; (*ajustado*) tight **♦** *adv* (*precisamente*) exactly, precisely; (*AM*: *apenas a tiempo*) just in time

juvenil [xuße'nil] *adj* youthful

juventud [xußen'tuð] *nf* (*adolescencia*) youth; (*jóvenes*) young people *pl*

juzgado [xuθ'ɣaðo] *nm* tribunal; (*JUR*) court

juzgar [xuθ'ɣar] *vt* to judge; **a ~ por** ... to judge by ..., judging by ...

K, k

kg *abr* (= *kilogramo*) kg

kilo ['kilo] *nm* kilo **♦** *pref*: **~gramo** *nm* kilogramme; **~metraje** *nm* distance in kilometres, ≈ mileage; **kilómetro** *nm* kilometre; **~vatio** *nm* kilowatt

kiosco ['kjosko] *nm* = **quiosco**

km *abr* (= *kilómetro*) km

Kosovo [ko'sovo] *nm* Kosovo

kv *abr* (= *kilovatio*) kw

L, l

l *abr* (= *litro*) l

la [la] *art def* the **♦** *pron* her; (*Ud.*) you; (*cosa*) it **♦** *nm* (*MUS*) la; **~ del sombrero rojo** the girl in the red hat; *tb ver* **el**

laberinto [laße'rinto] *nm* labyrinth

labia ['laßja] *nf* fluency; (*pey*) glib tongue

labio ['laßjo] *nm* lip

labor [la'ßor] *nf* labour; (*AGR*) farm work; (*tarea*) job, task; (*COSTURA*) needlework; **~able** *adj* (*AGR*) workable; **día ~able** working day; **~al** *adj* (*accidente*) at work; (*jornada*) working

laboratorio [laßora'torjo] *nm* laboratory

laborioso, a [laßo'rjoso, a] *adj* (*persona*) hard-working; (*trabajo*) tough

laborista [laßo'rista] *adj*: **Partido L~** Labour Party

labrado, a [la'ßraðo, a] *adj* worked; (*madera*) carved; (*metal*) wrought

labrador, a [laßra'ðor, a] *adj* farming *cpd* **♦** *nm/f* farmer

labranza [la'ßranθa] *nf* (*AGR*) cultivation

labrar [la'ßrar] *vt* (*gen*) to work; (*madera etc*) to carve; (*fig*) to cause, bring about

labriego, a [la'ßrjeɣo, a] *nm/f* peasant

laca ['laka] nf lacquer

lacayo [la'kajo] nm lackey

lacio, a [la'θjo, a] adj (pelo) lank, straight

lacón [la'kon] nm shoulder of pork

lacónico, a [la'koniko, a] adj laconic

lacra ['lakra] nf (fig) blot; **lacrar** vt (cerrar) to seal (with sealing wax); **lacre** nm sealing wax

lactancia [lak'tanθja] nf lactation

lactar [lak'tar] vt, vi to suckle

lácteo, a ['lakteo, a] adj: **productos ~s** dairy products

ladear [laðe'ar] vt to tip, tilt ♦ vi to tilt; **~se** vr to lean

ladera [la'ðera] nf slope

lado ['laðo] nm (gen) side; (fig) protection; (MIL) flank; **al ~ de** beside; **poner de ~** to put on its side; **poner a un ~** to put aside; **por todos ~s** on all sides, all round (BRIT)

ladrar [la'ðrar] vi to bark; **ladrido** nm bark, barking

ladrillo [la'ðriʎo] nm (gen) brick; (azulejo) tile

ladrón, ona [la'ðron, ona] nm/f thief

lagartija [laɣar'tixa] nf (ZOOL) (small) lizard

lagarto [la'ɣarto] nm (ZOOL) lizard

lago ['laɣo] nm lake

lágrima ['laɣrima] nf tear

laguna [la'ɣuna] nf (lago) lagoon; (hueco) gap

laico, a ['laiko, a] adj lay

lamentable [lamen'taßle] adj lamentable, regrettable; (miserable) pitiful

lamentar [lamen'tar] vt (sentir) to regret; (deplorar) to lament; **lo lamento mucho** I'm very sorry; **~se** vr to lament; **lamento** nm lament

lamer [la'mer] vt to lick

lámina ['lamina] nf (plancha delgada) sheet; (para estampar, estampa) plate

lámpara ['lampara] nf lamp; **~ de alcohol/gas** spirit/gas lamp; **~ de pie** standard lamp

lamparón [lampa'ron] nm grease spot

lana ['lana] nf wool

lancha ['lantʃa] nf launch; **~ de pesca** fishing boat; **~ salvavidas/torpedera** lifeboat/torpedo boat

langosta [lan'gosta] nf (crustáceo) lobster; (: de río) crayfish; **langostino** nm Dublin Bay prawn

languidecer [langiðe'θer] vi to languish; **languidez** nf langour; **lánguido, a** adj (gen) languid; (sin energía) listless

lanilla [la'niʎa] nf nap

lanza ['lanθa] nf (arma) lance, spear

lanzamiento [lanθa'mjento] nm (gen) throwing; (NAUT, COM) launch, launching; **~ de peso** putting the shot

lanzar [lan'θar] vt (gen) to throw; (DEPORTE:

---

pelota) to bowl; (NAUT, COM) to launch; (JUR) to evict; **~se** vr to throw o.s.

lapa ['lapa] nf limpet

lapicero [lapi'θero] nm pencil; (AM: bolígrafo) Biro ®

lápida ['lapiða] nf stone; **~ mortuoria** headstone; **~ conmemorativa** memorial stone; **lapidario, a** adj, nm lapidary

lápiz ['lapiθ] nm pencil; **~ de color** coloured pencil; **~ de labios** lipstick

lapón, ona [la'pon, ona] nm/f Laplander, Lapp

lapso ['lapso] nm (de tiempo) interval; (error) error

lapsus ['lapsus] nm inv error, mistake

largar [lar'xar] vt (soltar) to release; (aflojar) to loosen; (lanzar) to launch; (fam) to let fly; (velas) to unfurl; (AM) to throw; **~se** vr (fam) to beat it; **~se a** (AM) to start to

largo, a ['larɣo, a] adj (longitud) long; (tiempo) lengthy; (fig) generous ♦ nm length; (MUS) largo; **dos años ~s** two long years; **tiene 9 metros de ~** it is 9 metres long; **a lo ~ de** along; (tiempo) all through, throughout; **~metraje** nm feature film

laringe [la'rinxe] nf larynx; **laringitis** nf laryngitis

larva ['larßa] nf larva

las [las] art def the ♦ pron them; **~ que cantan** the ones/women/girls who sing; tb ver **el**

lascivo, a [las'θißo, a] adj lewd

láser ['laser] nm laser

lástima ['lastima] nf (pena) pity; **dar ~** to be pitiful; **es una ~ que** it's a pity that; **¡qué ~!** what a pity!; **ella está hecha una ~** she looks pitiful

lastimar [lasti'mar] vt (herir) to wound; (ofender) to offend; **~se** vr to hurt o.s.; **lastimero, a** adj pitiful, pathetic

lastre ['lastre] nm (TEC, NAUT) ballast; (fig) dead weight

lata ['lata] nf (metal) tin; (caja) tin (BRIT), can; (fam) nuisance; **en ~** tinned (BRIT), canned; **dar (la) ~** to be a nuisance

latente [la'tente] adj latent

lateral [late'ral] adj side cpd, lateral ♦ nm (TEATRO) wings

latido [la'tiðo] nm (del corazón) beat

latifundio [lati'fundjo] nm large estate; **latifundista** nm/f owner of a large estate

latigazo [lati'xaθo] nm (golpe) lash; (sonido) crack

látigo ['latixo] nm whip

latín [la'tin] nm Latin

latino, a [la'tino, a] adj Latin; **~americano, a** adj, nm/f Latin-American

latir [la'tir] vi (corazón, pulso) to beat

latitud [lati'tuð] nf (GEO) latitude

latón [la'ton] nm brass

latoso, a [la'toso, a] adj (*molesto*) annoying; (*aburrido*) boring

laúd [la'uð] nm lute

laurel [lau'rel] nm (*BOT*) laurel; (*CULIN*) bay

lava ['laβa] nf lava

lavabo [la'ßaßo] nm (*pila*) washbasin; (*tb: ~s*) toilet

lavado [la'ßaðo] nm washing; (*de ropa*) laundry; (*ARTE*) wash; **~ de cerebro** brainwashing; **~ en seco** dry-cleaning

lavadora [laßa'ðora] nf washing machine

lavanda [la'ßanda] nf lavender

lavandería [laßande'ria] nf laundry; (*automática*) launderette

lavaplatos [laßa'platos] nm inv dishwasher

lavar [la'ßar] vt to wash; (*borrar*) to wipe away; **~se** vr to wash o.s.; **~se las manos** to wash one's hands; **~se los dientes** to brush one's teeth; **~ y marcar** (*pelo*) to shampoo and set; **~ en seco** to dry-clean; **~ los platos** to wash the dishes

lavavajillas [laßaßa'xiλas] nm inv dishwasher

laxante [lak'sante] nm laxative

lazada [la'θaða] nf bow

lazarillo [laθa'riλo] nm: **perro ~** guide dog

lazo ['laθo] nm knot; (*lazada*) bow; (*para animales*) lasso; (*trampa*) snare; (*vínculo*) tie

le [le] pron (*directo*) him (o her); (: *usted*) you; (*indirecto*) to him (o her o it); (: *usted*) to you

leal [le'al] adj loyal; **~tad** nf loyalty

lección [lek'θjon] nf lesson

leche ['letʃe] nf milk; **tiene mala ~** (*fam!*) he's a swine (!); **~ condensada/en polvo** condensed/powdered milk; **~ desnatada** skimmed milk; **~ra** nf (*vendedora*) milkmaid; (*recipiente*) (milk) churn; (*AM*) cow; **~ro, a** adj dairy

lecho ['letʃo] nm (*cama, de río*) bed; (*GEO*) layer

lechón [le'tʃon] nm sucking (*BRIT*) o suckling (*US*) pig

lechoso, a [le'tʃoso, a] adj milky

lechuga [le'tʃuɣa] nf lettuce

lechuza [le'tʃuθa] nf owl

lector, a [lek'tor, a] nm/f reader ♦ nm: **~ de discos compactos** CD player

lectura [lek'tura] nf reading

leer [le'er] vt to read

legado [le'ɣaðo] nm (*don*) bequest; (*herencia*) legacy; (*enviado*) legate

legajo [le'xaxo] nm file

legal [le'ɣal] adj (*gen*) legal; (*persona*) trustworthy; **~idad** nf legality

legalizar [leɣali'θar] vt to legalize; (*documento*) to authenticate

legaña [le'ɣaɲa] nf sleep (*in eyes*)

legar [le'ɣar] vt to bequeath, leave

legendario, a [lexen'darjo, a] adj legendary

legión [le'xjon] nf legion; **legionario, a** adj legionary ♦ nm legionnaire

legislación [lexisla'θjon] nf legislation

legislar [lexis'lar] vi to legislate

legislatura [lexisla'tura] nf (*POL*) period of office

legitimar [lexiti'mar] vt to legitimize; **legítimo, a** adj (*genuino*) authentic; (*legal*) legitimate

lego, a ['leɣo, a] adj (*REL*) secular; (*ignorante*) ignorant ♦ nm layman

legua ['leɣwa] nf league

legumbres [le'ɣumbres] nfpl pulses

leído, a [le'iðo, a] adj well-read

lejanía [lexa'nia] nf distance; **lejano, a** adj far-off; (*en el tiempo*) distant; (*fig*) remote

lejía [le'xia] nf bleach

lejos ['lexos] adv far, far away; **a lo ~** in the distance; **de o desde ~** from afar; **~ de** far from

lelo, a ['lelo, a] adj silly ♦ nm/f idiot

lema ['lema] nm motto; (*POL*) slogan

lencería [lenθe'ria] nf linen, drapery

lengua ['leŋgwa] nf tongue; (*LING*) language; **morderse la ~** to hold one's tongue

lenguado [leŋ'gwaðo] nm sole

lenguaje [leŋ'gwaxe] nm language

lengüeta [leŋ'gweta] nf (*ANAT*) epiglottis; (*zapatos*) tongue; (*MUS*) reed

lente ['lente] nf lens; (*lupa*) magnifying glass; **~s** nfpl (*gafas*) glasses; **~s de contacto** contact lenses

lenteja [len'texa] nf lentil; **lentejuela** nf sequin

lentilla [len'tiλa] nf contact lens

lentitud [lenti'tuð] nf slowness; **con ~** slowly

lento, a ['lento, a] adj slow

leña ['leɲa] nf firewood; **~dor, a** nm/f woodcutter

leño ['leɲo] nm (*trozo de árbol*) log; (*madera*) timber; (*fig*) blockhead

Leo ['leo] nm Leo

león [le'on] nm lion; **~ marino** sea lion

leopardo [leo'parðo] nm leopard

leotardos [leo'tarðos] nmpl tights

lepra ['lepra] nf leprosy; **leproso, a** adj leper

lerdo, a ['lerðo, a] adj (*lento*) slow; (*patoso*) clumsy

les [les] pron (*directo*) them; (: *ustedes*) you; (*indirecto*) to them; (: *ustedes*) to you

lesbiana [les'ßjana] adj, nf lesbian

lesión [le'sjon] nf wound, lesion; (*DEPORTE*) injury; **lesionado, a** adj injured ♦ nm/f injured person

letal [le'tal] adj lethal

letanía [leta'nia] nf litany

letargo [le'tarɣo] nm lethargy

letra ['letra] nf letter; (*escritura*) handwriting;

letrina [le'trina] *nf* latrine

leucemia [leu'θemja] *nf* leukaemia

levadizo [leβa'ðiθo] *adj:* **puente ~** drawbridge

levadura [leβa'ðura] *nf* (*para el pan*) yeast; (*de la cerveza*) brewer's yeast

levantamiento [leβanta'mjento] *nm* raising, lifting; (*rebelión*) revolt, uprising; **~ de pesos** weight-lifting

levantar [leβan'tar] *vt* (*gen*) to raise; (*del suelo*) to pick up; (*hacia arriba*) to lift (up); (*plan*) to make, draw up; (*mesa*) to clear; (*campamento*) to strike; (*fig*) to cheer up, hearten; **~se** *vr* to get up; (*enderezarse*) to straighten up; (*rebelarse*) to rebel; **~ el ánimo** to cheer up

levante [le'βante] *nm* east coast; **el L~** region of Spain extending from Castellón to Murcia

levar [le'βar] *vt* to weigh

leve ['leβe] *adj* light; (*fig*) trivial; **~dad** *nf* lightness

levita [le'βita] *nf* frock coat

léxico ['leksiko] *nm* (*vocabulario*) vocabulary

ley [lei] *nf* (*gen*) law; (*metal*) standard

leyenda [le'jenda] *nf* legend

leyó etc *vb ver* **leer**

liar [li'ar] *vt* to tie (up); (*unir*) to bind; (*envolver*) to wrap (up); (*enredar*) to confuse; (*cigarrillo*) to roll; **~se** *vr* (*fam*) to get involved; **~se a palos** to get involved in a fight

Líbano ['liβano] *nm*: **el ~** (the) Lebanon

libelo [li'βelo] *nm* satire, lampoon

libélula [li'βelula] *nf* dragonfly

liberación [liβera'θjon] *nf* liberation; (*de la cárcel*) release

liberal [liβe'ral] *adj, nm/f* liberal; **~idad** *nf* liberality, generosity

liberar [liβe'rar] *vt* to liberate

libertad [liβer'tað] *nf* liberty, freedom; **~ de culto/de prensa/de comercio** freedom of worship/of the press/of trade; **~ condicional** probation; **~ bajo palabra** parole; **~ bajo fianza** bail

libertar [liβer'tar] *vt* (*preso*) to set free; (*de una obligación*) to release; (*eximir*) to exempt

libertino, a [liβer'tino, a] *adj* permissive ♦ *nm/f* permissive person

libra ['liβra] *nf* pound; (*ASTROLOGÍA*): **L~** Libra; **~ esterlina** pound sterling

librar [li'βrar] *vt* (*de peligro*) to save; (*batalla*) to wage, fight; (*de impuestos*) to exempt; (*cheque*) to make out; (*JUR*) to exempt; **~se** *vr*: **~se de** to escape from, free o.s. from

libre ['liβre] *adj* free; (*lugar*) unoccupied;

(*asiento*) vacant; (*de deudas*) free of debts; **~ de impuestos** free of tax; **tiro ~** free kick; **los 100 metros ~** the 100 metres free-style (*race*); **al aire ~** in the open air

librería [liβre'ria] *nf* (*tienda*) bookshop; **librero, a** *nm/f* bookseller

libreta [li'βreta] *nf* notebook; **~ de ahorros** savings book

libro ['liβro] *nm* book; **~ de bolsillo** paperback; **~ de caja** cashbook; **~ de cheques** chequebook (*BRIT*), checkbook (*US*); **~ de texto** textbook

Lic. *abr* = **licenciado, a**

licencia [li'θenθja] *nf* (*gen*) licence; (*permiso*) permission; **~ por enfermedad** sick leave; **~ de caza** game licence; **~do, a** *adj* licensed ♦ *nm/f* graduate; **licenciar** *vt* (*empleado*) to dismiss; (*permitir*) to permit, allow; (*soldado*) to discharge; (*estudiante*) to confer a degree upon; **licenciarse** *vr*: **licenciarse en letras** to graduate in arts

licencioso, a [liθen'θjoso, a] *adj* licentious

licitar [liθi'tar] *vt* to bid for; (*AM*) to sell by auction

lícito, a ['liθito, a] *adj* (*legal*) lawful; (*justo*) fair, just; (*permisible*) permissible

licor [li'kor] *nm* spirits *pl* (*BRIT*), liquor (*US*); (*de frutas etc*) liqueur

licuadora [likwa'ðora] *nf* blender

licuar [li'kwar] *vt* to liquidize

líder ['liðer] *nm/f* leader; **liderato** *nm* leadership; **liderazgo** *nm* leadership

lidia ['liðja] *nf* bullfighting; (*una ~*) bullfight; **toros de ~** fighting bulls; **lidiar** *vt*, *vi* to fight

liebre ['ljeβre] *nf* hare

lienzo ['ljenθo] *nm* linen; (*ARTE*) canvas; (*ARQ*) wall

liga ['liga] *nf* (*de medias*) garter, suspender; (*AM: gomita*) rubber band; (*confederación*) league

ligadura [liga'ðura] *nf* bond, tie; (*MED, MUS*) ligature

ligamento [liga'mento] *nm* ligament

ligar [li'xar] *vt* (*atar*) to tie; (*unir*) to join; (*MED*) to bind up; (*MUS*) to slur ♦ *vi* to mix, blend; (*fam*): (**él**) **liga mucho** he pulls a lot of women; **~se** *vr* to commit o.s.

ligereza [lixe'reθa] *nf* lightness; (*rapidez*) swiftness; (*agilidad*) agility; (*superficialidad*) flippancy

ligero, a [li'xero, a] *adj* (*de peso*) light; (*tela*) thin; (*rápido*) swift, quick; (*ágil*) agile, nimble; (*de importancia*) slight; (*de carácter*) flippant, superficial ♦ *adv*: **a la ligera** superficially

liguero [li'vero] *nm* suspender (*BRIT*) o garter (*US*) belt

lija ['lixa] *nf* (*ZOOL*) dogfish; (*tb: papel de ~*) sandpaper

lila ['lila] *nf* lilac

lima ['lima] *nf* file; (*BOT*) lime; ~ **de uñas** nailfile; **limar** *vt* to file

limitación [limita'θjon] *nf* limitation, limit; ~ **de velocidad** speed limit

limitar [limi'tar] *vt* to limit; (*reducir*) to reduce, cut down ♦ *vi*: ~ **con** to border on; ~**se** *vr*: ~**se a** to limit o.s. to

límite ['limite] *nm* (*gen*) limit; (*fin*) end; (*frontera*) border; ~ **de velocidad** speed limit

limítrofe [li'mitrofe] *adj* neighbouring

limón [li'mon] *nm* lemon ♦ *adj*: **amarillo** ~ lemon-yellow; **limonada** *nf* lemonade

limosna [li'mosna] *nf* alms *pl*; **vivir de** ~ to live on charity

limpiaparabrisas [limpjapara'βrisas] *nm inv* windscreen (*BRIT*) *o* windshield (*US*) wiper

limpiar [lim'pjar] *vt* to clean; (*con trapo*) to wipe; (*quitar*) to wipe away; (*zapatos*) to shine, polish; (*fig*) to clean up

limpieza [lim'pjeθa] *nf* (*estado*) cleanliness; (*acto*) cleaning; (: *de las calles*) cleansing; (: *de zapatos*) polishing; (*habilidad*) skill; (*fig: POLICÍA*) clean-up; (*pureza*) purity; (*MIL*): **operación de** ~ mopping-up operation; ~ **en seco** dry cleaning

limpio, a ['limpjo, a] *adj* clean; (*moralmente*) pure; (*COM*) clear, net; (*fam*) honest ♦ *adv*: **jugar** ~ to play fair; **pasar a** (*ESP*) *o* **en** (*AM*) ~ to make a clean copy

linaje [li'naxe] *nm* lineage, family

lince [' linθe] *nm* lynx

linchar [lin'tʃar] *vt* to lynch

lindar [lin'dar] *vi* to adjoin; ~ **con** to border on; **linde** *nm o f* boundary; **lindero, a** *adj* adjoining ♦ *nm* boundary

lindo, a ['lindo, a] *adj* pretty, lovely ♦ *adv*: **nos divertimos de lo** ~ we had a marvellous time; **canta muy** ~ (*AM*) he sings beautifully

línea ['linea] *nf* (*gen*) line; **en** ~ (*INFORM*) on line; ~ **aérea** airline; ~ **de meta** goal line; (*de carrera*) finishing line; ~ **recta** straight line

lingote [lin'gote] *nm* ingot

lingüista [lin'gwista] *nm/f* linguist; **lingüística** *nf* linguistics *sg*

lino ['lino] *nm* linen; (*BOT*) flax

linóleo [li'noleo] *nm* lino, linoleum

linterna [lin'terna] *nf* torch (*BRIT*), flashlight (*US*)

lío ['lio] *nm* bundle; (*fam*) fuss; (*desorden*) muddle, mess; **armar un** ~ to make a fuss

liquen ['liken] *nm* lichen

liquidación [likiða'θjon] *nf* liquidation; **venta de** ~ clearance sale

liquidar [liki'ðar] *vt* (*mercancías*) to liquidate; (*deudas*) to pay off; (*empresa*) to wind up

líquido, a ['likiðo, a] *adj* liquid; (*ganancia*) net ♦ *nm* liquid; ~ **imponible** net taxable income

lira ['lira] *nf* (*MUS*) lyre; (*moneda*) lira

lírico, a ['liriko, a] *adj* lyrical

lirio ['lirjo] *nm* (*BOT*) iris

lirón [li'ron] *nm* (*ZOOL*) dormouse; (*fig*) sleepyhead

Lisboa [lis'βoa] *n* Lisbon

lisiado, a [li'sjaðo, a] *adj* injured ♦ *nm/f* cripple

lisiar [li'sjar] *vt* to maim; ~**se** *vr* to injure o.s.

liso, a ['liso, a] *adj* (*terreno*) flat; (*cabello*) straight; (*superficie*) even; (*tela*) plain

lisonja [li'sonxa] *nf* flattery

lista ['lista] *nf* list; (*de alumnos*) school register; (*de libros*) catalogue; (*de platos*) menu; (*de precios*) price list; **pasar** ~ to call the roll; ~ **de correos** poste restante; ~ **de espera** waiting list; **tela de** ~**s** striped material; **listín** *nm*: ~ (**telefónico**) telephone directory

listo, a ['listo, a] *adj* (*perspicaz*) smart, clever; (*preparado*) ready

listón [lis'ton] *nm* (*de madera, metal*) strip

litera [li'tera] *nf* (*en barco, tren*) berth; (*en dormitorio*) bunk, bunk bed

literal [lite'ral] *adj* literal

literario, a [lite'rarjo, a] *adj* literary

literato, a [lite'rato, a] *adj* literary ♦ *nm/f* writer

literatura [litera'tura] *nf* literature

litigar [liti'ɣar] *vt* to fight ♦ *vi* (*JUR*) to go to law; (*fig*) to dispute, argue

litigio [li'tixjo] *nm* (*JUR*) lawsuit; (*fig*): **en** ~ **con** in dispute with

litografía [litoɣra'fia] *nf* lithography; (*una* ~) lithograph

litoral [lito'ral] *adj* coastal ♦ *nm* coast, seaboard

litro ['litro] *nm* litre

liviano, a [li'βjano, a] *adj* (*cosa, objeto*) trivial

lívido, a ['liβiðo, a] *adj* livid

llaga ['ʎaɣa] *nf* wound

llama ['ʎama] *nf* flame; (*ZOOL*) llama

llamada [ʎa'maða] *nf* call; ~ **al orden** call to order; ~ **a pie de página** reference note

llamamiento [ʎama'mjento] *nm* call

llamar [ʎa'mar] *vt* to call; (*atención*) to attract ♦ *vi* (*por teléfono*) to telephone; (*a la puerta*) to knock (*o* ring); (*por señas*) to beckon; (*MIL*) to call up; ~**se** *vr* to be called, be named; **¿cómo se llama usted?** what's your name?

llamarada [ʎama'raða] *nf* (*llamas*) blaze; (*rubor*) flush

llamativo, a [ʎama'tiβo, a] *adj* showy; (*color*) loud

llano, a ['ʎano, a] *adj* (*superficie*) flat; (*persona*) straightforward; (*estilo*) clear ♦ *nm* plain, flat ground

llanta ['ʎanta] *nf* (wheel) rim; (*AM*): ~ **(de**

goma) tyre; (: *cámara*) inner (tube)

llanto ['ʎanto] *nm* weeping

llanura [ʎa'nura] *nf* plain

llave ['ʎaβe] *nf* key; (*del agua*) tap; (*MECÁNICA*) spanner; (*de la luz*) switch; (*MUS*) key; ~ **inglesa** monkey wrench; ~ **maestra** master key; ~ **de contacto** (*AUTO*) ignition key; ~ **de paso** stopcock; **echar la ~ a** to lock up; **~ro** *nm* keyring

llegada [ʎe'ɣaða] *nf* arrival

llegar [ʎe'ɣar] *vi* to arrive; (*alcanzar*) to reach; (*bastar*) to be enough; **~se** *vr*: **~se a** to approach; **~ a** to manage to, succeed in; **~ a saber** to find out; **~ a ser** to become; **~ a las manos de** to come into the hands of

llenar [ʎe'nar] *vt* to fill; (*espacio*) to cover; (*formulario*) to fill in o up; (*fig*) to heap

lleno, a ['ʎeno, a] *adj* full, filled; (*repleto*) full up ♦ *nm* (*TEATRO*) full house; **dar de ~ contra un muro** to hit a wall head-on

llevadero, a [ʎeβa'ðero, a] *adj* bearable, tolerable

llevar [ʎe'βar] *vt* to take; (*ropa*) to wear; (*cargar*) to carry; (*quitar*) to take away; (*en coche*) to drive; (*transportar*) to transport; (*traer: dinero*) to carry; (*conducir*) to lead; (*MAT*) to carry ♦ *vi* (*suj: camino etc*): **~ a** to lead to; **~se** *vr* to carry off, take away; **llevamos dos días aquí** we have been here for two days; **él me lleva 2 años** he's 2 years older than me; (*COM*): **~ los libros** to keep the books; **~se bien** to get on well (together)

llorar [ʎo'rar] *vt, vi* to cry, weep; **~ de risa** to cry with laughter

lloriquear [ʎorike'ar] *vi* to snivel, whimper

lloro ['ʎoro] *nm* crying, weeping; **llorón, ona** *adj* tearful ♦ *nm/f* cry-baby; **~so, a** *adj* (*gen*) weeping, tearful; (*triste*) sad, sorrowful

llover [ʎo'βer] *vi* to rain

llovizna [ʎo'βiθna] *nf* drizzle; **lloviznar** *vi* to drizzle

llueve *etc vb ver* **llover**

lluvia ['ʎuβja] *nf* rain; ~ **radioactiva** (radioactive) fallout; **lluvioso, a** *adj* rainy

lo [lo] *art def*: ~ **bello** the beautiful, what is beautiful, that which is beautiful ♦ *pron* (*persona*) him; (*cosa*) it; *tb ver* **el**

loable [lo'aβle] *adj* praiseworthy; **loar** *vt* to praise

lobo ['loβo] *nm* wolf; ~ **de mar** (*fig*) sea dog; ~ **marino** seal

lóbrego, a ['loβreɣo, a] *adj* dark; (*fig*) gloomy

lóbulo ['loβulo] *nm* lobe

local [lo'kal] *adj* local ♦ *nm* place, site; (*oficinas*) premises *pl*; **~idad** *nf* (*barrio*) locality; (*lugar*) location; (*TEATRO*) seat, ticket; **~izar** *vt* (*ubicar*) to locate, find; (*restringir*) to localize; (*situar*) to place

loción [lo'θjon] *nf* lotion

loco, a ['loko, a] *adj* mad ♦ *nm/f* lunatic, mad person

locomotora [lokomo'tora] *nf* engine, locomotive

locuaz [lo'kwaθ] *adj* loquacious

locución [loku'θjon] *nf* expression

locura [lo'kura] *nf* madness; (*acto*) crazy act

locutor, a [loku'tor, a] *nm/f* (*RADIO*) announcer; (*comentarista*) commentator; (*TV*) newsreader

locutorio [loku'torjo] *nm* (*en telefónica*) telephone booth

lodo ['loðo] *nm* mud

lógica ['loxika] *nf* logic

lógico, a ['loxiko, a] *adj* logical

logística [lo'xistika] *nf* logistics *sg*

logotipo [loɣo'tipo] *nm* logo

logrado, a [lo'ɣraðo, a] *adj* (*interpretación, reproducción*) polished, excellent

lograr [lo'ɣrar] *vt* to achieve; (*obtener*) to get, obtain; ~ **hacer** to manage to do; ~ **que uno venga** to manage to get sb to come

logro ['loɣro] *nm* achievement, success

loma ['loma] *nf* hillock (*BRIT*), small hill

lombriz [lom'briθ] *nf* worm

lomo ['lomo] *nm* (*de animal*) back; (*CULIN: de cerdo*) pork loin; (: *de vaca*) rib steak; (*de libro*) spine

lona ['lona] *nf* canvas

loncha ['lontʃa] *nf* = **lonja**

lonche ['lontʃe] (*AM*) *nm* lunch; **~ría** (*AM*) *nf* snack bar, diner (*US*)

Londres ['londres] *n* London

longaniza [longa'niθa] *nf* pork sausage

longitud [lonxi'tuð] *nf* length; (*GEO*) longitude; **tener 3 metros de ~** to be 3 metres long; ~ **de onda** wavelength

lonja ['lonxa] *nf* slice; (*de tocino*) rasher; ~ **de pescado** fish market

loro ['loro] *nm* parrot

los [los] *art def* the ♦ *pron* them; (*ustedes*) you; **mis libros y ~ tuyos** my books and yours; *tb ver* **el**

losa ['losa] *nf* stone; ~ **sepulcral** gravestone

lote ['lote] *nm* portion; (*COM*) lot

lotería [lote'ria] *nf* lottery; (*juego*) lotto

loza ['loθa] *nf* crockery

lubina [lu'βina] *nf* sea bass

lubricante [luβri'kante] *nm* lubricant

lubricar [luβri'kar] *vt* to lubricate

lucha ['lutʃa] *nf* fight, struggle; ~ **de clases** class struggle; ~ **libre** wrestling; **luchar** *vi* to fight

lucidez [luθi'ðeθ] *nf* lucidity

lúcido, a ['luθiðo, a] *adj* (*persona*) lucid; (*mente*) logical; (*idea*) crystal-clear

luciérnaga [lu'θjernaɣa] *nf* glow-worm

lucir [lu'θir] *vt* to illuminate, light (up);

(*ostentar*) to show off ♦ *vi* (*brillar*) to shine; ~**se** *vr* (*irónico*) to make a fool of o.s.

lucro ['lukro] *nm* profit, gain

lúdico, a ['ludiko, a] *adj* (*aspecto, actividad*) play *cpd*

luego ['lwe o] *adv* (*después*) next; (*más tarde*) later, afterwards

lugar [lu'var] *nm* place; (*sitio*) spot; **en ~ de** instead of; **hacer ~** to make room; **fuera de ~** out of place; **tener ~** to take place; **~ común** commonplace

lugareño, a [luva'reno, a] *adj* village *cpd* ♦ *nm/f* villager

lugarteniente [luvarte'njente] *nm* deputy

lúgubre ['luvuβre] *adj* mournful

lujo ['luxo] *nm* luxury; (*fig*) profusion, abundance; **~so, a** *adj* luxurious

lujuria [lu'xurja] *nf* lust

lumbre ['lumbre] *nf* fire; (*para cigarrillo*) light

lumbrera [lum'brera] *nf* luminary

luminoso, a [lumi'noso, a] *adj* luminous, shining

luna ['luna] *nf* moon; (*de un espejo*) glass; (*de gafas*) lens; (*fig*) crescent; **~ llena/nueva** full/new moon; **estar en la ~** to have one's head in the clouds; **~ de miel** honeymoon

lunar [lu'nar] *adj* lunar ♦ *nm* (*ANAT*) mole; **tela de ~es** spotted material

lunes ['lunes] *nm inv* Monday

lupa ['lupa] *nf* magnifying glass

lustrar [lus'trar] *vt* (*mueble*) to polish; (*zapatos*) to shine; **lustre** *nm* polish; (*fig*) lustre; **dar lustre a** to polish; **lustroso, a** *adj* shining

luto ['luto] *nm* mourning; **llevar** o **vestirse de ~** to be in mourning

Luxemburgo [luksem'burvo] *nm* Luxembourg

luz [luθ] (*pl* **luces**) *nf* light; **dar a ~ un niño** to give birth to a child; **sacar a la ~** to bring to light; **dar** o **encender** (*ESP*) o **prender** (*AM*)/**apagar la ~** to switch the light on/off; **a todas luces** by any reckoning; **tener pocas luces** to be dim o stupid; **~ roja/verde** red/green light; **~ de freno** brake light; **luces de tráfico** traffic lights; **traje de luces** bullfighter's costume

M, m

m *abr* (= *metro*) m; (= *minuto*) m

macarrones [maka'rrones] *nmpl* macaroni *sg*

macedonia [maθe'ðonja] *nf*: **~ de frutas** fruit salad

macerar [maθe'rar] *vt* to macerate

maceta [ma'θeta] *nf* (*de flores*) pot of flowers; (*para plantas*) flowerpot

machacar [matʃa'kar] *vt* to crush, pound

♦ *vi* (*insistir*) to go on, keep on

machete [ma'tʃete] (*AM*) *nm* machete, (large) knife

machismo [ma'tʃismo] *nm* male chauvinism; **machista** *adj, nm* sexist

macho ['matʃo] *adj* male; (*fig*) virile ♦ *nm* male; (*fig*) he-man

macizo, a [ma'θiθo, a] *adj* (*grande*) massive; (*fuerte, sólido*) solid ♦ *nm* mass, chunk

madeja [ma'ðexa] *nf* (*de lana*) skein, hank; (*de pelo*) mass, mop

madera [ma'ðera] *nf* wood; (*fig*) nature, character; **una ~** a piece of wood

madero [ma'ðero] *nm* beam

madrastra [ma'ðrastra] *nf* stepmother

madre ['maðre] *adj* mother *cpd*; (*AM*) tremendous ♦ *nf* mother; (*de vino etc*) dregs *pl*; **~ política/soltera** mother-in-law/unmarried mother

Madrid [ma'ðrið] *n* Madrid

madriguera [maðri'vera] *nf* burrow

madrileño, a [maðri'leno, a] *adj* of o from Madrid ♦ *nm/f* native of Madrid

madrina [ma'ðrina] *nf* godmother; (*ARQ*) prop, shore; (*TEC*) brace; (*de boda*) bridesmaid

madrugada [maðru'vaða] *nf* early morning; (*alba*) dawn, daybreak

madrugador, a [maðruva'ðor, a] *adj* early-rising

madrugar [maðru'var] *vi* to get up early; (*fig*) to get ahead

madurar [maðu'rar] *vt, vi* (*fruta*) to ripen; (*fig*) to mature; **madurez** *nf* ripeness; maturity; **maduro, a** *adj* ripe; mature

maestra [ma'estra] *nf ver* **maestro**

maestría [maes'tria] *nf* mastery; (*habilidad*) skill, expertise

maestro, a [ma'estro, a] *adj* masterly; (*principal*) main ♦ *nm/f* master/mistress; (*profesor*) teacher ♦ *nm* (*autoridad*) authority; (*MUS*) maestro; (*AM*) skilled workman; **~ albañil** master mason

magdalena [maxða'lena] *nf* fairy cake

magia ['maxja] *nf* magic; **mágico, a** *adj* magic(al) ♦ *nm/f* magician

magisterio [maxis'terjo] *nm* (*enseñanza*) teaching; (*profesión*) teaching profession; (*maestros*) teachers *pl*

magistrado [maxis'traðo] *nm* magistrate

magistral [maxis'tral] *adj* magisterial; (*fig*) masterly

magnánimo, a [max'nanimo, a] *adj* magnanimous

magnate [max'nate] *nm* magnate, tycoon

magnético, a [max'netiko, a] *adj* magnetic; **magnetizar** *vt* to magnetize

magnetofón [maxneto'fon] *nm* tape recorder; **magnetofónico, a** *adj*: **cinta**

magnetofónica recording tape

magnetófono [maɣne'tofono] *nm* =
magnetofón

magnífico, a [maɣ'nifiko, a] *adj* splendid,
magnificent

magnitud [maɣni'tuð] *nf* magnitude

mago, a ['maɣo, a] *nm/f* magician; **los Reyes
M~s** the Magi, the Three Wise Men

magro, a ['maɣro, a] *adj* (*carne*) lean

maguey [ma'ɣei] *nm* agave

magullar [maɣu'ʎar] *vt* (*amoratar*) to bruise;
(*dañar*) to damage

mahometano, a [maome'tano, a] *adj*
Mohammedan

mahonesa [mao'nesa] *nf* mayonnaise

maíz [ma'iθ] *nm* maize (*BRIT*), corn (*US*);
sweet corn

majadero, a [maxa'ðero, a] *adj* silly, stupid

majestad [maxes'tað] *nf* majesty;
majestuoso, a *adj* majestic

majo, a ['maxo, a] *adj* nice; (*guapo*)
attractive, good-looking; (*elegante*) smart

mal [mal] *adv* badly; (*equivocadamente*)
wrongly ♦ *adj* = **malo** ♦ *nm* evil; (*desgracia*)
misfortune; (*daño*) harm, damage; (*MED*)
illness; **~ que bien** rightly or wrongly; **ir de
~ en peor** to get worse and worse

malabarismo [malaβa'rismo] *nm* juggling;
malabarista *nm/f* juggler

malaria [ma'larja] *nf* malaria

malcriado, a [mal'krjaðo, a] *adj* spoiled

maldad [mal'dað] *nf* evil, wickedness

maldecir [malde'θir] *vt* to curse ♦ *vi*: **~ de**
to speak ill of

maldición [maldi'θjon] *nf* curse

maldito, a [mal'dito, a] *adj* (*condenado*)
damned; (*perverso*) wicked; **¡~ sea!** damn it!

maleante [male'ante] *nm/f* criminal, crook

maledicencia [maleði'θenθja] *nf* slander,
scandal

maleducado, a [maleðu'kaðo, a] *adj* bad-
mannered, rude

malentendido [malenten'diðo] *nm*
misunderstanding

malestar [males'tar] *nm* (*gen*) discomfort;
(*fig: inquietud*) uneasiness; (*POL*) unrest

maleta [ma'leta] *nf* case, suitcase; (*AUTO*)
boot (*BRIT*), trunk (*US*); **hacer las ~s** to pack;
maletera (*AM*) *nf*, **maletero** *nm* (*AUTO*)
boot (*BRIT*), trunk (*US*); **maletín** *nm* small
case, bag

malévolo, a [ma'leβolo, a] *adj* malicious,
spiteful

maleza [ma'leθa] *nf* (*hierbas malas*) weeds *pl*;
(*arbustos*) thicket

malgastar [malɣas'tar] *vt* (*tiempo, dinero*) to
waste; (*salud*) to ruin

malhechor, a [male'tʃor, a] *nm/f* delinquent

malhumorado, a [malumo'raðo, a] *adj*
bad-tempered

malicia [ma'liθja] *nf* (*maldad*) wickedness;
(*astucia*) slyness, guile; (*mala intención*)
malice, spite; (*carácter travieso*)
mischievousness; **malicioso, a** *adj* wicked,
evil; sly, crafty; malicious, spiteful;
mischievous

maligno, a [ma'liɣno, a] *adj* evil; (*malévolo*)
malicious; (*MED*) malignant

malla ['maʎa] *nf* mesh; (*de baño*) swimsuit;
(*de ballet, gimnasia*) leotard; **~s** *nfpl* tights;
~ de alambre wire mesh

Mallorca [ma'ʎorka] *nf* Majorca

malo, a ['malo, a] *adj* bad; (*falso*) false
♦ *nm/f* villain; **estar ~** to be ill

malograr [malo'ɣrar] *vt* to spoil; (*plan*) to
upset; (*ocasión*) to waste; **~se** *vr* (*plan etc*) to
fail, come to grief; (*persona*) to die before
one's time

malparado, a [malpa'raðo, a] *adj*: **salir ~** to
come off badly

malpensado, a [malpen'saðo, a] *adj* nasty

malsano, a [mal'sano, a] *adj* unhealthy

malteada [malte'aða] (*AM*) *nf* milk shake

maltratar [maltra'tar] *vt* to ill-treat, mistreat

maltrecho, a [mal'tretʃo, a] *adj* battered,
damaged

malvado, a [mal'βaðo, a] *adj* evil, villainous

malversar [malβer'sar] *vt* to embezzle,
misappropriate

Malvinas [mal'βinas]: **Islas ~** *nfpl* Falkland
Islands

malvivir [malβi'βir] *vi* to live poorly

mama ['mama] *nf* (*de animal*) teat; (*de
mujer*) breast

mamá [ma'ma] (*pl* **~s**) (*fam*) *nf* mum,
mummy

mamar [ma'mar] *vt, vi* to suck

mamarracho [mama'ratʃo] *nm* sight, mess

mamífero [ma'mifero] *nm* mammal

mampara [mam'para] *nf* (*entre habitaciones*)
partition; (*biombo*) screen

mampostería [mamposte'ria] *nf* masonry

manada [ma'naða] *nf* (*ZOOL*) herd; (: *de
leones*) pride; (: *de lobos*) pack

manantial [manan'tjal] *nm* spring

manar [ma'nar] *vi* to run, flow

mancha ['mantʃa] *nf* stain, mark; (*ZOOL*)
patch; **manchar** *vt* (*gen*) to stain, mark;
(*ensuciar*) to soil, dirty

manchego, a [man'tʃeɣo, a] *adj* of o from
La Mancha

manco, a ['manko, a] *adj* (*de un brazo*)
one-armed; (*de una mano*) one-handed; (*fig*)
defective, faulty

mancomunar [mankomu'nar] *vt* to unite,
bring together; (*recursos*) to pool; (*JUR*) to
make jointly responsible; **mancomunidad** *nf*
union, association; (*comunidad*) community;

(*JUR*) joint responsibility

mandamiento [manda'mjento] *nm* (*orden*) order, command; (*REL*) commandment; ~ **judicial** warrant

mandar [man'dar] *vt* (*ordenar*) to order; (*dirigir*) to lead, command; (*enviar*) to send; (*pedir*) to order, ask for ♦ *vi* to be in charge; (*pey*) to be bossy; **¿mande?** pardon?, excuse me?; ~ **hacer un traje** to have a suit made

mandarina [manda'rina] *nf* tangerine, mandarin (orange)

mandato [man'dato] *nm* (*orden*) order; (*POL: período*) term of office; (*: territorio*) mandate; ~ **judicial** (*search*) warrant

mandíbula [man'diβula] *nf* jaw

mandil [man'dil] *nm* apron

mando ['mando] *nm* (*MIL*) command; (*de país*) rule; (*el primer lugar*) lead; (*POL*) term of office; (*TEC*) control; ~ **a la izquierda** left-hand drive

mandón, ona [man'don, ona] *adj* bossy, domineering

manejable [mane'xaβle] *adj* manageable

manejar [mane'xar] *vt* to manage; (*máquina*) to work, operate; (*caballo etc*) to handle; (*casa*) to run, manage; (*AM: AUTO*) to drive; ~**se** *vr* (*comportarse*) to act, behave; (*arreglárselas*) to manage; **manejo** *nm* management; handling; running; driving; (*facilidad de trato*) ease, confidence; **manejos** *nmpl* (*intrigas*) intrigues

manera [ma'nera] *nf* way, manner, fashion; ~**s** *nfpl* (*modales*) manners; **su ~ de ser** the way he is; (*aire*) his manner; **de ninguna ~** no way, by no means; **de otra ~** otherwise; **de todas ~s** at any rate; **no hay ~ de persuadirle** there's no way of convincing him

manga ['manga] *nf* (*de camisa*) sleeve; (*de riego*) hose

mangar [man'gar] (*fam*) *vt* to pinch, nick

mango ['mango] *nm* handle; (*BOT*) mango

mangonear [mangone'ar] *vi* (*meterse*) to meddle, interfere; (*ser mandón*) to boss people about

manguera [man'gera] *nf* hose

manía [ma'nia] *nf* (*MED*) mania; (*fig: moda*) rage, craze; (*disgusto*) dislike; (*malicia*) spite; **maníaco, a** *adj* maniac(al) ♦ *nm/f* maniac

maniatar [manja'tar] *vt* to tie the hands of

maniático, a [ma'njatiko, a] *adj* maniac(al) ♦ *nm/f* maniac

manicomio [mani'komjo] *nm* mental hospital (*BRIT*), insane asylum (*US*)

manifestación [manifesta'θjon] *nf* (*declaración*) statement, declaration; (*de emoción*) show, display; (*POL: desfile*) demonstration; (*: concentración*) mass meeting

manifestar [manifes'tar] *vt* to show,

manifest; (*declarar*) to state, declare; **manifiesto, a** *adj* clear, manifest ♦ *nm* manifesto

manillar [mani'ʎar] *nm* handlebars *pl*

maniobra [ma'njoβra] *nf* manoeuvre; ~**s** *nfpl* (*MIL*) manœuvres; **maniobrar** *vt* to manœuvre

manipulación [manipula'θjon] *nf* manipulation

manipular [manipu'lar] *vt* to manipulate; (*manejar*) to handle

maniquí [mani'ki] *nm* dummy ♦ *nm/f* model

manirroto, a [mani'rroto, a] *adj* lavish, extravagant ♦ *nm/f* spendthrift

manivela [mani'βela] *nf* crank

manjar [man'xar] *nm* (*tasty*) dish

mano ['mano] *nf* hand; (*ZOOL*) foot, paw; (*de pintura*) coat; (*serie*) lot, series; **a ~** by hand; **a ~ derecha/izquierda** on the right(-hand side)/left(-hand side); **de primera ~** (at) first hand; **de segunda ~** (at) second hand; **robo a ~ armada** armed robbery; ~ **de obra** labour, manpower; **estrechar la ~ a uno** to shake sb's hand

manojo [ma'noxo] *nm* handful, bunch; ~ **de llaves** bunch of keys

manopla [ma'nopla] *nf* mitten

manoseado, a [manose'aðo, a] *adj* well-worn

manosear [manose'ar] *vt* (*tocar*) to handle, touch; (*desordenar*) to mess up, rumple; (*insistir en*) to overwork; (*AM*) to caress, fondle

manotazo [mano'taθo] *nm* slap, smack

mansalva [man'salβa]: **a ~** *adv* indiscriminately

mansedumbre [manse'ðumbre] *nf* gentleness, meekness

mansión [man'sjon] *nf* mansion

manso, a ['manso, a] *adj* gentle, mild; (*animal*) tame

manta ['manta] *nf* blanket; (*AM: poncho*) poncho

manteca [man'teka] *nf* fat; (*AM*) butter; ~ **de cacahuete/cacao** peanut/cocoa butter; ~ **de cerdo** lard

mantecado [mante'kaðo] (*AM*) *nm* ice cream

mantel [man'tel] *nm* tablecloth

mantendré *etc vb ver* **mantener**

mantener [mante'ner] *vt* to support, maintain; (*alimentar*) to sustain; (*conservar*) to keep; (*TEC*) to maintain, service; ~**se** *vr* (*seguir de pie*) to be still standing; (*no ceder*) to hold one's ground; (*subsistir*) to sustain o.s., keep going; **mantenimiento** *nm* maintenance; sustenance; (*sustento*) support

mantequilla [mante'kiʎa] *nf* butter

mantilla [man'tiʎa] *nf* mantilla; ~**s** *nfpl* (*de*

bebé) baby clothes

manto ['manto] *nm (capa)* cloak; *(de ceremonia)* robe, gown

mantuve *etc vb ver* **mantener**

manual [ma'nwal] *adj* manual ♦ *nm* manual, handbook

manufactura [manufak'tura] *nf* manufacture; *(fábrica)* factory; **manufacturado, a** *adj (producto)* manufactured

manuscrito, a [manus'krito, a] *adj* handwritten ♦ *nm* manuscript

manutención [manuten'θjon] *nf* maintenance; *(sustento)* support

manzana [man'θana] *nf* apple; *(ARQ)* block (of houses)

manzanilla [manθa'niʎa] *nf (planta)* camomile; *(infusión)* camomile tea

manzano [man'θano] *nm* apple tree

maña ['maɲa] *nf (gen)* skill, dexterity; *(pey)* guile; *(destreza)* trick, knack

mañana [ma'ɲana] *adv* tomorrow ♦ *nm* future ♦ *nf* morning; **de** o **por la ~** in the morning; **¡hasta ~!** see you tomorrow!; **~ por la ~** tomorrow morning

mañoso, a [ma'ɲoso, a] *adj (hábil)* skilful; *(astuto)* smart, clever

mapa ['mapa] *nm* map

maqueta [ma'keta] *nf (scale)* model

maquillaje [maki'ʎaxe] *nm* make-up; *(acto)* making up

maquillar [maki'ʎar] *vt* to make up; **~se** *vr* to put on *(some)* make-up

máquina ['makina] *nf* machine; *(de tren)* locomotive, engine; *(FOTO)* camera; *(AM: coche)* car; *(fig)* machinery; **escrito a ~** typewritten; **~ de escribir** typewriter; **~ de coser/lavar** sewing/washing machine

maquinación [makina'θjon] *nf* machination, plot

maquinal [maki'nal] *adj (fig)* mechanical, automatic

maquinaria [maki'narja] *nf (máquinas)* machinery; *(mecanismo)* mechanism, works *pl*

maquinilla [maki'niʎa] *nf:* **~ de afeitar** razor

maquinista [maki'nista] *nm/f (de tren)* engine driver; *(TEC)* operator; *(NAUT)* engineer

mar [mar] *nm* o *f* sea; **~ adentro** o **afuera** out at sea; **en alta ~** on the high seas; **la ~ de** *(fam)* lots of; **el M~ Negro/Báltico** the Black/ Baltic Sea

maraña [ma'raɲa] *nf (maleza)* thicket; *(confusión)* tangle

maravilla [mara'βiʎa] *nf* marvel, wonder; *(BOT)* marigold; **maravillar** *vt* to astonish, amaze; **maravillarse** *vr* to be astonished, be amazed; **maravilloso, a** *adj* wonderful, marvellous

marca ['marka] *nf (gen)* mark; *(sello)* stamp; *(COM)* make, brand; **de ~** excellent, outstanding; **~ de fábrica** trademark; **~ registrada** registered trademark

marcado, a [mar'kaðo, a] *adj* marked, strong

marcador [marka'ðor] *nm (DEPORTE)* scoreboard; *(: persona)* scorer

marcapasos [marka'pasos] *nm inv* pacemaker

marcar [mar'kar] *vt (gen)* to mark; *(número de teléfono)* to dial; *(gol)* to score; *(números)* to record, keep a tally of; *(pelo)* to set ♦ *vi (DEPORTE)* to score; *(TEL)* to dial

marcha ['martʃa] *nf* march; *(TEC)* running, working; *(AUTO)* gear; *(velocidad)* speed; *(fig)* progress; *(dirección)* course; **poner en ~** to put into gear; *(fig)* to set in motion, get going; **dar ~ atrás** to reverse, put into reverse; **estar en ~** to be under way, be in motion

marchar [mar'tʃar] *vi (ir)* to go; *(funcionar)* to work, go; **~se** *vr* to go (away), leave

marchitar [martʃi'tar] *vt* to wither, dry up; **~se** *vr (BOT)* to wither; *(fig)* to fade away; **marchito, a** *adj* withered, faded; *(fig)* in decline

marcial [mar'θjal] *adj* martial, military

marciano, a [mar'θjano, a] *adj, nm/f* Martian

marco ['marko] *nm* frame; *(moneda)* mark; *(fig)* framework

marea [ma'rea] *nf* tide

marear [mare'ar] *vt (fig)* to annoy, upset; *(MED):* **~ a uno** to make sb feel sick; **~se** *vr (tener náuseas)* to feel sick; *(desvanecerse)* to feel faint; *(aturdirse)* to feel dizzy; *(fam: emborracharse)* to get tipsy

maremoto [mare'moto] *nm* tidal wave

mareo [ma'reo] *nm (náusea)* sick feeling; *(en viaje)* travel sickness; *(aturdimiento)* dizziness; *(fam: lata)* nuisance

marfil [mar'fil] *nm* ivory

margarina [marɣa'rina] *nf* margarine

margarita [marɣa'rita] *nf (BOT)* daisy; **(rueda) ~** daisywheel

margen ['marxen] *nm (borde)* edge, border; *(fig)* margin, space ♦ *nf (de río etc)* bank; **dar ~ para** to give an opportunity for; **mantenerse al ~** to keep out (of things)

marginar [marxi'nar] *vt (socialmente)* to marginalize, ostracize

marica [ma'rika] *(fam) nm* sissy

maricón [mari'kon] *(fam) nm* queer

marido [ma'riðo] *nm* husband

marihuana [mari'wana] *nf* marijuana, cannabis

marina [ma'rina] *nf* navy; **~ mercante** merchant navy

marinero, a |mari'nero, a| adj sea cpd ♦ nm sailor, seaman

marino, a |ma'rino, a| adj sea cpd, marine ♦ nm sailor

marioneta |marjo'neta| nf puppet

mariposa |mari'posa| nf butterfly

mariquita |mari'kita| nf ladybird (BRIT), ladybug (US)

mariscos |ma'riskos| nmpl shellfish inv, seafood(s)

marítimo, a |ma'ritimo, a| adj sea cpd, maritime

mármol ['marmol| nm marble

marqués, esa |mar'kes, esa| nm/f marquis/ marchioness

marrón |ma'rron| adj brown

marroquí |marro'ki| adj, nm/f Moroccan ♦ nm Morocco (leather)

Marruecos |ma'rrwekos| nm Morocco

martes ['martes| nm inv Tuesday

martillo |mar'tiʎo| nm hammer; ~ **neumático** pneumatic drill (BRIT), jackhammer

mártir ['martir| nm/f martyr; **martirio** nm martyrdom; (fig) torture, torment

marxismo |mark'sismo| nm Marxism; **marxista** adj, nm/f Marxist

marzo ['marθo| nm March

más |mas| adj, adv 1: ~ **(que, de)** (compar) more (than), ... + er (than); ~ **grande/ inteligente** bigger/more intelligent; **trabaja ~ (que yo)** he works more (than me); ver tb **cada**

2 (superl): **el ~** the most, ... + est; **el ~ grande/inteligente (de)** the biggest/most intelligent (in)

3 (negativo): **no tengo ~ dinero** I haven't got any more money; **no viene ~ por aquí** he doesn't come round here any more

4 (adicional): **no le veo ~ solución que** ... I see no other solution than to ...; **¿quién ~?** anybody else?

5 (+ adj: valor intensivo): **¡qué perro ~ sucio!** what a filthy dog!; **¡es ~ tonto!** he's so stupid!

6 (locuciones): ~ **o menos** more or less; **los ~** most people; **es ~** furthermore; ~ **bien** rather; **¡qué ~ da!** what does it matter!; ver tb **no**

7: **por ~: por ~ que te esfuerces** no matter how hard you try; **por ~ que quisiera** ... much as I should like to ...

8: **de ~: veo que aqui estoy de ~** I can see I'm not needed here; **tenemos uno de ~** we've got one extra

♦ prep: **2 ~ 2 son 4** 2 and o plus 2 are 4

♦ nm inv: **este trabajo tiene sus ~ y sus menos** this job's got its good points and its bad points

mas |mas| conj but

masa ['masa| nf (mezcla) dough; (volumen) volume, mass; (FÍSICA) mass; **en ~** en masse; **las ~s** (POL) the masses

masacre |ma'sakre| nf massacre

masaje |ma'saxe| nm massage

máscara ['maskara| nf mask; **mascarilla** nf (de belleza, MED) mask

masculino, a |masku'lino, a| adj masculine; (BIO) male

masía |ma'sia| nf farmhouse

masificación |masifika'θjon| nf overcrowding

masivo, a |ma'sißo, a| adj mass cpd

masón |ma'son| nm (free)mason

masoquista |maso'kista| nm/f masochist

masticar |masti'kar| vt to chew

mástil ['mastil| nm (de navío) mast; (de guitarra) neck

mastín |mas'tin| nm mastiff

masturbación |masturßa'θjon| nf masturbation

masturbarse |mastur'ßarse| vr to masturbate

mata ['mata| nf (arbusto) bush, shrub; (de hierba) tuft

matadero |mata'ðero| nm slaughterhouse, abattoir

matador, a |mata'ðor, a| adj killing ♦ nm/f killer ♦ nm (TAUR) matador, bullfighter

matamoscas |mata'moskas| nm inv (palo) fly swat

matanza |ma'tanθa| nf slaughter

matar |ma'tar| vt, vi to kill; ~**se** vr (suicidarse) to kill o.s., commit suicide; (morir) to be o get killed; ~ **el hambre** to stave off hunger

matasellos |mata'seʎos| nm inv postmark

mate ['mate| adj matt ♦ nm (en ajedrez) (check)mate; (AM: hierba) maté; (: vasija) gourd

matemáticas |mate'matikas| nfpl mathematics; **matemático, a** adj mathematical ♦ nm/f mathematician

materia |ma'terja| nf (gen) matter; (TEC) material; (ESCOL) subject; **en ~ de** on the subject of; ~ **prima** raw material; **material** adj material ♦ nm material; (TEC) equipment; **materialismo** nm materialism; **materialista** adj material(ic); **materialmente** adv materially; (fig) absolutely

maternal |mater'nal| adj motherly, maternal

maternidad |materni'ðað| nf motherhood, maternity; **materno, a** adj maternal; (lengua) mother cpd

matinal |mati'nal| adj morning cpd

matiz |ma'tiθ| nm shade; ~**ar** vt (variar) to vary; (ARTE) to blend; ~**ar de** to tinge with

matón |ma'ton| nm bully

matorral [mato'rral] nm thicket

matraca [ma'traka] nf rattle

matrícula [ma'trikula] nf (registro) register; (AUTO) registration number; (: placa) number plate; **matricular** vt to register, enrol

matrimonial [matrimo'njal] adj matrimonial

matrimonio [matri'monjo] nm (pareja) (married) couple; (unión) marriage

matriz [ma'triθ] nf (ANAT) womb; (TEC) mould; **casa ~** (COM) head office

matrona [ma'trona] nf (persona de edad) matron; (comadrona) midwife

maullar [mau'ʎar] vi to mew, miaow

maxilar [maksi'lar] nm jaw(bone)

máxima ['maksima] nf maxim

máxime ['maksime] adv especially

máximo, a ['maksimo, a] adj maximum; (más alto) highest; (más grande) greatest ♦ nm maximum

mayo ['majo] nm May

mayonesa [majo'nesa] nf mayonnaise

mayor [ma'jor] adj main, chief; (adulto) adult; (de edad avanzada) elderly; (MUS) major; (compar: de tamaño) bigger; (: de edad) older; (superl: de tamaño) biggest; (: de edad) oldest ♦ nm (adulto) adult; **al por ~** wholesale; **~ de edad** adult; **~es** nmpl (antepasados) ancestors

mayoral [majo'ral] nm foreman

mayordomo [major'ðomo] nm butler

mayoría [majo'ria] nf majority, greater part

mayorista [majo'rista] nm/f wholesaler

mayoritario, a [majori'tarjo, a] adj majority cpd

mayúscula [ma'juskula] nf capital letter

mayúsculo, a [ma'juskulo, a] adj (fig) big, tremendous

mazapán [maθa'pan] nm marzipan

mazo ['maθo] nm (martillo) mallet; (de flores) bunch; (DEPORTE) bat

me [me] pron (directo) me; (indirecto) (to) me; (reflexivo) (to) myself; ¡dámelo! give it to me!

mear [me'ar] (fam) vi to pee, piss (!)

mecánica [me'kanika] nf (ESCOL) mechanics sg; (mecanismo) mechanism; ver tb **mecánico**

mecánico, a [me'kaniko, a] adj mechanical ♦ nm/f mechanic

mecanismo [meka'nismo] nm mechanism; (marcha) gear

mecanografía [mekanoxra'fia] nf typewriting; **mecanógrafo, a** nm/f typist

mecate [me'kate] (AM) nm rope

mecedora [meθe'ðora] nf rocking chair

mecer [me'θer] vt (cuna) to rock; **~se** vr to rock; (ramo) to sway

mecha ['metʃa] nf (de vela) wick; (de bomba) fuse

mechero [me'tʃero] nm (cigarette) lighter

mechón [me'tʃon] nm (gen) tuft; (de pelo) lock

medalla [me'ðaʎa] nf medal

media ['meðja] nf (ESP) stocking; (AM) sock; (promedio) average

mediado, a [me'ðjaðo, a] adj half-full; (trabajo) half-completed; **a ~s de** in the middle of, halfway through

mediano, a [me'ðjano, a] adj (regular) medium, average; (mediocre) mediocre

medianoche [meðja'notʃe] nf midnight

mediante [me'ðjante] adv by (means of), through

mediar [me'ðjar] vi (interceder) to mediate, intervene

medicación [meðika'θjon] nf medication, treatment

medicamento [meðika'mento] nm medicine, drug

medicina [meði'θina] nf medicine

medición [meði'θjon] nf measurement

médico, a ['meðiko, a] adj medical ♦ nm/f doctor

medida [me'ðiða] nf measure; (medición) measurement; (prudencia) moderation, prudence; **en cierta/gran ~** up to a point/to a great extent; **un traje a la ~** made-to-measure suit; **~ de cuello** collar size; **a ~ de** in proportion to; (de acuerdo con) in keeping with; **a ~ que** (conforme) as

medio, a ['meðjo, a] adj half (a); (punto) mid, middle; (promedio) average ♦ adv half ♦ nm (centro) middle, centre; (promedio) average; (método) means, way; (ambiente) environment; **~s** nmpl means, resources; **~ litro** half a litre; **las tres y media** half past three; **medio ambiente** environment; **M~ Oriente** Middle East; **a ~ terminar** half finished; **pagar a medias** to share the cost; **~ambiental** adj (política, efectos) environmental

mediocre [me'ðjokre] adj mediocre

mediodía [meðjo'ðia] nm midday, noon

medir [me'ðir] vt, vi (gen) to measure

meditar [meði'tar] vt to ponder, think over, meditate on; (planear) to think out

mediterráneo, a [meðite'rraneo, a] adj Mediterranean ♦ nm: **el M~** the Mediterranean (Sea)

médula ['meðula] nf (ANAT) marrow; **~ espinal** spinal cord

medusa [me'ðusa] (ESP) nf jellyfish

megafonía [meðafo'nia] nf public address system, PA system; **megáfono** nm megaphone

megalómano, a [meɣa'lomano, a] nm/f megalomaniac

mejicano, a [mexi'kano, a] adj, nm/f Mexican

Méjico |'mexiko| nm Mexico
mejilla [me'xiʎa] nf cheek
mejillón [mexi'ʎon] nm mussel
mejor [me'xor] adj, adv (compar) better; (superl) best; **a lo ~** probably; (quizá) maybe; **~ dicho** rather; **tanto ~** so much the better
mejora [me'xora] nf improvement; **mejorar** vt to improve, make better ♦ vi to improve, get better; **mejorarse** vr to improve, get better
melancólico, a [melan'koliko, a] adj (triste) sad, melancholy; (soñador) dreamy
melena [me'lena] nf (de persona) long hair; (ZOOL) mane
mellizo, a [me'ʎiθo, a] adj, nm/f twin; **~s** nmpl (AM) cufflinks
melocotón [meloko'ton] (ESP) nm peach
melodía [melo'ðia] nf melody, tune
melodrama [melo'ðrama] nm melodrama; **melodramático, a** adj melodramatic
melón [me'lon] nm melon
membrete [mem'brete] nm letterhead
membrillo [mem'briʎo] nm quince; **carne de ~** quince jelly
memorable [memo'raβle] adj memorable
memoria [me'morja] nf (gen) memory; **~s** nfpl (de autor) memoirs; **memorizar** vt to memorize
menaje [me'naxe] nm: **~ de cocina** kitchenware
mencionar [menθjo'nar] vt to mention
mendigar [mendi'ɣar] vt to beg (for)
mendigo, a [men'diɣo, a] nm/f beggar
mendrugo [men'druɣo] nm crust
menear [mene'ar] vt to move; **~se** vr to shake; (balancearse) to sway; (moverse) to move; (fig) to get a move on
menestra [me'nestra] nf: **~ de verduras** vegetable stew
menguante [men'gwante] adj decreasing, diminishing
menguar [men'gwar] vt to lessen, diminish ♦ vi to diminish, decrease
menopausia [meno'pausja] nf menopause
menor [me'nor] adj (más pequeño: compar) smaller; (: superl) smallest; (más joven: compar) younger; (: superl) youngest; (MUS) minor ♦ nm/f (joven) young person, juvenile; **no tengo la ~ idea** I haven't the faintest idea; **al por ~** retail; **~ de edad** person under age
Menorca [me'norka] nf Minorca

PALABRA CLAVE

menos [menos] adj **1**: **~ (que, de)** (compar: cantidad) less (than); (: número) fewer (than); **con ~ entusiasmo** with less enthusiasm; **~ gente** fewer people; ver tb **cada**

2 (superl): **es el que ~ culpa tiene** he is the least to blame

♦ adv **1** (compar): **~ (que, de)** less (than); **me gusta ~ que el otro** I like it less than the other one

2 (superl): **es el ~ listo (de su clase)** he's the least bright in his class; **de todas ellas es la que ~ me agrada** out of all of them she's the one I like least; **(por) lo ~** at (the very) least

3 (locuciones): **no quiero verle y ~ visitarle** I don't want to see him let alone visit him; **tenemos 7 de ~** we're seven short

♦ prep except; (cifras) minus; **todos ~ él** everyone except (for) him; **5 ~ 2** 5 minus 2

♦ conj: **a ~ que: a ~ que venga mañana** unless he comes tomorrow

menospreciar [menospre'θjar] vt to underrate, undervalue; (despreciar) to scorn, despise
mensaje [men'saxe] nm message; **~ro, a** nm/f messenger
menstruación [menstrua'θjon] nf menstruation
menstruar [mens'trwar] vi to menstruate
mensual [men'swal] adj monthly; **1000 ptas ~es** 1000 ptas a month; **~idad** nf (salario) monthly salary; (COM) monthly payment, monthly instalment
menta ['menta] nf mint
mental [men'tal] adj mental; **~idad** nf mentality; **~izar** vt (sensibilizar) to make aware; (convencer) to convince; (padres) to prepare (mentally); **~izarse** vr (concienciarse) to become aware; **~izarse (de)** to get used to the idea (of); **~izarse de que ...** (convencerse) to get it into one's head that ...
mentar [men'tar] vt to mention, name
mente ['mente] nf mind
mentir [men'tir] vi to lie
mentira [men'tira] nf (una ~) lie; (acto) lying; (invención) fiction; **parece ~ que ...** it seems incredible that ..., I can't believe that ...
mentiroso, a [menti'roso, a] adj lying ♦ nm/f liar
menú [me'nu] (pl **~s**) nm menu; (AM) set meal; **~ del día** set menu
menudo, a [me'nuðo, a] adj (pequeño) small, tiny; (sin importancia) petty, insignificant; **¡~ negocio!** (fam) some deal!; **a ~** often, frequently
meñique [me'ɲike] nm little finger
meollo [me'oʎo] nm (fig) core
mercado [mer'kaðo] nm market
mercancía [merkan'θia] nf commodity; **~s** nfpl goods, merchandise sg
mercantil [merkan'til] adj mercantile, commercial
mercenario, a [merθe'narjo, a] adj, nm

mercenary

mercería [merθe'ria] *nf* haberdashery (*BRIT*), notions (*US*); (*tienda*) haberdasher's (*BRIT*), notions store (*US*); (*AM*) drapery

mercurio [mer'kurjo] *nm* mercury

merecer [mere'θer] *vt* to deserve, merit ♦ *vi* to be deserving, be worthy; **merece la pena** it's worthwhile; **merecido, a** *adj* (well) deserved; **llevar su merecido** to get one's deserts

merendar [meren'dar] *vt* to have for tea ♦ *vi* to have tea; (*en el campo*) to have a picnic; **merendero** *nm* open-air cafe

merengue [me'renge] *nm* meringue

meridiano [meri'ðjano] *nm* (*GEO*) meridian

merienda [me'rjenda] *nf* (light) tea, afternoon snack; (*de campo*) picnic

mérito ['merito] *nm* merit; (*valor*) worth, value

merluza [mer'luθa] *nf* hake

merma ['merma] *nf* decrease; (*pérdida*) wastage; **mermar** *vt* to reduce, lessen ♦ *vi* to decrease, dwindle

mermelada [merme'laða] *nf* jam

mero, a ['mero, a] *adj* mere; (*AM: fam*) very

merodear [meroðe'ar] *vi*: ~ **por** to prowl about

mes [mes] *nm* month

mesa ['mesa] *nf* table; (*de trabajo*) desk; (*GEO*) plateau; ~ **directiva** board; ~ **redonda** (*reunión*) round table; **poner/quitar la** ~ to lay/clear the table; **mesero, a** (*AM*) *nm/f* waiter/waitress

meseta [me'seta] *nf* (*GEO*) meseta, tableland

mesilla [me'siʎa] *nf*: ~ (**de noche**) bedside table

mesón [me'son] *nm* inn

mestizo, a [mes'tiθo, a] *adj* half-caste, of mixed race ♦ *nm/f* half-caste

mesura [me'sura] *nf* moderation, restraint

meta ['meta] *nf* goal; (*de carrera*) finish

metabolismo [metaβo'lismo] *nm* metabolism

metáfora [me'tafora] *nf* metaphor

metal [me'tal] *nm* (*materia*) metal; (*MUS*) brass; **metálico, a** *adj* metallic; (*de metal*) metal ♦ *nm* (*dinero contante*) cash

metalurgia [meta'lurxja] *nf* metallurgy

meteoro [mete'oro] *nm* meteor; ~**logía** *nf* meteorology

meter [me'ter] *vt* (*colocar*) to put, place; (*introducir*) to put in, insert; (*involucrar*) to involve; (*causar*) to make, cause; ~**se** *vr*: ~**se en** to go into, enter; (*fig*) to interfere in, meddle in; ~**se a** to start; ~**se a escritor** to become a writer; ~**se con uno** to provoke sb, pick a quarrel with sb

meticuloso, a [metiku'loso, a] *adj* meticulous, thorough

metódico, a [me'toðiko, a] *adj* methodical

método ['metoðo] *nm* method

metralleta [metra'ʎeta] *nf* sub-machine-gun

métrico, a ['metriko, a] *adj* metric

metro ['metro] *nm* metre; (*tren*) underground (*BRIT*), subway (*US*)

México ['mexiko] *nm* Mexico; **Ciudad de** ~ Mexico City

mezcla ['meθkla] *nf* mixture; **mezclar** *vt* to mix (up); **mezclarse** *vr* to mix, mingle; **mezclarse en** to get mixed up in, get involved in

mezquino, a [meθ'kino, a] *adj* mean

mezquita [meθ'kita] *nf* mosque

mg. *abr* (= *miligramo*) mg

mi [mi] *adj pos* my ♦ *nm* (*MUS*) E

mí [mi] *pron* me; myself

mía ['mia] *pron ver* **mío**

miaja ['mjaxa] *nf* crumb

michelín [mitʃe'lin] (*fam*) *nm* (*de grasa*) spare tyre

micro ['mikro] (*AM*) *nm* minibus

microbio [mi'kroβjo] *nm* microbe

micrófono [mi'krofono] *nm* microphone

microondas [mikro'ondas] *nm inv* (*tb: horno* ~) microwave (oven)

microscopio [mikro'skopjo] *nm* microscope

miedo ['mjeðo] *nm* fear; (*nerviosismo*) apprehension, nervousness; **tener** ~ to be afraid; **de** ~ wonderful, marvellous; **hace un frío de** ~ (*fam*) it's terribly cold; ~**so, a** *adj* fearful, timid

miel [mjel] *nf* honey

miembro ['mjembro] *nm* limb; (*socio*) member; ~ **viril** penis

mientras ['mjentras] *conj* while; (*duración*) as long as ♦ *adv* meanwhile; ~ **tanto** meanwhile; ~ **más tiene, más quiere** the more he has, the more he wants

miércoles ['mjerkoles] *nm inv* Wednesday

mierda ['mjerða] (*fam!*) *nf* shit (*!*)

miga ['miɣa] *nf* crumb; (*fig: meollo*) essence; **hacer buenas** ~**s** (*fam*) to get on well

migración [miɣra'θjon] *nf* migration

mil [mil] *num* thousand; **dos** ~ **libras** two thousand pounds

milagro [mi'laɣro] *nm* miracle; ~**so, a** *adj* miraculous

milésima [mi'lesima] *nf* (*de segundo*) thousandth

mili ['mili] (*fam*) *nf*: **hacer la** ~ to do one's military service

milicia [mi'liθja] *nf* militia; (*servicio militar*) military service

milímetro [mi'limetro] *nm* millimetre

militante [mili'tante] *adj* militant

militar [mili'tar] *adj* military ♦ *nm/f* soldier ♦ *vi* (*MIL*) to serve; (*en un partido*) to be a member

milla ['miʎa] nf mile

millar [mi'ʎar] nm thousand

millón [mi'ʎon] num million; **millonario, a** nm/f millionaire

mimar [mi'mar] vt to spoil, pamper

mimbre ['mimbre] nm wicker

mímica ['mimika] nf (para comunicarse) sign language; (imitación) mimicry

mimo ['mimo] nm (caricia) caress; (de niño) spoiling; (TEATRO) mime; (: actor) mime artist

mina ['mina] nf mine; **minar** vt to mine; (fig) to undermine

mineral [mine'ral] adj mineral ♦ nm (GEO) mineral; (mena) ore

minero, a [mi'nero, a] adj mining cpd ♦ nm/f miner

miniatura [minja'tura] adj inv, nf miniature

MiniDisc® [mini'ðisk] nm MiniDisc®

minifalda [mini'falda] nf miniskirt

mínimo, a ['minimo, a] adj, nm minimum

minino, a [mi'nino, a] (fam) nm/f puss, pussy

ministerio [minis'terjo] nm Ministry; **M~ de Hacienda/de Asuntos Exteriores** Treasury (BRIT), Treasury Department (US)/Foreign Office (BRIT), State Department (US)

ministro, a [mi'nistro, a] nm/f minister

minoría [mino'ria] nf minority

minucioso, a [minu'θjoso, a] adj thorough, meticulous; (prolijo) very detailed

minúscula [mi'nuskula] nf small letter

minúsculo, a [mi'nuskulo, a] adj tiny, minute

minusválido, a [minus'βaliðo, a] adj (physically) handicapped ♦ nm/f (physically) handicapped person

minuta [mi'nuta] nf (de comida) menu

minutero [minu'tero] nm minute hand

minuto [mi'nuto] nm minute

mío, a ['mio, a] pron: **el ~/la mía** mine; **un amigo ~** a friend of mine; **lo ~** what is mine

miope [mi'ope] adj short-sighted

mira ['mira] nf (de arma) sight(s) (pl); (fig) aim, intention

mirada [mi'raða] nf look, glance; (expresión) look, expression; **clavar la ~ en** to stare at; **echar una ~ a** to glance at

mirado, a [mi'raðo, a] adj (sensato) sensible; (considerado) considerate; **bien/mal ~** well/ not well thought of; **bien ~** all things considered

mirador [mira'ðor] nm viewpoint, vantage point

mirar [mi'rar] vt to look at; (observar) to watch; (considerar) to consider, think over; (vigilar, cuidar) to watch, look after ♦ vi to look; (ARQ) to face; **~se** vr (dos personas) to look at each other; **~ bien/mal** to think highly of/have a poor opinion of; **~se al espejo** to look at o.s. in the mirror

mirilla [mi'riʎa] nf spyhole, peephole

mirlo ['mirlo] nm blackbird

misa ['misa] nf mass

miserable [mise'raβle] adj (avaro) mean, stingy; (nimio) miserable, paltry; (lugar) squalid; (fam) vile, despicable ♦ nm/f (malvado) rogue

miseria [mi'serja] nf (pobreza) poverty; (tacañería) meanness, stinginess; (condiciones) squalor; **una ~** a pittance

misericordia [miseri'korðja] nf (compasión) compassion, pity; (piedad) mercy

misil [mi'sil] nm missile

misión [mi'sjon] nf mission; **misionero, a** nm/f missionary

mismo, a ['mismo, a] adj (semejante) same; (después de pron) -self; (para énfasis) very ♦ adv: **aquí/hoy ~** right here/this very day; **ahora ~** right now ♦ conj: **lo ~ que** just like, just as; **el ~ traje** the same suit; **en ese ~ momento** at that very moment; **vino el ~ Ministro** the minister himself came; **yo ~ lo vi** I saw it myself; **lo ~** the same (thing); **da lo ~** it's all the same; **quedamos en las mismas** we're no further forward; **por lo ~** for the same reason

misterio [mis'terjo] nm mystery; **~so, a** adj mysterious

mitad [mi'tað] nf (medio) half; (centro) middle; **a ~ de precio** (at) half-price; **en o a ~ del camino** halfway along the road; **cortar por la ~** to cut through the middle

mitigar [miti'ɣar] vt to mitigate; (dolor) to ease; (sed) to quench

mitin ['mitin] (pl **mítines**) nm meeting

mito ['mito] nm myth

mixto, a ['miksto, a] adj mixed

ml. abr (= mililitro) ml

mm. abr (= milímetro) mm

mobiliario [moβi'ljarjo] nm furniture

mochila [mo'tʃila] nf rucksack (BRIT), back-pack

moción [mo'θjon] nf motion

moco ['moko] nm mucus; **~s** nmpl (fam) snot; **limpiarse los ~s de la nariz** (fam) to wipe one's nose

moda ['moða] nf fashion; (estilo) style; **a la o de ~** in fashion, fashionable; **pasado de ~** out of fashion

modales [mo'ðales] nmpl manners

modalidad [moðali'ðað] nf kind, variety

modelar [moðe'lar] vt to model

modelo [mo'ðelo] adj inv, nm/f model

módem ['moðem] nm (INFORM) modem

moderado, a [moðe'raðo, a] adj moderate

moderar [moðe'rar] vt to moderate; (violencia) to restrain, control; (velocidad) to reduce; **~se** vr to restrain o.s., control o.s.

modernizar [moðerni'θar] vt to modernize

moderno, a [mo'ðerno, a] adj modern; (actual) present-day

modestia [mo'ðestja] nf modesty; **modesto, a** adj modest

módico, a ['moðiko, a] adj moderate, reasonable

modificar [moðifi'kar] vt to modify

modisto, a [mo'ðisto, a] nm/f (diseñador) couturier, designer; (que confecciona) dressmaker

modo ['moðo] nm way, manner; (MUS) mode; **~s** nmpl manners; **de ningún ~** in no way; **de todos ~s** at any rate; **~ de empleo** directions pl (for use)

modorra [mo'ðorra] nf drowsiness

mofa ['mofa] nf: **hacer ~ de** to mock; **mofarse** vr: **mofarse de** to mock, scoff at

mogollón [moγo'ʎon] (fam) adv a hell of a lot

moho ['moo] nm mould, mildew; (en metal) rust; **~so, a** adj mouldy; rusty

mojar [mo'xar] vt to wet; (humedecer) to damp(en), moisten; (calar) to soak; **~se** vr to get wet

mojón [mo'xon] nm boundary stone

molde ['molde] nm mould; (COSTURA) pattern; (fig) model; **~ado** nm soft perm; **~ar** vt to mould

mole ['mole] nf mass, bulk; (edificio) pile

moler [mo'ler] vt to grind, crush

molestar [moles'tar] vt to bother; (fastidiar) to annoy; (incomodar) to inconvenience, put out ♦ vi to be a nuisance; **~se** vr to bother; (incomodarse) to go to trouble; (ofenderse) to take offence; **¿(no) te molesta si ...?** do you mind if ...?

molestia [mo'lestja] nf bother, trouble; (incomodidad) inconvenience; (MED) discomfort; **es una ~** it's a nuisance; **molesto, a** adj (que fastidia) annoying; (incómodo) inconvenient; (inquieto) uncomfortable, ill at ease; (enfadado) annoyed

molido, a [mo'liðo, a] adj: **estar ~** (fig) to be exhausted o dead beat

molinillo [moli'niʎo] nm: **~ de carne/café** mincer/coffee grinder

molino [mo'lino] nm (edificio) mill; (máquina) grinder

momentáneo, a [momen'taneo, a] adj momentary

momento [mo'mento] nm moment; **de ~** at the moment, for the moment

momia ['momja] nf mummy

monarca [mo'narka] nm/f monarch, ruler; **monarquía** nf monarchy; **monárquico, a** nm/f royalist, monarchist

monasterio [monas'terjo] nm monastery

mondar [mon'dar] vt to peel; **~se** vr: **~se de risa** (fam) to split one's sides laughing

moneda [mo'neða] nf (tipo de dinero) currency, money; (pieza) coin; **una ~ de 5 pesetas** a 5 peseta piece; **monedero** nm purse; **monetario, a** adj monetary, financial

monitor, a [moni'tor, a] nm/f instructor, coach ♦ nm (TV) set; (INFORM) monitor

monja ['monxa] nf nun

monje ['monxe] nm monk

mono, a ['mono, a] adj (bonito) lovely, pretty; (gracioso) nice, charming ♦ nm/f monkey, ape ♦ nm dungarees pl; (overoles) overalls pl

monopatín [monopa'tin] nm skateboard

monopolio [mono'poljo] nm monopoly; **monopolizar** vt to monopolize

monotonía [monoto'nia] nf (sonido) monotone; (fig) monotony

monótono, a [mo'notono, a] adj monotonous

monstruo ['monstrwo] nm monster ♦ adj inv fantastic; **~so, a** adj monstrous

montaje [mon'taxe] nm assembly; (TEATRO) décor; (CINE) montage

montaña [mon'taɲa] nf (monte) mountain; (sierra) mountains pl, mountainous area; (AM: selva) forest; **~ rusa** roller coaster; **montañero, a** nm/f mountaineer; **montañés, esa** nm/f highlander; **montañismo** nm mountaineering

montar [mon'tar] vt (subir a) to mount, get on; (TEC) to assemble, put together; (negocio) to set up; (arma) to cock; (colocar) to lift on to; (CULIN) to beat ♦ vi to mount, get on; (sobresalir) to overlap; **~ en cólera** to get angry; **~ a caballo** to ride, go horseriding

monte ['monte] nm (montaña) mountain; (bosque) woodland; (área sin cultivar) wild area, wild country; **M~ de Piedad** pawnshop

montón [mon'ton] nm heap, pile; (fig): **un ~ de** heaps of, lots of

monumento [monu'mento] nm monument

monzón [mon'θon] nm monsoon

moño ['moɲo] nm bun

moqueta [mo'keta] nf fitted carpet

mora ['mora] nf blackberry; ver tb **moro**

morada [mo'raða] nf (casa) dwelling, abode

morado, a [mo'raðo, a] adj purple, violet ♦ nm bruise

moral [mo'ral] adj moral ♦ nf (ética) ethics pl; (moralidad) morals pl, morality; (ánimo) morale

moraleja [mora'lexa] nf moral

moralidad [morali'ðað] nf morals pl, morality

morboso, a [mor'ßoso, a] adj morbid

morcilla [mor'θiʎa] nf blood sausage, ≈ black pudding (BRIT)

mordaz [mor'ðaθ] *adj* (*crítica*) biting, scathing

mordaza [mor'ðaθa] *nf* (*para la boca*) gag; (*TEC*) clamp

morder [mor'ðer] *vt* to bite; (*fig: consumir*) to eat away, eat into; **mordisco** *nm* bite

moreno, a [mo'reno, a] *adj* (*color*) (dark) brown; (*de tez*) dark; (*de pelo ~*) dark-haired; (*negro*) black

morfina [mor'fina] *nf* morphine

moribundo, a [mori'ßundo, a] *adj* dying

morir [mo'rir] *vi* to die; (*fuego*) to die down; (*luz*) to go out; **~se** *vr* to die; (*fig*) to be dying; **murió en un accidente** he was killed in an accident; **~se por algo** to be dying for sth

moro, a [mo'ro, a] *adj* Moorish ♦ *nm/f* Moor

moroso, a [mo'roso, a] *nm/f* bad debtor, defaulter

morral [mo'rral] *nm* haversack

morro ['morro] *nm* (*ZOOL*) snout, nose; (*AUTO, AVIAT*) nose

morsa ['morsa] *nf* walrus

mortadela [morta'ðela] *nf* mortadella

mortaja [mor'taxa] *nf* shroud

mortal [mor'tal] *adj* mortal; (*golpe*) deadly; **~idad** *nf* mortality

mortero [mor'tero] *nm* mortar

mortífero, a [mor'tifero, a] *adj* deadly, lethal

mortificar [mortifi'kar] *vt* to mortify

mosca ['moska] *nf* fly

Moscú [mos'ku] *n* Moscow

mosquearse [moske'arse] (*fam*) *vr* (*enojarse*) to get cross; (*ofenderse*) to take offence

mosquitero [moski'tero] *nm* mosquito net

mosquito [mos'kito] *nm* mosquito

mostaza [mos'taθa] *nf* mustard

mosto ['mosto] *nm* (*unfermented*) grape juice

mostrador [mostra'ðor] *nm* (*de tienda*) counter; (*de café*) bar

mostrar [mos'trar] *vt* to show; (*exhibir*) to display, exhibit; (*explicar*) to explain; **~se** *vr*: **~se amable** to be kind; to prove to be kind; **no se muestra muy inteligente** he doesn't seem (to be) very intelligent

mota ['mota] *nf* speck, tiny piece; (*en diseño*) dot

mote ['mote] *nm* nickname

motín [mo'tin] *nm* (*del pueblo*) revolt, rising; (*del ejército*) mutiny

motivar [moti'ßar] *vt* (*causar*) to cause, motivate; (*explicar*) to explain, justify; **motivo** *nm* motive, reason

moto ['moto] (*fam*) *nf* = **motocicleta**

motocicleta [motoθi'kleta] *nf* motorbike (*BRIT*), motorcycle

motor [mo'tor] *nm* motor, engine; **~ a chorro**

o **de reacción/de explosión** jet engine/internal combustion engine

motora [mo'tora] *nf* motorboat

movedizo, a [moße'ðiθo, a] *adj* ver **arena**

mover [mo'ßer] *vt* to move; (*cabeza*) to shake; (*accionar*) to drive; (*fig*) to cause, provoke; **~se** *vr* to move; (*fig*) to get a move on

móvil ['moßil] *adj* mobile; (*pieza de máquina*) moving; (*mueble*) movable ♦ *nm* motive; **movilidad** *nf* mobility; **movilizar** *vt* to mobilize

movimiento [moßi'mjento] *nm* movement; (*TEC*) motion; (*actividad*) activity

mozo, a ['moθo, a] *adj* (*joven*) young ♦ *nm/f* youth, young man/girl

muchacho, a [mu'tʃatʃo, a] *nm/f* (*niño*) boy/girl; (*criado*) servant; (*criada*) maid

muchedumbre [mutʃe'ðumbre] *nf* crowd

PALABRA CLAVE

mucho, a ['mutʃo, a] *adj* **1** (*cantidad*) a lot of, much; (*número*) lots of, a lot of, many; **~ dinero** a lot of money; **hace ~ calor** it's very hot; **muchas amigas** lots o a lot of friends

2 (*sg: grande*): **ésta es mucha casa para él** this house is much too big for him

♦ *pron*: **tengo ~ que hacer** I've got a lot to do; **~s dicen que ...** a lot of people say that ...; *ver tb* **tener**

♦ *adv* **1**: **me gusta ~** I like it a lot; **lo siento ~** I'm very sorry; **come ~** he eats a lot; **¿te vas a quedar ~?** are you going to be staying long?

2 (*respuesta*) very; **¿estás cansado? – ¡~!** are you tired? – very!

3 (*locuciones*): **como ~** at (the) most; **con ~: el mejor con ~** by far the best; **ni ~ menos: no es rico ni ~ menos** he's far from being rich

4: **por ~ que: por ~ que le creas** no matter how o however much you believe her

---

muda ['muða] *nf* change of clothes

mudanza [mu'ðanθa] *nf* (*de casa*) move

mudar [mu'ðar] *vt* to change; (*ZOOL*) to shed ♦ *vi* to change; **~se** *vr* (*la ropa*) to change; **~se de casa** to move house

mudo, a ['muðo, a] *adj* dumb; (*callado, CINE*) silent

mueble ['mweßle] *nm* piece of furniture; **~s** *nmpl* furniture *sg*

mueca ['mweka] *nf* face, grimace; **hacer ~s a** to make faces at

muela ['mwela] *nf* (*back*) tooth

muelle ['mweʎe] *nm* spring; (*NAUT*) wharf; (*malecón*) pier

muero *etc vb ver* **morir**

muerte ['mwerte] *nf* death; (*homicidio*) murder; **dar ~ a** to kill

muerto, a ['mwerto, a] *adj pp de* **morir** ♦ *adj*

dead ♦ *nm/f* dead man/woman; (*difunto*) deceased; (*cadáver*) corpse; **estar ~ de cansancio** to be dead tired

muestra ['mwestra] *nf* (*señal*) indication, sign; (*demostración*) demonstration; (*prueba*) proof; (*estadística*) sample; (*modelo*) model, pattern; (*testimonio*) token

muestreo [mwes'treo] *nm* sample, sampling

muestro *etc vb ver* **mostrar**

muevo *etc vb ver* **mover**

mugir [mu'xir] *vi* (*vaca*) to moo

mugre ['muxre] *nf* dirt, filth; **mugriento, a** *adj* dirty, filthy

mujer [mu'xer] *nf* woman; (*esposa*) wife; **~iego** *nm* womanizer

mula ['mula] *nf* mule

muleta [mu'leta] *nf* (*para andar*) crutch; (*TAUR*) stick with red cape attached

mullido, a [mu'ʎiðo, a] *adj* (*cama*) soft; (*hierba*) soft, springy

multa ['multa] *nf* fine; **poner una ~ a** to fine; **multar** *vt* to fine

multicines [multi'θines] *nmpl* multiscreen cinema

multinacional [multinaθjo'nal] *nf* multinational

múltiple ['multiple] *adj* multiple; (*pl*) many, numerous

multiplicar [multipli'kar] *vt* (*MAT*) to multiply; (*fig*) to increase; **~se** *vr* (*BIO*) to multiply; (*fig*) to be everywhere at once

multitud [multi'tuð] *nf* (*muchedumbre*) crowd; **~ de** lots of

mundano, a [mun'dano, a] *adj* worldly

mundial [mun'djal] *adj* world-wide, universal; (*guerra, récord*) world *cpd*

mundo ['mundo] *nm* world; **todo el ~** everybody; **tener ~** to be experienced, know one's way around

munición [muni'θjon] *nf* ammunition

municipal [muniθi'pal] *adj* municipal, local

municipio [muni'θipjo] *nm* (*ayuntamiento*) town council, corporation; (*territorio administrativo*) town, municipality

muñeca [mu'ɲeka] *nf* (*ANAT*) wrist; (*juguete*) doll

muñeco [mu'ɲeko] *nm* (*figura*) figure; (*marioneta*) puppet; (*fig*) puppet, pawn

mural [mu'ral] *adj* mural, wall *cpd* ♦ *nm* mural

muralla [mu'raʎa] *nf* (*city*) wall(s) (*pl*)

murciélago [mur'θjelaxo] *nm* bat

murmullo [mur'muʎo] *nm* murmur(ing); (*cuchicheo*) whispering

murmuración [murmura'θjon] *nf* gossip; **murmurar** *vi* to murmur, whisper; (*cotillear*) to gossip

muro ['muro] *nm* wall

muscular [musku'lar] *adj* muscular

músculo ['muskulo] *nm* muscle

museo [mu'seo] *nm* museum; **~ de arte** art gallery

musgo ['musxo] *nm* moss

música ['musika] *nf* music; *ver tb* **músico**

músico, a ['musiko, a] *adj* musical ♦ *nm/f* musician

muslo ['muslo] *nm* thigh

mustio, a ['mustjo, a] *adj* (*persona*) depressed, gloomy; (*planta*) faded, withered

musulmán, ana [musul'man, ana] *nm/f* Moslem

mutación [muta'θjon] *nf* (*BIO*) mutation; (*cambio*) (sudden) change

mutilar [muti'lar] *vt* to mutilate; (*a una persona*) to maim

mutismo [mu'tismo] *nm* (*de persona*) uncommunicativeness; (*de autoridades*) silence

mutuamente [mutwa'mente] *adv* mutually

mutuo, a ['mutwo, a] *adj* mutual

muy [mwi] *adv* very; (*demasiado*) too; **M~ Señor mío** Dear Sir; **~ de noche** very late at night; **eso es ~ de él** that's just like him

N, n

N *abr* (= *norte*) N

nabo ['naβo] *nm* turnip

nácar ['nakar] *nm* mother-of-pearl

nacer [na'θer] *vi* to be born; (*de huevo*) to hatch; (*vegetal*) to sprout; (*río*) to rise; **nací en Barcelona** I was born in Barcelona; **nació una sospecha en su mente** a suspicion formed in her mind; **nacido, a** *adj* born; **recién nacido** newborn; **naciente** *adj* new, emerging; (*sol*) rising; **nacimiento** *nm* birth; (*de Navidad*) Nativity; (*de río*) source

nación [na'θjon] *nf* nation; **nacional** *adj* national; **nacionalismo** *nm* nationalism; **nacionalista** *nm/f* nationalist; **nacionalizar** *vt* to nationalize; **nacionalizarse** *vr* (*persona*) to become naturalized

nada ['naða] *pron* nothing ♦ *adv* not at all, in no way; **no decir ~** to say nothing, not to say anything; **~ más** nothing else; **de ~** don't mention it

nadador, a [naða'ðor, a] *nm/f* swimmer

nadar [na'ðar] *vi* to swim

nadie ['naðje] *pron* nobody, no-one; **~ habló** nobody spoke; **no había ~** there was nobody there, there wasn't anybody there

nado ['naðo]: **a ~** *adv*: **pasar a ~** to swim across

nafta ['nafta] (*AM*) *nf* petrol (*BRIT*), gas (*US*)

naipe ['naipe] *nm* (playing) card; **~s** *nmpl* cards

nalgas ['nalxas] *nfpl* buttocks

nana ['nana] nf lullaby

naranja [na'ranxa] adj inv, nf orange; **media ~** (fam) better half; **naranjada** nf orangeade; **naranjo** nm orange tree

narciso [nar'θiso] nm narcissus

narcótico, a [nar'kotiko, a] adj, nm narcotic; **narcotizar** vt to drug; **narcotráfico** nm drug trafficking o running

nardo ['narðo] nm lily

narigudo, a [nari'yuðo, a] adj big-nosed

nariz [na'riθ] nf nose

narración [narra'θjon] nf narration; **narrador, a** nm/f narrator

narrar [na'rrar] vt to narrate, recount; **narrativa** nf narrative

nata ['nata] nf cream

natación [nata'θjon] nf swimming

natal [na'tal] adj: **ciudad ~** home town; **~idad** nf birth rate

natillas [na'tiʎas] nfpl custard sg

nativo, a [na'tiβo, a] adj, nm/f native

nato, a ['nato, a] adj born; **un músico ~** a born musician

natural [natu'ral] adj natural; (fruta etc) fresh ♦ nm/f native ♦ nm (disposición) nature

naturaleza [natura'leθa] nf nature; (género) nature, kind; **~ muerta** still life

naturalidad [naturali'ðað] nf naturalness

naturalmente [natural'mente] adv (de modo natural) in a natural way; **¡~!** of course!

naufragar [naufra'yar] vi to sink; **naufragio** nm shipwreck; **náufrago, a** nm/f castaway, shipwrecked person

nauseabundo, a [nausea'βundo, a] adj nauseating, sickening

náuseas ['nauseas] nfpl nausea sg; **me da ~** it makes me feel sick

náutico, a ['nautiko, a] adj nautical

navaja [na'βaxa] nf knife; (de barbero, peluquero) razor

naval [na'βal] adj naval

Navarra [na'βarra] n Navarre

nave ['naβe] nf (barco) ship, vessel; (ARQ) nave; **~ espacial** spaceship

navegación [naβeya'θjon] nf navigation; (viaje) sea journey; **~ aérea** air traffic; **~ costera** coastal shipping; **navegador** nm (INFORM) browser; **navegante** nm/f navigator; **navegar** vi (barco) to sail; (avión) to fly

navidad [naβi'ðað] nf Christmas; **~es** nfpl Christmas time; **Feliz N~** Merry Christmas; **navideño, a** adj Christmas cpd

navío [na'βio] nm ship

nazca etc vb ver **nacer**

nazi ['naθi] adj, nm/f Nazi

NE abr (= nor(d)este) NE

neblina [ne'βlina] nf mist

nebulosa [neβu'losa] nf nebula

necesario, a [neθe'sarjo, a] adj necessary

neceser [neθe'ser] nm toilet bag; (bolsa grande) holdall

necesidad [neθesi'ðað] nf need; (lo inevitable) necessity; (miseria) poverty, need; **en caso de ~** in case of need o emergency; **hacer sus ~es** to relieve o.s.

necesitado, a [neθesi'taðo, a] adj needy, poor; **~ de** in need of

necesitar [neθesi'tar] vt to need, require

necio, a ['neθjo, a] adj foolish

necrópolis [ne'kropolis] nf inv cemetery

nectarina [nekta'rina] nf nectarine

nefasto, a [ne'fasto, a] adj ill-fated, unlucky

negación [neya'θjon] nf negation; (rechazo) refusal, denial

negar [ne'yar] vt (renegar, rechazar) to refuse; (prohibir) to refuse, deny; (desmentir) to deny; **~se** vr: **~se a** to refuse to

negativa [neya'tiβa] nf negative; (rechazo) refusal, denial

negativo, a [neya'tiβo, a] adj, nm negative

negligencia [neyli'xenθja] nf negligence; **negligente** adj negligent

negociado [neyo'θjaðo] nm department, section

negociante [neyo'θjante] nm/f businessman/woman

negociar [neyo'θjar] vt, vi to negotiate; **~ en** to deal in, trade in

negocio [ne'yoθjo] nm (COM) business; (asunto) affair, business; (operación comercial) deal, transaction; (AM) firm; (lugar) place of business; **los ~s** business sg; **hacer ~** to do business

negra ['neyra] nf (MUS) crotchet; ver tb **negro**

negro, a ['neyro, a] adj black; (suerte) awful ♦ nm black ♦ nm/f black man/woman

nene, a ['nene, a] nm/f baby, small child

nenúfar [ne'nufar] nm water lily

neologismo [neolo'xismo] nm neologism

neón [ne'on] nm: **luces/lámpara de ~** neon lights/lamp

neoyorquino, a [neojor'kino, a] adj (of) New York

nervio ['nerβjo] nm nerve; **nerviosismo** nm nervousness, nerves pl; **~so, a** adj nervous

neto, a ['neto, a] adj net

neumático, a [neu'matiko, a] adj pneumatic ♦ nm (ESP) tyre (BRIT), tire (US); **~ de recambio** spare tyre

neurastético, a [neuras'teniko, a] adj (fig) hysterical

neurólogo, a [neu'roloyo, a] nm/f neurologist

neurona [neu'rona] nf nerve cell

neutral [neu'tral] adj neutral; **~izar** vt to neutralize; (contrarrestar) to counteract

neutro, a ['neutro, a] adj (BIO, LING) neuter

neutrón [neu'tron] *nm* neutron

nevada [ne'βaða] *nf* snowstorm; (*caída de nieve*) snowfall

nevar [ne'βar] *vi* to snow

nevera [ne'βera] (*ESP*) *nf* refrigerator (*BRIT*), icebox (*US*)

nevería [neβe'ria] (*AM*) *nf* ice-cream parlour

nexo ['nekso] *nm* link, connection

ni [ni] *conj* nor, neither; (*tb: ~ siquiera*) not ... even; **~ aunque** que not even if; **~ blanco ~ negro** neither white nor black

Nicaragua [nika'raɣwa] *nf* Nicaragua; **nicaragüense** *adj, nm/f* Nicaraguan

nicho ['nitʃo] *nm* niche

nicotina [niko'tina] *nf* nicotine

nido ['niðo] *nm* nest

niebla ['njeβla] *nf* fog; (*neblina*) mist

niego *etc vb ver* **negar**

nieto, a ['njeto, a] *nm/f* grandson/daughter; **~s** *nmpl* grandchildren

nieve *etc* ['njeβe] *vb ver* **nevar** ♦ *nf* snow; (*AM*) icecream

N.I.F. *nm abr* (= *Número de Identificación Fiscal*) personal identification number used for financial and tax purposes

nimiedad [nimje'ðað] *nf* triviality

nimio, a ['nimjo, a] *adj* trivial, insignificant

ninfa ['ninfa] *nf* nymph

ningún [nin'gun] *adj ver* **ninguno**

ninguno, a [nin'guno, a] (*delante de nm*: **ningún**) *adj no* ♦ *pron* (*nadie*) nobody; (*ni uno*) none, not one; (*ni uno ni otro*) neither; **de ninguna manera** by no means, not at all

niña ['niɲa] *nf* (*ANAT*) pupil; *ver tb* **niño**

niñera [ni'ɲera] *nf* nursemaid, nanny; **niñería** *nf* childish act

niñez [ni'ɲeθ] *nf* childhood; (*infancia*) infancy

niño, a ['niɲo, a] *adj* (*joven*) young; (*inmaduro*) immature ♦ *nm/f* child, boy/girl

nipón, ona [ni'pon, ona] *adj, nm/f* Japanese

níquel ['nikel] *nm* nickel; **niquelar** *vt* (*TEC*) to nickel-plate

níspero ['nispero] *nm* medlar

nitidez [niti'ðeθ] *nf* (*claridad*) clarity; (: *de imagen*) sharpness; **nítido, a** *adj* clear; sharp

nitrato [ni'trato] *nm* nitrate

nitrógeno [ni'troxeno] *nm* nitrogen

nivel [ni'βel] *nm* (*GEO*) level; (*norma*) level, standard; (*altura*) height; **~ de aceite** oil level; **~ de aire** spirit level; **~ de vida** standard of living; **~ar** *vt* to level out; (*fig*) to even up; (*COM*) to balance

NN. UU. *nfpl abr* (= *Naciones Unidas*) UN *sg*

no [no] *adv* no; not; (*con verbo*) not ♦ *excl* no!; **~ tengo nada** I don't have anything, I have nothing; **~ es el mío** it's not mine; **ahora ~** not now; **¿~ lo sabes?** don't you know?; **~ mucho** not much; **~ bien termine, lo entregaré** as soon as I finish I'll hand it

over; **~ más: ayer ~ más** just yesterday; **¡pase ~ más!** come in!; **¡a que ~ lo sabes!** I bet you don't know!; **¡cómo ~!** of course!; **los países ~ alineados** the non-aligned countries; **la ~ intervención** non-intervention

noble ['noβle] *adj, nm/f* noble; **~za** *nf* nobility

noche ['notʃe] *nf* night, night-time; (*la tarde*) evening; **de ~, por la ~** at night; **es de ~** it's dark

nochebuena [notʃe'βwena] *nf* Christmas Eve

nochevieja [notʃe'βxexa] *nf* New Year's Eve

noción [no'θjon] *nf* notion

nocivo, a [no'θiβo, a] *adj* harmful

noctámbulo, a [nok'tambulo, a] *nm/f* sleepwalker

nocturno, a [nok'turno, a] *adj* (*de la noche*) nocturnal, night *cpd*; (*de la tarde*) evening *cpd* ♦ *nm* nocturne

nodriza [no'ðriθa] *nf* wet nurse; **buque o nave ~** supply ship

nogal [no'ɣal] *nm* walnut tree

nómada ['nomaða] *adj* nomadic ♦ *nm/f* nomad

nombramiento [nombra'mjento] *nm* naming; (*a un empleo*) appointment

nombrar [nom'brar] *vt* (*designar*) to name; (*mencionar*) to mention; (*dar puesto a*) to appoint

nombre ['nombre] *nm* name; (*sustantivo*) noun; **~ y apellidos** name in full; **~ común/ propio** common/proper noun; **~ de pila/de soltera** Christian/maiden name; **poner ~ a** to call, name

nómina ['nomina] *nf* (*lista*) payroll; (*hoja*) payslip

nominal [nomi'nal] *adj* nominal

nominar [nomi'nar] *vt* to nominate

nominativo, a [nomina'tiβo, a] *adj* (*COM*): **cheque ~ a X** cheque made out to X

nono, a ['nono, a] *adj* ninth

nordeste [nor'ðeste] *adj* north-east, north-eastern, north-easterly ♦ *nm* north-east

nórdico, a ['norðiko, a] *adj* Nordic

noreste [no'reste] *adj, nm* = **nordeste**

noria ['norja] *nf* (*AGR*) waterwheel; (*de carnaval*) big (*BRIT*) o Ferris (*US*) wheel

norma ['norma] *nf* rule (of thumb)

normal [nor'mal] *adj* (*corriente*) normal; (*habitual*) usual, natural; **~idad** *nf* normality; **restablecer la ~idad** to restore order; **~izar** *vt* (*reglamentar*) to normalize; (*TEC*) to standardize; **~izarse** *vr* to return to normal; **~mente** *adv* normally

normando, a [nor'mando, a] *adj, nm/f* Norman

normativa [norma'tiβa] *nf* (set of) rules *pl*, regulations *pl*

noroeste [noro'este] *adj* north-west, north-

western, north-westerly ♦ *nm* north-west
norte ['norte] *adj* north, northern, northerly
♦ *nm* north; (*fig*) guide
norteamericano, a [norteameri'kano, a]
adj, nm/f (North) American
Noruega [no'rweɣa] *nf* Norway
noruego, a [no'rweɣo, a] *adj, nm/f*
Norwegian
nos [nos] *pron* (*directo*) us; (*indirecto*) us; to
us; for us; from us; (*reflexivo*) (to) ourselves;
(*recíproco*) (to) each other; **~ levantamos a
las 7** we get up at 7
nosotros, as [no'sotros, as] *pron* (*sujeto*)
we; (*después de prep*) us
nostalgia [nos'talxja] *nf* nostalgia
nota ['nota] *nf* note; (*ESCOL*) mark
notable [no'taßle] *adj* notable; (*ESCOL*)
outstanding
notar [no'tar] *vt* to notice, note; **~se** *vr* to be
obvious; **se nota que ...** one observes that ...
notarial [nota'rjal] *adj*: **acta ~** affidavit
notario [no'tarjo] *nm* notary
noticia [no'tiθja] *nf* (*información*) piece of
news; **las ~s** the news *sg*; **tener ~s de alguien**
to hear from sb
noticiero [noti'θjero] (*AM*) *nm* news bulletin
notificación [notifika'θjon] *nf* notification;
notificar *vt* to notify, inform
notoriedad [notorje'ðað] *nf* fame, renown;
notorio, a *adj* (*público*) well-known;
(*evidente*) obvious
novato, a [no'ßato, a] *adj* inexperienced
♦ *nm/f* beginner, novice
novecientos, as [noße'θjentos, as] *num*
nine hundred
novedad [noße'ðað] *nf* (*calidad de nuevo*)
newness; (*noticia*) piece of news; (*cambio*)
change, (new) development
novel [no'ßel] *adj* new; (*inexperto*)
inexperienced ♦ *nm/f* beginner
novela [no'ßela] *nf* novel
noveno, a [no'ßeno, a] *adj* ninth
noventa [no'ßenta] *num* ninety
novia ['noßja] *nf ver* **novio**
noviazgo [no'ßjaθɣo] *nm* engagement
novicio, a [no'ßiθjo, a] *nm/f* novice
noviembre [no'ßjembre] *nm* November
novillada [noßi'ʎaða] *nf* (*TAUR*) bullfight with
young bulls; **novillero** *nm* novice bullfighter;
novillo *nm* young bull, bullock; **hacer
novillos** (*fam*) to play truant
novio, a ['noßjo, a] *nm/f* boyfriend/girlfriend;
(*prometido*) fiancé/fiancée; (*recién casado*)
bridegroom/bride; **los ~s** the newly-weds
nubarrón [nußa'rron] *nm* storm cloud
nube ['nuße] *nf* cloud
nublado, a [nu'ßlaðo, a] *adj* cloudy;
nublarse *vr* to grow dark
nubosidad [nußosi'ðað] *nf* cloudiness; **había**

mucha ~ it was very cloudy
nuca ['nuka] *nf* nape of the neck
nuclear [nukle'ar] *adj* nuclear
núcleo ['nukleo] *nm* (*centro*) core; (*FÍSICA*)
nucleus
nudillo [nu'ðiʎo] *nm* knuckle
nudista [nu'ðista] *adj* nudist
nudo ['nuðo] *nm* knot; **~so, a** *adj* knotty
nuera ['nwera] *nf* daughter-in-law
nuestro, a ['nwestro, a] *adj pos* our ♦ *pron*
ours; **~ padre** our father; **un amigo ~** a friend
of ours; **es el ~** it's ours
nueva ['nweßa] *nf* piece of news
nuevamente [nweßa'mente] *adv* (*otra vez*)
again; (*de nuevo*) anew
Nueva York [-jork] *n* New York
Nueva Zelanda [-θe'landa] *nf* New Zealand
nueve ['nweße] *num* nine
nuevo, a ['nweßo, a] *adj* (*gen*) new; **de ~**
again
nuez [nweθ] *nf* walnut; **~ de Adán** Adam's
apple; **~ moscada** nutmeg
nulidad [nuli'ðað] *nf* (*incapacidad*)
incompetence; (*abolición*) nullity
nulo, a ['nulo, a] *adj* (*inepto, torpe*) useless;
(*inválido*) (null and) void; (*DEPORTE*) drawn,
tied
núm. *abr* (= *número*) no
numeración [numera'θjon] *nf* (*cifras*)
numbers *pl*; (*arábiga, romana etc*) numerals
pl
numeral [nume'ral] *nm* numeral
numerar [nume'rar] *vt* to number
número ['numero] *nm* (*gen*) number;
(*tamaño: de zapato*) size; (*ejemplar: de diario*)
number, issue; **sin ~** numberless,
unnumbered; **~ de matrícula/de teléfono**
registration/telephone number; **~ atrasado**
back number
numeroso, a [nume'roso, a] *adj* numerous
nunca ['nunka] *adv* (*jamás*) never; **~ lo pensé**
I never thought it; **no viene ~** he never
comes; **~ más** never again; **más que ~** more
than ever
nupcias ['nupθjas] *nfpl* wedding *sg*, nuptials
nutria ['nutrja] *nf* otter
nutrición [nutri'θjon] *nf* nutrition
nutrido, a [nu'triðo, a] *adj* (*alimentado*)
nourished; (*fig: grande*) large; (*abundante*)
abundant
nutrir [nu'trir] *vt* (*alimentar*) to nourish; (*dar
de comer*) to feed; (*fig*) to strengthen;
nutritivo, a *adj* nourishing, nutritious
nylon [ni'lon] *nm* nylon

Ñ

ñato, a [ˈnato, a] (AM) adj snub-nosed
ñoñería [noneˈria] nf insipidness
ñoño, a [ˈnono, a] adj (AM: tonto) silly, stupid; (soso) insipid; (persona) spineless

O, o

O abr (= oeste) W
o [o] conj or
o/ abr (= orden) o.
oasis [oˈasis] nm inv oasis
obcecarse [oβθeˈkarse] vr to get o become stubborn
obedecer [oβeðeˈθer] vt to obey; **obediencia** nf obedience; **obediente** adj obedient
obertura [oβerˈtura] nf overture
obesidad [oβesiˈðað] nf obesity; **obeso, a** adj obese
obispo [oˈβispo] nm bishop
objeción [oβxeˈθjon] nf objection; **poner objeciones** to raise objections
objetar [oβxeˈtar] vt, vi to object
objetivo, a [oβxeˈtiβo, a] adj, nm objective
objeto [oβˈxeto] nm (cosa) object; (fin) aim
objetor, a [oβxeˈtor, a] nm/f objector
oblicuo, a [oˈβlikwo, a] adj oblique; (mirada) sidelong
obligación [oβlixaˈθjon] nf obligation; (COM) bond
obligar [oβliˈɣar] vt to force; ~**se** vr to bind o.s.; **obligatorio, a** adj compulsory, obligatory
oboe [oˈβoe] nm oboe
obra [ˈoβra] nf work; (ARQ) construction, building; (TEATRO) play; ~ **maestra** masterpiece; ~**s públicas** public works; **por ~ de** thanks to (the efforts of); **obrar** vt to work; (tener efecto) to have an effect on ♦ vi to act, behave; (tener efecto) to have an effect; **la carta obra en su poder** the letter is in his/her possession
obrero, a [oˈβrero, a] adj (clase) working; (movimiento) labour cpd ♦ nm/f (gen) worker; (sin oficio) labourer
obscenidad [oβsθeniˈðað] nf obscenity; **obsceno, a** adj obscene
obscu... = oscu...
obsequiar [oβseˈkjar] vt (ofrecer) to present with; (agasajar) to make a fuss of, lavish attention on; **obsequio** nm (regalo) gift; (cortesía) courtesy, attention
observación [oβserβaˈθjon] nf observation;

(reflexión) remark
observador, a [oβserβaˈðor, a] nm/f observer
observar [oβserˈβar] vt to observe; (anotar) to notice; ~**se** vr to keep to, observe
obsesión [oβseˈsjon] nf obsession; **obsesivo, a** adj obsessive
obsoleto, a [oβsoˈleto, a] adj obsolete
obstáculo [oβsˈtakulo] nm obstacle; (impedimento) hindrance, drawback
obstante [oβsˈtante]: **no ~** adv nevertheless
obstinado, a [oβstiˈnaðo, a] adj obstinate, stubborn
obstinarse [oβstiˈnarse] vr to be obstinate; ~ **en** to persist in
obstrucción [oβstrukˈθjon] nf obstruction; **obstruir** vt to obstruct
obtener [oβteˈner] vt (gen) to obtain; (premio) to win
obturador [oβturaˈðor] nm (FOTO) shutter
obvio, a [ˈoβjo, a] adj obvious
oca [ˈoka] nf (animal) goose; (juego) ≈ snakes and ladders
ocasión [okaˈsjon] nf (oportunidad) opportunity, chance; (momento) occasion, time; (causa) cause; **de ~** secondhand; **ocasionar** vt to cause
ocaso [oˈkaso] nm (fig) decline
occidente [okθiˈðente] nm west
OCDE nf abr (= Organización de Cooperación y Desarrollo Económico) OECD
océano [oˈθeano] nm ocean; **el ~ Índico** the Indian Ocean
ochenta [oˈtʃenta] num eighty
ocho [ˈotʃo] num eight; ~ **días** a week
ocio [ˈoθjo] nm (tiempo) leisure; (pey) idleness; ~**so, a** adj (inactivo) idle; (inútil) useless
octavilla [oktaˈviʎa] nf leaflet, pamphlet
octavo, a [okˈtaβo, a] adj eighth
octubre [okˈtuβre] nm October
ocular [okuˈlar] adj ocular, eye cpd; **testigo ~** eyewitness
oculista [okuˈlista] nm/f oculist
ocultar [okulˈtar] vt (esconder) to hide; (callar) to conceal; **oculto, a** adj hidden; (fig) secret
ocupación [okupaˈθjon] nf occupation
ocupado, a [okuˈpaðo, a] adj (persona) busy; (plaza) occupied, taken; (teléfono) engaged; **ocupar** vt (gen) to occupy; **ocuparse** vr: **ocuparse de o en** (gen) to concern o.s. with; (cuidar) to look after
ocurrencia [okuˈrrenθja] nf (idea) bright idea
ocurrir [okuˈrrir] vi to happen; ~**se** vr: **se me ocurrió que ...** it occurred to me that ...
odiar [oˈðjar] vt to hate; **odio** nm hate, hatred; **odioso, a** adj (gen) hateful; (malo)

nasty

odontólogo, a [oðon'toloxo, a] *nm/f*
dentist, dental surgeon

OEA *nf abr* (= *Organización de Estados
Americanos*) OAS

oeste [o'este] *nm* west; **una película del ~ a**
western

ofender [ofen'der] *vt* (*agraviar*) to offend;
(*insultar*) to insult; **~se** *vr* to take offence;
ofensa [o'fensa] *nf* offence; **ofensiva** *nf* offensive;
ofensivo, a *adj* offensive

oferta [o'ferta] *nf* offer; (*propuesta*) proposal;
la ~ y la demanda supply and demand;
artículos en ~ goods on offer

oficial [ofi'θjal] *adj* official ♦ *nm* (*MIL*) officer

oficina [ofi'θina] *nf* office; **~ de correos** post
office; **~ de turismo** tourist office; **oficinista**
nm/f clerk

oficio [o'fiθjo] *nm* (*profesión*) profession;
(*puesto*) post; (*REL*) service; **ser del ~** to be an
old hand; **tener mucho ~** to have a lot of
experience; **~ de difuntos** funeral service

oficioso, a [ofi'θjoso, a] *adj* (*pey*) officious;
(*no oficial*) unofficial, informal

ofimática [ofi'matika] *nf* office automation

ofrecer [ofre'θer] *vt* (*dar*) to offer; (*proponer*)
to propose; **~se** *vr* (*persona*) to offer o.s.,
volunteer; (*situación*) to present itself; **¿qué
se le ofrece?, ¿se le ofrece algo?** what can I
do for you?, can I get you anything?

ofrecimiento [ofreθi'mjento] *nm* offer

oftalmólogo, a [oftal'moloxo, a] *nm/f*
ophthalmologist

ofuscar [ofus'kar] *vt* (*por pasión*) to blind;
(*por luz*) to dazzle

oída [o'iða] *nf*: **de ~s** by hearsay

oído [o'iðo] *nm* (*ANAT*) ear; (*sentido*) hearing

oigo *etc vb ver* **oír**

oír [o'ir] *vt* (*gen*) to hear; (*atender a*) to listen
to; **¡oiga!** listen!; **~ misa** to attend mass

OIT *nf abr* (= *Organización Internacional del
Trabajo*) ILO

ojal [o'xal] *nm* buttonhole

ojalá [oxa'la] *excl* if only (it were so)!, some
hope! ♦ *conj* if only …!, would that …!;
~ (que) venga hoy I hope he comes today

ojeada [oxe'aða] *nf* glance

ojera [o'xera] *nf*: **tener ~s** to have bags under
one's eyes

ojeriza [oxe'riθa] *nf* ill-will

ojeroso, a [oxe'roso, a] *adj* haggard

ojo [o'xo] *nm* eye; (*de puente*) span; (*de
cerradura*) keyhole ♦ *excl* careful!; **tener
~ para** to have an eye for; **~ de buey** porthole

okupa [o'kupa] (*fam*) *nm/f* squatter

ola [o'la] *nf* wave

olé [o'le] *excl* bravo!, olé!

oleada [ole'aða] *nf* big wave, swell; (*fig*)
wave

oleaje [ole'axe] *nm* swell

óleo [o'leo] *nm* oil; **oleoducto** *nm* (oil)
pipeline

oler [o'ler] *vt* (*gen*) to smell; (*inquirir*) to pry
into; (*fig*: *sospechar*) to sniff out ♦ *vi* to
smell; **~ a** to smell of

olfatear [olfate'ar] *vt* to smell; (*inquirir*) to
pry into; **olfato** *nm* sense of smell

oligarquía [olivar'kia] *nf* oligarchy

olimpíada [olim'piaða] *nf*: **las O~s** the
Olympics; **olímpico, a** [o'limpiko, a] *adj*
Olympic

oliva [o'liβa] *nf* (*aceituna*) olive; **aceite de ~**
olive oil; **olivo** *nm* olive tree

olla [o'ʎa] *nf* pan; (*comida*) stew; **~ a presión**
o **exprés** pressure cooker; **~ podrida** *type of
Spanish stew*

olmo [o'lmo] *nm* elm (tree)

olor [o'lor] *nm* smell; **~oso, a** *adj* scented

olvidar [olβi'ðar] *vt* to forget; (*omitir*) to
omit; **~se** *vr* (*fig*) to forget o.s.; **se me olvidó**
forgot

olvido [ol'βiðo] *nm* oblivion; (*despiste*)
forgetfulness

ombligo [om'blivo] *nm* navel

omisión [omi'sjon] *nf* (*abstención*) omission;
(*descuido*) neglect

omiso, a [o'miso, a] *adj*: **hacer caso ~ de** to
ignore, pass over

omitir [omi'tir] *vt* to omit

omnipotente [omnipo'tente] *adj*
omnipotent

omóplato [o'moplato] *nm* shoulder blade

OMG *nm abr* (= *Organismo Modificado
Genéticamente*) GMO

OMS *nf abr* (= *Organización Mundial de la
Salud*) WHO

once ['onθe] *num* eleven; **~s** (*AM*) *nfpl* tea
break

onda ['onda] *nf* wave; **~ corta/larga/media**
short/long/medium wave; **ondear** *vt, vi* to
wave; (*tener ondas*) to be wavy; (*agua*) to
ripple; **ondearse** *vr* to swing, sway

ondulación [ondula'θjon] *nf* undulation;
ondulado, a *adj* wavy

ondular [ondu'lar] *vt* (*el pelo*) to wave ♦ *vi*
to undulate; **~se** *vr* to undulate

ONG *nf abr* (= *organización no guberna-
mental*) NGO

ONU ['onu] *nf abr* (= *Organización de las
Naciones Unidas*) UNO

opaco, a [o'pako, a] *adj* opaque

opción [op'θjon] *nf* (*gen*) option; (*derecho*)
right, option

OPEP ['opep] *nf abr* (= *Organización de Países
Exportadores de Petróleo*) OPEC

ópera ['opera] *nf* opera; **~ bufa** o **cómica**
comic opera

operación [opera'θjon] *nf* (*gen*) operation;

(*COM*) transaction, deal

operador, a [opera'ðor, a] *nm/f* operator; (*CINE: proyección*) projectionist; (: *rodaje*) cameraman

operar [ope'rar] *vt* (*producir*) to produce, bring about; (*MED*) to operate on ♦ *vi* (*COM*) to operate, deal; **~se** *vr* to occur; (*MED*) to have an operation

opereta [ope'reta] *nf* operetta

opinar [opi'nar] *vt* to think ♦ *vi* to give one's opinion; **opinión** *nf* (*creencia*) belief; (*criterio*) opinion

opio ['opjo] *nm* opium

oponente [opo'nente] *nm/f* opponent

oponer [opo'ner] *vt* (*resistencia*) to put up, offer; **~se** *vr* (*objetar*) to object; (*estar frente a frente*) to be opposed: (*dos personas*) to oppose each other; **~ A a B** to set A against B; **me opongo a pensar que** ... I refuse to believe o think that ...

oportunidad [oportuni'ðað] *nf* (*ocasión*) opportunity; (*posibilidad*) chance

oportuno, a [opor'tuno, a] *adj* (*en su tiempo*) opportune, timely; (*respuesta*) suitable; **en el momento ~** at the right moment

oposición [oposi'θjon] *nf* opposition; **oposiciones** *nfpl* (*ESCOL*) public examinations

opositor, a [oposi'tor, a] *nm/f* (*adversario*) opponent; (*candidato*): **~ (a)** candidate (for)

opresión [opre'sjon] *nf* oppression; **opresivo, a** *adj* oppressive; **opresor, a** *nm/f* oppressor

oprimir [opri'mir] *vt* to squeeze; (*fig*) to oppress

optar [op'tar] *vi* (*elegir*) to choose; **~ por** to opt for; **optativo, a** *adj* optional

óptico, a ['optiko, a] *adj* optic(al) ♦ *nm/f* optician; **óptica** *nf* optician's (shop); **desde esta óptica** from this point of view

optimismo [opti'mismo] *nm* optimism; **optimista** *nm/f* optimist

óptimo, a ['optimo, a] *adj* (*el mejor*) very best

opuesto, a [o'pwesto, a] *adj* (*contrario*) opposite; (*antagónico*) opposing

opulencia [opu'lenθja] *nf* opulence; **opulento, a** *adj* opulent

oración [ora'θjon] *nf* (*REL*) prayer; (*LING*) sentence

orador, a [ora'ðor, a] *nm/f* (*conferenciante*) speaker, orator

oral [o'ral] *adj* oral

orangután [orangu'tan] *nm* orangutan

orar [o'rar] *vi* to pray

oratoria [ora'torja] *nf* oratory

órbita ['orßita] *nf* orbit

orden ['orðen] *nm* (*gen*) order ♦ *nf* (*gen*) order; (*INFORM*) command; **~ del día** agenda;

de primer ~ first-rate; **en ~ de prioridad** in order of priority

ordenado, a [orðe'naðo, a] *adj* (*metódico*) methodical; (*arreglado*) orderly

ordenador [orðena'ðor] *nm* computer; **~ central** mainframe computer

ordenanza [orðe'nanθa] *nf* ordinance

ordenar [orðe'nar] *vt* (*mandar*) to order; (*poner orden*) to put in order, arrange; **~se** *vr* (*REL*) to be ordained

ordeñar [orðe'ɲar] *vt* to milk

ordinario, a [orði'narjo, a] *adj* (*común*) ordinary, usual; (*vulgar*) vulgar, common

orégano [o'reχano] *nm* oregano

oreja [o'rexa] *nf* ear; (*MECÁNICA*) lug, flange

orfanato [orfa'nato] *nm* orphanage

orfandad [orfan'dað] *nf* orphanhood

orfebrería [orfeßre'ria] *nf* gold/silver work

orgánico, a [or'ßaniko, a] *adj* organic

organigrama [orßani'ßrama] *nm* flow chart

organismo [orßa'nismo] *nm* (*BIO*) organism; (*POL*) organization

organización [orßaniθa'θjon] *nf* organization; **organizar** *vt* to organize

órgano ['orßano] *nm* organ

orgasmo [or'ßasmo] *nm* orgasm

orgía [or'xia] *nf* orgy

orgullo [or'ßuλo] *nm* pride; **orgulloso, a** *adj* (*gen*) proud; (*altanero*) haughty

orientación [orjenta'θjon] *nf* (*posición*) position; (*dirección*) direction

oriental [orjen'tal] *adj* eastern; (*del Lejano Oriente*) oriental

orientar [orjen'tar] *vt* (*situar*) to orientate; (*señalar*) to point; (*dirigir*) to direct; (*guiar*) to guide; **~se** *vr* to get one's bearings

oriente [o'rjente] *nm* east; **Cercano/ Medio/Lejano O~** Near/Middle/Far East

origen [o'rixen] *nm* origin

original [orixi'nal] *adj* (*nuevo*) original; (*extraño*) odd, strange; **~idad** *nf* originality

originar [orixi'nar] *vt* to start, cause; **~se** *vr* to originate; **~io, a** *adj* original; **~io de** native of

orilla [o'riλa] *nf* (*borde*) border; (*de río*) bank; (*de bosque, tela*) edge; (*de mar*) shore

orina [o'rina] *nf* urine; **orinal** *nm* (chamber) pot; **orinar** *vi* to urinate; **orinarse** *vr* to wet o.s.; **orines** *nmpl* urine

oriundo, a [o'rjundo, a] *adj*: **~ de** native of

ornitología [ornitolo'xia] *nf* ornithology, bird-watching

oro ['oro] *nm* gold; **~s** *nmpl* (*NAIPES*) hearts

oropel [oro'pel] *nm* tinsel

orquesta [or'kesta] *nf* orchestra; **~ de cámara/sinfónica** chamber/symphony orchestra

orquídea [or'kiðea] *nf* orchid

ortiga [or'tißa] *nf* nettle

ortodoxo, a [orto'ðokso, a] adj orthodox
ortografía [ortoɣra'fia] nf spelling
ortopedia [orto'peðja] nf orthopaedics sg;
  ortopédico, a adj orthopaedic
oruga [o'ruɣa] nf caterpillar
orzuelo [or'θwelo] nm stye
os [os] pron (gen) you; (a vosotros) to you
osa ['osa] nf (she-)bear; **O~ Mayor/Menor**
  Great/Little Bear
osadía [osa'ðia] nf daring
osar [o'sar] vi to dare
oscilación [osθila'θjon] nf (movimiento)
  oscillation; (fluctuación) fluctuation
oscilar [osθi'lar] vi to oscillate; to fluctuate
oscurecer [oskure'θer] vt to darken ♦ vi to
  grow dark; **~se** vr to grow o get dark
oscuridad [oskuri'ðað] nf obscurity;
  (tinieblas) darkness
oscuro, a [os'kuro, a] adj dark; (fig) obscure;
  a oscuras in the dark
óseo, a ['oseo, a] adj bone cpd
oso ['oso] nm bear; **~ de peluche** teddy bear;
  ~ hormiguero anteater
ostentación [ostenta'θjon] nf (gen)
  ostentation; (acto) display
ostentar [osten'tar] vt (gen) to show;
  (pey) to flaunt, show off; (poseer) to have,
  possess
ostra ['ostra] nf oyster
OTAN ['otan] nf abr (= Organización del
  Tratado del Atlántico Norte) NATO
otear [ote'ar] vt to observe; (fig) to look into
otitis [o'titis] nf earache
otoñal [oto'ɲal] adj autumnal
otoño [o'toɲo] nm autumn
otorgar [otor'ɣar] vt (conceder) to concede;
  (dar) to grant
otorrino, a [oto'rrino, a], **otorrinolarin-**
  gólogo, a [otorrinolarin'goloɣo, a] nm/f ear,
  nose and throat specialist

┌─────────────────────┐
│ *PALABRA CLAVE* │
└─────────────────────┘

otro, a ['otro, a] adj **1** (distinto: sg) another;
  (: pl) other; **con ~s amigos** with other o
  different friends
  2 (adicional): **tráigame ~ café (más), por**
  favor can I have another coffee please; **~s 10**
  días más another ten days
  ♦ pron **1: el ~** the other one; **(los) ~s** (the)
  others; **de ~** somebody else's; **que lo haga ~**
  let somebody else do it
  2 (recíproco): **se odian (la) una a (la) otra**
  they hate one another o each other
  3: ~ tanto: comer ~ tanto to eat the same o
  as much again; **recibió una decena de**
  telegramas y otras tantas llamadas he got
  about ten telegrams and as many calls

ovación [oßa'θjon] nf ovation

oval [o'ßal] adj oval; **~ado, a** adj oval; **óvalo**
  nm oval
ovario [o'ßarjo] nm ovary
oveja [o'ßexa] nf sheep
overol [oße'rol] (AM) nm overalls pl
ovillo [o'ßiʎo] nm (de lana) ball of wool;
  hacerse un ~ to curl up
OVNI ['oßni] nm abr (= objeto volante no
  identificado) UFO
ovulación [oßula'θjon] nf ovulation; **óvulo**
  nm ovum
oxidación [oksiða'θjon] nf rusting
oxidar [oksi'ðar] vt to rust; **~se** vr to go rusty
óxido ['oksiðo] nm oxide
oxigenado, a [oksixe'naðo, a] adj (QUÍM)
  oxygenated; (pelo) bleached
oxígeno [ok'sixeno] nm oxygen
oyente [o'jente] nm/f listener, hearer
oyes etc vb ver **oír**
ozono [o'θono] nm ozone

P, p

P abr (= padre) Fr.
pabellón [paße'ʎon] nm bell tent; (ARQ)
  pavilion; (de hospital etc) block, section;
  (bandera) flag
pacer [pa'θer] vi to graze
paciencia [pa'θjenθja] nf patience
paciente [pa'θjente] adj, nm/f patient
pacificación [paθifika'θjon] nf pacification
pacificar [paθifi'kar] vt to pacify;
  (tranquilizar) to calm
pacífico, a [pa'θifiko, a] adj (persona)
  peaceable; (existencia) peaceful; **el (océano)**
  P~ the Pacific (Ocean)
pacifismo [paθi'fismo] nm pacifism;
  pacifista nm/f pacifist
pacotilla [pako'tiʎa] nf: **de ~** (actor, escritor)
  third-rate; (mueble etc) cheap
pactar [pak'tar] vt to agree to o on ♦ vi to
  come to an agreement
pacto ['pakto] nm (tratado) pact; (acuerdo)
  agreement
padecer [paðe'θer] vt (sufrir) to suffer;
  (soportar) to endure, put up with;
  padecimiento nm suffering
padrastro [pa'ðrastro] nm stepfather
padre ['paðre] nm father ♦ adj (fam): **un**
  éxito ~ a tremendous success; **~s** nmpl
  parents
padrino [pa'ðrino] nm (REL) godfather; (tb:
  ~ de boda) best man; (fig) sponsor, patron;
  ~s nmpl godparents
padrón [pa'ðron] nm (censo) census, roll
paella [pa'eʎa] nf paella, dish of rice with
  meat, shellfish etc

paga ['paxa] *nf* (*pago*) payment; (*sueldo*) pay, wages *pl*

pagano, a [pa'xano, a] *adj, nm/f* pagan, heathen

pagar [pa'xar] *vt* to pay; (*las compras, crimen*) to pay for; (*fig: favor*) to repay ♦ *vi* to pay; **~ al contado/a plazos** to pay (in) cash/in instalments

pagaré [paxa're] *nm* I.O.U.

página ['paxina] *nf* page; **~ de inicio** (*INFORM*) home page

pago ['paxo] *nm* (*dinero*) payment; **~ anticipado/a cuenta/contra reembolso/en especie** advance payment/payment on account/cash on delivery/payment in kind; **en ~ de** in return for

pág(s). *abr* (= *página(s)*) p(p).

pague *etc vb ver* **pagar**

país [pa'is] *nm* (*gen*) country; (*región*) land; **los P~es Bajos** the Low Countries; **el P~ Vasco** the Basque Country

paisaje [pai'saxe] *nm* landscape, scenery

paisano, a [pai'sano, a] *adj* of the same country ♦ *nm/f* (*compatriota*) fellow countryman/woman; **vestir de ~** (*soldado*) to be in civvies; (*guardia*) to be in plain clothes

paja ['paxa] *nf* straw; (*fig*) rubbish (*BRIT*), trash (*US*)

pajarita [paxa'rita] *nf* (*corbata*) bow tie

pájaro ['paxaro] *nm* bird; **~ carpintero** woodpecker

pajita [pa'xita] *nf* (*drinking*) straw

pala ['pala] *nf* spade, shovel; (*raqueta etc*) bat; (: *de tenis*) racquet; (*CULIN*) slice; **~ matamoscas** fly swat

palabra [pa'laßra] *nf* word; (*facultad*) (power of) speech; (*derecho de hablar*) right to speak; **tomar la ~** (*en mitin*) to take the floor

palabrota [pala'brota] *nf* swearword

palacio [pa'laθjo] *nm* palace; (*mansión*) mansion, large house; **~ de justicia** courthouse; **~ municipal** town/city hall

paladar [pala'ðar] *nm* palate; **paladear** *vt* to taste

palanca [pa'lanka] *nf* lever; (*fig*) pull, influence

palangana [palan'gana] *nf* washbasin

palco ['palko] *nm* box

Palestina [pales'tina] *nf* Palestine; **palestino, a** *nm/f* Palestinian

paleta [pa'leta] *nf* (*de pintor*) palette; (*de albañil*) trowel; (*de ping-pong*) bat; (*AM*) ice lolly

paleto, a [pa'leto, a] (*fam, pey*) *nm/f* yokel

paliar [pa'ljar] *vt* (*mitigar*) to mitigate, alleviate; **paliativo** *nm* palliative

palidecer [paliðe'θer] *vi* to turn pale; **palidez** *nf* paleness; **pálido, a** *adj* pale

palillo [pa'liʎo] *nm* (*mondadientes*) toothpick; (*para comer*) chopstick

paliza [pa'liθa] *nf* beating, thrashing

palma ['palma] *nf* (*ANAT*) palm; (*árbol*) palm tree; **batir** o **dar ~s** to clap, applaud; **~da** *nf* slap; **~das** *nfpl* clapping *sg*, applause *sg*

palmar [pal'mar] (*fam*) *vi* (*tb: ~la*) to die, kick the bucket

palmear [palme'ar] *vi* to clap

palmera [pal'mera] *nf* (*BOT*) palm tree

palmo ['palmo] *nm* (*medida*) span; (*fig*) small amount; **~ a ~** inch by inch

palo ['palo] *nm* stick; (*poste*) post; (*de tienda de campaña*) pole; (*mango*) handle, shaft; (*golpe*) blow, hit; (*de golf*) club; (*de béisbol*) bat; (*NAUT*) mast; (*NAIPES*) suit

paloma [pa'loma] *nf* dove, pigeon

palomitas [palo'mitas] *nfpl* popcorn *sg*

palpar [pal'par] *vt* to touch, feel

palpitación [palpita'θjon] *nf* palpitation

palpitante [palpi'tante] *adj* palpitating; (*fig*) burning

palpitar [palpi'tar] *vi* to palpitate; (*latir*) to beat

palta ['palta] (*AM*) *nf* avocado (pear)

paludismo [palu'ðismo] *nm* malaria

pamela [pa'mela] *nf* picture hat, sun hat

pampa ['pampa] (*AM*) *nf* pampas, prairie

pan [pan] *nm* bread; (*una barra*) loaf; **~ integral** wholemeal (*BRIT*) o wholewheat (*US*) bread; **~ rallado** breadcrumbs *pl*

pana ['pana] *nf* corduroy

panadería [panaðe'ria] *nf* baker's (shop); **panadero, a** *nm/f* baker

Panamá [pana'ma] *nm* Panama; **panameño, a** *adj* Panamanian

pancarta [pan'karta] *nf* placard, banner

panda ['panda] *nm* (*ZOOL*) panda

pandereta [pande'reta] *nf* tambourine

pandilla [pan'diʎa] *nf* set, group; (*de criminales*) gang; (*pey: camarilla*) clique

panecillo [pane'θiʎo] *nm* (*bread*) roll

panel [pa'nel] *nm* panel; **~ solar** solar panel

panfleto [pan'fleto] *nm* pamphlet

pánico ['paniko] *nm* panic

panorama [pano'rama] *nm* panorama; (*vista*) view

pantalla [pan'taʎa] *nf* (*de cine*) screen; (*de lámpara*) lampshade

pantalón [panta'lon] *nm* trousers; **pantalones** *nmpl* trousers

pantano [pan'tano] *nm* (*ciénaga*) marsh, swamp; (*depósito: de agua*) reservoir; (*fig*) jam, difficulty

panteón [pante'on] *nm*: **~ familiar** family tomb

pantera [pan'tera] *nf* panther

panti(e)s ['pantis] *nmpl* tights

pantomima [panto'mima] *nf* pantomime

pantorrilla [panto'rriʎa] *nf* calf (of the leg)

pantufla [pan'tufla] *nf* slipper

panty(s) ['panti(s)] *nm(pl)* tights

panza ['panθa] *nf* belly, paunch

pañal [pa'ɲal] *nm* nappy (*BRIT*), diaper (*US*); **~es** *nmpl* (*fig*) early stages, infancy *sg*

paño ['paɲo] *nm* (*tela*) cloth; (*pedazo de tela*) (piece of) cloth; (*trapo*) duster, rag; **~ higiénico** sanitary towel; **~s menores** underclothes

pañuelo [pa'ɲwelo] *nm* handkerchief, hanky (*fam*); (*para la cabeza*) (head)scarf

papa ['papa] *nm*: **el P~** the Pope ♦ *nf* (*AM*) potato

papá [pa'pa] (*pl* **~s**) (*fam*) *nm* dad(dy), pa (*US*)

papada [pa'paða] *nf* double chin

papagayo [papa'xajo] *nm* parrot

papanatas [papa'natas] (*fam*) *nm inv* simpleton

paparrucha [papa'rrutʃa] *nf* piece of nonsense

papaya [pa'paja] *nf* papaya

papear [pape'ar] (*fam*) *vt, vi* to scoff

papel [pa'pel] *nm* paper; (*hoja de ~*) sheet of paper; (*TEATRO, fig*) role; **~ de calco/carbón/ de cartas** tracing paper/carbon paper/ stationery; **~ de envolver/pintado** wrapping paper/wallpaper; **~ de aluminio/higiénico** aluminium (*BRIT*) *o* aluminum (*US*) foil/toilet paper; **~ de estaño** *o* **plata** tinfoil; **~ de lija** sandpaper; **~ moneda** paper money; **~ secante** blotting paper

papeleo [pape'leo] *nm* red tape

papelera [pape'lera] *nf* wastepaper basket; (*en la calle*) litter bin

papelería [papele'ria] *nf* stationer's (shop)

papeleta [pape'leta] *nf* (*POL*) ballot paper; (*ESCOL*) report

paperas [pa'peras] *nfpl* mumps *sg*

papilla [pa'piʎa] *nf* (*para niños*) baby food

paquete [pa'kete] *nm* (*de cigarrillos etc*) packet; (*CORREOS etc*) parcel; (*AM*) package tour; (: *fam*) nuisance

par [par] *adj* (*igual*) like, equal; (*MAT*) even ♦ *nm* equal; (*de guantes*) pair; (*de veces*) couple; (*POL*) peer; (*GOLF, COM*) par; **abrir de ~ en ~** to open wide

para ['para] *prep* for; **no es ~ comer** it's not for eating; **decir ~ sí** to say to o.s.; **¿~ qué lo quieres?** what do you want it for?; **se casaron ~ separarse otra vez** they married only to separate again; **lo tendré ~ mañana** I'll have it (for) tomorrow; **ir ~ casa** to go home, head for home; **~ profesor es muy estúpido** he's very stupid for a teacher; **¿quién es usted ~ gritar así?** who are you to shout like that?; **tengo bastante ~ vivir** I have enough to live on; *ver tb* **con**

parabién [para'βjen] *nm* congratulations *pl*

parábola [pa'raβola] *nf* parable; (*MAT*) parabola; **parabólica** *nf* (*tb: antena ~*) satellite dish

parabrisas [para'βrisas] *nm inv* windscreen (*BRIT*), windshield (*US*)

paracaídas [paraka'iðas] *nm inv* parachute; **paracaidista** *nm/f* parachutist; (*MIL*) paratrooper

parachoques [para'tʃokes] *nm inv* (*AUTO*) bumper; (*MECÁNICA etc*) shock absorber

parada [pa'raða] *nf* stop; (*acto*) stopping; (*de industria*) shutdown, stoppage; (*lugar*) stopping place; **~ de autobús** bus stop

paradero [para'ðero] *nm* stopping-place; (*situación*) whereabouts

parado, a [pa'raðo, a] *adj* (*persona*) motionless, standing still; (*fábrica*) closed, at a standstill; (*coche*) stopped; (*AM*) standing (up); (*sin empleo*) unemployed, idle

paradoja [para'ðoxa] *nf* paradox

parador [para'ðor] *nm* parador, state-run hotel

paráfrasis [pa'rafrasis] *nf inv* paraphrase

paraguas [pa'raxwas] *nm inv* umbrella

Paraguay [para'xwai] *nm*: **el ~** Paraguay; **paraguayo, a** *adj, nm/f* Paraguayan

paraíso [para'iso] *nm* paradise, heaven

paraje [pa'raxe] *nm* place, spot

paralelo, a [para'lelo, a] *adj* parallel

parálisis [pa'ralisis] *nf inv* paralysis; **paralítico, a** *adj, nm/f* paralytic

paralizar [parali'θar] *vt* to paralyse; **~se** *vr* to become paralysed; (*fig*) to come to a standstill

paramilitar [paramili'tar] *adj* paramilitary

páramo ['paramo] *nm* bleak plateau

parangón [paran'gon] *nm*: **sin ~** incomparable

paranoico, a [para'noiko, a] *nm/f* paranoiac

parapente [para'pente] *nm* (*deporte*) paragliding; (*aparato*) paraglider

parapléjico, a [para'plexiko, a] *adj, nm/f* paraplegic

parar [pa'rar] *vt* to stop; (*golpe*) to ward off ♦ *vi* to stop; **~se** *vr* to stop; (*AM*) to stand up; **ha parado de llover** it has stopped raining; **van a ir a ~ a comisaria** they're going to end up in the police station; **~se en** to pay attention to

pararrayos [para'rrajos] *nm inv* lightning conductor

parásito, a [pa'rasito, a] *nm/f* parasite

parcela [par'θela] *nf* plot, piece of ground

parche ['partʃe] *nm* (*gen*) patch

parchís [par'tʃis] *nm* ludo

parcial [par'θjal] *adj* (*pago*) part-; (*eclipse*) partial; (*JUR*) prejudiced, biased; (*POL*) partisan; **~idad** *nf* prejudice, bias

pardillo, a [par'ðiʎo, a] (*pey*) *adj* yokel

parecer [pare'θer] nm (opinión) opinion, view; (aspecto) looks pl ♦ vi (tener apariencia) to seem, look; (asemejarse) to look o seem like; (aparecer, llegar) to appear; **~se** vr to look alike, resemble each other; **~se a** to look like, resemble; **según parece** evidently, apparently; **me parece que** I think (that), it seems to me that

parecido, a [pare'θiðo, a] adj similar ♦ nm similarity, likeness, resemblance; **bien ~** good-looking, nice-looking

pared [pa'reð] nf wall

pareja [pa'rexa] nf (par) pair; (dos personas) couple; (otro: de un par) other one (of a pair); (persona) partner

parentela [paren'tela] nf relations pl

parentesco [paren'tesko] nm relationship

paréntesis [pa'rentesis] nm inv parenthesis; (en escrito) bracket

parezco etc vb ver **parecer**

pariente, a [pa'rjente, a] nm/f relative, relation

parir [pa'rir] vt to give birth to ♦ vi (mujer) to give birth, have a baby

París [pa'ris] n Paris

parking [ˈparkin] nm car park (BRIT), parking lot (US)

parlamentar [parlamen'tar] vi to parley

parlamentario, a [parlamen'tarjo, a] adj parliamentary ♦ nm/f member of parliament

parlamento [parla'mento] nm parliament

parlanchín, ina [parlan'tʃin, ina] adj indiscreet ♦ nm/f chatterbox

parlar [par'lar] vi to chatter (away)

paro [ˈparo] nm (huelga) stoppage (of work), strike; (desempleo) unemployment; **subsidio de ~** unemployment benefit

parodia [pa'roðja] nf parody; **parodiar** vt to parody

parpadear [parpaðe'ar] vi (ojos) to blink; (luz) to flicker

párpado [ˈparpaðo] nm eyelid

parque [ˈparke] nm (lugar verde) park; **~ de atracciones/infantil/zoológico** fairground/playground/zoo

parqué [par'ke] nm parquet (flooring)

parquímetro [par'kimetro] nm parking meter

parra [ˈparra] nf (grape)vine

párrafo [ˈparrafo] nm paragraph; **echar un ~** (fam) to have a chat

parranda [pa'rranda] (fam) nf spree, binge

parrilla [pa'rriʎa] nf (CULIN) grill; (de coche) grille; **(carne a la) ~** barbecue; **~da** nf barbecue

párroco [ˈparroko] nm parish priest

parroquia [pa'rrokja] nf (iglesia) parish church; (COM) clientele, customers pl; **~no, a** nm/f parishioner; client, customer

parsimonia [parsi'monja] nf calmness, level-headedness

parte [ˈparte] nm message; (informe) report ♦ nf part; (lado, cara) side; (de reparto) share; (JUR) party; **en alguna ~ de Europa** somewhere in Europe; **en/por todas ~s** everywhere; **en gran ~** to a large extent; **la mayor ~ de los españoles** most Spaniards; **de un tiempo a esta ~** for some time past; **de ~ de alguien** on sb's behalf; **¿de ~ de quién?** (TEL) who is speaking?; **por ~ de** on the part of; **yo por mi ~** I for my part; **por otra ~** on the other hand; **dar ~ to** inform; **tomar ~ to** take part

partición [parti'θjon] nf division, sharing-out; (POL) partition

participación [partiθipa'θjon] nf (acto) participation, taking part; (parte, COM) share; (de lotería) shared prize; (aviso) notice, notification

participante [partiθi'pante] nm/f participant

participar [partiθi'par] vt to notify, inform ♦ vi to take part, participate

partícipe [par'tiθipe] nm/f participant

particular [partiku'lar] adj (especial) particular, special; (individual, personal) private, personal ♦ nm (punto, asunto) particular, point; (individuo) individual; **tiene coche ~** he has a car of his own

partida [par'tiða] nf (salida) departure; (COM) entry, item; (juego) game; (grupo de personas) band, group; **mala ~** dirty trick; **~ de nacimiento / matrimonio / defunción** birth/marriage/death certificate

partidario, a [parti'ðarjo, a] adj partisan ♦ nm/f supporter, follower

partido [par'tiðo] nm (POL) party; (DEPORTE) game, match; **sacar ~ de** to profit o benefit from; **tomar ~** to take sides

partir [par'tir] vt (dividir) to split, divide; (compartir, distribuir) to share (out), distribute; (romper) to break open, split open; (rebanada) to cut (off) ♦ vi (ponerse en camino) to set off o out; (comenzar) to start (off o out); **~se** vr to crack o split o break (in two etc); **a ~ de** (starting) from

partitura [parti'tura] nf (MUS) score

parto [ˈparto] nm birth; (fig) product, creation; **estar de ~** to be in labour

pasa [ˈpasa] nf raisin; **~ de Corinto/de Esmirna** currant/sultana

pasada [pa'saða] nf passing, passage; **de ~** in passing, incidentally; **una mala ~** a dirty trick

pasadizo [pasa'ðiθo] nm (pasillo) passage, corridor; (callejuela) alley

pasado, a [pa'saðo, a] adj past; (malo: comida, fruta) bad; (muy cocido) overdone; (anticuado) out of date ♦ nm past; **~ mañana** the day after tomorrow; **el mes ~** last month

pasador [pasa'ðor] nm (cerrojo) bolt; (de pelo) hair slide; (horquilla) grip

pasaje [pa'saxe] nm passage; (pago de viaje) fare; (los pasajeros) passengers pl; (pasillo) passageway

pasajero, a [pasa'xero, a] adj passing; (situación, estado) temporary; (amor, enfermedad) brief ♦ nm/f passenger

pasamontañas [pasamon'tapas] nm inv balaclava helmet

pasaporte [pasa'porte] nm passport

pasar [pa'sar] vt to pass; (tiempo) to spend; (desgracias) to suffer, endure; (noticia) to give, pass on; (río) to cross; (barrera) to pass through; (falta) to overlook, tolerate; (contrincante) to surpass, do better than; (coche) to overtake; (CINE) to show; (enfermedad) to give, infect with ♦ vi (gen) to pass; (terminarse) to be over; (ocurrir) to happen; **~se** vr (flores) to fade; (comida) to go bad o off; (fig) to overdo it, go too far; **~ de** to go beyond, exceed; **~ por** (AM) to fetch; **~lo bien/mal** to have a good/bad time; **¡pase!** come in!; **hacer ~** to show in; **~se al enemigo** to go over to the enemy; **se me pasó** I forgot; **no se le pasa nada** he misses nothing; **lo que pase** come what may; **¿qué pasa?** what's going on?, what's up?; **¿qué te pasa?** what's wrong?

pasarela [pasa'rela] nf footbridge; (en barco) gangway

pasatiempo [pasa'tjempo] nm pastime, hobby

Pascua ['paskwa] nf: **~ (de Resurrección)** Easter; **~ de Navidad** Christmas; **~s** nfpl Christmas (time); **¡felices ~s!** Merry Christmas!

pase ['pase] nm pass; (CINE) performance, showing

pasear [pase'ar] vt to take for a walk; (exhibir) to parade, show off ♦ vi to walk, go for a walk; **~se** vr to walk, go for a walk; **~ en coche** to go for a drive; **paseo** nm (avenida) avenue; (distancia corta) walk, stroll; **dar un o ir de paseo** to go for a walk

pasillo [pa'siʎo] nm passage, corridor

pasión [pa'sjon] nf passion

pasivo, a [pa'sißo, a] adj passive; (inactivo) inactive ♦ nm (COM) liabilities pl, debts pl

pasmar [pas'mar] vt (asombrar) to amaze, astonish; **pasmo** nm amazement, astonishment; (resfriado) chill; (fig) wonder, marvel; **pasmoso, a** adj amazing, astonishing

paso, a ['paso, a] adj dried ♦ nm step; (modo de andar) walk; (huella) footprint; (rapidez) speed, pace, rate; (camino accesible) way through, passage; (cruce) crossing; (pasaje) passing, passage; (GEO) pass; (estrecho) strait;

~ a nivel (FERRO) level-crossing; **~ de peatones** pedestrian crossing; **a ese ~** (fig) at that rate; **salir al ~ de** o **a** to waylay; **estar de ~** to be passing through; **~ elevado** flyover; **prohibido el ~** no entry; **ceda el ~** give way

pasota [pa'sota] (fam) adj, nm/f ≈ dropout; **ser un (tipo) ~** to be a bit of a dropout; (ser indiferente) not to care about anything

pasta ['pasta] nf paste; (CULIN: masa) dough; (: de bizcochos etc) pastry; (fam) dough; **~s** nfpl (bizcochos) pastries, small cakes; (fideos, espaguetis etc) pasta; **~ de dientes** o **dentífrica** toothpaste

pastar [pas'tar] vt, vi to graze

pastel [pas'tel] nm (dulce) cake; (ARTE) pastel; **~ de carne** meat pie; **~ería** nf cake shop

pasteurizado, a [pasteuri'θaðo, a] adj pasteurized

pastilla [pas'tiʎa] nf (de jabón, chocolate) bar; (píldora) tablet, pill

pasto ['pasto] nm (hierba) grass; (lugar) pasture, field

pastor, a [pas'tor, a] nm/f shepherd/ess ♦ nm (REL) clergyman, pastor; **~ alemán** Alsatian

pata ['pata] nf (pierna) leg; (pie) foot; (de muebles) leg; **~s arriba** upside down; **metedura de ~** (fam) gaffe; **meter la ~** (fam) to put one's foot in it; (TEC): **~ de cabra** crowbar; **tener buena/mala ~** to be lucky/unlucky; **~da** nf kick; (en el suelo) stamp

patalear [patale'ar] vi (en el suelo) to stamp one's feet

patata [pa'tata] nf potato; **~s fritas** chips, French fries; (de bolsa) crisps

paté [pa'te] nm pâté

patear [pate'ar] vt (pisar) to stamp on, trample (on); (pegar con el pie) to kick ♦ vi to stamp (with rage), stamp one's feet

patentar [paten'tar] vt to patent

patente [pa'tente] adj obvious, evident; (COM) patent ♦ nf patent

paternal [pater'nal] adj fatherly, paternal; **paterno, a** adj paternal

patético, a [pa'tetiko, a] adj pathetic, moving

patilla [pa'tiʎa] nf (de gafas) side(piece); **~s** nfpl sideburns

patín [pa'tin] nm skate; (de trineo) runner; **patinaje** nm skating; **patinar** vi to skate; (resbalarse) to skid, slip; (fam) to slip up, blunder

patio ['patjo] nm (de casa) patio, courtyard; **~ de recreo** playground

pato ['pato] nm duck; **pagar el ~** (fam) to take the blame, carry the can

patológico, a [pato'loxiko, a] adj pathological

patoso, a [pa'toso, a] (fam) adj clumsy

patraña [pa'traɲa] *nf* story, fib
patria ['patrja] *nf* native land, mother country
patrimonio [patri'monjo] *nm* inheritance; *(fig)* heritage
patriota [pa'trjota] *nm/f* patriot; **patriotismo** *nm* patriotism
patrocinar [patroθi'nar] *vt* to sponsor; **patrocinio** *nm* sponsorship
patrón, ona [pa'tron, ona] *nm/f (jefe)* boss, chief, master/mistress; *(propietario)* landlord/lady; *(REL)* patron saint ♦ *nm (TEC, COSTURA)* pattern
patronal [patro'nal] *adj:* **la clase ~** management
patronato [patro'nato] *nm* sponsorship; *(acto)* patronage; *(fundación benéfica)* trust, foundation
patrulla [pa'truʎa] *nf* patrol
pausa ['pausa] *nf* pause, break
pausado, a [pau'saðo, a] *adj* slow, deliberate
pauta ['pauta] *nf* line, guide line
pavimento [paβi'mento] *nm (con losas)* pavement, paving
pavo ['paβo] *nm* turkey; **~ real** peacock
pavor [pa'βor] *nm* dread, terror
payaso, a [pa'jaso, a] *nm/f* clown
payo, a ['pajo, a] *nm/f* non-gipsy
paz [paθ] *nf* peace; *(tranquilidad)* peacefulness, tranquillity; **hacer las paces** to make peace; *(fig)* to make up
pazo ['paθo] *nm* country house
P.D. *abr* (= *posdata*) P.S., p.s.
peaje [pe'axe] *nm* toll
peatón [pea'ton] *nm* pedestrian
peca ['peka] *nf* freckle
pecado [pe'kaðo] *nm* sin; **pecador, a** *adj* sinful ♦ *nm/f* sinner
pecaminoso, a [pekami'noso, a] *adj* sinful
pecar [pe'kar] *vi (REL)* to sin; **peca de generoso** he is generous to a fault
pecera [pe'θera] *nf* fish tank; *(redondo)* goldfish bowl
pecho ['petʃo] *nm (ANAT)* chest; *(de mujer)* breast; **dar el ~ a** to breast-feed; **tomar algo a ~** to take sth to heart
pechuga [pe'tʃuxa] *nf* breast
peculiar [peku'ljar] *adj* special, peculiar; *(característico)* typical, characteristic; **~idad** *nf* peculiarity; special feature, characteristic
pedal [pe'ðal] *nm* pedal; **~ear** *vi* to pedal
pedante [pe'ðante] *adj* pedantic ♦ *nm/f* pedant; **~ría** *nf* pedantry
pedazo [pe'ðaθo] *nm* piece, bit; **hacerse ~s** to smash, shatter
pedernal [peðer'nal] *nm* flint
pediatra [pe'ðjatra] *nm/f* paediatrician
pedido [pe'ðiðo] *nm (COM)* order; *(petición)* request
pedir [pe'ðir] *vt* to ask for, request; *(comida,*

COM: *mandar)* to order; *(necesitar)* to need, demand, require ♦ *vi* to ask; **me pidió que cerrara la puerta** he asked me to shut the door; **¿cuánto piden por el coche?** how much are they asking for the car?
pedo ['peðo] *(fam!) nm* fart
pega ['peɣa] *nf* snag; **poner ~s (a)** to complain (about)
pegadizo, a [peɣa'ðiθo, a] *adj (MUS)* catchy
pegajoso, a [peɣa'xoso, a] *adj* sticky, adhesive
pegamento [peɣa'mento] *nm* gum, glue
pegar [pe'ɣar] *vt (papel, sellos)* to stick (on); *(cartel)* to stick up; *(coser)* to sew (on); *(unir: partes)* to join, fix together; *(MED)* to give, infect with; *(dar: golpe)* to give, deal ♦ *vi (adherirse)* to stick, adhere; *(ir juntos: colores)* to match, go together; *(golpear)* to hit; *(quemar: el sol)* to strike hot, burn *(fig)*; **~se** *vr (gen)* to stick; *(dos personas)* to hit each other, fight; *(fam):* **~ un grito** to let out a yell; **~ un salto** to jump (with fright); **~ en** to touch; **~se un tiro** to shoot o.s.
pegatina [peɣa'tina] *nf* sticker
pegote [pe'ɣote] *(fam) nm* eyesore, sight
peinado [pei'naðo] *nm* hairstyle
peinar [pei'nar] *vt* to comb; *(hacer estilo)* to style; **~se** *vr* to comb one's hair
peine ['peine] *nm* comb; **~ta** *nf* ornamental comb
p.ej. *abr* (= *por ejemplo*) e.g.
Pekín [pe'kin] *n* Pekin(g)
pelado, a [pe'laðo, a] *adj (fruta, patata etc)* peeled; *(cabeza)* shorn; *(campo, fig)* bare; *(fam: sin dinero)* broke
pelaje [pe'laxe] *nm (ZOOL)* fur, coat; *(fig)* appearance
pelar [pe'lar] *vt (fruta, patatas etc)* to peel; *(cortar el pelo a)* to cut the hair of; *(quitar la piel: animal)* to skin; **~se** *vr (la piel)* to peel off; **voy a ~me** I'm going to get my hair cut
peldaño [pel'daɲo] *nm* step
pelea [pe'lea] *nf (lucha)* fight; *(discusión)* quarrel, row
peleado, a [pele'aðo, a] *adj:* **estar ~ (con uno)** to have fallen out (with sb)
pelear [pele'ar] *vi* to fight; **~se** *vr* to fight; *(reñirse)* to fall out, quarrel
peletería [pelete'ria] *nf* furrier's, fur shop
pelícano [pe'likano] *nm* pelican
película [pe'likula] *nf* film; *(cobertura ligera)* thin covering; *(FOTO: rollo)* roll o reel of film
peligro [pe'liɣro] *nm* danger; *(riesgo)* risk; **correr ~ de** to run the risk of; **~so, a** *adj* dangerous; risky
pelirrojo, a [peli'rroxo, a] *adj* red-haired, red-headed ♦ *nm/f* redhead
pellejo [pe'ʎexo] *nm (de animal)* skin, hide
pellizcar [peʎiθ'kar] *vt* to pinch, nip

pelma |'pelma| (fam) nm/f pain (in the neck)
pelmazo |pel'maθo| (fam) nm = **pelma**
pelo ['pelo] nm (cabellos) hair; (de barba, bigote) whisker; (de animal: pellejo) hair, fur, coat; **al ~** just right; **venir al ~** to be exactly what one needs; **un hombre de ~ en pecho** a brave man; **por los ~s** by the skin of one's teeth; **no tener ~s en la lengua** to be outspoken, not mince words; **tomar el ~ a uno** to pull sb's leg
pelota [pe'lota] nf ball; **en ~** stark naked; **hacer la ~ (a uno)** (fam) to creep (to sb); **~ vasca** pelota
pelotari [pelo'tari] nm pelota player
pelotón [pelo'ton] nm (MIL) squad, detachment
peluca [pe'luka] nf wig
peluche [pe'lutʃe] nm: **oso/muñeco de ~** teddy bear/soft toy
peludo, a [pe'luðo, a] adj hairy, shaggy
peluquería |peluke'ria| nf hairdresser's; **peluquero, a** nm/f hairdresser
pelusa [pe'lusa] nf (BOT) down; (en tela) fluff
pena ['pena] nf (congoja) grief, sadness; (remordimiento) regret; (dificultad) trouble; (dolor) pain; (JUR) sentence; **merecer o valer la ~** to be worthwhile; **a duras ~s** with great difficulty; **~ de muerte** death penalty; **~ pecuniaria** fine; **¡qué ~!** what a shame!
penal [pe'nal] adj penal ♦ nm (cárcel) prison
penalidad [penali'ðað] nf (problema, dificultad) trouble, hardship; (JUR) penalty, punishment; **~es** nfpl trouble, hardship
penalti, penalty [pe'nalti] (pl ~s o ~es) nm penalty (kick)
pendiente [pen'djente] adj pending, unsettled ♦ nm earring ♦ nf hill, slope
pene ['pene] nm penis
penetración [penetra'θjon] nf (acto) penetration; (agudeza) sharpness, insight
penetrante [pene'trante] adj (herida) deep; (persona, arma) sharp; (sonido) penetrating, piercing; (mirada) searching; (viento, ironía) biting
penetrar |pene'trar| vt to penetrate, pierce; (entender) to grasp ♦ vi to penetrate, go in; (entrar) to enter, go in; (líquido) to soak in; (fig) to pierce
penicilina [peniθi'lina] nf penicillin
península [pe'ninsula] nf peninsula; **peninsular** adj peninsular
penique [pe'nike] nm penny
penitencia [peni'tenθja] nf penance
penoso, a [pe'noso, a] adj (lamentable) distressing; (difícil) arduous, difficult
pensador, a [pensa'ðor, a] nm/f thinker
pensamiento [pensa'mjento] nm thought; (mente) mind; (idea) idea
pensar [pen'sar] vt to think; (considerar) to

think over, think out; (proponerse) to intend, plan; (imaginarse) to think up, invent ♦ vi to think; **~ en** to aim at, aspire to; **pensativo, a** adj thoughtful, pensive
pensión |pen'sjon| nf (casa) boarding o guest house; (dinero) pension; (cama y comida) board and lodging; **~ completa** full board; **media ~** half-board; **pensionista** nm/f (jubilado) (old-age) pensioner; (huésped) lodger
penúltimo, a [pe'nultimo, a] adj penultimate, last but one
penumbra [pe'numbra] nf half-light
penuria [pe'nurja] nf shortage, want
peña ['peɲa] nf (roca) rock; (cuesta) cliff, crag; (grupo) group, circle; (AM: club) folk club
peñasco [pe'ɲasko] nm large rock, boulder
peñón [pe'ɲon] nm wall of rock; **el P~** the Rock (of Gibraltar)
peón [pe'on] nm labourer; (AM) farm labourer, farmhand; (AJEDREZ) pawn
peonza [pe'onθa] nf spinning top
peor [pe'or] adj (comparativo) worse; (superlativo) worst ♦ adv worse; worst; **de mal en ~** from bad to worse
pepinillo [pepi'niʎo] nm gherkin
pepino [pe'pino] nm cucumber; **(no) me importa un ~** I don't care one bit
pepita [pe'pita] nf (BOT) pip; (MINERÍA) nugget
pepito [pe'pito] nm: **~ (de ternera)** steak sandwich
pequeñez [peke'neθ] nf smallness, littleness; (trivialidad) trifle, triviality
pequeño, a [pe'keɲo, a] adj small, little
pera ['pera] nf pear; **peral** nm pear tree
percance [per'kanθe] nm setback, misfortune
percatarse [perka'tarse] vr: **~ de** to notice, take note of
percebe [per'θeβe] nm barnacle
percepción [perθep'θjon] nf (vista) perception; (idea) notion, idea
percha ['pertʃa] nf (coat)hanger; (ganchos) coat hooks pl; (de ave) perch
percibir [perθi'βir] vt to perceive, notice; (COM) to earn, get
percusión [perku'sjon] nf percussion
perdedor, a |perðe'ðor, a| adj losing ♦ nm/f loser
perder [per'ðer] vt to lose; (tiempo, palabras) to waste; (oportunidad) to lose, miss; (tren) to miss ♦ vi to lose; **~se** vr (extraviarse) to get lost; (desaparecer) to disappear, be lost to view; (arruinarse) to be ruined; **echar a ~** (comida) to spoil, ruin; (oportunidad) to waste
perdición [perði'θjon] nf perdition, ruin
pérdida ['perðiða] nf loss; (de tiempo) waste;

~s nfpl (COM) losses

perdido, a [per'ðiðo, a] adj lost

perdiz [per'ðiθ] nf partridge

perdón [per'ðon] nm (disculpa) pardon, forgiveness; (clemencia) mercy; ¡~! sorry!, I beg your pardon!; **perdonar** vt to pardon, forgive; (la vida) to spare; (excusar) to exempt, excuse; ¡perdone (usted)! sorry!, I beg your pardon!

perdurar [perðu'rar] vi (resistir) to last, endure; (seguir existiendo) to stand, still exist

perecedero, a [pereθe'ðero, a] adj perishable

perecer [pere'θer] vi to perish, die

peregrinación [pereɣrina'θjon] nf (REL) pilgrimage

peregrino, a [pere'ɣrino, a] adj (idea) strange, absurd ♦ nm/f pilgrim

perejil [pere'xil] nm parsley

perenne [pe'renne] adj everlasting, perennial

pereza [pe're0a] nf laziness, idleness; **perezoso, a** adj lazy, idle

perfección [perfek'θjon] nf perfection; **perfeccionar** vt to perfect; (mejorar) to improve; (acabar) to complete, finish

perfectamente [perfekta'mente] adv perfectly

perfecto, a [per'fekto, a] adj perfect; (total) complete

perfil [per'fil] nm profile; (contorno) silhouette, outline; (ARQ) (cross) section; ~es nmpl features; ~ar vt (trazar) to outline; (fig) to shape, give character to

perforación [perfora'θjon] nf perforation; (con taladro) drilling; **perforadora** nf punch

perforar [perfo'rar] vt to perforate; (agujero) to drill, bore; (papel) to punch a hole in ♦ vi to drill, bore

perfume [per'fume] nm perfume, scent

pericia [pe'riθja] nf skill, expertise

periferia [peri'ferja] nf periphery; (de ciudad) outskirts pl

periférico [peri'feriko] (AM) nm ring road (BRIT), beltway (US)

perímetro [pe'rimetro] nm perimeter

periódico, a [pe'rjoðiko, a] adj periodic(al) ♦ nm newspaper

periodismo [perjo'ðismo] nm journalism; **periodista** nm/f journalist

periodo [pe'rjoðo] nm period

período [pe'rioðo] nm = **periodo**

periquito [peri'kito] nm budgerigar, budgie

perito, a [pe'rito, a] adj (experto) expert; (diestro) skilled, skilful ♦ nm/f expert; skilled worker; (técnico) technician

perjudicar [perxuði'kar] vt (gen) to damage, harm; **perjudicial** adj damaging, harmful; (en detrimento) detrimental; **perjuicio** nm damage, harm

perjurar [perxu'rar] vi to commit perjury

perla ['perla] nf pearl; **me viene de ~s** it suits me fine

permanecer [permane'θer] vi (quedarse) to stay, remain; (seguir) to continue to be

permanencia [perma'nenθja] nf permanence; (estancia) stay

permanente [perma'nente] adj permanent, constant ♦ nf perm

permiso [per'miso] nm permission; (licencia) permit, licence; **con ~** excuse me; **estar de ~** (MIL) to be on leave; **~ de conducir** driving licence (BRIT), driver's license (US)

permitir [permi'tir] vt to permit, allow

pernera [per'nera] nf trouser leg

pernicioso, a [perni'θjoso, a] adj pernicious

pero ['pero] conj but; (aún) yet ♦ nm (defecto) flaw, defect; (reparo) objection

perpendicular [perpendiku'lar] adj perpendicular

perpetrar [perpe'trar] vt to perpetrate

perpetuar [perpe'twar] vt to perpetuate; **perpetuo, a** adj perpetual

perplejo, a [per'plexo, a] adj perplexed, bewildered

perra ['perra] nf (ZOOL) bitch; **estar sin una ~** to be flat broke

perrera [pe'rrera] nf kennel

perrito [pe'rrito] nm: **~ caliente** hot dog

perro ['perro] nm dog

persa ['persa] adj, nm/f Persian

persecución [perseku'θjon] nf pursuit, chase; (REL, POL) persecution

perseguir [perse'ɣir] vt to pursue, hunt; (cortejar) to chase after; (molestar) to pester, annoy; (REL, POL) to persecute

perseverante [perseβe'rante] adj persevering, persistent

perseverar [perseβe'rar] vi to persevere, persist

persiana [per'sjana] nf (Venetian) blind

persignarse [persiɣ'narse] vr to cross o.s.

persistente [persis'tente] adj persistent

persistir [persis'tir] vi to persist

persona [per'sona] nf person; **~ mayor** elderly person

personaje [perso'naxe] nm important person, celebrity; (TEATRO etc) character

personal [perso'nal] adj (particular) personal; (para una persona) single, for one person ♦ nm personnel, staff; **~idad** nf personality

personarse [perso'narse] vr to appear in person

personificar [personifi'kar] vt to personify

perspectiva [perspek'tiβa] nf perspective; (vista, panorama) view, panorama; (posibilidad futura) outlook, prospect

perspicacia [perspi'kaθja] nf discernment, perspicacity

perspicaz [perspi'kaθ] *adj* shrewd
persuadir [perswa'ðir] *vt* (*gen*) to persuade; (*convencer*) to convince; **~se** *vr* to become convinced; **persuasión** *nf* persuasion; **persuasivo, a** *adj* persuasive; convincing
pertenecer [pertene'θer] *vi* to belong; (*fig*) to concern; **perteneciente** *adj*: **perteneciente a** belonging to; **pertenencia** *nf* ownership; **pertenencias** *nfpl* (*bienes*) possessions, property *sg*
pertenezca *etc vb ver* **pertenecer**
pértiga ['pertiya] *nf*: **salto de ~** pole vault
pertinente [perti'nente] *adj* relevant, pertinent; (*apropiado*) appropriate; **~ a** concerning, relevant to
perturbación [perturßa'θjon] *nf* (*POL*) disturbance; (*MED*) upset, disturbance
perturbado, a [pertur'ßaðo, a] *adj* mentally unbalanced
perturbar [pertur'ßar] *vt* (*el orden*) to disturb; (*MED*) to upset, disturb; (*mentalmente*) to perturb
Perú [pe'ru] *nm*: **el ~** Peru; **peruano, a** *adj, nm/f* Peruvian
perversión [perßer'sjon] *nf* perversion; **perverso, a** *adj* perverse; (*depravado*) depraved
pervertido, a [perßer'tiðo, a] *adj* perverted ♦ *nm/f* pervert
pervertir [perßer'tir] *vt* to pervert, corrupt
pesa ['pesa] *nf* weight; (*DEPORTE*) shot
pesadez [pesa'ðeθ] *nf* (*peso*) heaviness; (*lentitud*) slowness; (*aburrimiento*) tediousness
pesadilla [pesa'ðiʎa] *nf* nightmare, bad dream
pesado, a [pe'saðo, a] *adj* heavy; (*lento*) slow; (*difícil, duro*) tough, hard; (*aburrido*) boring, tedious; (*tiempo*) sultry
pésame ['pesame] *nm* expression of condolence, message of sympathy; **dar el ~** to express one's condolences
pesar [pe'sar] *vt* to weigh ♦ *vi* to weigh; (*ser pesado*) to weigh a lot, be heavy; (*fig: opinión*) to carry weight; **no pesa mucho** it is not very heavy ♦ *nm* (*arrepentimiento*) regret; (*pena*) grief, sorrow; **a ~ de** o **pese a (que)** in spite of, despite
pesca ['peska] *nf* (*acto*) fishing; (*lo pescado*) catch; **ir de ~** to go fishing
pescadería [peskaðe'ria] *nf* fish shop, fishmonger's (*BRIT*)
pescadilla [peska'ðiʎa] *nf* whiting
pescado [pes'kaðo] *nm* fish
pescador, a [peska'ðor, a] *nm/f* fisherman/woman
pescar [pes'kar] *vt* (*tomar*) to catch; (*intentar tomar*) to fish for; (*conseguir: trabajo*) to manage to get ♦ *vi* to fish, go fishing

pescuezo [pes'kweθo] *nm* neck
pesebre [pe'seßre] *nm* manger
peseta [pe'seta] *nf* peseta
pesimista [pesi'mista] *adj* pessimistic ♦ *nm/f* pessimist
pésimo, a ['pesimo, a] *adj* awful, dreadful
peso ['peso] *nm* weight; (*balanza*) scales *pl*; (*moneda*) peso; **~ bruto/neto** gross/net weight; **vender al ~** to sell by weight
pesquero, a [pes'kero, a] *adj* fishing *cpd*
pesquisa [pes'kisa] *nf* inquiry, investigation
pestaña [pes'taɲa] *nf* (*ANAT*) eyelash; (*borde*) rim; **pestañear** *vi* to blink
peste ['peste] *nf* plague; (*mal olor*) stink, stench
pesticida [pesti'θiða] *nm* pesticide
pestillo [pes'tiʎo] *nm* (*cerrojo*) bolt; (*picaporte*) doorhandle
petaca [pe'taka] *nf* (*de cigarros*) cigarette case; (*de pipa*) tobacco pouch; (*AM: maleta*) suitcase
pétalo ['petalo] *nm* petal
petardo [pe'tardo] *nm* firework, firecracker
petición [peti'θjon] *nf* (*pedido*) request, plea; (*memorial*) petition; (*JUR*) plea
petrificar [petrifi'kar] *vt* to petrify
petróleo [pe'troleo] *nm* oil, petroleum; **petrolero, a** *adj* petroleum *cpd* ♦ *nm* (oil) tanker
peyorativo, a [pejora'tißo, a] *adj* pejorative
pez [peθ] *nm* fish
pezón [pe'θon] *nm* teat, nipple
pezuña [pe'θuɲa] *nf* hoof
piadoso, a [pja'ðoso, a] *adj* (*devoto*) pious, devout; (*misericordioso*) kind, merciful
pianista [pja'nista] *nm/f* pianist
piano ['pjano] *nm* piano
piar [pjar] *vi* to cheep
pibe, a ['piße, a] (*AM*) *nm/f* boy/girl
picadero [pika'ðero] *nm* riding school
picadillo [pika'ðiʎo] *nm* mince, minced meat
picado, a [pi'kaðo, a] *adj* pricked, punctured; (*CULIN*) minced, chopped; (*mar*) choppy; (*diente*) bad; (*tabaco*) cut; (*enfadado*) cross
picador [pika'ðor] *nm* (*TAUR*) picador; (*minero*) faceworker
picadura [pika'ðura] *nf* (*pinchazo*) puncture; (*de abeja*) sting; (*de mosquito*) bite; (*tabaco picado*) cut tobacco
picante [pi'kante] *adj* hot; (*comentario*) racy, spicy
picaporte [pika'porte] *nm* (*manija*) doorhandle; (*pestillo*) latch
picar [pi'kar] *vt* (*agujerear, perforar*) to prick, puncture; (*abeja*) to sting; (*mosquito, serpiente*) to bite; (*CULIN*) to mince, chop; (*incitar*) to incite, goad; (*dañar, irritar*) to annoy, bother; (*quemar: lengua*) to burn,

sting ♦ vi (pez) to bite, take the bait; (sol) to burn, scorch; (abeja, MED) to sting; (mosquito) to bite; **~se** vr (agriarse) to turn sour, go off; (ofenderse) to take offence

picardía [pikar'ðia] nf villainy; (astucia) slyness, craftiness; (una ~) dirty trick; (palabra) rude/bad word o expression

pícaro, a ['pikaro, a] adj (malicioso) villainous; (travieso) mischievous ♦ nm (astuto) crafty sort; (sinvergüenza) rascal, scoundrel

pichón [pi'tʃon] nm young pigeon

pico ['piko] nm (de ave) beak; (punta) sharp point; (TEC) pick, pickaxe; (GEO) peak, summit; **y ~** and a bit

picor [pi'kor] nm itch

picotear [pikote'ar] vt to peck ♦ vi to nibble, pick

picudo, a [pi'kuðo, a] adj pointed, with a point

pidió etc vb ver **pedir**

pido etc vb ver **pedir**

pie [pje] (pl ~s) nm foot; (fig: motivo) motive, basis; (: fundamento) foothold; **ir a ~** to go on foot, walk; **estar de ~** to be standing (up); **ponerse de ~** to stand up; **de ~s a cabeza** from top to bottom; **al ~ de la letra** (citar) literally, verbatim; (copiar) exactly, word for word; **en ~ de guerra** on a war footing; **dar ~ a** to give cause for; **hacer ~** (en el agua) to touch (the) bottom

piedad [pje'ðað] nf (lástima) pity, compassion; (clemencia) mercy; (devoción) piety, devotion

piedra ['pjeðra] nf stone; (roca) rock; (de mechero) flint; (METEOROLOGÍA) hailstone

piel [pjel] nf (ANAT) skin; (ZOOL) skin, hide, fur; (cuero) leather; (BOT) skin, peel

pienso etc vb ver **pensar**

pierdo etc vb ver **perder**

pierna ['pjerna] nf leg

pieza ['pjeθa] nf piece; (habitación) room; **~ de recambio o repuesto** spare (part)

pigmeo, a [piɣ'meo, a] adj, nm/f pigmy

pijama [pi'xama] nm pyjamas pl

pila ['pila] nf (ELEC) battery; (montón) heap, pile; (lavabo) sink

píldora ['pildora] nf pill; **la ~ (anticonceptiva)** the (contraceptive) pill

pileta [pi'leta] nf basin, bowl; (AM) swimming pool

pillaje [pi'ʎaxe] nm pillage, plunder

pillar [pi'ʎar] vt (saquear) to pillage, plunder; (fam: coger) to catch; (: agarrar) to grasp, seize; (: entender) to grasp, catch on to; **~se** vr: **~se un dedo con la puerta** to catch one's finger in the door

pillo, a ['piʎo, a] adj villainous; (astuto) sly, crafty ♦ nm/f rascal, rogue, scoundrel

piloto [pi'loto] nm pilot; (de aparato) (pilot) light; (AUTO: luz) tail o rear light; (: conductor) driver

pimentón [pimen'ton] nm paprika

pimienta [pi'mjenta] nf pepper

pimiento [pi'mjento] nm pepper, pimiento

pin [pin] (pl pins) nm badge

pinacoteca [pinako'teka] nf art gallery

pinar [pi'nar] nm pine forest (BRIT), pine grove (US)

pincel [pin'θel] nm paintbrush

pinchadiscos [pintʃa'ðiskos] nm/f inv disc-jockey, DJ

pinchar [pin'tʃar] vt (perforar) to prick, pierce; (neumático) to puncture; (fig) to prod

pinchazo [pin'tʃaθo] nm (perforación) prick; (de neumático) puncture; (fig) prod

pincho ['pintʃo] nm savoury (snack); **~ moruno** shish kebab; **~ de tortilla** small slice of omelette

ping-pong ['pin'pon] nm table tennis

pingüino [pin'gwino] nm penguin

pino ['pino] nm pine (tree)

pinta ['pinta] nf spot; (de líquidos) spot, drop; (aspecto) appearance, look(s) (pl); **~do, a** adj spotted; (de colores) colourful; **~das** nfpl graffiti sg

pintar [pin'tar] vt to paint ♦ vi to paint; (fam) to count, be important; **~se** vr to put on make-up

pintor, a [pin'tor, a] nm/f painter

pintoresco, a [pinto'resko, a] adj picturesque

pintura [pin'tura] nf painting; **~ a la acuarela** watercolour; **~ al óleo** oil painting

pinza ['pinθa] nf (ZOOL) claw; (para colgar ropa) clothes peg; (TEC) pincers pl; **~s** nfpl (para depilar etc) tweezers pl

piña ['piɲa] nf (fruto del pino) pine cone; (fruta) pineapple; (fig) group

piñón [pi'ɲon] nm (fruto) pine nut; (TEC) pinion

pío, a ['pio, a] adj (devoto) pious, devout; (misericordioso) merciful

piojo ['pjoxo] nm louse

pionero, a [pjo'nero, a] adj pioneering ♦ nm/f pioneer

pipa ['pipa] nf pipe; **~s** nfpl (BOT) (edible) sunflower seeds

pipí [pi'pi] (fam) nm: **hacer ~** to have a wee(-wee) (BRIT), to have to go (wee-wee) (US)

pique ['pike] nm (resentimiento) pique, resentment; (rivalidad) rivalry, competition; **irse a ~** to sink; (esperanza, familia) to be ruined

piqueta [pi'keta] nf pick(axe)

piquete [pi'kete] nm (MIL) squad, party; (de obreros) picket

pirado, a [pi'raðo, a] (fam) adj round the

bend ♦ nm/f nutter

piragua [pi'raɣwa] nf canoe; **piragüismo** nm canoeing

pirámide [pi'ramiðe] nf pyramid

pirata [pi'rata] adj, nm pirate ♦ nm/f: ~ **informático/a** hacker

Pirineo(s) [piri'neo(s)] nm(pl) Pyrenees pl

pirómano, a [pi'romano, a] nm/f (MED, JUR) arsonist

piropo [pi'ropo] nm compliment, (piece of) flattery

pirueta [pi'rweta] nf pirouette

pis [pis] (fam) nm pee, piss; **hacer ~** to have a pee; (para niños) to wee-wee

pisada [pi'saða] nf (paso) footstep; (huella) footprint

pisar [pi'sar] vt (caminar sobre) to walk on, tread on; (apretar con el pie) to press; (fig) to trample on, walk all over ♦ vi to tread, step, walk

piscina [pis'θina] nf swimming pool

Piscis [pis'θis] nm Pisces

piso ['piso] nm (suelo, planta) floor; (apartamento) flat (BRIT), apartment; **primer ~** (ESP) first floor; (AM) ground floor

pisotear [pisote'ar] vt to trample (on o underfoot)

pista ['pista] nf track, trail; (indicio) clue; ~ **de aterrizaje** runway; ~ **de baile** dance floor; ~ **de hielo** ice rink; ~ **de tenis** tennis court

pistola [pis'tola] nf pistol; (TEC) spray-gun; **pistolero, a** nm/f gunman/woman, gangster

pistón [pis'ton] nm (TEC) piston; (MUS) key

pitar [pi'tar] vt (silbato) to blow; (rechiflar) to whistle at, boo ♦ vi to whistle; (AUTO) to sound o toot one's horn; (AM) to smoke

pitillo [pi'tiʎo] nm cigarette

pito ['pito] nm whistle; (de coche) horn

pitonisa [pito'nisa] nf fortune-teller

pitorreo [pito'rreo] nm joke; **estar de ~** to be joking

pizarra [pi'θarra] nf (piedra) slate; (encerado) blackboard

pizca ['piθka] nf pinch, spot; (fig) spot, speck; **ni ~** not a bit

placa ['plaka] nf plate; (distintivo) badge, insignia; ~ **de matrícula** number plate

placentero, a [plaθen'tero, a] adj pleasant, agreeable

placer [pla'θer] nm pleasure ♦ vt to please

plácido, a [pla'θiðo, a] adj placid

plaga ['plaɣa] nf pest; (MED) plague; (abundancia) abundance; **plagar** vt to infest, plague; (llenar) to fill

plagio ['plaxjo] nm plagiarism

plan [plan] nm (esquema, proyecto) plan; (idea, intento) idea, intention; **tener ~** (fam) to have a date; **tener un ~** (fam) to have an affair; **en ~ económico** (fam) on the cheap; **vamos en ~ de turismo** we're going as tourists; **si te pones en ese ~** ... if that's your attitude ...

plana ['plana] nf sheet (of paper), page; (TEC) trowel; **en primera ~** on the front page; ~ **mayor** staff

plancha ['plantʃa] nf (para planchar) iron; (rótulo) plate, sheet; (NAUT) gangway; **a la ~** (CULIN) grilled; ~**do** nm ironing; **planchar** vt to iron ♦ vi to do the ironing

planeador [planea'ðor] nm glider

planear [plane'ar] vt to plan ♦ vi to glide

planeta [pla'neta] nm planet

planicie [pla'niθje] nf plain

planificación [planifika'θjon] nf planning; ~ **familiar** family planning

plano, a ['plano, a] adj flat, level, even ♦ nm (MAT, TEC) plane; (FOTO) shot; (ARQ) plan; (GEO) map; (de ciudad) map, street plan; **primer ~** close-up; **caer de ~** to fall flat

planta ['planta] nf (BOT, TEC) plant; (ANAT) sole of the foot, foot; (piso) floor; (AM: personal) staff; ~ **baja** ground floor

plantación [planta'θjon] nf (AGR) plantation; (acto) planting

plantar [plan'tar] vt (BOT) to plant; (levantar) to erect, set up; ~**se** vi to stand firm; ~ **a uno en la calle** to throw sb out; **dejar plantado a uno** (fam) to stand sb up

plantear [plante'ar] vt (problema) to pose; (dificultad) to raise

plantilla [plan'tiʎa] nf (de zapato) insole; (personal) personnel; **ser de ~** to be on the staff

plantón [plan'ton] nm (MIL) guard, sentry; (fam) long wait; **dar (un) ~ a uno** to stand sb up

plasmar [plas'mar] vt (dar forma) to mould, shape; (representar) to represent; ~**se** vr: ~**se en** to take the form of

plasta ['plasta] (fam) adj inv boring ♦ nm/f bore

plástico, a ['plastiko, a] adj plastic ♦ nm plastic

Plastilina ® [plasti'lina] nf Plasticine ®

plata ['plata] nf (metal) silver; (cosas hechas de ~) silverware; (AM) cash, dough; **hablar en ~** to speak bluntly o frankly

plataforma [plata'forma] nf platform; ~ **de lanzamiento/perforación** launch(ing) pad/drilling rig

plátano ['platano] nm (fruta) banana; (árbol) plane tree; banana tree

platea [pla'tea] nf (TEATRO) pit

plateado, a [plate'aðo, a] adj silver; (TEC) silver-plated

plática ['platika] nf talk, chat; **platicar** vi to talk, chat

platillo [pla'tiʎo] nm saucer; **~s** nmpl (MUS) cymbals; **~ volador** o **volante** flying saucer

platino [pla'tino] nm platinum; **~s** nmpl (AUTO) contact points

plato ['plato] nm plate, dish; (parte de comida) course; (comida) dish; **~ combinado** set main course (served on one plate); **~ fuerte** main course; **primer ~** first course

playa ['plaja] nf beach; (costa) seaside; **~ de estacionamiento** (AM) car park

playera [pla'jera] nf (AM: camiseta) T-shirt; **~s** nfpl (zapatos) canvas shoes

plaza ['plaθa] nf square; (mercado) market(place); (sitio) room, space; (en vehículo) seat, place; (colocación) post, job; **~ de toros** bullring

plazo ['plaθo] nm (lapso de tiempo) time, period; (fecha de vencimiento) expiry date; (pago parcial) instalment; **a corto/largo ~** short-/long-term; **comprar algo a ~s** to buy sth on hire purchase (BRIT) o on time (US)

plazoleta [plaθo'leta] nf small square

pleamar [plea'mar] nf high tide

plebe ['pleβe] nf: **la ~** the common people pl, the masses pl; (pey) the plebs pl; **~yo, a** adj plebeian; (pey) coarse, common

plebiscito [pleβis'θito] nm plebiscite

plegable [ple'ɣaβle] adj collapsible; (silla) folding

plegar [ple'ɣar] vt (doblar) to fold, bend; (COSTURA) to pleat; **~se** vr to yield, submit

pleito ['pleito] nm (JUR) lawsuit, case; (fig) dispute, feud

plenilunio [pleni'lunjo] nm full moon

plenitud [pleni'tuð] nf plenitude, fullness; (abundancia) abundance

pleno, a ['pleno, a] adj full; (completo) complete ♦ nm plenum; **en ~ día** in broad daylight; **en ~ verano** at the height of summer; **en plena cara** full in the face

pliego etc ['pljeɣo] vb ver **plegar** ♦ nm (hoja) sheet (of paper); (carta) sealed letter/document; **~ de condiciones** details pl, specifications pl

pliegue etc ['pljeɣe] vb ver **plegar** ♦ nm fold, crease; (de vestido) pleat

plomero [plo'mero] nm (AM) plumber

plomo ['plomo] nm (metal) lead; (ELEC) fuse; **sin ~** unleaded

pluma ['pluma] nf feather; (para escribir): **~ (estilográfica)** ink pen; **~ fuente** (AM) fountain pen

plumero [plu'mero] nm (para el polvo) feather duster

plumón [plu'mon] nm (de ave) down; (AM: fino) felt-tip pen; (: ancho) marker

plural [plu'ral] adj plural; **~idad** nf plurality

pluriempleo [pluriem'pleo] nm having more than one job

plus [plus] nm bonus; **~valía** nf (COM) appreciation

población [poβla'θjon] nf population; (pueblo, ciudad) town, city

poblado, a [po'βlaðo, a] adj inhabited ♦ nm (aldea) village; (pueblo) (small) town; **densamente ~** densely populated

poblador, a [poβla'ðor, a] nm/f settler, colonist

poblar [po'βlar] vt (colonizar) to colonize; (fundar) to found; (habitar) to inhabit

pobre ['poβre] adj poor ♦ nm/f poor person; **~za** nf poverty

pocilga [po'θilɣa] nf pigsty

pócima ['poθima] nf = **poción**

PALABRA CLAVE
---

poco, a ['poko, a] adj 1 (sg) little, not much; **~ tiempo** little o not much time; **de ~ interés** of little interest, not very interesting; **poca cosa** not much

2 (pl) few, not many; **unos ~s** a few, some; **~s niños comen lo que les conviene** few children eat what they should

♦ adv 1 little, not much; **cuesta ~** it doesn't cost much

2 (+ adj: = negativo, antónimo): **~ amable/inteligente** not very nice/intelligent

3: **por ~ me caigo** I almost fell

4: **a ~: a ~ de haberse casado** shortly after getting married

5: **~ a ~** little by little

♦ nm a little, a bit; **un ~ triste/de dinero** a little sad/money

---

podar [po'ðar] vt to prune

PALABRA CLAVE
---

poder [po'ðer] vi 1 (capacidad) can, be able to; **no puedo hacerlo** I can't do it, I'm unable to do it

2 (permiso) can, may, be allowed to; **¿se puede?** may I (o we)?; **puedes irte ahora** you may go now; **no se puede fumar en este hospital** smoking is not allowed in this hospital

3 (posibilidad) may, might, could; **puede llegar mañana** he may o might arrive tomorrow; **pudiste haberte hecho daño** you might o could have hurt yourself; **¡podías habérmelo dicho antes!** you might have told me before!

4: **puede ser: puede ser** perhaps; **puede ser que lo sepa Tomás** Tomás may o might know

5: **¡no puedo más!** I've had enough!; **no pude menos que dejarlo** I couldn't help but leave it; **es tonto a más no ~** he's as stupid as they come

6: **~ con: no puedo con este crío** this kid's too

much for me
♦ *nm* power; ~ **adquisitivo** purchasing power; **detentar** *o* **ocupar** *o* **estar en el** ~ to be in power

poderoso, a |poðeroso, a| *adj* (*político, país*) powerful

podio |'poðjo| *nm* (*DEPORTE*) podium

podium |'poðjum| = **podio**

podrido, a |po'ðriðo, a| *adj* rotten, bad; (*fig*) rotten, corrupt

podrir |po'ðrir| = **pudrir**

poema |po'ema| *nm* poem

poesía |poe'sia| *nf* poetry

poeta |po'eta| *nm/f* poet; **poético, a** *adj* poetic(al)

poetisa |poe'tisa| *nf* (woman) poet

póker |'poker| *nm* poker

polaco, a |po'lako, a| *adj* Polish ♦ *nm/f* Pole

polar |po'lar| *adj* polar; ~**idad** *nf* polarity; ~**izarse** *vr* to polarize

polea |po'lea| *nf* pulley

polémica |po'lemika| *nf* polemics *sg*; (*una* ~) controversy, polemic

polen |'polen| *nm* pollen

policía |poli'θia| *nm/f* policeman/woman ♦ *nf* police; ~**co, a** *adj* police *cpd*; **novela policiaca** detective story; **policial** *adj* police *cpd*

polideportivo |poliðepor'tiβo| *nm* sports centre *o* complex

poligamia |poli'γamja| *nf* polygamy

polígono |po'liγono| *nm* (*MAT*) polygon; ~ **industrial** industrial estate

polilla |po'liʎa| *nf* moth

polio |'poljo| *nf* polio

política |po'litika| *nf* politics *sg*; (*económica, agraria etc*) policy; *ver tb* **político**

político, a |po'litiko, a| *adj* political; (*discreto*) tactful; (*de familia*) -in-law ♦ *nm/f* politician; **padre** ~ father-in-law

póliza |'poliθa| *nf* certificate, voucher; (*impuesto*) tax stamp; ~ **de seguros** insurance policy

polizón |poli'θon| *nm* stowaway

pollera |po'ʎera| (*AM*) *nf* skirt

pollería |poʎe'ria| *nf* poulterer's (shop)

pollo |'poʎo| *nm* chicken

polo |'polo| *nm* (*GEO, ELEC*) pole; (*helado*) ice lolly; (*DEPORTE*) polo; (*suéter*) polo-neck; ~ **Norte/Sur** North/South Pole

Polonia |po'lonja| *nf* Poland

poltrona |pol'trona| *nf* easy chair

polución |polu'θjon| *nf* pollution

polvera |pol'βera| *nf* powder compact

polvo |'polβo| *nm* dust; (*QUÍM, CULIN, MED*) powder; ~**s** *nmpl* (*maquillaje*) powder *sg*; **quitar el** ~ to dust; ~ **de talco** talcum powder;

estar hecho ~ (*fam*) to be worn out *o* exhausted

pólvora |'polβora| *nf* gunpowder; (*fuegos artificiales*) fireworks *pl*

polvoriento, a |polβo'rjento, a| *adj* (*superficie*) dusty; (*sustancia*) powdery

pomada |po'maða| *nf* cream, ointment

pomelo |po'melo| *nm* grapefruit

pómez |'pomeθ| *nf*: **piedra** ~ pumice stone

pomo |'pomo| *nm* doorknob

pompa |'pompa| *nf* (*burbuja*) bubble; (*bomba*) pump; (*esplendor*) pomp, splendour; **pomposo, a** *adj* splendid, magnificent; (*pey*) pompous

pómulo |'pomulo| *nm* cheekbone

pon |pon| *vb ver* **poner**

ponche |'pontʃe| *nm* punch

poncho |'pontʃo| *nm* poncho

ponderar |ponde'rar| *vt* (*considerar*) to weigh up, consider; (*elogiar*) to praise highly, speak in praise of

pondré *etc vb ver* **poner**

──── PALABRA CLAVE ────

poner |po'ner| *vt* **1** (*colocar*) to put; (*telegrama*) to send; (*obra de teatro*) to put on; (*película*) to show; **ponlo más fuerte** turn it up; **¿qué ponen en el Excelsior?** what's on at the Excelsior?

2 (*tienda*) to open; (*instalar: gas etc*) to put in; (*radio, TV*) to switch *o* turn on

3 (*suponer*): **pongamos que ...** let's suppose that ...

4 (*contribuir*): **el gobierno ha puesto otro millón** the government has contributed another million

5 (*TELEC*): **póngame con el Sr. López** can you put me through to Mr. López?

6: ~ **de**: **le han puesto de director general** they've appointed him general manager

7 (+ *adj*) to make; **me estás poniendo nerviosa** you're making me nervous

8 (*dar nombre*): **al hijo le pusieron Diego** they called their son Diego

♦ *vi* (*gallina*) to lay

♦ ~**se** *vr* **1** (*colocarse*): **se puso a mi lado** he came and stood beside me; **tú ponte en esa silla** you go and sit on that chair

2 (*vestido, cosméticos*) to put on; **¿por qué no te pones el vestido nuevo?** why don't you put on *o* wear your new dress?

3 (+ *adj*) to turn; to get, become; **se puso muy serio** he got very serious; **después de lavarla la tela se puso azul** after washing it the material turned blue

4: ~**se a**: **se puso a llorar** he started to cry; **tienes que ~te a estudiar** you must get down to studying

5: ~**se a bien con uno** to make it up with sb;

~se a mal con uno to get on the wrong side of sb

pongo etc vb ver **poner**
poniente [po'njente] nm (occidente) west; (viento) west wind
pontífice [pon'tifiθe] nm pope, pontiff
popa ['popa] nf stern
popular [popu'lar] adj popular; (cultura) of the people, folk cpd; **~idad** nf popularity; **~izarse** vr to become popular

---

PALABRA CLAVE

---

por [por] prep **1** (objetivo) for; **luchar ~ la patria** to fight for one's country
2 (+ infin): **~ no llegar tarde** so as not to arrive late; **~ citar unos ejemplos** to give a few examples
3 (causa) out of, because of; **~ escasez de fondos** through o for lack of funds
4 (tiempo): **~ la mañana/noche** in the morning/at night; **se queda ~ una semana** she's staying (for) a week
5 (lugar): **pasar ~ Madrid** to pass through Madrid; **ir a Guayaquil ~ Quito** to go to Guayaquil via Quito; **caminar ~ la calle** to walk along the street; ver tb **todo**
6 (cambio, precio): **te doy uno nuevo ~ el que tienes** I'll give you a new one (in return) for the one you've got
7 (valor distributivo): **550 pesetas ~ hora/cabeza** 550 pesetas an o per hour/a o per head
8 (modo, medio) by; **~ correo/avión** by post/air; **día ~ día** day by day; **entrar ~ la entrada principal** to go in through the main entrance
9: **10 ~ 10 son 100** 10 times 10 is 100
10 (en lugar de): **vino él ~ su jefe** he came instead of his boss
11: **~ mí que revienten** as far as I'm concerned they can drop dead
12: **¿~ qué?** why?; **¿~ qué no?** why not?

---

porcelana [porθe'lana] nf porcelain; (china) china
porcentaje [porθen'taxe] nm percentage
porción [por'θjon] nf (parte) portion, share; (cantidad) quantity, amount
pordiosero, a [pordjo'sero, a] nm/f beggar
porfiar [por'fjar] vi to persist, insist; (disputar) to argue stubbornly
pormenor [porme'nor] nm detail, particular
pornografía [pornoɣra'fia] nf pornography
poro ['poro] nm pore; **~so, a** adj porous
porque ['porke] conj (a causa de) because; (ya que) since; (con el fin de) so that, in order that
porqué [por'ke] nm reason, cause
porquería [porke'ria] nf (suciedad) filth, dirt;

(acción) dirty trick; (objeto) small thing, trifle; (fig) rubbish
porra ['porra] nf (arma) stick, club
porrazo [po'rraθo] nm blow, bump
porro ['porro] nm (fam) (droga) joint (fam)
porrón [po'rron] nm glass wine jar with a long spout
portaaviones [porta(a)ßjones] nm inv aircraft carrier
portada [por'taða] nf (de revista) cover
portador, a [porta'ðor, a] nm/f carrier, bearer; (COM) bearer, payee
portaequipajes [portaeki'paxes] nm inv (AUTO: maletero) boot; (: baca) luggage rack
portal [por'tal] nm (entrada) vestibule, hall; (portada) porch, doorway; (puerta de entrada) main door
portamaletas [portama'letas] nm inv (AUTO: maletero) boot; (: baca) roof rack
portarse [por'tarse] vr to behave, conduct o.s.
portátil [por'tatil] adj portable
portavoz [porta'ßoθ] nm/f spokesman/woman
portazo [por'taθo] nm: **dar un ~** to slam the door
porte ['porte] nm (COM) transport; (precio) transport charges pl
portento [por'tento] nm marvel, wonder; **~so, a** adj marvellous, extraordinary
porteño, a [por'teno, a] adj of o from Buenos Aires
portería [porte'ria] nf (oficina) porter's office; (DEPORTE) goal
portero, a [por'tero, a] nm/f porter; (conserje) caretaker; (ujier) doorman; (DEPORTE) goalkeeper; **~ automático** intercom
pórtico ['portiko] nm (patio) portico, porch; (fig) gateway; (arcada) arcade
portorriqueño, a [portorri'keno, a] adj Puerto Rican
Portugal [portu'val] nm Portugal; **portugués, esa** adj, nm/f Portuguese ♦ nm (LING) Portuguese
porvenir [porße'nir] nm future
pos [pos] prep: **en ~ de** after, in pursuit of
posada [po'saða] nf (refugio) shelter, lodging; (mesón) guest house; **dar ~ a** to give shelter to, take in
posaderas [posa'ðeras] nfpl backside sg, buttocks
posar [po'sar] vt (en el suelo) to lay down, put down; (la mano) to place, put gently ♦ vi (modelo) to sit, pose; **~se** vr to settle; (pájaro) to perch; (avión) to land, come down
posavasos [posa'basos] nm inv coaster; (para cerveza) beermat
posdata [pos'ðata] nf postscript
pose ['pose] nf pose
poseedor, a [posee'ðor, a] nm/f owner,

possessor; (*de récord, puesto*) holder

poseer |pose'er| *vt* to possess, own; (*ventaja*) to enjoy; (*récord, puesto*) to hold

posesión [pose'sjon] *nf* possession; **posesionarse** *vr*: **posesionarse de** to take possession of, take over

posesivo, a [pose'siβo, a] *adj* possessive

posgrado [pos'graðo] *nm*: **curso de ~** postgraduate course

posibilidad [posiβili'ðað] *nf* possibility; (*oportunidad*) chance; **posibilitar** *vt* to make possible; (*hacer realizable*) to make feasible

posible [po'siβle] *adj* possible; (*realizable*) feasible; **de ser ~** if possible; **en lo ~** as far as possible

posición [posi'θjon] *nf* position; (*rango social*) status

positivo, a [posi'tiβo, a] *adj* positive

poso ['poso] *nm* sediment; (*heces*) dregs *pl*

posponer [pospo'ner] *vt* (*relegar*) to put behind/below; (*aplazar*) to postpone

posta ['posta] *nf*: **a ~** deliberately, on purpose

postal [pos'tal] *adj* postal ♦ *nf* postcard

poste ['poste] *nm* (*de telégrafos etc*) post, pole; (*columna*) pillar

póster ['poster] (*pl* **pósteres, pósters**) *nm* poster

postergar [poster'γar] *vt* to postpone, delay

posteridad |posteri'ðað| *nf* posterity

posterior [poste'rjor] *adj* back, rear; (*siguiente*) following, subsequent; (*más tarde*) later; **~idad** *nf*: **con ~idad** later, subsequently

postgrado [post'graðo] *nm* = **posgrado**

postizo, a [pos'tiθo, a] *adj* false, artificial ♦ *nm* hairpiece

postor, a [pos'tor, a] *nm/f* bidder

postre ['postre] *nm* sweet, dessert

postrero, a [pos'trero, a] (*delante de nmsg*: **postrer**) *adj* (*último*) last; (*que viene detrás*) rear

postulado [postu'laðo] *nm* postulate

póstumo, a ['postumo, a] *adj* posthumous

postura [pos'tura] *nf* (*del cuerpo*) posture, position; (*fig*) attitude, position

potable [po'taβle] *adj* drinkable; **agua ~** drinking water

potaje [po'taxe] *nm* thick vegetable soup

pote ['pote] *nm* pot, jar

potencia |po'tenθja| *nf* power; **~l** |poten'θjal| *adj, nm* potential; **~r** *vt* to boost

potente |po'tente| *adj* powerful

potro, a ['potro, a] *nm/f* (*ZOOL*) colt/filly ♦ *nm* (*de gimnasia*) vaulting horse

pozo ['poθo] *nm* well; (*de río*) deep pool; (*de mina*) shaft

P.P. *abr* (= *porte pagado*) CP

práctica ['praktika] *nf* practice; (*método*) method; (*arte, capacidad*) skill; **en la ~** in practice

practicable [prakti'kaβle] *adj* practicable; (*camino*) passable

practicante [prakti'kante] *nm/f* (*MED*: *ayudante de doctor*) medical assistant; (: *enfermero*) nurse; (*quien practica algo*) practitioner ♦ *adj* practising

practicar [prakti'kar] *vt* to practise; (*DEPORTE*) to play; (*realizar*) to carry out, perform

práctico, a [a 'praktiko, a] *adj* practical; (*instruído*: *persona*) skilled, expert

practique *etc vb ver* **practicar**

pradera [pra'ðera] *nf* meadow; (*US etc*) prairie

prado ['praðo] *nm* (*campo*) meadow, field; (*pastizal*) pasture

Praga ['praγa] *n* Prague

pragmático, a [praγ'matiko, a] *adj* pragmatic

preámbulo [pre'ambulo] *nm* preamble, introduction

precario, a [pre'karjo, a] *adj* precarious

precaución [prekau'θjon] *nf* (*medida preventiva*) preventive measure, precaution; (*prudencia*) caution, wariness

precaver [preka'βer] *vt* to guard against; (*impedir*) to forestall; **~se** *vr*: **~se de** *o* **contra algo** to (be on one's) guard against sth; **precavido, a** *adj* cautious, wary

precedente [preθe'ðente] *adj* preceding; (*anterior*) former ♦ *nm* precedent

preceder [preθe'ðer] *vt*, *vi* to precede, go before, come before

precepto [pre'θepto] *nm* precept

preciado, a [pre'θjaðo, a] *adj* (*estimado*) esteemed, valuable

preciarse [pre'θjarse] *vr* to boast; **~se de** to pride o.s. on, boast of being

precinto [pre'θinto] *nm* (*tb*: **~ de garantía**) seal

precio ['preθjo] *nm* price; (*costo*) cost; (*valor*) value, worth; (*de viaje*) fare; **~ al contado/de coste/de oportunidad** cash/cost/bargain price; **~ al detalle** *o* **al por menor** retail price; **~ tope** top price

preciosidad [preθjosi'ðað] *nf* (*valor*) (high) value, (great) worth; (*encanto*) charm; (*cosa bonita*) beautiful thing; **es una ~** it's lovely, it's really beautiful

precioso, a [pre'θjoso, a] *adj* precious; (*de mucho valor*) valuable; (*fam*) lovely, beautiful

precipicio [preθi'piθjo] *nm* cliff, precipice; (*fig*) abyss

precipitación [preθipita'θjon] *nf* haste; (*lluvia*) rainfall

precipitado, a [preθipi'taðo, a] *adj* (*conducta*) hasty, rash; (*salida*) hasty, sudden

precipitar [preθipi'tar] *vt* (*arrojar*) to hurl down, throw; (*apresurar*) to hasten; (*acelerar*) to speed up, accelerate; **~se** *vr* to throw o.s.; (*apresurarse*) to rush; (*actuar sin pensar*) to act rashly

precisamente [preθisa'mente] *adv* precisely; (*exactamente*) precisely, exactly

precisar [preθi'sar] *vt* (*necesitar*) to need, require; (*fijar*) to determine exactly, fix; (*especificar*) to specify

precisión [preθi'sjon] *nf* (*exactitud*) precision

preciso, a [pre'θiso, a] *adj* (*exacto*) precise; (*necesario*) necessary, essential

preconcebido, a [prekonθe'ßiðo, a] *adj* preconceived

precoz [pre'koθ] *adj* (*persona*) precocious; (*calvicie etc*) premature

precursor, a [prekur'sor, a] *nm/f* predecessor, forerunner

predecir [preðe'θir] *vt* to predict, forecast

predestinado, a [preðesti'naðo, a] *adj* predestined

predicar [preði'kar] *vt, vi* to preach

predicción [preðik'θjon] *nf* prediction

predilecto, a [preði'lekto, a] *adj* favourite

predisponer [preðispo'ner] *vt* to predispose; (*pey*) to prejudice; **predisposición** *nf* inclination; prejudice, bias

predominante [preðomi'nante] *adj* predominant

predominar [preðomi'nar] *vt* to dominate ♦ *vi* to predominate; (*prevalecer*) to prevail; **predominio** *nm* predominance; prevalence

preescolar [pre(e)sko'lar] *adj* preschool

prefabricado, a [prefaßri'kaðo, a] *adj* prefabricated

prefacio [pre'faθjo] *nm* preface

preferencia [prefe'renθja] *nf* preference; **de ~** preferably, for preference

preferible [prefe'rißle] *adj* preferable

preferir [prefe'rir] *vt* to prefer

prefiero *etc vb ver* **preferir**

prefijo [pre'fixo] *nm* (*TELEC*) (dialling) code

pregonar [preɣo'nar] *vt* to proclaim, announce

pregunta [pre'ɣunta] *nf* question; **hacer una ~** to ask a question

preguntar [preɣun'tar] *vt* to ask; (*cuestionar*) to question ♦ *vi* to ask; **~se** *vr* to wonder; **~ por alguien** to ask for sb

preguntón, ona [preɣun'ton, ona] *adj* inquisitive

prehistórico, a [preis'toriko, a] *adj* prehistoric

prejuicio [pre'xwiθjo] *nm* (*acto*) prejudgement; (*idea preconcebida*) preconception; (*parcialidad*) prejudice, bias

preliminar [prelimi'nar] *adj* preliminary

preludio [pre'luðjo] *nm* prelude

prematuro, a [prema'turo, a] *adj* premature

premeditación [premeðita'θjon] *nf* premeditation

premeditar [premeði'tar] *vt* to premeditate

premiar [pre'mjar] *vt* to reward; (*en un concurso*) to give a prize to

premio ['premjo] *nm* reward; prize; (*COM*) premium

premonición [premoni'θjon] *nf* premonition

prenatal [prena'tal] *adj* antenatal, prenatal

prenda ['prenda] *nf* (*ropa*) garment, article of clothing; (*garantía*) pledge; **~s** *nfpl* (*talentos*) talents, gifts

prendedor [prende'ðor] *nm* brooch

prender [pren'der] *vt* (*captar*) to catch, capture; (*detener*) to arrest; (*COSTURA*) to pin, attach; (*sujetar*) to fasten ♦ *vi* to catch; (*arraigar*) to take root; **~se** *vr* (*encenderse*) to catch fire

prendido, a [pren'diðo, a] (*AM*) *adj* (*luz etc*) on

prensa ['prensa] *nf* press; **la ~** the press; **prensar** *vt* to press

preñado, a [pre'ɲaðo, a] *adj* pregnant; **~ de** pregnant with, full of

preocupación [preokupa'θjon] *nf* worry, concern; (*ansiedad*) anxiety

preocupado, a [preoku'paðo, a] *adj* worried, concerned; (*ansioso*) anxious

preocupar [preoku'par] *vt* to worry; **~se** *vr* to worry; **~se de algo** (*hacerse cargo*) to take care of sth

preparación [prepara'θjon] *nf* (*acto*) preparation; (*estado*) readiness; (*entrenamiento*) training

preparado, a [prepa'raðo, a] *adj* (*dispuesto*) prepared; (*CULIN*) ready (to serve) ♦ *nm* preparation

preparar [prepa'rar] *vt* (*disponer*) to prepare, get ready; (*TEC: tratar*) to prepare, process; (*entrenar*) to teach, train; **~se** *vr*: **~se a** o **para** to prepare to o for, get ready to o for; **preparativo, a** *adj* preparatory, preliminary; **preparativos** *nmpl* preparations; **preparatoria** (*AM*) *nf* sixth-form college (*BRIT*), senior high school (*US*)

prerrogativa [prerroɣa'tißa] *nf* prerogative, privilege

presa ['presa] *nf* (*cosa apresada*) catch; (*víctima*) victim; (*de animal*) prey; (*de agua*) dam

presagiar [presa'xjar] *vt* to presage, forebode; **presagio** *nm* omen

prescindir [presθin'dir] *vi*: **~ de** (*privarse de*) to do without, go without; (*descartar*) to dispense with

prescribir [preskri'ßir] *vt* to prescribe; **prescripción** *nf* prescription

presencia [pre'senθja] *nf* presence; **presencial** *adj*: **testigo presencial** eyewitness; **presenciar** *vt* to be present at;

(*asistir a*) to attend; (*ver*) to see, witness

presentación [presenta'θjon] *nf* presentation; (*introducción*) introduction

presentador, a [presenta'ðor, a] *nm/f* presenter, compère

presentar [presen'tar] *vt* to present; (*ofrecer*) to offer; (*mostrar*) to show, display; (*a una persona*) to introduce; **~se** *vr* (*llegar inesperadamente*) to appear, turn up; (*ofrecerse como candidato*) to run, stand; (*aparecer*) to show, appear; (*solicitar empleo*) to apply

presente [pre'sente] *adj* present ♦ *nm* present; **hacer ~** to state, declare; **tener ~** to remember, bear in mind

presentimiento [presenti'mjento] *nm* premonition, presentiment

presentir [presen'tir] *vt* to have a premonition of

preservación [preserßa'θjon] *nf* protection, preservation

preservar [preser'ßar] *vt* to protect, preserve; **preservativo** *nm* sheath, condom

presidencia [presi'ðenθja] *nf* presidency; (*de comité*) chairmanship

presidente [presi'ðente] *nm/f* president; (*de comité*) chairman/woman

presidiario [presi'ðjarjo] *nm* convict

presidio [pre'sidjo] *nm* prison, penitentiary

presidir [presi'ðir] *vt* (*dirigir*) to preside at, preside over; (: *comité*) to take the chair at; (*dominar*) to dominate, rule ♦ *vi* to preside; to take the chair

presión [pre'sjon] *nf* pressure; **presionar** *vt* to press; (*fig*) to press, put pressure on ♦ *vi*: **presionar para** to press for

preso, a ['preso, a] *nm/f* prisoner; **tomar o llevar ~ a uno** to arrest sb, take sb prisoner

prestación [presta'θjon] *nf* service; (*subsidio*) benefit; **prestaciones** *nfpl* (*TEC, AUT*) performance features

prestado, a [pres'taðo, a] *adj* on loan; **pedir ~** to borrow

prestamista [presta'mista] *nm/f* moneylender

préstamo ['prestamo] *nm* loan; **~ hipotecario** mortgage

prestar [pres'tar] *vt* to lend, loan; (*atención*) to pay; (*ayuda*) to give

presteza [pres'teθa] *nf* speed, promptness

prestigio [pres'tixjo] *nm* prestige; (*honorable*) prestigious; (*famoso, renombrado*) renowned, famous

presumido, a [presu'miðo, a] *adj* (*persona*) vain

presumir [presu'mir] *vt* to presume ♦ *vi* (*tener aires*) to be conceited; **según cabe ~** as may be presumed, presumably; **presunción** *nf* presumption; **presunto, a** *adj* (*supuesto*)

supposed, presumed; (*así llamado*) so-called;

presuntuoso, a *adj* conceited, presumptuous

presuponer [presupo'ner] *vt* to presuppose

presupuesto [presu'pwesto] *pp de* **presuponer** ♦ *nm* (*FINANZAS*) budget; (*estimación: de costo*) estimate

pretencioso, a [preten'θjoso, a] *adj* pretentious

pretender [preten'der] *vt* (*intentar*) to try to, seek to; (*reivindicar*) to claim; (*buscar*) to seek, try for; (*cortejar*) to woo, court; **~ que** to expect that; **pretendiente** *nm/f* (*amante*) suitor; (*al trono*) pretender; **pretensión** *nf* (*aspiración*) aspiration; (*reivindicación*) claim; (*orgullo*) pretension

pretexto [pre'teksto] *nm* pretext; (*excusa*) excuse

prevalecer [preßale'θer] *vi* to prevail

prevención [preßen'θjon] *nf* prevention; (*precaución*) precaution

prevenido, a [preße'niðo, a] *adj* prepared, ready; (*cauteloso*) cautious

prevenir [preße'nir] *vt* (*impedir*) to prevent; (*predisponer*) to prejudice, bias; (*avisar*) to warn; (*preparar*) to prepare, get ready; **~se** *vr* to get ready, prepare; **~se contra** to take precautions against; **preventivo, a** *adj* preventive, precautionary

prever [pre'ßer] *vt* to foresee

previo, a ['preßjo, a] *adj* (*anterior*) previous; (*preliminar*) preliminary ♦ *prep*: **~ acuerdo de los otros** subject to the agreement of the others

previsión [preßi'sjon] *nf* (*perspicacia*) foresight; (*predicción*) forecast; **previsto, a** *adj* anticipated, forecast

prima ['prima] *nf* (*COM*) bonus; **~ de seguro** insurance premium; *ver tb* **primo**

primacía [prima'θia] *nf* primacy

primario, a [pri'marjo, a] *adj* primary

primavera [prima'ßera] *nf* spring(-time)

primera [pri'mera] *nf* (*AUTO*) first gear; (*FERRO: tb*: **~ clase**) first class; **de ~** (*fam*) first-class, first-rate

primero, a [pri'mero, a] (*delante de nmsg:* **primer**) *adj* first; (*principal*) prime ♦ *adv* first; (*más bien*) sooner, rather; **primera plana** front page

primicia [pri'miθja] *nf* (*tb*: **~ informativa**) scoop

primitivo, a [primi'tißo, a] *adj* primitive; (*original*) original

primo, a ['primo, a] *adj* prime ♦ *nm/f* cousin; (*fam*) fool, idiot; **~ hermano** first cousin; **materias primas** raw materials

primogénito, a [primo'xenito, a] *adj* first-born

primordial [primor'ðjal] *adj* basic,

fundamental

primoroso, a |primoˈroso, a| *adj* exquisite, delicate

princesa |prinˈθesa| *nf* princess

principal |prinθiˈpal| *adj* principal, main ♦ *nm* (*jefe*) chief, principal

príncipe |ˈprinθipe| *nm* prince

principiante |prinθiˈpjante| *nm/f* beginner

principio |prinˈθipjo| *nm* (*comienzo*) beginning, start; (*origen*) origin; (*primera etapa*) rudiment, basic idea; (*moral*) principle; **a ~s de** at the beginning of

pringoso, a |prinˈɣoso, a| *adj* (*grasiento*) greasy; (*pegajoso*) sticky

pringue |ˈpringe| *nm* (*grasa*) grease, fat, dripping

prioridad |prioriˈðað| *nf* priority

prisa |ˈprisa| *nf* (*apresuramiento*) hurry, haste; (*rapidez*) speed; (*urgencia*) (sense of) urgency; **a o de ~** quickly; **correr ~** to be urgent; **darse ~** to hurry up; **estar de o tener ~** to be in a hurry

prisión |priˈsjon| *nf* (*cárcel*) prison; (*período de cárcel*) imprisonment; **prisionero, a** *nm/f* prisoner

prismáticos |prisˈmatikos| *nmpl* binoculars

privación |priβaˈθjon| *nf* deprivation; (*falta*) want, privation

privado, a |priˈβaðo, a| *adj* private

privar |priˈβar| *vt* to deprive; **privativo, a** *adj* exclusive

privilegiado, a |priβileˈxjaðo, a| *adj* privileged; (*memoria*) very good

privilegiar |priβileˈxjar| *vt* to grant a privilege to; (*favorecer*) to favour

privilegio |priβiˈlexjo| *nm* privilege; (*concesión*) concession

pro |pro| *nm o f* profit, advantage ♦ *prep*: **asociación ~ ciegos** association for the blind ♦ *prefijo*: **~ soviético/americano** pro-Soviet/American; **en ~ de** on behalf of, for; **los ~s y los contras** the pros and cons

proa |ˈproa| *nf* bow, prow; **de ~** bow *cpd*, fore

probabilidad |proβaβiliˈðað| *nf* probability, likelihood; (*oportunidad, posibilidad*) chance, prospect; **probable** *adj* probable, likely

probador |proβaˈðor| *nm* (*en tienda*) fitting room

probar |proˈβar| *vt* (*demostrar*) to prove; (*someter a prueba*) to test, try out; (*ropa*) to try on; (*comida*) to taste ♦ *vi* to try; **~se un traje** to try on a suit

probeta |proˈβeta| *nf* test tube

problema |proˈβlema| *nm* problem

procedente |proθeˈðente| *adj* (*razonable*) reasonable; (*conforme a derecho*) proper, fitting; **~ de** coming from, originating in

proceder |proθeˈðer| *vi* (*avanzar*) to proceed; (*actuar*) to act; (*ser correcto*) to be

right (and proper), be fitting ♦ *nm* (*comportamiento*) behaviour, conduct; **~ de** to come from, originate in; **procedimiento** *nm* procedure; (*proceso*) process; (*método*) means *pl*, method

procesado, a |proθeˈsaðo, a| *nm/f* accused

procesador |proθesaˈðor| *nm*: **~ de textos** word processor

procesar |proθeˈsar| *vt* to try, put on trial

procesión |proθeˈsjon| *nf* procession

proceso |proˈθeso| *nm* process; (*JUR*) trial

proclamar |proklaˈmar| *vt* to proclaim

procreación |prokreaˈθjon| *nf* procreation

procrear |prokreˈar| *vt, vi* to procreate

procurador, a |prokuraˈðor, a| *nm/f* attorney

procurar |prokuˈrar| *vt* (*intentar*) to try, endeavour; (*conseguir*) to get, obtain; (*asegurar*) to secure; (*producir*) to produce

prodigio |proˈðixjo| *nm* prodigy; (*milagro*) wonder, marvel; **~so, a** *adj* prodigious, marvellous

pródigo, a |ˈproðixo, a| *adj*: **hijo ~** prodigal son

producción |proðukˈθjon| *nf* (*gen*) production; (*producto*) output; **~ en serie** mass production

producir |proðuˈθir| *vt* to produce; (*causar*) to cause, bring about; **~se** *vr* (*cambio*) to come about; (*accidente*) to take place; (*problema etc*) to arise; (*hacerse*) to be produced, be made; (*estallar*) to break out

productividad |proðuktiβiˈðað| *nf* productivity; **productivo, a** *adj* productive; (*provechoso*) profitable

producto |proˈðukto| *nm* product

productor, a |proðukˈtor, a| *adj* productive, producing ♦ *nm/f* producer

proeza |proˈeθa| *nf* exploit, feat

profanar |profaˈnar| *vt* to desecrate, profane; **profano, a** *adj* profane ♦ *nm/f* layman/woman

profecía |profeˈθia| *nf* prophecy

proferir |profeˈrir| *vt* (*palabra, sonido*) to utter; (*injuria*) to hurl, let fly

profesión |profeˈsjon| *nf* profession; **profesional** *adj* professional

profesor, a |profeˈsor, a| *nm/f* teacher; **~ado** *nm* teaching profession

profeta |proˈfeta| *nm/f* prophet; **profetizar** *vt, vi* to prophesy

prófugo, a |ˈprofuxo, a| *nm/f* fugitive; (*MIL*: *desertor*) deserter

profundidad |profundiˈðað| *nf* depth; **profundizar** *vi*: **profundizar en** to go deeply into; **profundo, a** *adj* deep; (*misterio, pensador*) profound

progenitor |proxeniˈtor| *nm* ancestor; **~es** *nmpl* (*padres*) parents

programa [pro'ɣrama] nm programme
(BRIT), program (US); **~ción** nf programming;
~dor, a nm/f programmer; **programar** vt to
program

progresar [proɣre'sar] vi to progress, make
progress; **progresista** adj, nm/f progressive;
progresivo, a adj progressive; (gradual)
gradual; (continuo) continuous; **progreso**
nm progress

prohibición [proiβi'θjon] nf prohibition, ban

prohibir [proi'βir] vt to prohibit, ban, forbid;
se prohibe fumar, prohibido fumar no
smoking; **"prohibido el paso"** "no entry"

prójimo, a ['proximo, a] nm/f fellow man;
(vecino) neighbour

proletariado [proleta'rjaðo] nm proletariat

proletario, a [prole'tarjo, a] adj, nm/f
proletarian

proliferación [prolifera'θjon] nf proliferation

proliferar [prolife'rar] vi to proliferate;
prolífico, a adj prolific

prólogo ['proloɣo] nm prologue

prolongación [prolonga'θjon] nf extension;
prolongado, a adj (largo) long; (alargado)
lengthy

prolongar [prolon'gar] vt to extend;
(reunión etc) to prolong; (calle, tubo) to
extend

promedio [pro'meðjo] nm average; (de
distancia) middle, mid-point

promesa [pro'mesa] nf promise

prometer [prome'ter] vt to promise ♦ vi to
show promise; **~se** vr (novios) to get
engaged; **prometido, a** adj promised;
engaged ♦ nm/f fiancé/fiancée

prominente [promi'nente] adj prominent

promiscuo, a [pro'miskwo, a] adj
promiscuous

promoción [promo'θjon] nf promotion

promotor [promo'tor] nm promoter;
(instigador) instigator

promover [promo'βer] vt to promote;
(causar) to cause; (instigar) to instigate, stir
up

promulgar [promul'ɣar] vt to promulgate;
(anunciar) to proclaim

pronombre [pro'nombre] nm pronoun

pronosticar [pronosti'kar] vt to predict,
foretell, forecast; **pronóstico** nm prediction,
forecast; **pronóstico del tiempo** weather
forecast

pronto, a ['pronto, a] adj (rápido) prompt,
quick; (preparado) ready ♦ adv quickly,
promptly; (en seguida) at once, right away;
(dentro de poco) soon; (temprano) early
♦ nm: **tener ~s de enojo** to be quick-
tempered; **de ~** suddenly; **por lo ~**
meanwhile, for the present

pronunciación [pronunθja'θjon] nf

pronunciation

pronunciar [pronun'θjar] vt to pronounce;
(discurso) to make, deliver; **~se** vr to revolt,
rebel; (declararse) to declare o.s.

propagación [propaɣa'θjon] nf propagation

propaganda [propa'ɣanda] nf (política)
propaganda; (comercial) advertising

propagar [propa'ɣar] vt to propagate

propensión [propen'sjon] nf inclination,
propensity; **propenso, a** adj inclined to; **ser
propenso a** to be inclined to, have a tendency
to

propicio, a [pro'piθjo, a] adj favourable,
propitious

propiedad [propje'ðað] nf property;
(posesión) possession, ownership; **~ particular**
private property

propietario, a [propje'tarjo, a] nm/f owner,
proprietor

propina [pro'pina] nf tip

propio, a ['propjo, a] adj own, of one's own;
(característico) characteristic, typical; (debido)
proper; (mismo) selfsame, very; **el ~ ministro**
the minister himself; **¿tienes casa propia?**
have you a house of your own?

proponer [propo'ner] vt to propose, put
forward; (problema) to pose; **~se** vr to
propose, intend

proporción [propor'θjon] nf proportion;
(MAT) ratio; **proporciones** nfpl (dimensiones)
dimensions; (fig) size sg; **proporcionado, a**
adj proportionate; (regular) medium,
middling; (justo) just right; **proporcionar** vt
(dar) to give, supply, provide

proposición [proposi'θjon] nf proposition;
(propuesta) proposal

propósito [pro'posito] nm purpose; (intento)
aim, intention ♦ adv: **a ~** by the way,
incidentally; (a posta) on purpose,
deliberately; **a ~ de** about, with regard to

propuesta [pro'pwesta] vb ver **proponer** ♦ nf
proposal

propulsar [propul'sar] vt to drive, propel;
(fig) to promote, encourage; **propulsión** nf
propulsion; **propulsión a chorro** o **por reacción**
jet propulsion

prórroga ['prorroɣa] nf extension; (JUR) stay;
(COM) deferment; (DEPORTE) extra time;
prorrogar vt (período) to extend; (decisión)
to defer, postpone

prorrumpir [prorrum'pir] vi to burst forth,
break out

prosa ['prosa] nf prose

proscrito, a [pro'skrito, a] adj banned

proseguir [prose'ɣir] vt to continue, carry on
♦ vi to continue, go on

prospección [prospek'θjon] nf exploration;
(del oro) prospecting

prospecto [pros'pekto] nm prospectus

prosperar [prospe'rar] *vi* to prosper, thrive, flourish; **prosperidad** *nf* prosperity; (*éxito*) success; **próspero, a** *adj* prosperous, flourishing; (*que tiene éxito*) successful

~tíbulo [pros'tiβulo] *nm* brothel (BRIT), prostitution (US)

prostitución [prostitu'θjon] *nf* prostitution

prostituir [prosti'twir] *vt* to prostitute; **~se** *vr* to prostitute o.s., become a prostitute

prostituta [prosti'tuta] *nf* prostitute

protagonista [protaɣo'nista] *nm/f* protagonist

protagonizar [protaɣoni'θar] *vt* to take the chief rôle in

protección [protek'θjon] *nf* protection

protector, a [protek'tor, a] *adj* protective, protecting ♦ *nm/f* protector

proteger [prote'xer] *vt* to protect; **protegido, a** *nm/f* protégé/protégée

proteína [prote'ina] *nf* protein

protesta [pro'testa] *nf* protest; (*declaración*) protestation

protestante [protes'tante] *adj* Protestant

protestar [protes'tar] *vt* to protest, declare ♦ *vi* to protest

protocolo [proto'kolo] *nm* protocol

prototipo [proto'tipo] *nm* prototype

prov. *abr* (= *provincia*) prov

provecho [pro'βetʃo] *nm* advantage, benefit; (FINANZAS) profit; **¡buen ~!** bon appétit!; **en ~ de** to the benefit of; **sacar ~ de** to benefit from, profit by

proveer [proβe'er] *vt* to provide, supply ♦ *vi*: **~ a** to provide for

provenir [proβe'nir] *vi*: **~ de** to come from, stem from

proverbio [pro'βerβjo] *nm* proverb

providencia [proβi'ðenθja] *nf* providence

provincia [pro'βinθja] *nf* province; **~no, a** *adj* provincial; (*del campo*) country *cpd*

provisión [proβi'sjon] *nf* provision; (*abastecimiento*) provision, supply; (*medida*) measure, step

provisional [proβisjo'nal] *adj* provisional

provocación [proβoka'θjon] *nf* provocation

provocar [proβo'kar] *vt* to provoke; (*alentar*) to tempt, invite; (*causar*) to bring about, lead to; (*promover*) to promote; (*estimular*) to rouse, stimulate; **¿te provoca un café?** (AM) would you like a coffee?; **provocativo, a** *adj* provocative

próximamente [proksima'mente] *adv* shortly, soon

proximidad [proksimi'ðað] *nf* closeness, proximity; **próximo, a** *adj* near, close; (*vecino*) neighbouring; (*siguiente*) next

proyectar [projek'tar] *vt* (*objeto*) to hurl, throw; (*luz*) to cast, shed; (CINE) to screen, show; (*planear*) to plan

proyectil [projek'til] *nm* projectile, missile

proyecto [pro'jekto] *nm* plan; (*estimación de costo*) detailed estimate

proyector [projek'tor] *nm* (CINE) projector

prudencia [pru'ðenθja] *nf* (*sabiduría*) wisdom; (*cuidado*) care; **prudente** *adj* sensible, wise; (*conductor*) careful

prueba *etc* ['prweβa] *vb ver* **probar** ♦ *nf* proof; (*ensayo*) test, trial; (*degustación*) tasting, sampling; (*de ropa*) fitting; **a ~** on trial; **a ~ de** proof against; **a ~ de agua/fuego** waterproof/fireproof; **someter a ~** to put to the test

prurito [pru'rito] *nm* itch; (*de bebé*) nappy (BRIT) o diaper (US) rash

psico... [siko] *prefijo* psycho...; **~análisis** *nm inv* psychoanalysis; **~logía** *nf* psychology; **~lógico, a** *adj* psychological; **psicólogo, a** *nm/f* psychologist; **psicópata** *nm/f* psychopath; **~sis** *nf inv* psychosis

psiquiatra [si'kjatra] *nm/f* psychiatrist; **psiquiátrico, a** *adj* psychiatric

psíquico, a ['sikiko, a] *adj* psychic(al)

PSOE [pe'soe] *nm abr* = **Partido Socialista Obrero Español**

pta(s) *abr* = **peseta(s)**

pts *abr* = **pesetas**

púa ['pua] *nf* (BOT, ZOOL) prickle, spine; (*para guitarra*) plectrum (BRIT), pick (US); **alambre de ~** barbed wire

pubertad [puβer'tað] *nf* puberty

publicación [puβlika'θjon] *nf* publication

publicar [puβli'kar] *vt* (*editar*) to publish; (*hacer público*) to publicize; (*divulgar*) to make public, divulge

publicidad [puβliθi'ðað] *nf* publicity; (COM: *propaganda*) advertising; **publicitario, a** *adj* publicity *cpd*; advertising *cpd*

público, a ['puβliko, a] *adj* public ♦ *nm* public; (TEATRO *etc*) audience

puchero [pu'tʃero] *nm* (CULIN: *guiso*) stew; (: *olla*) cooking pot; **hacer ~s** to pout

pude *etc vb ver* **poder**

púdico, a ['puðiko, a] *adj* modest

pudiente [pu'ðjente] *adj* (*rico*) wealthy, well-to-do

pudiera *etc vb ver* **poder**

pudor [pu'ðor] *nm* modesty

pudrir [pu'ðrir] *vt* to rot; **~se** *vr* to rot, decay

pueblo ['pweβlo] *nm* people; (*nación*) nation; (*aldea*) village

puedo *etc vb ver* **poder**

puente ['pwente] *nm* bridge; **hacer ~** (*inf*) to take extra days off work between 2 public holidays; to take a long weekend; **~ aéreo** shuttle service; **~ colgante** suspension bridge

puerco, a ['pwerko, a] *nm/f* pig/sow ♦ *adj* (*sucio*) dirty, filthy; (*obsceno*) disgusting; **~ de mar** porpoise; **~ marino** dolphin

pueril [pwe'ril] *adj* childish

puerro ['pwerro] *nm* leek

puerta ['pwerta] *nf* door; (*de jardín*) gate; (*portal*) doorway; (*fig*) gateway; (*portería*) goal; **a la ~** at the door; **a ~ cerrada** behind closed doors; **~ giratoria** revolving door

puerto ['pwerto] *nm* port; (*paso*) pass; (*fig*) haven, refuge

Puerto Rico |pwerto'riko] *nm* Puerto Rico; **puertorriqueño, a** *adj, nm/f* Puerto Rican

pues [pwes] *adv* (*entonces*) then; (*bueno*) well, well then; (*así que*) so ♦ *conj* (*ya que*) since; **¡~!** (*sí*) yes!, certainly!

puesta ['pwesta] *nf* (*apuesta*) bet, stake; **~ en marcha** starting; **~ del sol** sunset

puesto, a ['pwesto, a] *pp de* **poner** ♦ *adj*: **tener algo ~** to have sth on, be wearing sth ♦ *nm* (*lugar, posición*) place; (*trabajo*) post, job; (*COM*) stall ♦ *conj*: **~ que** since, as

púgil ['puxil] *nm* boxer

pugna ['puɣna] *nf* battle, conflict; **pugnar** *vi* (*luchar*) to struggle, fight; (*pelear*) to fight

pujar [pu'xar] *vi* (*en subasta*) to bid; (*esforzarse*) to struggle, strain

pulcro, a ['pulkro, a] *adj* neat, tidy

pulga ['pulɣa] *nf* flea

pulgada [pul'ɣaða] *nf* inch

pulgar [pul'ɣar] *nm* thumb

pulir [pu'lir] *vt* to polish; (*alisar*) to smooth; (*fig*) to polish up, touch up

pulla ['puʎa] *nf* cutting remark

pulmón [pul'mon] *nm* lung; **pulmonía** *nf* pneumonia

pulpa ['pulpa] *nf* pulp; (*de fruta*) flesh, soft part

pulpería [pulpe'ria] (*AM*) *nf* (*tienda*) small grocery store

púlpito ['pulpito] *nm* pulpit

pulpo |'pulpo] *nm* octopus

pulsación [pulsa'θjon] *nf* beat; **pulsaciones** pulse rate

pulsar [pul'sar] *vt* (*tecla*) to touch, tap; (*MUS*) to play; (*botón*) to press, push ♦ *vi* to pulsate; (*latir*) to beat, throb; (*MED*): **~ a uno** to take sb's pulse

pulsera [pul'sera] *nf* bracelet

pulso ['pulso] *nm* (*ANAT*) pulse; (*fuerza*) strength; (*firmeza*) steadiness, steady hand

pulverizador [pulβeriθa'ðor] *nm* spray, spray gun

pulverizar [pulβeri'θar] *vt* to pulverize; (*líquido*) to spray

puna ['puna] (*AM*) *nf* mountain sickness

punitivo, a [puni'tiβo, a] *adj* punitive

punta ['punta] *nf* point, tip; (*extremidad*) end; (*fig*) touch, trace; **horas ~s** peak hours, rush hours; **sacar ~ a** to sharpen

puntada |pun'taða] *nf* (*COSTURA*) stitch

puntal |pun'tal] *nm* prop, support

puntapié [punta'pje] *nm* kick

puntear [punte'ar] *vt* to tick, mark

puntería [punte'ria] *nf* (*de arma*) aim, aiming; (*destreza*) marksmanship

puntero, a [pun'tero, a] *adj* leading; (*palo*) pointer

puntiagudo, a [puntja'ɣuðo, a] *adj* sharp, pointed

puntilla [pun'tiʎa] *nf* (*encaje*) lace edging o trim; (**andar) de ~s** (to walk) on tiptoe

punto ['punto] *nm* (*gen*) point; (*señal diminuta*) spot, dot; (*COSTURA, MED*) stitch; (*lugar*) spot, place; (*momento*) point, moment; **a ~** ready; **estar a ~ de** to be on the point of o about to; **en ~** on the dot; **~ muerto** dead centre; (*AUTO*) neutral (gear); **~ final** full stop (*BRIT*), period (*US*); **~ y coma** semicolon; **~ de interrogación** question mark; **~ de vista** point of view, viewpoint; **hacer ~** (*tejer*) to knit

puntuación [puntwa'θjon] *nf* punctuation; (*puntos: en examen*) mark(s) (*pl*); (*: DEPORTE*) score

puntual [pun'twal] *adj* (*a tiempo*) punctual; (*exacto*) exact, accurate; **~idad** *nf* punctuality; exactness, accuracy; **~izar** *vt* to fix, specify

puntuar [pun'twar] *vi* (*DEPORTE*) to score, count

punzada [pun'θaða] *nf* (*de dolor*) twinge

punzante [pun'θante] *adj* (*dolor*) shooting, sharp; (*herramienta*) sharp; **punzar** *vt* to prick, pierce ♦ *vi* to shoot, stab

puñado [pu'ɲaðo] *nm* handful

puñal [pu'ɲal] *nm* dagger; **~ada** *nf* stab

puñetazo [puɲe'taθo] *nm* punch

puño ['puɲo] *nm* (*ANAT*) fist; (*cantidad*) fistful, handful; (*COSTURA*) cuff; (*de herramienta*) handle

pupila [pu'pila] *nf* pupil

pupitre [pu'pitre] *nm* desk

puré [pu're] *nm* puree; (*sopa*) (thick) soup; **~ de patatas** mashed potatoes

pureza [pu'reθa] *nf* purity

purga ['purɣa] *nf* purge; **purgante** *adj, nm* purgative; **purgar** *vt* to purge

purgatorio [purɣa'torjo] *nm* purgatory

purificar [purifi'kar] *vt* to purify; (*refinar*) to refine

puritano, a [puri'tano, a] *adj* (*actitud*) puritanical; (*iglesia, tradición*) puritan ♦ *nm/f* puritan

puro, a ['puro, a] *adj* pure; (*verdad*) simple, plain ♦ *adv*: **de ~ cansado** out of sheer tiredness ♦ *nm* cigar

púrpura ['purpura] *nf* purple; **purpúreo, a** *adj* purple

pus [pus] *nm* pus

puse *etc vb ver* **poner**

pusiera etc vb ver **poner**

pústula ['pustula] nf pimple, sore

puta ['puta] (fam!) nf whore, prostitute

putrefacción [putrefak'θjon] nf rotting, putrefaction

PVP abr (ESP: = precio venta al público) RRP

pyme, PYME ['pime] nf abr (= Pequeña y Mediana Empresa) SME

Q, q

que [ke] conj 1 (con oración subordinada: muchas veces no se traduce) that; **dijo ~ vendría** he said (that) he would come; **espero ~ lo encuentres** I hope (that) you find it; ver tb **el**

2 (en oración independiente): **¡~ entre!** send him in; **¡~ se mejore tu padre!** I hope your father gets better

3 (enfático): **¿me quieres? – ¡~ sí!** do you love me? – of course!

4 (consecutivo: muchas veces no se traduce) that; **es tan grande ~ no lo puedo levantar** it's so big (that) I can't lift it

5 (comparaciones) than; **yo ~ tú/él** if I were you/him; ver tb **más; menos; mismo**

6 (valor disyuntivo): **~ le guste o no** whether he likes it or not; **~ venga o ~ no venga** whether he comes or not

7 (porque): **no puedo, ~ tengo ~ quedarme en casa** I can't, I've got to stay in

♦ pron 1 (cosa) that, which; (+ prep) which; **el sombrero ~ te compraste** the hat (that o which) you bought; **la cama en ~ dormí** the bed (that o which) I slept in

2 (persona: suj) that, who; (: objeto) that, whom; **el amigo ~ me acompañó al museo** the friend that o who went to the museum with me: **la chica ~ invité** the girl (that o whom) I invited

qué [ke] adj what?, which? ♦ pron what?; **¡~ divertido!** how funny!; **¿~ edad tienes?** how old are you?; **¿de ~ me hablas?** what are you saying to me?; **¿~ tal?** how are you?, how are things?; **¿~ hay (de nuevo)?** what's new?

quebradizo, a [keßra'ðiθo, a] adj fragile; (persona) frail

quebrado, a [ke'ßraðo, a] adj (roto) broken ♦ nm/f bankrupt ♦ nm (MAT) fraction

quebrantar [keßran'tar] vt (infringir) to violate, transgress; **~se** vr (persona) to fail in health

quebranto [ke'ßranto] nm damage, harm; (dolor) grief, pain

quebrar [ke'ßrar] vt to break, smash ♦ vi to go bankrupt; **~se** vr to break, get broken; (MED) to be ruptured

quedar [ke'ðar] vi to stay, remain; (encontrarse: sitio) to be; (haber aún) to remain, be left; **~se** vr to remain, stay (behind); **~se (con) algo** to keep sth; **~ en** (acordar) to agree on/to; **~ en nada** to come to nothing; **~ por hacer** to be still to be done; **~ ciego/mudo** to be left blind/dumb; **no te queda bien ese vestido** that dress doesn't suit you; **eso queda muy lejos** that's a long way (away); **quedamos a las seis** we agreed to meet at six

quedo, a ['keðo, a] adj still ♦ adv softly, gently

quehacer [kea'θer] nm task, job; **~es (domésticos)** nmpl household chores

queja ['kexa] nf complaint; **quejarse** vr (enfermo) to moan, groan; (protestar) to complain; **quejarse de que** to complain (about the fact) that; **quejido** nm moan

quemado, a [ke'maðo, a] adj burnt

quemadura [kema'ðura] nf burn, scald

quemar [ke'mar] vt to burn; (fig: malgastar) to burn up, squander ♦ vi to be burning hot; **~se** vr (consumirse) to burn (up); (del sol) to get sunburnt

quemarropa [kema'rropa]: **a ~** adv point-blank

quepo etc vb ver **caber**

querella [ke'reʎa] nf (JUR) charge; (disputa) dispute; **~rse** vr (JUR) to file a complaint

querer [ke'rer] vt 1 (desear) to want; **quiero más dinero** I want more money; **quisiera o querría un té** I'd like a tea; **sin ~** unintentionally; **quiero ayudar/que vayas** I want to help/you to go

2 (preguntas: para pedir algo): **¿quiere abrir la ventana?** could you open the window?; **¿quieres echarme una mano?** can you give me a hand?

3 (amar) to love; (tener cariño a) to be fond of; **quiere mucho a sus hijos** he's very fond of his children

4 (requerir): **esta planta quiere más luz** this plant needs more light

5: **le pedí que me dejara ir pero no quiso** I asked him to let me go but he refused

querido, a [ke'riðo, a] adj dear ♦ nm/f darling; (amante) lover

queso ['keso] nm cheese

quicio ['kiθjo] nm hinge; **sacar a uno de ~** to get on sb's nerves

quiebra ['kjeßra] nf break, split; (COM) bankruptcy; (ECON) slump

quiebro ['kjeβro] nm (del cuerpo) swerve

quien [kjen] pron who; **hay ~ piensa que** there are those who think that; **no hay ~ lo haga** no-one will do it

quién [kjen] pron who, whom; ¿**~ es?** who's there?

quienquiera [kjen'kjera] (pl **quienesquiera**) pron whoever

quiero etc vb ver **querer**

quieto, a ['kjeto, a] adj still; (carácter) placid; **quietud** nf stillness

quilate [ki'late] nm carat

quilla ['kiʎa] nf keel

quimera [ki'mera] nf chimera; **quimérico, a** adj fantastic

químico, a ['kimiko, a] adj chemical ♦ nm/f chemist ♦ nf chemistry

quincalla [kin'kaʎa] nf hardware, ironmongery (BRIT)

quince ['kinθe] num fifteen; **~ días** a fortnight; **~añero, a** nm/f teenager; **~na** nf fortnight; (pago) fortnightly pay; **~nal** adj fortnightly

quiniela [ki'njela] nf football pools pl; **~s** nfpl (impreso) pools coupon sg

quinientos, as [ki'njentos, as] adj, num five hundred

quinina [ki'nina] nf quinine

quinto, a ['kinto, a] adj fifth ♦ nf country house; (MIL) call-up, draft

quiosco ['kjosko] nm (de música) bandstand; (de periódicos) news stand

quirófano [ki'rofano] nm operating theatre

quirúrgico, a [ki'rurxiko, a] adj surgical

quise etc vb ver **querer**

quisiera etc vb ver **querer**

quisquilloso, a [kiski'ʎoso, a] adj (susceptible) touchy; (meticuloso) pernickety

quiste ['kiste] nm cyst

quitaesmalte [kitaes'malte] nm nail-polish remover

quitamanchas [kita'mantʃas] nm inv stain remover

quitanieves [kita'njeβes] nm inv snowplough (BRIT), snowplow (US)

quitar [ki'tar] vt to remove, take away; (ropa) to take off; (dolor) to relieve; ¡**quita de ahí!** get away!; **~se** vr to withdraw; (ropa) to take off; **se quitó el sombrero** he took off his hat

quite ['kite] nm (esgrima) parry; (evasión) dodge

Quito ['kito] n Quito

quizá(s) [ki'θa(s)] adv perhaps, maybe

R, r

rábano ['raβano] nm radish; **me importa un ~** I don't give a damn

rabia ['raβja] nf (MED) rabies sg; (ira) fury, rage; **rabiar** vi to have rabies; to rage, be furious; **rabiar por algo** to long for sth

rabieta [ra'βjeta] nf tantrum, fit of temper

rabino [ra'βino] nm rabbi

rabioso, a [ra'βjoso, a] adj rabid; (fig) furious

rabo ['raβo] nm tail

racha ['ratʃa] nf gust of wind: **buena/mala ~** spell of good/bad luck

racial [ra'θjal] adj racial, race cpd

racimo [ra'θimo] nm bunch

raciocinio [raθjo'θinjo] nm reason

ración [ra'θjon] nf portion; **raciones** nfpl rations

racional [raθjo'nal] adj (razonable) reasonable; (lógico) rational; **~izar** vt to rationalize

racionar [raθjo'nar] vt to ration (out)

racismo [ra'θismo] nm racism; **racista** adj, nm/f racist

radar [ra'ðar] nm radar

radiactivo, a [raðiak'tiβo, a] adj = **radioactivo**

radiador [raðja'ðor] nm radiator

radiante [ra'ðjante] adj radiant

radical [raði'kal] adj, nm/f radical

radicar [raði'kar] vi: **~ en** (dificultad, problema) to lie in; (solución) to consist in; **~se** vr to establish o.s., put down (one's) roots

radio ['raðjo] nf radio; (aparato) radio (set) ♦ nm (MAT) radius; (QUÍM) radium; **~actividad** nf radioactivity; **~activo, a** adj radioactive; **~difusión** nf broadcasting; **~emisora** nf transmitter, radio station; **~escucha** nm/f listener; **~grafía** nf X-ray; **~grafiar** vt to X-ray; **~terapia** nf radiotherapy; **~yente** nm/f listener

ráfaga ['rafaxa] nf gust; (de luz) flash; (de tiros) burst

raído, a [ra'iðo, a] adj (ropa) threadbare

raigambre [rai'xambre] nf (BOT) roots pl; (fig) tradition

raíz [ra'iθ] nf root; **~ cuadrada** square root; **a ~ de** as a result of

raja ['raxa] nf (de melón etc) slice; (grieta) crack; **rajar** vt to split; (fam) to slash; **rajarse** vr to split, crack; **rajarse de** to back out of

rajatabla [raxa'taβla]: **a ~** adv (estrictamente) strictly, to the letter

rallador [raʎa'ðor] nm grater

rallar [ra'ʎar] vt to grate

rama ['rama] nf branch; **~je** nm branches pl, foliage; **ramal** nm (de cuerda) strand; (FERRO) branch line (BRIT); (AUTO) branch (road) (BRIT)

rambla ['rambla] nf (avenida) avenue

ramificación [ramifika'θjon] nf ramification

ramificarse [ramifiˈkarse] *vr* to branch out

ramillete [ramiˈʎete] *nm* bouquet

ramo [ˈramo] *nm* branch; (*sección*) department, section

rampa [ˈrampa] *nf* ramp

ramplón, ona [ramˈplon, ona] *adj* uncouth, coarse

rana [ˈrana] *nf* frog; **salto de ~** leapfrog

ranchero [ranˈtʃero] *nm* (*AM*) rancher; smallholder

rancho [ˈrantʃo] *nm* (*grande*) ranch; (*pequeño*) small farm

rancio, a [ˈranθjo, a] *adj* (*comestibles*) rancid; (*vino*) aged, mellow; (*fig*) ancient

rango [ˈrango] *nm* rank, standing

ranura [raˈnura] *nf* groove; (*de teléfono etc*) slot

rapar [raˈpar] *vt* to shave; (*los cabellos*) to crop

rapaz [raˈpaθ] (*nf*: **rapaza**) *nm/f* young boy/girl ♦ *adj* (*ZOOL*) predatory

rape [ˈrape] *nm* (*pez*) monkfish; **al ~** cropped

rapé [raˈpe] *nm* snuff

rapidez [rapiˈðeθ] *nf* speed, rapidity; **rápido, a** *adj* fast, quick ♦ *adv* quickly ♦ *nm* (*FERRO*) express; **rápidos** *nmpl* rapids

rapiña [raˈpiɲa] *nm* robbery; **ave de ~** bird of prey

raptar [rapˈtar] *vt* to kidnap; **rapto** *nm* kidnapping; (*impulso*) sudden impulse; (*éxtasis*) ecstasy, rapture

raqueta [raˈketa] *nf* racquet

raquítico, a [raˈkitiko, a] *adj* stunted; (*fig*) poor, inadequate; **raquitismo** *nm* rickets *sg*

rareza [raˈreθa] *nf* rarity; (*fig*) eccentricity

raro, a [ˈraro, a] *adj* (*poco común*) rare; (*extraño*) odd, strange; (*excepcional*) remarkable

ras [ras] *nm*: **a ~ de** level with; **a ~ de tierra** at ground level

rasar [raˈsar] *vt* (*igualar*) to level

rascacielos [raskaˈθjelos] *nm inv* skyscraper

rascar [rasˈkar] *vt* (*con las uñas etc*) to scratch; (*raspar*) to scrape; **~se** *vr* to scratch (o.s.)

rasgar [rasˈɣar] *vt* to tear, rip (up)

rasgo [ˈrasɣo] *nm* (*con pluma*) stroke; **~s** *nmpl* (*facciones*) features, characteristics; **a grandes ~s** in outline, broadly

rasguñar [rasɣuˈɲar] *vt* to scratch; **rasguño** *nm* scratch

raso, a [ˈraso, a] *adj* (*liso*) flat, level; (*a baja altura*) very low ♦ *nm* satin; **cielo ~** clear sky

raspadura [raspaˈðura] *nf* (*acto*) scrape, scraping; (*marca*) scratch; **~s** *nfpl* (*de papel etc*) scrapings

raspar [rasˈpar] *vt* to scrape; (*arañar*) to scratch; (*limar*) to file

rastra [ˈrastra] *nf* (*AGR*) rake; **a ~s** by dragging; (*fig*) unwillingly

rastreador [rastreaˈðor] *nm* tracker; **~ de minas** minesweeper

rastrear [rastreˈar] *vt* (*seguir*) to track

rastrero, a [rasˈtrero, a] *adj* (*BOT, ZOOL*) creeping; (*fig*) despicable, mean

rastrillo [rasˈtriʎo] *nm* rake

rastro [ˈrastro] *nm* (*AGR*) rake; (*pista*) track, trail; (*vestigio*) trace; **el R~** the Madrid fleamarket

rastrojo [rasˈtroxo] *nm* stubble

rasurador [rasuraˈðor] (*AM*) *nm* electric shaver

rasuradora [rasuraˈðora] (*AM*) *nf* = **rasurador**

rasurarse [rasuˈrarse] *vr* to shave

rata [ˈrata] *nf* rat

ratear [rateˈar] *vt* (*robar*) to steal

ratero, a [raˈtero, a] *adj* light-fingered ♦ *nm/f* (*carterista*) pickpocket; (*AM*: *de casas*) burglar

ratificar [ratifiˈkar] *vt* to ratify

rato [ˈrato] *nm* while, short time; **a ~s** from time to time; **hay para ~** there's still a long way to go; **al poco ~** soon afterwards; **pasar el ~** to kill time; **pasar un buen/mal ~** to have a good/rough time; **en mis ~s libres** in my spare time

ratón [raˈton] *nm* mouse; **ratonera** *nf* mousetrap

raudal [rauˈðal] *nm* torrent; **a ~es** in abundance

raya [ˈraja] *nf* line; (*marca*) scratch; (*en tela*) stripe; (*de pelo*) parting; (*límite*) boundary; (*pez*) ray; (*puntuación*) ray; (*punto*) dash; **pasarse de la ~** to go too far; **tener a ~** to keep in check; **rayar** *vt* to line; to scratch; (*subrayar*) to underline ♦ *vi*: **rayar en** o **con** to border on

rayo [ˈrajo] *nm* (*del sol*) ray, beam; (*de luz*) shaft; (*en una tormenta*) (flash of) lightning; **~s X** X-rays

raza [ˈraθa] *nf* race; **~ humana** human race

razón [raˈθon] *nf* reason; (*justicia*) right, justice; (*razonamiento*) reasoning; (*motivo*) reason, motive; (*MAT*) ratio; **a ~ de 10 cada día** at the rate of 10 a day; **"~: ..."** "inquiries to ..."; **en ~ de** with regard to; **dar ~ a uno** to agree that sb is right; **tener ~** to be right; **~ directa/inversa** direct/inverse proportion; **~ de ser** raison d'être; **razonable** *adj* reasonable; (*justo, moderado*) fair; **razonamiento** *nm* (*juicio*) judg(e)ment; (*argumento*) reasoning; **razonar** *vt, vi* to reason, argue

reacción [reakˈθjon] *nf* reaction; **avión a ~** jet plane; **~ en cadena** chain reaction; **reaccionar** *vi* to react; **reaccionario, a** *adj* reactionary

reacio, a [reˈaθjo, a] *adj* stubborn

reactivar [reakti'βar] vt to revitalize
reactor [reak'tor] nm reactor
readaptación [reaðapta'θjon] nf:
~ **profesional** industrial retraining
reajuste [rea'xuste] nm readjustment
real [re'al] adj real; (del rey, fig) royal
realce [re'alθe] nm (lustre, fig) splendour;
poner de ~ to emphasize
realidad [reali'ðað] nf reality, fact; (verdad)
truth
realista [rea'lista] nm/f realist
realización [realiθa'θjon] nf fulfilment
realizador, a [realiθa'ðor, a] nm/f film-
maker
realizar [reali'θar] vt (objetivo) to achieve;
(plan) to carry out; (viaje) to make,
undertake; ~**se** vr to come about, come
true
realmente [real'mente] adv really, actually
realquilar [realki'lar] vt to sublet
realzar [real'θar] vt to enhance; (acentuar) to
highlight
reanimar [reani'mar] vt to revive; (alentar)
to encourage; ~**se** vr to revive
reanudar [reanu'ðar] vt (renovar) to renew;
(historia, viaje) to resume
reaparición [reapari'θjon] nf reappearance
rearme [re'arme] nm rearmament
rebaja [re'βaxa] nf (COM) reduction; (: descuento) discount; ~**s** nfpl (COM) sale; **rebajar**
vt (bajar) to lower; (reducir) to reduce;
(disminuir) to lessen; (humillar) to humble
rebanada [reβa'naða] nf slice
rebañar [reβa'ɲar] vt (comida) to scrape up;
(plato) to scrape clean
rebaño [re'βaɲo] nm herd; (de ovejas) flock
rebasar [reβa'sar] vt (tb: ~ **de**) to exceed
rebatir [reβa'tir] vt to refute
rebeca [re'βeka] nf cardigan
rebelarse [reβe'larse] vr to rebel, revolt
rebelde [re'βelde] adj rebellious; (niño)
unruly ♦ nm/f rebel; **rebeldía** nf
rebelliousness; (desobediencia) disobedience
rebelión [reβe'ljon] nf rebellion
reblandecer [reβlande'θer] vt to soften
rebobinar [reβoβi'nar] vt (cinta, película de
video) to rewind
rebosante [reβo'sante] adj overflowing
rebosar [reβo'sar] vi (líquido, recipiente) to
overflow; (abundar) to abound, be plentiful
rebotar [reβo'tar] vt to bounce; (rechazar) to
repel ♦ vi (pelota) to bounce; (bala) to
ricochet; **rebote** nm rebound; **de rebote** on
the rebound
rebozado, a [reβo'θaðo, a] adj fried in
batter o breadcrumbs
rebozar [reβo'θar] vt to wrap up; (CULIN) to
fry in batter o breadcrumbs
rebuscado, a [reβus'kaðo, a] adj

(amanerado) affected; (palabra) recherché;
(idea) far-fetched
rebuscar [reβus'kar] vi: ~ **(en/por)** to search
carefully (in/for)
rebuznar [reβuθ'nar] vi to bray
recado [re'kaðo] nm (mensaje) message;
(encargo) errand; **tomar un** ~ (TEL) to take a
message
recaer [reka'er] vi to relapse; ~ **en** to fall to o
on; (criminal etc) to fall back into, relapse
into; **recaída** nf relapse
recalcar [rekal'kar] vt (fig) to stress,
emphasize
recalcitrante [rekalθi'trante] adj recalcitrant
recalentar [rekalen'tar] vt (volver a calentar)
to reheat; (calentar demasiado) to overheat
recámara [re'kamara] (AM) nf bedroom
recambio [re'kambjo] nm spare; (de pluma)
refill
recapacitar [rekapaθi'tar] vi to reflect
recargado, a [rekar'vaðo, a] adj overloaded
recargar [rekar'var] vt to overload; (batería)
to recharge; **recargo** nm surcharge;
(aumento) increase
recatado, a [reka'taðo, a] adj (modesto)
modest, demure; (prudente) cautious
recato [re'kato] nm (modestia) modesty,
demureness; (cautela) caution
recaudación [rekauða'θjon] nf (acción)
collection; (cantidad) takings pl; (en deporte)
gate; **recaudador, a** nm/f tax collector
recelar [reθe'lar] vt: ~ **que** (sospechar) to
suspect that; (temer) to fear that ♦ vi: ~ **de**
distrust; **recelo** nm distrust, suspicion;
receloso, a adj distrustful, suspicious
recepción [reθep'θjon] nf reception;
recepcionista nm/f receptionist
receptáculo [reθep'takulo] nm receptacle
receptivo, a [reθep'tiβo, a] adj receptive
receptor, a [reθep'tor, a] nm/f recipient
♦ nm (TEL) receiver
recesión [reθe'sjon] nf (COM) recession
receta [re'θeta] nf (CULIN) recipe; (MED)
prescription
rechazar [retʃa'θar] vt to reject; (oferta) to
turn down; (ataque) to repel
rechazo [re'tʃaθo] nm rejection
rechifla [re'tʃifla] nf hissing, booing; (fig)
derision
rechinar [retʃi'nar] vi to creak; (dientes) to
grind
rechistar [retʃis'tar] vi: **sin** ~ without a
murmur
rechoncho, a [re'tʃontʃo, a] (fam) adj
thickset (BRIT), heavy-set (US)
rechupete [retʃu'pete]: **de** ~ (comida)
delicious, scrumptious
recibidor, a [reθiβi'ðor, a] nm entrance hall
recibimiento [reθiβi'mjento] nm reception,

welcome

recibir [reθiˈβir] vt to receive; (*dar la bienvenida*) to welcome ♦ vi to entertain; **~se** vr: **~se de** to qualify as; **recibo** nm receipt

reciclar [reθiˈklar] vt to recycle

recién [reˈθjen] adv recently, newly; **los ~ casados** the newly-weds; **el ~ llegado** the newcomer; **el ~ nacido** the newborn child

reciente [reˈθjente] adj recent; (*fresco*) fresh; **~mente** adv recently

recinto [reˈθinto] nm enclosure; (*área*) area, place

recio, a [ˈreθjo, a] adj strong, tough; (*voz*) loud ♦ adv hard; loud(ly)

recipiente [reθiˈpjente] nm receptacle

reciprocidad [reθiproθiˈðað] nf reciprocity; **recíproco, a** adj reciprocal

recital [reθiˈtal] nm (MUS) recital; (LITERATURA) reading

recitar [reθiˈtar] vt to recite

reclamación [reklamaˈθjon] nf claim, demand; (*queja*) complaint

reclamar [reklaˈmar] vt to claim, demand ♦ vi: **~ contra** to complain about; **~ a uno en justicia** to take sb to court; **reclamo** nm (*anuncio*) advertisement; (*tentación*) attraction

reclinar [rekliˈnar] vt to recline, lean; **~se** vr to lean back

recluir [rekluˈir] vt to intern, confine

reclusión [rekluˈsjon] nf (*prisión*) prison; (*refugio*) seclusion; **~ perpetua** life imprisonment

recluta [reˈkluta] nm/f recruit ♦ nf recruitment; **reclutar** vt (*datos*) to collect; (*dinero*) to collect up; **~miento** [reklutaˈmjento] nm recruitment

recobrar [rekoˈβrar] vt (*salud*) to recover; (*rescatar*) to get back; **~se** vr to recover

recodo [reˈkoðo] nm (*de río, camino*) bend

recogedor [rekoxeˈðor] nm dustpan

recoger [rekoˈxer] vt to collect; (AGR) to harvest; (*levantar*) to pick up; (*juntar*) to gather; (*pasar a buscar*) to come for, get; (*dar asilo*) to give shelter to; (*faldas*) to gather up; (*pelo*) to put up; **~se** vr (*retirarse*) to retire; **recogido, a** adj (*lugar*) quiet, secluded; (*pequeño*) small ♦ nf (CORREOS) collection; (AGR) harvest

recolección [rekolekˈθjon] nf (AGR) harvesting; (*colecta*) collection

recomendación [rekomendaˈθjon] nf (*sugerencia*) suggestion, recommendation; (*referencia*) reference

recomendar [rekomenˈdar] vt to suggest, recommend; (*confiar*) to entrust

recompensa [rekomˈpensa] nf reward, recompense; **recompensar** vt to reward, recompense

recomponer [rekompoˈner] vt to mend

reconciliación [rekonθiljaˈθjon] nf reconciliation

reconciliar [rekonθiˈljar] vt to reconcile; **~se** vr to become reconciled

recóndito, a [reˈkondito, a] adj (*lugar*) hidden, secret

reconfortar [rekonforˈtar] vt to comfort

reconocer [rekonoˈθer] vt to recognize; (*registrar*) to search; (MED) to examine; **reconocido, a** adj recognized; (*agradecido*) grateful; **reconocimiento** nm recognition; search; examination; gratitude; (*confesión*) admission

reconquista [rekonˈkista] nf reconquest; **la R~** the Reconquest (of Spain)

reconstituyente [rekonstituˈjente] nm tonic

reconstruir [rekonstruˈir] vt to reconstruct

reconversión [rekonβerˈsjon] nf: **~ industrial** industrial rationalization

recopilación [rekopilaˈθjon] nf (*resumen*) summary; (*compilación*) compilation; **recopilar** vt to compile

récord [ˈrekorð] (pl **~s**) adj inv, nm record

recordar [rekorˈðar] vt (*acordarse de*) to remember; (*acordar a otro*) to remind ♦ vi to remember

recorrer [rekoˈrrer] vt (*país*) to cross, travel through; (*distancia*) to cover; (*registrar*) to search; (*repasar*) to look over; **recorrido** nm run, journey; **tren de largo recorrido** main-line train

recortado, a [rekorˈtaðo, a] adj uneven, irregular

recortar [rekorˈtar] vt to cut out; **recorte** nm (*acción, de prensa*) cutting; (*de telas, chapas*) trimming; **recorte presupuestario** budget cut

recostado, a [rekosˈtaðo, a] adj leaning; **estar ~** to be lying down

recostar [rekosˈtar] vt to lean; **~se** vr to lie down

recoveco [rekoˈβeko] nm (*de camino, río etc*) bend; (*en casa*) cubby hole

recreación [rekreaˈθjon] nf recreation

recrear [rekreˈar] vt (*entretener*) to entertain; (*volver a crear*) to recreate; **recreativo, a** adj recreational; **recreo** nm recreation; (ESCOL) break, playtime

recriminar [rekrimiˈnar] vt to reproach ♦ vi to recriminate; **~se** vr to reproach each other

recrudecer [rekruðeˈθer] vt, vi to worsen; **~se** vr to worsen

recrudecimiento [rekruðeθiˈmjento] nm upsurge

recta [ˈrekta] nf straight line

rectángulo, a [rekˈtangulo, a] adj rectangular ♦ nm rectangle

rectificar [rektifiˈkar] vt to rectify; (*volverse*

recto) to straighten ♦ vi to correct o.s.

rectitud [rekti'tuð] nf straightness; (fig) rectitude

recto, a ['rekto, a] adj straight; (persona) honest, upright ♦ nm rectum

rector, a [rek'tor, a] adj governing

recuadro [re'kwaðro] nm box; (TIPOGRAFÍA) inset

recubrir [reku'ßrir] vt: ~ (con) (pintura, crema) to cover (with)

recuento [re'kwento] nm inventory; **hacer el ~ de** to count o reckon up

recuerdo [re'kwerðo] nm souvenir; ~s nmpl (memorias) memories; ¡~s a tu madre! give my regards to your mother!

recular [reku'lar] vi to back down

recuperable [rekupe'raßle] adj recoverable

recuperación [rekupera'θjon] nf recovery

recuperar [rekupe'rar] vt to recover; (tiempo) to make up; ~se vr to recuperate

recurrir [reku'rrir] vi (JUR) to appeal; ~ a to resort to; (persona) to turn to; **recurso** nm resort; (medios) means pl, resources pl; (JUR) appeal

recusar [reku'sar] vt to reject, refuse

red [reð] nf net, mesh; (FERRO etc) network; (trampa) trap; **la R~** (Internet) the Net

redacción [reðak'θjon] nf (acción) editing; (personal) editorial staff; (ESCOL) essay, composition

redactar [reðak'tar] vt to draw up, draft; (periódico) to edit

redactor, a [reðak'tor, a] nm/f editor

redada [re'ðaða] nf: ~ **policial** police raid, round-up

rededor [reðe'ðor] nm: **al o en ~** around, round about

redención [reðen'θjon] nf redemption

redicho, a [re'ðitʃo, a] adj affected

redil [re'ðil] nm sheepfold

redimir [reði'mir] vt to redeem

rédito ['reðito] nm interest, yield

redoblar [reðo'ßlar] vt to redouble ♦ vi (tambor) to roll

redomado, a [reðo'maðo, a] adj (astuto) sly, crafty; (perfecto) utter

redonda [re'ðonda] nf: **a la ~** around, round about

redondear [reðonde'ar] vt to round, round off

redondel [reðon'del] nm (círculo) circle; (TAUR) bullring, arena

redondo, a [re'ðondo, a] adj (circular) round; (completo) complete

reducción [reðuk'θjon] nf reduction

reducido, a [reðu'θiðo, a] adj reduced; (limitado) limited; (pequeño) small

reducir [reðu'θir] vt to reduce; to limit; ~se vr to diminish

redundancia [reðun'danθja] nf redundancy

reembolsar [re(e)mbol'sar] vt (persona) to reimburse; (dinero) to repay, pay back; (depósito) to refund; **reembolso** nm reimbursement; refund

reemplazar [re(e)mpla'θar] vt to replace; **reemplazo** nm replacement; **de reemplazo** (MIL) reserve

reencuentro [re(e)n'kwentro] nm reunion

referencia [refe'renθja] nf reference; **con ~ a** with reference to

referéndum [refe'rendum] (pl ~s) nm referendum

referente [refe'rente] adj: ~ **a** concerning, relating to

referir [refe'rir] vt (contar) to tell, recount; (relacionar) to refer, relate; ~se vr: ~se a to refer to

refilón [refi'lon]: **de ~** adv obliquely

refinado, a [refi'naðo, a] adj refined

refinamiento [refina'mjento] nm refinement

refinar [refi'nar] vt to refine; **refinería** nf refinery

reflejar [refle'xar] vt to reflect; **reflejo, a** adj reflected; (movimiento) reflex ♦ nm reflection; (ANAT) reflex

reflexión [reflek'sjon] nf reflection; **reflexionar** vt to reflect on ♦ vi to reflect; (detenerse) to pause (to think)

reflexivo, a [reflek'siβo, a] adj thoughtful; (LING) reflexive

reflujo [re'fluxo] nm ebb

reforma [re'forma] nf reform; (ARQ etc) repair; ~ **agraria** agrarian reform

reformar [refor'mar] vt to reform; (modificar) to change, alter; (ARQ) to repair; ~se vr to mend one's ways

reformatorio [reforma'torjo] nm reformatory

reforzar [refor'θar] vt to strengthen; (ARQ) to reinforce; (fig) to encourage

refractario, a [refrak'tarjo, a] adj (TEC) heat-resistant

refrán [re'fran] nm proverb, saying

refregar [refre'xar] vt to scrub

refrenar [refre'nar] vt to check, restrain

refrendar [refren'dar] vt (firma) to endorse, countersign; (ley) to approve

refrescante [refres'kante] adj refreshing, cooling

refrescar [refres'kar] vt to refresh ♦ vi to cool down; ~se vr to get cooler; (tomar aire fresco) to go out for a breath of fresh air; (beber) to have a drink

refresco [re'fresko] nm soft drink, cool drink; "~s" "refreshments"

refriega [re'frjexa] nf scuffle, brawl

refrigeración [refrixera'θjon] nf

refrigeration; (*de sala*) air-conditioning

refrigerador [refrixera'ðor] *nm* refrigerator (*BRIT*), icebox (*US*)

refrigerar [refrixe'rar] *vt* to refrigerate; (*sala*) to air-condition

refuerzo [re'fwerθo] *nm* reinforcement; (*TEC*) support

refugiado, a [refu'xjaðo, a] *nm/f* refugee

refugiarse [refu'xjarse] *vr* to take refuge, shelter

refugio [re'fuxjo] *nm* refuge; (*protección*) shelter

refunfuñar [refunfu'nar] *vi* to grunt, growl; (*quejarse*) to grumble

refutar [refu'tar] *vt* to refute

regadera [reγa'ðera] *nf* watering can

regadío [reγa'ðio] *nm* irrigated land

regalado, a [reγa'laðo, a] *adj* comfortable, luxurious; (*gratis*) free, for nothing

regalar [reγa'lar] *vt* (*dar*) to give (as a present); (*entregar*) to give away; (*mimar*) to pamper, make a fuss of

regaliz [reγa'liθ] *nm* liquorice

regalo [re'γalo] *nm* (*obsequio*) gift, present; (*gusto*) pleasure

regañadientes [reγaɲa'ðjentes]: **a ~** *adv* reluctantly

regañar [reγa'nar] *vt* to scold ♦ *vi* to grumble; **regañón, ona** *adj* nagging

regar [re'γar] *vt* to water, irrigate; (*fig*) to scatter, sprinkle

regatear [reγate'ar] *vt* (*COM*) to bargain over; (*escatimar*) to be mean with ♦ *vi* to bargain, haggle; (*DEPORTE*) to dribble; **regateo** *nm* bargaining; dribbling; (*del cuerpo*) swerve, dodge

regazo [re'γaθo] *nm* lap

regeneración [rexenera'θjon] *nf* regeneration

regenerar [rexene'rar] *vt* to regenerate

regentar [rexen'tar] *vt* to direct, manage; **regente** (*COM*) manager; (*POL*) regent

régimen ['reximen] (*pl* **regímenes**) *nm* regime; (*MED*) diet

regimiento [rexi'mjento] *nm* regiment

regio, a ['rexjo, a] *adj* royal, regal; (*fig: suntuoso*) splendid; (*AM: fam*) great, terrific

región [re'xjon] *nf* region

regir [re'xir] *vt* to govern, rule; (*dirigir*) to manage, run ♦ *vi* to apply, be in force

registrar [rexis'trar] *vt* (*buscar*) to search; (: *en cajón*) to look through; (*inspeccionar*) to inspect; (*anotar*) to register, record; (*INFORM*) to log; **~se** *vr* to register; (*ocurrir*) to happen

registro [re'xistro] *nm* (*acto*) registration; (*MUS, libro*) register; (*inspección*) inspection, search; ~ **civil** registry office

regla ['reγla] *nf* (*ley*) rule, regulation; (*de medir*) ruler, rule; (*MED: período*) period

reglamentación [reγlamenta'θjon] *nf* (*acto*) regulation; (*lista*) rules *pl*

reglamentar [reγlamen'tar] *vt* to regulate; **reglamentario, a** *adj* statutory; **reglamento** *nm* rules *pl*, regulations *pl*

regocijarse [reγoθi'xarse] *vr*: ~ **de** to rejoice at, be happy about; **regocijo** *nm* joy, happiness

regodearse [reγoðe'arse] *vr* to be glad, be delighted; **regodeo** *nm* delight

regresar [reγre'sar] *vi* to come back, go back, return; **regresivo, a** *adj* backward; (*fig*) regressive; **regreso** *nm* return

reguero [re'γero] *nm* (*de sangre etc*) trickle; (*de humo*) trail

regulador [reγula'ðor] *nm* regulator; (*de radio etc*) knob, control

regular [reγu'lar] *adj* regular; (*normal*) normal, usual; (*común*) ordinary; (*organizado*) regular, orderly; (*mediano*) average; (*fam*) not bad, so-so ♦ *adv* so-so, alright ♦ *vt* (*controlar*) to control, regulate; (*TEC*) to adjust; **por lo ~** as a rule; **~idad** *nf* regularity; **~izar** *vt* to regularize

regusto [re'γusto] *nm* aftertaste

rehabilitación [reaβilita'θjon] *nf* rehabilitation; (*ARQ*) restoration

rehabilitar [reaβili'tar] *vt* to rehabilitate; (*ARQ*) to restore; (*reintegrar*) to reinstate

rehacer [rea'θer] *vt* (*reparar*) to mend, repair; (*volver a hacer*) to redo, repeat; **~se** *vr* (*MED*) to recover

rehén [re'en] *nm* hostage

rehuir [reu'ir] *vt* to avoid, shun

rehusar [reu'sar] *vt, vi* to refuse

reina ['reina] *nf* queen; **~do** *nm* reign

reinante [rei'nante] *adj* (*fig*) prevailing

reinar [rei'nar] *vi* to reign

reincidir [reinθi'ðir] *vi* to relapse

reincorporarse [reinkorpo'rarse] *vr*: ~ **a** to rejoin

reino ['reino] *nm* kingdom; **el R~ Unido** the United Kingdom

reintegrar [reinte'γrar] *vt* (*reconstituir*) to reconstruct; (*persona*) to reinstate; (*dinero*) to refund, pay back; **~se** *vr*: **~se a** to return to

reír [re'ir] *vi* to laugh; **~se** *vr* to laugh; **~se de** to laugh at

reiterar [reite'rar] *vt* to reiterate

reivindicación [reiβindika'θjon] *nf* (*demanda*) claim, demand; (*justificación*) vindication

reivindicar [reiβindi'kar] *vt* to claim

reja ['rexa] *nf* (*de ventana*) grille, bars *pl*; (*en la calle*) grating

rejilla [re'xiʎa] *nf* grating, grille; (*muebles*) wickerwork; (*de ventilación*) vent; (*de coche etc*) luggage rack

rejoneador [rexonea'ðor] *nm* mounted

bullfighter

rejuvenecer |rexußene'θer| vt, vi to rejuvenate

relación |rela'θjon| nf relation, relationship; (MAT) ratio; (narración) report; **relaciones públicas** public relations; **con ~ a, en ~ con** in relation to; **relacionar** vt to relate, connect; **relacionarse** vr to be connected, be linked

relajación |relaxa'θjon| nf relaxation

relajado, a |rela'xaðo, a| adj (disoluto) loose; (cómodo) relaxed; (MED) ruptured

relajar |rela'xar| vt to relax; **~se** vr to relax

relamerse |rela'merse| vr to lick one's lips

relamido, a |rela'miðo, a| adj (pulcro) overdressed; (afectado) affected

relámpago |re'lampaxo| nm flash of lightning; **visita/huelga ~** lightning visit/strike; **relampaguear** vi to flash

relatar |rela'tar| vt to tell, relate

relativo, a |rela'tißo, a| adj relative; **en lo ~ a** concerning

relato |re'lato| nm (narración) story, tale

relegar |rele'xar| vt to relegate

relevante |rele'ßante| adj eminent, outstanding

relevar |rele'ßar| vt (sustituir) to relieve; **~se** vr to relay; **~ a uno de un cargo** to relieve sb of his post

relevo |re'leßo| nm relief; **carrera de ~s** relay race

relieve |re'ljeße| nm (ARTE, TEC) relief; (fig) prominence, importance; **bajo ~** bas-relief

religión |reli'xjon| nf religion; **religioso, a** adj religious ♦ nm/f monk/nun

relinchar |relin'tʃar| vi to neigh; **relincho** nm neigh; (acto) neighing

reliquia |re'likja| nf relic; **~ de familia** heirloom

rellano |re'ʎano| nm (ARQ) landing

rellenar |reʎe'nar| vt (llenar) to fill up; (CULIN) to stuff; (COSTURA) to pad; **relleno, a** adj full up; stuffed ♦ nm stuffing; (de tapicería) padding

reloj |re'lo(x)| nm clock; **~ (de pulsera)** wristwatch; **~ despertador** alarm (clock); **poner el ~** to set one's watch (o the clock); **~ero, a** nm/f clockmaker; watchmaker

reluciente |relu'θjente| adj brilliant, shining

relucir |relu'θir| vi to shine; (fig) to excel

relumbrar |relum'brar| vi to dazzle, shine brilliantly

remachar |rema'tʃar| vt to rivet; (fig) to hammer home, drive home; **remache** nm rivet

remanente |rema'nente| nm remainder; (COM) balance; (de producto) surplus

remangar |reman'gar| vt to roll up

remanso |re'manso| nm pool

remar |re'mar| vi to row

rematado, a |rema'taðo, a| adj complete, utter

rematar |rema'tar| vt to finish off; (COM) to sell off cheap ♦ vi to end, finish off; (DEPORTE) to shoot

remate |re'mate| nm end, finish; (punta) tip; (DEPORTE) shot; (ARQ) top; **de o para ~** to crown it all (BRIT), to top it off

remedar |reme'ðar| vt to imitate

remediar |reme'ðjar| vt to remedy; (subsanar) to make good, repair; (evitar) to avoid

remedio |re'meðjo| nm remedy; (alivio) relief, help; (JUR) recourse, remedy; **poner ~ a** to correct, stop; **no tener más ~** to have no alternative; **¡qué ~!** there's no choice!; **sin ~** hopeless

remedo |re'meðo| nm imitation; (pey) parody

remendar |remen'dar| vt to repair; (con parche) to patch

remesa |re'mesa| nf remittance; (COM) shipment

remiendo |re'mjendo| nm mend; (con parche) patch; (cosido) darn

remilgado, a |remil'xaðo, a| adj prim; (afectado) affected

remilgo |re'milxo| nm primness; (afectación) affectation

reminiscencia |reminis'θenθja| nf reminiscence

remiso, a |re'miso, a| adj slack, slow

remite |re'mite| nm (en sobre) name and address of sender

remitir |remi'tir| vt to remit, send ♦ vi to slacken; (en carta): **remite: X** sender: X; **remitente** nm/f sender

remo |'remo| nm (de barco) oar; (DEPORTE) rowing

remojar |remo'xar| vt to steep, soak; (galleta etc) to dip, dunk

remojo |re'moxo| nm: **dejar la ropa en ~** to leave clothes to soak

remolacha |remo'latʃa| nf beet, beetroot

remolcador |remolka'ðor| nm (NAUT) tug; (AUTO) breakdown lorry

remolcar |remol'kar| vt to tow

remolino |remo'lino| nm eddy; (de agua) whirlpool; (de viento) whirlwind; (de gente) crowd

remolque |re'molke| nm tow, towing; (cuerda) towrope; **llevar a ~** to tow

remontar |remon'tar| vt to mend; **~se** vr to soar; **~se a** (COM) to amount to; **~ el vuelo** to soar

remorder |remor'ðer| vt to distress, disturb; **~le la conciencia a uno** to have a guilty conscience; **remordimiento** nm remorse

remoto, a |re'moto, a| adj remote

remover [remo'ßer] vt to stir; (*tierra*) to turn over; (*objetos*) to move round

remozar [remo'θar] vt (*ARQ*) to refurbish

remuneración [remunera'θjon] nf remuneration

remunerar [remune'rar] vt to remunerate; (*premiar*) to reward

renacer [rena'θer] vi to be reborn; (*fig*) to revive; **renacimiento** nm rebirth; **el Renacimiento** the Renaissance

renacuajo [rena'kwaxo] nm (*ZOOL*) tadpole

renal [re'nal] adj renal, kidney cpd

rencilla [ren'θiʎa] nf quarrel

rencor [ren'kor] nm rancour, bitterness; **~oso, a** adj spiteful

rendición [rendi'θjon] nf surrender

rendido, a [ren'diðo, a] adj (*sumiso*) submissive; (*cansado*) worn-out, exhausted

rendija [ren'dixa] nf (*hendedura*) crack, cleft

rendimiento [rendi'mjento] nm (*producción*) output; (*TEC, COM*) efficiency

rendir [ren'dir] vt (*vencer*) to defeat; (*producir*) to produce; (*dar beneficio*) to yield; (*agotar*) to exhaust ♦ vi to pay; **~se** vr (*someterse*) to surrender; (*cansarse*) to wear o.s. out; **~ homenaje** o **culto a** to pay homage to

renegar [rene'var] vi (*renunciar*) to renounce; (*blasfemar*) to blaspheme; (*quejarse*) to complain

RENFE ['renfe] nf abr (= *Red Nacional de los Ferrocarriles Españoles*) ≈ BR (*BRIT*)

renglón [ren'glon] nm (*línea*) line; (*COM*) item, article; **a ~ seguido** immediately after

renombrado, a [renom'braðo, a] adj renowned

renombre [re'nombre] nm renown

renovación [renoßa'θjon] nf (*de contrato*) renewal; (*ARQ*) renovation

renovar [reno'ßar] vt to renew; (*ARQ*) to renovate

renta ['renta] nf (*ingresos*) income; (*beneficio*) profit; (*alquiler*) rent; **~ vitalicia** annuity; **rentable** adj profitable; **rentar** vt to produce, yield

renuncia [re'nunθja] nf resignation

renunciar [renun'θjar] vt to renounce; (*tabaco, alcohol etc*): **~ a** to give up; (*oferta, oportunidad*) to turn down; (*puesto*) to resign ♦ vi to resign

reñido, a [re'niðo, a] adj (*batalla*) bitter, hard-fought; **estar ~ con uno** to be on bad terms with sb

reñir [re'nir] vt (*regañar*) to scold ♦ vi (*estar peleado*) to quarrel, fall out; (*combatir*) to fight

reo ['reo] nm/f culprit, offender; **~ de muerte** prisoner condemned to death

reojo [re'oxo] **de ~** adv out of the corner of one's eye

reparación [repara'θjon] nf (*acto*) mending, repairing; (*TEC*) repair; (*fig*) amends, reparation

reparar [repa'rar] vt to repair; (*fig*) to make amends for; (*observar*) to observe ♦ vi: **~ en** (*darse cuenta de*) to notice; (*prestar atención a*) to pay attention to

reparo [re'paro] nm (*advertencia*) observation; (*duda*) doubt; (*dificultad*) difficulty; **poner ~s (a)** to raise objections (to)

repartición [reparti'θjon] nf distribution; (*división*) division; **repartidor, a** nm/f distributor

repartir [repar'tir] vt to distribute, share out; (*CORREOS*) to deliver; **reparto** nm distribution; delivery; (*TEATRO, CINE*) cast; (*AM: urbanización*) housing estate (*BRIT*), real estate development (*US*)

repasar [repa'sar] vt (*ESCOL*) to revise; (*MECÁNICA*) to check, overhaul; (*COSTURA*) to mend; **repaso** nm revision; overhaul, checkup; mending

repatriar [repa'trjar] vt to repatriate

repecho [re'petʃo] nm steep incline

repelente [repe'lente] adj repellent, repulsive

repeler [repe'ler] vt to repel

repensar [repen'sar] vt to reconsider

repente [re'pente] nm: **de ~** suddenly; **~ de ira** fit of anger

repentino, a [repen'tino, a] adj sudden

repercusión [reperku'sjon] nf repercussion

repercutir [reperku'tir] vi (*objeto*) to rebound; (*sonido*) to echo; **~ en** (*fig*) to have repercussions on

repertorio [reper'torjo] nm list; (*TEATRO*) repertoire

repetición [repeti'θjon] nf repetition

repetir [repe'tir] vt to repeat; (*plato*) to have a second helping of ♦ vi to repeat; (*sabor*) to come back; **~se** vr (*volver sobre un tema*) to repeat o.s.

repetitivo, a [repeti'tißo, a] adj repetitive, repetitious

repicar [repi'kar] vt (*campanas*) to ring

repique [re'pike] nm pealing, ringing; **~teo** nm pealing; (*de tambor*) drumming

repisa [re'pisa] nf ledge, shelf; (*de ventana*) windowsill; **~ de chimenea** mantelpiece

repito etc vb ver **repetir**

replantearse [replante'arse] vr: **~ un problema** to reconsider a problem

replegarse [reple'varse] vr to fall back, retreat

repleto, a [re'pleto, a] adj replete, full up

réplica ['replika] nf answer; (*ARTE*) replica

replicar [repli'kar] vi to answer; (*objetar*) to argue, answer back

repliegue [re'pljeve] nm (*MIL*) withdrawal

repoblación [repoβla'θjon] nf repopulation; (de río) restocking; **~ forestal** reafforestation

repoblar [repo'βlar] vt to repopulate; (con árboles) to reafforest

repollo [re'poʎo] nm cabbage

reponer [repo'ner] vt to replace, put back; (TEATRO) to revive; **~se** vr to recover; **~ que** to reply that

reportaje [repor'taxe] nm report, article

reportero, a [repor'tero, a] nm/f reporter

reposacabezas [reposaka'ßeθas] nm inv headrest

reposado, a [repo'saðo, a] adj (descansado) restful; (tranquilo) calm

reposar [repo'sar] vi to rest, repose

reposición [reposi'θjon] nf replacement; (CINE) remake

reposo [re'poso] nm rest

repostar [repos'tar] vt to replenish; (AUTO) to fill up (with petrol (BRIT) o gasoline (US))

repostería [reposte'ria] nf confectioner's (shop); **repostero, a** nm/f confectioner

reprender [repren'der] vt to reprimand

represa [re'presa] nf dam; (lago artificial) lake, pool

represalia [repre'salja] nf reprisal

representación [representa'θjon] nf representation; (TEATRO) performance; **representante** nm/f representative; performer

representar [represen'tar] vt to represent; (TEATRO) to perform; (edad) to look; **~se** vr to imagine; **representativo, a** adj representative

represión [repre'sjon] nf repression

reprimenda [repri'menda] nf reprimand, rebuke

reprimir [repri'mir] vt to repress

reprobar [repro'βar] vt to censure, reprove

reprochar [repro'tʃar] vt to reproach; **reproche** nm reproach

reproducción [reproðuk'θjon] nf reproduction

reproducir [reproðu'θir] vt to reproduce; **~se** vr to breed; (situación) to recur

reproductor, a [reproðuk'tor, a] adj reproductive

reptil [rep'til] nm reptile

república [re'puβlika] nf republic; **R~ Dominicana** Dominican Republic; **republicano, a** adj, nm/f republican

repudiar [repu'ðjar] vt to repudiate; (fe) to renounce

repuesto [re'pwesto] nm (pieza de recambio) spare (part); (abastecimiento) supply; **rueda de ~** spare wheel

repugnancia [repux'nanθja] nf repugnance; **repugnante** adj repugnant, repulsive

repugnar [repux'nar] vt to disgust

repulsa [re'pulsa] nf rebuff

repulsión [repul'sjon] nf repulsion, aversion; **repulsivo, a** adj repulsive

reputación [reputa'θjon] nf reputation

requemado, a [reke'maðo, a] adj (quemado) scorched; (bronceado) tanned

requerimiento [rekeri'mjento] nm request; (JUR) summons

requerir [reke'rir] vt (pedir) to ask, request; (exigir) to require; (llamar) to send for, summon

requesón [reke'son] nm cottage cheese

requete... [re'kete] prefijo extremely

réquiem ['rekjem] (pl **~s**) nm requiem

requisito [reki'sito] nm requirement, requisite

res [res] nf beast, animal

resaca [re'saka] nf (en el mar) undertow, undercurrent; (fam) hangover

resaltar [resal'tar] vi to project, stick out; (fig) to stand out

resarcir [resar'θir] vt to compensate; **~se** vr to make up for

resbaladizo, a [resβala'ðiθo, a] adj slippery

resbalar [resβa'lar] vi to slip, slide; (fig) to slip (up); **~se** vr to slip, slide; to slip (up); **resbalón** nm (acción) slip

rescatar [reska'tar] vt (salvar) to save, rescue; (objeto) to get back, recover; (cautivos) to ransom

rescate [res'kate] nm rescue; (de objeto) recovery; **pagar un ~** to pay a ransom

rescindir [resθin'dir] vt to rescind

rescisión [resθi'sjon] nf cancellation

rescoldo [res'koldo] nm embers pl

resecar [rese'kar] vt to dry thoroughly; (MED) to cut out, remove; **~se** vr to dry up

reseco, a [re'seko, a] adj very dry; (fig) skinny

resentido, a [resen'tiðo, a] adj resentful

resentimiento [resenti'mjento] nm resentment, bitterness

resentirse [resen'tirse] vr (debilitarse: persona) to suffer; **~ de** (consecuencias) to feel the effects of; **~ de (o por) algo** to resent sth, be bitter about sth

reseña [re'seɲa] nf (cuenta) account; (informe) report; (LITERATURA) review

reseñar [rese'ɲar] vt to describe; (LITERATURA) to review

reserva [re'serβa] nf reserve; (reservación) reservation; **a ~ de que ...** unless ...; **con toda ~** in strictest confidence

reservado, a [reser'βaðo, a] adj reserved; (retraído) cold, distant ♦ nm private room

reservar [reser'βar] vt (guardar) to keep; (habitación, entrada) to reserve; **~se** vr to save o.s.; (callar) to keep to o.s.

resfriado [resfri'aðo] nm cold; **resfriarse** vr

to cool; (MED) to catch (a) cold

resguardar [reswar'ðar] vt to protect,
shield; **~se** vr: **~se de** to guard against;
resguardo nm defence; (vale) voucher;
(recibo) receipt, slip

residencia [resi'ðenθja] nf residence; **~l** nf
(urbanización) housing estate

residente [resi'ðente] adj, nm/f resident

residir [resi'ðir] vi to reside, live; **~ en** to
reside in, lie in

residuo [re'siðwo] nm residue

resignación [resixna'θjon] nf resignation;
resignarse vr: **resignarse a** o **con** to resign
o.s. to, be resigned to

resina [re'sina] nf resin

resistencia [resis'tenθja] nf (dureza)
endurance, strength; (oposición, ELEC)
resistance; **resistente** adj strong, hardy;
resistant

resistir [resis'tir] vt (soportar) to bear;
(oponerse a) to withstand, oppose; (aguantar) to
put up with ♦ vi to resist; (aguantar) to last,
endure; **~se** vr: **~se a** to refuse to, resist

resolución [resolu'θjon] nf resolution;
(decisión) decision; **resoluto, a** adj resolute

resolver [resol'ßer] vt to resolve; (solucionar)
to solve, resolve; (decidir) to decide, settle;
~se vr to make up one's mind

resonancia [reso'nanθja] nf (del sonido)
resonance; (repercusión) repercussion

resonar [reso'nar] vi to ring, echo

resoplar [reso'plar] vi to snort; **resoplido**
nm heavy breathing

resorte [re'sorte] nm spring; (fig) lever

respaldar [respal'dar] vt to back (up),
support; **~se** vr to lean back; **~se con** o **en**
(fig) to take one's stand on; **respaldo** nm
(de sillón) back; (fig) support, backing

respectivo, a [respek'tißo, a] adj respective;
en lo ~ a with regard to

respecto [res'pekto] nm: **al ~ on** this matter;
con ~ a, ~ de with regard to, in relation to

respetable [respe'taßle] adj respectable

respetar [respe'tar] vt to respect; **respeto**
nm respect; (acatamiento) deference;
respetos nmpl respects; **respetuoso, a** adj
respectful

respingo [res'pingo] nm start, jump

respiración [respira'θjon] nf breathing;
(MED) respiration; (ventilación) ventilation

respirar [respi'rar] vi to breathe;
respiratorio, a adj respiratory; **respiro** nm
breathing; (fig: descanso) respite

resplandecer [resplande'θer] vi to shine;
resplandeciente adj resplendent, shining;
resplandor nm brilliance, brightness; (de
luz, fuego) blaze

responder [respon'der] vt to answer ♦ vi to
answer; (fig) to respond; (pey) to answer

back; **~ de** o **por** to answer for; **respondón,
ona** adj cheeky

responsabilidad [responsaßili'ðað] nf
responsibility

responsabilizarse [responsaßili'θarse] vr
to make o.s. responsible, take charge

responsable [respon'saßle] adj responsible

respuesta [res'pwesta] nf answer, reply

resquebrajar [reskeßra'xar] vt to crack,
split; **~se** vr to crack, split

resquemor [reske'mor] nm resentment

resquicio [res'kiθjo] nm chink; (hendedura)
crack

resta ['resta] nf (MAT) remainder

restablecer [restaßle'θer] vt to re-establish,
restore; **~se** vr to recover

restallar [resta'ʎar] vi to crack

restante [res'tante] adj remaining; **lo ~** the
remainder

restar [res'tar] vt (MAT) to subtract; (fig) to
take away ♦ vi to remain, be left

restauración [restaura'θjon] nf restoration

restaurante [restau'rante] nm restaurant

restaurar [restau'rar] vt to restore

restitución [restitu'θjon] nf return,
restitution

restituir [restitu'ir] vt (devolver) to return,
give back; (rehabilitar) to restore

resto ['resto] nm (residuo) rest, remainder;
(apuesta) stake; **~s** nmpl remains

restregar [restre'xar] vt to scrub, rub

restricción [restrik'θjon] nf restriction

restrictivo, a [restrik'tißo, a] adj restrictive

restringir [restrin'xir] vt to restrict, limit

resucitar [resuθi'tar] vt, vi to resuscitate,
revive

resuello [re'sweʎo] nm (aliento) breath; **estar
sin ~** to be breathless

resuelto, a [re'swelto, a] pp de **resolver**
♦ adj resolute, determined

resultado [resul'taðo] nm result; (conclusión)
outcome; **resultante** adj resulting, resultant

resultar [resul'tar] vi (ser) to be; (llegar a ser)
to turn out to be; (salir bien) to turn out
well; (COM) to amount to; **~ de** to stem from;
me resulta difícil hacerlo it's difficult for me to
do it

resumen [re'sumen] (pl resúmenes) nm
summary, résumé; **en ~** in short

resumir [resu'mir] vt to sum up; (cortar) to
abridge, cut down; (condensar) to summarize

resurgir [resur'xir] vi (reaparecer) to reappear

resurrección [resurre(k)'θjon] nf
resurrection

retablo [re'taßlo] nm altarpiece

retaguardia [reta'xwarðja] nf rearguard

retahíla [reta'ila] nf series, string

retal [re'tal] nm remnant

retar [re'tar] vt to challenge; (desafiar) to

defy, dare

retardar [retar'ðar] vt (demorar) to delay; (hacer más lento) to slow down; (retener) to hold back

retazo [re'taθo] nm snippet (BRIT), fragment

retener [rete'ner] vt (intereses) to withhold

reticente [reti'θente] adj (tono) insinuating; (postura) reluctant; **ser ~ a hacer algo** to be reluctant o unwilling to do sth

retina [re'tina] nf retina

retintín [retin'tin] nm jangle, jingle

retirada [reti'raða] nf (MIL, refugio) retreat; (de dinero) withdrawal; (de embajador) recall; **retirado, a** (lugar) remote; (vida) quiet; (jubilado) retired

retirar [reti'rar] vt to withdraw; (quitar) to remove; (jubilar) to retire, pension off; **~se** vr to retreat, withdraw; to retire; (acostarse) to retire, go to bed; **retiro** nm retreat; retirement; (pago) pension

reto ['reto] nm dare, challenge

retocar [reto'kar] vt (fotografía) to touch up, retouch

retoño [re'toɲo] nm sprout, shoot; (fig) offspring, child

retoque [re'toke] nm retouching

retorcer [retor'θer] vt to twist; (manos, lavado) to wring; **~se** vr to become twisted; (mover el cuerpo) to writhe

retorcido, a [retor'θiðo, a] adj (persona) devious

retórica [re'torika] nf rhetoric; (pey) affectedness; **retórico, a** adj rhetorical

retornar [retor'nar] vt to return, give back ♦ vi to return, go/come back; **retorno** nm return

retortijón [retorti'xon] nm twist, twisting

retozar [reto'θar] vi (juguetear) to frolic, romp; (saltar) to gambol; **retozón, ona** adj playful

retracción [retrak'θjon] nf retraction

retractarse [retrak'tarse] vr to retract; **me retracto** I take that back

retraerse [retra'erse] vr to retreat, withdraw; **retraído, a** adj shy, retiring; **retraimiento** nm retirement; (timidez) shyness

retransmisión [retransmi'sjon] nf repeat (broadcast)

retransmitir [retransmi'tir] vt (mensaje) to relay; (TV etc) to repeat, retransmit; (: en vivo) to broadcast live

retrasado, a [retra'saðo, a] adj late; (MED) mentally retarded; (país etc) backward, underdeveloped

retrasar [retra'sar] vt (demorar) to postpone, put off; (retardar) to slow down ♦ vi (atrasarse) to be late; (reloj) to be slow; (producción) to fall (off); (quedarse atrás) to lag behind; **~se** vr to be late; to be slow; to

fall (off); to lag behind

retraso [re'traso] nm (demora) delay; (lentitud) slowness; (tardanza) lateness; (atraso) backwardness; **~s** (FINANZAS) nmpl arrears; **llegar con ~** to arrive late; **~ mental** mental deficiency

retratar [retra'tar] vt (ARTE) to paint the portrait of; (fotografiar) to photograph; (fig) to depict, describe; **~se** vr to have one's portrait painted; to have one's photograph taken; **retrato** nm portrait; (fig) likeness; **retrato-robot** nm Identikit ® picture

retreta [re'treta] nf retreat

retrete [re'trete] nm toilet

retribución [retriβu'θjon] nf (recompensa) reward; (pago) pay, payment

retribuir [retri'ßwir] vt (recompensar) to reward; (pagar) to pay

retro... ['retro] prefijo retro...

retroactivo, a [retroak'tiβo, a] adj retroactive, retrospective

retroceder [retroθe'ðer] vi (echarse atrás) to move back(wards); (fig) to back down

retroceso [retro'θeso] nm backward movement; (MED) relapse; (fig) backing down

retrógrado, a [re'troɣraðo, a] adj retrograde, retrogressive; (POL) reactionary

retrospectivo, a [retrospek'tiβo, a] adj retrospective

retrovisor [retroβi'sor] nm (tb: espejo ~) rear-view mirror

retumbar [retum'bar] vi to echo, resound

reúma [re'uma], **reuma** ['reuma] nm rheumatism

reumatismo [reuma'tismo] nm = **reúma**

reunificar [reunifi'kar] vt to reunify

reunión [reu'njon] nf (asamblea) meeting; (fiesta) party

reunir [reu'nir] vt (juntar) to reunite, join (together); (recoger) to gather (together); (personas) to get together; (cualidades) to combine; **~se** vr (personas: en asamblea) to meet, gather

revalidar [reβali'ðar] vt (ratificar) to confirm, ratify

revalorizar [reβalori'θar] vt to revalue, reassess

revancha [re'βantʃa] nf revenge

revelación [reβela'θjon] nf revelation

revelado [reβe'laðo] nm developing

revelar [reβe'lar] vt to reveal; (FOTO) to develop

reventa [re'βenta] nf (de entradas: para concierto) touting

reventar [reβen'tar] vt to burst, explode

reventón [reβen'ton] nm (AUTO) blow-out (BRIT), flat (US)

reverencia [reβe'renθja] nf reverence;

reverenciar [reβeren'θjar] vt to revere

reverendo, a [reβe'rendo, a] adj reverend

reverente [reβe'rente] adj reverent

reversible [reβer'siβle] adj (prenda) reversible

reverso [re'βerso] nm back, other side; (de moneda) reverse

revertir [reβer'tir] vi to revert

revés [re'βes] nm back, wrong side; (fig) reverse, setback; (DEPORTE) backhand; **al ~** the wrong way round; (de arriba abajo) upside down; (ropa) inside out; **volver algo del ~** to turn sth round; (ropa) to turn sth inside out

revestir [reβes'tir] vt (cubrir) to cover, coat

revisar [reβi'sar] vt (examinar) to check; (texto etc) to revise; **revisión** nf revision

revisor, a [reβi'sor, a] nm/f inspector; (FERRO) ticket collector

revista [re'βista] nf magazine, review; (TEATRO) revue; (inspección) inspection; **pasar ~ a** to review, inspect

revivir [reβi'βir] vi to revive

revocación [reβoka'θjon] nf repeal

revocar [reβo'kar] vt to revoke

revolcarse [reβol'karse] vr to roll about

revolotear [reβolote'ar] vi to flutter

revoltijo [reβol'tixo] nm mess, jumble

revoltoso, a [reβol'toso, a] adj (travieso) naughty, unruly

revolución [reβolu'θjon] nf revolution; **revolucionar** vt to revolutionize; **revolucionario, a** adj, nm/f revolutionary

revolver [reβol'βer] vt (desordenar) to disturb, mess up; (mover) to move about ♦ vi: **~ en** to go through, rummage (about) in; **~se** vr (volver contra) to turn on o against

revólver [re'βolβer] nm revolver

revuelo [re'βwelo] nm fluttering; (fig) commotion

revuelta [re'βwelta] nf (motín) revolt; (agitación) commotion

revuelto, a [re'βwelto, a] pp de **revolver** ♦ adj (mezclado) mixed-up, in disorder

rey [rei] nm king; **Día de R~es** Twelfth Night

reyerta [re'jerta] nf quarrel, brawl

rezagado, a [reθa'xaðo, a] nm/f straggler

rezagar [reθa'xar] vt (dejar atrás) to leave behind; (retrasar) to delay, postpone

rezar [re'θar] vi to pray; **~ con** (fam) to concern, have to do with; **rezo** nm prayer

rezongar [reθon'gar] vi to grumble

rezumar [reθu'mar] vt to ooze

ría ['ria] nf estuary

riada [ri'aða] nf flood

ribera [ri'βera] nf (de río) bank; (: área) riverside

ribete [ri'βete] nm (de vestido) border; (fig) addition; **~ar** vt to edge, border

ricino [ri'θino] nm: **aceite de ~** castor oil

rico, a ['riko, a] adj rich; (adinerado) wealthy, rich; (lujoso) luxurious; (comida) delicious; (niño) lovely, cute ♦ nm/f rich person

rictus ['riktus] nm (mueca) sneer, grin

ridiculez [riðiku'leθ] nf absurdity

ridiculizar [riðikuli'θar] vt to ridicule

ridículo, a [ri'ðikulo, a] adj ridiculous; **hacer el ~** to make a fool of o.s.; **poner a uno en ~** to make a fool of sb

riego ['rjexo] nm (aspersión) watering; (irrigación) irrigation

riel [rjel] nm rail

rienda ['rjenda] nf rein; **dar ~ suelta a** to give free rein to

riesgo ['rjesxo] nm risk; **correr el ~ de** to run the risk of

rifa ['rifa] nf (lotería) raffle; **rifar** vt to raffle

rifle ['rifle] nm rifle

rigidez [rixi'ðeθ] nf rigidity, stiffness; (fig) strictness; **rígido, a** adj rigid, stiff; strict, inflexible

rigor [ri'xor] nm strictness, rigour; (inclemencia) harshness; **de ~** de rigueur, essential; **riguroso, a** adj rigorous; harsh; (severo) severe

rimar [ri'mar] vi to rhyme

rimbombante [rimbom'bante] adj pompous

rímel ['rimel] nm mascara

rímmel ['rimel] nm = **rímel**

rincón [rin'kon] nm corner (inside)

rinoceronte [rinoθe'ronte] nm rhinoceros

riña ['riɲa] nf (disputa) argument; (pelea) brawl

riñón [ri'ɲon] nm kidney

río etc ['rio] vb ver **reir** ♦ nm river; (fig) torrent, stream; **~ abajo/arriba** downstream/upstream; **~ de la Plata** River Plate

rioja [ri'oxa] nm (vino) rioja (wine)

rioplatense [riopla'tense] adj of o from the River Plate region

riqueza [ri'keθa] nf wealth, riches pl; (cualidad) richness

risa ['risa] nf laughter; (una ~) laugh; **¡qué ~!** what a laugh!

risco ['risko] nm crag, cliff

risible [ri'siβle] adj ludicrous, laughable

risotada [riso'taða] nf guffaw, loud laugh

ristra ['ristra] nf string

risueño, a [ri'sweɲo, a] adj (sonriente) smiling; (contento) cheerful

ritmo ['ritmo] nm rhythm; **a ~ lento** slowly; **trabajar a ~ lento** to go slow

rito ['rito] nm rite

ritual [ri'twal] adj, nm ritual

rival [ri'βal] adj, nm/f rival; **~idad** nf rivalry; **~izar** vi: **~izar con** to rival, vie with

rizado, a [ri'θaðo, a] adj curly ♦ nm curls pl

rizar [ri'θar] vt to curl; **~se** vr (pelo) to curl;

(*agua*) to ripple; **rizo** *nm* curl; ripple
RNE *nf abr* = **Radio Nacional de España**
robar [ro'βar] *vt* to rob; (*objeto*) to steal; (*casa etc*) to break into; (*NAIPES*) to draw
roble ['roβle] *nm* oak; **~dal** *nm* oakwood
robo ['roβo] *nm* robbery, theft
robot [ro'βot] *nm* robot; **~ (de cocina)** food processor
robustecer [roβuste'θer] *vt* to strengthen
robusto, a [ro'βusto, a] *adj* robust, strong
roca ['roka] *nf* rock
roce ['roθe] *nm* (*caricia*) brush; (*TEC*) friction; (*en la piel*) graze; **tener ~ con** to be in close contact with
rociar [ro'θjar] *vt* to spray
rocín [ro'θin] *nm* nag, hack
rocío [ro'θio] *nm* dew
rocoso, a [ro'koso, a] *adj* rocky
rodaballo [roδa'βaʎo] *nm* turbot
rodado, a [ro'δaδo, a] *adj* (*con ruedas*) wheeled
rodaja [ro'δaxa] *nf* slice
rodaje [ro'δaxe] *nm* (*CINE*) shooting, filming; (*AUTO*) running in
rodar [ro'δar] *vt* (*vehículo*) to wheel (along); (*escalera*) to roll down; (*viajar por*) to travel (over) ♦ *vi* to roll; (*coche*) to go, run; (*CINE*) to shoot, film
rodear [roδe'ar] *vt* to surround ♦ *vi* to go round; **se** *vr*: **~se de amigos** to surround o.s. with friends
rodeo [ro'δeo] *nm* (*ruta indirecta*) detour; (*evasión*) evasion; (*AM*) rodeo; **hablar sin ~s** to come to the point, speak plainly
rodilla [ro'δiʎa] *nf* knee; **de ~s** kneeling; **ponerse de ~s** to kneel (down)
rodillo [ro'δiʎo] *nm* roller; (*CULIN*) rolling-pin
roedor, a [roe'δor, a] *adj* gnawing ♦ *nm* rodent
roer [ro'er] *vt* (*masticar*) to gnaw; (*corroer, fig*) to corrode
rogar [ro'xar] *vt, vi* (*pedir*) to ask for; (*suplicar*) to beg, plead; **se ruega no fumar** please do not smoke
rojizo, a [ro'xiθo, a] *adj* reddish
rojo, a ['roxo, a] *adj, nm* red; **al ~ vivo** red-hot
rol [rol] *nm* list, roll; (*papel*) role
rollito [ro'ʎito] *nm*: **~ de primavera** spring roll
rollizo, a [ro'ʎiθo, a] *adj* (*objeto*) cylindrical; (*persona*) plump
rollo ['roʎo] *nm* roll; (*de cuerda*) coil; (*madera*) log; (*fam*) bore; **¡qué ~!** what a carry-on!
Roma ['roma] *ñ* Rome
romance [ro'manθe] *nm* (*amoroso*) romance; (*LITERATURA*) ballad
romano, a [ro'mano, a] *adj, nm/f* Roman; **a la romana** in batter

romanticismo [romanti'θismo] *nm* romanticism
romántico, a [ro'mantiko, a] *adj* romantic
rombo ['rombo] *nm* (*GEOM*) rhombus
romería [rome'ria] *nf* (*REL*) pilgrimage; (*excursión*) trip, outing
romero, a [ro'mero, a] *nm/f* pilgrim ♦ *nm* rosemary
romo, a ['romo, a] *adj* blunt; (*fig*) dull
rompecabezas [rompeka'βeθas] *nm inv* riddle, puzzle; (*juego*) jigsaw (puzzle)
rompeolas [rompe'olas] *nm inv* breakwater
romper [rom'per] *vt* to break; (*hacer pedazos*) to smash; (*papel, tela etc*) to tear, rip ♦ *vi* (*olas*) to break; (*sol, diente*) to break through; **~ un contrato** to break a contract; **~ a** (*empezar a*) to start (suddenly) to; **~ a llorar** to burst into tears; **~ con uno** to fall out with sb
ron [ron] *nm* rum
roncar [ron'kar] *vi* to snore
ronco, a ['ronko, a] *adj* (*afónico*) hoarse; (*áspero*) raucous
ronda ['ronda] *nf* (*gen*) round; (*patrulla*) patrol; **rondar** *vt* to patrol ♦ *vi* to patrol; (*fig*) to prowl round
ronquido [ron'kiδo] *nm* snore, snoring
ronronear [ronrone'ar] *vi* to purr; **ronroneo** *nm* purr
roña ['roɲa] *nf* (*VETERINARIA*) mange; (*mugre*) dirt, grime; (*óxido*) rust
roñoso, a [ro'ɲoso, a] *adj* (*mugriento*) filthy; (*tacaño*) mean
ropa ['ropa] *nf* clothes *pl*, clothing; **~ blanca** linen; **~ de cama** bed linen; **~ interior** underwear; **~ para lavar** washing; **~je** *nm* gown, robes *pl*
ropero [ro'pero] *nm* linen cupboard; (*guardarropa*) wardrobe
rosa ['rosa] *adj* pink ♦ *nf* rose; **~ de los vientos** the compass
rosado, a [ro'saδo, a] *adj* pink ♦ *nm* rosé
rosal [ro'sal] *nm* rosebush
rosario [ro'sarjo] *nm* (*REL*) rosary; **rezar el ~** to say the rosary
rosca ['roska] *nf* (*de tornillo*) thread; (*de humo*) coil, spiral; (*pan, postre*) ring-shaped roll/pastry
rosetón [rose'ton] *nm* rosette; (*ARQ*) rose window
rosquilla [ros'kiʎa] *nf* doughnut-shaped fritter
rostro ['rostro] *nm* (*cara*) face
rotación [rota'θjon] *nf* rotation; **~ de cultivos** crop rotation
rotativo, a [rota'tiβo, a] *adj* rotary
roto, a ['roto, a] *pp de* **romper** ♦ *adj* broken
rotonda [ro'tonda] *nf* roundabout
rótula ['rotula] *nf* kneecap; (*TEC*) ball-and-

socket joint

rotulador [rotula'ðor] nm felt-tip pen

rotular [rotu'lar] vt (carta, documento) to head, entitle; (objeto) to label; **rótulo** nm heading, title; label; (letrero) sign

rotundamente [rotunda'mente] adv (negar) flatly; (responder, afirmar) emphatically; **rotundo, a** adj round; (enfático) emphatic

rotura [ro'tura] nf (acto) breaking; (MED) fracture

roturar [rotu'rar] vt to plough

rozadura [roθa'ðura] nf abrasion, graze

rozar [ro'θar] vt (frotar) to rub; (arañar) to scratch; (tocar ligeramente) to shave, touch lightly; **~se** vr to rub (together); **~se con** (fam) to rub shoulders with

rte. abr (= remite, remitente) sender

RTVE nf abr = **Radiotelevisión Española**

rubí [ru'ßi] nm ruby; (de reloj) jewel

rubio, a [ˈrußjo, a] adj fair-haired, blond(e) ♦ nm/f blond/blonde; **tabaco ~** Virginia tobacco

rubor [ru'ßor] nm (sonrojo) blush; (timidez) bashfulness; **~izarse** vr to blush

rúbrica [ˈrußrika] nf (de la firma) flourish; **rubricar** vt (firmar) to sign with a flourish; (concluir) to sign and seal

rudimentario, a [ruðimen'tarjo, a] adj rudimentary; **rudimento** nm rudiment

rudo, a [ˈruðo, a] adj (sin pulir) unpolished; (grosero) coarse; (violento) violent; (sencillo) simple

rueda [ˈrweða] nf wheel; (círculo) ring, circle; (rodaja) slice, round; **~ delantera/trasera/de repuesto** front/back/spare wheel; **~ de prensa** press conference

ruedo [ˈrweðo] nm (círculo) circle; (TAUR) arena, bullring

ruego etc [ˈrweɣo] vb ver **rogar** ♦ nm request

rufián [ruˈfjan] nm scoundrel

rugby [ˈrußßi] nm rugby

rugido [ruˈxiðo] nm roar

rugir [ruˈxir] vi to roar

rugoso, a [ruˈɣoso, a] adj (arrugado) wrinkled; (áspero) rough; (desigual) ridged

ruido [ˈrwiðo] nm noise; (sonido) sound; (alboroto) racket, row; (escándalo) commotion, rumpus; **~so, a** adj noisy, loud; (fig) sensational

ruin [rwin] adj contemptible, mean

ruina [ˈrwina] nf ruin; (colapso) collapse; (de persona) ruin, downfall

ruindad [rwinˈdað] nf lowness, meanness; (acto) low o mean act

ruinoso, a [rwiˈnoso, a] adj ruinous; (destartalado) dilapidated, tumbledown; (COM) disastrous

ruiseñor [rwiseˈɲor] nm nightingale

ruleta [ruˈleta] nf roulette

rulo [ˈrulo] nm (para el pelo) curler

Rumanía [rumaˈnia] nf Rumania

rumba [ˈrumba] nf rumba

rumbo [ˈrumbo] nm (ruta) route, direction; (ángulo de dirección) course, bearing; (fig) course of events; **ir con ~ a** to be heading for

rumboso, a [rumˈboso, a] adj generous

rumiante [ruˈmjante] nm ruminant

rumiar [ruˈmjar] vt to chew; (fig) to chew over ♦ vi to chew the cud

rumor [ruˈmor] nm (ruido sordo) low sound; (murmuración) murmur, buzz

rumorearse vr: **se rumorea que** it is rumoured that

runrún [runˈrun] nm (voces) murmur, sound of voices; (fig) rumour

rupestre [ruˈpestre] adj rock cpd

ruptura [rupˈtura] nf rupture

rural [ruˈral] adj rural

Rusia [ˈrusja] nf Russia; **ruso, a** adj, nm/f Russian

rústica [ˈrustika] nf: **libro en ~** paperback (book); ver tb **rústico**

rústico, a [ˈrustiko, a] adj rustic; (ordinario) coarse, uncouth ♦ nm/f yokel

ruta [ˈruta] nf route

rutina [ruˈtina] nf routine; **~rio, a** adj routine

S, s

S abr (= santo, a) St; (= sur) S

s. abr (= siglo) C.; (= siguiente) foll

S.A. abr (= Sociedad Anónima) Ltd. (BRIT), Inc. (US)

sábado [ˈsaßaðo] nm Saturday

sábana [ˈsaßana] nf sheet

sabandija [saßanˈdixa] nf bug, insect

sabañón [saßaˈɲon] nm chilblain

saber [saˈßer] vt to know; (llegar a conocer) to find out, learn; (tener capacidad de) to know how to ♦ vi: **~ a** to taste of, taste like ♦ nm knowledge, learning; **a ~** namely; **¿sabes conducir/nadar?** can you drive/swim?; **¿sabes francés?** do you speak French?; **~ de memoria** to know by heart; **hacer ~ algo a uno** to inform sb of sth, let sb know sth

sabiduría [saßiðuˈria] nf (conocimientos) wisdom; (instrucción) learning

sabiendas [saˈßjendas]: **a ~** adv knowingly

sabio, a [ˈsaßjo, a] adj (docto) learned; (prudente) wise, sensible

sabor [saˈßor] nm taste, flavour; **~ear** vt to taste, savour; (fig) to relish

sabotaje [saßoˈtaxe] nm sabotage

saboteador, a [saßoteaˈðor, a] nm/f saboteur

sabotear [saßoteˈar] vt to sabotage

sabré etc vb ver **saber**

sabroso, a [sa'ßroso, a] adj tasty; (fig: fam) racy, salty

sacacorchos [saka'kortʃos] nm inv corkscrew

sacapuntas [saka'puntas] nm inv pencil sharpener

sacar [sa'kar] vt to take out; (fig: extraer) to get (out); (quitar) to remove, get out; (hacer salir) to bring out; (conclusión) to draw; (novela etc) to publish, bring out; (ropa) to take off; (obra) to make; (premio) to receive; (entradas) to get; (TENIS) to serve; ~ adelante una foto to take a photo; ~ la lengua to stick out one's tongue; ~ buenas/ malas notas to get good/bad marks

sacarina [saka'rina] nf saccharin(e)

sacerdote [saθer'ðote] nm priest

saciar [sa'θjar] vt (hambre, sed) to satisfy; ~se vr (de comida) to get full up; comer hasta ~se to eat one's fill

saco ['sako] nm bag; (grande) sack; (su contenido) bagful; (AM) jacket; ~ de dormir sleeping bag

sacramento [sakra'mento] nm sacrament

sacrificar [sakrifi'kar] vt to sacrifice; **sacrificio** nm sacrifice

sacrilegio [sakri'lexjo] nm sacrilege; **sacrílego, a** adj sacrilegious

sacristía [sakris'tia] nf sacristy

sacro, a ['sakro, a] adj sacred

sacudida [saku'ðiða] nf (agitación) shake, shaking; (sacudimiento) jolt, bump; ~ eléctrica electric shock

sacudir [saku'ðir] vt to shake; (golpear) to hit

sádico, a ['saðiko, a] adj sadistic ♦ nm/f sadist; **sadismo** nm sadism

saeta [sa'eta] nf (flecha) arrow

sagacidad [sayaθi'ðað] nf shrewdness, cleverness; **sagaz** adj shrewd, clever

sagitario [saxi'tarjo] nm Sagittarius

sagrado, a [sa'yraðo, a] adj sacred, holy

Sáhara ['saara] nm: **el** ~ the Sahara (desert)

sal [sal] vb ver **salir** ♦ nf salt

sala ['sala] nf room; (~ de estar) living room; (TEATRO) house, auditorium; (de hospital) ward; ~ de apelación court; ~ de espera waiting room; ~ de estar living room; ~ de fiestas dance hall

salado, a [sa'laðo, a] adj salty; (fig) witty, amusing; **agua salada** salt water

salar [sa'lar] vt to salt, add salt to

salarial [sala'rjal] adj (aumento, revisión) wage cpd, salary cpd

salario [sa'larjo] nm wage, pay

salchicha [sal'tʃitʃa] nf (pork) sausage; **salchichón** nm (salami-type) sausage

saldar [sal'dar] vt to pay; (vender) to sell off; (fig) to settle, resolve; **saldo** nm (pago) settlement; (de una cuenta) balance; (lo restante) remnant(s) (pl), remainder; **saldos** nmpl (en tienda) sale

saldré etc vb ver **salir**

salero [sa'lero] nm salt cellar

salgo etc vb ver **salir**

salida [sa'liða] nf (puerta etc) exit, way out; (acto) leaving, going out; (de tren, AVIAT) departure; (TEC) output, production; (fig) way out; (COM) opening; (GEO, válvula) outlet; (de gas) leak; **calle sin** ~ cul-de-sac; ~ **de incendios** fire escape

saliente [sa'ljente] adj (ARQ) projecting; (sol) rising; (fig) outstanding

---
PALABRA CLAVE
---

salir [sa'lir] vi 1 (partir: tb: ~ de) to leave; **Juan ha salido** Juan is out; **salió de la cocina** he came out of the kitchen

2 (aparecer) to appear; (disco, libro) to come out; **anoche salió en la tele** she appeared o was on TV last night; **salió en todos los periódicos** it was in all the papers

3 (resultar): **la muchacha nos salió muy trabajadora** the girl turned out to be a very hard worker; **la comida te ha salido exquisita** the food was delicious; **sale muy caro** it's very expensive

4: ~**le a uno algo: la entrevista que hice me salió bien/mal** the interview I did went o turned out well/badly

5: ~ **adelante**: **no sé como haré para** ~ **adelante** I don't know how I'll get by

♦ ~**se** vr (líquido) to spill; (animal) to escape

---

salmo ['salmo] nm psalm

salmón [sal'mon] nm salmon

salmonete [salmo'nete] nm red mullet

salmuera [sal'mwera] nf pickle, brine

salón [sa'lon] nm (de casa) living room, lounge; (muebles) lounge suite; ~ **de belleza** beauty parlour; ~ **de baile** dance hall

salpicadero [salpika'ðero] nm (AUTO) dashboard

salpicar [salpi'kar] vt (rociar) to sprinkle, spatter; (esparcir) to scatter

salpicón [salpi'kon] nm: ~ **de mariscos** seafood salad

salsa ['salsa] nf sauce; (con carne asada) gravy; (fig) spice

saltamontes [salta'montes] nm inv grasshopper

saltar [sal'tar] vt to jump (over), leap (over); (dejar de lado) to skip, miss out ♦ vi to jump, leap; (pelota) to bounce; (al aire) to fly up; (quebrarse) to break; (al agua) to dive; (fig) to explode, blow up

salto ['salto] nm jump, leap; (al agua) dive; ~ **de agua** waterfall; ~ **de altura** high jump

saltón, ona [sal'ton, ona] adj (ojos) bulging, popping; (dientes) protruding

salud [sa'luð] nf health; ¡(a su) ~! cheers!, good health!; **~able** adj (de buena ~) healthy; (provechoso) good, beneficial

saludar [salu'ðar] vt to greet; (MIL) to salute; **saludo** nm greeting; "**saludos**" (en carta) "best wishes", "regards"

salva ['salβa] nf: ~ **de aplausos** ovation

salvación [salβa'θjon] nf salvation; (rescate) rescue

salvado [sal'βaðo] nm bran

salvaguardar [salβaɣwar'ðar] vt to safeguard

salvajada [salβa'xaða] nf atrocity

salvaje [sal'βaxe] adj wild; (tribu) savage; **salvajismo** nm savagery

salvamento [salβa'mento] nm rescue

salvar [sal'βar] vt (rescatar) to save, rescue; (resolver) to overcome, resolve; (cubrir distancias) to cover, travel; (hacer excepción) to except, exclude; (barco) to salvage

salvavidas [salβa'βiðas] adj inv: **bote/ chaleco/cinturón ~** lifeboat/life jacket/life belt

salvo, a ['salβo, a] adj safe ♦ adv except (for), save; **a ~** out of danger; **~ que** unless; **~conducto** nm safe-conduct

san [san] adj saint; **S~** Juan St John

sanar [sa'nar] vt (herida) to heal; (persona) to cure ♦ vi (persona) to get well, recover; (herida) to heal

sanatorio [sana'torjo] nm sanatorium

sanción [san'θjon] nf sanction; **sancionar** vt to sanction

sandalia [san'dalja] nf sandal

sandez [san'deθ] nf foolishness

sandía [san'dia] nf watermelon

sandwich ['sandwitʃ] (pl ~s, ~es) nm sandwich

saneamiento [sanea'mjento] nm sanitation

sanear [sane'ar] vt to clean up; (terreno) to drain

sangrar [san'grar] vt, vi to bleed; **sangre** nf blood

sangría [san'gria] nf sangria, sweetened drink of red wine with fruit

sangriento, a [san'grjento, a] adj bloody

sanguijuela [sangi'xwela] nf (ZOOL, fig) leech

sanguinario, a [sangi'narjo, a] adj bloodthirsty

sanguíneo, a [san'gineo, a] adj blood cpd

sanidad [sani'ðað] nf: ~ **(pública)** public health

sanitario, a [sani'tarjo, a] adj health cpd; **~s** nmpl toilets (BRIT), washroom (US)

sano, a ['sano, a] adj healthy; (sin daños)

sound; (comida) wholesome; (entero) whole, intact; ~ **y salvo** safe and sound

Santiago [san'tjaɣo] nm: ~ **(de Chile)** Santiago

santiamén [santja'men] nm: **en un ~** in no time at all

santidad [santi'ðað] nf holiness, sanctity

santiguarse [santi'ɣwarse] vr to make the sign of the cross

santo, a ['santo, a] adj holy; (fig) wonderful, miraculous ♦ nm/f saint ♦ nm saint's day; ~ **y seña** password

santuario [san'twarjo] nm sanctuary; shrine

saña ['saɲa] nf rage, fury

sapo ['sapo] nm toad

saque ['sake] nm (TENIS) service, serve; (FÚTBOL) throw-in; ~ **de esquina** corner (kick)

saquear [sake'ar] vt (MIL) to sack; (robar) to loot, plunder; (fig) to ransack; **saqueo** nm sacking; looting, plundering; ransacking

sarampión [saram'pjon] nm measles sg

sarcasmo [sar'kasmo] nm sarcasm; **sarcástico, a** adj sarcastic

sardina [sar'ðina] nf sardine

sargento [sar'xento] nm sergeant

sarmiento [sar'mjento] nm (BOT) vine shoot

sarna ['sarna] nf itch; (MED) scabies

sarpullido [sarpu'ʎiðo] nm (MED) rash

sarro ['sarro] nm (en dientes) tartar, plaque

sartén [sar'ten] nf frying pan

sastre ['sastre] nm tailor; **~ría** nf (arte) tailoring; (tienda) tailor's (shop)

Satanás [sata'nas] nm Satan

satélite [sa'telite] nm satellite

sátira ['satira] nf satire

satisfacción [satisfak'θjon] nf satisfaction

satisfacer [satisfa'θer] vt to satisfy; (gastos) to meet; (pérdida) to make good; **~se** vr to satisfy o.s., be satisfied; (vengarse) to take revenge; **satisfecho, a** adj satisfied; (contento) content(ed), happy; (tb: satisfecho de sí mismo) self-satisfied, smug

saturar [satu'rar] vt to saturate; **~se** vr (mercado, aeropuerto) to reach saturation point

sauce ['sauθe] nm willow; ~ **llorón** weeping willow

sauna ['sauna] nf sauna

savia ['saβja] nf sap

saxofón [sakso'fon] nm saxophone

sazonar [saθo'nar] vt to ripen; (CULIN) to flavour, season

SE abr (= sudeste) SE

PALABRA CLAVE

se [se] pron **1** (reflexivo: sg: m) himself; (: f) herself; (: pl) themselves; (: cosa) itself; (: de Vd) yourself; (: de Vds) yourselves; ~ **está preparando** she's preparing herself; **para usos**

léxicos del pron ver el vb en cuestión, p.ej.
arrepentirse
2 (con complemento indirecto) to him; to her;
to them; to it; to you; a usted ~ lo dije ayer I
told you yesterday; ~ compró un sombrero he
bought himself a hat; ~ rompió la pierna he
broke his leg
3 (uso recíproco) each other, one another;
~ miraron (el uno al otro) they looked at each
other o one another
4 (en oraciones pasivas): se han vendido
muchos libros a lot of books have been sold
5 (impers): ~ dice que people say that, it is
said that; allí ~ come muy bien the food there
is very good, you can eat very well there

sé vb ver **saber; ser**
sea etc vb ver **ser**
sebo ['seβo] nm fat, grease
secador [seka'ðor] nm: ~ de pelo hair-dryer
secadora [seka'ðora] nf tumble dryer
secar [se'kar] vt to dry; ~se vr to dry (off);
(río, planta) to dry up
sección [sek'θjon] nf section
seco, a ['seko, a] adj dry; (carácter) cold;
(respuesta) sharp, curt; habrá pan a secas
there will be just bread; decir algo a secas to
say sth curtly; parar en ~ to stop dead
secretaría [sekreta'ria] nf secretariat
secretario, a [sekre'tarjo, a] nm/f secretary
secreto, a [se'kreto, a] adj secret; (persona)
secretive ♦ nm secret; (calidad) secrecy
secta ['sekta] nf sect; ~rio, a adj sectarian
sector [sek'tor] nm sector
secuela [se'kwela] nf consequence
secuencia [se'kwenθja] nf sequence
secuestrar [sekwes'trar] vt to kidnap;
(bienes) to seize, confiscate; **secuestro** nm
kidnapping; seizure, confiscation
secular [seku'lar] adj secular
secundar [sekun'dar] vt to second, support
secundario, a [sekun'darjo, a] adj
secondary
sed [seð] nf thirst; tener ~ to be thirsty
seda ['seða] nf silk
sedal [se'ðal] nm fishing line
sedante [se'ðante] nm sedative
sede ['seðe] nf (de gobierno) seat; (de
compañía) headquarters pl; Santa S~ Holy
See
sedentario, a [seðen'tarjo, a] adj sedentary
sediento, a [se'ðjento, a] adj thirsty
sedimento [seði'mento] nm sediment
sedoso, a [se'ðoso, a] adj silky, silken
seducción [seðuk'θjon] nf seduction
seducir [seðu'θir] vt to seduce; (cautivar) to
charm, fascinate; (atraer) to attract;
seductor, a adj seductive; charming,
fascinating; attractive ♦ nm/f seducer

segar [se'xar] vt (mies) to reap, cut; (hierba)
to mow, cut
seglar [se'xlar] adj secular, lay
segregación [sexreɣa'θjon] nf segregation.
~ racial racial segregation
segregar [sexre'xar] vt to segregate, separate
seguida [se'xiða] nf: en ~ at once, right away
seguido, a [se'xiðo, a] adj (continuo)
continuous, unbroken; (recto) straight ♦ adv
(directo) straight (on); (después) after; (AM: a
menudo) often; ~s consecutive, successive; 5
días ~s 5 days running, 5 days in a row
seguimiento [sexi'mjento] nm chase,
pursuit; (continuación) continuation
seguir [se'xir] vt to follow; (venir después) to
follow on, come after; (proseguir) to
continue; (perseguir) to chase, pursue ♦ vi
(gen) to follow; (continuar) to continue, carry
o go on; ~se vr to follow; sigo sin
comprender I still don't understand; sigue
lloviendo it's still raining
según [se'xun] prep according to ♦ adv:
¿irás? — ~ are you going? — it all depends
♦ conj as; ~ caminamos while we walk
segundo, a [se'xundo, a] adj second ♦ nm
second ♦ nf second meaning; de segunda
mano second-hand; segunda (clase) second
class; segunda enseñanza secondary
education; segunda (marcha) (AUT) second
(gear)
seguramente [sexura'mente] adv surely;
(con certeza) for sure, with certainty
seguridad [sexuri'ðað] nf safety; (del estado,
de casa etc) security; (certidumbre) certainty;
(confianza) confidence; (estabilidad) stability;
~ social social security
seguro, a [se'xuro, a] adj (cierto) sure,
certain; (fiel) trustworthy; (libre de peligro)
safe; (bien defendido, firme) secure ♦ adv for
sure, certainly ♦ nm (COM) insurance;
~ contra terceros/a todo riesgo third party/
comprehensive insurance; ~s sociales social
security sg
seis [seis] num six
seísmo [se'ismo] nm tremor, earthquake
selección [selek'θjon] nf selection;
seleccionar vt to pick, choose, select
selectividad [selektiβi'ðað] (ESP) nf
university entrance examination
selecto, a [se'lekto, a] adj select, choice;
(escogido) selected
sellar [se'ʎar] vt (documento oficial) to seal;
(pasaporte, visado) to stamp
sello ['seʎo] nm stamp; (precinto) seal
selva ['selβa] nf (bosque) forest, woods pl;
(jungla) jungle
semáforo [se'maforo] nm (AUTO) traffic lights
pl; (FERRO) signal
semana [se'mana] nf week; entre ~ during

the week; **S~ Santa** Holy Week; **semanal** *adj*
weekly; **~rio** *nm* weekly magazine
semblante [sem'blante] *nm* face; *(fig)* look
sembrar [sem'brar] *vt* to sow; *(objetos)* to
sprinkle, scatter about; *(noticias etc)* to spread
semejante [seme'xante] *adj (parecido)*
similar ♦ *nm* fellow man, fellow creature; **~s**
alike, similar; **nunca hizo cosa ~** he never did
any such thing; **semejanza** *nf* similarity,
resemblance
semejar [seme'xar] *vi* to seem like, resemble;
~se *vr* to look alike, be similar
semen ['semen] *nm* semen
semestral [semes'tral] *adj* half-yearly, bi-
annual
semicírculo [semi'θirkulo] *nm* semicircle
semidesnatado, a [semiðesna'taðo, a] *adj*
semi-skimmed
semifinal [semifi'nal] *nf* semifinal
semilla [se'miʎa] *nf* seed
seminario [semi'narjo] *nm (REL)* seminary;
(ESCOL) seminar
sémola ['semola] *nf* semolina
Sena ['sena] *nm*: **el ~** the (river) Seine
senado [se'naðo] *nm* senate; **senador, a**
nm/f senator
sencillez [senθi'ʎeθ] *nf* simplicity; *(de
persona)* naturalness; **sencillo, a** *adj* simple;
natural, unaffected
senda ['senda] *nf* path, track
senderismo [sende'rismo] *nm* hiking
sendero [sen'dero] *nm* path, track
sendos, as ['sendos, as] *adj pl*: **les dio
~ golpes** he hit both of them
senil [se'nil] *adj* senile
seno ['seno] *nm (ANAT)* bosom, bust; *(fig)*
bosom; **~s** breasts
sensación [sensa'θjon] *nf* sensation;
(sentido) sense; *(sentimiento)* feeling;
sensacional *adj* sensational
sensato, a [sen'sato, a] *adj* sensible
sensible [sen'sible] *adj* sensitive; *(apreciable)*
perceptible, appreciable; *(pérdida)*
considerable; **~ro, a** *adj* sentimental
sensitivo, a [sensi'tiβo, a] *adj* sense *cpd*
sensorial [senso'rjal] *adj* sensory
sensual [sen'swal] *adj* sensual
sentada [sen'taða] *nf* sitting; *(protesta)* sit-in
sentado, a [sen'taðo, a] *adj*: **estar ~** to sit,
be sitting (down); **dar por ~** to take for
granted, assume
sentar [sen'tar] *vt* to sit, seat; *(fig)* to
establish ♦ *vi (vestido)* to suit; *(alimento)*:
~ bien/mal a to agree/disagree with; **~se** *vr
(persona)* to sit, sit down; *(los depósitos)* to
settle
sentencia [sen'tenθja] *nf (máxima)* maxim,
saying; *(JUR)* sentence; **sentenciar** *vt* to
sentence

sentido, a [sen'tiðo, a] *adj (pérdida)*
regrettable; *(carácter)* sensitive ♦ *nm* sense;
(sentimiento) feeling; *(significado)* sense,
meaning; *(dirección)* direction; **mi más
~ pésame** my deepest sympathy; **~ del humor**
sense of humour; **~ único** one-way (street);
tener ~ to make sense
sentimental [sentimen'tal] *adj* sentimental;
vida ~ love life
sentimiento [senti'mjento] *nm* feeling
sentir [sen'tir] *vt* to feel; *(percibir)* to
perceive, sense; *(lamentar)* to regret, be sorry
for ♦ *vi (tener la sensación)* to feel;
(lamentarse) to feel sorry ♦ *nm* opinion,
judgement; **~se bien/mal** to feel well/ill; **lo
siento** I'm sorry
seña ['seŋa] *nf* sign; *(MIL)* password; **~s** *nfpl
(dirección)* address *sg*; **~s personales** personal
description *sg*
señal [se'ŋal] *nf* sign; *(síntoma)* symptom;
(FERRO, TELEC) signal; *(marca)* mark; *(COM)*
deposit; **en ~ de** as a token of, as a sign of;
~ar *vt* to mark; *(indicar)* to point out,
indicate
señor [se'ŋor] *nm (hombre)* man; *(caballero)*
gentleman; *(dueño)* owner, master; *(trato:
antes de nombre propio)* Mr; (: *hablando
directamente)* sir; **muy ~ mío** Dear Sir; **el
~ alcalde/presidente** the mayor/president
señora [se'ŋora] *nf (dama)* lady; *(trato: antes
de nombre propio)* Mrs; (: *hablando
directamente)* madam; *(esposa)* wife; **Nuestra
S~** Our Lady
señorita [seŋo'rita] *nf (con nombre y/o
apellido)* Miss; *(mujer joven)* young lady
señorito [seŋo'rito] *nm* young gentleman;
(pey) rich kid
señuelo [se'ŋwelo] *nm* decoy
sepa *etc vb ver* **saber**
separación [separa'θjon] *nf* separation;
(división) division; *(hueco)* gap
separar [sepa'rar] *vt* to separate; *(dividir)* to
divide; **~se** *vr (parte)* to come away; *(partes)*
to come apart; *(persona)* to leave, go away;
(matrimonio) to separate; **separatismo** *nm*
separatism
sepia ['sepja] *nf* cuttlefish
septentrional [septentrjo'nal] *adj* northern
septiembre [sep'tjembre] *nm* September
séptimo, a ['septimo, a] *adj, nm* seventh
sepulcral [sepul'kral] *adj (fig: silencio,
atmósfera)* deadly; **sepulcro** *nm* tomb, grave
sepultar [sepul'tar] *vt* to bury; **sepultura** *nf
(acto)* burial; *(tumba)* grave, tomb
sequedad [seke'ðað] *nf* dryness; *(fig)*
brusqueness, curtness
sequía [se'kia] *nf* drought
séquito ['sekito] *nm (de rey etc)* retinue;
(seguidores) followers *pl*

ser [ser] *vi* **1** (*descripción*) to be; **es médica/muy alta** she's a doctor/very tall; **la familia es de Cuzco** his (*o* her *etc*) family is from Cuzco; **soy Ana** (*TELEC*) Ana speaking *o* here **2** (*propiedad*): **es de Joaquín** it's Joaquín's, it belongs to Joaquín **3** (*horas, fechas, números*): **es la una** it's one o'clock; **son las seis y media** it's half-past six; **es el 1 de junio** it's the first of June; **somos/son seis** there are six of us/them **4** (*en oraciones pasivas*): **ha sido descubierto ya** it's already been discovered **5**: **es de esperar que ...** it is to be hoped *o* I *etc* hope that ... **6** (*locuciones con sub*): **o sea** that is to say; **sea él sea su hermana** either him or his sister **7**: **a no ~ por él ...** but for him ... **8**: **a no ~ que: a no ~ que tenga uno ya** unless he's got one already
♦ *nm* being; **~ humano** human being

serenarse [sere'narse] *vr* to calm down
sereno, a [se'reno, a] *adj* (*persona*) calm, unruffled; (*el tiempo*) fine, settled; (*ambiente*) calm, peaceful ♦ *nm* night watchman
serial [ser'jal] *nm* serial
serie [serje] *nf* series; (*cadena*) sequence, succession; **fuera de ~** out of order; (*fig*) special, out of the ordinary; **fabricación en ~** mass production
seriedad [serje'ðað] *nf* seriousness; (*formalidad*) reliability; **serio, a** *adj* serious; reliable, dependable; grave, serious; **en serio** *adv* seriously
serigrafía [serixra'fia] *nf* silk-screen printing
sermón [ser'mon] *nm* (*REL*) sermon
seropositivo, a [seroposi'tiβo] *adj* HIV positive
serpentear [serpente'ar] *vi* to wriggle; (*camino, río*) to wind, snake
serpentina [serpen'tina] *nf* streamer
serpiente [ser'pjente] *nf* snake; **~ de cascabel** rattlesnake
serranía [serra'nia] *nf* mountainous area
serrar [se'rrar] *vt* = **aserrar**
serrín [se'rrin] *nm* = **aserrín**
serrucho [se'rrutʃo] *nm* saw
servicio [ser'βiθjo] *nm* service; **~s** *nmpl* toilet(s); **~ incluido** service charge included; **~ militar** military service
servidumbre [serβi'ðumbre] *nf* (*sujeción*) servitude; (*criados*) servants *pl*, staff
servil [ser'βil] *adj* servile
servilleta [serβi'ʎeta] *nf* serviette, napkin
servir [ser'βir] *vt* to serve ♦ *vi* to serve; (*tener utilidad*) to be of use, be useful; **~se** *vr* to serve *o* help o.s.; **~se de algo** to make use of

sth, use sth; **sírvase pasar** please come in
sesenta [se'senta] *num* sixty
sesgo ['sesxo] *nm* slant; (*fig*) slant, twist
sesión [se'sjon] *nf* (*POL*) session, sitting; (*CINE*) showing
seso ['seso] *nm* brain; **sesudo, a** *adj* sensible, wise
seta ['seta] *nf* mushroom; **~ venenosa** toadstool
setecientos, as [sete'θjentos, as] *adj, num* seven hundred
setenta [se'tenta] *num* seventy
seto ['seto] *nm* hedge
seudónimo [seu'ðonimo] *nm* pseudonym
severidad [seβeri'ðað] *nf* severity; **severo, a** *adj* severe
Sevilla [se'βiʎa] *n* Seville; **sevillano, a** *adj* of *o* from Seville ♦ *nm/f* native *o* inhabitant of Seville
sexo ['sekso] *nm* sex
sexto, a ['seksto, a] *adj, nm* sixth
sexual [sek'swal] *adj* sexual; **vida ~** sex life
si [si] *conj* if; **me pregunto ~ ...** I wonder if *o* whether ...
sí [si] *adv* yes ♦ *nm* consent ♦ *pron* (*uso impersonal*) oneself; (*sg: m*) himself; (*: f*) herself; (*: de cosa*) itself; (*de usted*) yourself; (*pl*) themselves; (*de ustedes*) yourselves; (*recíproco*) each other; **él no quiere pero yo ~** he doesn't want to but I do; **ella ~ vendrá** she will certainly come, she is sure to come; **claro que ~** of course; **creo que ~** I think so
siamés, esa [sja'mes, esa] *adj, nm/f* Siamese
SIDA ['siða] *nm abr* (= *Síndrome de Inmunodeficiencia Adquirida*) AIDS
siderúrgico, a [siðe'rurxico, a] *adj* iron and steel *cpd*
sidra ['siðra] *nf* cider
siembra ['sjembra] *nf* sowing
siempre ['sjempre] *adv* always; (*todo el tiempo*) all the time; **~ que** (*cada vez*) whenever; (*dado que*) provided that; **como ~** as usual; **para ~** for ever
sien [sjen] *nf* temple
siento *etc vb ver* **sentar; sentir**
sierra ['sjerra] *nf* (*TEC*) saw; (*cadena de montañas*) mountain range
siervo, a ['sjerβo, a] *nm/f* slave
siesta ['sjesta] *nf* siesta, nap; **echar la ~** to have an afternoon nap *o* a siesta
siete ['sjete] *num* seven
sífilis ['sifilis] *nf* syphilis
sifón [si'fon] *nm* syphon; **whisky con ~** whisky and soda
sigla ['sixla] *nf* abbreviation; acronym
siglo ['sixlo] *nm* century; (*fig*) age
significación [sixnifika'θjon] *nf* significance
significado [sixnifi'kaðo] *nm* (*de palabra etc*) meaning

significar [siɣnifi'kar] vt to mean, signify; (*notificar*) to make known, express; **significativo, a** adj significant

signo ['siɣno] nm sign; **~ de admiración** o **exclamación** exclamation mark; **~ de interrogación** question mark

sigo etc vb ver **seguir**

siguiente [si'ɣjente] adj next, following

siguió etc vb ver **seguir**

sílaba ['silaβa] nf syllable

silbar [sil'βar] vt, vi to whistle; **silbato** nm whistle; **silbido** nm whistle, whistling

silenciador [silenθja'ðor] nm silencer

silenciar [silen'θjar] vt (*persona*) to silence; (*escándalo*) to hush up; **silencio** nm silence, quiet; **silencioso, a** adj silent, quiet

silla ['siʎa] nf (*asiento*) chair; (*tb: ~ de montar*) saddle; **~ de ruedas** wheelchair

sillón [si'ʎon] nm armchair, easy chair

silueta [si'lweta] nf silhouette; (*de edificio*) outline; (*figura*) figure

silvestre [sil'βestre] adj wild

simbólico, a [sim'boliko, a] adj symbolic(al)

simbolizar [simboli'θar] vt to symbolize

símbolo ['simbolo] nm symbol

simetría [sime'tria] nf symmetry

simiente [si'mjente] nf seed

similar [simi'lar] adj similar

simio ['simjo] nm ape

simpatía [simpa'tia] nf liking; (*afecto*) affection; (*amabilidad*) kindness; **simpático, a** adj nice, pleasant; kind

simpatizante [simpati'θante] nm/f sympathizer

simpatizar [simpati'θar] vi: **~ con** to get on well with

simple ['simple] adj simple; (*elemental*) simple, easy; (*mero*) mere; (*puro*) pure, sheer ♦ nm/f simpleton; **~za** nf simpleness; (*necedad*) silly thing; **simplificar** vt to simplify

simposio [sim'posjo] nm symposium

simular [simu'lar] vt to simulate

simultáneo, a [simul'taneo, a] adj simultaneous

sin [sin] prep without; **la ropa está ~ lavar** the clothes are unwashed; **~ que** without; **~ embargo** however, still

sinagoga [sina'ɣoɣa] nf synagogue

sinceridad [sinθeri'ðað] nf sincerity; **sincero, a** adj sincere

sincronizar [sinkroni'θar] vt to synchronize

sindical [sindi'kal] adj trade-union cpd, trade-union cpd; **~ista** adj, nm/f trade unionist

sindicato [sindi'kato] nm (*de trabajadores*) trade(s) union; (*de negociantes*) syndicate

síndrome ['sindrome] nm (*MED*) syndrome; **~ de abstinencia** (*MED*) withdrawal symptoms

sinfín [sin'fin] nm: **un ~ de** a great many, no

end of

sinfonía [sinfo'nia] nf symphony

singular [singu'lar] adj singular; (*fig*) outstanding, exceptional; (*raro*) peculiar, odd; **~idad** nf singularity, peculiarity; **~izarse** vr to distinguish o.s., stand out

siniestro, a [si'njestro, a] adj sinister ♦ nm (*accidente*) accident

sinnúmero [sin'numero] nm = **sinfín**

sino ['sino] nm fate, destiny ♦ conj (*pero*) but; (*salvo*) except, save

sinónimo, a [si'nonimo, a] adj synonymous ♦ nm synonym

síntesis ['sintesis] nf synthesis; **sintético, a** adj synthetic

sintetizar [sinteti'θar] vt to synthesize

sintió vb ver **sentir**

síntoma ['sintoma] nm symptom

sintonía [sinto'nia] nf (*RADIO, MUS: de programa*) tuning; **sintonizar** vt (*RADIO: emisora*) to tune (in)

sinvergüenza [simber'ɣwenθa] nm/f rogue, scoundrel; **¡es un ~!** he's got a nerve!

siquiera [si'kjera] conj even if, even though ♦ adv at least; **ni ~** not even

sirena [si'rena] nf siren

Siria ['sirja] nf Syria

sirviente, a [sir'βjente, a] nm/f servant

sirvo etc vb ver **servir**

sisear [sise'ar] vt, vi to hiss

sistema [sis'tema] nm system; (*método*) method; **sistemático, a** adj systematic

sitiar [si'tjar] vt to besiege, lay siege to

sitio ['sitjo] nm (*lugar*) place; (*espacio*) room, space; (*MIL*) siege; **~ Web** (*INFORM*) website

situación [sitwa'θjon] nf situation, position; (*estatus*) position, standing

situado, a [situ'aðo] adj situated, placed

situar [si'twar] vt to place, put; (*edificio*) to locate, situate

slip [slip] nm pants pl, briefs pl

smoking ['smokin, es'mokin] (pl **~s**) nm dinner jacket (*BRIT*), tuxedo (*US*)

snob [es'nob] = **esnob**

SO abr (= *suroeste*) SW

sobaco [so'βako] nm armpit

sobar [so'βar] vt (*ropa*) to rumple; (*comida*) to play around with

soberanía [soβera'nia] nf sovereignty; **soberano, a** adj sovereign; (*fig*) supreme ♦ nm/f sovereign

soberbia [so'βerβja] nf pride; haughtiness, arrogance; magnificence

soberbio, a [so'βerβjo, a] adj (*orgulloso*) proud; (*altivo*) haughty, arrogant; (*estupendo*) magnificent, superb

sobornar [soβor'nar] vt to bribe; **soborno** nm bribe

sobra [so'βra] nf excess, surplus; **~s** nfpl leftovers, scraps; **de ~** surplus, extra; **tengo de ~** I've more than enough; **~do, a** adj (*más que suficiente*) more than enough; (*superfluo*) excessive; **sobrante** adj remaining, extra ♦ *nm* surplus, remainder

sobrar [so'βrar] *vt* to exceed, surpass ♦ *vi* (*tener de más*) to be more than enough; (*quedar*) to remain, be left (over)

sobrasada [soβra'saða] *nf* pork sausage spread

sobre ['soβre] *prep* (*gen*) on; (*encima*) on (top of); (*por encima de, arriba de*) over, above; (*más que*) more than; (*además*) in addition to, besides; (*alrededor de*) about ♦ *nm* envelope; **~ todo** above all

sobrecama [soβre'kama] *nf* bedspread

sobrecargar [soβrekar'var] *vt* (*camión*) to overload; (*COM*) to surcharge

sobredosis [soβre'ðosis] *nf inv* overdose

sobreentender [soβre(e)nten'der] *vt* to deduce, infer; **~se** *vr*: **se sobreentiende que ...** it is implied that ...

sobrehumano, a [soβreu'mano, a] *adj* superhuman

sobrellevar [soβreʎe'βar] *vt* to bear, endure

sobremesa [soβre'mesa] *nf*: **durante la ~** after dinner; **ordenador de ~** desktop computer

sobrenatural [soβrenatu'ral] *adj* supernatural

sobrenombre [soβre'nombre] *nm* nickname

sobrepasar [soβrepa'sar] *vt* to exceed, surpass

sobreponerse [soβrepo'nerse] *vr*: **~ a** to overcome

sobresaliente [soβresa'ljente] *adj* outstanding, excellent

sobresalir [soβresa'lir] *vi* to project, jut out; (*fig*) to stand out, excel

sobresaltar [soβresal'tar] *vt* (*asustar*) to scare, frighten; (*sobrecoger*) to startle; **sobresalto** *nm* (*movimiento*) start; (*susto*) scare; (*turbación*) sudden shock

sobretodo [soβre'toðo] *nm* overcoat

sobrevenir [soβreβe'nir] *vi* (*ocurrir*) to happen (unexpectedly); (*resultar*) to follow, ensue

sobreviviente [soβreβi'βjente] *adj* surviving ♦ *nm/f* survivor

sobrevivir [soβreβi'βir] *vi* to survive

sobrevolar [soβreβo'lar] *vt* to fly over

sobriedad [soβrje'ðað] *nf* sobriety, soberness; (*moderación*) moderation, restraint

sobrino, a [so'βrino, a] *nm/f* nephew/niece

sobrio, a ['soβrjo, a] *adj* sober; (*moderado*) moderate, restrained

socarrón, ona [soka'rron, ona] *adj* (*sarcástico*) sarcastic, ironic(al)

socavar [soka'βar] *vt* (*tb fig*) to undermine

socavón [soka'βon] *nm* (*hoyo*) hole

sociable [so'θjaβle] *adj* (*persona*) sociable, friendly; (*animal*) social

social [so'θjal] *adj* social; (*COM*) company *cpd*

socialdemócrata [soθjalde'mokrata] *nm/f* social democrat

socialista [soθja'lista] *adj, nm/f* socialist

socializar [soθjali'θar] *vt* to socialize

sociedad [soθje'ðað] *nf* society; (*COM*) company; **~ anónima** limited company; **~ de consumo** consumer society

socio, a ['soθjo, a] *nm/f* (*miembro*) member; (*COM*) partner

sociología [soθjolo'xia] *nf* sociology; **sociólogo, a** *nm/f* sociologist

socorrer [soko'rrer] *vt* to help; **socorrista** *nm/f* first aider; (*en piscina, playa*) lifeguard; **socorro** *nm* (*ayuda*) help, aid; (*MIL*) relief; **¡socorro!** help!

soda ['soða] *nf* (*sosa*) soda; (*bebida*) soda (water)

sofá [so'fa] (*pl* **~s**) *nm* sofa, settee; **~-cama** *nm* studio couch; sofa bed

sofisticación [sofistika'θjon] *nf* sophistication

sofocar [sofo'kar] *vt* to suffocate; (*apagar*) to smother, put out; **~se** *vr* to suffocate; (*fig*) to blush, feel embarrassed; **sofoco** *nm* suffocation; embarrassment

sofreír [sofre'ir] *vt* (*CULIN*) to fry lightly

soga ['soxa] *nf* rope

sois *vb ver* **ser**

soja ['soxa] *nf* soya

sol [sol] *nm* sun; (*luz*) sunshine, sunlight; **hace ~** it is sunny

solamente [sola'mente] *adv* only, just

solapa [so'lapa] *nf* (*de chaqueta*) lapel; (*de libro*) jacket

solapado, a [sola'paðo, a] *adj* (*intenciones*) underhand; (*gestos, movimiento*) sly

solar [so'lar] *adj* solar, sun *cpd*

solaz [so'laθ] *nm* recreation, relaxation; **~ar** *vt* (*divertir*) to amuse

soldado [sol'daðo] *nm* soldier; **~ raso** private

soldador [solda'ðor] *nm* soldering iron; (*persona*) welder

soldar [sol'dar] *vt* to solder, weld

soleado, a [sole'aðo, a] *adj* sunny

soledad [sole'ðað] *nf* solitude; (*estado infeliz*) loneliness

solemne [so'lemne] *adj* solemn; **solemnidad** *nf* solemnity

soler [so'ler] *vi* to be in the habit of, be accustomed to; **suele salir a las ocho** she usually goes out at 8 o'clock

solfeo [sol'feo] *nm* solfa

solicitar [soliθi'tar] *vt* (*permiso*) to ask for, seek; (*puesto*) to apply for; (*votos*) to canvass for; (*atención*) to attract

solícito, a [so'liθito, a] *adj (diligente)* diligent; *(cuidadoso)* careful; **solicitud** *nf (calidad)* great care; *(petición)* request; *(a un puesto)* application

solidaridad [soliðari'ðað] *nf* solidarity; **solidario, a** *adj (participación)* joint, common; *(compromiso)* mutually binding

solidez [soli'ðeθ] *nf* solidity; **sólido, a** *adj* solid

soliloquio [soli'lokjo] *nm* soliloquy

solista [so'lista] *nm/f* soloist

solitario, a [soli'tarjo, a] *adj (persona)* lonely, solitary; *(lugar)* lonely, desolate ♦ *nm/f (reclusa)* recluse; *(en la sociedad)* loner ♦ *nm* solitaire

sollozar [soʎo'θar] *vi* to sob; **sollozo** *nm* sob

solo, a ['solo, a] *adj (único)* single, sole; *(sin compañía)* alone; *(solitario)* lonely; **hay una sola dificultad** there is just one difficulty; **a solas** alone, by oneself

sólo ['solo] *adv* only, just

solomillo [solo'miʎo] *nm* sirloin

soltar [sol'tar] *vt (dejar ir)* to let go of; *(desprender)* to unfasten, loosen; *(librar)* to release, set free; *(risa etc)* to let out

soltero, a [sol'tero, a] *adj* single, unmarried ♦ *nm/f* bachelor/single woman; **solterón, ona** *nm/f* old bachelor/spinster

soltura [sol'tura] *nf* looseness, slackness; *(de los miembros)* agility, ease of movement; *(en el hablar)* fluency, ease

soluble [so'luβle] *adj (QUÍM)* soluble; *(problema)* solvable; **~ en agua** soluble in water

solución [solu'θjon] *nf* solution; **solucionar** *vt (problema)* to solve; *(asunto)* to settle, resolve

solventar [solβen'tar] *vt (pagar)* to settle, pay; *(resolver)* to resolve; **solvente** *adj (ECON: empresa, persona)* solvent

sombra ['sombra] *nf* shadow; *(como protección)* shade; **~s** *nfpl (oscuridad)* darkness *sg*, shadows; **tener buena/mala ~** to be lucky/unlucky

sombrero [som'brero] *nm* hat .

sombrilla [som'briʎa] *nf* parasol, sunshade

sombrío, a [som'brio, a] *adj (oscuro)* dark; *(triste)* sombre, sad; *(persona)* gloomy

somero, a [so'mero, a] *adj* superficial

someter [some'ter] *vt (país)* to conquer; *(persona)* to subject to one's will; *(informe)* to present, submit; **~se** *vr* to give in, yield, submit; **~ a** to subject to

somier [so'mjer] *(pl somiers)* *n* spring mattress

somnífero [som'nifero] *nm* sleeping pill

somnolencia [somno'lenθja] *nf* sleepiness, drowsiness

somos *vb ver* ser

son [son] *vb ver* ser ♦ *nm* sound; **en ~ de broma** as a joke

sonajero [sona'xero] *nm* (baby's) rattle

sonambulismo [sonambu'lismo] *nm* sleepwalking; **sonámbulo, a** *nm/f* sleepwalker

sonar [so'nar] *vt* to ring ♦ *vi* to sound; *(hacer ruido)* to make a noise; *(pronunciarse)* to be sounded, be pronounced; *(ser conocido)* to sound familiar; *(campana)* to ring; *(reloj)* to strike, chime; **~se** *vr:* **~se (las narices)** to blow one's nose; **me suena ese nombre** that name rings a bell

sonda ['sonda] *nf (NAUT)* sounding; *(TEC)* bore, drill; *(MED)* probe

sondear [sonde'ar] *vt* to sound; to bore (into), drill; to probe, sound; *(fig)* to sound out; **sondeo** *nm* sounding; boring, drilling; *(fig)* poll, enquiry

sonido [so'niðo] *nm* sound

sonoro, a [so'noro, a] *adj* sonorous; *(resonante)* loud, resonant

sonreír [sonre'ir] *vi* to smile; **~se** *vr* to smile; **sonriente** *adj* smiling; **sonrisa** *nf* smile

sonrojarse [sonro'xarse] *vr* to blush, go red; **sonrojo** *nm* blush

soñador, a [soɲa'ðor, a] *nm/f* dreamer

soñar [so'ɲar] *vt, vi* to dream; **~ con** to dream about o of

soñoliento, a [soɲo'ljento, a] *adj* sleepy, drowsy

sopa ['sopa] *nf* soup

sopesar [sope'sar] *vt* to consider, weigh up

soplar [so'plar] *vt (polvo)* to blow away, blow off; *(inflar)* to blow up; *(vela)* to blow out ♦ *vi* to blow; **soplo** *nm* blow, puff; *(de viento)* puff, gust

soplón, ona [so'plon, ona] *(fam)*, *nm/f (niño)* telltale; *(de policía)* grass *(fam)*

sopor [so'por] *nm* drowsiness

soporífero [sopo'rifero] *nm* sleeping pill

soportable [sopor'taβle] *adj* bearable

soportar [sopor'tar] *vt* to bear, carry; *(fig)* to bear, put up with; **soporte** *nm* support; *(fig)* pillar, support

soprano [so'prano] *nf* soprano

sorber [sor'βer] *vt (chupar)* to sip; *(absorber)* to soak up, absorb

sorbete [sor'βete] *nm* iced fruit drink

sorbo ['sorβo] *nm (trago: grande)* gulp, swallow; *(: pequeño)* sip

sordera [sor'ðera] *nf* deafness

sórdido, a ['sorðiðo, a] *adj* dirty, squalid

sordo, a ['sorðo, a] *adj (persona)* deaf ♦ *nm/f* deaf person; **~mudo, a** *adj* deaf and dumb

sorna ['sorna] *nf* sarcastic tone

soroche [so'rotʃe] *(AM)* *nm* mountain sickness

sorprendente [sorpren'dente] *adj* surprising

sorprender [sorpren'der] *vt* to surprise;

sorpresa nf surprise

sortear [sorte'ar] vt to draw lots for; (*rifar*) to raffle; (*dificultad*) to avoid; **sorteo** nm (*en lotería*) draw; (*rifa*) raffle

sortija [sor'tixa] nf ring; (*rizo*) ringlet, curl

sosegado, a [sose'γaðo, a] adj quiet, calm

sosegar [sose'γar] vt to quieten, calm; (*el ánimo*) to reassure ♦ vi to rest; **sosiego** nm quiet(ness), calm(ness)

soslayo [sos'lajo]: **de ~** adv obliquely, sideways

soso, a ['soso, a] adj (*CULIN*) tasteless; (*aburrido*) dull, uninteresting

sospecha [sos'petʃa] nf suspicion; **sospechar** vt to suspect; **sospechoso, a** adj suspicious; (*testimonio, opinión*) suspect ♦ nm/f suspect

sostén [sos'ten] nm (*apoyo*) support; (*sujetador*) bra; (*alimentación*) sustenance, food

sostener [soste'ner] vt to support; (*mantener*) to keep up, maintain; (*alimentar*) to sustain, keep going; **~se** vr to support o.s.; (*seguir*) to continue, remain; **sostenido, a** adj continuous, sustained; (*prolongado*) prolonged

sotana [so'tana] nf (*REL*) cassock

sótano ['sotano] nm basement

soviético, a [so'βjetiko, a] adj Soviet; **los ~s** the Soviets

soy vb ver **ser**

Sr. abr (= Señor) Mr

Sra. abr (= Señora) Mrs

S.R.C. abr (= se ruega contestación) R.S.V.P.

Sres. abr (= Señores) Messrs

Srta. abr (= Señorita) Miss

Sta. abr (= Santa) St

status ['status, e'status] nm inv status

Sto. abr (= Santo) St

su [su] pron (*de él*) his; (*de ella*) her; (*de una cosa*) its; (*de ellos, ellas*) their; (*de usted, ustedes*) your

suave ['swaβe] adj gentle; (*superficie*) smooth; (*trabajo*) easy; (*música, voz*) soft, sweet; **suavidad** nf gentleness; smoothness; softness, sweetness; **suavizante** nm (*de ropa*) softener; (*del pelo*) conditioner; **suavizar** vt to soften; (*quitar la aspereza*) to smooth (out)

subalimentado, a [suβalimen'taðo, a] adj undernourished

subasta [su'βasta] nf auction; **subastar** vt to auction (off)

subcampeón, ona [suβkampe'on, ona] nm/f runner-up

subconsciente [suβkon'sθjente] adj, nm subconscious

subdesarrollado, a [suβðesarro'ʎaðo, a] adj underdeveloped

subdesarrollo [suβðesa'rroʎo] nm underdevelopment

subdirector, a [suβðirek'tor, a] nm/f assistant director

súbdito, a ['suβðito, a] nm/f subject

subestimar [suβesti'mar] vt to underestimate, underrate

subida [su'βiða] nf (*de montaña etc*) ascent, climb; (*de precio*) rise, increase; (*pendiente*) slope, hill

subir [su'βir] vt (*objeto*) to raise, lift up; (*cuesta, calle*) to go up; (*colina, montaña*) to climb; (*precio*) to raise, put up ♦ vi to go up, come up; (*a un coche*) to get in; (*a un autobús, tren o avión*) to get on, board; (*precio*) to rise, go up; (*río, marea*) to rise; **~se** vr to get up, climb

súbito, a ['suβito, a] adj (*repentino*) sudden; (*imprevisto*) unexpected

subjetivo, a [suβxe'tiβo, a] adj subjective

sublevación [suβleβa'θjon] nf revolt, rising

sublevar [suβle'βar] vt to rouse to revolt; **~se** vr to revolt, rise

sublime [su'βlime] adj sublime

submarinismo [suβmari'nismo] nm scuba diving

submarino, a [suβma'rino, a] adj underwater ♦ nm submarine

subnormal [suβnor'mal] adj subnormal ♦ nm/f subnormal person

subordinado, a [suβorði'naðo, a] adj, nm/f subordinate

subrayar [suβra'jar] vt to underline

subsanar [suβsa'nar] vt to recitfy

subscribir [suβskri'βir] vt = suscribir

subsidio [suβ'siðjo] nm (*ayuda*) aid, financial help; (*subvención*) subsidy, grant; (*de enfermedad, paro etc*) benefit, allowance

subsistencia [suβsis'tenθja] nf subsistence

subsistir [suβsis'tir] vi to subsist; (*sobrevivir*) to survive, endure

subterráneo, a [suβte'rraneo, a] adj underground, subterranean ♦ nm underpass, underground passage

subtítulo [suβ'titulo] nm (*CINE*) subtitle

suburbano, a [suβur'βano, a] adj suburban

suburbio [su'βurβjo] nm (*barrio*) slum quarter

subvención [suββen'θjon] nf (*ECON*) subsidy, grant; **subvencionar** vt to subsidize

subversión [suββer'sjon] nf subversion; **subversivo, a** adj subversive

subyugar [suβju'βar] vt (*país*) to subjugate, subdue; (*enemigo*) to overpower; (*voluntad*) to dominate

sucedáneo, a [suθe'ðaneo, a] adj substitute ♦ nm substitute (food)

suceder [suθe'ðer] vt, vi to happen; (*seguir*) to succeed, follow; **lo que sucede es que ...**

the fact is that ...; **sucesión** nf succession; (serie) sequence, series

sucesivamente [suθesiβa'mente] adv: **y así ~** and so on

sucesivo, a [suθe'siβo, a] adj successive, following; **en lo ~** in future, from now on

suceso [su'θeso] nm (hecho) event, happening; (incidente) incident

suciedad [suθje'ðað] nf (estado) dirtiness; (mugre) dirt, filth

sucinto, a [su'θinto, a] adj (conciso) succinct, concise

sucio, a ['suθjo, a] adj dirty

suculento, a [suku'lento, a] adj succulent

sucumbir [sukum'bir] vi to succumb

sucursal [sukur'sal] nf branch (office)

sudadera [suða'ðera] nf sweatshirt

Sudáfrica [suð'afrika] nf South Africa

Sudamérica [suða'merika] nf South America; **sudamericano, a** adj, nm/f South American

sudar [su'ðar] vt, vi to sweat

sudeste [su'ðeste] nm south-east

sudoeste [suðo'este] nm south-west

sudor [su'ðor] nm sweat; **~oso, a** adj sweaty, sweating

Suecia ['sweθja] nf Sweden; **sueco, a** adj Swedish ♦ nm/f Swede

suela ['swela] nf sole

sueldo ['sweldo] nm pay, wage(s) (pl)

suele etc vb ver **soler**

suelo ['swelo] nm (tierra) ground; (de casa) floor

suelto, a ['swelto, a] adj loose; (libre) free; (separado) detached; (ágil) quick, agile ♦ nm (loose) change, small change

sueño etc ['sweɲo] vb ver **soñar** ♦ nm sleep; (somnolencia) sleepiness, drowsiness; (lo soñado, fig) dream; **tener ~** to be sleepy

suero ['swero] nm (MED) serum; (de leche) whey

suerte ['swerte] nf (fortuna) luck; (azar) chance; (destino) fate, destiny; (especie) sort, kind; **tener ~** to be lucky; **de otra ~** otherwise, if not; **de ~ que** so that, in such a way that

suéter ['sweter] nm sweater

suficiente [sufi'θjente] adj enough, sufficient ♦ nm (ESCOL) pass

sufragio [su'fraxjo] nm (voto) vote; (derecho de voto) suffrage

sufrido, a [su'friðo, a] adj (persona) tough; (paciente) long-suffering, patient

sufrimiento [sufri'mjento] nm (dolor) suffering

sufrir [su'frir] vt (padecer) to suffer; (soportar) to bear, put up with; (apoyar) to hold up, support ♦ vi to suffer

sugerencia [suxe'renθja] nf suggestion

sugerir [suxe'rir] vt to suggest; (sutilmente) to hint

sugestión [suxes'tjon] nf suggestion; (sutil) hint; **sugestionar** vt to influence

sugestivo, a [suxes'tiβo, a] adj stimulating; (fascinante) fascinating

suicida [sui'θiða] adj suicidal ♦ nm/f suicidal person; (muerto) suicide, person who has committed suicide; **suicidarse** vr to commit suicide, kill o.s.; **suicidio** nm suicide

Suiza ['swiθa] nf Switzerland; **suizo, a** adj, nm/f Swiss

sujeción [suxe'θjon] nf subjection

sujetador [suxeta'ðor] nm (sostén) bra

sujetar [suxe'tar] vt (fijar) to fasten; (detener) to hold down; **~se** vr to subject o.s.; **sujeto, a** adj fastened, secure ♦ nm subject; (individuo) individual; **sujeto a** subject to

suma ['suma] nf (cantidad) total, sum; (de dinero) sum; (acto) adding (up), addition; **en ~** in short

sumamente [suma'mente] adv extremely, exceedingly

sumar [su'mar] vt to add (up) ♦ vi to add up

sumario, a [su'marjo, a] adj brief, concise ♦ nm summary

sumergir [sumer'xir] vt to submerge; (hundir) to sink

suministrar [sumini'strar] vt to supply, provide; **suministro** nm supply; (acto) supplying, providing

sumir [su'mir] vt to sink, submerge; (fig) to plunge

sumisión [sumi'sjon] nf (acto) submission; (calidad) submissiveness, docility; **sumiso, a** adj submissive, docile

sumo, a ['sumo, a] adj great, extreme; (autoridad) highest, supreme

suntuoso, a [sun'twoso, a] adj sumptuous, magnificent

supe etc vb ver **saber**

supeditar [supeði'tar] vt: **~ algo a algo** to subordinate sth to sth

super... [super] prefijo super..., over...; **~bueno** adj great, fantastic

súper ['super] nf (gasolina) three-star (petrol)

superar [supe'rar] vt (sobreponerse a) to overcome; (rebasar) to surpass, do better than; (pasar) to go beyond; **~se** vr to excel o.s.

superávit [supe'raβit] nm inv surplus

superficial [superfi'θjal] adj superficial; (medida) surface cpd, of the surface

superficie [super'fiθje] nf surface; (área) area

superfluo, a [su'perflwo, a] adj superfluous

superior [supe'rjor] adj (piso, clase) upper; (temperatura, número, nivel) higher; (mejor:

calidad, producto) superior, better ♦ nm/f
superior; **~idad** nf superiority
supermercado [supermer'kaðo] nm
supermarket
superponer [superpo'ner] vt to superimpose
supersónico, a [super'soniko, a] adj
supersonic
superstición [supersti'θjon] nf superstition;
supersticioso, a adj superstitious
supervisar [superßi'sar] vt to supervise
supervivencia [superßi'ßenθja] nf survival
superviviente [superßi'ßjente] adj surviving
supiera etc vb ver **saber**
suplantar [suplan'tar] vt to supplant
suplemento [suple'mento] nm supplement
suplente [su'plente] adj, nm/f substitute
supletorio, a [suple'torjo, a] adj
supplementary ♦ nm supplement; **teléfono ~**
extension
súplica ['suplika] nf request; (JUR) petition
suplicar [supli'kar] vt (cosa) to beg (for),
plead for; (persona) to beg, plead with
suplicio [su'pliθjo] nm torture
suplir [su'plir] vt (compensar) to make good,
make up for; (reemplazar) to replace,
substitute ♦ vi: **~ a** to take the place of,
substitute for
supo etc vb ver **saber**
suponer [supo'ner] vt to suppose;
suposición nf supposition
supremacía [suprema'θia] nf supremacy
supremo, a [su'premo, a] adj supreme
supresión [supre'sjon] nf suppression; (de
derecho) abolition; (de palabra etc) deletion;
(de restricción) cancellation, lifting
suprimir [supri'mir] vt to suppress; (derecho,
costumbre) to abolish; (palabra etc) to delete;
(restricción) to cancel, lift
supuesto, a [su'pwesto, a] pp de **suponer**
♦ adj (hipotético) supposed ♦ nm
assumption, hypothesis; **~ que** since; **por ~** of
course
sur [sur] nm south
surcar [sur'kar] vt to plough; **surco** nm (en
metal, disco) groove; (AGR) furrow
surgir [sur'xir] vi to arise, emerge; (dificultad)
to come up, crop up
suroeste [suro'este] nm south-west
surtido, a [sur'tiðo, a] adj mixed, assorted
♦ nm (selección) selection, assortment;
(abastecimiento) supply, stock; **~r** nm (also:
~r de gasolina) petrol pump (BRIT), gas pump
(US)
surtir [sur'tir] vt to supply, provide ♦ vi to
spout, spurt
susceptible [susθep'tißle] adj susceptible;
(sensible) sensitive; **~ de** capable of
suscitar [susθi'tar] vt to cause, provoke;
(interés, sospechas) to arouse

suscribir [suskri'ßir] vt (firmar) to sign;
(respaldar) to subscribe to, endorse; **~se** vr to
subscribe; **suscripción** nf subscription
susodicho, a [suso'ðitʃo, a] adj above-
mentioned
suspender [suspen'der] vt (objeto) to hang
(up), suspend; (trabajo) to stop, suspend;
(ESCOL) to fail; (interrumpir) to adjourn;
(atrasar) to postpone; **suspensión** nf
suspension; (fig) stoppage, suspension
suspenso, a [sus'penso, a] adj hanging,
suspended; (vestido) failed; (ESCOL) fail;
quedar o **estar en ~** to be pending
suspicacia [suspi'kaθja] nf suspicion,
mistrust; **suspicaz** adj suspicious, distrustful
suspirar [suspi'rar] vi to sigh; **suspiro** nm
sigh
sustancia [sus'tanθja] nf substance
sustentar [susten'tar] vt (alimentar) to
sustain, nourish; (objeto) to hold up, support;
(idea, teoría) to maintain, uphold; (fig) to
sustain, keep going; **sustento** nm support;
(alimento) sustenance, food
sustituir [sustitu'ir] vt to substitute, replace;
sustituto, a nm/f substitute, replacement
susto ['susto] nm fright, scare
sustraer [sustra'er] vt to remove, take away;
(MAT) to subtract
susurrar [susu'rrar] vi to whisper; **susurro**
nm whisper
sutil [su'til] adj (aroma, diferencia) subtle;
(tenue) thin; (inteligencia, persona) sharp;
~eza nf subtlety; thinness
suyo, a ['sujo, a] (con artículo o después del
verbo **ser**) adj (de él) his; (de ella) hers; (de
ellos, ellas) theirs; (de Ud, Uds) yours; **un
amigo ~** a friend of his (o hers o theirs o
yours)

T, t

tabacalera [taßaka'lera] nf: **T~** Spanish state
tobacco monopoly
tabaco [ta'ßako] nm tobacco; (fam)
cigarettes pl
taberna [ta'ßerna] nf bar, pub (BRIT)
tabique [ta'ßike] nm partition (wall)
tabla ['taßla] nf (de madera) plank; (estante)
shelf; (de vestido) pleat; (ARTE) panel; **~s** nfpl:
estar o **quedar en ~s** to draw; **~do** nm
(plataforma) platform; (TEATRO) stage
tablao [ta'ßlao] nm (tb: **~ flamenco**) flamenco
show
tablero [ta'ßlero] nm (de madera) plank,
board; (de ajedrez, damas) board; **~ de
anuncios** notice (BRIT) o bulletin (US) board
tableta [ta'ßleta] nf (MED) tablet; (de
chocolate) bar

tablón |ta'βlon| *nm* (*de suelo*) plank; (*de techo*) beam; ~ **de anuncios** notice board (*BRIT*), bulletin board (*US*)

tabú |ta'βu| *nm* taboo

tabular |taβu'lar| *vt* to tabulate

taburete |taβu'rete| *nm* stool

tacaño, a |ta'kaɲo, a| *adj* mean

tacha |'tatʃa| *nf* flaw; (*TEC*) stud; **tachar** *vt* (*borrar*) to cross out; **tachar de** to accuse of

tácito, a |'taθito, a| *adj* tacit

taciturno, a |taθi'turno, a| *adj* silent

taco |'tako| *nm* (*BILLAR*) cue; (*libro de billetes*) book; (*AM: de zapato*) heel; (*tarugo*) peg; (*palabrota*) swear word

tacón |ta'kon| *nm* heel; **de ~ alto** high-heeled; **taconeo** *nm* (*heel*) stamping

táctica |'taktika| *nf* tactics *pl*

táctico, a |'taktiko, a| *adj* tactical

tacto |'takto| *nm* touch; (*fig*) tact

taimado, a |tai'maðo, a| *adj* (*astuto*) sly

tajada |ta'xaða| *nf* slice

tajante |ta'xante| *adj* sharp

tajo |'taxo| *nm* (*corte*) cut; (*GEO*) cleft

tal |tal| *adj* such; ~ **vez** perhaps ♦ *pron* (*persona*) someone, such a one; (*cosa*) something, such a thing; ~ **como** such as; ~ **para cual** (*dos iguales*) two of a kind ♦ *adv*: ~ **como** (*igual*) just as; ~ **cual** (*como es*) just as it is; ¿**qué ~?** how are things?; ¿**qué ~ te gusta?** how do you like it? ♦ *conj*: **con ~ de que** provided that

taladrar |tala'ðrar| *vt* to drill; **taladro** *nm* drill

talante |ta'lante| *nm* (*humor*) mood; (*voluntad*) will, willingness

talar |ta'lar| *vt* to fell, cut down; (*devastar*) to devastate

talco |'talko| *nm* (*polvos*) talcum powder

talego |ta'leɣo| *nm* sack

talento |ta'lento| *nm* talent; (*capacidad*) ability

TALGO |'talɣo| (*ESP*) *nm abr* (= *tren articulado ligero Goicoechea-Oriol*) ≈ HST (*BRIT*)

talismán |talis'man| *nm* talisman

talla |'taʎa| *nf* (*estatura, fig, MED*) height, stature; (*palo*) measuring rod; (*ARTE*) carving; (*medida*) size

tallado, a |ta'ʎaðo, a| *adj* carved ♦ *nm* carving

tallar |ta'ʎar| *vt* (*madera*) to carve; (*metal etc*) to engrave; (*medir*) to measure

tallarines |taʎa'rines| *nmpl* noodles

talle |'taʎe| *nm* (*ANAT*) waist; (*fig*) appearance

taller |ta'ʎer| *nm* (*TEC*) workshop; (*de artista*) studio

tallo |'taʎo| *nm* (*de planta*) stem; (*de hierba*) blade; (*brote*) shoot

talón |ta'lon| *nm* (*ANAT*) heel; (*COM*) counterfoil; (*cheque*) cheque (*BRIT*), check (*US*)

talonario |talo'narjo| *nm* (*de cheques*) chequebook (*BRIT*), checkbook (*US*); (*de recibos*) receipt book

tamaño, a |ta'maɲo, a| *adj* (*tan grande*) such a big; (*tan pequeño*) such a small ♦ *nm* size; **de ~ natural** full-size

tamarindo |tama'rindo| *nm* tamarind

tambalearse |tambale'arse| *vr* (*persona*) to stagger; (*vehículo*) to sway

también |tam'bjen| *adv* (*igualmente*) also, too, as well; (*además*) besides

tambor |tam'bor| *nm* drum; (*ANAT*) eardrum; ~ **del freno** brake drum

tamiz |ta'miθ| *nm* sieve; ~**ar** *vt* to sieve

tampoco |tam'poko| *adv* nor, neither; **yo ~ lo compré** I didn't buy it either

tampón |tam'pon| *nm* tampon

tan |tan| *adv* so; ~ **es así que ...** so much so that ....

tanda |'tanda| *nf* (*gen*) series; (*turno*) shift

tangente |tan'xente| *nf* tangent

Tánger |'tanxer| *n* Tangier(s)

tangible |tan'xiβle| *adj* tangible

tanque |'tanke| *nm* (*cisterna, MIL*) tank; (*AUTO*) tanker

tantear |tante'ar| *vt* (*calcular*) to reckon (up); (*medir*) to take the measure of; (*probar*) to test, try out; (*tomar la medida: persona*) to take the measurements of; (*situación*) to weigh up; (*persona: opinión*) to sound out ♦ *vi* (*DEPORTE*) to score; **tanteo** *nm* (*cálculo*) (rough) calculation; (*prueba*) test, trial; (*DEPORTE*) scoring

tanto, a |'tanto, a| *adj* (*cantidad*) so much, as much; ~**s** so many, as many; **20 y ~s** 20-odd ♦ *adv* (*cantidad*) so much, as much; (*tiempo*) so long, as long ♦ *conj*: **en ~ que** while; **hasta ~ (que)** until such time as ♦ *nm* (*suma*) certain amount; (*proporción*) so much; (*punto*) point; (*gol*) goal; **un ~ perezoso** somewhat lazy ♦ *pron*: **cada uno paga ~** each one pays so much; ~ **tú como yo** both you and I; ~ **como eso** as much as that; ~ **más ... cuanto que** all the more ... because; ~ **mejor/peor** so much the better/the worse; ~ **si viene como si va** whether he comes or whether he goes; ~ **es así que** so much so that; **por o por lo ~** therefore; **me he vuelto ronco de o con ~ hablar** I have become hoarse with so much talking; **a ~s de agosto** on such and such a day in August

tapa |'tapa| *nf* (*de caja, olla*) lid; (*de botella*) top; (*de libro*) cover; (*comida*) snack

tapadera |tapa'ðera| *nf* lid, cover

tapar |ta'par| *vt* (*cubrir*) to cover; (*envolver*) to wrap o cover up; (*la vista*) to obstruct; (*persona, falta*) to conceal; (*AM*) to fill; ~**se** *vr* to wrap o.s. up

taparrabo [tapa'rraβo] nm loincloth

tapete [ta'pete] nm table cover

tapia ['tapja] nf (garden) wall; **tapiar** vt to wall in

tapicería [tapiθe'ria] nf tapestry; (para muebles) upholstery; (tienda) upholsterer's (shop)

tapiz [ta'piθ] nm (alfombra) carpet; (tela tejida) tapestry; **~ar** vt (muebles) to upholster

tapón [ta'pon] nm (de botella) top; (de lavabo) plug; **~ de rosca** screw-top

taquigrafía [takivra'fia] nf shorthand; **taquígrafo, a** nm/f shorthand writer, stenographer

taquilla [ta'kiʎa] nf (donde se compra) booking office; (suma recogida) takings pl; **taquillero, a** adj: **función taquillera** box office success ♦ nm/f ticket clerk

tara ['tara] nf (defecto) defect; (COM) tare

tarántula [ta'rantula] nf tarantula

tararear [tarare'ar] vi to hum

tardar [tar'ðar] vi (tomar tiempo) to take a long time; (llegar tarde) to be late; (demorar) to delay; **¿tarda mucho el tren?** does the train take (very) long?; **a más ~** at the latest; **no tardes en venir** come soon

tarde ['tarðe] adv late ♦ nf (de día) afternoon; (al anochecer) evening; **de ~ en ~** from time to time; **¡buenas ~s!** good afternoon!; **a o por la ~** in the afternoon; in the evening

tardío, a [tar'ðio, a] adj (retrasado) late; (lento) slow (to arrive)

tarea [ta'rea] nf task; (faena) chore; (ESCOL) homework

tarifa [ta'rifa] nf (lista de precios) price list; (precio) tariff

tarima [ta'rima] nf (plataforma) platform

tarjeta [tar'xeta] nf card; **~ postal/de crédito/de Navidad** postcard/credit card/Christmas card; **~ cliente** loyalty card

tarro ['tarro] nm jar, pot

tarta ['tarta] nf (pastel) cake; (de base dura) tart

tartamudear [tartamuðe'ar] vi to stammer; **tartamudo, a** adj stammering ♦ nm/f stammerer

tártaro, a ['tartaro, a] adj: **salsa tártara** tartar(e) sauce

tasa ['tasa] nf (precio) (fixed) price, rate; (valoración) valuation; (medida, norma) measure, standard; **~ de cambio/interés** exchange/interest rate; **~s universitarias** university fees; **~s de aeropuerto** airport tax; **~ción** nf valuation; **~dor, a** nm/f valuer

tasar [ta'sar] vt (arreglar el precio) to fix a price for; (valorar) to value, assess

tasca ['taska] nf (fam) pub

tatarabuelo, a [tatara'βwelo, a] nm/f great-

great-grandfather/mother

tatuaje [ta'twaxe] nm (dibujo) tattoo; (acto) tattooing

tatuar [ta'twar] vt to tattoo

taurino, a [tau'rino, a] adj bullfighting cpd

Tauro ['tauro] nm Taurus

tauromaquia [tauro'makja] nf tauromachy, (art of) bullfighting

taxi ['taksi] nm taxi

taxista [tak'sista] nm/f taxi driver

taza ['taθa] nf cup; (de retrete) bowl; **~ para café** coffee cup; **tazón** nm (taza grande) mug, large cup; (de fuente) basin

te [te] pron (complemento de objeto) you; (complemento indirecto) (to) you; (reflexivo) (to) yourself; **¿~ duele mucho el brazo?** does your arm hurt a lot?; **~ equivocas** you're wrong; **¡cálma~!** calm down!

té [te] nm tea

tea ['tea] nf torch

teatral [tea'tral] adj theatre cpd; (fig) theatrical

teatro [te'atro] nm theatre; (LITERATURA) plays pl, drama

tebeo [te'βeo] nm comic

techo ['tetʃo] nm (externo) roof; (interno) ceiling; **~ corredizo** sunroof

tecla ['tekla] nf key; **~do** nm keyboard; **teclear** vi (MUS) to strum; (con los dedos) to tap ♦ vt (INFORM) to key in

técnica ['teknika] nf technique; (tecnología) technology; ver tb **técnico**

técnico, a ['tekniko, a] adj technical ♦ nm/f technician; (experto) expert

tecnología [teknolo'xia] nf technology; **tecnológico, a** adj technological

tedio ['teðjo] nm boredom, tedium; **~so, a** adj boring, tedious

teja ['texa] nf tile; (BOT) lime (tree); **~do** nm (tiled) roof

tejemaneje [texema'nexe] nm (lío) fuss; (intriga) intrigue

tejer [te'xer] vt to weave; (hacer punto) to knit; (fig) to fabricate; **tejido** nm (tela) material, fabric; (telaraña) web; (ANAT) tissue

tel [tel] abr (= teléfono) tel

tela ['tela] nf (tejido) material; (telaraña) web; (en líquido) skin; **telar** nm (máquina) loom

telaraña [tela'raɲa] nf cobweb

tele ['tele] (fam) nf telly (BRIT), tube (US)

tele... ['tele] pref tele...; **~comunicación** nf telecommunication; **~control** nm remote control; **~diario** nm television news; **~difusión** nf (television) broadcast; **~dirigido, a** adj remote-controlled

teléf abr (= teléfono) tel

teleférico [tele'feriko] nm (de esquí) ski-lift

telefonear [telefone'ar] vi to telephone

telefónico, a [tele'foniko, a] adj telephone

cpd

telefonillo [telefo'niʎo] *nm* (*de puerta*) intercom

telefonista [telefo'nista] *nm/f* telephonist

teléfono [te'lefono] *nm* (tele)phone; **estar hablando al ~** to be on the phone; **llamar o llamar a uno por ~** to ring sb (up) o phone sb (up); **~ móvil** car phone; **~ portátil** mobile phone

telegrafía [televra'fia] *nf* telegraphy

telégrafo [te'levrafo] *nm* telegraph

telegrama [tele'vrama] *nm* telegram

tele: **~impresor** *nm* teleprinter (*BRIT*), teletype (*US*); **~novela** *nf* soap (opera); **~objetivo** *nm* telephoto lens; **~patía** *nf* telepathy; **~pático, a** *adj* telepathic; **~scópico, a** *adj* telescopic; **~scopio** *nm* telescope; **~silla** *nm* chairlift; **~spectador, a** *nm/f* viewer; **~squí** *nm* ski-lift; **~tarjeta** *nf* phonecard; **~tipo** *nm* teletype; **~ventas** *nfpl* telesales

televidente [teleßi'ðente] *nm/f* viewer

televisar [teleßi'sar] *vt* to televise

televisión [teleßi'sjon] *nf* television; **~ en colores** colour television; **~ digital** digital television

televisor [teleßi'sor] *nm* television set

télex ['teleks] *nm inv* telex

telón [te'lon] *nm* curtain; **~ de acero** (*POL*) iron curtain; **~ de fondo** backcloth, background

tema ['tema] *nm* (*asunto*) subject, topic; (*MUS*) theme; **temática** *nf* (*social, histórica, artística*) range of topics; **temático, a** *adj* thematic

temblar [tem'blar] *vi* to shake, tremble; (*de frío*) to shiver; **temblón, ona** *adj* shaking; **temblor** *nm* trembling; (*de tierra*) earthquake; **tembloroso, a** *adj* trembling

temer [te'mer] *vt* to fear ♦ *vi* to be afraid; **temo que llegue tarde** I am afraid he may be late

temerario, a [teme'rarjo, a] *adj* (*descuidado*) reckless; (*irreflexivo*) hasty; **temeridad** *nf* (*imprudencia*) rashness; (*audacia*) boldness

temeroso, a [teme'roso, a] *adj* (*miedoso*) fearful; (*que inspira temor*) frightful

temible [te'mißle] *adj* fearsome

temor [te'mor] *nm* (*miedo*) fear; (*duda*) suspicion

témpano ['tempano] *nm*: **~ de hielo** ice-floe

temperamento [tempera'mento] *nm* temperament

temperatura [tempera'tura] *nf* temperature

tempestad [tempes'taθ] *nf* storm; **tempestuoso, a** *adj* stormy

templado, a [tem'plaðo, a] *adj* (*moderado*) moderate; (*frugal*) frugal; (*agua*) lukewarm; (*clima*) mild; (*MUS*) well-tuned; **templanza** *nf* moderation; mildness

templar [tem'plar] *vt* (*moderar*) to moderate; (*furia*) to restrain; (*calor*) to reduce; (*afinar*) to tune (up); (*acero*) to temper; (*tuerca*) to tighten up; **temple** *nm* (*ajuste*) tempering; (*afinación*) tuning; (*pintura*) tempera

templo ['templo] *nm* (*iglesia*) church; (*pagano etc*) temple

temporada [tempo'raða] *nf* time, period; (*estación*) season

temporal [tempo'ral] *adj* (*no permanente*) temporary; (*REL*) temporal ♦ *nm* storm

tempranero, a [tempra'nero, a] *adj* (*BOT*) early; (*persona*) early-rising

temprano, a [tem'prano, a] *adj* early; (*demasiado pronto*) too soon, too early

ten *vb ver* **tener**

tenaces [te'naθes] *adj pl ver* **tenaz**

tenacidad [tenaθi'ðaθ] *nf* tenacity; (*dureza*) toughness; (*terquedad*) stubbornness

tenacillas [tena'θiʎas] *nfpl* tongs; (*para el pelo*) curling tongs (*BRIT*) o iron *sg* (*US*); (*MED*) forceps

tenaz [te'naθ] *adj* (*material*) tough; (*persona*) tenacious; (*creencia, resistencia*) stubborn

tenaza(s) [te'naθa(s)] *nf(pl)* (*MED*) forceps; (*TEC*) pliers; (*ZOOL*) pincers

tendedero [tende'ðero] *nm* (*para ropa*) drying place; (*cuerda*) clothes line

tendencia [ten'denθja] *nf* tendency; **tener ~ a** to tend to, have a tendency to; **tendencioso, a** *adj* tendentious

tender [ten'der] *vt* (*extender*) to spread out; (*colgar*) to hang out; (*vía férrea, cable*) to lay; (*estirar*) to stretch ♦ *vi*: **~ a** to tend to, have a tendency towards; **~se** *vr* to lie down; **~ la cama/la mesa** (*AM*) to make the bed/lay (*BRIT*) o set (*US*) the table

tenderete [tende'rete] *nm* (*puesto*) stall; (*exposición*) display of goods

tendero, a [ten'dero, a] *nm/f* shopkeeper

tendido, a [ten'diðo, a] *adj* (*acostado*) lying down, flat; (*colgado*) hanging ♦ *nm* (*TAUR*) front rows of seats; **a galope ~** flat out

tendón [ten'don] *nm* tendon

tendré *etc vb ver* **tener**

tenebroso, a [tene'ßroso, a] *adj* (*oscuro*) dark; (*fig*) gloomy

tenedor [tene'ðor] *nm* (*CULIN*) fork; **~ de libros** book-keeper

tenencia [te'nenθja] *nf* (*de casa*) tenancy; (*de oficio*) tenure; (*de propiedad*) possession

---

PALABRA CLAVE

---

tener [te'ner] *vt* **1** (*poseer, gen*) to have; (*en la mano*) to hold; **¿tienes un boli?** have you got a pen?; **va a ~ un niño** she's going to have a baby; **¡ten** (*o* **tenga**)!, **¡aquí tienes** (*o* **tiene**)! here you are!

2 (*edad, medidas*) to be; **tiene 7 años** she's 7

(years old); **tiene 15 cm de largo** it's 15 cm long; *ver* **calor; hambre** *etc*
3 (*considerar*): **lo tengo por brillante** I consider him to be brilliant; **~ en mucho a uno** to think very highly of sb
4 (+ *pp*: = *pretérito*): **tengo terminada ya la mitad del trabajo** I've done half the work already
5: **~ que hacer algo** to have to do sth; **tengo que acabar este trabajo hoy** I have to finish this job today
6: **¿qué tienes, estás enfermo?** what's the matter with you, are you ill?
♦ **~se** *vr* **1**: **~se en pie** to stand up
2: **~se por** to think o.s.; **se tiene por muy listo** he thinks himself very clever

tengo *etc vb ver* **tener**
tenia [ˈtenja] *nf* tapeworm
teniente [teˈnjente] *nm* (*rango*) lieutenant; (*ayudante*) deputy
tenis [ˈtenis] *nm* tennis; **~ de mesa** table tennis; **~ta** *nm/f* tennis player
tenor [teˈnor] *nm* (*sentido*) meaning; (*MUS*) tenor; **a ~ de** on the lines of
tensar [tenˈsar] *vt* to tighten; (*arco*) to draw
tensión [tenˈsjon] *nf* tension; (*TEC*) stress; (*MED*): **~ arterial** blood pressure; **tener la ~ alta** to have high blood pressure
tenso, a [ˈtenso, a] *adj* tense
tentación [tentaˈθjon] *nf* temptation
tentáculo [tenˈtakulo] *nm* tentacle
tentador, a [tentaˈðor, a] *adj* tempting
tentar [tenˈtar] *vt* (*seducir*) to tempt; (*atraer*) to attract; **tentativa** *nf* attempt; **tentativa de asesinato** attempted murder
tentempié [tentemˈpje] *nm* snack
tenue [ˈtenwe] *adj* (*delgado*) thin, slender; (*neblina*) light; (*lazo, vínculo*) slight
teñir [teˈɲir] *vt* to dye; (*fig*) to tinge; **~se** *vr* to dye; **~se el pelo** to dye one's hair
teología [teoloˈxia] *nf* theology
teoría [teoˈria] *nf* theory; **en ~** in theory; **teóricamente** *adv* theoretically; **teórico, a** *adj* theoretic(al) ♦ *nm/f* theoretician, theorist; **teorizar** *vi* to theorize
terapéutico, a [teraˈpeutiko, a] *adj* therapeutic
terapia [teˈrapja] *nf* therapy
tercer [terˈθer] *adj ver* **tercero**
tercermundista [terθermunˈdista] *adj* Third World *cpd*
tercero, a [terˈθero, a] *adj* (*delante de nmsg*: **tercer**) third ♦ *nm* (*JUR*) third party
terceto [terˈθeto] *nm* trio
terciar [terˈθjar] *vi* (*participar*) to take part; (*hacer de árbitro*) to mediate; **~se** *vr* to come up; **~io, a** *adj* tertiary
tercio [ˈterθjo] *nm* third

terciopelo [terθjoˈpelo] *nm* velvet
terco, a [ˈterko, a] *adj* obstinate
tergal ® [terˈval] *nm* type of polyester
tergiversar [terxiβerˈsar] *vt* to distort
termal [terˈmal] *adj* thermal
termas [ˈtermas] *nfpl* hot springs
térmico, a [ˈtermiko, a] *adj* thermal
terminación [terminaˈθjon] *nf* (*final*) end; (*conclusión*) conclusion, ending
terminal [termiˈnal] *adj, nm, nf* terminal
terminante [termiˈnante] *adj* (*final*) final, definitive; (*tajante*) categorical; **~mente** *adv*: **~mente prohibido** strictly forbidden
terminar [termiˈnar] *vt* (*completar*) to complete, finish; (*concluir*) to end ♦ *vi* (*llegar a su fin*) to end; (*parar*) to stop; (*acabar*) to finish; **~se** *vr* to come to an end; **~ por hacer algo** to end up (by) doing sth
término [ˈtermino] *nm* end, conclusion; (*parada*) terminus; (*límite*) boundary; **~ medio** average; (*fig*) middle way; **en último ~** (*a fin de cuentas*) in the last analysis; (*como último recurso*) as a last resort
terminología [terminoloˈxia] *nf* terminology
termodinámico, a [termoðiˈnamiko, a] *adj* thermodynamic
termómetro [terˈmometro] *nm* thermometer
termonuclear [termonukleˈar] *adj* thermonuclear
termo(s) ® [ˈtermo(s)] *nm* Thermos ® (flask)
termostato [termoˈstato] *nm* thermostat
ternero, a [terˈnero, a] *nm/f* (*animal*) calf ♦ *nf* (*carne*) veal
ternura [terˈnura] *nf* (*trato*) tenderness; (*palabra*) endearment; (*cariño*) fondness
terquedad [terkeˈðað] *nf* obstinacy
terrado [teˈrraðo] *nm* terrace
terraplén [terraˈplen] *nm* embankment
terrateniente [terrateˈnjente] *nm/f* landowner
terraza [teˈrraθa] *nf* (*balcón*) balcony; (*tejado*) (flat) roof; (*AGR*) terrace
térremoto [terreˈmoto] *nm* earthquake
terrenal [terreˈnal] *adj* earthly
terreno [teˈrreno] *nm* (*tierra*) land; (*parcela*) plot; (*suelo*) soil; (*fig*) field; **un ~** a piece of land
terrestre [teˈrrestre] *adj* terrestrial; (*ruta*) land *cpd*
terrible [teˈrriβle] *adj* terrible, awful
territorio [terriˈtorjo] *nm* territory
terrón [teˈrron] *nm* (*de azúcar*) lump; (*de tierra*) clod, lump
terror [teˈrror] *nm* terror; **~ífico, a** *adj* terrifying; **~ista** *adj, nm/f* terrorist
terso, a [ˈterso, a] *adj* (*liso*) smooth; (*pulido*)

polished; **tersura** nf smoothness

tertulia [ter'tulja] nf (reunión informal) social gathering; (grupo) group, circle

tesis ['tesis] nf inv thesis

tesón [te'son] nm (firmeza) firmness; (tenacidad) tenacity

tesorero, a [teso'rero, a] nm/f treasurer

tesoro [te'soro] nm treasure; (COM, POL) treasury

testaferro [testa'ferro] nm figurehead

testamentario, a [testamen'tarjo, a] adj testamentary ♦ nm/f executor/executrix

testamento [testa'mento] nm will

testar [tes'tar] vi to make a will

testarudo, a [testa'ruðo, a] adj stubborn

testículo [tes'tikulo] nm testicle

testificar [testifi'kar] vt to testify; (fig) to attest ♦ vi to give evidence

testigo [tes'tiɣo] nm/f witness; ~ de cargo/ descargo witness for the prosecution/defence; ~ ocular eye witness

testimoniar [testimo'njar] vt to testify to; (fig) to show; **testimonio** nm testimony

teta ['teta] nf (de biberón) teat; (ANAT: fam) breast

tétanos ['tetanos] nm tetanus

tetera [te'tera] nf teapot

tétrico, a ['tetriko, a] adj gloomy, dismal

textil [teks'til] adj textile

texto ['teksto] nm text; **textual** adj textual

textura [teks'tura] nf (de tejido) texture

tez [teθ] nf (cutis) complexion

ti [ti] pron you; (reflexivo) yourself

tía ['tia] nf (pariente) aunt; (fam) chick, bird

tibieza [ti'βjeθa] nf (temperatura) tepidness; (actitud) coolness; **tibio, a** adj lukewarm

tiburón [tiβu'ron] nm shark

tic [tik] nm (ruido) click; (de reloj) tick; (MED) ~ nervioso nervous tic

tictac [tik'tak] nm (de reloj) tick tock

tiempo ['tjempo] nm time; (época, período) age, period; (METEOROLOGÍA) weather; (LING) tense; (DEPORTE) half; a ~ in time; a un o al mismo ~ at the same time; al poco ~ very soon (after); se quedó poco ~ he didn't stay very long; hace poco ~ not long ago; mucho ~ a long time; de ~ en ~ from time to time; hace buen/mal ~ the weather is fine/bad; estar a ~ to be in time; hace ~ some time ago; hacer ~ to while away the time; motor de 2 ~s two-stroke engine; primer ~ first half

tienda ['tjenda] nf shop, store; ~ (de campaña) tent; ~ de alimentación o comestibles grocer's (BRIT), grocery store (US)

tienes etc vb ver **tener**

tienta etc ['tjenta] vb ver **tentar** ♦ nf: andar a ~s to grope one's way along

tiento ['tjento] vb ver **tentar** ♦ nm (tacto) touch; (precaución) wariness

tierno, a ['tjerno, a] adj (blando) tender; (fresco) fresh; (amable) sweet

tierra ['tjerra] nf earth; (suelo) soil; (mundo) earth, world; (país) country, land; ~ adentro inland

tieso, a ['tjeso, a] adj (rígido) rigid; (duro) stiff; (fam: orgulloso) conceited

tiesto ['tjesto] nm flowerpot

tifoidea [tifoi'ðea] nf typhoid

tifón [ti'fon] nm typhoon

tifus ['tifus] nm typhus

tigre ['tiɣre] nm tiger

tijera [ti'xera] nf scissors pl; (ZOOL) claw; ~s nfpl scissors; (para plantas) shears

tijeretear [tixerete'ar] vt to snip

tila ['tila] nf lime blossom tea

tildar [til'dar] vt: ~ de to brand as

tilde ['tilde] nf (TIP) tilde

tilín [ti'lin] nm tinkle

tilo ['tilo] nm lime tree

timar [ti'mar] vt (estafar) to swindle

timbal [tim'bal] nm small drum

timbrar [tim'brar] vt to stamp

timbre ['timbre] nm (sello) stamp; (campanilla) bell; (tono) timbre; (COM) stamp duty

timidez [timi'ðeθ] nf shyness; **tímido, a** adj shy

timo ['timo] nm swindle

timón [ti'mon] nm helm, rudder; **timonel** nm helmsman

tímpano ['timpano] nm (ANAT) eardrum; (MUS) small drum

tina ['tina] nf tub; (baño) bath(tub); **tinaja** nf large jar

tinglado [tin'glaðo] nm (cobertizo) shed; (fig: truco) trick; (intriga) intrigue

tinieblas [ti'njeβlas] nfpl darkness sg; (sombras) shadows

tino ['tino] nm (habilidad) skill; (juicio) insight

tinta ['tinta] nf ink; (TEC) dye; (ARTE) colour

tinte ['tinte] nm dye

tintero [tin'tero] nm inkwell

tintinear [tintine'ar] vt to tinkle

tinto ['tinto] nm red wine

tintorería [tintore'ria] nf dry cleaner's

tintura [tin'tura] nf (QUÍM) dye; (farmacéutico) tincture

tío ['tio] nm (pariente) uncle; (fam: individuo) bloke (BRIT), guy

tiovivo [tio'βiβo] nm merry-go-round

típico, a ['tipiko, a] adj typical

tipo ['tipo] nm (clase) type, kind; (hombre) fellow; (ANAT: de hombre) build; (: de mujer) figure; (IMPRENTA) type; ~ bancario/de descuento/de interés/de cambio bank/ discount/interest/exchange rate

tipografía [tipoɣra'fia] nf printing cpd; **tipográfico, a** adj printing cpd

tíquet ['tiket] (pl ~s) nm ticket; (en tienda) cash slip

tiquismiquis |tikis'mikis| nm inv fussy person ♦ nmpl (querellas) squabbling sg; (escrúpulos) silly scruples

tira ['tira] nf strip; (fig) abundance; ~ y afloja give and take

tirabuzón [tiraβu'θon] nm (rizo) curl

tirachinas [tira'tʃinas] nm inv catapult

tirada [ti'raða] nf (acto) cast, throw; (serie) series; (TIP) printing, edition; de una ~ at one go

tirado, a [ti'raðo, a] adj (barato) dirt-cheap; (fam: fácil) very easy

tirador [tira'ðor] nm (mango) handle

tiranía [tira'nia] nf tyranny; **tirano, a** adj tyrannical ♦ nm/f tyrant

tirante [ti'rante] adj (cuerda etc) tight, taut; (relaciones) strained ♦ nm (ARQ) brace; (TEC) stay; ~s nmpl (de pantalón) braces (BRIT), suspenders (US); **tirantez** nf tightness; (fig) tension

tirar [ti'rar] vt to throw; (dejar caer) to drop; (volcar) to upset; (derribar) to knock down o over; (desechar) to throw out o away; (dinero) to squander; (imprimir) to print ♦ vi (disparar) to shoot; (de la puerta etc) to pull; (fam: andar) to go; (tender a, buscar realizar) to tend to; (DEPORTE) to shoot; ~se vr to throw o.s.; ~ abajo to bring down, destroy; **tira más a su padre** he takes more after his father; **ir tirando** to manage; **a todo ~** at the most

tirita [ti'rita] nf (sticking) plaster (BRIT), bandaid (US)

tiritar [tiri'tar] vi to shiver

tiro ['tiro] nm (lanzamiento) throw; (disparo) shot; (DEPORTE) shot; (GOLF, TENIS) drive; (alcance) range; ~ al blanco target practice; **caballo de ~** cart-horse; **andar de ~s largos** to be all dressed up; **al ~** (AM) at once

tirón [ti'ron] nm (sacudida) pull, tug; de un ~ in one go, all at once

tiroteo [tiro'teo] nm exchange of shots, shooting

tísico, a ['tisiko, a] adj consumptive

tisis ['tisis] nf inv consumption, tuberculosis

títere ['titere] nm puppet

titiritero, a |titiri'tero, a| nm/f puppeteer

titubeante [tituße'ante| adj (al andar) shaky, tottering; (al hablar) stammering; (dudoso) hesitant

titubear [tituße'ar] vi to stagger; to stammer; (fig) to hesitate; **titubeo** nm staggering; stammering; hesitation

titulado, a [titu'laðo, a] adj (libro) entitled; (persona) titled

titular [titu'lar] adj titular ♦ nm/f holder ♦ nm headline ♦ vt to title; ~se vr to be entitled;

título nm title; (de diario) headline; (certificado) professional qualification; (universitario) (university) degree; **a título de** in the capacity of

tiza ['tiθa] nf chalk

tiznar [tiθ'nar] vt to blacken

tizón [ti'θon] nm brand

toalla [to'aʎa] nf towel

tobillo [to'βiʎo] nm ankle

tobogán [toßo'xan] nm (montaña rusa) roller-coaster; (de niños) chute, slide

tocadiscos [toka'ðiskos] nm inv record player

tocado, a [to'kaðo, a] adj (fam) touched ♦ nm headdress

tocador [toka'ðor] nm (mueble) dressing table; (cuarto) boudoir; (fam) ladies' toilet (BRIT) o room (US)

tocante [to'kante]: ~ a prep with regard to

tocar [to'kar] vt to touch; (MUS) to play; (referirse a) to allude to; (timbre) to ring ♦ vi (a la puerta) to knock (on o at the door); (ser de turno) to fall to, be the turn of; (ser hora) to be due; ~se vr (cubrirse la cabeza) to cover one's head; (tener contacto) to touch (each other); **por lo que a mí me toca** as far as I am concerned; **te toca a ti** it's your turn

tocayo, a [to'kajo, a] nm/f namesake

tocino [to'θino] nm bacon

todavía [toða'ßia] adv (aun) even; (aún) still, yet; ~ **más** yet more; ~ **no** not yet

> PALABRA CLAVE

todo, a ['toðo, a] adj **1** (con artículo sg) all; **toda la carne** all the meat; **toda la noche** all night, the whole night; ~ **el libro** the whole book; **toda una botella** a whole bottle; ~ **lo contrario** quite the opposite; **está toda sucia** she's all dirty; **por** ~ **el país** throughout the whole country

2 (con artículo pl) all; every; ~**s los libros** all the books; **todas las noches** every night; ~**s los que quieran salir** all those who want to leave

♦ pron **1** everything, all; ~**s** everyone, everybody; **lo sabemos** ~ we know everything; ~**s querían más tiempo** everybody o everyone wanted more time; **nos marchamos** ~**s** all of us left

2: con ~: **con** ~ **él me sigue gustando** even so I still like him

♦ adv all; **vaya** ~ **seguido** keep straight on o ahead

♦ nm: **como un** ~ as a whole; **del** ~: **no me agrada del** ~ I don't entirely like it

todopoderoso, a [toðopoðe'roso, a] adj all powerful; (REL) almighty

toga ['toxa] nf toga; (ESCOL) gown

Tokio ['tokjo] n Tokyo

toldo ['toldo] nm (para el sol) sunshade
(BRIT), parasol; (tienda) marquee

tolerancia [tole'ranθja] nf tolerance;
tolerante adj (sociedad) liberal; (persona)
open-minded

tolerar [tole'rar] vt to tolerate; (resistir) to
endure

toma ['toma] nf (acto) taking; (MED) dose;
~ **(de corriente)** socket

tomar [to'mar] vt to take; (aspecto) to take
on; (beber) to drink ♦ vi to take; (AM) to
drink; **~se** vr to take; **~se** to consider o.s.
to be; **~ a bien/a mal** to take well/badly; **~ en
serio** to take seriously; **~ el pelo a alguien** to
pull sb's leg; **~la con uno** to pick a quarrel
with sb; **¡tome!** here you are!; **~ el sol** to
sunbathe

tomate [to'mate] nm tomato

tomillo [to'miʎo] nm thyme

tomo ['tomo] nm (libro) volume

ton [ton] abr = **tonelada** ♦ nm: **sin ~ ni son**
without rhyme or reason

tonada [to'naða] nf tune

tonalidad [tonali'ðað] nf tone

tonel [to'nel] nm barrel

tonelada [tone'laða] nf ton; **tonelaje** nm
tonnage

tónica ['tonika] nf (MUS) tonic; (fig) keynote

tónico, a ['toniko, a] adj tonic ♦ nm (MED)
tonic

tonificar [tonifi'kar] vt to tone up

tono ['tono] nm tone; **fuera de ~**
inappropriate; **darse ~** to put on airs

tontería [tonte'ria] nf (estupidez) foolishness;
(cosa) stupid thing; (acto) foolish act; **~s** nfpl
(disparates) rubbish sg, nonsense sg

tonto, a ['tonto, a] adj stupid, silly ♦ nm/f
fool

topar [to'par] vi: **~ contra** o **en** to run into;
~ con to run up against

tope ['tope] adj maximum ♦ nm (fin) end;
(límite) limit; (FERRO) buffer; (AUTO) bumper;
al ~ end to end

tópico, a ['topiko, a] adj topical ♦ nm
platitude

topo ['topo] nm (ZOOL) mole; (fig) blunderer

topografía [topoɣra'fia] nf topography;
topógrafo, a nm/f topographer

toque etc ['toke] vb ver **tocar** ♦ nm touch;
(MUS) beat; (de campana) peal; **dar un ~ a** to
warn; **~ de queda** curfew

toqué vb ver **tocar**

toquetear [tokete'ar] vt to finger

toquilla [to'kiʎa] nf (pañuelo) headscarf;
(chal) shawl

tórax ['toraks] nm thorax

torbellino [torbe'ʎino] nm whirlwind; (fig)
whirl

torcedura [torθe'ðura] nf twist; (MED) sprain

torcer [tor'θer] vt to twist; (la esquina) to
turn; (MED) to sprain ♦ vi (desviar) to turn
off; **~se** vr (ladearse) to bend; (desviarse) to
go astray; (fracasar) to go wrong; **torcido,
a** adj twisted; (fig) crooked ♦ nm curl

tordo, a ['torðo, a] adj dappled ♦ nm thrush

torear [tore'ar] vt (fig: evadir) to avoid; (jugar
con) to tease ♦ vi to fight bulls; **toreo** nm
bullfighting; **torero, a** nm/f bullfighter

tormenta [tor'menta] nf storm; (fig:
confusión) turmoil

tormento [tor'mento] nm torture; (fig)
anguish

tornar [tor'nar] vt (devolver) to return, give
back; (transformar) to transform ♦ vi to go
back; **~se** vr (ponerse) to become

tornasolado, a [tornaso'laðo, a] adj
(brillante) iridescent; (reluciente) shimmering

torneo [tor'neo] nm tournament

tornillo [tor'niʎo] nm screw

torniquete [torni'kete] nm (MED) tourniquet

torno ['torno] nm (TEC) winch; (tambor)
drum; **en ~ (a)** round, about

toro ['toro] nm bull; (fam) he-man; **los ~s**
bullfighting

toronja [to'ronxa] nf grapefruit

torpe ['torpe] adj (poco hábil) clumsy,
awkward; (necio) dim; (lento) slow

torpedo [tor'peðo] nm torpedo

torpeza [tor'peθa] nf (falta de agilidad)
clumsiness; (lentitud) slowness; (error)
mistake

torre ['torre] nf tower; (de petróleo) derrick

torrefacto, a [torre'fakto, a] adj roasted

torrente [to'rrente] nm torrent

tórrido, a ['torriðo, a] adj torrid

torrija [to'rrixa] nf French toast

torsión [tor'sjon] nf twisting

torso ['torso] nm torso

torta ['torta] nf cake; (fam) slap

tortícolis [tor'tikolis] nm inv stiff neck

tortilla [tor'tiʎa] nf omelette; (AM) maize
pancake; **~ francesa/española** plain/potato
omelette

tórtola ['tortola] nf turtledove

tortuga [tor'tuɣa] nf tortoise

tortuoso, a [tor'twoso, a] adj winding

tortura [tor'tura] nf torture; **torturar** vt to
torture

tos [tos] nf cough; **~ ferina** whooping cough

tosco, a ['tosko, a] adj coarse

toser [to'ser] vi to cough

tostada [tos'taða] nf piece of toast; **tostado,
a** adj toasted; (por el sol) dark brown; (piel)
tanned

tostador [tosta'ðor] nm toaster

tostar [tos'tar] vt to toast; (café) to roast;
(persona) to tan; **~se** vr to get brown

total [to'tal] *adj* total ♦ *adv* in short; (*al fin y al cabo*) when all is said and done ♦ *nm* total; **~ que** to cut (*BRIT*) o make (*US*) a long story short

totalidad [totali'ðað] *nf* whole

totalitario, a [totali'tarjo, a] *adj* totalitarian

tóxico, a ['toksiko, a] *adj* toxic ♦ *nm* poison; **toxicómano, a** *nm/f* drug addict

toxina [to'ksina] *nf* toxin

tozudo, a [to'θuðo, a] *adj* obstinate

traba ['traßa] *nf* bond, tie; (*cadena*) shackle

trabajador, a [traßaxa'ðor, a] *adj* hard-working ♦ *nm/f* worker

trabajar [traßa'xar] *vt* to work; (*AGR*) to till; (*empeñarse en*) to work at; (*convencer*) to persuade ♦ *vi* to work; (*esforzarse*) to strive; **trabajo** *nm* work; (*tarea*) task; (*POL*) labour; (*fig*) effort; **tomarse el trabajo de** to take the trouble to; **trabajo por turno/a destajo** shift work/piecework; **trabajoso, a** *adj* hard

trabalenguas [traßa'lengwas] *nm inv* tongue twister

trabar [tra'ßar] *vt* (*juntar*) to join, unite; (*atar*) to tie down, fetter; (*agarrar*) to seize; (*amistad*) to strike up; **~se** *vr* to become entangled; **trabársele a uno la lengua** to be tongue-tied

tracción [trak'θjon] *nf* traction; **~ delantera/trasera** front-wheel/rear-wheel drive

tractor [trak'tor] *nm* tractor

tradición [traði'θjon] *nf* tradition; **tradicional** *adj* traditional

traducción [traðuk'θjon] *nf* translation

traducir [traðu'θir] *vt* to translate; **traductor, a** *nm/f* translator

traer [tra'er] *vt* (*llevar*) to bring; (*llevar puesto*) to wear; (*incluir*) to carry; (*causar*) to cause; **~se** *vr*: **~se algo** to be up to sth

traficar [trafi'kar] *vi* to trade

tráfico ['trafiko] *nm* (*COM*) trade; (*AUTO*) traffic

tragaluz [traxa'luθ] *nm* skylight

tragaperras [traxa'perras] *nm o f inv* slot machine

tragar [tra'xar] *vt* to swallow; (*devorar*) to devour, bolt down; **~se** *vr* to swallow

tragedia [tra'xeðja] *nf* tragedy; **trágico, a** *adj* tragic

trago ['traxo] *nm* (*líquido*) drink; (*bocado*) gulp; (*fam: de bebida*) swig; (*desgracia*) blow

traición [trai'θjon] *nf* treachery; (*JUR*) treason; (*una ~*) act of treachery; **traicionar** *vt* to betray

traicionero, a [traiθjo'nero, a] *adj* treacherous

traidor, a [trai'ðor, a] *adj* treacherous ♦ *nm/f* traitor

traigo etc *vb ver* **traer**

traje ['traxe] *vb ver* **traer** ♦ *nm* (*de hombre*) suit; (*de mujer*) dress; (*vestido típico*) costume; **~ de baño** swimsuit; **~ de luces** bullfighter's costume

trajera etc *vb ver* **traer**

trajín [tra'xin] *nm* (*fam: movimiento*) bustle; **trajinar** *vi* (*moverse*) to bustle about

trama ['trama] *nf* (*intriga*) plot; (*de tejido*) weft (*BRIT*), woof (*US*); **tramar** *vt* to plot; (*TEC*) to weave

tramitar [trami'tar] *vt* (*asunto*) to transact; (*negociar*) to negotiate

trámite ['tramite] *nm* (*paso*) step; (*JUR*) transaction; **~s** *nmpl* (*burocracia*) procedure *sg*; (*JUR*) proceedings

tramo ['tramo] *nm* (*de tierra*) plot; (*de escalera*) flight; (*de vía*) section

tramoya [tra'moja] *nf* (*TEATRO*) piece of stage machinery; **tramoyista** *nm/f* scene shifter; (*fig*) trickster

trampa ['trampa] *nf* trap; (*en el suelo*) trapdoor; (*truco*) trick; (*engaño*) fiddle; **trampear** *vt, vi* to cheat

trampolín [trampo'lin] *nm* (*de piscina etc*) diving board

tramposo, a [tram'poso, a] *adj* crooked, cheating ♦ *nm/f* crook, cheat

tranca ['tranka] *nf* (*palo*) stick; (*de puerta, ventana*) bar; **trancar** *vt* to bar

trance ['tranθe] *nm* (*momento difícil*) difficult moment o juncture; (*estado hipnotizado*) trance

tranquilidad [trankili'ðað] *nf* (*calma*) calmness, stillness; (*paz*) peacefulness

tranquilizar [trankili'θar] *vt* (*calmar*) to calm (down); (*asegurar*) to reassure; **~se** *vr* to calm down; **tranquilo, a** *adj* (*calmado*) calm; (*apacible*) peaceful; (*mar*) calm; (*mente*) untroubled

transacción [transak'θjon] *nf* transaction

transbordador [transßorða'ðor] *nm* ferry

transbordar [transßor'ðar] *vt* to transfer; **transbordo** *nm* transfer; **hacer transbordo** to change (trains *etc*)

transcurrir [transku'rrir] *vi* (*tiempo*) to pass; (*hecho*) to take place

transcurso [trans'kurso] *nm*: **~ del tiempo** lapse (of time)

transeúnte [transe'unte] *nm/f* passer-by

transferencia [transfe'renθja] *nf* transference; (*COM*) transfer

transferir [transfe'rir] *vt* to transfer

transformador [transforma'ðor] *nm* (*ELEC*) transformer

transformar [transfor'mar] *vt* to transform; (*convertir*) to convert

tránsfuga ['transfuxa] *nm/f* (*MIL*) deserter; (*POL*) turncoat

transfusión [transfu'sjon] *nf* transfusion

transgénico, a [trans'xeniko, a] *adj* genetically modified, GM

transición [transi'θjon] *nf* transition

transigir [transi'xir] *vi* to compromise, make concessions

transistor [transis'tor] *nm* transistor

transitar [transi'tar] *vi* to go (from place to place); **tránsito** *nm* transit; (*AUTO*) traffic; **transitorio, a** *adj* transitory

transmisión [transmi'sjon] *nf* (*TEC*) transmission; (*transferencia*) transfer; ~ **en directo/exterior** live/outside broadcast

transmitir [transmi'tir] *vt* to transmit; (*RADIO, TV*) to broadcast

transparencia [transpa'renθja] *nf* transparency; (*claridad*) clearness, clarity; (*foto*) slide

transparentar [transparen'tar] *vt* to reveal ♦ *vi* to be transparent; **transparente** *adj* transparent; (*claro*) clear

transpirar [transpi'rar] *vi* to perspire

transportar [transpor'tar] *vt* to transport; (*llevar*) to carry; **transporte** *nm* transport; (*COM*) haulage

transversal [transβer'sal] *adj* transverse, cross

tranvía [tram'bia] *nm* tram

trapecio [tra'peθjo] *nm* trapeze; **trapecista** *nm/f* trapeze artist

trapero, a [tra'pero, a] *nm/f* ragman

trapicheo [trapi'tʃeo] (*fam*) *nm* scheme, fiddle

trapo ['trapo] *nm* (*tela*) rag; (*de cocina*) cloth

tráquea ['trakea] *nf* windpipe

traqueteo [trake'teo] *nm* rattling

tras [tras] *prep* (*detrás*) behind; (*después*) after

trasatlántico [trasat'lantiko] *nm* (*barco*) (cabin) cruiser

trascendencia [trasθen'denθja] *nf* (*importancia*) importance; (*FILOSOFÍA*) transcendence

trascendental [trasθenden'tal] *adj* important; (*FILOSOFÍA*) transcendental

trascender [trasθen'der] *vi* (*noticias*) to come out; (*suceso*) to have a wide effect

trasero, a [tra'sero, a] *adj* back, rear ♦ *nm* (*ANAT*) bottom

trasfondo [tras'fondo] *nm* background

trasgredir [trasɣre'ðir] *vt* to contravene

trashumante [trasu'mante] *adj* (*animales*) migrating

trasladar [trasla'ðar] *vt* to move; (*persona*) to transfer; (*postergar*) to postpone; (*copiar*) to copy; **~se** *vr* (*mudarse*) to move; **traslado** *nm* move; (*mudanza*) move, removal

traslucir [traslu'θir] *vt* to show; **~se** *vr* to be translucent; (*fig*) to be revealed

trasluz [tras'luθ] *nm* reflected light; **al ~** against *o* up to the light

trasnochador, a [trasnotʃa'ðor, a] *nm/f* night owl

trasnochar [trasno'tʃar] *vi* (*acostarse tarde*) to stay up late

traspapelar [traspape'lar] *vt* (*document, carta*) to mislay, misplace

traspasar [traspa'sar] *vt* (*suj: bala etc*) to pierce, go through; (*propiedad*) to sell, transfer; (*calle*) to cross over; (*límites*) to go beyond; (*ley*) to break; **traspaso** *nm* (*venta*) transfer, sale

traspié [tras'pje] *nm* (*tropezón*) trip; (*error*) blunder

trasplantar [trasplan'tar] *vt* to transplant

traste ['traste] *nm* (*MUS*) fret; **dar al ~ con algo** to ruin sth

trastero [tras'tero] *nm* storage room

trastienda [tras'tjenda] *nf* back of shop

trasto ['trasto] (*pey*) *nm* (*cosa*) piece of junk; (*persona*) dead loss

trastornado, a [trastor'naðo, a] *adj* (*loco*) mad, crazy

trastornar [trastor'nar] *vt* (*fig: planes*) to disrupt; (: *nervios*) to shatter; (: *persona*) to drive crazy; **~se** *vr* (*volverse loco*) to go mad *o* crazy; **trastorno** *nm* (*acto*) overturning; (*confusión*) confusion

tratable [tra'taβle] *adj* friendly

tratado [tra'taðo] *nm* (*POL*) treaty; (*COM*) agreement

tratamiento [trata'mjento] *nm* treatment; ~ **de textos** (*INFORM*) word processing *cpd*

tratar [tra'tar] *vt* (*ocuparse de*) to treat; (*manejar, TEC*) to handle; (*MED*) to treat; (*dirigirse a: persona*) to address ♦ *vi*: ~ **de** (*hablar sobre*) to deal with, be about; (*intentar*) to try to; **~se** *vr* to treat each other; ~ **con** (*COM*) to trade in; (*negociar*) to negotiate with; (*tener contactos*) to have dealings with; **¿de qué se trata?** what's it about?; **trato** *nm* dealings *pl*; (*relaciones*) relationship; (*comportamiento*) manner; (*COM*) agreement

trauma ['trauma] *nm* trauma

través [tra'βes] *nm* (*fig*) reverse; **al ~** across, crossways; **a ~ de** across; (*sobre*) over; (*por*) through

travesaño [traβe'saɲo] *nm* (*ARQ*) crossbeam; (*DEPORTE*) crossbar

travesía [traβe'sia] *nf* (*calle*) cross-street; (*NAUT*) crossing

travesura [traβe'sura] *nf* (*broma*) prank; (*ingenio*) wit

traviesa [tra'βjesa] *nf* (*ARQ*) crossbeam

travieso, a [tra'βjeso, a] *adj* (*niño*) naughty

trayecto [tra'jekto] *nm* (*ruta*) road, way; (*viaje*) journey; (*tramo*) stretch; **~ria** *nf* trajectory; (*fig*) path

traza ['traθa] *nf* (*aspecto*) looks *pl*; (*señal*)

sign; ~**do, a** adj: **bien ~do** shapely, well-formed ♦ nm (ARQ) plan, design; (fig) outline
trazar [tra'θar] vt (ARQ) to plan; (ARTE) to sketch; (fig) to trace; (plan) to draw up; **trazo** nm (línea) line; (bosquejo) sketch
trébol ['treßol] nm (BOT) clover
trece ['treθe] num thirteen
trecho ['tretʃo] nm (distancia) distance; (de tiempo) while; **de ~ en ~** at intervals
tregua ['trewxa] nf (MIL) truce; (fig) respite
treinta ['treinta] num thirty
tremendo, a [tre'mendo, a] adj (terrible) terrible; (imponente: cosa) imposing; (fam: fabuloso) tremendous
trémulo, a ['tremulo, a] adj quivering
tren [tren] nm train; **~ de aterrizaje** undercarriage
trenca ['trenka] nf duffel coat
trenza ['trenθa] nf (de pelo) plait (BRIT), braid (US); **trenzar** vt (pelo) to plait, braid; **trenzarse** vr (AM) to become involved
trepadora [trepa'ðora] nf (BOT) climber
trepar [tre'par] vt, vi to climb
trepidante [trepi'ðante] adj (acción) fast; (ritmo) hectic
tres [tres] num three
tresillo [tre'siʎo] nm three-piece suite; (MUS) triplet
treta ['treta] nf trick
triángulo ['trjangulo] nm triangle
tribu ['trißu] nf tribe
tribuna [tri'ßuna] nf (plataforma) platform; (DEPORTE) (grand)stand
tribunal [trißu'nal] nm (JUR) court; (comisión, fig) tribunal
tributar [trißu'tar] vt (gen) to pay; **tributo** nm (COM) tax
tricotar [triko'tar] vi to knit
trigal [tri'xal] nm wheat field
trigo ['trixo] nm wheat
trigueño, a [tri'xeno, a] adj (pelo) corn-coloured
trillado, a [tri'ʎaðo, a] adj threshed; (asunto) trite, hackneyed; **trilladora** nf threshing machine
trillar [tri'ʎar] vt (AGR) to thresh
trimestral [trimes'tral] adj quarterly; (ESCOL) termly
trimestre [tri'mestre] nm (ESCOL) term
trinar [tri'nar] vi (pájaros) to sing; (rabiar) to fume, be angry
trinchar [trin'tʃar] vt to carve
trinchera [trin'tʃera] nf (fosa) trench
trineo [tri'neo] nm sledge
trinidad [trini'ðað] nf trio; (REL): **la T~** the Trinity
trino ['trino] nm trill
tripa ['tripa] nf (ANAT) intestine; (fam: tb: ~s) insides pl

triple ['triple] adj triple
triplicado, a [tripli'kaðo, a] adj: **por ~** in triplicate
tripulación [tripula'θjon] nf crew
tripulante [tripu'lante] nm/f crewman/woman
tripular [tripu'lar] vt (barco) to man; (AUTO) to drive
triquiñuela [triki'nwela] nf trick
tris [tris] nm inv crack; **en un ~** in an instant
triste ['triste] adj sad; (lamentable) sorry, miserable; **~za** nf (aflicción) sadness; (melancolía) melancholy
triturar [tritu'rar] vt (moler) to grind; (mascar) to chew
triunfar [trjun'far] vi (tener éxito) to triumph; (ganar) to win; **triunfo** nm triumph
trivial [tri'ßjal] adj trivial; **~izar** vt to minimize, play down
triza ['triθa] nf: **hacer ~s** to smash to bits; (papel) to tear to shreds
trocar [tro'kar] vt to exchange
trocear [troθe'ar] vt (carne, manzana) to cut up, cut into pieces
trocha ['trotʃa] nf short cut
troche ['trotʃe]: **a ~ y moche** adv helter-skelter, pell-mell
trofeo [tro'feo] nm (premio) trophy; (éxito) success
tromba ['tromba] nf downpour
trombón [trom'bon] nm trombone
trombosis [trom'bosis] nf inv thrombosis
trompa ['trompa] nf horn; (trompo) humming top; (hocico) snout; (fam): **cogerse una ~** to get tight
trompazo [trom'paθo] nm bump, bang
trompeta [trom'peta] nf trumpet; (clarín) bugle
trompicón [trompi'kon]: **a ~es** adv in fits and starts
trompo ['trompo] nm spinning top
trompón [trom'pon] nm bump
tronar [tro'nar] vt (AM) to shoot ♦ vi to thunder; (fig) to rage
tronchar [tron'tʃar] vt (árbol) to chop down; (fig: vida) to cut short; (: esperanza) to shatter; (persona) to tire out; **~se** vr to fall down
tronco ['tronko] nm (de árbol, ANAT) trunk
trono ['trono] nm throne
tropa ['tropa] nf (MIL) troop; (soldados) soldiers pl
tropel [tro'pel] nm (muchedumbre) crowd
tropezar [trope'θar] vi to trip, stumble; (error) to slip up; **~ con** to run into; (topar con) to bump into; **tropezón** nm trip; (fig) blunder
tropical [tropi'kal] adj tropical
trópico ['tropiko] nm tropic

tropiezo [tro'pjeθo] *vb ver* **tropezar ♦** *nm* (*error*) slip, blunder; (*desgracia*) misfortune; (*obstáculo*) snag

trotamundos [trota'mundos] *nm inv* globetrotter

trotar [tro'tar] *vi* to trot; **trote** *nm* trot; (*fam*) travelling; **de mucho trote** hard-wearing

trozo ['troθo] *nm* bit, piece

trucha ['trutʃa] *nf* trout

truco ['truko] *nm* (*habilidad*) knack; (*engaño*) trick

trueno ['trweno] *nm* thunder; (*estampido*) bang

trueque *etc* ['trweke] *vb ver* **trocar ♦** *nm* exchange; (*COM*) barter

trufa ['trufa] *nf* (*BOT*) truffle

truhán, ana [tru'an, ana] *nm/f* rogue

truncar [trun'kar] *vt* (*cortar*) to truncate; (*fig: la vida etc*) to cut short; (: *el desarrollo*) to stunt

tu [tu] *adj* your

tú [tu] *pron* you

tubérculo [tu'ßerkulo] *nm* (*BOT*) tuber

tuberculosis [tußerku'losis] *nf inv* tuberculosis

tubería [tuße'ria] *nf* pipes *pl*; (*conducto*) pipeline

tubo ['tußo] *nm* tube, pipe; ~ **de ensayo** test tube; ~ **de escape** exhaust (pipe)

tuerca ['twerka] *nf* nut

tuerto, a ['twerto, a] *adj* blind in one eye ♦ *nm/f* one-eyed person

tuerza *etc vb ver* **torcer**

tuétano ['twetano] *nm* marrow; (*BOT*) pith

tufo ['tufo] *nm* (*hedor*) stench

tul [tul] *nm* tulle

tulipán [tuli'pan] *nm* tulip

tullido, a [tu'ʎiðo, a] *adj* crippled

tumba ['tumba] *nf* (*sepultura*) tomb

tumbar [tum'bar] *vt* to knock down; ~**se** *vr* (*echarse*) to lie down; (*extenderse*) to stretch out

tumbo ['tumbo] *nm*: **dar** ~**s** to stagger

tumbona [tum'bona] *nf* (*butaca*) easy chair; (*de playa*) deckchair (*BRIT*), beach chair (*US*)

tumor [tu'mor] *nm* tumour

tumulto [tu'multo] *nm* turmoil

tuna ['tuna] *nf* (*MUS*) student music group; *ver tb* **tuno**

tunante [tu'nante] *nm/f* rascal

tunda ['tunda] *nf* (*golpeo*) beating

túnel ['tunel] *nm* tunnel

Túnez ['tuneθ] *nm* Tunisia; (*ciudad*) Tunis

tuno, a ['tuno, a] *nm/f* (*fam*) rogue ♦ *nm* member of student music group

tupido, a [tu'piðo, a] *adj* (*denso*) dense; (*tela*) close-woven

turba ['turßa] *nf* crowd

turbante [tur'ßante] *nm* turban

turbar [tur'ßar] *vt* (*molestar*) to disturb; (*incomodar*) to upset; ~**se** *vr* to be disturbed

turbina [tur'ßina] *nf* turbine

turbio, a ['turßjo, a] *adj* cloudy; (*tema etc*) confused

turbulencia [turßu'lenθja] *nf* turbulence; (*fig*) restlessness; **turbulento, a** *adj* turbulent; (*fig: intranquilo*) restless; (: *ruidoso*) noisy

turco, a ['turko, a] *adj* Turkish ♦ *nm/f* Turk

turismo [tu'rismo] *nm* tourism; (*coche*) car; **turista** *nm/f* tourist; **turístico, a** *adj* tourist *cpd*

turnar [tur'nar] *vi* to take (it in) turns; ~**se** *vr* to take (it in) turns; **turno** *nm* (*de trabajo*) shift; (*juegos etc*) turn

turquesa [tur'kesa] *nf* turquoise

Turquía [tur'kia] *nf* Turkey

turrón [tu'rron] *nm* (*dulce*) nougat

tutear [tute'ar] *vt* to address as familiar "tú"; ~**se** *vr* to be on familiar terms

tutela [tu'tela] *nf* (*legal*) guardianship; **tutelar** *adj* tutelary ♦ *vt* to protect

tutor, a [tu'tor, a] *nm/f* (*legal*) guardian; (*ESCOL*) tutor

tuve *etc vb ver* **tener**

tuviera *etc vb ver* **tener**

tuyo, a ['tujo, a] *adj* yours, of yours ♦ *pron* yours; **un amigo** ~ a friend of yours; **los** ~**s** (*fam*) your relations, your family

TV ['te'ße] *nf abr* (= *televisión*) TV

TVE *nf abr* = **Televisión Española**

U, u

u [u] *conj* or

ubicar [ußi'kar] *vt* to place, situate; (*AM: encontrar*) to find; ~**se** *vr* to lie, be located

ubre ['ußre] *nf* udder

UCI *nf abr* (= *Unidad de Cuidados Intensivos*) ICU

Ud(s) *abr* = **usted(es)**

UE *nf abr* (= *Unión Europea*) EU

ufanarse [ufa'narse] *vr* to boast; ~ **de** to pride o.s. on; **ufano, a** *adj* (*arrogante*) arrogant; (*presumido*) conceited

UGT *nf abr* = **Unión General de Trabajadores**

ujier [u'xjer] *nm* usher; (*portero*) doorkeeper

úlcera ['ulθera] *nf* ulcer

ulcerar [ulθe'rar] *vt* to make sore; ~**se** *vr* to ulcerate

ulterior [ulte'rjor] *adj* (*más allá*) farther, further; (*subsecuente, siguiente*) subsequent

últimamente ['ultimamente] *adv* (*recientemente*) lately, recently

ultimar [ulti'mar] *vt* to finish; (*finalizar*) to finalize; (*AM: rematar*) to finish off

ultimátum [ulti'matum] (*pl* ~**s**) ultimatum

último, a ['ultimo, a] adj last; (más reciente)
latest, most recent; (más bajo) bottom; (más
alto) top; **en las últimas** on one's last legs;
por ♦ finally
ultra ['ultra] adj ultra **♦** nm/f extreme right-
winger
ultrajar [ultra'xar] vt (ofender) to outrage;
(insultar) to insult, abuse; **ultraje** nm
outrage; insult
ultramar [ultra'mar] nm: **de o en ~** abroad,
overseas
ultramarinos [ultrama'rinos] nmpl
groceries; **tienda de ~** grocer's (shop)
ultranza [ul'tranθa]: **a ~** adv (a todo trance)
at all costs; (completo) outright
ultratumba [ultra'tumba] nf: **la vida de ~**
the next life
umbral [um'bral] nm (gen) threshold
umbrío, a [um'brio, a] adj shady

un, una [un, 'una] art indef a; (antes de
vocal) an; **una mujer/naranja** a woman/an
orange
♦ adj: **unos** (o **unas**): **hay unos regalos para ti**
there are some presents for you; **hay unas
cervezas en la nevera** there are some beers in
the fridge

└────────────────────────────────────┘

unánime [u'nanime] adj unanimous;
unanimidad nf unanimity
undécimo, a [un'deθimo, a] adj eleventh
ungir [un'xir] vt to anoint
ungüento [un'gwento] nm ointment
únicamente ['unikamente] adv solely, only
único, a ['uniko, a] adj only, sole; (sin par)
unique
unidad [uni'ðað] nf unity; (COM, TEC etc) unit
unido, a [u'niðo, a] adj joined, linked; (fig)
united
unificar [unifi'kar] vt to unite, unify
uniformar [unifor'mar] vt to make uniform,
level up; (persona) to put into uniform
uniforme [uni'forme] adj uniform, equal;
(superficie) even **♦** nm uniform;
uniformidad nf uniformity; (de terreno)
levelness, evenness
unilateral [unilate'ral] adj unilateral
unión [u'njon] nf union; (acto) uniting,
joining; (unidad) unity; (TEC) joint; **la
U~ Europea** the European Union; **la
U~ Soviética** the Soviet Union
unir [u'nir] vt (juntar) to join, unite; (atar) to
tie, fasten; (combinar) to combine; **~se** vr to
join together, unite; (empresas) to merge
unísono [u'nisono] nm: **al ~** in unison
universal [uniβer'sal] adj universal;
(mundial) world cpd
universidad [uniβersi'ðað] nf university

universitario, a [uniβersi'tarjo, a] adj
university cpd **♦** nm/f (profesor) lecturer;
(estudiante) (university) student; (graduado)
graduate
universo [uni'βerso] nm universe

uno, a ['uno, a] adj one; **es todo ~** it's all one
and the same; **~s pocos** a few; **~s cien** about
a hundred
♦ pron **1** one; **quiero sólo ~** I only want one;
~ de ellos one of them
2 (alguien) somebody, someone; **conozco a
~ que se te parece** I know somebody o
someone who looks like you; **~ mismo**
oneself; **~s querían quedarse** some (people)
wanted to stay
3: **(los) ~s ... (los) otros ...** some ... others;
una y otra son muy agradables they're both
very nice
♦ nf one; **es la una** it's one o'clock
♦ nm (number) one

└────────────────────────────────────┘

untar [un'tar] vt (mantequilla) to spread;
(engrasar) to grease, oil
uña ['uɲa] nf (ANAT) nail; (garra) claw; (casco)
hoof; (arrancaclavos) claw
uranio [u'ranjo] nm uranium
urbanidad [urβani'ðað] nf courtesy,
politeness
urbanismo [urβa'nismo] nm town planning
urbanización [urβaniθa'θjon] nf (barrio,
colonia) housing estate
urbanizar [urβani'θar] vt (zona) to develop,
urbanize
urbano, a [ur'βano, a] adj (de ciudad)
urban; (cortés) courteous, polite
urbe ['urβe] nf large city
urdimbre [ur'ðimbre] nf (de tejido) warp;
(intriga) intrigue
urdir [ur'ðir] vt to warp; (complot) to plot,
contrive
urgencia [ur'xenθja] nf urgency; (prisa)
haste, rush; (emergencia) emergency;
servicios de ~ emergency services;
"Urgencias" "Casualty"; **urgente** adj urgent
urgir [ur'xir] vi to be urgent; **me urge** I'm in a
hurry for it
urinario, a [uri'narjo, a] adj urinary **♦** nm
urinal
urna ['urna] nf urn; (POL) ballot box
urraca [u'rraka] nf magpie
URSS nf: **la ~** the USSR
Uruguay [uru'ɣwai] nm: **el ~** Uruguay;
uruguayo, a adj, nm/f Uruguayan
usado, a [u'saðo, a] adj used; (de segunda
mano) secondhand
usar [u'sar] vt to use; (ropa) to wear; (tener
costumbre) to be in the habit of; **~se** vr to be

used; **uso** nm use; wear; (costumbre) usage, custom; (moda) fashion; **al uso** in keeping with custom; **al uso de** in the style of

usted [us'teð] pron (sg) you sg; (pl): **~es** you pl

usual [u'swal] adj usual

usuario, a [usu'arjo, a] nm/f user

usura [u'sura] nf usury; **usurero, a** nm/f usurer

usurpar [usur'par] vt to usurp

utensilio [uten'siljo] nm tool; (CULIN) utensil

útero ['utero] nm uterus, womb

útil ['util] adj useful ♦ nm tool; **utilidad** nf usefulness; (COM) profit; **utilizar** vt to use, utilize

utopía [uto'pia] nf Utopia; **utópico, a** adj Utopian

uva ['ußa] nf grape

V, v

v abr (= voltio) v

va vb ver **ir**

vaca ['baka] nf (animal) cow; **carne de ~** beef

vacaciones [baka'θjones] nfpl holidays

vacante [ba'kante] adj vacant, empty ♦ nf vacancy

vaciar [ba'θjar] vt to empty out; (ahuecar) to hollow out; (moldear) to cast; **~se** vr to empty

vacilante [baθi'lante] adj unsteady; (habla) faltering; (dudoso) hesitant

vacilar [baθi'lar] vi to be unsteady; (al hablar) to falter; (dudar) to hesitate, waver; (memoria) to fail

vacío, a [ba'θio, a] adj empty; (puesto) vacant; (desocupado) idle; (vano) vain ♦ nm emptiness; (FÍSICA) vacuum; (un ~) (empty) space

vacuna [ba'kuna] nf vaccine; **vacunar** vt to vaccinate

vacuno, a [ba'kuno, a] adj cow cpd; **ganado ~** cattle

vacuo, a ['bakwo, a] adj empty

vadear [baðe'ar] vt (río) to ford; **vado** nm ford

vagabundo, a [baɣa'ßundo, a] adj wandering ♦ nm tramp

vagamente [baɣa'mente] adv vaguely

vagancia [ba'ɣanθja] nf (pereza) idleness, laziness

vagar [ba'ɣar] vi to wander; (no hacer nada) to idle

vagina [ba'xina] nf vagina

vago, a ['baɣo, a] adj vague; (perezoso) lazy ♦ nm/f (vagabundo) tramp; (flojo) lazybones sg, idler

vagón [ba'ɣon] nm (FERRO: de pasajeros)

carriage; (: de mercancías) wagon

vaguedad [baɣe'ðað] nf vagueness

vaho ['bao] nm (vapor) vapour, steam; (respiración) breath

vaina ['baina] nf sheath

vainilla [bai'niʎa] nf vanilla

vainita [bai'nita] (AM) nf green o French bean

vais vb ver **ir**

vaivén [bai'ßen] nm to-and-fro movement; (de tránsito) coming and going; **vaivenes** nmpl (fig) ups and downs

vajilla [ba'xiʎa] nf crockery, dishes pl; **lavar la ~** to do the washing-up (BRIT), wash the dishes (US)

valdré etc vb ver **valer**

vale ['bale] nm voucher; (recibo) receipt; (pagaré) IOU

valedero, a [bale'ðero, a] adj valid

valenciano, a [balen'θjano, a] adj Valencian

valentía [balen'tia] nf courage, bravery

valer [ba'ler] vt to be worth; (MAT) to equal; (costar) to cost ♦ vi (ser útil) to be useful; (ser válido) to be valid; **~se** vr to take care of oneself; **~se de** to make use of, take advantage of; **~ la pena** to be worthwhile; **¿vale?** (ESP) OK?

valeroso, a [bale'roso, a] adj brave, valiant

valgo etc vb ver **valer**

valía [ba'lia] nf worth, value

validar [bali'ðar] vt to validate; **validez** nf validity; **válido, a** adj valid

valiente [ba'ljente] adj brave, valiant ♦ nm hero

valioso, a [ba'ljoso, a] adj valuable

valla ['baʎa] nf fence; (DEPORTE) hurdle; **~ publicitaria** hoarding; **vallar** vt to fence in

valle ['baʎe] nm valley

valor [ba'lor] nm value, worth; (precio) price; (valentía) valour, courage; (importancia) importance; **~es** nmpl (COM) securities; **~ar** vt to value

vals [bals] nm inv waltz

válvula ['balßula] nf valve

vamos vb ver **ir**

vampiro, resa [bam'piro, 'resa] nm/f vampire

van vb ver **ir**

vanagloriarse [banaɣlo'rjarse] vr to boast

vandalismo [banda'lismo] nm vandalism; **vándalo, a** nm/f vandal

vanguardia [ban'gwardja] nf vanguard; (ARTE etc) avant-garde

vanidad [bani'ðað] nf vanity; **vanidoso, a** adj vain, conceited

vano, a ['bano, a] adj vain

vapor [ba'por] nm vapour; (vaho) steam; **al ~** (CULIN) steamed; **~izador** nm atomizer; **~izar** vt to vaporize; **~oso, a** adj vaporous

vapulear [bapule'ar] vt to beat, thrash

vaquero, a [ba'kero, a] *adj* cattle *cpd* ♦ *nm* cowboy; **~s** *nmpl* (*pantalones*) jeans

vaquilla [ba'kiʎa] *nf* (*ZOOL*) heifer

vara ['bara] *nf* stick; (*TEC*) rod; **~ mágica** magic wand

variable [ba'rjaβle] *adj*, *nf* variable

variación [baria'θjon] *nf* variation

variar [bar'jar] *vt* to vary; (*modificar*) to modify; (*cambiar de posición*) to switch around ♦ *vi* to vary

varicela [bari'θela] *nf* chickenpox

varices [ba'riθes] *nfpl* varicose veins

variedad [barje'ðað] *nf* variety

varilla [ba'riʎa] *nf* stick; (*BOT*) twig; (*TEC*) rod; (*de rueda*) spoke

vario, a ['barjo, a] *adj* varied; **~s** various, several

varita [ba'rita] *nf*: **~ mágica** magic wand

varón [ba'ron] *nm* male, man; **varonil** *adj* manly, virile

Varsovia [bar'soβja] *n* Warsaw

vas *vb ver* **ir**

vasco, a ['basko, a] *adj*, *nm/f* Basque

vascongado, a [baskon'gaðo, a] *adj* Basque; **las Vascongadas** the Basque Country

vascuence [bas'kwenθe] *adj* = **vascongado**

vaselina [base'lina] *nf* Vaseline ®

vasija [ba'sixa] *nf* container, vessel

vaso ['baso] *nm* glass, tumbler; (*ANAT*) vessel

vástago ['bastaɣo] *nm* (*BOT*) shoot; (*TEC*) rod; (*fig*) offspring

vasto, a ['basto, a] *adj* vast, huge

Vaticano [bati'kano] *nm*: **el ~** the Vatican

vatio ['batjo] *nm* (*ELEC*) watt

vaya *etc vb ver* **ir**

Vd(s) *abr* = **usted(es)**

ve *vb ver* **ir**; **ver**

vecindad [beθin'dað] *nf* neighbourhood; (*habitantes*) residents *pl*

vecindario [beθin'darjo] *nm* neighbourhood; residents *pl*

vecino, a [be'θino, a] *adj* neighbouring ♦ *nm/f* neighbour; (*residente*) resident

veda ['beða] *nf* prohibition

vedar [be'ðar] *vt* (*prohibir*) to ban, prohibit; (*impedir*) to stop, prevent

vegetación [bexeta'θjon] *nf* vegetation

vegetal [bexe'tal] *adj*, *nm* vegetable

vegetariano, a [bexeta'rjano, a] *adj*, *nm/f* vegetarian

vehemencia [be(e)'menθja] *nf* vehemence; **vehemente** *adj* vehement

vehículo [be'ikulo] *nm* vehicle; (*MED*) carrier

veía *etc vb ver* **ver**

veinte ['beinte] *num* twenty

vejación [bexa'θjon] *nf* vexation; (*humillación*) humiliation

vejar [be'xar] *vt* (*irritar*) to annoy, vex; (*humillar*) to humiliate

vejez [be'xeθ] *nf* old age

vejiga [be'xixa] *nf* (*ANAT*) bladder

vela ['bela] *nf* (*de cera*) candle; (*NAUT*) sail; (*insomnio*) sleeplessness; (*vigilia*) vigil; (*MIL*) sentry duty; **estar a dos ~s** (*fam*: *sin dinero*) to be skint

velado, a [be'laðo, a] *adj* veiled; (*sonido*) muffled; (*FOTO*) blurred ♦ *nf* soirée

velar [be'lar] *vt* (*vigilar*) to keep watch over ♦ *vi* to stay awake; **~ por** to watch over, look after

velatorio [bela'torjo] *nm* (*funeral*) wake

veleidad [belei'ðað] *nf* (*ligereza*) fickleness; (*capricho*) whim

velero [be'lero] *nm* (*NAUT*) sailing ship; (*AVIAT*) glider

veleta [be'leta] *nf* weather vane

veliz [be'lis] (*AM*) *nm* suitcase

vello ['beʎo] *nm* down, fuzz

velo ['belo] *nm* veil

velocidad [beloθi'ðað] *nf* speed; (*TEC*, *AUTO*) gear

velocímetro [belo'θimetro] *nm* speedometer

veloz [be'loθ] *adj* fast

ven *vb ver* **venir**

vena ['bena] *nf* vein

venado [be'naðo] *nm* deer

vencedor, a [benθe'ðor, a] *adj* victorious ♦ *nm/f* victor, winner

vencer [ben'θer] *vt* (*dominar*) to defeat, beat; (*derrotar*) to vanquish; (*superar*, *controlar*) to overcome, master ♦ *vi* (*triunfar*) to win (through), triumph; (*plazo*) to expire; **vencido, a** *adj* (*derrotado*) defeated, beaten; (*COM*) due ♦ *adv*: **pagar vencido** to pay in arrears; **vencimiento** *nm* (*COM*) maturity

venda ['benda] *nf* bandage; **vendaje** *nm* bandage, dressing; **vendar** *vt* to bandage; **vendar los ojos** to blindfold

vendaval [benda'βal] *nm* (*viento*) gale

vendedor, a [bende'ðor, a] *nm/f* seller

vender [ben'der] *vt* to sell; **~ al contado/al por mayor/al por menor** to sell for cash/wholesale/retail

vendimia [ben'dimja] *nf* grape harvest

vendré *etc vb ver* **venir**

veneno [be'neno] *nm* poison; (*de serpiente*) venom; **~so, a** *adj* poisonous; venomous

venerable [bene'raβle] *adj* venerable; **venerar** *vt* (*respetar*) to revere; (*adorar*) to worship

venéreo, a [be'nereo, a] *adj*: **enfermedad venérea** venereal disease

venezolano, a [beneθo'lano, a] *adj* Venezuelan

Venezuela [bene'θwela] *nf* Venezuela

venganza [ben'ganθa] *nf* vengeance, revenge; **vengar** *vt* to avenge; **vengarse** *vr*

to take revenge; **vengativo, a** adj (persona)
vindictive

vengo etc vb ver **venir**

venia ['benja] nf (perdón) pardon; (permiso)
consent

venial [be'njal] adj venial

venida [be'niða] nf (llegada) arrival; (regreso)
return

venidero, a [beni'ðero, a] adj coming, future

venir [be'nir] vi to come; (llegar) to arrive;
(ocurrir) to happen; (fig): ~ **de** to stem from;
~ **bien/mal** to be suitable/unsuitable; **el año
que viene** next year; **~se abajo** to collapse

venta ['benta] nf (COM) sale; ~ **a plazos** hire
purchase; ~ **al contado/al por mayor/al por
menor** o **al detalle** cash sale/wholesale/retail;
~ **con derecho a retorno** sale or return; **"en ~"**
"for sale"

ventaja [ben'taxa] nf advantage; **ventajoso,
a** adj advantageous

ventana [ben'tana] nf window; **ventanilla**
nf (de taquilla) window (of booking office etc)

ventilación [bentila'θjon] nf ventilation;
(corriente) draught

ventilador [bentila'ðor] nm fan

ventilar [benti'lar] vt to ventilate; (para
secar) to put out to dry; (asunto) to air,
discuss

ventisca [ben'tiska] nf blizzard

ventrílocuo, a [ben'trilokwo, a] nm/f
ventriloquist

ventura [ben'tura] nf (felicidad) happiness;
(buena suerte) luck; (destino) fortune; **a la
(buena) ~** at random; **venturoso, a** adj
happy; (afortunado) lucky, fortunate

veo etc vb ver **ver**

ver [ber] vt to see; (mirar) to look at, watch;
(entender) to understand; (investigar) to look
into; ♦ vi to see; to understand; **~se** vr
(encontrarse) to meet; (dejarse ~) to be seen;
(hallarse: en un apuro) to find o.s., be; **a ~**
let's see; **no tener nada que ~ con** to have
nothing to do with; **a mi modo de ~** as I see it

vera ['bera] nf edge, verge; (de río) bank

veracidad [beraθi'ðað] nf truthfulness

veranear [berane'ar] vi to spend the
summer; **veraneo** nm summer holiday;
veraniego, a adj summer cpd

verano [be'rano] nm summer

veras ['beras] nfpl truth sg; **de ~** really, truly

veraz [be'raθ] adj truthful

verbal [ber'ßal] adj verbal

verbena [ber'ßena] nf (baile) open-air dance

verbo ['berßo] nm verb; **~so, a** adj verbose

verdad [ber'ðað] nf truth; (fiabilidad)
reliability; **de ~** real, proper; **a decir ~** to tell
the truth; **~ero, a** adj (veraz) true, truthful;
(fiable) reliable; (fig) real

verde ['berðe] adj green; (chiste) blue, dirty

♦ nm green; **viejo ~** dirty old man; **~ar** vi to
turn green; **verdor** nm greenness

verdugo [ber'ðuɣo] nm executioner

verdulero, a [berðu'lero, a] nm/f
greengrocer

verduras [ber'ðuras] nfpl (CULIN) greens

vereda [be'reða] nf path; (AM) pavement
(BRIT), sidewalk (US)

veredicto [bere'ðikto] nm verdict

vergonzoso, a [berxon'θoso, a] adj
shameful; (tímido) timid, bashful

vergüenza [ber'xwenθa] nf shame, sense of
shame; (timidez) bashfulness; (pudor)
modesty; **me da ~** I'm ashamed

verídico, a [be'riðiko, a] adj true, truthful

verificar [berifi'kar] vt to check; (corroborar)
to verify; (llevar a cabo) to carry out; **~se** vr
(predicción) to prove to be true

verja ['berxa] nf (cancela) iron gate; (valla)
iron railings pl; (de ventana) grille

vermut [ber'mut] (pl **~s**) nm vermouth

verosímil [bero'simil] adj likely, probable;
(relato) credible

verruga [be'rruɣa] nf wart

versado, a [ber'saðo, a] adj: ~ **en** versed in

versátil [ber'satil] adj versatile

versión [ber'sjon] nf version

verso ['berso] nm verse; **un ~** a line of poetry

vértebra ['berteßra] nf vertebra

verter [ber'ter] vt (líquido: adrede) to empty,
pour (out); (: sin querer) to spill; (basura) to
dump ♦ vi to flow

vertical [berti'kal] adj vertical

vértice ['bertiθe] nm vertex, apex

vertidos [ber'tiðos] nmpl waste sg

vertiente [ber'tjente] nf slope; (fig) aspect

vertiginoso, a [bertixi'noso, a] adj giddy,
dizzy

vértigo ['bertiɣo] nm vertigo; (mareo)
dizziness

vesícula [be'sikula] nf blister

vespino ® [bes'pino] nm o nf moped

vestíbulo [bes'tißulo] nm hall; (de teatro)
foyer

vestido [bes'tiðo] pp de **vestir**; ~ **de azul/
marinero** dressed in blue/as a sailor ♦ nm
(ropa) clothes pl, clothing; (de mujer) dress,
frock

vestigio [bes'tixjo] nm (huella) trace; **~s**
nmpl (restos) remains

vestimenta [besti'menta] nf clothing

vestir [bes'tir] vt (poner: ropa) to put on;
(llevar: ropa) to wear; (proveer de ropa) to
clothe; (suj: sastre) to make clothes for ♦ vi
to dress; (verse bien) to look good; **~se** vr to
get dressed, dress o.s.

vestuario [bes'twarjo] nm clothes pl,
wardrobe; (TEATRO: cuarto) dressing room;
(DEPORTE) changing room

veta ['beta] nf (vena) vein, seam; (en carne) streak; (de madera) grain

vetar [be'tar] vt to veto

veterano, a [bete'rano, a] adj, nm veteran

veterinaria [beteri'narja] nf veterinary science; ver tb **veterinario**

veterinario, a [beteri'narjo, a] nm/f vet(erinary surgeon)

veto ['beto] nm veto

vez [beθ] nf time; (turno) turn; **a la ~ que** at the same time as; **a su ~** in its turn; **otra ~** again; **una ~** once; **de una ~** in one go; **de una ~ para siempre** once and for all; **en ~ de** instead of; **a o algunas veces** sometimes; **una y otra ~** repeatedly; **de ~ en cuando** from time to time; **7 veces 9** 7 times 9; **hacer las veces de** to stand in for; **tal ~** perhaps

vía ['bia] nf track, route; (FERRO) line; (fig) way; (ANAT) passage, tube ♦ prep via, by way of; **por ~ judicial** by legal means; **por ~ oficial** through official channels; **en ~s de** in the process of; **~ aérea** airway; **V~ Láctea** Milky Way; **~ pública** public road o thoroughfare

viable ['bjaβle] adj (solución, plan, alternativa) feasible

viaducto [bja'ðukto] nm viaduct

viajante [bja'xante] nm commercial traveller

viajar [bja'xar] vi to travel; **viaje** nm journey; (gira) tour; (NAUT) voyage; **estar de viaje** to be on a trip; **viaje de ida y vuelta** round trip; **viaje de novios** honeymoon; **viajero, a** adj travelling; (ZOOL) migratory ♦ nm/f (quien viaja) traveller; (pasajero) passenger

vial [bjal] adj road cpd, traffic cpd

víbora ['biβora] nf viper; (AM) poisonous snake

vibración [biβra'θjon] nf vibration

vibrar [bi'βrar] vt, vi to vibrate

vicario [bi'karjo] nm curate

vicepresidente [biθepresi'ðente] nm/f vice-president

viceversa [biθe'βersa] adv vice versa

viciado, a [bi'θjaðo, a] adj (corrompido) corrupt; (contaminado) foul, contaminated; **viciar** vt (pervertir) to pervert; (JUR) to nullify; (estropear) to spoil; **viciarse** vr to become corrupted

vicio ['biθjo] nm vice; (mala costumbre) bad habit; **~so, a** adj (muy malo) vicious; (corrompido) depraved ♦ nm/f depraved person

vicisitud [biθisi'tuð] nf vicissitude

víctima ['biktima] nf victim

victoria [bik'torja] nf victory; **victorioso, a** adj victorious

vid [bið] nf vine

vida ['biða] nf (gen) life; (duración) lifetime; **de por ~** for life; **en la/mi ~** never; **estar con ~** to be still alive; **ganarse la ~** to earn one's living

vídeo ['biðeo] nm video ♦ adj inv: **película ~** video film; **~cámara** nf camcorder; **~casete** nm video cassette, videotape; **~club** nm video club; **~juego** nm video game

vidriero, a [bi'ðrjero, a] nm/f glazier ♦ nf (ventana) stained-glass window; (AM: de tienda) shop window; (puerta) glass door

vidrio ['biðrjo] nm glass

vieira ['bjeira] nf scallop

viejo, a ['bjexo, a] adj old ♦ nm/f old man/woman; **hacerse ~** to get old

Viena ['bjena] n Vienna

vienes etc vb ver **venir**

vienés, esa [bje'nes, esa] adj Viennese

viento ['bjento] nm wind; **hacer ~** to be windy

vientre ['bjentre] nm belly; (matriz) womb

viernes ['bjernes] nm inv Friday; **V~ Santo** Good Friday

Vietnam [bjet'nam] nm: **el ~** Vietnam; **vietnamita** adj Vietnamese

viga ['biɣa] nf beam, rafter; (de metal) girder

vigencia [bi'xenθja] nf validity; **estar en ~** to be in force; **vigente** adj valid, in force; (imperante) prevailing

vigésimo, a [bi'xesimo, a] adj twentieth

vigía [bi'xia] nm look-out

vigilancia [bixi'lanθja] nf: **tener a uno bajo ~** to keep watch on sb

vigilar [bixi'lar] vt to watch over ♦ vi (gen) to be vigilant; (hacer guardia) to keep watch; **~ por** to take care of

vigilia [vi'xilja] nf wakefulness, being awake; (REL) fast

vigor [bi'ɣor] nm vigour, vitality; **en ~** in force; **entrar/poner en ~** to come/put into effect; **~oso, a** adj vigorous

VIH nm abr (= virus de la inmunodeficiencia humana) HIV; **~ positivo/negativo** HIV-positive/-negative

vil [bil] adj vile, low; **~eza** nf vileness; (acto) base deed

vilipendiar [bilipen'djar] vt to vilify, revile

villa ['biʎa] nf (casa) villa; (pueblo) small town; (municipalidad) municipality; **~ miseria** (AM) shantytown

villancico [biʎan'θiko] nm (Christmas) carol

villorrio [bi'ʎorrjo] nm shantytown

vilo ['bilo]: **en ~** adv in the air, suspended; (fig) on tenterhooks, in suspense

vinagre [bi'naɣre] nm vinegar

vinagreta [bina'ɣreta] nf vinaigrette, French dressing

vinculación [binkula'θjon] nf (lazo) link, bond; (acción) linking

vincular [binku'lar] vt to link, bind; **vínculo** nm link, bond

vine etc vb ver **venir**

vinicultura [binikul'tura] nf wine growing

viniera etc vb ver **venir**

vino ['bino] vb ver **venir** ♦ nm wine; ~ **blanco/tinto** white/red wine

viña ['bija] nf vineyard; **viñedo** nm vineyard

viola ['bjola] nf viola

violación [bjola'θjon] nf violation; ~ **(sexual)** rape

violar [bjo'lar] vt to violate; (sexualmente) to rape

violencia [bjo'lenθja] nf violence, force; (incomodidad) embarrassment; (acto injusto) unjust act; **violentar** vt to force; (casa) to break into; (agredir) to assault; (violar) to violate; **violento, a** adj violent; (furioso) furious; (situación) embarrassing; (acto) forced, unnatural

violeta [bjo'leta] nf violet

violín [bjo'lin] nm violin

violón [bjo'lon] nm double bass

viraje [bi'raxe] nm turn; (de vehículo) swerve; (fig) change of direction; **virar** vi to change direction

virgen ['birxen] adj, nf virgin

Virgo ['birxo] nm Virgo

viril [bi'ril] adj virile; ~**idad** nf virility

virtud [bir'tuð] nf virtue; **en ~ de** by virtue of; **virtuoso, a** adj virtuous ♦ nm/f virtuoso

viruela [bi'rwela] nf smallpox

virulento, a [biru'lento, a] adj virulent

virus ['birus] nm inv virus

visa ['bisa] (AM) nf = **visado**

visado [bi'saðo] nm visa

víscera ['bisθera] nf (ANAT, ZOOL) gut, bowel; ~**s** nfpl entrails

visceral [bisθe'ral] adj (odio) intense; **reacción ~** gut reaction

viscoso, a [bis'koso, a] adj viscous

visera [bi'sera] nf visor

visibilidad [bisiβili'ðað] nf visibility; **visible** adj visible; (fig) obvious

visillos [bi'siʎos] nmpl lace curtains

visión [bi'sjon] nf (ANAT) vision, (eye)sight; (fantasía) vision, fantasy

visita [bi'sita] nf call, visit; (persona) visitor; **hacer una ~** to pay a visit

visitar [bisi'tar] vt to visit, call on

vislumbrar [bislum'brar] vt to glimpse, catch a glimpse of

viso ['biso] nm (del metal) glint, gleam; (de tela) sheen; (aspecto) appearance

visón [bi'son] nm mink

visor [bi'sor] nm (FOTO) viewfinder

víspera ['bispera] nf: **la ~ de ...** the day before ...

vista ['bista] nf sight, vision; (capacidad de ver) (eye)sight; (mirada) look(s) (pl); **a primera ~** at first glance; **hacer la ~ gorda** to turn a blind eye; **volver la ~** to look back;

está a la ~ que it's obvious that; **en ~ de** in view of; **en ~ de que** in view of the fact that; **¡hasta la ~!** so long!, see you!; **con ~s a** with a view to; ~**zo** nm glance; **dar o echar un ~zo a** to glance at

visto, a ['bisto, a] pp de **ver** ♦ vb ver **vestir** ♦ adj seen; (considerado) considered ♦ nm: ~ **bueno** approval; "~ **bueno**" "approved"; **por lo ~** apparently; **está ~ que** it's clear that; **está bien/mal ~** it's acceptable/unacceptable; ~ **que** since, considering that

vistoso, a [bis'toso, a] adj colourful

visual [bi'swal] adj visual

vital [bi'tal] adj life cpd, living cpd; (fig) vital; (persona) lively, vivacious; ~**icio, a** adj for life; ~**idad** nf (de persona, negocio) energy; (de ciudad) liveliness

vitamina [bita'mina] nf vitamin

viticultor, a [bitikul'tor, a] nm/f wine grower; **viticultura** nf wine growing

vitorear [bitore'ar] vt to cheer, acclaim

vitrina [bi'trina] nf show case; (AM) shop window

viudez nf widowhood

viudo, a ['bjuðo, a] nm/f widower/widow

viva ['biβa] excl hurrah!: **¡~ el rey!** long live the king!

vivacidad [biβaθi'ðað] nf (vigor) vigour; (vida) liveliness

vivaracho, a [biβa'ratʃo, a] adj jaunty, lively; (ojos) bright, twinkling

vivaz [bi'βaθ] adj lively

víveres ['biβeres] nmpl provisions

vivero [bi'βero] nm (para plantas) nursery; (para peces) fish farm; (fig) hotbed

viveza [bi'βeθa] nf liveliness; (agudeza: mental) sharpness

vivienda [bi'βjenda] nf housing; (una ~) house; (piso) flat (BRIT), apartment (US)

viviente [bi'βjente] adj living

vivir [bi'βir] vt, vi to live ♦ nm life, living

vivo, a ['biβo, a] adj living, alive; (fig: descripción) vivid; (persona: astuto) smart, clever; **en ~** (transmisión etc) live

vocablo [bo'kaβlo] nm (palabra) word; (término) term

vocabulario [bokaβu'larjo] nm vocabulary

vocación [boka'θjon] nf vocation; **vocacional** (AM) nf ≈ technical college

vocal [bo'kal] adj vocal ♦ nf vowel; ~**izar** vt to vocalize

vocear [boθe'ar] vt (para vender) to cry; (aclamar) to acclaim; (fig) to proclaim ♦ vi to yell; **vocerío** nm shouting

vocero [bo'θero] nm/f spokesman/woman

voces [bo'θes] pl de **voz**

vociferar [boθife'rar] vt to shout ♦ vi to yell

vodka ['boðka] nm o f vodka

vol abr = **volumen**

volador, a [bola'ðor, a] *adj* flying
volandas [bo'landas]: **en** ~ *adv* in the air
volante [bo'lante] *adj* flying ♦ *nm* (*de coche*) steering wheel; (*de reloj*) balance
volar [bo'lar] *vt* (*edificio*) to blow up ♦ *vi* to fly
volátil [bo'latil] *adj* volatile
volcán [bol'kan] *nm* volcano; ~**ico, a** *adj* volcanic
volcar [bol'kar] *vt* to upset, overturn; (*tumbar, derribar*) to knock over; (*vaciar*) to empty out ♦ *vi* to overturn; ~**se** *vr* to tip over
voleibol [bolei'ßol] *nm* volleyball
volqué *etc vb ver* **volcar**
voltaje [bol'taxe] *nm* voltage
voltear [bolte'ar] *vt* to turn over; (*volcar*) to turn upside down
voltereta [bolte'reta] *nf* somersault
voltio ['boltjo] *nm* volt
voluble [bo'lußle] *adj* fickle
volumen [bo'lumen] (*pl* **volúmenes**) *nm* volume; **voluminoso, a** *adj* voluminous; (*enorme*) massive
voluntad [bolun'taθ] *nf* will; (*resolución*) willpower; (*deseo*) desire, wish
voluntario, a [bolun'tarjo, a] *adj* voluntary ♦ *nm/f* volunteer
voluntarioso, a [bolunta'rjoso, a] *adj* headstrong
voluptuoso, a [bolup'twoso, a] *adj* voluptuous
volver [bol'ßer] *vt* (*gen*) to turn; (*dar vuelta a*) to turn (over); (*voltear*) to turn round, turn upside down; (*poner al revés*) to turn inside out; (*devolver*) to return ♦ *vi* to return, go back, come back; ~**se** *vr* to turn round; ~ **la espalda** to turn one's back; ~ **triste** *etc* **a uno** to make sb sad *etc*; ~ **a hacer** to do again; ~ **en sí** to come to; ~**se insoportable/ muy caro** to get o become unbearable/very expensive; ~**se loco** to go mad
vomitar [bomi'tar] *vt, vi* to vomit; **vómito** *nm* vomit
voraz [bo'raθ] *adj* voracious
vos [bos] (*AM*) *pron* you
vosotros, as [bo'sotros, as] *pron* you; (*reflexivo*): **entre/para** ~ among/for yourselves
votación [bota'θjon] *nf* (*acto*) voting; (*voto*) vote
votar [bo'tar] *vi* to vote; **voto** *nm* vote; (*promesa*) vow; **votos** (good) wishes
voy *vb ver* **ir**
voz [boθ] *nf* voice; (*grito*) shout; (*rumor*) rumour; (*LING*) word; **dar voces** to shout, yell; **a media** ~ in a low voice; **a ~ en cuello o en grito** at the top of one's voice; **de viva** ~ verbally; **en** ~ **alta** aloud; ~ **de mando** command
vuelco ['bwelko] *vb ver* **volcar** ♦ *nm* spill, overturning

vuelo ['bwelo] *vb ver* **volar** ♦ *nm* flight; (*encaje*) lace, frill; **coger al** ~ to catch in flight; ~ **charter/regular** charter/scheduled flight; ~ **libre** (*DEPORTE*) hang-gliding
vuelque *etc vb ver* **volcar**
vuelta ['bwelta] *nf* (*gen*) turn; (*curva*) bend, curve; (*regreso*) return; (*revolución*) revolution; (*de circuito*) lap; (*de papel, tela*) reverse; (*cambio*) change; **a la** ~ on one's return; **a** ~ **de correo** by return of post; **dar** ~**s** (*suj: cabeza*) to spin; **dar** ~**s a una idea** to turn over an idea (in one's head); **estar de** ~ to be back; **dar una** ~ to go for a walk; (*en coche*) to go for a drive; ~ **ciclista** (*DEPORTE*) (cycle) tour
vuelto *pp de* **volver**
vuelvo *etc vb ver* **volver**
vuestro, a ['bwestro, a] *adj* your; **un amigo** ~ a friend of yours ♦ *pron*: **el** ~/**la vuestra, los** ~**s**/**las vuestras** yours
vulgar [bul'xar] *adj* (*ordinario*) vulgar; (*común*) common; ~**idad** *nf* commonness; (*acto*) vulgarity; (*expresión*) coarse expression; ~**izar** *vt* to popularize
vulgo ['bulxo] *nm* common people
vulnerable [bulne'raßle] *adj* vulnerable
vulnerar [bulne'rar] *vt* (*ley, acuerdo*) to violate, breach; (*derechos, intimidad*) to violate; (*reputación*) to damage

W, w

Walkman ® [wak'man] *nm* Walkman ®
wáter ['bater] *nm* toilet
whisky ['wiski] *nm* whisky, whiskey
WWW *nm o nf abr* (*INFORM*: = *World Wide Web*) WWW

X, x

xenofobia [kseno'foßja] *nf* xenophobia
xilófono [ksi'lofono] *nm* xylophone

Y, y

y [i] *conj* and
ya [ja] *adv* (*gen*) already; (*ahora*) now; (*en seguida*) at once; (*pronto*) soon ♦ *excl* all right! ♦ *conj* (*ahora que*) now that; ~ **lo sé** I know; ~ **que** since
yacer [ja'θer] *vi* to lie
yacimiento [jaθi'mjento] *nm* (*de mineral*) deposit; (*arqueológico*) site
yanqui ['janki] *adj, nm/f* Yankee
yate ['jate] *nm* yacht

yazco etc vb ver **yacer**

yedra ['jeðɾa] nf ivy

yegua ['jeɣwa] nf mare

yema ['jema] nf (del huevo) yolk; (BOT) leaf bud; (fig) best part; ~ **del dedo** fingertip

yergo etc vb ver **erguir**

yermo, a ['jermo, a] adj (estéril, fig) barren ♦ nm wasteland

yerno ['jerno] nm son-in-law

yerro etc vb ver **errar**

yeso ['jeso] nm plaster

yo [jo] pron I; **soy ~** it's me, it is I

yodo ['joðo] nm iodine

yoga ['joɣa] nm yoga

yogur(t) [jo'ɣur(t)] nm yoghurt

yugo ['juɣo] nm yoke

Yugoslavia [juɣos'laßja] nf Yugoslavia

yugular [juɣu'lar] adj jugular

yunque ['junke] nm anvil

yunta ['junta] nf yoke

yuxtaponer [jukstapo'ner] vt to juxtapose; **yuxtaposición** nf juxtaposition

Z, z

zafar [θa'far] vt (soltar) to untie; (superficie) to clear; **~se** vr (escaparse) to escape; (TEC) to slip off

zafio, a ['θafjo, a] adj coarse

zafiro [θa'firo] nm sapphire

zaga ['θaɣa] nf: **a la ~** behind, in the rear

zaguán [θa'ɣwan] nm hallway

zaherir [θae'rir] vt (criticar) to criticize

zaino, a ['θaino, a] adj (caballo) chestnut

zalamería [θalame'ria] nf flattery; **zalamero, a** adj flattering; (cobista) suave

zamarra [θa'marra] nf (chaqueta) sheepskin jacket

zambullirse [θambu'ʎirse] vr to dive

zampar [θam'par] vt to gobble down

zanahoria [θana'orja] nf carrot

zancada [θan'kaða] nf stride

zancadilla [θanka'ðiʎa] nf trip

zanco ['θanko] nm stilt

zancudo, a [θan'kuðo, a] adj long-legged ♦ nm (AM) mosquito

zángano ['θangano] nm drone

zanja ['θanxa] nf ditch; **zanjar** vt (resolver) to resolve

zapata [θa'pata] nf (MECÁNICA) shoe

zapatear [θapate'ar] vi to tap with one's feet

zapatería [θapate'ria] nf (oficio) shoemaking; (tienda) shoe shop; (fábrica) shoe factory; **zapatero, a** nm/f shoemaker

zapatilla [θapa'tiʎa] nf slipper; **~ de deporte** training shoe

zapato [θa'pato] nm shoe

zapping ['θapin] nm channel-hopping; **hacer ~** to flick through the channels

zar [θar] nm tsar, czar

zarandear [θarande'ar] (fam) vt to shake vigorously

zarpa ['θarpa] nf (garra) claw

zarpar [θar'par] vi to weigh anchor

zarza ['θarθa] nf (BOT) bramble; **zarzal** nm (matorral) bramble patch

zarzamora [θarθa'mora] nf blackberry

zarzuela [θar'θwela] nf Spanish light opera

zigzag [θiɣ'θaɣ] nm zigzag; **zigzaguear** vi to zigzag

zinc [θink] nm zinc

zócalo ['θokalo] nm (ARQ) plinth, base

zodíaco [θo'ðiako] nm (ASTRO) zodiac

zona ['θona] nf zone; **~ fronteriza** border area

zoo ['θoo] nm zoo

zoología [θoolo'xia] nf zoology; **zoológico, a** adj zoological ♦ nm (tb: parque ~) zoo; **zoólogo, a** nm/f zoologist

zoom [θum] nm zoom lens

zopilote [θopi'lote] (AM) nm buzzard

zoquete [θo'kete] nm (fam) blockhead

zorro, a ['θorro, a] adj crafty ♦ nm/f fox/vixen

zozobra [θo'θoßra] nf (fig) anxiety; **zozobrar** vi (hundirse) to capsize; (fig) to fail

zueco ['θweko] nm clog

zumbar [θum'bar] vt (golpear) to hit ♦ vi to buzz; **zumbido** nm buzzing

zumo ['θumo] nm juice

zurcir [θur'θir] vt (coser) to darn

zurdo, a ['θurðo, a] adj (persona) left-handed

zurrar [θu'rrar] (fam) vt to wallop

A, a

A [eɪ] n (MUS) la m

KEYWORD

a [ə] indef art (before vowel or silent h: an)
1 un(a); **~ book** un libro; **an apple** una manzana; **she's ~ doctor** (ella) es médica
2 (instead of the number "one") un(a); **~ year ago** hace un año; **~ hundred/thousand** etc **pounds** cien/mil etc libras
3 (in expressing ratios, prices etc): **3 ~ day/week** 3 al día/a la semana; **10 km an hour** 10 km por hora; **£5 ~ person** £5 por persona; **30p ~ kilo** 30p el kilo

A.A. n abbr (= Automobile Association: BRIT) ≈ RACE m (SP); (= Alcoholics Anonymous) Alcohólicos Anónimos

A.A.A. (US) n abbr (= American Automobile Association) ≈ RACE m (SP)

aback [ə'bæk] adv: **to be taken ~** quedar desconcertado

abandon [ə'bændən] vt abandonar; (give up) renunciar a

abate [ə'beɪt] vi (storm) amainar; (anger) aplacarse; (terror) disminuir

abattoir ['æbətwɑ:*] (BRIT) n matadero

abbey ['æbɪ] n abadía

abbot ['æbət] n abad m

abbreviation [ə'bri:vɪ'eɪʃən] n (short form) abreviatura

abdicate ['æbdɪkeɪt] vt renunciar a ♦ vi abdicar

abdomen ['æbdəmən] n abdomen m

abduct [æb'dʌkt] vt raptar, secuestrar

abeyance [ə'beɪəns] n: **in ~** (law) en desuso; (matter) en suspenso

abide [ə'baɪd] vt: **I can't ~ it/him** no lo/le puedo ver; **~ by** vt fus atenerse a

ability [ə'bɪlɪtɪ] n habilidad f, capacidad f; (talent) talento

abject ['æbdʒekt] adj (poverty) miserable; (apology) rastrero

ablaze [ə'bleɪz] adj en llamas, ardiendo

able ['eɪbl] adj capaz; (skilled) hábil; **to be ~ to do sth** poder hacer algo; **~-bodied** adj sano; **ably** adv hábilmente

abnormal [æb'nɔ:məl] adj anormal

aboard [ə'bɔ:d] adv a bordo ♦ prep a bordo de

abode [ə'bəud] n: **of no fixed ~** sin domicilio fijo

abolish [ə'bɔlɪʃ] vt suprimir, abolir

aborigine [æbə'rɪdʒɪnɪ] n aborigen m/f

abort [ə'bɔ:t] vt, vi abortar; **~ion** [ə'bɔ:ʃən] n aborto; **to have an ~ion** abortar, hacerse abortar; **~ive** adj malogrado

KEYWORD

about [ə'baut] adv **1** (approximately) más o menos, aproximadamente; **~ a hundred/thousand** etc unos(unas) cien/mil etc; **it takes ~ 10 hours** se tarda unas or más o menos 10 horas; **at ~ 2 o'clock** sobre las dos; **I've just ~ finished** casi he terminado
2 (referring to place) por todas partes; **to leave things lying ~** dejar las cosas (tiradas) por ahí; **to run ~** correr por todas partes; **to walk ~** pasearse, ir y venir
3: **to be ~ to do sth** estar a punto de hacer algo
♦ prep **1** (relating to) de, sobre, acerca de; **a book ~ London** un libro sobre or acerca de Londres; **what is it ~?** ¿de qué se trata?, ¿qué pasa?; **we talked ~ it** hablamos de eso or ello; **what** or **how ~ doing this?** ¿qué tal si hacemos esto?
2 (referring to place) por; **to walk ~ the town** caminar por la ciudad

above [ə'bʌv] adv encima, por encima, arriba
♦ prep encima de; (greater than: in number) más de; (: in rank) superior a; **mentioned ~** susodicho; **~ all** sobre todo; **~ board** adj legítimo

abrasive [ə'breɪzɪv] adj abrasivo; (manner) brusco

abreast [ə'brest] adv de frente; **to keep ~ of** (fig) mantenerse al corriente de

abroad [ə'brɔ:d] adv (to be) en el extranjero; (to go) al extranjero

abrupt [ə'brʌpt] adj (sudden) brusco; (curt) áspero

abruptly [ə'brʌptlɪ] adv (leave) repentinamente; (speak) bruscamente

abscess ['æbsɪs] n absceso

abscond [əb'skɔnd] vi (thief): **to ~ with** fugarse con; (prisoner): **to ~ (from)** escaparse (de)

absence ['æbsəns] n ausencia

absent ['æbsənt] adj ausente; **~ee** [-'ti:] n

ausente *m/f*; **~-minded** *adj* distraído

absolute ['æbsəlu:t] *adj* absoluto; **~ly**
[-'lu:tlı] *adv* (*totally*) totalmente; (*certainly!*)
¡por supuesto (que sí)!

absolve [əb'zɔlv] *vt*: **to ~ sb (from)** absolver
a alguien (de)

absorb [əb'zɔ:b] *vt* absorber; **to be ~ed in a
book** estar absorto en un libro; **~ent cotton**
(*US*) *n* algodón *m* hidrófilo; **~ing** *adj*
absorbente

absorption [əb'zɔ:pʃən] *n* absorción *f*

abstain [əb'steın] *vi*: **to ~ (from)** abstenerse
(de)

abstinence ['æbstınəns] *n* abstinencia

abstract ['æbstrækt] *adj* abstracto

absurd [əb'sə:d] *adj* absurdo

abundance [ə'bʌndəns] *n* abundancia

abuse [*n* ə'bju:s, *vb* ə'bju:z] *n* (*insults*) insultos
mpl, injurias *fpl*; (*ill-treatment*) malos tratos
mpl; (*misuse*) abuso ♦ *vt* insultar; maltratar;
abusar de; **abusive** *adj* ofensivo

abysmal [ə'bızməl] *adj* pésimo; (*failure*)
garrafal; (*ignorance*) supino

abyss [ə'bıs] *n* abismo

AC *abbr* (= alternating current) corriente *f*
alterna

academic [ækə'demık] *adj* académico,
universitario; (*pej: issue*) puramente teórico
♦ *n* estudioso/a; profesor(a) *m/f*
universitario/a

academy [ə'kædəmı] *n* (*learned body*)
academia; (*school*) instituto, colegio; **~ of
music** conservatorio

accelerate [æk'seləreıt] *vt, vi* acelerar;
accelerator (*BRIT*) *n* acelerador *m*

accent ['æksɛnt] *n* acento; (*fig*) énfasis *m*

accept [ək'sɛpt] *vt* aceptar; (*responsibility,
blame*) admitir; **~able** *adj* aceptable; **~ance**
n aceptación *f*

access ['æksɛs] *n* acceso; **to have ~ to** tener
libre acceso a; **~ible** [-'sɛsəbl] *adj* (*place,
person*) accesible; (*knowledge etc*) asequible

accessory [æk'sɛsərı] *n* accesorio; (*LAW*):
~ to cómplice de

accident ['æksıdənt] *n* accidente *m*; (*chance
event*) casualidad *f*; **by ~** (*unintentionally*) sin
querer; (*by chance*) por casualidad; **~al**
[-'dɛntl] *adj* accidental, fortuito; **~ally**
[-'dɛntəlı] *adv* sin querer; por casualidad;
~ insurance *n* seguro contra accidentes;
~-prone *adj* propenso a los accidentes

acclaim [ə'kleım] *vt* aclamar, aplaudir ♦ *n*
aclamación *f*, aplausos *mpl*

acclimatize [ə'klaımətaız] (*US*: **acclimate**) *vt*:
to become ~d aclimatarse

accommodate [ə'kɔmədeıt] *vt* (*subj:
person*) alojar, hospedar; (: *car, hotel etc*)
tener cabida para; (*oblige, help*) complacer;
accommodating *adj* servicial, complaciente

accommodation [əkɔmə'deıʃən] *n* (*US*
accommodations *npl*) alojamiento

accompany [ə'kʌmpənı] *vt* acompañar

accomplice [ə'kʌmplıs] *n* cómplice *m/f*

accomplish [ə'kʌmplıʃ] *vt* (*finish*) concluir;
(*achieve*) lograr; **~ed** *adj* experto, hábil;
~ment *n* (*skill: gen pl*) talento; (*completion*)
realización *f*

accord [ə'kɔ:d] *n* acuerdo ♦ *vt* conceder; **of
his own ~** espontáneamente; **~ance** *n*: **in
~ance with** de acuerdo con; **~ing**: **~ing to**
prep según; (*in accordance with*) conforme a;
~ingly *adv* (*appropriately*) de acuerdo con
esto; (*as a result*) en consecuencia

accordion [ə'kɔ:dıən] *n* acordeón *m*

accost [ə'kɔst] *vt* abordar, dirigirse a

account [ə'kaunt] *n* (*COMM*) cuenta; (*report*)
informe *m*; **~s** *npl* (*COMM*) cuentas *fpl*; **of no ~**
de ninguna importancia; **on ~** a cuenta; **on
no ~** bajo ningún concepto; **on ~ of** a causa
de, por motivo de; **to take into ~, take ~ of**
tener en cuenta; **~ for** *vt fus* (*explain*)
explicar; (*represent*) representar; **~able** *adj*:
~able (to) responsable (ante); **~ancy** *n*
contabilidad *f*; **~ant** *n* contable *m/f*,
contador(a) *m/f*; **~ number** *n* (*at bank etc*)
número de cuenta

accrued interest [ə'kru:d-] *n* interés *m*
acumulado

accumulate [ə'kju:mjuleıt] *vt* acumular ♦ *vi*
acumularse

accuracy ['ækjurəsı] *n* (*of total*) exactitud *f*;
(*of description etc*) precisión *f*

accurate ['ækjurıt] *adj* (*total*) exacto;
(*description*) preciso; (*person*) cuidadoso;
(*device*) de precisión; **~ly** *adv* con precisión

accusation [ækju'zeıʃən] *n* acusación *f*

accuse [ə'kju:z] *vt*: **to ~ sb (of sth)** acusar a
uno (de algo); **~d** *n* (*LAW*) acusado/a

accustom [ə'kʌstəm] *vt* acostumbrar; **~ed**
adj: **~ed to** acostumbrado a

ace [eıs] *n* as *m*

ache [eık] *n* dolor *m* ♦ *vi* doler; **my head ~s**
me duele la cabeza

achieve [ə'tʃi:v] *vt* (*aim, result*) alcanzar;
(*success*) lograr, conseguir; **~ment** *n*
(*completion*) realización *f*; (*success*) éxito

acid ['æsıd] *adj* ácido; (*taste*) agrio ♦ *n* (*CHEM,
inf: LSD*) ácido; **~ rain** *n* lluvia ácida

acknowledge [ək'nɔlıdʒ] *vt* (*letter: also*:
~ receipt of) acusar recibo de; (*fact, situation,
person*) reconocer; **~ment** *n* acuse *m* de
recibo

acne ['æknı] *n* acné *m*

acorn ['eıkɔ:n] *n* bellota

acoustic [ə'ku:stık] *adj* acústico; **~s** *n, npl*
acústica *sg*

acquaint [ə'kweınt] *vt*: **to ~ sb with sth**
(*inform*) poner a uno al corriente de algo; **to**

be ~ed with conocer; **~ance** n (person) conocido/a; (with person, subject) conocimiento

acquire [ə'kwaɪə*] vt adquirir; **acquisition** [ækwɪ'zɪʃən] n adquisición f

acquit [ə'kwɪt] vt absolver, exculpar; **to ~ o.s. well** salir con éxito

acre ['eɪkə*] n acre m

acrid ['ækrɪd] adj acre

acrobat ['ækrəbæt] n acróbata m/f

across [ə'krɔs] prep (on the other side of) al otro lado de, del otro lado de; (crosswise) a través de ♦ adv de un lado a otro, de una parte a otra; a través, al través; (measurement): **the road is 10m ~** la carretera tiene 10m de ancho; **to run/swim ~** atravesar corriendo/nadando; **~ from** enfrente de

acrylic [ə'krɪlɪk] adj acrílico ♦ n acrílica f

act [ækt] n acto, acción f; (of play) acto; (in music hall etc) número; (LAW) decreto, ley f ♦ vi (behave) comportarse; (have effect: drug, chemical) hacer efecto; (THEATRE) actuar; (pretend) fingir; (take action) obrar ♦ vt (part) hacer el papel de; **in the ~ of:** **to catch sb in the ~ of ...** pillar a uno en el momento en que ...; **to ~ as** actuar or hacer de; **~ing** adj suplente ♦ n (activity) actuación f; (profession) profesión f de actor

action ['ækʃən] n acción f, acto; (MIL) acción f, batalla; (LAW) proceso, demanda; **out of ~** (person) fuera de combate; (thing) estropeado; **to take ~** tomar medidas; **~ replay** n (TV) repetición f

activate ['æktɪveɪt] vt activar

active ['æktɪv] adj activo, enérgico; (volcano) en actividad; **~ly** adv (participate) activamente; (discourage, dislike) enérgicamente; **activity** [-'tɪvɪtɪ] n actividad f; **activity holiday** n vacaciones fpl con actividades organizadas

actor ['æktə*] n actor m

actress ['æktrɪs] n actriz f

actual ['æktjuəl] adj verdadero, real; (emphatic use) propiamente dicho; **~ly** adv realmente, en realidad; (even) incluso

acumen ['ækjumən] n perspicacia

acute [ə'kjuːt] adj agudo

ad [æd] n abbr = **advertisement**

A.D. adv abbr (= anno Domini) A.C.

adamant ['ædəmənt] adj firme, inflexible

adapt [ə'dæpt] vt adaptar ♦ vi: **to ~ (to)** adaptarse (a), ajustarse (a); **~able** adj adaptable; **~er, ~or** n (ELEC) adaptador m

add [æd] vt añadir, agregar; (figures: also: **~ up**) sumar ♦ vi: **to ~ to** (increase) aumentar, acrecentar; **it doesn't ~ up** (fig) no tiene sentido

adder ['ædə*] n víbora

addict ['ædɪkt] n adicto/a; (enthusiast)

entusiasta m/f; **~ed** [ə'dɪktɪd] adj: **to be ~ed to** ser adicto a; (football etc) ser fanático de; **~ion** [ə'dɪkʃən] n (to drugs etc) adicción f; **~ive** [ə'dɪktɪv] adj que causa adicción

addition [ə'dɪʃən] n (adding up) adición f; (thing added) añadidura, añadido; **in ~** además, por añadidura; **in ~ to** además de; **~al** adj adicional

additive ['ædɪtɪv] n aditivo

address [ə'drɛs] n dirección f, señas fpl; (speech) discurso ♦ vt (letter) dirigir; (speak to) dirigirse a, dirigir la palabra a; (problem) tratar

adept ['ædɛpt] adj: **~ at** experto or hábil en

adequate ['ædɪkwɪt] adj (satisfactory) adecuado; (enough) suficiente

adhere [əd'hɪə*] vi: **to ~ to** (stick to) pegarse a; (fig: abide by) observar; (: belief etc) ser partidario de

adhesive [əd'hiːzɪv] n adhesivo; **~ tape** n (BRIT) cinta adhesiva; (US: MED) esparadrapo

ad hoc [æd'hɔk] adj ad hoc

adjacent [ə'dʒeɪsənt] adj: **~ to** contiguo a, inmediato a

adjective ['ædʒɛktɪv] n adjetivo

adjoining [ə'dʒɔɪnɪŋ] adj contiguo, vecino

adjourn [ə'dʒɜːn] vt aplazar ♦ vi suspenderse

adjudicate [ə'dʒuːdɪkeɪt] vi sentenciar

adjust [ə'dʒʌst] vt (change) modificar; (clothing) arreglar; (machine) ajustar ♦ vi: **to ~ (to)** adaptarse (a); **~able** adj ajustable; **~ment** n adaptación f; (to machine, prices) ajuste m

ad-lib [æd'lɪb] vt, vi improvisar; **ad lib** adv de forma improvisada

administer [əd'mɪnɪstə*] vt administrar; **administration** [-'treɪʃən] n (management) administración f; (government) gobierno; **administrative** [-trətɪv] adj administrativo

admiral ['ædmərəl] n almirante m; **A~ty** (BRIT) n Ministerio de Marina, Almirantazgo

admiration [ædmə'reɪʃən] n admiración f

admire [əd'maɪə*] vt admirar; **~r** n (fan) admirador(a) m/f

admission [əd'mɪʃən] n (to university, club) ingreso; (entry fee) entrada; (confession) confesión f

admit [əd'mɪt] vt (confess) confesar; (permit to enter) dejar entrar, dar entrada a; (to club, organization) admitir; (accept: defeat) reconocer; **to be ~ted to hospital** ingresar en el hospital; **~ to** vt fus confesarse culpable de; **~tance** n entrada; **~tedly** adv es cierto or verdad que

admonish [əd'mɔnɪʃ] vt amonestar

ad nauseam [æd'nɔːsɪæm] adv hasta el cansancio

ado [ə'duː] n: **without (any) more ~** sin más (ni más)

adolescent [ædəu'lesnt] adj, n adolescente m/f

adopt [ə'dɒpt] vt adoptar; **~ed** adj adoptivo; **~ion** [ə'dɒpʃən] n adopción f

adore [ə'dɔ:*] vt adorar

Adriatic [eɪdrɪ'ætɪk] n: **the ~ (Sea)** el (Mar) Adriático

adrift [ə'drɪft] adv a la deriva

adult ['ædʌlt] n adulto/a ♦ adj (grown-up) adulto; (for adults) para adultos

adultery [ə'dʌltərɪ] n adulterio

advance [əd'vɑ:ns] n (progress) adelanto, progreso; (money) anticipo, préstamo; (MIL) avance m ♦ adj: **~ booking** venta anticipada; **~ notice, ~ warning** previo aviso ♦ vt (money) anticipar; (theory, idea) proponer (para la discusión) ♦ vi avanzar, adelantarse; **to make ~s (to sb)** hacer proposiciones (a alguien); **in ~** por adelantado; **~d** adj avanzado; (SCOL: studies) adelantado

advantage [əd'vɑ:ntɪdʒ] n (also TENNIS) ventaja; **to take ~ of** (person) aprovecharse de; (opportunity) aprovechar

Advent ['ædvənt] n (REL) Adviento

adventure [əd'ventʃə*] n aventura; **adventurous** [-tʃərəs] adj atrevido; aventurero

adverb ['ædvə:b] n adverbio

adverse ['ædvə:s] adj adverso, contrario

adversity [əd'və:sɪtɪ] n infortunio

advert ['ædvə:t] (BRIT) n abbr = **advertisement**

advertise ['ædvətaɪz] vi (in newspaper etc) anunciar, hacer publicidad; **to ~ for** (staff, accommodation etc) buscar por medio de anuncios ♦ vt anunciar; **~ment** [əd'və:tɪsmənt] n (COMM) anuncio; **~r** n anunciante m/f; **advertising** n publicidad f, anuncios mpl; (industry) industria publicitaria

advice [əd'vaɪs] n consejo, consejos mpl; (notification) aviso; **a piece of ~** un consejo; **to take legal ~** consultar con un abogado

advisable [əd'vaɪzəbl] adj aconsejable, conveniente

advise [əd'vaɪz] vt aconsejar; (inform): **to ~ sb of sth** informar a uno de algo; **to ~ sb against sth/doing sth** desaconsejar algo a uno/aconsejar a uno que no haga algo; **~dly** [əd'vaɪzdlɪ] adv (deliberately) deliberadamente; **~r** n = **advisor; advisor** n consejero/a; (consultant) asesor(a) m/f; **advisory** adj consultivo

advocate ['ædvəkeɪt] vt abogar por ♦ n [-kɪt] (lawyer) abogado/a; (supporter): **~ of** defensor(a) m/f de

Aegean [iː'dʒiːən] n: **the ~ (Sea)** el (Mar) Egeo

aerial ['eərɪəl] n antena ♦ adj aéreo

aerobics [eə'rəubɪks] n aerobic m

aeroplane ['eərəpleɪn] (BRIT) n avión m

aerosol ['eərəsɒl] n aerosol m

aesthetic [iːs'θetɪk] adj estético

afar [ə'fɑ:*] adv: **from ~** desde lejos

affair [ə'feə*] n asunto; (also: love ~) aventura (amorosa)

affect [ə'fekt] vt (influence) afectar, influir en; (afflict, concern) afectar; (move) conmover; **~ed** adj afectado

affection [ə'fekʃən] n afecto, cariño; **~ate** adj afectuoso, cariñoso

affinity [ə'fɪnɪtɪ] n (bond, rapport): **to feel an ~ with** sentirse identificado con; (resemblance) afinidad f

afflict [ə'flɪkt] vt afligir

affluence ['æfluəns] n opulencia, riqueza

affluent ['æfluənt] adj (wealthy) acomodado; **the ~ society** la sociedad opulenta

afford [ə'fɔ:d] vt (provide) proporcionar; **can we ~ (to buy) it?** ¿tenemos bastante dinero para comprarlo?

Afghanistan [æf'gænɪstæn] n Afganistán m

afield [ə'fiːld] adv: **far ~** muy lejos

afloat [ə'fləut] adv (floating) a flote

afoot [ə'fut] adv: **there is something ~** algo se está tramando

afraid [ə'freɪd] adj: **to be ~ of** (person) tener miedo a; (thing) tener miedo de; **to be ~ to** tener miedo de, temer; **I am ~ that** me temo que; **I am ~ so/no** lo siento, pero no/es así

afresh [ə'freʃ] adv de nuevo, otra vez

Africa ['æfrɪkə] n África; **~n** adj, n africano/a m/f

after ['ɑ:ftə*] prep (time) después de; (place, order) detrás de, tras ♦ adv después ♦ conj después (de) que; **what/who are you ~?** ¿qué/a quién busca usted?; **~ having done/he left** después de haber hecho/después de que se marchó; **to name sb ~ sb** llamar a uno por uno; **it's twenty ~ eight** (US) son las ocho y veinte; **to ask ~ sb** preguntar por alguien; **~ all** después de todo, al fin y al cabo; **~ you!** ¡pase usted!; **~-effects** npl consecuencias fpl, efectos mpl; **~math** n consecuencias fpl, resultados mpl; **~noon** n tarde f; **~s** (inf) n (dessert) postre m; **~-sales service** (BRIT) n servicio de asistencia pos-venta; **~-shave (lotion)** n aftershave m; **~sun (lotion/cream)** n loción f/crema para después del sol, aftersun m; **~thought** n ocurrencia (tardía); **~wards** (US **~ward**) adv después, más tarde

again [ə'gen] adv otra vez, de nuevo; **to do sth ~** volver a hacer algo; **~ and ~** una y otra vez

against [ə'genst] prep (in opposition to) en contra de; (leaning on, touching) contra, junto a

age [eɪdʒ] n edad f; (period) época ♦ vi

envejecer(se) ♦ vt envejecer; **she is 20 years of ~** tiene 20 años; **to come of ~** llegar a la mayoría de edad; **it's been ~s since I saw you** hace siglos que no te veo; **~d 10 de 10 años de edad; the ~d** ['eɪdʒɪd] npl los ancianos; **~ group** n: **to be in the same ~ group** tener la misma edad; **~ limit** n edad f mínima (or máxima)

agency ['eɪdʒənsɪ] n agencia

agenda [ə'dʒɛndə] n orden m del día

agent ['eɪdʒənt] n agente m/f; (COMM: holding concession) representante m/f, delegado/a; (CHEM, fig) agente m

aggravate ['ægrəveɪt] vt (situation) agravar; (person) irritar

aggregate ['ægrɪgeɪt] n conjunto

aggressive [ə'grɛsɪv] adj (belligerent) agresivo; (assertive) enérgico

aggrieved [ə'griːvd] adj ofendido, agraviado

aghast [ə'gɑːst] adj horrorizado

agile ['ædʒaɪl] adj ágil

agitate ['ædʒɪteɪt] vt (trouble) inquietar ♦ vi: **to ~ for/against** hacer campaña pro or en favor de/en contra de

AGM n abbr (= annual general meeting) asamblea anual

ago [ə'gəʊ] adv: **2 days ~** hace 2 días; **not long ~** hace poco; **how long ~?** ¿hace cuánto tiempo?

agog [ə'gɒg] adj (eager) ansioso; (excited) emocionado

agonizing ['ægənaɪzɪŋ] adj (pain) atroz; (decision, wait) angustioso

agony ['ægənɪ] n (pain) dolor m agudo; (distress) angustia; **to be in ~** retorcerse de dolor

agree [ə'griː] vt (price, date) acordar, quedar en ♦ vi (have same opinion): **to ~ (with/that)** estar de acuerdo (con/que); (correspond) coincidir, concordar; (consent) acceder; **to ~ with** (subj: person) estar de acuerdo con, ponerse de acuerdo con; (: food) sentar bien a; (LING) concordar con; **to ~ to sth/to do sth** consentir en algo/aceptar hacer algo; **to ~ that** (admit) estar de acuerdo en que; **~able** adj (sensation) agradable; (person) simpático; (willing) de acuerdo, conforme; **~d** adj (time, place) convenido; **~ment** n acuerdo; (contract) contrato; **in ~ment** de acuerdo, conforme

agricultural [ægrɪ'kʌltʃərəl] adj agrícola

agriculture ['ægrɪkʌltʃə*] n agricultura

aground [ə'graʊnd] adv: **to run ~** (NAUT) encallar, embarrancar

ahead [ə'hɛd] adv (in front) delante; (into the future): **she had no time to think ~** no tenía tiempo de hacer planes para el futuro; **~ of** delante de; (in advance of) antes de; **~ of time** antes de la hora; **go right or straight ~**

(direction) siga adelante; (permission) hazlo (or hágalo)

aid [eɪd] n ayuda, auxilio; (device) aparato ♦ vt ayudar, auxiliar; **in ~ of** a beneficio de

aide [eɪd] n (person, also: MIL) ayudante m/f

AIDS [eɪdz] n abbr (= acquired immune deficiency syndrome) SIDA m

ailment ['eɪlmənt] n enfermedad f, achaque m

aim [eɪm] vt (gun, camera) apuntar; (missile, remark) dirigir; (blow) asestar ♦ vi (also: take ~) apuntar ♦ n (in shooting: skill) puntería; (objective) propósito, meta; **to ~ at** (with weapon) apuntar a; (objective) aspirar a, pretender; **to ~ to do** tener la intención de hacer; **~less** adj sin propósito, sin objeto

ain't [eɪnt] (inf) = am not; aren't; isn't

air [ɛə*] n aire m; (appearance) aspecto ♦ vt (room) ventilar; (clothes, ideas) airear ♦ cpd aéreo; **to throw sth into the ~** (ball etc) lanzar algo al aire; **by ~** (travel) en avión; **to be on the ~** (RADIO, TV) estar en antena; **~bed** (BRIT) n colchón m neumático; **~-conditioned** adj climatizado; **~ conditioning** n aire acondicionado; **~craft** n inv avión m; **~craft carrier** n porta(a)viones m inv; **~field** n campo de aviación; **A~ Force** n fuerzas fpl aéreas, aviación f; **~ freshener** n ambientador m; **~gun** n escopeta de aire comprimido; **~ hostess** (BRIT) n azafata; **~ letter** (BRIT) n carta aérea; **~lift** n puente m aéreo; **~line** n línea aérea; **~liner** n avión m de pasajeros; **~mail** n: **by ~mail** por avión; **~plane** (US) n avión m; **~port** n aeropuerto; **~ raid** n ataque m aéreo; **~sick** adj: **to be ~sick** marearse (en avión); **~space** n espacio aéreo; **~tight** adj hermético; **~-traffic controller** n controlador(a) m/f aéreo/a; **~y** adj (room) bien ventilado; (fig: manner) desenfadado

aisle [aɪl] n (of church) nave f; (of theatre, supermarket) pasillo; **~ seat** n (on plane) asiento de pasillo

ajar [ə'dʒɑː*] adj entreabierto

alarm [ə'lɑːm] n (in shop, bank) alarma; (anxiety) inquietud f ♦ vt asustar, inquietar; **~ call** n (in hotel etc) alarma; **~ clock** n despertador m

alas [ə'læs] adv desgraciadamente

albeit [ɔːl'biːɪt] conj aunque

album ['ælbəm] n álbum m; (L.P.) elepé m

alcohol ['ælkəhɒl] n alcohol m; **~ic** [-'hɒlɪk] adj, n alcohólico/a m/f

ale [eɪl] n cerveza

alert [ə'lɜːt] adj (attentive) atento; (to danger, opportunity) alerta ♦ n alerta m, alarma ♦ vt poner sobre aviso; **to be on the ~** (also MIL) estar alerta o sobre aviso

algebra ['ældʒɪbrə] n álgebra

Algeria |ælˈdʒɪərɪə| n Argelia

alias |ˈeɪlɪəs| adv alias, conocido por ♦ n (of criminal) apodo; (of writer) seudónimo

alibi |ˈælɪbaɪ| n coartada

alien |ˈeɪlɪən| n (foreigner) extranjero/a; (extraterrestrial) extraterrestre m/f ♦ adj: ~ to ajeno a; ~ate vt enajenar, alejar

alight |əˈlaɪt| adj ardiendo; (eyes) brillante ♦ vi (person) apearse, bajar; (bird) posarse

align |əˈlaɪn| vt alinear

alike |əˈlaɪk| adj semejantes, iguales ♦ adv igualmente, del mismo modo; **to look ~** parecerse

alimony |ˈælɪmənɪ| n manutención f

alive |əˈlaɪv| adj vivo; (lively) alegre

KEYWORD

---

all |ɔːl| adj (sg) todo/a; (pl) todos/as; ~ **day** todo el día; ~ **night** toda la noche; ~ **men** todos los hombres; ~ **five came** vinieron los cinco; ~ **the books** todos los libros; ~ **his life** toda su vida
♦ pron **1** todo; **I ate it ~, I ate ~ of it** me lo comí todo; ~ **of us went** fuimos todos; ~ **the boys went** fueron todos los chicos; **is that ~?** ¿eso es todo?, ¿algo más?; (in shop) ¿algo más?, ¿alguna cosa más?
2 (in phrases): **above ~** sobre todo; por encima de todo; **after ~** después de todo; **at ~: not at ~** (in answer to question) en absoluto; (in answer to thanks) ¡de nada!, ¡no hay de qué!; **I'm not at ~ tired** no estoy nada cansado/a; **anything at ~ will do** cualquier cosa viene bien; ~ **in ~** a fin de cuentas
♦ adv: ~ **alone** completamente solo/a; **it's not as hard as ~ that** no es tan difícil como lo pintas; **~ the more/the better** tanto más/mejor; ~ **but** casi; **the score is 2 ~** están empatados a 2

---

all clear n (after attack etc) fin m de la alerta; (fig) luz f verde

allege |əˈledʒ| vt pretender; **~dly** |əˈledʒɪdlɪ| adv supuestamente, según se afirma

allegiance |əˈliːdʒəns| n lealtad f

allergy |ˈælədʒɪ| n alergia

alleviate |əˈliːvɪeɪt| vt aliviar

alley |ˈælɪ| n callejuela

alliance |əˈlaɪəns| n alianza

allied |ˈælaɪd| adj aliado

alligator |ˈælɪɡeɪtə*| n (ZOOL) caimán m

all-in (BRIT) adj, adv (charge) todo incluido

all-night adj (café, shop) abierto toda la noche; (party) que dura toda la noche

allocate |ˈæləkeɪt| vt (money etc) asignar

allot |əˈlɒt| vt asignar; **~ment** n ración f; (garden) parcela

all-out adj (effort etc) supremo; **all out** adv con todas las fuerzas

allow |əˈlau| vt permitir, dejar; (a claim) admitir; (sum, time etc) dar, conceder; (concede): **to ~ that** reconocer que; **to ~ sb to do** permitir a alguien hacer; **he is ~ed to ...** se le permite ...; ~ **for** vt fus tener en cuenta; **~ance** n subvención f; (welfare payment) subsidio, pensión f; (pocket money) dinero de bolsillo; (tax ~ance) desgravación f; **to make ~ances for** (person) disculpar a; (thing) tener en cuenta

alloy |ˈælɔɪ| n mezcla

all: ~ right adv bien; (as answer) ¡conforme!, ¡está bien!; **~-rounder** n: **he's a good ~-rounder** se le da bien todo; **~-time** adj (record) de todos los tiempos

alluring |əˈljuərɪŋ| adj atractivo, tentador(a)

ally |ˈælaɪ| n aliado/a ♦ vt: **to ~ o.s. with** aliarse con

almighty |ɔːlˈmaɪtɪ| adj todopoderoso; (row etc) imponente

almond |ˈɑːmənd| n almendra

almost |ˈɔːlməust| adv casi

alone |əˈləun| adj, adv solo; **to leave sb ~** dejar a uno en paz; **to leave sth ~** no tocar algo, dejar algo sin tocar; **let ~ ...** y mucho menos ...

along |əˈlɒŋ| prep a lo largo de, por ♦ adv: **is he coming ~ with us?** ¿viene con nosotros?; **he was limping ~** iba cojeando; ~ **with** junto con; **all ~** (all the time) desde el principio; **~side** prep al lado de ♦ adv al lado

aloof |əˈluːf| adj reservado ♦ adv: **to stand ~** mantenerse apartado

aloud |əˈlaud| adv en voz alta

alphabet |ˈælfəbet| n alfabeto

Alps |ælps| npl: **the ~** los Alpes

already |ɔːlˈredɪ| adv ya

alright |ˈɔːlˈraɪt| (BRIT) adv = **all right**

Alsatian |ælˈseɪʃən| n (dog) pastor m alemán

also |ˈɔːlsəu| adv también, además

altar |ˈɔːltə*| n altar m

alter |ˈɔːltə*| vt cambiar, modificar ♦ vi cambiar; **~ation** |ɔːltəˈreɪʃən| n cambio; (to clothes) arreglo; (to building) arreglos mpl

alternate |adj ɔlˈtəːnɪt, vb ˈɔːltəːneɪt| adj (actions etc) alternativo; (events) alterno; (US) = **alternative** ♦ vi: **to ~ (with)** alternar (con); **on ~ days** un día sí y otro no; **alternating current** |-neɪtɪŋ| n corriente f alterna

alternative |ɔlˈtəːnətɪv| adj alternativo ♦ n alternativa; ~ **medicine** medicina alternativa; **~ly** adv: **~ly one could ...** por otra parte se podría ...

although |ɔːlˈðəu| conj aunque

altitude |ˈæltɪtjuːd| n altura

alto |ˈæltəu| n (female) contralto f; (male) alto

altogether |ɔːltəˈɡeðə*| adv completamente, del todo; (on the whole) en total, en conjunto

aluminium |æljuˈmɪnɪəm| (BRIT), alumi-

num [ə'lu:mɪnəm] (*US*) *n* aluminio
always ['ɔ:lweɪz] *adv* siempre
Alzheimer's (disease) ['æltshaɪməz-] *n* enfermedad *f* de Alzheimer
AM *n abbr* (= *Assembly Member*) parlamentario/a *m/f*
am [æm] *vb see* **be**
a.m. *adv abbr* (= *ante meridiem*) de la mañana
amalgamate [ə'mælgəmeɪt] *vi* amalgamarse ♦ *vt* amalgamar, unir
amateur ['æmətə*] *n* aficionado/a, amateur *m/f*; **~ish** *adj* inexperto, superficial
amaze [ə'meɪz] *vt* asombrar, pasmar; **to be ~d (at)** quedar pasmado (de); **~ment** *n* asombro, sorpresa; **amazing** *adj* extraordinario; (*fantastic*) increíble
Amazon ['æməzən] *n* (*GEO*) Amazonas *m*
ambassador [æm'bæsədə*] *n* embajador(a) *m/f*
amber ['æmbə*] *n* ámbar *m*; **at ~** (*BRIT: AUT*) en el amarillo
ambiguous [æm'bɪgjuəs] *adj* ambiguo
ambition [æm'bɪʃən] *n* ambición *f*; **ambitious** [-ʃəs] *adj* ambicioso
ambulance ['æmbjuləns] *n* ambulancia
ambush ['æmbuʃ] *n* emboscada ♦ *vt* tender una emboscada a
amenable [ə'mi:nəbl] *adj*: **to be ~ to** dejarse influir por
amend [ə'mend] *vt* enmendar; **to make ~s** dar cumplida satisfacción
amenities [ə'mi:nɪtɪz] *npl* comodidades *fpl*
America [ə'merɪkə] *n* (*USA*) Estados *mpl* Unidos; **~n** *adj*, *n* norteamericano/a *m/f*; estadounidense *m/f*
amiable ['eɪmɪəbl] *adj* amable, simpático
amicable ['æmɪkəbl] *adj* amistoso, amigable
amid(st) [ə'mɪd(st)] *prep* entre, en medio de
amiss [ə'mɪs] *adv*: **to take sth ~** tomar algo a mal; **there's something ~** pasa algo
ammonia [ə'məunɪə] *n* amoníaco
ammunition [æmju'nɪʃən] *n* municiones *fpl*
amnesty ['æmnɪstɪ] *n* amnistía
amok [ə'mɔk] *adv*: **to run ~** enloquecerse, desbocarse
among(st) [ə'mʌŋ(st)] *prep* entre, en medio de
amorous ['æmərəs] *adj* amoroso
amount [ə'maunt] *n* (*gen*) cantidad *f*; (*of bill etc*) suma, importe *m* ♦ *vi*: **to ~ to** sumar; (*be same as*) equivaler a, significar
amp(ère) ['æmp(eə*)] *n* amperio
ample ['æmpl] *adj* (*large*) grande; (*abundant*) abundante; (*enough*) bastante, suficiente
amplifier ['æmplɪfaɪə*] *n* amplificador *m*
amuse [ə'mju:z] *vt* divertir; (*distract*) distraer, entretener; **~ment** *n* diversión *f*; (*pastime*) pasatiempo; (*laughter*) risa; **~ment arcade** *n* salón *m* de juegos; **~ment park** *n* parque *m* de

atracciones
an [æn] *indef art see* **a**
anaemic [ə'ni:mɪk] (*US* **anemic**) *adj* anémico; (*fig*) soso, insípido
anaesthetic [ænɪs'θetɪk] *n* (*US* **anesthetic**) anestesia
analog(ue) ['ænəlɔg] *adj* (*computer, watch*) analógico
analyse ['ænəlaɪz] (*US* **analyze**) *vt* analizar; **analysis** [ə'næləsɪs] (*pl* **analyses**) *n* análisis *m inv*; **analyst** [-lɪst] *n* (*political analyst, psychoanalyst*) analista *m/f*
analyze ['ænəlaɪz] (*US*) *vt* = **analyse**
anarchist ['ænəkɪst] *n* anarquista *m/f*
anatomy [ə'nætəmɪ] *n* anatomía
ancestor ['ænsɪstə*] *n* antepasado
anchor ['æŋkə*] *n* ancla, áncora ♦ *vi* (*also*: **to drop ~**) anclar ♦ *vt* anclar; **to weigh ~** levar anclas
anchovy ['æntʃəvɪ] *n* anchoa
ancient ['eɪnʃənt] *adj* antiguo
ancillary [æn'sɪlərɪ] *adj* auxiliar
and [ænd] *conj* y; (*before i-, hi- + consonant*) e; **men ~ women** hombres y mujeres; **father ~ son** padre e hijo; **trees ~ grass** árboles y hierba; **~ so on** etcétera, y así sucesivamente; **try ~ come** procura venir; **he talked ~ talked** habló sin parar; **better ~ better** cada vez mejor
Andes ['ændi:z] *npl*: **the ~** los Andes
anemic *etc* [ə'ni:mɪk] (*US*) = **anaemic** *etc*
anesthetic *etc* [ænɪs'θetɪk] (*US*) = **anaesthetic** *etc*
anew [ə'nju:] *adv* de nuevo, otra vez
angel ['eɪndʒəl] *n* ángel *m*
anger ['æŋgə*] *n* cólera
angina [æn'dʒaɪnə] *n* angina (del pecho)
angle ['æŋgl] *n* ángulo; **from their ~** desde su punto de vista
angler ['æŋglə*] *n* pescador(a) *m/f* (de caña)
Anglican ['æŋglɪkən] *adj*, *n* anglicano/a *m/f*
angling ['æŋglɪŋ] *n* pesca con caña
Anglo... [æŋgləu] *prefix* anglo...
angrily ['æŋgrɪlɪ] *adv* coléricamente, airadamente
angry ['æŋgrɪ] *adj* enfadado, airado; (*wound*) inflamado; **to be ~ with sb/at sth** estar enfadado con alguien/por algo; **to get ~** enfadarse, enojarse
anguish ['æŋgwɪʃ] *n* (*physical*) tormentos *mpl*; (*mental*) angustia
animal ['ænɪməl] *n* animal *m*; (*pej: person*) bestia ♦ *adj* animal
animate ['ænɪmɪt] *adj* vivo; **~d** [-meɪtɪd] *adj* animado
aniseed ['ænɪsi:d] *n* anís *m*
ankle ['æŋkl] *n* tobillo *m*; **~ sock** *n* calcetín *m* corto
annex [*n* 'æneks, *vb* æ'neks] *n* (*also*: *BRIT*: **annexe**) (*building*) edificio anexo ♦ *vt*

(*territory*) anexionar
annihilate [əˈnaɪəleɪt] *vt* aniquilar
anniversary [ænɪˈvɜːsərɪ] *n* aniversario
announce [əˈnaʊns] *vt* anunciar;
anuncio; (*official*) declaración *f*; **~r** *n* (*RADIO*)
locutor(a) *m/f*; (*TV*) presentador(a) *m/f*
annoy [əˈnɔɪ] *vt* molestar, fastidiar; **don't get**
~ed! ¡no se enfade!; **~ance** *n* enojo; **~ing** *adj*
molesto, fastidioso; (*person*) pesado
annual [ˈænjʊəl] *adj* anual ♦ *n* (*BOT*) anual *m*;
(*book*) anuario; **~ly** *adv* anualmente, cada
año
annul [əˈnʌl] *vt* anular
annum [ˈænəm] *n see* **per**
anonymous [əˈnɒnɪməs] *adj* anónimo
anorak [ˈænəræk] *n* anorak *m*
anorexia [ænəˈrɛksɪə] *n* (*MED: also:*
~ *nervosa*) anorexia
another [əˈnʌðə*] *adj* (*one more, a different*
one) otro ♦ *pron* otro; *see* **one**
answer [ˈɑːnsə*] *n* contestación *f*, respuesta;
(*to problem*) solución *f* ♦ *vi* contestar,
responder ♦ *vt* (*reply to*) contestar a,
responder a; (*problem*) resolver; (*prayer*)
escuchar; **in ~ to your letter** contestando *or*
en contestación a su carta; **to ~ the phone**
contestar *or* coger el teléfono; **to ~ the bell** *or*
the door acudir a la puerta; **~ back** *vi*
replicar, ser respondón/ona; **~ for** *vt fus*
responder de *or* por; **~ to** *vt fus* (*description*)
corresponder a; **~able** *adj:* **~able to sb for sth**
responsable ante uno de algo; **~ing**
machine *n* contestador *m* automático
ant [ænt] *n* hormiga
antagonism [ænˈtæɡənɪzm] *n* antagonismo,
hostilidad *f*
antagonize [ænˈtæɡənaɪz] *vt* provocar la
enemistad de
Antarctic [æntˈɑːktɪk] *n:* **the ~** el Antártico
antelope [ˈæntɪləʊp] *n* antílope *m*
antenatal [ˈæntɪˈneɪtl] *adj* antenatal,
prenatal; **~ clinic** *n* clínica prenatal
anthem [ˈænθəm] *n:* **national ~** himno
nacional
anthropology [ænθrəˈpɒlədʒɪ] *n*
antropología
anti... [æntɪ] *prefix* anti...; **~-aircraft**
[-ˈɛəkrɑːft] *adj* antiaéreo; **~biotic** [-baɪˈɒtɪk] *n*
antibiótico; **~body** [ˈæntɪbɒdɪ] *n* anticuerpo
anticipate [ænˈtɪsɪpeɪt] *vt* prever; (*expect*)
esperar, contar con; (*look forward to*) esperar
con ilusión; (*do first*) anticiparse a,
adelantarse a; **anticipation** [-ˈpeɪʃən] *n*
(*expectation*) previsión *f*; (*eagerness*) ilusión *f*,
expectación *f*
anticlimax [æntɪˈklaɪmæks] *n* decepción *f*
anticlockwise [æntɪˈklɒkwaɪz] (*BRIT*) *adv* en
dirección contraria a la de las agujas del reloj
antics [ˈæntɪks] *npl* gracias *fpl*

anticyclone [æntɪˈsaɪkləʊn] *n* anticiclón *m*
antidepressant [ˈæntɪdɪˈprɛsnt] *n*
antidepresivo
antidote [ˈæntɪdəʊt] *n* antídoto
antifreeze [ˈæntɪfriːz] *n* anticongelante *m*
antihistamine [æntɪˈhɪstəmiːn] *n*
antihistamínico
antiquated [ˈæntɪkweɪtd] *adj* anticuado
antique [ænˈtiːk] *n* antigüedad *f* ♦ *adj*
antiguo; **~ dealer** *n* anticuario/a; **~ shop** *n*
tienda de antigüedades
antiquity [ænˈtɪkwɪtɪ] *n* antigüedad *f*
antiseptic [æntɪˈsɛptɪk] *adj, n* antiséptico
antlers [ˈæntləz] *npl* cuernas *fpl*, cornamenta
sg
anus [ˈeɪnəs] *n* ano
anvil [ˈænvɪl] *n* yunque *m*
anxiety [æŋˈzaɪətɪ] *n* inquietud *f*; (*MED*)
ansiedad *f*; **~ to do** deseo de hacer
anxious [ˈæŋkʃəs] *adj* inquieto, preocupado;
(*worrying*) preocupante; (*keen*): **to be ~ to do**
tener muchas ganas de hacer

KEYWORD
---

any [ˈɛnɪ] *adj* **1** (*in questions etc*) algún/
alguna; **have you ~ butter/children?** ¿tienes
mantequilla/hijos?; **if there are ~ tickets left** si
quedan billetes, si queda algún billete
2 (*with negative*): **I haven't ~ money/books**
no tengo dinero/libros
3 (*no matter which*) cualquier; **~ excuse will**
do valdrá *or* servirá cualquier excusa; **choose**
~ book you like escoge el libro que quieras;
~ teacher you ask will tell you cualquier
profesor al que preguntes te lo dirá
4 (*in phrases*): **in ~ case** de todas formas, en
cualquier caso; **~ day now** cualquier día (de
estos); **at ~ moment** en cualquier momento,
de un momento a otro; **at ~ rate** en todo
caso; **~ time: come (at) ~ time** ven cuando
quieras; **he might come (at) ~ time** podría
llegar de un momento a otro
♦ *pron* **1** (*in questions etc*): **have you got ~?**
¿tienes alguno(s)/a(s)?; **can ~ of you sing?**
¿sabe cantar alguno de vosotros/ustedes?
2 (*with negative*): **I haven't ~ (of them)** no
tengo ninguno
3 (*no matter which one(s)*): **take ~ of those**
books (you like) toma el libro que quieras de
ésos
♦ *adv* **1** (*in questions etc*): **do you want**
~ more soup/sandwiches? ¿quieres más
sopa/bocadillos?; **are you feeling ~ better?** ¿te
sientes algo mejor?
2 (*with negative*): **I can't hear him ~ more** ya
no le oigo; **don't wait ~ longer** no esperes
más

anybody [ˈɛnɪbɒdɪ] *pron* cualquiera; (*in*

interrogative sentences) alguien; (*in negative sentences*): **I don't see** ~ no veo a nadie; **if ~ should phone ...** si llama alguien ...

anyhow ['enɪhaʊ] *adv* (*at any rate*) de todos modos, de todas formas; (*haphazard*): **do it ~ you like** hazlo como quieras; **she leaves things just** ~ deja las cosas como quiera *or* de cualquier modo; **I shall go** ~ de todos modos iré

anyone ['enɪwʌn] *pron* = **anybody**

anything ['enɪθɪŋ] *pron* (*in questions etc*) algo, alguna cosa; (*with negative*) nada; **can you see** ~? ¿ves algo?; **if ~ happens to me ...** si algo me ocurre ...; (*no matter what*): **you can say ~ you like** puedes decir lo que quieras; ~ **will do** vale todo *or* cualquier cosa; **he'll eat** ~ come de todo *or* lo que sea

anyway ['enɪweɪ] *adv* (*at any rate*) de todos modos, de todas formas; **I shall go** ~ iré de todos modos; (*besides*): ~, **I couldn't come even if I wanted to** además, no podría venir aunque quisiera; **why are you phoning,** ~? ¿entonces, por qué llamas?, ¿por qué llamas, pues?

anywhere ['enɪweə*] *adv* (*in questions etc*): **can you see him** ~? ¿le ves por algún lado?; **are you going** ~? ¿vas a algún sitio?; (*with negative*): **I can't see him** ~ no le veo por ninguna parte; ~ **in the world** (*no matter where*) en cualquier parte (del mundo); **put the books down** ~ deja los libros donde quieras

apart [ə'pɑːt] *adv* (*aside*) aparte; (*situation*): ~ (**from**) separado (de); (*movement*): **to pull ~** separar; **10 miles** ~ separados por 10 millas; **to take** ~ desmontar; ~ **from** *prep* aparte de

apartheid [ə'pɑːteɪt] *n* apartheid *m*

apartment [ə'pɑːtmənt] *n* (*US*) piso (*SP*), departamento (*AM*), apartamento; (*room*) cuarto; ~ **building** (*US*) *n* edificio de apartamentos

apathetic [æpə'θetɪk] *adj* apático, indiferente

ape [eɪp] *n* mono ♦ *vt* imitar, remedar

aperitif [ə'perɪtiːf] *n* aperitivo

aperture ['æpətʃʊə*] *n* rendija, resquicio; (*PHOT*) abertura

APEX ['eɪpeks] *n abbr* (= *Advanced Purchase Excursion Fare*) tarifa APEX *f*

apex *n* ápice *m*; (*fig*) cumbre *f*

apiece [ə'piːs] *adv* cada uno

aplomb [ə'plɒm] *n* aplomo

apologetic [əpɒlə'dʒetɪk] *adj* de disculpa; (*person*) arrepentido

apologize [ə'pɒlədʒaɪz] *vi*: **to ~** (**for sth to sb**) disculparse (con alguien de algo)

apology [ə'pɒlədʒɪ] *n* disculpa, excusa

apostrophe [ə'pɒstrəfɪ] *n* apóstrofo *m*

appal [ə'pɔːl] *vt* horrorizar, espantar; ~**ling** *adj* espantoso; (*awful*) pésimo

apparatus [æpə'reɪtəs] *n* (*equipment*) equipo; (*organization*) aparato; (*in gymnasium*) aparatos *mpl*

apparel [ə'pærəl] (*US*) *n* ropa

apparent [ə'pærənt] *adj* aparente; (*obvious*) evidente; ~**ly** *adv* por lo visto, al parecer

appeal [ə'piːl] *vi* (*LAW*) apelar ♦ *n* (*LAW*) apelación *f*; (*request*) llamamiento; (*plea*) petición *f*; (*charm*) atractivo; **to ~ for** reclamar; **to ~ to** (*be attractive to*) atraer; **it doesn't ~ to me** no me atrae, no me llama la atención; ~**ing** *adj* (*attractive*) atractivo

appear [ə'pɪə*] *vi* aparecer, presentarse; (*LAW*) comparecer; (*publication*) salir (a luz), publicarse; (*seem*) parecer; **to ~ on TV/in "Hamlet"** salir por la tele/hacer un papel en "Hamlet"; **it would ~ that** parecería que; ~**ance** *n* aparición *f*; (*look*) apariencia, aspecto

appease [ə'piːz] *vt* (*pacify*) apaciguar; (*satisfy*) satisfacer

appendices [ə'pendɪsiːz] *npl of* **appendix**

appendicitis [əpendɪ'saɪtɪs] *n* apendicitis *f*

appendix [ə'pendɪks] (*pl* **appendices**) *n* apéndice *m*

appetite ['æpɪtaɪt] *n* apetito; (*fig*) deseo, anhelo

appetizer ['æpɪtaɪzə*] *n* (*drink*) aperitivo; (*food*) tapas *fpl* (*SP*)

applaud [ə'plɔːd] *vt, vi* aplaudir

applause [ə'plɔːz] *n* aplausos *mpl*

apple ['æpl] *n* manzana; ~ **tree** *n* manzano

appliance [ə'plaɪəns] *n* aparato

applicable [ə'plɪkəbl] *adj* (*relevant*): **to be ~ (to)** referirse (a)

applicant ['æplɪkənt] *n* candidato/a; solicitante *m/f*

application [æplɪ'keɪʃən] *n* aplicación *f*; (*for a job etc*) solicitud *f*, petición *f*; ~ **form** *n* solicitud *f*

applied [ə'plaɪd] *adj* aplicado

apply [ə'plaɪ] *vt* (*paint etc*) poner; (*law etc*: *put into practice*) poner en vigor ♦ *vi*: **to ~ to** (*ask*) dirigirse a; (*be applicable*) ser aplicable a; **tn ~ for** (*permit, grant, job*) solicitar; **to ~ o.s. to** aplicarse a, dedicarse a

appoint [ə'pɔɪnt] *vt* (*to post*) nombrar; ~**ed** *adj*: **at the** ~**ed time** a la hora señalada; ~**ment** *n* (*with client*) cita; (*act*) nombramiento; (*post*) puesto; (*at hairdresser etc*): **to have an** ~**ment** tener hora; **to make an** ~**ment** (*with sb*) citarse (con uno)

appraisal [ə'preɪzl] *n* valoración *f*

appreciate [ə'priːʃɪeɪt] *vt* apreciar, tener en mucho; (*be grateful for*) agradecer; (*be aware of*) comprender ♦ *vi* (*COMM*) aumentar(se) en valor; **appreciation** [-'eɪʃən] *n* apreciación *f*; (*gratitude*) reconocimiento, agradecimiento; (*COMM*) aumento en valor

appreciative [ə'pri:ʃiətɪv] adj apreciativo; (*comment*) agradecido

apprehensive [æprɪ'hɛnsɪv] adj aprensivo

apprentice [ə'prɛntɪs] n aprendiz/a m/f; **~ship** n aprendizaje m

approach [ə'prəutʃ] vi acercarse ♦ vt acercarse a; (*ask, apply to*) dirigirse a; (*situation, problem*) abordar ♦ n acercamiento; (*access*) acceso; (*to problem, situation*): **~ (to)** actitud f (ante); **~able** adj (*person*) abordable; (*place*) accesible

appropriate [adj ə'prəuprɪɪt, vb ə'prəuprɪeɪt] adj apropiado, conveniente ♦ vt (*take*) apropiarse de

approval [ə'pru:vəl] n aprobación f, visto bueno; (*permission*) consentimiento; **on ~** (*COMM*) a prueba

approve [ə'pru:v] vt aprobar; **~ of** vt fus (*thing*) aprobar; (*person*): **they don't ~ of her** (ella) no les parece bien

approximate [ə'prɒksɪmɪt] adj aproximado; **~ly** adv aproximadamente, más o menos

apricot ['eɪprɪkɒt] n albaricoque m (*SP*), damasco (*AM*)

April ['eɪprəl] n abril m; **~ Fools' Day** n el primero de abril; ≈ día m de los Inocentes (*28 December*)

apron ['eɪprən] n delantal m

apt [æpt] adj acertado, apropiado; (*likely*): **~ to do** propenso a hacer

aquarium [ə'kwɛərɪəm] n acuario

Aquarius [ə'kwɛərɪəs] n Acuario

Arab ['ærəb] adj, n árabe m/f

Arabian [ə'reɪbɪən] adj árabe

Arabic ['ærəbɪk] adj árabe; (*numerals*) arábigo ♦ n árabe m

arable ['ærəbl] adj cultivable

Aragon ['ærəgən] n Aragón m

arbitrary ['ɑːbɪtrərɪ] adj arbitrario

arbitration [ɑːbɪ'treɪʃən] n arbitraje m

arcade [ɑː'keɪd] n (*round a square*) soportales mpl; (*shopping mall*) galería comercial

arch [ɑːtʃ] n arco; (*of foot*) arco del pie ♦ vt arquear

archaeologist [ɑːkɪ'ɒlədʒɪst] (*US* **archeologist**) n arqueólogo/a

archaeology [ɑːkɪ'ɒlədʒɪ] (*US* **archeology**) n arqueología

archbishop [ɑːtʃ'bɪʃəp] n arzobispo

archeology etc [ɑːkɪ'ɒlədʒɪ] (*US*) = **archaeology** etc

archery ['ɑːtʃərɪ] n tiro al arco

architect ['ɑːkɪtɛkt] n arquitecto/a; **~ure** n arquitectura

archives ['ɑːkaɪvz] npl archivo

Arctic ['ɑːktɪk] adj ártico ♦ n: **the ~** el Ártico

ardent ['ɑːdənt] adj ardiente, apasionado

arduous ['ɑːdjuəs] adj (*task*) arduo; (*journey*) agotador(a)

are [ɑː*] vb see **be**

area ['ɛərɪə] n área, región f; (*part of place*) zona; (*MATH etc*) área, superficie f; (*in room: e.g. dining ~*) parte f; (*of knowledge, experience*) campo

arena [ə'ri:nə] n estadio; (*of circus*) pista

aren't [ɑːnt] = **are not**

Argentina [ɑːdʒən'ti:nə] n Argentina; **Argentinian** [-'tɪnɪən] adj, n argentino/a m/f

arguably ['ɑːgjuəblɪ] adv posiblemente

argue ['ɑːgju:] vi (*quarrel*) discutir, pelearse; (*reason*) razonar, argumentar; **to ~ that** sostener que

argument ['ɑːgjumənt] n discusión f, pelea; (*reasons*) argumento; **~ative** [-'mɛntətɪv] adj discutidor(a)

Aries ['ɛəriːz] n Aries m

arise [ə'raɪz] (*pt* **arose**, *pp* **arisen**) vi surgir, presentarse

arisen [ə'rɪzn] pp of **arise**

aristocrat ['ærɪstəkræt] n aristócrata m/f

arithmetic [ə'rɪθmətɪk] n aritmética

ark [ɑːk] n: **Noah's A~** el Arca f de Noé

arm [ɑːm] n brazo ♦ vt armar; **~s** npl armas fpl; **~ in ~** cogidos del brazo

armaments ['ɑːməmənts] npl armamento

armchair ['ɑːmtʃeə*] n sillón m, butaca

armed [ɑːmd] adj armado; **~ robbery** n robo a mano armada

armour ['ɑːmə*] (*US* **armor**) n armadura; (*MIL: tanks*) blindaje m; **~ed car** n coche m (*SP*) or carro (*AM*) blindado

armpit ['ɑːmpɪt] n sobaco, axila

armrest ['ɑːmrɛst] n apoyabrazos m inv

army ['ɑːmɪ] n ejército; (*fig*) multitud f

aroma [ə'rəumə] n aroma m, fragancia; **~therapy** n aromaterapia

arose [ə'rəuz] pt of **arise**

around [ə'raund] adv alrededor; (*in the area*): **there is no one else ~** no hay nadie más por aquí ♦ prep alrededor de

arouse [ə'rauz] vt despertar; (*anger*) provocar

arrange [ə'reɪndʒ] vt arreglar, ordenar; (*organize*) organizar; **to ~ to do sth** quedar en hacer algo; **~ment** n arreglo; (*agreement*) acuerdo; **~ments** npl (*preparations*) preparativos mpl

array [ə'reɪ] n: **~ of** (*things*) serie f de; (*people*) conjunto de

arrears [ə'rɪəz] npl atrasos mpl; **to be in ~ with one's rent** estar retrasado en el pago del alquiler

arrest [ə'rɛst] vt detener; (*sb's attention*) llamar ♦ n detención f; **under ~** detenido

arrival [ə'raɪvəl] n llegada; **new ~** recién llegado/a; (*baby*) recién nacido

arrive [ə'raɪv] vi llegar; (*baby*) nacer

arrogant ['ærəgənt] adj arrogante

arrow ['ærəu] n flecha

arse [ɑːs] (*BRIT: inf!*) *n* culo, trasero

arson [ˈɑːsn] *n* incendio premeditado

art [ɑːt] *n* arte *m*; (*skill*) destreza; **A~s** *npl* (*SCOL*) Letras *fpl*

artery [ˈɑːtərɪ] *n* arteria

art gallery *n* pinacoteca; (*saleroom*) galería de arte

arthritis [ɑːˈθraɪtɪs] *n* artritis *f*

artichoke [ˈɑːtɪtʃəuk] *n* alcachofa; **Jerusalem ~** aguaturma

article [ˈɑːtɪkl] *n* artículo; (*BRIT: LAW: training*): **~s** *npl* contrato de aprendizaje; **~ of clothing** prenda de vestir

articulate [*adj* ɑːˈtɪkjulɪt, *vb* ɑːˈtɪkjuleɪt] *adj* claro, bien expresado ♦ *vt* expresar; **~d lorry** (*BRIT*) *n* trailer *m*

artificial [ɑːtɪˈfɪʃəl] *adj* artificial; (*affected*) afectado

artillery [ɑːˈtɪlərɪ] *n* artillería

artisan [ˈɑːtɪzæn] *n* artesano

artist [ˈɑːtɪst] *n* artista *m/f*; (*MUS*) intérprete *m/f*; **~ic** [ɑːˈtɪstɪk] *adj* artístico; **~ry** *n* arte *m*, habilidad *f* (artística)

art school *n* escuela de bellas artes

KEYWORD
---

as [æz] *conj* **1** (*referring to time*) cuando, mientras; a medida que; **~ the years went by** con el paso de los años; **he came in ~ I was leaving** entró cuando me marchaba; **~ from tomorrow** desde *or* a partir de mañana

2 (*in comparisons*): **~ big ~** tan grande como; **twice ~ big ~** el doble de grande que; **~ much money/many books ~** tanto dinero/ tantos libros como; **~ soon ~** en cuanto

3 (*since, because*) como, ya que; **he left early ~ he had to be home by 10** se fue temprano ya que tenía que estar en casa a las 10

4 (*referring to manner, way*): **do ~ you wish** haz lo que quieras; **~ she said** como dijo; **he gave it to me ~ a present** me lo dio de regalo

5 (*in the capacity of*): **he works ~ a barman** trabaja de barman; **~ chairman of the company, he ...** como presidente de la compañía, ...

6 (*concerning*): **~ for or to that** por *or* en lo que respecta a eso

7 : **~ if or though** como si; **he looked ~ if he was ill** parecía como si estuviera enfermo, tenía aspecto de enfermo; *see also* **long**; **such**; **well**

---

a.s.a.p. *abbr* (= *as soon as possible*) cuanto antes

asbestos [æzˈbestəs] *n* asbesto, amianto

ascend [əˈsend] *vt* subir; (*throne*) ascender *or* subir a

ascent [əˈsent] *n* subida; (*slope*) cuesta, pendiente *f*

ascertain [æsəˈteɪn] *vt* averiguar

ash [æʃ] *n* ceniza; (*tree*) fresno

ashamed [əˈʃeɪmd] *adj* avergonzado, apenado (*AM*); **to be ~ of** avergonzarse de

ashore [əˈʃɔː*] *adv* en tierra; (*swim etc*) a tierra

ashtray [ˈæʃtreɪ] *n* cenicero

Ash Wednesday *n* miércoles *m* de Ceniza

Asia [ˈeɪʃə] *n* Asia; **~n** *adj*, *n* asiático/a *m/f*

aside [əˈsaɪd] *adv* a un lado ♦ *n* aparte *m*

ask [ɑːsk] *vt* (*question*) preguntar; (*invite*) invitar; **to ~ sb sth/to do sth** preguntar algo a alguien/pedir a alguien que haga algo; **to ~ sb about sth** preguntar algo a alguien; **to ~ (sb) a question** hacer una pregunta (a alguien); **to ~ sb out to dinner** invitar a cenar a uno; **~ after** *vt fus* preguntar por; **~ for** *vt fus* pedir; (*trouble*) buscar

asking price *n* precio inicial

asleep [əˈsliːp] *adj* dormido; **to fall ~** dormirse, quedarse dormido

asparagus [əsˈpærəgəs] *n* (*plant*) espárrago; (*food*) espárragos *mpl*

aspect [ˈæspekt] *n* aspecto, apariencia; (*direction in which a building etc faces*) orientación *f*

aspersions [əsˈpəːʃənz] *npl*: **to cast ~ on** difamar a, calumniar a

asphyxiation [æsfɪksɪˈeɪʃən] *n* asfixia

aspire [əsˈpaɪə*] *vi*: **to ~ to** aspirar a, ambicionar

aspirin [ˈæsprɪn] *n* aspirina

ass [æs] *n* asno, burro; (*inf: idiot*) imbécil *m/f*; (*US: inf!*) culo, trasero

assailant [əˈseɪlənt] *n* asaltador(a) *m/f*, agresor(a) *m/f*

assassinate [əˈsæsɪneɪt] *vt* asesinar; **assassination** [əsæsɪˈneɪʃən] *n* asesinato

assault [əˈsɔːlt] *n* asalto; (*LAW*) agresión *f* ♦ *vt* asaltar, atacar; (*sexually*) violar

assemble [əˈsembl] *vt* reunir, juntar; (*TECH*) montar ♦ *vi* reunirse, juntarse

assembly [əˈsemblɪ] *n* reunión *f*, asamblea; (*parliament*) parlamento; (*construction*) montaje *m*; **~ line** *n* cadena de montaje

assent [əˈsent] *n* asentimiento, aprobación *f*

assert [əˈsəːt] *vt* afirmar; (*authority*) hacer valer; **~ion** [-ʃən] *n* afirmación *f*

assess [əˈses] *vt* valorar, calcular; (*tax, damages*) fijar; (*for tax*) gravar; **~ment** *n* valoración *f*; (*for tax*) gravamen *m*; **~or** *n* asesor(a) *m/f*

asset [ˈæset] *n* ventaja; **~s** *npl* (*COMM*) activo; (*property, funds*) fondos *mpl*

assign [əˈsaɪn] *vt*: **to ~ (to)** (*date*) fijar (para); (*task*) asignar (a); (*resources*) destinar (a); **~ment** *n* tarea

assist [əˈsɪst] *vt* ayudar; **~ance** *n* ayuda, auxilio; **~ant** *n* ayudante *m/f*; (*BRIT: also*:

shop ~ant) dependiente/a *m/f*

associate [*adj, n* ə'səuʃɪɪt, *vb* ə'səuʃɪeɪt] *adj* asociado ♦ *n* (*at work*) colega *m/f* ♦ *vt* asociar; (*ideas*) relacionar ♦ *vi*: **to ~ with sb** tratar con alguien

association [əsəusɪ'eɪʃən] *n* asociación *f*

assorted [ə'sɔ:tɪd] *adj* surtido, variado

assortment [ə'sɔ:tmənt] *n* (*of shapes, colours*) surtido; (*of books*) colección *f*; (*of people*) mezcla

assume [ə'sju:m] *vt* suponer; (*responsibilities*) asumir; (*attitude*) adoptar, tomar

assumption [ə'sʌmpʃən] *n* suposición *f*, presunción *f*; (*of power etc*) toma

assurance [ə'ʃuərəns] *n* garantía, promesa; (*confidence*) confianza, aplomo; (*insurance*) seguro

assure [ə'ʃuə*] *vt* asegurar

asthma [ˈæsmə] *n* asma

astonish [ə'stɔnɪʃ] *vt* asombrar, pasmar; **~ment** *n* asombro, sorpresa

astound [ə'staund] *vt* asombrar, pasmar

astray [ə'streɪ] *adv*: **to go ~** extraviarse; **to lead ~** (*morally*) llevar por mal camino

astride [ə'straɪd] *prep* a caballo *or* horcajadas sobre

astrology [æs'trɔlədʒɪ] *n* astrología

astronaut [ˈæstrənɔ:t] *n* astronauta *m/f*

astronomy [æs'trɔnəmɪ] *n* astronomía

asylum [ə'saɪləm] *n* (*refuge*) asilo; (*mental hospital*) manicomio

---

KEYWORD

---

at [æt] *prep* **1** (*referring to position*) en; (*direction*) a; **~ the top** en lo alto; **~ home/ school** en casa/la escuela; **to look ~ sth/sb** mirar algo/a uno

2 (*referring to time*): **~ 4 o'clock** a las 4; **~ night** por la noche; **~ Christmas** en Navidad; **~ times** a veces

3 (*referring to rates, speed etc*): **~ £1 a kilo** a una libra el kilo; **two ~ a time** de dos en dos; **~ 50 km/h** a 50 km/h

4 (*referring to manner*): **~ a stroke** de un golpe; **~ peace** en paz

5 (*referring to activity*): **to be ~ work** estar trabajando; (*in the office etc*) estar en el trabajo; **to play ~ cowboys** jugar a los vaqueros; **to be good ~ sth** ser bueno en algo

6 (*referring to cause*): **shocked/surprised/ annoyed ~ sth** asombrado/sorprendido/ fastidiado por algo; **I went ~ his suggestion** fui a instancias suyas

---

ate [eɪt] *pt of* **eat**

atheist [ˈeɪθɪɪst] *n* ateo/a

Athens [ˈæθɪnz] *n* Atenas

athlete [ˈæθli:t] *n* atleta *m/f*

athletic [æθ'letɪk] *adj* atlético; **~s** *n* atletismo

Atlantic [ət'læntɪk] *adj* atlántico ♦ *n*: **the ~ (Ocean)** el (Océano) Atlántico

atlas [ˈætləs] *n* atlas *m*

A.T.M. *n abbr* (= *automated telling machine*) cajero automático

atmosphere [ˈætməsfɪə*] *n* atmósfera; (*of place*) ambiente *m*

atom [ˈætəm] *n* átomo; **~ic** [ə'tɔmɪk] *adj* atómico; **~(ic) bomb** *n* bomba atómica; **~izer** [ˈætəmaɪzə*] *n* atomizador *m*

atone [ə'təun] *vi*: **to ~ for** expiar

atrocious [ə'trəuʃəs] *adj* atroz

attach [ə'tætʃ] *vt* (*fasten*) atar; (*join*) unir, sujetar; (*document, letter*) adjuntar; (*importance etc*) dar, conceder; **to be ~ed to sb/sth** (*to like*) tener cariño a alguien/algo

attaché case [ə'tæʃeɪ-] *n* maletín *m*

attachment [ə'tætʃmənt] *n* (*tool*) accesorio; (*love*): **~** (**to**) apego (a)

attack [ə'tæk] *vt* (*MIL*) atacar; (*subj: criminal*) agredir, asaltar; (*criticize*) criticar; (*task*) emprender ♦ *n* ataque *m*, asalto; (*on sb's life*) atentado; (*fig: criticism*) crítica; (*of illness*) ataque *m*; **heart ~** infarto (de miocardio); **~er** *n* agresor(a) *m/f*, asaltante *m/f*

attain [ə'teɪn] *vt* (*also*: **~ to**) alcanzar; (*achieve*) lograr, conseguir

attempt [ə'tempt] *n* tentativa, intento; (*attack*) atentado ♦ *vt* intentar; **~ed** *adj*: **~ed burglary/murder/suicide** tentativa *or* intento de robo/asesinato/suicidio

attend [ə'tend] *vt* asistir a; (*patient*) atender; **~ to** *vt fus* ocuparse de; (*customer, patient*) atender a; **~ance** *n* asistencia, presencia; (*people present*) concurrencia; **~ant** *n* ayudante *m/f*; (*in garage etc*) encargado/a ♦ *adj* (*dangers*) concomitante

attention [ə'tenʃən] *n* atención *f*; (*care*) atenciones *fpl* ♦ *excl* (*MIL*) ¡firme(s)!; **for the ~ of ...** (*ADMIN*) atención ...

attentive [ə'tentɪv] *adj* atento

attic [ˈætɪk] *n* desván *m*

attitude [ˈætɪtju:d] *n* actitud *f*; (*disposition*) disposición *f*

attorney [ə'tə:nɪ] *n* (*lawyer*) abogado/a; **A~ General** *n* (*BRIT*) ≈ Presidente *m* del Consejo del Poder Judicial (*SP*); (*US*) ≈ ministro de Justicia

attract [ə'trækt] *vt* atraer; (*sb's attention*) llamar; **~ion** [ə'trækʃən] *n* encanto; (*gen pl: amusements*) diversiones *fpl*; (*PHYSICS*) atracción *f*; (*fig: towards sb, sth*) atractivo; **~ive** *adj* guapo; (*interesting*) atrayente

attribute [*n* ˈætrɪbju:t, *vb* ə'trɪbju:t] *n* atributo ♦ *vt*: **to ~ sth to** atribuir algo a

attrition [ə'trɪʃən] *n*: **war of ~** guerra de agotamiento

aubergine [ˈəubəʒi:n] (*BRIT*) *n* berenjena; (*colour*) morado

auburn ['ɔːbən] *adj* color castaño rojizo

auction ['ɔːkʃən] *n* (*also: sale by ~*) subasta ♦ *vt* subastar; **~eer** [-'nɪə*] *n* subastador(a) *m/f*

audible ['ɔːdɪbl] *adj* audible, que se puede oír

audience ['ɔːdɪəns] *n* público; (*RADIO*) radioescuchas *mpl*; (*TV*) telespectadores *mpl*; (*interview*) audiencia

audio-visual [ɔːdɪəu'vɪzjuəl] *adj* audiovisual; **~ aid** *n* ayuda audiovisual

audit ['ɔːdɪt] *vt* revisar, intervenir

audition [ɔː'dɪʃən] *n* audición *f*

auditor ['ɔːdɪtə*] *n* interventor(a) *m/f*, censor(a) *m/f* de cuentas

augment [ɔːg'mɛnt] *vt* aumentar

augur ['ɔːgə*] *vi*: **it ~s well** es un buen augurio

August ['ɔːgəst] *n* agosto

aunt [ɑːnt] *n* tía; **~ie** *n* diminutive of **aunt**; **~y** *n* diminutive of **aunt**

au pair ['əu'pɛə*] *n* (*also: ~ girl*) (chica) au pair *f*

auspicious [ɔːs'pɪʃəs] *adj* propicio, de buen augurio

Australia [ɔs'treɪlɪə] *n* Australia; **~n** *adj, n* australiano/a *m/f*

Austria ['ɔstrɪə] *n* Austria; **~n** *adj, n* austríaco/a *m/f*

authentic [ɔː'θɛntɪk] *adj* auténtico

author ['ɔːθə] *n* autor(a) *m/f*

authoritarian [ɔːθɔrɪ'tɛərɪən] *adj* autoritario

authoritative [ɔː'θɔrɪtətɪv] *adj* autorizado; (*manner*) autoritario

authority [ɔː'θɔrɪtɪ] *n* autoridad *f*; (*official permission*) autorización *f*; **the authorities** *npl* las autoridades

authorize ['ɔːθəraɪz] *vt* autorizar

auto ['ɔːtəu] (*US*) *n* coche *m* (*SP*), carro (*AM*), automóvil *m*

auto: **~biography** [ɔːtəbaɪˈɔgrəfɪ] *n* autobiografía; **~graph** ['ɔːtəgrɑːf] *n* autógrafo ♦ *vt* (*photo etc*) dedicar; (*programme*) firmar; **~mated** ['ɔːtəmeɪtɪd] *adj* automatizado; **~matic** [ɔːtə'mætɪk] *adj* automático ♦ *n* (*gun*) pistola automática; (*car*) coche *m* automático; **~matically** *adv* automáticamente; **~mation** [ɔː'təmeɪʃən] *n* reconversión *f*; **~mobile** ['ɔːtəməbiːl] (*US*) *n* coche *m* (*SP*), carro (*AM*), automóvil *m*; **~nomy** [ɔː'tɔnəmɪ] *n* autonomía

autumn ['ɔːtəm] *n* otoño

auxiliary [ɔːg'zɪlɪərɪ] *adj, n* auxiliar *m/f*

avail [ə'veɪl] *vt*: **to ~ o.s. of** aprovechar(se) de ♦ *n*: **to no ~** en vano, sin resultado

available [ə'veɪləbl] *adj* disponible; (*unoccupied*) libre; (*person: unattached*) soltero y sin compromiso

avalanche ['ævəlɑːnʃ] *n* alud *m*, avalancha

avant-garde ['ævɑ̃'gɑːd] *adj* de vanguardia

Ave. *abbr* = **avenue**

avenge [ə'vɛndʒ] *vt* vengar

avenue ['ævənjuː] *n* avenida; (*fig*) camino

average ['ævərɪdʒ] *n* promedio, término medio ♦ *adj* medio, de término medio; (*ordinary*) regular, corriente ♦ *vt* sacar un promedio de; **on ~** por regla general; **~ out** *vi*: **to ~ out at** salir en un promedio de

averse [ə'vɜːs] *adj*: **to be ~ to sth/doing** sentir aversión or antipatía por algo/por hacer

avert [ə'vɜːt] *vt* prevenir; (*blow*) desviar; (*one's eyes*) apartar

aviary ['eɪvɪərɪ] *n* pajarera, avería

avocado [ævə'kɑːdəu] *n* (*also: BRIT: ~ pear*) aguacate *m* (*SP*), palta (*AM*)

avoid [ə'vɔɪd] *vt* evitar, eludir

await [ə'weɪt] *vt* esperar, aguardar

awake [ə'weɪk] (*pt* **awoke**, *pp* **awoken** or **awaked**) *adj* despierto ♦ *vt* despertar ♦ *vi* despertarse; **to be ~** estar despierto; **~ning** *n* el despertar

award [ə'wɔːd] *n* premio; (*LAW: damages*) indemnización *f* ♦ *vt* otorgar, conceder; (*LAW: damages*) adjudicar

aware [ə'wɛə*] *adj*: **~ (of)** consciente (de); **to become ~ of/that** (*realize*) darse cuenta de/de que; (*learn*) enterarse de/de que; **~ness** *n* conciencia; (*knowledge*) conocimiento

away [ə'weɪ] *adv* fuera; (*movement*): **she went ~** se marchó; (*far ~*) lejos; **two kilometres ~** a dos kilómetros de distancia; **two hours ~ by car** a dos horas en coche; **the holiday was two weeks ~** faltaban dos semanas para las vacaciones; **he's ~ for a week** estará ausente una semana; **to take ~ (from)** quitar (a); (*subtract*) substraer (de); **to work/pedal ~** seguir trabajando/ pedaleando; **to fade ~** (*colour*) desvanecerse; (*sound*) apagarse; **~ game** *n* (*SPORT*) partido de fuera

awe [ɔː] *n* admiración *f* respetuosa; **~-inspiring** *adj* imponente

awful ['ɔːfəl] *adj* horroroso; (*quantity*): **an ~ lot (of)** cantidad (de); **~ly** *adv* (*very*) terriblemente

awkward ['ɔːkwəd] *adj* desmañado, torpe; (*shape*) incómodo; (*embarrassing*) delicado, difícil

awning ['ɔːnɪŋ] *n* (*of tent, caravan, shop*) toldo

awoke [ə'wəuk] *pt of* **awake**

awoken [ə'wəukən] *pp of* **awake**

awry [ə'raɪ] *adv*: **to be ~** estar descolocado or mal puesto

axe [æks] (*US* **ax**) *n* hacha ♦ *vt* (*project*) cortar; (*jobs*) reducir

axes ['æksiːz] *npl of* **axis**

axis ['æksɪs] (*pl* **axes**) *n* eje *m*

axle ['æksl] *n* eje *m*, árbol *m*

ay(e) [aɪ] *excl* sí

B, b

B [biː] *n* (MUS) si *m*

B.A. *abbr* = **Bachelor of Arts**

baby ['beɪbɪ] *n* bebé *m/f*; (US: *inf*: *darling*) mi amor; ~ **carriage** (US) *n* cochecito; **~-sit** *vi* hacer de canguro; **~-sitter** *n* canguro/a; ~ **wipe** *n* toallita húmeda (*para bebés*)

bachelor ['bætʃələ*] *n* soltero; **B~ of Arts/ Science** licenciado/a en Filosofía y Letras/ Ciencias

back [bæk] *n* (*of person*) espalda; (*of animal*) lomo; (*of hand*) dorso; (*as opposed to front*) parte *f* de atrás; (*of chair*) respaldo; (*of page*) reverso; (*of book*) final *m*; (FOOTBALL) defensa *m*; (*of crowd*): **the ones at the ~** los del fondo ♦ *vt* (*candidate: also*: ~ **up**) respaldar, apoyar; (*horse: at races*) apostar a; (*car*) dar marcha atrás a or con ♦ *vi* (*car etc*) ir (or salir or entrar) marcha atrás ♦ *adj* (*payment, rent*) atrasado; (*seats, wheels*) de atrás ♦ *adv* (*not forward*) (*hacia*) atrás; (*returned*): **he's ~** está de vuelta, ha vuelto; **he ran ~** volvió corriendo; (*restitution*): **throw the ball ~** devuelve la pelota; **can I have it ~?** ¿me lo devuelve?; (*again*): **he called ~** llamó de nuevo; ~ **down** *vi* echarse atrás; ~ **out** *vi* (*of promise*) volverse atrás; ~ **up** *vt* (*person*) apoyar, respaldar; (*theory*) defender; (COMPUT) hacer una copia preventiva or de reserva; **~bencher** (BRIT) *n* miembro del parlamento sin cargo relevante; **~bone** *n* columna vertebral; **~date** *vt* (*pay rise*) dar efecto retroactivo a; (*letter*) poner fecha atrasada a; **~drop** *n* telón *m* de fondo; **~fire** *vi* (AUT) petardear; (*plans*) fallar, salir mal; **~ground** *n* fondo; (*of events*) antecedentes *mpl*; (*basic knowledge*) bases *fpl*; (*experience*) conocimientos *mpl*, educación *f*; **family ~ground** origen *m*, antecedentes *mpl*; **~hand** *n* (TENNIS: *also*: ~hand stroke*) revés *m*; **~hander** (BRIT) *n* (*bribe*) soborno; **~ing** *n* (*fig*) apoyo, respaldo; **~lash** *n* reacción *f*; **~log** *n*: **~log of work** trabajo atrasado; ~ **number** *n* (*of magazine etc*) número atrasado; **~pack** *n* mochila; **~packer** *n* mochilero(a); ~ **pay** *n* pago atrasado; **~side** (*inf*) *n* trasero, culo; **~stage** *adv* entre bastidores; **~stroke** *n* espalda; **~up** *adj* suplementario; (COMPUT) de reserva ♦ *n* (*support*) apoyo; (*also*: ~-up file*) copia preventiva or de reserva; **~ward** *adj* (*person, country*) atrasado; **~wards** *adv* hacia atrás; (*read a list*) al revés; (*fall*) de espaldas; **~yard** *n* traspatio

bacon ['beɪkən] *n* tocino, beicon *m*

bad [bæd] *adj* malo; (*mistake, accident*) grave; (*food*) podrido, pasado; **his ~ leg** su pierna lisiada; **to go ~** (*food*) pasarse

badge [bædʒ] *n* insignia; (*policeman's*) chapa, placa

badger ['bædʒə*] *n* tejón *m*

badly ['bædlɪ] *adv* mal; **to reflect ~ on sb** influir negativamente en la reputación de uno; ~ **wounded** gravemente herido; **he needs it ~** le hace gran falta; **to be ~ off (for money)** andar mal de dinero

badminton ['bædmɪntən] *n* bádminton *m*

bad-tempered *adj* de mal genio or carácter; (*temporarily*) de mal humor

bag [bæg] *n* bolsa; (*handbag*) bolso; (*satchel*) mochila; (*case*) maleta; **~s of** (*inf*) un montón de; **~gage** *n* equipaje *m*; **~gage allowance** *n* límite *m* de equipaje; **~gage reclaim** *n* recogida de equipajes; **~gy** *adj* amplio; **~pipes** *npl* gaita

Bahamas [bə'hɑːməz] *npl*: **the ~** las Islas Bahamas

bail [beɪl] *n* fianza ♦ *vt* (*prisoner: gen: grant* ~ *to*) poner en libertad bajo fianza; (*boat: also*: ~ **out**) achicar; **on ~** (*prisoner*) bajo fianza; **to ~ sb out** obtener la libertad de uno bajo fianza; *see also* **bale**

bailiff ['beɪlɪf] *n* alguacil *m*

bait [beɪt] *n* cebo ♦ *vt* poner cebo en; (*tease*) tomar el pelo a

bake [beɪk] *vt* cocer (al horno) ♦ *vi* cocerse; **~d beans** *npl* judías *fpl* en salsa de tomate; **~d potato** *n* patata al horno; **~r** *n* panadero; **~ry** *n* panadería; (*for cakes*) pastelería; **baking** *n* (*act*) amasar *m*; (*batch*) hornada; **baking powder** *n* levadura (*en polvo*)

balance ['bæləns] *n* equilibrio; (COMM: *sum*) balance *m*; (*remainder*) resto; (*scales*) balanza ♦ *vt* equilibrar; (*budget*) nivelar; (*account*) saldar; (*make equal*) equilibrar; ~ **of trade/ payments** balanza de comercio/pagos; **~d** *adj* (*personality, diet*) equilibrado; (*report*) objetivo; ~ **sheet** *n* balance *m*

balcony ['bælkənɪ] *n* (*open*) balcón *m*; (*closed*) galería; (*in theatre*) anfiteatro

bald [bɔːld] *adj* calvo; (*tyre*) liso

bale [beɪl] *n* (AGR) paca, fardo; (*of papers etc*) fajo; ~ **out** *vi* lanzarse en paracaídas

Balearics [bælɪ'ærɪks] *npl*: **the ~** las Baleares

ball [bɔːl] *n* pelota; (*football*) balón *m*; (*of wool, string*) ovillo; (*dance*) baile *m*; **to play ~** (*fig*) cooperar

ballast ['bæləst] *n* lastre *m*

ball bearings *npl* cojinetes *mpl* de bolas

ballerina [bælə'riːnə] *n* bailarina

ballet ['bæleɪ] *n* ballet *m*; ~ **dancer** *n* bailarín/ina *m/f*

balloon [bə'luːn] *n* globo

ballot ['bælət] n votación f; ~ **paper** n papeleta (para votar)

ballpoint (pen) ['bɔːlpɔɪnt-] n bolígrafo

ballroom ['bɔːlrum] n salón m de baile

Baltic ['bɔːltɪk] n: **the ~ (Sea)** el (Mar) Báltico

ban [bæn] n prohibición f, proscripción f ♦ vt prohibir, proscribir

banal [bəˈnɑːl] adj banal, vulgar

banana [bəˈnɑːnə] n plátano (SP), banana (AM)

band [bænd] n grupo; (strip) faja, tira; (stripe) lista; (MUS: jazz) orquesta; (: rock) grupo; (: MIL) banda; ~ **together** vi juntarse, asociarse

bandage ['bændɪdʒ] n venda, vendaje m ♦ vt vendar

Bandaid ® ['bændeɪd] (US) n tirita

bandit ['bændɪt] n bandido

bandy-legged ['bændɪˈlɛɡd] adj estevado

bang [bæŋ] n (of gun, exhaust) estallido, detonación f; (of door) portazo; (blow) golpe m ♦ vt (door) cerrar de golpe; (one's head) golpear ♦ vi estallar; (door) cerrar de golpe

Bangladesh [bɑːŋɡləˈdɛʃ] n Bangladesh m

bangs [bæŋz] (US) npl flequillo

banish ['bænɪʃ] vt desterrar

banister(s) ['bænɪstə(z)] n(pl) barandilla, pasamanos m inv

bank [bæŋk] n (COMM) banco; (of river, lake) ribera, orilla; (of earth) terraplén m ♦ vi (AVIAT) ladearse; ~ **on** vt fus contar con; ~ **account** n cuenta de banco; ~ **card** n tarjeta bancaria; ~**er** n banquero; ~**er's card** (BRIT) n = ~ **card**; B~ **holiday** (BRIT) n día m festivo; ~**ing** n banca; ~**note** n billete m de banco; ~ **rate** n tipo de interés bancario

bankrupt ['bæŋkrʌpt] adj quebrado, insolvente; **to go** ~ hacer bancarrota; **to be** ~ estar en quiebra; ~**cy** n quiebra

bank statement n balance m or detalle m de cuenta

banner ['bænə*] n pancarta

bannister(s) ['bænɪstə(z)] n(pl) = **banister(s)**

baptism ['bæptɪzəm] n bautismo; (act) bautizo

bar [bɑː*] n (pub) bar m; (counter) mostrador m; (rod) barra; (of window, cage) reja; (of soap) pastilla; (of chocolate) tableta; (fig: hindrance) obstáculo; (prohibition) proscripción f; (MUS) barra ♦ vt (road) obstruir; (person) excluir; (activity) prohibir; **the B~** (LAW) la abogacía; **behind ~s** entre rejas; ~ **none** sin excepción

barbaric [bɑːˈbærɪk] adj bárbaro

barbecue ['bɑːbɪkjuː] n barbacoa

barbed wire ['bɑːbd-] n alambre m de púas

barber ['bɑːbə*] n peluquero, barbero

bar code n código de barras

bare [bɛə*] adj desnudo; (trees) sin hojas; (necessities etc) básico ♦ vt desnudar; (teeth) enseñar; ~**back** adv a pelo, sin silla; ~**faced** adj descarado; ~**foot** adj, adv descalzo; ~**ly** adv apenas

bargain ['bɑːɡɪn] n pacto, negocio; (good buy) ganga ♦ vi (to negociar; (haggle) regatear; **into the** ~ además, por añadidura; ~ **for** vt fus: **he got more than he** ~**ed for** le resultó peor de lo que esperaba

barge [bɑːdʒ] n barcaza; ~ **in** vi irrumpir; (interrupt: conversation) interrumpir

bark [bɑːk] n (of tree) corteza; (of dog) ladrido ♦ vi ladrar

barley ['bɑːlɪ] n cebada

barmaid ['bɑːmeɪd] n camarera

barman ['bɑːmən] n camarero, barman m

barn [bɑːn] n granero

barometer [bəˈrɒmɪtə*] n barómetro

baron ['bærən] n barón m; (press ~ etc) magnate m; ~**ess** n baronesa

barracks ['bærəks] npl cuartel m

barrage ['bærɑːʒ] n (MIL) descarga, bombardeo; (dam) presa; (of criticism) lluvia, aluvión m

barrel ['bærəl] n barril m; (of gun) cañón m

barren ['bærən] adj estéril

barricade [bærɪˈkeɪd] n barricada

barrier ['bærɪə*] n barrera

barring ['bɑːrɪŋ] prep excepto, salvo

barrister ['bærɪstə*] (BRIT) n abogado/a

barrow ['bærəʊ] n (cart) carretilla (de mano)

bartender ['bɑːtɛndə*] (US) n camarero, barman m

barter ['bɑːtə*] vt: **to** ~ **sth for sth** trocar algo por algo

base [beɪs] n base f ♦ vt: **to** ~ **sth on** basar or fundar algo en ♦ adj bajo, infame

baseball ['beɪsbɔːl] n béisbol m

basement ['beɪsmənt] n sótano

bases[1] ['beɪsiːz] npl of **basis**

bases[2] ['beɪsɪz] npl of **base**

bash [bæʃ] (inf) vt golpear

bashful ['bæʃful] adj tímido, vergonzoso

basic ['beɪsɪk] adj básico; ~**ally** adv fundamentalmente, en el fondo; (simply) sencillamente; ~**s** npl: **the ~s** los fundamentos

basil ['bæzl] n albahaca

basin ['beɪsn] n cuenco, tazón m; (GEO) cuenca; (also: wash~) lavabo

basis ['beɪsɪs] (pl **bases**) n base f; **on a part-time/trial** ~ a tiempo parcial/a prueba

bask [bɑːsk] vi: **to** ~ **in the sun** tomar el sol

basket ['bɑːskɪt] n cesta, cesto; canasta; ~**ball** n baloncesto

Basque [bæsk] adj, n vasco/a m/f; ~ **Country** n Euskadi m, País m Vasco

bass [beɪs] n (MUS: instrument) bajo; (double ~) contrabajo; (singer) bajo

bassoon [bə'su:n] n fagot m
bastard ['bɑ:stəd] n bastardo; (inf!) hijo de puta (!)
bat [bæt] n (ZOOL) murciélago; (for ball games) palo; (BRIT: for table tennis) pala ♦ vt: **he didn't ~ an eyelid** ni pestañeó
batch [bætʃ] n (of bread) hornada; (of letters etc) lote m
bated ['beɪtɪd] adj: **with ~ breath** sin respirar
bath [bɑ:θ, pl bɑ:ðz] n (action) baño; (~tub) baño (SP), bañera (SP), tina (AM) ♦ vt bañar; **to have a ~** bañarse, tomar un baño; see also **baths**
bathe [beɪð] vi bañarse ♦ vt (wound) lavar; **~r** n bañista m/f
bathing ['beɪðɪŋ] n el bañarse; **~ costume** (US = **suit**) n traje m de baño
bath: **~robe** n (man's) batín m; (woman's) bata; **~room** n (cuarto de) baño; **~s** [bɑ:ðz] npl (also: swimming ~s) piscina; **~ towel** n toalla de baño
baton ['bætən] n (MUS) batuta; (ATHLETICS) testigo; (weapon) porra
batter ['bætə*] vt maltratar; (subj: rain etc) azotar ♦ n masa (para rebozar); **~ed** adj (hat, pan) estropeado
battery ['bætərɪ] n (AUT) batería; (of torch) pila
battle ['bætl] n batalla; (fig) lucha ♦ vi luchar; **~ship** n acorazado
bawl [bɔ:l] vi chillar, gritar; (child) berrear
bay [beɪ] n (GEO) bahía; **B~ of Biscay** ≈ mar Cantábrico; **to hold sb at ~** mantener a alguien a raya; **~ leaf** n hoja de laurel
bay window n ventana savediza
bazaar [bə'zɑ:*] n bazar m; (fete) venta con fines benéficos
B. & B. n abbr (= bed and breakfast) cama y desayuno
BBC n abbr (= British Broadcasting Corporation) cadena de radio y televisión estatal británica
B.C. adv abbr (= before Christ) a. de C.

──────────
KEYWORD
──────────

be [bi:] (pt was, were, pp been) aux vb 1 (with present participle: forming continuous tenses): **what are you doing?** ¿qué estás haciendo?, ¿qué haces?; **they're coming tomorrow** vienen mañana; **I've been waiting for you for hours** llevo horas esperándote
2 (with pp: forming passives) ser (but often replaced by active or reflective constructions): **to ~ murdered** ser asesinado; **the box had been opened** habían abierto la caja; **the thief was nowhere to ~ seen** no se veía al ladrón por ninguna parte
3 (in tag questions): **it was fun, wasn't it?** fue divertido, ¿no? or ¿verdad?; **he's good-**

looking, isn't he? es guapo, ¿no te parece?; **she's back again, is she?** entonces, ¿ha vuelto?
4 (+ to + infin): **the house is to ~ sold** (necessity) hay que vender la casa; (future) van a vender la casa; **he's not to open it** no tiene que abrirlo
♦ vb + complement 1 (with n or num complement, but see also 3, 4, 5 and impers vb below) ser; **he's a doctor** es médico; **2 and 2 are 4** 2 y 2 son 4
2 (with adj complement: expressing permanent or inherent quality) ser; (: expressing state seen as temporary or reversible) estar; **I'm English** soy inglés/esa; **she's tall/pretty** es alta/bonita; **he's young** es joven; **~ careful/good/quiet** ten cuidado/pórtate bien/cállate; **I'm tired** estoy cansado/a; **it's dirty** está sucio/a
3 (of health) estar; **how are you?** ¿cómo estás?; **he's very ill** está muy enfermo; **I'm better now** ya estoy mejor
4 (of age) tener; **how old are you?** ¿cuántos años tienes?; **I'm sixteen (years old)** tengo dieciséis años
5 (cost) costar; ser; **how much was the meal?** ¿cuánto fue or costó la comida?; **that'll ~ £5.75, please** son £5.75, por favor; **this shirt is £17** esta camisa cuesta £17
♦ vi 1 (exist, occur etc) existir, haber; **the best singer that ever was** el mejor cantante que existió jamás; **is there a God?** ¿hay un Dios?, ¿existe Dios?; **~ that as it may** sea como sea; **so ~ it** así sea
2 (referring to place) estar; **I won't ~ here tomorrow** no estaré aquí mañana
3 (referring to movement): **where have you been?** ¿dónde has estado?
♦ impers vb 1 (referring to time): **it's 5 o'clock** son las 5; **it's the 28th of April** estamos a 28 de abril
2 (referring to distance): **it's 10 km to the village** el pueblo está a 10 km
3 (referring to the weather): **it's too hot/cold** hace demasiado calor/frío; **it's windy today** hace viento hoy
4 (emphatic): **it's me** soy yo; **it was Maria who paid the bill** fue María la que pagó la cuenta

beach [bi:tʃ] n playa ♦ vt varar
beacon ['bi:kən] n (lighthouse) faro; (marker) guía
bead [bi:d] n cuenta; (of sweat etc) gota
beak [bi:k] n pico
beaker ['bi:kə*] n vaso de plástico
beam [bi:m] n (ARCH) viga, travesaño; (of light) rayo, haz m de luz ♦ vi brillar; (smile) sonreír
bean [bi:n] n judía; **runner/broad ~**

225 **bear → believe**

habichuela/haba; **coffee ~** grano de café;
~sprouts npl brotes mpl de soja
bear [beə*] (pt **bore**, pp **borne**) n oso ♦ vt
(weight etc) llevar; (cost) pagar;
(responsibility) tener; (endure) soportar,
aguantar; (children) parir, tener; (fruit) dar
♦ vi: **to ~ right/left** torcer a la derecha/
izquierda; **~ out** vt (suspicions) corroborar,
confirmar; (person) dar la razón a; **~ up** vi
(remain cheerful) mantenerse animado
beard [bɪəd] n barba; **~ed** adj con barba,
barbudo
bearer ['beərə*] n portador(a) m/f
bearing ['beərɪŋ] n porte m,
comportamiento; (connection) relación f; **~s**
npl (also: **ball ~s**) cojinetes mpl a bolas; **to
take a ~** tomar marcaciones; **to find one's ~s**
orientarse
beast [bi:st] n bestia; (inf) bruto, salvaje m;
~ly (inf) adj horrible
beat [bi:t] (pt **beat**, pp **beaten**) n (of heart)
latido; (MUS) ritmo, compás m; (of
policeman) ronda ♦ vt pegar, golpear; (eggs)
batir; (defeat: opponent) vencer, derrotar;
(: record) sobrepasar ♦ vi (heart) latir; (drum)
redoblar; (rain, wind) azotar; **off the ~en
track** aislado; **to ~ it** (inf) largarse; **~ off** vt
rechazar; **~ up** vt (attack) dar una paliza a;
~ing n paliza
beautiful ['bju:tɪful] adj precioso, hermoso,
bello; **~ly** adv maravillosamente
beauty ['bju:tɪ] n belleza; **~ salon** n salón m
de belleza; **~ spot** n (TOURISM) lugar m
pintoresco
beaver ['bi:və*] n castor m
became [bɪ'keɪm] pt of **become**
because [bɪ'kɒz] conj porque; **~ of** debido a,
a causa de
beckon ['bekən] vt (also: **~ to**) llamar con
señas
become [bɪ'kʌm] (irreg: like **come**) vt (suit)
favorecer, sentar bien a ♦ vi (+ n) hacerse,
llegar a ser; (+ adj) ponerse, volverse; **to
~ fat** engordar
becoming [bɪ'kʌmɪŋ] adj (behaviour)
decoroso; (clothes) favorecedor(a)
bed [bed] n cama; (of flowers) macizo; (of
coal, clay) capa; (of river) lecho; (of sea)
fondo; **to go to ~** acostarse; **~ and
breakfast** n (place) pensión f; (terms) cama
y desayuno; **~clothes** npl ropa de cama;
~ding n ropa de cama
bedraggled [bɪ'dræɡld] adj (untidy: person)
desastrado; (clothes, hair) desordenado
bed: **~ridden** adj postrado (en cama);
~room n dormitorio; **~side** n: **at the ~side
of** a la cabecera de; **~sit(ter)** (BRIT) n estudio
(SP), suite m (AM); **~spread** n cubrecama m,
colcha; **~time** n hora de acostarse

bee [bi:] n abeja
beech [bi:tʃ] n haya
beef [bi:f] n carne f de vaca; **roast ~** rosbif m;
~burger n hamburguesa; **B~eater** n
alabardero de la Torre de Londres
beehive ['bi:haɪv] n colmena
beeline ['bi:laɪn] n: **to make a ~ for** ir
derecho a
been [bi:n] pp of **be**
beer [bɪə*] n cerveza
beet [bi:t] (US) n (also: **red ~**) remolacha
beetle ['bi:tl] n escarabajo
beetroot ['bi:tru:t] (BRIT) n remolacha
before [bɪ'fɔ:*] prep (of time) antes de; (of
space) delante de ♦ conj antes (de) que
♦ adv antes, anteriormente; delante,
adelante; **~ going** antes de marcharse; **~ she
goes** antes de que se vaya; **the week ~** la
semana anterior; **I've never seen it ~** no lo he
visto nunca; **~hand** adv de antemano, con
anticipación
beg [beɡ] vi pedir limosna ♦ vt pedir, rogar;
(entreat) suplicar; **to ~ sb to do sth** rogar a
uno que haga algo; see also **pardon**
began [bɪ'ɡæn] pt of **begin**
beggar ['beɡə*] n mendigo/a
begin [bɪ'ɡɪn] (pt **began**, pp **begun**) vt, vi
empezar, comenzar; **to ~ doing** or **to do sth**
empezar a hacer algo; **~ner** n principiante
m/f; **~ning** n principio, comienzo
begun [bɪ'ɡʌn] pp of **begin**
behalf [bɪ'hɑ:f] n: **on ~ of** en nombre de, por;
(for benefit of) en beneficio de; **on my/his ~**
por mí/él
behave [bɪ'heɪv] vi (person) portarse,
comportarse; (well: also: **~ o.s.**) portarse
bien; **behaviour** (US **behavior**) n
comportamiento, conducta
behind [bɪ'haɪnd] prep detrás de;
(supporting): **to be ~ sb** apoyar a alguien
♦ adv detrás, por detrás, atrás ♦ n trasero; **to
be ~ (schedule)** ir retrasado; **~ the scenes**
(fig) entre bastidores
behold [bɪ'həʊld] (irreg: like **hold**) vt
contemplar
beige [beɪʒ] adj color beige
Beijing ['beɪ'dʒɪŋ] n Pekín m
being ['bi:ɪŋ] n ser m; (existence): **in ~**
existente; **to come into ~** aparecer
Beirut [beɪ'ru:t] n Beirut m
Belarus [belə'rus] n Bielorrusia
belated [bɪ'leɪtɪd] adj atrasado, tardío
belch [beltʃ] vi eructar ♦ vt (gen: **~ out:** smoke
etc) arrojar
Belgian ['beldʒən] adj, n belga m/f
Belgium ['beldʒəm] n Bélgica
belief [bɪ'li:f] n opinión f; (faith) fe f
believe [bɪ'li:v] vt, vi creer; **to ~ in** creer en;
~r n partidario/a; (REL) creyente m/f, fiel m/f

belittle [bɪˈlɪtl] vt quitar importancia a

bell [bel] n campana; (small) campanilla; (on door) timbre m

belligerent [bɪˈlɪdʒərənt] adj agresivo

bellow [ˈbeləu] vi bramar; (person) rugir

belly [ˈbelɪ] n barriga, panza

belong [bɪˈlɔŋ] vi: to ~ to pertenecer a; (club etc) ser socio de a; this book ~s here este libro va aquí; ~ings npl pertenencias fpl

beloved [bɪˈlʌvɪd] adj querido/a

below [bɪˈləu] prep bajo, debajo de; (less than) inferior a ♦ adv abajo, (por) debajo; see ~ véase más abajo

belt [belt] n cinturón m; (TECH) correa, cinta ♦ vt (thrash) pegar con correa; ~way (US) n (AUT) carretera de circunvalación

bench [bentʃ] n banco; (BRIT: POL): the Government/Opposition ~es (los asientos de) los miembros del Gobierno/de la Oposición; the B~ (LAW: judges) magistratura

bend [bend] (pt, pp bent) vt doblar ♦ vi inclinarse ♦ n (BRIT: in road, river) curva; (in pipe) codo; ~ down vi inclinarse, doblarse; ~ over vi inclinarse

beneath [bɪˈniːθ] prep bajo, debajo de; (unworthy of) indigno de ♦ adv abajo, (por) debajo

benefactor [ˈbenɪfæktə*] n bienhechor m

beneficial [benɪˈfɪʃəl] adj beneficioso

benefit [ˈbenɪfɪt] n beneficio; (allowance of money) subsidio ♦ vt beneficiar ♦ vi: he'll ~ from it le sacará provecho

benevolent [bɪˈnevələnt] adj (person) benévolo

benign [bɪˈnaɪn] adj benigno; (smile) afable

bent [bent] pt, pp of bend ♦ n inclinación f ♦ adj: to be ~ on estar empeñado en

bequest [bɪˈkwest] n legado

bereaved [bɪˈriːvd] npl: the ~ los íntimos de una persona afligidos por su muerte

beret [ˈbereɪ] n boina

Berlin [bəːˈlɪn] n Berlín

berm [bəːm] (US) n (AUT) arcén m

Bermuda [bəːˈmjuːdə] n las Bermudas

berry [ˈberɪ] n baya

berserk [bəˈsəːk] adj: to go ~ perder los estribos

berth [bəːθ] n (bed) litera; (cabin) camarote m; (for ship) amarradero ♦ vi atracar, amarrar

beseech [bɪˈsiːtʃ] (pt, pp besought) vt suplicar

beset [bɪˈset] (pt, pp beset) vt (person) acosar

beside [bɪˈsaɪd] prep junto a, al lado de; to be ~ o.s. with anger estar fuera de sí; that's ~ the point eso no tiene nada que ver; ~s adv además ♦ prep además de

besiege [bɪˈsiːdʒ] vt sitiar; (fig) asediar

best [best] adj (el/la) mejor ♦ adv (lo) mejor; the ~ part of (quantity) la mayor parte de; at ~ en el mejor de los casos; to make the ~ of sth sacar el mejor partido de algo; to do one's ~ hacer todo lo posible; to the ~ of my knowledge que yo sepa; to the ~ of my ability como mejor puedo; ~-before date n fecha de consumo preferente; ~ man n padrino de boda

bestow [bɪˈstəu] vt (title) otorgar

bestseller [ˈbestˈselə*] n éxito de librería, bestseller m

bet [bet] (pt, pp bet or betted) n apuesta ♦ vt: to ~ money on apostar dinero por; to ~ sb sth apostar algo a uno ♦ vi apostar

betray [bɪˈtreɪ] vt traicionar; (trust) faltar a; ~al n traición f

better [ˈbetə*] adj, adv mejor ♦ vt superar ♦ n: to get the ~ of sb quedar por encima de alguien; you had ~ do it más vale que lo hagas; he thought ~ of it cambió de parecer; to get ~ (MED) mejorar(se); ~ off adj mejor; (wealthier) más acomodado

betting [ˈbetɪŋ] n juego, el apostar; ~ shop (BRIT) n agencia de apuestas

between [bɪˈtwiːn] prep entre ♦ adv (time) mientras tanto; (place) en medio

beverage [ˈbevərɪdʒ] n bebida

beware [bɪˈweə*] vi: to ~ (of) tener cuidado (con); "~ of the dog" "perro peligroso"

bewildered [bɪˈwɪldəd] adj aturdido, perplejo

beyond [bɪˈjɔnd] prep más allá de; (past: understanding) fuera de; (after: date) después de, más allá de; (above) superior a ♦ adv (in space) más allá; (in time) posteriormente; ~ doubt fuera de toda duda; ~ repair irreparable

bias [ˈbaɪəs] n (prejudice) prejuicio, pasión f; (preference) predisposición f; ~(s)ed adj parcial

bib [bɪb] n babero

Bible [ˈbaɪbl] n Biblia

bicarbonate of soda [baɪˈkɑːbənɪt-] n bicarbonato sódico

bicker [ˈbɪkə*] vi pelearse

bicycle [ˈbaɪsɪkl] n bicicleta

bid [bɪd] (pt bade or bid, pp bidden or bid) n oferta, postura; (in tender) licitación f; (attempt) tentativa, conato ♦ vi hacer una oferta ♦ vt (offer) ofrecer; to ~ sb good day dar a uno los buenos días; ~der n: the highest ~der el mejor postor; ~ding n (at auction) ofertas fpl

bide [baɪd] vt: to ~ one's time esperar el momento adecuado

bifocals [baɪˈfəuklz] npl gafas fpl (SP) or anteojos mpl (AM) bifocales

big [bɪg] adj grande; (brother, sister) mayor

bigheaded [ˈbɪgˈhedɪd] adj engreído

bigot [ˈbɪgət] n fanático/a, intolerante m/f;

~ed adj fanático, intolerante; **~ry** n
  fanatismo, intolerancia

big top n (at circus) carpa

bike [baɪk] n bici f

bikini [bɪˈkiːnɪ] n bikini m

bilingual [baɪˈlɪŋgwəl] adj bilingüe

bill [bɪl] n cuenta; (invoice) factura; (POL)
  proyecto de ley; (US: banknote) billete m; (of
  bird) pico; (of show) programa m; **"post no
  ~s"** "prohibido fijar carteles"; **to fit or fill the
  ~** (fig) cumplir con los requisitos; **~board**
  (US) n cartelera

billet [ˈbɪlɪt] n alojamiento

billfold [ˈbɪlfəʊld] (US) n cartera

billiards [ˈbɪljədz] n billar m

billion [ˈbɪljən] n (BRIT) billón m (millón de
  millones); (US) mil millones mpl

bimbo [ˈbɪmbəʊ] (inf) n tía buena sin seso

bin [bɪn] n (for rubbish) cubo (SP) or bote m
  (AM) de la basura; (container) recipiente m

bind [baɪnd] (pt, pp **bound**) vt atar; (book)
  encuadernar; (oblige) obligar ♦ n (inf:
  nuisance) lata; **~ing** adj (contract) obligatorio

binge [bɪndʒ] (inf) n: **to go on a ~** ir de
  juerga

bingo [ˈbɪŋgəʊ] n bingo m

binoculars [bɪˈnɔkjʊləz] npl prismáticos mpl

bio... [baɪə] prefix: **~chemistry** n
  bioquímica; **~degradable** [baɪəʊdɪˈgreɪdəbl]
  adj biodegradable; **~graphy** [baɪˈɔgrəfɪ] n
  biografía; **~logical** adj biológico; **~logy**
  [baɪˈɔlədʒɪ] n biología

birch [bəːtʃ] n (tree) abedul m

bird [bəːd] n ave f, pájaro; (BRIT: inf: girl)
  chica; **~'s eye view** n (aerial view) vista de
  pájaro; (overview) visión f de conjunto;
  ~ watcher n ornitólogo/a

Biro ® [ˈbaɪrəʊ] n bolígrafo

birth [bəːθ] n nacimiento; **to give ~ to** parir,
  dar a luz; **~ certificate** n partida de
  nacimiento; **~ control** n (policy) control m
  de natalidad; (methods) métodos mpl
  anticonceptivos; **~day** n cumpleaños m inv
  ♦ cpd (cake, card etc) de cumpleaños; **~
  place** n lugar m de nacimiento; **~ rate** n
  (tasa de) natalidad f

biscuit [ˈbɪskɪt] (BRIT) n galleta, bizcocho (AM)

bisect [baɪˈsɛkt] vt bisecar

bishop [ˈbɪʃəp] n obispo; (CHESS) alfil m

bit [bɪt] pt of **bite** ♦ n trozo, pedazo, pedacito;
  (COMPUT) bit m, bitio; (for horse) freno,
  bocado; **a ~ of** un poco de; **a ~ mad** un poco
  loco; **~ by ~** poco a poco

bitch [bɪtʃ] n perra; (inf!: woman) zorra (!)

bite [baɪt] (pt **bit**, pp **bitten**) vt, vi morder;
  (insect etc) picar ♦ n (insect ~) picadura;
  (mouthful) bocado; **to ~ one's nails** comerse
  las uñas; **let's have a ~ (to eat)** (inf) vamos a
  comer algo

bitter [ˈbɪtə*] adj amargo; (wind) cortante,
  penetrante; (battle) encarnizado ♦ n (BRIT:
  beer) cerveza típica británica a base de lúpulos;
  ~ness n lo amargo, amargura; (anger)
  rencor m

bizarre [bɪˈzɑː*] adj raro, extraño

black [blæk] adj negro; (tea, coffee) solo ♦ n
  color m negro; (person): **B~** negro/a ♦ vt
  (BRIT: INDUSTRY) boicotear; **to give sb a ~ eye**
  ponerle a uno el ojo morado; **~ and blue**
  (bruised) amoratado; **to be in the ~** (bank
  account) estar en números negros; **~berry** n
  zarzamora; **~bird** n mirlo; **~board** n pizarra;
  ~ coffee n café m solo; **~currant** n grosella
  negra; **~en** vt (fig) desacreditar; **~ ice** n
  hielo invisible en la carretera; **~leg** (BRIT) n
  esquirol m, rompehuelgas m inv; **~list** n lista
  negra; **~mail** n chantaje m ♦ vt chantajear;
  ~ market n mercado negro; **~out** n (MIL)
  oscurecimiento; (power cut) apagón m; (TV,
  RADIO) interrupción f de programas; (fainting)
  desvanecimiento; **B~ Sea** n: **the B~ Sea** el
  Mar Negro; **~ sheep** n (fig) oveja negra;
  ~smith n herrero; **~ spot** n (AUT) lugar m
  peligroso; (for unemployment etc) punto
  negro

bladder [ˈblædə*] n vejiga

blade [bleɪd] n hoja; (of propeller) paleta; **a
  ~ of grass** una brizna de hierba

blame [bleɪm] n culpa ♦ vt: **to ~ sb for sth**
  echar a uno la culpa de algo; **to be to ~** tener
  la culpa de

bland [blænd] adj (music, taste) soso

blank [blæŋk] adj en blanco; (look) sin
  expresión ♦ n (of memory): **my mind is a ~**
  no puedo recordar nada; (on form) blanco,
  espacio en blanco; (cartridge) cartucho sin
  bala or de fogueo; **~ cheque** n cheque m en
  blanco

blanket [ˈblæŋkɪt] n manta (SP), cobija (AM);
  (of snow) capa; (of fog) manto

blare [blɛə*] vi sonar estrepitosamente

blasé [ˈblɑːzeɪ] adj hastiado

blast [blɑːst] n (of wind) ráfaga, soplo; (of
  explosive) explosión f ♦ vt (blow up) volar;
  ~-off n (SPACE) lanzamiento

blatant [ˈbleɪtənt] adj descarado

blaze [bleɪz] n (fire) fuego; (fig: of colour)
  despliegue m; (: of glory) esplendor m ♦ vi
  arder en llamas; (fig) brillar ♦ vt: **to ~ a trail**
  (fig) abrir (un) camino; **in a ~ of publicity** con
  gran publicidad

blazer [ˈbleɪzə*] n chaqueta de uniforme de
  colegial o de socio de club

bleach [bliːtʃ] n (also: household ~) lejía ♦ vt
  blanquear; **~ed** adj (hair) teñido de (rubio);
  ~ers (US) npl (SPORT) gradas fpl al sol

bleak [bliːk] adj (countryside) desierto;
  (prospect) poco prometedor(a); (weather)

crudo; (smile) triste

bleat [bli:t] vi balar

bleed [bli:d] (pt, pp **bled**) vt, vi sangrar; **my nose is ~ing** me está sangrando la nariz

bleeper ['bli:pə*] n busca m

blemish ['blemiʃ] n marca, mancha; (on reputation) tacha

blend [blend] n mezcla ♦ vt mezclar; (colours etc) combinar, mezclar ♦ vi (colours etc: also: ~ in) combinarse, mezclarse

bless [bles] (pt, pp **blessed** or **blest**) vt bendecir; **~ you!** (after sneeze) ¡Jesús!; **~ing** n (approval) aprobación f; (godsend) don m del cielo, bendición f; (advantage) beneficio, ventaja

blew [blu:] pt of **blow**

blind [blaɪnd] adj ciego; (fig): **~ (to)** ciego (a) ♦ n (for window) persiana ♦ vt cegar; (dazzle) deslumbrar; (deceive): **to ~ sb to ...** cegar a uno a ...; **the ~** npl los ciegos; **~ alley** n callejón m sin salida; **~ corner** (BRIT) n esquina escondida; **~fold** n venda ♦ adv con los ojos vendados ♦ vt vendar los ojos a; **~ly** adv a ciegas, ciegamente; **~ness** n ceguera; **~ spot** n (AUT) ángulo ciego

blink [blɪŋk] vi parpadear, pestañear; (light) oscilar; **~ers** npl anteojeras fpl

bliss [blɪs] n felicidad f

blister ['blɪstə*] n ampolla ♦ vi (paint) ampollarse

blizzard ['blɪzəd] n ventisca

bloated ['bləʊtɪd] adj hinchado; (person: full) ahíto

blob [blɒb] n (drop) gota; (indistinct object) bulto

bloc [blɒk] n (POL) bloque m

block [blɒk] n bloque m; (in pipes) obstáculo; (of buildings) manzana (SP), cuadra (AM) ♦ vt obstruir, cerrar; (progress) estorbar; **~ of flats** (BRIT) bloque m de pisos; **mental ~** bloqueo mental; **~ade** [-'keɪd] n bloqueo ♦ vt bloquear; **~age** n estorbo, obstrucción f; **~buster** n (book) bestseller m; (film) éxito de público; **~ letters** npl letras fpl de molde

bloke [bləʊk] (BRIT: inf) n tipo, tío

blond(e) [blɒnd] adj, n rubio/a m/f

blood [blʌd] n sangre f; **~ donor** n donante m/f de sangre; **~ group** n grupo sanguíneo; **~hound** n sabueso; **~ poisoning** n envenenamiento de la sangre; **~ pressure** n presión f sanguínea; **~shed** n derramamiento de sangre; **~shot** adj inyectado en sangre; **~stream** n corriente f sanguínea; **~ test** n análisis m inv de sangre; **~thirsty** adj sanguinario; **~ vessel** n vaso sanguíneo; **~y** adj sangriento; (nose etc) lleno de sangre; (BRIT: inf!): **this ~y...** este condenado o puñetero ... (!) ♦ adv: **~y strong/good** (BRIT: inf!) terriblemente fuerte/bueno; **~y-minded**

(BRIT: inf) adj puñetero (!)

bloom [blu:m] n flor f ♦ vi florecer

blossom ['blɒsəm] n flor f ♦ vi (also fig) florecer

blot [blɒt] n borrón m; (fig) mancha ♦ vt (stain) manchar; **~ out** vt (view) tapar

blotchy ['blɒtʃɪ] adj (complexion) lleno de manchas

blotting paper ['blɒtɪŋ-] n papel m secante

blouse [blauz] n blusa

blow [bləʊ] (pt **blew**, pp **blown**) n golpe m; (with sword) espadazo ♦ vi soplar; (dust, sand etc) volar; (fuse) fundirse ♦ vt (subj: wind) llevarse; (fuse) quemar; (instrument) tocar; **to ~ one's nose** sonarse; **~ away** vi llevarse, arrancar; **~ down** vt derribar; **~ off** vt arrebatar; **~ out** vi apagarse; **~ over** vi amainar; **~ up** vi estallar ♦ vt volar; (tyre) inflar; (PHOT) ampliar; **~-dry** n moldeado (con secador) n; **~lamp** (BRIT) n soplete m, lámpara de soldar; **~-out** n (of tyre) pinchazo; **~torch** n = **~lamp**

blue [blu:] adj azul; (depressed) deprimido; **~ film/joke** película/chiste m verde; **out of the ~** (fig) de repente; **~bell** n campanilla, campánula azul; **~bottle** n moscarda, mosca azul; **~print** n (fig) anteproyecto

bluff [blʌf] vi tirarse un farol, farolear ♦ n farol m; **to call sb's ~** coger a uno la palabra

blunder ['blʌndə*] n patinazo, metedura de pata ♦ vi cometer un error, meter la pata

blunt [blʌnt] adj (pencil) despuntado; (knife) desafilado, romo; (person) franco, directo

blur [blə:*] n (shape): **to become a ~** hacerse borroso ♦ vt (vision) enturbiar; (distinction) borrar

blush [blʌʃ] vi ruborizarse, ponerse colorado ♦ n rubor m

blustery ['blʌstərɪ] adj (weather) tempestuoso, tormentoso

boar [bɔ:*] n verraco, cerdo

board [bɔ:d] n (card~) cartón m; (wooden) tabla, tablero; (on wall) tablón m; (for chess etc) tablero; (committee) junta, consejo; (in firm) mesa or junta directiva; (NAUT, AVIAT): **on ~** a bordo ♦ vt (ship) embarcarse en; (train) subir a; **full ~** (BRIT) pensión completa; **half ~** (BRIT) media pensión; **to go by the ~** (fig) ser abandonado or olvidado; **~ up** vt (door) tapiar; **~ and lodging** n casa y comida; **~er** n (SCOL) interno/a; **~ing card** (BRIT) n tarjeta de embarque; **~ing house** n casa de huéspedes; **~ing pass** (US) n = **~ing card**; **~ing school** n internado; **~ room** n sala de juntas

boast [bəʊst] vi: **to ~ (about or of)** alardear (de)

boat [bəʊt] n barco, buque m; (small) barca, bote m

bob [bɔb] vi (also: ~ up and down) menearse, balancearse; ~ up vi (re)aparecer de repente

bobby ['bɔbɪ] (BRIT: inf) n poli m

bobsleigh ['bɔbsleɪ] n bob m

bode [bəud] vi: to ~ well/ill (for) ser prometedor/poco prometedor (para)

bodily ['bɔdɪlɪ] adj corporal ♦ adv (move: person) en peso

body ['bɔdɪ] n cuerpo; (corpse) cadáver m; (of car) caja, carrocería; (fig: group) grupo; (: organization) organismo; ~-building n culturismo; ~guard n guardaespaldas m inv; ~work n carrocería

bog [bɔg] n pantano, ciénaga ♦ vt: to get ~ged down (fig) empantanarse, atascarse

bogus ['bəugəs] adj falso, fraudulento

boil [bɔɪl] vt (water) hervir; (eggs) pasar por agua, cocer ♦ vi hervir; (fig: with anger) estar furioso; (: with heat) asfixiarse ♦ n (MED) furúnculo, divieso; to come to the ~, to come to a ~ (US) comenzar a hervir; to ~ down to (fig) reducirse a; ~ over vi salirse, rebosar; (anger etc) llegar al colmo; ~ed egg n huevo cocido (SP) or pasado (AM); ~ed potatoes npl patatas fpl (SP) or papas fpl (AM) hervidas; ~er n caldera; ~er suit (BRIT) n mono; ~ing point n punto de ebullición

boisterous ['bɔɪstərəs] adj (noisy) bullicioso; (excitable) exuberante; (crowd) tumultuoso

bold [bəuld] adj valiente, audaz; (pej) descarado; (colour) llamativo

Bolivia [bə'lɪvɪə] n Bolivia; ~n adj, n boliviano/a m/f

bollard ['bɔlɑd] (BRIT) n (AUT) poste m

bolt [bəult] n (lock) cerrojo; (with nut) perno, tornillo ♦ adv: ~ upright rígido, erguido ♦ vt (door) echar el cerrojo a; (also: ~ together) sujetar con tornillos; (food) engullir ♦ vi fugarse; (horse) desbocarse

bomb [bɔm] n bomba ♦ vt bombardear; ~ disposal n desmontaje m de explosivos; ~er n (AVIAT) bombardero; ~shell n (fig) bomba

bond [bɔnd] n (promise) fianza; (FINANCE) bono; (link) vínculo, lazo; (COMM): in ~ en depósito bajo fianza

bondage ['bɔndɪdʒ] n esclavitud f

bone [bəun] n hueso; (of fish) espina ♦ vt deshuesar; quitar las espinas a; ~ idle adj gandul; ~ marrow n médula

bonfire ['bɔnfaɪə*] n hoguera, fogata

bonnet ['bɔnɪt] n gorra; (BRIT: of car) capó m

bonus ['bəunəs] n (payment) paga extraordinaria, plus m; (fig) bendición f

bony ['bəunɪ] adj (arm, face) huesudo; (MED: tissue) óseo; (meat) lleno de huesos; (fish) lleno de espinas

boo [bu:] excl ¡uh! ♦ vt abuchear, rechiflar

booby trap ['bu:bɪ-] n trampa explosiva

book [buk] n libro; (of tickets) taco; (of stamps etc) librito ♦ vt (ticket) sacar; (seat, room) reservar; ~s npl (COMM) cuentas fpl, contabilidad f; ~case n librería, estante m para libros; ~ing office n (BRIT: RAIL) despacho de billetes (SP) or boletos (AM); (THEATRE) taquilla (SP), boletería (AM); ~keeping n contabilidad f; ~let n folleto; ~maker n corredor m de apuestas; ~seller n librero; ~shop, ~ store n librería

boom [bu:m] n (noise) trueno, estampido; (in prices etc) alza rápida; (ECON, in population) boom m ♦ vi (cannon) hacer gran estruendo, retumbar; (ECON) estar en alza

boon [bu:n] n favor m, beneficio

boost [bu:st] n estímulo, empuje m ♦ vt estimular, empujar; ~er n (MED) reinyección f

boot [bu:t] n bota; (BRIT: of car) maleta, maletero ♦ vt (COMPUT) arrancar; to ~ (in addition) además, por añadidura

booth [bu:ð] n (telephone ~, voting ~) cabina

booze [bu:z] (inf) n bebida

border ['bɔ:də*] n borde m, margen m; (of a country) frontera; (for flowers) arriate m ♦ vt (road) bordear; (another country: also: ~ on) lindar con; B~s n: the B~s región fronteriza entre Escocia e Inglaterra; ~ on vt fus (insanity etc) rayar en; ~line n: on the ~line en el límite; ~line case n caso dudoso

bore [bɔ:*] pt of bear ♦ vt (hole) hacer un agujero en; (well) perforar; (person) aburrir ♦ n (person) pelmazo, pesado; (of gun) calibre m; to be ~d estar aburrido; ~dom n aburrimiento

boring ['bɔ:rɪŋ] adj aburrido

born [bɔ:n] adj: to be ~ nacer; I was ~ in 1960 nací en 1960

borne [bɔ:n] pp of bear

borough ['bʌrə] n municipio

borrow ['bɔrəu] vt: to ~ sth (from sb) tomar algo prestado (a alguien)

Bosnia(-Herzegovina) ['bɔsnɪə(hɜ:zə'gəuvɪnə)] n Bosnia (-Herzegovina)

bosom ['buzəm] n pecho

boss [bɔs] n jefe m ♦ vt (also: ~ about or around) mangonear; ~y adj mandón/ona

bosun ['bəusn] n contramaestre m

botany ['bɔtənɪ] n botánica

botch [bɔtʃ] vt (also: ~ up) arruinar, estropear

both [bəuθ] adj, pron ambos/as, los/las dos; ~ of us went, we ~ went fuimos los dos, ambos fuimos ♦ adv: ~ A and B tanto A como B

bother ['bɔðə*] vt (worry) preocupar; (disturb) molestar, fastidiar ♦ vi (also: ~ o.s.) molestarse ♦ n (trouble) dificultad f; (nuisance) molestia, lata; to ~ doing tomarse la molestia de hacer

bottle ['bɔtl] n botella; (*small*) frasco; (*baby's*) biberón m ♦ vt embotellar; ~ **up** vt suprimir; ~ **bank** n contenedor m de vidrio; **~neck** n (AUT) embotellamiento; (*in supply*) obstáculo; **~-opener** n abrebotellas m inv

bottom ['bɔtəm] n (*of box, sea*) fondo; (*buttocks*) trasero, culo; (*of page*) pie m; (*of list*) final m; (*of class*) último/a ♦ adj (*lowest*) más bajo; (*last*) último

bough [bau] n rama

bought [bɔːt] pt, pp of **buy**

boulder ['bəuldə*] n canto rodado

bounce [bauns] vi (*ball*) (re)botar; (*cheque*) ser rechazado ♦ vt hacer (re)botar ♦ n (*rebound*) (re)bote m; **~r** (*inf*) n gorila m (*que echa a los alborotadores de un bar, club etc*)

bound [baund] pt, pp of **bind** ♦ n (*leap*) salto; (*gen pl: limit*) límite m ♦ vi (*leap*) saltar ♦ vt (*border*) rodear ♦ adj: **~ by** rodeado de; **to be ~ to do sth** (*obliged*) tener el deber de hacer algo; **he's ~ to come** es seguro que vendrá; **out of ~s** prohibido el paso; **~ for** con destino a

boundary ['baundrɪ] n límite m

bouquet ['bukeɪ] n (*of flowers*) ramo

bourgeois ['buəʒwaː] adj burgués/esa m/f

bout [baut] n (*of malaria etc*) ataque m; (*of activity*) período; (*BOXING etc*) combate m, encuentro

bow¹ [bəu] n (*knot*) lazo; (*weapon, MUS*) arco

bow² [bau] n (*of the head*) reverencia; (NAUT: *also: ~s*) proa ♦ vi inclinarse, hacer una reverencia; (*yield*): **to ~ to** or **before** ceder ante, someterse a

bowels [bauəlz] npl intestinos mpl, vientre m; (*fig*) entrañas fpl

bowl [bəul] n tazón m, cuenco; (*ball*) bola ♦ vi (CRICKET) arrojar la pelota; *see also* **bowls**

bow-legged ['bəu'legɪd] adj estevado

bowler ['bəulə*] n (CRICKET) lanzador m (de la pelota); (BRIT: *also: ~ hat*) hongo, bombín m

bowling ['bəulɪŋ] n (*game*) bochas fpl, bolos mpl; **~ alley** n bolera; **~ green** n pista para bochas

bowls [bəulz] n juego de las bochas, bolos mpl

bow tie ['bəu-] n corbata de lazo, pajarita

box [bɔks] n (*also: cardboard ~*) caja, cajón m; (THEATRE) palco ♦ vt encajonar ♦ vi (SPORT) boxear; **~er** ['bɔksə*] n (*person*) boxeador m; **~ing** ['bɔksɪŋ] n (SPORT) boxeo; **B~ing Day** (BRIT) n día en que se dan los aguinaldos, 26 de diciembre; **~ing gloves** npl guantes mpl de boxeo; **~ing ring** n ring m, cuadrilátero; **~ office** n taquilla (SP), boletería (AM); **~room** n trastero

boy [bɔɪ] n (*young*) niño; (*older*) muchacho, chico; (*son*) hijo

boycott ['bɔɪkɔt] n boicot m ♦ vt boicotear

boyfriend ['bɔɪfrend] n novio

boyish ['bɔɪɪʃ] adj juvenil; (*girl*) con aspecto de muchacho

B.R. n abbr (*formerly = British Rail*) ≈ RENFE f (SP)

bra [braː] n sostén m, sujetador m

brace [breɪs] n (BRIT: *also: ~s: on teeth*) corrector m, aparato; (*tool*) berbiquí m ♦ vt (*knees, shoulders*) tensionar; **~s** npl (BRIT) tirantes mpl; **to ~ o.s.** (*fig*) prepararse

bracelet ['breɪslɪt] n pulsera, brazalete m

bracing ['breɪsɪŋ] adj vigorizante, tónico

bracket ['brækɪt] n (TECH) soporte m, puntal m; (*group*) clase f, categoría; (*also: brace ~*) soporte m, abrazadera; (*also: round ~*) paréntesis m inv; (*also: square ~*) corchete m ♦ vt (*word etc*) poner entre paréntesis

brag [bræg] vi jactarse

braid [breɪd] n (*trimming*) galón m; (*of hair*) trenza

brain [breɪn] n cerebro; **~s** npl sesos mpl; **she's got ~s** es muy lista; **~wash** vt lavar el cerebro; **~wave** n idea luminosa; **~y** adj muy inteligente

braise [breɪz] vt cocer a fuego lento

brake [breɪk] n (*on vehicle*) freno ♦ vi frenar; **~ light** n luz f de frenado

bran [bræn] n salvado

branch [braːntʃ] n rama; (COMM) sucursal f; **~ out** vi (*fig*) extenderse

brand [brænd] n marca; (*fig: type*) tipo ♦ vt (*cattle*) marcar con hierro candente; **~-new** adj flamante, completamente nuevo

brandy ['brændɪ] n coñac m

brash [bræʃ] adj (*forward*) descarado

brass [braːs] n latón m; **the ~** (MUS) los cobres; **~ band** n banda de metal

brat [bræt] (*pej*) n mocoso/a

brave [breɪv] adj valiente, valeroso ♦ vt (*face up to*) desafiar; **~ry** n valor m, valentía

brawl [brɔːl] n pelea, reyerta

brazen ['breɪzn] adj descarado, cínico ♦ vt: **to ~ it out** echarle cara

Brazil [brə'zɪl] n (el) Brasil; **~ian** adj, n brasileño/a m/f

breach [briːtʃ] vt abrir brecha en ♦ n (*gap*) brecha; (*breaking*): **~ of contract** infracción f de contrato; **~ of the peace** perturbación f del órden público

bread [bred] n pan m; **~ and butter** n pan con mantequilla; (*fig*) pan (de cada día); **~bin** n panera; **~crumbs** npl migajas fpl; (CULIN) pan rallado; **~line** n: **on the ~line** en la miseria

breadth [bretθ] n anchura; (*fig*) amplitud f

breadwinner ['bredwɪnə*] n sustento m de la familia

break [breɪk] (*pt* **broke**, *pp* **broken**) vt romper;

(*promise*) faltar a; (*law*) violar, infringir; (*record*) batir ♦ *vi* romperse, quebrarse; (*storm*) estallar; (*weather*) cambiar; (*dawn*) despuntar; (*news etc*) darse a conocer ♦ *n* (*gap*) abertura; (*fracture*) fractura; (*time*) intervalo; (: *at school*) (*período de*) recreo; (*chance*) oportunidad *f*; **to ~ the news to sb** comunicar la noticia a uno; **~ down** *vt* (*figures, data*) analizar, descomponer ♦ *vi* (*machine*) estropearse; (*AUT*) averiarse; (*person*) romper a llorar; (*talks*) fracasar; **~ even** *vi* cubrir los gastos; **~ free** or **loose** *vi* escaparse; **~ in** *vt* (*horse etc*) domar ♦ *vi* (*burglar*) forzar una entrada; (*interrupt*) interrumpir; **~ into** *vt fus* (*house*) forzar; **~ off** *vi* (*speaker*) pararse, detenerse; (*branch*) partir; **~ open** *vt* (*door etc*) abrir por la fuerza, forzar; **~ out** *vi* estallar; (*prisoner*) escaparse; **to ~ out in spots** salirle a uno granos; **~ up** *vi* (*ship*) hacerse pedazos; (*crowd, meeting*) disolverse; (*marriage*) deshacerse; (*SCOL*) terminar (el curso) ♦ *vt* (*rocks etc*) partir; (*journey*) partir; (*fight etc*) acabar con; **~age** *n* rotura; **~down** *n* (*AUT*) avería; (*in communications*) interrupción *f*; (*MED: also: nervous ~down*) colapso, crisis *f* nerviosa; (*of marriage, talks*) fracaso; (*of statistics*) análisis *m inv*; **~down van** (*BRIT*) *n* (*camión m*) grúa; **~er** *n* (*ola*) rompiente *f*

breakfast ['brɛkfəst] *n* desayuno

break: **~-in** *n* robo con allanamiento de morada; **~ing and entering** *n* (*LAW*) violación *f* de domicilio, allanamiento de morada; **~through** *n* (*also fig*) avance *m*; **~water** *n* rompeolas *m inv*

breast [brɛst] *n* (*of woman*) pecho, seno; (*chest*) pecho; (*of bird*) pechuga; **~-feed** (*irreg: like feed*) *vt*, *vi* amamantar, criar a los pechos; **~-stroke** *n* braza (de pecho)

breath [brɛθ] *n* aliento, respiración *f*; **to take a deep ~** respirar hondo; **out of ~** sin aliento, sofocado

Breathalyser ® ['brɛθəlaɪzə*] (*BRIT*) *n* alcoholímetro *m*

breathe [briːð] *vt, vi* respirar; **~ in** *vt, vi* aspirar; **~ out** *vt, vi* espirar; **~r** *n* respiro; **breathing** *n* respiración *f*

breath: **~less** *adj* sin aliento, jadeante; **~taking** *adj* imponente, pasmoso

breed [briːd] (*pt, pp bred*) *vt* criar ♦ *vi* reproducirse, procrear ♦ *n* (*ZOOL*) raza, casta; (*type*) tipo; **~ing** *n* (*of person*) educación *f*

breeze [briːz] *n* brisa

breezy ['briːzɪ] *adj* de mucho viento, ventoso; (*person*) despreocupado

brevity ['brevɪtɪ] *n* brevedad *f*

brew [bruː] *vt* (*tea*) hacer; (*beer*) elaborar ♦ *vi* (*fig: trouble*) prepararse; (*storm*) amenazar; **~ery** *n* fábrica de cerveza,

cervecería

bribe [braɪb] *n* soborno ♦ *vt* sobornar, cohechar; **~ry** *n* soborno, cohecho

bric-a-brac ['brɪkəbræk] *n inv* baratijas *fpl*

brick [brɪk] *n* ladrillo; **~layer** *n* albañil *m*

bridal ['braɪdl] *adj* nupcial

bride [braɪd] *n* novia; **~groom** *n* novio; **~smaid** *n* dama de honor

bridge [brɪdʒ] *n* puente *m*; (*NAUT*) puente *m* de mando; (*of nose*) caballete *m*; (*CARDS*) bridge *m* ♦ *vt* (*fig*): **to ~ a gap** llenar un vacío

bridle ['braɪdl] *n* brida, freno; **~ path** *n* camino de herradura

brief [briːf] *adj* breve, corto ♦ *n* (*LAW*) escrito; (*task*) cometido, encargo ♦ *vt* informar; **~s** *npl* (*for men*) calzoncillos *mpl*; (*for women*) bragas *fpl*; **~case** *n* cartera (*SP*), portafolio (*AM*); **~ing** *n* (*PRESS*) informe *m*; **~ly** *adv* (*glance*) fugazmente; (*say*) en pocas palabras

brigadier [brɪgə'dɪə*] *n* general *m* de brigada

bright [braɪt] *adj* brillante; (*room*) luminoso; (*day*) de sol; (*person: clever*) listo, inteligente; (: *lively*) alegre; (*colour*) vivo; (*future*) prometedor(a); **~en** (*also: ~en up*) *vt* (*room*) hacer más alegre; (*event*) alegrar ♦ *vi* (*weather*) despejarse; (*person*) animarse, alegrarse; (*prospects*) mejorar

brilliance ['brɪljəns] *n* brillo, brillantez *f*; (*of talent etc*) brillantez

brilliant ['brɪljənt] *adj* brillante; (*inf*) fenomenal

brim [brɪm] *n* borde *m*; (*of hat*) ala

brine [braɪn] *n* (*CULIN*) salmuera

bring [brɪŋ] (*pt, pp brought*) *vt* (*thing, person: with you*) traer; (: *to sb*) llevar, conducir; (*trouble, satisfaction*) causar; **~ about** *vt* ocasionar, producir; **~ back** *vt* volver a traer; (*return*) devolver; **~ down** *vt* (*government, plane*) derribar; (*price*) rebajar; **~ forward** *vt* adelantar; **~ off** *vt* (*task, plan*) lograr, conseguir; **~ out** *vt* sacar; (*book etc*) publicar; (*meaning*) subrayar; **~ round** *vt* (*unconscious person*) hacer volver en sí; **~ up** *vt* subir; (*person*) educar, criar; (*question*) sacar a colación; (*food: vomit*) devolver, vomitar

brink [brɪŋk] *n* borde *m*

brisk [brɪsk] *adj* (*abrupt: tone*) brusco; (*person*) enérgico, vigoroso; (*pace*) rápido; (*trade*) activo

bristle ['brɪsl] *n* cerda ♦ *vi*: **to ~ in anger** temblar de rabia

Britain ['brɪtən] *n* (*also: Great ~*) Gran Bretaña

British ['brɪtɪʃ] *adj* británico ♦ *npl*: **the ~** los británicos; **~ Isles** *npl*: **the ~ Isles** las Islas Británicas; **~ Rail** *n* ≈ RENFE *f* (*SP*)

Briton ['brɪtən] *n* británico/a

brittle ['brɪtl] *adj* quebradizo, frágil

broach [brəʊtʃ] vt (subject) abordar
broad [brɔːd] adj (range) amplio;
(smile) abierto; (general: outlines etc) general;
(accent) cerrado; **in ~ daylight** en pleno día;
~cast (irreg: like cast) n emisión f ♦ vt
(RADIO) emitir; (TV) transmitir ♦ vi emitir;
transmitir; **~en** vt ampliar ♦ vi ensancharse;
to ~en one's mind hacer más tolerante a uno;
~ly adv en general; **~-minded** adj tolerante,
liberal
broccoli [ˈbrɔkəlɪ] n brécol m
brochure [ˈbrəʊʃjʊə*] n folleto
broil [brɔɪl] vt (CULIN) asar a la parrilla
broke [brəʊk] pt of break ♦ adj (inf) pelado,
sin blanca
broken [ˈbrəʊkən] pp of break ♦ adj roto;
(machine: also: ~ down) averiado; **~ leg**
pierna rota; **in ~ English** en un inglés
imperfecto; **~-hearted** adj con el corazón
partido
broker [ˈbrəʊkə*] n agente m/f, bolsista m/f;
(insurance ~) agente de seguros
brolly [ˈbrɔlɪ] (BRIT: inf) n paraguas m inv
bronchitis [brɔŋˈkaɪtɪs] n bronquitis f
bronze [brɔnz] n bronce m
brooch [brəʊtʃ] n prendedor m, broche m
brood [bruːd] n camada, cría ♦ vi (person)
dejarse obsesionar
broom [brum] n escoba; (BOT) retama
Bros. abbr (= Brothers) Hnos
broth [brɔθ] n caldo
brothel [ˈbrɔθl] n burdel m
brother [ˈbrʌðə*] n hermano; **~-in-law** n
cuñado
brought [brɔːt] pt, pp of bring
brow [braʊ] n (forehead) frente m; (eye~)
ceja; (of hill) cumbre f
brown [braʊn] adj (colour) marrón; (hair)
castaño; (tanned) bronceado, moreno ♦ n
(colour) color m marrón or pardo ♦ vt (CULIN)
dorar; **~ bread** n pan integral
Brownie [ˈbraʊnɪ] n niña exploradora; **b~**
(US: cake) pastel de chocolate con nueces
brown paper n papel m de estraza
brown sugar n azúcar m terciado
browse [braʊz] vi (through book) hojear;
(in shop) mirar; **~r** n (COMPUT) navegador
m
bruise [bruːz] n cardenal m (SP), moretón m
(AM) ♦ vt magullar
brunch [brʌntʃ] n desayuno-almuerzo
brunette [bruːˈnet] n morena
brunt [brʌnt] n: **to bear the ~ of** llevar el peso
de
brush [brʌʃ] n cepillo; (for painting, shaving
etc) brocha; (artist's) pincel m; (with police
etc) roce m ♦ vt (sweep) barrer; (groom)
cepillar; (also: ~ against) rozar al pasar;
~ aside vt rechazar, no hacer caso a; **~ up**

vt (knowledge) repasar, refrescar; **~wood** n
(sticks) leña
Brussels [ˈbrʌslz] n Bruselas; **~ sprout** n col
f de Bruselas
brute [bruːt] n bruto; (person) bestia ♦ adj:
by ~ force a fuerza bruta
B.Sc. abbr (= Bachelor of Science) licenciado en
Ciencias
BSE n abbr (= bovine spongiform en-
cephalopathy) encefalopatía espongiforme
bovina
bubble [ˈbʌbl] n burbuja ♦ vi burbujear,
borbotar; **~ bath** n espuma para el baño;
~ gum n chicle m de globo
buck [bʌk] n (rabbit) conejo macho; (deer)
gamo; (US: inf) dólar m ♦ vi corcovear; **to
pass the ~ (to sb)** echar (a uno) el muerto;
~ up vi (cheer up) animarse, cobrar ánimo
bucket [ˈbʌkɪt] n cubo, balde m
buckle [ˈbʌkl] n hebilla ♦ vt abrochar con
hebilla ♦ vi combarse
bud [bʌd] n (of plant) brote m, yema; (of
flower) capullo ♦ vi brotar, echar brotes
Buddhism [ˈbʊdɪzm] n Budismo
budding [ˈbʌdɪŋ] adj en ciernes, en embrión
buddy [ˈbʌdɪ] (US) n compañero, compinche
m
budge [bʌdʒ] vt mover; (fig) hacer ceder ♦ vi
moverse, ceder
budgerigar [ˈbʌdʒərɪgɑː*] n periquito
budget [ˈbʌdʒɪt] n presupuesto ♦ vi: **to ~ for**
sth presupuestar algo
budgie [ˈbʌdʒɪ] n = budgerigar
buff [bʌf] adj (colour) color de ante ♦ n (inf:
enthusiast) entusiasta m/f
buffalo [ˈbʌfələʊ] (pl ~ or ~es) n (BRIT)
búfalo; (US: bison) bisonte m
buffer [ˈbʌfə*] n (COMPUT) memoria
intermedia; (RAIL) tope m
buffet1 [ˈbʊfeɪ] n (BRIT: in station) bar m,
cafetería; (food) buffet m; **~ car** (BRIT) n
(RAIL) coche-comedor m
buffet2 [ˈbʌfɪt] vt golpear
bug [bʌg] n (esp US: insect) bicho, sabandija;
(COMPUT) error m; (germ) microbio, bacilo;
(spy device) micrófono oculto ♦ vt (inf:
annoy) fastidiar; (room) poner micrófono
oculto en
buggy [ˈbʌgɪ] n cochecito de niño
bugle [ˈbjuːgl] n corneta, clarín m
build [bɪld] (pt, pp built) n (of person) tipo
♦ vt construir, edificar; **~ up** vt (morale,
forces, production) acrecentar; (stocks)
acumular; **~er** n (contractor) contratista m/f;
~ing n construcción f; (structure) edificio;
~ing society (BRIT) n sociedad f inmobiliaria
built [bɪlt] pt, pp of build ♦ adj: **~-in** (wardrobe
etc) empotrado; **~-up area** n zona
urbanizada

bulb [bʌlb] n (BOT) bulbo; (ELEC) bombilla (SP), foco (AM)

Bulgaria [bʌl'gɛərɪə] n Bulgaria; **~n** adj, n búlgaro/a m/f

bulge [bʌldʒ] n bulto, protuberancia ♦ vi bombearse, pandearse; (pocket etc): **to ~ (with)** rebosar (de)

bulk [bʌlk] n masa, mole f; **in ~** (COMM) a granel; **the ~ of** la mayor parte de; **~y** adj voluminoso, abultado

bull [bul] n toro; (male elephant, whale) macho; **~dog** n dogo

bulldozer ['buldəʊzə*] n bulldozer m

bullet ['bulɪt] n bala

bulletin ['bulɪtɪn] n anuncio, parte m; (journal) boletín m; **~ board** n (US) tablón m de anuncios; (COMPUT) tablero de noticias

bulletproof ['bulɪtpru:f] adj a prueba de balas

bullfight ['bulfaɪt] n corrida de toros; **~er** n torero; **~ing** n los toros, el toreo

bullion ['buljən] n oro (or plata) en barras

bullock ['bulək] n novillo

bullring ['bulrɪŋ] n plaza de toros

bull's-eye n centro del blanco

bully ['bulɪ] n valentón m, matón m ♦ vt intimidar, tiranizar

bum [bʌm] n (inf: backside) culo; (esp US: tramp) vagabundo

bumblebee ['bʌmblbi:] n abejorro

bump [bʌmp] n (blow) tope m, choque m; (jolt) sacudida; (on road etc) bache m; (on head etc) chichón m ♦ vt (strike) chocar contra; **~ into** vt fus chocar contra, tropezar con; (person) topar con; **~er** n (AUT) parachoques m inv ♦ adj: **~er crop/harvest** cosecha abundante; **~er cars** npl coches mpl de choque; **~y** adj (road) lleno de baches

bun [bʌn] n (BRIT: cake) pastel m; (US: bread) bollo; (of hair) moño

bunch [bʌntʃ] n (of flowers) ramo; (of keys) manojo; (of bananas) piña; (of people) grupo; (pej) pandilla; **~es** npl (in hair) coletas fpl

bundle ['bʌndl] n bulto, fardo; (of sticks) haz m; (of papers) legajo ♦ vt (also: ~ up) atar, envolver; **to ~ sth/sb into** meter algo/a alguien precipitadamente en

bungalow ['bʌŋgələu] n bungalow m, chalé m

bungle ['bʌŋgl] vt hacer mal

bunion ['bʌnjən] n juanete m

bunk [bʌŋk] n litera; **~ beds** npl literas fpl

bunker ['bʌŋkə*] n (coal store) carbonera; (MIL) refugio; (GOLF) bunker m

bunny ['bʌnɪ] n (also: ~ rabbit) conejito

buoy [bɔɪ] n boya; **~ant** adj (ship) capaz de flotar; (economy) boyante; (person) optimista

burden ['bɜ:dn] n carga ♦ vt cargar

bureau [bjuə'rəu] (pl **bureaux**) n (BRIT: writing desk) escritorio, buró m; (US: chest of drawers) cómoda; (office) oficina, agencia

bureaucracy [bjuə'rɔkrəsɪ] n burocracia

burglar ['bɜ:glə*] n ladrón/ona m/f; **~ alarm** n alarma f antirrobo; **~y** n robo con allanamiento, robo de una casa

burial ['berɪəl] n entierro

burly ['bɜ:lɪ] adj fornido, membrudo

Burma ['bɜ:mə] n Birmania

burn [bɜ:n] (pt, pp **burned** or **burnt**) vt quemar; (house) incendiar ♦ vi quemarse, arder; incendiarse; (sting) escocer ♦ n quemadura; **~ down** vt incendiar; **~er** n (on cooker etc) quemador m; **~ing** adj (building etc) en llamas; (hot: sand etc) abrasador(a); (ambition) ardiente

burrow ['bʌrəu] n madriguera ♦ vi hacer una madriguera; (rummage) hurgar

bursary ['bɜ:sərɪ] (BRIT) n beca

burst [bɜ:st] (pt, pp **burst**) vt reventar; (subj: river: banks etc) romper ♦ vi reventarse; (tyre) pincharse ♦ n (of gunfire) ráfaga; (also: ~ pipe) reventón m; **a ~ of energy/speed/enthusiasm** una explosión de energía/un ímpetu de velocidad/un arranque de entusiasmo; **to ~ into flames** estallar en llamas; **to ~ into tears** deshacerse en lágrimas; **to ~ out laughing** soltar la carcajada; **to ~ open** abrirse de golpe; **to be ~ing with** (subj: container) estar lleno a rebosar de; (person) reventar por or de; **~ into** vt fus (room etc) irrumpir en

bury ['berɪ] vt enterrar; (body) enterrar, sepultar

bus [bʌs] (pl **~es**) n autobús m

bush [buʃ] n arbusto; (scrub land) monte m; **to beat about the ~** andar(se) con rodeos

bushy ['buʃɪ] adj (thick) espeso, poblado

busily ['bɪzɪlɪ] adv afanosamente

business ['bɪznɪs] n (matter) asunto; (trading) comercio, negocios mpl; (firm) empresa, casa; (occupation) oficio; **to be away on ~** estar en viaje de negocios; **it's my ~ to ...** me toca or corresponde ...; **it's none of my ~** yo no tengo nada que ver; **he means ~** habla en serio; **~like** adj eficiente; **~man** n hombre m de negocios; **~ trip** n viaje m de negocios; **~woman** n mujer f de negocios

busker ['bʌskə*] (BRIT) n músico/a ambulante

bus: ~ shelter n parada cubierta; **~ station** n estación f de autobuses; **~-stop** n parada de autobús

bust [bʌst] n (ANAT) pecho; (sculpture) busto ♦ adj (inf: broken) roto, estropeado; **to go ~** quebrar

bustle ['bʌsl] n bullicio, movimiento ♦ vi menearse, apresurarse; **bustling** adj (town) animado, bullicioso

busy ['bɪzɪ] adj ocupado, atareado; (shop, street) concurrido, animado; (TEL: line) comunicando ♦ vt: **to ~ o.s. with** ocuparse en; **~body** n entrometido/a; **~ signal** (US) n (TEL) señal f de comunicando

---

KEYWORD

but [bʌt] conj 1 pero; **he's not very bright, ~ he's hard-working** no es muy inteligente, pero es trabajador
2 (in direct contradiction) sino; **he's not English ~ French** no es inglés sino francés; **he didn't sing ~ he shouted** no cantó sino que gritó 3 (showing disagreement, surprise etc): **~ that's far too expensive!** ¡pero eso es carísimo!; **~ it does work!** ¡(pero) sí que funciona!
♦ prep (apart from, except) menos, salvo; **we've had nothing ~ trouble** no hemos tenido más que problemas; **no-one ~ him can do it** nadie más que él puede hacerlo; **who ~ a lunatic would do such a thing?** ¡sólo un loco haría una cosa así!; **~ for you/your help** si no fuera por ti/tu ayuda; **anything ~ that** cualquier cosa menos eso
♦ adv (just, only): **she's ~ a child** no es más que una niña; **had I ~ known** si lo hubiera sabido; **I can ~ try** al menos lo puedo intentar; **it's all ~ finished** está casi acabado

---

butcher ['butʃə*] n carnicero ♦ vt hacer una carnicería con; (cattle etc) matar; **~'s (shop)** n carnicería

butler ['bʌtlə*] n mayordomo

butt [bʌt] n (barrel) tonel m; (of gun) culata; (of cigarette) colilla; (BRIT: fig: target) blanco ♦ vt dar cabezadas contra, top(et)ar; **~ in** vi (interrupt) interrumpir

butter ['bʌtə*] n mantequilla ♦ vt untar con mantequilla; **~cup** n botón m de oro

butterfly ['bʌtəflaɪ] n mariposa; (SWIMMING: also: **~ stroke**) braza de mariposa

buttocks ['bʌtəks] npl nalgas fpl

button ['bʌtn] n botón m; (US) placa, chapa ♦ vt (also: **~ up**) abotonar, abrochar ♦ vi abrocharse

buttress ['bʌtrɪs] n contrafuerte m

buy [baɪ] (pt, pp **bought**) vt comprar ♦ n compra; **to ~ sb sth/sth from sb** comprarle algo a alguien; **to ~ sb a drink** invitar a alguien a tomar algo; **~er** n comprador(a) m/f

buzz [bʌz] n zumbido; (inf: phone call) llamada (por teléfono) ♦ vi zumbar; **~er** n timbre m; **~ word** n palabra que está de moda

---

KEYWORD

by [baɪ] prep 1 (referring to cause, agent) por; de; **killed ~ lightning** muerto por un relámpago; **a painting ~ Picasso** un cuadro de Picasso
2 (referring to method, manner, means): **~ bus/car/train** en autobús/coche/tren; **to pay ~ cheque** pagar con un cheque; **~ moonlight/candlelight** a la luz de la luna/una vela; **~ saving hard, he ...** ahorrando, ...
3 (via, through) por; **we came ~ Dover** vinimos por Dover
4 (close to, past): **the house ~ the river** la casa junto al río; **she rushed ~ me** pasó a mi lado como una exhalación; **I go ~ the post office every day** paso por delante de Correos todos los días
5 (time: not later than) para; (: during): **~ daylight** de día; **~ 4 o'clock** para las cuatro; **~ this time tomorrow** mañana a estas horas; **~ the time I got here it was too late** cuando llegué ya era demasiado tarde
6 (amount): **~ the metre/kilo** por metro/kilo; **paid ~ the hour** pagado por hora
7 (MATH, measure): **to divide/multiply ~ 3** dividir/multiplicar por 3; **a room 3 metres ~ 4** una habitación de 3 metros por 4; **it's broader ~ a metre** es un metro más ancho
8 (according to) según, de acuerdo con; **it's 3 o'clock ~ my watch** según mi reloj, son las tres; **it's all right ~ me** por mí, está bien
9: **(all) ~ oneself** etc todo solo; **he did it (all) ~ himself** lo hizo él solo; **he was standing (all) ~ himself in a corner** estaba de pie solo en un rincón
10: **~ the way** a propósito, por cierto; **this wasn't my idea, ~ the way** pues, no fue idea mía
♦ adv 1 see **go; pass** etc
2: **~ and ~** finalmente; **they'll come back ~ and ~** acabarán volviendo; **~ and large** en líneas generales, en general

---

bye(-bye) ['baɪ('baɪ)] excl adiós, hasta luego

by(e)-law n ordenanza municipal

by-: **~-election** (BRIT) n elección f parcial; **~gone** ['baɪɡɒn] adj pasado, del pasado ♦ n: **let ~gones be ~gones** lo pasado, pasado está; **~pass** ['baɪpɑːs] n carretera de circunvalación; (MED) (operación f de) by-pass m ♦ vt evitar; **~-product** n subproducto, derivado; (of situation) consecuencia; **~stander** ['baɪstændə*] n espectador(a) m/f

byte [baɪt] n (COMPUT) byte m, octeto

byword ['baɪwɜːd] n: **to be a ~ for** ser conocidísimo por

C, c

C [si:] *n* (*MUS*) do *m*

C. *abbr* (= *centigrade*) C.

C.A. *abbr* = **chartered accountant**

cab [kæb] *n* taxi *m*; (*of truck*) cabina

cabbage ['kæbɪdʒ] *n* col *f*, berza

cabin ['kæbɪn] *n* cabaña; (*on ship*) camarote *m*; (*on plane*) cabina; ~ **crew** *n* tripulación *f* de cabina; ~ **cruiser** *n* yate *m* de motor

cabinet ['kæbɪnɪt] *n* (*POL*) consejo de ministros; (*furniture*) armario; (*also: display* ~) vitrina

cable ['keɪbl] *n* cable *m* ♦ *vt* cablegrafiar; ~-**car** *n* teleférico; ~ **television** *n* televisión *f* por cable

cache [kæʃ] *n* (*of arms, drugs etc*) alijo

cackle ['kækl] *vi* lanzar risotadas; (*hen*) cacarear

cactus ['kæktəs] (*pl* **cacti**) *n* cacto

cadge [kædʒ] (*inf*) *vt* gorronear

Caesarean [si:'zeərɪən] *adj*: ~ (**section**) cesárea

café ['kæfeɪ] *n* café *m*

cafeteria [kæfɪ'tɪərɪə] *n* cafetería

cage [keɪdʒ] *n* jaula

cagey ['keɪdʒɪ] (*inf*) *adj* cauteloso, reservado

cagoule [kə'gu:l] *n* chubasquero

cajole [kə'dʒəʊl] *vt* engatusar

cake [keɪk] *n* (*CULIN: large*) tarta; (: *small*) pastel *m*; (*of soap*) pastilla; ~**d** *adj*: ~**d with** cubierto de

calculate ['kælkjuleɪt] *vt* calcular; **calculation** [-'leɪʃən] *n* cálculo, cómputo; **calculator** *n* calculadora

calendar ['kæləndə*] *n* calendario; ~ **month/year** *n* mes *m*/año civil

calf [kɑ:f] (*pl* **calves**) *n* (*of cow*) ternero, becerro; (*of other animals*) cría; (*also:* ~**skin**) piel *f* de becerro; (*ANAT*) pantorrilla

calibre ['kælɪbə*] (*US* **caliber**) *n* calibre *m*

call [kɔ:l] *vt* llamar; (*meeting*) convocar ♦ *vi* (*shout*) llamar; (*TEL*) llamar (por teléfono), telefonear (*esp AM*); (*visit: also:* ~ **in**, ~ **round**) hacer una visita ♦ *n* llamada; (*of bird*) canto; **to be ~ed** llamarse; **on** ~ (*on duty*) de guardia; ~ **back** *vi* (*return*) volver; (*TEL*) volver a llamar; ~ **for** *vt fus* (*demand*) pedir, exigir; (*fetch*) venir por (*SP*), pasar por (*AM*); ~ **off** *vt* (*cancel: meeting, race*) cancelar; (: *deal*) anular; (: *strike*) desconvocar; ~ **on** *vt fus* (*visit*) visitar; (*turn to*) acudir a; ~ **out** *vi* gritar; ~ **up** *vt* (*MIL*) llamar al servicio militar; (*TEL*) llamar; ~**box** (*BRIT*) *n* cabina telefónica; ~ **centre** *n* (*BRIT*) centro de llamadas; ~**er** *n* visita; (*TEL*) usuario/a; ~ **girl** *n* prostituta; ~**in** (*US*) *n*

(*programa m*) coloquio (por teléfono); ~**ing** *n* vocación *f*; (*occupation*) profesión *f*; ~**ing card** (*US*) *n* tarjeta de visita

callous ['kæləs] *adj* insensible, cruel

calm [kɑ:m] *adj* tranquilo; (*sea*) liso, en calma ♦ *n* calma, tranquilidad *f* ♦ *vt* calmar, tranquilizar; ~ **down** *vi* calmarse, tranquilizarse ♦ *vt* calmar, tranquilizar

Calor gas ® ['kælə*-] *n* butano

calorie ['kælərɪ] *n* caloría

calves [kɑ:vz] *npl of* **calf**

Cambodia [kæm'bəudjə] *n* Camboya

camcorder ['kæmkɔ:də*] *n* videocámara

came [keɪm] *pt of* **come**

camel ['kæməl] *n* camello

camera ['kæmərə] *n* máquina fotográfica; (*CINEMA, TV*) cámara; **in** ~ (*LAW*) a puerta cerrada; ~**man** *n* cámara *m*

camouflage ['kæməflɑ:ʒ] *n* camuflaje *m* ♦ *vt* camuflar

camp [kæmp] *n* campamento, camping *m*; (*MIL*) campamento; (*for prisoners*) campo; (*fig: faction*) bando ♦ *vi* acampar ♦ *adj* afectado, afeminado

campaign [kæm'peɪn] *n* (*MIL, POL etc*) campaña ♦ *vi* hacer campaña

camp: ~**bed** (*BRIT*) *n* cama de campaña; ~**er** *n* campista *m/f*; (*vehicle*) caravana; ~**ing** *n* camping *m*; **to go** ~**ing** hacer camping; ~**site** *n* camping *m*

campus ['kæmpəs] *n* ciudad *f* universitaria

can¹ [kæn] *n* (*of oil, water*) bidón *m*; (*tin*) lata, bote *m* ♦ *vt* enlatar

---

KEYWORD

can² [kæn] (*negative* **cannot, can't**; *conditional and pt* **could**) *aux vb* 1 (*be able to*) poder; **you ~ do it if you try** puedes hacerlo si lo intentas; **I ~'t see you** no te veo

2 (*know how to*) saber; **I ~ swim/play tennis/drive** sé nadar/jugar al tenis/conducir; ~ **you speak French?** ¿hablas *or* sabes hablar francés?

3 (*may*) poder; ~ **I use your phone?** ¿me dejas *or* puedo usar tu teléfono?

4 (*expressing disbelief, puzzlement etc*): **it ~'t be true!** ¡no puede ser (verdad)!; **what CAN he want?** ¿qué querrá?

5 (*expressing possibility, suggestion etc*): **he could be in the library** podría estar en la biblioteca; **she could have been delayed** pudo haberse retrasado

---

Canada ['kænədə] *n* (el) Canadá; **Canadian** [kə'neɪdɪən] *adj, n* canadiense *m/f*

canal [kə'næl] *n* canal *m*

canary [kə'neərɪ] *n* canario; **the C~ Islands** *npl* las (Islas) Canarias

cancel ['kænsəl] *vt* cancelar; (*train*) suprimir;

(cross out) tachar, borrar; **~lation** [-'leɪʃən] n cancelación f; supresión f

cancer ['kænsə*] n cáncer m; **C~** (ASTROLOGY) Cáncer m

candid ['kændɪd] adj franco, abierto

candidate ['kændɪdeɪt] n candidato/a

candle ['kændl] n vela; (in church) cirio; **~light** n: **by ~light** a la luz de una vela; **~stick** n (single) candelero; (low) palmatoria; (bigger, ornate) candelabro

candour ['kændə*] (US candor) n franqueza

candy ['kændɪ] n azúcar m cande; (US) caramelo; **~floss** (BRIT) n algodón m (azucarado)

cane [keɪn] n (BOT) caña; (stick) vara, palmeta; (for furniture) mimbre f ♦ (BRIT) vt (SCOL) castigar (con vara)

canister ['kænɪstə*] n bote m, lata; (of gas) bombona

cannabis ['kænəbɪs] n marijuana

canned [kænd] adj en lata, de lata

cannon ['kænən] (pl ~ or ~s) n cañón m

cannot ['kænɔt] = **can not**

canoe [kə'nuː] n canoa; (SPORT) piragua; **~ing** n piragüismo

canon ['kænən] n (clergyman) canónigo; (standard) canon m

can-opener n abrelatas m inv

canopy ['kænəpɪ] n dosel m; toldo

can't [kænt] = **can not**

canteen [kæn'tiːn] n (eating place) cantina; (BRIT: of cutlery) juego

canter ['kæntə*] vi ir a medio galope

canvas ['kænvəs] n (material) lona; (painting) lienzo; (NAUT) velas fpl

canvass ['kænvəs] vi (POL): **to ~ for** solicitar votos por ♦ vt (COMM) sondear

canyon ['kænjən] n cañón m

cap [kæp] n (hat) gorra; (of pen) capuchón m; (of bottle) tapa, tapón m; (contraceptive) diafragma m; (for toy gun) cápsula ♦ vt (outdo) superar; (limit) recortar

capability [keɪpə'bɪlɪtɪ] n capacidad f

capable ['keɪpəbl] adj capaz

capacity [kə'pæsɪtɪ] n capacidad f; (position) calidad f

cape [keɪp] n capa; (GEO) cabo

caper ['keɪpə*] n (CULIN: gen: ~s) alcaparra; (prank) broma

capital ['kæpɪtl] n (also: ~ city) capital f; (money) capital m; (also: ~ letter) mayúscula; **~ gains tax** n impuesto sobre las ganancias de capital; **~ism** n capitalismo; **~ist** adj, n capitalista m/f; **~ize** on vt fus aprovechar; **~ punishment** n pena de muerte

Capricorn ['kæprɪkɔːn] n (ASTROLOGY) Capricornio

capsize [kæp'saɪz] vt volcar, hacer zozobrar ♦ vi volcarse, zozobrar

capsule ['kæpsjuːl] n cápsula

captain ['kæptɪn] n capitán m

caption ['kæpʃən] n (heading) título; (to picture) leyenda

captive ['kæptɪv] adj, n cautivo/a m/f

capture ['kæptʃə*] vt prender, apresar; (animal, COMPUT) capturar; (place) tomar; (attention) captar, llamar ♦ n apresamiento; captura; toma; (data ~) formulación f de datos

car [kɑː*] n coche m, carro (AM), automóvil m (US: RAIL) vagón m

carafe [kə'ræf] n jarra

carat ['kærət] n quilate m

caravan ['kærəvæn] n (BRIT) caravana, ruló f; (in desert) caravana; **~ning** n: **to go ~ning** ir de vacaciones en caravana, viajar en caravana; **~ site** (BRIT) n camping m para caravanas

carbohydrate [kɑːbəu'haɪdreɪt] n hidrato de carbono; (food) fécula

carbon ['kɑːbən] n carbono; **~ paper** n papel m carbón

car boot sale n mercadillo organizado en un aparcamiento, en el que se exponen las mercancías en el maletero del coche

carburettor [kɑːbju'retə*] (US carburetor) n carburador m

card [kɑːd] n (material) cartulina; (index ~ etc) ficha; (playing ~) carta, naipe m; (visiting ~, greetings ~ etc) tarjeta; **~board** n cartón m

cardiac ['kɑːdɪæk] adj cardíaco

cardigan ['kɑːdɪgən] n rebeca

cardinal ['kɑːdɪnl] adj cardinal; (importance, principal) esencial ♦ n cardenal m

card index n fichero

care [keə*] n cuidado; (worry) inquietud f; (charge) cargo, custodia ♦ vi: **to ~ about** (person, animal) tener cariño a; (thing, idea) preocuparse por; **~ of** en casa de, al cuidado de; **in sb's ~** a cargo de uno; **to take ~** to cuidarse de, tener cuidado de; **to take ~ of** cuidar; (problem etc) ocuparse de; **I don't ~** no me importa; **I couldn't ~ less** eso me trae sin cuidado; **~ for** vt fus cuidar a; (like) querer

career [kə'rɪə*] n profesión f; (in work, school) carrera ♦ vi (also: ~ along) correr a toda velocidad; **~ woman** n mujer f dedicada a su profesión

care: ~free adj despreocupado; **~ful** adj cuidadoso; (cautious) cauteloso; **(be) ~ful!** ¡tenga cuidado!; **~fully** adv con cuidado, cuidadosamente; con cautela; **~less** adj descuidado; (heedless) poco atento; **~lessness** n descuido; falta de atención; **~r** ['keərə*] n enfermero/a m/f (official); (unpaid) persona que cuida a un pariente o *vecino*

caress [kə'res] *n* caricia ♦ *vt* acariciar

caretaker ['keəteɪkə*] *n* portero/a, conserje *m/f*

car-ferry *n* transbordador *m* para coches

cargo ['kɑ:gəu] (*pl* **-es**) *n* cargamento, carga

car hire *n* alquiler *m* de automóviles

Caribbean [kærɪ'bi:ən] *n*: **the ~ (Sea)** el (Mar) Caribe

caring ['keərɪŋ] *adj* humanitario; (*behaviour*) afectuoso

carnation [kɑ:'neɪʃən] *n* clavel *m*

carnival ['kɑ:nɪvəl] *n* carnaval *m*; (*US: funfair*) parque *m* de atracciones

carol ['kærəl] *n*: (**Christmas**) ~ villancico

carp [kɑ:p] *n* (*fish*) carpa

car park (*BRIT*) *n* aparcamiento, parking *m*

carpenter ['kɑ:pɪntə*] *n* carpintero/a

carpet ['kɑ:pɪt] *n* alfombra; (*fitted*) moqueta ♦ *vt* alfombrar

car phone *n* teléfono movil

car rental (*US*) *n* alquiler *m* de coches

carriage ['kærɪdʒ] *n* (*BRIT: RAIL*) vagón *m*; (*horse-drawn*) coche *m*; (*of goods*) transporte *m*; (: *cost*) porte *m*, flete *m*; **~way** (*BRIT*) *n* (*part of road*) calzada

carrier ['kærɪə*] *n* (*transport company*) transportista, empresa de transportes; (*MED*) portador *m*; **~ bag** (*BRIT*) *n* bolsa de papel or plástico

carrot ['kærət] *n* zanahoria

carry ['kærɪ] *vt* (*subj: person*) llevar; (*transport*) transportar; (*involve: responsibilities etc*) entrañar, implicar; (*MED*) ser portador de ♦ *vi* (*sound*) oírse; **to get carried away** (*fig*) entusiasmarse; **~ on** *vi* (*continue*) seguir (adelante), continuar ♦ *vt* proseguir, continuar; **~ out** *vt* (*orders*) cumplir; (*investigation*) llevar a cabo, realizar; **~ cot** (*BRIT*) *n* cuna portátil; **~-on** (*inf*) *n* (*fuss*) lío

cart [kɑ:t] *n* carro, carreta ♦ *vt* (*inf: transport*) acarrear

carton ['kɑ:tən] *n* (*box*) caja (de cartón), (*of milk etc*) bote *m*; (*of yogurt*) tarrina

cartoon [kɑ:'tu:n] *n* (*PRESS*) caricatura; (*comic strip*) tira cómica; (*film*) dibujos *mpl* animados

cartridge ['kɑ:trɪdʒ] *n* cartucho; (*of pen*) recambio; (*of record player*) cápsula

carve [kɑ:v] *vt* (*meat*) trinchar; (*wood, stone*) cincelar, esculpir; (*initials etc*) grabar; **~ up** *vt* dividir, repartir; **carving** *n* (*object*) escultura; (*design*) talla; (*art*) tallado; **carving knife** *n* trinchante *m*

car wash *n* lavado de coches

case [keɪs] *n* (*container*) caja; (*MED*) caso; (*for jewels etc*) estuche *m*; (*LAW*) causa, proceso; (*BRIT: also: suit~*) maleta; **in ~ of** en caso de;

in any ~ en todo caso; **just in ~** por si acaso

cash [kæʃ] *n* dinero en efectivo, dinero contante ♦ *vt* cobrar, hacer efectivo; **to pay (in) ~** pagar al contado; **~ on delivery** al entregar; **~book** *n* libro de caja; **~ card** *n* tarjeta *f* dinero; **~ desk** (*BRIT*) *n* caja; **~ dispenser** *n* cajero automático

cashew [kæ'ʃu:] *n* (*also*: ~ **nut**) anacardo

cash flow *n* flujo de fondos, cash-flow *m*

cashier [kæ'ʃɪə*] *n* cajero/a

cashmere ['kæʃmɪə*] *n* cachemira

cash register *n* caja

casing ['keɪsɪŋ] *n* revestimiento

casino [kə'si:nəu] *n* casino

casket ['kɑ:skɪt] *n* cofre *m*, estuche *m*; (*US: coffin*) ataúd *m*

casserole ['kæsərəul] *n* (*food, pot*) cazuela

cassette [kæ'set] *n* cassette *f*; **~ player/ recorder** *n* tocacassettes *m inv*, cassette *m*

cast [kɑ:st] (*pt, pp* **cast**) *vt* (*throw*) echar, arrojar, lanzar; (*glance, eyes*) dirigir; (*THEATRE*): **to ~ sb as Othello** dar a uno el papel de Otelo ♦ *vi* (*FISHING*) lanzar ♦ *n* (*THEATRE*) reparto; (*also: plaster* ~) vaciado; **to ~ one's vote** votar; **to ~ doubt on** suscitar dudas acerca de; **~ off** *vi* (*NAUT*) desamarrar; (*KNITTING*) cerrar (los puntos); **~ on** *vi* (*KNITTING*) poner los puntos

castanets [kæstə'nets] *npl* castañuelas *fpl*

castaway ['kɑ:stəwəɪ] *n* náufrago/a

caster sugar ['kɑ:stə*-] (*BRIT*) *n* azúcar *m* extrafino

Castile [kæs'ti:l] *n* Castilla; **Castilian** *adj, n* castellano/a *m/f*

casting vote ['kɑ:stɪŋ-] (*BRIT*) *n* voto decisivo

cast iron *n* hierro fundido

castle ['kɑ:sl] *n* castillo; (*CHESS*) torre *f*

castor oil ['kɑ:stə*-] *n* aceite *m* de ricino

casual ['kæʒjul] *adj* fortuito; (*irregular: work etc*) eventual, temporero; (*unconcerned*) despreocupado; (*clothes*) de sport; **~ly** *adv* de manera despreocupada; (*dress*) de sport

casualty ['kæʒjultɪ] *n* víctima, herido; (*dead*) muerto; (*MED: department*) urgencias *fpl*

cat [kæt] *n* gato; (*big* ~) felino

Catalan ['kætəlæn] *adj, n* catalán/ana *m/f*

catalogue ['kætəlɔg] (*US* **catalog**) *n* catálogo ♦ *vt* catalogar

Catalonia [kætə'ləunɪə] *n* Cataluña

catalyst ['kætəlɪst] *n* catalizador *m*

catalytic convertor [kætə'lɪtɪk kən'vɜ:tə*] *n* catalizador *m*

catapult ['kætəpʌlt] *n* tirachinas *m inv*

catarrh [kə'tɑ:*] *n* catarro

catastrophe [kə'tæstrəfɪ] *n* catástrofe *f*

catch [kætʃ] (*pt, pp* **caught**) *vt* coger (*SP*), agarrar (*AM*); (*arrest*) detener; (*grasp*) asir; (*breath*) contener; (*surprise: person*) sorprender; (*attract: attention*) captar; (*hear*) oír; (*MED*) contagiarse de, coger; (*also:* ~ up) alcanzar ♦ vi (*fire*) encenderse; (*in branches etc*) enredarse ♦ n (*fish etc*) pesca; (*act of catching*) cogida; (*hidden problem*) dificultad f; (*game*) pilla-pilla; (*of lock*) pestillo, cerradura; **to ~ fire** encenderse; **to ~ sight of** divisar; ~ **on** vi (*understand*) caer en la cuenta; (*grow popular*) hacerse popular; ~ **up** vi (*fig*) ponerse al día; ~**ing** ['kætʃɪŋ] adj (*MED*) contagioso; ~**ment area** ['kætʃmənt-] (*BRIT*) n zona de captación; ~**phrase** ['kætʃfreɪz] n lema m, eslogan m; ~**y** ['kætʃɪ] adj (*tune*) pegadizo

category ['kætɪgən] n categoría, clase f

cater ['keɪtə*] vi: **to ~ for** (*BRIT*) abastecer a; (*needs*) atender a; (*COMM: parties etc*) proveer comida a; ~**er** n abastecedor(a) m/f, proveedor(a) m/f; ~**ing** n (*trade*) hostelería

caterpillar ['kætəpɪlə*] n oruga, gusano

cathedral [kə'θiːdrəl] n catedral f

catholic ['kæθəlɪk] adj (*tastes etc*) amplio; **C~** adj, n (*REL*) católico/a m/f

CAT scan [kæt-] n TAC f, tomografía

Cat'seye ® ['kæts'aɪ] (*BRIT*) n (*AUT*) catafoto

cattle ['kætl] npl ganado

catty ['kætɪ] adj malicioso, rencoroso

caucus ['kɔːkəs] n (*POL*) camarilla política; (*: US: to elect candidates*) comité m electoral

caught [kɔːt] pt, pp of **catch**

cauliflower ['kɔlɪflauə*] n coliflor f

cause [kɔːz] n causa, motivo, razón f; (*principle: also: POL*) causa ♦ vt causar

caution ['kɔːʃən] n cautela, prudencia; (*warning*) advertencia, amonestación f ♦ vt amonestar; **cautious** adj cauteloso, prudente, precavido

cavalry ['kævəlrɪ] n caballería

cave [keɪv] n cueva, caverna; ~ **in** vi (*roof etc*) derrumbarse, hundirse

caviar(e) ['kævɪɑː*] n caviar m

CB n abbr (= *Citizens' Band (Radio)*) banda ciudadana

CBI n abbr (= *Confederation of British Industry*) ≈ C.E.O.E. f (*SP*)

cc abbr = **cubic centimetres**; = **carbon copy**

CD n abbr (= *compact disc*) DC m; (*player*) (reproductor m de) disco compacto; ~ **player** n lector m de discos compactos; ~-**ROM** [siːdiːˈrɔm] n abbr CD-ROM m

cease [siːs] vt, vi cesar; ~**fire** n alto m el fuego; ~**less** adj incesante

cedar ['siːdə*] n cedro

ceiling ['siːlɪŋ] n techo; (*fig*) límite m

celebrate ['selɪbreɪt] vt celebrar ♦ vi divertirse; ~**d** adj célebre; **celebration** [-'breɪʃən] n fiesta, celebración f

celery ['selərɪ] n apio

cell [sel] n celda; (*BIOL*) célula; (*ELEC*) elemento

cellar ['selə*] n sótano; (*for wine*) bodega

cello ['tʃeləu] n violoncelo

Cellophane ® ['seləfeɪn] n celofán m

cellphone ['selfəun] n teléfono celular

Celt [kelt, selt] adj, n celta m/f; ~**ic** adj celta

cement [sə'ment] n cemento; ~ **mixer** n hormigonera

cemetery ['semɪtrɪ] n cementerio

censor ['sensə*] n censor m ♦ vt (*cut*) censurar; ~**ship** n censura

censure ['senʃə*] vt censurar

census ['sensəs] n censo

cent [sent] n (*unit of dollar*) centavo, céntimo; (*unit of euro*) céntimo; *see also* **per**

centenary [sen'tiːnərɪ] n centenario

center ['sentə*] (*US*) = **centre**

centi... [sentɪ] prefix: ~**grade** adj centígrado; ~**litre** (*US* ~**liter**) n centilitro; ~**metre** (*US* ~**meter**) n centímetro

centipede ['sentɪpiːd] n ciempiés m inv

central ['sentrəl] adj central; (*of house etc*) céntrico; **C~ America** n Centroamérica; ~ **heating** n calefacción f central; ~**ize** vt centralizar

centre ['sentə*] (*US* **center**) n centro; (*fig*) núcleo ♦ vt centrar; ~-**forward** n (*SPORT*) delantero centro; ~-**half** n (*SPORT*) medio centro

century ['sentjurɪ] n siglo; **20th** ~ siglo veinte

ceramic [sɪ'ræmɪk] adj cerámico; ~**s** n cerámica

cereal ['siːrɪəl] n cereal m

ceremony ['serɪmənɪ] n ceremonia; **to stand on** ~ hacer ceremonias, estar de cumplido

certain ['sɜːtən] adj seguro; (*person*): **a ~ Mr Smith** un tal Sr Smith; (*particular, some*) cierto; **for** ~ a ciencia cierta; ~**ly** adv (*undoubtedly*) ciertamente; (*of course*) desde luego, por supuesto; ~**ty** n certeza, certidumbre f, seguridad f; (*inevitability*) certeza

certificate [sə'tɪfɪkɪt] n certificado

certified ['sɜːtɪfaɪd]: ~ **mail** (*US*) n correo certificado; ~ **public accountant** (*US*) n contable m/f diplomado/a

certify ['sɜːtɪfaɪ] vt certificar; (*award diploma to*) conceder un diploma a; (*declare insane*) declarar loco

cervical ['sɜːvɪkl] adj cervical

cervix ['sɜːvɪks] n cuello del útero

cf. abbr (= *compare*) cfr

CFC n abbr (= *chlorofluorocarbon*) CFC m

ch. abbr (= *chapter*) cap

chain [tʃeɪn] n cadena; (*of mountains*) cordillera; (*of events*) sucesión f ♦ vt (*also:* ~ up) encadenar; ~ **reaction** n reacción f en cadena; ~-**smoke** vi fumar un cigarrillo tras otro; ~ **store** n tienda de una cadena, ≈

gran almacén

chair [tʃeə*] n silla; (armchair) sillón m,
butaca; (of university) cátedra; (of meeting
etc) presidencia ♦ vt (meeting) presidir; **~lift**
n telesilla; **~man** n presidente m

chalk [tʃɔ:k] n (GEO) creta; (for writing) tiza
(SP), gis m (AM)

challenge ['tʃælɪndʒ] n desafío, reto ♦ vt
desafiar, retar; (statement, right) poner en
duda; **to ~ sb to do sth** retar a uno a que
haga algo; **challenging** adj exigente; (tone)
de desafío

chamber ['tʃeɪmbə*] n cámara, sala; (POL)
cámara; (BRIT: LAW: gen pl) despacho; **~ of
commerce** cámara de comercio; **~maid** n
camarera; **~ music** n música de cámara

chamois ['ʃæmwɑ:] n gamuza

champagne [ʃæm'peɪn] n champaña m,
champán m

champion ['tʃæmpɪən] n campeón/ona m/f;
(of cause) defensor(a) m/f; **~ship** n
campeonato

chance [tʃɑ:ns] n (opportunity) ocasión f,
oportunidad f; (likelihood) posibilidad f; (risk)
riesgo ♦ vt arriesgar, probar ♦ adj fortuito,
casual; **to ~ it** arriesgarse, intentarlo; **to take a
~** arriesgarse; **by ~** por casualidad

chancellor ['tʃɑ:nsələ*] n canciller m; **C~ of
the Exchequer** (BRIT) n Ministro de
Hacienda

chandelier [ʃændə'lɪə*] n araña (de luces)

change [tʃeɪndʒ] vt cambiar; (replace)
cambiar, reemplazar; (gear, clothes, job)
cambiar de; (transform) transformar ♦ vi
cambiar(se); (trains) hacer transbordo;
(traffic lights) cambiar de color; (coins)
transformed) **to ~ into** transformarse en ♦ n
cambio; (alteration) modificación f,
transformación f; (of clothes) muda; (coins)
suelto, sencillo; (money returned) vuelta; **to
~ gear** (AUT) cambiar de marcha; **to ~ one's
mind** cambiar de opinión o idea; **for a ~** para
variar; **~able** adj (weather) cambiable;
~ machine n máquina de cambio; **~over** n
(to new system) cambio; **changing** adj
cambiante; **changing room** (BRIT) n
vestuario

channel ['tʃænl] n (TV) canal m; (of river)
cauce m; (groove) conducto; (fig: medium)
medio ♦ vt (river etc) encauzar; **the (English)
C~** el Canal (de la Mancha); **the C~ Islands**
las Islas Normandas; **the C~ Tunnel** el túnel
del Canal de la Mancha, el Eurotúnel; **~-
hopping** n (TV) zapping m

chant [tʃɑ:nt] n (of crowd) gritos mpl; (REL)
canto ♦ vt (slogan, word) repetir a gritos

chaos ['keɪɔs] n caos m

chap [tʃæp] (BRIT: inf) n (man) tío, tipo

chapel ['tʃæpəl] n capilla

chaperone ['ʃæpərəun] n carabina

chaplain ['tʃæplɪn] n capellán m

chapped [tʃæpt] adj agrietado

chapter ['tʃæptə*] n capítulo

char [tʃɑ:*] vt (burn) carbonizar, chamuscar

character ['kærɪktə*] n carácter m,
naturaleza, índole f; (moral strength,
personality) carácter; (in novel, film) personaje
m; **~istic** [-'rɪstɪk] adj característico ♦ n
característica

charcoal ['tʃɑ:kəul] n carbón m vegetal;
(ART) carboncillo

charge [tʃɑ:dʒ] n (LAW) cargo, acusación f;
(cost) precio, coste m; (responsibility) cargo
♦ vt (LAW): **to ~ (with)** acusar de (de); (battery)
cargar; (price) pedir; (customer) cobrar ♦ vi
precipitarse; (MIL) cargar, atacar; **~s** npl: **to
reverse the ~s** (BRIT: TEL) revertir el cobro; **to
take ~ of** hacerse cargo de, encargarse de; **to
be in ~ of** estar encargado de; (business)
mandar; **how much do you ~?** ¿cuánto cobra
usted?; **to ~ an expense (up) to sb's account**
cargar algo a cuenta de alguien; **~ card** n
tarjeta de cuenta

charity ['tʃærɪtɪ] n caridad f; (organization)
sociedad f benéfica; (money, gifts) limosnas
fpl

charm [tʃɑ:m] n encanto, atractivo;
(talisman) hechizo; (on bracelet) dije m ♦ vt
encantar; **~ing** adj encantador(a)

chart [tʃɑ:t] n (diagram) cuadro; (graph)
gráfica; (map) carta de navegación ♦ vt
(course) trazar; (progress) seguir; **~s** npl (Top
40): **the ~s** ≈ los 40 principales (SP)

charter ['tʃɑ:tə*] vt (plane) alquilar; (ship)
fletar ♦ n (document) carta; (of university,
company) estatutos mpl; **~ed accountant**
(BRIT) n contable m/f diplomado/a; **~ flight** n
vuelo chárter

chase [tʃeɪs] vt (pursue) perseguir; (also:
~ away) ahuyentar ♦ n persecución f

chasm ['kæzəm] n sima

chassis ['ʃæsɪ] n chasis m

chat [tʃæt] vi (also: **have a ~**) charlar ♦ n
charla; **~ show** (BRIT) n programa m de
entrevistas

chatter ['tʃætə*] vi (person) charlar; (teeth)
castañetear ♦ n (of birds) parloteo; (of
people) charla, cháchara; **~box** (inf) n
parlanchín/ina m/f

chatty ['tʃætɪ] adj (style) informal; (person)
hablador(a)

chauffeur ['ʃəufə*] n chófer m

chauvinist ['ʃəuvɪnɪst] n (male:) machista
m; (nationalist) chovinista m/f

cheap [tʃi:p] adj barato; (joke) de mal gusto;
(poor quality) de mala calidad ♦ adv barato;
~ day return n billete m de ida y vuelta el
mismo día; **~er** adj más barato; **~ly** adv

barato, a bajo precio

cheat [tʃi:t] vi hacer trampa ♦ vt: **to ~ sb (out of sth)** estafar (algo) a uno ♦ n (person) tramposo/a

check [tʃɛk] vt (examine) controlar; (facts) comprobar; (halt) parar, detener; (restrain) refrenar, restringir ♦ n (inspection) control m, inspección f; (curb) freno; (US: bill) nota, cuenta; (US) = **cheque**; (pattern: gen pl) cuadro ♦ adj (also: ~ed: pattern, cloth) a cuadros; **~ in** vi (at hotel) firmar el registro; (at airport) facturar el equipaje ♦ vt (luggage) facturar; **~ out** vi (of hotel) marcharse; **~ up** vi: **to ~ up on sth** comprobar algo; **to ~ up on sb** investigar a alguien; **~ered** (US) adj = **check**; **~ered; ~ers** (US) n juego de damas; **~in (desk)** n mostrador m de facturación; **~ing account** (US) n cuenta corriente; **~mate** n jaque m mate; **~out** n caja; **~point** n (punto de) control m; **~room** n consigna; **~up** n (MED) reconocimiento general

cheek [tʃi:k] n mejilla; (impudence) descaro; **what a ~!** ¡qué cara!; **~bone** n pómulo; **~y** adj fresco, descarado

cheep [tʃi:p] vi piar

cheer [tʃɪə*] vt vitorear, aplaudir; (gladden) alegrar, animar ♦ vi dar vivas ♦ n viva m; **~s** npl aplausos mpl; **~s!** ¡salud!; **~ up** vi animarse ♦ vt alegrar, animar; **~ful** adj alegre

cheerio [tʃɪərɪ'əu] (BRIT) excl ¡hasta luego!

cheese [tʃi:z] n queso; **~board** n tabla de quesos

cheetah ['tʃi:tə] n leopardo cazador

chef [ʃɛf] n jefe/a m/f de cocina

chemical ['kɛmɪkəl] adj químico ♦ n producto químico

chemist ['kɛmɪst] n (BRIT: pharmacist) farmacéutico/a; (scientist) químico/a; **~ry** n química; **~'s (shop)** (BRIT) n farmacia

cheque [tʃɛk] (US **check**) n cheque m; **~book** n talonario de cheques (SP), chequera (AM); **~ card** n tarjeta de cheque

chequered ['tʃɛkəd] (US **checkered**) adj (fig) accidentado

cherish ['tʃɛrɪʃ] vt (love) querer, apreciar; (protect) cuidar; (hope etc) abrigar

cherry ['tʃɛrɪ] n cereza; (also: ~ tree) cerezo

chess [tʃɛs] n ajedrez m; **~board** n tablero (de ajedrez)

chest [tʃɛst] n (ANAT) pecho; (box) cofre m, cajón m; **~ of drawers** n cómoda

chestnut ['tʃɛsnʌt] n castaña; **~ (tree)** n castaño

chew [tʃu:] vt mascar, masticar; **~ing gum** n chicle m

chic [ʃi:k] adj elegante

chick [tʃɪk] n pollito, polluelo; (inf: girl) chica

chicken ['tʃɪkɪn] n gallina, pollo; (food) pollo;

(inf: coward) gallina m/f; **~ out** (inf) vi rajarse; **~pox** n varicela

chicory ['tʃɪkərɪ] n (for coffee) achicoria; (salad) escarola

chief [tʃi:f] n jefe/a m/f ♦ adj principal; **~ executive** n director(a) m/f general; **~ly** adv principalmente

chilblain ['tʃɪlbleɪn] n sabañón m

child [tʃaɪld] (pl **children**) n niño/a; (offspring) hijo/a; **~birth** n parto; **~hood** n niñez f, infancia; **~ish** adj pueril, aniñado; **~like** adj de niño; **~ minder** (BRIT) n madre f de día; **~ren** ['tʃɪldrən] npl of **child**

Chile ['tʃɪli] n Chile m; **~an** adj, n chileno/a m/f

chill [tʃɪl] n frío; (MED) resfriado ♦ vt enfriar; (CULIN) congelar

chil(l)i ['tʃɪli] (BRIT) n chile m (SP), ají m (AM)

chilly ['tʃɪli] adj frío

chime [tʃaɪm] n repique m; (of clock) campanada ♦ vi repicar; sonar

chimney ['tʃɪmnɪ] n chimenea; **~ sweep** n deshollinador m

chimpanzee [tʃɪmpæn'zi:] n chimpancé m

chin [tʃɪn] n mentón m, barbilla

china ['tʃaɪnə] n porcelana; (crockery) loza

China ['tʃaɪnə] n China m; **Chinese** [tʃaɪ'ni:z] adj chino ♦ n inv chino/a; (LING) chino

chink [tʃɪŋk] n (opening) grieta, hendedura; (noise) tintineo

chip [tʃɪp] n (gen pl: CULIN: BRIT) patata (SP) or papa (AM) frita; (: US: also: potato ~) patata or papa frita; (of wood) astilla; (of glass, stone) lasca; (at poker) ficha; (COMPUT) chip m ♦ vt (cup, plate) desconchar

chiropodist [kɪ'rɔpədɪst] (BRIT) n pedicuro/a, callista m/f

chirp [tʃə:p] vi (bird) gorjear, piar

chisel ['tʃɪzl] n (for wood) escoplo; (for stone) cincel m

chit [tʃɪt] n nota

chitchat ['tʃɪttʃæt] n chismes mpl, habladurías fpl

chivalry ['ʃɪvəlrɪ] n caballerosidad f

chives [tʃaɪvz] npl cebollinos mpl

chlorine ['klɔ:ri:n] n cloro

chock-a-block ['tʃɔkə'blɔk] adj atestado

chock-full ['tʃɔk'ful] adj atestado

chocolate ['tʃɔklɪt] n chocolate m; (sweet) bombón m

choice [tʃɔɪs] n elección f, selección f; (option) opción f; (preference) preferencia ♦ adj escogido

choir ['kwaɪə*] n coro; **~boy** n niño de coro

choke [tʃəuk] vi ahogarse; (on food) atragantarse ♦ vt estrangular, ahogar; (block): **to be ~d with** estar atascado de ♦ n (AUT) estárter m

cholesterol [kə'lɛstərɔl] n colesterol m

choose [tʃuːz] (pt **chose**, pp **chosen**) vt escoger, elegir; (team) seleccionar; **to ~ to do sth** optar por hacer algo

choosy ['tʃuːzɪ] adj delicado

chop [tʃɔp] vt (wood) cortar, tajar; (CULIN: also: ~ up) picar ♦ n (CULIN) chuleta; **~s** npl (jaws) boca, labios mpl

chopper ['tʃɔpə*] n (helicopter) helicóptero

choppy ['tʃɔpɪ] adj (sea) picado, agitado

chopsticks ['tʃɔpstɪks] npl palillos mpl

chord [kɔːd] n (MUS) acorde m

chore [tʃɔː*] n faena, tarea; (routine task) trabajo rutinario

chorus ['kɔːrəs] n coro; (repeated part of song) estribillo

chose [tʃəuz] pt of **choose**

chosen ['tʃəuzn] pp of **choose**

chowder ['tʃaudə*] n (esp US) sopa de pescado

Christ [kraist] n Cristo

christen ['krɪsn] vt bautizar

Christian ['krɪstɪən] adj, n cristiano/a m/f; **~ity** |-'ænɪtɪ] n cristianismo; **~ name** n nombre m de pila

Christmas ['krɪsməs] n Navidad f; **Merry ~!** ¡Felices Pascuas!; **~ card** n crismas m inv, tarjeta de Navidad; **~ Day** n día m de Navidad; **~ Eve** n Nochebuena; **~ tree** n árbol m de Navidad

chrome [krəum] n cromo

chronic ['krɔnɪk] adj crónico

chronological [krɔnə'lɔdʒɪkəl] adj cronológica

chubby ['tʃʌbɪ] adj regordete

chuck [tʃʌk] (inf) vt lanzar, arrojar; (BRIT: also: ~ up) abandonar; **~ out** vt (person) echar (fuera); (rubbish etc) tirar

chuckle ['tʃʌkl] vi reírse entre dientes

chug [tʃʌg] vi resoplar; (car, boat: also: ~ along) avanzar traqueteando

chum [tʃʌm] n compañero/a

chunk [tʃʌŋk] n pedazo, trozo

church [tʃəːtʃ] n iglesia; **~yard** n cementerio

churn [tʃəːn] n (for butter) mantequera; (for milk) lechera; **~ out** vt producir en serie

chute [ʃuːt] n (also: rubbish ~) vertedero; (for coal etc) rampa de caída

chutney ['tʃʌtnɪ] n condimento a base de frutas de la India

CIA (US) n abbr (= Central Intelligence Agency) CIA f

CID (BRIT) n abbr (= Criminal Investigation Department) ≈ B.I.C. f (SP)

cider ['saɪdə*] n sidra

cigar [sɪ'gɑː*] n puro

cigarette [sɪgə'ret] n cigarrillo (SP), cigarro (AM); pitillo; **~ case** n pitillera; **~ end** n colilla

Cinderella |sɪndə'relə] n Cenicienta

cinders ['sɪndəz] npl cenizas fpl

cine camera ['sɪnɪ-] (BRIT) n cámara cinematográfica

cinema ['sɪnəmə] n cine m

cinnamon ['sɪnəmən] n canela

circle ['səːkl] n círculo; (in theatre) anfiteatro ♦ vi dar vueltas ♦ vt (surround) rodear, cercar; (move round) dar la vuelta a

circuit ['səːkɪt] n circuito; (tour) gira; (track) pista; (lap) vuelta; **~ous** [səː'kjuɪtəs] adj indirecto

circular ['səːkjulə*] adj circular ♦ n circular f

circulate ['səːkjuleɪt] vi circular; (person: at party etc) hablar con los invitados ♦ vt poner en circulación; **circulation** [-'leɪʃən] n circulación f; (of newspaper) tirada

circumstances ['səːkəmstənsɪz] npl circunstancias fpl; (financial condition) situación f económica

circus ['səːkəs] n circo

CIS n abbr (= Commonwealth of Independent States) CEI f

cistern ['sɪstən] n tanque m, depósito; (in toilet) cisterna

citizen ['sɪtɪzn] n (POL) ciudadano/a; (of city) vecino/a, habitante m/f; **~ship** n ciudadanía

citrus fruits ['sɪtrəs-] npl agrios mpl

city ['sɪtɪ] n ciudad f; **the C~** centro financiero de Londres

civic ['sɪvɪk] adj cívico: (authorities) municipal; **~ centre** (BRIT) n centro público

civil ['sɪvɪl] adj civil; (polite) atento, cortés; **~ engineer** n ingeniero de caminos(, canales y puertos); **~ian** [sɪ'vɪlɪən] adj civil (no militar) ♦ n civil m/f, paisano/a

civilization [sɪvɪlaɪ'zeɪʃən] n civilización f

civilized ['sɪvɪlaɪzd] adj civilizado

civil: ~ law n derecho civil; **~ servant** n funcionario/a del Estado; **C~ Service** n administración f pública; **~ war** n guerra civil

claim [kleɪm] vt exigir, reclamar; (rights etc) reivindicar; (assert) pretender ♦ vi (for insurance) reclamar ♦ n reclamación f; pretensión f; **~ant** n demandante m/f

clairvoyant [klɛə'vɔɪənt] n clarividente m/f

clam [klæm] n almeja

clamber ['klæmbə*] vi trepar

clammy ['klæmɪ] adj frío y húmedo

clamour ['klæmə*] (US **clamor**) vi: **to ~ for** clamar por, pedir a voces

clamp [klæmp] n abrazadera, grapa ♦ vt (2 things together) cerrar fuertemente; (one thing on another) afianzar (con abrazadera); (AUT: wheel) poner el cepo a; **~ down on** vt fus (subj: government, police) reforzar la lucha contra

clang [klæŋ] vi sonar, hacer estruendo

clap [klæp] vi aplaudir; **~ping** n aplausos mpl

claret ['klærət] n burdeos m inv

clarify ['klærɪfaɪ] vt aclarar

clarinet [klærɪ'net] n clarinete m

clash [klæʃ] n enfrentamiento; choque m; desacuerdo; estruendo ♦ vi (fight) enfrentarse; (beliefs) chocar; (disagree) estar en desacuerdo; (colours) desentonar; (two events) coincidir

clasp [klɑːsp] n (hold) apretón m; (of necklace, bag) cierre m ♦ vt apretar; abrazar

class [klɑːs] n clase f ♦ vt clasificar

classic ['klæsɪk] adj, n clásico; **~al** adj clásico

classified ['klæsɪfaɪd] adj (information) reservado; **~ advertisement** n anuncio por palabras

classmate ['klɑːsmeɪt] n compañero/a de clase

classroom ['klɑːsrum] n aula

clatter ['klætə*] n estrépito ♦ vi hacer ruido or estrépito

clause [klɔːz] n cláusula; (LING) oración f

claw [klɔː] n (of cat) uña; (of bird of prey) garra; (of lobster) pinza

clay [kleɪ] n arcilla

clean [kliːn] adj limpio; (record, reputation) bueno, intachable; (joke) decente ♦ vt limpiar; (hands etc) lavar; **~ out** vt limpiar; **~ up** vt limpiar, asear; **~-cut** adj (person) bien parecido; **~er** n (person) asistenta; (substance) producto para la limpieza; **~er's** n tintorería; **~ing** n limpieza; **~liness** ['klenlɪnɪs] n limpieza

cleanse [klenz] vt limpiar; **~r** n (for face) crema limpiadora

clean-shaven adj sin barba, afeitado

cleansing department (BRIT) n departamento de limpieza

clear [klɪə*] adj claro; (road, way) libre; (conscience) limpio, tranquilo; (skin) terso; (sky) despejado ♦ vt (space) despejar, limpiar; (LAW: suspect) absolver; (obstacle) salvar, saltar por encima de; (cheque) aceptar ♦ vi (fog etc) despejarse ♦ adv: **~ of** a distancia de; **to ~ the table** recoger or levantar la mesa; **~ up** vt limpiar; (mystery) aclarar, resolver; **~ance** n (removal) despeje m; (permission) acreditación f; **~-cut** adj bien definido, nítido; **~ing** n (in wood) claro; **~ing bank** (BRIT) n cámara de compensación; **~ly** adv claramente; (evidently) sin duda; **~way** (BRIT) n carretera donde no se puede parar

clef [klef] n (MUS) clave f

cleft [kleft] n (in rock) grieta, hendedura

clench [klentʃ] vt apretar, cerrar

clergy ['klɜːdʒɪ] n clero; **~man** n clérigo

clerical ['klerɪkəl] adj de oficina; (REL) clerical

clerk [klɑːk, (US) klɜːrk] n (BRIT) oficinista m/f; (US) dependiente/a m/f

clever ['klevə*] adj (intelligent) inteligente,

listo; (skilful) hábil; (device, arrangement) ingenioso

click [klɪk] vt (tongue) chasquear; (heels) taconear ♦ vi (COMPUT) hacer clic

client ['klaɪənt] n cliente m/f

cliff [klɪf] n acantilado

climate ['klaɪmɪt] n clima m

climax ['klaɪmæks] n (of battle, career) apogeo; (of film, book) punto culminante; (sexual) orgasmo

climb [klaɪm] vi subir; (plant) trepar; (move with effort): **to ~ over a wall/into a car** trepar a una tapia/subir a un coche ♦ vt (stairs) subir; (tree) trepar a; (mountain) escalar ♦ n subida; **~-down** n vuelta atrás; **~er** n alpinista m/f (SP), andinista m/f (AM); **~ing** n alpinismo (SP), andinismo (AM)

clinch [klɪntʃ] vt (deal) cerrar; (argument) remachar

cling [klɪŋ] (pt, pp clung) vi: **to ~ to** agarrarse a; (clothes) pegarse a

clinic ['klɪnɪk] n clínica; **~al** adj clínico; (fig) frío

clink [klɪŋk] vi tintinar

clip [klɪp] n (for hair) horquilla; (also: paper ~) sujetapapeles m inv, clip m; (TV, CINEMA) fragmento ♦ vt (cut) cortar; (also: ~ together) unir; **~pers** npl (for gardening) tijeras fpl; **~ping** n (newspaper) recorte m

clique [kliːk] n camarilla

cloak [kləuk] n capa, manto ♦ vt (fig) encubrir, disimular; **~room** n guardarropa; (BRIT: WC) lavabo (SP), aseos mpl (SP), baño (AM)

clock [klɔk] n reloj m; **~ in** or **on** vi fichar, picar; **~ off** or **out** vi fichar or picar la salida; **~wise** adv en el sentido de las agujas del reloj; **~work** n aparato de relojería ♦ adj (toy) de cuerda

clog [klɔg] n zueco, chanclo ♦ vt atascar ♦ vi (also: ~ up) atascarse

cloister ['klɔɪstə*] n claustro

close¹ [kləus] adj (near): **~ (to)** cerca (de); (friend) íntimo; (connection) estrecho; (examination) detallado, minucioso; (weather) bochornoso; **to have a ~ shave** (fig) escaparse por un pelo ♦ adv cerca; **~ by**, **~ at hand** muy cerca; **~ to** prep cerca de

close² [kləuz] vt (shut) cerrar; (end) concluir, terminar ♦ vi (shop etc) cerrarse; (end) concluirse, terminarse ♦ n (end) fin m, final m, conclusión f; **~ down** vi cerrarse definitivamente; **~d** adj (shop etc) cerrado; **~d shop** n taller m gremial

close-knit [kləus'nɪt] adj (fig) muy unido

closely ['kləuslɪ] adv (study) con detalle; (watch) de cerca; (resemble) estrechamente

closet ['klɔzɪt] n armario

close-up ['kləusʌp] n primer plano

closure ['kləʊʒə*] n cierre m

clot [klɔt] n (gen: blood ~) coágulo; (inf: idiot) imbécil m/f ♦ vi (blood) coagularse

cloth [klɔθ] n (material) tela, paño; (rag) trapo

clothe [kləʊð] vt vestir; ~s npl ropa; ~s brush n cepillo (para la ropa); ~s line n cuerda (para tender la ropa); ~s peg (US ~s pin) n pinza

clothing ['kləʊðɪŋ] n = **clothes**

cloud [klaʊd] n nube f; ~burst n aguacero; ~y adj nublado, nubloso; (liquid) turbio

clout [klaʊt] vt dar un tortazo a

clove [kləʊv] n clavo; ~ of garlic diente m de ajo

clover ['kləʊvə*] n trébol m

clown [klaʊn] n payaso ♦ vi (also: ~ about, ~ around) hacer el payaso

cloying ['klɔɪɪŋ] adj empalagoso

club [klʌb] n (society) club m; (weapon) porra, cachiporra; (also: golf ~) palo ♦ vt aporrear ♦ vi: to ~ together (for gift) comprar entre todos; ~s npl (CARDS) tréboles mpl; ~ class n (AVIAT) clase f preferente; ~house n local social, sobre todo en clubs deportivos

cluck [klʌk] vi cloquear

clue [klu:] n pista; (in crosswords) indicación f; I haven't a ~ no tengo ni idea

clump [klʌmp] n (of trees) grupo

clumsy ['klʌmzɪ] adj (person) torpe, desmañado; (tool) difícil de manejar; (movement) desgarbado

clung [klʌŋ] pt, pp of **cling**

cluster ['klʌstə*] n grupo ♦ vi agruparse, apiñarse

clutch [klʌtʃ] n (AUT) embrague m; (grasp): ~es garras fpl ♦ vt asir; agarrar

clutter ['klʌtə*] vt atestar

cm abbr (= centimetre) cm

CND n abbr (= Campaign for Nuclear Disarmament) plataforma pro desarme nuclear

Co. abbr = county; company

c/o abbr (= care of) c/a, a/c

coach [kəʊtʃ] n autocar m (SP), coche m de línea; (horse-drawn) coche m; (of train) vagón m, coche m; (SPORT) entrenador(a) m/f, instructor(a) m/f; (tutor) profesor(a) m/f particular ♦ vt (SPORT) entrenar; (student) preparar, enseñar; ~ trip n excursión f en autocar

coal [kəʊl] n carbón m; ~ face n frente m de carbón; ~field n yacimiento de carbón

coalition [kəʊə'lɪʃən] n coalición f

coalman ['kəʊlmən] (irreg) n carbonero

coalmine ['kəʊlmaɪn] n mina de carbón

coarse [kɔ:s] adj basto, burdo; (vulgar) grosero, ordinario

coast [kəʊst] n costa, litoral m ♦ vi (AUT) ir en punto muerto; ~al adj costero, costanero;

~guard n guardacostas m inv; ~line n litoral m

coat [kəʊt] n abrigo; (of animal) pelaje m, lana; (of paint) mano f, capa ♦ vt cubrir, revestir; ~ of arms n escudo de armas; ~ hanger n percha (SP), gancho (AM); ~ing n capa, baño

coax [kəʊks] vt engatusar

cobbler ['kɔblə] n zapatero (remendón)

cobbles ['kɔblz] npl, **cobblestones** ['kɔblstəʊnz] npl adoquines mpl

cobweb ['kɔbweb] n telaraña

cocaine [kə'keɪn] n cocaína

cock [kɔk] n (rooster) gallo; (male bird) macho ♦ vt (gun) amartillar; ~erel n gallito

cockle ['kɔkl] n berberecho

cockney ['kɔknɪ] n habitante de ciertos barrios de Londres

cockpit ['kɔkpɪt] n cabina

cockroach ['kɔkrəʊtʃ] n cucaracha

cocktail ['kɔkteɪl] n coctel m, cóctel m; ~ cabinet n mueble-bar m; ~ party n coctel m, cóctel m

cocoa ['kəʊkəʊ] n cacao; (drink) chocolate m

coconut ['kəʊkənʌt] n coco

cod [kɔd] n bacalao

C.O.D. abbr (= cash on delivery) C.A.E.

code [kəʊd] n código; (cipher) clave f; (dialling ~) prefijo; (post ~) código postal

cod-liver oil ['kɔdlɪvər–] n aceite m de hígado de bacalao

coercion [kəʊ'ə:ʃən] n coacción f

coffee ['kɔfɪ] n café m; ~ bar n (BRIT) n cafetería; ~ bean n grano de café; ~ break n descanso (para tomar café); ~pot n cafetera; ~ table n mesita (para servir el café)

coffin ['kɔfɪn] n ataúd m

cog [kɔg] n (wheel) rueda dentada; (tooth) diente m

cogent ['kəʊdʒənt] adj convincente

cognac ['kɔnjæk] n coñac m

coil [kɔɪl] n rollo; (ELEC) bobina, carrete m; (contraceptive) espiral f ♦ vt enrollar

coin [kɔɪn] n moneda ♦ vt (word) inventar, idear; ~age n moneda; ~-box n (BRIT) n cabina telefónica

coincide [kəʊɪn'saɪd] vi coincidir; (agree) estar de acuerdo; **coincidence** [kəʊ'ɪn-sɪdəns] n casualidad f

Coke ® [kəʊk] n Coca-Cola ®

coke [kəʊk] n (coal) coque m

colander ['kɔləndə*] n colador m, escurridor m

cold [kəʊld] adj frío ♦ n frío; (MED) resfriado; it's ~ hace frío; to be ~ (person) tener frío; to catch ~ enfriarse; to catch a ~ resfriarse, acatarrarse; in ~ blood a sangre fría; ~-shoulder vt dar or volver la espalda a;

~ sore n herpes mpl or fpl
coleslaw ['kəulslɔː] n especie de ensalada de
col
colic ['kɔlɪk] n cólico
collapse [kə'læps] vi hundirse, derrumbarse;
(MED) sufrir un colapso ♦ n hundimiento,
derrumbamiento; (MED) colapso; **collapsible**
adj plegable
collar ['kɔlə*] n (of coat, shirt) cuello; (of dog
etc) collar; **~bone** n clavícula
collateral [kɔ'lætərəl] n garantía colateral
colleague ['kɔliːg] n colega m/f; (at work)
compañero, a
collect [kə'lɛkt] vt (litter, mail etc) recoger;
(as a hobby) coleccionar; (BRIT: call and pick
up) recoger; (debts, subscriptions etc)
recaudar ♦ vi reunirse; (dust) acumularse; **to
call ~** (US: TEL) llamar a cobro revertido; **~ion**
[kə'lɛkʃən] n colección f; (of mail, for charity)
recogida; **~or** n coleccionista m/f
college ['kɔlɪdʒ] n colegio mayor; (of
agriculture, technology) escuela universitaria
collide [kə'laɪd] vi chocar
colliery ['kɔlɪərɪ] (BRIT) n mina de carbón
collision [kə'lɪʒən] n choque m
colloquial [kə'ləukwɪəl] adj familiar,
coloquial
Colombia [kə'lɔmbɪə] n Colombia; **~n** adj, n
colombiano/a
colon ['kəulən] n (sign) dos puntos; (MED)
colon m
colonel ['kəːnl] n coronel m
colonial [kə'ləunɪəl] adj colonial
colony ['kɔlənɪ] n colonia
colour(e) ['kʌlə*] (US **color**) n color m ♦ vt
color(e)ar; (dye) teñir; (fig: account) adornar;
(: judgement) distorsionar ♦ vi (blush)
sonrojarse; **~s** npl (of party, club) colores mpl;
in ~ en color; **~ in** vt colorear; **~ bar** n
segregación f racial; **~-blind** adj daltónico;
~ed adj de color; (photo) en color; **~ film** n
película en color; **~ful** adj lleno de color;
(story) fantástico; (person) excéntrico; **~ing** n
(complexion) tez f; (in food) colorante m;
~ scheme n combinación f de colores;
~ television n televisión f en color
colt [kəult] n potro
column ['kɔləm] n columna; **~ist**
['kɔləmnɪst] n columnista m/f
coma ['kəumə] n coma m
comb [kəum] n peine m; (ornamental)
peineta ♦ vt (hair) peinar; (area) registrar a
fondo
combat ['kɔmbæt] n combate m ♦ vt
combatir
combination [kɔmbɪ'neɪʃən] n combinación
f
combine [vb kəm'baɪn, n 'kɔmbaɪn] vt
combinar; (qualities) reunir ♦ vi combinarse

♦ n (ECON) cartel m; **~ (harvester)** n
cosechadora

come [kʌm] (pt came, pp come) vi **1** (movement towards) venir; **to ~ running** venir
corriendo
2 (arrive) llegar; **he's ~ here to work** ha
venido aquí para trabajar; **to ~ home** volver a
casa
3 (reach): **to ~ to** llegar a; **the bill came to
£40** la cuenta ascendía a cuarenta libras
4 (occur): **an idea came to me** se me ocurrió
una idea
5 (be, become): **to ~ loose/undone** etc
aflojarse/desabrocharse, desatarse etc; **I've
~ to like him** por fin ha llegado a gustarme
come about vi suceder, ocurrir
come across vt fus (person) topar con;
(thing) dar con
come away vi (leave) marcharse; (become
detached) desprenderse
come back vi (return) volver
come by vt fus (acquire) conseguir
come down vi (price) bajar; (tree, building)
ser derribado
come forward vi presentarse
come from vt fus (place, source) ser de
come in vi (visitor) entrar; (train, report)
llegar; (fashion) ponerse de moda; (on deal
etc) entrar
come in for vt fus (criticism etc) recibir
come into vt fus (money) heredar; (be
involved) tener que ver con; **to ~ into fashion**
ponerse de moda
come off vi (button) soltarse, desprenderse;
(attempt) salir bien
come on vi (pupil) progresar; (work, project)
desarrollarse; (lights) encenderse; (electricity)
volver; **~ on!** ¡vamos!
come out vi (fact) salir a la luz; (book, sun)
salir; (stain) quitarse
come round vi (after faint, operation) volver
en sí
come to vi (wake) volver en sí
come up vi (sun) salir; (problem) surgir;
(event) aproximarse; (in conversation)
mencionarse
come up against vt fus (resistance etc)
tropezar con
come up with vt fus (idea) sugerir; (money)
conseguir
come upon vt fus (find) dar con

comeback ['kʌmbæk] n: **to make a ~**
(THEATRE) volver a las tablas
comedian [kə'miːdɪən] n cómico;
comedienne [-'ɛn] n cómica
comedy ['kɔmɪdɪ] n comedia; (humour)

comicidad f

comet ['kɔmɪt] n cometa m

comeuppance [kʌm'ʌpəns] n: **to get one's ~** llevar su merecido

comfort ['kʌmfət] n bienestar m; (relief) alivio ♦ vt consolar; **~s** npl (of home etc) comodidades fpl; **~able** adj cómodo; (financially) acomodado; (easy) fácil; **~ably** adv (sit) cómodamente; (live) holgadamente; **~ station** (US) n servicios mpl

comic ['kɔmɪk] adj (also: **~al**) cómico ♦ n (comedian) cómico; (BRIT: for children) tebeo; (BRIT: for adults) comic m; **~ strip** n tira cómica

coming ['kʌmɪŋ] n venida, llegada ♦ adj que viene; **~(s) and going(s)** n(pl) ir y venir m, ajetreo

comma ['kɔmə] n coma f

command [kə'mɑːnd] n orden f, mandato; (MIL: authority) mando; (mastery) dominio ♦ vt (troops) mandar; (give orders to): **to ~ sb to do** mandar or ordenar a uno hacer; **~eer** [kɔmən'dɪə*] vt requisar; **~er** n (MIL) comandante m/f, jefe/a m/f

commemorate [kə'mɛməreɪt] vt conmemorar

commence [kə'mɛns] vt, vi comenzar, empezar

commend [kə'mɛnd] vt elogiar, alabar; (recommend) recomendar

commensurate [kə'mɛnʃərɪt] adj: **~ with** en proporción a, que corresponde a

comment ['kɔmɛnt] n comentario ♦ vi: **to ~ on** hacer comentarios sobre; **"no ~"** (written) "sin comentarios"; (spoken) "no tengo nada que decir"; **~ary** ['kɔməntərɪ] n comentario; **~ator** ['kɔməntɛɪtə*] n comentarista m/f

commerce ['kɔmə:s] n comercio

commercial [kə'mə:ʃəl] adj comercial ♦ n (TV, RADIO) anuncio

commiserate [kə'mɪzəreɪt] vi: **to ~ with** compadecerse de, condolerse de

commission [kə'mɪʃən] n (committee, fee) comisión f ♦ vt (work of art) encargar; **out of ~** fuera de servicio; **~aire** [kəmɪʃə'nɛə*] (BRIT) n portero; **~er** n (POLICE) comisario de policía

commit [kə'mɪt] vt (act) cometer; (resources) dedicar; (to sb's care) entregar; **to ~ o.s. (to do)** comprometerse (a hacer); **to ~ suicide** suicidarse; **~ment** n compromiso; (to ideology etc) entrega

committee [kə'mɪtɪ] n comité m

commodity [kə'mɔdɪtɪ] n mercancía

common ['kɔmən] adj común; (pej) ordinario ♦ n campo común; **the C~s** npl (BRIT) (la Cámara de) los Comunes mpl; **in ~** en común; **~er** n plebeyo; **~ law** n ley f consuetudinaria; **~ly** adv comúnmente;

C~ Market n Mercado Común; **~place** adj de lo más común; **~room** n sala común; **~ sense** n sentido común; **the C~wealth** n la Commonwealth

commotion [kə'məuʃən] n tumulto, confusión f

commune [n 'kɔmjuːn, vb kə'mjuːn] n (group) comuna f ♦ vi: **to ~ with** comulgar or conversar con

communicate [kə'mjuːnɪkeɪt] vt comunicar ♦ vi: **to ~ (with)** comunicarse (con); (in writing) estar en contacto (con)

communication [kəmjuːnɪ'keɪʃən] n comunicación f; **~ cord** (BRIT) n timbre m de alarma

communion [kə'mjuːnɪən] n (also: Holy C~) comunión f

communiqué [kə'mjuːnɪkeɪ] n comunicado, parte f

communism ['kɔmjunɪzəm] n comunismo; **communist** adj, n comunista m/f

community [kə'mjuːnɪtɪ] n comunidad f; (large group) colectividad f; **~ centre** n centro social; **~ chest** (US) n arca comunitaria, fondo común

commutation ticket [kɔmjuː'teɪʃən-] (US) n billete m de abono

commute [kə'mjuːt] vi viajar a diario de la casa al trabajo ♦ vt conmutar; **~r** n persona (que viaja ... see vi)

compact [adj kəm'pækt, n 'kɔmpækt] adj compacto ♦ n (also: powder ~) polvera; **~ disc** n compact disc m; **~ disc player** n reproductor m de disco compacto, compact disc m

companion [kəm'pænɪən] n compañero/a; **~ship** n compañerismo

company ['kʌmpənɪ] n compañía; (COMM) sociedad f, compañía; **to keep sb ~** acompañar a uno; **~ secretary** (BRIT) n secretario/a de compañía

comparative [kəm'pærətɪv] adj relativo; (study) comparativo; **~ly** adv (relatively) relativamente

compare [kəm'pɛə*] vt: **to ~ sth/sb with/to** comparar algo/a uno con ♦ vi: **to ~ (with)** compararse (con); **comparison** [-'pærɪsn] n comparación f

compartment [kəm'pɑːtmənt] n (also: RAIL) compartim(i)ento

compass ['kʌmpəs] n brújula; **~es** npl (MATH) compás m

compassion [kəm'pæʃən] n compasión f; **~ate** adj compasivo

compatible [kəm'pætɪbl] adj compatible

compel [kəm'pɛl] vt obligar

compensate ['kɔmpənseɪt] vt compensar ♦ vi: **to ~ for** compensar; **compensation** [-'seɪʃən] n (for loss) indemnización f

compère ['kɔmpɛə*] n presentador m
compete [kəm'pi:t] vi (take part) tomar
parte, concurrir; (vie with): **to ~ with**
competir con, hacer competencia a
competent ['kɔmpɪtənt] adj competente,
capaz
competition [kɔmpɪ'tɪʃən] n (contest)
concurso; (rivalry) competencia
competitive [kəm'petɪtɪv] adj (ECON, SPORT)
competitivo
competitor [kəm'petɪtə*] n (rival)
competidor(a) m/f; (participant) concursante
m/f
complacency [kəm'pleɪsnsɪ] n
autosatisfacción f
complacent [kəm'pleɪsənt] adj
autocomplaciente
complain [kəm'pleɪn] vi quejarse; (COMM)
reclamar; **~t** n queja; reclamación f; (MED)
enfermedad f
complement [n 'kɔmplɪmənt, vb
'kɔmplɪment] n complemento; (esp of ship's
crew) dotación f ♦ vt (enhance)
complementar; **~ary** [kɔmplɪ'mentərɪ] adj
complementario
complete [kəm'pli:t] adj (full) completo;
(finished) acabado ♦ vt (fulfil) completar;
(finish) acabar; (a form) llenar; **~ly** adv
completamente; **completion** [-'pli:ʃən] n
terminación f; (of contract) realización f
complex ['kɔmpleks] adj, n complejo
complexion [kəm'plekʃən] n (of face) tez f,
cutis m
compliance [kəm'plaɪəns] n (submission)
sumisión f; (agreement) conformidad f; **in
~ with** de acuerdo con
complicate ['kɔmplɪkeɪt] vt complicar; **~d**
adj complicado; **complication** [-'keɪʃən] n
complicación f
compliment ['kɔmplɪmənt] n (formal)
cumplido ♦ vt felicitar; **~s** npl (regards)
saludos mpl; **to pay sb a ~** hacer cumplidos a
uno; **~ary** [-'mentərɪ] adj lisonjero; (free) de
favor
comply [kəm'plaɪ] vi: **to ~ with** cumplir con
component [kəm'pəunənt] adj componente
♦ n (TECH) pieza
compose [kəm'pəuz] vt: **to be ~d of**
componerse de; (music etc) componer; **to
~ o.s.** tranquilizarse; **~d** adj sosegado; **~r** n
(MUS) compositor(a) m/f; **composition**
[kɔmpə'zɪʃən] n composición f
compost ['kɔmpɔst] n abono (vegetal)
composure [kəm'pəuʒə*] n serenidad f,
calma
compound ['kɔmpaund] n (CHEM)
compuesto; (LING) palabra compuesta;
(enclosure) recinto ♦ adj compuesto;
(fracture) complicado

comprehend [kɔmprɪ'hend] vt comprender;
comprehension [-'henʃən] n comprensión f
comprehensive [kɔmprɪ'hensɪv] adj
exhaustivo; (INSURANCE) contra todo riesgo;
~ (school) n centro estatal de enseñanza
secundaria; ≈ Instituto Nacional de
Bachillerato (SP)
compress [vb kəm'pres, n 'kɔmpres] vt
comprimir; (information) condensar ♦ n
(MED) compresa
comprise [kəm'praɪz] vt (also: be ~d of)
comprender, constar de; (constitute)
constituir
compromise ['kɔmprəmaɪz] n (agreement)
arreglo ♦ vt comprometer ♦ vi transigir
compulsion [kəm'pʌlʃən] n compulsión f;
(force) obligación f
compulsive [kəm'pʌlsɪv] adj compulsivo;
(viewing, reading) obligado
compulsory [kəm'pʌlsərɪ] adj obligatorio
computer [kəm'pju:tə*] n ordenador m,
computador m, computadora f; **~ game** n
juego para ordenador; **~-generated** adj
realizado por ordenador, creado por
ordenador; **~ize** vt (data) computerizar;
(system) informatizar; **~ programmer** n
programador(a) m/f; **~ programming** n
programación f; **~ science** n informática; **computing** [kəm'pju:tɪŋ] n (activity, science)
informática
comrade ['kɔmrɪd] n (POL, MIL) camarada;
(friend) compañero/a; **~ship** n camaradería,
compañerismo
con [kɔn] vt (deceive) engañar; (cheat) estafar
♦ n estafa
conceal [kən'si:l] vt ocultar
conceit [kən'si:t] n presunción f; **~ed** adj
presumido
conceive [kən'si:v] vt, vi concebir
concentrate ['kɔnsəntreɪt] vi concentrarse
♦ vt concentrar
concentration [kɔnsən'treɪʃən] n
concentración f
concept ['kɔnsept] n concepto
concern [kən'sə:n] n (matter) asunto;
(COMM) empresa; (anxiety) preocupación f
♦ vt (worry) preocupar; (involve) afectar;
(relate to) tener que ver con; **to be ~ed
(about)** interesarse (por), preocuparse (por);
~ing prep sobre, acerca de
concert ['kɔnsət] n concierto; **~ed**
[kən'sə:tɪd] adj (efforts etc) concertado;
~ hall n sala de conciertos
concerto [kən'tʃə:təu] n concierto
concession [kən'seʃən] n concesión f; **tax ~**
privilegio fiscal
conclude [kən'klu:d] vt concluir; (treaty etc)
firmar; (agreement) llegar a; (decide) llegar a
la conclusión de; **conclusion** [-'klu:ʒən] n

conclusión f; firma; **conclusive** [-'klu:sɪv] adj decisivo, concluyente

concoct [kən'kɔkt] vt confeccionar; (plot) tramar; (fig) concreto

concourse ['kɔnkɔːs] n vestíbulo

concrete ['kɔnkriːt] n hormigón m ♦ adj de hormigón; (fig) concreto

concur [kən'kəː*] vi estar de acuerdo, asentir

concurrently [kən'kʌrntlɪ] adv al mismo tiempo

concussion [kən'kʌʃən] n conmoción f cerebral

condemn [kən'dɛm] vt condenar; (building) declarar en ruina

condense [kən'dɛns] vi condensarse ♦ vt condensar, abreviar; **~d milk** n leche f condensada

condition [kən'dɪʃən] n condición f, estado; (requirement) condición f ♦ vt condicionar; **on ~ that** a condición (de) que; **~er** n suavizante

condolences [kən'dəulənsɪz] npl pésame m

condom ['kɔndəm] n condón m

condone [kən'dəun] vt condonar

conducive [kən'djuːsɪv] adj: **~ to** conducente a

conduct [n 'kɔndʌkt, vb kən'dʌkt] n conducta, comportamiento ♦ vt (lead) conducir; (manage) llevar a cabo, dirigir; (MUS) dirigir; **to ~ o.s.** comportarse; **~ed tour** (BRIT) n visita acompañada; **~or** n (of orchestra) director m; (US: on train) revisor(a) m/f; (on bus) cobrador m; (ELEC) conductor m; **~ress** n (on bus) cobradora

cone [kəun] n cono m; (pine ~) piña; (on road) pivote m; (for ice-cream) cucurucho

confectioner [kən'fɛkʃənə*] n repostero/a; **~'s (shop)** n confitería; **~y** n dulces mpl

confer [kən'fəː*] vt: **to ~ sth on** otorgar algo a ♦ vi conferenciar

conference ['kɔnfərəns] n (meeting) reunión f; (convention) congreso

confess [kən'fɛs] vt confesar ♦ vi admitir; **~ion** [-'fɛʃən] n confesión f

confetti [kən'fɛtɪ] n confeti m

confide [kən'faɪd] vi: **to ~ in** confiar en

confidence ['kɔnfɪdns] n (also: self-~) confianza; (secret) confidencia; **in ~** (speak, write) en confianza; **~ trick** n timo; **confident** adj seguro de sí mismo; (certain) seguro; **confidential** [kɔnfɪ'dɛnʃəl] adj confidencial

confine [kən'faɪn] vt (limit) limitar; (shut up) encerrar; **~d** adj (space) reducido; **~ment** n (prison) prisión f; **~s** ['kɔnfaɪnz] npl confines mpl

confirm [kən'fəːm] vt confirmar; **~ation** [kɔnfə'meɪʃən] n confirmación f; **~ed** adj empedernido

confiscate ['kɔnfɪskeɪt] vt confiscar

conflict [n 'kɔnflɪkt, vb kən'flɪkt] n conflicto ♦ vi (opinions) chocar; **~ing** adj contradictorio

conform [kən'fɔːm] vi conformarse; **to ~ to** ajustarse a

confound [kən'faund] vt confundir

confront [kən'frʌnt] vt (problems) hacer frente a; (enemy, danger) enfrentarse con; **~ation** [kɔnfrən'teɪʃən] n enfrentamiento

confuse [kən'fjuːz] vt (perplex) aturdir, desconcertar; (mix up) confundir; (complicate) complicar; **~d** adj confuso; (person) perplejo; **confusing** adj confuso; **confusion** [-'fjuːʒən] n confusión f

congeal [kən'dʒiːl] vi (blood) coagularse; (sauce etc) cuajarse

congested [kən'dʒɛstɪd] adj congestionado; **congestion** n congestión f

congratulate [kən'grætjuleɪt] vt: **to ~ sb (on)** felicitar a uno (por); **congratulations** [-'leɪʃənz] npl felicitaciones fpl; **congratulations!** ¡enhorabuena!

congregate ['kɔngrɪgeɪt] vi congregarse; **congregation** [-'geɪʃən] n (of a church) feligreses mpl

congress ['kɔngrɛs] n congreso; (US): **C~** Congreso; **C~man** (irreg) (US) n miembro del Congreso

conifer ['kɔnɪfə*] n conífera

conjunctivitis [kəndʒʌŋktɪ'vaɪtɪs] n conjuntivitis f

conjure ['kʌndʒə*] vi hacer juegos de manos; **~ up** vt (ghost, spirit) hacer aparecer; (memories) evocar; **~r** n ilusionista m/f

con man ['kɔn-] n estafador m

connect [kə'nɛkt] vt juntar, unir; (ELEC) conectar; (TEL: subscriber) poner; (: caller) poner al habla; (fig) relacionar, asociar ♦ vi: **to ~ with** (train) enlazar con; **to be ~ed with** (associated) estar relacionado con; **~ion** [-ʃən] n juntura, unión f; (ELEC) conexión f; (RAIL) enlace m; (TEL) comunicación f; (fig) relación f

connive [kə'naɪv] vi: **to ~ at** hacer la vista gorda a

connoisseur [kɔnɪ'sə*] n experto/a, entendido/a

conquer ['kɔŋkə*] vt (territory) conquistar; (enemy, feelings) vencer; **~or** n conquistador m

conquest ['kɔŋkwɛst] n conquista

cons [kɔnz] npl see **convenience**; **pro**

conscience ['kɔnʃəns] n conciencia

conscientious [kɔnʃɪ'ɛnʃəs] adj concienzudo; (objection) de conciencia

conscious ['kɔnʃəs] adj (deliberate) deliberado; (awake, aware) consciente; **~ness** n conciencia; (MED) conocimiento

conscript ['kɔnskrɪpt] n recluta m; **~ion** [kən'skrɪpʃən] n servicio militar (obligatorio)

consensus [kən'sɛnsəs] n consenso

consent [kən'sɛnt] n consentimiento ♦ vi: to ~ (to) consentir (en)

consequence ['kɔnsɪkwəns] n consecuencia; (significance) importancia

consequently ['kɔnsɪkwəntlɪ] adv por consiguiente

conservation [kɔnsə'veɪʃən] n conservación f

conservative [kən'sə:vətɪv] adj conservador(a); (estimate etc) cauteloso; **C~** (BRIT) adj, n (POL) conservador(a) m/f

conservatory [kən'sə:vətrɪ] n invernadero, (MUS) conservatorio

conserve [kən'sə:v] vt conservar ♦ n conserva

consider [kən'sɪdə*] vt considerar; (take into account) tener en cuenta; (study) estudiar, examinar; **to ~ doing sth** pensar en (la posibilidad de) hacer algo; **~able** adj considerable; **~ably** adv notablemente; **~ate** adj considerado; **consideration** [-'reɪʃən] n consideración f; (factor) factor m; **to give sth further consideration** estudiar algo más a fondo; **~ing** prep teniendo en cuenta

consign [kən'saɪn] vt: **to ~ to** (sth unwanted) relegar a; (person) destinar a; **~ment** n envío

consist [kən'sɪst] vi: **to ~ of** consistir en

consistency [kən'sɪstənsɪ] n (of argument etc) coherencia; consecuencia; (thickness) consistencia

consistent [kən'sɪstənt] adj (person) consecuente; (argument etc) coherente

consolation [kɔnsə'leɪʃən] n consuelo

console¹ [kən'səul] vt consolar

console² ['kɔnsəul] n consola

consonant ['kɔnsənənt] n consonante f

consortium [kən'sɔ:tɪəm] n consorcio

conspicuous [kən'spɪkjuəs] adj (visible) visible

conspiracy [kən'spɪrəsɪ] n conjura, complot m

constable ['kʌnstəbl] (BRIT) n policía m/f; **chief ~ ≈** jefe m de policía

constabulary [kən'stæbjulərɪ] n ≈ policía

constant ['kɔnstənt] adj constante; **~ly** adv constantemente

constipated ['kɔnstɪpeɪtəd] adj estreñido; **constipation** [kɔnstɪ'peɪʃən] n estreñimiento

constituency [kən'stɪtjuənsɪ] n (POL: area) distrito electoral; (: electors) electorado; **constituent** [-ənt] n (POL) elector(a) m/f; (part) componente m

constitution [kɔnstɪ'tju:ʃən] n constitución f; **~al** adj constitucional

constraint [kən'streɪnt] n obligación f; (limit) restricción f

construct [kən'strʌkt] vt construir; **~ion** [-ʃən] n construcción f; **~ive** adj constructivo

consul ['kɔnsl] n cónsul m/f; **~ate** ['kɔnsjulɪt] n consulado

consult [kən'sʌlt] vt consultar; **~ant** n (BRIT: MED) especialista m/f; (other specialist) asesor(a) m/f; **~ation** [kɔnsəl'teɪʃən] n consulta; **~ing room** (BRIT) n consultorio

consume [kən'sju:m] vt (eat) comerse; (drink) beberse; (fire etc, COMM) consumir; **~r** n consumidor(a) m/f; **~r goods** npl bienes mpl de consumo

consummate ['kɔnsʌmeɪt] vt consumar

consumption [kən'sʌmpʃən] n consumo

cont. abbr (= continued) sigue

contact ['kɔntækt] n contacto; (person) contacto; (: pej) enchufe m ♦ vt ponerse en contacto con; **~ lenses** npl lentes fpl de contacto

contagious [kən'teɪdʒəs] adj contagioso

contain [kən'teɪn] vt contener; **to ~ o.s.** contenerse; **~er** n recipiente m; (for shipping etc) contenedor m

contaminate [kən'tæmɪneɪt] vt contaminar

cont'd abbr (= continued) sigue

contemplate ['kɔntəmpleɪt] vt contemplar; (reflect upon) considerar

contemporary [kən'tɛmpərərɪ] adj, n contemporáneo,a m/f

contempt [kən'tɛmpt] n desprecio; **~ of court** (LAW) desacato (a los tribunales); **~ible** adj despreciable; **~uous** adj desdeñoso

contend [kən'tɛnd] vt (argue) afirmar ♦ vi: **to ~ with/for** luchar contra/por; **~er** n (SPORT) contendiente m/f

content [adj, vb kən'tɛnt, n 'kɔntɛnt] adj (happy) contento; (satisfied) satisfecho ♦ vt contentar; satisfacer ♦ n contenido; **~s** npl contenido; (table of) **~s** índice m de materias; **~ed** adj contento; satisfecho

contention [kən'tɛnʃən] n (assertion) aseveración f; (disagreement) discusión f

contest [n 'kɔntɛst, vb kən'tɛst] n lucha; (competition) concurso ♦ vt (dispute) impugnar; (POL) presentar como candidato/a en; **~ant** [kən'tɛstənt] n concursante m/f; (in fight) contendiente m/f

context ['kɔntɛkst] n contexto

continent ['kɔntɪnənt] n continente m; **the C~** (BRIT) el continente europeo; **~al** [-'nɛntl] adj continental; **~al breakfast** n desayuno estilo europeo; **~al quilt** (BRIT) n edredón m

contingency [kən'tɪndʒənsɪ] n contingencia

continual [kən'tɪnjuəl] adj continuo; **~ly** adv constantemente

continuation [kəntɪnju'eɪʃən] n prolongación f; (after interruption) reanudación f

continue [kən'tɪnju:] vi, vt seguir, continuar

continuous [kən'tɪnjuəs] *adj* continuo

contort [kən'tɔːt] *vt* retorcer

contour ['kɔntuə*] *n* contorno; (*also*: ~ line) curva de nivel

contraband ['kɔntrəbænd] *n* contrabando

contraceptive [kɔntrə'septɪv] *adj, n* anticonceptivo

contract [*n* 'kɔntrækt, *vb* kən'trækt] *n* contrato ♦ *vi* (*COMM*): **to ~ to do sth** comprometerse por contrato a hacer algo; (*become smaller*) contraerse, encogerse ♦ *vt* contraer; **~ion** [kən'trækʃən] *n* contracción *f*; **~or** *n* contratista *m/f*

contradict [kɔntrə'dɪkt] *vt* contradecir; **~ion** [-ʃən] *n* contradicción *f*

contraption [kən'træpʃən] (*pej*) *n* artilugio *m*

contrary¹ ['kɔntrərɪ] *adj* contrario ♦ *n* lo contrario; **on the ~** al contrario; **unless you hear to the ~** a no ser que le digan lo contrario

contrary² [kən'treərɪ] *adj* (*perverse*) terco

contrast [*n* 'kɔntrɑːst, *vt* kən'trɑːst] *n* contraste *m* ♦ *vt* comparar; **in ~ to** en contraste con

contravene [kɔntrə'viːn] *vt* infringir

contribute [kən'trɪbjuːt] *vi* contribuir ♦ *vt*: **to ~ £10/an article to** contribuir con 10 libras/un artículo a; **to ~ to** (*charity*) donar a; (*newspaper*) escribir para; (*discussion*) intervenir en; **contribution** [kɔntrɪ'bjuːʃən] *n* (*donation*) donativo; (*BRIT: for social security*) cotización *f*; (*to debate*) intervención *f*; (*to journal*) colaboración *f*; **contributor** *n* contribuyente *m/f*; (*to newspaper*) colaborador(a) *m/f*

contrive [kən'traɪv] *vt* (*invent*) idear ♦ *vi*: **to ~ to do** lograr hacer

control [kən'trəul] *vt* controlar; (*process etc*) dirigir; (*machinery*) manejar; (*temper*) dominar; (*disease*) contener ♦ *n* control *m*; **~s** *npl* (*of vehicle*) instrumentos *mpl* de mando; (*of radio*) controles *mpl*; (*governmental*) medidas *fpl* de control; **under ~** bajo control; **to be in ~ of** tener el mando de; **the car went out of ~** se perdió el control del coche; **~led substance** *n* sustancia controlada; **~ panel** *n* tablero de instrumentos; **~ room** *n* sala de mando; **~ tower** *n* (*AVIAT*) torre *f* de control

controversial [kɔntrə'vəːʃl] *adj* polémico

controversy ['kɔntrəvəːsɪ] *n* polémica

convalesce [kɔnvə'les] *vi* convalecer

convector [kən'vektə*] *n* calentador *m* de aire

convene [kən'viːn] *vt* convocar ♦ *vi* reunirse

convenience [kən'viːnɪəns] *n* (*easiness*) comodidad *f*; (*suitability*) idoneidad *f*; (*advantage*) ventaja; **at your ~** cuando le sea conveniente; **all modern ~s, all mod cons** (*BRIT*) todo confort

convenient [kən'viːnɪənt] *adj* (*useful*) útil; (*place, time*) conveniente

convent ['kɔnvənt] *n* convento

convention [kən'venʃən] *n* convención *f*; (*meeting*) asamblea; (*agreement*) convenio; **~al** *adj* convencional

converge [kən'vəːdʒ] *vi* convergir; (*people*): **to ~ on** dirigirse todos a

conversant [kən'vəːsnt] *adj*: **to be ~ with** estar al tanto de

conversation [kɔnvə'seɪʃən] *n* conversación *f*; **~al** *adj* familiar; **~al skill** facilidad *f* de palabra

converse [*n* 'kɔnvəːs, *vb* kən'vəːs] *n* inversa ♦ *vi* conversar; **~ly** [-'vəːslɪ] *adv* a la inversa

conversion [kən'vəːʃən] *n* conversión *f*

convert [*vb* kən'vəːt, *n* 'kɔnvəːt] *vt* (*REL, COMM*) convertir; (*alter*): **to ~ sth into/to** transformar algo en/convertir algo a ♦ *n* converso/a; **~ible** *adj* convertible ♦ *n* descapotable *m*

convey [kən'veɪ] *vt* llevar; (*thanks*) comunicar; (*idea*) expresar; **~or belt** *n* cinta transportadora

convict [*vb* kən'vɪkt, *n* 'kɔnvɪkt] *vt* (*find guilty*) declarar culpable a ♦ *n* presidiario/a; **~ion** [-ʃən] *n* condena; (*belief, certainty*) convicción *f*

convince [kən'vɪns] *vt* convencer; **~d** *adj*: **~d of/that** convencido de/de que; **convincing** *adj* convincente

convoluted ['kɔnvəluːtɪd] *adj* (*argument etc*) enrevesado

convoy ['kɔnvɔɪ] *n* convoy *m*

convulse [kən'vʌls] *vt*: **to be ~d with laughter** desternillarse de risa; **convulsion** [-'vʌlʃən] *n* convulsión *f*

cook [kuk] *vt* (*stew etc*) guisar; (*meal*) preparar ♦ *vi* cocer; (*person*) cocinar ♦ *n* cocinero/a; **~ book** *n* libro de cocina; **~er** *n* cocina; **~ery** *n* cocina; **~ery book** (*BRIT*) *n* = ~ **book**; **~ie** (*US*) *n* galleta; **~ing** *n* cocina

cool [kuːl] *adj* fresco; (*not afraid*) tranquilo; (*unfriendly*) frío ♦ *vt* enfriar ♦ *vi* enfriarse; **~ness** *n* frescura; tranquilidad *f*; (*indifference*) falta de entusiasmo

coop [kuːp] *n* gallinero ♦ *vt*: **to ~ up** (*fig*) encerrar

cooperate [kəu'ɔpəreɪt] *vi* cooperar, colaborar; **cooperation** [-'reɪʃən] *n* cooperación *f*, colaboración *f*; **cooperative** [-rətɪv] *adj* (*business*) cooperativo; (*person*) servicial ♦ *n* cooperativa

coordinate [*vb* kəu'ɔːdɪneɪt, *n* kəu'ɔːdɪnət] *vt* coordinar ♦ *n* (*MATH*) coordenada; **~s** *npl* (*clothes*) coordinados *mpl*; **coordination** [-'neɪʃən] *n* coordinación *f*

co-ownership [kəʊ'əʊnəʃɪp] n co-propiedad f

cop [kɔp] (inf) n poli m (SP), tira m (AM)

cope [kəʊp] vi: to ~ with (problem) hacer frente a

copper ['kɔpə*] n (metal) cobre m; (BRIT: inf) poli m; ~s npl (money) calderilla f (SP), centavos mpl (AM)

copulate ['kɔpjʊleɪt] vi copularse

copy ['kɔpɪ] n copia f; (of book etc) ejemplar m ♦ vt copiar; ~right n derechos mpl de autor

coral ['kɔrəl] n coral m

cord [kɔːd] n cuerda; (ELEC) cable m; (fabric) pana

cordial ['kɔːdɪəl] adj cordial ♦ n cordial m

cordon ['kɔːdn] n cordón m; ~ off vt acordonar

corduroy ['kɔːdərɔɪ] n pana

core [kɔː*] n centro, núcleo; (of fruit) corazón m; (of problem) meollo ♦ vt quitar el corazón de

coriander [kɔrɪ'ændə*] n culantro

cork [kɔːk] n corcho; (tree) alcornoque m; ~screw n sacacorchos pl inv

corn [kɔːn] n (BRIT: cereal crop) trigo; (US: maize) maíz m; (on foot) callo; ~ on the cob (CULIN) maíz en la mazorca (SP), choclo (AM)

corned beef ['kɔːnd-] n carne f acecinada (en lata)

corner ['kɔːnə*] n (outside) esquina; (inside) rincón m; (in road) curva; (FOOTBALL) córner m; (BOXING) esquina ♦ vt (trap) arrinconar; (COMM) acaparar ♦ vi (in car) tomar las curvas; ~stone n (also fig) piedra angular

cornet ['kɔːnɪt] n (MUS) corneta; (BRIT: of ice-cream) cucurucho

cornflakes ['kɔːnfleɪks] npl copos mpl de maíz, cornflakes mpl

cornflour ['kɔːnflaʊə*] (BRIT), **cornstarch** ['kɔːnstɑːtʃ] (US) n harina de maíz

Cornwall ['kɔːnwəl] n Cornualles m

corny ['kɔːnɪ] (inf) adj gastado

coronary ['kɔrənərɪ] n (also: ~ thrombosis) infarto

coronation [kɔrə'neɪʃən] n coronación f

coroner ['kɔrənə*] n juez m (de instrucción)

corporal ['kɔːpərl] n cabo ♦ adj: ~ punishment castigo corporal

corporate ['kɔːpərɪt] adj (action, ownership) colectivo; (finance, image) corporativo

corporation [kɔːpə'reɪʃən] n (of town) ayuntamiento; (COMM) corporación f

corps [kɔː*, pl kɔːz] n inv cuerpo; **diplomatic ~** cuerpo diplomático; **press ~** gabinete m de prensa

corpse [kɔːps] n cadáver m

correct [kə'rekt] adj justo, exacto; (proper) correcto ♦ vt corregir; (exam) corregir, calificar; ~ion [-ʃən] n (act) corrección f;

(instance) rectificación f

correspond [kɔrɪs'pɔnd] vi (write): to ~ (with) escribirse (con); (be equivalent to): to ~ (to) corresponder (a); (be in accordance): to ~ (with) corresponder (con); ~ence n correspondencia f; ~ence course n curso por correspondencia; ~ent n corresponsal m/f

corridor ['kɔrɪdɔː*] n pasillo

corrode [kə'rəʊd] vt corroer ♦ vi corroerse

corrugated ['kɔrəgeɪtɪd] adj ondulado; ~ iron n chapa ondulada

corrupt [kə'rʌpt] adj (person) corrupto; (COMPUT) corrompido ♦ vt corromper; (COMPUT) degradar

Corsica ['kɔːsɪkə] n Córcega

cosmetic [kɔz'metɪk] adj, n cosmético

cosmopolitan [kɔzmə'pɔlɪtn] adj cosmopolita

cost [kɔst] (pt, pp cost) n (price) precio; ~s npl (COMM) costes mpl; (LAW) costas fpl ♦ vi costar, valer ♦ vt preparar el presupuesto de; **how much does it ~?** ¿cuánto cuesta?; **to ~ sb time/effort** costarle a uno tiempo/esfuerzo; **it ~ him his life** le costó la vida; **at all ~s** cueste lo que cueste

co-star ['kəʊstɑː*] n coprotagonista m/f

Costa Rica ['kɔstə'riːkə] n Costa Rica; ~n adj, n costarriqueño/a m/f

cost-effective [kɔstɪ'fektɪv] adj rentable

costly ['kɔstlɪ] adj costoso

cost-of-living [kɔstəv'lɪvɪŋ] adj: ~ allowance plus m de carestía de vida; ~ index índice m del costo de vida

cost price (BRIT) n precio de coste

costume ['kɔstjuːm] n traje m; (BRIT: also: swimming ~) traje de baño; ~ jewellery n bisutería

cosy ['kəʊzɪ] (US cozy) adj (person) cómodo; (room) acogedor(a)

cot [kɔt] n (BRIT: child's) cuna; (US: campbed) cama de campaña

cottage ['kɔtɪdʒ] n casita de campo; (rustic) barraca; ~ cheese n requesón m

cotton ['kɔtn] n algodón m; (thread) hilo; ~ on to (inf) vt fus caer en la cuenta de; ~ candy (US) n algodón m (azucarado); ~ wool (BRIT) n algodón m (hidrófilo)

couch [kautʃ] n sofá m; (doctor's etc) diván m

couchette [ku:'ʃet] n litera

cough [kɔf] vi toser ♦ n tos f; ~ drop n pastilla para la tos

could [kud] pt of can²; ~n't = could not

council ['kaunsl] n consejo; **city** or **town ~** consejo municipal; ~ **estate** (BRIT) n urbanización f de viviendas municipales de alquiler; ~ **house** (BRIT) n vivienda municipal de alquiler; ~**lor** n concejal(a) m/f

counsel ['kaunsl] n (advice) consejo; (lawyer)

abogado/a ♦ vt aconsejar; **~lor** n consejero/
a; **~or** n (US) n abogado/a

count [kaunt] vt contar; (include) incluir ♦ vi
contar ♦ n cuenta; (of votes) escrutinio;
(level) nivel m; (nobleman) conde m; **~ on** vt
fus contar con; **~down** n cuenta atrás

countenance ['kauntinəns] n semblante m,
rostro ♦ vt (tolerate) aprobar, tolerar

counter ['kauntə*] n (in shop) mostrador m;
(in games) ficha ♦ vt contrarrestar ♦ adv: **to
run ~ to** ser contrario a, ir en contra de; **~act**
vt contrarrestar

counterfeit ['kauntəfit] n falsificación f,
simulación f ♦ vt falsificar ♦ adj falso,
falsificado

counterfoil ['kauntəfɔil] n talón m

counterpart ['kauntəpɑ:t] n homólogo/a

counter-productive [kauntəprə'dʌktiv]
adj contraproducente

countersign ['kauntəsain] vt refrendar

countess ['kauntis] n condesa

countless ['kauntlis] adj innumerable

country ['kʌntri] n país m; (native land)
patria; (as opposed to town) campo; (region)
región f, tierra; ~ **dancing** (BRIT) n baile m
regional; ~ **house** n casa de campo; **~man**
n (irreg) (compatriot) compatriota m; (rural)
campesino, paisano; **~side** n campo

county ['kaunti] n condado

coup [ku:] (pl **~s**) n (also: ~ d'état) golpe m
(de estado); (achievement) éxito

couple ['kʌpl] n (of things) par m; (of people)
pareja; (married ~) matrimonio; **a ~ of** un par
de

coupon ['ku:pɔn] n cupón m; (voucher) valé
m

courage ['kʌridʒ] n valor m, valentía; **~ous**
[kə'reidʒəs] adj valiente

courgette [kuə'ʒɛt] (BRIT) n calabacín m (SP),
calabacita (AM)

courier ['kuriə*] n mensajero/a; (for tourists)
guía m/f (de turismo)

course [kɔ:s] n (direction) dirección f; (of
river, SCOL) curso; (process) transcurso; (MED):
~ **of treatment** tratamiento; (of ship) rumbo;
(part of meal) plato; (GOLF) campo; **of ~**
desde luego, naturalmente; **of ~!** ¡claro!

court [kɔ:t] n (royal) corte f; (LAW) tribunal m,
juzgado; (TENNIS etc) pista, cancha ♦ vt
(woman) cortejar a; **to take to ~** demandar

courteous ['kɜ:tiəs] adj cortés

courtesy ['kɜ:təsi] n cortesía; **(by) ~ of** por
cortesía de; ~ **bus**, ~ **coach** n autobús m
gratuito

court-house ['kɔ:thaus] (US) n palacio de
justicia

courtier ['kɔ:tiə*] n cortesano

court-martial (pl **courts-martial**) n consejo
de guerra

courtroom ['kɔ:trum] n sala de justicia

courtyard ['kɔ:tjɑ:d] n patio

cousin ['kʌzn] n primo/a; **first ~** primo/a
carnal, primo/a hermano/a

cove [kəuv] n cala, ensenada

covenant ['kʌvənənt] n pacto

cover ['kʌvə*] vt cubrir; (feelings, mistake)
ocultar; (with lid) tapar; (book etc) forrar;
(distance) recorrer; (include) abarcar;
(protect: also: INSURANCE) cubrir; (PRESS)
investigar; (discuss) tratar ♦ n cubierta; (lid)
tapa; (for chair etc) funda; (envelope) sobre
m; (for book) forro; (of magazine) portada;
(shelter) abrigo; (INSURANCE) cobertura; (of
spy) cobertura; **~s** npl (on bed) sábanas;
mantas; **to take ~** (shelter) protegerse,
resguardarse; **under ~** (indoors) bajo techo;
under ~ of darkness al amparo de la
oscuridad; **under separate ~** (COMM) por
separado; ~ **up** vi: **to ~ up for sb** encubrir a
uno; **~age** n (TV, PRESS) cobertura; **~alls** (US)
npl mono; ~ **charge** n precio del cubierto;
~ing n capa; **~ing letter** (US ~ **letter**) n
carta de explicación; ~ **note** n (INSURANCE)
póliza provisional

covert ['kəuvət] adj secreto, encubierto

cover-up n encubrimiento

cow [kau] n vaca; (inf!: woman) bruja ♦ vt
intimidar

coward ['kauəd] n cobarde m/f; **~ice** [-is] n
cobardía; **~ly** adj cobarde

cowboy ['kaubɔi] n vaquero

cower ['kauə*] vi encogerse (de miedo)

coy [kɔi] adj tímido

cozy ['kəuzi] (US) adj = **cosy**

CPA (US) n abbr = **certified public accountant**

crab [kræb] n cangrejo; ~ **apple** n manzana
silvestre

crack [kræk] n grieta; (noise) crujido; (drug)
crack m ♦ vt agrietar, romper; (nut) cascar;
(solve: problem) resolver; (: code) descifrar;
(whip etc) chasquear; (knuckles) crujir; (joke)
contar ♦ adj (expert) de primera; ~ **down
on** vt fus adoptar fuertes medidas contra;
~ **up** vi (MED) sufrir una crisis nerviosa; **~er** n
(biscuit) cráquer m; (Christmas ~er) petardo
sorpresa

crackle ['krækl] vi crepitar

cradle ['kreidl] n cuna

craft [krɑ:ft] n (skill) arte m; (trade) oficio;
(cunning) astucia; (boat: pl inv) barco;
(plane: pl inv) avión m

craftsman ['krɑ:ftsmən] n artesano; **~ship** n
(quality) destreza

crafty ['krɑ:fti] adj astuto

crag [kræg] n peñasco

cram [kræm] vt (fill): **to ~ sth with** llenar algo
(a reventar) de; (put): **to ~ sth into** meter
algo a la fuerza en ♦ vi (for exams) empollar

cramp [kræmp] n (MED) calambre m; ~**ed**
adj apretado, estrecho

cranberry ['krænbərı] n arándano agrio

crane [kreın] n (TECH) grúa; (bird) grulla

crank [kræŋk] n manivela; (person) chiflado

cranny ['krænı] n see **nook**

crash [kræʃ] n (noise) estrépito; (of cars etc)
choque m; (of plane) accidente m de
aviación; (COMM) quiebra ♦ vt (car, plane)
estrellar ♦ vi (car, plane) estrellarse; (two
cars) chocar; (COMM) quebrar; ~ **course** n
curso acelerado; ~ **helmet** n casco
(protector); ~ **landing** n aterrizaje m forzado

crass [kræs] adj grosero, maleducado

crate [kreıt] n cajón m de embalaje; (for
bottles) caja

cravat(e) [krə'væt] n pañuelo

crave [kreıv] vt, vi: **to** ~ (**for**) ansiar, anhelar

crawl [krɔːl] vi (drag o.s.) arrastrarse; (child)
andar a gatas, gatear; (vehicle) avanzar
(lentamente) ♦ n (SWIMMING) crol m

crayfish ['kreıfıʃ] n inv (freshwater) cangrejo
de río; (saltwater) cigala

crayon ['kreıən] n lápiz m de color

craze [kreız] n (fashion) moda

crazy ['kreızı] adj (person) loco; (idea)
disparatado; (inf: keen): ~ **about sb/sth** loco
por uno/algo

creak [kriːk] vi (floorboard) crujir; (hinge etc)
chirriar, rechinar

cream [kriːm] n (of milk) nata, crema; (lotion)
crema; (fig) flor f y nata ♦ adj (colour) color
crema; ~ **cake** n pastel m de nata;
~ **cheese** n queso blanco; ~**y** adj cremoso;
(colour) color crema

crease [kriːs] n (fold) pliegue m; (in trousers)
raya; (wrinkle) arruga ♦ vt (wrinkle) arrugar
♦ vi (wrinkle up) arrugarse

create [kriː'eıt] vt crear; **creation** [-ʃən] n
creación f; **creative** adj creativo; **creator** n
creador(a) m/f

creature ['kriːtʃə*] n (animal) animal m,
bicho; (person) criatura

crèche [kreʃ] n guardería (infantil)

credence ['kriːdəns] n: **to lend** or **give** ~ **to**
creer en, dar crédito a

credentials [krı'denʃlz] npl (references)
referencias fpl; (identity papers) documentos
mpl de identidad

credible ['kredıbl] adj creíble; (trustworthy)
digno de confianza

credit ['kredıt] n crédito; (merit) honor m,
mérito ♦ vt (COMM) abonar; (believe: also:
give ~ **to**) creer, prestar fe a ♦ adj crediticio;
~**s** npl (CINEMA) fichas fpl técnicas; **to be in** ~
(person) tener saldo a favor; **to** ~ **sb with** (fig)
reconocer a uno el mérito de; ~ **card** n
tarjeta de crédito; ~**or** n acreedor(a) m/f

creed [kriːd] n credo

creek [kriːk] n cala, ensenada; (US) riachuelo

creep [kriːp] (pt, pp **crept**) vi arrastrarse; ~**er**
n enredadera; ~**y** adj (frightening)
horripilante

cremate [krı'meıt] vt incinerar

crematorium [kremə'tɔːrıəm] (pl
crematoria) n crematorio

crêpe [kreıp] n (fabric) crespón m; (also:
~ rubber) crepé m; ~ **bandage** (BRIT) n
venda de crepé

crept [krept] pt, pp of **creep**

crescent ['kresnt] n media luna; (street) calle
f (en forma de semicírculo)

cress [kres] n berro

crest [krest] n (of bird) cresta; (of hill) cima,
cumbre f; (of coat of arms) blasón m; ~**fallen**
adj alicaído

crevice ['krevıs] n grieta, hendedura

crew [kruː] n (of ship etc) tripulación f; (TV,
CINEMA) equipo; ~**-cut** n corte m al rape; ~-
neck n cuello a la caja

crib [krıb] n cuna ♦ vt (inf) plagiar

crick [krık] n (in neck) tortícolis f

cricket ['krıkıt] n (insect) grillo; (game)
críquet m

crime [kraım] n (no pl: illegal activities)
crimen m; (illegal action) delito; **criminal**
['krımınl] n criminal m/f, delincuente m/f
♦ adj criminal; (illegal) delictivo; (law) penal

crimson ['krımzn] adj carmesí

cringe [krındʒ] vi agacharse, encogerse

crinkle ['krıŋkl] vt arrugar

cripple ['krıpl] n lisiado/a, cojo/a ♦ vt lisiar,
mutilar

crisis ['kraısıs] (pl **crises**) n crisis f inv

crisp [krısp] adj fresco; (vegetables etc)
crujiente; (manner) seco; ~**s** (BRIT) npl
patatas fpl (SP) or papas fpl (AM) fritas

crisscross ['krıskrɔs] adj entrelazado

criterion [kraı'tıərıən] (pl **criteria**) n criterio

critic ['krıtık] n crítico/a; ~**al** adj crítico;
(illness) grave; ~**ally** adv (speak etc) en tono
crítico; (ill) gravemente; ~**ism** ['krıtısızm] n
crítica; ~**ize** ['krıtısaız] vt criticar

croak [krəuk] vi (frog) croar; (raven) graznar;
(person) gruñir

Croatia [krəu'eıʃə] n Croacia

crochet ['krəuʃeı] n ganchillo

crockery ['krɔkərı] n loza, vajilla

crocodile ['krɔkədaıl] n cocodrilo

crocus ['krəukəs] n croco, crocus m

croft [krɔft] n granja pequeña

crony ['krəunı] (inf: pej) n compinche m/f

crook [kruk] n ladrón/ona m/f; (of shepherd)
cayado; ~**ed** ['krukıd] adj torcido; (dishonest)
nada honrado

crop [krɔp] n (produce) cultivo; (amount
produced) cosecha; (riding ~) látigo de
montar ♦ vt cortar, recortar; ~ **up** vi surgir,

presentarse
cross [krɔs] n cruz f; (hybrid) cruce m ♦ vt
(street etc) cruzar, atravesar ♦ adj de mal
humor, enojado; **~ out** vt tachar; **~ over** vi
cruzar; **~bar** n travesaño; **~country (race)**
n carrera a campo traviesa, cross m; **~-**
examine vt interrogar; **~-eyed** adj bizco;
~fire n fuego cruzado; **~ing** n (sea passage)
travesía; (also: pedestrian ~ing) paso para
peatones; **~ing guard** (US) n persona
encargada de ayudar a los niños a cruzar la
calle; **~ purposes** npl: **to be at ~ purposes**
no comprenderse uno a otro; **~-reference** n
referencia, llamada; **~roads** n cruce m,
encrucijada; **~ section** n corte m transversal;
(of population) muestra (representativa);
~walk (US) n paso de peatones; **~wind** n
viento de costado; **~word** n crucigrama m
crotch [krɔtʃ] n (ANAT, of garment)
entrepierna
crotchet ['krɔtʃɪt] n (MUS) negra
crouch [krautʃ] vi agacharse, acurrucarse
crow [krəu] n (bird) cuervo; (of cock) canto,
cacareo ♦ vi (cock) cantar
crowbar ['krəubɑ:*] n palanca
crowd [kraud] n muchedumbre f, multitud f
♦ vt (fill) llenar ♦ vi (gather): **to ~ round**
reunirse en torno a; (cram): **to ~ in** entrar en
tropel; **~ed** adj (full) atestado; (densely
populated) superpoblado
crown [kraun] n corona; (of head) coronilla;
(for tooth) funda; (of hill) cumbre f ♦ vt
coronar; (fig) completar, rematar; **~ jewels**
npl joyas fpl reales; **~ prince** n príncipe m
heredero
crow's feet npl patas fpl de gallo
crucial ['kru:ʃl] adj decisivo
crucifix ['kru:sɪfɪks] n crucifijo; **~ion** [-'fɪkʃən]
n crucifixión f
crude [kru:d] adj (materials) bruto; (fig:
basic) tosco; (: vulgar) ordinario; **~ (oil)** n
(petróleo) crudo
cruel ['kruəl] adj cruel; **~ty** n crueldad f
cruise [kru:z] n crucero ♦ vi (ship) hacer un
crucero; (car) ir a velocidad de crucero; **~r** n
(motorboat) yate m de motor; (warship)
crucero
crumb [krʌm] n miga, migaja
crumble ['krʌmbl] vt desmenuzar ♦ vi
(building, also fig) desmoronarse; **crumbly**
adj que se desmigaja fácilmente
crumpet ['krʌmpɪt] n ≈ bollo para tostar
crumple ['krʌmpl] vt (paper) estrujar;
(material) arrugar
crunch [krʌntʃ] vt (with teeth) mascar;
(underfoot) hacer crujir ♦ n (fig) hora o
momento de la verdad; **~y** adj crujiente
crusade [kru:'seɪd] n cruzada
crush [krʌʃ] n (crowd) aglomeración f;

(infatuation): **to have a ~ on sb** estar loco por
uno; (drink): **lemon ~** limonada ♦ vt aplastar;
(paper) estrujar; (cloth) arrugar; (fruit)
exprimir; (opposition) aplastar; (hopes)
destruir
crust [krʌst] n corteza; (of snow, ice) costra
crutch [krʌtʃ] n muleta
crux [krʌks] n: **the ~ of** lo esencial de, el quid
de
cry [kraɪ] vi llorar; (shout: also: ~ out) gritar
♦ n (shriek) chillido; (shout) grito; **~ off** vi
echarse atrás
cryptic ['krɪptɪk] adj enigmático, secreto
crystal ['krɪstl] n cristal m; **~-clear** adj claro
como el agua
cub [kʌb] n cachorro; (also: ~ scout) niño
explorador
Cuba ['kju:bə] n Cuba; **~n** adj, n cubano/a
m/f
cube [kju:b] n cubo ♦ vt (MATH) cubicar;
cubic adj cúbico
cubicle ['kju:bɪkl] n (at pool) caseta; (for
bed) cubículo
cuckoo ['kuku:] n cuco; **~ clock** n reloj m de
cucú
cucumber ['kju:kʌmbə*] n pepino
cuddle ['kʌdl] vt abrazar ♦ vi abrazarse
cue [kju:] n (snooker ~) taco; (THEATRE etc)
señal f
cuff [kʌf] n (of sleeve) puño; (US: of trousers)
vuelta; (blow) bofetada; **off the ~** adv de
improviso; **~links** npl gemelos mpl
cuisine [kwɪ'zi:n] n cocina
cul-de-sac ['kʌldəsæk] n callejón m sin salida
cull [kʌl] vt (idea) sacar ♦ n (of animals)
matanza selectiva
culminate ['kʌlmɪneɪt] vi: **to ~ in** terminar
en; **culmination** [-'neɪʃən] n culminación f,
colmo
culottes [ku:'lɔts] npl falda pantalón f
culprit ['kʌlprɪt] n culpable m/f
cult [kʌlt] n culto
cultivate ['kʌltɪveɪt] vt (also fig) cultivar; **~d**
adj culto; **cultivation** [-'veɪʃən] n cultivo
cultural ['kʌltʃərəl] adj cultural
culture ['kʌltʃə*] n (also fig) cultura; (BIO)
cultivo; **~d** adj culto
cumbersome ['kʌmbəsəm] adj de mucho
bulto, voluminoso; (process) enrevesado
cunning ['kʌnɪŋ] n astucia ♦ adj astuto
cup [kʌp] n taza; (as prize) copa
cupboard ['kʌbəd] n armario; (kitchen)
alacena
cup tie (BRIT) n partido de copa
curate ['kjuərɪt] n cura m
curator [kjuə'reɪtə*] n director(a) m/f
curb [kə:b] vt refrenar; (person) reprimir ♦ n
freno; (US) bordillo
curdle ['kə:dl] vi cuajarse

cure [kjuə*] vt curar ♦ n cura, curación f; (fig: solution) remedio

curfew ['kə:fju:] n toque m de queda

curiosity [kjuərɪ'ɔsɪtɪ] n curiosidad f

curious ['kjuərɪəs] adj curioso; (person: interested): **to be** ~ sentir curiosidad

curl [kə:l] n rizo ♦ vt (hair) rizar ♦ vi rizarse; ~ **up** vi (person) hacerse un ovillo; ~**er** n rulo; ~**y** adj rizado

currant ['kʌrnt] n pasa (de Corinto); (black~, red~) grosella

currency ['kʌrnsɪ] n moneda; **to gain** ~ (fig) difundirse

current ['kʌrnt] n corriente f ♦ adj (accepted) corriente; (present) actual; ~ **account** (BRIT) n cuenta corriente; ~ **affairs** npl noticias fpl de actualidad; ~**ly** adv actualmente

curriculum [kə'rɪkjuləm] (pl ~s or curricula) n plan m de estudios; ~ **vitae** n currículum m

curry ['kʌrɪ] n curry m ♦ vt: **to** ~ **favour with** buscar favores con; ~ **powder** n curry m en polvo

curse [kə:s] vi soltar tacos ♦ vt maldecir ♦ n maldición f; (swearword) palabrota, taco

cursor ['kə:sə*] n (COMPUT) cursor m

cursory ['kə:sərɪ] adj rápido, superficial

curt [kə:t] adj corto, seco

curtail [kə:'teɪl] vt (visit etc) acortar; (freedom) restringir; (expenses etc) reducir

curtain ['kə:tn] n cortina; (THEATRE) telón m

curts(e)y ['kə:tsɪ] vi hacer una reverencia

curve [kə:v] n curva ♦ vi (road) hacer una curva; (line etc) curvarse

cushion ['kuʃən] n cojín m; (of air) colchón m ♦ vt (shock) amortiguar

custard ['kʌstəd] n natillas fpl

custody ['kʌstədɪ] n custodia; **to take into** ~ detener

custom ['kʌstəm] n costumbre f; (COMM) clientela; ~**ary** adj acostumbrado

customer ['kʌstəmə*] n cliente m/f

customized ['kʌstəmaɪzd] adj (car etc) hecho a encargo

custom-made adj hecho a la medida

customs ['kʌstəmz] npl aduana; ~ **officer** n aduanero/a

cut [kʌt] (pt, pp cut) vt cortar; (price) rebajar; (text, programme) acortar; (reduce) reducir ♦ vi cortar ♦ n (of garment) corte m; (in skin) cortadura; (in salary etc) rebaja; (in spending) reducción f, recorte m; (slice of meat) tajada; **to** ~ **a tooth** echar un diente; ~ **down** vt (tree) derribar; (reduce) reducir; ~ **off** vt cortar; (person, place) aislar; (TEL) desconectar; ~ **out** vt (shape) recortar; (stop: activity etc) dejar; (remove) quitar; ~ **up** vt cortar (en pedazos); ~**back** n reducción f

cute [kju:t] adj mono

cuticle ['kju:tɪkl] n cutícula

cutlery ['kʌtlərɪ] n cubiertos mpl

cutlet ['kʌtlɪt] n chuleta; (nut etc ~) plato vegetariano hecho con nueces y verdura en forma de chuleta

cut: ~**out** n (switch) dispositivo de seguridad, disyuntor m; (cardboard ~out) recortable m; ~**-price** (US ~**-rate**) adj a precio reducido; ~**throat** n asesino/a ♦ adj feroz

cutting ['kʌtɪŋ] adj (remark) mordaz ♦ n (BRIT: from newspaper) recorte m; (from plant) esqueje m

CV n abbr = curriculum vitae

cwt abbr = hundredweight(s)

cyanide ['saɪənaɪd] n cianuro

cybercafé ['saɪbəkæfeɪ] n cibercafé m

cycle ['saɪkl] n ciclo; (bicycle) bicicleta ♦ vi ir en bicicleta; ~ **lane** n carril-bici m; ~ **path** n carril-bici m; **cycling** n ciclismo; **cyclist** n ciclista m/f

cyclone ['saɪkləun] n ciclón m

cygnet ['sɪgnɪt] n pollo de cisne

cylinder ['sɪlɪndə*] n cilindro; (of gas) bombona; ~**head gasket** n junta de culata

cymbals ['sɪmblz] npl platillos mpl

cynic ['sɪnɪk] n cínico/a; ~**al** adj cínico; ~**ism** ['sɪnɪsɪzəm] n cinismo

Cyprus ['saɪprəs] n Chipre f

cyst [sɪst] n quiste m; ~**itis** [-'taɪtɪs] n cistitis f

czar [za:*] n zar m

Czech [tʃek] adj, n checo/a m/f; ~ **Republic** n la República Checa

D, d

D [di:] n (MUS) re m

dab [dæb] vt (eyes, wound) tocar (ligeramente); (paint, cream) poner un poco de

dabble ['dæbl] vi: **to** ~ **in** ser algo aficionado a

dad [dæd] n = daddy

daddy ['dædɪ] n papá m

daffodil ['dæfədɪl] n narciso

daft [da:ft] adj tonto

dagger ['dægə*] n puñal m, daga

daily ['deɪlɪ] adj diario, cotidiano ♦ adv todos los días, cada día

dainty ['deɪntɪ] adj delicado

dairy ['deərɪ] n (shop) lechería; (on farm) vaquería; ~ **farm** n granja; ~ **products** npl productos mpl lácteos; ~ **store** (US) n lechería

daisy ['deɪzɪ] n margarita

dale [deɪl] n valle m

dam [dæm] n presa ♦ vt construir una presa sobre, represar

damage ['dæmɪdʒ] n lesión f; daño; (dents etc) desperfectos mpl; (fig) perjuicio ♦ vt dañar, perjudicar; (*spoil, break*) estropear; **~s** *npl* (*LAW*) daños *mpl* y perjuicios

damn [dæm] *vt* condenar; (*curse*) maldecir ♦ *n* (*inf*): **I don't give a ~** me importa un pito ♦ *adj* (*inf: also:* ~**ed**) maldito; **~ (it)!** ¡maldito sea!; **~ing** *adj* (*evidence*) irrecusable

damp [dæmp] *adj* húmedo, mojado ♦ *n* humedad *f* ♦ *vt* (*also:* ~**en**: *cloth, rag*) mojar; (: *enthusiasm*) enfriar

damson ['dæmzən] *n* ciruela damascena

dance [dɑːns] *n* baile *m* ♦ *vi* bailar; **~ hall** *n* salón *m* de baile; **~r** *n* bailador(a) *m/f*; (*professional*) bailarín/ina *m/f*; **dancing** *n* baile *m*

dandelion ['dændɪlaɪən] *n* diente *m* de león

dandruff ['dændrəf] *n* caspa

Dane [deɪn] *n* danés/esa *m/f*

danger ['deɪndʒə*] *n* peligro; (*risk*) riesgo; **~!** (*on sign*) ¡peligro de muerte!; **to be in ~ of** correr riesgo de; **~ous** *adj* peligroso; **~ously** *adv* peligrosamente

dangle ['dæŋgl] *vt* colgar ♦ *vi* pender, colgar

Danish ['deɪnɪʃ] *adj* danés/esa ♦ *n* (*LING*) danés *m*

dare [dɛə*] *vt*: **to ~ sb to do** desafiar a uno a hacer ♦ *vi*: **to ~ (to) do sth** atreverse a hacer algo; **I ~ say** (*I suppose*) puede ser (que); **daring** *adj* atrevido, osado ♦ *n* atrevimiento, osadía

dark [dɑːk] *adj* oscuro; (*hair, complexion*) moreno ♦ *n*: **in the ~** a oscuras; **to be in the ~ about** (*fig*) no saber nada de; **after ~** después del anochecer; **~en** *vt* (*colour*) hacer más oscuro ♦ *vi* oscurecerse; **~ glasses** *npl* gafas *fpl* negras (*SP*), anteojos *mpl* negros (*AM*); **~ness** *n* oscuridad *f*; **~room** *n* cuarto oscuro

darling ['dɑːlɪŋ] *adj, n* querido/a *m/f*

darn [dɑːn] *vt* zurcir

dart [dɑːt] *n* dardo; (*in sewing*) sisa ♦ *vi* precipitarse; **~ away/along** *vi* salir/marchar disparado; **~board** *n* diana; **~s** *n* dardos *mpl*

dash [dæʃ] *n* (*small quantity: of liquid*) gota, chorrito; (: *of solid*) pizca; (*sign*) raya ♦ *vt* (*throw*) tirar; (*hopes*) defraudar ♦ *vi* precipitarse, ir de prisa; **~ away** *or* **off** *vi* marcharse apresuradamente

dashboard ['dæʃbɔːd] *n* (*AUT*) salpicadero

dashing ['dæʃɪŋ] *adj* gallardo

data ['deɪtə] *npl* datos *mpl*; **~ processing** *n* proceso de datos

date [deɪt] *n* (*day*) fecha; (*with friend*) cita; (*fruit*) dátil *m* ♦ *vt* fechar; (*person*) salir con; **~ of birth** fecha de nacimiento; **to ~** *adv* hasta la fecha; **~d** *adj* anticuado; **~ rape** *n* violación ocurrida durante una cita con un conocido

daub [dɔːb] *vt* embadurnar

daughter ['dɔːtə*] *n* hija; **~-in-law** *n* nuera,

hija política

daunting ['dɔːntɪŋ] *adj* desalentador(a)

dawdle ['dɔːdl] *vi* (*go slowly*) andar muy despacio

dawn [dɔːn] *n* alba, amanecer *m*; (*fig*) nacimiento ♦ *vi* (*day*) amanecer; (*fig*): **it ~ed on him that ...** cayó en la cuenta de que ...

day [deɪ] *n* día *m*; (*working* ~) jornada; (*hey*~) tiempos *mpl*, días *mpl*; **the ~ before/after** el día anterior/siguiente; **the ~ after tomorrow** pasado mañana; **the ~ before yesterday** anteayer; **the following ~** el día siguiente; **by ~** de día; **~break** *n* amanecer *m*; **~dream** *vi* soñar despierto; **~light** *n* luz *f* (del día); **~ return** (*BRIT*) *n* billete *m* de ida y vuelta (en un día); **~time** *n* día *m*; **~-to-~** *adj* cotidiano

daze [deɪz] *vt* (*stun*) aturdir ♦ *n*: **in a ~** aturdido

dazzle ['dæzl] *vt* deslumbrar

DC *abbr* (= *direct current*) corriente *f* continua

dead [ded] *adj* muerto; (*limb*) dormido; (*telephone*) cortado; (*battery*) agotado ♦ *adv* (*completely*) totalmente; (*exactly*) exactamente; **to shoot sb ~** matar a uno a tiros; **~ tired** muerto (de cansancio); **to stop ~** parar en seco; **the ~** *npl* los muertos; **to be a ~ loss** (*inf: person*) ser un inútil; **~en** *vt* (*blow, sound*) amortiguar; (*pain etc*) aliviar; **~ end** *n* callejón *m* sin salida; **~ heat** *n* (*SPORT*) empate *m*; **~line** *n* fecha (*or* hora) tope; **~lock** *n*: **to reach ~lock** llegar a un punto muerto; **~ly** *adj* mortal, fatal; **~pan** *adj* sin expresión; **the D~ Sea** *n* el Mar Muerto

deaf [def] *adj* sordo; **~en** *vt* ensordecer; **~ness** *n* sordera

deal [diːl] (*pt, pp* **dealt**) *n* (*agreement*) pacto, convenio; (*business* ~) trato ♦ *vt* dar; (*card*) repartir; **a great ~ (of)** bastante, mucho; **~ in** *vt fus* tratar en, comerciar en; **~ with** *vt fus* (*people*) tratar con; (*problem*) ocuparse de; (*subject*) tratar de; **~ings** *npl* (*COMM*) transacciones *fpl*; (*relations*) relaciones *fpl*

dealt [delt] *pt, pp* de **deal**

dean [diːn] *n* (*REL*) deán *m*; (*SCOL: BRIT*) decano; (: *US*) decano; rector *m*

dear [dɪə*] *adj* querido; (*expensive*) caro ♦ *n*: **my ~** mi querido/a ♦ *excl*: **~ me!** ¡Dios mío!; **D~ Sir/Madam** (*in letter*) Muy Señor Mío, Estimado Señor/Estimada Señora; **D~ Mr/Mrs X** Estimado/a Señor(a) X; **~ly** *adv* (*love*) mucho; (*pay*) caro

death [deθ] *n* muerte *f*; **~ certificate** *n* partida de defunción; **~ly** *adj* (*white*) como un muerto; (*silence*) sepulcral; **~ penalty** *n* pena de muerte; **~ rate** *n* mortalidad *f*; **~ toll** *n* número de víctimas

debacle [deɪ'bɑːkl] *n* desastre *m*

debase [dɪˈbeɪs] vt degradar
debatable [dɪˈbeɪtəbl] adj discutible
debate [dɪˈbeɪt] n debate m ♦ vt discutir
debit [ˈdebɪt] n debe m ♦ vt: **to ~ a sum to sb** or **to sb's account** cargar una suma en cuenta a alguien
debris [ˈdebriː] n escombros mpl
debt [det] n deuda; **to be in ~** tener deudas; **~or** n deudor(a) m/f
début [ˈdeɪbjuː] n presentación f
decade [ˈdekeɪd] n decenio, década
decadence [ˈdekədəns] n decadencia
decaff [ˈdiːkæf] (inf) n descafeinado
decaffeinated [dɪˈkæfɪneɪtɪd] adj descafeinado
decanter [dɪˈkæntə*] n garrafa
decay [dɪˈkeɪ] n (of building) desmoronamiento; (of tooth) caries f inv ♦ vi (rot) pudrirse
deceased [dɪˈsiːst] n: **the ~** el/la difunto/a
deceit [dɪˈsiːt] n engaño; **~ful** adj engañoso; **deceive** [dɪˈsiːv] vt engañar
December [dɪˈsembə*] n diciembre m
decent [ˈdiːsənt] adj (proper) decente; (person: kind) amable, bueno
deception [dɪˈsepʃən] n engaño
deceptive [dɪˈseptɪv] adj engañoso
decibel [ˈdesɪbel] n decibel(io) m
decide [dɪˈsaɪd] vt (person) decidir; (question, argument) resolver ♦ vi decidir; **to ~ to do/that** decidir hacer/que; **to ~ on sth** decidirse por algo; **~d** adj (resolute) decidido; (clear, definite) indudable; **~dly** [-dɪdlɪ] adv decididamente; (emphatically) con resolución
deciduous [dɪˈsɪdjuəs] adj de hoja caduca
decimal [ˈdesɪməl] adj decimal ♦ n decimal m; **~ point** n coma decimal
decipher [dɪˈsaɪfə*] vt descifrar
decision [dɪˈsɪʒən] n decisión f
decisive [dɪˈsaɪsɪv] adj decisivo; (person) decidido
deck [dek] n (NAUT) cubierta; (of bus) piso; (record ~) platina; (of cards) baraja; **~chair** n tumbona
declaration [dekləˈreɪʃən] n declaración f
declare [dɪˈkleə*] vt declarar
decline [dɪˈklaɪn] n disminución f, descenso ♦ vt rehusar ♦ vi (person, business) decaer; (strength) disminuir
decoder [diːˈkəʊdə*] n (TV) decodificador m
décor [ˈdeɪkɔː*] n decoración f; (THEATRE) decorado
decorate [ˈdekəreɪt] vt (adorn): **to ~ (with)** adornar (de), decorar (de); (paint) pintar; (paper) empapelar; **decoration** [-ˈreɪʃən] n adorno; (act) decoración f; (medal) condecoración f; **decorator** n (workman) pintor m (decorador)
decorum [dɪˈkɔːrəm] n decoro

decoy [ˈdiːkɔɪ] n señuelo
decrease [n ˈdiːkriːs, vb dɪˈkriːs] n: **~ (in)** disminución f (de) ♦ vt disminuir, reducir ♦ vi reducirse
decree [dɪˈkriː] n decreto; **~ nisi** n sentencia provisional de divorcio
dedicate [ˈdedɪkeɪt] vt dedicar; **dedication** [-ˈkeɪʃən] n (devotion) dedicación f; (in book) dedicatoria
deduce [dɪˈdjuːs] vt deducir
deduct [dɪˈdʌkt] vt restar; descontar; **~ion** [dɪˈdʌkʃən] n (amount deducted) descuento; (conclusion) deducción f, conclusión f
deed [diːd] n hecho, acto; (feat) hazaña; (LAW) escritura
deep [diːp] adj profundo; (expressing measurements) de profundidad; (voice) bajo; (breath) profundo; (colour) intenso ♦ adv: **the spectators stood 20 ~** los espectadores se formaron de 20 en fondo; **to be 4 metres ~** tener 4 metros de profundidad; **~en** vt ahondar, profundizar ♦ vi aumentar, crecer; **~-freeze** n congelador m; **~-fry** vt freír en aceite abundante; **~ly** adv (breathe) a pleno pulmón; (interested, moved, grateful) profundamente, hondamente; **~-sea diving** n buceo de altura; **~-seated** adj (beliefs) (profundamente) arraigado
deer [dɪə*] n inv ciervo
deface [dɪˈfeɪs] vt (wall, surface) estropear, pintarrajear
default [dɪˈfɔːlt] n: **by ~** (win) por incomparecencia ♦ adj (COMPUT) por defecto
defeat [dɪˈfiːt] n derrota ♦ vt derrotar, vencer; **~ist** adj, n derrotista m/f
defect [n ˈdiːfekt, vb dɪˈfekt] n defecto ♦ vi: **~ to the enemy** pasarse al enemigo; **~ive** [dɪˈfektɪv] adj defectuoso
defence [dɪˈfens] (US **defense**) n defensa; **~less** adj indefenso
defend [dɪˈfend] vt defender; **~ant** n acusado/a; (in civil case) demandado/a; **~er** n defensor(a) m/f; (SPORT) defensa m/f
defense [dɪˈfens] (US) n = **defence**
defensive [dɪˈfensɪv] adj defensivo ♦ n: **on the ~** a la defensiva
defer [dɪˈfɜː*] vt aplazar
defiance [dɪˈfaɪəns] n desafío; **in ~ of** en contra de; **defiant** [dɪˈfaɪənt] adj (challenging) desafiante, retador(a)
deficiency [dɪˈfɪʃənsɪ] n (lack) falta; (defect) defecto; **deficient** [dɪˈfɪʃənt] adj deficiente
deficit [ˈdefɪsɪt] n déficit m
define [dɪˈfaɪn] vt (word etc) definir; (limits etc) determinar
definite [ˈdefɪnɪt] adj (fixed) determinado; (obvious) claro; (certain) indudable; **he was ~ about it** no dejó lugar a dudas (sobre ello); **~ly** adv desde luego, por supuesto

definition [dɛfɪˈnɪʃən] n definición f; (clearness) nitidez f

deflate [diːˈfleɪt] vt desinflar

deflect [dɪˈflɛkt] vt desviar

defraud [dɪˈfrɔːd] vt: to ~ sb of sth estafar algo a uno

defrost [diːˈfrɔst] vt descongelar; ~er (US) n (demister) eliminador m de vaho

deft [dɛft] adj diestro, hábil

defunct [dɪˈfʌŋkt] adj difunto; (organization etc) ya que no existe

defuse [diːˈfjuːz] vt desactivar; (situation) calmar

defy [dɪˈfaɪ] vt (resist) oponerse a; (challenge) desafiar; (fig): **it defies description** resulta imposible describirlo

degenerate [vb dɪˈdʒɛnəreɪt, adj dɪˈdʒɛnərɪt] vi degenerar ♦ adj degenerado

degree [dɪˈgriː] n grado; (SCOL) título; **to have a ~ in maths** tener una licenciatura en matemáticas; **by ~s** (gradually) poco a poco, por etapas; **to some ~** hasta cierto punto

dehydrated [diːhaɪˈdreɪtɪd] adj deshidratado; (milk) en polvo

de-ice [diːˈaɪs] vt deshelar

deign [deɪn] vi: **to ~ to do** dignarse hacer

dejected [dɪˈdʒɛktɪd] adj abatido, desanimado

delay [dɪˈleɪ] vt demorar, aplazar; (person) entretener; (train) retrasar ♦ vi tardar ♦ n demora, retraso; **to be ~ed** retrasarse; **without ~** en seguida, sin tardar

delectable [dɪˈlɛktəbl] adj (person) encantador(a); (food) delicioso

delegate [n ˈdɛlɪgɪt, vb ˈdɛlɪgeɪt] n delegado/a ♦ vt (person) delegar en; (task) delegar

delete [dɪˈliːt] vt suprimir, tachar

deliberate [adj dɪˈlɪbərɪt, vb dɪˈlɪbəreɪt] adj (intentional) intencionado; (slow) pausado, lento ♦ vi deliberar; ~ly adv (on purpose) a propósito

delicacy [ˈdɛlɪkəsɪ] n delicadeza; (choice food) manjar m

delicate [ˈdɛlɪkɪt] adj delicado; (fragile) frágil

delicatessen [dɛlɪkəˈtɛsn] n ultramarinos mpl finos

delicious [dɪˈlɪʃəs] adj delicioso

delight [dɪˈlaɪt] n (feeling) placer m, deleite m; (person, experience etc) encanto, delicia ♦ vt encantar, deleitar; **to take ~ in** deleitarse en; ~ed adj: ~ed (at or with/to do) encantado (con/de hacer); ~ful adj encantador(a), delicioso

delinquent [dɪˈlɪŋkwənt] adj, n delincuente m/f

delirious [dɪˈlɪrɪəs] adj: **to be ~** delirar, desvariar; **to be ~ with** estar loco de

deliver [dɪˈlɪvə*] vt (distribute) repartir; (hand over) entregar; (message) comunicar;

(speech) pronunciar; (MED) asistir al parto de; ~y n reparto; entrega; (of speaker) modo de expresarse; (MED) parto, alumbramiento; **to take ~y of** recibir

delude [dɪˈluːd] vt engañar

deluge [ˈdɛljuːdʒ] n diluvio

delusion [dɪˈluːʒən] n ilusión f, engaño

de luxe [dəˈlʌks] adj de lujo

demand [dɪˈmɑːnd] vt (gen) exigir; (rights) reclamar ♦ n exigencia; (claim) reclamación f; (ECON) demanda; **to be in ~** ser muy solicitado; **on ~** a solicitud; ~ing adj (boss) exigente; (work) absorbente

demean [dɪˈmiːn] vt: **to ~ o.s.** rebajarse

demeanour [dɪˈmiːnə*] (US **demeanor**) n porte m, conducta

demented [dɪˈmɛntɪd] adj demente

demise [dɪˈmaɪz] n (death) fallecimiento

demister [diːˈmɪstə*] n (AUT) eliminador m de vaho

demo [ˈdɛməu] (inf) n abbr (= demonstration) manifestación f

democracy [dɪˈmɔkrəsɪ] n democracia; **democrat** [ˈdɛməkræt] n demócrata m/f; **democratic** [dɛməˈkrætɪk] adj democrático; (US) demócrata

demolish [dɪˈmɔlɪʃ] vt derribar, demoler; (fig: argument) destruir

demon [ˈdiːmən] n (evil spirit) demonio

demonstrate [ˈdɛmənstreɪt] vt demostrar; (skill, appliance) mostrar ♦ vi manifestarse; **demonstration** [-ˈstreɪʃən] n (POL) manifestación f; (proof, exhibition) demostración f; **demonstrator** n (POL) manifestante m/f; (COMM) demostrador(a) m/f; vendedor(a) m/f

demote [dɪˈməut] vt degradar

demure [dɪˈmjuə*] adj recatado

den [dɛn] n (of animal) guarida; (room) habitación f

denial [dɪˈnaɪəl] n (refusal) negativa; (of report etc) negación f

denim [ˈdɛnɪm] n tela vaquera; ~s npl vaqueros mpl

Denmark [ˈdɛnmɑːk] n Dinamarca

denomination [dɪnɔmɪˈneɪʃən] n valor m; (REL) confesión f

denounce [dɪˈnauns] vt denunciar

dense [dɛns] adj (crowd) denso; (thick) espeso; (: foliage etc) tupido; (inf: stupid) torpe; ~ly adv: ~ly populated con una alta densidad de población

density [ˈdɛnsɪtɪ] n densidad f; **single/double-~ disk** n (COMPUT) disco de densidad sencilla/doble densidad

dent [dɛnt] n abolladura ♦ vt (also: make a ~ in) abollar

dental [ˈdɛntl] adj dental; ~ **surgeon** n odontólogo/a

dentist ['dentist] n dentista m/f
dentures ['dentʃəz] npl dentadura (postiza)
deny [dɪ'naɪ] vt negar; (charge) rechazar
deodorant [diː'əʊdərənt] n desodorante m
depart [dɪ'pɑːt] vi irse, marcharse; (train)
salir; to ~ from (fig: differ from) apartarse de
department [dɪ'pɑːtmənt] n (COMM) sección
f; (SCOL) departamento; (POL) ministerio;
~ **store** n gran almacén m
departure [dɪ'pɑːtʃə*] n partida, ida; (of
train) salida; (of employee) marcha; a new ~
un nuevo rumbo; ~ **lounge** n (at airport)
sala de embarque
depend [dɪ'pend] vi: to ~ on depender de;
(rely on) contar con; it ~s depende, según;
~ing on the result según el resultado; ~able
adj (person) formal, serio; (watch) exacto;
(car) seguro; ~ant n dependiente m/f; ~ent
adj: to be ~ent on depender de ♦ n =
dependant
depict |dɪ'pɪkt] vt (in picture) pintar;
(describe) representar
depleted [dɪ'pliːtɪd] adj reducido
deploy [dɪ'plɔɪ] vt desplegar
deport [dɪ'pɔːt] vt deportar
deposit [dɪ'pɒzɪt] n depósito; (CHEM)
sedimento; (of ore, oil) yacimiento ♦ vt (gen)
depositar; ~ **account** n (BRIT) cuenta de
ahorros
depot ['depəʊ] n (storehouse) depósito; (for
vehicles) parque m; (US) estación f
depreciate [dɪ'priːʃɪeɪt] vi depreciarse, perder
valor
depress [dɪ'pres] vt deprimir; (wages etc)
hacer bajar; (press down) apretar; ~ed adj
deprimido; ~ing adj deprimente; ~ion
[dɪ'preʃən] n depresión f
deprivation [depri'veɪʃən] n privación f
deprive [dɪ'praɪv] vt: to ~ sb of privar a uno
de; ~d adj necesitado
depth [depθ] n profundidad f; (of cupboard)
fondo; to be in the ~s of despair sentir la
mayor desesperación; to be out of one's ~ (in
water) no hacer pie; (fig) sentirse totalmente
perdido
deputize ['depjutaɪz] vi: to ~ for sb suplir a
uno
deputy ['depjutɪ] adj: ~ head subdirector(a)
m/f ♦ n sustituto/a, suplente m/f; (US: POL)
diputado/a; (US: also: ~ sheriff) agente m
(del sheriff)
derail [dɪ'reɪl] vt: to be ~ed descarrilarse
deranged [dɪ'reɪndʒd] adj trastornado
derby ['dɑːbɪ] (US) n (hat) hongo
derelict ['derɪlɪkt] adj abandonado
derisory [dɪ'raɪzərɪ] adj (sum) irrisorio
derive [dɪ'raɪv] vt (benefit etc) obtener ♦ vi:
to ~ from derivarse de
derogatory [dɪ'rɔgətərɪ] adj despectivo

descend [dɪ'send] vt, vi descender, bajar; to
~ from descender de; to ~ to rebajarse a;
~ant n descendiente m/f
descent [dɪ'sent] n descenso; (origin)
descendencia
describe [dɪs'kraɪb] vt describir; **description**
[-'krɪpʃən] n descripción f; (sort) clase f,
género
desecrate ['desɪkreɪt] vt profanar
desert [n 'dezət, vb dɪ'zɜːt] n desierto ♦ vt
abandonar ♦ vi (MIL) desertar; ~er [dɪ'zɜːtə*]
n desertor(a) m/f; ~ion [dɪ'zɜːʃən] n
deserción f; (LAW) abandono; ~ **island** n isla
desierta; ~s [dɪ'zɜːts] npl: to get one's just ~s
llevar su merecido
deserve [dɪ'zɜːv] vt merecer, ser digno de;
deserving adj (person) digno; (action,
cause) meritorio
design [dɪ'zaɪn] n (sketch) bosquejo; (layout,
shape) diseño; (pattern) dibujo; (intention)
intención f ♦ vt diseñar
designate [vb 'dezɪgneɪt, adj 'dezɪgnɪt] vt
(appoint) nombrar; (destine) designar ♦ adj
designado
designer [dɪ'zaɪnə*] n diseñador(a) m/f;
(fashion ~) modisto/a, diseñador(a) m/f de
moda
desirable [dɪ'zaɪərəbl] adj (proper) deseable;
(attractive) atractivo
desire [dɪ'zaɪə*] n deseo ♦ vt desear
desk [desk] n (in office) escritorio; (for pupil)
pupitre m; (in hotel, at airport) recepción f;
(BRIT: in shop, restaurant) caja
desk-top publishing ['desktɒp-] n
autoedición f
desolate ['desəlɪt] adj (place) desierto;
(person) afligido
despair [dɪs'peə*] n desesperación f ♦ vi: to
~ of perder la esperanza de
despatch [dɪs'pætʃ] n, vt = **dispatch**
desperate ['despərɪt] adj desesperado;
(fugitive) peligroso; to be ~ for sth/to do
necesitar urgentemente algo/hacer; ~ly adv
desesperadamente; (very) terriblemente,
gravemente
desperation [despə'reɪʃən] n desesperación
f; in (sheer) ~ (absolutamente) desesperado
despicable [dɪs'pɪkəbl] adj vil, despreciable
despise [dɪs'paɪz] vt despreciar
despite [dɪs'paɪt] prep a pesar de, pese a
despondent [dɪs'pɒndənt] adj deprimido,
abatido
dessert [dɪ'zɜːt] n postre m; ~spoon n
cuchara (de postre)
destination [destɪ'neɪʃən] n destino
destiny ['destɪnɪ] n destino
destitute ['destɪtjuːt] adj desamparado,
indigente
destroy [dɪs'trɔɪ] vt destruir; (animal)

sacrificar; **~er** n (NAUT) destructor m

destruction [dɪs'trʌkʃən] n destrucción f

detach [dɪ'tætʃ] vt separar; (unstick) despegar; **~ed** adj (attitude) objetivo, imparcial; **~ed house** n ≈ chalé m, ≈ chalet m; **~ment** n (aloofness) frialdad f; (MIL) destacamento

detail ['diːteɪl] n detalle m; (no pl: in picture etc) detalles mpl; (trifle) pequeñez f ♦ vt detallar; (MIL) destacar; **in ~** detalladamente; **~ed** adj detallado

detain [dɪ'teɪn] vt retener; (in captivity) detener

detect [dɪ'tɛkt] vt descubrir; (MED, POLICE) identificar; (MIL, RADAR, TECH) detectar; **~ion** [dɪ'tɛkʃən] n descubrimiento; identificación f; **~ive** n detective m/f; **~ive story** n novela policíaca; **~or** n detector m

detention [dɪ'tɛnʃən] n detención f, arresto; (SCOL) castigo

deter [dɪ'tə:*] vt (dissuade) disuadir

detergent [dɪ'tə:dʒənt] n detergente m

deteriorate [dɪ'tɪərɪəreɪt] vi deteriorarse; **deterioration** [-'reɪʃən] n deterioro

determination [dɪtə:mɪ'neɪʃən] n resolución f

determine [dɪ'tə:mɪn] vt determinar; **~d** adj (person) resuelto, decidido; **~d to do** resuelto a hacer

deterrent [dɪ'tɛrənt] n (MIL) fuerza de disuasión

detest [dɪ'tɛst] vt aborrecer

detonate ['dɛtəneɪt] vi estallar ♦ vt hacer detonar

detour ['diːtuə*] n (gen, US: AUT) desviación f

detract [dɪ'trækt] vt: **to ~ from** quitar mérito a, desvirtuar

detriment ['dɛtrɪmənt] n: **to the ~ of** en perjuicio de; **~al** [dɛtrɪ'mɛntl] adj: **~al (to)** perjudicial (a)

devaluation [dɪvælju'eɪʃən] n devaluación f

devalue [diː'væljuː] vt (currency) devaluar; (fig) quitar mérito a

devastate ['dɛvəsteɪt] vt devastar; (fig): **to be ~d by** quedar destrozado por; **devastating** adj devastador(a); (fig) arrollador(a)

develop [dɪ'vɛləp] vt desarrollar; (PHOT) revelar; (disease) coger; (habit) adquirir; (fault) empezar a tener ♦ vi desarrollarse; (advance) progresar; (facts, symptoms) aparecer; **~er** n promotor m; **~ing country** n país m en (vías de) desarrollo; **~ment** n desarrollo; (advance) progreso; (of affair, case) desenvolvimiento; (of land) urbanización f

deviation [diːvɪ'eɪʃən] n desviación f

device [dɪ'vaɪs] n (apparatus) aparato, mecanismo

devil ['dɛvl] n diablo, demonio

devious ['diːvɪəs] adj taimado

devise [dɪ'vaɪz] vt idear, inventar

devoid [dɪ'vɔɪd] adj: **~ of** desprovisto de

devolution [diːvə'luːʃən] n (POL) descentralización f

devote [dɪ'vəut] vt: **to ~ sth to** dedicar algo a; **~d** adj (loyal) leal, fiel; **to be ~d to sb** querer con devoción a alguien; **the book is ~d to politics** el libro trata de la política; **~e** [dɛvəu'tiː] n entusiasta m/f; (REL) devoto/a; **devotion** n dedicación f; (REL) devoción f

devour [dɪ'vauə*] vt devorar

devout [dɪ'vaut] adj devoto

dew [djuː] n rocío

diabetes [daɪə'biːtiːz] n diabetes f; **diabetic** [-'bɛtɪk] adj, n diabético/a m/f

diabolical [daɪə'bɔlɪkəl] (inf) adj (weather, behaviour) pésimo

diagnosis [daɪəg'nəusɪs] (pl **-ses**) n diagnóstico

diagonal [daɪ'ægənl] adj, n diagonal f

diagram ['daɪəgræm] n diagrama m, esquema m

dial ['daɪəl] n esfera, cuadrante m, cara (AM); (on radio etc) selector m; (of phone) disco ♦ vt (number) marcar

dialling ['daɪəlɪŋ]: **~ code** n prefijo; **~ tone** (US **dial tone**) n (BRIT) señal f or tono de marcar

dialogue ['daɪəlɔg] (US **dialog**) n diálogo

diameter [daɪ'æmɪtə*] n diámetro

diamond ['daɪəmənd] n diamante m; (shape) rombo; **~s** npl (CARDS) diamantes mpl

diaper ['daɪəpə*] (US) n pañal m

diaphragm ['daɪəfræm] n diafragma m

diarrhoea [daɪə'riːə] (US **diarrhea**) n diarrea

diary ['daɪərɪ] n (daily account) diario; (book) agenda

dice [daɪs] n inv dados mpl ♦ vt (CULIN) cortar en cuadritos

Dictaphone ® ['dɪktəfəun] n dictáfono ®

dictate [dɪk'teɪt] vt dictar; (conditions) imponer; **dictation** [-'teɪʃən] n dictado; (giving of orders) órdenes fpl

dictator [dɪk'teɪtə*] n dictador m; **~ship** n dictadura

dictionary ['dɪkʃənrɪ] n diccionario

did [dɪd] pt of **do**

didn't ['dɪdənt] = **did not**

die [daɪ] vi morir; (fig: fade) desvanecerse, desaparecer; **to be dying for sth/to do sth** morirse por algo/de ganas de hacer algo; **~ away** vi (sound, light) perderse; **~ down** vi apagarse; (wind) amainar; **~ out** vi desaparecer

diesel ['diːzəl] n vehículo con motor Diesel; **~ engine** n motor m Diesel; **~ (oil)** n gasoil m

diet ['daɪət] n dieta; (*restricted food*) régimen m ♦ vi (*also*: be on a ~) estar a dieta, hacer régimen

differ ['dɪfə*] vi: **to ~ (from)** (*be different*) ser distinto (a), diferenciarse (de); (*disagree*) discrepar (de); **~ence** n diferencia; (*disagreement*) desacuerdo; **~ent** adj diferente, distinto; **~entiate** [-'renʃɪeɪt] vi: **to ~entiate (between)** distinguir (entre); **~ently** adv de otro modo, en forma distinta

difficult ['dɪfɪkəlt] adj difícil; **~y** n dificultad f

diffident ['dɪfɪdənt] adj tímido

dig [dɪg] (*pt, pp* dug) vt (*hole, ground*) cavar ♦ n (*prod*) empujón m; (*archaeological*) excavación f; (*remark*) indirecta; **to ~ one's nails into** clavar las uñas en; **~ into** vt fus (*savings*) consumir; **~ up** vt (*information*) desenterrar; (*plant*) desarraigar

digest [vb daɪ'dʒest, n 'daɪdʒest] vt (*food*) digerir; (*facts*) asimilar ♦ n resumen m; **~ion** [dɪ'dʒestʃən] n digestión f

digit ['dɪdʒɪt] n (*number*) dígito; (*finger*) dedo; **~al** adj digital; **~al TV** n televisión f digital

dignified ['dɪgnɪfaɪd] adj grave, solemne

dignity ['dɪgnɪtɪ] n dignidad f

digress [daɪ'gres] vi: **to ~ from** apartarse de

digs [dɪgz] (*BRIT: inf*) npl pensión f, alojamiento

dilapidated [dɪ'læpɪdeɪtɪd] adj desmoronado, ruinoso

dilemma [daɪ'lemə] n dilema m

diligent ['dɪlɪdʒənt] adj diligente

dilute [daɪ'luːt] vt diluir

dim [dɪm] adj (*light*) débil; (*outline*) indistinto; (*room*) oscuro; (*inf: stupid*) lerdo ♦ vt (*light*) bajar

dime [daɪm] (*US*) n moneda de diez centavos

dimension [dɪ'menʃən] n dimensión f

diminish [dɪ'mɪnɪʃ] vt, vi disminuir

diminutive [dɪ'mɪnjʊtɪv] adj diminuto ♦ n (*LING*) diminutivo

dimmers ['dɪməz] (*US*) npl (*AUT: dipped headlights*) luces fpl cortas; (: *parking lights*) luces fpl de posición

dimple ['dɪmpl] n hoyuelo

din [dɪn] n estruendo, estrépito

dine [daɪn] vi cenar; **~r** n (*person*) comensal m/f; (*US*) restaurante m económico

dinghy ['dɪŋgɪ] n bote m; (*also*: rubber ~) lancha (neumática)

dingy ['dɪndʒɪ] adj (*room*) sombrío; (*colour*) sucio

dining car ['daɪnɪŋ-] (*BRIT*) n (*RAIL*) coche-comedor m

dining room n comedor m

dinner ['dɪnə*] n (*evening meal*) cena; (*lunch*) comida; (*public*) cena, banquete m; **~ jacket** n smoking m; **~ party** n cena; **~ time** n

(*evening*) hora de cenar; (*midday*) hora de comer

dinosaur ['daɪnəsɔː*] n dinosaurio

diocese ['daɪəsɪs] n diócesis f inv

dip [dɪp] n (*slope*) pendiente m; (*in sea*) baño; (*CULIN*) salsa ♦ vt (*in water*) mojar; (*ladle etc*) meter; (*BRIT: AUT*): **to ~ one's lights** poner luces de cruce ♦ vi (*road etc*) descender, bajar

diploma [dɪ'pləumə] n diploma m

diplomacy [dɪ'pləuməsɪ] n diplomacia

diplomat ['dɪpləmæt] n diplomático/a; **~ic** [dɪplə'mætɪk] adj diplomático

diprod ['dɪprɒd] (*US*) n = dipstick

dipstick ['dɪpstɪk] (*BRIT*) n (*AUT*) varilla de nivel (del aceite)

dipswitch ['dɪpswɪtʃ] (*BRIT*) n (*AUT*) interruptor m

dire [daɪə*] adj calamitoso

direct [daɪ'rekt] adj directo; (*challenge*) claro; (*person*) franco ♦ vt dirigir; (*order*): **to ~ sb to do sth** mandar a uno hacer algo ♦ adv derecho; **can you ~ me to...?** ¿puede indicarme dónde está...?; **~ debit** (*BRIT*) n domiciliación f bancaria de recibos

direction [dɪ'rekʃən] n dirección f; **sense of ~** sentido de la dirección; **~s** npl (*instructions*) instrucciones fpl; **~s for use** modo de empleo

directly [dɪ'rektlɪ] adv (*in straight line*) directamente; (*at once*) en seguida

director [dɪ'rektə*] n director(a) m/f

directory [dɪ'rektərɪ] n (*TEL*) guía (telefónica); (*COMPUT*) directorio; **~ enquiries** (*BRIT*), **~ assistance** (*US*) n (servicio de) información f

dirt [dɜːt] n suciedad f; (*earth*) tierra; **~-cheap** adj baratísimo; **~y** adj sucio; (*joke*) verde (*SP*), colorado (*AM*) ♦ vt ensuciar; (*stain*) manchar; **~y trick** n juego sucio

disability [dɪsə'bɪlɪtɪ] n incapacidad f

disabled [dɪs'eɪbld] adj: **to be physically ~** ser minusválido/a; **to be mentally ~** ser deficiente mental

disadvantage [dɪsəd'vɑːntɪdʒ] n desventaja, inconveniente m

disagree [dɪsə'griː] vi (*differ*) discrepar; **to ~ (with)** no estar de acuerdo (con); **~able** adj desagradable; (*person*) antipático; **~ment** n desacuerdo

disallow [dɪsə'lau] vt (*goal*) anular; (*claim*) rechazar

disappear [dɪsə'pɪə*] vi desaparecer; **~ance** n desaparición f

disappoint [dɪsə'pɔɪnt] vt decepcionar, defraudar; **~ed** adj decepcionado; **~ing** adj decepcionante; **~ment** n decepción f

disapproval [dɪsə'pruːvəl] n desaprobación f

disapprove [dɪsə'pruːv] vi: **to ~ of** ver mal

disarmament [dɪs'ɑːməmənt] n desarme m

disarray [dɪsə'reɪ] n: **in ~** (*army, organization*)

desorganizado; (*hair, clothes*) desarreglado
disaster [dɪˈzɑːstə*] *n* desastre *m*
disband [dɪsˈbænd] *vt* disolver ♦ *vi*
desbandarse
disbelief [dɪsbəˈliːf] *n* incredulidad *f*
disc [dɪsk] *n* disco; (*COMPUT*) = **disk**
discard [dɪsˈkɑːd] *vt* (*old things*) tirar; (*fig*)
descartar
discern [dɪˈsəːn] *vt* percibir, discernir;
(*understand*) comprender; **~ing** *adj* perspicaz
discharge [*vb* dɪsˈtʃɑːdʒ, *n* ˈdɪstʃɑːdʒ] *vt*
(*task, duty*) cumplir; (*waste*) verter; (*patient*)
dar de alta; (*employee*) despedir; (*soldier*)
licenciar; (*defendant*) poner en libertad ♦ *n*
(*ELEC*) descarga; (*MED*) supuración *f*;
(*dismissal*) despedida; (*of duty*) desempeño;
(*of debt*) pago, descargo
discipline [ˈdɪsɪplɪn] *n* disciplina ♦ *vt*
disciplinar; (*punish*) castigar
disc jockey *n* pinchadiscos *m/f inv*
disclaim [dɪsˈkleɪm] *vt* negar
disclose [dɪsˈkləʊz] *vt* revelar; **disclosure**
[-ˈkləʊʒə*] *n* revelación *f*
disco [ˈdɪskəʊ] *n abbr* = **discothèque**
discomfort [dɪsˈkʌmfət] *n* incomodidad *f*;
(*unease*) inquietud *f*; (*physical*) malestar *m*
disconcert [dɪskənˈsəːt] *vt* desconcertar
disconnect [dɪskəˈnekt] *vt* separar; (*ELEC etc*)
desconectar
discontent [dɪskənˈtent] *n* descontento;
~ed *adj* descontento
discontinue [dɪskənˈtɪnjuː] *vt* interrumpir;
(*payments*) suspender; "**~d**" (*COMM*) "ya no
se fabrica"
discord [ˈdɪskɔːd] *n* discordia; (*MUS*)
disonancia
discothèque [ˈdɪskəʊtek] *n* discoteca
discount [*n* ˈdɪskaunt, *vb* dɪsˈkaunt] *n*
descuento ♦ *vt* descontar
discourage [dɪsˈkʌrɪdʒ] *vt* desalentar; (*advise
against*): **to ~ sb from doing** disuadir a uno
de hacer
discover [dɪsˈkʌvə*] *vt* descubrir; (*error*)
darse cuenta de; **~y** *n* descubrimiento
discredit [dɪsˈkredɪt] *vt* desacreditar
discreet [dɪˈskriːt] *adj* (*tactful*) discreto;
(*careful*) circunspecto, prudente
discrepancy [dɪˈskrepənsɪ] *n* diferencia
discretion [dɪˈskreʃən] *n* (*tact*) discreción *f*;
at the ~ of a criterio de
discriminate [dɪˈskrɪmɪneɪt] *vi*: **to
~ between** distinguir entre; **to ~ against**
discriminar contra; **discriminating** *adj*
entendido; **discrimination** [-ˈneɪʃən] *n*
(*discernment*) perspicacia; (*bias*)
discriminación *f*
discuss [dɪsˈkʌs] *vt* discutir; (*a theme*) tratar;
~ion [dɪˈskʌʃən] *n* discusión *f*
disdain [dɪsˈdeɪn] *n* desdén *m*

disease [dɪˈziːz] *n* enfermedad *f*
disembark [dɪsɪmˈbɑːk] *vt, vi* desembarcar
disentangle [dɪsɪnˈtæŋgl] *vt* soltar; (*wire,
thread*) desenredar
disfigure [dɪsˈfɪgə*] *vt* (*person*) desfigurar;
(*object*) afear
disgrace [dɪsˈgreɪs] *n* ignominia; (*shame*)
vergüenza, escándalo ♦ *vt* deshonrar; **~ful**
adj vergonzoso
disgruntled [dɪsˈgrʌntld] *adj* disgustado,
descontento
disguise [dɪsˈgaɪz] *n* disfraz *m* ♦ *vt* disfrazar;
in ~ disfrazado
disgust [dɪsˈgʌst] *n* repugnancia ♦ *vt*
repugnar, dar asco a; **~ing** *adj* repugnante,
asqueroso; (*behaviour etc*) vergonzoso
dish [dɪʃ] *n* (*gen*) plato; **to do** *or* **wash the ~es**
fregar los platos; **~ out** *vt* repartir; **~ up** *vt*
servir; **~cloth** *n* estropajo
dishearten [dɪsˈhɑːtn] *vt* desalentar
dishevelled [dɪˈʃevəld] (*US* **disheveled**) *adj*
(*hair*) despeinado; (*appearance*) desarreglado
dishonest [dɪsˈɒnɪst] *adj* (*person*) poco
honrado, tramposo; (*means*) fraudulento; **~y**
n falta de honradez
dishonour [dɪsˈɒnə*] (*US* **dishonor**) *n*
deshonra; **~able** *adj* deshonroso
dishtowel [ˈdɪʃtaʊəl] (*US*) *n* estropajo
dishwasher [ˈdɪʃwɒʃə*] *n* lavaplatos *m inv*
disillusion [dɪsɪˈluːʒən] *vt* desilusionar
disinfect [dɪsɪnˈfekt] *vt* desinfectar; **~ant** *n*
desinfectante *m*
disintegrate [dɪsˈɪntɪgreɪt] *vi* disgregarse,
desintegrarse
disinterested [dɪsˈɪntrəstɪd] *adj*
desinteresado
disjointed [dɪsˈdʒɔɪntɪd] *adj* inconexo
disk [dɪsk] *n* (*esp US*) = **disc**; (*COMPUT*) disco,
disquete *m*; **single-/double-sided ~** disco de
una cara/dos caras; **~ drive** *n* disc drive *m*;
~ette *n* = **disk**
dislike [dɪsˈlaɪk] *n* antipatía, aversión *f* ♦ *vt*
tener antipatía a
dislocate [ˈdɪsləkeɪt] *vt* dislocar
dislodge [dɪsˈlɒdʒ] *vt* sacar
disloyal [dɪsˈlɔɪəl] *adj* desleal
dismal [ˈdɪzml] *adj* (*gloomy*) deprimente,
triste; (*very bad*) malísimo, fatal
dismantle [dɪsˈmæntl] *vt* desmontar,
desarmar
dismay [dɪsˈmeɪ] *n* consternación *f* ♦ *vt*
consternar
dismiss [dɪsˈmɪs] *vt* (*worker*) despedir;
(*pupils*) dejar marchar; (*soldiers*) dar permiso
para irse; (*idea, LAW*) rechazar; (*possibility*)
descartar; **~al** *n* despido
dismount [dɪsˈmaunt] *vi* apearse
disobedient [dɪsəˈbiːdɪənt] *adj* desobediente
disobey [dɪsəˈbeɪ] *vt* desobedecer

disorder |dɪsˈɔːdə*| n desorden m; (*rioting*) disturbios mpl; (*MED*) trastorno; **~ly** adj desordenado; (*meeting*) alborotado; (*conduct*) escandaloso

disorientated |dɪsˈɔːrɪenteɪtəd| adj desorientado

disown |dɪsˈəun| vt (*action*) renegar de; (*person*) negar cualquier tipo de relación con

disparaging |dɪsˈpærɪdʒɪŋ| adj despreciativo

dispassionate |dɪsˈpæʃənɪt| adj (*unbiased*) imparcial

dispatch |dɪsˈpætʃ| vt enviar ♦ n (*sending*) envío; (*PRESS*) informe m; (*MIL*) parte m

dispel |dɪsˈpel| vt disipar

dispense |dɪsˈpens| vt (*medicines*) preparar; **~ with** vt fus prescindir de; **~r** n (*container*) distribuidor m automático; **dispensing chemist** (*BRIT*) n farmacia

disperse |dɪsˈpɜːs| vt dispersar ♦ vi dispersarse

dispirited |dɪˈspɪrɪtɪd| adj desanimado, desalentado

displace |dɪsˈpleɪs| vt desplazar, reemplazar; **~d person** n (*POL*) desplazado/a

display |dɪsˈpleɪ| n (*in shop window*) escaparate m; (*exhibition*) exposición f; (*COMPUT*) visualización f; (*of feeling*) manifestación f ♦ vt exponer; manifestar; (*ostentatiously*) lucir

displease |dɪsˈpliːz| vt (*offend*) ofender; (*annoy*) fastidiar; **~d** adj: **~d with** disgustado con; **displeasure** |-ˈpleʒə*| n disgusto

disposable |dɪsˈpəuzəbl| adj desechable; (*income*) disponible; **~ nappy** n pañal m desechable

disposal |dɪsˈpəuzl| n (*of rubbish*) destrucción f; **at one's ~** a su disposición

dispose |dɪsˈpəuz| vi: **to ~ of** (*unwanted goods*) deshacerse de; (*problem etc*) resolver; **~d** adj: **~d to do** dispuesto a hacer; **to be well-~d towards sb** estar bien dispuesto hacia uno; **disposition** |dɪspəˈzɪʃən| n (*nature*) temperamento; (*inclination*) propensión f

disprove |dɪsˈpruːv| vt refutar

dispute |dɪsˈpjuːt| n disputa; (*also: industrial ~*) conflicto (laboral) ♦ vt (*argue*) disputar, discutir; (*question*) cuestionar

disqualify |dɪsˈkwɒlɪfaɪ| vt (*SPORT*) desclasificar; **to ~ sb for sth/from doing sth** incapacitar a alguien para algo/hacer algo

disquiet |dɪsˈkwaɪət| n preocupación f, inquietud f

disregard |dɪsrɪˈgɑːd| vt (*ignore*) no hacer caso de

disrepair |dɪsrɪˈpeə*| n: **to fall into ~** (*building*) desmoronarse

disreputable |dɪsˈrepjutəbl| adj (*person*) de mala fama; (*behaviour*) vergonzoso

disrespectful |dɪsrɪˈspektful| adj irrespetuoso

disrupt |dɪsˈrʌpt| vt (*plans*) desbaratar, trastornar; (*conversation*) interrumpir

dissatisfaction |dɪssætɪsˈfækʃən| n disgusto, descontento

dissect |dɪˈsekt| vt disecar

dissent |dɪˈsent| n disensión f

dissertation |dɪsəˈteɪʃən| n tesina

disservice |dɪsˈsɜːvɪs| n: **to do sb a ~** perjudicar a alguien

dissimilar |dɪˈsɪmɪlə*| adj distinto

dissipate |ˈdɪsɪpeɪt| vt disipar; (*waste*) desperdiciar

dissolve |dɪˈzɒlv| vt disolver ♦ vi disolverse; **to ~ in(to) tears** deshacerse en lágrimas

dissuade |dɪˈsweɪd| vt: **to ~ sb (from)** disuadir a uno (de)

distance |ˈdɪstəns| n distancia; **in the ~** a lo lejos

distant |ˈdɪstənt| adj lejano; (*manner*) reservado, frío

distaste |dɪsˈteɪst| n repugnancia; **~ful** adj repugnante, desagradable

distended |dɪsˈtendɪd| adj (*stomach*) hinchado

distil |dɪsˈtɪl| (*US* **distill**) vt destilar; **~lery** n destilería

distinct |dɪsˈtɪŋkt| adj (*different*) distinto; (*clear*) claro; (*unmistakeable*) inequívoco; **as ~ from** a diferencia de; **~ion** |dɪsˈtɪŋkʃən| n distinción f; (*honour*) honor m; (*in exam*) sobresaliente m; **~ive** adj distintivo

distinguish |dɪsˈtɪŋgwɪʃ| vt distinguir; **to ~ o.s.** destacarse; **~ed** adj (*eminent*) distinguido; **~ing** adj (*feature*) distintivo

distort |dɪsˈtɔːt| vt distorsionar; (*shape, image*) deformar; **~ion** |dɪsˈtɔːʃən| n distorsión f; deformación f

distract |dɪsˈtrækt| vt distraer; **~ed** adj distraído; **~ion** |dɪsˈtrækʃən| n distracción f; (*confusion*) aturdimiento

distraught |dɪsˈtrɔːt| adj loco de inquietud

distress |dɪsˈtres| n (*anguish*) angustia, aflicción f ♦ vt afligir; **~ing** adj angustioso; doloroso; **~ signal** n señal f de socorro

distribute |dɪsˈtrɪbjuːt| vt distribuir; (*share out*) repartir; **distribution** |-ˈbjuːʃən| n distribución f, reparto; **distributor** n (*AUT*) distribuidor m; (*COMM*) distribuidora

district |ˈdɪstrɪkt| n (*of country*) zona, región f; (*of town*) barrio; (*ADMIN*) distrito; **~ attorney** (*US*) n fiscal m/f; **~ nurse** (*BRIT*) n enfermera que atiende a pacientes a domicilio

distrust |dɪsˈtrʌst| n desconfianza ♦ vt desconfiar de

disturb |dɪsˈtɜːb| vt (*person: bother, interrupt*) molestar; (: *upset*) perturbar, inquietar; (*disorganize*) alterar; **~ance** n (*upheaval*) perturbación f; (*political etc: gen pl*) disturbio; (*of mind*) trastorno; **~ed** *adj* (*worried, upset*) preocupado, angustiado; **emotionally ~ed** trastornado; (*childhood*) inseguro; **~ing** *adj* inquietante, perturbador(a)

disuse [dɪs'juːs] *n*: **to fall into ~** caer en desuso

disused [dɪs'juːzd] *adj* abandonado

ditch [dɪtʃ] *n* zanja; (*irrigation ~*) acequia ♦ *vt* (*inf: partner*) deshacerse de; (: *plan, car etc*) abandonar

dither ['dɪðə*] (*pej*) *vi* vacilar

ditto ['dɪtəu] *adv* ídem, lo mismo

divan [dɪ'væn] *n* (*also: ~ bed*) cama turca

dive [daɪv] *n* (*from board*) salto; (*underwater*) buceo; (*of submarine*) sumersión *f* ♦ *vi* (*swimmer: into water*) saltar; (: *under water*) zambullirse, bucear; (*fish, submarine*) sumergirse; (*bird*) lanzarse en picado; **to ~ into** (*bag etc*) meter la mano en; (*place*) meterse de prisa en; **~r** *n* (*underwater*) buzo

diverse [daɪ'vɔːs] *adj* diversos/as, varios/as

diversion [daɪ'vɔːʃən] *n* (*BRIT: AUT*) desviación *f*; (*distraction, MIL*) diversión *f*; (*of funds*) distracción *f*

divert [daɪ'vɔːt] *vt* (*turn aside*) desviar

divide [dɪ'vaɪd] *vt* (*separate*) separar ♦ *vi* dividirse; (*road*) bifurcarse; **~d highway** (*US*) *n* carretera de doble calzada

dividend ['dɪvɪdɛnd] *n* dividendo; (*fig*): **to pay ~s** proporcionar beneficios

divine [dɪ'vaɪn] *adj* (*also fig*) divino

diving ['daɪvɪŋ] *n* (*SPORT*) salto; (*underwater*) buceo; **~ board** *n* trampolín *m*

divinity [dɪ'vɪnɪtɪ] *n* divinidad *f*; (*SCOL*) teología

division [dɪ'vɪʒən] *n* división *f*; (*sharing out*) reparto; (*disagreement*) diferencias *fpl*; (*COMM*) sección *f*

divorce [dɪ'vɔːs] *n* divorcio ♦ *vt* divorciarse de; **~d** *adj* divorciado; **~e** [-'siː] *n* divorciado/a

divulge [daɪ'vʌldʒ] *vt* divulgar, revelar

D.I.Y. (*BRIT*) *adj, n abbr* = **do-it-yourself**

dizzy ['dɪzɪ] *adj* (*spell*) de mareo; **to feel ~** marearse

DJ *n abbr* = **disc jockey**

KEYWORD

do [duː] (*pt* **did**, *pp* **done**) *n* (*inf: party etc*): **we're having a little ~ on Saturday** damos una fiestecita el sábado; **it was rather a grand ~** fue un acontecimiento a lo grande
♦ *aux vb* 1 (*in negative constructions: not translated*) **I don't understand** no entiendo
2 (*to form questions: not translated*) **didn't you know?** ¿no lo sabías?; **what ~ you think?** ¿qué opinas?
3 (*for emphasis, in polite expressions*): **people**

~ make mistakes sometimes sí que se cometen errores a veces; **she does seem rather late** a mí también me parece que se ha retrasado; **~ sit down/help yourself** siéntate/ sírvete por favor; **~ take care!** ¡ten cuidado (, te pido)!
4 (*used to avoid repeating vb*): **she sings better than I ~** canta mejor que yo; **~ you agree? — yes, I ~/no, I don't** ¿estás de acuerdo? — sí (lo estoy)/no (lo estoy); **she lives in Glasgow — so ~ I** vive en Glasgow — yo también; **he didn't like it and neither did we** no le gustó y a nosotros tampoco; **who made this mess? — I did** ¿quién hizo esta chapuza? — yo; **he asked me to help him and I did** me pidió que le ayudara y lo hice
5 (*in question tags*): **you like him, don't you?** te gusta, ¿verdad? *or* ¿no?; **I don't know him, ~ I?** creo que no le conozco
♦ *vt* 1 (*gen, carry out, perform etc*): **what are you ~ing tonight?** ¿qué haces esta noche?; **what can I ~ for you?** ¿en qué puedo servirle?; **to ~ the washing-up/cooking** fregar los platos/cocinar; **to ~ one's teeth/hair/nails** lavarse los dientes/arreglarse el pelo/arreglarse las uñas
2 (*AUT etc*): **the car was ~ing 100** el coche iba a 100; **we've done 200 km already** ya hemos hecho 200 km; **he can ~ 100 in that car** puede ir a 100 en ese coche
♦ *vi* 1 (*act, behave*) hacer; **~ as I ~** haz como yo
2 (*get on, fare*): **he's ~ing well/badly at school** va bien/mal en la escuela; **the firm is ~ing well** la empresa anda *or* va bien; **how ~ you ~?** mucho gusto; (*less formal*) ¿qué tal?
3 (*suit*): **will it ~?** ¿sirve?, ¿está *or* va bien?
4 (*be sufficient*) bastar; **will £10 ~?** ¿será bastante con £10?; **that'll ~** así está bien; **that'll ~!** (*in annoyance*) ¡ya está bien!, ¡basta ya!; **to make ~ (with)** arreglárselas (con)

do away with *vt fus* (*kill, disease*) eliminar; (*abolish: law etc*) abolir; (*withdraw*) retirar

do up *vt* (*laces*) atar; (*zip, dress, shirt*) abrochar; (*renovate: room, house*) renovar

do with *vt fus* (*need*): **I could ~ with a drink/some help** no me vendría mal un trago/un poco de ayuda; (*be connected*) tener que ver con; **what has it got to ~ with you?** ¿qué tiene que ver contigo?

do without *vi* pasar sin; **if you're late for tea then you'll ~ without** si llegas tarde tendrás que quedarte sin cenar ♦ *vt fus* pasar sin; **I can ~ without a car** puedo pasar sin coche

dock [dɔk] *n* (*NAUT*) muelle *m*; (*LAW*) banquillo (de los acusados); **~s** *npl* (*NAUT*) muelles *mpl*, puerto *sg* ♦ *vi* (*enter ~*) atracar (la) muelle; (*SPACE*) acoplarse; **~er** *n* trabajador *m* portuario, estibador *m*; **~yard** *n* astillero

doctor ['dɔktə*] *n* médico/a; (*Ph.D. etc*) doctor(a) *m/f* ♦ *vt* (*drink etc*) adulterar; **D~ of Philosophy** *n* Doctor en Filosofía y Letras

document ['dɔkjumənt] *n* documento; **~ary** |-'mentərɪ] *adj* documental ♦ *n* documental *m*

dodge [dɔdʒ] *n* (*fig*) truco ♦ *vt* evadir; (*blow*) esquivar

dodgems ['dɔdʒəmz] (*BRIT*) *npl* coches *mpl* de choque

doe [dəu] *n* (*deer*) cierva, gama; (*rabbit*) coneja

does [dʌz] *vb see* do; **~n't = does not**

dog [dɔg] *n* perro ♦ *vt* seguir los pasos de; (*subj: bad luck*) perseguir; **~ collar** *n* collar *m* de perro; (*of clergyman*) alzacuellos *m inv*; **~-eared** *adj* sobado

dogged ['dɔgɪd] *adj* tenaz, obstinado

dogsbody ['dɔgzbɔdɪ] (*BRIT: inf*) *n* burro de carga

doings ['duɪŋz] *npl* (*activities*) actividades *fpl*

do-it-yourself *n* bricolaje *m*

doldrums ['dɔldrəmz] *npl*: **to be in the ~** (*person*) estar abatido; (*business*) estar estancado

dole [dəul] (*BRIT*) *n* (*payment*) subsidio de paro; **on the ~** parado; **~ out** *vt* repartir

doll [dɔl] *n* muñeca; (*US: inf: woman*) muñeca, gachí *f*

dollar ['dɔlə*] *n* dólar *m*

dolled up (*inf*) *adj* arreglado

dolphin ['dɔlfɪn] *n* delfín *m*

domain [də'meɪn] *n* (*fig*) campo, competencia; (*land*) dominios *mpl*

dome [dəum] *n* (*ARCH*) cúpula

domestic [də'mestɪk] *adj* (*animal, duty*) doméstico; (*flight, policy*) nacional; **~ated** *adj* domesticado; (*home-loving*) casero, hogareño

dominate ['dɔmɪneɪt] *vt* dominar

domineering [dɔmɪ'nɪərɪŋ] *adj* dominante

dominion [də'mɪnɪən] *n* dominio

domino ['dɔmɪnəu] (*pl* **~es**) *n* ficha de dominó; **~es** *n* (*game*) dominó

don [dɔn] (*BRIT*) *n* profesor(a) *m/f* universitario/a

donate [də'neɪt] *vt* donar; **donation** |də'neɪʃən] *n* donativo

done [dʌn] *pp of* do

donkey ['dɔŋkɪ] *n* burro

donor ['dəunə*] *n* donante *m/f*; **~ card** *n* carnet *m* de donante de órganos

don't [dəunt] = do not

donut ['dəunʌt] (*US*) *n* = doughnut

doodle ['du:dl] *vi* hacer dibujitos or garabatos

doom [du:m] *n* (*fate*) suerte *f* ♦ *vt*: **to be ~ed to failure** estar condenado al fracaso

door [dɔ:*] *n* puerta; **~bell** *n* timbre *m*;

~ handle *n* tirador *m*; (*of car*) manija; **~man** (*irreg*) *n* (*in hotel*) portero; **~mat** *n* felpudo, estera; **~step** *n* peldaño; **~-to-~** *adj* de puerta en puerta; **~way** *n* entrada, puerta

dope [dəup] *n* (*inf: illegal drug*) droga; (: *person*) imbécil *m/f* ♦ *vt* (*horse etc*) drogar

dormant ['dɔ:mənt] *adj* inactivo

dormitory ['dɔ:mɪtrɪ] *n* (*BRIT*) dormitorio; (*US*) colegio mayor

dormouse ['dɔ:maus] (*pl* **-mice**) *n* lirón *m*

DOS *n abbr* (= *disk operating system*) DOS *m*

dosage ['dəusɪdʒ] *n* dosis *f inv*

dose [dəus] *n* dósis *f inv*

doss house ['dɔs-] (*BRIT*) *n* pensión *f* de mala muerte

dossier ['dɔsɪeɪ] *n* expediente *m*, dosier *m*

dot [dɔt] *n* punto ♦ *vi*: **~ted with** salpicado de; **on the ~** en punto

double ['dʌbl] *adj* doble ♦ *adv* (*twice*): **to cost ~** costar el doble ♦ *vt* n doble *m* ♦ *vt* doblar ♦ *vi* doblarse; **on the ~, at the ~** (*BRIT*) corriendo; **~ bass** *n* contrabajo; **~ bed** *n* cama de matrimonio; **~ bend** (*BRIT*) *n* doble curva; **~-breasted** *adj* cruzado; **~-click** *vi* (*COMPUT*) hacer doble clic; **~cross** *vt* (*trick*) engañar; (*betray*) traicionar; **~decker** *n* autobús *m* de dos pisos; **~ glazing** (*BRIT*) *n* doble acristalamiento; **~ room** *n* habitación *f* doble; **~s** *n* (*TENNIS*) juego de dobles; **doubly** *adv* doblemente

doubt [daut] *n* duda ♦ *vt* dudar; (*suspect*) dudar de; **to ~ that** dudar que; **~ful** *adj* dudoso; (*person*): **to be ~ful about sth** tener dudas sobre algo; **~less** *adv* sin duda

dough [dəu] *n* masa, pasta; **~nut** (*US* donut) *n* ≈ rosquilla

dove [dʌv] *n* paloma

dovetail ['dʌvteɪl] *vi* (*fig*) encajar

dowdy ['daudɪ] *adj* (*person*) mal vestido; (*clothes*) pasado de moda

down [daun] *n* (*feathers*) plumón *m*, flojel *m* ♦ *adv* (*~wards*) abajo, hacia abajo; (*on the ground*) por o en tierra ♦ *prep* abajo ♦ *vt* (*inf: drink*) beberse; **~ with X!** ¡abajo X!; **~-and-out** *n* vagabundo/a; **~-at-heel** *adj* venido a menos; (*appearance*) desaliñado; **~cast** *adj* abatido; **~fall** *n* caída, ruina; **~hearted** *adj* desanimado; **~hill** *adv*: **to go ~hill** (*also fig*) ir cuesta abajo; **~ payment** *n* entrada, pago al contado; **~pour** *n* aguacero; **~right** *adj* (*nonsense, lie*) manifiesto; (*refusal*) terminante; **~size** *vi* (*ECON: company*) reducir la plantilla de

Down's syndrome ['daunz-] *n* síndrome *m* de Down

down-: ~stairs *adv* (*below*) (en la casa de) abajo; (*~wards*) escaleras abajo; **~stream** *adv* aguas or río abajo; **~-to-earth** *adj* práctico; **~town** *adv* en el centro de la ciudad; **~ under** adv en Australia (or Nueva Zelanda); **~ward** [-wəd] adj, adv hacia abajo; **~wards** [-wədz] adv hacia abajo

dowry ['dauri] n dote f

doz. abbr = **dozen**

doze [dəuz] vi dormitar; **~ off** vi quedarse medio dormido

dozen ['dʌzn] n docena; **a ~ books** una docena de libros; **~s of** cantidad de

Dr. abbr = **doctor; drive**

drab [dræb] adj gris, monótono

draft [drɑ:ft] n (first copy) borrador m; (POL: of bill) anteproyecto; (US: call-up) quinta ♦ vt (plan) preparar; (write roughly) hacer un borrador de; see also **draught**

draftsman ['drɑ:ftsmən] (US) n = **draughtsman**

drag [dræg] vt arrastrar; (river) dragar, rastrear ♦ vi (time) pasar despacio; (play, film etc) hacerse pesado ♦ n (inf) lata; (women's clothing): **in ~** vestido de travesti; **~ on** vi ser interminable; **~ and drop** vt (COMPUT) arrastrar y soltar

dragon ['drægən] n dragón m

dragonfly ['drægənflaɪ] n libélula

drain [dreɪn] n desaguadero; (in street) sumidero; (source of loss): **to be a ~ on** consumir, agotar ♦ vt (land, marshes) desaguar; (reservoir) desecar; (vegetables) escurrir ♦ vi escurrirse; **~age** n (act) desagüe m; (MED, AGR) drenaje m; (sewage) alcantarillado; **~ing board** (US **~board**) n escurridera, escurridor m; **~pipe** n tubo de desagüe

drama ['drɑ:mə] n (art) teatro; (play) drama m; (excitement) emoción f; **~tic** [drə'mætɪk] adj dramático; (sudden, marked) espectacular; **~tist** ['dræmətɪst] n dramaturgo/a; **~tize** ['dræmətaɪz] vt (events) dramatizar

drank [dræŋk] pt of **drink**

drape [dreɪp] vt (cloth) colocar; (flag) colgar; **~s** (US) npl cortinas fpl

drastic ['dræstɪk] adj (measure) severo; (change) radical, drástico

draught [drɑ:ft] (US **draft**) n (of air) corriente f de aire; (NAUT) calado; **on ~** (beer) de barril; **~ beer** n cerveza de barril; **~board** (BRIT) n tablero de damas; **~s** (BRIT) n (game) juego de damas

draughtsman ['drɑ:ftsmən] (US **draftsman**) (irreg) n delineante m

draw [drɔ:] (pt **drew**, pp **drawn**) vt (picture) dibujar; (cart) tirar de; (curtain) correr; (take out) sacar; (attract) atraer; (money) retirar; (wages) cobrar ♦ vi (SPORT) empatar ♦ n (SPORT) empate m; (lottery) sorteo; **~ near** vi acercarse; **~ out** vi (lengthen) alargarse ♦ vt sacar; **~ up** vi (stop) pararse ♦ vt (chair)

acercar; (document) redactar; **~back** n inconveniente m, desventaja; **~bridge** n puente m levadizo

drawer [drɔ:*] n cajón m

drawing ['drɔ:ɪŋ] n dibujo; **~ board** n tablero (de dibujante); **~ pin** (BRIT) n chincheta; **~ room** n salón m

drawl [drɔ:l] n habla lenta y cansina

drawn [drɔ:n] pp of **draw**

dread [drɛd] n pavor m, terror m ♦ vt temer, tener miedo or pavor a; **~ful** adj horroroso

dream [dri:m] (pt, pp **dreamed** or **dreamt**) n sueño ♦ vt, vi soñar; **~y** adj (distracted) soñador(a), distraído; (music) suave

dreary ['drɪəri] adj monótono

dredge [drɛdʒ] vt dragar

dregs [drɛgz] npl posos mpl; (of humanity) hez f

drench [drɛntʃ] vt empapar

dress [drɛs] n vestido; (clothing) ropa ♦ vt vestir; (wound) vendar ♦ vi vestirse; **to get ~ed** vestirse; **~ up** vi vestirse de etiqueta; (in fancy dress) disfrazarse; **~ circle** (BRIT) n principal m; **~er** n (furniture) aparador m; (: US) cómoda (con espejo); **~ing** n (MED) vendaje m; (CULIN) aliño; **~ing gown** (BRIT) n bata; **~ing room** n (THEATRE) camarín m; (SPORT) vestuario; **~ing table** n tocador m; **~maker** n modista, costurera; **~ rehearsal** n ensayo general

drew [dru:] pt of **draw**

dribble ['drɪbl] vi (baby) babear ♦ vt (ball) regatear

dried [draɪd] adj (fruit) seco; (milk) en polvo

drier ['draɪə*] n = **dryer**

drift [drɪft] n (of current etc) flujo; (of snow) ventisquero; (meaning) significado ♦ vi (boat) ir a la deriva; (sand, snow) amontonarse; **~wood** n madera de deriva

drill [drɪl] n (~ bit) broca; (tool for DIY etc) taladro; (of dentist) fresa; (for mining etc) perforadora, barrena; (MIL) instrucción f ♦ vt perforar, taladrar; (troops) enseñar la instrucción a ♦ vi (for oil) perforar

drink [drɪŋk] (pt **drank**, pp **drunk**) n bebida; (sip) trago ♦ vt, vi beber; **to have a ~** tomar algo; tomar una copa or un trago; **a ~ of water** un trago de agua; **~er** n bebedor(a) m/f; **~ing water** n agua potable

drip [drɪp] n (act) goteo; (one ~) gota; (MED) gota a gota m ♦ vi gotear; **~-dry** adj (shirt) inarrugable; **~ping** n (animal fat) pringue m

drive [draɪv] (pt **drove**, pp **driven**) n (journey) viaje m (en coche); (also: **~way**) entrada; (energy) energía, vigor m; (COMPUT: also: disk **~**) drive m ♦ vt (car) conducir (SP), manejar (AM); (nail) clavar; (push) empujar; (TECH: motor) impulsar ♦ vi (AUT: at controls) conducir; (: travel) pasearse en coche; **left-/**

right-hand ~ conducción f a la izquierda/
derecha; to ~ sb mad volverle loco a uno
drivel ['drɪvl] (inf) n tonterías fpl
driven ['drɪvn] pp of drive
driver ['draɪvə*] n conductor(a) m/f (SP),
chofer m (AM); (of taxi, bus) chofer; ~'s
license (US) n carnet m de conducir
driveway ['draɪvweɪ] n entrada
driving ['draɪvɪŋ] n el conducir (SP), el
manejar (AM); ~ instructor n instructor(a)
m/f de conducción or manejo; ~ lesson n
clase f de conducción or manejo; ~ licence
(BRIT) n permiso de conducir; ~ school n
autoescuela; ~ test n examen m de
conducción or manejo
drizzle ['drɪzl] n llovizna
drool [druːl] vi babear
droop [druːp] vi (flower) marchitarse;
(shoulders) encorvarse; (head) inclinarse
drop [drɔp] n (of water) gota; (lessening)
baja; (fall) caída ♦ vt dejar caer; (voice, eyes,
price) bajar; (passenger) dejar; (omit) omitir
♦ vi (object) caer; (wind) amainar; ~s npl
(MED) gotas fpl; ~ off vi (sleep) dormirse ♦ vt
(passenger) dejar; ~ out vi (withdraw)
retirarse; ~-out n marginado/a; (SCOL)
estudiante que abandona los estudios; ~per n
cuentagotas m inv; ~pings npl excremento
drought [draut] n sequía
drove [drəuv] pt of drive
drown [draun] vt ahogar ♦ vi ahogarse
drowsy ['drauzɪ] adj soñoliento; to be ~ tener
sueño
drug [drʌg] n medicamento; (narcotic) droga
♦ vt drogar; to be on ~s drogarse; ~ addict
n drogadicto/a; ~gist (US) n farmacéutico;
~store (US) n farmacia
drum [drʌm] n tambor m; (for oil, petrol)
bidón m; ~s npl batería; ~mer n tambor m
drunk [drʌŋk] pp of drink ♦ adj borracho ♦ n
(also: ~ard) borracho/a; ~en adj borracho;
(laughter, party) de borrachos
dry [draɪ] adj seco; (day) sin lluvia; (climate)
árido, seco ♦ vt secar; (tears) enjugarse ♦ vi
secarse; ~ up vi (river) secarse; ~-cleaner's
n tintorería; ~-cleaning n lavado en seco;
~er n (for hair) secador m; (US: for clothes)
secadora; ~ rot n putrefacción f fungoide
DSS n abbr = Department of Social Security
DTP n abbr (= desk-top publishing) autoedición
f
dual ['djuəl] adj doble; ~ carriageway (BRIT)
n carretera de doble calzada; ~-purpose adj
de doble uso
dubbed [dʌbd] adj (CINEMA) doblado
dubious ['djuːbɪəs] adj indeciso; (reputation,
company) sospechoso
duchess ['dʌtʃɪs] n duquesa
duck [dʌk] n pato ♦ vi agacharse; ~ling n

patito
duct [dʌkt] n conducto, canal m
dud [dʌd] n (object, tool) engaño, engañifa
♦ adj: ~ cheque (BRIT) cheque m sin fondos
due [djuː] adj (owed): he is ~ £10 se le deben
10 libras; (expected: event): the meeting is
~ on Wednesday la reunión tendrá lugar el
miércoles; (: arrival) the train is ~ at 8am el
tren tiene su llegada para las 5; (proper)
debido ♦ n: to give sb his (or her) ~ ser justo
con alguien ♦ adv: ~ north derecho al norte;
~s npl (for club, union) cuota; (in harbour)
derechos mpl; in ~ course a su debido
tiempo; ~ to debido a; to be ~ to deberse a
duet [djuː'ɛt] n dúo
duffel bag ['dʌfəl] n bolsa de lona
duffel coat n trenca, abrigo de tres cuartos
dug [dʌg] pt, pp of dig
duke [djuːk] n duque m
dull [dʌl] adj (light) débil; (stupid) torpe;
(boring) pesado; (sound, pain) sordo;
(weather, day) gris ♦ vt (pain, grief) aliviar;
(mind, senses) entorpecer
duly ['djuːlɪ] adv debidamente; (on time) a su
debido tiempo
dumb [dʌm] adj mudo; (pej: stupid)
estúpido; ~founded [dʌm'faundɪd] adj
pasmado
dummy ['dʌmɪ] n (tailor's ~) maniquí m;
(mock-up) maqueta; (BRIT: for baby) chupete
m ♦ adj falso, postizo
dump [dʌmp] n (also: rubbish ~) basurero,
vertedero; (inf: place) cuchitril m ♦ vt (put
down) dejar; (get rid of) deshacerse de;
(COMPUT: data) transferir
dumpling ['dʌmplɪŋ] n bola de masa hervida
dumpy ['dʌmpɪ] adj regordete/a
dunce [dʌns] n estiércol m
dung [dʌŋ] n estiércol m
dungarees [dʌŋgə'riːz] npl mono
dungeon ['dʌndʒən] n calabozo
duplex ['djuːpleks] n dúplex m
duplicate [n 'djuːplɪkət, vb 'djuːplɪkeɪt] n
duplicado ♦ vt duplicar; (photocopy)
fotocopiar; (repeat) repetir; in ~ por
duplicado
durable ['djuərəbl] adj duradero
duration [djuə'reɪʃən] n duración f
during ['djuərɪŋ] prep durante
dusk [dʌsk] n crepúsculo, anochecer m
dust [dʌst] n polvo ♦ vt quitar el polvo a,
desempolvar; (cake etc): to ~ with
espolvorear de; ~bin (BRIT) n cubo de la
basura (SP), balde m (AM); ~er n paño,
trapo; ~man (BRIT irreg) n basurero; ~y adj
polvoriento
Dutch [dʌtʃ] adj holandés/esa ♦ n (LING)
holandés m; the ~ npl los holandeses; to go ~
(inf) pagar cada uno lo suyo; ~man/

woman (*irreg*) *n* holandés/esa *m/f*
duty ['djuːtɪ] *n* deber *m*; (*tax*) derechos *mpl* de aduana; **on ~** de servicio; (*at night etc*) de guardia; **off ~** libre (de servicio); **~-free** *adj* libre de impuestos
duvet ['duːveɪ] (*BRIT*) *n* edredón *m*
DVD *n abbr* (= *digital versatile or video disc*) DVD *m*
dwarf [dwɔːf] (*pl* **dwarves**) *n* enano/a ♦ *vt* empequeñecer
dwell [dwel] (*pt*, *pp* **dwelt**) *vi* morar; **~ on** *vt fus* explayarse en
dwindle ['dwɪndl] *vi* menguar, disminuir
dye [daɪ] *n* tinte *m* ♦ *vt* teñir
dying ['daɪɪŋ] *adj* moribundo, agonizante
dyke [daɪk] (*BRIT*) *n* dique *m*
dynamic [daɪ'næmɪk] *adj* dinámico
dynamite ['daɪnəmaɪt] *n* dinamita
dynamo ['daɪnəməʊ] *n* dinamo *f*
dynasty ['dɪnəstɪ] *n* dinastía

E, e

E [iː] *n* (*MUS*) mi *m*
each [iːtʃ] *adj* cada *inv* ♦ *pron* cada uno; **~ other** el uno al otro; **they hate ~ other** se odian (entre ellos *or* mutuamente); **they have 2 books ~** tienen 2 libros por persona
eager ['iːgə*] *adj* (*keen*) entusiasmado; **to be ~ to do sth** tener muchas ganas de hacer algo, impacientarse por hacer algo; **to be ~ for** tener muchas ganas de
eagle ['iːgl] *n* águila
ear [ɪə*] *n* oreja; oído; (*of corn*) espiga; **~ache** *n* dolor *m* de oídos; **~drum** *n* tímpano
earl [əːl] *n* conde *m*
earlier ['əːlɪə*] *adj* anterior ♦ *adv* antes
early ['əːlɪ] *adv* temprano; (*before time*) con tiempo, con anticipación ♦ *adj* temprano; (*settlers etc*) primitivo; (*death, departure*) prematuro; (*reply*) pronto; **to have an ~ night** acostarse temprano; **in the ~ or ~ in the spring/19th century** a principios de primavera/del siglo diecinueve; **~ retirement** *n* jubilación *f* anticipada
earmark ['ɪəmɑːk] *vt*: **to ~ (for)** reservar (para), destinar (a)
earn [əːn] *vt* (*salary*) percibir; (*interest*) devengar; (*praise*) merecerse
earnest ['əːnɪst] *adj* (*wish*) fervoroso; (*person*) serio, formal; **in ~** en serio
earnings ['əːnɪŋz] *npl* (*personal*) sueldo, ingresos *mpl*; (*company*) ganancias *fpl*
ear: **~phones** *npl* auriculares *mpl*; **~ring** *n* pendiente *m*, arete *m*; **~shot** *n*: **within ~shot** al alcance del oído
earth [əːθ] *n* tierra; (*BRIT: ELEC*) cable *m* de toma de tierra ♦ *vt* (*BRIT: ELEC*) conectar a

tierra; **~enware** *n* loza (de barro); **~quake** *n* terremoto; **~y** *adj* (*fig*: *vulgar*) grosero
ease [iːz] *n* facilidad *f*; (*comfort*) comodidad *f* ♦ *vt* (*lessen*: *problem*) mitigar; (: *pain*) aliviar; (: *tension*) reducir; **to ~ sth in/out** meter/sacar algo con cuidado; **at ~!** (*MIL*) ¡descansen!; **~ off** *or* **up** *vi* (*wind, rain*) amainar; (*slow down*) aflojar la marcha
easel ['iːzl] *n* caballete *m*
easily ['iːzɪlɪ] *adv* fácilmente
east [iːst] *n* este *m* ♦ *adj* del este, oriental; (*wind*) este ♦ *adv* al este, hacia el este; **the E~** el Oriente; (*POL*) los países del Este
Easter ['iːstə*] *n* Pascua (de Resurrección); **~ egg** *n* huevo de Pascua
east: **~erly** ['iːstəlɪ] *adj* (*to the east*) al este; (*from the east*) del este; **~ern** ['iːstən] *adj* del este, oriental; (*oriental*) oriental; (*communist*) del este; **~ward(s)** ['iːstwəd(z)] *adv* hacia el este
easy ['iːzɪ] *adj* fácil; (*simple*) sencillo; (*comfortable*) holgado, cómodo; (*relaxed*) tranquilo ♦ *adv*: **to take it** *or* **things ~** (*not worry*) tomarlo con calma; (*rest*) descansar; **~ chair** *n* sillón *m*; **~-going** *adj* acomodadizo
eat [iːt] (*pt* **ate**, *pp* **eaten**) *vt* comer; **~ away at** *vt fus* corroer; mermar; **~ into** *vt fus* corroer; (*savings*) mermar
eaves [iːvz] *npl* alero
eavesdrop ['iːvzdrɔp] *vi*: **to ~ (on)** escuchar a escondidas
ebb [eb] *n* reflujo ♦ *vi* bajar; (*fig*: *also*: **~ away**) decaer
ebony ['ebənɪ] *n* ébano
EC *n abbr* (= *European Community*) CE *f*
ECB *n abbr* (= *European Central Bank*) BCE *m*
eccentric [ɪk'sentrɪk] *adj*, *n* excéntrico/a *m/f*
echo ['ekəʊ] (*pl* **~es**) *n* eco *m* ♦ *vt* (*sound*) repetir ♦ *vi* resonar, hacer eco
éclair [ɪ'kleə*] *n* pastelillo relleno de crema y con chocolate por encima
eclipse [ɪ'klɪps] *n* eclipse *m*
ecology [ɪ'kɔlədʒɪ] *n* ecología
e-commerce *n abbr* (= *electronic commerce*) comercio electrónico
economic [iːkə'nɔmɪk] *adj* económico; (*business etc*) rentable; **~al** *adj* económico; **~s** *n* (*SCOL*) economía ♦ *npl* (*of project etc*) rentabilidad *f*
economize [ɪ'kɔnəmaɪz] *vi* economizar, ahorrar
economy [ɪ'kɔnəmɪ] *n* economía; **~ class** *n* (*AVIAT*) clase *f* económica; **~ size** *n* tamaño económico
ecstasy ['ekstəsɪ] *n* éxtasis *m inv*; (*drug*) éxtasis *m inv*; **ecstatic** [eks'tætɪk] *adj* extático
ECU ['eɪkjuː] *n* (= *European Currency Unit*) ECU *m*
Ecuador ['ekwədɔː*r*] *n* Ecuador *m*; **~ian** *adj*, *n* ecuatoriano/a *m/f*

eczema [ˈɛksɪmə] n eczema m
edge [edʒ] n (of knife) filo; (of object) borde m; (of lake) orilla ♦ vt (SEWING) ribetear; **on ~** (fig) = edgy; **to ~ away from** alejarse poco a poco de; **~ways** adv: **he couldn't get a word in ~ways** no pudo meter ni baza
edgy [ˈɛdʒɪ] adj nervioso, inquieto
edible [ˈɛdɪbl] adj comestible
Edinburgh [ˈɛdɪnbərə] n Edimburgo
edit [ˈɛdɪt] vt (be editor of) dirigir; (text, report) corregir, preparar; **~ion** [ɪˈdɪʃən] n edición f; **~or** n (of newspaper) director(a) m/f; (of column): **foreign/political ~or** encargado de la sección de extranjero/política; (of book) redactor(a) m/f; **~orial** [-ˈtɔːrɪəl] adj editorial ♦ n editorial m
educate [ˈɛdjukeɪt] vt (gen) educar; (instruct) instruir
education [ɛdjuˈkeɪʃən] n educación f; (schooling) enseñanza; (SCOL) pedagogía; **~al** adj (policy etc) educacional; (experience) docente; (toy) educativo
EEC n abbr (= European Economic Community) CEE f
eel [iːl] n anguila
eerie [ˈɪərɪ] adj misterioso
effect [ɪˈfɛkt] n efecto ♦ vt efectuar, llevar a cabo; **to take ~** (law) entrar en vigor or vigencia; (drug) surtir efecto; **in ~** en realidad; **~ive** adj eficaz; (actual) verdadero; **~ively** adv eficazmente; (in reality) efectivamente; **~iveness** n eficacia
effeminate [ɪˈfɛmɪnɪt] adj afeminado
efficiency [ɪˈfɪʃənsɪ] n eficiencia; rendimiento
efficient [ɪˈfɪʃənt] adj eficiente; (machine) de buen rendimiento
effort [ˈɛfət] n esfuerzo; **~less** sin ningún esfuerzo; (style) natural
effusive [ɪˈfjuːsɪv] adj efusivo
e.g. adv abbr (= exempli gratia) p. ej.
egg [ɛg] n huevo; **hard-boiled/soft-boiled ~** huevo duro/pasado por agua; **~ on** vt incitar; **~cup** n huevera; **~ plant** (esp US) n berenjena; **~shell** n cáscara de huevo
ego [ˈiːgəu] n ego; **~tism** n egoísmo; **~tist** n egoísta m/f
Egypt [ˈiːdʒɪpt] n Egipto, **~ian** [ɪˈdʒɪpʃən] adj, n egipcio/a m/f
eiderdown [ˈaɪdədaun] n edredón m
eight [eɪt] num ocho; **~een** num diez y ocho, dieciocho; **eighth** [eɪtθ] num octavo; **~y** num ochenta
Eire [ˈɛərə] n Eire m
either [ˈaɪðə*] adj cualquiera de los dos; (both, each) cada ♦ pron: **~ (of them)** cualquiera de los dos ♦ adv tampoco; **on ~ side** en ambos lados; **I don't like ~** no me gusta ninguno/a de los/las dos; **no, I don't ~** no, yo tampoco ♦ conj: **~ yes or no** o sí o no

eject [ɪˈdʒɛkt] vt echar, expulsar; (tenant) desahuciar; **~or seat** n asiento proyectable
elaborate [adj ɪˈlæbərɪt, vb ɪˈlæbəreɪt] adj (complex) complejo ♦ vt (expand) ampliar; (refine) refinar ♦ vi explicar con más detalles
elastic [ɪˈlæstɪk] n elástico ♦ adj elástico; (fig) flexible; **~ band** (BRIT) n gomita
elated [ɪˈleɪtɪd] adj: **to be ~** regocijarse
elbow [ˈɛlbəu] n codo
elder [ˈɛldə*] adj mayor ♦ n (tree) saúco; (person) mayor; **~ly** adj de edad, mayor ♦ npl: **the ~ly** los mayores
eldest [ˈɛldɪst] adj, n el/la mayor
elect [ɪˈlɛkt] vt elegir ♦ adj: **the president ~** el presidente electo; **to ~ to do** optar por hacer; **~ion** [ɪˈlɛkʃən] n elección f; **~ioneering** [ɪlɛkʃə-ˈnɪərɪŋ] n campaña electoral; **~or** n elector(a) m/f; **~oral** adj electoral; **~orate** n electorado
electric [ɪˈlɛktrɪk] adj eléctrico; **~al** adj eléctrico; **~ blanket** n manta eléctrica; **~ fire** n estufa eléctrica; **~ian** [ɪlɛkˈtrɪʃən] n electricista m/f; **~ity** [ɪlɛkˈtrɪsɪtɪ] n electricidad f; **electrify** [ɪˈlɛktrɪfaɪ] vt (RAIL) electrificar; (fig: audience) electrizar
electronic [ɪlɛkˈtrɔnɪk] adj electrónico; **~ mail** n correo electrónico; **~s** n electrónica
elegant [ˈɛlɪgənt] adj elegante
element [ˈɛlɪmənt] n elemento; (of kettle etc) resistencia; **~ary** [-ˈmɛntərɪ] adj elemental; (primitive) rudimentario; (school) primario
elephant [ˈɛlɪfənt] n elefante m
elevation [ɛlɪˈveɪʃən] n elevación f; (height) altura
elevator [ˈɛlɪveɪtə*] n (US) ascensor m; (in warehouse etc) montacargas m inv
eleven [ɪˈlɛvn] num once; **~ses** (BRIT) npl café m de las once; **~th** num undécimo
elicit [ɪˈlɪsɪt] vt: **to ~ (from)** sacar (de)
eligible [ˈɛlɪdʒəbl] adj: **a ~ young man/woman** un buen partido; **to be ~ for sth** llenar los requisitos para algo
elm [ɛlm] n olmo
elongated [ˈiːlɔŋgeɪtɪd] adj alargado
elope [ɪˈləup] vi fugarse (para casarse)
eloquent [ˈɛləkwənt] adj elocuente
else [ɛls] adv: **something ~** otra cosa; **somewhere ~** en otra parte; **everywhere ~** en todas partes menos aquí; **where ~?** ¿dónde más?, ¿en qué otra parte?; **there was little ~ to do** apenas quedaba otra cosa que hacer; **nobody ~ spoke** no habló nadie más; **~where** adv (be) en otra parte; (go) a otra parte
elude [ɪˈluːd] vt (subj: idea etc) escaparse a; (capture) esquivar
elusive [ɪˈluːsɪv] adj esquivo; (quality) difícil de encontrar
emaciated [ɪˈmeɪsɪeɪtɪd] adj demacrado
E-mail, e-mail [ˈiːmeɪl] n abbr (= electronic mail) correo electrónico, e-mail m

emancipate [ɪ'mænsɪpeɪt] vt emancipar
embankment [ɪm'bæŋkmənt] n terraplén m
embark [ɪm'bɑːk] vi embarcarse ♦ vt embarcar; **to ~ on** (journey) emprender; (course of action) lanzarse a; **~ation** [embɑː'keɪʃən] n (people) embarco; (goods) embarque m
embarrass [ɪm'bærəs] vt avergonzar; (government etc) dejar en mal lugar; **~ed** adj (laugh, silence) embarazoso; **~ing** adj (situation) violento; (question) embarazoso; **~ment** n (shame) vergüenza; (problem): **to be an ~ment for sb** poner en un aprieto a uno
embassy ['embəsɪ] n embajada
embedded [ɪm'bedɪd] adj (object) empotrado; (thorn etc) clavado
embellish [ɪm'belɪʃ] vt embellecer; (story) adornar
embers ['embəz] npl rescoldo, ascua
embezzle [ɪm'bezl] vt desfalcar, malversar
embitter [ɪm'bɪtə*] vt (fig: sour) amargar
embody [ɪm'bɒdɪ] vt (spirit) encarnar; (include) incorporar
embossed [ɪm'bɒst] adj realzado
embrace [ɪm'breɪs] vt abrazar, dar un abrazo a; (include) abarcar ♦ vi abrazarse ♦ n abrazo
embroider [ɪm'brɔɪdə*] vt bordar; **~y** n bordado
embryo ['embrɪəʊ] n embrión m
emerald ['emərəld] n esmeralda
emerge [ɪ'mɜːdʒ] vi salir; (arise) surgir
emergency [ɪ'mɜːdʒənsɪ] n crisis f inv; **in an ~** en caso de urgencia; **state of ~** estado de emergencia; **~ cord** (US) n timbre m de alarma; **~ exit** n salida de emergencia; **~ landing** n aterrizaje m forzoso; **~ services** npl (fire, police, ambulance) servicios mpl de urgencia or emergencia
emery board ['emərɪ-] n lima de uñas
emigrate ['emɪgreɪt] vi emigrar
emissions [ɪ'mɪʃənz] npl emisión f
emit [ɪ'mɪt] vt emitir; (smoke) arrojar; (smell) despedir; (sound) producir
emotion [ɪ'məʊʃən] n emoción f; **~al** adj (needs) emocional; (person) sentimental; (scene) conmovedor(a), emocionante; (speech) emocionado
emperor ['empərə*] n emperador m
emphasis ['emfəsɪs] (pl **-ses**) n énfasis m inv
emphasize ['emfəsaɪz] vt (word, point) subrayar, recalcar; (feature) hacer resaltar
emphatic [em'fætɪk] adj (reply) categórico; (person) insistente
empire ['empaɪə*] n (also fig) imperio
employ [ɪm'plɔɪ] vt emplear; **~ee** [-'iː] n empleado/a; **~er** n patrón/ona m/f; empresario; **~ment** n (work) trabajo; **~ment agency** n agencia de colocaciones
empower [ɪm'paʊə*] vt: **to ~ sb to do sth**

autorizar a uno para hacer algo
empress ['empris] n emperatriz f
emptiness ['emptɪnɪs] n vacío; (of life etc) vaciedad f
empty ['emptɪ] adj vacío; (place) desierto; (house) desocupado; (threat) vano ♦ vt vaciar; (place) dejar vacío ♦ vi vaciarse; (house etc) quedar desocupado; **~-handed** adj con las manos vacías
EMU n abbr (= European Monetary Union) UME f
emulate ['emjuleɪt] vt emular
emulsion [ɪ'mʌlʃən] n emulsión f; (also: ~ paint) pintura emulsión
enable [ɪ'neɪbl] vt: **to ~ sb to do sth** permitir a uno hacer algo
enamel [ɪ'næməl] n esmalte m; (also: ~ paint) pintura esmaltada
enchant [ɪn'tʃɑːnt] vt encantar; **~ing** adj encantador(a)
encl. abbr (= enclosed) adj
enclose [ɪn'kləʊz] vt (land) cercar; (letter etc) adjuntar; **please find ~d** le mandamos adjunto
enclosure [ɪn'kləʊʒə*] n cercado, recinto
encompass [ɪn'kʌmpəs] vt abarcar
encore [ɔŋ'kɔː*] excl ¡otra!, ¡bis! ♦ n bis m
encounter [ɪn'kaʊntə*] n encuentro ♦ vt encontrar, encontrarse con; (difficulty) tropezar con
encourage [ɪn'kʌrɪdʒ] vt alentar, animar; (activity) fomentar; (growth) estimular; **~ment** n estímulo, (of industry) fomento
encroach [ɪn'krəʊtʃ] vi: **to ~ (up)on** invadir; (rights) usurpar; (time) adueñarse de
encyclop(a)edia [ensaɪkləʊ'piːdɪə] n enciclopedia
end [end] n (gen, also aim) fin m; (of table) extremo; (of street) final m; (SPORT) lado ♦ vt terminar, acabar; (also: bring to an ~, put an ~ to) acabar con ♦ vi terminar, acabar; **in the ~** al fin; **on ~** (object) de punta, de cabeza; **to stand on ~** (hair) erizarse; **for hours on ~** hora tras hora; **~ up** vi: **to ~ up in** terminar en; (place) a parar en
endanger [ɪn'deɪndʒə*] vt poner en peligro; **an ~ed species** una especie en peligro de extinción
endearing [ɪn'dɪərɪŋ] adj simpático, atractivo
endeavour [ɪn'devə*] (US **endeavor**) n esfuerzo; (attempt) tentativa ♦ vi: **to ~ to do** esforzarse por hacer; (try) procurar hacer
ending ['endɪŋ] n (of book) desenlace m; (LING) terminación f
endive ['endaɪv] n (chicory) endibia; (curly) escarola
endless ['endlɪs] adj interminable, inacabable
endorse [ɪn'dɔːs] vt (cheque) endosar; (approve) aprobar; **~ment** n (on driving licence) nota de inhabilitación

endure [ɪn'djuə*] vt (bear) aguantar, soportar ♦ vi (last) durar

enemy ['ɛnəmɪ] adj, n enemigo/a m/f

energetic [ɛnə'dʒɛtɪk] adj enérgico

energy ['ɛnədʒɪ] n energía

enforce [ɪn'fɔːs] vt (LAW) hacer cumplir

engage [ɪn'geɪdʒ] vt (attention) llamar; (interest) ocupar; (in conversation) abordar; (worker) contratar; (AUT): **to ~ the clutch** embragar ♦ vi (TECH) engranar; **to ~ in** dedicarse a, ocuparse en; **~d** adj (BRIT: busy, in use) ocupado; (betrothed) prometido; **to get ~d** prometerse; **~d tone** (BRIT) n (TEL) señal f de comunicando; **~ment** n (appointment) compromiso, cita; (booking) contratación f; (to marry) compromiso; (period) noviazgo; **~ment ring** n anillo de prometida

engaging [ɪn'geɪdʒɪŋ] adj atractivo

engine ['ɛndʒɪn] n (AUT) motor m; (RAIL) locomotora; **~ driver** n maquinista m/f

engineer [ɛndʒɪ'nɪə*] n ingeniero; (BRIT: for repairs) mecánico; (on ship, US: RAIL) maquinista m; **~ing** n ingeniería

England ['ɪŋglənd] n Inglaterra

English ['ɪŋglɪʃ] adj inglés/esa ♦ n (LING) inglés m; **the ~** npl los ingleses mpl; **the ~ Channel** n (el Canal de) la Mancha; **~man/woman** (irreg) n inglés/esa m/f

engraving [ɪn'greɪvɪŋ] n grabado

engrossed [ɪn'grəust] adj: **~ in** absorto en

engulf [ɪn'gʌlf] vt (subj: water) sumergir, hundir; (: fire) prender; (: fear) apoderarse de

enhance [ɪn'hɑːns] vt (gen) aumentar; (beauty) realzar

enjoy [ɪn'dʒɔɪ] vt (health, fortune) disfrutar de, gozar de; (like) gustarle a uno; **to ~ o.s.** divertirse; **~able** adj agradable; (amusing) divertido; **~ment** n (joy) placer m; (activity) diversión f

enlarge [ɪn'lɑːdʒ] vt aumentar; (broaden) extender; (PHOT) ampliar ♦ vi: **to ~ on** (subject) tratar con más detalles; **~ment** n (PHOT) ampliación f

enlighten [ɪn'laɪtn] vt (inform) informar; **~ed** adj comprensivo; **the E~ment** n (HISTORY) ≈ la Ilustración, ≈ el Siglo de las Luces

enlist [ɪn'lɪst] vt alistar; (support) conseguir ♦ vi alistarse

enmity ['ɛnmɪtɪ] n enemistad f

enormous [ɪ'nɔːməs] adj enorme

enough [ɪ'nʌf] adj: **~ time/books** bastante tiempo/bastantes libros ♦ pron bastante(s) ♦ adv: **big ~** bastante grande; **he has not worked ~** no ha trabajado bastante; **have you got ~?** ¿tiene usted bastante(s)?; **~ to eat** (lo) suficiente or (lo) bastante para comer; **~!** ¡basta ya!; **that's ~, thanks** con eso basta,

gracias; **I've had ~ of him** estoy harto de él; ... **which, funnily or oddly ~** ... ... lo que, por extraño que parezca ...

enquire [ɪn'kwaɪə*] vt, vi = inquire

enrage [ɪn'reɪdʒ] vt enfurecer

enrol [ɪn'rəul] (US enroll) vt (members) inscribir; (SCOL) matricular ♦ vi inscribirse; matricularse; **~ment** (US enrollment) n inscripción f; matriculación f

en route [ɔn'ruːt] adv durante el viaje

en suite [ɔn'swiːt] adj: **with ~ bathroom** con baño

ensure [ɪn'ʃuə*] vt asegurar

entail [ɪn'teɪl] vt suponer

entangled [ɪn'tæŋgld] adj: **to become ~ (in)** quedarse enredado (en) or enmarañado (en)

enter ['ɛntə*] vt (room) entrar en; (club) hacerse socio de; (army) alistarse en; (sb for a competition) inscribir; (write down) anotar, apuntar; (COMPUT) meter ♦ vi entrar; **~ for** vt fus presentarse para; **~ into** vt fus (discussion etc) entablar; (agreement) llegar a, firmar

enterprise ['ɛntəpraɪz] n empresa; (spirit) iniciativa; **free ~** la libre empresa; **private ~** la iniciativa privada; **enterprising** adj emprendedor(a)

entertain [ɛntə'teɪn] vt (amuse) divertir; (invite: guest) invitar (a casa); (idea) abrigar; **~er** n artista m/f; **~ing** adj divertido, entretenido; **~ment** n (amusement) diversión f; (show) espectáculo

enthralled [ɪn'θrɔːld] adj encantado

enthusiasm [ɪn'θuːzɪæzəm] n entusiasmo

enthusiast [ɪn'θuːzɪæst] n entusiasta m/f; **~ic** [-'æstɪk] adj entusiasta; **to be ~ic about** entusiasmarse por

entire [ɪn'taɪə*] adj entero; **~ly** adv totalmente; **~ty** [ɪn'taɪərətɪ] n: **in its ~ty** en su totalidad

entitle [ɪn'taɪtl] vt: **to ~ sb to sth** dar a uno derecho a algo; **~d** adj (book) titulado; **to be ~d to do** tener derecho a hacer

entrance [n 'ɛntrəns, vb ɪn'trɑːns] n entrada ♦ vt encantar, hechizar; **to gain ~ to** (university etc) ingresar en; **~ examination** n examen m de ingreso; **~ fee** n cuota; **~ ramp** (US) n (AUT) rampa de acceso

entrant ['ɛntrənt] n (in race, competition) participante m/f; (in examination) candidato/a

entrenched [ɛn'trɛntʃd] adj inamovible

entrepreneur [ɔntrəprə'nəː] n empresario

entrust [ɪn'trʌst] vt: **to ~ sth to sb** confiar algo a uno

entry ['ɛntrɪ] n entrada; (in competition) participación f; (in register) apunte m; (in account) partida; (in reference book) artículo; **"no ~"** "prohibido el paso"; (AUT) "dirección prohibida"; **~ form** n hoja de inscripción; **~ phone** n portero automático

envelop [ɪnˈvɛləp] vt envolver
envelope [ˈɛnvələʊp] n sobre m
envious [ˈɛnvɪəs] adj envidioso; (look) de envidia
environment [ɪnˈvaɪərnmənt] n (surroundings) entorno; (natural world): **the ~** el medio ambiente; **~al** [-ˈmɛntl] adj ambiental; medioambiental; **~-friendly** adj no perjudicial para el medio ambiente
envisage [ɪnˈvɪzɪdʒ] vt prever
envoy [ˈɛnvɔɪ] n enviado
envy [ˈɛnvɪ] n envidia ♦ vt tener envidia a; **to ~ sb sth** envidiar algo a uno
epic [ˈɛpɪk] n épica ♦ adj épico
epidemic [ɛpɪˈdɛmɪk] n epidemia
epilepsy [ˈɛpɪlɛpsɪ] n epilepsia
episode [ˈɛpɪsəʊd] n episodio
epitomize [ɪˈpɪtəmaɪz] vt epitomar, resumir
equal [ˈiːkwl] adj igual; (treatment) equitativo ♦ n igual m/f ♦ vt ser igual a; (fig) igualar; **to be ~ to** (task) estar a la altura de; **~ity** [iːˈkwɔlɪtɪ] n igualdad f; **~ize** vi (SPORT) empatar; **~ly** adv igualmente; (share etc) a partes iguales
equate [ɪˈkweɪt] vt: **to ~ sth with** equiparar algo con; **equation** [ɪˈkweɪʒən] n (MATH) ecuación f
equator [ɪˈkweɪtə*] n ecuador m
equilibrium [iːkwɪˈlɪbrɪəm] n equilibrio
equip [ɪˈkwɪp] vt equipar; (person) proveer; **to be well ~ped** estar bien equipado; **~ment** n equipo; (tools) avíos mpl
equities [ˈɛkwɪtɪz] (BRIT) npl (COMM) derechos mpl sobre or en el activo
equivalent [ɪˈkwɪvələnt] adj: **~ (to)** equivalente (a) ♦ n equivalente m
era [ˈɪərə] n era, época
eradicate [ɪˈrædɪkeɪt] vt erradicar
erase [ɪˈreɪz] vt borrar; **~r** n goma de borrar
erect [ɪˈrɛkt] adj erguido ♦ vt erigir, levantar; (assemble) montar; **~ion** [-ʃən] n construcción f; (assembly) montaje m; (PHYSIOL) erección f
ERM n abbr (= Exchange Rate Mechanism) tipo de cambio europeo
erode [ɪˈrəʊd] vt (GEO) erosionar; (metal) corroer, desgastar; (fig) desgastar
erotic [ɪˈrɔtɪk] adj erótico
errand [ˈɛrnd] n recado (SP), mandado (AM)
erratic [ɪˈrætɪk] adj desigual, poco uniforme
error [ˈɛrə*] n error m, equivocación f
erupt [ɪˈrʌpt] vi entrar en erupción; (fig) estallar; **~ion** [ɪˈrʌpʃən] n erupción f; (of war) estallido
escalate [ˈɛskəleɪt] vi extenderse, intensificarse
escalator [ˈɛskəleɪtə*] n escalera móvil
escapade [ɛskəˈpeɪd] n travesura
escape [ɪˈskeɪp] n fuga ♦ vi escaparse; (flee) huir, evadirse; (leak) fugarse ♦ vt (respon-

sibility etc) evitar, eludir; (consequences) escapar a; (elude): **his name ~s me** no me sale su nombre; **to ~ from** (place) escaparse de; (person) escaparse a
escort [n ˈɛskɔːt, vb ɪˈskɔːt] n acompañante m/f; (MIL) escolta ♦ vt acompañar
Eskimo [ˈɛskɪməʊ] n esquimal m/f
especially [ɪˈspɛʃlɪ] adv (above all) sobre todo; (particularly) en particular, especialmente
espionage [ˈɛspɪənɑːʒ] n espionaje m
esplanade [ɛspləˈneɪd] n (by sea) paseo marítimo
Esquire [ɪˈskwaɪə] n (abbr Esq.) n: **J. Brown, ~** Sr. D. J. Brown
essay [ˈɛseɪ] n (LITERATURE) ensayo; (SCOL: short) redacción f; (: long) trabajo
essence [ˈɛsns] n esencia
essential [ɪˈsɛnʃl] adj (necessary) imprescindible; (basic) esencial; **~s** npl lo imprescindible, lo esencial; **~ly** adv esencialmente
establish [ɪˈstæblɪʃ] vt establecer; (prove) demostrar; (relations) entablar; (reputation) ganarse; **~ed** adj (business) conocido; (practice) arraigado; **~ment** n establecimiento; **the E~ment** la clase dirigente
estate [ɪˈsteɪt] n (land) finca, hacienda; (inheritance) herencia; (BRIT: also: housing ~) urbanización f; **~ agent** (BRIT) n agente m/f inmobiliario/a; **~ car** (BRIT) n furgoneta
esteem [ɪˈstiːm] n: **to hold sb in high ~** estimar en mucho a uno
esthetic [ɪsˈθɛtɪk] (US) adj = aesthetic
estimate [n ˈɛstɪmət, vb ˈɛstɪmeɪt] n estimación f, apreciación f; (assessment) tasa, cálculo; (COMM) presupuesto ♦ vt estimar, tasar; calcular; **estimation** [-ˈmeɪʃən] n opinión f, juicio; cálculo
estranged [ɪˈstreɪndʒd] adj separado
estuary [ˈɛstjʊərɪ] n estuario, ría
etc abbr (= et cetera) etc
eternal [ɪˈtɜːnl] adj eterno
eternity [ɪˈtɜːnɪtɪ] n eternidad f
ethical [ˈɛθɪkl] adj ético; **ethics** [ˈɛθɪks] n ética ♦ npl moralidad f
Ethiopia [iːθɪˈəʊpɪə] n Etiopia
ethnic [ˈɛθnɪk] adj étnico; **~ minority** n minoría étnica
ethos [ˈiːθɔs] n genio, carácter m
etiquette [ˈɛtɪkɛt] n etiqueta
EU n abbr (= European Union) UE f
euro n euro
Eurocheque [ˈjʊərəʊtʃɛk] n Eurocheque m
Euroland [ˈjʊərəʊlænd] n Eurolandia
Europe [ˈjʊərəp] n Europa; **~an** [-ˈpiːən] adj, n europeo/a m/f; **~an Community** n Comunidad f Europea; **~an Union** n Unión f Europea

evacuate [ɪ'vækjueɪt] vt (people) evacuar; (place) desocupar

evade [ɪ'veɪd] vt evadir, eludir

evaporate [ɪ'væpəreɪt] vi evaporarse; (fig) desvanecerse; **~d milk** n leche f evaporada

evasion [ɪ'veɪʒən] n evasión f

eve [iːv] n: **on the ~ of** en vísperas de

even ['iːvn] adj (level) llano; (smooth) liso; (speed, temperature) uniforme; (number) par ♦ adv hasta, incluso; (introducing a comparison) aún, todavía; **~ if, ~ though** aunque + sub; **~ more** aun más; **~ so** aun así; **not ~** ni siquiera; **~ he was there** hasta él estuvo allí; **~ on Sundays** incluso los domingos; **to get ~ with sb** ajustar cuentas con uno

evening ['iːvnɪŋ] n tarde f; (late) noche f; **in the ~** por la tarde; **~ class** n clase f nocturna; **~ dress** n (no pl: formal clothes) traje m de etiqueta; (woman's) traje m de noche

event [ɪ'vent] n suceso, acontecimiento; (SPORT) prueba; **in the ~ of** en caso de; **~ful** adj (life) activo; (day) ajetreado

eventual [ɪ'ventʃuəl] adj final; **~ity** [-'ælɪtɪ] n eventualidad f; **~ly** adv (finally) finalmente; (in time) con el tiempo

ever ['evə*] adv (at any time) nunca, jamás; (at all times) siempre; (in question): **why ~ not?** ¿y por qué no?; **the best ~** lo nunca visto; **have you ~ seen it?** ¿lo ha visto usted alguna vez?; **better than ~** mejor que nunca; **~ since** adv desde entonces ♦ conj después de que; **~green** n árbol m de hoja perenne; **~lasting** adj eterno, perpetuo

---

KEYWORD

every ['evrɪ] adj **1** (each) cada; **~ one of them** (persons) todos ellos/as; (objects) cada uno de ellos/as; **~ shop in the town was closed** todas las tiendas de la ciudad estaban cerradas

2 (all possible) todo/a; **I gave you ~ assistance** te di toda la ayuda posible; **I have ~ confidence in him** tiene toda mi confianza; **we wish you ~ success** te deseamos toda suerte de éxitos

3 (showing recurrence) todo/a; **~ day/week** todos los días/todas las semanas; **~ other car had been broken into** habían forzado uno de cada dos coches; **she visits me ~ other/third day** me visita cada dos/tres días; **~ now and then** de vez en cuando

every: **~body** pron = everyone; **~day** adj (daily) cotidiano, de todos los días; (usual) acostumbrado; **~one** pron todos/as, todo el mundo; **~thing** pron todo; **this shop sells ~thing** esta tienda vende de todo; **~where** adv: **I've been looking for you ~where** te he

estado buscando por todas partes; **~where you go you meet ... en** todas partes encuentras ...

evict [ɪ'vɪkt] vt desahuciar; **~ion** [ɪ'vɪkʃən] n desahucio

evidence ['evɪdəns] n (proof) prueba; (of witness) testimonio; (sign) indicios mpl; **to give ~** prestar declaración, dar testimonio

evident ['evɪdənt] adj evidente, manifiesto; **~ly** adv por lo visto

evil ['iːvl] adj malo; (influence) funesto ♦ n mal m

evoke [ɪ'vəuk] vt evocar

evolution [iːvə'luːʃən] n evolución f

evolve [ɪ'vɔlv] vt desarrollar ♦ vi evolucionar, desarrollarse

ewe [juː] n oveja

ex- [eks] prefix ex

exact [ɪg'zækt] adj exacto; (person) meticuloso ♦ vt: **to ~ sth (from)** exigir algo (de); **~ing** adj exigente; (conditions) arduo; **~ly** adv exactamente; (indicating agreement) exacto

exaggerate [ɪg'zædʒəreɪt] vt, vi exagerar; **exaggeration** [-'reɪʃən] n exageración f

exalted [ɪg'zɔːltɪd] adj eminente

exam [ɪg'zæm] n abbr (SCOL) = **examination**

examination [ɪgzæmɪ'neɪʃən] n examen m; (MED) reconocimiento

examine [ɪg'zæmɪn] vt examinar; (inspect) inspeccionar, escudriñar; (MED) reconocer; **~r** n examinador(a) m/f

example [ɪg'zɑːmpl] n ejemplo; **for ~** por ejemplo

exasperate [ɪg'zɑːspəreɪt] vt exasperar, irritar; **exasperation** [-'ʃən] n exasperación f, irritación f

excavate ['ekskəveɪt] vt excavar

exceed [ɪk'siːd] vt (amount) exceder; (number) pasar de; (speed limit) sobrepasar; (powers) excederse en; (hopes) superar; **~ingly** adv sumamente, sobremanera

excellent ['eksələnt] adj excelente

except [ɪk'sept] prep (also: ~ for, ~ing) excepto, salvo ♦ vt exceptuar, excluir; **~ if/ when** excepto si/cuando; **~ that** salvo que; **~ion** [ɪk'sepʃən] n excepción f; **to take ~ion to** ofenderse por; **~ional** [ɪk'sepʃənl] adj excepcional

excerpt ['eksəːpt] n extracto

excess [ɪk'ses] n exceso; **~es** npl (of cruelty etc) atrocidades fpl; **~ baggage** n exceso de equipaje; **~ fare** n suplemento; **~ive** adj excesivo

exchange [ɪks'tʃeɪndʒ] n intercambio; (conversation) diálogo; (also: telephone ~) central f (telefónica) ♦ vt: **to ~ (for)** cambiar (por); **~ rate** n tipo de cambio

exchequer [ɪks'tʃekə*] (BRIT) n: **the E~** la

Hacienda del Fisco

excise [ˈeksaɪz] n impuestos mpl sobre el alcohol y el tabaco

excite [ɪkˈsaɪt] vt (*stimulate*) estimular; (*arouse*) excitar; **~d** adj: **to get ~d** emocionarse; **~ment** n (*agitation*) excitación f; (*exhilaration*) emoción f; **exciting** adj emocionante

exclaim [ɪkˈskleɪm] vi exclamar; **exclamation** [ekskləˈmeɪʃən] n exclamación f; **exclamation mark** n punto de admiración

exclude [ɪkˈskluːd] vt excluir; exceptuar

exclusive [ɪkˈskluːsɪv] adj exclusivo; (*club, district*) selecto; **~ of tax** excluyendo impuestos; **~ly** adv únicamente

excruciating [ɪkˈskruːʃieɪtɪŋ] adj (*pain*) agudísimo, atroz; (*noise, embarrassment*) horrible

excursion [ɪkˈskəːʃən] n (*tourist ~*) excursión f

excuse [n ɪkˈskjuːs, vb ɪkˈskjuːz] n disculpa, excusa; (*pretext*) pretexto ♦ vt (*justify*) justificar; (*forgive*) disculpar, perdonar; **to ~ sb from doing sth** dispensar a uno de hacer algo; **~ me!** (*attracting attention*) ¡por favor!; (*apologizing*) ¡perdón!; **if you will ~ me** con su permiso

ex-directory [ˈeksdɪˈrektərɪ] (*BRIT*) adj que no consta en la guía

execute [ˈeksɪkjuːt] vt (*plan*) realizar; (*order*) cumplir; (*person*) ajusticiar, ejecutar; **execution** [-ˈkjuːʃən] n realización f; cumplimiento; ejecución f

executive [ɪgˈzekjutɪv] n (*person, committee*) ejecutivo; (*POL: committee*) poder m ejecutivo ♦ adj ejecutivo

exemplify [ɪgˈzemplɪfaɪ] vt ejemplificar; (*illustrate*) ilustrar

exempt [ɪgˈzempt] adj: **~ from** exento de ♦ vt: **to ~ sb from** eximir a uno de; **~ion** [-ʃən] n exención f

exercise [ˈeksəsaɪz] n ejercicio ♦ vt (*patience*) usar de; (*right*) valerse de; (*dog*) llevar de paseo; (*mind*) preocupar ♦ vi (*also: to take ~*) hacer ejercicio(s); **~ bike** n ciclostático ®️ m, bicicleta estática; **~ book** n cuaderno

exert [ɪgˈzəːt] vt ejercer; **to ~ o.s.** esforzarse; **~ion** [-ʃən] n esfuerzo

exhale [eksˈheɪl] vt despedir ♦ vi exhalar

exhaust [ɪgˈzɔːst] n (*AUT: also: ~ pipe*) escape m; (: *fumes*) gases mpl de escape ♦ vt agotar; **~ed** adj agotado; **~ion** [ɪgˈzɔːstʃən] n agotamiento; **nervous ~ion** postración f nerviosa; **~ive** adj exhaustivo

exhibit [ɪgˈzɪbɪt] n (*ART*) obra expuesta; (*LAW*) objeto expuesto ♦ vt (*show: emotions*) manifestar; (: *courage, skill*) demostrar; (*paintings*) exponer; **~ion** [eksɪˈbɪʃən] n

exposición f; (*of talent etc*) demostración f

exhilarating [ɪgˈzɪləreɪtɪŋ] adj estimulante, tónico

exile [ˈeksaɪl] n exilio; (*person*) exiliado/a ♦ vt desterrar, exiliar

exist [ɪgˈzɪst] vi existir; (*live*) vivir; **~ence** n existencia; **~ing** adj existente, actual

exit [ˈeksɪt] n salida ♦ vi (*THEATRE*) hacer mutis; (*COMPUT*) salir (al sistema); **~ poll** n encuesta a la salida de los colegios electorales; **~ ramp** (*US*) n (*AUT*) vía de acceso

exodus [ˈeksədəs] n éxodo

exonerate [ɪgˈzɔnəreɪt] vt: **to ~ from** exculpar de

exotic [ɪgˈzɔtɪk] adj exótico

expand [ɪkˈspænd] vt ampliar; (*number*) aumentar ♦ vi (*population*) aumentar; (*trade etc*) expandirse; (*gas, metal*) dilatarse

expanse [ɪkˈspæns] n extensión f

expansion [ɪkˈspænʃən] n (*of population*) aumento; (*of trade*) expansión f

expect [ɪkˈspekt] vt esperar; (*require*) contar con; (*suppose*) suponer ♦ vi: **to be ~ing** (*pregnant woman*) estar embarazada; **~ancy** n (*anticipation*) esperanza; **life ~ancy** esperanza de vida; **~ant mother** n futura madre f; **~ation** [ekspekˈteɪʃən] n (*hope*) esperanza; (*belief*) expectativa

expedient [ɪkˈspiːdɪənt] adj conveniente, oportuno ♦ n recurso, expediente m

expedition [ekspəˈdɪʃən] n expedición f

expel [ɪkˈspel] vt arrojar; (*from place*) expulsar

expend [ɪkˈspend] vt (*money*) gastar; (*time, energy*) consumir; **~iture** n gastos mpl, desembolso; consumo

expense [ɪkˈspens] n gasto, gastos mpl; (*high cost*) costa; **~s** npl (*COMM*) gastos mpl; **at the ~ of** a costa de; **~ account** n cuenta de gastos

expensive [ɪkˈspensɪv] adj caro, costoso

experience [ɪkˈspɪərɪəns] n experiencia ♦ vt experimentar; (*suffer*) sufrir; **~d** adj experimentado

experiment [ɪkˈsperɪmənt] n experimento ♦ vi hacer experimentos

expert [ˈekspəːt] adj experto, perito ♦ n experto/a, perito/a; (*specialist*) especialista m/f; **~ise** [-ˈtiːz] n pericia

expire [ɪkˈspaɪə*] vi caducar, vencer; **expiry** n vencimiento

explain [ɪkˈspleɪn] vt explicar; **explanation** [ekspləˈneɪʃən] n explicación f; **explanatory** [ɪkˈsplænətrɪ] adj explicativo; aclaratorio

explicit [ɪkˈsplɪsɪt] adj explícito

explode [ɪkˈspləud] vi estallar, explotar; (*population*) crecer rápidamente; (*with anger*) reventar

exploit [n ˈeksplɔɪt, vb ɪkˈsplɔɪt] n hazaña ♦ vt explotar; **~ation** [-ˈteɪʃən] n explotación f

exploratory [ɪk'splɔrətrɪ] adj de exploración; (fig: talks) exploratorio, preliminar

explore [ɪk'splɔː*] vt explorar; (fig) examinar; investigar; **~r** n explorador(a) m/f

explosion [ɪk'spləuʒən] n (also fig) explosión f; **explosive** [ɪks'pləusɪv] adj, n explosivo

exponent [ɪk'spəunənt] n (of theory etc) partidario/a; (of skill etc) exponente m/f

export [vb ɛk'spɔːt, n 'ɛkspɔːt] vt exportar ♦ n (process) exportación f; (product) producto de exportación ♦ cpd de exportación; **~er** n exportador m

expose [ɪk'spəuz] vt exponer; (unmask) desenmascarar; **~d** adj expuesto

exposure [ɪk'spəuʒə*] n exposición f; (publicity) publicidad f; (PHOT: speed) velocidad f de obturación; (: shot) fotografía; **to die from ~** (MED) morir de frío; **~ meter** n fotómetro

express [ɪk'spres] adj (definite) expreso, explícito; (BRIT: letter etc) urgente ♦ n (train) rápido ♦ vt expresar; **~ion** [ɪk'spreʃən] n expresión f; (of actor etc) sentimiento; **~ly** adv expresamente; **~way** (US) n (urban motorway) autopista

exquisite [ɛk'skwɪzɪt] adj exquisito

extend [ɪk'stend] vt (visit, street) prolongar; (building) ampliar; (invitation) ofrecer ♦ vi (land) extenderse; (period of time) prolongarse

extension [ɪk'stenʃən] n extensión f; (building) ampliación f; (of time) prolongación f; (TEL: in private house) línea derivada; (: in office) extensión f

extensive [ɪk'stensɪv] adj extenso; (damage) importante; (knowledge) amplio; **~ly** adv: **he's travelled ~ly** ha viajado por muchos países

extent [ɪk'stent] n (breadth) extensión f; (scope) alcance m; **to some ~** hasta cierto punto; **to the ~ of...** hasta el punto de...; **to such an ~ that...** hasta tal punto que...; **to what ~?** ¿hasta qué punto?

extenuating [ɪk'stenjueɪtɪŋ] adj: **~ circumstances** circunstancias fpl atenuantes

exterior [ɛk'stɪərɪə*] adj exterior, externo ♦ n exterior m

external [ɛk'stɜːnl] adj externo

extinct [ɪk'stɪŋkt] adj (volcano) extinguido; (race) extinto

extinguish [ɪk'stɪŋgwɪʃ] vt extinguir, apagar; **~er** n extintor m

extort [ɪk'stɔːt] vt obtener por fuerza; **~ionate** adj excesivo, exorbitante

extra ['ekstrə] adj adicional ♦ adv (in addition) de más ♦ n (luxury, addition) extra m; (CINEMA, THEATRE) extra m/f, comparsa m/f

extra... ['ekstrə] prefix extra...

extract [vb ɪk'strækt, n 'ekstrækt] vt sacar; (tooth) extraer; (money, promise) obtener ♦ n extracto

extracurricular [ekstrəkə'rɪkjulə*] adj extraescolar, extra-académico

extradite ['ekstrədaɪt] vt extraditar

extra: **~-marital** adj extramatrimonial; **~mural** [ekstrə'mjuərl] adj extraescolar; **~ordinary** [ɪk'strɔːdnrɪ] adj extraordinario; (odd) raro

extravagance [ɪk'strævəgəns] n derroche m, despilfarro; (thing bought) extravagancia

extravagant [ɪk'strævəgənt] adj (lavish: person) pródigo; (: gift) (demasiado) caro; (wasteful) despilfarrador/a

extreme [ɪk'striːm] adj extremo, extremado ♦ n extremo; **~ly** adv sumamente, extremadamente

extricate ['ekstrɪkeɪt] vt: **to ~ sth/sb from** librar algo/a uno de

extrovert ['ekstrəvɜːt] n extrovertido/a

eye [aɪ] n ojo ♦ vt mirar de soslayo, ojear; **to keep an ~ on** vigilar; **~bath** n ojera; **~brow** n ceja; **~drops** npl gotas fpl para los ojos, colino; **~lash** n pestaña; **~lid** n párpado; **~liner** n lápiz m de ojos; **~-opener** n revelación f, gran sorpresa; **~shadow** n sombreador m de ojos; **~sight** n vista; **~sore** n monstruosidad f; **~ witness** n testigo m/f presencial

F, f

F [ef] n (MUS) fa m

F. abbr = **Fahrenheit**

fable ['feɪbl] n fábula

fabric ['fæbrɪk] n tejido, tela

fabulous ['fæbjuləs] adj fabuloso

façade [fə'sɑːd] n fachada

face [feɪs] n (ANAT) cara, rostro; (of clock) esfera (SP), cara (AM); (of mountain) cara, ladera; (of building) fachada ♦ vt (direction) estar de cara a; (situation) hacer frente a; (facts) aceptar; **~ down** (person, card) boca abajo; **to lose ~** desprestigiarse; **to make** or **pull a ~** hacer muecas; **in the ~ of** (difficulties etc) ante; **on the ~ of it** a primera vista; **~ to ~ cara a cara; ~ up to** vt fus hacer frente a, arrostrar; **~ cloth** (BRIT) n manopla; **~ cream** n crema (de belleza); **~ lift** n estirado facial; (of building) renovación f; **~ powder** n polvos mpl; **~-saving** adj para salvar las apariencias; **~ value** n (of stamp) valor m nominal; **to take sth at ~ value** (fig) tomar algo en sentido literal

facilities [fə'sɪlɪtɪz] npl (buildings) instalaciones fpl; (equipment) servicios mpl; **credit ~** facilidades fpl de crédito

facing ['feɪsɪŋ] prep frente a

facsimile [fæk'sımılı] n (*replica*) facsímil(e) m; (*machine*) telefax m; (*fax*) fax m
fact [fækt] n hecho; **in ~** en realidad
factor ['fæktə*] n factor m
factory ['fæktərɪ] n fábrica
factual ['fæktjʊəl] adj basado en los hechos
faculty ['fækəltɪ] n facultad f; (*US: teaching staff*) personal m docente
fad [fæd] n novedad f, moda
fade [feɪd] vi desteñirse; (*sound, smile*) desvanecerse; (*light*) apagarse; (*flower*) marchitarse; (*hope, memory*) perderse
fag [fæg] (*BRIT: inf*) n (*cigarette*) pitillo (*SP*), cigarro
fail [feɪl] vt (*candidate*) suspender; (*exam*) no aprobar (*SP*), reprobar (*AM*); (*subj: memory etc*) fallar a ♦ vi suspender; (*be unsuccessful*) fracasar; (*strength, brakes*) fallar; (*light*) acabarse; **to ~ to do sth** (*neglect*) dejar de hacer algo; (*be unable*) no poder hacer algo; **without ~** sin falta; **~ing** n falta, defecto ♦ prep a falta de; **~ure** ['feɪljə*] n fracaso; (*person*) fracasado/a; (*mechanical etc*) fallo
faint [feɪnt] adj débil; (*recollection*) vago; (*mark*) apenas visible ♦ n desmayo ♦ vi desmayarse; **to feel ~** estar mareado, marearse
fair [feə*] adj justo; (*hair, person*) rubio; (*weather*) bueno; (*good enough*) regular; (*considerable*) considerable ♦ adv (*play*) limpio ♦ n feria; (*BRIT: funfair*) parque m de atracciones; **~ly** adv (*justly*) con justicia; (*quite*) bastante; **~ness** n justicia, imparcialidad f; **~ play** n juego limpio
fairy ['feərɪ] n hada; **~ tale** n cuento de hadas
faith [feɪθ] n fe f; (*trust*) confianza; (*sect*) religión f; **~ful** adj (*loyal: troops etc*) leal; (*spouse*) fiel; (*account*) exacto; **~fully** adv fielmente; **yours ~fully** (*BRIT: in letters*) le saluda atentamente
fake [feɪk] n (*painting etc*) falsificación f; (*person*) impostor/a m/f ♦ adj falso ♦ vt fingir; (*painting etc*) falsificar
falcon ['fɔːlkən] n halcón m
fall [fɔːl] (*pt fell, pp fallen*) n caída; (*in price etc*) descenso; (*US*) otoño ♦ vi caer(se); (*price*) bajar, descender; **~s** npl (*water~*) cascada, salto de agua; **to ~ flat** (*on one's face*) caerse (boca abajo); (*plan*) fracasar; (*joke, story*) no hacer gracia; **~ back** vi retroceder; **~ back on** vt fus (*remedy etc*) recurrir a; **~ behind** vi quedarse atrás; **~ down** vi (*person*) caerse; (*building, hopes*) derrumbarse; **~ for** vt fus (*trick*) dejarse engañar por; (*person*) enamorarse de; **~ in** vi (*roof*) hundirse; (*MIL*) alinearse; **~ off** vi caerse; (*diminish*) disminuir; **~ out** vi (*friends etc*) reñir; (*hair, teeth*) caerse; **~ through** vi (*plan, project*) fracasar

fallacy ['fæləsɪ] n error m
fallen ['fɔːlən] pp of **fall**
fallout ['fɔːlaut] n lluvia radioactiva
fallow ['fæləu] adj en barbecho
false [fɔːls] adj falso; **under ~ pretences** con engaños; **~ alarm** n falsa alarma; **~ teeth** (*BRIT*) npl dentadura postiza
falter ['fɔːltə*] vi vacilar; (*engine*) fallar
fame [feɪm] n fama
familiar [fə'mɪlɪə*] adj conocido, familiar; (*tone*) de confianza; **to be ~ with** (*subject*) conocer (bien)
family ['fæmɪlɪ] n familia; **~ business** n negocio familiar; **~ doctor** n médico/a de cabecera
famine ['fæmɪn] n hambre f, hambruna
famished ['fæmɪʃt] adj hambriento
famous ['feɪməs] adj famoso, célebre; **~ly** adv (*get on*) estupendamente
fan [fæn] n abanico; (*ELEC*) ventilador m; (*of pop star*) fan m/f; (*SPORT*) hincha m/f ♦ vt abanicar; (*fire, quarrel*) atizar
fanatic [fə'nætɪk] n fanático/a
fan belt n correa del ventilador
fanciful ['fænsɪful] adj (*design, name*) fantástico
fancy ['fænsɪ] n (*whim*) capricho, antojo; (*imagination*) imaginación f ♦ adj (*luxury*) lujoso, de lujo ♦ vt (*feel like, want*) tener ganas de; (*imagine*) imaginarse; (*think*) creer; **to take a ~ to sb** tomar cariño a uno; **he fancies her** (*inf*) le gusta (ella) mucho; **~ dress** n disfraz m; **~-dress ball** n baile m de disfraces
fanfare ['fænfeə*] n fanfarria (de trompeta)
fang [fæŋ] n colmillo
fantastic [fæn'tæstɪk] adj (*enormous*) enorme; (*strange, wonderful*) fantástico
fantasy ['fæntəzɪ] n (*dream*) sueño; (*unreality*) fantasía
far [fɑː*] adj (*distant*) lejano ♦ adv lejos; (*much, greatly*) mucho; **~ away, ~ off** (a lo) lejos; **~ better** mucho mejor; **~ from** lejos de; **by ~** con mucho; **go as ~ as the farm** vaya hasta la granja; **as ~ as I know** que yo sepa; **how ~?** ¿hasta dónde?; (*fig*) ¿hasta qué punto?; **~away** adj remoto; (*look*) distraído
farce [fɑːs] n farsa
fare [feə*] n (*on trains, buses*) precio (del billete); (*in taxi: cost*) tarifa; (*food*) comida; **half ~** medio pasaje m; **full ~** pasaje completo
Far East n: **the ~** el Extremo Oriente
farewell [feə'wel] excl, n adiós m
farm [fɑːm] n granja (*SP*), finca (*AM*), estancia (*AM*) ♦ vt cultivar; **~er** n granjero (*SP*), estanciero (*AM*); **~hand** n peón m; **~house** n granja, casa de hacienda (*AM*); **~ing** n agricultura; (*of crops*) cultivo; (*of animals*) cría; **~land** n tierra de cultivo; **~ worker** n

= ~**hand**; ~**yard** n corral m
far-reaching [fɑːˈriːtʃɪŋ] adj (reform, effect) de gran alcance
fart [fɑːt] (inf!) vi tirarse un pedo (!)
farther [ˈfɑːðə*] adv más lejos, más allá ♦ adj más lejano
farthest [ˈfɑːðɪst] superlative of far
fascinate [ˈfæsɪneɪt] vt fascinar; **fascination** [-ˈneɪʃən] n fascinación f
fascism [ˈfæʃɪzəm] n fascismo
fashion [ˈfæʃən] n moda; (~ industry) industria de la moda; (manner) manera ♦ vt formar; **in** ~ a la moda; **out of** ~ pasado de moda; ~**able** adj de moda; ~ **show** n desfile m de modelos
fast [fɑːst] adj rápido; (dye, colour) resistente; (clock): **to be** ~ estar adelantado ♦ adv rápidamente, de prisa; (stuck, held) firmemente ♦ n ayuno ♦ vi ayunar; ~ **asleep** profundamente dormido
fasten [ˈfɑːsn] vt atar, sujetar; (coat, belt) abrochar ♦ vi atarse; abrocharse; ~**er**, ~**ing** n cierre m; (of door etc) cerrojo
fast food n comida rápida, platos mpl preparados
fastidious [fæsˈtɪdɪəs] adj (fussy) quisquilloso
fat [fæt] adj gordo; (book) grueso; (profit) grande, pingüe ♦ n grasa; (on person) carnes fpl; (lard) manteca
fatal [ˈfeɪtl] adj (mistake) fatal; (injury) mortal; ~**ity** [fəˈtælɪtɪ] n (road death etc) víctima f; ~**ly** adv fatalmente; mortalmente
fate [feɪt] n destino; (of person) suerte f; ~**ful** adj fatídico
father [ˈfɑːðə*] n padre m; ~-**in-law** n suegro; ~**ly** adj paternal
fathom [ˈfæðəm] n braza ♦ vt (mystery) desentrañar; (understand) lograr comprender
fatigue [fəˈtiːg] n fatiga, cansancio
fatten [ˈfætn] vt, vi engordar
fatty [ˈfætɪ] adj (food) graso ♦ n (inf) gordito/a, gordinflón/ona m/f
fatuous [ˈfætjuəs] adj fatuo, necio
faucet [ˈfɔːsɪt] (US) n grifo (SP), llave f (AM)
fault [fɔːlt] n (blame) culpa; (defect: in person, machine) defecto; (GEO) falla ♦ vt criticar; **it's my** ~ es culpa mía; **to find** ~ **with** criticar, poner peros a; **at** ~ culpable; ~**y** adj defectuoso
fauna [ˈfɔːnə] n fauna
favour [ˈfeɪvə*] (US favor) n favor m; (approval) aprobación f ♦ vt (proposition) estar a favor de, aprobar; (assist) ser propicio a; **to do sb a** ~ hacer un favor a uno; **to find** ~ **with sb** caer en gracia a uno; **in** ~ **of** a favor de; ~**able** adj favorable; ~**ite** [ˈfeɪvrɪt] adj, n favorito, preferido
fawn [fɔːn] n cervato ♦ adj (also: ~-coloured) color de cervato, leonado ♦ vi: **to** ~ **(up)on**

adular
fax [fæks] n (document) fax m; (machine) telefax m ♦ vt mandar por telefax
FBI (US) n abbr (= Federal Bureau of Investigation) ≈ BIC f (SP)
fear [fɪə*] n miedo, temor m ♦ vt tener miedo de, temer; **for** ~ **of** por si; ~**ful** adj temeroso, miedoso; (awful) terrible; ~**less** adj audaz
feasible [ˈfiːzəbl] adj factible
feast [fiːst] n banquete m; (REL: also: ~ day) fiesta ♦ vi festejar
feat [fiːt] n hazaña
feather [ˈfeðə*] n pluma
feature [ˈfiːtʃə*] n característica; (article) artículo de fondo ♦ vt (subj: film) presentar ♦ vi: **to** ~ **in** tener un papel destacado en; ~**s** npl (of face) facciones fpl; ~ **film** n largometraje m
February [ˈfebruərɪ] n febrero
fed [fed] pt, pp of feed
federal [ˈfedərəl] adj federal
fed up [fedˈʌp] adj: **to be** ~ **(with)** estar harto (de)
fee [fiː] n pago; (professional) derechos mpl, honorarios mpl; (of club) cuota; **school** ~**s** matrícula
feeble [ˈfiːbl] adj débil; (joke) flojo
feed [fiːd] (pt, pp fed) n comida; (of animal) pienso; (on printer) dispositivo de alimentación ♦ vt alimentar; (BRIT: baby: breast~) dar el pecho a; (animal) dar de comer a; (data, information): **to** ~ **into** meter en; ~ **on** vt fus alimentarse de; ~**back** n reacción f, feedback m
feel [fiːl] (pt, pp felt) n (sensation) sensación f; (sense of touch) tacto; (impression): **to have the** ~ **of** parecerse a ♦ vt tocar; (pain etc) sentir; (think, believe) creer; **to** ~ **hungry/cold** tener hambre/frío; **to** ~ **lonely/better** sentirse solo/mejor; **I don't** ~ **well** no me siento bien; **it** ~**s soft** es suave al tacto; **to** ~ **like** (want) tener ganas de; ~ **about** or **around** vi tantear; ~**er** n (of insect) antena; ~**ing** n (physical) sensación f; (foreboding) presentimiento; (emotion) sentimiento
feet [fiːt] npl of foot
feign [feɪn] vt fingir
fell [fel] pt of fall ♦ vt (tree) talar
fellow [ˈfeləʊ] n tipo, tío (SP); (comrade) compañero; (of learned society) socio/a ♦ cpd: ~ **citizen** n conciudadano/a; ~ **countryman** (irreg) n compatriota m; ~ **men** npl semejantes mpl; ~**ship** n compañerismo; (grant) beca
felony [ˈfelənɪ] n crimen m
felt [felt] pt, pp of feel ♦ n fieltro; ~-**tip pen** n rotulador m
female [ˈfiːmeɪl] n (pej: woman) mujer f, tía; (ZOOL) hembra ♦ adj femenino; hembra

feminine ['feminin] adj femenino
feminist ['feminist] n feminista
fence [fens] n valla, cerca ♦ vt (also: ~ in)
cercar ♦ vi (SPORT) hacer esgrima; **fencing** n
esgrima
fend [fend] vi: **to ~ for o.s.** valerse por sí
mismo; **~ off** vt (attack) rechazar; (questions)
evadir
fender ['fendə*] n guardafuego; (US: AUT)
parachoques m inv
ferment [vb fə'ment, n 'fə:ment] vi fermentar
♦ n (fig) agitación f
fern [fə:n] n helecho
ferocious [fə'rəuʃəs] adj feroz
ferret ['ferit] n hurón m
ferry ['feri] n (small) barca (de pasaje), balsa;
(large: also: ~boat) transbordador m (SP),
embarcadero (AM) ♦ vt transportar
fertile ['fə:tail] adj fértil; (BIOL) fecundo;
fertilize ['fə:tilaiz] vt (BIOL) fecundar; (AGR)
abonar; **fertilizer** n abono
fester ['festə*] vi ulcerarse
festival ['festivəl] n (REL) fiesta; (ART, MUS)
festival m
festive ['festiv] adj festivo; **the ~ season** (BRIT:
Christmas) las Navidades
festivities [fes'tiviti:z] npl fiestas fpl
festoon [fes'tu:n] vt: **to ~ with** engalanar de
fetch [fetʃ] vt ir a buscar; (sell for) venderse
por
fête [feit] n fiesta
fetus ['fi:təs] (US) n = **foetus**
feud [fju:d] n (hostility) enemistad f; (quarrel)
disputa
fever ['fi:və*] n fiebre f; **~ish** adj febril
few [fju:] adj (not many) pocos ♦ pron pocos;
algunos; **a ~** adj unos pocos, algunos; **~er**
adj menos; **~est** adj los/las menos
fiancé [fi'ā:ŋsei] n novio, prometido; **~e** n
novia, prometida
fib [fib] n mentirilla
fibre ['faibə*] (US fiber) n fibra; **~glass**
(Fiberglass ®) US) n fibra de vidrio
fickle ['fikl] adj inconstante
fiction ['fikʃən] n ficción f; **~al** adj novelesco;
fictitious [fik'tiʃəs] adj ficticio
fiddle ['fidl] n (MUS) violín m; (cheating)
trampa ♦ vt (BRIT: accounts) falsificar; **~ with**
vt fus juguetear con
fidget ['fidʒit] vi enredar; **stop ~ing!** ¡estáte
quieto!
field [fi:ld] n campo; (fig) campo, esfera;
(SPORT) campo, cancha (AM); **~ marshal** n
mariscal m; **~work** n trabajo de campo
fiend [fi:nd] n demonio
fierce [fiəs] adj feroz; (wind, heat) fuerte;
(fighting, enemy) encarnizado
fiery ['faiəri] adj (burning) ardiente;
(temperament) apasionado

fifteen [fif'ti:n] num quince
fifth [fifθ] num quinto
fifty ['fifti] num cincuenta; **~-~** adj (deal, split)
a medias ♦ adv a medias, mitad por mitad
fig [fig] n higo
fight [fait] (pt, pp fought) n (gen) pelea; (MIL)
combate m; (struggle) lucha ♦ vt luchar
contra; (cancer, alcoholism) combatir;
(election) intentar ganar; (emotion) resistir
♦ vi pelear, luchar; **~er** n combatiente m/f;
(plane) caza m; **~ing** n combate m, pelea
figment ['figmənt] n: **a ~ of the imagination**
una quimera
figurative ['figjurətiv] adj (meaning)
figurado; (style) figurativo
figure ['figə*] n (DRAWING, GEOM) figura,
dibujo; (number, cipher) cifra; (body, outline)
tipo; (personality) figura ♦ vt (esp US)
imaginar ♦ vi (appear) figurar; **~ out** vt
(work out) resolver; **~head** n (NAUT)
mascarón m de proa; (pej: leader) figura
decorativa; **~ of speech** n figura retórica
file [fail] n (tool) lima; (dossier) expediente m;
(folder) carpeta; (COMPUT) fichero; (row) fila
♦ vt limar; (LAW: claim) presentar; (store)
archivar; **~ in/out** vi entrar/salir en fila;
filing cabinet n fichero, archivador m
fill [fil] vt (space): **to ~ (with)** llenar (de);
(vacancy, need) cubrir ♦ n: **to eat one's ~**
llenarse; **~ in** vt rellenar; **~ up** vt llenar
(hasta el borde) ♦ vi (AUT) poner gasolina
fillet ['filit] n filete m; **~ steak** n filete m de
ternera
filling ['filiŋ] n (CULIN) relleno; (for tooth)
empaste m; **~ station** n estación f de
servicio
film [film] n película ♦ vt (scene) filmar ♦ vi
rodar (una película); **~ star** n astro, estrella
de cine
filter ['filtə*] n filtro ♦ vt filtrar; **~ lane** (BRIT)
n carril m de selección; **~-tipped** adj con
filtro
filth [filθ] n suciedad f; **~y** adj sucio;
(language) obsceno
fin [fin] n (gen) aleta
final ['fainl] adj (last) final, último; (definitive)
definitivo, terminante ♦ n (BRIT: SPORT) final f;
~s npl (SCOL) examen m final; (US: SPORT)
final f
finale [fi'nɑ:li] n final m
final: ~ist n (SPORT) finalista m/f; **~ize** vt
concluir, completar; **~ly** adv (lastly) por
último, finalmente; (eventually) por fin
finance [fai'næns] n (money) fondos mpl; **~s**
npl finanzas fpl; (personal ~s) situación f económica ♦ vt financiar; **financial** [-'nænʃəl]
adj financiero
find [faind] (pt, pp found) vt encontrar, hallar;
(come upon) descubrir ♦ n hallazgo;

descubrimiento; **to ~ sb guilty** (*LAW*) declarar culpable a uno; **~ out** *vt* averiguar; (*truth*, *secret*) descubrir; **to ~ out about** (*subject*) informarse sobre; (*by chance*) enterarse de; **~ings** *npl* (*LAW*) veredicto, fallo; (*of report*) recomendaciones *fpl*

fine [faɪn] *adj* excelente; (*thin*) fino ♦ *adv* (*well*) bien ♦ *n* (*LAW*) multa ♦ *vt* (*LAW*) multar; **to be ~** (*person*) estar bien; (*weather*) hacer buen tiempo; **~ arts** *npl* bellas artes *fpl*

finery ['faɪnərɪ] *n* adornos *mpl*

finger ['fɪŋgə*] *n* dedo ♦ *vt* (*touch*) manosear; **little/index ~** (dedo) meñique *m*/ índice *m*; **~nail** *n* uña; **~print** *n* huella dactilar; **~tip** *n* yema del dedo

finish ['fɪnɪʃ] *n* (*end*) fin *m*; (*SPORT*) meta; (*polish etc*) acabado ♦ *vt*, *vi* terminar; **to ~ doing sth** acabar de hacer algo; **to ~ third** llegar el tercero; **~ off** *vt* acabar, terminar; (*kill*) acabar con; **~ up** *vt* acabar, terminar ♦ *vi* ir a parar, terminar; **~ing line** *n* línea de llegada *or* meta

finite ['faɪnaɪt] *adj* finito; (*verb*) conjugado

Finland ['fɪnlənd] *n* Finlandia

Finn [fɪn] *n* finlandés/esa *m/f*; **~ish** *adj* finlandés/esa ♦ *n* (*LING*) finlandés *m*

fir [fɜː*] *n* abeto

fire ['faɪə*] *n* fuego; (*in hearth*) lumbre *f*; (*accidental*) incendio; (*heater*) estufa ♦ *vt* (*gun*) disparar; (*interest*) despertar; (*inf: dismiss*) despedir ♦ *vi* (*shoot*) disparar; **on ~** ardiendo, en llamas; **~ alarm** *n* alarma de incendios; **~arm** *n* arma de fuego; **~ brigade** (*US* ~ **department**) *n* (cuerpo de) bomberos *mpl*; **~ engine** *n* coche *m* de bomberos; **~ escape** *n* escalera de incendios; **~ extinguisher** *n* extintor *m* (de incendios); **~guard** *n* rejilla de protección; **~man** (*irreg*) *n* bombero; **~place** *n* chimenea; **~side** *n*: **by the ~side** al lado de la chimenea; **~ station** *n* parque *m* de bomberos; **~wood** *n* leña; **~works** *npl* fuegos *mpl* artificiales

firing squad ['faɪrɪŋ-] *n* pelotón *m* de ejecución

firm [fɜːm] *adj* firme; (*look*, *voice*) resuelto ♦ *n* firma, empresa; **~ly** *adv* firmemente; resueltamente

first [fɜːst] *adj* primero ♦ *adv* (*before others*) primero; (*when listing reasons etc*) en primer lugar, primeramente ♦ *n* (*person: in race*) primero/a; (*AUT*) primera; (*BRIT: SCOL*) título de licenciado con calificación de sobresaliente; **at ~** al principio; **~ of all** ante todo; **~ aid** *n* primera ayuda, primeros auxilios *mpl*; **~-aid kit** *n* botiquín *m*; **~-class** *adj* (*excellent*) de primera (categoría); (*ticket etc*) de primera clase; **~-hand** *adj* de primera mano; **F~ Lady** *n* (*esp US*) *n* primera dama; **~ly** *adv*

en primer lugar; **~ name** *n* nombre *m* (de pila); **~-rate** *adj* estupendo

fish [fɪʃ] *n inv* pez *m*; (*food*) pescado ♦ *vt*, *vi* pescar; **to go ~ing** ir de pesca; **~erman** (*irreg*) *n* pescador *m*; **~ farm** *n* criadero de peces; **~ fingers** (*BRIT*) *npl* croquetas *fpl* de pescado; **~ing boat** *n* barca de pesca; **~ing line** *n* sedal *m*; **~ing rod** *n* caña de pescar); **~ing rod** *n* caña de pescar); **~monger's (shop)** (*BRIT*) *n* pescadería; **~ sticks** (*US*) *npl* = **~ fingers**; **~y** (*inf*) *adj* sospechoso

fist [fɪst] *n* puño

fit [fɪt] *adj* (*healthy*) en (buena) forma; (*proper*) adecuado, apropiado ♦ *vt* (*subj: clothes*) estar *or* sentar bien a; (*instal*) poner; (*equip*) proveer, dotar; (*facts*) cuadrar *or* corresponder con ♦ *vi* (*clothes*) sentar bien; (*in space*, *gap*) caber; (*facts*) coincidir ♦ *n* (*MED*) ataque *m*; **~ to** (*ready*) a punto de; **~ for** apropiado para; **a ~ of anger/pride** un arranque de cólera/orgullo; **this dress is a good ~** este vestido me sienta bien; **by ~s and starts** a rachas; **~ in** *vi* (*fig: person*) llevarse bien (con todos); **~ful** *adj* espasmódico, intermitente; **~ment** *n* módulo adosable; **~ness** *n* (*MED*) salud *f*; **~ted carpet** *n* moqueta; **~ted kitchen** *n* cocina amueblada; **~ter** *n* ajustador *m*; **~ting** *adj* apropiado ♦ *n* (*of dress*) prueba; (*of piece of equipment*) instalación *f*; **~ting room** *n* probador *m*; **~tings** *npl* instalaciones *fpl*

five [faɪv] *num* cinco; **~r** (*inf*) *n* (*BRIT*) billete *m* de cinco libras; (*US*) billete *m* de cinco dólares

fix [fɪks] *vt* (*secure*) fijar, asegurar; (*mend*) arreglar; (*prepare*) preparar ♦ *n*: **to be in a ~** estar en un aprieto; **~ up** *vt* (*meeting*) arreglar; **to ~ sb up with sth** proveer a uno de algo; **~ation** [fɪkˈseɪʃən] *n* obsesión *f*; **~ed** *adj* (*prices etc*) fijo; **~ture** *n* (*SPORT*) encuentro; **~tures** *npl* (*cupboards etc*) instalaciones *fpl* fijas

fizzy ['fɪzɪ] *adj* (*drink*) gaseoso

fjord [fjɔːd] *n* fiordo

flabbergasted ['flæbəgɑːstɪd] *adj* pasmado, alucinado

flabby ['flæbɪ] *adj* gordo

flag [flæg] *n* bandera; (*stone*) losa ♦ *vi* decaer; **to ~ sb down** hacer señas a uno para que se pare; **~pole** *n* asta de bandera; **~ship** *n* buque *m* insignia; (*fig*) bandera

flair [flɛə*] *n* aptitud *f* especial

flak [flæk] *n* (*MIL*) fuego antiaéreo; (*inf: criticism*) lluvia de críticas

flake [fleɪk] *n* (*of rust, paint*) escama; (*of snow, soap powder*) copo ♦ *vi* (*also*: **~ off**) desconcharse

flamboyant [flæmˈbɔɪənt] *adj* (*dress*) vistoso; (*person*) extravagante

flame [fleɪm] n llama
flamingo [fləˈmɪŋɡəu] n flamenco
flammable [ˈflæməbl] adj inflamable
flan [flæn] (BRIT) n tarta
flank [flæŋk] n (of animal) ijar m; (of army) flanco ♦ vt flanquear
flannel [ˈflænl] n (BRIT: also: face ~) manopla; (fabric) franela
flap [flæp] n (of pocket, envelope) solapa ♦ vt (wings, arms) agitar ♦ vi (sail, flag) ondear
flare [fleə*] n (llamarada; (MIL) bengala; (in skirt etc) vuelo; ~ **up** vi encenderse; (fig: person) encolerizarse; (: revolt) estallar
flash [flæʃ] n relámpago; (also: news ~) noticias fpl de última hora; (PHOT) flash m ♦ vt (light, headlights) lanzar un destello con; (news, message) transmitir; (smile) lanzar ♦ vi brillar; (hazard light etc) lanzar destellos; **in a ~** en un instante; **he ~ed by** or **past** pasó como un rayo; **~back** n (CINEMA) flashback m; **~bulb** n bombilla fusible; **~ cube** n cubo de flash; **~light** n linterna
flashy [ˈflæʃi] (pej) adj ostentoso
flask [flɑːsk] n frasco; (also: vacuum ~) termo
flat [flæt] adj llano; (smooth) liso; (tyre) desinflado; (battery) descargado; (beer) muerto; (refusal etc) rotundo; (MUS) desafinado; (rate) fijo ♦ n (BRIT: apartment) piso (SP), departamento (AM), apartamento; (AUT) pinchazo; (MUS) bemol m; **to work ~ out** trabajar a toda mecha; **~ly** adv terminantemente, de plano; **~ten** vt (also: ~ten out) allanar; (smooth out) alisar; (building, plants) arrasar
flatter [ˈflætə*] vt adular, halagar; **~ing** adj halagüeño; (dress) que favorece; **~y** n adulación f
flaunt [flɔːnt] vt ostentar, lucir
flavour [ˈfleɪvə*] (US **flavor**) n sabor m, gusto ♦ vt sazonar, condimentar; **strawberry-~ed** con sabor a fresa; **~ing** n (in product) aromatizante m
flaw [flɔː] n defecto; **~less** adj impecable
flax [flæks] n lino
flea [fliː] n pulga
fleck [flɛk] n (mark) mota
flee [fliː] (pt, pp **fled**) vt huir de ♦ vi huir, fugarse
fleece [fliːs] n vellón m; (wool) lana ♦ vt (inf) desplumar
fleet [fliːt] n flota; (of lorries etc) escuadra
fleeting [ˈfliːtɪŋ] adj fugaz
Flemish [ˈflemɪʃ] adj flamenco
flesh [fleʃ] n carne f; (skin) piel f; (of fruit) pulpa; **~ wound** n herida superficial
flew [fluː] pt of **fly**
flex [fleks] n cordón m ♦ vt (muscles) tensar; **~ible** adj flexible
flick [flɪk] n capirotazo; chasquido ♦ vt (with

hand) dar un capirotazo a; (whip etc) chasquear; (switch) accionar; **~ through** vt fus hojear
flicker [ˈflɪkə*] vi (light) parpadear; (flame) vacilar
flier [ˈflaɪə*] n aviador(a) m/f
flight [flaɪt] n vuelo; (escape) huida, fuga; (also: ~ of steps) tramo (de escaleras); **~ attendant** (US) n camarero/azafata; **~ deck** n (AVIAT) cabina de mandos; (NAUT) cubierta de aterrizaje
flimsy [ˈflɪmzi] adj (thin) muy ligero; (building) endeble; (excuse) flojo
flinch [flɪntʃ] vi encogerse; **to ~ from** retroceder ante
fling [flɪŋ] (pt, pp **flung**) vt arrojar
flint [flɪnt] n pedernal m; (in lighter) piedra
flip [flɪp] vt dar la vuelta a; (switch: turn on) encender; (: turn off) apagar; (coin) echar a cara o cruz
flippant [ˈflɪpənt] adj poco serio
flipper [ˈflɪpə*] n aleta
flirt [flɜːt] vi coquetear, flirtear ♦ n coqueta
float [fləut] n flotador m; (in procession) carroza; (money) reserva ♦ vi flotar; (swimmer) hacer la plancha
flock [flɒk] n (of sheep) rebaño; (of birds) bandada ♦ vi: **to ~ to** acudir en tropel a
flog [flɒg] vt azotar
flood [flʌd] n inundación f; (of letters, imports etc) avalancha ♦ vt inundar ♦ vi (place) inundarse; (people): **to ~ into** inundar; **~ing** n inundaciones fpl; **~light** n foco
floor [flɔː*] n suelo; (storey) piso; (of sea) fondo ♦ vt (subj: question) dejar sin respuesta; (: blow) derribar; **ground ~**, **first ~** (US) planta baja; **first ~**, **second ~** (US) primer piso; **~board** n tabla; **~ show** n cabaret m
flop [flɒp] n fracaso ♦ vi (fail) fracasar; (fall) derrumbarse; **~py** adj flojo ♦ n (COMPUT: also: ~py disk) floppy m
flora [ˈflɔːrə] n flora
floral [ˈflɔːrl] adj (pattern) floreado
florid [ˈflɒrɪd] adj florido; (complexion) rubicundo
florist [ˈflɒrɪst] n florista m/f; **~'s (shop)** n florería
flounder [ˈflaundə*] vi (swimmer) patalear; (fig: economy) estar en dificultades ♦ n (ZOOL) platija
flour [ˈflauə*] n harina
flourish [ˈflʌrɪʃ] vi florecer ♦ n ademán m, movimiento (ostentoso)
flout [flaut] vt burlarse de
flow [fləu] n (movement) flujo; (of traffic) circulación f; (tide) corriente f ♦ vi (river, blood) fluir; (traffic) circular; **~ chart** n organigrama m
flower [ˈflauə*] n flor f ♦ vi florecer; **~ bed** n

macizo; **~pot** n tiesto; **~y** adj (fragrance)
floral; (pattern) floreado; (speech) florido
flown [fləʊn] pp of **fly**
flu [fluː] n: **to have ~** tener la gripe
fluctuate ['flʌktjʊeɪt] vi fluctuar
fluent ['fluːənt] adj (linguist) que habla
perfectamente; (speech) elocuente; **he speaks
~ French, he's ~ in French** domina el francés;
~ly adv con fluidez
fluff [flʌf] n pelusa; **~y** adj de pelo suave
fluid ['fluːɪd] adj (movement) fluido, líquido;
(situation) inestable ♦ n fluido, líquido
fluke [fluːk] (inf) n chiripa
flung [flʌŋ] pt, pp of **fling**
fluoride ['flʊəraɪd] n fluoruro
flurry ['flʌrɪ] n (of snow) temporal m; **~ of
activity** frenesí m de actividad
flush [flʌʃ] n rubor m; (fig: of youth etc)
resplandor m ♦ vt limpiar con agua ♦ vi
ruborizarse ♦ adj: **~ with** a ras de; **to ~ the
toilet** hacer funcionar la cisterna; **~ed** adj
ruborizado
flustered ['flʌstəd] adj aturdido
flute [fluːt] n flauta
flutter ['flʌtə*] n (of wings) revoloteo, aleteo;
a ~ of panic/excitement una oleada de
pánico/excitación ♦ vi revolotear
flux [flʌks] n: **to be in a state of ~** estar
continuamente cambiando
fly [flaɪ] (pt **flew**, pp **flown**) n mosca; (on
trousers: also: **flies**) bragueta ♦ vt (plane)
pilot(e)ar; (cargo) transportar (en avión);
(distances) recorrer (en avión) ♦ vi volar;
(passengers) ir en avión; (escape) evadirse;
(flag) ondear; **~ away or off** vi emprender
el vuelo; **~-drive** n: **~-drive holiday**
vacaciones que incluyen vuelo y alquiler de
coche; **~ing** n (activity) (el) volar; (action)
vuelo ♦ adj: **~ing visit** visita relámpago; **with
~ing colours** con lucimiento; **~ing saucer** n
platillo volante; **~ing start** n: **to get off to a
~ing start** empezar con buen pie; **~over**
(BRIT) n paso a desnivel or superior; **~sheet** n
(for tent) doble techo
foal [fəʊl] n potro
foam [fəʊm] n espuma ♦ vi hacer espuma;
~ rubber n goma espuma
fob [fɒb] vt: **to ~ sb off with sth** despachar a
uno con algo
focal point ['fəʊkl-] n (fig) centro de
atención
focus ['fəʊkəs] (pl **~es**) n foco; (centre) centro
♦ vt (field glasses etc) enfocar ♦ vi: **to ~ (on)**
enfocar (a); (issue etc) centrarse en; **in/out of
~** enfocado/desenfocado
fodder ['fɒdə*] n pienso
foetus ['fiːtəs] (US **fetus**) n feto
fog [fɒg] n niebla; **~gy** adj: **it's ~gy** hay niebla,
está brumoso; **~ lamp** (US **~ light**) n (AUT)

faro de niebla
foil [fɔɪl] vt frustrar ♦ n hoja; (kitchen ~) papel
m (de) aluminio; (complement)
complemento; (FENCING) florete m
fold [fəʊld] n (bend, crease) pliegue m; (AGR) redil
m ♦ vt doblar; (arms) cruzar; **~ up** vi plegarse,
doblarse; (business) quebrar ♦ vt (map etc)
plegar; **~er** n (for papers) carpeta; (COMPUT)
directorio; **~ing** adj (chair, bed) plegable
foliage ['fəʊlɪdʒ] n follaje m
folk [fəʊk] npl gente f ♦ adj popular,
folklórico; **~s** npl (family) familia sg, parientes
mpl; **~lore** ['fəʊklɔː*] n folklore m; **~ song** n
canción f popular or folklórica
follow ['fɒləʊ] vt seguir ♦ vi seguir; (result)
resultar; **to ~ suit** hacer lo mismo; **~ up** vt
(letter, offer) responder a; (case) investigar;
~er n (of person, belief) partidario/a; **~ing**
adj siguiente ♦ n afición f, partidarios mpl
folly ['fɒlɪ] n locura
fond [fɒnd] adj (memory, smile etc) cariñoso;
(hopes) ilusorio; **to be ~ of** tener cariño a;
(pastime, food) ser aficionado a
fondle ['fɒndl] vt acariciar
font [fɒnt] n pila bautismal; (TYP) fundición f
food [fuːd] n comida; **~ mixer** n batidora;
~ poisoning n intoxicación f alimenticia;
~ processor n robot m de cocina; **~stuffs**
npl comestibles mpl
fool [fuːl] n tonto/a; (CULIN) puré m de frutas
con nata ♦ vt engañar ♦ vi (gen: ~ around)
bromear; **~hardy** adj temerario; **~ish** adj
tonto; (careless) imprudente; **~proof** adj
(plan etc) infalible
foot [fʊt] (pl **feet**) n pie m; (measure) pie m
(= 304 mm); (of animal) pata ♦ vt (bill)
pagar; **on ~** a pie; **~age** n (CINEMA) imágenes
fpl; **~ball** n balón m; (game: BRIT) fútbol m;
(: US) fútbol m americano; **~ball player** n
(BRIT: also: **~baller**) futbolista m; (US) jugador
m de fútbol americano; **~brake** n freno de
pie; **~bridge** n puente m para peatones;
~hills npl estribaciones fpl; **~hold** n pie m
firme; **~ing** n (fig) posición f; **to lose one's
~ing** perder el pie; **~lights** npl candilejas fpl;
~note n nota (al pie de la página); **~path** n
sendero; **~print** n huella, pisada; **~step** n
paso; **~wear** n calzado

KEYWORD

for [fɔː*] prep **1** (indicating destination,
intention) para; **the train ~ London** el tren con
destino a or de Londres; **he left ~ Rome**
marchó para Roma; **he went ~ the paper** fue
por el periódico; **is this ~ me?** ¿es esto para
mí?; **it's time ~ lunch** es la hora de comer
2 (indicating purpose) para; **what('s it) ~?**
¿para qué (es)?; **to pray ~ peace** rezar por la
paz

3 (*on behalf of, representing*): **the MP ~ Hove** el diputado por Hove; **he works ~ the government/a local firm** trabaja para el gobierno/en una empresa local; **I'll ask him ~ you** se lo pediré por ti; **G ~ George** G de Gerona
4 (*because of*) por esta razón; **~ fear of being criticized** por temor a ser criticado
5 (*with regard to*) para; **it's cold ~ July** hace frío para julio; **he has a gift ~ languages** tiene don de lenguas
6 (*in exchange for*) por; **I sold it ~ £5** lo vendí por £5; **to pay 50 pence ~ a ticket** pagar 50 peniques por un billete
7 (*in favour of*): **are you ~ or against us?** ¿estás con nosotros o contra nosotros?; **I'm all ~ it** estoy totalmente a favor; **vote ~ X** vote (a) X
8 (*referring to distance*): **there are roadworks ~ 5 km** hay obras en 5 km; **we walked ~ miles** caminamos kilómetros y kilómetros
9 (*referring to time*): **he was away ~ 2 years** estuvo fuera (durante) dos años; **it hasn't rained ~ 3 weeks** no ha llovido durante o en 3 semanas; **I have known her ~ years** la conozco desde hace años; **can you do it ~ tomorrow?** ¿lo podrás hacer para mañana?
10 (*with infinitive clauses*): **it is not ~ me to decide** la decisión no es cosa mía; **it would be best ~ you to leave** sería mejor que te fueras; **there is still time ~ you to do it** todavía te queda tiempo para hacerlo; **~ this to be possible ...** para que esto sea posible ...
11 (*in spite of*) a pesar de; **~ all his complaints** a pesar de sus quejas ♦ *conj* (*since, as: rather formal*) puesto que

forage ['fɒrɪdʒ] *vi* (*animal*) forrajear; (*person*): **to ~ for** hurgar en busca de
foray ['fɒreɪ] *n* incursión *f*
forbid [fə'bɪd] (*pt* forbad(e), *pp* forbidden) *vt* prohibir; **to ~ sb to do sth** prohibir a uno hacer algo; **~ding** *adj* amenazador(a)
force [fɔːs] *n* fuerza ♦ *vt* forzar; (*push*) meter a la fuerza; **to ~ o.s. to do** hacer un esfuerzo por hacer; **the F~s** *npl* (*BRIT*) las Fuerzas Armadas; **in ~** en vigor; **~d** [fɔːst] *adj* forzado; **~-feed** *vt* alimentar a la fuerza; **~ful** *adj* enérgico
forcibly ['fɔːsəblɪ] *adv* a la fuerza; (*speak*) enérgicamente
ford [fɔːd] *n* vado
fore [fɔː*] *n*: **to come to the ~** empezar a destacar
fore: **~arm** *n* antebrazo; **~boding** *n* presentimiento; **~cast** *n* pronóstico ♦ *vt* (*irreg: like cast*) pronosticar; **~court** *n* patio; **~finger** *n* (dedo) índice *m*; **~front** *n*: **in the ~front of** en la vanguardia de

forego *vt* = forgo
foregone ['fɔːgɒn] *pp of* forego ♦ *adj*: **it's a ~ conclusion** es una conclusión evidente
foreground ['fɔːgraund] *n* primer plano
forehead ['fɒrɪd] *n* frente *f*
foreign ['fɒrɪn] *adj* extranjero; (*trade*) exterior; (*object*) extraño; **~er** *n* extranjero/a; **~ exchange** *n* divisas *fpl*; **F~ Office** (*BRIT*) *n* Ministerio de Asuntos Exteriores; **F~ Secretary** (*BRIT*) *n* Ministro de Asuntos Exteriores
fore: **~leg** *n* pata delantera; **~man** (*irreg*) *n* capataz *m*; (*in construction*) maestro de obras; **~most** *adj* principal ♦ *adv*: **first and ~most** ante todo
forensic [fə'rensɪk] *adj* forense
fore: **~runner** *n* precursor(a) *m/f*; **~see** (*pt* foresaw, *pp* foreseen) *vt* prever; **~seeable** *adj* previsible; **~shadow** *vt* prefigurar, anunciar; **~sight** *n* previsión *f*
forest ['fɒrɪst] *n* bosque *m*
forestry ['fɒrɪstrɪ] *n* silvicultura
foretaste ['fɔːteɪst] *n* muestra
foretell [fɔː'tel] (*pt, pp* foretold) *vt* predecir, pronosticar
forever [fə'revə*] *adv* para siempre; (*endlessly*) constantemente
foreword ['fɔːwəːd] *n* prefacio
forfeit ['fɔːfɪt] *vt* perder
forgave [fə'geɪv] *pt of* forgive
forge [fɔːdʒ] *n* herrería ♦ *vt* (*signature, money*) falsificar; (*metal*) forjar; **~ ahead** *vi* avanzar mucho; **~ry** *n* falsificación *f*
forget [fə'get] (*pt* forgot, *pp* forgotten) *vt* olvidar ♦ *vi* olvidarse; **~ful** *adj* despistado; **~-me-not** *n* nomeolvides *f inv*
forgive [fə'gɪv] (*pt* forgave, *pp* forgiven) *vt* perdonar; **to ~ sb for sth** perdonar algo a uno; **~ness** *n* perdón *m*
forgo [fɔː'gəu] (*pt* forwent, *pp* forgone) *vt* (*give up*) renunciar a; (*go without*) privarse de
forgot [fə'gɒt] *pt of* forget
forgotten [fə'gɒtn] *pp of* forget
fork [fɔːk] *n* (*for eating*) tenedor *m*; (*for gardening*) horca; (*of roads*) bifurcación *f* ♦ *vi* (*road*) bifurcarse; **~ out** (*inf*) *vt* (*pay*) desembolsar; **~-lift truck** *n* máquina elevadora
forlorn [fə'lɔːn] *adj* (*person*) triste, melancólico; (*place*) abandonado; (*attempt, hope*) desesperado
form [fɔːm] *n* forma; (*BRIT: SCOL*) clase *f*; (*document*) formulario ♦ *vt* formar; (*idea*) concebir; (*habit*) adquirir; **in top ~** en plena forma; **to ~ a queue** hacer cola
formal ['fɔːməl] *adj* (*offer, receipt*) por escrito; (*person etc*) correcto; (*occasion, dinner*) de etiqueta; (*dress*) correcto; (*garden*) (de estilo) clásico; **~ity** [-'mælɪtɪ] *n* (*procedure*)

trámite *m*; corrección *f*; etiqueta; **~ly** *adv* oficialmente

format ['fɔ:mæt] *n* formato ♦ *vt* (COMPUT) formatear

formative ['fɔ:mətɪv] *adj* (years) de formación; (influence) formativo

former ['fɔ:mə*] *adj* anterior; (earlier) antiguo; (ex) ex; **the ~ ... the latter** ... aquél ... éste ...; **~ly** *adv* antes

formula ['fɔ:mjulə] *n* fórmula

forsake [fə'seɪk] (*pt* forsook, *pp* forsaken) *vt* (gen) abandonar; (plan) renunciar a

fort [fɔ:t] *n* fuerte *m*

forte ['fɔ:tɪ] *n* fuerte *m*

forth [fɔ:θ] *adv*: **back and ~** de acá para allá; **and so ~** y así sucesivamente; **~coming** *adj* próximo, venidero; (help, information) disponible; (character) comunicativo; **~right** *adj* franco ♦ *adv* en el acto

fortify ['fɔ:tɪfaɪ] *vt* (city) fortificar; (person) fortalecer

fortitude ['fɔ:tɪtjuːd] *n* fortaleza

fortnight ['fɔ:tnaɪt] (BRIT) *n* quince días *mpl*; quincena; **~ly** *adj* de cada quince días, quincenal ♦ *adv* cada quince días, quincenalmente

fortress ['fɔ:trɪs] *n* fortaleza

fortunate ['fɔ:tʃənɪt] *adj* afortunado; **it is ~ that** ... (es una) suerte que ...; **~ly** *adv* afortunadamente

fortune ['fɔ:tʃən] *n* suerte *f*; (wealth) fortuna; **~-teller** *n* adivino/a

forty ['fɔ:tɪ] *num* cuarenta

forum ['fɔ:rəm] *n* foro

forward ['fɔ:wəd] *adj* (movement, position) avanzado; (front) delantero; (in time) adelantado; (not shy) atrevido ♦ *n* (SPORT) delantero ♦ *vt* (letter) remitir; (career) promocionar; **to move ~** avanzar; **~(s)** *adv* (hacia) adelante

fossil ['fɔsl] *n* fósil *m*

foster ['fɔstə*] *vt* (child) acoger en una familia; fomentar; **~ child** *n* hijo/a adoptivo/a

fought [fɔ:t] *pt, pp* of fight

foul [faul] *adj* sucio, puerco; (weather, smell etc) asqueroso; (language) grosero; (temper) malísimo ♦ *n* (SPORT) falta ♦ *vt* (dirty) ensuciar; **~ play** *n* (LAW) muerte *f* violenta

found [faund] *pt, pp* of find ♦ *vt* fundar; **~ation** [-'deɪʃən] *n* (act) fundación *f*; (basis) base *f*; (also: ~ation cream) crema base; **~ations** *npl* (of building) cimientos *mpl*

founder ['faundə*] *n* fundador(a) *m/f* ♦ *vi* hundirse

foundry ['faundrɪ] *n* fundición *f*

fountain ['fauntɪn] *n* fuente *f*; **~ pen** *n* pluma (estilográfica) (SP), pluma-fuente *f* (AM)

four [fɔ:*] *num* cuatro; **on all ~s** a gatas; **~-poster (bed)** *n* cama de dosel; **~teen** *num* catorce; **~th** *num* cuarto

fowl [faul] *n* ave *f* (de corral)

fox [fɔks] *n* zorro ♦ *vt* confundir

foyer ['fɔɪeɪ] *n* vestíbulo

fraction ['frækʃən] *n* fracción *f*

fracture ['fræktʃə*] *n* fractura

fragile ['frædʒaɪl] *adj* frágil

fragment ['frægmənt] *n* fragmento

fragrant ['freɪɡrənt] *adj* fragante, oloroso

frail [freɪl] *adj* frágil; (person) débil

frame [freɪm] *n* (TECH) armazón *m*; (of person) cuerpo; (of picture, door etc) marco; (of spectacles: also: ~s) montura ♦ *vt* enmarcar; **~ of mind** *n* estado de ánimo; **~work** *n* marco

France [frɑ:ns] *n* Francia

franchise ['fræntʃaɪz] *n* (POL) derecho de votar, sufragio; (COMM) licencia, concesión *f*

frank [fræŋk] *adj* franco ♦ *vt* (letter) franquear; **~ly** *adv* francamente

frantic ['fræntɪk] *adj* (distraught) desesperado; (hectic) frenético

fraternity [frə'tɜ:nɪtɪ] *n* (feeling) fraternidad *f*; (group of people) círculos *mpl*

fraud [frɔ:d] *n* fraude *m*; (person) impostor(a) *m/f*

fraught [frɔ:t] *adj*: **~ with** lleno de

fray [freɪ] *vi* deshilacharse

freak [fri:k] *n* (person) fenómeno; (event) suceso anormal

freckle ['frekl] *n* peca

free [fri:] *adj* libre; (gratis) gratuito ♦ *vt* (prisoner etc) poner en libertad; (jammed object) soltar; **~ (of charge), for ~** gratis; **~dom** ['fri:dəm] *n* libertad *f*; **F~fone** ® ['fri:fəun] *n* número gratuito; **~-for-all** *n* riña general; **~ gift** *n* prima; **~hold** *n* propiedad *f* vitalicia; **~ kick** *n* tiro libre; **~lance** *adj* independiente ♦ *adv* por cuenta propia; **~ly** *adv* libremente; (liberally) generosamente; **F~mason** *n* francmasón *m*; **F~post** ® *n* porte *m* pagado; **~-range** *adj* (hen, eggs) de granja; **~ trade** *n* libre comercio; **~way** (US) *n* autopista; **~ will** *n* libre albedrío; **of one's own ~ will** por su propia voluntad

freeze [fri:z] (*pt* froze, *pp* frozen) *vi* (weather) helar; (liquid, pipe, person) helarse, congelarse ♦ *vt* helar; (food, prices, salaries) congelar ♦ *n* helada; (on arms, wages) congelación *f*; **~-dried** *adj* liofilizado; **~r** *n* congelador *m* (SP), congeladora (AM)

freezing ['fri:zɪŋ] *adj* helado; **3 degrees below ~** tres grados bajo cero; **~ point** *n* punto de congelación

freight [freɪt] *n* (goods) carga; (money charged) flete *m*; **~ train** (US) *n* tren *m* de mercancías

French [frɛntʃ] *adj* francés/esa ♦ *n* (LING)
francés *m*; **the ~** *npl* los franceses; **~ bean** *n*
judía verde; **~ fried potatoes** *npl* patatas *fpl*
(SP) or papas *fpl* (AM) fritas; **~ fries** (US) *npl*
= **~ fried potatoes**; **~man/woman** (*irreg*) *n*
francés/esa *m/f*; **~ window** *n* puerta de
cristal

frenzy ['frɛnzɪ] *n* frenesí *m*

frequent [*adj* 'friːkwənt, *vb* frɪ'kwɛnt] *adj*
frecuente ♦ *vt* frecuentar; **~ly** [-əntlɪ] *adv*
frecuentemente, a menudo

fresh [frɛʃ] *adj* fresco; (*bread*) tierno; (*new*)
nuevo; **~en** *vi* (*wind, air*) soplar más recio;
~en up *vi* (*person*) arreglarse, lavarse; **~er**
(BRIT: *inf*) *n* (UNIV) estudiante *m/f* de primer
año; **~ly** *adv* (*made, painted etc*) recién;
~man (US *irreg*) *n* = **~er**; **~ness** *n* frescura;
~water *adj* (*fish*) de agua dulce

fret [frɛt] *vi* inquietarse

friar ['fraɪə*] *n* fraile *m*; (*before name*) fray *m*

friction ['frɪkʃən] *n* fricción *f*

Friday ['fraɪdɪ] *n* viernes *m inv*

fridge [frɪdʒ] (BRIT) *n* nevera (SP),
refrigeradora (AM)

fried [fraɪd] *adj* frito

friend [frɛnd] *n* amigo/a; **~ly** *adj* simpático;
(*government*) amigo; (*place*) acogedor(a);
(*match*) amistoso; **~ly fire** fuego amigo,
disparos *mpl* del propio bando; **~ship** *n*
amistad *f*

frieze [friːz] *n* friso

fright [fraɪt] *n* (*terror*) terror *m*; (*scare*) susto;
to take ~ asustarse; **~en** *vt* asustar; **~ened**
adj asustado; **~ening** *adj* espantoso; **~ful** *adj*
espantoso, horrible

frill [frɪl] *n* volante *m*

fringe [frɪndʒ] *n* (BRIT: *of hair*) flequillo; (*on
lampshade etc*) flecos *mpl*; (*of forest etc*)
borde *m*, margen *m*; **~ benefits** *npl*
beneficios *mpl* marginales

frisk [frɪsk] *vt* cachear, registrar

frisky ['frɪskɪ] *adj* juguetón/ona

fritter ['frɪtə*] *n* buñuelo; **~ away** *vt*
desperdiciar

frivolous ['frɪvələs] *adj* frívolo

frizzy ['frɪzɪ] *adj* rizado

fro [frəu] *see* **to**

frock [frɔk] *n* vestido

frog [frɔg] *n* rana; **~man** *n* hombre-rana *m*

frolic ['frɔlɪk] *vi* juguetear

from [frɔm] *prep* **1** (*indicating starting place*)
de, desde; **where do you come ~?** ¿de dónde
eres?; **~ London to Glasgow** de Londres a
Glasgow; **to escape ~ sth/sb** escaparse de
algo/alguien

2 (*indicating origin etc*) de; **a letter/telephone
call ~ my sister** una carta/llamada de mi

hermana; **tell him ~ me that ...** dígale de mi
parte que ...

3 (*indicating time*): **~ one o'clock to** or **until** or
till two de la(s) una a or hasta las dos;
~ January (on) a partir de enero

4 (*indicating distance*) de; **the hotel is 1 km
~ the beach** el hotel está a 1 km de la playa

5 (*indicating price, number etc*) de; **prices
range ~ £10 to £50** los precios van desde £10
a or hasta £50; **the interest rate was
increased ~ 9% to 10%** el tipo de interés fue
incrementado un 9% a un 10%

6 (*indicating difference*) de; **he can't tell red
~ green** no sabe distinguir el rojo del verde;
to be different ~ sb/sth ser diferente a algo/
alguien

7 (*because of, on the basis of*): **~ what he
says** por lo que dice; **weak ~ hunger**
debilitado por el hambre

front [frʌnt] *n* (*foremost part*) parte *f*
delantera; (*of house*) fachada; (*of dress*)
delantero; (*promenade: also: sea ~*) paseo
marítimo; (MIL, POL, METEOROLOGY) frente *m*;
(*fig: appearances*) apariencias *fpl* ♦ *adj*
(*wheel, leg*) delantero; (*row, line*) primero; **in
~ (of)** delante (de); **~ door** *n* puerta
principal; **~ier** ['frʌntɪə*] *n* frontera; **~ page**
n primera plana; **~ room** (BRIT) *n* salón *m*,
sala; **~-wheel drive** *n* tracción *f* delantera

frost [frɔst] *n* helada; (*also: hoar~*) escarcha;
~bite *n* congelación *f*; **~ed** *adj* (*glass*)
deslustrado; **~y** *adj* (*weather*) de helada;
(*welcome etc*) glacial

froth [frɔθ] *n* espuma

frown [fraun] *vi* fruncir el ceño

froze [frəuz] *pt of* **freeze**

frozen ['frəuzn] *pp of* **freeze**

fruit [fruːt] *n inv* fruta; fruto; (*fig*) fruto;
resultados *mpl*; **~erer** *n* frutero/a; **~erer's
(shop)** *n* frutería; **~ful** *adj* provechoso; **~ion**
[fruː'ɪʃən] *n*: **to come to ~ion** realizarse;
~ juice *n* zumo (SP) or jugo (AM) de fruta;
~ machine (BRIT) *n* máquina *f* tragaperras;
~ salad *n* macedonia (SP) or ensalada (AM)
de frutas

frustrate [frʌs'treɪt] *vt* frustrar

fry [fraɪ] (*pt, pp* **fried**) *vt* freír; **small ~** gente *f*
menuda; **~ing pan** *n* sartén *f*

ft. *abbr* = **foot**; **feet**

fudge [fʌdʒ] *n* (CULIN) caramelo blando

fuel [fjuəl] *n* (*for heating*) combustible *m*;
(*coal*) carbón *m*; (*wood*) leña; (*for engine*)
carburante *m*; **~ oil** *n* fuel oil *m*; **~ tank** *n*
depósito (de combustible)

fugitive ['fjuːdʒɪtɪv] *n* fugitivo/a

fulfil [ful'fɪl] *vt* (*function*) cumplir con;
(*condition*) satisfacer; (*wish, desire*) realizar;
~ment (US **fulfillment**) *n* satisfacción *f*; (*of*

promise, desire) realización f
full [ful] *adj* lleno; (*fig*) pleno; (*complete*)
completo; (*maximum*) máximo; (*information*)
detallado; (*price*) íntegro; (*skirt*) amplio
♦ *adv*: **to know ~ well that** saber
perfectamente que; **I'm ~ (up)** no puedo
más; **~ employment** pleno empleo; **a ~ two
hours** dos horas completas; **at ~ speed** a
máxima velocidad; **in ~** (*reproduce, quote*)
íntegramente; **~-length** *adj* (*novel etc*)
entero; (*coat*) largo; (*portrait*) de cuerpo
entero; **~ moon** *n* luna llena; **~-scale** *adj*
(*attack, war*) en gran escala; (*model*) de
tamaño natural; **~ stop** *n* punto; **~-time** *adj*
(*work*) de tiempo completo ♦ *adv*: **to work
~-time** trabajar a tiempo completo; **~y** *adv*
completamente; (*at least*) por lo menos; **~y-
fledged** *adj* (*teacher, barrister*) diplomado
fumble ['fʌmbl] *vi*: **to ~ with** manejar
torpemente
fume [fjuːm] *vi* (*rage*) estar furioso; **~s** *npl*
humo, gases *mpl*
fun [fʌn] *n* (*amusement*) diversión f; **to have ~**
divertirse; **for ~** en broma; **to make ~ of**
burlarse de
function ['fʌŋkʃən] *n* función f ♦ *vi*
funcionar; **~al** *adj* (*operational*) en buen
estado; (*practical*) funcional
fund [fʌnd] *n* fondo; (*reserve*) reserva; **~s** *npl*
(*money*) fondos *mpl*
fundamental [fʌndə'mɛntl] *adj*
fundamental
funeral ['fjuːnərəl] *n* (*burial*) entierro;
(*ceremony*) funerales *mpl*; **~ parlour** (*BRIT*) *n*
funeraria; **~ service** *n* misa de difuntos,
funeral *m*
funfair ['fʌnfɛə*] (*BRIT*) *n* parque *m* de
atracciones
fungus ['fʌŋgəs] (*pl* fungi) *n* hongo; (*mould*)
moho
funnel ['fʌnl] *n* embudo; (*of ship*) chimenea
funny ['fʌnɪ] *adj* gracioso, divertido; (*strange*)
curioso, raro
fur [fəː*] *n* piel f; (*BRIT: in kettle etc*) sarro;
~ coat *n* abrigo de pieles
furious ['fjuəriəs] *adj* furioso; (*effort*) violento
furlong ['fəːlɔŋ] *n* octava parte de una milla,
= 201.17 m
furnace ['fəːnɪs] *n* horno
furnish ['fəːnɪʃ] *vt* amueblar; (*supply*)
suministrar; (*information*) facilitar; **~ings** *npl*
muebles *mpl*
furniture ['fəːnɪtʃə*] *n* muebles *mpl*; **piece of
~** mueble *m*
furrow ['fʌrəu] *n* surco
furry ['fəːrɪ] *adj* peludo
further ['fəːðə*] *adj* (*new*) nuevo, adicional
♦ *adv* más lejos; (*more*) más; (*moreover*)
además ♦ *vt* promover, adelantar;

~ education *n* educación f superior; **~more**
[fəːðə'mɔː*] *adv* además
furthest ['fəːðɪst] *superlative* of **far**
fury ['fjuərɪ] *n* furia
fuse [fjuːz] (*US* **fuze**) *n* fusible *m*; (*for bomb
etc*) mecha ♦ *vt* (*metal*) fundir; (*fig*) fusionar
♦ *vi* fundirse; fusionarse; (*BRIT: ELEC*): **to ~ the
lights** fundir los plomos; **~ box** *n* caja de
fusibles
fuss [fʌs] *n* (*excitement*) conmoción f;
(*trouble*) alboroto; **to make a ~** armar un lío
or jaleo; **to make a ~ of sb** mimar a uno; **~y**
adj (*person*) exigente; (*too ornate*) recargado
futile ['fjuːtaɪl] *adj* vano
future ['fjuːtʃə*] *adj* futuro; (*coming*) venidero
♦ *n* futuro; (*prospects*) porvenir; **in ~** de
ahora en adelante
fuze [fjuːz] (*US*) = **fuse**
fuzzy ['fʌzɪ] *adj* (*PHOT*) borroso; (*hair*) muy
rizado

G, g

G [dʒiː] *n* (*MUS*) sol *m*
g. *abbr* (= *gram(s)*) gr.
G8 *abbr* (= *Group of Eight*) el grupo de los 8
gabble ['gæbl] *vi* hablar atropelladamente
gable ['geɪbl] *n* aguilón m
gadget ['gædʒɪt] *n* aparato
Gaelic ['geɪlɪk] *adj, n* (*LING*) gaélico
gag [gæg] *n* (*on mouth*) mordaza; (*joke*) chiste
m ♦ *vt* amordazar
gaiety ['geɪɪtɪ] *n* alegría
gaily ['geɪlɪ] *adv* alegremente
gain [geɪn] *n*: **~ (in)** aumento (de); (*profit*)
ganancia ♦ *vt* ganar ♦ *vi* (*watch*) adelantarse;
to ~ from/by sth sacar provecho de algo; **to
~ on sb** ganar terreno a uno; **to ~ 3 lbs (in
weight)** engordar 3 libras
gal. *abbr* = **gallon**
gala ['gɑːlə] *n* fiesta
gale [geɪl] *n* (*wind*) vendaval *m*
gallant ['gælənt] *adj* valiente; (*towards ladies*)
atento
gall bladder ['gɔːl-] *n* vesícula biliar
gallery ['gælərɪ] *n* (*also: art ~: public*)
pinacoteca; (*: private*) galería de arte; (*for
spectators*) tribuna
gallon ['gælən] *n* galón *m* (*BRIT = 4,546 litros,
US = 3,785 litros*)
gallop ['gæləp] *n* galope *m* ♦ *vi* galopar
gallows ['gæləuz] *n* horca
gallstone ['gɔːlstəun] *n* cálculo biliar
galore [gə'lɔː*] *adv* en cantidad, en
abundancia
gambit ['gæmbɪt] *n* (*fig*): (*opening*) **~**
estrategia (inicial)
gamble ['gæmbl] *n* (*risk*) riesgo ♦ *vt* jugar,

apostar ♦ vi (*take a risk*) jugárselas; (*bet*) apostar; **to ~ on** apostar a; (*success etc*) contar con; **~r** n jugador(a) m/f; **gambling** n juego

game [geɪm] n juego; (*match*) partido; (*of cards*) partida; (*HUNTING*) caza ♦ adj (*willing*): **to be ~ for anything** atreverse a todo; **big ~** caza mayor; **~keeper** n guardabosques m inv

gammon ['gæmən] n (*bacon*) tocino ahumado; (*ham*) jamón m ahumado

gamut ['gæmət] n gama

gang [gæŋ] n (*of criminals*) pandilla; (*of friends etc*) grupo; (*of workmen*) brigada; **~ up** vi: **to ~ up on sb** aliarse contra uno

gangster ['gæŋstə*] n gángster m

gangway ['gæŋweɪ] n (*on ship*) pasarela; (*BRIT: in theatre, bus etc*) pasillo

gaol [dʒeɪl] (*BRIT*) n, vt = **jail**

gap [gæp] n vacío, hueco (*AM*); (*in trees, traffic*) claro; (*in time*) intervalo; (*difference*): **~** (*between*) diferencia (*entre*)

gape [geɪp] vi mirar boquiabierto; (*shirt etc*) abrirse (completamente); **gaping** adj (completamente) abierto

garage ['gærɑ:ʒ] n garaje m; (*for repairs*) taller m

garbage ['gɑ:bɪdʒ] (*US*) n basura; (*inf: nonsense*) tonterías fpl; **~ can** n cubo (*SP*) or bote m (*AM*) de la basura

garbled ['gɑ:bld] adj (*distorted*) falsificado, amañado

garden ['gɑ:dn] n jardín m; **~s** npl (*park*) parque m; **~er** n jardinero/a; **~ing** n jardinería

gargle ['gɑ:gl] vi hacer gárgaras, gargarear (*AM*)

garish ['geərɪʃ] adj chillón/ona

garland ['gɑ:lənd] n guirnalda

garlic ['gɑ:lɪk] n ajo

garment ['gɑ:mənt] n prenda (de vestir)

garnish ['gɑ:nɪʃ] vt (*CULIN*) aderezar

garrison ['gærɪsn] n guarnición f

garter ['gɑ:tə*] n (*for sock*) liga; (*US*) liguero

gas [gæs] n gas m; (*fuel*) combustible m; (*US: gasoline*) gasolina ♦ vt asfixiar con gas; **~ cooker** (*BRIT*) n cocina de gas; **~ cylinder** n bombona de gas; **~ fire** n estufa de gas

gash [gæʃ] n raja; (*wound*) cuchillada ♦ vt rajar; acuchillar

gasket ['gæskɪt] n (*AUT*) junta de culata

gas mask n careta antigás

gas meter n contador m de gas

gasoline ['gæsəli:n] (*US*) n gasolina

gasp [gɑ:sp] n boqueada; (*of shock etc*) grito sofocado ♦ vi (*pant*) jadear

gas station (*US*) n gasolinera

gastric ['gæstrɪk] adj gástrico

gate [geɪt] n puerta; (*iron ~*) verja; **~crash** (*BRIT*) vt colarse en; **~way** n (*also fig*) puerta

gather ['gæðə*] vt (*flowers, fruit*) coger (*SP*), recoger; (*assemble*) reunir; (*pick up*) recoger; (*SEWING*) fruncir; (*understand*) entender ♦ vi (*assemble*) reunirse; **to ~ speed** ganar velocidad; **~ing** n reunión f, asamblea

gaudy ['gɔ:dɪ] adj chillón/ona

gauge [geɪdʒ] n (*instrument*) indicador m ♦ vt medir; (*fig*) juzgar

gaunt [gɔ:nt] adj (*haggard*) demacrado; (*stark*) desolado

gauntlet ['gɔ:ntlɪt] n (*fig*): **to run the ~ of** exponerse a; **to throw down the ~** arrojar el guante

gauze [gɔ:z] n gasa

gave [geɪv] pt of **give**

gay [geɪ] adj (*homosexual*) gay; (*joyful*) alegre; (*colour*) vivo

gaze [geɪz] n mirada fija ♦ vi: **to ~ at sth** mirar algo fijamente

gazelle [gə'zɛl] n gacela

gazumping [gə'zʌmpɪŋ] (*BRIT*) n la subida del precio de una casa una vez que ya ha sido apalabrado

GB abbr = **Great Britain**

GCE n abbr (*BRIT*) = General Certificate of Education

GCSE (*BRIT*) n abbr (= General Certificate of Secondary Education) examen de reválida que se hace a los 16 años

gear [gɪə*] n equipo, herramientas fpl; (*TECH*) engranaje m; (*AUT*) velocidad f, marcha ♦ vt (*fig: adapt*): **to ~ sth to** adaptar ar ajustar algo a; **top** or **high** (*US*)/**low ~** cuarta/primera velocidad; **in ~** en marcha; **~ box** n caja de cambios; **~ lever** n palanca de cambio; **~ shift** (*US*) n = **~ lever**

geese [gi:s] npl of **goose**

gel [dʒɛl] n gel m

gem [dʒɛm] n piedra preciosa

Gemini ['dʒɛmɪnaɪ] n Géminis m, Gemelos mpl

gender ['dʒɛndə*] n género

gene [dʒi:n] n gen(e) m

general ['dʒɛnərl] n general m ♦ adj general; **in ~** en general; **~ delivery** (*US*) n lista de correos; **~ election** n elecciones fpl generales; **~ly** adv generalmente, en general; **~ practitioner** n médico general

generate ['dʒɛnəreɪt] vt (*ELEC*) generar; (*jobs, profits*) producir

generation [dʒɛnə'reɪʃən] n generación f

generator ['dʒɛnəreɪtə*] n generador m

generosity [dʒɛnə'rɔsɪtɪ] n generosidad f

generous ['dʒɛnərəs] adj generoso

genetic [dʒɪ'netɪk] adj: **~ engineering** ingeniería genética; **~ fingerprinting** identificación f genética

Geneva [dʒɪ'ni:və] n Ginebra

genial ['dʒi:nɪəl] adj afable, simpático

genitals ['dʒenɪtlz] npl (órganos mpl) genitales mpl

genius ['dʒiːnɪəs] n genio

genteel [dʒen'tiːl] adj fino, elegante

gentle ['dʒentl] adj apacible, dulce; (animal) manso; (breeze, curve etc) suave

gentleman ['dʒentlmən] (irreg) n señor m; (well-bred man) caballero

gently ['dʒentlɪ] adv dulcemente; suavemente

gentry ['dʒentrɪ] n alta burguesía

gents [dʒents] n aseos mpl (de caballeros)

genuine ['dʒenjuɪn] adj auténtico; (person) sincero

geography [dʒɪ'ɔɡrəfɪ] n geografía

geology [dʒɪ'ɔlədʒɪ] n geología

geometric(al) [dʒɪə'metrɪk(l)] adj geométrico

geranium [dʒɪ'reɪnjəm] n geranio

geriatric [dʒerɪ'ætrɪk] adj, n geriátrico/a m/f

germ [dʒəːm] n (microbe) microbio, bacteria; (seed, fig) germen m

German ['dʒəːmən] adj alemán/ana ♦ n alemán/ana m/f; (LING) alemán m; ~ **measles** n rubéola

Germany ['dʒəːmənɪ] n Alemania

gesture ['dʒestjəˀ] n gesto; (symbol) muestra

KEYWORD

get [ɡet] (pt, pp **got**, pp **gotten** (US)) vi
1 (become, be) ponerse, volverse; to ~ **old/tired** envejecer/cansarse; to ~ **drunk** emborracharse; to ~ **dirty** ensuciarse; to ~ **married** casarse; **when do I ~ paid?** ¿cuándo me pagan or se me paga?; **it's ~ting late** se está haciendo tarde
2 (go): to ~ **to/from** llegar a/de; to ~ **home** llegar a casa
3 (begin) empezar a; to ~ **to know sb** (llegar a) conocer a uno; **I'm ~ting to like him** me está empezando a gustar; **let's ~ going** or **started** ¡vamos (a empezar)!
4 (modal aux vb): **you've got to do it** tienes que hacerlo
♦ vt 1: to ~ **sth done** (finish) terminar algo; (have done) mandar hacer algo; to ~ **one's hair cut** cortarse el pelo; to ~ **the car going** or **to go** arrancar el coche; to ~ **sb to do sth** conseguir or hacer que alguien haga algo; to ~ **sth/sb ready** preparar algo/a alguien
2 (obtain: money, permission, results) conseguir; (find: job, flat) encontrar; (fetch: person, doctor) buscar; (object) ir a buscar, traer; to ~ **sth for sb** conseguir algo para alguien; ~ **me Mr Jones, please** (TEL) póngame or comuníqueme (AM) con el Sr. Jones, por favor; **can I ~ you a drink?** ¿quieres algo de beber?
3 (receive: present, letter) recibir; (acquire: reputation) alcanzar; (: prize) ganar; **what did

you ~ for your birthday? ¿qué te regalaron por tu cumpleaños?; **how much did you ~ for the painting?** ¿cuánto sacaste por el cuadro?
4 (catch) coger (SP), agarrar (AM); (hit: target etc) dar en; to ~ **sb by the arm/throat** coger or agarrar a uno por el brazo/cuello; ~ **him!** ¡cógelo! (SP), ¡atrápalo! (AM); **the bullet got him in the leg** la bala le dio en la pierna
5 (take, move) llevar; to ~ **sth to sb** hacer llegar algo a alguien; **do you think we'll ~ it through the door?** ¿crees que lo podremos meter por la puerta?
6 (catch, take: plane, bus etc) coger (SP), tomar (AM); **where do I ~ the train for Birmingham?** ¿dónde se coge or se toma el tren para Birmingham?
7 (understand) entender; (hear) oír; **I've got it!** ¡ya lo tengo!, ¡eureka!; **I don't ~ your meaning** no te entiendo; **I'm sorry, I didn't ~ your name** lo siento, no cogí tu nombre
8 (have, possess): to **have got** tener

get about vi salir mucho; (news) divulgarse
get along vi (agree) llevarse bien; (depart) marcharse; (manage) = **get by**
get at vt fus (attack) atacar; (reach) alcanzar
get away vi marcharse; (escape) escaparse
get away with vt fus hacer impunemente
get back vi (return) volver ♦ vt recobrar
get by vi (pass) (lograr) pasar; (manage) arreglárselas
get down vi bajarse ♦ vt fus bajar ♦ vt bajar; (depress) deprimir
get down to vt fus (work) ponerse a
get in vi entrar; (train) llegar; (arrive home) volver a casa, regresar
get into vt fus entrar en; (vehicle) subir a; to ~ **into a rage** enfadarse
get off vi (from train etc) bajar; (depart: person, car) marcharse ♦ vt (remove) quitar ♦ vt fus (train, bus) bajar de
get on vi (at exam etc): **how are you ~ting on?** ¿cómo te va?; (agree): to ~ **on (with)** llevarse bien (con) ♦ vt fus subir a
get out vi salir; (of vehicle) bajar ♦ vt sacar
get out of vt fus salir de; (duty etc) escaparse de
get over vt fus (illness) recobrarse de
get round vt fus rodear; (fig: person) engatusar a
get through vi (TEL) (lograr) comunicarse
get through to vt fus (TEL) comunicar con
get together vi reunirse ♦ vt reunir, juntar
get up vi (rise) levantarse ♦ vt fus subir
get up to vt fus (reach) llegar a; (prank) hacer

geyser ['ɡiːzəˀ] n (water heater) calentador m de agua; (GEO) géiser m

ghastly ['ɡɑːstlɪ] adj horrible

gherkin ['gɔːkɪn] n pepinillo

ghetto blaster ['gɛtəʊblɑːstə*] n cassette m portátil de gran tamaño

ghost [gəʊst] n fantasma m

giant ['dʒaɪənt] n gigante m/f ♦ adj gigantesco, gigante

gibberish ['dʒɪbərɪʃ] n galimatías m

giblets ['dʒɪblɪts] npl menudillos mpl

Gibraltar [dʒɪ'brɔːltə*] n Gibraltar m

giddy ['gɪdɪ] adj mareado

gift [gɪft] n regalo; (ability) talento; **~ed** adj dotado; **~ token** or **voucher** n vale m canjeable por un regalo

gigantic [dʒaɪ'gæntɪk] adj gigantesco

giggle ['gɪgl] vi reírse tontamente

gill [dʒɪl] n (measure) = 0.25 pints (BRIT = 0.148l, US = 0.118l)

gills [gɪlz] npl (of fish) branquias fpl, agallas fpl

gilt [gɪlt] adj, n dorado; **~-edged** adj (COMM) de máxima garantía

gimmick ['gɪmɪk] n truco

gin [dʒɪn] n ginebra

ginger ['dʒɪndʒə*] n jengibre m; **~ ale** = **~ beer**; **~ beer** (BRIT) n gaseosa de jengibre; **~bread** n pan m (or galleta) de jengibre

gingerly ['dʒɪndʒəlɪ] adv con cautela

gipsy ['dʒɪpsɪ] n = **gypsy**

giraffe [dʒɪ'rɑːf] n jirafa

girder ['gɔːdə*] n viga

girl [gɔːl] n (small) niña; (young woman) chica, joven f, muchacha; (daughter) hija; **an English ~** una (chica) inglesa; **~friend** n (of girl) amiga; (of boy) novia; **~ish** adj de niña

giro ['dʒaɪrəʊ] n (BRIT: bank ~) giro bancario; (post office ~) giro postal; (state benefit) cheque quincenal del subsidio de desempleo

gist [dʒɪst] n lo esencial

give [gɪv] (pt **gave**, pp **given**) vt dar; (deliver) entregar; (as gift) regalar ♦ vi (break) romperse; (stretch: fabric) dar de sí; **to ~ sb sth, ~ sth to sb** dar algo a uno; **~ away** vt (give free) regalar; (betray) traicionar; (disclose) revelar; **~ back** vt devolver; **~ in** vi ceder ♦ vt entregar; **~ off** vt despedir; **~ out** vt distribuir; **~ up** vi rendirse, darse por vencido ♦ vt renunciar a; **to ~ up smoking** dejar de fumar; **to ~ o.s. up** entregarse; **~ way** vi ceder; (BRIT: AUT) ceder el paso

glacier ['glæsɪə*] n glaciar m

glad [glæd] adj contento

gladly ['glædlɪ] adv con mucho gusto

glamorous ['glæmərəs] adj encantador(a), atractivo; **glamour** ['glæmə*] n encanto, atractivo

glance [glɑːns] n ojeada, mirada ♦ vi: **to ~ at** echar una ojeada a; **glancing** adj (blow) oblicuo

gland [glænd] n glándula

glare [glɛə*] n (of anger) mirada feroz; (of light) deslumbramiento, brillo; **to be in the ~ of publicity** ser el foco de la atención pública ♦ vi deslumbrar; **to ~ at** mirar con odio a; **glaring** adj (mistake) manifiesto

glass [glɑːs] n vidrio, cristal m; (for drinking) vaso; (: with stem) copa; **~es** npl (spectacles) gafas fpl; **~house** n invernadero; **~ware** n cristalería

glaze [gleɪz] vt (window) poner cristales a; (pottery) vidriar ♦ n vidriado; **glazier** ['gleɪzɪə*] n vidriero/a

gleam [gliːm] vi brillar

glean [gliːn] vt (information) recoger

glee [gliː] n alegría, regocijo

glen [glɛn] n cañada

glib [glɪb] adj de mucha labia; (promise, response) poco sincero

glide [glaɪd] vi deslizarse; (AVIAT, birds) planear; **~r** n (AVIAT) planeador m; **gliding** n (AVIAT) vuelo sin motor

glimmer ['glɪmə*] n luz f tenue; (of interest) muestra; (of hope) rayo

glimpse [glɪmps] n vislumbre m ♦ vt vislumbrar, entrever

glint [glɪnt] vi centellear

glisten ['glɪsn] vi relucir, brillar

glitter ['glɪtə*] vi relucir, brillar

gloat [gləʊt] vi: **to ~ over** recrearse en

global ['gləʊbl] adj mundial; **~ warming** (re)calentamiento global or de la tierra

globe [gləʊb] n globo; (model) globo terráqueo

gloom [gluːm] n tinieblas fpl, oscuridad f; (sadness) tristeza, melancolía; **~y** adj (dark) oscuro; (sad) triste; (pessimistic) pesimista

glorious ['glɔːrɪəs] adj glorioso; (weather etc) magnífico

glory ['glɔːrɪ] n gloria

gloss [glɔs] n (shine) brillo; (paint) pintura de aceite; **~ over** vt fus disimular

glossary ['glɔsərɪ] n glosario

glossy ['glɔsɪ] adj lustroso; (magazine) de lujo

glove [glʌv] n guante m; **~ compartment** n (AUT) guantera

glow [gləʊ] vi brillar

glower ['glaʊə*] vi: **to ~ at** mirar con ceño

glue [gluː] n goma (de pegar), cemento ♦ vt pegar

glum [glʌm] adj (person, tone) melancólico

glut [glʌt] n superabundancia

glutton ['glʌtn] n glotón/ona m/f; **a ~ for work** un(a) trabajador(a) incansable

GM adj abbr (= genetically modified) transgénico

gnat [næt] n mosquito

gnaw [nɔː] vt roer

gnome [nəʊm] n gnomo

go [gəʊ] (pt **went**, pp **gone**; pl **~es**) vi ir; (travel) viajar; (depart) irse, marcharse; (work) funcionar, marchar; (be sold) venderse; (time) pasar; (fit, suit): **to ~ with**

hacer juego con; (*become*) ponerse; (*break etc*) estropearse, romperse ♦ *n*: **to have a ~ (at)** probar suerte (con); **to be on the ~** no parar; **whose ~ is it?** ¿a quién le toca?; **he's going to do it** va a hacerlo; **to ~ for a walk** ir de paseo; **to ~ dancing** ir a bailar; **how did it ~?** ¿qué tal salió o resultó?, ¿cómo ha ido?; **to ~ round the back** pasar por detrás; **~ about** *vi* (*rumour*) propagarse ♦ *vt fus*: **how do I ~ about this?** ¿cómo me las arreglo para hacer esto?; **~ ahead** *vi* seguir adelante; **~ along** *vi* ir ♦ *vt fus* bordear; **to ~ along with** (*agree*) estar de acuerdo con; **~ away** *vi* irse, marcharse; **~ back** *vi* volver; **~ back on** *vt fus* (*promise*) faltar a; **~ by** *vi* (*time*) pasar ♦ *vt fus* guiarse por; **~ down** *vi* bajar; (*ship*) hundirse; (*sun*) ponerse ♦ *vt fus* bajar; **~ for** *vt fus* (*fetch*) ir por; (*like*) gustar; (*attack*) atacar; **~ in** *vi* entrar; **~ in for** *vt fus* (*competition*) presentarse a; **~ into** *vt fus* entrar en; (*investigate*) investigar; (*embark on*) dedicarse a; **~ off** *vi* irse, marcharse; (*food*) pasarse; (*explode*) estallar; (*event*) realizarse ♦ *vt fus* dejar de gustar; **I'm going off him/the idea** ya no me gusta tanto él/la idea; **~ on** *vi* (*continue*) seguir, continuar; (*happen*) pasar, ocurrir; **to ~ on doing sth** seguir haciendo algo; **~ out** *vi* salir; (*fire, light*) apagarse; **~ over** *vi* (*ship*) zozobrar ♦ *vt fus* (*check*) revisar; **~ through** *vt fus* (*town etc*) atravesar; **~ up** *vi, vt fus* subir; **~ without** *vt fus* pasarse sin

goad [gəud] *vt* aguijonear

go-ahead *adj* (*person*) dinámico; (*firm*) innovador(a) ♦ *n* luz f verde

goal [gəul] *n* meta; (*score*) gol m; **~keeper** *n* portero; **~-post** *n* poste m (de la portería)

goat [gəut] *n* cabra

gobble ['gɔbl] *vt* (*also*: **~ down**, **~ up**) tragarse, engullir

go-between *n* intermediario/a

god [gɔd] *n* dios m; **G~** *n* Dios m; **~child** *n* ahijado/a; **~daughter** *n* ahijada; **~dess** *n* diosa; **~father** *n* padrino; **~-forsaken** *adj* dejado de la mano de Dios; **~mother** *n* madrina; **~send** *n* don m del cielo; **~son** *n* ahijado

goggles ['gɔglz] *npl* gafas fpl

going ['gəuiŋ] *n* (*conditions*) estado del terreno ♦ *adj*: **the ~ rate** la tarifa corriente or en vigor

gold [gəuld] *n* oro ♦ *adj* de oro; **~en** *adj* (*made of ~*) de oro; (*~ in colour*) dorado; **~fish** *n* pez m de colores; **~mine** *n* (*also fig*) mina de oro; **~-plated** *adj* chapado en oro; **~smith** *n* orfebre m/f

golf [gɔlf] *n* golf m; **~ ball** *n* (*for game*) pelota de golf; (*on typewriter*) esfera; **~ club** *n* club m de golf; (*stick*) palo (de golf);

~ course *n* campo de golf; **~er** *n* golfista m/f

gone [gɔn] *pp* of **go**

good [gud] *adj* bueno; (*pleasant*) agradable; (*kind*) bueno, amable; (*well-behaved*) educado ♦ *n* bien m, provecho; **~s** *npl* (*COMM*) mercancías fpl; **~!** ¡qué bien!; **to be ~ at** tener aptitud para; **to be ~ for** servir para; **it's ~ for you** te hace bien; **would you be ~ enough to ...?** ¿podría hacerme el favor de ...?, ¿sería tan amable de ...?; **a ~ deal (of)** mucho; **a ~ many** muchos; **to make ~** reparar; **it's no ~ complaining** no vale la pena (de) quejarse; **for ~** para siempre, definitivamente; **~ morning/afternoon** ¡buenos días/buenas tardes!; **~ evening!** ¡buenas noches!; **~ night!** ¡buenas noches!; **~bye!** ¡adiós!; **to say ~bye** despedirse; **G~ Friday** *n* Viernes m Santo; **~-looking** *adj* guapo; **~-natured** *adj* amable, simpático; **~ness** *n* (*of person*) bondad f; **for ~ness sake!** ¡por Dios!; **~ness gracious!** ¡Dios mío!; **~s train** (*BRIT*) *n* tren m de mercancías; **~will** *n* buena voluntad f

goose [gu:s] (*pl* **geese**) *n* ganso, oca

gooseberry ['guzbəri] *n* grosella espinosa; **to play ~** hacer de carabina

gooseflesh ['gu:sfleʃ] *n* = **goose pimples**

goose pimples *npl* carne f de gallina

gore [gɔ:*] *vt* cornear ♦ *n* sangre f

gorge [gɔ:dʒ] *n* barranco ♦ *vr*: **to ~ o.s. (on)** atracarse (de)

gorgeous ['gɔ:dʒəs] *adj* (*thing*) precioso; (*weather*) espléndido; (*person*) guapísimo

gorilla [gə'rilə] *n* gorila m

gorse [gɔ:s] *n* tojo

gory ['gɔ:ri] *adj* sangriento

go-slow (*BRIT*) *n* huelga de manos caídas

gospel ['gɔspl] *n* evangelio

gossip ['gɔsip] *n* (*scandal*) cotilleo, chismes mpl; (*chat*) charla; (*scandalmonger*) cotilla m/f, chismoso/a ♦ *vi* cotillear

got [gɔt] *pt, pp* of **get**; **~ten** (*US*) *pp* of **get**

gout [gaut] *n* gota

govern ['gʌvən] *vt* gobernar; (*influence*) dominar; **~ess** *n* institutriz f; **~ment** *n* gobierno; **~or** *n* gobernador(a) m/f; (*of school etc*) miembro del consejo; (*of jail*) director(a) m/f

gown [gaun] *n* traje m; (*of teacher*, *BRIT: of judge*) toga

G.P. *n abbr* = **general practitioner**

grab [græb] *vt* coger (*SP*) o agarrar (*AM*), arrebatar ♦ *vi*: **to ~ at** intentar agarrar

grace [greis] *n* gracia ♦ *vt* honrar; (*adorn*) adornar; **5 days' ~** un plazo de 5 días; **~ful** *adj* grácil, ágil; (*style, shape*) elegante, gracioso; **gracious** ['greiʃəs] *adj* amable

grade [greid] *n* (*quality*) clase f, calidad f; (*in*

hierarchy) grado; (*SCOL*: *mark*) nota; (*US*: *school class*) curso ♦ *vt* clasificar; ~ **crossing** (*US*) *n* paso a nivel; ~ **school** (*US*) *n* escuela primaria

gradient ['greidiənt] *n* pendiente *f*

gradual ['grædjuəl] *adj* paulatino; ~**ly** *adv* paulatinamente

graduate [*n* 'grædjuit, *vb* 'grædjueit] *n* (*US*: *of high school*) graduado/a; (*of university*) licenciado/a ♦ *vi* graduarse; licenciarse; **graduation** |-'eɪʃən| *n* (*ceremony*) entrega del título

graffiti [grə'fi:tɪ] *n* pintadas *fpl*

graft [grɑːft] *n* (*AGR, MED*) injerto; (*BRIT*: *inf*) trabajo duro; (*bribery*) corrupción *f* ♦ *vt* injertar

grain [greɪn] *n* (*single particle*) grano; (*corn*) granos *mpl*, cereales *mpl*; (*of wood*) fibra

gram [græm] *n* gramo

grammar ['græmə*] *n* gramática; ~ **school** (*BRIT*) *n* ≈ instituto de segunda enseñanza, liceo (*SP*)

grammatical [grə'mætɪkl] *adj* gramatical

gramme [græm] *n* = **gram**

gramophone ['græməfəun] (*BRIT*) *n* tocadiscos *m inv*

grand [grænd] *adj* magnífico, imponente; (*wonderful*) estupendo; (*gesture etc*) grandioso; ~**children** *npl* nietos *mpl*; ~**dad** (*inf*) *n* yayo, abuelito; ~**daughter** *n* nieta; ~**eur** ['grændjə*] *n* magnificencia, lo grandioso; ~**father** *n* abuelo; ~**ma** (*inf*) *n* yaya, abuelita; ~**mother** *n* abuela; ~**pa** (*inf*) *n* = ~**dad**; ~**parents** *npl* abuelos *mpl*; ~ **piano** *n* piano de cola; ~**son** *n* nieto; ~**stand** (*SPORT*) *n* tribuna

granite ['grænɪt] *n* granito

granny ['grænɪ] (*inf*) *n* abuelita, yaya

grant [grɑːnt] *vt* (*concede*) conceder; (*admit*) reconocer ♦ *n* (*SCOL*) beca; (*ADMIN*) subvención *f*; **to take sth/sb for ~ed** dar algo por sentado/no hacer ningún caso a uno

granulated sugar ['grænju:leɪtɪd-] (*BRIT*) *n* azúcar *m* blanquilla

grape [greɪp] *n* uva

grapefruit ['greɪpfru:t] *n* pomelo (*SP*), toronja (*AM*)

graph [grɑːf] *n* gráfica; ~**ic** ['græfɪk] *adj* gráfico; ~**ics** *n* artes *fpl* gráficas ♦ *npl* (*drawings*) dibujos *mpl*

grapple ['græpl] *vi*: **to ~ with sth/sb** agarrar a algo/uno

grasp [grɑːsp] *vt* agarrar, asir; (*understand*) comprender ♦ *n* (*grip*) asimiento; (*understanding*) comprensión *f*; ~**ing** *adj* (*mean*) avaro

grass [grɑːs] *n* hierba; (*lawn*) césped *m*; ~**hopper** *n* saltamontes *m inv*; ~**roots** *adj* (*fig*) popular

grate [greɪt] *n* parrilla de chimenea ♦ *vi*: **to ~ (on)** chirriar (sobre) ♦ *vt* (*CULIN*) rallar

grateful ['greɪtful] *adj* agradecido

grater ['greɪtə*] *n* rallador *m*

gratifying ['grætɪfaɪɪŋ] *adj* grato

grating ['greɪtɪŋ] *n* (*iron bars*) reja ♦ *adj* (*noise*) áspero

gratitude ['grætɪtjuːd] *n* agradecimiento

gratuity [grə'tjuːɪtɪ] *n* gratificación *f*

grave [greɪv] *n* tumba ♦ *adj* serio, grave

gravel ['grævl] *n* grava

gravestone ['greɪvstəun] *n* lápida

graveyard ['greɪvjɑːd] *n* cementerio

gravity ['grævɪtɪ] *n* gravedad *f*

gravy ['greɪvɪ] *n* salsa de carne

gray [greɪ] *adj* = **grey**

graze [greɪz] *vi* pacer ♦ *vt* (*touch lightly*) rozar; (*scrape*) raspar ♦ *n* (*MED*) abrasión *f*

grease [griːs] *n* (*fat*) grasa; (*lubricant*) lubricante *m* ♦ *vt* engrasar; lubrificar; ~**proof paper** (*BRIT*) *n* papel *m* apergaminado; **greasy** *adj* grasiento

great [greɪt] *adj* grande; (*inf*) magnífico, estupendo; **G~ Britain** *n* Gran Bretaña; ~**grandfather** *n* bisabuelo; ~**grandmother** *n* bisabuela; ~**ly** *adv* muy; (*with verb*) mucho; ~**ness** *n* grandeza

Greece [griːs] *n* Grecia

greed [griːd] *n* (*also*: ~*iness*) codicia, avaricia; (*for food*) gula; (*for power etc*) avidez *f*; ~**y** *adj* avaro; (*for food*) glotón/ona

Greek [griːk] *adj* griego ♦ *n* griego/a; (*LING*) griego

green [griːn] *adj* (*also POL*) verde; (*inexperienced*) novato ♦ *n* verde *m*; (*stretch of grass*) césped *m*; (*GOLF*) green *m*; ~**s** *npl* (*vegetables*) verduras *fpl*; ~ **belt** *n* zona verde; ~ **card** *n* (*AUT*) carta verde; (*US*: *work permit*) permiso de trabajo para los extranjeros en EE. UU.; ~**ery** *n* verdura; ~**grocer** (*BRIT*) *n* verdulero/a; ~**house** *n* invernadero; ~**house effect** *n* efecto invernadero; ~**house gas** *n* gases *mpl* de invernadero; ~**ish** *adj* verdoso

Greenland ['griːnlənd] *n* Groenlandia

greet [griːt] *vt* (*welcome*) dar la bienvenida a; (*receive*: *news*) recibir; ~**ing** *n* (*welcome*) bienvenida; ~**ing(s) card** *n* tarjeta de felicitación

grenade [grə'neɪd] *n* granada

grew [gruː] *pt of* **grow**

grey [greɪ] *adj* gris; (*weather*) sombrío; ~**haired** *adj* canoso; ~**hound** *n* galgo

grid [grɪd] *n* reja; (*ELEC*) red *f*; ~**lock** *n* (*traffic jam*) retención *f*

grief [griːf] *n* dolor *m*, pena

grievance ['griːvəns] *n* motivo de queja, agravio

grieve [griːv] *vi* afligirse, acongojarse ♦ *vt* dar pena a; **to ~ for** llorar por

grievous |'griːvəs| adj: ~ **bodily harm** (LAW) daños mpl corporales graves

grill |grɪl| n (on cooker) parrilla; (also: mixed ~) parrillada ♦ vt (BRIT) asar a la parrilla; (inf: question) interrogar

grille |grɪl| n reja; (AUT) rejilla

grim |grɪm| adj (place) sombrío; (situation) triste; (person) ceñudo

grimace |grɪ'meɪs| n mueca ♦ vi hacer muecas

grime |graɪm| n mugre f, suciedad f

grin |grɪn| n sonrisa abierta ♦ vi sonreír abiertamente

grind |graɪnd| (pt, pp **ground**) vt (coffee, pepper etc) moler; (US: meat) picar; (make sharp) afilar ♦ n (work) rutina

grip |grɪp| n (hold) asimiento; (control) control m, dominio; (of tyre etc): **to have a good/bad ~** agarrarse bien/mal; (handle) asidero; (holdall) maletín m ♦ vt agarrar; (viewer, reader) fascinar; **to get to ~s with** enfrentarse con; **~ping** adj absorbente

grisly |'grɪzlɪ| adj horripilante, horrible

gristle |'grɪsl| n ternilla

grit |grɪt| n gravilla; (courage) valor m ♦ vt (road) poner gravilla en; **to ~ one's teeth** apretar los dientes

groan |grəun| n gemido; quejido ♦ vi gemir; quejarse

grocer |'grəusə*| n tendero (de ultramarinos (SP)); **~ies** npl comestibles mpl; **~'s (shop)** n tienda de ultramarinos or de abarrotes (AM)

groin |grɔɪn| n ingle f

groom |gruːm| n mozo/a de cuadra; (also: bride~) novio ♦ vt (horse) almohazar; (fig): **to ~ sb for** preparar a uno para; **well-~ed** de buena presencia

groove |gruːv| n ranura, surco

grope |grəup| vt: **to ~ for** vt fus buscar a tientas

gross |grəus| adj (neglect, injustice) grave; (vulgar: behaviour) grosero; (: appearance) de mal gusto; (COMM) bruto; **~ly** adv (greatly) enormemente

grotto |'grɔtəu| n gruta

grotty |'grɔtɪ| (inf) adj horrible

ground |graund| pt, pp of **grind** ♦ n suelo, tierra; (SPORT) campo, terreno; (reason: gen pl) causa, razón f; (US: also: ~ wire) tierra ♦ vt (plane) mantener en tierra; (US: ELEC) conectar con tierra; **~s** npl (of coffee etc) poso; (gardens etc) jardines mpl, parque m; **on the ~** en el suelo; **to the ~** al suelo; **to gain/lose ~** ganar/perder terreno; **~ cloth** (US) n = **~sheet**; **~ing** n (in education) conocimientos mpl básicos; **~less** adj infundado; **~sheet** (BRIT) n tela impermeable; suelo; **~ staff** n personal m de tierra; **~work** n preparación f

group |gruːp| n grupo; (musical) conjunto ♦ vt (also: ~ together) agrupar ♦ vi (also: ~ together) agruparse

grouse |graus| n inv (bird) urogallo ♦ vi (complain) quejarse

grove |grəuv| n arboleda

grovel |'grɔvl| vi (fig): **to ~ before** humillarse ante

grow |grəu| (pt grew, pp grown) vi crecer; (increase) aumentar; (expand) desarrollarse; (become) volverse; **to ~ rich/weak** enriquecerse/debilitarse ♦ vt cultivar; (hair, beard) dejar crecer; **~ up** vi crecer, hacerse hombre/mujer; **~er** n cultivador(a) m/f, productor(a) m/f; **~ing** adj creciente

growl |graul| vi gruñir

grown |grəun| pp of **grow**; **~-up** n adulto, mayor m/f

growth |grəuθ| n crecimiento, desarrollo; (what has grown) brote m; (MED) tumor m

grub |grʌb| n larva, gusano; (inf: food) comida

grubby |'grʌbɪ| adj sucio, mugriento

grudge |grʌdʒ| n (motivo de) rencor m ♦ vt: **to ~ sb sth** dar algo a uno de mala gana; **to bear sb a ~** guardar rencor a uno

gruelling |'gruəlɪŋ| (US **grueling**) adj penoso, duro

gruesome |'gruːsəm| adj horrible

gruff |grʌf| adj (voice) ronco; (manner) brusco

grumble |'grʌmbl| vi refunfuñar, quejarse

grumpy |'grʌmpɪ| adj gruñón/ona

grunt |grʌnt| vi gruñir

G-string |'dʒiːstrɪŋ| n taparrabo

guarantee |gærən'tiː| n garantía ♦ vt garantizar

guard |gɑːd| n (squad) guardia; (one man) guardia m; (BRIT: RAIL) jefe m de tren; (on machine) dispositivo de seguridad; (also: fire~) rejilla de protección ♦ vt guardar; (prisoner) vigilar; **to be on one's ~** estar alerta; **~ against** vt fus (prevent) protegerse de; **~ed** adj (fig) cauteloso; **~ian** n guardián/ana m/f; (of minor) tutor(a) m/f; **~'s van** n (BRIT: RAIL) furgón m

Guatemala |gwætɪ'mɑːlə| n Guatemala; **~n** adj, n guatemalteco/a m/f

guerrilla |gə'rɪlə| n guerrillero/a

guess |ges| vi adivinar; (US) suponer ♦ vt adivinar; suponer ♦ n suposición f, conjetura; **to take** or **have a ~** tratar de adivinar; **~work** n conjeturas fpl

guest |gest| n invitado/a; (in hotel) huésped/a m/f; **~ house** n casa de huéspedes, pensión f; **~ room** n cuarto de huéspedes

guffaw |gʌ'fɔː| vi reírse a carcajadas

guidance |'gaɪdəns| n (advice) consejos mpl

guide |gaɪd| n (person) guía m/f; (book, fig) guía ♦ vt (round museum etc) guiar; (lead)

conducir; (*direct*) orientar; (*girl*) ~ *n*
exploradora; **~book** *n* guía; **~ dog** *n* perro
m guía; **~lines** *npl* (*advice*) directrices *fpl*

guild [gɪld] *n* gremio

guilt [gɪlt] *n* culpabilidad *f*; **~y** *adj* culpable

guinea pig ['gɪnɪ-] *n* cobaya; (*fig*) conejillo
de Indias

guise [gaɪz] *n*: **in** or **under the ~ of** bajo
apariencia de

guitar [gɪ'tɑ:*] *n* guitarra

gulf [gʌlf] *n* golfo; (*abyss*) abismo

gull [gʌl] *n* gaviota

gullible ['gʌlɪbl] *adj* créduio

gully ['gʌlɪ] *n* barranco

gulp [gʌlp] *vi* tragar saliva ♦ *vt* (*also*: ~ **down**)
tragarse

gum [gʌm] *n* (*ANAT*) encía; (*glue*) goma,
cemento; (*sweet*) caramelo de goma; (*also*:
chewing-~) chicle *m* ♦ *vt* pegar con goma;
~boots (*BRIT*) *npl* botas *fpl* de goma

gun [gʌn] *n* (*small*) pistola, revólver *m*;
(*shotgun*) escopeta; (*rifle*) fusil *m*; (*cannon*)
cañón *m*; **~man** *n* cañonero; **~fire** *n*
disparos *mpl*; **~man** *n* pistolero; **~point** *n*:
at ~point a mano armada; **~powder** *n*
pólvora; **~shot** *n* escopetazo

gurgle ['gə:gl] *vi* (*baby*) gorgotear; (*water*)
borbotear

gush [gʌʃ] *vi* salir a raudales; (*person*)
deshacerse en efusiones

gust [gʌst] *n* (*of wind*) ráfaga

gusto ['gʌstəu] *n* entusiasmo

gut [gʌt] *n* intestino; **~s** *npl* (*ANAT*) tripas *fpl*;
(*courage*) valor *m*

gutter ['gʌtə*] *n* (*of roof*) canalón *m*; (*in
street*) cuneta

guy [gaɪ] *n* (*also*: ~*rope*) cuerda; (*inf*: *man*) tío
(*SP*), tipo; (*figure*) monigote *m*

guzzle ['gʌzl] *vi* tragar ♦ *vt* engullir

gym [dʒɪm] *n* (*also*: *gymnasium*) gimnasio;
(*also*: *gymnastics*) gimnasia; **~nast** *n*
gimnasta *m/f*; **~ shoes** *npl* zapatillas *fpl* de
deporte); **~ slip** (*BRIT*) *n* túnica de colegiala

gynaecologist [gaɪnɪ'kɔlədʒɪst] (*US* **gyne-
cologist**) *n* ginecólogo/a

gypsy ['dʒɪpsɪ] *n* gitano/a

H, h

haberdashery [hæbə'dæʃərɪ] (*BRIT*) *n*
mercería

habit ['hæbɪt] *n* hábito, costumbre *f*; (*drug ~*)
adicción *f*; (*costume*) hábito

habitual [hə'bɪtjuəl] *adj* acostumbrado,
habitual; (*drinker, liar*) empedernido

hack [hæk] *vt* (*cut*) cortar; (*slice*) tajar ♦ *n*
(*pej: writer*) escritor(a) *m/f* a sueldo; **~er** *n*
(*COMPUT*) pirata *m/f* informático/a

hackneyed ['hæknɪd] *adj* trillado

had [hæd] *pt, pp of* **have**

haddock ['hædək] (*pl* ~ *or* ~**s**) *n especie de*
merluza

hadn't ['hædnt] = **had not**

haemorrhage ['hemərɪdʒ] (*US* **hemorrhage**)
n hemorragia

haemorrhoids ['hemərɔɪdz] (*US* **hemorrhoids**) *npl* hemorroides *fpl*

haggle ['hægl] *vi* regatear

Hague [heɪg] *n*: **The ~** La Haya

hail [heɪl] *n* granizo; (*fig*) lluvia ♦ *vt* saludar;
(*taxi*) llamar a; (*acclaim*) aclamar ♦ *vi*
granizar; **~stone** *n* (piedra de) granizo

hair [heə*] *n* pelo, cabellos *mpl*; (*one ~*) pelo,
cabello; (*on legs etc*) vello; **to do one's ~**
arreglarse el pelo; **to have grey ~** tener canas
fpl; **~brush** *n* cepillo (para el pelo); **~cut** *n*
corte *m* (de pelo); **~do** *n* peinado; **~dresser**
n peluquero/a; **~dresser's** *n* peluquería;
~ dryer *n* secador *m* de pelo; **~grip** *n*
horquilla; **~net** *n* redecilla; **~piece** *n* postizo;
~pin *n* horquilla; **~pin bend** (*US* ~**pin curve**)
n curva de horquilla; **~raising** *adj*
espeluznante; **~ removing cream** *n* crema
depilatoria; **~ spray** *n* laca; **~style** *n*
peinado; **~y** *adj* peludo; velludo; (*inf*:
frightening) espeluznante

hake [heɪk] (*pl inv or* ~**s**) *n* merluza

half [hɑ:f] (*pl* **halves**) *n* mitad *f*; (*of beer*) ≈
caña (*SP*), media pinta; (*RAIL, BUS*) billete *m*
de niño ♦ *adj* medio ♦ *adv* medio, a medias;
two and a ~ dos y media; **~ a dozen** media
docena; **~ a pound** media libra; **to cut sth in
~** cortar algo por la mitad; **~-caste**
['hɑ:fkɑ:st] *n* mestizo/a; **~-hearted** *adj*
indiferente, poco entusiasta; **~-hour** *n* media
hora; **~-mast** *n*: **at ~-mast** (*flag*) a media
asta; **~-price** *adj, adv* a mitad de precio;
~ term (*BRIT*) *n* (*SCOL*) vacaciones de
mediados del trimestre; **~-time** *n* descanso;
~way *adv* a medio camino; (*in period of
time*) a mitad de

hall [hɔ:l] *n* (*for concerts*) sala; (*entrance way*)
hall *m*; vestíbulo; **~ of residence** (*BRIT*) *n*
residencia

hallmark ['hɔ:lmɑ:k] *n* sello

hallo [hə'ləu] *excl* = **hello**

Hallowe'en [hæləu'i:n] *n* víspera de Todos
los Santos

hallucination [həlu:sɪ'neɪʃən] *n* alucinación
f

hallway ['hɔ:lweɪ] *n* vestíbulo

halo ['heɪləu] *n* (*of saint*) halo, aureola

halt [hɔ:lt] *n* (*stop*) alto, parada ♦ *vt* parar;
interrumpir ♦ *vi* pararse

halve [hɑ:v] *vt* partir por la mitad

halves [hɑ:vz] *npl of* **half**

ham [hæm] *n* jamón *m* (cocido)

hamburger ['hæmbə:gə*] n hamburguesa

hamlet ['hæmlɪt] n aldea

hammer ['hæmə*] n martillo ♦ vt (nail) clavar; (force): **to ~ an idea into sb/a message across** meter una idea en la cabeza a uno/ machacar una idea ♦ vi dar golpes

hammock ['hæmək] n hamaca

hamper ['hæmpə*] vt estorbar ♦ n cesto

hand [hænd] n mano f; (of clock) aguja; (writing) letra; (worker) obrero ♦ vt dar, pasar; **to give or lend sb a ~** echar una mano a uno, ayudar a uno; **at ~** a mano; (time) libre; (job etc) entre manos; **on ~** (person, services) a mano, al alcance; **to ~** (information etc) a mano; **on the one ~ ..., on the other ~ ...** por una parte ... por otra (parte) ...; **~ in** vt entregar; **~ out** vt distribuir; **~ over** vt (deliver) entregar; **~bag** n bolso (SP), cartera (AM); **~book** n manual m; **~brake** n freno de mano; **~cuffs** npl esposas fpl; **~ful** n puñado

handicap ['hændɪkæp] n minusvalía; (disadvantage) desventaja; (SPORT) handicap m ♦ vt estorbar; **mentally/physically ~ped** deficiente m/f (mental)/minusválido/a (físico/a)

handicraft ['hændɪkrɑːft] n artesanía; (object) objeto de artesanía

handiwork ['hændɪwɔ:k] n obra

handkerchief ['hæŋkətʃɪf] n pañuelo

handle ['hændl] n (of door etc) tirador m; (of cup etc) asa; (of knife etc) mango; (for winding) manivela ♦ vt (touch) tocar; (deal with) encargarse de; (treat: people) manejar; **"~ with care"** "(manéjese) con cuidado"; **to fly off the ~** perder los estribos; **~bar(s)** n(pl) manillar m

hand-: **~ luggage** n equipaje m de mano; **~made** adj hecho a mano; **~out** n (money etc) limosna; (leaflet) folleto; **~rail** n pasamanos m inv; **~shake** n apretón m de manos

handsome ['hænsəm] adj guapo; (building) bello; (fig: profit) considerable

handwriting ['hændraɪtɪŋ] n letra

handy ['hændɪ] adj (close at hand) a la mano; (tool etc) práctico; (skilful) hábil, diestro

hang [hæŋ] (pt, pp hung) vt colgar; (criminal: pt, pp hanged) ahorcar ♦ vi (painting, coat etc) colgar; (hair, drapery) caer; **to get the ~ of sth** (inf) lograr dominar algo; **~ about** or **around** vi haraganear; **~ on** vi (wait) esperar; **~ up** vi (TEL) colgar ♦ vt colgar

hanger ['hæŋə*] n percha; **~-on** n parásito

hang-: **~-gliding** ['glaɪdɪŋ] n vuelo libre; **~over** n (after drinking) resaca; **~-up** n complejo

hanker ['hæŋkə*] vi: **to ~ after** añorar

hankie ['hæŋkɪ], **hanky** ['hæŋkɪ] n abbr = **handkerchief**

haphazard [hæp'hæzəd] adj fortuito

happen ['hæpən] vi suceder, ocurrir; (chance): **he ~ed to hear/see** dió la casualidad de que oyó/vió; **as it ~s** da la casualidad de que; **~ing** n suceso, acontecimiento

happily ['hæpɪlɪ] adv (luckily) afortunadamente; (cheerfully) alegremente

happiness ['hæpɪnɪs] n felicidad f; (cheerfulness) alegría

happy ['hæpɪ] adj feliz; (cheerful) alegre; **to be ~ (with)** estar contento (con); **to be ~ to do** estar encantado de hacer; **~ birthday!** ¡feliz cumpleaños!; **~-go-lucky** adj despreocupado; **~ hour** n horas en las que la bebida es más barata, happy hour f

harass ['hærəs] vt acosar, hostigar; **~ment** n persecución f

harbour ['hɑ:bə*] (US harbor) n puerto ♦ vt (fugitive) dar abrigo a; (hope etc) abrigar

hard [hɑ:d] adj duro; (difficult) difícil; (work) arduo; (person) severo; (fact) innegable ♦ adv (work) mucho, duro; (think) profundamente; **to look ~ at** clavar los ojos en; **to try ~** esforzarse; **no ~ feelings!** ¡sin rencor(es)!; **to be ~ of hearing** ser duro de oído; **to be ~ done by** ser tratado injustamente; **~back** n libro en cartoné; **~ cash** n dinero contante; **~ disk** n (COMPUT) disco duro or rígido; **~en** vt endurecer; (fig) curtir ♦ vi endurecerse; curtirse; **~-headed** adj realista; **~ labour** n trabajos mpl forzados

hardly ['hɑ:dlɪ] adv apenas; **~ ever** casi nunca

hard-: **~ship** n privación f; **~ shoulder** (BRIT) n (AUT) arcén m; **~-up** (inf) adj sin un duro (SP), sin plata (AM); **~ware** n ferretería; (COMPUT) hardware m, (MIL) armamento; **~ware shop** n ferretería; **~-wearing** adj resistente, duradero; **~-working** adj trabajador(a)

hardy ['hɑ:dɪ] adj fuerte; (plant) resistente

hare [heə*] n liebre f; **~-brained** adj descabellado

harm [hɑ:m] n daño, mal m ♦ vt (person) hacer daño a; (health, interests) perjudicar; (thing) dañar; **out of ~'s way** a salvo; **~ful** adj dañino; **~less** adj (person) inofensivo; (joke etc) inocente

harmony ['hɑ:mənɪ] n armonía

harness ['hɑ:nɪs] n arreos mpl; (for child) arnés m; (safety ~) arneses mpl ♦ vt (horse) enjaezar; (resources) aprovechar

harp [hɑ:p] n arpa ♦ vi: **to ~ on (about)** machacar (con)

harrowing ['hærəʊɪŋ] adj angustioso

harsh [hɑ:ʃ] adj (cruel) duro, cruel; (severe) severo; (sound) áspero; (light) deslumbrador(a)

harvest ['hɑːvɪst] n (~ time) siega; (of cereals etc) cosecha; (of grapes) vendimia ♦ vt cosechar

has [hæz] vb see **have**

hash [hæʃ] n (CULIN) picadillo; (fig: mess) lío

hashish ['hæʃɪʃ] n hachís m

hasn't ['hæznt] = **has not**

hassle ['hæsl] (inf) n lata

haste [heɪst] n prisa; **~n** ['heɪsn] vt acelerar ♦ vi darse prisa; **hastily** adv de prisa; precipitadamente; **hasty** adj apresurado; (rash) precipitado

hat [hæt] n sombrero

hatch [hætʃ] n (NAUT: also: ~way) escotilla; (also: service ~) ventanilla ♦ vi (bird) salir del cascarón ♦ vt incubar; (plot) tramar; **5 eggs have ~ed** han salido 5 pollos

hatchback ['hætʃbæk] n (AUT) tres or cinco puertas m

hatchet ['hætʃɪt] n hacha

hate [heɪt] vt odiar, aborrecer ♦ n odio; **~ful** adj odioso; **hatred** ['heɪtrɪd] n odio

haughty ['hɔːtɪ] adj altanero

haul [hɔːl] vt tirar ♦ n (of fish) redada; (of stolen goods etc) botín m; **~age** (BRIT) n transporte m; (costs) gastos mpl de transporte; **~ier** (US **~er**) n transportista m/f

haunch [hɔːntʃ] n anca; (of meat) pierna

haunt [hɔːnt] vt (subj: ghost) aparecerse en; (obsess) obsesionar ♦ n guarida

have [hæv] (pt, pp had) aux vb **1** (gen) haber; **to ~ arrived/eaten** haber llegado/comido; **having finished** or **when he had finished, he left** cuando hubo acabado, se fue
2 (in tag questions): **you've done it, ~n't you?** lo has hecho, ¿verdad? or ¿no?
3 (in short answers and questions): **I ~n't** no; **so I ~** pues, es verdad; **we ~n't paid — yes we ~!** no hemos pagado — ¡sí que hemos pagado!; **I've been there before, ~ you?** he estado allí antes, ¿y tú?
♦ modal aux vb (be obliged): **to ~ (got) to do sth** tener que hacer algo; **you ~n't to tell her** no hay que or no debes decírselo
♦ vt **1** (possess): **he has (got) blue eyes/dark hair** tiene los ojos azules/el pelo negro
2 (referring to meals etc): **to ~ breakfast/lunch/dinner** desayunar/comer/cenar; **to ~ a drink/a cigarette** tomar algo/fumar un cigarrillo
3 (receive) recibir; (obtain) obtener; **may I ~ your address?** ¿puedes darme tu dirección?; **you can ~ it for £5** te lo puedes quedar por £5; **I must ~ it by tomorrow** lo necesito para mañana; **to ~ a baby** tener un niño or bebé
4 (maintain, allow): **I won't ~ it/this**

nonsense! ¡no lo permitiré!/¡no permitiré estas tonterías!; **we can't ~ that** no podemos permitir eso
5: **to ~ sth done** hacer or mandar hacer algo; **to ~ one's hair cut** cortarse el pelo; **to ~ sb do sth** hacer que alguien haga algo
6 (experience, suffer): **to ~ a cold/flu** tener un resfriado/la gripe; **she had her bag stolen/her arm broken** le robaron el bolso/se rompió un brazo; **to ~ an operation** operarse
7 (+ noun): **to ~ a swim/walk/bath/rest** nadar/dar un paseo/darse un baño/descansar; **let's ~ a look** vamos a ver; **to ~ a meeting/party** celebrar una reunión/una fiesta; **let me ~ a try** déjame intentarlo
have out vt: **to ~ it out with sb** (settle a problem etc) dejar las cosas en claro con alguien

haven ['heɪvn] n puerto; (fig) refugio

haven't ['hævnt] = **have not**

havoc ['hævək] n estragos mpl

hawk [hɔːk] n halcón m

hay [heɪ] n heno; **~ fever** n fiebre f del heno; **~stack** n almiar m

haywire ['heɪwaɪə*] (inf) adj: **to go ~** (plan) embrollarse

hazard ['hæzəd] n peligro ♦ vt aventurar; **~ous** adj peligroso; **~ warning lights** npl (AUT) señales fpl de emergencia

haze [heɪz] n neblina

hazelnut ['heɪzlnʌt] n avellana

hazy ['heɪzɪ] adj brumoso; (idea) vago

he [hiː] pron él; **~ who ...** él que ..., quien ...

head [hɛd] n cabeza; (leader) jefe/a m/f; (of school) director(a) m/f ♦ vt (list) encabezar; (group) capitanear; (company) dirigir; **~s (or tails)** cara (o cruz); **~ first** de cabeza; **~ over heels** (in love) perdidamente; **to ~ the ball** cabecear (la pelota); **~ for** vt fus dirigirse a; (disaster) ir camino de; **~ache** n dolor m de cabeza; **~dress** n tocado; **~ing** n título; **~lamp** (BRIT) n = **~light**; **~land** n promontorio; **~light** n faro; **~line** n titular m; **~long** adv (fall) de cabeza; (rush) precipitadamente; **~master/mistress** n director(a) m/f (de escuela); **~ office** n oficina central, central f; **~-on** adj (collision) de frente; **~phones** npl auriculares mpl; **~quarters** npl sede f central; (MIL) cuartel n general; **~rest** n reposa-cabezas m inv; **~room** n (in car) altura interior; (under bridge) (límite m de) altura; **~scarf** n pañuelo; **~strong** adj testarudo; **~ waiter** n maître m; **~way** n: **to make ~way** (fig) hacer progresos; **~wind** n viento contrario; **~y** adj (experience, period) apasionante; (wine) cabezón; (atmosphere) embriagador(a)

heal [hiːl] vt curar ♦ vi cicatrizarse

health [hɛlθ] n salud f; **~ food** n alimentos mpl orgánicos; **the H~ Service** (BRIT) n el servicio de salud pública; ≈ el Insalud (SP); **~y** adj sano, saludable

heap [hi:p] n montón m ♦ vt: **to ~ (up)** amontonar; **to ~ sth with** llenar algo hasta arriba de; **~s of** un montón de

hear [hɪə*] (pt, pp **heard**) vt (also LAW) oír; (news) saber ♦ vi oír; **to ~ about** oír hablar de; **to ~ from sb** tener noticias de uno; **~ing** n (sense) oído; (LAW) vista; **~ing aid** n audífono; **~say** n rumores mpl, hablillas fpl

hearse [hɜːs] n coche m fúnebre

heart [hɑːt] n corazón m; (fig) valor m; (of lettuce) cogollo; **~s** npl (CARDS) corazones mpl; **to lose/take ~** descorazonarse/cobrar ánimo; **at ~** en el fondo; **by ~** (learn, know) de memoria; **~ attack** n infarto (de miocardio); **~beat** n latido (del corazón); **~breaking** adj desgarrador(a); **~broken** adj: **she was ~broken about it** esto le partió el corazón; **~burn** n acedía; **~ failure** n fallo cardíaco; **~felt** adj (deeply felt) más sentido

hearth [hɑːθ] n (fireplace) chimenea

hearty ['hɑːtɪ] adj (person) campechano; (laugh) sano; (dislike, support) absoluto

heat [hiːt] n calor m; (SPORT: also: qualifying ~) prueba eliminatoria ♦ vt calentar; **~ up** vi calentarse ♦ vt calentar; **~ed** adj caliente; (fig) acalorado; **~er** n estufa; (in car) calefacción f

heath [hiːθ] (BRIT) n brezal m

heather ['hɛðə*] n brezo

heating ['hiːtɪŋ] n calefacción f

heatstroke ['hiːtstrəʊk] n insolación f

heatwave ['hiːtweɪv] n ola de calor

heave [hiːv] vt (pull) tirar; (push) empujar con esfuerzo; (lift) levantar (con esfuerzo) ♦ vi (chest) palpitar; (retch) tener náuseas ♦ n tirón m; empujón m; **to ~ a sigh** suspirar

heaven ['hɛvn] n cielo; (fig) una maravilla; **~ly** adj celestial; (fig) maravilloso

heavily ['hɛvɪlɪ] adv pesadamente; (drink, smoke) con exceso; (sleep, sigh) profundamente; (depend) mucho

heavy ['hɛvɪ] adj pesado; (work, blow) duro; (sea, rain, meal) fuerte; (drinker, smoker) grande; (responsibility) grave; (schedule) ocupado; (weather) bochornoso; **~ goods vehicle** n vehículo pesado; **~weight** n (SPORT) peso pesado

Hebrew ['hiːbruː] adj, n (LING) hebreo

heckle ['hɛkl] vt interrumpir

hectic ['hɛktɪk] adj agitado

he'd [hiːd] = **he would**; **he had**

hedge [hɛdʒ] n seto ♦ vi contestar con evasivas; **to ~ one's bets** (fig) cubrirse

hedgehog ['hɛdʒhɒg] n erizo

heed [hiːd] vt (also: **take ~ of**) (pay attention to) hacer caso de; **~less** adj: **to be ~less (of)** no hacer caso (de)

heel [hiːl] n talón m; (of shoe) tacón m ♦ vt (shoe) poner tacón a

hefty ['hɛftɪ] adj (person) fornido; (parcel, profit) gordo

heifer ['hɛfə*] n novilla, ternera

height [haɪt] n (of person) estatura; (of building) altura; (high ground) cerro; (altitude) altitud f; (fig: of season): **at the ~ of summer** en los días más calurosos del verano; (: of power etc) cúspide f; (: of stupidity etc) colmo; **~en** vt elevar; (fig) aumentar

heir [ɛə*] n heredero; **~ess** n heredera; **~loom** n reliquia de familia

held [hɛld] pt, pp of **hold**

helicopter ['hɛlɪkɒptə*] n helicóptero

hell [hɛl] n infierno; **~!** (inf) ¡demonios!

he'll [hiːl] = **he will**; **he shall**

hello [hə'ləʊ] excl ¡hola!; (to attract attention) ¡oiga!; (surprise) ¡caramba!

helm [hɛlm] n (NAUT) timón m

helmet ['hɛlmɪt] n casco

help [hɛlp] n ayuda; (cleaner etc) criada, asistenta ♦ vt ayudar; **~!** ¡socorro!; **~ yourself** sírvete; **he can't ~ it** no es culpa suya; **~er** n ayudante m/f; **~ful** adj útil; (person) servicial; (advice) útil; **~ing** n ración f; **~less** adj (incapable) incapaz; (defenceless) indefenso

hem [hɛm] n dobladillo ♦ vt poner or coser el dobladillo; **~ in** vt cercar

hemorrhage ['hɛmərɪdʒ] (US) n = **haemorrhage**

hemorrhoids ['hɛmərɔɪdz] (US) npl = **haemorrhoids**

hen [hɛn] n gallina; (female bird) hembra

hence [hɛns] adv (therefore) por lo tanto; **2 years ~** de aquí a 2 años; **~forth** adv de hoy en adelante

hepatitis [hɛpə'taɪtɪs] n hepatitis f

her [hɜː*] pron (direct) la; (indirect) le; (stressed, after prep) ella ♦ adj su; see also **me**; **my**

herald ['hɛrəld] n heraldo ♦ vt anunciar; **~ry** n heráldica

herb [hɜːb] n hierba

herd [hɜːd] n rebaño

here [hɪə*] adv aquí; (at this point) en este punto; **~!** (present) ¡presente!; **~ is/are** aquí está/están; **~ she is** aquí está; **~after** adv en el futuro; **~by** adv (in letter) por la presente

heritage ['hɛrɪtɪdʒ] n patrimonio

hermit ['hɜːmɪt] n ermitaño/a

hernia ['hɜːnɪə] n hernia

hero ['hɪərəʊ] (pl **~es**) n héroe m; (in book, film) protagonista m

heroin ['hɛrəʊɪn] n heroína

heroine ['hɛrəʊɪn] n heroína; (in book, film) protagonista

heron ['herən] n garza

herring ['herɪŋ] n arenque m

hers [həːz] pron (el) suyo/(la) suya etc; see also **mine**[1]

herself [həːˈself] pron (reflexive) se; (emphatic) ella misma; (after prep) sí (misma); see also **oneself**

he's [hiːz] = he is; he has

hesitant ['hezɪtənt] adj vacilante

hesitate ['hezɪteɪt] vi vacilar; (in speech) titubear; (be unwilling) resistirse a; **hesitation** ['-teɪʃən] n indecisión f; titubeo; dudas fpl

heterosexual [hetərəuˈseksjuəl] adj heterosexual

heyday ['heɪdeɪ] n: **the ~ of** el apogeo de

HGV n abbr = **heavy goods vehicle**

hi [haɪ] excl ¡hola!; (to attract attention) ¡oiga!

hiatus [haɪˈeɪtəs] n vacío

hibernate ['haɪbəneɪt] vi invernar

hiccough ['hɪkʌp] = **hiccup**

hiccup ['hɪkʌp] vi hipar; **~s** npl hipo

hide [haɪd] (pt **hid**, pp **hidden**) n (skin) piel f ♦ vt esconder, ocultar ♦ vi: **to ~ (from sb)** esconderse or ocultarse (de uno); **~-and-seek** n escondite m

hideous ['hɪdɪəs] adj horrible

hiding ['haɪdɪŋ] n (beating) paliza; **to be in ~** (concealed) estar escondido

hierarchy ['haɪərɑːkɪ] n jerarquía

hi-fi ['haɪfaɪ] n estéreo, hifi m ♦ adj de alta fidelidad

high [haɪ] adj alto; (speed, number) grande; (price) elevado; (wind) fuerte; (voice) agudo ♦ adv alto, a gran altura; **it is 20 m ~** tiene 20 m de altura; **~ in the air** en las alturas; **~brow** adj intelectual; **~chair** n silla alta; **~er education** n educación f or enseñanza superior; **~-handed** adj despótico; **~-heeled** adj de tacón alto; **~ jump** n (SPORT) salto de altura; **the H~lands** npl las tierras altas de Escocia; **~light** n (fig: of event) punto culminante; (in hair) reflejo ♦ vt subrayar; **~ly** adv (paid) muy bien; (critical, confidential) sumamente; (a lot): **to speak/think ~ly of** hablar muy bien de/tener en mucho a; **~ly strung** adj hipertenso; **~ness** n altura; **Her** or **His H~ness** Su Alteza; **~-pitched** adj agudo; **~-rise block** n torre f de pisos; **~ school** n ≈ Instituto Nacional de Bachillerato (SP); **~ season** (BRIT) n temporada alta; **~ street** (BRIT) n calle f mayor; **~way** n carretera; (US) carretera nacional; autopista; **H~way Code** (BRIT) n código de la circulación

hijack ['haɪdʒæk] vt secuestrar; **~er** n secuestrador(a) m/f

hike [haɪk] vi (go walking) ir de excursión (a pie) ♦ n caminata; **~r** n excursionista m/f;

hiking n senderismo

hilarious [hɪˈleərɪəs] adj divertidísimo

hill [hɪl] n colina; (high) montaña; (slope) cuesta; **~side** n ladera; **~ walking** n senderismo (de montaña); **~y** adj montañoso

hilt [hɪlt] n (of sword) empuñadura; **to the ~** (fig: support) incondicionalmente

him [hɪm] pron (direct) le, lo; (indirect) le; (stressed, after prep) él; see also **me**; **~self** pron (reflexive) se; (emphatic) él mismo; (after prep) sí (mismo); see also **oneself**

hinder ['hɪndə*] vt estorbar, impedir; **hindrance** ['hɪndrəns] n estorbo

hindsight ['haɪndsaɪt] n: **with ~** en retrospectiva

Hindu ['hɪnduː] n hindú m/f

hinge [hɪndʒ] n bisagra, gozne m ♦ vi (fig): **to ~ on** depender de

hint [hɪnt] n indirecta; (advice) consejo; (sign) dejo ♦ vt: **to ~ that** insinuar que ♦ vi: **to ~ at** hacer alusión a

hip [hɪp] n cadera

hippopotamus [hɪpəˈpɔtəməs] n (pl **~es** or **hippopotami**) n hipopótamo

hire ['haɪə*] vt (BRIT: car, equipment) alquilar; (worker) contratar ♦ n alquiler m; **for ~** se alquila; (taxi) libre; **~(d) car** (BRIT) n coche m de alquiler; **~ purchase** (BRIT) n compra a plazos

his [hɪz] pron (el) suyo/(la) suya etc ♦ adj su; see also **mine**[1]; **my**

Hispanic [hɪsˈpænɪk] adj hispánico

hiss [hɪs] vi silbar

historian [hɪˈstɔːrɪən] n historiador(a) m/f

historic(al) [hɪˈstɔrɪk(l)] adj histórico

history ['hɪstərɪ] n historia

hit [hɪt] (pt, pp **hit**) vt (strike) golpear, pegar; (reach: target) alcanzar; (collide with: car) chocar contra; (fig: affect) afectar ♦ n golpe m; (success) éxito; **to ~ it off with sb** llevarse bien con uno; **~-and-run driver** n conductor(a) que atropella y huye

hitch [hɪtʃ] vt (fasten) atar, amarrar; (also: ~ up) remangar ♦ n (difficulty) dificultad f; **to ~ a lift** hacer autostop

hitch-hike vi hacer autostop; **~hiking** n autostop m

hi-tech [haɪˈtek] adj de alta tecnología

hitherto ['hɪðəˈtuː] adv hasta ahora

HIV n abbr (= human immunodeficiency virus) VIH m; **~-negative/positive** adj VIH negativo/positivo

hive [haɪv] n colmena

HMS abbr = **His (Her) Majesty's Ship**

hoard [hɔːd] n (treasure) tesoro; (stockpile) provisión f ♦ vt acumular; (goods in short supply) acaparar; **~ing** n (for posters) cartelera

hoarse [hɔːs] adj ronco

hoax [həʊks] n trampa
hob [hɔb] n quemador m
hobble ['hɔbl] vi cojear
hobby ['hɔbɪ] n pasatiempo, afición f
hobo ['həʊbəʊ] (US) n vagabundo
hockey ['hɔkɪ] n hockey m
hog [hɔg] n cerdo, puerco ♦ vt (fig) acaparar;
to go the whole ~ poner toda la carne en el
asador
hoist [hɔɪst] n (crane) grúa ♦ vt levantar,
alzar; (flag, sail) izar
hold [həʊld] (pt, pp held) vt sostener;
(contain) contener; (have: power,
qualification) tener; (keep back) retener; (keep
in position): **to ~ one's head up** mantener la
cabeza alta; (meeting) celebrar ♦ vi
(withstand pressure) resistir; (be valid) valer
♦ n (grasp) asimiento; (fig) dominio; **~ the
line!** (TEL) ¡no cuelgue!; **to ~ one's own** (fig)
defenderse; **to catch or get (a) ~ of** agarrarse
or asirse de; **~ back** vt retener; (secret)
ocultar; **~ down** vt (person) sujetar; (job)
mantener; **~ off** vt (enemy) rechazar; **~ on** vi
agarrarse bien; (wait) esperar; **~ on!** (TEL)
¡(espere) un momento!; **~ on to** vt fus
agarrarse a; (keep) guardar; **~ out** vt ofrecer
♦ vi (resist) resistir; **~ up** vt (raise) levantar;
(support) apoyar; (delay) retrasar; (rob)
asaltar; **~all** (BRIT) n bolsa; **~er** n (container)
receptáculo; (of ticket, record) poseedor(a)
m/f; (of office, title etc) titular m/f; **~ing** n
(share) interés m; (farmland) parcela; **~up** n
(robbery) atraco; (delay) retraso; (BRIT: in
traffic) embotellamiento
hole [həʊl] n agujero
holiday ['hɔlɪdɪ] n vacaciones fpl; (public ~)
(día m de) fiesta, día m feriado; **on ~** de
vacaciones; **~ camp** (BRIT: also: ~ centre)
centro de vacaciones; **~-maker** (BRIT) n
turista m/f; **~ resort** n centro turístico
holiness ['həʊlɪnɪs] n santidad f
Holland ['hɔlənd] n Holanda
hollow ['hɔləʊ] adj hueco, (claim) vacío;
(eyes) hundido; (sound) sordo ♦ n hueco;
(in ground) hoyo ♦ vt: **to ~ out** excavar
holly ['hɔlɪ] n acebo
holocaust ['hɔləkɔːst] n holocausto
holy ['həʊlɪ] adj santo, sagrado; (water)
bendito
homage ['hɔmɪdʒ] n homenaje m
home [həʊm] n casa; (country) patria;
(institution) asilo ♦ cpd (domestic) casero, de
casa; (ECON, POL) nacional ♦ adv (direction) a
casa; (right in: nail etc) a fondo; **at ~** en casa;
(in country) en el país; (fig) como pez en el
agua; **to go/come ~** ir/volver a casa; **make
yourself at ~** ¡estás en tu casa!; **~ address** n
domicilio; **~land** n tierra natal; **~less** adj sin

hogar, sin casa; **~ly** adj (simple) sencillo; **~-
made** adj casero; **H~ Office** (BRIT) n
Ministerio del Interior; **~ page** n página de
inicio; **~ rule** n autonomía; **H~ Secretary**
(BRIT) n Ministro del Interior; **~sick** adj: **to be
~sick** tener morriña, sentir nostalgia; **~ town**
n ciudad f natal; **~ward** ['həʊmwəd] adj
(journey) hacia casa; **~work** n deberes mpl
homoeopathic [həʊmɪə'pæθɪk] (US homeo-
pathic) adj homeopático
homosexual [hɔməʊ'seksjuəl] adj, n
homosexual m/f
Honduran [hɔn'djuərən] adj, n hondureño/a
m/f
Honduras [hɔn'djuərəs] n Honduras f
honest ['ɔnɪst] adj honrado; (sincere) franco,
sincero; **~ly** adv honradamente,
francamente; **~y** n honradez f
honey ['hʌnɪ] n miel f; **~comb** n panal m;
~moon n luna de miel; **~suckle** n
madreselva
honk [hɔŋk] vi (AUT) tocar el pito, pitar
honorary ['ɔnərərɪ] adj (member, president)
de honor; (title) honorífico; **~ degree** n
doctorado honoris causa
honour ['ɔnə*] (US honor) vt honrar;
(commitment, promise) cumplir con ♦ n honor
m, honra; **~able** adj honorable; **~s degree**
n (SCOL) título de licenciado con calificación
alta
hood [hud] n capucha; (BRIT: AUT) capota;
(US: AUT) capó m; (of cooker) campana de
humos
hoof [huːf] (pl hooves) n pezuña
hook [huk] n gancho; (on dress) corchete m,
broche m; (for fishing) anzuelo ♦ vt
enganchar; (fish) pescar
hooligan ['huːlɪgən] n gamberro
hoop [huːp] n aro
hooray [huː'reɪ] excl = hurray
hoot [huːt] (BRIT) vi (AUT) tocar el pito, pitar;
(siren) sonar la sirena; (owl) ulular; **~er** (BRIT)
n (AUT) pito, claxon m; (NAUT) sirena
Hoover ® ['huːvə*] (BRIT) n aspiradora ♦ vt:
h~ pasar la aspiradora por
hooves [huːvz] npl of hoof
hop [hɔp] vi saltar, brincar; (on one foot) saltar
con un pie
hope [həʊp] vt, vi esperar ♦ n esperanza; **I
~ so/not** espero que sí/no; **~ful** adj (person)
optimista; (situation) prometedor(a); **~fully**
adv con esperanza; (one hopes): **~fully he will
recover** esperamos que se recupere; **~less**
adj desesperado; (person): **to be ~less** ser un
desastre
hops [hɔps] npl lúpulo
horizon [hə'raɪzn] n horizonte m; **~tal**
[hɔrɪ'zɔntl] adj horizontal
hormone ['hɔːməʊn] n hormona

horn [hɔːn] n cuerno; (MUS: also: French ~)
trompa; (AUT) pito, claxon m
hornet ['hɔːnɪt] n avispón m
horoscope ['hɔrəskəup] n horóscopo
horrible ['hɔrɪbl] adj horrible
horrid ['hɔrɪd] adj horrible, horroroso
horrify ['hɔrɪfaɪ] vt horrorizar
horror ['hɔrə*] n horror m; ~ **film** n película
de horror
hors d'œuvre [ɔː'dəːvrə] n entremeses mpl
horse [hɔːs] n caballo; ~**back** n: on ~**back** a
caballo; ~-**chestnut** n (tree) castaño de
Indias; (nut) castaña de Indias; ~**man/
woman** (irreg) n jinete a m/f; ~**power** n
caballo de (fuerza); ~-**racing** n carreras fpl
de caballos; ~**radish** n rábano picante;
~**shoe** n herradura
hose [həuz] n (also: ~pipe) manguera
hospitable [hɔs'pɪtəbl] adj hospitalario
hospital ['hɔspɪtl] n hospital m
hospitality [hɔspɪ'tælɪtɪ] n hospitalidad f
host [həust] n anfitrión m; (TV, RADIO)
presentador m; (REL) hostia; (large number):
a ~ of multitud de
hostage ['hɔstɪdʒ] n rehén m
hostel ['hɔstl] n hostal m; (youth) ~ albergue
m juvenil
hostess ['həustɪs] n anfitriona; (BRIT: air ~)
azafata; (TV, RADIO) presentadora
hostile ['hɔstaɪl] adj hostil
hot [hɔt] adj caliente; (weather) caluroso, de
calor; (as opposed to warm) muy caliente;
(spicy) picante; **to be ~** (person) tener calor;
(object) estar caliente; (weather) hacer calor;
~**bed** n (fig) semillero; ~ **dog** n perro
caliente
hotel [həu'tel] n hotel m
hot: ~**house** n invernadero; ~ **line** n (POL)
teléfono rojo; ~**ly** adv con pasión,
apasionadamente; ~-**water bottle** n bolsa
de agua caliente
hound [haund] vt acosar ♦ n perro (de caza)
hour ['auə*] n hora; ~**ly** adj (de) cada hora
house [n haus, pl 'hauzɪz, vb hauz] n (gen,
firm) casa; (POL) cámara; (THEATRE) sala ♦ vt
(person) alojar; (collection) albergar; **on the ~**
(fig) la casa invita; ~ **arrest** n arresto
domiciliario; ~**boat** n casa flotante; ~**bound**
adj confinado en casa; ~**breaking** n
allanamiento de morada; ~**hold** n familia;
(home) casa; ~**keeper** n ama de llaves;
~**keeping** n (work) trabajos mpl domésticos;
~**keeping** (money) n dinero para gastos
domésticos; ~-**warming party** n fiesta de
estreno de una casa; ~**wife** (irreg) n ama de
casa; ~**work** n faenas fpl (de la casa)
housing ['hauzɪŋ] n (act) alojamiento;
(houses) viviendas fpl; ~ **development** n
urbanización f; ~ **estate** (BRIT) n =

~ development
hovel ['hɔvl] n casucha
hover ['hɔvə*] vi flotar (en el aire); ~**craft** n
aerodeslizador m
how [hau] adv (in what way) cómo; ~ **are
you?** ¿cómo estás?; ~ **much milk/many
people?** ¿cuánta leche/gente?; ~ **much does it
cost?** ¿cuánto cuesta?; ~ **long have you been
here?** ¿cuánto hace que estás aquí?; ~ **old are
you?** ¿cuántos años tienes?; ~ **tall is he?**
¿cómo es de alto?; ~ **is school?** ¿cómo (te)
va (en) la escuela?; ~ **was the film?** ¿qué tal
la película?; ~ **lovely/awful!** ¡qué bonito/
horror!
however [hau'evə*] adv: ~ **I do it** lo haga
como lo haga; ~ **cold it is** por mucho frío que
haga; ~ **fast he runs** por muy rápido que
corra; ~ **did you do it?** ¿cómo lo hiciste?
♦ conj sin embargo, no obstante
howl [haul] n aullido ♦ vi aullar; (person) dar
alaridos; (wind) ulular
H.P. n abbr = hire purchase
h.p. abbr = horse power
HQ n abbr = headquarters
hub [hʌb] n (of wheel) cubo; (fig) centro
hubcap ['hʌbkæp] n tapacubos m inv
huddle ['hʌdl] vi: **to ~ together** acurrucarse
hue [hju:] n color m, matiz m
huff [hʌf] n: **in a ~** enojado
hug [hʌg] vt abrazar; (thing) apretar con los
brazos
huge [hju:dʒ] adj enorme
hull [hʌl] n (of ship) casco
hullo [hə'ləu] excl = hello
hum [hʌm] vt tararear, canturrear ♦ vi
tararear, canturrear; (insect) zumbar
human ['hju:mən] adj, n humano; ~**e**
[hju:'meɪn] adj humano, humanitario;
~**itarian** [hju:mænɪ'teərɪən] adj humanitario;
~**ity** [hju:'mænɪtɪ] n humanidad f
humble ['hʌmbl] adj humilde
humdrum ['hʌmdrʌm] adj (boring)
monótono, aburrido
humid ['hju:mɪd] adj húmedo
humiliate [hju:'mɪlɪeɪt] vt humillar
humorous ['hju:mərəs] adj gracioso,
divertido
humour ['hju:mə*] (US **humor**) n humorismo,
sentido del humor; (mood) humor m ♦ vt
(person) complacer
hump [hʌmp] n (in ground) montículo;
(camel's) giba
hunch [hʌntʃ] n (premonition) presentimiento; ~**back** n joroba m/f; ~**ed** adj jo-
robado
hundred ['hʌndrəd] num ciento; (before n)
cien; ~**s of** centenares de; ~**weight** n (BRIT)
= 50.8 kg; 112 lb; (US) = 45.3 kg; 100 lb
hung [hʌŋ] pt, pp of hang

Hungarian [hʌŋˈgeərɪən] adj, n húngaro/a m/f

Hungary [ˈhʌŋgərɪ] n Hungría

hunger [ˈhʌŋgə*] n hambre f ♦ vi: **to ~ for** (fig) tener hambre de, anhelar; **~ strike** n huelga de hambre

hungry [ˈhʌŋgrɪ] adj: **~ (for)** hambriento (de); **to be ~** tener hambre

hunk [hʌŋk] n (of bread etc) trozo, pedazo

hunt [hʌnt] vt (seek) buscar; (SPORT) cazar ♦ vi (search): **to ~ (for)** buscar; (SPORT) cazar ♦ n búsqueda; caza, cacería; **~er** n cazador(a) m/f; **~ing** n caza

hurdle [ˈhəːdl] n (SPORT) valla; (fig) obstáculo

hurl [həːl] vt lanzar, arrojar

hurrah [huˈrɑː] excl = **hurray**

hurray [huˈreɪ] excl ¡viva!

hurricane [ˈhʌrɪkən] n huracán m

hurried [ˈhʌrɪd] adj (rushed) hecho de prisa; **~ly** adv con prisa, apresuradamente

hurry [ˈhʌrɪ] n prisa ♦ vi (also: ~ up) apresurarse, darse prisa ♦ vt (also: ~ up: person) dar prisa a; (: work) apresurar, hacer de prisa; **to be in a ~** tener prisa

hurt [həːt] (pt, pp hurt) vt hacer daño a ♦ vi doler ♦ adj lastimado; **~ful** adj (remark etc) hiriente

hurtle [ˈhəːtl] vi: **to ~ past** pasar como un rayo; **to ~ down** ir a toda velocidad

husband [ˈhʌzbənd] n marido

hush [hʌʃ] n silencio ♦ vt hacer callar; **~!** ¡chitón!, ¡cállate!; **~ up** vt encubrir

husk [hʌsk] n (of wheat) cáscara

husky [ˈhʌskɪ] adj ronco ♦ n perro esquimal

hustle [ˈhʌsl] vt (hurry) dar prisa a ♦ n: **~ and bustle** ajetreo

hut [hʌt] n cabaña; (shed) cobertizo

hutch [hʌtʃ] n conejera

hyacinth [ˈhaɪəsɪnθ] n jacinto

hydrant [ˈhaɪdrənt] n (also: fire ~) boca de incendios

hydraulic [haɪˈdrɔːlɪk] adj hidráulico

hydroelectric [haɪdrəʊˈlektrɪk] adj hidroeléctrico

hydrofoil [ˈhaɪdrəfɔɪl] n aerodeslizador m

hydrogen [ˈhaɪdrədʒən] n hidrógeno

hygiene [ˈhaɪdʒiːn] n higiene f; **hygienic** [-ˈdʒiːnɪk] adj higiénico

hymn [hɪm] n himno

hype [haɪp] (inf) n bombardeo publicitario

hypermarket [ˈhaɪpəmɑːkɪt] n hipermercado

hyphen [ˈhaɪfn] n guión m

hypnotize [ˈhɪpnətaɪz] vt hipnotizar

hypocrisy [hɪˈpɔkrɪsɪ] n hipocresía; **hypocrite** [ˈhɪpəkrɪt] n hipócrita m/f; **hypocritical** [hɪpəˈkrɪtɪkl] adj hipócrita

hypothesis [haɪˈpɔθɪsɪs] (pl hypotheses) n hipótesis f inv

hysteria [hɪˈstɪərɪə] n histeria; **hysterical** [-ˈsterɪkl] adj histérico; (funny) para morirse de risa; **hysterics** [-ˈsterɪks] npl histeria; **to be in hysterics** (fig) morirse de risa

I, i

I [aɪ] pron yo

ice [aɪs] n hielo; (~ cream) helado ♦ vt (cake) alcorzar ♦ vi (also: ~ over, ~ up) helarse; **~berg** n iceberg m; **~box** n (BRIT) congelador m; (US) nevera (SP), refrigeradora (AM); **~ cream** n helado; **~ cube** n cubito de hielo; **~d** adj (cake) escarchado; (drink) helado; **~ hockey** n hockey m sobre hielo

Iceland [ˈaɪslənd] n Islandia

ice: ~ lolly (BRIT) n polo; **~ rink** n pista de hielo; **~ skating** n patinaje m sobre hielo

icicle [ˈaɪsɪkl] n carámbano

icing [ˈaɪsɪŋ] n (CULIN) alcorza; **~ sugar** (BRIT) n azúcar m glas(eado)

icy [ˈaɪsɪ] adj helado

I'd [aɪd] = **I would; I had**

idea [aɪˈdɪə] n idea

ideal [aɪˈdɪəl] n ideal m ♦ adj ideal

identical [aɪˈdentɪkl] adj idéntico

identification [aɪdentɪfɪˈkeɪʃən] n identificación f; **(means of) ~** documentos mpl personales

identify [aɪˈdentɪfaɪ] vt identificar

Identikit ® [aɪˈdentɪkɪt] n: **~ (picture)** retrato-robot m

identity [aɪˈdentɪtɪ] n identidad f; **~ card** n carnet m de identidad

ideology [aɪdɪˈɔlədʒɪ] n ideología

idiom [ˈɪdɪəm] n modismo; (style of speaking) lenguaje m

idiosyncrasy [ɪdɪəʊˈsɪŋkrəsɪ] n idiosincrasia

idiot [ˈɪdɪət] n idiota m/f; **~ic** [-ˈɔtɪk] adj tonto

idle [ˈaɪdl] adj (inactive) ocioso; (lazy) holgazán/ana; (unemployed) parado, desocupado; (machinery etc) parado; (talk etc) frívolo ♦ vi (machine) marchar en vacío

idol [ˈaɪdl] n ídolo; **~ize** vt idolatrar

i.e. abbr (= that is) esto es

if [ɪf] conj si; **~ necessary** si fuera necesario, si hiciese falta; **~ I were you** yo en tu lugar; **~ so/not** de ser así/si no; **~ only I could!** ¡ojalá pudiera!; see also **as; even**

igloo [ˈɪgluː] n iglú m

ignite [ɪgˈnaɪt] vt (set fire to) encender ♦ vi encenderse

ignition [ɪgˈnɪʃən] n (AUT: process) ignición f; (: mechanism) encendido; **to switch on/off the ~** arrancar/apagar el motor; **~ key** n (AUT) llave f de contacto

ignorant [ˈɪgnərənt] adj ignorante; **to be ~ of** ignorar

ignore [ɪgˈnɔ:ʳ] vt (person, advice) no hacer caso de; (fact) pasar por alto

I'll [aɪl] = I will; I shall

ill [ɪl] adj enfermo, malo ♦ n mal m ♦ adv mal; **to be taken ~** ponerse enfermo; **~-advised** adj (decision) imprudente; **~-at-ease** adj incómodo

illegal [ɪˈli:gl] adj ilegal

illegible [ɪˈledʒɪbl] adj ilegible

illegitimate [ɪlɪˈdʒɪtɪmət] adj ilegítimo

ill-fated adj malogrado

ill feeling n rencor m

illicit [ɪˈlɪsɪt] adj ilícito

illiterate [ɪˈlɪtərət] adj analfabeto

ill: ~-mannered adj mal educado; **~ness** n enfermedad f; **~-treat** vt maltratar

illuminate [ɪˈlu:mɪneɪt] vt (room, street) iluminar, alumbrar; **illumination** [-ˈneɪʃən] n alumbrado; **illuminations** npl (decorative lights) iluminaciones fpl, luces fpl

illusion [ɪˈlu:ʒən] n ilusión f; (trick) truco

illustrate [ˈɪləstreɪt] vt ilustrar

illustration [ɪləˈstreɪʃən] n (act of illustrating) ilustración f; (example) ejemplo, ilustración f; (in book) lámina

illustrious [ɪˈlʌstrɪəs] adj ilustre

I'm [aɪm] = I am

image [ˈɪmɪdʒ] n imagen f; **~ry** [-ərɪ] n imágenes fpl

imaginary [ɪˈmædʒɪnərɪ] adj imaginario

imagination [ɪmædʒɪˈneɪʃən] n imaginación f; (inventiveness) inventiva

imaginative [ɪˈmædʒɪnətɪv] adj imaginativo

imagine [ɪˈmædʒɪn] vt imaginarse

imbalance [ɪmˈbæləns] n desequilibrio

imitate [ˈɪmɪteɪt] vt imitar; **imitation** [ɪmɪˈteɪʃən] n imitación f; (copy) copia

immaculate [ɪˈmækjulət] adj inmaculado

immaterial [ɪməˈtɪərɪəl] adj (unimportant) sin importancia

immature [ɪməˈtjuəʳ] adj (person) inmaduro

immediate [ɪˈmi:dɪət] adj inmediato; (pressing) urgente, apremiante; (nearest: family) próximo; (: neighbourhood) inmediato; **~ly** adv (at once) en seguida; (directly) inmediatamente; **~ly next to** muy junto a

immense [ɪˈmɛns] adj inmenso, enorme; (importance) enorme

immerse [ɪˈmɜ:s] vt (submerge) sumergir; **to be ~d in** (fig) estar absorto en

immersion heater [ɪˈmɜ:ʃən-] (BRIT) n calentador m de inmersión

immigrant [ˈɪmɪgrənt] n inmigrante m/f; **immigration** [ɪmɪˈgreɪʃən] n inmigración f

imminent [ˈɪmɪnənt] adj inminente

immobile [ɪˈməubaɪl] adj inmóvil

immoral [ɪˈmɔrl] adj inmoral

immortal [ɪˈmɔːtl] adj inmortal

immune [ɪˈmju:n] adj: **~ (to)** inmune (a); **immunity** n (MED, of diplomat) inmunidad f

immunize [ˈɪmjunaɪz] vt inmunizar

impact [ˈɪmpækt] n impacto

impair [ɪmˈpɛəʳ] vt perjudicar

impart [ɪmˈpɑ:t] vt comunicar; (flavour) proporcionar

impartial [ɪmˈpɑ:ʃl] adj imparcial

impassable [ɪmˈpɑ:səbl] adj (barrier) infranqueable; (river, road) intransitable

impassive [ɪmˈpæsɪv] adj impasible

impatience [ɪmˈpeɪʃəns] n impaciencia

impatient [ɪmˈpeɪʃənt] adj impaciente; **to get or grow ~** impacientarse

impeccable [ɪmˈpɛkəbl] adj impecable

impede [ɪmˈpi:d] vt estorbar

impediment [ɪmˈpɛdɪmənt] n obstáculo, estorbo; (also: speech ~) defecto (del habla)

impending [ɪmˈpɛndɪŋ] adj inminente

imperative [ɪmˈpɛrətɪv] adj (tone) imperioso; (need) imprescindible

imperfect [ɪmˈpə:fɪkt] adj (goods etc) defectuoso ♦ n (LING: also: ~ tense) imperfecto

imperial [ɪmˈpɪərɪəl] adj imperial

impersonal [ɪmˈpə:sənl] adj impersonal

impersonate [ɪmˈpə:səneɪt] vt hacerse pasar por; (THEATRE) imitar

impertinent [ɪmˈpə:tɪnənt] adj impertinente, insolente

impervious [ɪmˈpə:vɪəs] adj impermeable; (fig): **~ to** insensible a

impetuous [ɪmˈpɛtjuəs] adj impetuoso

impetus [ˈɪmpətəs] n ímpetu m; (fig) impulso

impinge [ɪmˈpɪndʒ]: **to ~ on** vt fus (affect) afectar a

implement [n ˈɪmplɪmənt, vb ˈɪmplɪment] n herramienta; (for cooking) utensilio ♦ vt (regulation) hacer efectivo; (plan) realizar

implicit [ɪmˈplɪsɪt] adj implícito; (belief, trust) absoluto

imply [ɪmˈplaɪ] vt (involve) suponer; (hint) dar a entender que

impolite [ɪmpəˈlaɪt] adj mal educado

import [vb ɪmˈpɔ:t, n ˈɪmpɔ:t] vt importar ♦ n (COMM) importación f; (: article) producto importado; (meaning) significado, sentido

importance [ɪmˈpɔ:təns] n importancia

important [ɪmˈpɔ:tənt] adj importante; **it's not ~** no importa, no tiene importancia

importer [ɪmˈpɔ:təʳ] n importador(a) m/f

impose [ɪmˈpəuz] vt imponer ♦ vi: **to ~ on sb** abusar de uno; **imposing** adj imponente, impresionante

imposition [ɪmpəˈzɪʃn] n (of tax etc) imposición f; **to be an ~ on** (person) molestar a

impossible [ɪmˈpɔsɪbl] adj imposible; (person) insoportable

impotent ['ɪmpətənt] adj impotente

impound [ɪm'paund] vt embargar

impoverished [ɪm'pɔvərɪʃt] adj necesitado

impractical [ɪm'præktɪkl] adj (person, plan) poco práctico

imprecise [ɪmprɪ'saɪs] adj impreciso

impregnable [ɪm'pregnəbl] adj (castle) inexpugnable

impress [ɪm'pres] vt impresionar; (mark) estampar; **to ~ sth on sb** hacer entender algo a uno

impression [ɪm'preʃən] n impresión f; (imitation) imitación f; **to be under the ~ that** tener la impresión de que; **~ist** n impresionista m/f

impressive [ɪm'presɪv] adj impresionante

imprint ['ɪmprɪnt] n (outline) huella; (PUBLISHING) pie m de imprenta

imprison [ɪm'prɪzn] vt encarcelar; **~ment** n encarcelamiento; (term of ~ment) cárcel f

improbable [ɪm'prɔbəbl] adj improbable, inverosímil

improper [ɪm'prɔpə*] adj (unsuitable: conduct etc) incorrecto; (: activities) deshonesto

improve [ɪm'pru:v] vt mejorar; (foreign language) perfeccionar ♦ vi mejorarse; **~ment** n mejoramiento; perfección f; progreso

improvise ['ɪmprəvaɪz] vt, vi improvisar

impulse ['ɪmpʌls] n impulso; **to act on ~** obrar sin reflexión; **impulsive** [-'pʌlsɪv] adj irreflexivo

impure [ɪm'pjuə*] adj (adulterated) adulterado; (morally) impuro; **impurity** n impureza

KEYWORD

in [ɪn] prep 1 (indicating place, position, with place names) en; **~ the house/garden** en (la) casa/el jardín; **~ here/there** aquí/ahí or allí dentro; **~ London/England** en Londres/Inglaterra

2 (indicating time) en; **~ spring** en (la) primavera; **~ the afternoon** por la tarde; **at 4 o'clock ~ the afternoon** a las 4 de la tarde; **I did it ~ 3 hours/days** lo hice en 3 horas/días; **I'll see you ~ 2 weeks** or **~ 2 weeks' time** te veré dentro de 2 semanas

3 (indicating manner etc) en; **~ a loud/soft voice** en voz alta/baja; **~ pencil/ink** a lápiz/bolígrafo; **the boy ~ the blue shirt** el chico de la camisa azul

4 (indicating circumstances): **~ the sun/shade/rain** al sol/a la sombra/bajo la lluvia; **a change ~ policy** un cambio de política

5 (indicating mood, state): **~ tears** en lágrimas, llorando; **~ anger/despair** enfadado/desesperado; **to live ~ luxury** vivir lujosamente

6 (with ratios, numbers): **1 ~ 10 households, 1 household ~ 10** una de cada 10 familias; **20 pence ~ the pound** 20 peniques por libra; **they lined up ~ twos** se alinearon de dos en dos

7 (referring to people, works) en; entre; **the disease is common ~ children** la enfermedad es común entre los niños; **~ (the works of) Dickens** en (las obras de) Dickens

8 (indicating profession etc): **to be ~ teaching** estar en la enseñanza

9 (after superlative) de; **the best pupil ~ the class** el/la mejor alumno/a de la clase

10 (with present participle): **~ saying this** al decir esto

♦ adv: **to be ~** (person: at home) estar en casa; (work) estar; (train, ship, plane) haber llegado; (in fashion) estar de moda; **she'll be ~ later today** llegará más tarde hoy; **to ask sb ~** hacer pasar a uno; **to run/limp etc ~** entrar corriendo/cojeando etc

♦ n: **the ~s and outs** (of proposal, situation etc) los detalles

in. abbr = inch

inability [ɪnə'bɪlɪtɪ] n: **~ (to do)** incapacidad f (de hacer)

inaccurate [ɪn'ækjurət] adj inexacto, incorrecto

inadequate [ɪn'ædɪkwət] adj (income, reply etc) insuficiente; (person) incapaz

inadvertently [ɪnəd'və:tntlɪ] adv por descuido

inadvisable [ɪnəd'vaɪzəbl] adj poco aconsejable

inane [ɪ'neɪn] adj necio, fatuo

inanimate [ɪn'ænɪmət] adj inanimado

inappropriate [ɪnə'prəuprɪət] adj inadecuado; (improper) poco oportuno

inarticulate [ɪnɑ:'tɪkjulət] adj (person) incapaz de expresarse; (speech) mal pronunciado

inasmuch as [ɪnəz'mʌtʃ-] conj puesto que, ya que

inauguration [ɪnɔ:gju'reɪʃən] n ceremonia de apertura

inborn [ɪn'bɔ:n] adj (quality) innato

inbred [ɪn'bred] adj innato; (family) engendrado por endogamia

Inc. abbr (US: = incorporated) S.A.

incapable [ɪn'keɪpəbl] adj incapaz

incapacitate [ɪnkə'pæsɪteɪt] vt: **to ~ sb** incapacitar a uno

incense [n 'ɪnsens, vb ɪn'sens] n incienso ♦ vt (anger) indignar, encolerizar

incentive [ɪn'sentɪv] n incentivo, estímulo

incessant [ɪn'sesnt] adj incesante, continuo; **~ly** adv constantemente

incest ['ɪnsɛst] *n* incesto
inch [ɪntʃ] *n* pulgada; **to be within an ~ of** estar a dos dedos de; **he didn't give an ~** no dio concesión alguna
incident ['ɪnsɪdnt] *n* incidente *m*
incidental [ɪnsɪ'dɛntl] *adj* accesorio; **~ to** relacionado con; **~ly** [-'dɛntəlɪ] *adv* (*by the way*) a propósito
incite [ɪn'saɪt] *vt* provocar
inclination [ɪnklɪ'neɪʃən] *n* (*tendency*) tendencia, inclinación *f*; (*desire*) deseo; (*disposition*) propensión *f*
incline [*n* 'ɪnklaɪn, *vb* ɪn'klaɪn] *n* pendiente *m*, cuesta ♦ *vt* (*head*) poner de lado ♦ *vi* inclinarse; **to be ~d to** (*tend*) ser propenso a
include [ɪn'kluːd] *vt* (*incorporate*) incluir; (*in letter*) adjuntar; **including** *prep* incluso, inclusive
inclusion [ɪn'kluːʒən] *n* inclusión *f*
inclusive [ɪn'kluːsɪv] *adj* inclusivo; **~ of tax** incluidos los impuestos
income ['ɪnkʌm] *n* (*earned*) ingresos *mpl*; (*from property etc*) renta; (*from investment etc*) rédito; **~ tax** *n* impuesto sobre la renta
incoming ['ɪnkʌmɪŋ] *adj* (*flight, government etc*) entrante
incomparable [ɪn'kɔmpərəbl] *adj* incomparable, sin par
incompatible [ɪnkəm'pætɪbl] *adj* incompatible
incompetent [ɪn'kɔmpɪtənt] *adj* incompetente
incomplete [ɪnkəm'pliːt] *adj* (*partial: achievement etc*) incompleto; (*unfinished: painting etc*) inacabado
incongruous [ɪn'kɔŋgruəs] *adj* (*strange*) discordante; (*inappropriate*) incongruente
inconsiderate [ɪnkən'sɪdərət] *adj* desconsiderado
inconsistent [ɪnkən'sɪstənt] *adj* inconsecuente; (*contradictory*) incongruente; **~ with** (que) no concuerda con
inconspicuous [ɪnkən'spɪkjuəs] *adj* (*colour, building etc*) discreto; (*person*) que llama poco la atención
inconvenience [ɪnkən'viːnjəns] *n* inconvenientes *mpl*; (*trouble*) molestia, incomodidad *f* ♦ *vt* incomodar
inconvenient [ɪnkən'viːnjənt] *adj* incómodo, poco práctico; (*time, place, visitor*) inoportuno
incorporate [ɪn'kɔːpəreɪt] *vt* incorporar; (*contain*) comprender; (*add*) agregar; **~d** *adj*: **~d company** (*US*) ≈ sociedad *f* anónima
incorrect [ɪnkə'rɛkt] *adj* incorrecto
increase [*n* 'ɪnkriːs, *vb* ɪn'kriːs] *n* aumento ♦ *vi* aumentar; (*grow*) crecer; (*price*) subir ♦ *vt* aumentar; (*price*) subir; **increasing** *adj* creciente; **increasingly** *adv* cada vez más,

más y más
incredible [ɪn'krɛdɪbl] *adj* increíble
incubator ['ɪnkjubeɪtə*] *n* incubadora
incumbent [ɪn'kʌmbənt] *adj*: **it is ~ on him to ...** le incumbe ...
incur [ɪn'kəː*] *vt* (*expenditure*) incurrir; (*loss*) sufrir; (*anger, disapproval*) provocar
indebted [ɪn'dɛtɪd] *adj*: **to be ~ to sb** estar agradecido a uno
indecent [ɪn'diːsnt] *adj* indecente; **~ assault** (*BRIT*) *n* atentado contra el pudor; **~ exposure** *n* exhibicionismo
indecisive [ɪndɪ'saɪsɪv] *adj* indeciso
indeed [ɪn'diːd] *adv* efectivamente, en realidad; (*in fact*) en efecto; (*furthermore*) es más; **yes ~!** ¡claro que sí!
indefinitely [ɪn'dɛfɪnɪtlɪ] *adv* (*wait*) indefinidamente
indemnity [ɪn'dɛmnɪtɪ] *n* (*insurance*) indemnidad *f*; (*compensation*) indemnización *f*
independence [ɪndɪ'pɛndns] *n* independencia
independent [ɪndɪ'pɛndənt] *adj* independiente
index ['ɪndɛks] (*pl* **~es**) *n* (*in book*) índice *m*; (: *in library etc*) catálogo; (*pl* **indices**: *ratio, sign*) exponente *m*; **~ card** *n* ficha; **~ed** (*US*) *adj* = **~-linked**; **~ finger** *n* índice *m*; **~-linked** (*BRIT*) *adj* vinculado al índice del coste de la vida
India ['ɪndɪə] *n* la India; **~n** *adj, n* indio/a *m/f*; **Red ~n** piel roja *m/f*; **~n Ocean** *n*: **the ~n Ocean** el Océano Índico
indicate ['ɪndɪkeɪt] *vt* indicar; **indication** [-'keɪʃən] *n* indicio, señal *f*; **indicative** [ɪn'dɪkətɪv] *adj*: **to be indicative of** indicar; **indicator** *n* indicador *m*; (*AUT*) intermitente *m*
indices ['ɪndɪsiːz] *npl of* **index**
indictment [ɪn'daɪtmənt] *n* acusación *f*
indifferent [ɪn'dɪfrənt] *adj* indiferente; (*mediocre*) regular
indigenous [ɪn'dɪdʒɪnəs] *adj* indígena
indigestion [ɪndɪ'dʒɛstʃən] *n* indigestión *f*
indignant [ɪn'dɪgnənt] *adj*: **to be ~ at sth/ with sb** indignarse por algo/con uno
indigo ['ɪndɪgəu] *adj* de color añil ♦ *n* añil *m*
indirect [ɪndɪ'rɛkt] *adj* indirecto
indiscreet [ɪndɪ'skriːt] *adj* indiscreto, imprudente
indiscriminate [ɪndɪ'skrɪmɪnət] *adj* indiscriminado
indisputable [ɪndɪ'spjuːtəbl] *adj* incontestable
indistinct [ɪndɪ'stɪŋkt] *adj* (*noise, memory etc*) confuso
individual [ɪndɪ'vɪdjuəl] *n* individuo ♦ *adj* individual; (*personal*) personal; (*particular*)

particular; **~ly** adv (singly) individualmente
indoctrinate [ɪnˈdɔktrɪneɪt] vt adoctrinar
indoor [ˈɪndɔːʳ] adj (swimming pool) cubierto; (plant) de interior; (sport) bajo cubierta; **~s** [ɪnˈdɔːz] adv dentro
induce [ɪnˈdjuːs] vt inducir, persuadir; (bring about) producir; (birth) provocar; **~ment** n (incentive) incentivo; (pej: bribe) soborno
indulge [ɪnˈdʌldʒ] vt (whim) satisfacer; (person) complacer; (child) mimar ♦ vi: to **~ in** darse el gusto de; **~nce** n vicio; (leniency) indulgencia; **~nt** adj indulgente
industrial [ɪnˈdʌstrɪəl] adj industrial; **~ action** n huelga; **~ estate** (BRIT) n polígono (SP) or zona (AM) industrial; **~ist** n industrial m/f; **~ize** vt industrializar; **~ park** (US) n = **~ estate**
industrious [ɪnˈdʌstrɪəs] adj trabajador(a); (student) aplicado
industry [ˈɪndʌstrɪ] n industria; (diligence) aplicación f
inebriated [ɪˈniːbrɪeɪtɪd] adj borracho
inedible [ɪnˈedɪbl] adj incomible; (poisonous) no comestible
ineffective [ɪnɪˈfektɪv] adj ineficaz, inútil
ineffectual [ɪnɪˈfektjuəl] adj = **ineffective**
inefficient [ɪnɪˈfɪʃənt] adj ineficaz, ineficiente
inept [ɪˈnept] adj incompetente
inequality [ɪnɪˈkwɔlɪtɪ] n desigualdad f
inert [ɪˈnɜːt] adj inerte, inactivo; (immobile) inmóvil
inescapable [ɪnɪˈskeɪpəbl] adj ineludible
inevitable [ɪnˈevɪtəbl] adj inevitable; **inevitably** adv inevitablemente
inexcusable [ɪnɪksˈkjuːzəbl] adj imperdonable
inexpensive [ɪnɪkˈspensɪv] adj económico
inexperienced [ɪnɪkˈspɪərɪənst] adj inexperto
infallible [ɪnˈfælɪbl] adj infalible
infamous [ˈɪnfəməs] adj infame
infancy [ˈɪnfənsɪ] n infancia
infant [ˈɪnfənt] n niño/a; (baby) niño pequeño, bebé m; (pej) aniñado
infantry [ˈɪnfəntrɪ] n infantería
infant school (BRIT) n parvulario
infatuated [ɪnˈfætjueɪtɪd] adj: **~ with** (in love) loco por
infatuation [ɪnfætuˈeɪʃən] n enamoramiento, pasión f
infect [ɪnˈfekt] vt (wound) infectar; (food) contaminar; (person, animal) contagiar; **~ion** [ɪnˈfekʃən] n infección f; (fig) contagio; **~ious** [ɪnˈfekʃəs] adj (also fig) contagioso
infer [ɪnˈfɜːʳ] vt deducir, inferir
inferior [ɪnˈfɪərɪəʳ] adj, n inferior m/f; **~ity** [-rɪˈɔrɪtɪ] n inferioridad f
infertile [ɪnˈfɜːtaɪl] adj estéril; (person) infecundo

infested [ɪnˈfestɪd] adj: **~ with** plagado de
in-fighting n (fig) lucha(s) f(pl) interna(s)
infinite [ˈɪnfɪnɪt] adj infinito
infinitive [ɪnˈfɪnɪtɪv] n infinitivo
infinity [ɪnˈfɪnɪtɪ] n infinito; (an ~) infinidad f
infirmary [ɪnˈfɜːmərɪ] n hospital m
inflamed [ɪnˈfleɪmd] adj: **to become ~** inflamarse
inflammable [ɪnˈflæməbl] adj inflamable
inflammation [ɪnfləˈmeɪʃən] n inflamación f
inflatable [ɪnˈfleɪtəbl] adj (ball, boat) inflable
inflate [ɪnˈfleɪt] vt (tyre, price etc) inflar; (fig) hinchar; **inflation** [ɪnˈfleɪʃən] n (ECON) inflación f
inflexible [ɪnˈfleksəbl] adj (rule) rígido; (person) inflexible
inflict [ɪnˈflɪkt] vt: **to ~ sth on sb** infligir algo en uno
influence [ˈɪnfluəns] n influencia ♦ vt influir en, influenciar; **under the ~ of alcohol** en estado de embriaguez; **influential** [-ˈenʃl] adj influyente
influenza [ɪnfluˈenzə] n gripe f
influx [ˈɪnflʌks] n afluencia
inform [ɪnˈfɔːm] vt: **to ~ sb of sth** informar a uno sobre or de algo ♦ vi: **to ~ on sb** delatar a uno
informal [ɪnˈfɔːməl] adj (manner, tone) familiar; (dress, interview, occasion) informal; (visit, meeting) extraoficial; **~ity** [-ˈmælɪtɪ] n informalidad f; sencillez f
informant [ɪnˈfɔːmənt] n informante m/f
information [ɪnfəˈmeɪʃən] n información f; (knowledge) conocimientos mpl; **a piece of ~** un dato; **~ desk** n (mostrador m de) información f; **~ office** n información f
informative [ɪnˈfɔːmətɪv] adj informativo
informer [ɪnˈfɔːməʳ] n (also: police ~) soplón/ona m/f
infra-red [ɪnfrəˈred] adj infrarrojo
infrastructure [ˈɪnfrəstrʌktʃəʳ] n (of system etc) infraestructura
infringe [ɪnˈfrɪndʒ] vt infringir, violar ♦ vi: **to ~ on** abusar de; **~ment** n infracción f; (of rights) usurpación f
infuriating [ɪnˈfjuərɪeɪtɪŋ] adj (habit, noise) enloquecedor(a)
ingenious [ɪnˈdʒiːnjəs] adj ingenioso; **ingenuity** [-dʒɪˈnjuːɪtɪ] n ingeniosidad f
ingenuous [ɪnˈdʒenjuəs] adj ingenuo
ingot [ˈɪŋgət] n lingote m, barra
ingrained [ɪnˈgreɪnd] adj arraigado
ingratiate [ɪnˈgreɪʃɪeɪt] vt: **to ~ o.s. with** congraciarse con
ingredient [ɪnˈgriːdɪənt] n ingrediente m
inhabit [ɪnˈhæbɪt] vt vivir en; **~ant** n habitante m/f
inhale [ɪnˈheɪl] vt inhalar ♦ vi (breathe in) aspirar; (in smoking) tragar

inherent [ɪn'hɪərənt] adj: ~ **in** or **to** inherente a

inherit [ɪn'hɛrɪt] vt heredar; **~ance** n herencia; (fig) patrimonio

inhibit [ɪn'hɪbɪt] vt inhibir, impedir; **~ed** adj (PSYCH) cohibido; **~ion** [-'bɪʃən] n cohibición f

inhospitable [ɪnhɔs'pɪtəbl] adj (person) inhospitalario; (place) inhóspito

inhuman [ɪn'hju:mən] adj inhumano

initial [ɪ'nɪʃl] adj primero ♦ n inicial f ♦ vt firmar con las iniciales; **~s** npl (as signature) iniciales fpl; (abbreviation) siglas fpl; **~ly** adv al principio

initiate [ɪ'nɪʃɪeɪt] vt iniciar; **to ~ proceedings against sb** (LAW) entablar proceso contra uno

initiative [ɪ'nɪʃətɪv] n iniciativa

inject [ɪn'dʒɛkt] vt inyectar; **to ~ sb with sth** inyectar algo a uno; **~ion** [ɪn'dʒɛkʃən] n inyección f

injunction [ɪn'dʒʌŋkʃən] n interdicto

injure ['ɪndʒə*] vt (hurt) herir, lastimar; (fig: reputation etc) perjudicar; **~d** adj (person, arm) herido, lastimado; **injury** n herida, lesión f; (wrong) perjuicio, daño; **injury time** n (SPORT) (tiempo de) descuento

injustice [ɪn'dʒʌstɪs] n injusticia

ink [ɪŋk] n tinta

inkling ['ɪŋklɪŋ] n sospecha; (idea) idea

inlaid ['ɪnleɪd] adj (with wood, gems etc) incrustado

inland [adj 'ɪnlənd, adv ɪn'lænd] adj (waterway, port etc) interior ♦ adv tierra adentro; **I~ Revenue** (BRIT) n departamento de impuestos; ≈ Hacienda (SP)

in-laws npl suegros mpl

inlet ['ɪnlɛt] n (GEO) ensenada, cala; (TECH) admisión f, entrada

inmate ['ɪnmeɪt] n (in prison) preso/a; presidiario/a; (in asylum) internado/a

inn [ɪn] n posada, mesón m

innate [ɪ'neɪt] adj innato

inner ['ɪnə*] adj (courtyard, calm) interior; (feelings) íntimo; **~ city** n barrios deprimidos del centro de una ciudad; **~ tube** n (of tyre) cámara (SP), llanta (AM)

innings ['ɪnɪŋz] n (CRICKET) entrada, turno

innocent ['ɪnəsnt] adj inocente

innocuous [ɪ'nɔkjuəs] adj inocuo

innovation [ɪnəu'veɪʃən] n novedad f

innuendo [ɪnju:'ɛndəu] (pl **~es**) n indirecta

inoculation [ɪnɔkju'leɪʃən] n inoculación f

in-patient n paciente m/f interno/a

input ['ɪnput] n (resources) inversión f; (COMPUT) entrada de datos

inquest ['ɪnkwɛst] n (coroner's) encuesta judicial

inquire [ɪn'kwaɪə*] vi preguntar ♦ vt: **to ~ whether** preguntar si; **to ~ about** (person)

preguntar por; (fact) informarse de; **~ into** vt fus investigar, indagar; **inquiry** n pregunta; (investigation) investigación f, pesquisa; **"Inquiries"** "Información"; **inquiry office** (BRIT) n oficina de información

inquisitive [ɪn'kwɪzɪtɪv] adj (curious) curioso

ins. abbr = inches

insane [ɪn'seɪn] adj loco; (MED) demente

insanity [ɪn'sænɪtɪ] n demencia, locura

inscription [ɪn'skrɪpʃən] n inscripción f; (in book) dedicatoria

inscrutable [ɪn'skru:təbl] adj inescrutable, insondable

insect ['ɪnsɛkt] n insecto; **~icide** [ɪn'sɛktɪsaɪd] n insecticida m; **~ repellent** n loción f contra insectos

insecure [ɪnsɪ'kjuə*] adj inseguro

insemination [ɪnsɛmɪ'neɪʃn] n: **artificial ~** inseminación f artificial

insensitive [ɪn'sɛnsɪtɪv] adj insensible

insert [vb ɪn'sə:t, n 'ɪnsə:t] vt (into sth) introducir ♦ n encarte m; **~ion** [ɪn'sə:ʃən] n inserción f

in-service ['ɪnsə:vɪs] adj (training, course) a cargo de la empresa

inshore [ɪn'ʃɔ:*] adj de bajura ♦ adv (be) cerca de la orilla; (move) hacia la orilla

inside ['ɪn'saɪd] n interior m ♦ adj interior, interno ♦ adv (be) (por) dentro; (go) hacia dentro ♦ prep dentro de; (of time): **~ 10 minutes** en menos de 10 minutos; **~s** npl (inf: stomach) tripas fpl; **~ information** n información f confidencial; **~ lane** n (AUT: in Britain) carril m izquierdo; (: in US, Europe etc) carril m derecho; **~ out** adv (turn) al revés; (know) a fondo

insider dealing, insider trading n (STOCK EXCHANGE) abuso de información privilegiada

insight ['ɪnsaɪt] n perspicacia

insignificant [ɪnsɪg'nɪfɪknt] adj insignificante

insincere [ɪnsɪn'sɪə*] adj poco sincero

insinuate [ɪn'sɪnjueɪt] vt insinuar

insipid [ɪn'sɪpɪd] adj soso, insulso

insist [ɪn'sɪst] vi insistir; **to ~ on** insistir en; **to ~ that** insistir en que; (claim) exigir que; **~ent** adj insistente; (noise, action) persistente

insole ['ɪnsəul] n plantilla

insolent ['ɪnsələnt] adj insolente, descarado

insomnia [ɪn'sɔmnɪə] n insomnio

inspect [ɪn'spɛkt] vt inspeccionar, examinar; (troops) pasar revista a; **~ion** [ɪn'spɛkʃən] n inspección f, examen m; (of troops) revista; **~or** n inspector(a) m/f; (BRIT: on buses, trains) revisor(a) m/f

inspiration [ɪnspə'reɪʃən] n inspiración f; **inspire** [ɪn'spaɪə*] vt inspirar

instability [ɪnstə'bɪlɪtɪ] n inestabilidad f

install [ɪn'stɔ:l] vt instalar; (official) nombrar;

~ation [ɪnstə'leɪʃən] n instalación f
instalment [ɪn'stɔ:lmənt] (US **installment**) n
plazo; (of story) entrega; (of TV serial etc)
capítulo; **in ~s** (pay, receive) a plazos
instance ['ɪnstəns] n ejemplo, caso; **for ~** por
ejemplo; **in the first ~** en primer lugar
instant ['ɪnstənt] n instante m, momento
♦ adj inmediato; (coffee etc) instantáneo;
~ly adv en seguida
instead [ɪn'stɛd] adv en cambio; **~ of** en
lugar de, en vez de
instep ['ɪnstɛp] n empeine m
instil [ɪn'stɪl] vt: **to ~ sth into** inculcar algo a
instinct ['ɪnstɪŋkt] n instinto
institute ['ɪnstɪtju:t] n instituto; (professional
body) colegio ♦ vt (begin) iniciar, empezar;
(proceedings) entablar; (system, rule)
establecer
institution [ɪnstɪ'tju:ʃən] n institución f;
(MED: home) asilo; (: asylum) manicomio; (of
system etc) establecimiento; (of custom)
iniciación f
instruct [ɪn'strʌkt] vt: **to ~ sb in sth** instruir a
uno en or sobre algo; **to ~ sb to do sth** dar
instrucciones a uno de hacer algo; **~ion**
[ɪn'strʌkʃən] n (teaching) instrucción f; **~ions**
npl (orders) órdenes fpl; **~ions** (for use) modo
de empleo; **~or** n instructor(a) m/f
instrument ['ɪnstrəmənt] n instrumento;
~al [-'mɛntl] adj (MUS) instrumental; **to be
~al in** ser (el) artífice de; **~ panel** n tablero
(de instrumentos)
insufficient [ɪnsə'fɪʃənt] adj insuficiente
insular ['ɪnsjulə*] adj insular; (person)
estrecho de miras
insulate ['ɪnsjuleɪt] vt aislar; **insulation**
[-'leɪʃən] n aislamiento
insulin ['ɪnsjulɪn] n insulina
insult [n 'ɪnsʌlt, vb ɪn'sʌlt] n insulto ♦ vt
insultar; **~ing** adj insultante
insurance [ɪn'ʃuərəns] n seguro; **fire/life ~**
seguro contra incendios/sobre la vida;
~ agent n agente m/f de seguros; **~ policy**
n póliza (de seguros)
insure [ɪn'ʃuə*] vt asegurar
intact [ɪn'tækt] adj íntegro; (unharmed)
intacto
intake ['ɪnteɪk] n (of food) ingestión f; (of air)
consumo; (BRIT: SCOL): **an ~ of 200 a year** 200
matriculados al año
integral ['ɪntɪɡrəl] adj (whole) íntegro; (part)
integrante
integrate ['ɪntɪɡreɪt] vt integrar ♦ vi
integrarse
integrity [ɪn'tɛɡrɪtɪ] n honradez f, rectitud f
intellect ['ɪntəlɛkt] n intelecto; **~ual**
[-'lɛktjuəl] adj, n intelectual m/f
intelligence [ɪn'tɛlɪdʒəns] n inteligencia
intelligent [ɪn'tɛlɪdʒənt] adj inteligente

intelligible [ɪn'tɛlɪdʒɪbl] adj inteligible,
comprensible
intend [ɪn'tɛnd] vt (gift etc): **to ~ sth for**
destinar algo a; **to ~ to do sth** tener intención
de or pensar hacer algo
intense [ɪn'tɛns] adj intenso; **~ly** adv
(extremely) sumamente
intensify [ɪn'tɛnsɪfaɪ] vt intensificar;
(increase) aumentar
intensive [ɪn'tɛnsɪv] adj intensivo; **~ care
unit** n unidad f de vigilancia intensiva
intent [ɪn'tɛnt] n propósito; (LAW)
premeditación f ♦ adj (absorbed) absorto;
(attentive) atento; **to all ~s and purposes**
prácticamente; **to be ~ on doing sth** estar
resuelto a hacer algo
intention [ɪn'tɛnʃən] n intención f,
propósito; **~al** adj deliberado; **~ally** adv a
propósito
intently [ɪn'tɛntlɪ] adv atentamente,
fijamente
interact [ɪntər'ækt] vi influirse mutuamente;
~ive adj (COMPUT) interactivo
interchange ['ɪntətʃeɪndʒ] n intercambio;
(on motorway) intersección f; **~able** adj
intercambiable
intercom ['ɪntəkɔm] n interfono
intercourse ['ɪntəkɔ:s] n (sexual) relaciones
fpl sexuales
interest ['ɪntrɪst] n (also COMM) interés m
♦ vt interesar; **to be ~ed in** interesarse por;
~ing adj interesante; **~ rate** n tipo or tasa de
interés
interface ['ɪntəfeɪs] n (COMPUT) junción f
interfere [ɪntə'fɪə*] vi: **to ~ in** (quarrel, other
people's business) entrometerse en; **to ~ with**
(hinder) estorbar; (damage) estropear
interference [ɪntə'fɪərəns] n intromisión f;
(RADIO, TV) interferencia
interim ['ɪntərɪm] n: **in the ~** en el ínterin
♦ adj provisional
interior [ɪn'tɪərɪə*] n interior m ♦ adj interior;
~ designer n interiorista m/f
interjection [ɪntə'dʒɛkʃən] n interposición f;
(LING) interjección f
interlock [ɪntə'lɔk] vi entrelazarse
interlude ['ɪntəlu:d] n intervalo; (THEATRE)
intermedio
intermediate [ɪntə'mi:dɪət] adj intermedio
intermission [ɪntə'mɪʃən] n intermisión f;
(THEATRE) descanso
intern [vb ɪn'tə:n, n 'ɪntə:n] vt internar ♦ n
(US) interno/a
internal [ɪn'tə:nl] adj (layout, pipes, security)
interior; (injury, structure, memo) internal; **~ly**
adv: **"not to be taken ~ly"** "uso externo";
I~ Revenue Service (US) n departamento
de impuestos; ≈ Hacienda (SP)
international [ɪntə'næʃənl] adj internacional

♦ n (BRIT: match) partido internacional
Internet ['ɪntənet] n: the ~ Internet m or f;
  ~ **café** n cibercafé m; ~ **Service Provider** n
  proveedor m de (acceso a) Internet
interplay ['ɪntəpleɪ] n interacción f
interpret [ɪn'tɜːprɪt] vt interpretar; (translate)
  traducir; (understand) entender ♦ vi hacer de
  intérprete; **~er** n intérprete m/f
interrogate [ɪn'terəugeɪt] vt interrogar;
  interrogation [-'geɪʃən] n interrogatorio
interrupt [ɪntə'rʌpt] vt, vi interrumpir; **~ion**
  [-'rʌpʃən] n interrupción f
intersect [ɪntə'sekt] vi (roads) cruzarse; **~ion**
  [-'sekʃən] n (of roads) cruce m
intersperse [ɪntə'spɜːs] vt: to ~ **with** salpicar
  de
intertwine [ɪntə'twaɪn] vt entrelazarse
interval ['ɪntəvl] n intervalo; (BRIT: THEATRE,
  SPORT) descanso; (: SCOL) recreo; **at ~s** a
  ratos, de vez en cuando
intervene [ɪntə'viːn] vi intervenir; (event)
  interponerse; (time) transcurrir;
  intervention n intervención f
interview ['ɪntəvjuː] n entrevista ♦ vt
  entrevistarse con; **~er** n entrevistador(a) m/f
intestine [ɪn'testɪn] n intestino
intimacy ['ɪntɪməsɪ] n intimidad f
intimate [adj 'ɪntɪmət, vb 'ɪntɪmeɪt] adj
  íntimo; (friendship) estrecho; (knowledge)
  profundo ♦ vt dar a entender
into ['ɪntuː] prep en; (towards) a; (inside)
  hacia el interior de; ~ **3 pieces/French** en 3
  pedazos/al francés
intolerable [ɪn'tɔlərəbl] adj intolerable,
  insoportable
intolerant [ɪn'tɔlərənt] adj: ~ **(of)** intolerante
  (con or para)
intoxicated [ɪn'tɔksɪkeɪtɪd] adj embriagado
intractable [ɪn'træktəbl] adj (person)
  intratable; (problem) espinoso
intranet ['ɪntrənet] n intranet f
intransitive [ɪn'trænsɪtɪv] adj intransitivo
intravenous [ɪntrə'viːnəs] adj intravenoso
in-tray n bandeja de entrada
intricate ['ɪntrɪkət] adj (design, pattern)
  intrincado
intrigue [ɪn'triːg] n intriga ♦ vt fascinar;
  intriguing adj fascinante
intrinsic [ɪn'trɪnsɪk] adj intrínseco
introduce [ɪntrə'djuːs] vt introducir, meter;
  (speaker, TV show etc) presentar; **to ~ sb (to**
  sb) presentar uno (a otro); **to ~ sb to**
  (pastime, technique) introducir a uno a;
  introduction [-'dʌkʃən] n introducción f; (of
  person) presentación f; **introductory**
  [-'dʌktərɪ] adj introductorio; (lesson, offer) de
  introducción
introvert ['ɪntrəvɜːt] n introvertido/a ♦ adj
  (also: ~ed) introvertido

intrude [ɪn'truːd] vi (person) entrometerse;
  to ~ on estorbar; **~r** n intruso/a; **intrusion**
  [-ʒən] n invasión f
intuition [ɪntjuː'ɪʃən] n intuición f
inundate ['ɪnʌndeɪt] vt: **to ~ with** inundar de
invade [ɪn'veɪd] vt invadir
invalid [n 'ɪnvəlɪd, adj ɪn'vælɪd] n (MED)
  minusválido/a ♦ adj (not valid) inválido, nulo
invaluable [ɪn'væljuəbl] adj inestimable
invariable [ɪn'veərɪəbl] adj invariable
invent [ɪn'vent] vt inventar; **~ion** [ɪn'venʃən]
  n invento; (lie) ficción f, mentira; **~ive** adj
  inventivo; **~or** n inventor(a) m/f
inventory ['ɪnvəntrɪ] n inventario
invert [ɪn'vɜːt] vt invertir
inverted commas (BRIT) npl comillas fpl
invest [ɪn'vest] vt invertir ♦ vi: **to ~ in**
  (company etc) invertir dinero en; (fig: sth
  useful) comprar
investigate [ɪn'vestɪgeɪt] vt investigar;
  investigation [-'geɪʃən] n investigación f,
  pesquisa
investment [ɪn'vestmənt] n inversión f
investor [ɪn'vestə*] n inversionista m/f
invigilator [ɪn'vɪdʒɪleɪtə*] n persona que
  vigila un examen
invigorating [ɪn'vɪgəreɪtɪŋ] adj vigorizante
invisible [ɪn'vɪzɪbl] adj invisible
invitation [ɪnvɪ'teɪʃən] n invitación f
invite [ɪn'vaɪt] vt invitar; (opinions etc) solicitar,
  pedir; **inviting** adj atractivo; (food) apetitoso
invoice ['ɪnvɔɪs] n factura ♦ vt facturar
involuntary [ɪn'vɔləntrɪ] adj involuntario
involve [ɪn'vɔlv] vt suponer, implicar; tener
  que ver con; (concern, affect) corresponder;
  to ~ sb (in sth) comprometer a uno (con
  algo); **~d** adj complicado; **to be ~d in** (take
  part) tomar parte en; (be engrossed) estar
  muy metido en; **~ment** n participación f;
  dedicación f
inward ['ɪnwəd] adj (movement) interior,
  interno; (thought, feeling) íntimo; **~(s)** adv
  hacia dentro
I/O abbr (COMPUT = input/output) entrada/
  salida
iodine ['aɪəudiːn] n yodo
ion ['aɪən] n ion m; **ioniser** ['aɪənaɪzə*] n
  ionizador m
iota [aɪ'əutə] n jota, ápice m
IOU n abbr (= I owe you) pagaré m
IQ n abbr (= intelligence quotient) cociente m
  intelectual
IRA n abbr (= Irish Republican Army) IRA m
Iran [ɪ'rɑːn] n Irán m; **~ian** [ɪ'reɪnɪən] adj, n
  iraní m/f
Iraq [ɪ'rɑːk] n Iraq; **~i** adj, n iraquí m/f
irate [aɪ'reɪt] adj enojado, airado
Ireland ['aɪələnd] n Irlanda
iris ['aɪrɪs] (pl **~es**) n (ANAT) iris m; (BOT) lirio

Irish [ˈaɪrɪʃ] adj irlandés/esa ♦ npl: **the ~** los
irlandeses; **~man/woman** (irreg) n
irlandés/esa m/f; **~ Sea** n: **the ~ Sea** el mar
de Irlanda

iron [ˈaɪən] n hierro; (for clothes) plancha
♦ cpd de hierro ♦ vt (clothes) planchar;
~ out vt (fig) allanar

ironic(al) [aɪˈrɔnɪk(l)] adj irónico

ironing [ˈaɪənɪŋ] n (activity) planchado;
(clothes: ironed) ropa planchada; (: to be
ironed) ropa por planchar; **~ board** n tabla
de planchar

ironmonger's (shop) [ˈaɪənmʌŋgəz]
(BRIT) n ferretería, quincallería

irony [ˈaɪrənɪ] n ironía

irrational [ɪˈræʃənl] adj irracional

irreconcilable [ɪrekənˈsaɪləbl] adj (ideas)
incompatible; (enemies) irreconciliable

irregular [ɪˈregjulə*] adj irregular; (surface)
desigual; (action, event) anómalo; (behaviour)
poco ortodoxo

irrelevant [ɪˈreləvənt] adj fuera de lugar,
inoportuno

irresolute [ɪˈrezəluːt] adj indeciso

irrespective [ɪrɪˈspektɪv]: **~ of** prep sin tener
en cuenta, no importa

irresponsible [ɪrɪˈspɔnsɪbl] adj (act)
irresponsable; (person) poco serio

irrigate [ˈɪrɪgeɪt] vt regar; **irrigation**
[-ˈgeɪʃən] n riego

irritable [ˈɪrɪtəbl] adj (person) de mal humor

irritate [ˈɪrɪteɪt] vt fastidiar; (MED) picar;
irritating adj fastidioso; **irritation** [-ˈteɪʃən]
n fastidio; irritación; picazón f, picor m

IRS (US) n abbr = **Internal Revenue Service**

is [ɪz] vb see be

Islam [ˈɪzlɑːm] n Islam m; **~ic** [ɪzˈlæmɪk] adj
islámico

island [ˈaɪlənd] n isla; **~er** n isleño/a

isle [aɪl] n isla

isn't [ˈɪznt] = **is not**

isolate [ˈaɪsəleɪt] vt aislar; **~d** adj aislado;
isolation [-ˈleɪʃən] n aislamiento

ISP n abbr = **Internet Service Provider**

Israel [ˈɪzreɪl] n Israel m; **~i** [ɪzˈreɪlɪ] adj, n
israelí m/f

issue [ˈɪʃuː] n (problem, subject, most
important part) cuestión f; (outcome)
resultado; (of banknotes etc) emisión f; (of
newspaper etc) edición f ♦ vt (rations,
equipment) distribuir, repartir; (orders) dar;
(certificate, passport) expedir; (decree)
promulgar; (magazine) publicar; (cheques)
extender; (banknotes, stamps) emitir; **at ~** en
cuestión; **to take ~ with sb (over)** estar en
desacuerdo con uno (sobre); **to make an ~ of
sth** hacer una cuestión de algo

Istanbul [ɪstænˈbuːl] n Estambul m

it [ɪt] pron 1 (specific: subject: not generally
translated) él/ella; (: direct object) lo, la;
(: indirect object) le; (after prep) él/ella;
(abstract concept) ello; **~'s on the table** está
en la mesa; **I can't find ~** no lo (or la)
encuentro; **give ~ to me** dámelo (or dámela);
I spoke to him about ~ le hablé del asunto;
what did you learn from ~? ¿qué aprendiste
de él (or ella)?; **did you go to ~?** (party,
concert etc) ¿fuiste?
2 (impersonal): **~'s raining** llueve, está
lloviendo; **~'s 6 o'clock/the 10th of August**
son las 6/es el 10 de agosto; **how far is ~?** —
~'s 10 miles/2 hours on the train ¿a qué
distancia está? — a 10 millas/2 horas en tren;
who is ~? — **~'s me** ¿quién es? — soy yo

Italian [ɪˈtæljən] adj italiano ♦ n italiano/a;
(LING) italiano

italics [ɪˈtælɪks] npl cursiva

Italy [ˈɪtəlɪ] n Italia

itch [ɪtʃ] n picazón f ♦ vi (part of body) picar;
to ~ to do sth rabiar por hacer algo; **~y** adj:
my hand is ~y me pica la mano

it'd [ˈɪtd] = **it would; it had**

item [ˈaɪtəm] n artículo; (on agenda) asunto
(a tratar); (also: news ~) noticia; **~ize** vt
detallar

itinerary [aɪˈtɪnərərɪ] n itinerario

it'll [ˈɪtl] = **it will; it shall**

its [ɪts] adj su; sus pl

it's [ɪts] = **it is; it has**

itself [ɪtˈself] pron (reflexive) sí mismo/a;
(emphatic) él mismo/ella misma

ITV n abbr (BRIT: = Independent Television)
cadena de televisión comercial independiente
del Estado

I.U.D. n abbr (= intra-uterine device) DIU m

I've [aɪv] = **I have**

ivory [ˈaɪvərɪ] n marfil m

ivy [ˈaɪvɪ] n (BOT) hiedra

J, j

jab [dʒæb] vt: **to ~ sth into sth** clavar algo en
algo ♦ n (inf) (MED) pinchazo

jack [dʒæk] n (AUT) gato; (CARDS) sota; **~ up**
vt (AUT) levantar con gato

jackal [ˈdʒækɔːl] n (ZOOL) chacal m

jacket [ˈdʒækɪt] n chaqueta, americana, saco
(AM); (of book) sobrecubierta

jack: ~-knife vi colear; **~ plug** n (ELEC)
enchufe m de clavija; **~pot** n premio gordo

jaded [ˈdʒeɪdɪd] adj (tired) cansado; (fed-up)
hastiado

jagged [ˈdʒægɪd] adj dentado

jail |dʒeɪl| n cárcel f ♦ vt encarcelar

jam |dʒæm| n mermelada; (also: traffic ~) embotellamiento; (inf: difficulty) apuro ♦ vt (passage etc) obstruir; (mechanism, drawer etc) atascar; (RADIO) interferir ♦ vi atascarse, trabarse; **to ~ sth into sth** meter algo a la fuerza en algo

Jamaica |dʒə'meɪkə| n Jamaica

jangle |'dʒæŋgl| vi entrechocar (ruidosamente)

janitor |'dʒænɪtə*| n (caretaker) portero, conserje m

January |'dʒænjuərɪ| n enero

Japan |dʒə'pæn| n (el) Japón; **~ese** |dʒæpə'niːz| adj japonés/esa ♦ n inv japonés/ esa m/f; (LING) japonés m

jar |dʒɑː*| n tarro, bote m ♦ vi (sound) chirriar; (colours) desentonar

jargon |'dʒɑːgən| n jerga

jasmine |'dʒæzmɪn| n jazmín m

jaundice |'dʒɔːndɪs| n ictericia

jaunt |dʒɔːnt| n excursión f

javelin |'dʒævlɪn| n jabalina

jaw |dʒɔː| n mandíbula

jay |dʒeɪ| n (ZOOL) arrendajo

jaywalker |'dʒeɪwɔːkə*| n peatón/ona m/f imprudente

jazz |dʒæz| n jazz m; **~ up** vt (liven up) animar, avivar

jealous |'dʒeləs| adj celoso; (envious) envidioso; **~y** n celos mpl; envidia

jeans |dʒiːnz| npl vaqueros mpl, tejanos mpl

Jeep ® |dʒiːp| n jeep m

jeer |dʒɪə*| vi: **to ~ (at)** (mock) mofarse (de)

jelly |'dʒelɪ| n (jam) jalea; (dessert etc) gelatina; **~fish** n inv medusa (SP), aguaviva (AM)

jeopardy |'dʒepədɪ| n: **to be in ~** estar en peligro

jerk |dʒɜːk| n (jolt) sacudida; (wrench) tirón m; (inf) imbécil m/f ♦ vt tirar bruscamente de ♦ vi (vehicle) traquetear

jersey |'dʒɜːzɪ| n jersey m; (fabric) (tejido de) punto

Jesus |'dʒiːzəs| n Jesús m

jet |dʒet| n (of gas, liquid) chorro; (AVIAT) avión m a reacción; **~-black** adj negro como el azabache; **~ engine** n motor m a reacción; **~ lag** n desorientación f después de un largo vuelo

jettison |'dʒetɪsn| vt desechar

jetty |'dʒetɪ| n muelle m, embarcadero

Jew |dʒuː| n judío

jewel |'dʒuːəl| n joya; (in watch) rubí m; **~ler** (US **~er**) n joyero/a; **~ler's (shop)** (US **~ry store**) n joyería; **~lery** (US **~ry**) n joyas fpl, alhajas fpl

Jewess |'dʒuːɪs| n judía

Jewish |'dʒuːɪʃ| adj judío

jibe |dʒaɪb| n mofa

jiffy |'dʒɪfɪ| (inf) n: **in a ~** en un santiamén

jigsaw |'dʒɪgsɔː| n (also: ~ puzzle) rompecabezas m inv, puzle m

jilt |dʒɪlt| vt dejar plantado a

jingle |'dʒɪŋgl| n musiquilla ♦ vi tintinear

jinx |dʒɪŋks| n: **there's a ~ on it** está gafado

jitters |'dʒɪtəz| (inf) npl: **to get the ~** ponerse nervioso

job |dʒɔb| n (task) tarea; (post) empleo; **it's not my ~** no me incumbe a mí; **it's a good ~ that ...** menos mal que ...; **just the ~!** ¡estupendo!; **~ centre** (BRIT) n oficina estatal de colocaciones; **~less** adj sin trabajo

jockey |'dʒɔkɪ| n jockey m/f ♦ vi: **to ~ for position** maniobrar para conseguir una posición

jog |dʒɔg| vt empujar (ligeramente) ♦ vi (run) hacer footing; **to ~ sb's memory** refrescar la memoria a uno; **~ along** vi (fig) ir tirando; **~ging** n footing m

join |dʒɔɪn| vt (things) juntar, unir; (club) hacerse socio de; (POL: party) afiliarse a; (queue) ponerse en; (meet: people) reunirse con ♦ vi (roads) juntarse; (rivers) confluir ♦ n juntura; **~ in** vi tomar parte, participar ♦ vt fus tomar parte or participar en; **~ up** vi reunirse; (MIL) alistarse

joiner |'dʒɔɪnə*| (BRIT) n carpintero/a; **~y** n carpintería

joint |dʒɔɪnt| n (TECH) junta, unión f; (ANAT) articulación f; (BRIT: CULIN) pieza de carne (para asar); (inf: place) tugurio; (: of cannabis) porro ♦ adj (common) común; (combined) combinado; **~ account** (with bank etc) cuenta común

joke |dʒəuk| n chiste m; (also: practical ~) broma ♦ vi bromear; **to play a ~ on** gastar una broma a; **~r** n (CARDS) comodín m

jolly |'dʒɔlɪ| adj (merry) alegre; (enjoyable) divertido ♦ adv (BRIT: inf) muy, terriblemente

jolt |dʒəult| n (jerk) sacudida; (shock) susto ♦ vt (physically) sacudir; (emotionally) asustar

jostle |'dʒɔsl| vt dar empellones a, codear

jot |dʒɔt| n: **not one** ~ ni jota, ni pizca; **~ down** vt apuntar; **~ter** (BRIT) n bloc m

journal |'dʒɜːnl| n (magazine) revista; (diary) periódico, diario; **~ism** n periodismo; **~ist** n periodista m/f, reportero/a

journey |'dʒɜːnɪ| n viaje m; (distance covered) trayecto

jovial |'dʒəuvɪəl| adj risueño, jovial

joy |dʒɔɪ| n alegría; **~ful** adj alegre; **~ous** adj alegre; **~ ride** n (illegal) paseo en coche robado; **~rider** n gamberro que roba un coche para dar una vuelta y luego abandonarlo; **~ stick** n (AVIAT) palanca de mando; (COMPUT) palanca de control

JP n abbr = **Justice of the Peace**

Jr abbr = **junior**

jubilant ['dʒuːbɪlnt] adj jubiloso

judge [dʒʌdʒ] n juez m/f; (fig: expert) perito
♦ vt juzgar; (consider) considerar;
judg(e)ment n juicio

judiciary [dʒuː'dɪʃɪərɪ] n poder m judicial

judicious [dʒuː'dɪʃəs] adj juicioso

judo ['dʒuːdəu] n judo

jug [dʒʌg] n jarra

juggernaut ['dʒʌgənɔːt] (BRIT) n (huge truck)
trailer m

juggle ['dʒʌgl] vi hacer juegos malabares; **~r**
n malabarista m/f

juice [dʒuːs] n zumo, jugo (esp AM); **juicy** adj
jugoso

jukebox ['dʒuːkbɔks] n máquina de discos

July [dʒuː'laɪ] n julio

jumble ['dʒʌmbl] n revoltijo ♦ vt (also: ~ up)
revolver; **~ sale** (BRIT) n venta de objetos
usados con fines benéficos

jumbo (jet) ['dʒʌmbəu-] n jumbo

jump [dʒʌmp] vi saltar, dar saltos; (with fear
etc) pegar un bote; (increase) aumentar ♦ vt
saltar ♦ n salto; aumento; **to ~ the queue**
(BRIT) colarse

jumper ['dʒʌmpə*] n (BRIT: pullover) suéter m,
jersey m; (US: dress) mandil m; **~ cables**
(US) npl = **jump leads**

jump leads (BRIT) npl cables mpl puente de
batería

jumpy ['dʒʌmpɪ] (inf) adj nervioso

Jun. abbr = **junior**

junction ['dʒʌŋkʃən] n (BRIT: of roads) cruce
m; (RAIL) empalme m

juncture ['dʒʌŋktʃə*] n: **at this ~** en este
momento, en esta coyuntura

June [dʒuːn] n junio

jungle ['dʒʌŋgl] n selva, jungla

junior ['dʒuːnɪə*] adj (in age) menor, más
joven; (brother/sister etc): **7 years her ~** siete
años menor que ella; (position) subalterno
♦ n menor m/f, joven m/f; **~ school** (BRIT) n
escuela primaria

junk [dʒʌŋk] n (cheap goods) baratijas fpl;
(rubbish) basura; **~ food** n alimentos
preparados y envasados de escaso valor
nutritivo

junkie ['dʒʌŋkɪ] (inf) n drogadicto/a, yonqui
m/f

junk mail n propaganda de buzón

junk shop n tienda de objetos usados

Junr abbr = **junior**

juror ['dʒuərə*] n jurado

jury ['dʒuərɪ] n jurado

just [dʒʌst] adj justo ♦ adv (exactly)
exactamente; (only) sólo, solamente; **he's
~ done it/left** acaba de hacerlo/irse; **~ right**
perfecto; **~ two o'clock** las dos en punto;
she's ~ as clever as you (ella) es tan lista

como tú; **~ as well that ...** menos mal que ...;
~ as he was leaving en el momento en que se
marchaba; **~ before/enough** justo antes/lo
suficiente; **~ here** aquí mismo; **he ~ missed**
ha fallado por poco; **~ listen to this** escucha
esto un momento

justice ['dʒʌstɪs] n justicia; (US: judge) juez m;
to do ~ to (fig) hacer justicia a; **J~ of the
Peace** n juez m de paz

justify ['dʒʌstɪfaɪ] vt justificar; (text) alinear

jut [dʒʌt] vi (also: ~ out) sobresalir

juvenile ['dʒuːvənaɪl] adj (court) de menores;
(humour, mentality) infantil ♦ n menor m de
edad

K, k

K abbr (= one thousand) mil; (= kilobyte)
kilobyte m; (COMPUT) kilooocteto

kangaroo [kæŋgə'ruː] n canguro

karate [kə'rɑːtɪ] n karate m

kebab [kə'bæb] n pincho moruno

keel [kiːl] n quilla; **on an even ~** (fig) en
equilibrio

keen [kiːn] adj (interest, desire) grande, vivo;
(eye, intelligence) agudo; (competition)
reñido; (edge) afilado; (eager) entusiasta; **to
be ~ to do** or **on doing sth** tener muchas
ganas de hacer algo; **to be ~ on sth/sb**
interesarse por algo/uno

keep [kiːp] (pt, pp **kept**) vt (preserve, store)
guardar; (hold back) quedarse con;
(maintain) mantener; (detain) detener;
(shop) ser propietario de; (feed: family etc)
mantener; (promise) cumplir; (chickens, bees
etc) criar; (accounts) llevar; (diary) escribir;
(prevent): **to ~ sb from doing sth** impedir a
uno hacer algo ♦ vi (food) conservarse;
(remain) seguir, continuar ♦ n (of castle)
torreón m; (food etc) comida, subsistencia;
(inf): **for ~s** para siempre; **to ~ doing sth**
seguir haciendo algo; **to ~ sb happy** tener a
uno contento; **to ~ a place tidy** mantener un
lugar limpio; **to ~ sth to o.s.** guardar algo
para sí mismo; **to ~ sth (back) from sb** ocultar
algo a uno; **to ~ time** (clock) mantener la
hora exacta; **~ on** vi: **to ~ on doing** seguir or
continuar haciendo; **to ~ on (about sth)** no
parar de hablar (de algo); **~ out** vi (stay out)
permanecer fuera; "**~ out**" "prohibida la
entrada"; **~ up** vt mantener, conservar ♦ vi
no retrasarse; **to ~ up with** (pace) ir al paso
de; (level) mantenerse a la altura de; **~er** n
guardián/ana m/f; **~-fit** n gimnasia (para
mantenerse en forma); **~ing** n (care)
cuidado; **in ~ing with** de acuerdo con; **~sake**
n recuerdo

kennel ['kɛnl] n perrera; **~s** npl residencia

canina

Kenya ['kɛnjə] *n* Kenia

kept [kɛpt] *pt, pp of* **keep**

kerb [kə:b] (*BRIT*) *n* bordillo

kernel ['kə:nl] *n* (*nut*) almendra; (*fig*) meollo

ketchup ['kɛtʃəp] *n* salsa de tomate, catsup *m*

kettle ['kɛtl] *n* hervidor *m* de agua; **~ drum** *n* (*MUS*) timbal *m*

key [ki:] *n* llave *f*; (*MUS*) tono; (*of piano, typewriter*) tecla ♦ *adj* (*issue etc*) clave *inv* ♦ *vt* (*also:* ~ *in*) teclear; **~board** *n* teclado; **~ed up** *adj* (*person*) nervioso; **~hole** *n* ojo (de la cerradura); **~hole surgery** *n* cirugía cerrada, cirugía no invasiva; **~note** *n* (*MUS*) tónica; (*of speech*) punto principal *or* clave; **~ring** *n* llavero

khaki ['kɑːkɪ] *n* caqui

kick [kɪk] *vt* dar una patada *or* un puntapié a; (*inf: habit*) quitarse de ♦ *vi* (*horse*) dar coces ♦ *n* patada; puntapié *m*; (*of animal*) coz *f*; (*thrill*): **he does it for ~s** lo hace por pura diversión; **~ off** *vi* (*SPORT*) hacer el saque inicial

kid [kɪd] *n* (*inf: child*) chiquillo/a; (*animal*) cabrito; (*leather*) cabritilla ♦ *vi* (*inf*) bromear

kidnap ['kɪdnæp] *vt* secuestrar; **~per** *n* secuestrador(a) *m/f*; **~ping** *n* secuestro

kidney ['kɪdnɪ] *n* riñón *m*

kill [kɪl] *vt* matar; (*murder*) asesinar ♦ *n* matanza; **to ~ time** matar el tiempo; **~er** *n* asesino/a; **~ing** *n* (*one*) asesinato; (*several*) matanza; **to make a ~ing** (*fig*) hacer su agosto; **~joy** (*BRIT*) *n* aguafiestas *m/f inv*

kiln [kɪln] *n* horno

kilo ['ki:ləu] *n* kilo; **~byte** *n* (*COMPUT*) kilobyte *m*, kilococteto; **~gram(me)** ['kɪləugræm] *n* kilo, kilogramo; **~metre** ['kɪləmi:tə*] (*US* **~meter**) *n* kilómetro; **~watt** ['kɪləuwɔt] *n* kilovatio

kilt [kɪlt] *n* falda escocesa

kin [kɪn] *n see* **next**

kind [kaɪnd] *adj* amable, atento ♦ *n* clase *f*, especie *f*; (*species*) género; **in ~** (*COMM*) en especie; **a ~ of** una especie de; **to be two of a ~** ser tal para cual

kindergarten ['kɪndəgɑ:tn] *n* jardín *m* de la infancia

kind-hearted *adj* bondadoso, de buen corazón

kindle ['kɪndl] *vt* encender; (*arouse*) despertar

kindly ['kaɪndlɪ] *adj* bondadoso; cariñoso ♦ *adv* bondadosamente, amablemente; **will you ~ ...** sea usted tan amable de ...

kindness ['kaɪndnɪs] *n* (*quality*) bondad *f*, amabilidad *f*; (*act*) favor *m*

king [kɪŋ] *n* rey *m*; **~dom** *n* reino; **~fisher** *n* martín *m* pescador; **~-size** *adj* de tamaño extra

kiosk ['ki:ɔsk] *n* quiosco; (*BRIT: TEL*) cabina

kipper ['kɪpə*] *n* arenque *m* ahumado

kiss [kɪs] *n* beso ♦ *vt* besar; **to ~ (each other)** besarse; **~ of life** respiración *f* boca a boca

kit [kɪt] *n* (*equipment*) equipo; (*tools etc*) (caja de) herramientas *fpl*; (*assembly ~*) juego de armar

kitchen ['kɪtʃɪn] *n* cocina; **~ sink** *n* fregadero

kite [kaɪt] *n* (*toy*) cometa

kitten ['kɪtn] *n* gatito/a

kitty ['kɪtɪ] *n* (*pool of money*) fondo común

km *abbr* (= *kilometre*) km

knack [næk] *n*: **to have the ~ of doing sth** tener el don de hacer algo

knapsack ['næpsæk] *n* mochila

knead [ni:d] *vt* amasar

knee [ni:] *n* rodilla; **~cap** *n* rótula

kneel [ni:l] (*pt, pp* **knelt**) *vi* (*also:* ~ *down*) arrodillarse

knew [nju:] *pt of* **know**

knickers ['nɪkəz] (*BRIT*) *npl* bragas *fpl*

knife [naɪf] (*pl* **knives**) *n* cuchillo ♦ *vt* acuchillar

knight [naɪt] *n* caballero; (*CHESS*) caballo; **~hood** (*BRIT*) *n* (*title*): **to receive a ~hood** recibir el título de Sir

knit [nɪt] *vt* tejer, tricotar ♦ *vi* hacer punto, tricotar; (*bones*) soldarse; **to ~ one's brows** fruncir el ceño; **~ting** *n* labor *f* de punto; **~ting machine** *n* máquina de tricotar; **~ting needle** *n* aguja de hacer punto; **~wear** *n* prendas *fpl* de punto

knives [naɪvz] *npl of* **knife**

knob [nɔb] *n* (*of door*) tirador *m*; (*of stick*) puño; (*on radio, TV*) botón *m*

knock [nɔk] *vt* (*strike*) golpear; (*bump into*) chocar contra; (*inf*) criticar ♦ *vi* (*at door etc*): **to ~ at/on** llamar a ♦ *n* golpe *m*; (*on door*) llamada; **~ down** *vt* atropellar; **~ off** (*inf*) *vi* (*finish*) salir del trabajo ♦ *vt* (*from price*) descontar; (*inf: steal*) birlar; **~ out** *vt* dejar sin sentido; (*BOXING*) poner fuera de combate, dejar K.O.; (*in competition*) eliminar; **~ over** *vt* (*object*) tirar; (*person*) atropellar; **~er** *n* (*on door*) aldabón *m*; **~out** *n* (*BOXING*) K.O. *m*, knockout *m* ♦ *cpd* (*competition etc*) eliminatorio

knot [nɔt] *n* nudo ♦ *vt* anudar

know [nəu] (*pt* **knew**, *pp* **known**) *vt* (*facts*) saber; (*be acquainted with*) conocer; (*recognize*) reconocer, conocer; **to ~ how to swim** saber nadar; **to ~ about** *or* **of sb/sth** saber de uno/algo; **~-all** *n* sabelotodo *m/f*; **~-how** *n* conocimientos *mpl*; **~ing** *adj* (*look*) de complicidad; **~ingly** *adv* (*purposely*) adrede; (*smile, look*) con complicidad

knowledge ['nɔlɪdʒ] *n* conocimiento; (*learning*) saber *m*, conocimientos *mpl*; **~able** *adj* entendido

knuckle [ˈnʌkl] n nudillo
Koran [kɔˈrɑːn] n Corán m
Korea [kaˈrɪə] n Corea
kosher [ˈkəʊʃə*] adj autorizado por la ley judía
Kosovo [ˈkɒsəvəʊ] n Kosovo m

L, l

L (BRIT) abbr = **learner driver**
l. abbr (= litre) l
lab [læb] n abbr = **laboratory**
label [ˈleɪbl] n etiqueta ♦ vt poner etiqueta a
labor etc [ˈleɪbə*] (US) = **labour**
laboratory [ləˈbɒrətərɪ] n laboratorio
laborious [ləˈbɔːrɪəs] adj penoso
labour [ˈleɪbə*] (US **labor**) n (hard work) trabajo; (~ force) mano f de obra; (MED): **to be in ~** estar de parto ♦ vi: **to ~ (at sth)** trabajar (en algo) ♦ vt: **to ~ a point** insistir en un punto; **L~, the L~ party** (BRIT) el partido laborista, los laboristas mpl; **~ed** adj (breathing) fatigoso; **~er** n peón m; **farm ~er** peón m; (day ~er) jornalero
lace [leɪs] n encaje m; (of shoe etc) cordón m ♦ vt (shoes: also: ~ up) atarse (los zapatos)
lack [læk] n (absence) falta ♦ vt faltarle a uno, carecer de; **through** or **for ~ of** por falta de; **to be ~ing** faltar, no haber; **to be ~ing in sth** faltarle a uno algo
lacquer [ˈlækə*] n laca
lad [læd] n muchacho, chico
ladder [ˈlædə*] n escalera (de mano); (BRIT: in tights) carrera
laden [ˈleɪdn] adj: **~ (with)** cargado (de)
ladle [ˈleɪdl] n cucharón m
lady [ˈleɪdɪ] n señora; (dignified, graceful) dama; **"ladies and gentlemen ..."** "señoras y caballeros ..."; **young ~** señorita; **the ladies' (room)** los servicios de señoras; **~bird** (US **~bug**) n mariquita; **~like** adj fino; **L~ship** n: **your L~ship** su Señoría
lag [læg] n retraso ♦ vi (also: ~ behind) retrasarse, quedarse atrás ♦ vt (pipes) revestir
lager [ˈlɑːgə*] n cerveza (rubia)
lagoon [ləˈguːn] n laguna
laid [leɪd] pt, pp of **lay**; **~ back** (inf) adj relajado; **~ up** adj: **to be ~ up (with)** tener que guardar cama (a causa de)
lain [leɪn] pp of **lie**
lake [leɪk] n lago
lamb [læm] n cordero; (meat) (carne f de) cordero; **~ chop** n chuleta de cordero; **lambswool** n lana de cordero
lame [leɪm] adj cojo; (excuse) poco convincente
lament [ləˈmɛnt] n quejo ♦ vt lamentarse de
laminated [ˈlæmɪneɪtɪd] adj (metal) laminado; (wood) contrachapado; (surface) plastificado
lamp [læmp] n lámpara; **~post** (BRIT) n (poste m de) farol m; **~shade** n pantalla
lance [lɑːns] vt (MED) abrir con lanceta
land [lænd] n tierra; (country) país m; (piece of ~) terreno; (estate) tierras fpl, finca ♦ vi (from ship) desembarcar; (AVIAT) aterrizar; (fig: fall) caer, terminar ♦ vt (passengers, goods) desembarcar; **to ~ sb with sth** (inf) hacer cargar a uno con algo; **~ up** vi: **to ~ up in/at** ir a parar a/en; **~fill site** [ˈlændfɪl-] n vertedero; **~ing** n aterrizaje m; (of staircase) rellano; **~ing gear** n (AVIAT) tren m de aterrizaje; **~lady** n (of rented house, pub etc) dueña; **~lord** n propietario; (of pub etc) patrón m; **~mark** n lugar m conocido; **to be a ~mark** (fig) marcar un hito histórico; **~owner** n terrateniente m/f; **~scape** n paisaje m; **~scape gardener** n arquitecto de jardines; **~slide** n (GEO) corrimiento de tierras; (fig: POL) victoria arrolladora
lane [leɪn] n (in country) camino; (AUT) carril m; (in race) calle f
language [ˈlæŋgwɪdʒ] n lenguaje m; (national tongue) idioma m, lengua; **bad ~** palabrotas fpl; **~ laboratory** n laboratorio de idiomas
lank [læŋk] adj (hair) lacio
lanky [ˈlæŋkɪ] adj larguirucho
lantern [ˈlæntn] n linterna, farol m.
lap [læp] n (of track) vuelta; (of body) regazo; **to sit on sb's ~** sentarse en las rodillas de uno ♦ vt (also: ~ up) beber a lengüetadas ♦ vi (waves) chapotear; **~ up** vt (fig) tragarse
lapel [ləˈpɛl] n solapa
Lapland [ˈlæplænd] n Laponia
lapse [læps] n fallo; (moral) desliz m; (of time) intervalo ♦ vi (expire) caducar; (time) pasar, transcurrir; **to ~ into bad habits** caer en malos hábitos
laptop (computer) [ˈlæptɒp-] n (ordenador m) portátil m
larch [lɑːtʃ] n alerce m
lard [lɑːd] n manteca (de cerdo)
larder [ˈlɑːdə*] n despensa
large [lɑːdʒ] adj grande; **at ~** (free) en libertad; (generally) en general; **~ly** adv (mostly) en su mayor parte; (introducing reason) en gran parte; **~-scale** adj (map) en gran escala; (fig) importante
lark [lɑːk] n (bird) alondra; (joke) broma
laryngitis [lærɪnˈdʒaɪtɪs] n laringitis f
laser [ˈleɪzə*] n láser m; **~ printer** n impresora (por) láser
lash [læʃ] n latigazo; (also: eye~) pestaña ♦ vt azotar; (tie: to ~ to/together atar a/atar; ~ out vi: **to ~ out (at sb)** (hit) arremeter (contra uno); **to ~ out against sb** lanzar invectivas contra uno

lass [læs] (*BRIT*) *n* chica
lasso [læˈsuː] *n* lazo
last [lɑːst] *adj* (*far on: end: of series etc*) final
♦ *adv* (*most recently*) la última vez; (*finally*)
por último ♦ *vi* durar; (*continue*) continuar,
seguir; **~ night** anoche; **~ week** la semana
pasada; **at ~** por fin; **~ but one** penúltimo;
~-ditch *adj* (*attempt*) último, desesperado;
~ing *adj* duradero; **~ly** *adv* por último,
finalmente; **~-minute** *adj* de última hora
latch [lætʃ] *n* pestillo
late [leɪt] *adj* (*far on: in time, process etc*) al
final de; (*not on time*) tarde, atrasado; (*dead*)
fallecido ♦ *adv* tarde; (*behind time, schedule*)
con retraso; **of ~** últimamente; **~ at night** a
última hora de la noche; **in ~ May** hacia fines
de mayo; **the ~ Mr X** el difunto Sr X;
~comer *n* recién llegado/a; **~ly** *adv*
últimamente; **~r** *adj* (*date etc*) posterior;
(*version etc*) más reciente ♦ *adv* más tarde,
después; **~st** [ˈleɪtɪst] *adj* último; **at the ~st** a
más tardar
lathe [leɪð] *n* torno
lather [ˈlɑːðə*] *n* espuma (de jabón) ♦ *vt*
enjabonar
Latin [ˈlætɪn] *n* latín *m* ♦ *adj* latino;
~ America *n* América latina; **~-American**
adj, *n* latinoamericano/a
latitude [ˈlætɪtjuːd] *n* latitud *f*; (*fig*) libertad *f*
latter [ˈlætə*] *adj* último; (*of two*) segundo
♦ *n*: **the ~** el último, éste; **~ly** *adv*
últimamente
laudable [ˈlɔːdəbl] *adj* loable
laugh [lɑːf] *n* risa ♦ *vi* reír(se); (**to do sth**) **for
a ~** (*hacer algo*) en broma; **~ at** *vt fus* reírse
de; **~ off** *vt* tomar algo a risa; **~able** *adj*
ridículo; **~ing stock** *n*: **the ~ing stock of** el
hazmerreír de; **~ter** *n* risa
launch [lɔːntʃ] *n* lanzamiento; (*boat*) lancha
♦ *vt* (*ship*) botar; (*rocket etc*) lanzar; (*fig*)
comenzar; **~ into** *vt fus* lanzarse a; **~(ing)
pad** *n* plataforma de lanzamiento
launder [ˈlɔːndə*] *vt* lavar
Launderette ® [lɔːnˈdrɛt] (*BRIT*) *n*
lavandería (automática)
Laundromat ® [ˈlɔːndrəmæt] (*US*) *n* =
Launderette
laundry [ˈlɔːndrɪ] *n* (*dirty*) ropa sucia; (*clean*)
colada; (*room*) lavadero
lavatory [ˈlævətərɪ] *n* wáter *m*
lavender [ˈlævəndə*] *n* lavanda
lavish [ˈlævɪʃ] *adj* (*amount*) abundante;
(*person*): **~ with** pródigo en ♦ *vt*: **to ~ sth on
sb** colmar a uno de algo
law [lɔː] *n* ley *f*; (*SCOL*) derecho; (*a rule*) regla;
(*professions connected with ~*) jurisprudencia;
~-abiding *adj* respetuoso de la ley; **~ and
order** *n* orden *m* público; **~ court** *n* tribunal
m (de justicia); **~ful** *adj* legítimo, lícito;

~less *adj* (*action*) criminal
lawn [lɔːn] *n* césped *m*; **~mower** *n*
cortacésped *m*; **~ tennis** *n* tenis *m* sobre
hierba
law school (*US*) *n* (*SCOL*) facultad *f* de
derecho
lawsuit [ˈlɔːsuːt] *n* pleito
lawyer [ˈlɔːjə*] *n* abogado/a; (*for sales, wills
etc*) notario/a
lax [læks] *adj* laxo
laxative [ˈlæksətɪv] *n* laxante *m*
lay [leɪ] (*pt, pp laid*) *pt of* **lie** ♦ *adj* laico; (*not
expert*) lego ♦ *vt* (*place*) colocar; (*eggs, table*)
poner; (*cable*) tender; (*carpet*) extender;
~ aside *or* **by** *vt* dejar a un lado; **~ down** *vt*
(*pen etc*) dejar; (*rules etc*) establecer; **to
~ down the law** (*pej*) imponer las normas;
~ off *vt* (*workers*) despedir; **~ on** *vt* (*meal,
facilities*) proveer; **~ out** *vt* (*spread out*)
disponer, exponer; **~about** (*inf*) *n* vago/a;
~-by *n* (*BRIT: AUT*) área de aparcamiento
layer [ˈleɪə*] *n* capa
layman [ˈleɪmən] (*irreg*) *n* lego
layout [ˈleɪaut] *n* (*design*) plan *m*, trazado;
(*PRESS*) composición *f*
laze [leɪz] *vi* (*also: ~ about*) holgazanear
lazy [ˈleɪzɪ] *adj* perezoso, vago; (*movement*)
lento
lb. *abbr* = **pound** (*weight*)
lead[1] [liːd] (*pt, pp led*) *n* (*front position*)
delantera; (*clue*) pista; (*ELEC*) cable *m*; (*for
dog*) correa; (*THEATRE*) papel *m* principal ♦ *vt*
(*walk etc in front of*) ir a la cabeza de;
(*guide*): **to ~ sb somewhere** conducir a uno a
algún sitio; (*be leader of*) dirigir; (*start, guide:
activity*) protagonizar ♦ *vi* conducir a; (*road, pipe etc*)
conducir a; (*SPORT*) ir primero; **to be in the ~**
(*SPORT*) llevar la delantera; (*fig*) ir a la cabeza;
to ~ the way (*also fig*) llevar la delantera;
~ away *vt* llevar; **~ back** *vt* (*person, route*)
llevar de vuelta; **~ on** *vt* (*tease*) engañar;
~ to *vt fus* producir, provocar; **~ up to** *vt fus*
(*events*) conducir a; (*in conversation*) preparar
el terreno para
lead[2] [lɛd] *n* (*metal*) plomo; (*in pencil*) mina;
~ed petrol *n* gasolina con plomo
leader [ˈliːdə*] *n* jefe/a *m/f*, líder *m*; (*SPORT*)
líder *m*; **~ship** *n* dirección *f*; (*position*)
mando; (*quality*) iniciativa
leading [ˈliːdɪŋ] *adj* (*main*) principal; (*first*)
primero; (*front*) delantero; **~ lady** *n*
(*THEATRE*) primera actriz *f*; **~ light** *n* (*person*)
figura principal; **~ man** (*irreg*) *n* (*THEATRE*)
primer galán *m*
lead singer [liːd-] *n* cantante *m/f*
leaf [liːf] (*pl leaves*) *n* hoja ♦ *vi*: **to ~ through**
hojear; **to turn over a new ~** reformarse
leaflet [ˈliːflɪt] *n* folleto
league [liːg] *n* sociedad *f*; (*FOOTBALL*) liga; **to**

be in ~ with haberse confabulado con

leak [li:k] n (of liquid, gas) escape m, fuga; (in pipe) agujero; (in roof) gotera; (in security) filtración f ♦ vi (shoes, ship) hacer agua; (pipe) tener (un) escape; (roof) gotear; (liquid, gas) escaparse, fugarse; (fig) divulgarse ♦ vt (fig) filtrar

lean [li:n] (pt, pp leaned or leant) adj (thin) flaco; (meat) magro ♦ vt: to ~ sth on sth apoyar algo en algo ♦ vi (slope) inclinarse; to ~ against apoyarse contra; to ~ on apoyarse en; ~ back/forward vi inclinarse hacia atrás/adelante; ~ out vi asomarse; ~ over vi inclinarse; ~ing n: ~ing (towards) inclinación f (hacia); **leant** [lɛnt] pt, pp of lean

leap [li:p] (pt, pp leaped or leapt) n salto ♦ vi saltar; ~frog n pídola; ~ year n año bisiesto

learn [lɜːn] (pt, pp learned or learnt) vt aprender ♦ vi aprender; to ~ about sth enterarse de algo; to ~ to do sth aprender a hacer algo; ~ed ['lɜːnɪd] adj erudito; ~er n (BRIT: also: ~er driver) principiante m/f; ~ing n el saber m, conocimientos mpl

lease [li:s] n arriendo ♦ vt arrendar

leash [li:ʃ] n correa

least [li:st] adj: the ~ (slightest) el menor, el más pequeño; (smallest amount of) mínimo ♦ adv (+ vb) menos; (+ adj): the ~ expensive el/la menos costoso/a; the ~ possible effort el menor esfuerzo posible; at ~ por lo menos, al menos; you could at ~ have written por lo menos podías haber escrito; not in the ~ en absoluto

leather ['lɛðə*] n cuero

leave [li:v] (pt, pp left) vt dejar; (go away from) abandonar; (place etc: permanently) salir de ♦ vi irse; (train etc) salir ♦ n permiso; to ~ sth to sb (money etc) legar algo a uno; (responsibility etc) encargar a uno de algo; to be left quedar, sobrar; there's some milk left over sobra or queda algo de leche; on ~ de permiso; ~ behind vt (on purpose) dejar; (accidentally) dejarse; ~ out vt omitir; ~ of absence n permiso de ausentarse

leaves [li:vz] npl of leaf

Lebanon ['lɛbənən] n: the ~ el Líbano

lecherous ['lɛtʃərəs] (pej) adj lascivo

lecture ['lɛktʃə*] n conferencia; (SCOL) clase f ♦ vi dar una clase ♦ vt (scold): to ~ sb on or about sth echar una reprimenda a uno por algo; to give a ~ on dar una conferencia sobre; ~r n conferenciante m/f; (BRIT: at university) profesor(a) m/f

led [lɛd] pt, pp of lead

ledge [lɛdʒ] n repisa; (of window) alféizar m; (of mountain) saliente m

ledger ['lɛdʒə*] n libro mayor

leech [li:tʃ] n sanguijuela

leek [li:k] n puerro

leer [lɪə*] vi: to ~ at sb mirar de manera lasciva a uno

leeway ['li:weɪ] n (fig): to have some ~ tener cierta libertad de acción

left [lɛft] pt, pp of leave ♦ adj izquierdo; (remaining): there are 2 ~ quedan dos ♦ n izquierda ♦ adv a la izquierda; on or to the ~ a la izquierda; the L~ (POL) la izquierda; ~-handed adj zurdo; the ~-hand side n la izquierda; ~-luggage (office) (BRIT) n consigna; ~-overs npl sobras fpl; ~-wing adj (POL) de izquierdas, izquierdista

leg [lɛg] n pierna; (of animal, chair) pata; (trouser ~) pernera; (CULIN: of lamb) pierna; (of chicken) pata; (of journey) etapa

legacy ['lɛgəsɪ] n herencia

legal ['li:gl] adj (permitted by law) lícito; (of law) legal; ~ holiday (US) n fiesta oficial; ~ize vt legalizar; ~ly adv legalmente; ~ tender n moneda de curso legal

legend ['lɛdʒənd] n (also fig: person) leyenda

legislation [lɛdʒɪs'leɪʃən] n legislación f

legislature ['lɛdʒɪslətʃə*] n cuerpo legislativo

legitimate [lɪ'dʒɪtɪmət] adj legítimo

leg-room n espacio para las piernas

leisure ['lɛʒə*] n ocio, tiempo libre; at ~ con tranquilidad; ~ centre n centro de recreo; ~ly adj sin prisa; lento

lemon ['lɛmən] n limón m; ~ade n (fizzy) gaseosa; ~ tea n té m con limón

lend [lɛnd] (pt, pp lent) vt: to ~ sth to sb prestar algo a alguien; ~ing library n biblioteca de préstamo

length [lɛŋθ] n (size) largo, longitud f; (distance): the ~ of todo lo largo de; (of swimming pool, cloth) largo; (of wood, string) trozo; (amount of time) duración f; at ~ (at last) por fin, finalmente; (lengthily) largamente; ~en vt alargar ♦ vi alargarse; ~ways adv a lo largo; ~y adj largo, extenso

lenient ['li:nɪənt] adj indulgente

lens [lɛnz] n (of spectacles) lente f; (of camera) objetivo

Lent [lɛnt] n Cuaresma

lent [lɛnt] pt, pp of lend

lentil ['lɛntl] n lenteja

Leo ['li:əu] n Leo

leotard ['li:ətɑːd] n mallas fpl

leprosy ['lɛprəsɪ] n lepra

lesbian ['lɛzbɪən] n lesbiana

less [lɛs] adj (in size, degree etc) menor; (in quality) menos ♦ pron, adv menos ♦ prep: ~ tax/10% discount menos impuestos/el 10 por ciento de descuento; ~ than half menos de la mitad; ~ than ever menos que nunca; ~ and ~ cada vez menos; the ~ he works ... cuanto menos trabaja ...; ~en vi disminuir, reducirse ♦ vt disminuir, reducir; ~er ['lɛsə*] adj menor; to a ~er extent en menor grado

lesson ['lɛsn] n clase f; (warning) lección f

let [lɛt] (pt, pp **let**) vt (allow) dejar, permitir; (BRIT: lease) alquilar; **to ~ sb do sth** dejar que uno haga algo; **to ~ sb know sth** comunicar algo a uno; **~'s go** ¡vamos!; **~ him come** que venga; **"to ~" "se alquila"; ~ down** vt (tyre) desinflar; (disappoint) defraudar; **~ go** vi, vt soltar; **~ in** vt dejar entrar; (visitor etc) hacer pasar; **~ off** vt (culprit) dejar escapar; (gun) disparar; (bomb) accionar; (firework) hacer estallar; **~ on** (inf) vi divulgar; **~ out** vt dejar salir; (sound) soltar; **~ up** vi amainar, disminuir

lethal ['liːθl] adj (weapon) mortífero; (poison, wound) mortal

letter ['lɛtə*] n (of alphabet) letra; (correspondence) carta; **~ bomb** n carta-bomba; **~box** (BRIT) n buzón m; **~ing** n letras fpl

lettuce ['lɛtɪs] n lechuga

let-up n disminución f

leukaemia [luːˈkiːmɪə] (US **leukemia**) n leucemia

level ['lɛvl] adj (flat) llano ♦ adv: **to draw ~ with** llegar a la altura de ♦ n nivel m; (height) altura ♦ vt nivelar; allanar; (destroy: building) derribar; (: forest) arrasar; **to be ~ with** estar a nivel de; "A" **~s** (BRIT) npl ≈ exámenes mpl de bachillerato superior, B.U.P.; "O" **~s** (BRIT) npl ≈ exámenes mpl de octavo de básica; **on the ~** (fig: honest) serio; **~ off** or **out** vt (prices etc) estabilizarse; **~ crossing** (BRIT) n paso a nivel; **~-headed** adj sensato

lever ['liːvə*] n (also fig) palanca ♦ vt: **to ~ up** levantar con palanca; **~age** n (using bar etc) apalancamiento; (fig: influence) influencia

levy ['lɛvɪ] n impuesto ♦ vt exigir, recaudar

lewd [luːd] adj lascivo; (joke) obsceno, colorado (AM)

liability [laɪəˈbɪlətɪ] n (pej: person, thing) estorbo, lastre m; (JUR: responsibility) responsabilidad f; **liabilities** npl (COMM) pasivo

liable ['laɪəbl] adj (subject): **~ to** sujeto a; (responsible): **~ for** responsable de; (likely): **~ to do** propenso a hacer

liaise [lɪˈeɪz] vi: **to ~ with** enlazar con; **liaison** [liːˈeɪzɒn] n (coordination) enlace m; (affair) relaciones fpl amorosas

liar ['laɪə*] n mentiroso/a

libel ['laɪbl] n calumnia ♦ vt calumniar

liberal ['lɪbərəl] adj liberal; (offer, amount etc) generoso

liberate ['lɪbəreɪt] vt (people: from poverty etc) librar; (prisoner) libertar; (country) liberar

liberty ['lɪbətɪ] n libertad f; (criminal): **to be at ~** estar en libertad; **to be at ~ to do** estar libre para hacer; **to take the ~ of doing sth** tomarse la libertad de hacer algo

Libra ['liːbrə] n Libra

librarian [laɪˈbrɛərɪən] n bibliotecario/a

library ['laɪbrərɪ] n biblioteca

libretto [lɪˈbrɛtəʊ] n libreto

Libya ['lɪbɪə] n Libia; **~n** adj, n libio/a m/f

lice [laɪs] npl of **louse**

licence ['laɪsəns] (US **license**) n licencia; (permit) permiso; (also: driving ~, (US) driver's ~) carnet m de conducir (SP), permiso (AM)

license ['laɪsəns] n (US) = **licence** ♦ vt autorizar, dar permiso a; **~d** adj (for alcohol) autorizado para vender bebidas alcohólicas; (car) matriculado; **~ plate** (US) n placa (de matrícula)

lick [lɪk] vt lamer; (inf: defeat) dar una paliza a; **to ~ one's lips** relamerse

licorice ['lɪkərɪs] (US) n = **liquorice**

lid [lɪd] n (of box, case) tapa; (of pan) tapadera

lido ['laɪdəʊ] n (BRIT) piscina

lie [laɪ] (pt **lay**, pp **lain**) vi (rest) estar echado, estar acostado; (of object: be situated) estar, encontrarse; (tell lies: pt, pp **lied**) mentir ♦ n mentira; **to ~ low** (fig) mantenerse a escondidas; **~ about** or **around** vi (things) estar tirado; (BRIT: people) estar tumbado; **~-down** (BRIT) n: **to have a ~-down** echarse (una siesta); **~-in** (BRIT) n: **to have a ~-in** quedarse en la cama

lieu [luː]: **in ~ of** prep en lugar de

lieutenant [lɛfˈtɛnənt, (US) luːˈtɛnənt] n (MIL) teniente m

life [laɪf] (pl **lives**) n vida; **to come to ~** animarse; **~ assurance** (BRIT) n seguro de vida; **~belt** (BRIT) n salvavidas m inv; **~boat** n lancha de socorro; **~guard** n vigilante m/f, socorrista m/f; **~ insurance** n = **~ assurance**; **~ jacket** n chaleco salvavidas; **~less** adj sin vida; (dull) soso; **~like** adj (model etc) que parece vivo; (realistic) realista; **~long** adj de toda la vida; **~ preserver** (US) n cinturón m/chaleco salvavidas; **~ sentence** n cadena perpetua; **~-size** adj de tamaño natural; **~ span** n vida; **~style** n estilo de vida; **~ support system** n (MED) sistema m de respiración asistida; **~time** n (of person) vida; (of thing) período de vida

lift [lɪft] vt levantar; (end: ban, rule) levantar, suprimir ♦ vi (fog) disiparse ♦ n (BRIT: machine) ascensor m; **to give sb a ~** (BRIT) llevar a uno en el coche; **~-off** n despegue m

light [laɪt] (pt, pp **lighted** or **lit**) n luz f; (lamp) luz f, lámpara; (AUT) faro; (for cigarette etc): **have you got a ~?** ¿tienes fuego? ♦ vt (candle, cigarette, fire) encender (SP), prender (AM); (room) alumbrar ♦ adj (colour) claro; (not heavy, also fig) ligero; (room) con mucha luz; (gentle, graceful) ágil; **~s** npl (traffic ~s) semáforos mpl; **to come to ~** salir a luz; **in the ~ of** (new evidence etc) a la luz de; **~ up** vi (smoke) encender un cigarrillo; (face) iluminarse ♦ vt (illuminate) iluminar, alumbrar; (set fire to) encender; **~ bulb** n bombilla (SP), foco (AM); **~en** vt (make less heavy) aligerar; **~er** n (also: **cigarette ~er**) encendedor m, mechero; **~-headed** adj (dizzy) mareado; (excited) exaltado; **~-hearted** adj (person) alegre; (remark etc) divertido; **~house** n faro; **~ing** n (system) alumbrado; **~ly** adv ligeramente; (not seriously) con poca seriedad; **to get off ~ly** ser castigado con poca severidad; **~ness** n (in weight) ligereza

lightning ['laɪtnɪŋ] n relámpago, rayo; **~ conductor** (US = **rod**) n pararrayos m inv

light: **~ pen** n lápiz m óptico; **~weight** adj (suit) ligero ♦ n (BOXING) peso ligero; **~ year** n año luz

like [laɪk] vt gustarle a uno ♦ prep como ♦ adj parecido, semejante ♦ n: **and the ~** y otros por el estilo; **his ~s and dislikes** sus gustos y aversiones; **I would ~, I'd ~** me gustaría; (for purchase) quisiera; **would you ~ a coffee?** ¿te apetece un café?; **I ~ swimming** me gusta nadar; **she ~s apples** le gustan las manzanas; **to be or look ~ sb/sth** parecerse a alguien/ algo; **what does it look/taste/sound ~?** ¿cómo es/a qué sabe/cómo suena?; **that's just ~ him** es muy de él, es característico de él; **do it ~ this** hazlo así; **it is nothing ~ ...** no tiene parecido alguno con ...; **~able** adj simpático, agradable

likelihood ['laɪklɪhʊd] n probabilidad f

likely ['laɪklɪ] adj probable; **he's ~ to leave** es probable que se vaya; **not ~!** ¡ni hablar!

likeness ['laɪknɪs] n semejanza, parecido; **that's a good ~** se parece mucho

likewise ['laɪkwaɪz] adv igualmente; **to do ~** hacer lo mismo

liking ['laɪkɪŋ] n: **~ (for)** (person) cariño (a); (thing) afición (a); **to be to sb's ~** ser del gusto de uno

lilac ['laɪlək] n (tree) lilo; (flower) lila

lily ['lɪlɪ] n lirio, azucena; **~ of the valley** n lirio de los valles

limb [lɪm] n miembro

limber ['lɪmbə*]: **to ~ up** vi (SPORT) hacer ejercicios de calentamiento

limbo ['lɪmbəʊ] n: **to be in ~** (fig) quedar a la expectativa

lime [laɪm] n (tree) limero; (fruit) lima; (GEO) cal f

limelight ['laɪmlaɪt] n: **to be in the ~** (fig) ser el centro de atención

limerick ['lɪmərɪk] n especie de poema humorístico

limestone ['laɪmstəʊn] n piedra caliza

limit ['lɪmɪt] n límite m ♦ vt limitar; **~ed** adj limitado; **to be ~ed to** limitarse a; **~ed (liability) company** (BRIT) n sociedad f anónima

limousine ['lɪməziːn] n limusina

limp [lɪmp] n: **to have a ~** tener cojera ♦ vi cojear ♦ adj flojo; (material) fláccido

limpet ['lɪmpɪt] n lapa

line [laɪn] n línea; (rope) cuerda; (for fishing) sedal m; (wire) hilo; (row, series) fila, hilera; (of writing) renglón m, línea; (of song) verso; (on face) arruga; (RAIL) vía ♦ vt (road etc) llenar; (SEWING) forrar; **to ~ the streets** llenar las aceras; **in ~ with** alineado con; (according to) de acuerdo con; **~ up** vi hacer cola ♦ vt alinear; (prepare) preparar; organizar

lined [laɪnd] adj (face) arrugado; (paper) rayado

linen ['lɪnɪn] n ropa blanca; (cloth) lino

liner ['laɪnə*] n vapor m de línea, transatlántico m; (for bin) bolsa (de basura)

linesman ['laɪnzmən] n (SPORT) juez m de línea

line-up n (US: queue) cola; (SPORT) alineación f

linger ['lɪŋgə*] vi retrasarse, tardar en marcharse; (smell, tradition) persistir

lingerie ['lænʒəriː] n lencería

linguist ['lɪŋgwɪst] n lingüista m/f; **~ics** n lingüística

lining ['laɪnɪŋ] n forro; (ANAT) (membrana) mucosa

link [lɪŋk] n (of a chain) eslabón m; (relationship) relación f, vínculo ♦ vt vincular, unir; (associate): **to ~ with** or **to** relacionar con; **~s** npl (GOLF) campo de golf; **~ up** vt acoplar ♦ vi unirse

lino ['laɪnəʊ] n = **linoleum**

linoleum [lɪ'nəʊlɪəm] n linóleo

lion ['laɪən] n león m; **~ess** n leona

lip [lɪp] n labio

liposuction ['lɪpəʊsʌkʃn] n liposucción f

lip: **~read** vi leer los labios; **~ salve** n crema protectora para labios; **~ service** n: **to pay ~ service to sth** (pej) prometer algo de boquilla; **~stick** n lápiz m de labios, carmín m

liqueur [lɪ'kjʊə*] n licor m

liquid ['lɪkwɪd] adj, n líquido; **~ize** [-aɪz] vt (CULIN) licuar; **~izer** n licuadora

liquor ['lɪkə*] n licor m, bebidas fpl alcohólicas

liquorice ['lɪkərɪs] (BRIT) n regaliz m

liquor store (US) n bodega, tienda de vinos y bebidas alcohólicas

Lisbon ['lɪzbən] n Lisboa

lisp [lɪsp] n ceceo ♦ vi cecear

list [lɪst] n lista ♦ vt (mention) enumerar; (put on a list) poner en una lista; **~ed building** (BRIT) n monumento declarado de interés *histórico-artístico*

listen ['lɪsn] *vi* escuchar, oír; **to ~ to** sb/sth escuchar a uno/algo; **~er** *n* oyente *m/f*; (*RADIO*) radioyente *m/f*

listless ['lɪstlɪs] *adj* apático, indiferente

lit [lɪt] *pt, pp of* **light**

liter ['liːtə*] (*US*) *n* = **litre**

literacy ['lɪtərəsɪ] *n* capacidad *f* de leer y escribir

literal ['lɪtərl] *adj* literal

literary ['lɪtərərɪ] *adj* literario

literate ['lɪtərət] *adj* que sabe leer y escribir; (*educated*) culto

literature ['lɪtərɪtʃə*] *n* literatura; (*brochures etc*) folletos *mpl*

lithe [laɪð] *adj* ágil

litigation [lɪtɪ'geɪʃən] *n* litigio

litre ['liːtə*] (*US* **liter**) *n* litro

litter ['lɪtə*] *n* (*rubbish*) basura; (*young animals*) camada, cría; **~ bin** (*BRIT*) *n* papelera; **~ed** *adj*: **~ed with** (*scattered*) lleno de

little ['lɪtl] *adj* (*small*) pequeño; (*not much*) poco ♦ *adv* poco; **a ~** un poco (de); **~ house/bird** casita/pajarito; **a ~ bit** un poquito; **~ by ~** poco a poco; **~ finger** *n* dedo meñique

live¹ [laɪv] *adj* (*animal*) vivo; (*wire*) conectado; (*broadcast*) en directo; (*shell*) cargado

live² [lɪv] *vi* vivir; **~ down** *vt* hacer olvidar; **~ on** *vt fus* (*food, salary*) vivir de; **~ together** *vi* vivir juntos; **~ up to** *vt fus* (*fulfil*) cumplir con

livelihood ['laɪvlɪhud] *n* sustento

lively ['laɪvlɪ] *adj* vivo; (*interesting: place, book etc*) animado

liven up ['laɪvn-] *vt* animar ♦ *vi* animarse

liver ['lɪvə*] *n* hígado

lives [laɪvz] *npl of* **life**

livestock ['laɪvstɔk] *n* ganado

livid ['lɪvɪd] *adj* lívido; (*furious*) furioso

living ['lɪvɪŋ] *adj* (*alive*) vivo ♦ *n*: **to earn** or **make a ~** ganarse la vida; **~ conditions** *npl* condiciones *fpl* de vida; **~ room** *n* sala (de estar); **~ standards** *npl* nivel *m* de vida; **~ wage** *n* jornal *m* suficiente para vivir

lizard ['lɪzəd] *n* lagarto; (*small*) lagartija

load [laud] *n* carga; (*weight*) peso ♦ *vt* (*COMPUT*) cargar; (*also: ~ up*): **to ~ (with)** cargar (con or de); **a ~ of rubbish** (*inf*) tonterías *fpl*; **a ~ of, ~s of** (*fig*) (gran) cantidad de, montones de; **~ed** *adj* (*vehicle*): **to be ~ed with** estar cargado de; (*question*) intencionado; (*inf: rich*) forrado (de dinero)

loaf [lauf] (*pl* **loaves**) *n* (barra de) pan *m*

loan [laun] *n* préstamo ♦ *vt* prestar; **on ~** prestado

loath [lauθ] *adj*: **to be ~ to do** sth estar poco

dispuesto a hacer algo

loathe [lauð] *vt* aborrecer; (*person*) odiar; **loathing** *n* aversión *f*; odio

loaves [lauvz] *npl of* **loaf**

lobby ['lɔbɪ] *n* vestíbulo, sala de espera; (*POL: pressure group*) grupo de presión ♦ *vt* presionar

lobster ['lɔbstə*] *n* langosta

local ['laukl] *adj* local ♦ *n* (*pub*) bar *m*; **the ~s** los vecinos, los del lugar; **~ anaesthetic** *n* (*MED*) anestesia local; **~ authority** *n* municipio, ayuntamiento (*SP*); **~ call** *n* (*TEL*) llamada local; **~ government** *n* gobierno municipal; **~ity** [-'kælɪtɪ] *n* localidad *f*; **~ly** [-kəlɪ] *adv* en la vecindad; por aquí

locate [lau'keɪt] *vt* (*find*) localizar; (*situate*): **to be ~d in** estar situado en

location [lau'keɪʃən] *n* situación *f*; **on ~** (*CINEMA*) en exteriores

loch [lɔx] *n* lago

lock [lɔk] *n* (*of door, box*) cerradura; (*of canal*) esclusa; (*of hair*) mechón *m* ♦ *vt* (*with key*) cerrar (con llave) ♦ *vi* (*door etc*) cerrarse (con llave); (*wheels*) trabarse; **~ in** *vt* encerrar; **~ out** *vt* (*person*) cerrar la puerta a; **~ up** *vt* (*criminal*) meter en la cárcel; (*mental patient*) encerrar; (*house*) cerrar (con llave) ♦ *vi* echar la llave

locker ['lɔkə*] *n* casillero

locket ['lɔkɪt] *n* medallón *m*

locksmith ['lɔksmɪθ] *n* cerrajero/a

lockup ['lɔkʌp] *n* (*jail, cell*) cárcel *f*

locum ['laukəm] *n* (*MED*) (médico/a) interino/a

locust ['laukəst] *n* langosta

lodge [lɔdʒ] *n* casita (del guarda) ♦ *vi* (*person*): **to ~ (with)** alojarse (en casa de); (*bullet, bone*) incrustarse ♦ *vt* (*complaint*) presentar; **~r** *n* huésped(a) *m/f*

lodgings ['lɔdʒɪŋz] *npl* alojamiento

loft [lɔft] *n* desván *m*

lofty ['lɔftɪ] *adj* (*noble*) sublime; (*haughty*) altanero

log [lɔg] *n* (*of wood*) leño, tronco; (*written account*) diario ♦ *vt* anotar

logbook ['lɔgbuk] *n* (*NAUT*) diario de a bordo; (*AVIAT*) libro de vuelo; (*of car*) documentación *f* (del coche (*SP*) or carro (*AM*))

loggerheads ['lɔgəhɛdz] *npl*: **to be at ~ (with)** estar en desacuerdo (con)

logic ['lɔdʒɪk] *n* lógica; **~al** *adj* lógico

logo ['laugəu] *n* logotipo

loin [lɔɪn] *n* (*CULIN*) lomo, solomillo

loiter ['lɔɪtə*] *vi* (*linger*) entretenerse

loll [lɔl] *vi* (*also: ~ about*) repantigarse

lollipop ['lɔlɪpɔp] *n* chupa-chups ® *m inv*, piruli *m*; **~ man/lady** (*BRIT irreg*) *n* persona encargada de ayudar a los niños a cruzar la *calle*

London ['lʌndən] *n* Londres; **~er** *n* londinense *m/f*

lone [ləun] *adj* solitario

loneliness ['ləunlınıs] *n* soledad *f*; aislamiento

lonely ['ləunlı] *adj* (*situation*) solitario; (*person*) solo; (*place*) aislado

long [lɒŋ] *adj* largo ♦ *adv* mucho tiempo, largamente ♦ *vi*: **to ~ for sth** anhelar algo; **so or as ~ as** mientras, con tal que; **don't be ~!** ¡no tardes!, ¡vuelve pronto!; **how ~ is the street?** ¿cuánto tiene la calle de largo?; **how ~ is the lesson?** ¿cuánto dura la clase?; **6 metres ~** que mide 6 metros, de 6 metros de largo; **6 months ~** que dura 6 meses, de 6 meses de duración; **all night ~** toda la noche; **he no ~er comes** ya no viene; **~ before** mucho antes; **before ~** (+ *future*) dentro de poco; (+ *past*) poco tiempo después; **at ~ last** al fin, por fin; **~-distance** *adj* (*race*) de larga distancia; (*call*) interurbano; **~-haired** *adj* de pelo largo; **~hand** *n* escritura sin abreviaturas; **~ing** *n* anhelo, ansia; (*nostalgia*) nostalgia ♦ *adj* anhelante

longitude ['lɒŋgıtjuːd] *n* longitud *f*

long-: ~ jump *n* salto de longitud; **~-life** *adj* (*batteries*) de larga duración; (*milk*) uperizado; **~-lost** *adj* desaparecido hace mucho tiempo; **~-range** *adj* (*plan*) de gran alcance; (*missile*) de largo alcance; **~-sighted** (*BRIT*) *adj* présbita; **~-standing** *adj* de mucho tiempo; **~-suffering** *adj* sufrido; **~-term** *adj* a largo plazo; **~ wave** *n* onda larga; **~-winded** *adj* prolijo

loo [luː] (*BRIT*: *inf*) *n* wáter *m*

look [luk] *vi* mirar; (*seem*) parecer; (*building etc*): **to ~ south/on to the sea** dar al sur/al mar ♦ *n* (*gen*): **to have a ~** mirar; (*glance*) mirada; (*appearance*) aire *m*, aspecto; **~s** *npl* (*good ~s*) belleza; **~ (here)!** (*expressing annoyance etc*) ¡oye!; **~!** (*expressing surprise*) ¡mira!; **~ after** *vt fus* (*care for*) cuidar a; (*deal with*) encargarse de; **~ at** *vt fus* mirar; (*read quickly*) echar un vistazo a; **~ back** *vi* mirar hacia atrás; **~ down on** *vt fus* (*fig*) despreciar, mirar con desprecio; **~ for** *vt fus* buscar; **~ forward to** *vt fus* esperar con ilusión; (*in letters*): **we ~ forward to hearing from you** quedamos a la espera de sus gratas noticias; **~ into** *vt* investigar; **~ on** *vi* mirar (como espectador); **~ out** *vi* (*beware*): **to ~ out (for)** tener cuidado (de); **~ out for** *vt fus* (*seek*) buscar; (*await*) esperar; **~ round** *vi* volver la cabeza; **~ through** *vt fus* (*examine*) examinar; **~ to** *vt fus* (*rely on*) contar con; **~ up** *vi* mirar hacia arriba; (*improve*) mejorar ♦ *vt* (*word*) buscar; **~ up to** *vt fus* admirar; **~-out** *n* (*tower etc*) puesto de observación;

(*person*) vigía *m/f*; **to be on the ~-out for sth** estar al acecho de algo

loom [luːm] *vi*: **~ (up)** (*threaten*) surgir, amenazar; (*event*: *approach*) aproximarse

loony ['luːnı] (*inf*) *n*, *adj* loco/a *m/f*

loop [luːp] *n* lazo ♦ *vt*: **to ~ sth round sth** pasar algo alrededor de algo; **~hole** *n* escapatoria

loose [luːs] *adj* suelto; (*clothes*) ancho; (*morals*, *discipline*) relajado; **to be on the ~** estar en libertad; **to be at a ~ end** or **at ~ ends** (*US*) no saber qué hacer; **~ change** *n* cambio; **~ chippings** *npl* (*on road*) gravilla suelta; **~ly** *adv* libremente, aproximadamente; **~n** *vt* aflojar

loot [luːt] *n* botín *m* ♦ *vt* saquear

lop off [lɒp-] *vt* (*branches*) podar

lop-sided *adj* torcido

lord [lɔːd] *n* señor *m*; **L~ Smith** Lord Smith; **the L~** el Señor; **my ~** (*to bishop*) Ilustrísima; (*to noble etc*) Señor; **good L~!** ¡Dios mío!; **the (House of) L~s** (*BRIT*) la Cámara de los Lores; **~ship** *n*: **your L~ship** su Señoría

lore [lɔː] *n* tradiciones *fpl*

lorry ['lɒrı] (*BRIT*) *n* camión *m*; **~ driver** *n* camionero/a

lose [luːz] (*pt*, *pp* **lost**) *vt* perder ♦ *vi* perder, ser vencido; **to ~ (time)** (*clock*) atrasarse; **~r** *n* perdedor(a) *m/f*

loss [lɒs] *n* pérdida; **heavy ~es** (*MIL*) grandes pérdidas; **to be at a ~** no saber qué hacer; **to make a ~** sufrir pérdidas

lost [lɒst] *pt*, *pp* of **lose** ♦ *adj* perdido; **~ property** (*US* **~ and found**) *n* objetos *mpl* perdidos

lot [lɒt] *n* (*group*: *of things*) grupo; (*at auctions*) lote *m*; **the ~** el todo, todos; **a ~** (*large number*: *of books etc*) muchos; (*a great deal*) mucho, bastante; **a ~ of**, **~s of** mucho(s) (*pl*); **I read a ~** leo bastante; **to draw ~s (for sth)** echar suertes (para decidir algo)

lotion ['ləuʃən] *n* loción *f*

lottery ['lɒtərı] *n* lotería

loud [laud] *adj* (*voice*, *sound*) fuerte; (*laugh*, *shout*) estrepitoso; (*condemnation etc*) enérgico; (*gaudy*) chillón/ona ♦ *adv* (*speak etc*) fuerte; **out ~** en voz alta; **~hailer** (*BRIT*) *n* megáfono; **~ly** *adv* (*noisily*) fuerte; (*aloud*) en voz alta; **~speaker** *n* altavoz *m*

lounge [laundʒ] *n* salón *m*, sala (de estar); (*at airport etc*) sala; (*BRIT*: *also*: **~-bar**) salón-bar *m* ♦ *vi* (*also*: **~ about** or **around**) reposar, holgazanear

louse [laus] (*pl* **lice**) *n* piojo

lousy ['lauzı] (*inf*) *adj* (*bad quality*) malísimo, asqueroso; (*ill*) fatal

lout [laut] *n* gamberro/a

lovable ['lʌvəbl] *adj* amable, simpático

love [lʌv] n (romantic, sexual) amor m; (kind, caring) cariño ♦ vt amar, querer; (thing, activity) encantarle a uno; "~ from Anne" (on letter) "un abrazo (de) Anne"; **to ~ to do** encantarle a uno hacer; **to be/fall in ~ with** estar enamorado/enamorarse de; **to make ~** hacer el amor; **for the ~ of** por amor de; "**15 ~**" (TENNIS) "15 a cero"; **I ~ paella** me encanta la paella; **~ affair** n aventura sentimental; **~ letter** n carta de amor; **~ life** n vida sentimental

lovely [ˈlʌvlɪ] adj (delightful) encantador(a); (beautiful) precioso

lover [ˈlʌvə*] n amante m/f; (person in love) enamorado; (amateur): **a ~ of** un(a) aficionado/a or un(a) amante de

loving [ˈlʌvɪŋ] adj amoroso, cariñoso; (action) tierno

low [ləʊ] adj, ad bajo ♦ n (METEOROLOGY) área de baja presión; **to be ~ on** (supplies etc) andar mal de; **to feel ~** sentirse deprimido; **to turn (down) ~** bajar; **~-alcohol** adj de bajo contenido en alcohol; **~-calorie** adj bajo en calorías; **~-cut** (dress) escotado

lower [ˈləʊə*] adj más bajo; (less important) menos importante ♦ vt bajar; (reduce) reducir ♦ vr: **to ~ o.s. to** (fig) rebajarse a

low: **~-fat** adj (milk, yoghurt) desnatado; (diet) bajo en calorías; **~lands** npl (GEO) tierras fpl bajas; **~ly** adj humilde, inferior; **~ season** n la temporada baja

loyal [ˈlɔɪəl] adj leal; **~ty** n lealtad f; **~ty card** n tarjeta cliente

lozenge [ˈlɔzɪndʒ] n (MED) pastilla

L.P. n abbr (= long-playing record) elepé m

L-plates [ˈɛl-] (BRIT) npl placas fpl de aprendiz de conductor

Ltd abbr (= limited company) S.A.

lubricate [ˈluːbrɪkeɪt] vt lubricar, engrasar

luck [lʌk] n suerte f; **bad ~** mala suerte; **good ~!** ¡que tengas suerte!, ¡suerte!; **bad or hard or tough ~!** ¡qué pena!; **~ily** adv afortunadamente; **~y** adj afortunado; (at cards etc) que tiene suerte; (object) que trae suerte

ludicrous [ˈluːdɪkrəs] adj absurdo

lug [lʌg] vt (drag) arrastrar

luggage [ˈlʌgɪdʒ] n equipaje m; **~ rack** n (on car) baca, portaequipajes m inv

lukewarm [ˈluːkwɔːm] adj tibio

lull [lʌl] n tregua ♦ vt: **to ~ sb to sleep** arrullar a uno; **to ~ sb into a false sense of security** dar a alguien una falsa sensación de seguridad

lullaby [ˈlʌləbaɪ] n nana

lumbago [lʌmˈbeɪgəʊ] n lumbago

lumber [ˈlʌmbə*] n (junk) trastos mpl viejos; (wood) maderos mpl; **~ with** vt: **to be ~ed with** tener que cargar con algo; **~jack** n maderero

luminous [ˈluːmɪnəs] adj luminoso

lump [lʌmp] n terrón m; (fragment) trozo; (swelling) bulto ♦ vt (also: **~ together**) juntar; **~ sum** n suma global; **~y** adj (sauce) lleno de grumos; (mattress) lleno de bultos

lunatic [ˈluːnətɪk] adj loco

lunch [lʌntʃ] n almuerzo, comida ♦ vi almorzar

luncheon [ˈlʌntʃən] n almuerzo; **~ voucher** (BRIT) n vale m de comida

lunch time n hora de comer

lung [lʌŋ] n pulmón m

lunge [lʌndʒ] vi (also: **~ forward**) abalanzarse; **to ~ at** arremeter contra

lurch [lɜːtʃ] vi dar sacudidas ♦ n sacudida; **to leave sb in the ~** dejar a uno plantado

lure [luə*] n (attraction) atracción f ♦ vt tentar

lurid [ˈluərɪd] adj (colour) chillón/ona; (account) espeluznante

lurk [lɜːk] vi (person, animal) estar al acecho; (fig) acechar

luscious [ˈlʌʃəs] adj (attractive: person, thing) precioso; (food) delicioso

lush [lʌʃ] adj exuberante

lust [lʌst] n lujuria; (greed) codicia

lustre [ˈlʌstə*] (US luster) n lustre m, brillo

lusty [ˈlʌstɪ] adj robusto, fuerte

Luxembourg [ˈlʌksəmbɜːg] n Luxemburgo

luxuriant [lʌgˈzjuərɪənt] adj exuberante

luxurious [lʌgˈzjuərɪəs] adj lujoso

luxury [ˈlʌkʃərɪ] n lujo ♦ cpd de lujo

lying [ˈlaɪɪŋ] n mentiras fpl ♦ adj mentiroso

lyrical [ˈlɪrɪkl] adj lírico

lyrics [ˈlɪrɪks] npl (of song) letra

M, m

m. abbr = metre; mile; million

M.A. abbr = Master of Arts

mac [mæk] (BRIT) n impermeable m

macaroni [mækəˈrəʊnɪ] n macarrones mpl

machine [məˈʃiːn] n máquina ♦ vt (dress etc) coser a máquina; (TECH) hacer a máquina; **~ gun** n ametralladora; **~ language** n (COMPUT) lenguaje m máquina; **~ry** n maquinaria; (fig) mecanismo

macho [ˈmætʃəʊ] adj machista

mackerel [ˈmækrl] n inv caballa

mackintosh [ˈmækɪntɔʃ] (BRIT) n impermeable m

mad [mæd] adj loco; (idea) disparatado; (angry) furioso; (keen): **to be ~ about sth** volverle loco a uno algo

madam [ˈmædəm] n señora

madden [ˈmædn] vt volver loco

made [meɪd] pt, pp of make

Madeira [məˈdɪərə] n (GEO) Madera; (wine) vino de Madera

made-to-measure (BRIT) adj hecho a la

medida

madly ['mædlɪ] adv locamente

madman ['mædmən] (irreg) n loco

madness ['mædnɪs] n locura

Madrid [mə'drɪd] n Madrid

magazine [mægə'ziːn] n revista; (RADIO, TV) programa m magazina

maggot ['mægət] n gusano

magic ['mædʒɪk] n magia ♦ adj mágico; **~ian** [mə'dʒɪʃən] n mago/a; (conjurer) presti-digitador(a) m/f

magistrate ['mædʒɪstreɪt] n juez m/f (municipal)

magnet ['mægnɪt] n imán m; **~ic** [-'nɛtɪk] adj magnético; (personality) atrayente

magnificent [mæg'nɪfɪsənt] adj magnífico

magnify ['mægnɪfaɪ] vt (object) ampliar; (sound) aumentar; **~ing glass** n lupa

magpie ['mægpaɪ] n urraca

mahogany [mə'hɔgənɪ] n caoba

maid [meɪd] n criada; **old ~** (pej) solterona

maiden ['meɪdn] n doncella ♦ adj (aunt etc) solterona; (speech, voyage) inaugural; **~ name** n nombre m de soltera

mail [meɪl] n correo; (letters) cartas fpl ♦ vt echar al correo; **~box** (US) n buzón m; **~ing list** n lista de direcciones; **~-order** n pedido postal

maim [meɪm] vt mutilar, lisiar

main [meɪn] adj principal, mayor ♦ n (pipe) cañería maestra; (US) red f eléctrica; **the ~s** npl (BRIT: ELEC) la red eléctrica; **in the ~** en general; **~frame** n (COMPUT) ordenador m central; **~land** n tierra firme; **~ly** adv principalmente; **~ road** n carretera; **~stay** n (fig) pilar m; **~stream** n corriente f principal

maintain [meɪn'teɪn] vt mantener; **maintenance** ['meɪntənəns] n manteni-miento; (LAW) manutención f

maize [meɪz] n (BRIT) n maíz m (SP), choclo (AM)

majestic [mə'dʒɛstɪk] adj majestuoso

majesty ['mædʒɪstɪ] n majestad f; (title): **Your M~** Su Majestad

major ['meɪdʒə*] n (MIL) comandante m ♦ adj principal; (MUS) mayor

Majorca [mə'jɔːkə] n Mallorca

majority [mə'dʒɒrɪtɪ] n mayoría

make [meɪk] (pt, pp made) vt hacer; (manufacture) fabricar; (mistake) cometer; (speech) pronunciar; (cause to be): **to ~ sb sad** poner triste a alguien; (force): **to ~ sb do sth** obligar a alguien a hacer algo; (earn) ganar; (equal): **2 and 2 ~ 4** 2 y 2 son 4 ♦ n marca; **to ~ the bed** hacer la cama; **to ~ a fool of sb** poner a alguien en ridículo; **to ~ a profit/loss** obtener ganancias/sufrir pérdidas; **to ~ it** (arrive) llegar; (achieve sth) tener éxito; **what time do you ~ it?** ¿qué hora

tienes?; **to ~ do with** contentarse con; **~ for** vt fus (place) dirigirse a; **~ out** vt (decipher) descifrar; (understand) entender; (see) distinguir; (cheque) extender; **~ up** vt (invent) inventar; (prepare) hacer; (constitute) constituir ♦ vi reconciliarse; (with cosmetics) maquillarse; **~ up for** vt fus compensar; **~-believe** n ficción f, invención f; **~r** n fabricante m/f; (of film, programme) autor(a) m/f; **~shift** adj improvisado; **~-up** n maquillaje m; **~-up remover** n desmaquillador m

making ['meɪkɪŋ] n (fig): **in the ~** en vías de formación; **to have the ~s of** (person) tener madera de

Malaysia [mə'leɪzɪə] n Malasia, Malaysia

male [meɪl] n (BIOL) macho ♦ adj (sex, attitude) masculino; (child etc) varón

malfunction [mæl'fʌŋkʃən] n mal funcionamiento

malice ['mælɪs] n malicia; **malicious** [mə'lɪʃəs] adj malicioso; rencoroso

malignant [mə'lɪgnənt] adj (MED) maligno

mall [mɔːl] (US) n (also: shopping ~) centro comercial

mallet ['mælɪt] n mazo

malnutrition [mælnjuː'trɪʃən] n desnutrición f

malpractice [mæl'præktɪs] n negligencia profesional

malt [mɔːlt] n malta; (whisky) whisky m de malta

Malta ['mɔːltə] n Malta; **Maltese** [-'tiːz] adj, n inv maltés/esa m/f

mammal ['mæml] n mamífero

mammoth ['mæməθ] n mamut m ♦ adj gigantesco

man [mæn] (pl **men**) n hombre m; (~kind) el hombre ♦ vt (NAUT) tripular; (MIL) guarnecer; (operate: machine) manejar; **an old ~** un viejo; **~ and wife** marido y mujer

manage ['mænɪdʒ] vi arreglárselas, ir tirando ♦ vt (be in charge of) dirigir; (control: person) manejar; (: ship) gobernar; **~able** adj manejable; **~ment** n dirección f; **~r** n director(a) m/f; (of pop star) mánayer m/f; (SPORT) entrenador(a) m/f; **~ress** n directora, entrenadora; **~rial** [-ə'dʒɪərɪəl] adj directivo; **managing director** n director(a) m/f general

mandarin ['mændərɪn] n (also: ~ orange) mandarina; (person) mandarín m

mandatory ['mændətərɪ] adj obligatorio

mane [meɪn] n (of horse) crin f; (of lion) melena

maneuver [mə'nuːvə*] (US) = **manoeuvre**

manfully ['mænfəlɪ] adv valientemente

mangle ['mæŋgl] vt mutilar, destrozar

man: ~handle vt maltratar; **~hole** n agujero

de acceso; **~hood** n edad f viril; (*state*) virilidad f; **~-hour** n hora-hombre f; **~hunt** n (*POLICE*) búsqueda y captura

mania ['meɪnɪə] n manía; **~c** ['meɪnɪæk] n maníaco/a; (*fig*) maníático

manic ['mænɪk] adj frenético; **~-depressive** n maníaco/a depresivo/a

manicure ['mænɪkjuə*] n manicura

manifest ['mænɪfest] vt manifestar, mostrar ♦ adj manifiesto

manifesto [mænɪ'festəu] n manifiesto

manipulate [mə'nɪpjuleɪt] vt manipular

man: ~kind [mæn'kaɪnd] n humanidad f, género humano; **~ly** adj varonil; **~-made** adj artificial

manner ['mænə*] n manera, modo; (*behaviour*) conducta, manera de ser; (*type*): **all ~ of things** toda clase de cosas; **~s** npl (*behaviour*) modales mpl; **bad ~s** mala educación; **~ism** n peculiaridad f de lenguaje (*or de comportamiento*)

manoeuvre [mə'nu:və*] (*US* **maneuver**) vt, vi maniobrar ♦ n maniobra

manor ['mænə*] n (*also*: ~ **house**) casa solariega

manpower ['mænpauə*] n mano f de obra

mansion ['mænʃən] n palacio, casa grande

manslaughter ['mænslɔ:tə*] n homicidio no premeditado

mantelpiece ['mæntlpi:s] n repisa, chimenea

manual ['mænjuəl] adj manual ♦ n manual m

manufacture [mænju'fæktʃə*] vt fabricar ♦ n fabricación f; **~r** n fabricante m/f

manure [mə'njuə*] n estiércol m

manuscript ['mænjuskrɪpt] n manuscrito

many ['menɪ] adj, pron muchos/as; **a great ~** muchísimos, un buen número de; **~ a time** muchas veces

map [mæp] n mapa m; **to ~ out** vt proyectar

maple ['meɪpl] n arce m (*SP*), maple m (*AM*)

mar [ma:*] vt estropear

marathon ['mærəθən] n maratón m

marble ['ma:bl] n mármol m; (*toy*) canica

March [ma:tʃ] n marzo

march [ma:tʃ] vi (*MIL*) marchar; (*demonstrators*) manifestarse ♦ n marcha; (*demonstration*) manifestación f

mare [meə*] n yegua

margarine [ma:dʒə'ri:n] n margarina

margin ['ma:dʒɪn] n margen m; (*COMM: profit*) ~) margen m de beneficios; **~al** adj marginal; **~al seat** n (*POL*) escaño electoral difícil de asegurar

marigold ['mærɪɡəuld] n caléndula

marijuana [mærɪ'wa:nə] n marijuana

marina [mə'ri:nə] n puerto deportivo

marinate ['mærɪneɪt] vt marinar

marine [mə'ri:n] adj marino ♦ n soldado de marina

marital ['mærɪtl] adj matrimonial; **~ status** estado civil

marjoram ['ma:dʒərəm] n mejorana

mark [ma:k] n marca, señal f; (*in snow, mud etc*) huella; (*stain*) mancha; (*BRIT: SCOL*) nota; (*currency*) marco ♦ vt marcar; manchar; (*damage: furniture*) rayar; (*indicate: place etc*) señalar; (*BRIT: SCOL*) calificar, corregir; **to ~ time** marcar el paso; (*fig*) marcar(se) un ritmo; **~ed** adj (*obvious*) marcado, acusado; **~er** n (*sign*) marcador m; (*bookmark*) señal f (de libro)

market ['ma:kɪt] n mercado ♦ vt (*COMM*) comercializar; **~ garden** n (*BRIT*) n huerto; **~ing** n márketing m; **~place** n mercado; **~ research** n análisis m inv de mercados

marksman ['ma:ksmən] n tirador m

marmalade ['ma:məleɪd] n mermelada de naranja

maroon [mə'ru:n] vt: **to be ~ed** quedar aislado; (*fig*) quedar abandonado

marquee [ma:'ki:] n entoldado

marriage ['mærɪdʒ] n (*relationship, institution*) matrimonio; (*wedding*) boda; (*act*) casamiento; **~ certificate** n partida de casamiento

married ['mærɪd] adj casado; (*life, love*) conyugal

marrow ['mærəu] n médula; (*vegetable*) calabacín m

marry ['mærɪ] vt casarse con; (*subj: father, priest etc*) casar ♦ vi (*also*: **get married**) casarse

Mars [ma:z] n Marte m

marsh [ma:ʃ] n pantano; (*salt ~*) marisma

marshal ['ma:ʃl] n (*MIL*) mariscal m; (*at sports meeting etc*) oficial m; (*US: of police, fire department*) jefe/a m/f ♦ vt (*thoughts etc*) ordenar; (*soldiers*) formar

marshy ['ma:ʃɪ] adj pantanoso

martial law ['ma:ʃl-] n ley f marcial

martyr ['ma:tə*] n mártir m/f; **~dom** n martirio

marvel ['ma:vl] n maravilla, prodigio ♦ vi: **to ~ (at)** maravillarse (de); **~lous** (*US* **~ous**) adj maravilloso

Marxist ['ma:ksɪst] adj, n marxista m/f

marzipan ['ma:zɪpæn] n mazapán m

mascara [mæs'ka:rə] n rímel m

masculine ['mæskjulɪn] adj masculino

mash [mæʃ] vt machacar; **~ed potatoes** npl puré m de patatas (*SP*) or papas (*AM*)

mask [ma:sk] n máscara ♦ vt (*cover*): **to ~ one's face** ocultarse la cara; (*hide: feelings*) esconder

mason ['meɪsn] n (*also*: **stone~**) albañil m; (*also*: **free~**) masón m; **~ry** n (*in building*) mampostería

masquerade [mæskə'reɪd] vi: **to ~ as** disfrazarse de, hacerse pasar por

mass [mæs] n (people) muchedumbre f; (of air, liquid etc) masa; (of detail, hair etc) gran cantidad f; (REL) misa ♦ cpd masivo ♦ vi reunirse; concentrarse; **the ~es** npl las masas; **~es of** (inf) montones de

massacre ['mæsəkə*] n masacre f

massage ['mæsɑːʒ] n masaje m ♦ vt dar masaje en

masseur [mæ'sɜː*] n masajista m

masseuse [mæ'sɜːz] n masajista f

massive ['mæsɪv] adj enorme; (support, changes) masivo

mass media npl medios mpl de comunicación

mass production n fabricación f en serie

mast [mɑːst] n (NAUT) mástil m; (RADIO etc) torre f

master ['mɑːstə*] n (of servant) amo; (of situation) dueño, maestro; (in primary school) maestro; (in secondary school) profesor m; (title for boys): **M~ X** Señorito X ♦ vt dominar; **M~ of Arts/Science** n licenciatura superior en Letras/Ciencias; **~ly** adj magistral; **~mind** n inteligencia superior ♦ vt dirigir, planear; **~piece** n obra maestra; **~y** n maestría

mat [mæt] n estera; (also: door~) felpudo; (also: table ~) salvamanteles m inv, posavasos m inv ♦ adj = **matt**

match [mætʃ] n cerilla, fósforo; (game) partido; (equal) igual m/f ♦ vt (go well with) hacer juego con; (equal) igualar; (correspond to) corresponderse con; (pair: also: ~ up) casar con ♦ vi hacer juego; **to be a good ~** hacer juego; **~box** n caja de cerillas; **~ing** adj que hace juego

mate [meɪt] n (work~) colega m/f; (inf: friend) amigo/a; (animal) macho m/hembra f; (in merchant navy) segundo de a bordo ♦ vi acoplarse, aparearse ♦ vt aparear

material [mə'tɪərɪəl] n (substance) materia; (information) material m; (cloth) tela, tejido ♦ adj material; (important) esencial; **~s** npl materiales mpl

maternal [mə'tɜːnl] adj maternal

maternity [mə'tɜːnɪtɪ] n maternidad f; **~ dress** n vestido premamá

math [mæθ] (US) n = **mathematics**

mathematical [mæθə'mætɪkl] adj matemático

mathematician [mæθəmə'tɪʃən] n matemático/a

mathematics [mæθə'mætɪks] n matemáticas fpl

maths [mæθs] (BRIT) n = **mathematics**

matinée ['mætɪneɪ] n sesión f de tarde

matrices ['meɪtrɪsiːz] npl of **matrix**

matriculation [mətrɪkju'leɪʃən] n (formalización f de) matrícula

matrimony ['mætrɪmənɪ] n matrimonio

matrix ['meɪtrɪks] (pl matrices) n matriz f

matron ['meɪtrən] n enfermera f jefe; (in school) ama de llaves

mat(t) [mæt] adj mate

matted ['mætɪd] adj enmarañado

matter ['mætə*] n cuestión f, asunto; (PHYSICS) sustancia, materia; (reading ~) material m; (MED: pus) pus m ♦ vi importar; **~s** npl (affairs) asuntos mpl, temas mpl; **it doesn't ~** no importa; **what's the ~?** ¿qué pasa?; **no ~ what** pase lo que pase; **as a ~ of course** por rutina; **as a ~ of fact** de hecho; **~-of-fact** adj prosaico, práctico

mattress ['mætrɪs] n colchón m

mature [mə'tjuə*] adj maduro ♦ vi madurar; **maturity** n madurez f

maul [mɔːl] vt magullar

mauve [məuv] adj de color malva (SP) or guinda (AM)

maximum ['mæksɪməm] (pl maxima) adj máximo ♦ n máximo

May [meɪ] n mayo

may [meɪ] (conditional: might) vi (indicating possibility): **he ~ come** puede que venga; (be allowed to): **~ I smoke?** ¿puedo fumar?; (wishes): **~ God bless you!** ¡que Dios le bendiga!; **you ~ as well go** bien puedes irte

maybe ['meɪbiː] adv quizá(s)

May Day n el primero de Mayo

mayhem ['meɪhɛm] n caos m total

mayonnaise [meɪə'neɪz] n mayonesa

mayor [mɛə*] n alcalde m; **~ess** n alcaldesa

maze [meɪz] n laberinto

M.D. abbr = **Doctor of Medicine**

me [miː] pron (direct) me; (stressed, after pron) mí; **can you hear ~?** ¿me oyes?; **he heard ME!** me oyó a mí; **it's ~** soy yo; **give them to ~** dámelos/las; **with/without ~** conmigo/sin mí

meadow ['mɛdəu] n prado, pradera

meagre ['miːgə*] (US **meager**) adj escaso, pobre

meal [miːl] n comida; (flour) harina; **~time** n hora de comer

mean [miːn] (pt, pp **meant**) adj (with money) tacaño; (unkind) mezquino, malo; (shabby) humilde; (average) medio ♦ vt (signify) querer decir, significar; (refer to) referirse a; (intend): **to ~ to do sth** pensar or pretender hacer algo ♦ n medio, término medio; **~s** npl (way) medio, manera; (money) recursos mpl, medios mpl; **by ~s of** mediante, por medio de; **by all ~s!** ¡naturalmente!, ¡claro que sí!; **do you ~ it?** ¿lo dices en serio?; **what do you ~?** ¿qué quiere decir?; **to be meant for sb/sth** ser para uno/algo

meander [mɪ'ændə*] vi (river) serpentear

meaning ['mi:nɪŋ] n significado, sentido; (*purpose*) sentido, propósito; **~ful** adj significativo; **~less** adj sin sentido

meanness ['mi:nnɪs] n (*with money*) tacañería; (*unkindness*) maldad f, mezquindad f; (*shabbiness*) humildad f

meant [mɛnt] pt, pp of **mean**

meantime ['mi:ntaɪm] adv (*also: in the ~*) mientras tanto

meanwhile ['mi:nwaɪl] adv = **meantime**

measles ['mi:zlz] n sarampión m

measure ['mɛʒə*] vt, vi medir ♦ n medida; (*ruler*) regla; **~ments** npl medidas fpl

meat [mi:t] n carne f; **cold ~** fiambre m; **~ball** n albóndiga; **~ pie** n pastel m de carne

Mecca ['mɛkə] n La Meca

mechanic [mɪ'kænɪk] n mecánico/a; **~s** n mecánica ♦ npl mecanismo; **~al** adj mecánico

mechanism ['mɛkənɪzəm] n mecanismo

medal ['mɛdl] n medalla; **~lion** [mɪ'dælɪən] n medallón m; **~list** (US **~ist**) n (*SPORT*) medallista m/f

meddle ['mɛdl] vi: **to ~ in** entrometerse en; **to ~ with sth** manosear algo

media ['mi:dɪə] npl medios mpl de comunicación ♦ npl of **medium**

mediaeval [mɛdɪ'i:vl] adj = **medieval**

mediate ['mi:dɪeɪt] vi mediar; **mediator** n intermediario/a, mediador(a) m/f

Medicaid ® ['mɛdɪkeɪd] (US) n programa de ayuda médica para los pobres

medical ['mɛdɪkl] adj médico ♦ n reconocimiento médico

Medicare ® ['mɛdɪkeə*] (US) n programa de ayuda médica para los ancianos

medication [mɛdɪ'keɪʃən] n medicación f

medicine ['mɛdsɪn] n medicina; (*drug*) medicamento

medieval [mɛdɪ'i:vl] adj medieval

mediocre [mi:dɪ'əukə*] adj mediocre

meditate ['mɛdɪteɪt] vi meditar

Mediterranean [mɛdɪtə'reɪnɪən] adj mediterráneo; **the ~ (Sea)** el (Mar) Mediterráneo

medium ['mi:dɪəm] (pl **media**) adj mediano, regular ♦ n (*means*) medio; (pl **mediums**: *person*) médium m/f; **~ wave** n onda media

meek [mi:k] adj manso, sumiso

meet [mi:t] (pt, pp **met**) vt encontrar; (*accidentally*) encontrarse con, tropezar con; (*by arrangement*) reunirse con; (*for the first time*) conocer; (*go and fetch*) ir a buscar; (*opponent*) enfrentarse con; (*obligations*) cumplir; (*encounter: problem*) hacer frente a; (*need*) satisfacer ♦ vi encontrarse; (*in session*) reunirse; (*join: objects*) unirse; (*for the first time*) conocerse; **~ with** vt fus (*difficulty*) tropezar con; **to ~ with success** tener éxito; **~ing** n

encuentro; (*arranged*) cita, compromiso; (*business ~ing*) reunión f; (*POL*) mitin m

megabyte ['mɛgəbaɪt] n (*COMPUT*) megabyte m, megaocteto

megaphone ['mɛgəfəun] n megáfono

melancholy ['mɛlənkəlɪ] n melancolía ♦ adj melancólico

mellow ['mɛləu] adj (*wine*) añejo; (*sound, colour*) suave ♦ vi (*person*) ablandar

melody ['mɛlədɪ] n melodía

melon ['mɛlən] n melón m

melt [mɛlt] vi (*metal*) fundirse; (*snow*) derretirse ♦ vt fundir; **~down** n (*in nuclear reactor*) fusión f de un reactor (nuclear); **~ing pot** n (*fig*) crisol m

member ['mɛmbə*] n (*gen, ANAT*) miembro; (*of club*) socio/a; **M~ of Parliament** (*BRIT*) diputado/a; **M~ of the European Parliament** (*BRIT*) eurodiputado/a; **M~ of the Scottish Parliament** (*BRIT*) diputado/a del Parlamento escocés; **~ship** n (*members*) número de miembros; (*state*) filiación f; **~ship card** n carnet m de socio

memento [mə'mɛntəu] n recuerdo

memo ['mɛməu] n apunte m, nota

memoirs ['mɛmwɑ:z] npl memorias fpl

memorandum [mɛmə'rændəm] (pl **memoranda**) n apunte m, nota; (*official note*) acta

memorial [mɪ'mɔ:rɪəl] n monumento conmemorativo ♦ adj conmemorativo

memorize ['mɛməraɪz] vt aprender de memoria

memory ['mɛmərɪ] n (*also: COMPUT*) memoria; (*instance*) recuerdo; (*of dead person*): **in ~ of** a la memoria de

men [mɛn] npl of **man**

menace ['mɛnəs] n amenaza ♦ vt amenazar; **menacing** adj amenazador(a)

mend [mɛnd] vt reparar, arreglar; (*darn*) zurcir ♦ vi reponerse ♦ n arreglo, reparación f; zurcido ♦ n: **to be on the ~** ir mejorando; **to ~ one's ways** enmendarse; **~ing** n reparación f; (*clothes*) ropa por remendar

meningitis [mɛnɪn'dʒaɪtɪs] n meningitis f

menopause ['mɛnəupɔ:z] n menopausia

menstruation [mɛnstru'eɪʃən] n menstruación f

mental ['mɛntl] adj mental; **~ity** [-'tælɪtɪ] n mentalidad f

mention ['mɛnʃən] n mención f ♦ vt mencionar; (*speak of*) hablar de; **don't ~ it!** ¡de nada!

menu ['mɛnju:] n (*set ~*) menú m; (*printed*) carta; (*COMPUT*) menú m

MEP n abbr = **Member of the European Parliament**

merchandise ['mə:tʃəndaɪz] n mercancías fpl

merchant ['mə:tʃənt] n comerciante m/f;

~ bank (BRIT) n banco comercial; **~ navy** (US **~ marine**) n marina mercante

merciful ['mə:sɪful] adj compasivo; (fortunate) afortunado

merciless ['mə:sɪlɪs] adj despiadado

mercury ['mə:kjurɪ] n mercurio

mercy ['mə:sɪ] n compasión f; (REL) misericordia; **at the ~ of** a la merced de

merely ['mɪəlɪ] adv simplemente, sólo

merge [mə:dʒ] vt (join) unir ♦ vi unirse; (COMM) fusionarse; (colours etc) fundirse; **~r** n (COMM) fusión f

meringue [mə'ræŋ] n merengue m

merit ['merɪt] n mérito ♦ vt merecer

mermaid ['mə:meɪd] n sirena

merry ['merɪ] adj alegre; **M~ Christmas!** ¡Felices Pascuas!; **~-go-round** n tiovivo

mesh [meʃ] n malla

mesmerize ['mezməraɪz] vt hipnotizar

mess [mes] n (muddle: of situation) confusión f; (: of room) revoltijo; (dirt) porquería; (MIL) comedor m; **~ about** or **around** (inf) vi perder el tiempo; (pass the time) entretenerse; **~ about** or **around with** (inf) vt fus divertirse con; **~ up** vt (spoil) estropear; (dirty) ensuciar

message ['mesɪdʒ] n recado, mensaje m

messenger ['mesɪndʒə*] n mensajero/a

Messrs abbr (on letters: = Messieurs) Sres

messy ['mesɪ] adj (dirty) sucio; (untidy) desordenado

met [met] pt, pp of **meet**

metal ['metl] n metal m; **~lic** [-'tælɪk] adj metálico

metaphor ['metəfə*] n metáfora

meteor ['mi:tɪə*] n meteoro; **~ite** [-aɪt] n meteorito

meteorology [mi:tɪə'rɔlədʒɪ] n meteorología

meter ['mi:tə*] n (instrument) contador m; (US: unit) = **metre** ♦ vt (US: POST) franquear

method ['meθəd] n método

meths [meθs] (BRIT) n, **methylated spirit** ['meθɪleɪtɪd-] (BRIT) n alcohol m metilado or desnaturalizado

metre ['mi:tə*] (US **meter**) n metro

metric ['metrɪk] adj métrico

metropolitan [metrə'pɔlɪtən] adj metropolitano; **the M~ Police** (BRIT) la policía londinense

mettle ['metl] n: **to be on one's ~** estar dispuesto a mostrar todo lo que uno vale

mew [mju:] vi (cat) maullar

mews [mju:z] n: **~ flat** (BRIT) piso acondicionado en antiguos establos o cocheras

Mexican ['meksɪkən] adj, n mejicano/a m/f, mexicano/a m/f

Mexico ['meksɪkəu] n Méjico (SP), México (AM); **~ City** n Ciudad f de Méjico or México

miaow [mi:'au] vi maullar

mice [maɪs] npl of **mouse**

micro... [maɪkrəu] prefix micro...; **~chip** n microplaqueta; **~(computer)** n microordenador m; **~phone** n micrófono; **~processor** n microprocesador m; **~scope** n microscopio; **~wave** n (also: **~wave oven**) horno microondas

mid [mɪd] adj: **in ~ May** a mediados de mayo; **in ~ afternoon** a media tarde; **in ~ air** en el aire; **~day** n mediodía m

middle ['mɪdl] n centro; (half-way point) medio; (waist) cintura ♦ adj de en medio; (course, way) intermedio; **in the ~ of the night** en plena noche; **~-aged** adj de mediana edad; **the M~ Ages** npl la Edad Media; **~ class** adj de clase media; **the ~ class(es)** n(pl) la clase media; **M~ East** n Oriente m Medio; **~man** n intermediario; **~ name** n segundo nombre; **~-of-the-road** adj moderado; **~weight** n (BOXING) peso medio

middling ['mɪdlɪŋ] adj mediano

midge [mɪdʒ] n mosquito

midget ['mɪdʒɪt] n enano/a

Midlands ['mɪdləndz] npl: **the ~** la región central de Inglaterra

midnight ['mɪdnaɪt] n medianoche f

midst [mɪdst] n: **in the ~ of** (crowd) en medio de; (situation, action) en mitad de

midsummer [mɪd'sʌmə*] n: **in ~** en pleno verano

midway [mɪd'weɪ] adj, adv: **~ (between)** a medio camino (entre); **~ through** a la mitad (de)

midweek [mɪd'wi:k] adv entre semana

midwife ['mɪdwaɪf] (pl **midwives**) n comadrona, partera

might [maɪt] vb see **may** ♦ n fuerza, poder m; **~y** adj fuerte, poderoso

migraine ['mi:greɪn] n jaqueca

migrant ['maɪgrənt] n adj (bird) migratorio; (worker) emigrante

migrate [maɪ'greɪt] vi emigrar

mike [maɪk] n abbr (= microphone) micro

mild [maɪld] adj (person) apacible; (climate) templado; (slight) ligero; (taste) suave; (illness) leve; **~ly** adv ligeramente; **to put it ~ly** para no decir más

mile [maɪl] n milla; **~age** n número de millas, ≈ kilometraje m; **~ometer** [maɪ'lɔmɪtə*] n ≈ cuentakilómetros m inv; **~stone** n mojón m

militant ['mɪlɪtnt] adj, n militante m/f

military ['mɪlɪtərɪ] adj militar

militia [mɪ'lɪʃə] n milicia

milk [mɪlk] n leche f ♦ vt (cow) ordeñar; (fig) chupar; **~ chocolate** n chocolate m con leche; **~man** (irreg) n lechero; **~ shake** n batido, malteada (AM); **~y** adj lechoso; **M~y Way** n Vía Láctea

mill [mɪl] n (windmill etc) molino; (coffee ~) molinillo; (factory) fábrica ♦ vt moler ♦ vi (also: ~ about) arremolinarse

millennium [mɪˈlenɪəm] (pl ~s or millennia) n milenio, milenario; **the ~ bug** el (problema del) efecto 2000

miller [ˈmɪlə*] n molinero

milli... [ˈmɪlɪ] prefix: **~gram(me)** n miligramo; **~metre** (US **~meter**) n milímetro

million [ˈmɪljən] n millón m; **a ~ times** un millón de veces; **~aire** [-jəˈneə*] n millonario/a

milometer [maɪˈlɒmɪtə*] (BRIT) n = **mileometer**

mime [maɪm] n mímica; (actor) mimo/a ♦ vt remedar ♦ vi actuar de mimo

mimic [ˈmɪmɪk] n imitador(a) m/f ♦ adj mímico ♦ vt remedar, imitar

min. abbr = **minimum; minute(s)**

mince [mɪns] vt picar ♦ n (BRIT: CULIN) carne f picada; **~meat** n conserva de fruta picada; (US: meat) carne f picada; **~ pie** n empanadilla rellena de fruta picada; **~r** n picadora de carne

mind [maɪnd] n mente f; (intellect) intelecto; (contrasted with matter) espíritu m ♦ vt (attend to, look after) ocuparse de, cuidar; (be careful to) tener cuidado con; (object to): **I don't ~ the noise** no me molesta el ruido; **it is on my ~** me preocupa; **to bear sth in ~** tomar or tener algo en cuenta; **to make up one's ~** decidirse; **I don't ~** me es igual; **~ you, ...** te advierto que ...; **never ~!** ¡es igual!, ¡no importa!; (don't worry) ¡no te preocupes!; **"~ the step"** "cuidado con el escalón"; **~er** n guardaespaldas m inv; (child ~er) ≈ niñera; **~ful** adj: **~ful of** consciente de; **~less** adj (crime) sin motivo; (work) de autómata

mine¹ [maɪn] pron el mío/la mía etc; **a friend of ~** un(a) amigo/a mío/mía ♦ adj: **this book is ~** este libro es mío

mine² [maɪn] n mina ♦ vt (coal) extraer; (bomb: beach etc) minar; **~field** n campo de minas; **miner** n minero/a

mineral [ˈmɪnərəl] adj mineral ♦ n mineral m; **~s** npl (BRIT: soft drinks) refrescos mpl; **~ water** n agua mineral

mingle [ˈmɪŋgl] vi: **to ~ with** mezclarse con

miniature [ˈmɪnətʃə*] adj (en) miniatura ♦ n miniatura

minibus [ˈmɪnɪbʌs] n microbús m

minimal [ˈmɪnɪml] adj mínimo

minimize [ˈmɪnɪmaɪz] vt minimizar; (play down) empequeñecer

minimum [ˈmɪnɪməm] (pl minima) n, adj mínimo

mining [ˈmaɪnɪŋ] n explotación f minera

miniskirt [ˈmɪnɪskɜːt] n minifalda

minister [ˈmɪnɪstə*] n (BRIT: POL) ministro/a

(SP), secretario/a (AM); (REL) pastor m ♦ vi: **to ~ to** atender a

ministry [ˈmɪnɪstrɪ] n (BRIT: POL) ministerio (SP), secretaria (AM); (REL) sacerdocio

mink [mɪŋk] n visón m

minnow [ˈmɪnəu] n pececillo (de agua dulce)

minor [ˈmaɪnə*] adj (repairs, injuries) leve; (poet, planet) menor; (MUS) menor ♦ n (LAW) menor m de edad

Minorca [mɪˈnɔːkə] n Menorca

minority [maɪˈnɒrɪtɪ] n minoría

mint [mɪnt] n (plant) menta, hierbabuena; (sweet) caramelo de menta ♦ vt (coins) acuñar; **the (Royal) M~, the (US) M~** la Casa de la Moneda; **in ~ condition** en perfecto estado

minus [ˈmaɪnəs] n (also: ~ sign) signo de menos ♦ prep menos; **12 ~ 6 equals 6** 12 menos 6 son 6; **~ 24°C** menos 24 grados

minute¹ [ˈmɪnɪt] n minuto; (fig) momento; **~s** npl (of meeting) actas fpl; **at the last ~** a última hora

minute² [maɪˈnjuːt] adj diminuto; (search) minucioso

miracle [ˈmɪrəkl] n milagro

mirage [ˈmɪrɑːʒ] n espejismo

mirror [ˈmɪrə*] n espejo; (in car) retrovisor m

mirth [mɜːθ] n alegría

misadventure [mɪsədˈventʃə*] n desgracia

misapprehension [mɪsæprɪˈhenʃən] n equivocación f

misappropriate [mɪsəˈprəuprɪeɪt] vt malversar

misbehave [mɪsbɪˈheɪv] vi portarse mal

miscalculate [mɪsˈkælkjuleɪt] vt calcular mal

miscarriage [ˈmɪskærɪdʒ] n (MED) aborto; **~ of justice** error m judicial

miscellaneous [mɪsɪˈleɪnɪəs] adj varios/as, diversos/as

mischief [ˈmɪstʃɪf] n travesuras fpl, diabluras fpl; (maliciousness) malicia; **mischievous** [-tʃɪvəs] adj travieso

misconception [mɪskənˈsepʃən] n idea equivocada; equivocación f

misconduct [mɪsˈkɒndʌkt] n mala conducta; **professional ~** falta profesional

misdemeanour [mɪsdɪˈmiːnə*] (US **misdemeanor**) n delito, ofensa

miser [ˈmaɪzə*] n avaro/a

miserable [ˈmɪzərəbl] adj (unhappy) triste, desgraciado; (unpleasant, contemptible) miserable

miserly [ˈmaɪzəlɪ] adj avariento, tacaño

misery [ˈmɪzərɪ] n tristeza; (wretchedness) miseria, desdicha

misfire [mɪsˈfaɪə*] vi fallar

misfit [ˈmɪsfɪt] n inadaptado/a

misfortune [mɪsˈfɔːtʃən] n desgracia

misgiving [mɪsˈgɪvɪŋ] n (apprehension) presentimiento; **to have ~s about sth** tener dudas acerca de algo

misguided [mɪsˈgaɪdɪd] *adj* equivocado

mishandle [mɪsˈhændl] *vt* (*mismanage*) manejar mal

mishap [ˈmɪshæp] *n* desgracia, contratiempo

misinform [mɪsɪnˈfɔːm] *vt* informar mal

misinterpret [mɪsɪnˈtɜːprɪt] *vt* interpretar mal

misjudge [mɪsˈdʒʌdʒ] *vt* juzgar mal

mislay [mɪsˈleɪ] (*irreg*) *vt* extraviar, perder

mislead [mɪsˈliːd] (*irreg*) *vt* llevar a conclusiones erróneas; **~ing** *adj* engañoso

mismanage [mɪsˈmænɪdʒ] *vt* administrar mal

misplace [mɪsˈpleɪs] *vt* extraviar

misprint [ˈmɪsprɪnt] *n* errata, error *m* de imprenta

Miss [mɪs] *n* Señorita

miss [mɪs] *vt* (*train etc*) perder; (*fail to hit: target*) errar; (*regret the absence of*): **I ~ him** (yo) le echo de menos or a faltar; (*fail to see*): **you can't ~ it** no tiene pérdida ♦ *vi* fallar ♦ *n* (*shot*) tiro fallido *or* perdido; **~ out** (*BRIT*) *vt* omitir

misshapen [mɪsˈʃeɪpən] *adj* deforme

missile [ˈmɪsaɪl] *n* (*AVIAT*) mísil *m*; (*object thrown*) proyectil *m*

missing [ˈmɪsɪŋ] *adj* (*pupil*) ausente; (*thing*) perdido; (*MIL*): **~ in action** desaparecido en combate

mission [ˈmɪʃən] *n* misión *f*; (*official representation*) delegación *f*; **~ary** *n* misionero/a

mist [mɪst] *n* (*light*) neblina; (*heavy*) niebla; (*at sea*) bruma ♦ *vi* (*eyes: also: ~ over, ~ up*) llenarse de lágrimas; (*BRIT: windows: also: ~ over, ~ up*) empañarse

mistake [mɪsˈteɪk] (*vt: irreg*) *n* error *m* ♦ *vt* entender mal; **by ~** por equivocación; **to make a ~** equivocarse; **to ~ A for B** confundir A con B; **mistaken** *pp* of **mistake** ♦ *adj* equivocado; **to be mistaken** equivocarse, engañarse

mister [ˈmɪstə*] (*inf*) *n* señor *m*; *see* **Mr**

mistletoe [ˈmɪsltəʊ] *n* muérdago

mistook [mɪsˈtʊk] *pt* of **mistake**

mistress [ˈmɪstrɪs] *n* (*lover*) amante *f*; (*of house*) señora (de la casa); (*BRIT: in primary school*) maestra; (*in secondary school*) profesora; (*of situation*) dueña

mistrust [mɪsˈtrʌst] *vt* desconfiar de

misty [ˈmɪstɪ] *adj* (*day*) de niebla; (*glasses etc*) empañado

misunderstand [mɪsʌndəˈstænd] (*irreg*) *vt, vi* entender mal; **~ing** *n* malentendido

misuse [*n* mɪsˈjuːs, *vb* mɪsˈjuːz] *n* mal uso; (*of power*) abuso; (*of funds*) malversación *f* ♦ *vt* abusar de; malversar

mitt(en) [ˈmɪt(n)] *n* manopla

mix [mɪks] *vt* mezclar; (*combine*) unir ♦ *vi* mezclarse; (*people*) llevarse bien ♦ *n* mezcla; **~ up** *vt* mezclar; (*confuse*) confundir; **~ed** *adj* mixto; (*feelings etc*) encontrado; **~ed-up** *adj* (*confused*) confuso, revuelto; **~er** *n* (*for food*) licuadora; (*for drinks*) coctelera; (*person*): **he's a good ~er** tiene don de gentes; **~ture** *n* mezcla; (*also: cough ~ture*) jarabe *m*; **~-up** *n* confusión *f*

mm *abbr* (= *millimetre*) mm

moan [məʊn] *n* gemido ♦ *vi* gemir; (*inf: complain*): **to ~ (about)** quejarse (de)

moat [məʊt] *n* foso

mob [mɔb] *n* multitud *f* ♦ *vt* acosar

mobile [ˈməʊbaɪl] *adj* móvil ♦ *n* móvil *m*; **~ home** *n* caravana; **~ phone** *n* teléfono portátil

mock [mɔk] *vt* (*ridicule*) ridiculizar; (*laugh at*) burlarse de ♦ *adj* fingido; **~ exam** *examen preparatorio antes de los exámenes oficiales*; **~ery** *n* burla; **~-up** *n* maqueta

mod [mɔd] *adj* see **convenience**

mode [məʊd] *n* modo

model [ˈmɔdl] *n* modelo; (*fashion ~, artist's ~*) modelo *m/f* ♦ *adj* modelo ♦ *vt* (*with clay etc*) modelar (*copy*); **to ~ o.s. on** tomar como modelo a ♦ *vi* ser modelo; **to ~ clothes** pasar modelos, ser modelo; **~ railway** *n* ferrocarril *m* de juguete

modem [ˈməʊdəm] *n* modem *m*

moderate [*adj* ˈmɔdərət, *vb* ˈmɔdəreɪt] *adj* moderado/a ♦ *vi* moderarse, calmarse ♦ *vt* moderar

modern [ˈmɔdən] *adj* moderno; **~ize** *vt* modernizar

modest [ˈmɔdɪst] *adj* modesto; (*small*) módico; **~y** *n* modestia

modify [ˈmɔdɪfaɪ] *vt* modificar

mogul [ˈməʊɡəl] *n* (*fig*) magnate *m*

mohair [ˈməʊhɛə*] *n* mohair *m*

moist [mɔɪst] *adj* húmedo; **~en** [ˈmɔɪsn] *vt* humedecer; **~ure** [ˈmɔɪstʃə*] *n* humedad *f*; **~urizer** [ˈmɔɪstʃəraɪzə*] *n* crema hidratante

molar [ˈməʊlə*] *n* muela

mold [məʊld] (*US*) *n, vt* = **mould**

mole [məʊl] *n* (*animal, spy*) topo; (*spot*) lunar *m*

molest [məʊˈlest] *vt* importunar; (*assault sexually*) abusar sexualmente de

mollycoddle [ˈmɔlɪkɔdl] *vt* mimar

molt [məʊlt] (*US*) *vi* = **moult**

molten [ˈməʊltən] *adj* fundido; (*lava*) líquido

mom [mɔm] (*US*) *n* = **mum**

moment [ˈməʊmənt] *n* momento; **at the ~** de momento, por ahora; **~ary** *adj* momentáneo; **~ous** [-ˈmentəs] *adj* trascendental, importante

momentum [məʊˈmentəm] *n* momento; (*fig*) ímpetu *m*; **to gather ~** cobrar velocidad;

(fig) ganar fuerza
mommy ['mɒmi] *(US)* n = **mummy**
Monaco ['mɒnəkəu] n Mónaco
monarch ['mɒnək] n monarca m/f; **~y** n
monarquía
monastery ['mɒnəstəri] n monasterio
Monday ['mʌndɪ] n lunes m inv
monetary ['mʌnɪtəri] adj monetario
money ['mʌni] n dinero; *(currency)* moneda;
to make ~ ganar dinero; **~ order** n giro; **~-
spinner** *(inf)* n: **to be a ~spinner** dar mucho
dinero
mongrel ['mʌŋgrəl] n *(dog)* perro mestizo
monitor ['mɒnɪtə*] n *(SCOL)* monitor m;
(also: television ~) receptor m de control; *(of
computer)* monitor m ♦ vt controlar
monk [mʌŋk] n monje m
monkey ['mʌŋkɪ] n mono; **~ nut** *(BRIT)* n
cacahuete m *(SP)*, maní m *(AM)*; **~ wrench**
n llave f inglesa
monopoly [mə'nɒpəlɪ] n monopolio
monotone ['mɒnətəun] n voz f *(or tono)*
monocorde
monotonous [mə'nɒtənəs] adj monótono
monsoon [mɒn'suːn] n monzón m
monster ['mɒnstə*] n monstruo
monstrous ['mɒnstrəs] adj *(huge)* enorme;
(atrocious, ugly) monstruoso
month [mʌnθ] n mes m; **~ly** adj mensual
♦ adv mensualmente
monument ['mɒnjumənt] n monumento
moo [muː] vi mugir
mood [muːd] n humor m; *(of crowd, group)*
clima m; **to be in a good/bad ~** estar de
buen/mal humor; **~y** adj *(changeable)* de
humor variable; *(sullen)* malhumorado
moon [muːn] n luna; **~light** n luz f de la
luna; **~lighting** n pluriempleo; **~lit** adj: **a
~lit night** una noche de luna
Moor [muə*] n moro/a
moor [muə*] n páramo ♦ vt *(ship)* amarrar
♦ vi echar las amarras
Moorish ['muərɪʃ] adj moro; *(architecture)*
árabe, morisco
moorland ['muələnd] n páramo, brezal m
moose [muːs] n inv alce m
mop [mɒp] n fregona; *(of hair)* greña, melena
♦ vt fregar; **~ up** vt limpiar
mope [məup] vi estar or andar deprimido
moped ['məupɛd] n ciclomotor m
moral ['mɒrl] adj moral ♦ n moraleja; **~s** npl
moralidad f, moral f
morale [mɒ'rɑːl] n moral f
morality [mə'rælɪtɪ] n moralidad f
morass [mə'ræs] n pantano

KEYWORD

more [mɔː*] adj 1 *(greater in number etc)*
más; **~ people/work than before** más gente/

trabajo que antes
2 *(additional)* más; **do you want (some)
~ tea?** ¿quieres más té?; **is there any ~ wine?**
¿queda vino?; **it'll take a few ~ weeks** tardará
unas semanas más; **it's 2 kms ~ to the house**
faltan 2 kms para la casa; **~ time/letters than
we expected** más tiempo del que/más cartas
de las que esperábamos
♦ pron *(greater amount, additional amount)*
más; **~ than 10** más de 10; **it cost ~ than the
other one/than we expected** costó más que el
otro/más de lo que esperábamos; **is there any
~?** ¿hay más?; **many/much ~** muchos(as)/
mucho(a) más
♦ adv más; **~ dangerous/easily (than)** más
peligroso/fácilmente (que); **~ and
~ expensive** cada vez más caro; **~ or less** más
o menos; **~ than ever** más que nunca

moreover [mɔː'rəuvə*] adv además, por otra
parte
morning ['mɔːnɪŋ] n mañana; *(early ~)*
madrugada ♦ cpd matutino, de la mañana; **in
the ~** por la mañana; **7 o'clock in the ~** las 7
de la mañana; **~ sickness** n náuseas fpl
matutinas
Morocco [mə'rɒkəu] n Marruecos m
moron ['mɔːrɒn] *(inf)* n imbécil m/f
morphine ['mɔːfiːn] n morfina
Morse [mɔːs] n *(also: ~ code)* (código) Morse
morsel ['mɔːsl] n *(of food)* bocado
mortar ['mɔːtə*] n argamasa
mortgage ['mɔːgɪdʒ] n hipoteca ♦ vt
hipotecar; **~ company** *(US)* n ≈ banco
hipotecario
mortuary ['mɔːtjuəri] n depósito de
cadáveres
Moscow ['mɒskəu] n Moscú
Moslem ['mɒzləm] adj, n = **Muslim**
mosque [mɒsk] n mezquita
mosquito [mɒs'kiːtəu] *(pl ~es)* n mosquito
(SP), zancudo *(AM)*
moss [mɒs] n musgo
most [məust] adj la mayor parte de, la
mayoría de ♦ pron la mayor parte, la mayoría
♦ adv el más; *(very)* muy; **the ~** *(also: + adj)*
el más; **~ of them** la mayor parte de ellos; **I
saw the ~** yo vi el que más; **at the (very) ~** a
lo sumo, todo lo más; **to make the ~ of**
aprovechar (al máximo); **a ~ interesting book**
un libro interesantísimo; **~ly** adv en su mayor
parte, principalmente
MOT *(BRIT)* n abbr (= Ministry of Transport):
the ~ (test) inspección *(anual)* obligatoria de
coches y camiones
motel [məu'tel] n motel m
moth [mɒθ] n mariposa nocturna; *(clothes ~)*
polilla
mother ['mʌðə*] n madre f ♦ adj materno

♦ vt (care for) cuidar (como una madre); ~hood n maternidad f; ~-in-law n suegra; ~ly adj maternal; ~-of-pearl n nácar m; ~to-be n futura madre f; ~ tongue n lengua materna

motion ['məʊʃən] n movimiento; (gesture) ademán m, señal f; (at meeting) moción f ♦ vt, vi: to ~ (to) sb to do sth hacer señas a uno para que haga algo; ~less adj inmóvil; ~ picture n película

motivated ['məʊtɪveɪtɪd] adj motivado

motive ['məʊtɪv] n motivo

motley ['mɒtlɪ] adj variado

motor ['məʊtəʳ] n motor m; (BRIT: inf: vehicle) coche m (SP), carro (AM), automóvil m ♦ adj motor (f: motora or motriz); ~bike n moto f; ~boat n lancha motora, ~car (BRIT) n coche m, carro, automóvil m; ~cycle n motocicleta; ~cycle racing n motociclismo; ~cyclist n motociclista m/f; ~ing (BRIT) n automovilismo; ~ist n conductor(a) m/f, automovilista m/f; ~ racing (BRIT) n carreras fpl de coches, automovilismo; ~ vehicle n automóvil m; ~way (BRIT) n autopista

mottled ['mɒtld] adj abigarrado, multicolor

motto ['mɒtəʊ] (pl ~es) n lema m; (watchword) consigna

mould [məʊld] (US **mold**) n molde m; (mildew) moho ♦ vt moldear; (fig) formar; ~y adj enmohecido

moult [məʊlt] (US **molt**) vi mudar la piel (or las plumas)

mound [maʊnd] n montón m, montículo

mount [maʊnt] n monte m ♦ vt montar, subir a; (jewel) engarzar; (picture) enmarcar; (exhibition etc) organizar ♦ vi (increase) aumentar; ~ up vi aumentar

mountain ['maʊntɪn] n montaña ♦ cpd de montaña; ~ bike n bicicleta de montaña; ~eer [-'nɪəʳ] n montañero/a (SP), andinista m/f (AM); ~eering [-'nɪərɪŋ] n montañismo, andinismo; ~ous adj montañoso; ~ rescue team n equipo de rescate de montaña; ~side n ladera de la montaña

mourn [mɔːn] vt llorar, lamentar ♦ vi: to ~ for llorar la muerte de; ~er n doliente m/f; dolorido/a; ~ing n luto; in ~ing de luto

mouse [maʊs] (pl mice) n (ZOOL, COMPUT) ratón m; ~ mat n (COMPUT) alfombrilla; ~trap n ratonera

mousse [muːs] n (CULIN) crema batida; (for hair) espuma (moldeadora)

moustache [məs'tɑːʃ] (US **mustache**) n bigote m

mousy ['maʊsɪ] adj (hair) pardusco

mouth [maʊθ, pl maʊðz] n boca; (of river) desembocadura; ~ful n bocado; ~ organ n armónica; ~piece n (of musical instrument) boquilla; (spokesman) portavoz m/f; ~wash

n enjuague m; ~watering adj apetitoso

movable ['muːvəbl] adj movible

move [muːv] n (movement) movimiento; (in game) jugada; (: turn to play) turno; (change: of house) mudanza; (: of job) cambio de trabajo ♦ vt mover; (emotionally) conmover; (POL: resolution etc) proponer ♦ vi moverse; (traffic) circular; (also: ~ house). trasladarse, mudarse; to ~ sb to do sth mover a uno a hacer algo; to get a ~ on darse prisa; ~ about or around vi moverse; (travel) viajar; ~ along vi avanzar, adelantarse; ~ away vi alejarse; ~ back vi retroceder; ~ forward vi avanzar; ~ in vi (to a house) instalarse; (police, soldiers) intervenir; ~ on vi ponerse en camino; ~ out vi (of house) mudarse; ~ over vi apartarse, hacer sitio; ~ up vi (employee) ser ascendido

moveable ['muːvəbl] adj = movable

movement ['muːvmənt] n movimiento

movie ['muːvɪ] n película; to go to the ~s ir al cine

moving ['muːvɪŋ] adj (emotional) conmovedor(a); (that moves) móvil

mow [maʊ] (pt mowed, pp mowed or mown) vt (grass, corn) cortar, segar; ~ down vt (shoot) acribillar; ~er n (also: lawn~er) cortacéspedes m inv, segadora

MP n abbr = Member of Parliament

m.p.h. abbr = miles per hour (60 m.p.h. = 96 k.p.h.)

Mr ['mɪstəʳ] (US **Mr.**) n: ~ Smith (el) Sr. Smith

Mrs ['mɪsɪz] (US **Mrs.**) n: ~ Smith (la) Sra. Smith

Ms [mɪz] (US **Ms.**) n (= Miss or Mrs): ~ Smith (la) Sr(t)a. Smith

M.Sc. abbr = Master of Science

MSP n abbr = Member of the Scottish Parliament

much [mʌtʃ] adj mucho ♦ adv mucho; (before pp) muy ♦ n or pron mucho; how ~ is it? ¿cuánto es?, ¿cuánto cuesta?; too ~ demasiado; it's not ~ es mucho; as ~ as tanto como; however ~ he tries por mucho que se esfuerce

muck [mʌk] n suciedad f; ~ about or around (inf) vi perder el tiempo; (enjoy o.s.) entretenerse; ~ up (inf) vt arruinar, estropear

mud [mʌd] n barro, lodo

muddle ['mʌdl] n desorden m, confusión f; (mix-up) embrollo, lío ♦ vt (also: ~ up) embro-llar, confundir; ~ through vi salir del paso

muddy ['mʌdɪ] adj fangoso, cubierto de lodo

mudguard ['mʌdgɑːd] n guardabarros m inv

muffin ['mʌfɪn] n panecillo dulce

muffle ['mʌfl] vt (sound) amortiguar; (against cold) embozar; ~d adj (noise etc) amortiguado, apagado; ~r n (US AUT) silenciador m

mug [mʌg] n taza grande (sin platillo); (for beer) jarra; (inf: face) jeta; (: fool) bobo ♦ vt (*assault*) asaltar; **~ging** *n* asalto

muggy ['mʌgɪ] *adj* bochornoso

mule [mju:l] *n* mula

multi... [mʌltɪ] *prefix* multi...

multi-level [mʌltɪ'levl] (*US*) *adj* = **multi-storey**

multiple ['mʌltɪpl] *adj* múltiple ♦ *n* múltiplo; **~ sclerosis** *n* esclerosis *f* múltiple

multiplex cinema ['mʌltɪpleks-] *n* multicines *mpl*

multiplication [mʌltɪplɪ'keɪʃən] *n* multiplicación *f*

multiply ['mʌltɪplaɪ] *vt* multiplicar ♦ *vi* multiplicarse

multistorey [mʌltɪ'stɔːrɪ] (*BRIT*) *adj* de muchos pisos

multitude ['mʌltɪtjuːd] *n* multitud *f*

mum [mʌm] (*BRIT*: *inf*) *n* mamá ♦ *adj*: **to keep ~** mantener la boca cerrada

mumble ['mʌmbl] *vt*, *vi* hablar entre dientes, refunfuñar

mummy ['mʌmɪ] *n* (*BRIT*: *mother*) mamá; (*embalmed*) momia

mumps [mʌmps] *n* paperas *fpl*

munch [mʌntʃ] *vt*, *vi* mascar

mundane [mʌn'deɪn] *adj* trivial

municipal [mju:'nɪsɪpl] *adj* municipal

murder ['mə:də*] *n* asesinato; (*in law*) homicidio ♦ *vt* asesinar, matar; **~er/ess** *n* asesino/a; **~ous** *adj* homicida

murky ['mə:kɪ] *adj* (*water*) turbio; (*street*, *night*) lóbrego

murmur ['mə:mə*] *n* murmullo ♦ *vt*, *vi* murmurar

muscle ['mʌsl] *n* músculo; (*fig*: *strength*) garra, fuerza; **~ in** *vi* entrometerse; **muscular** ['mʌskjulə*] *adj* muscular; (*person*) musculoso

muse [mju:z] *vi* meditar ♦ *n* musa

museum [mju:'zɪəm] *n* museo

mushroom ['mʌʃrum] *n* seta, hongo; (*CULIN*) champiñón *m* ♦ *vi* crecer de la noche a la mañana

music ['mju:zɪk] *n* música; **~al** *adj* musical; (*sound*) melodioso; (*person*) con talento musical ♦ *n* (*show*) comedia musical; **~al instrument** *n* instrumento musical; **~ hall** *n* teatro de variedades; **~ian** [-'zɪʃən] *n* músico/a

Muslim ['mʌzlɪm] *adj*, *n* musulmán/ana *m/f*

muslin ['mʌzlɪn] *n* muselina

mussel ['mʌsl] *n* mejillón *m*

must [mʌst] *aux vb* (*obligation*): **I ~ do it** debo hacerlo, tengo que hacerlo; (*probability*): **he ~ be there by now** ya debe (de) estar allí ♦ *n*: **it's a ~** es imprescindible

mustache ['mʌstæʃ] (*US*) *n* = **moustache**

mustard ['mʌstəd] *n* mostaza

muster ['mʌstə*] *vt* juntar, reunir

mustn't ['mʌsnt] = **must not**

mute [mju:t] *adj*, *n* mudo/a *m/f*

muted ['mju:tɪd] *adj* callado; (*colour*) apagado

mutiny ['mju:tɪnɪ] *n* motín *m* ♦ *vi* amotinarse

mutter ['mʌtə*] *vt*, *vi* murmurar

mutton ['mʌtn] *n* carne *f* de cordero

mutual ['mju:tʃuəl] *adj* mutuo; (*interest*) común; **~ly** *adv* mutuamente

muzzle ['mʌzl] *n* hocico; (*for dog*) bozal *m*; (*of gun*) boca ♦ *vt* (*dog*) poner un bozal a

my [maɪ] *adj* mi(s); **~ house/brother/sisters** mi casa/mi hermano/mis hermanas; **I've washed ~ hair/cut ~ finger** me he lavado el pelo/ cortado un dedo; **is this ~ pen or yours?** ¿es este bolígrafo mío o tuyo?

myself [maɪ'self] *pron* (*reflexive*) me; (*emphatic*) yo mismo; (*after prep*) mí (mismo); *see also* **oneself**

mysterious [mɪs'tɪərɪəs] *adj* misterioso

mystery ['mɪstərɪ] *n* misterio

mystify ['mɪstɪfaɪ] *vt* (*perplex*) dejar perplejo

myth [mɪθ] *n* mito

N, n

n/a *abbr* (= *not applicable*) no interesa

nag [næg] *vt* (*scold*) regañar; **~ging** *adj* (*doubt*) persistente; (*pain*) continuo

nail [neɪl] *n* (*human*) uña; (*metal*) clavo ♦ *vt* clavar; **to ~ sth to sth** clavar algo en algo; **to ~ sb down to doing sth** comprometer a uno a que haga algo; **~brush** *n* cepillo para las uñas; **~file** *n* lima para las uñas; **~ polish** *n* esmalte *m* or laca para las uñas; **~ polish remover** *n* quitaesmalte *m*; **~ scissors** *npl* tijeras *fpl* para las uñas; **~ varnish** (*BRIT*) *n* = **~ polish**

naïve [naɪ'i:v] *adj* ingenuo

naked ['neɪkɪd] *adj* (*nude*) desnudo; (*flame*) expuesto al aire

name [neɪm] *n* nombre *m*; (*surname*) apellido; (*reputation*) fama, renombre *m* ♦ *vt* (*child*) poner nombre a; (*criminal*) identificar; (*price*, *date etc*) fijar; **what's your ~?** ¿cómo se llama?; **by ~** de nombre; **in the ~ of** en nombre de; **to give one's ~ and address** dar sus señas; **~ly** *adv* a saber; **~sake** *n* tocayo/a

nanny ['nænɪ] *n* niñera

nap [næp] *n* (*sleep*) sueñecito, siesta

nape [neɪp] *n*: **~ of the neck** nuca, cogote *m*

napkin ['næpkɪn] *n* (*also*: **table ~**) servilleta

nappy ['næpɪ] (*BRIT*) *n* pañal *m*; **~ rash** *n* prurito

narcotic [nɑ:'kɔtɪk] *adj*, *n* narcótico

narrow ['nærəʊ] *adj* estrecho, angosto; (*fig*: *majority etc*) corto; (: *ideas etc*) estrecho ♦ *vi* (*road*) estrecharse; (*diminish*) reducirse; **to**

have a ~ escape escaparse por los pelos; **to ~ sth down** reducir algo; **~ly** adv (miss) por poco; **~-minded** adj de miras estrechas

nasty ['nɑːstɪ] adj (remark) feo; (person) antipático; (revolting: taste, smell) asqueroso; (wound, disease etc) peligroso, grave

nation ['neɪʃən] n nación f

national ['næʃənl] adj, n nacional m/f; **~ dress** n vestido nacional; **N~ Health Service** (BRIT) n servicio nacional de salud pública; ≈ Insalud m (SP); **N~ Insurance** (BRIT) n seguro social nacional; **~ism** n nacionalismo; **~ist** adj, n nacionalista m/f; **~ity** [-'nælɪtɪ] n nacionalidad f; **~ize** vt nacionalizar; **~ly** adv (nationwide) en escala nacional; (as a nation) nacionalmente, como nación; **~ park** (BRIT) n parque m nacional

nationwide ['neɪʃənwaɪd] adj en escala or a nivel nacional

native ['neɪtɪv] n (local inhabitant) natural m/f, nacional m/f ♦ adj (indigenous) indígena; (country) natal; (innate) natural, innato; **a ~ of Russia** un(a) natural m/f de Rusia; **a ~ speaker of French** un hablante nativo de francés; **N~ American** adj, n americano/a indígena, amerindio/a; **~ language** n lengua materna

Nativity [nə'tɪvɪtɪ] n: **the ~** Navidad f

NATO ['neɪtəʊ] n abbr (= North Atlantic Treaty Organization) OTAN f

natural ['nætʃrəl] adj natural; **~ly** adv (speak etc) naturalmente; (of course) desde luego, por supuesto

nature ['neɪtʃə*] n (also: N~) naturaleza; (group, sort) género, clase f; (character) carácter m, genio; **by ~** por or de naturaleza

naught [nɔːt] = nought

naughty ['nɔːtɪ] adj (child) travieso

nausea ['nɔːsɪə] npl fpl

nautical ['nɔːtɪkl] adj náutico, marítimo; (mile) marino

naval ['neɪvl] adj naval, de marina; **~ officer** n oficial m/f de marina

nave [neɪv] n nave f

navel ['neɪvl] n ombligo

navigate ['nævɪgeɪt] vt gobernar ♦ vi navegar; (AUT) ir de copiloto; **navigation** [-'geɪʃən] n (action) navegación f; (science) náutica; **navigator** n navegador(a) m/f, navegante m/f; (AUT) copiloto m/f

navvy ['nævɪ] (BRIT) n peón m caminero

navy ['neɪvɪ] n marina de guerra; (ships) armada, flota; **~(-blue)** adj azul marino

Nazi ['nɑːtsɪ] n nazi m/f

NB abbr (= nota bene) nótese

near [nɪə*] adj (place, relation) cercano; (time) próximo ♦ adv cerca ♦ prep (also: ~ to: space) cerca de, junto a; (: time) cerca de ♦ vt acercarse a, aproximarse a; **~by** [nɪə'baɪ]

adj cercano, próximo ♦ adv cerca; **~ly** adv casi, por poco; **I ~ly fell** por poco me caigo; **~ miss** n tiro cercano; **~side** n (AUT: in Britain) lado izquierdo; (: in US, Europe etc) lado derecho; **~-sighted** adj miope, corto de vista

neat [niːt] adj (place) ordenado, bien cuidado; (person) pulcro; (plan) ingenioso; (spirits) solo; **~ly** adv (tidily) con esmero; (skilfully) ingeniosamente

necessarily ['nesɪsrɪlɪ] adv necesariamente

necessary ['nesɪsrɪ] adj necesario, preciso

necessitate [nɪ'sesɪteɪt] vt hacer necesario

necessity [nɪ'sesɪtɪ] n necesidad f; **necessities** npl artículos mpl de primera necesidad

neck [nek] n (of person, garment, bottle) cuello; (of animal) pescuezo ♦ vi (inf) besuquearse; **~ and ~** parejos; **~lace** ['neklɪs] n collar m; **~line** n escote m; **~tie** ['nektaɪ] n corbata

née [neɪ] adj: **~ Scott** de soltera Scott

need [niːd] n (lack) escasez f, falta; (necessity) necesidad f ♦ vt (require) necesitar; **I ~ to do it** tengo que o debo hacerlo; **you don't ~ to go** no hace falta que (te) vayas

needle ['niːdl] n aguja ♦ vt (fig: inf) picar, fastidiar

needless ['niːdlɪs] adj innecesario; **~ to say** huelga decir que

needlework ['niːdlwɜːk] n (activity) costura, labor f de aguja

needn't ['niːdnt] = need not

needy ['niːdɪ] adj necesitado

negative ['negətɪv] n (PHOT) negativo; (LING) negación f ♦ adj negativo; **~ equity** n situación que se da cuando el valor de la vivienda es menor que el de la hipoteca que pesa sobre ella

neglect [nɪ'glekt] vt (one's duty) faltar a, no cumplir con; (child) descuidar, desatender ♦ n (of house, garden etc) abandono; (of child) desatención f; (of duty) incumplimiento

negligee ['neglɪʒeɪ] n (nightgown) salto de cama

negotiate [nɪ'gəʊʃɪeɪt] vt (treaty, loan) negociar; (obstacle) franquear; (bend in road) tomar ♦ vi: **to ~ (with)** negociar (con); **negotiation** [-'eɪʃən] n negociación f, gestión f

neigh [neɪ] vi relinchar

neighbour ['neɪbə*] (US **neighbor**) n vecino/a; **~hood** n (place) vecindad f, barrio; (people) vecindario; **~ing** adj vecino; **~ly** adj (person) amable; (attitude) de buen vecino

neither ['naɪðə*] adj ni ♦ conj: **I didn't move and ~ did John** no me he movido, ni Juan tampoco ♦ pron ninguno ♦ adv: **~ good nor bad** ni bueno ni malo; **~ is true** ninguno/a de los/las dos es cierto/a

neon ['niːɔn] n neón m; ~ **light** n lámpara de neón

nephew ['nevjuː] n sobrino

nerve [nəːv] n (ANAT) nervio; (courage) valor m; (impudence) descaro, frescura; **a fit of ~s** un ataque de nervios; **~-racking** adj desquiciante

nervous ['nəːvəs] adj (anxious, ANAT) nervioso; (timid) tímido, miedoso; ~ **breakdown** n crisis f nerviosa

nest [nest] n (of bird) nido; (wasps' ~) avispero ♦ vi anidar; ~ **egg** n (fig) ahorros mpl

nestle ['nesl] vi: **to ~ down** acurrucarse

net [net] n (gen) red f; (fabric) tul m ♦ adj (COMM) neto, líquido ♦ vt coger (SP) or agarrar (AM) con red; (SPORT) marcar; **the N~** (Internet) la Red; **~ball** n básquet m

Netherlands ['neðələndz] npl: **the ~** los Países Bajos

nett [net] adj = **net**

netting ['netɪŋ] n red f, redes fpl

nettle ['netl] n ortiga

network ['netwəːk] n red f

neurotic [njuə'rɔtɪk] adj, n neurótico/a m/f

neuter ['njuːtə*] adj (LING) neutro ♦ vt castrar, capar

neutral ['njuːtrəl] adj (person) neutral; (colour etc, ELEC) neutro ♦ n (AUT) punto muerto; **~ize** vt neutralizar

never ['nevə*] adv nunca, jamás; **I ~ went** no fui nunca; ~ **in my life** jamás en la vida; see also **mind**; **~-ending** adj interminable, sin fin; **~theless** [nevəðə'les] adv sin embargo, no obstante

new [njuː] adj nuevo; (brand new) a estrenar; (recent) reciente; **N~ Age** n Nueva Era; **~born** adj recién nacido; **~comer** ['njuːkʌmə*] n recién venido/a or llegado/a; **~-fangled** (pej) adj modernísimo; **~found** adj (friend) nuevo; (enthusiasm) recién adquirido; **~ly** adv nuevamente, recién; **~ly-weds** npl recién casados mpl

news [njuːz] n noticias fpl; **a piece of ~** una noticia; **the ~** (RADIO, TV) las noticias fpl; ~ **agency** n agencia de noticias; **~agent** (BRIT) n vendedor(a) m/f de periódicos; **~caster** n presentador(a) m/f, locutor(a) m/f; ~ **flash** n noticia de última hora; **~letter** n hoja informativa, boletín m; **~paper** n periódico, diario; **~print** n papel m de periódico; **~reader** n = **~caster**; **~reel** n noticiario; ~ **stand** n quiosco or puesto de periódicos

newt [njuːt] n tritón m

New Year n Año Nuevo; **~'s Day** n Día m de Año Nuevo; **~'s Eve** n Nochevieja

New York ['njuː'jɔːk] n Nueva York

New Zealand [njuː'ziːlənd] n Nueva Zelanda; **~er** n neozelandés/esa m/f

next [nekst] adj (house, room) vecino; (bus stop, meeting) próximo; (following: page etc) siguiente ♦ adv después; **the ~ day** el día siguiente; ~ **time** la próxima vez; ~ **year** el año próximo or que viene; ~ **to** junto a, al lado de; ~ **to nothing** casi nada; ~ **please!** ¡el siguiente! ~ **door** adv en la casa de al lado ♦ adj vecino, de al lado; **~-of-kin** n pariente m más cercano

NHS n abbr = **National Health Service**

nib [nɪb] n plumilla

nibble ['nɪbl] vt mordisquear, mordiscar

Nicaragua [nɪkə'rægjuə] n Nicaragua; **~n** adj, n nicaragüense m/f

nice [naɪs] adj (likeable) simpático; (kind) amable; (pleasant) agradable; (attractive) bonito, mono, lindo (AM); **~ly** adv amablemente; bien

nick [nɪk] n (wound) rasguño; (cut, indentation) mella, muesca ♦ vt (inf) birlar, robar; **in the ~ of time** justo a tiempo

nickel ['nɪkl] n níquel m; (US) moneda de 5 centavos

nickname ['nɪkneɪm] n apodo, mote m ♦ vt apodar

nicotine ['nɪkətiːn] n nicotina

niece [niːs] n sobrina

Nigeria [naɪ'dʒɪərɪə] n Nigeria; **~n** adj, n nigeriano/a m/f

niggling ['nɪglɪŋ] adj (trifling) nimio, insignificante; (annoying) molesto

night [naɪt] n noche f; (evening) tarde f; **the ~ before last** anteanoche; **at ~, by ~** de noche, por la noche; **~cap** n (drink) bebida que se toma antes de acostarse; ~ **club** n cabaret m; **~dress** (BRIT) n camisón m; **~fall** n anochecer m; **~gown** n = **~dress**; **~ie** ['naɪtɪ] n = **~dress**

nightingale ['naɪtɪŋgeɪl] n ruiseñor m

night: ~life n vida nocturna; **~ly** adj de todas las noches ♦ adv todas las noches, cada noche; **~mare** n pesadilla; ~ **porter** n portero de noche; ~ **school** n clase(s) f(pl) nocturna(s); ~ **shift** n turno nocturno or de noche; **~-time** n noche f; ~ **watchman** n vigilante m nocturno

nil [nɪl] (BRIT) n (SPORT) cero, nada

Nile [naɪl] n: **the ~** el Nilo

nimble ['nɪmbl] adj (agile) ágil, ligero; (skilful) diestro

nine [naɪn] num nueve; **~teen** num diecinueve, diez y nueve; **~ty** num noventa

ninth [naɪnθ] adj noveno

nip [nɪp] vt (pinch) pellizcar; (bite) morder

nipple ['nɪpl] n (ANAT) pezón m

nitrogen ['naɪtrədʒən] n nitrógeno

KEYWORD

no [nəu] (pl ~es) adv (opposite of "yes") no; are you coming? — ~ (I'm not) ¿vienes? — no; would you like some more? — ~ thank you ¿quieres más? — no gracias
♦ adj (not any): I have ~ money/time/books no tengo dinero/tiempo/libros; ~ other man would have done it ningún otro lo hubiera hecho; "~ entry" "prohibido el paso"; "~ smoking" "prohibido fumar"
♦ n no m

nobility [nəu'bɪlɪtɪ] n nobleza
noble ['nəubl] adj noble
nobody ['nəubədɪ] pron nadie
nod [nɔd] vi saludar con la cabeza; (in agreement) decir que sí con la cabeza; (doze) dar cabezadas ♦ vt: to ~ one's head inclinar la cabeza ♦ n inclinación f de cabeza; ~ off vi dar cabezadas
noise [nɔɪz] n ruido; (din) escándalo, estrépito; **noisy** adj ruidoso; (child) escandaloso
nominate ['nɔmɪneɪt] vt (propose) proponer; (appoint) nombrar; **nominee** [-'niː] n candidato/a
non... [nɔn] prefix no, des..., in...; **~alcoholic** adj no alcohólico; **~chalant** adj indiferente; **~committal** adj evasivo; **~descript** adj soso
none [nʌn] pron ninguno/a ♦ adv de ninguna manera; ~ of you ninguno de vosotros; I've ~ left no me queda ninguno/a; he's ~ the worse for it no le ha hecho ningún mal
nonentity [nɔ'nɛntɪtɪ] n cero a la izquierda, nulidad f
nonetheless [nʌnðə'lɛs] adv sin embargo, no obstante
non-existent adj inexistente
non-fiction n literatura no novelesca
nonplussed [nɔn'plʌst] adj perplejo
nonsense ['nɔnsəns] n tonterías fpl, disparates fpl; ~! ¡qué tonterías!
non-: **~smoker** n no fumador(a) m/f; **~smoking** adj (de) no fumador; **~stick** adj (pan, surface) antiadherente; **~stop** adj continuo; (RAIL) directo ♦ adv sin parar
noodles ['nuːdlz] npl tallarines mpl
nook [nuk] n: ~s and crannies escondrijos mpl
noon [nuːn] n mediodía m
no-one pron = nobody
noose [nuːs] n (hangman's) dogal m
nor [nɔː*] conj = neither ♦ adv see neither
norm [nɔːm] n norma
normal ['nɔːml] adj normal; **~ly** adv normalmente
north [nɔːθ] n norte m ♦ adj del norte, norteño ♦ adv al o hacia el norte; **N~**

Africa n África del Norte; **N~ America** n América del Norte; **~east** n nor(d)este m; **~erly** ['nɔːðəlɪ] adj (point, direction) norteño; **~ern** ['nɔːðən] adj norteño, del norte; **N~ern Ireland** n Irlanda del Norte; **N~ Pole** n Polo Norte; **N~ Sea** n Mar m del Norte; **~ward(s)** ['nɔːθwəd(z)] adv hacia el norte; **~west** n nor(d)oeste m
Norway ['nɔːweɪ] n Noruega; **Norwegian** [-'wiːdʒən] adj noruego/a ♦ n noruego/a; (LING) noruego
nose [nəuz] n (ANAT) nariz f; (ZOOL) hocico; (sense of smell) olfato ♦ vi: to ~ about curiosear; **~bleed** n hemorragia nasal; **~dive** n (of plane: deliberate) picado vertical; (: involuntary) caída en picado; **~y** (inf) adj curioso, fisgón/ona
nostalgia [nɔs'tældʒɪə] n nostalgia
nostril ['nɔstrɪl] n ventana de la nariz
nosy ['nəuzɪ] (inf) adj = nosey
not [nɔt] adv no; ~ that ... no es que ...; it's too late, isn't it? es demasiado tarde, ¿verdad or no?; ~ yet/now todavía/ahora no; why ~? ¿por qué no?; see also all; only
notably ['nəutəblɪ] adv especialmente
notary ['nəutərɪ] n notario/a
notch [nɔtʃ] n muesca, corte m
note [nəut] n (MUS, record, letter) nota; (banknote) billete m; (tone) tono ♦ vt (observe) notar, observar; (write down) apuntar, anotar; **~book** n libreta, cuaderno; **~d** ['nəutɪd] adj célebre, conocido; **~pad** n bloc m; **~paper** n papel m para cartas
nothing ['nʌθɪŋ] n nada; (zero) cero; he does ~ no hace nada; ~ new nada nuevo; ~ much no mucho; for ~ (free) gratis, sin pago; (in vain) en balde
notice ['nəutɪs] n (announcement) anuncio; (warning) aviso; (dismissal) despido; (resignation) dimisión f; (period of time) plazo ♦ vt (observe) notar, observar; to bring sth to sb's ~ (attention) llamar la atención de uno sobre algo; to take ~ of tomar nota de, prestar atención a; at short ~ con poca anticipación; until further ~ hasta nuevo aviso; to hand in one's ~ dimitir; **~able** adj evidente, obvio; ~ board (BRIT) n tablón m de anuncios
notify ['nəutɪfaɪ] vt: to ~ sb (of sth) comunicar (algo) a uno
notion ['nəuʃən] n idea; (opinion) opinión f
notorious [nəu'tɔːrɪəs] adj notorio
nougat ['nuːgaː] n turrón m
nought [nɔːt] n cero
noun [naun] n nombre m, sustantivo
nourish ['nʌrɪʃ] vt nutrir; (fig) alimentar; **~ing** adj nutritivo; **~ment** n alimento, sustento
novel ['nɔvl] n novela ♦ adj (new) nuevo,

original; (*unexpected*) insólito; **~ist** *n*
novelista *m/f*; **~ty** *n* novedad *f*
November [nəu'vembə*] *n* noviembre
m
novice ['nɒvɪs] *n* (*REL*) novicio/a
now [nau] *adv* (*at the present time*) ahora;
(*these days*) actualmente, hoy día ♦ *conj*:
~ (that) ya que, ahora que; **right ~** ahora
mismo; **by ~** ya; **just ~** ahora mismo; **~
and then, ~ and again** de vez en cuando;
from ~ on de ahora en adelante;
~adays ['nauədeɪz] *adv* hoy (en) día,
actualmente
nowhere ['nəuweə*] *adv* (*direction*) a
ninguna parte; (*location*) en ninguna parte
nozzle ['nɒzl] *n* boquilla
nuance ['njuːɑːns] *n* matiz *m*
nuclear ['njuːklɪə*] *adj* nuclear
nucleus ['njuːklɪəs] (*pl* **nuclei**) *n* núcleo
nude [njuːd] *adj*, *n* desnudo/a *m/f*; **in the ~**
desnudo
nudge [nʌdʒ] *vt* dar un codazo a
nudist ['njuːdɪst] *n* nudista *m/f*
nuisance ['njuːsns] *n* molestia, fastidio;
(*person*) pesado, latoso; **what a ~!** ¡qué lata!
null [nʌl] *adj*: **~ and void** nulo y sin efecto
numb [nʌm] *adj*: **~ with cold/fear**
entumecido por el frío/paralizado de miedo
number ['nʌmbə*] *n* (*quantity*) número;
cantidad *f* ♦ *vt* (*pages etc*) numerar, poner
número a; (*amount to*) sumar, ascender a;
to be ~ed among figurar entre; **a ~ of** varios,
algunos; **they were ten in ~** eran diez;
~ plate (*BRIT*) *n* matrícula, placa
numeral ['njuːmərəl] *n* número, cifra
numerate ['njuːmərɪt] *adj* competente en la
aritmética
numerous ['njuːmərəs] *adj* numeroso
nun [nʌn] *n* monja, religiosa
nurse [nəːs] *n* enfermero/a; (*also:* **~maid**)
niñera *f* ♦ *vt* (*patient*) cuidar, atender
nursery ['nəːsəri] *n* (*institution*) guardería
infantil; (*room*) cuarto de los niños; (*for
plants*) criadero, semillero; **~ rhyme** *n*
canción *f* infantil; **~ school** *n* parvulario,
escuela de párvulos; **~ slope** (*BRIT*) *n* (*SKI*)
cuesta para principiantes
nursing ['nəːsɪŋ] *n* (*profession*) profesión *f* de
enfermera; (*care*) asistencia, cuidado;
~ home *n* clínica de reposo
nut [nʌt] *n* (*TECH*) tuerca; (*BOT*) nuez *f*;
~crackers *npl* cascanueces *m* *inv*
nutmeg ['nʌtmeg] *n* nuez *f* moscada
nutritious [nju:'trɪʃəs] *adj* nutritivo,
alimenticio
nuts [nʌts] (*inf*) *adj* loco
nutshell ['nʌtʃel] *n*: **in a ~** en resumidas
cuentas
nylon ['naɪlɒn] *n* nilón *m* ♦ *adj* de nilón

O, o

oak [əuk] *n* roble *m* ♦ *adj* de roble
O.A.P. (*BRIT*) *n* *abbr* = **old-age pensioner**
oar [ɔː*] *n* remo
oasis [əu'eɪsɪs] (*pl* **oases**) *n* oasis *m* *inv*
oath [əuθ] *n* juramento; (*swear word*)
palabrota; **on** (*BRIT*) or **under ~** bajo
juramento
oatmeal ['əutmiːl] *n* harina de avena
oats [əuts] *n* avena
obedience [ə'biːdɪəns] *n* obediencia
obedient [ə'biːdɪənt] *adj* obediente
obey [ə'beɪ] *vt* obedecer; (*instructions,
regulations*) cumplir
obituary [ə'bɪtjuəri] *n* necrología
object [*n* 'ɒbdʒɪkt, *vb* əb'dʒɛkt] *n* objeto;
(*purpose*) objeto, propósito; (*LING*)
complemento ♦ *vi*: **to ~ to** estar en contra
de; (*proposal*) oponerse a; **to ~ that** objetar
que; **expense is no ~** no importa cuánto
cuesta; **I ~!** ¡yo protesto!; **I have no ~ion to ...** no tengo
inconveniente en que ...; **~ionable**
[əb'dʒɛkʃənəbl] *adj* desagradable; (*conduct*)
censurable; **~ive** *adj*, *n* objetivo
obligation [ɒblɪ'geɪʃən] *n* obligación *f*; (*debt*)
deber *m*; **without ~** sin compromiso
oblige [ə'blaɪdʒ] *vt* (*do a favour for*)
complacer, hacer un favor a; **to ~ sb to do
sth** forzar or obligar a uno a hacer algo; **to be
~d to sb for sth** estarle agradecido a uno por
algo; **obliging** *adj* servicial, atento
oblique [ə'bliːk] *adj* oblicuo; (*allusion*)
indirecto
obliterate [ə'blɪtəreɪt] *vt* borrar
oblivion [ə'blɪvɪən] *n* olvido; **oblivious** [-ɪəs]
adj: **oblivious of** inconsciente de
oblong ['ɒblɒŋ] *adj* rectangular ♦ *n*
rectángulo
obnoxious [əb'nɒkʃəs] *adj* odioso,
detestable; (*smell*) nauseabundo
oboe ['əubəu] *n* oboe *m*
obscene [əb'siːn] *adj* obsceno
obscure [əb'skjuə*] *adj* oscuro ♦ *vt*
oscurecer; (*hide: sun*) esconder
observant [əb'zəːvnt] *adj* observador(a)
observation [ɒbzə'veɪʃən] *n* observación *f*;
(*MED*) examen *m*
observe [əb'zəːv] *vt* observar; (*rule*) cumplir;
~r *n* observador(a) *m/f*
obsess [əb'ses] *vt* obsesionar; **~ive** *adj*
obsesivo; obsesionante
obsolete ['ɒbsəliːt] *adj*: **to be ~** estar en
desuso
obstacle ['ɒbstəkl] *n* obstáculo; (*nuisance*)
estorbo; **~ race** *n* carrera de obstáculos

obstinate ['ɔbstɪnɪt] adj terco, porfiado; (determined) obstinado

obstruct [əb'strʌkt] vt obstruir; (hinder) estorbar, obstaculizar; **~ion** [əb'strʌkʃən] n (action) obstrucción f; (object) estorbo, obstáculo

obtain [əb'teɪn] vt obtener; (achieve) conseguir

obvious ['ɔbvɪəs] adj obvio, evidente; **~ly** adv evidentemente; **~ly not** por supuesto que no

occasion [ə'keɪʒən] n oportunidad f, ocasión f; (event) acontecimiento; **~al** adj poco frecuente, ocasional; **~ally** adv de vez en cuando

occupant ['ɔkjupənt] n (of house) inquilino/a; (of car) ocupante m/f

occupation [ɔkju'peɪʃən] n ocupación f; (job) trabajo; (pastime) ocupaciones fpl; **~al hazard** n riesgo profesional

occupier ['ɔkjupaɪə*] n inquilino/a

occupy ['ɔkjupaɪ] vt (seat, post, time) ocupar; (house) habitar; **to ~ o.s. in doing** pasar el tiempo haciendo

occur [ə'kə:*] vi pasar, suceder; **to ~ to sb** ocurrírsele a uno; **~rence** [ə'kʌrəns] n acontecimiento; (existence) existencia

ocean ['əuʃən] n océano

o'clock [ə'klɔk] adv: **it is 5 ~** son las 5

OCR n abbr = **optical character recognition/reader**

October [ɔk'təubə*] n octubre m

octopus ['ɔktəpəs] n pulpo

odd [ɔd] adj extraño, raro; (number) impar; (sock, shoe etc) suelto; **60~** 60 y pico; at **~ times** de vez en cuando; **to be the ~ one out** estar de más; **~ity** n rareza; (person) excéntrico; **~-job man** n chico para todo; **~ jobs** npl bricolaje m; **~ly** adv curiosamente, extrañamente; see also **enough; ~ments** npl (COMM) retales mpl; **~s** npl (in betting) puntos mpl de ventaja; **it makes no ~s** da lo mismo; **at ~s** reñidos/as; **~s and ends** minucias fpl

odometer [ɔ'dɔmɪtə*] (US) n cuenta-kilómetros m inv

odour ['əudə*] (US **odor**) n olor m; (un-pleasant) hedor m

of [ɔv, əv] prep **1** (gen) de; **a friend ~ ours** un amigo nuestro; **a boy ~ 10** un chico de 10 años; **that was kind ~ you** eso fue muy amable por o de tu parte

2 (expressing quantity, amount, dates etc) de; **a kilo ~ flour** un kilo de harina; **there were 3 ~ them** había tres; **3 ~ us went** tres de nosotros fuimos; **the 5th ~ July** el 5 de julio

3 (from, out of) de; **made ~ wood** (hecho de) madera

off [ɔf] adj, adv (engine) desconectado; (light) apagado; (tap) cerrado; (BRIT: food: bad) pasado, malo; (: milk) cortado; (cancelled) cancelado ♦ prep de; **to be ~** (to leave) irse, marcharse; **to be ~ sick** estar enfermo o de baja; **a day ~** un día libre o sin trabajar; **to have an ~ day** tener un día malo; **he had his coat ~** se había quitado el abrigo; **10% ~** (COMM) (con el) 10% de descuento; **5 km ~ (the road)** a 5 km (de la carretera); **~ the coast** frente a la costa; **I'm ~ meat** (no longer eat/like it) paso de la carne; **on the ~ chance** por si acaso; **~ and on** de vez en cuando

offal ['ɔfl] (BRIT) n (CULIN) menudencias fpl

off-colour ['ɔf'kʌlə*] (BRIT) adj (ill) indispuesto

offence [ə'fens] (US **offense**) n (crime) delito; **to take ~ at** ofenderse por

offend [ə'fend] vt (person) ofender; **~er** n delincuente m/f

offensive [ə'fensɪv] adj ofensivo; (smell etc) repugnante ♦ n (MIL) ofensiva

offer ['ɔfə*] n oferta, ofrecimiento; (proposal) propuesta ♦ vt ofrecer; (opportunity) facilitar; **"on ~"** (COMM) "en oferta"; **~ing** n ofrenda

offhand [ɔf'hænd] adj informal ♦ adv de improviso

office ['ɔfɪs] n (place) oficina; (room) despacho; (position) carga, oficio; **doctor's ~** (US) consultorio; **to take ~** entrar en funciones; **~ block** (US **~ building**) n bloque m de oficinas; **~ hours** npl horas fpl de oficina; (US: MED) horas fpl de consulta

officer ['ɔfɪsə*] n (MIL etc) oficial m/f; (also: **police ~**) agente m/f de policía; (of organization) director(a) m/f

office worker n oficinista m/f

official [ə'fɪʃl] adj oficial, autorizado ♦ n funcionario, oficial m

offing ['ɔfɪŋ] n: **in the ~** (fig) en perspectiva

off-: ~licence (BRIT) n (shop) bodega, tienda de vinos y bebidas alcohólicas; **~line** adj, adv (COMPUT) fuera de línea; **~-peak** adj (electricity) de banda económica; (ticket) billete de precio reducido por viajar fuera de las horas punta; **~-putting** (BRIT) adj (person) asqueroso; (remark) desalentador(a); **~-season** adj, adv fuera de temporada

offset ['ɔfset] (irreg) vt contrarrestar, compensar

offshoot ['ɔfʃu:t] n (fig) ramificación f

offshore [ɔf'ʃɔ:*] adj (breeze, island) costera; (fishing) de bajura

offside ['ɔf'saɪd] adj (SPORT) fuera de juego; (AUT: in UK) del lado derecho; (: in US, Europe etc) del lado izquierdo

333 offspring → one-sided

offspring ['ɔfsprɪŋ] *n inv* descendencia

off: **~stage** *adv* entre bastidores; **~-the-peg** (*US* **~-the-rack**) *adv* confeccionado; **~-white** *adj* color crudo

often ['ɔfn] *adv* a menudo, con frecuencia; **how ~ do you go?** ¿cada cuánto vas?

oh [əu] *excl* ¡ah!

oil [ɔɪl] *n* aceite *m*; (*petroleum*) petróleo; (*for heating*) aceite *m* combustible ♦ *vt* engrasar; **~can** *n* lata de aceite; **~field** *n* campo petrolífero; **~ filter** *n* (*AUT*) filtro de aceite; **~ painting** *n* pintura al óleo; **~ rig** *n* torre *f* de perforación; **~ tanker** *n* petrolero; (*truck*) camión *m* cisterna; **~ well** *n* pozo (de petróleo); **~y** *adj* aceitoso; (*food*) grasiento

ointment ['ɔɪntmənt] *n* ungüento

O.K., okay [əu'keɪ] *excl* O.K., ¡está bien!, ¡vale! (*SP*) ♦ *adj* bien ♦ *vt* dar el visto bueno a

old [əuld] *adj* viejo; (*former*) antiguo; **how ~ are you?** ¿cuántos años tienes?, ¿qué edad tienes?; **he's 10 years ~** tiene 10 años; **~er brother** hermano mayor; **~ age** *n* vejez *f*; **~-age pensioner** *n* (*BRIT*) jubilado/a; **~-fashioned** *adj* anticuado, pasado de moda

olive ['ɔlɪv] *n* (*fruit*) aceituna; (*tree*) olivo ♦ *adj* (*also*: **~-green**) verde oliva; **~ oil** *n* aceite *m* de oliva

Olympic [əu'lɪmpɪk] *adj* olímpico; **the ~ Games, the ~s** las Olimpíadas

omelet(te) ['ɔmlɪt] *n* tortilla (*SP*), tortilla de huevo (*AM*)

omen ['əumən] *n* presagio

ominous ['ɔmɪnəs] *adj* de mal agüero, amenazador(a)

omit [əu'mɪt] *vt* omitir

KEYWORD

on [ɔn] *prep* **1** (*indicating position*) en; sobre; **~ the wall** en la pared; **it's ~ the table** está sobre or en la mesa; **~ the left** a la izquierda **2** (*indicating means, method, condition etc*): **~ foot** a pie; **~ the train/plane** (*go*) en tren/avión; (*be*) en el tren/el avión; **~ the radio/television/telephone** por or en la radio/televisión/al teléfono; **to be ~ drugs** drogarse; (*MED*) estar a tratamiento; **to be ~ holiday/business** estar de vacaciones/en viaje de negocios **3** (*referring to time*): **~ Friday** el viernes; **~ Fridays** los viernes; **~ June 20th** el 20 de junio; **a week ~ Friday** del viernes en una semana; **~ arrival** al llegar; **~ seeing this** al ver esto **4** (*about, concerning*) sobre, acerca de; **a book ~ physics** un libro de or sobre física ♦ *adv* **1** (*referring to dress*): **to have one's coat ~** tener or llevar el abrigo puesto; **she put her gloves ~** se puso los guantes

2 (*referring to covering*): **"screw the lid ~ tightly"** "cerrar bien la tapa" **3** (*further, continuously*): **to walk** *etc* **~** seguir caminando *etc*
♦ *adj* **1** (*functioning, in operation*: *machine, radio, TV, light*) encendido/a (*SP*), prendido/a (*AM*); (: *tap*) abierto/a; (: *brakes*) echado/a, puesto/a; **is the meeting still ~?** (*in progress*) ¿todavía continúa la reunión?; (*not cancelled*) ¿va a haber reunión al fin?; **there's a good film ~ at the cinema** ponen una buena película en el cine **2**: **that's not ~!** (*inf*: *not possible*) ¡eso ni hablar!; (: *not acceptable*) ¡eso no se hace!

once [wʌns] *adv* una vez; (*formerly*) antiguamente ♦ *conj* una vez que; **~ he had left/it was done** una vez que se había marchado/se hizo; **at ~** en seguida, inmediatamente; (*simultaneously*) a la vez; **~ a week** una vez por semana; **~ more** otra vez; **~ and for all** de una vez por todas; **~ upon a time** érase una vez

oncoming ['ɔnkʌmɪŋ] *adj* (*traffic*) que viene de frente

KEYWORD

one [wʌn] *num* un(o)/una; **~ hundred and fifty** ciento cincuenta; **~ by ~** uno a uno ♦ *adj* **1** (*sole*) único; **the ~ book which** el único libro que; **the ~ man who** el único que **2** (*same*) mismo/a; **they came in the ~ car** vinieron en un solo coche ♦ *pron* **1**: **this ~** éste/ésta; **that ~** ése/ésa; (*more remote*) aquél/aquella; **I've already got (a red) ~** ya tengo uno/a (rojo/a); **~ by ~** uno/a por uno/a **2**: **~ another** os (*SP*), se (+ *el uno al otro, unos a otros etc*); **do you two ever see ~ another?** ¿vosotros dos os veis alguna vez? (*SP*), ¿se ven ustedes dos alguna vez?; **the boys didn't dare look at ~ another** los chicos no se atrevieron a mirarse (el uno al otro); **they all kissed ~ another** se besaron unos a otros **3** (*impers*): **~ never knows** nunca se sabe; **to cut ~'s finger** cortarse el dedo; **~ needs to eat** hay que comer

one: **~-day excursion** (*US*) *n* billete *m* de ida y vuelta en un día; **~-man** *adj* (*business*) individual; **~-man band** *n* hombre-orquesta *m*; **~-off** (*BRIT*: *inf*) *n* (*event*) acontecimiento único

oneself [wʌn'sɛlf] *pron* (*reflexive*) se; (*after prep*) sí; (*emphatic*) uno/a mismo/a; **to hurt ~** hacerse daño; **to keep sth for ~** guardarse algo; **to talk to ~** hablar solo

one: **~-sided** *adj* (*argument*) parcial; **~-to-~**

adj (relationship) de dos; **~-way** *adj (street)* de sentido único

ongoing [ˈɒnɡəʊɪŋ] *adj* continuo

onion [ˈʌnjən] *n* cebolla

on-line *adj, adv (COMPUT)* en línea

onlooker [ˈɒnlʊkə*] *n* espectador(a) *m/f*

only [ˈəʊnlɪ] *adv* solamente, sólo ♦ *adj* único, solo ♦ *conj* solamente que, pero; **an ~ child** un hijo único; **not ~ ... but also ...** no sólo ... sino también ...

onset [ˈɒnsɛt] *n* comienzo

onshore [ˈɒnʃɔː*] *adj (wind)* que sopla del mar hacia la tierra

onslaught [ˈɒnslɔːt] *n* ataque *m*, embestida

onto [ˈɒntu] *prep* = **on to**

onward(s) [ˈɒnwəd(z)] *adv (move)* (hacia) adelante; **from that time ~** desde entonces en adelante

onyx [ˈɒnɪks] *n* ónice *m*

ooze [uːz] *vi* rezumar

opaque [əʊˈpeɪk] *adj* opaco

OPEC [ˈəʊpɛk] *n abbr* (= *Organization of Petroleum-Exporting Countries*) OPEP *f*

open [ˈəʊpn] *adj* abierto; *(car)* descubierto; *(road, view)* despejado; *(meeting)* público; *(admiration)* manifiesto ♦ *vt* abrir ♦ *vi* abrirse; *(book etc: commence)* comenzar; **in the ~ (air)** al aire libre; **~ on to** *vt fus (subj: room, door)* dar a; **~ up** *vt* abrir; *(blocked road)* despejar ♦ *vi* abrirse, empezar; **~ing** *n* abertura; *(start)* comienzo; *(opportunity)* oportunidad *f*; **~ing hours** *npl* horario de apertura; **~ learning** *n* enseñanza flexible a tiempo parcial; **~ly** *adv* abiertamente; **~-minded** *adj* imparcial; **~-necked** *adj (shirt)* desabrochado; sin corbata; **~-plan** *adj*: **~-plan office** gran oficina sin particiones

opera [ˈɒprə] *n* ópera; **~ house** *n* teatro de la ópera

operate [ˈɒpəreɪt] *vt (machine)* hacer funcionar; *(company)* dirigir ♦ *vi* funcionar; **to ~ on sb** *(MED)* operar a uno

operatic [ɒpəˈrætɪk] *adj* de ópera

operating table [ˈɒpəreɪtɪŋ-] *n* mesa de operaciones

operating theatre *n* sala de operaciones

operation [ɒpəˈreɪʃən] *n* operación *f*; *(of machine)* funcionamiento; **to be in ~** estar funcionando *or* en funcionamiento; **to have an ~** *(MED)* ser operado; **~al** *adj* operacional, en buen estado

operative [ˈɒpərətɪv] *adj* en vigor

operator [ˈɒpəreɪtə*] *n (of machine)* maquinista *m/f*, operario/a; *(TEL)* operador(a) *m/f*, telefonista *m/f*

opinion [əˈpɪnɪən] *n* opinión *f*; **in my ~** en mi opinión, a mi juicio; **~ated** *adj* testarudo; **~ poll** *n* encuesta, sondeo

opponent [əˈpəʊnənt] *n* adversario/a, contrincante *m/f*

opportunity [ɒpəˈtjuːnɪtɪ] *n* oportunidad *f*; **to take the ~ of doing** aprovechar la ocasión para hacer

oppose [əˈpəʊz] *vt* oponerse a; **to be ~d to sth** oponerse a algo; **as ~d to** a diferencia de; **opposing** *adj* opuesto, contrario

opposite [ˈɒpəzɪt] *adj* opuesto, contrario a; *(house etc)* de enfrente ♦ *adv* en frente ♦ *prep* en frente de, frente a ♦ *n* lo contrario

opposition [ɒpəˈzɪʃən] *n* oposición *f*

oppressive [əˈprɛsɪv] *adj* opresivo; *(weather)* agobiante

opt [ɒpt] *vi*: **to ~ for** optar por; **to ~ to do** optar por hacer; **~ out** *vi*: **to ~ out of** optar por no hacer

optical [ˈɒptɪkl] *adj* óptico

optician [ɒpˈtɪʃən] *n* óptico *m/f*

optimist [ˈɒptɪmɪst] *n* optimista *m/f*; **~ic** [-ˈmɪstɪk] *adj* optimista

option [ˈɒpʃən] *n* opción *f*; **~al** *adj* facultativo, discrecional

or [ɔː*] *conj* o; *(before o, ho)* u; *(with negative)*: **he hasn't seen ~ heard anything** no ha visto ni oído nada; **~ else** si no

oral [ˈɔːrəl] *adj* oral ♦ *n* examen *m* oral

orange [ˈɒrɪndʒ] *n (fruit)* naranja ♦ *adj* color naranja

orbit [ˈɔːbɪt] *n* órbita ♦ *vt, vi* orbitar

orchard [ˈɔːtʃəd] *n* huerto

orchestra [ˈɔːkɪstrə] *n* orquesta; *(US: seating)* platea

orchid [ˈɔːkɪd] *n* orquídea

ordain [ɔːˈdeɪn] *vt (REL)* ordenar, decretar

ordeal [ɔːˈdiːl] *n* experiencia horrorosa

order [ˈɔːdə*] *n* orden *m*; *(command)* orden *f*; *(good ~)* buen estado; *(COMM)* pedido ♦ *vt (also: put in ~)* arreglar, poner en orden; *(COMM)* pedir; *(command)* mandar, ordenar; **in ~** en orden; *(of document)* en regla; **in (working) ~** en funcionamiento; **in ~ to do/ that** para hacer/que; **on ~** *(COMM)* pedido; **to be out of ~** estar desordenado; *(not working)* no funcionar; **to ~ sb to do sth** mandar a uno hacer algo; **~ form** *n* hoja de pedido; **~ly** *n (MIL)* ordenanza *m*; *(MED)* enfermero/a (auxiliar) ♦ *adj* ordenado

ordinary [ˈɔːdnrɪ] *adj* corriente, normal; *(pej)* común y corriente; **out of the ~** fuera de lo común

Ordnance Survey [ˈɔːdnəns-] *(BRIT) n* servicio oficial de topografía

ore [ɔː*] *n* mineral *m*

organ [ˈɔːɡən] *n* órgano; **~ic** [ɔːˈɡænɪk] *adj* orgánico; **~ism** *n* organismo

organization [ɔːɡənaɪˈzeɪʃən] *n* organización *f*

organize [ˈɔːɡənaɪz] *vt* organizar; **~r** *n* organizador(a) *m/f*

orgasm ['ɔːgæzəm] *n* orgasmo
orgy ['ɔːdʒɪ] *n* orgía
Orient ['ɔːrɪənt] *n* Oriente *m*; **oriental** [-'entl] *adj* oriental
orientate ['ɔːrɪənteɪt] *vt*: **to ~ o.s.** orientarse
origin ['ɔrɪdʒɪn] *n* origen *m*
original [ə'rɪdʒɪnl] *adj* original; (*first*) primero; (*earlier*) primitivo ♦ *n* original *m*; **~ly** *adv* al principio
originate [ə'rɪdʒɪneɪt] *vi*: **to ~ from, to ~ in** surgir de, tener su origen en
Orkneys ['ɔːknɪz] *npl*: **the ~** (*also: the Orkney Islands*) las Orcadas
ornament ['ɔːnəmənt] *n* adorno; (*trinket*) chuchería; **~al** [-'mentl] *adj* decorativo, de adorno
ornate [ɔː'neɪt] *adj* muy ornado, vistoso
orphan ['ɔːfn] *n* huérfano/a
orthopaedic [ɔːθə'piːdɪk] (*US* **orthopedic**) *adj* ortopédico
ostensibly [ɔs'tensɪblɪ] *adv* aparentemente
ostentatious [ɔsten'teɪʃəs] *adj* ostentoso
osteopath ['ɔstɪəpæθ] *n* osteópata *m/f*
ostracize ['ɔstrəsaɪz] *vt* hacer el vacío a
ostrich ['ɔstrɪtʃ] *n* avestruz *m*
other ['ʌðə*] *adj* otro ♦ *pron*: **the ~ (one)** el/la otro/a ♦ *adv*: **~ than** aparte de; **~s** (**~ people**) otros; **the ~ day** el otro día; **~wise** *adv* de otra manera ♦ *conj* (*if not*) si no
otter ['ɔtə*] *n* nutria
ouch [autʃ] *excl* ¡ay!
ought [ɔːt] (*pt* **ought**) *aux vb*: **I ~ to do it** debería hacerlo; **this ~ to have been corrected** esto debiera haberse corregido; **he ~ to win** (*probability*) debe or debiera ganar
ounce [auns] *n* onza (28.35*g*)
our ['auə*] *adj* nuestro; *see also* **my**; **~s** *pron* (el) nuestro/(la) nuestra *etc*; *see also* **mine**[1]; **~selves** *pron pl* (*reflexive, after prep*) nosotros; (*emphatic*) nosotros mismos; *see also* **oneself**
oust [aust] *vt* desalojar
out [aut] *adv* fuera, afuera; (*not at home*) fuera (de casa); (*light, fire*) apagado; **~ there** allí (fuera); **he's ~** (*absent*) no está, ha salido; **to be ~ in one's calculations** equivocarse (en sus cálculos); **to run ~** salir corriendo; **~ loud** en alta voz; **~ of** (*outside*) fuera de; (*because of*: *anger etc*) por; **~ of petrol** sin gasolina; **"~ of order"** "no funciona"; **~-and-~** *adj* (*liar, thief etc*) redomado, empedernido; **~back** *n* interior *m*; **~board** *adj*: **~board motor** (motor *m*) fuera borda *m*; **~break** *n* (*of war*) comienzo; (*of disease*) epidemia; (*of violence etc*) ola; **~burst** *n* explosión *f*, arranque *m*; **~cast** *n* paria *m/f*; **~come** *n* resultado; **~crop** *n* (*of rock*) afloramiento; **~cry** *n* protestas *fpl*; **~dated** *adj* anticuado, fuera de moda; **~do** (*irreg*) *vt* superar;

~door *adj* exterior, de aire libre; (*clothes*) de calle; **~doors** *adv* al aire libre
outer ['autə*] *adj* exterior, externo; **~ space** *n* espacio exterior
outfit ['autfɪt] *n* (*clothes*) conjunto
out: **~going** *adj* (*character*) extrovertido; (*retiring*: *president etc*) saliente; **~goings** (*BRIT*) *npl* gastos *mpl*; **~grow** (*irreg*) *vt*: **he has ~grown his clothes** su ropa le queda pequeña ya; **~house** *n* dependencia; **~ing** ['autɪŋ] *n* excursión *f*, paseo
out: **~law** *n* proscrito ♦ *vt* proscribir; **~lay** *n* inversión *f*; **~let** *n* salida; (*of pipe*) desagüe *m*; (*US*: *ELEC*) toma de corriente; (*also: retail ~let*) punto de venta; **~line** *n* (*shape*) contorno, perfil *m*; (*sketch, plan*) esbozo ♦ *vt* (*plan etc*) esbozar; **in ~line** (*fig*) a grandes rasgos; **~live** *vt* sobrevivir a; **~look** *n* (*fig*: *prospects*) perspectivas *fpl*; (: *for weather*) pronóstico; **~lying** *adj* remoto, aislado; **~moded** *adj* anticuado, pasado de moda; **~number** *vt* superar en número; **~-of-date** *adj* (*passport*) caducado; (*clothes*) pasado de moda; **~-of-the-way** *adj* apartado; **~patient** *n* paciente *m/f* externo/a; **~post** *n* puesto avanzado; **~put** *n* (volumen *m* de) producción *f*, rendimiento; (*COMPUT*) salida
outrage ['autreɪdʒ] *n* escándalo; (*atrocity*) atrocidad *f* ♦ *vt* ultrajar; **~ous** [-'reɪdʒəs] *adj* monstruoso
outright [*adv* aut'raɪt, *adj* 'autraɪt] *cdv* (*ask, deny*) francamente; (*refuse*) rotundamente; (*win*) de manera absoluta; (*be killed*) en el acto ♦ *adj* franco; rotundo
outset ['autset] *n* principio
outside [aut'saɪd] *n* exterior *m* ♦ *adj* exterior, externo ♦ *adv* fuera ♦ *prep* fuera de; (*beyond*) más allá de; **at the ~** (*fig*) a lo sumo; **~ lane** *n* (*AUT*: *in Britain*) carril *m* de la derecha; (: *in US, Europe etc*) carril *m* de la izquierda; **~ line** *n* (*TEL*) línea (exterior); **~r** *n* (*stranger*) extraño, forastero
out: **~size** *adj* (*clothes*) de talla grande; **~skirts** *npl* alrededores *mpl*, afueras *fpl*; **~spoken** *adj* muy franco; **~standing** *adj* excepcional, destacado; (*remaining*) pendiente; **~stay** *vt*: **to ~stay one's welcome** quedarse más de la cuenta; **~stretched** *adj* (*hand*) extendido; **~strip** *vt* (*competitors, demand*) dejar atrás, aventajar; **~-tray** *n* bandeja de salida
outward ['autwəd] *adj* externo; (*journey*) de ida
outweigh [aut'weɪ] *vt* pesar más que
outwit [aut'wɪt] *vt* ser más listo que
oval ['əuvl] *adj* ovalado ♦ *n* óvalo
ovary ['əuvərɪ] *n* ovario
oven ['ʌvn] *n* horno; **~proof** *adj* resistente al horno

over [ˈəuvə*] adv encima, por encima ♦ adj (or adv) (finished) terminado; (surplus) de sobra ♦ prep (por) encima de; (above) sobre; (on the other side of) al otro lado de; (more than) más de; (during) durante; ~ here (por) aquí; ~ there (por) allí or allá; all ~ (everywhere) por todas partes; ~ and ~ (again) una y otra vez; ~ and above además de; to ask sb ~ invitar a uno a casa; to bend ~ inclinarse

overall [adj, n ˈəuvərɔːl; adv əuvəˈrɔːl] adj (length etc) total; (study) de conjunto ♦ adv en conjunto ♦ n (BRIT) guardapolvo; ~s npl mono (SP), overol m (AM)

over: ~**awe** vt to be ~awed (by) quedar impresionado (con); ~**balance** vi perder el equilibrio; ~**board** adv (NAUT) por la borda; ~**book** [əuvəˈbuk] vt sobrereservar

overcast [ˈəuvəkɑːst] adj encapotado

overcharge [əuvəˈtʃɑːdʒ] vt: to ~ sb cobrar un precio excesivo a uno

overcoat [ˈəuvəkəut] n abrigo, sobretodo

overcome [əuvəˈkʌm] (irreg) vt vencer; (difficulty) superar

over: ~**crowded** adj atestado de gente; (city, country) superpoblado; ~**do** (irreg) vt exagerar; (overcook) cocer demasiado; to ~do it (work etc) pasarse; ~**dose** n sobredosis f inv; ~**draft** n saldo deudor; ~**drawn** adj (account) en descubierto; ~**due** adj retrasado; ~**estimate** [əuvərˈestimeit] vt sobreestimar

overflow [vb əuvəˈfləu, n ˈəuvəfləu] vi desbordarse ♦ n (also: ~ pipe) (cañería de) desagüe m

overgrown [əuvəˈgrəun] adj (garden) invadido por la vegetación

overhaul [vb əuvəˈhɔːl, n ˈəuvəhɔːl] vt revisar, repasar ♦ n revisión f

overhead [adv əuvəˈhed, adj, n ˈəuvəhed] adv por arriba or encima ♦ adj (cable) aéreo ♦ n (US) ~s; ~s npl (expenses) gastos mpl generales

over: ~**hear** (irreg) vt oír por casualidad; ~**heat** vi (engine) recalentarse; ~**joyed** adj encantado, lleno de alegría

overland [ˈəuvəlænd] adj, adv por tierra

overlap [əuvəˈlæp] vi traslaparse

over: ~**leaf** adv al dorso; ~**load** vt sobrecargar; ~**look** vt (have view of) dar a, tener vistas a; (miss: by mistake) pasar por alto; (excuse) perdonar

overnight [əuvəˈnait] adv durante la noche; (fig) de la noche a la mañana ♦ adj de noche; to stay ~ pasar la noche

overpass [ˈəuvəpɑːs] (US) n paso superior

overpower [əuvəˈpauə*] vt dominar; (fig) embargar; ~**ing** adj (heat) agobiante; (smell) penetrante

over: ~**rate** vt sobreestimar; ~**ride** (irreg) vt no hacer caso de; ~**riding** adj predominante; ~**rule** vt (decision) anular; (claim) denegar; ~**run** (irreg) vt (country) invadir; (time limit) rebasar, exceder

overseas [əuvəˈsiːz] adv (abroad: live) en el extranjero; (: travel) al extranjero ♦ adj (trade) exterior; (visitor) extranjero

overshadow [əuvəˈʃædəu] vt: to be ~ed by estar a la sombra de

overshoot [əuvəˈʃuːt] (irreg) vt excederse

oversight [ˈəuvəsait] n descuido

oversleep [əuvəˈsliːp] (irreg) vi quedarse dormido

overstep [əuvəˈstep] vt: to ~ the mark pasarse de la raya

overt [əuˈvɜːt] adj abierto

overtake [əuvəˈteik] (irreg) vt sobrepasar; (BRIT: AUT) adelantar

over: ~**throw** (irreg) vt (government) derrocar; ~**time** n horas fpl extraordinarias; ~**tone** n (fig) tono

overture [ˈəuvətʃuə*] n (MUS) obertura; (fig) preludio

over: ~**turn** vt volcar; (fig: plan) desbaratar; (: government) derrocar ♦ vi volcar; ~**weight** adj demasiado gordo or pesado; ~**whelm** vt aplastar; (subj: emotion) sobrecoger; ~**whelming** adj (victory, defeat) arrollador(a); (feeling) irresistible; ~**work** vi trabajar demasiado; ~**wrought** [əuvəˈrɔːt] adj sobreexcitado

owe [əu] vt: to ~ sb sth, to ~ sth to sb deber algo a uno; **owing to** prep debido a, por causa de

owl [aul] n búho, lechuza

own [əun] vt tener, poseer ♦ adj propio; **a room of my** ~ una habitación propia; **to get one's** ~ **back** tomar revancha; **on one's** ~ solo, a solas; ~ **up** vi confesar; ~**er** n dueño/a; ~**ership** n posesión f

ox [ɔks] (pl ~**en**) n buey m; ~**tail** n: ~**tail soup** sopa de rabo de buey

oxygen [ˈɔksidʒən] n oxígeno

oyster [ˈɔistə*] n ostra

oz. abbr = **ounce(s)**

ozone [ˈəuzəun]: ~ **friendly** adj que no daña la capa de ozono; ~ **hole** n agujero m de/en la capa de ozono; ~ **layer** n capa f de ozono

P, p

p [piː] abbr = **penny; pence**

P.A. n abbr = **personal assistant; public address system**

p.a. abbr = **per annum**

pa [pɑː] (inf) n papá m

pace [peis] n paso ♦ vi: to ~ up and down

pasearse de un lado a otro; **to keep ~ with**
llevar el mismo paso que; **~maker** n (MED)
regulador m cardíaco, marcapasos m inv;
(SPORT: also: **~setter**) liebre f
Pacific [pə'sɪfɪk] n: **the ~ (Ocean)** el (Océano)
Pacífico
pack [pæk] n (packet) paquete m; (of hounds)
jauría; (of people) manada, bando; (of cards)
baraja; (bundle) fardo; (US: of cigarettes)
paquete m; (back ~) mochila ♦ vt (fill) llenar;
(in suitcase etc) meter, poner; (cram) llenar,
atestar; **to ~ (one's bags)** hacerse la maleta;
to ~ sb off despachar a uno; **~ it in!** (inf)
¡déjalo!
package ['pækɪdʒ] n paquete m; (bulky)
bulto; (also: ~ deal) acuerdo global;
~ holiday n vacaciones fpl organizadas;
~ tour n viaje m organizado
packed lunch n almuerzo frío
packet ['pækɪt] n paquete m
packing ['pækɪŋ] n embalaje m; **~ case** n
cajón m de embalaje
pact [pækt] n pacto
pad [pæd] n (of paper) bloc m; (cushion)
cojinete m; (inf: home) casa ♦ vt rellenar;
~ding n (material) relleno
paddle ['pædl] n (oar) canalete m; (US: for
table tennis) paleta ♦ vt impulsar con canalete
♦ vi (with feet) chapotear; **paddling pool**
(BRIT) n estanque m de juegos
paddock ['pædək] n corral m
padlock ['pædlɔk] n candado
paediatrics [piːdɪ'ætrɪks] (US **pediatrics**) n
pediatría
pagan ['peɪgən] adj, n pagano/a m/f
page [peɪdʒ] n (of book) página; (of
newspaper) plana; (also: ~ boy) paje m ♦ vt
(in hotel etc) llamar por altavoz a
pageant ['pædʒənt] n (procession) desfile m;
(show) espectáculo; **~ry** n pompa
pager ['peɪdʒə*] n (TEL) busca m
paging device ['peɪdʒɪŋ-] n = **pager**
paid [peɪd] pt, pp of **pay** ♦ adj (work)
remunerado; (holiday) pagado; (official etc) a
sueldo; **to put ~ to** (BRIT) acabar con
pail [peɪl] n cubo, balde m
pain [peɪn] n dolor m; **to be in ~** sufrir; **to take
~s to do sth** tomarse grandes molestias en
hacer algo; **~ed** adj (expression) afligido;
~ful adj doloroso; (difficult) penoso;
(disagreeable) desagradable; **~fully** adv (fig:
very) terriblemente; **~killer** n analgésico;
~less adj que no causa dolor; **~staking**
['peɪnzteɪkɪŋ] adj (person) concienzudo,
esmerado
paint [peɪnt] n pintura ♦ vt pintar; **to ~ the
door blue** pintar la puerta de azul; **~brush** n
(artist's) pincel m; (decorator's) brocha; **~er**
n pintor(a) m/f; **~ing** n pintura; **~work** n

pintura
pair [peə*] n (of shoes, gloves etc) par m; (of
people) pareja; **a ~ of scissors** unas tijeras; **a
~ of trousers** unos pantalones, un pantalón
pajamas [pə'dʒɑːməz] (US) npl pijama m
Pakistan [pɑːkɪ'stɑːn] n Paquistán m; **~i** adj,
n paquistaní m/f
pal [pæl] (inf) n compinche m/f, compañero/a
palace ['pæləs] n palacio
palatable ['pælɪtəbl] adj sabroso
palate ['pælɪt] n paladar m
pale [peɪl] adj (gen) pálido; (colour) claro ♦ n:
to be beyond the ~ pasarse de la raya
Palestine ['pælɪstaɪn] n Palestina;
Palestinian [-'tɪnɪən] adj, n palestino/a m/f
palette ['pælɪt] n paleta
pall [pɔːl] vi perder el sabor
pallet ['pælɪt] n (for goods) pallet m
pallid ['pælɪd] adj pálido
palm [pɑːm] n (ANAT) palma; (also: ~ tree)
palmera, palma ♦ vt: **to ~ sth off on sb** (inf)
encajar algo a uno; **P~ Sunday** n Domingo
de Ramos
paltry ['pɔːltrɪ] adj irrisorio
pamper ['pæmpə*] vt mimar
pamphlet ['pæmflət] n folleto
pan [pæn] n (also: sauce~) cacerola, cazuela,
olla; (also: frying ~) sartén f
Panama ['pænəmɑː] n Panamá m; **the
~ Canal** el Canal de Panamá
pancake ['pænkeɪk] n crepe f
panda ['pændə] n panda m; **~ car** (BRIT) n
coche m Z (SP)
pandemonium [pændɪ'məunɪəm] n jaleo
pander ['pændə*] vi: **to ~ to** complacer a
pane [peɪn] n cristal m
panel ['pænl] n (of wood etc) panel m; (RADIO,
TV) panel m de invitados; **~ling** (US **~ing**) n
paneles mpl
pang [pæŋ] n: **a ~ of regret** (una punzada de)
remordimiento; **hunger ~s** dolores mpl del
hambre
panic ['pænɪk] n (terror m) pánico ♦ vi
dejarse llevar por el pánico; **~ky** adj (person)
asustadizo; **~-stricken** adj preso de pánico
pansy ['pænzɪ] n (BOT) pensamiento; (inf:
pej) maricón m
pant [pænt] vi jadear
panther ['pænθə*] n pantera
panties ['pæntɪz] npl bragas fpl, pantis mpl
pantihose ['pæntɪhəuz] (US) n pantimedias
fpl
pantomime ['pæntəmaɪm] (BRIT) n revista
musical representada en Navidad, basada en
cuentos de hadas
pantry ['pæntrɪ] n despensa
pants [pænts] n (BRIT: underwear: woman's)
bragas fpl; (: man's) calzoncillos mpl; (US:
trousers) pantalones mpl

paper ['peɪpə*] n papel m; (also: news~)
periódico, diario; (academic essay) ensayo;
(exam) examen m ♦ adj de papel ♦ vt
empapelar (SP), tapizar (AM); ~s npl (also:
identity ~s) papeles mpl, documentos mpl;
~back n libro en rústica; ~ bag n bolsa de
papel; ~ clip n clip m; ~ hankie n pañuelo
de papel; ~weight n pisapapeles m inv;
~work n trabajo administrativo

paprika ['pæprɪkə] n pimentón m

par [pɑː*] n par f; (GOLF) par m; to be on a
~ with estar a la par con

parachute ['pærəʃuːt] n paracaídas m inv

parade [pə'reɪd] n desfile m ♦ vt (show off)
hacer alarde de ♦ vi desfilar; (MIL) pasar
revista

paradise ['pærədaɪs] n paraíso

paradox ['pærədɔks] n paradoja; ~ically
[-'dɔksɪklɪ] adv paradójicamente

paraffin ['pærəfɪn] (BRIT) n (also: ~ oil)
parafina

paragon ['pærəgən] n modelo

paragraph ['pærəgrɑːf] n párrafo

parallel ['pærəlel] adj en paralelo; (fig)
semejante ♦ n (line) paralela; (fig, GEO)
paralelo

paralyse ['pærəlaɪz] vt paralizar

paralysis [pə'rælɪsɪs] n parálisis f inv

paralyze ['pærəlaɪz] (US) vt = paralyse

paramount ['pærəmaunt] adj: of
~ importance de suma importancia

paranoid ['pærənɔɪd] adj (person, feeling)
paranoico

paraphernalia [pærəfə'neɪlɪə] n (gear) avíos
mpl

parasite ['pærəsaɪt] n parásito/a

parasol ['pærəsɔl] n sombrilla, quitasol m

paratrooper ['pærətruːpə*] n paracaidista
m/f

parcel ['pɑːsl] n paquete m ♦ vt (also: ~ up)
empaquetar, embalar

parched [pɑːtʃt] adj (person) muerto de sed

parchment ['pɑːtʃmənt] n pergamino

pardon ['pɑːdn] n (LAW) indulto ♦ vt
perdonar; ~ me!, I beg your ~! (I'm sorry!)
¡perdone usted!; (I beg your) ~?, ~ me? (US)
(what did you say?) ¿cómo?

parent ['peərənt] n (mother) madre f; (father)
padre m; ~s npl padres mpl; ~al [pə'rentl] adj
paternal/maternal

parenthesis [pə'renθɪsɪs] (pl parentheses) n
paréntesis m inv

Paris ['pærɪs] n París

parish ['pærɪʃ] n parroquia

Parisian [pə'rɪzɪən] adj, n parisiense m/f

park [pɑːk] n parque m ♦ vt aparcar,
estacionar ♦ vi aparcar, estacionarse

parking ['pɑːkɪŋ] n aparcamiento,
estacionamiento; "no ~" "prohibido

estacionarse"; ~ lot (US) n parking m;
~ meter n parquímetro; ~ ticket n multa de
aparcamiento

parliament ['pɑːləmənt] n parlamento;
(Spanish) Cortes fpl; ~ary [-'mentəri] adj
parlamentario

parlour ['pɑːlə*] (US parlor) n sala de recibo,
salón m, living m (AM)

parochial [pə'rəukɪəl] (pej) adj de miras
estrechas

parole [pə'rəul] n: on ~ libre bajo palabra

parquet ['pɑːkeɪ] n: ~ floor(ing) parquet m

parrot ['pærət] n loro, papagayo

parry ['pærɪ] vt parar

parsley ['pɑːslɪ] n perejil m

parsnip ['pɑːsnɪp] n chirivía

parson ['pɑːsn] n cura m

part [pɑːt] n (gen, MUS) parte f; (bit) trozo;
(of machine) pieza; (THEATRE etc) papel m; (of
serial) entrega; (US: in hair) raya ♦ adv =
partly ♦ vt separar ♦ vi (people) separarse;
(crowd) apartarse; to take ~ in tomar parte or
participar en; to take sth in good ~ tomar
algo en buena parte; to take sb's ~ defender
a uno; for my ~ por mi parte; for the most ~
en su mayor parte; to ~ one's hair hacerse la
raya; ~ with vt fus ceder, entregar; (money)
pagar; ~ exchange (BRIT) n: in ~ exchange
como parte del pago

partial ['pɑːʃl] adj parcial; to be ~ to ser
aficionado a

participant [pɑː'tɪsɪpənt] n (in competition)
concursante m/f; (in campaign etc)
participante m/f

participate [pɑː'tɪsɪpeɪt] vi: to ~ in participar
en; **participation** [-'peɪʃən] n participación f

participle ['pɑːtɪsɪpl] n participio

particle ['pɑːtɪkl] n partícula; (of dust) grano

particular [pə'tɪkjulə*] adj (special)
particular; (concrete) concreto; (given)
determinado; (fussy) quisquilloso;
(demanding) exigente; ~s npl (information)
datos mpl; (details) pormenores mpl; in ~ en
particular; ~ly adv (in particular) sobre todo;
(difficult, good etc) especialmente

parting ['pɑːtɪŋ] n (act of) separación f;
(farewell) despedida; (BRIT: in hair) raya ♦ adj
de despedida

partisan [pɑːtɪ'zæn] adj partidista ♦ n
partidario/a

partition [pɑː'tɪʃən] n (POL) división f; (wall)
tabique m

partly ['pɑːtlɪ] adv en parte

partner ['pɑːtnə*] n (COMM) socio/a; (SPORT,
at dance) pareja; (spouse) cónyuge m/f;
(lover) compañero/a; ~ship n asociación f;
(COMM) sociedad f

partridge ['pɑːtrɪdʒ] n perdiz f

part-time adj, adv a tiempo parcial

party ['pɑ:tɪ] n (POL) partido; (celebration) fiesta; (group) grupo; (LAW) parte f interesada ♦ cpd (POL) de partido; ~ **dress** n vestido de fiesta

pass [pɑ:s] vt (time, object) pasar; (place) pasar por; (overtake) rebasar; (exam) aprobar; (approve) aprobar ♦ vi pasar; (SCOL) aprobar, ser aprobado ♦ n (permit) permiso; (membership card) carnet m; (in mountains) puerto, desfiladero; (SPORT) pase m; (SCOL: also: ~ mark): **to get a ~** in aprobar en; **to ~ sth through sth** pasar algo por algo; **to make a ~ at sb** (inf) hacer proposiciones a uno; ~ **away** vi fallecer; ~ **by** vi pasar ♦ vt (ignore) pasar por alto; ~ **for** fus pasar por; ~ **on** vt transmitir; ~ **out** vi desmayarse; ~ **up** vt (opportunity) renunciar a; ~**able** adj (road) transitable; (tolerable) pasable

passage ['pæsɪdʒ] n (also: ~way) pasillo; (act of passing) tránsito; (fare, in book) pasaje m; (by boat) travesía; (ANAT) tubo

passbook ['pɑ:sbʊk] n libreta de banco

passenger ['pæsɪndʒə*] n pasajero/a, viajero/a

passer-by [pɑ:sə'baɪ] n transeúnte m/f

passing ['pɑ:sɪŋ] adj pasajero; **in ~** de paso; ~ **place** n (AUT) apartadero

passion ['pæʃən] n pasión f; ~**ate** adj apasionado

passive ['pæsɪv] adj (gen, also LING) pasivo; ~ **smoking** n efectos del tabaco en fumadores pasivos

Passover ['pɑ:səʊvə*] n Pascua (de los judíos)

passport ['pɑ:spɔ:t] n pasaporte m; ~ **control** n control m de pasaporte; ~ **office** n oficina de pasaportes

password ['pɑ:swɜ:d] n contraseña

past [pɑ:st] prep (in front of) por delante de; (further than) más allá de; (later than) después de ♦ adj pasado; (president etc) antiguo ♦ n (time) pasado; (of person) antecedentes mpl; **he's ~** forty tiene más de cuarenta años; **ten/quarter ~ eight** las ocho y diez/cuarto; **for the ~ few/3 days** durante los últimos días/últimos 3 días; **to run ~ sb** pasar a uno corriendo

pasta ['pæstə] n pasta

paste [peɪst] n pasta; (glue) engrudo ♦ vt pegar

pasteurized ['pæstəraɪzd] adj pasteurizado

pastille ['pæstl] n pastilla

pastime ['pɑ:staɪm] n pasatiempo

pastry ['peɪstrɪ] n (dough) pasta; (cake) pastel m

pasture ['pɑ:stʃə*] n pasto

pasty[1] ['pæstɪ] n empanada

pasty[2] ['peɪstɪ] adj (complexion) pálido

pat [pæt] vt dar una palmadita a; (dog etc)
acariciar

patch [pætʃ] n (of material, eye ~) parche m; (mended part) remiendo; (of land) terreno ♦ vt remendar; **(to go through) a bad ~** (pasar por) una mala racha; ~ **up** vt reparar; (quarrel) hacer las paces en; ~**work** n labor m de retazos; ~**y** adj desigual

pâté ['pæteɪ] n paté m

patent ['peɪtnt] n patente f ♦ vt patentar ♦ adj patente, evidente; ~ **leather** n charol m

paternal [pə'tɜ:nl] adj paternal; (relation) paterno

path [pɑ:θ] n camino, sendero; (trail, track) pista; (of missile) trayectoria

pathetic [pə'θetɪk] adj patético, lastimoso; (very bad) malísimo

pathological [pæθə'lɒdʒɪkəl] adj patológico

pathway ['pɑ:θweɪ] n sendero, vereda

patience ['peɪʃns] n paciencia; (BRIT: CARDS) solitario

patient ['peɪʃnt] n paciente m/f ♦ adj paciente, sufrido

patio ['pætɪəʊ] n patio

patriot ['peɪtrɪət] n patriota m/f; ~**ic** [pætrɪ'ɒtɪk] adj patriótico

patrol [pə'trəʊl] n patrulla ♦ vt patrullar por; ~ **car** n coche m patrulla; ~**man** (US irreg) n policía m

patron ['peɪtrən] n (in shop) cliente m/f; (of charity) patrocinador(a) m/f; ~ **of the arts** mecenas m; ~**ize** ['pætrənaɪz] vt (shop) ser cliente de; (artist etc) proteger; (look down on) condescender con; ~ **saint** n santo/a patrón/ona m/f

patter ['pætə*] n golpeteo; (sales talk) labia ♦ vi (rain) tamborilear

pattern ['pætən] n (SEWING) patrón m; (design) dibujo

pauper ['pɔ:pə*] n pobre m/f

pause [pɔ:z] n pausa ♦ vi hacer una pausa

pave [peɪv] vt pavimentar; **to ~ the way for** preparar el terreno para

pavement ['peɪvmənt] (BRIT) n acera (SP), vereda (AM)

pavilion [pə'vɪlɪən] n (SPORT) caseta

paving ['peɪvɪŋ] n pavimento, enlosado; ~ **stone** n losa

paw [pɔ:] n pata

pawn [pɔ:n] n (CHESS) peón m; (fig) instrumento ♦ vt empeñar; ~ **broker** n prestamista m/f; ~**shop** n monte m de piedad

pay [peɪ] (pt, pp **paid**) n (wage etc) sueldo, salario ♦ vt pagar ♦ vi (be profitable) rendir; **to ~ attention (to)** prestar atención (a); **to ~ sb a visit** hacer una visita a uno; **to ~ one's respects to sb** presentar sus respetos a uno; ~ **back** vt (money) reembolsar; (person) pagar; ~ **for** vt fus pagar; ~ **in** vt ingresar; ~ **off** vt saldar ♦ vi (scheme, decision) dar resultado; ~ **up** vt pagar (de mala gana); **~able** adj: **~able** to pagadero a; ~ **day** n día m de paga; **~ee** n portador(a) m/f; ~ **envelope** (US) n = ~ **packet**; **~ment** n pago; **monthly ~ment** mensualidad f; ~ **packet** (BRIT) n sobre m (de paga); ~ **phone** n teléfono público; **~roll** n nómina; ~ **slip** n recibo de sueldo; ~ **television** n televisión f de pago

PC n abbr = **personal computer**; (BRIT) = **police constable** ♦ adv abbr = **politically correct**

p.c. abbr = **per cent**

pea [piː] n guisante m (SP), chícharo (AM), arveja (AM)

peace [piːs] n paz f; (calm) paz f, tranquilidad f; **~ful** adj (gentle) pacífico; (calm) tranquilo, sosegado

peach [piːtʃ] n melocotón m (SP), durazno (AM)

peacock ['piːkɔk] n pavo real

peak [piːk] n (of mountain) cumbre f, cima; (of cap) visera; (fig) cumbre f; ~ **hours** npl, ~ **period** n horas fpl punta

peal [piːl] n (of bells) repique m; ~ **of laughter** carcajada

peanut ['piːnʌt] n cacahuete m (SP), maní m (AM); ~ **butter** manteca de cacahuete or maní

pear [pɛə*] n pera

pearl [pɜːl] n perla

peasant ['pɛznt] n campesino/a

peat [piːt] n turba

pebble ['pɛbl] n guijarro

peck [pɛk] vt (also: ~ **at**) picotear ♦ n picotazo; (kiss) besito; **~ing order** n orden m de jerarquía; **~ish** (BRIT: inf) adj: **I feel ~ish** tengo ganas de picar algo

peculiar [pɪˈkjuːlɪə*] adj (odd) extraño, raro; (typical) propio, característico; ~ **to** propio de

pedal ['pɛdl] n pedal m ♦ vi pedalear

pedantic [pɪˈdæntɪk] adj pedante

peddler ['pɛdlə*] n: **drug ~** traficante m/f; camello

pedestrian [pɪˈdɛstrɪən] n peatón/ona m/f ♦ adj pedestre; ~ **crossing** (BRIT) n paso de peatones; ~ **precinct** (BRIT), ~ **zone** (US) n zona peatonal

pediatrics [piːdɪˈætrɪks] (US) n = **paediatrics**

pedigree ['pɛdɪɡriː] n genealogía; (of animal) raza, pedigrí m ♦ cpd (animal) de raza, de casta

pee [piː] (inf) vi mear

peek [piːk] vi mirar a hurtadillas

peel [piːl] n piel f; (of orange, lemon) cáscara; (: removed) peladuras fpl ♦ vt pelar ♦ vi (paint etc) desconcharse; (wallpaper)

despegarse, desprenderse; (skin) pelar

peep [piːp] n (BRIT: look) mirada furtiva; (sound) pío ♦ vi (BRIT: look) mirar furtivamente; ~ **out** vi salir (un poco); **~hole** n mirilla

peer [pɪə*] vi: **to ~ at** escudriñar ♦ n (noble) par m; (equal) igual m; (contemporary) contemporáneo/a; **~age** n nobleza

peeved [piːvd] adj enojado

peg [pɛɡ] n (for coat etc) gancho, colgadero; (BRIT: also: **clothes ~**) pinza

Pekingese [piːkɪˈniːz] n (dog) pequinés/esa m/f

pelican ['pɛlɪkən] n pelícano; ~ **crossing** (BRIT) n (AUT) paso de peatones señalizado

pellet ['pɛlɪt] n bolita; (bullet) perdigón m

pelt [pɛlt] vt: **to ~ sb with sth** arrojarle algo a uno ♦ vi (rain) llover a cántaros; (inf: run) correr ♦ n pellejo

pen [pɛn] n (fountain ~) pluma; (ballpoint ~) bolígrafo; (for sheep) redil m

penal ['piːnl] adj penal; **~ize** vt castigar

penalty ['pɛnltɪ] n (gen) pena; (fine) multa; ~ **(kick)** n (FOOTBALL) penalty m; (RUGBY) golpe m de castigo

penance ['pɛnəns] n penitencia

pence [pɛns] npl of **penny**

pencil ['pɛnsl] n lápiz m, lapicero (AM); ~ **case** n estuche m; ~ **sharpener** n sacapuntas m inv

pendant ['pɛndnt] n pendiente m

pending ['pɛndɪŋ] prep antes de ♦ adj pendiente

pendulum ['pɛndjuləm] n péndulo

penetrate ['pɛnɪtreɪt] vt penetrar

penfriend ['pɛnfrɛnd] (BRIT) n amigo/a por carta

penguin ['pɛŋɡwɪn] n pingüino

penicillin [pɛnɪˈsɪlɪn] n penicilina

peninsula [pəˈnɪnsjulə] n península

penis ['piːnɪs] n pene m

penitentiary [pɛnɪˈtɛnʃərɪ] (US) n cárcel f, presidio

penknife ['pɛnnaɪf] n navaja

pen name n seudónimo

penniless ['pɛnɪlɪs] adj sin dinero

penny ['pɛnɪ] (pl **pennies** or (BRIT) **pence**) n penique m; (US) centavo

penpal ['pɛnpæl] n amigo/a por carta

pension ['pɛnʃən] n (state benefit) jubilación f; **~er** (BRIT) n jubilado/a; ~ **fund** n caja or fondo de pensiones

pentagon ['pɛntəɡən] n: **the P~** (US: POL) el Pentágono

Pentecost ['pɛntɪkɔst] n Pentecostés m

penthouse ['pɛnthaus] n ático de lujo

pent-up ['pɛntʌp] adj reprimido

people ['piːpl] npl gente f; (citizens) pueblo, ciudadanos mpl; (POL): **the ~** el pueblo ♦ n

(*nation, race*) pueblo, nación f; **several**
~ **came** vinieron varias personas; ~ **say that ...**
dice la gente que ...
pep [pep] (*inf*): ~ **up** *vt* animar
pepper ['pepə*] *n* (*spice*) pimienta;
(*vegetable*) pimiento ♦ *vt*: **to ~ with** (*fig*)
salpicar de; ~**mint** *n* (*sweet*) pastilla de
menta
peptalk ['peptɔːk] *n*: **to give sb a** ~ darle a
uno una inyección de ánimo
per [pəː*] *prep* por; ~ **day/person** por día/
persona; ~ **annum** al año; ~ **capita** *adj, adv*
per cápita
perceive [pə'siːv] *vt* percibir; (*realize*) darse
cuenta de
per cent *n* por ciento
percentage [pə'sentɪdʒ] *n* porcentaje *m*
perception [pə'sepʃən] *n* percepción f;
(*insight*) perspicacia; (*opinion etc*) opinión f;
perceptive [-'septɪv] *adj* perspicaz
perch [pəːtʃ] *n* (*fish*) perca; (*for bird*) percha
♦ *vi*: **to ~ (on)** (*bird*) posarse (en); (*person*)
encaramarse (en)
percolator ['pəːkəleɪtə*] *n* (*also: coffee ~*)
cafetera de filtro
perennial [pə'renɪəl] *adj* perenne
perfect [*adj, n* 'pəːfɪkt, *vb* pə'fekt] *adj*
perfecto ♦ *n* (*also:* ~ *tense*) perfecto ♦ *vt*
perfeccionar; ~**ly** ['pəːfɪktlɪ] *adv*
perfectamente
perforate ['pəːfəreɪt] *vt* perforar
perform [pə'fɔːm] *vt* (*carry out*) realizar,
llevar a cabo; (*THEATRE*) representar; (*piece of
music*) interpretar ♦ *vi* (*well, badly*) funcionar;
~**ance** *n* (*of a play*) representación f; (*of
actor, athlete etc*) actuación f; (*of car, engine,
company*) rendimiento *m*; (*of economy*)
resultados *mpl*; ~**er** *n* (*actor*) actor *m*, actriz f
perfume ['pəːfjuːm] *n* perfume *m*
perhaps [pə'hæps] *adv* quizá(s), tal vez
peril ['perɪl] *n* peligro, riesgo
perimeter [pə'rɪmɪtə*] *n* perímetro
period ['pɪərɪəd] *n* período; (*SCOL*) clase f;
(*full stop*) punto; (*MED*) regla ♦ *adj* (*costume,
furniture*) de época; ~**ic(al)** [-'ɔdɪk(l)] *adj*
periódico; ~**ical** [-'ɔdɪkl] *n* periódico; ~**ically**
[-'ɔdɪklɪ] *adv* de vez en cuando, cada cierto
tiempo
peripheral [pə'rɪfərəl] *adj* periférico ♦ *n*
(*COMPUT*) periférico, unidad f periférica
perish ['perɪʃ] *vi* perecer; (*decay*) echarse a
perder; ~**able** *adj* perecedero
perjury ['pəːdʒərɪ] *n* (*LAW*) perjurio
perk [pəːk] *n* extra *m*; ~ **up** *vi* (*cheer up*)
animarse
perm [pəːm] *n* permanente f
permanent ['pəːmənənt] *adj* permanente
permeate ['pəːmɪeɪt] *vi* penetrar, trascender
♦ *vt* penetrar, trascender a

permissible [pə'mɪsɪbl] *adj* permisible, lícito
permission [pə'mɪʃən] *n* permiso
permissive [pə'mɪsɪv] *adj* permisivo
permit [*n* 'pəːmɪt, *vt* pə'mɪt] *n* permiso,
licencia ♦ *vt* permitir
perplex [pə'pleks] *vt* dejar perplejo
persecute ['pəːsɪkjuːt] *vt* perseguir
persevere [pəːsɪ'vɪə*] *vi* persistir
Persian ['pəːʃən] *adj, n* persa *m/f*; **the ~ Gulf**
el Golfo Pérsico
persist [pə'sɪst] *vi*: **to ~ (in doing sth)** persistir
(en hacer algo); ~**ence** *n* empeño; ~**ent** *adj*
persistente; (*determined*) porfiado
person ['pəːsn] *n* persona; **in ~** en persona;
~**al** *adj* personal; individual; (*visit*) en
persona; ~**al assistant** *n* ayudante *m/f*
personal; ~**al column** *n* anuncios *mpl*
personales; ~**al computer** *n* ordenador *m*
personal; ~**ality** [-'nælɪtɪ] *n* personalidad f;
~**ally** *adv* personalmente; (*in person*) en
persona; **to take sth ~ally** tomarse algo a mal;
~**al organizer** *n* agenda; ~**al stereo** *n*
Walkman ® *m*; ~**ify** [-'sɔnɪfaɪ] *vt* encarnar
personnel [pəːsə'nel] *n* personal *m*
perspective [pə'spektɪv] *n* perspectiva
Perspex ® ['pəːspeks] *n* plexiglás ® *m*
perspiration [pəːspɪ'reɪʃən] *n* transpiración f
persuade [pə'sweɪd] *vt*: **to ~ sb to do sth**
persuadir a uno para que haga algo
Peru [pə'ruː] *n* el Perú *m*; **Peruvian** *adj, n*
peruano/a *m/f*
perverse [pə'vəːs] *adj* perverso; (*wayward*)
travieso
pervert [*n* 'pəːvəːt, *vb* pə'vəːt] *n* pervertido/a
♦ *vt* pervertir; (*truth, sb's words*) tergiversar
pessimist ['pesɪmɪst] *n* pesimista *m/f*; ~**ic**
[-'mɪstɪk] *adj* pesimista
pest [pest] *n* (*insect*) insecto nocivo; (*fig*) lata,
molestia
pester ['pestə*] *vt* molestar, acosar
pesticide ['pestɪsaɪd] *n* pesticida *m*
pet [pet] *n* animal *m* doméstico ♦ *cpd* favorito
♦ *vt* acariciar; **teacher's ~** favorito/a (del
profesor); ~ **hate** manía
petal ['petl] *n* pétalo
peter ['piːtə*]: **to ~ out** *vi* agotarse, acabarse
petite [pə'tiːt] *adj* chiquita
petition [pə'tɪʃən] *n* petición f
petrified ['petrɪfaɪd] *adj* horrorizado
petrol ['petrəl] (*BRIT*) *n* gasolina; **two/four-star**
~ gasolina normal/súper; ~ **can** *n* bidón *m* de
gasolina
petroleum [pə'trəʊlɪəm] *n* petróleo
petrol: ~ **pump** (*BRIT*) *n* (*in garage*) surtidor
m de gasolina; ~ **station** (*BRIT*) *n* gasolinera;
~ **tank** (*BRIT*) *n* depósito (de gasolina)
petticoat ['petɪkəʊt] *n* enaguas *fpl*
petty ['petɪ] *adj* (*mean*) mezquino;
(*unimportant*) insignificante; ~ **cash** *n* dinero

para gastos menores; **~ officer** *n* contramaestre *m*

petulant ['pɛtjulənt] *adj* malhumorado

pew [pjuː] *n* banco

pewter ['pjuːtə*] *n* peltre *m*

phantom ['fæntəm] *n* fantasma *m*

pharmacist ['faːməsɪst] *n* farmacéutico/a

pharmacy ['faːməsɪ] *n* farmacia

phase [feɪz] *n* fase *f* ♦ *vt:* **to ~ sth in/out** introducir/retirar algo por etapas

Ph.D. *abbr* = **Doctor of Philosophy**

pheasant ['fɛznt] *n* faisán *m*

phenomenon [fəˈnɔmɪnən] (*pl* **phenomena**) *n* fenómeno

philanthropist [fɪˈlænθrəpɪst] *n* filántropo/a

Philippines ['fɪlɪpiːnz] *npl:* **the ~** las Filipinas

philosopher [fɪˈlɔsəfə*] *n* filósofo/a

philosophy [fɪˈlɔsəfɪ] *n* filosofía

phobia ['fəubjə] *n* fobia

phone [fəun] *n* teléfono ♦ *vt* telefonear, llamar por teléfono; **to be on the ~** tener teléfono; (*be calling*) estar hablando por teléfono; **~ back** *vt, vi* volver a llamar; **~ up** *vt, vi* llamar por teléfono; **~ book** *n* guía telefónica; **~ booth** *n* cabina telefónica; **~ box** (*BRIT*) *n* = **~ booth**; **~ call** *n* llamada (telefónica); **~card** *n* teletarjeta; **~-in** (*BRIT*) *n* (*RADIO, TV*) programa *m* de participación (telefónica)

phonetics [fəˈnɛtɪks] *n* fonética

phoney ['fəunɪ] *adj* falso

photo ['fəutəu] *n* foto *f*; **~copier** *n* fotocopiadora; **~copy** *n* fotocopia ♦ *vt* fotocopiar

photograph ['fəutəgraːf] *n* fotografía ♦ *vt* fotografiar; **~er** [fəˈtɔgrəfə*] *n* fotógrafo/a; **~y** [fəˈtɔgrəfɪ] *n* fotografía

phrase [freɪz] *n* frase *f* ♦ *vt* expresar; **~ book** *n* libro de frases

physical ['fɪzɪkl] *adj* físico; **~ education** *n* educación *f* física; **~ly** *adv* físicamente

physician [fɪˈzɪʃən] *n* médico/a

physicist ['fɪzɪsɪst] *n* físico/a

physics ['fɪzɪks] *n* física

physiotherapy [fɪzɪəuˈθɛrəpɪ] *n* fisioterapia

physique [fɪˈziːk] *n* físico

pianist ['piːənɪst] *n* pianista *m/f*

piano [pɪˈænəu] *n* piano

pick [pɪk] *n* (*tool: also:* **~-axe**) pico, piqueta ♦ *vt* (*select*) elegir, escoger; (*gather*) coger (*SP*), recoger; (*remove, take out*) sacar, quitar; (*lock*) abrir con ganzúa; **take your ~** escoja lo que quiera; **the ~ of** lo mejor de; **to ~ one's nose/teeth** hurgarse las narices/limpiarse los dientes; **to ~ a quarrel with sb** meterse con alguien; **~ at** *vt fus:* **to ~ at one's food** comer con poco apetito; **~ on** *vt fus* (*person*) meterse con; **~ out** *vt* escoger; (*distinguish*) identificar; **~ up** *vi* (*improve: sales*) ir mejor;

(*: patient*) reponerse; (*: FINANCE*) recobrarse ♦ *vt* recoger; (*learn*) aprender; (*POLICE: arrest*) detener; (*person: for sex*) ligar; (*RADIO*) captar; **to ~ up speed** acelerarse; **to ~ o.s. up** levantarse

picket ['pɪkɪt] *n* piquete *m* ♦ *vt* piquetear

pickle ['pɪkl] *n* (*also:* **~s:** *as condiment*) escabeche *m*; (*fig: mess*) apuro ♦ *vt* encurtir

pickpocket ['pɪkpɔkɪt] *n* carterista *m/f*

pickup ['pɪkʌp] *n* (*small truck*) furgoneta

picnic ['pɪknɪk] *n* merienda ♦ *vi* ir de merienda; **~ area** *n* zona de picnic; (*AUT*) área de descanso

picture ['pɪktʃə*] *n* cuadro; (*painting*) pintura; (*photograph*) fotografía; (*TV*) imagen *f*; (*film*) película; (*fig: description*) descripción *f*; (*: situation*) situación *f* ♦ *vt* (*imagine*) imaginar; **~s** *npl* (*BRIT*) el cine; **~ book** *n* libro de dibujos

picturesque [pɪktʃəˈrɛsk] *adj* pintoresco

pie [paɪ] *n* pastel *m*; (*open*) tarta; (*small: meat*) empanada

piece [piːs] *n* pedazo, trozo; (*of cake*) trozo; (*item*): **a ~ of clothing/furniture/advice** una prenda (de vestir)/un mueble/un consejo ♦ *vt:* **to ~ together** juntar; (*TECH*) armar; **to take to ~s** desmontar; **~meal** *adv* poco a poco; **~work** *n* trabajo a destajo

pie chart *n* gráfico de sectores *or* tarta

pier [pɪə*] *n* muelle *m*, embarcadero

pierce [pɪəs] *vt* perforar

piercing ['pɪəsɪŋ] *adj* penetrante

pig [pɪg] *n* cerdo (AM), puerco (SP), chancho (AM); (*pej: unkind person*) asqueroso; (*: greedy person*) glotón/ona *m/f*

pigeon ['pɪdʒən] *n* paloma; (*as food*) pichón *m*; **~hole** *n* casilla

piggy bank ['pɪgɪ-] *n* hucha (*en forma de cerdito*)

pig: ~headed ['pɪgˈhɛdɪd] *adj* terco, testarudo; **~let** ['pɪglɪt] *n* cochinillo; **~skin** *n* piel *f* de cerdo; **~sty** ['pɪgstaɪ] *n* pocilga; **~tail** *n* (*girl's*) trenza; (*Chinese, TAUR*) coleta

pike [paɪk] *n* (*fish*) lucio

pilchard ['pɪltʃəd] *n* sardina

pile [paɪl] *n* montón *m*; (*of carpet, cloth*) pelo ♦ *vt* (*also:* **~ up**) amontonar; (*fig*) acumular ♦ *vi* (*also:* **~ up**) amontonarse; acumularse; **~ into** *vt fus* (*car*) meterse en; **~s** [paɪlz] *npl* (*MED*) almorranas *fpl*, hemorroides *mpl*; **~-up** *n* (*AUT*) accidente *m* múltiple

pilfering ['pɪlfərɪŋ] *n* ratería

pilgrim ['pɪlgrɪm] *n* peregrino/a; **~age** *n* peregrinación *f*, romería

pill [pɪl] *n* píldora; **the ~** la píldora

pillage ['pɪlɪdʒ] *vt* pillar, saquear

pillar ['pɪlə*] *n* pilar *m*; **~ box** (*BRIT*) *n* buzón *m*

pillion ['pɪljən] *n* (*of motorcycle*) asiento

trasero
pillow ['pɪləu] n almohada; **~case** n funda
pilot ['paɪlət] n piloto ♦ cpd (scheme etc)
piloto ♦ vt pilotar; **~ light** n piloto
pimp [pɪmp] n chulo (SP), cafiche m (AM)
pimple ['pɪmpl] n grano
PIN n abbr (= personal identification number)
número personal
pin [pɪn] n alfiler m ♦ vt prender (con alfiler);
~s and needles hormigueo; **to ~ sb down** (fig)
hacer que uno concrete; **to ~ sth on sb** (fig)
colgarle a uno el sambenito de algo
pinafore ['pɪnəfɔ:*] n delantal m; **~ dress**
(BRIT) n mandil m
pinball ['pɪnbɔ:l] n mesa americana
pincers ['pɪnsəz] npl pinzas fpl, tenazas fpl
pinch [pɪntʃ] n (of salt etc) pizca ♦ vt
pellizcar; (inf: steal) birlar; **at a ~** en caso de
apuro
pincushion ['pɪnkuʃən] n acerico
pine [paɪn] n (also: ~ tree, wood) pino ♦ vi: **to
~ for** suspirar por; **~ away** vi morirse de
pena
pineapple ['paɪnæpl] n piña, ananás m
ping [pɪŋ] n (noise) sonido agudo; **~-pong** ®
n pingpong ® m
pink [pɪŋk] adj rosado, (color de) rosa ♦ n
(colour) rosa; (BOT) clavel m, clavellina f
pinpoint ['pɪnpɔɪnt] vt precisar
pint [paɪnt] n pinta (BRIT = 568cc; US =
473cc); (BRIT: inf: of beer) pinta de cerveza,
≈ jarra (SP)
pin-up n fotografía erótica
pioneer [paɪə'nɪə*] n pionero/a
pious ['paɪəs] adj piadoso, devoto
pip [pɪp] n (seed) pepita; **the ~s** (BRIT) la señal
pipe [paɪp] n tubo, caño; (for smoking) pipa
♦ vt conducir en cañerías; **~s** npl (gen)
cañería; (also: bag~s) gaita; **~ cleaner** n
limpiapipas m inv; **~ dream** n sueño
imposible; **~line** n (for oil) oleoducto; (for
gas) gasoducto; **~r** n gaitero/a
piping ['paɪpɪŋ] adv: **to be ~ hot** estar que
quema
piquant ['pi:kənt] adj picante; (fig) agudo
pique [pi:k] n pique m, resentimiento
pirate ['paɪərət] n pirata m/f ♦ vt (cassette,
book) piratear; **~ radio** (BRIT) n emisora
pirata
Pisces ['paɪsi:z] n Piscis m
piss [pɪs] (inf!) vi mear; **~ed** (inf!) adj (drunk)
borracho
pistol ['pɪstl] n pistola
piston ['pɪstən] n pistón m, émbolo
pit [pɪt] n hoyo; (also: coal ~) mina; (in
garage) foso de inspección; (also: orchestra
~) platea ♦ vt: **to ~ one's wits against sb**
medir fuerzas con uno; **~s** npl (AUT) box m
pitch [pɪtʃ] n (MUS) tono; (BRIT: SPORT) campo;

terreno; (fig) punto; (tar) brea ♦ vt (throw)
arrojar, lanzar ♦ vi (fall) caer(se); **to ~ a tent**
montar una tienda (de campaña); **~-black**
adj negro como boca de lobo; **~ed battle** n
batalla campal
pitfall ['pɪtfɔ:l] n riesgo
pith [pɪθ] n (of orange) médula
pithy ['pɪθɪ] adj (fig) jugoso
pitiful ['pɪtɪful] adj (touching) lastimoso,
conmovedor(a)
pitiless ['pɪtɪlɪs] adj despiadado
pittance ['pɪtns] n miseria
pity ['pɪtɪ] n compasión f, piedad f ♦ vt
compadecer(se de); **what a ~!** ¡qué pena!
pizza ['pi:tsə] n pizza
placard ['plækɑ:d] n letrero; (in march etc)
pancarta
placate [plə'keɪt] vt apaciguar
place [pleɪs] n lugar m, sitio; (seat) plaza,
asiento; (post) puesto; (home): **at/to his ~**
en/a su casa; (role: in society etc) papel m
♦ vt (object) poner, colocar; (identify)
reconocer; **to take ~** tener lugar; **to be ~d** (in
race, exam) colocarse; **out of ~** (not suitable)
fuera de lugar; **in the first ~** en primer lugar;
to change ~s with sb cambiarse de sitio con
uno; **~ of birth** lugar m de nacimiento
placid ['plæsɪd] adj apacible
plague [pleɪg] n plaga; (MED) peste f ♦ vt
(fig) acosar, atormentar
plaice [pleɪs] n inv platija
plaid [plæd] n (material) tartán m
plain [pleɪn] adj (unpatterned) liso; (clear)
claro, evidente; (simple) sencillo; (not
handsome) poco atractivo ♦ adv claramente
♦ n llano, llanura; **~ chocolate** n chocolate
m amargo; **~-clothes** adj (police) vestido de
paisano; **~ly** adv claramente
plaintiff ['pleɪntɪf] n demandante m/f
plait [plæt] n trenza
plan [plæn] n (drawing) plano; (scheme) plan
m, proyecto ♦ vt proyectar, planificar ♦ vi
hacer proyectos; **to ~ to do** pensar hacer
plane [pleɪn] n (AVIAT) avión m; (MATH, fig)
plano; (also: ~ tree) plátano; (tool) cepillo
planet ['plænɪt] n planeta m
plank [plæŋk] n tabla
planner ['plænə*] n planificador(a) m/f
planning ['plænɪŋ] n planificación f; **family ~**
planificación familiar; **~ permission** n
permiso para realizar obras
plant [plɑ:nt] n planta; (machinery)
maquinaria; (factory) fábrica ♦ vt plantar;
(field) sembrar; (bomb) colocar
plaster ['plɑ:stə*] n (for walls) yeso; (also:
~ of Paris) yeso mate; (BRIT: also: sticking ~)
tirita (SP), esparadrapo, curita (AM) ♦ vt
enyesar; (cover): **to ~ with** llenar or cubrir de;
~ed (inf) adj borracho; **~er** n yesero

plastic ['plæstɪk] n plástico ♦ adj de plástico; **~ bag** n bolsa de plástico

Plasticine ® ['plæstɪsi:n] n (BRIT) n plastilina ®

plastic surgery n cirujía plástica

plate [pleɪt] n (dish) plato; (metal, in book) lámina; (dental) placa de dentadura postiza

plateau ['plætəu] (pl **~s** or **~x**) n meseta, altiplanicie f

plateaux ['plætəuz] npl of **plateau**

plate glass n vidrio cilindrado

platform ['plætfɔ:m] n (RAIL) andén m; (stage, BRIT: on bus) plataforma; (at meeting) tribuna; (POL) programa m (electoral)

platinum ['plætɪnəm] adj, n platino

platoon [plə'tu:n] n pelotón m

platter ['plætə*] n fuente f

plausible ['plɔ:zɪbl] adj verosímil; (person) convincente

play [pleɪ] n (THEATRE) obra, comedia ♦ vt (game) jugar; (compete against) jugar contra; (instrument) tocar; (part: in play etc) hacer el papel de; (tape, record) poner ♦ vi jugar; (band) tocar; (tape, record) sonar; **to ~ safe** ir a lo seguro; **~ down** vt quitar importancia a; **~ up** vi (cause trouble to) dar guerra; **~boy** n playboy m; **~er** n jugador(a) m/f; (THEATRE) actor/actriz m/f; (MUS) músico/a; **~ful** adj juguetón/ona; **~ground** n (in school) patio de recreo; (in park) parque m infantil; **~group** n jardín m de niños; **~ing card** n naipe m, carta; **~ing field** n campo de deportes; **~mate** n compañero/a de juego; **~-off** n (SPORT) (partido de) desempate m; **~pen** n corral m; **~thing** n juguete m; **~time** n (SCOL) recreo; **~wright** n dramaturgo/a

plc abbr (= public limited company) ≈ S.A.

plea [pli:] n súplica, petición f; (LAW) alegato, defensa; **~ bargaining** n (LAW) acuerdo entre fiscal y defensor para agilizar los trámites judiciales

plead [pli:d] vt (LAW): **to ~ sb's case** defender a uno; (give as excuse) poner como pretexto ♦ vi (LAW) declararse; (beg): **to ~ with sb** suplicar or rogar a uno

pleasant ['plɛznt] adj agradable; **~ries** npl cortesías fpl

please [pli:z] excl ¡por favor! ♦ vt (give pleasure to) dar gusto a, agradar ♦ vi (think fit): **do as you ~** haz lo que quieras; **~ yourself!** (inf) ¡haz lo que quieras!, ¡como quieras!; **~d** adj (happy) alegre, contento; **~d (with)** satisfecho (de); **~d to meet you** ¡encantado!, ¡tanto gusto!; **pleasing** adj agradable, grato

pleasure ['plɛʒə*] n placer m, gusto; "it's a **~**" "el gusto es mío"

pleat [pli:t] n pliegue m

pledge [plɛdʒ] n (promise) promesa, voto ♦ vt prometer

plentiful ['plɛntɪful] adj copioso, abundante

plenty ['plɛntɪ] n: **~ of** mucho(s)/a(s)

pliable ['plaɪəbl] adj flexible

pliers ['plaɪəz] npl alicates mpl, tenazas fpl

plight [plaɪt] n situación f difícil

plimsolls ['plɪmsəlz] (BRIT) npl zapatos mpl de tenis

plinth [plɪnθ] n plinto

plod [plɔd] vi caminar con paso pesado; (fig) trabajar laboriosamente

plonk [plɔŋk] (inf) n (BRIT: wine) vino peleón ♦ vt: **to ~ sth down** dejar caer algo

plot [plɔt] n (scheme) complot m, conjura; (of story, play) argumento; (of land) terreno, lote m (AM) ♦ vt (mark out) trazar; (conspire) tramar, urdir ♦ vi conspirar

plough [plau] (US **plow**) n arado ♦ vt (earth) arar; **to ~ money into** invertir dinero en; **~ through** vt fus (crowd) abrirse paso por la fuerza por; **~man's lunch** (BRIT) n almuerzo de pub a base de pan, queso y encurtidos

pluck [plʌk] vt (fruit) coger (SP), recoger (AM); (musical instrument) puntear; (bird) desplumar; (eyebrows) depilar; **to ~ up courage** hacer de tripas corazón

plug [plʌg] n tapón m; (ELEC) enchufe m, clavija; (AUT: also: **spark(ing) ~**) bujía ♦ vt (hole) tapar; (inf: advertise) dar publicidad a; **~ in** vt (ELEC) enchufar

plum [plʌm] n (fruit) ciruela

plumb [plʌm] vt: **to ~ the depths of** alcanzar los mayores extremos de

plumber ['plʌmə*] n fontanero/a (SP), plomero/a (AM)

plumbing ['plʌmɪŋ] n (trade) fontanería, plomería; (piping) cañería

plummet ['plʌmɪt] vi: **to ~ (down)** caer a plomo

plump [plʌmp] adj rechoncho, rollizo ♦ vi: **to ~ for** (inf: choose) optar por; **~ up** vt mullir

plunder ['plʌndə*] vt pillar, saquear

plunge [plʌndʒ] n zambullida ♦ vt sumergir, hundir ♦ vi (fall) caer; (dive) saltar; (person) arrojarse; **to take the ~** lanzarse; **plunging** adj: **plunging neckline** escote m pronunciado

pluperfect [plu:'pə:fɪkt] n pluscuamperfecto

plural ['pluərl] adj plural ♦ n plural m

plus [plʌs] n (also: **~ sign**) signo más ♦ prep más, y, además de; **ten/twenty ~** más de diez/veinte

plush [plʌʃ] adj lujoso

plutonium [plu:'təunɪəm] n plutonio

ply [plaɪ] vt (a trade) ejercer ♦ vi (ship) ir y venir ♦ n (of wool, rope) cabo; **to ~ sb with drink** insistir en ofrecer a uno muchas copas; **~wood** n madera contrachapada

P.M. n abbr = **Prime Minister**

p.m. adv abbr (= post meridiem) de la tarde or noche

pneumatic [nju:'mætɪk] adj neumático; **~ drill** n martillo neumático

pneumonia [nju:'məunɪə] n pulmonía

poach [pəutʃ] vt (cook) escalfar; (steal) cazar (or pescar) en vedado ♦ vi cazar (or pescar) en vedado; **~ed** adj escalfado; **~er** n cazador(a) m/f furtivo/a

P.O. Box n abbr = Post Office Box

pocket ['pɔkɪt] n bolsillo; (fig: small area) bolsa ♦ vt meter en el bolsillo; (steal) embolsar; **to be out of ~** (BRIT) salir perdiendo; **~book** (US) n cartera; **~ calculator** n calculadora de bolsillo; **~ knife** n navaja; **~ money** n asignación f

pod [pɔd] n vaina

podgy ['pɔdʒɪ] adj gordinflón/ona

podiatrist [pɔ'di:ətrɪst] (US) n pedicuro/a

poem ['pəuɪm] n poema m

poet ['pəuɪt] n poeta m/f; **~ic** [-'etɪk] adj poético; **~ry** n poesía

poignant ['pɔɪnjənt] adj conmovedor(a)

point [pɔɪnt] n punto; (tip) punta; (purpose) fin m, propósito; (use) utilidad f; (significant part) lo significativo; (moment) momento; (ELEC) toma (de corriente); (also: decimal ~): **2 ~ 3 (2.3)** dos coma tres (2,3) ♦ vt señalar; (gun etc): **to ~ sth at sb** apuntar algo a uno ♦ vi: **to ~ at** señalar; **~s** npl (AUT) contactos mpl; (RAIL) agujas fpl; **to be on the ~ of doing sth** estar a punto de hacer algo; **to make a ~ of** poner empeño en; **to get/miss the ~** comprender/no comprender; **to come to the ~** ir al meollo; **there's no ~ (in doing)** no tiene sentido (hacer); **~ out** vt señalar; **~ to** vt fus (fig) indicar, señalar; **~-blank** adv (say, refuse) sin más hablar; (also: at ~-blank range) a quemarropa; **~ed** adj (shape) puntiagudo, afilado; (remark) intencionado; **~edly** adv intencionadamente; **~er** n (needle) aguja, indicador m; **~less** adj sin sentido; **~ of view** n punto de vista

poise [pɔɪz] n aplomo, elegancia

poison ['pɔɪzn] n veneno ♦ vt envenenar; **~ing** n envenenamiento; **~ous** adj venenoso; (fumes etc) tóxico

poke [pəuk] vt (jab with finger, stick etc) empujar; (put): **to ~ sth in(to)** introducir algo en; **~ about** vi fisgonear

poker ['pəukə*] n atizador m; (CARDS) póker m

poky ['pəukɪ] adj estrecho

Poland ['pəulənd] n Polonia

polar ['pəulə*] adj polar; **~ bear** n oso polar

Pole [pəul] n polaco/a

pole [pəul] n (of wood) palo; (fixed) poste m; (GEO) polo; **~ bean** (US) n ≈ judía verde; **~ vault** n salto con pértiga

police [pə'li:s] n policía ♦ vt vigilar; **~ car** n coche-patrulla m; **~man** (irreg) n policía m, guardia m; **~ state** n estado policial; **~ station** n comisaría; **~woman** (irreg) n mujer f policía

policy ['pɔlɪsɪ] n política; (also: insurance ~) póliza

polio ['pəulɪəu] n polio f

Polish ['pəulɪʃ] adj polaco ♦ n (LING) polaco

polish ['pɔlɪʃ] n (for shoes) betún m; (for floor) cera (de lustrar); (shine) brillo, lustre m; (fig: refinement) educación f ♦ vt (shoes) limpiar; (make shiny) pulir, sacar brillo a; **~ off** vt (food) despachar; **~ed** adj (fig: person) elegante

polite [pə'laɪt] adj cortés, atento; **~ness** n cortesía

political [pə'lɪtɪkl] adj político; **~ly** adv políticamente; **~ly correct** políticamente correcto

politician [pɔlɪ'tɪʃən] n político/a

politics ['pɔlɪtɪks] n política

poll [pəul] n (election) votación f; (also: opinion ~) sondeo, encuesta ♦ vt encuestar; (votes) obtener

pollen ['pɔlən] n polen m

polling day ['pəulɪn-] n día m de elecciones

polling station n centro electoral

pollute [pə'lu:t] vt contaminar

pollution [pə'lu:ʃən] n polución f, contaminación f del medio ambiente

polo ['pəuləu] n (sport) polo; **~-necked** adj de cuello vuelto; **~ shirt** n polo, niqui m

polyester [pɔlɪ'estə*] n poliéster m

polystyrene [pɔlɪ'staɪri:n] n poliestireno

polythene ['pɔlɪθi:n] (BRIT) n politeno

pomegranate ['pɔmɪgrænɪt] n granada

pomp [pɔmp] n pompa

pompous ['pɔmpəs] adj pomposo

pond [pɔnd] n (natural) charca; (artificial) estanque m

ponder ['pɔndə*] vt meditar

ponderous ['pɔndərəs] adj pesado

pong [pɔn] (BRIT: inf) n hedor m

pony ['pəunɪ] n poney m, jaca, potro (AM); **~tail** n cola de caballo; **~ trekking** (BRIT) n excursión f a caballo

poodle ['pu:dl] n caniche m

pool [pu:l] n (natural) charca; (also: swimming ~) piscina (SP), alberca (AM); (fig: of light etc) charco; (SPORT) chapolín m ♦ vt juntar; **~s** npl (football ~s) quinielas fpl; **~ typing** n servicio de mecanografía

poor [puə*] adj pobre; (bad) de mala calidad ♦ npl: **the ~** los pobres; **~ly** adj mal, enfermo ♦ adv mal

pop [pɔp] n (sound) ruido seco; (MUS) (música) pop m; (inf: father) papá m; (drink) gaseosa ♦ vt (put quickly) meter (de prisa)

♦ vi reventar; (cork) saltar; ~ in/out vi entrar/salir un momento; ~ up vi aparecer inesperadamente; ~corn n palomitas fpl

pope [pəup] n papa m

poplar ['pɒplə*] n álamo

popper ['pɒpə*] (BRIT) n automático

poppy ['pɒpɪ] n amapola

Popsicle ® ['pɒpsɪkl] (US) n polo

pop star n estrella del pop

populace ['pɒpjuləs] n pueblo, plebe f

popular ['pɒpjulə*] adj popular

population [pɒpju'leɪʃən] n población f

porcelain ['pɒːslɪn] n porcelana

porch [pɔːtʃ] n pórtico, entrada; (US) veranda

porcupine ['pɔːkjupaɪn] n puerco m espín

pore [pɔː*] n poro ♦ vi: to ~ over engolfarse en

pork [pɔːk] n carne f de cerdo (SP) or chancho (AM)

pornography [pɔː'nɒgrəfɪ] n pornografía

porpoise ['pɔːpəs] n marsopa

porridge ['pɒrɪdʒ] n gachas fpl de avena

port [pɔːt] n puerto; (NAUT: left side) babor m; (wine) vino de Oporto; ~ of call puerto de escala

portable ['pɔːtəbl] adj portátil

porter ['pɔːtə*] n (for luggage) maletero m; (doorkeeper) portero/a, conserje m/f

portfolio [pɔːt'fəuliəu] n cartera

porthole ['pɔːthəul] n portilla

portion ['pɔːʃən] n porción f; (of food) ración f

portrait ['pɔːtreɪt] n retrato

portray [pɔː'treɪ] vt retratar; (subj: actor) representar

Portugal ['pɔːtjugl] n Portugal m

Portuguese [pɔːtju'giːz] adj portugués/esa ♦ n inv portugués/esa m/f; (LING) portugués m

pose [pəuz] n postura, actitud f ♦ vi (pretend): to ~ as hacerse pasar por ♦ vt (question) plantear; to ~ for posar para

posh [pɒʃ] (inf) adj elegante, de lujo

position [pə'zɪʃən] n posición f; (job) puesto; (situation) situación f ♦ vt colocar

positive ['pɒzɪtɪv] adj positivo; (certain) seguro; (definite) definitivo

possess [pə'zes] vt poseer; ~ion [pə'zeʃən] n posesión f; ~ions npl (belongings) pertenencias fpl

possibility [pɒsɪ'bɪlɪtɪ] n posibilidad f

possible ['pɒsɪbl] adj posible; as big as ~ lo más grande posible; possibly adv posiblemente; I cannot possibly come me es imposible venir

post [pəust] n (BRIT: system) correos mpl; (BRIT: letters, delivery) correo; (job, situation) puesto; (pole) poste m ♦ vt (BRIT: send by post) echar al correo; (BRIT: appoint): to ~ to enviar a; ~age n porte m, franqueo; ~age stamp n sello de correos; ~al adj postal, de correos; ~al order n giro postal; ~box (BRIT) n buzón m; ~card n tarjeta postal; ~code (BRIT) n código postal

postdate [pəust'deɪt] vt (cheque) poner fecha adelantada a

poster ['pəustə*] n cartel m

poste restante [pəust'restɔ̃t] (BRIT) n lista de correos

postgraduate ['pəust'grædjuət] n posgraduado/a

posthumous ['pɒstjuməs] adj póstumo

postman ['pəustmən] (irreg) n cartero

postmark ['pəustmɑːk] n matasellos m inv

post-mortem [-'mɔːtəm] n autopsia

post office n (building) (oficina de) correos m; (organization): the Post Office Administración f General de Correos; Post Office Box n apartado postal (SP), casilla de correos (AM)

postpone [pəs'pəun] vt aplazar

postscript ['pəustskrɪpt] n posdata

posture ['pɒstʃə*] n postura, actitud f

postwar [pəust'wɔː*] adj de la posguerra

posy ['pəuzɪ] n ramillete m (de flores)

pot [pɒt] n (for cooking) olla; (tea~) tetera; (coffee~) cafetera; (for flowers) maceta; (for jam) tarro, pote m; (inf: marijuana) chocolate m ♦ vt (plant) poner en tiesto; to go to ~ (inf) irse al traste

potato [pə'teɪtəu] (pl ~es) n patata (SP), papa (AM); ~ peeler n pelapatatas m inv

potent ['pəutnt] adj potente, poderoso; (drink) fuerte

potential [pə'tenʃl] adj potencial, posible ♦ n potencial m; ~ly adv en potencia

pothole ['pɒthəul] n (in road) bache m; (BRIT: underground) gruta; potholing (BRIT) n: to go potholing dedicarse a la espeleología

potluck [pɒt'lʌk] n: to take ~ tomar lo que haya

potted ['pɒtɪd] adj (food) en conserva; (plant) en tiesto or maceta; (shortened) resumido

potter ['pɒtə*] n alfarero/a ♦ vi: to ~ around, ~ about (BRIT) hacer trabajitos; ~y n cerámica; (factory) alfarería

potty ['pɒtɪ] n orinal m de niño

pouch [pautʃ] n (ZOOL) bolsa; (for tobacco) petaca

poultry ['pəultrɪ] n aves fpl de corral; (meat) pollo

pounce [pauns] vi: to ~ on precipitarse sobre

pound [paund] n libra (weight = 453g or 16oz; money = 100 pence) ♦ vt (beat) golpear; (crush) machacar ♦ vi (heart) latir; ~ sterling n libra esterlina

pour [pɔː*] vt echar; (tea etc) servir ♦ vi

correr, fluir; **to ~ sb a drink** servirle a uno una copa; **~ away** or **off** vt vaciar, verter; **~ in** vi (people) entrar en tropel; **~ out** vi salir en tropel ♦ vt (drink) echar, servir; (fig): to **~ out one's feelings** desahogarse; **~ing** adj: **~ing rain** lluvia torrencial

pout [paut] vi hacer pucheros

poverty ['pɔvətɪ] n pobreza, miseria; **~-stricken** adj necesitada

powder ['paudə*] n polvo; (face ~) polvos mpl ♦ vt polvorear; **to ~ one's face** empolvarse la cara; **~ compact** n polvera; **~ed milk** n leche f en polvo; **~ room** n aseos mpl

power ['pauə*] n poder m; (strength) fuerza; (nation, TECH) potencia; (drive) empuje m; (ELEC) fuerza, energía ♦ vt impulsar; **to be in ~** (POL) estar en el poder; **~ cut** (BRIT) n apagón m; **~ed** adj: **~ed by** impulsado por; **~ failure** n = **~ cut**; **~ful** adj poderoso; (engine) potente; (speech etc) convincente; **~less** adj: **~less (to do)** incapaz (de hacer); **~ point** (BRIT) n enchufe m; **~ station** n central f eléctrica

p.p. abbr (= per procurationem): **~ J. Smith** p.p. (por poder de) J. Smith; (= pages) págs

PR n abbr = **public relations**

practical ['præktɪkl] adj práctico; **~ity** [-'kælɪtɪ] n factibilidad f; **~ joke** n broma pesada; **~ly** adv (almost) casi

practice ['præktɪs] n (habit) costumbre f; (exercise) práctica, ejercicio; (training) adiestramiento; (MED: of profession) práctica, ejercicio; (MED, LAW: business) consulta ♦ vt, vi (US) = **practise**; **in ~** (in reality) en la práctica; **out of ~** desentrenado

practise ['præktɪs] (US **practice**) vt (carry out) practicar; (profession) ejercer; (train at) practicar ♦ vi ejercer; (train) practicar; **practising** adj (Christian etc) practicante; (lawyer) en ejercicio

practitioner [præk'tɪʃənə*] n (MED) médico/a

prairie ['prɛərɪ] n pampa

praise [preɪz] n alabanza(s) f(pl), elogio(s) m(pl) ♦ vt alabar, elogiar; **~worthy** adj loable

pram [præm] (BRIT) n cochecito de niño

prank [præŋk] n travesura

prawn [prɔːn] n gamba; **~ cocktail** n cóctel m de gambas

pray [preɪ] vi rezar

prayer [prɛə*] n oración f, rezo; (entreaty) ruego, súplica

preach [priːtʃ] vi (also fig) predicar; **~er** n predicador(a) m/f

precaution [prɪ'kɔːʃən] n precaución f

precede [prɪ'siːd] vt, vi preceder

precedent ['presɪdənt] n precedente m

preceding [prɪ'siːdɪŋ] adj anterior

precinct ['priːsɪŋkt] n recinto; **~s** npl contornos mpl; **pedestrian ~** (BRIT) zona peatonal; **shopping ~** (BRIT) centro comercial

precious ['preʃəs] adj precioso

precipitate [prɪ'sɪpɪteɪt] vt precipitar

precise [prɪ'saɪs] adj preciso, exacto; **~ly** adv precisamente, exactamente

precocious [prɪ'kəuʃəs] adj precoz

precondition [priːkən'dɪʃən] n condición f previa

predecessor ['priːdɪsesə*] n antecesor(a) m/f

predicament [prɪ'dɪkəmənt] n apuro

predict [prɪ'dɪkt] vt pronosticar; **~able** adj previsible; **~ion** [-'dɪkʃən] n predicción f

predominantly [prɪ'dɔmɪnəntlɪ] adv en su mayoría

pre-empt [priː'emt] vt adelantarse a

preen [priːn] vt: **to ~ itself** (bird) limpiarse (las plumas); **to ~ o.s.** pavonearse

preface ['prefəs] n prefacio

prefect ['priːfekt] (BRIT) n (in school) monitor(a) m/f

prefer [prɪ'fəː*] vt preferir; **to ~ doing** or **to do** preferir hacer; **~able** ['prefrəbl] adj preferible; **~ably** ['prefrəblɪ] adv de preferencia; **~ence** ['prefrəns] n preferencia; (priority) prioridad f; **~ential** [prefə'renʃəl] adj preferente

prefix ['priːfɪks] n prefijo

pregnancy ['pregnənsɪ] n (of woman) embarazo; (of animal) preñez f

pregnant ['pregnənt] adj (woman) embarazada; (animal) preñada

prehistoric ['priːhɪs'tɔrɪk] adj prehistórico

prejudice ['predʒudɪs] n prejuicio; **~d** adj (person) predispuesto

premarital ['priː'mærɪtl] adj premarital

premature ['premətʃuə*] adj prematuro

premier ['premɪə*] adj primero, principal ♦ n (POL) primer(a) ministro/a

première ['premɪɛə*] n estreno

premise ['premɪs] n premisa; **~s** npl (of business etc) local m; **on the ~s** en el lugar mismo

premium ['priːmɪəm] n premio; (insurance) prima; **to be at a ~** ser muy solicitado; **~ bond** (BRIT) n bono del estado que participa en una lotería nacional

premonition [premə'nɪʃən] n presentimiento

preoccupied [priː'ɔkjupaɪd] adj ensimismado

prep [prep] n (SCOL: study) deberes mpl

prepaid [priː'peɪd] adj porte pagado

preparation [prepə'reɪʃən] n preparación f; **~s** npl preparativos mpl

preparatory [prɪ'pærətərɪ] adj preparatorio,

preliminar; **~ school** n escuela preparatoria
prepare [prɪ'peə*] vt preparar, disponer;
(CULIN) preparar ♦ vi: **to ~ for** (action)
prepararse or disponerse para; (event) hacer
preparativos para; **~d to** dispuesto a; **~d for**
listo para
preposition [prepə'zɪʃən] n preposición f
preposterous [prɪ'pɔstərəs] adj absurdo,
ridículo
prep school n = **preparatory school**
prerequisite [priː'rekwɪzɪt] n requisito
Presbyterian [prezbɪ'tɪərɪən] adj, n
presbiteriano/a m/f
preschool ['priː'skuːl] adj preescolar
prescribe [prɪ'skraɪb] vt (MED) recetar
prescription [prɪ'skrɪpʃən] n (MED) receta
presence ['prezns] n presencia; **in sb's ~** en
presencia de uno; **~ of mind** aplomo
present [adj, n 'preznt, vb prɪ'zent] adj (in
attendance) presente; (current) actual ♦ n
(gift) regalo; (actuality): **the ~** la actualidad,
el presente ♦ vt (introduce, describe)
presentar; (expound) exponer; (give)
presentar, dar, ofrecer; (THEATRE) representar;
to give sb a ~ regalar algo a uno; **at ~**
actualmente; **~able** [prɪ'zentəbl] adj: **to
make o.s. ~able** arreglarse; **~ation** [-'teɪʃən]
n presentación f; (of report etc) exposición f;
(formal ceremony) entrega de un regalo; **~-
day** adj actual; **~er** [prɪ'zentə*] n (RADIO, TV)
locutor(a) m/f; **~ly** adv (soon) dentro de
poco; (now) ahora
preservative [prɪ'zəːvətɪv] n conservante m
preserve [prɪ'zəːv] vt (keep safe) preservar,
proteger; (maintain) mantener; (food)
conservar ♦ n (for game) coto, vedado; (often
pl: jam) conserva, confitura
president ['prezɪdənt] n presidente m/f; **~ial**
[-'denʃl] adj presidencial
press [pres] n (newspapers): **the P~** la prensa;
(printer's) imprenta; (of button) pulsación f
♦ vt empujar; (button etc) apretar; (clothes:
iron) planchar; (put pressure on: person)
presionar; (insist): **to ~ sth on sb** insistir en
que uno acepte algo ♦ vi (squeeze) apretar;
(pressurize): **to ~ for** presionar por; **we are
~ed for time/money** estamos apurados de
tiempo/dinero; **~ on** vi avanzar; (hurry)
apretar el paso; **~ agency** n agencia de
prensa; **~ conference** n rueda de prensa;
~ing adj apremiante; **~ stud** (BRIT) n botón
m de presión; **~-up** (BRIT) n plancha
pressure ['preʃə*] n presión f; **to put ~ on sb**
presionar a uno; **~ cooker** n olla a presión;
~ gauge n manómetro; **~ group** n grupo
de presión; **pressurized** adj (container) a
presión
prestige [pres'tiːʒ] n prestigio
presumably [prɪ'zjuːməblɪ] adv es de

suponer que, cabe presumir que
presume [prɪ'zjuːm] vt: **to ~ (that)** presumir
(que), suponer (que)
pretence [prɪ'tens] (US **pretense**) n
fingimiento; **under false ~s** con engaños
pretend [prɪ'tend] vt, vi (feign) fingir
pretentious [prɪ'tenʃəs] adj presumido;
(ostentatious) ostentoso, aparatoso
pretext ['priːtekst] n pretexto
pretty ['prɪtɪ] adj bonito (SP), lindo (AM)
♦ adv bastante
prevail [prɪ'veɪl] vi (gain mastery) prevalecer;
(be current) predominar; **~ing** adj (dominant)
predominante
prevalent ['prevələnt] adj (widespread)
extendido
prevent [prɪ'vent] vt: **to ~ sb from doing sth**
impedir a uno hacer algo; **to ~ sth from
happening** evitar que ocurra algo; **~ative** adj
= **preventive**; **~ive** adj preventivo
preview ['priːvjuː] n (of film) preestreno
previous ['priːvɪəs] adj previo, anterior; **~ly**
adv antes
prewar [priː'wɔː*] adj de antes de la guerra
prey [preɪ] n presa ♦ vi: **to ~ on** (feed on)
alimentarse de; **it was ~ing on his mind** le
preocupaba, le obsesionaba
price [praɪs] n precio ♦ vt (goods) fijar el
precio de; **~less** adj que no tiene precio;
~ list n tarifa
prick [prɪk] n (sting) picadura ♦ vt pinchar;
(hurt) picar; **to ~ up one's ears** aguzar el oído
prickle ['prɪkl] n (sensation) picor m; (BOT)
espina; **prickly** adj espinoso; (fig: person)
enojadizo; **prickly heat** n sarpullido causado
por exceso de calor
pride [praɪd] n orgullo; (pej) soberbia ♦ vt: **to
~ o.s.** on enorgullecerse de
priest [priːst] n sacerdote m; **~hood** n
sacerdocio
prim [prɪm] adj (demure) remilgado; (prudish)
gazmoño
primarily ['praɪmərɪlɪ] adv ante todo
primary ['praɪmərɪ] adj (first in importance)
principal ♦ n (US: POL) (elección f) primaria;
~ school (BRIT) n escuela primaria
prime [praɪm] adj primero, principal;
(excellent) selecto, de primera clase ♦ n: **in
the ~ of life** en la flor de la vida ♦ vt (wood,
fig) preparar; **~ example** ejemplo típico;
P~ Minister n primer(a) ministro/a
primeval [praɪ'miːvəl] adj primitivo
primitive ['prɪmɪtɪv] adj primitivo; (crude)
rudimentario
primrose ['prɪmrəuz] n primavera, prímula
Primus (stove) ® ['praɪməs-] (BRIT) n
hornillo de camping
prince [prɪns] n príncipe m
princess [prɪn'ses] n princesa

principal ['prɪnsɪpl] *adj* principal, mayor ♦ *n* director(a) *m/f*; **~ity** [-'pælɪtɪ] *n* principado

principle ['prɪnsɪpl] *n* principio; **in ~** en principio; **on ~** por principio

print [prɪnt] *n* (*foot~*) huella; (*finger~*) huella dactilar; (*letters*) letra de molde; (*fabric*) estampado; (*ART*) grabado; (*PHOT*) impresión *f* ♦ *vt* imprimir; (*cloth*) estampar; (*write in capitals*) escribir en letras de molde; **out of ~** agotado; **~ed matter** *n* impresos *mpl*; **~er** *n* (*person*) impresor(a) *m/f*; (*machine*) impresora; **~ing** *n* (*art*) imprenta; (*act*) impresión *f*; **~out** *n* (*COMPUT*) impresión *f*

prior ['praɪə*] *adj* anterior, previo; (*more important*) más importante; **~ to** antes de

priority [praɪ'ɒrɪtɪ] *n* prioridad *f*; **to have ~** (*over*) tener prioridad (sobre)

prison ['prɪzn] *n* cárcel *f*, prisión *f* ♦ *cpd* carcelario; **~er** *n* (*in prison*) preso/a; (*captured person*) prisionero; **~er-of-war** *n* prisionero de guerra

privacy ['prɪvəsɪ] *n* intimidad *f*

private ['praɪvɪt] *adj* (*personal*) particular; (*property, industry, discussion etc*) privado; (*person*) reservado; (*place*) tranquilo ♦ *n* soldado raso; **"~"** (*on envelope*) "confidencial"; (*on door*) "prohibido el paso"; **in ~** en privado; **~ enterprise** *n* empresa privada; **~ eye** *n* detective *m/f* privado/a; **~ property** *n* propiedad *f* privada; **~ school** *n* colegio particular

privet ['prɪvɪt] *n* alheña

privilege ['prɪvɪlɪdʒ] *n* privilegio; (*prerogative*) prerrogativa

privy ['prɪvɪ] *adj*: **to be ~ to** estar enterado de

prize [praɪz] *n* premio ♦ *adj* de primera clase ♦ *vt* apreciar, estimar; **~-giving** *n* distribución *f* de premios; **~winner** *n* premiado/a

pro [prəu] *n* (*SPORT*) profesional *m/f* ♦ *prep* a favor de; **the ~s and cons** los pros y los contras

probability [prɒbə'bɪlɪtɪ] *n* probabilidad *f*; **in all ~** con toda probabilidad

probable ['prɒbəbl] *adj* probable

probably ['prɒbəblɪ] *adv* probablemente

probation [prə'beɪʃən] *n*: **on ~** (*employee*) a prueba; (*LAW*) en libertad condicional

probe [prəub] *n* (*MED, SPACE*) sonda; (*enquiry*) encuesta, investigación *f* ♦ *vt* sondar; (*investigate*) investigar

problem ['prɒbləm] *n* problema *m*

procedure [prə'si:dʒə*] *n* procedimiento; (*bureaucratic*) trámites *mpl*

proceed [prə'si:d] *vi* (*do afterwards*): **to ~ to do sth** proceder a hacer algo; (*continue*): **to ~** (**with**) continuar *or* seguir (con); **~ings** *npl* acto(s) (*pl*); (*LAW*) proceso; **~s** ['prəusi:dz] *npl* (*money*) ganancias *fpl*, ingresos *mpl*

process ['prəuses] *n* proceso ♦ *vt* tratar, elaborar; **~ing** *n* tratamiento, elaboración *f*; (*PHOT*) revelado

procession [prə'seʃən] *n* desfile *m*; **funeral ~** cortejo fúnebre

pro-choice [prəu'tʃɔɪs] *adj* en favor del derecho a elegir de la madre

proclaim [prə'kleɪm] *vt* (*announce*) anunciar

procrastinate [prəu'kræstɪneɪt] *vi* demorarse

procure [prə'kjuə*] *vt* conseguir

prod [prɒd] *vt* empujar ♦ *n* empujón *m*

prodigy ['prɒdɪdʒɪ] *n* prodigio

produce [*n* 'prɒdju:s, *vt* prə'dju:s] *n* (*AGR*) productos *mpl* agrícolas ♦ *vt* producir; (*play, film, programme*) presentar; **~r** *n* productor(a) *m/f*; (*of film, programme*) director(a) *m/f*; (*of record*) productor(a) *m/f*

product ['prɒdʌkt] *n* producto

production [prə'dʌkʃən] *n* producción *f*; (*THEATRE*) presentación *f*; **~ line** *n* línea de producción

productivity [prɒdʌk'tɪvɪtɪ] *n* productividad *f*

profession [prə'feʃən] *n* profesión *f*; **~al** *adj* profesional ♦ *n* profesional *m/f*; (*skilled person*) perito

professor [prə'fesə*] *n* (*BRIT*) catedrático/a; (*US, Canada*) profesor(a) *m/f*

proficient [prə'fɪʃənt] *adj* experto, hábil

profile ['prəufaɪl] *n* perfil *m*

profit ['prɒfɪt] *n* (*COMM*) ganancia ♦ *vi*: **to ~ by** *or* **from** aprovechar *or* sacar provecho de; **~ability** [-ə'bɪlɪtɪ] *n* rentabilidad *f*; **~able** *adj* (*ECON*) rentable

profound [prə'faund] *adj* profundo

profusely [prə'fju:slɪ] *adv* profusamente

programme ['prəugræm] (*US* **program**) *n* programa *m* ♦ *vt* programar; **~r** (*US* **programer**) *n* programador(a) *m/f*; **programming** (*US* **programing**) *n* programación *f*

progress [*n* 'prəugres, *vi* prə'gres] *n* progreso; (*development*) desarrollo ♦ *vi* progresar, avanzar; **in ~** en curso; **~ive** [-'gresɪv] *adj* progresivo; (*person*) progresista

prohibit [prə'hɪbɪt] *vt* prohibir; **to ~ sb from doing sth** prohibir a uno hacer algo; **~ion** [-'bɪʃn] *n* prohibición *f*; (*US*): **P~ion** Ley *f* Seca

project [*n* 'prɒdʒekt, *vb* prə'dʒekt] *n* proyecto ♦ *vt* proyectar ♦ *vi* (*stick out*) salir, sobresalir; **~ion** [prə'dʒekʃən] *n* proyección *f*; (*overhang*) saliente *m*; **~or** [prə'dʒektə*] *n* proyector *m*

pro-life [prəu'laɪf] *adj* pro-vida

prolong [prə'lɒŋ] *vt* prolongar, extender

prom [prɒm] *n abbr* = **promenade**; (*US*: *ball*) baile *m* de gala

promenade [prɒmə'nɑ:d] *n* (*by sea*) paseo

marítimo; ~ **concert** (*BRIT*) n concierto (en que parte del público permanece de pie)

prominence ['prɒmɪnəns] n importancia

prominent ['prɒmɪnənt] adj (*standing out*) saliente; (*important*) eminente, importante

promiscuous [prə'mɪskjuəs] adj (*sexually*) promiscuo

promise ['prɒmɪs] n promesa ♦ vt, vi prometer; **promising** adj prometedor(a)

promote [prə'məut] vt (*employee*) ascender; (*product, pop star*) hacer propaganda por; (*ideas*) fomentar; ~**r** n (*of event*) promotor(a) m/f; (*of cause etc*) impulsor(a) m/f; **promotion** [-'məuʃən] n (*advertising campaign*) campaña de promoción f; (*in rank*) ascenso

prompt [prɒmpt] adj rápido ♦ adv: **at 6 o'clock ~** a las seis en punto ♦ n (*COMPUT*) aviso ♦ vt (*urge*) mover, incitar; (*when talking*) instar; (*THEATRE*) apuntar; **to ~ sb to do sth** instar a uno a hacer algo; ~**ly** adv rápidamente; (*exactly*) puntualmente

prone [prəun] adj (*lying*) postrado; ~ **to** propenso a

prong [prɒŋ] n diente m, punta

pronoun ['prəunaun] n pronombre m

pronounce [prə'nauns] vt pronunciar; ~**d** adj (*marked*) marcado

pronunciation [prənʌnsɪ'eɪʃən] n pronunciación f

proof [pruːf] n prueba ♦ adj: ~ **against** a prueba de

prop [prɒp] n apoyo; (*fig*) sostén m ♦ vt (*also: ~ up*) apoyar; (*lean*): **to ~ sth against** apoyar algo contra

propaganda [prɒpə'gændə] n propaganda

propel [prə'pɛl] vt impulsar, propulsar; ~**ler** n hélice f

propensity [prə'pɛnsɪtɪ] n propensión f

proper ['prɒpə*] adj (*suited, right*) propio; (*exact*) justo; (*seemly*) correcto, decente; (*authentic*) verdadero; (*referring to place*): **the village ~** el pueblo mismo; ~**ly** adv (*adequately*) correctamente; (*decently*) decentemente; ~ **noun** n nombre m propio

property ['prɒpətɪ] n propiedad f; (*personal*) bienes mpl muebles; ~ **owner** n dueño/a de propiedades

prophecy ['prɒfɪsɪ] n profecía

prophesy ['prɒfɪsaɪ] vt (*fig*) predecir

prophet ['prɒfɪt] n profeta m

proportion [prə'pɔːʃən] n proporción f; (*share*) parte f; ~**al** adj: ~**al (to)** en proporción (con); ~**al representation** n representación f proporcional; ~**ate** adj: ~**ate (to)** en proporción (con)

proposal [prə'pəuzl] n (*offer of marriage*) oferta de matrimonio; (*plan*) proyecto

propose [prə'pəuz] vt proponer ♦ vi

declararse; **to ~ to do** tener intención de hacer

proposition [prɒpə'zɪʃən] n propuesta

proprietor [prə'praɪətə*] n propietario/a, dueño/a

propriety [prə'praɪətɪ] n decoro

pro rata [-'rɑːtə] adv a prorrateo

prose [prəuz] n prosa

prosecute ['prɒsɪkjuːt] vt (*LAW*) procesar; **prosecution** [-'kjuːʃən] n proceso, causa; (*accusing side*) acusación f; **prosecutor** n acusador(a) m/f; (*also: public prosecutor*) fiscal m

prospect [n 'prɒspɛkt, vb prə'spɛkt] n (*possibility*) posibilidad f; (*outlook*) perspectiva ♦ vi: **to ~ for** buscar; ~**s** npl (*for work etc*) perspectivas fpl; ~**ing** n prospección f; ~**ive** [prə'spɛktɪv] adj futuro

prospectus [prə'spɛktəs] n prospecto

prosper ['prɒspə*] vi prosperar; ~**ity** [-'spɛrɪtɪ] n prosperidad f; ~**ous** adj próspero

prostitute ['prɒstɪtjuːt] n prostituta f; (*male*) hombre que se dedica a la prostitución

protect [prə'tɛkt] vt proteger; ~**ion** [-'tɛkʃən] n protección f; ~**ive** adj protector(a)

protein ['prəutiːn] n proteína

protest [n 'prəutɛst, vb prə'tɛst] n protesta ♦ vi: **to ~ about** or **at/against** protestar de/contra ♦ vt (*insist*): **to ~ (that)** insistir en (que)

Protestant ['prɒtɪstənt] adj, n protestante m/f

protester [prə'tɛstə*] n manifestante m/f

protracted [prə'træktɪd] adj prolongado

protrude [prə'truːd] vi salir, sobresalir

proud [praud] adj orgulloso; (*pej*) soberbio, altanero

prove [pruːv] vt probar; (*show*) demostrar ♦ vi: **to ~ (to be) correct** resultar correcto; **to ~ o.s.** probar su valía

proverb ['prɒvɜːb] n refrán m

provide [prə'vaɪd] vt proporcionar, dar; **to ~ sb with sth** proveer a uno de algo; ~**d (that)** conj con tal de que, a condición de que; ~ **for** vt fus (*person*) mantener a; (*problem etc*) tener en cuenta; **providing** [prə'vaɪdɪŋ] conj: **providing (that)** a condición de que, con tal de que

province ['prɒvɪns] n provincia; (*fig*) esfera; **provincial** [prə'vɪnʃəl] adj provincial; (*pej*) provinciano

provision [prə'vɪʒən] n (*supplying*) suministro, abastecimiento; (*of contract etc*) disposición f; ~**s** npl (*food*) comestibles mpl; ~**al** adj provisional

proviso [prə'vaɪzəu] n condición f, estipulación f

provocative [prə'vɒkətɪv] adj provocativo

provoke [prə'vəuk] vt (*cause*) provocar,

incitar; (*anger*) enojar

prowess ['prauis] *n* destreza

prowl [praul] *vi* (*also:* ~ *about,* ~ *around*) merodear ♦ *n*: **on the ~** de merodeo; **~er** *n* merodeador(a) *m/f*

proxy ['prɒksi] *n*: **by ~** por poderes

prudent ['pru:dənt] *adj* prudente

prune [pru:n] *n* ciruela pasa ♦ *vt* podar

pry [prai] *vi*: **to ~ (into)** entrometerse (en)

PS *n abbr* (= *postscript*) P.D.

psalm [sɑ:m] *n* salmo

pseudonym ['sju:dəunim] *n* seudónimo

psyche ['saiki] *n* psique *f*

psychiatric [saiki'ætrik] *adj* psiquiátrico

psychiatrist [sai'kaiətrist] *n* psiquiatra *m/f*

psychic ['saikik] *adj* (*also:* ~*al*) psíquico

psychoanalyse [saikəu'ænəlaiz] *vt* psicoanalizar; **psychoanalysis** [-ə'nælisis] *n* psicoanálisis *m inv*

psychological [saikə'lɒdʒikl] *adj* psicológico

psychologist [sai'kɒlədʒist] *n* psicólogo/a

psychology [sai'kɒlədʒi] *n* psicología

PTO *abbr* (= *please turn over*) sigue

pub [pʌb] *n abbr* (= *public house*) pub *m*, bar *m*

puberty ['pju:bəti] *n* pubertad *f*

public ['pʌblik] *adj* público ♦ *n*: **the ~** el público; **in ~** en público; **to make ~** hacer público; **~ address system** *n* megafonía

publican ['pʌblikən] *n* tabernero/a

publication [pʌbli'keiʃən] *n* publicación *f*

public: ~ company *n* sociedad *f* anónima; **~ convenience** (*BRIT*) *n* aseos *mpl* públicos (*SP*), sanitarios *mpl* (*AM*); **~ holiday** *n* día de fiesta (*SP*), (día) feriado (*AM*); **~ house** (*BRIT*) *n* bar *m*, pub *m*

publicity [pʌb'lisiti] *n* publicidad *f*

publicize ['pʌblisaiz] *vt* publicitar

publicly ['pʌblikli] *adv* públicamente, en público

public: ~ opinion *n* opinión *f* pública; **~ relations** *n* relaciones *fpl* públicas; **~ school** *n* (*BRIT*) escuela privada; (*US*) instituto; **~-spirited** *adj* que tiene sentido del deber ciudadano; **~ transport** *n* transporte *m* público

publish ['pʌbliʃ] *vt* publicar; **~er** *n* (*person*) editor(a) *m/f*; (*firm*) editorial *f*; **~ing** *n* (*industry*) industria del libro

pub lunch *n* almuerzo que se sirve en un pub; **to go for a ~** almorzar o comer en un pub

pucker ['pʌkə*] *vt* (*pleat*) arrugar; (*brow etc*) fruncir

pudding ['pudiŋ] *n* pudín *m*; (*BRIT: dessert*) postre *m*; **black ~** morcilla

puddle ['pʌdl] *n* charco

puff [pʌf] *n* soplo; (*of smoke, air*) bocanada; (*of breathing*) resoplido ♦ *vt*: **to ~ one's pipe** chupar la pipa ♦ *vi* (*pant*) jadear; **~ out** *vt*

hinchar; **~ pastry** *n* hojaldre *m*; **~y** *adj* hinchado

pull [pul] *n* (*tug*): **to give sth a ~** dar un tirón a algo ♦ *vt* tirar de; (*press: trigger*) apretar; (*haul*) tirar, arrastrar; (*close: curtain*) echar ♦ *vi* tirar; **to ~ to pieces** hacer pedazos; **to not ~ one's punches** no andarse con bromas; **to ~ one's weight** hacer su parte; **to ~ o.s. together** sobreponerse; **to ~ sb's leg** tomar el pelo a uno; **~ apart** *vt* (*break*) romper; **~ down** *vt* (*building*) derribar; **~ in** *vi* (*car etc*) parar (junto a la acera); (*train*) llegar a la estación; **~ off** *vt* (*deal etc*) cerrar; **~ out** *vi* (*car, train etc*) salir ♦ *vt* sacar, arrancar; **~ over** *vi* (*AUT*) hacerse a un lado; **~ through** *vi* (*MED*) reponerse; **~ up** *vi* (*stop*) parar ♦ *vt* (*raise*) levantar; (*uproot*) arrancar, desarraigar

pulley ['puli] *n* polea

pullover ['puləuvə*] *n* jersey *m*, suéter *m*

pulp [pʌlp] *n* (*of fruit*) pulpa

pulpit ['pulpit] *n* púlpito

pulsate [pʌl'seit] *vi* pulsar, latir

pulse [pʌls] *n* (*ANAT*) pulso; (*rhythm*) pulsación *f*; (*BOT*) legumbre *f*

pump [pʌmp] *n* bomba; (*shoe*) zapatilla ♦ *vt* sacar con una bomba; **~ up** *vt* inflar

pumpkin ['pʌmpkin] *n* calabaza

pun [pʌn] *n* juego de palabras

punch [pʌntʃ] *n* (*blow*) golpe *m*, puñetazo; (*tool*) punzón *m*; (*drink*) ponche *m* ♦ *vt* (*hit*): **to ~ sb/sth** dar un puñetazo or golpear a uno/algo; **~line** *n* palabras que rematan un chiste; **~-up** (*BRIT: inf*) *n* riña

punctual ['pʌŋktjuəl] *adj* puntual

punctuation [pʌŋktju'eiʃən] *n* puntuación *f*

puncture ['pʌŋktʃə*] (*BRIT*) *n* pinchazo ♦ *vt* pinchar

pungent ['pʌndʒənt] *adj* acre

punish ['pʌniʃ] *vt* castigar; **~ment** *n* castigo

punk [pʌŋk] *n* (*also:* ~ *rocker*) punki *m/f*; (*also:* ~ *rock*) música punk; (*US: inf*: *hoodlum*) rufián *m*

punt [pʌnt] *n* (*boat*) batea

punter ['pʌntə*] (*BRIT*) *n* (*gambler*) jugador(a) *m/f*; (*inf*) cliente *m/f*

puny ['pju:ni] *adj* débil

pup [pʌp] *n* cachorro

pupil ['pju:pl] *n* alumno/a; (*of eye*) pupila

puppet ['pʌpit] *n* títere *m*

puppy ['pʌpi] *n* cachorro, perrito

purchase ['pə:tʃis] *n* compra ♦ *vt* comprar; **~r** *n* comprador(a) *m/f*

pure [pjuə*] *adj* puro

purée ['pjuərei] *n* puré *m*

purely ['pjuəli] *adv* puramente

purge [pə:dʒ] *n* (*MED, POL*) purga ♦ *vt* purgar

purify ['pjuərifai] *vt* purificar, depurar

purple ['pə:pl] *adj* purpúreo; morado

purpose ['pə:pəs] n propósito; **on ~ a**
propósito, adrede; **~ful** adj resuelto,
determinado

purr [pə:*] vi ronronear

purse [pə:s] n monedero; (US) bolsa (SP),
cartera (AM) ♦ vt fruncir

pursue [pə'sju:] vt seguir; **~r** n
perseguidor(a) m/f

pursuit [pə'sju:t] n (chase) caza; (occupation)
actividad f

push [puʃ] n empuje m, empujón m; (of
button) presión f; (drive) empuje m ♦ vt
empujar; (button) apretar; (promote)
promover ♦ vi empujar; (demand): **to ~ for**
luchar por; **~ aside** vt apartar con la mano;
~ off (inf) vi largarse; **~ on** vi seguir
adelante; **~ through** vi (crowd) abrirse paso
a empujones ♦ vt (measure) despachar; **~ up**
vt (total, prices) hacer subir; **~chair** (BRIT) n
sillita de ruedas; **~er** n (drug ~er) traficante
m/f de drogas; **~over** (inf) n: **it's a ~over**
está tirado; **~-up** (US) n plancha; **~y** (pej) adj
agresivo

puss [pus] (inf) n minino

pussy(-cat) ['pusɪ-] (inf) n = **puss**

put [put] (pt, pp put) vt (place) poner,
colocar; (~ into) meter; (say) expresar; (a
question) hacer; (estimate) estimar; **~ about**,
or **around** vt (rumour) diseminar; **~ across**
vt (ideas etc) comunicar; **~ away** vt (store)
guardar; **~ back** vt (replace) devolver a su
lugar; (postpone) aplazar; **~ by** vt (money)
guardar; **~ down** vt (on ground) poner en el
suelo; (animal) sacrificar; (in writing)
apuntar; (revolt etc) sofocar; (attribute): **to ~
sth down** to atribuir algo a; **~ forward** vt
(ideas) presentar, proponer; **~ in** vt
(complaint) presentar; (time) dedicar; **~ off**
vt (postpone) aplazar; (discourage) desanimar;
~ on vt ponerse; (light etc) encender; (play
etc) presentar; (gain): **to ~ on weight**
engordar; (brake) echar; (record, kettle etc)
poner; (assume) adoptar; **~ out** vt (fire,
light) apagar; (rubbish etc) sacar; (cat etc)
echar; (one's hand) alargar; (inf: person): **to
be ~ out** alterarse; **~ through** vt (TEL) poner;
(plan etc) hacer aprobar; **~ up** vt (raise)
levantar, alzar; (hang) colgar; (build)
construir; (increase) aumentar;
(accommodate) alojar; **~ up with** vt fus
aguantar

putt [pʌt] n putt m, golpe m corto; **~ing
green** n green m; minigolf m

putty ['pʌtɪ] n masilla

put-up ['putʌp] adj: **~ job** (BRIT) amaño

puzzle ['pʌzl] n rompecabezas m inv; (also:
crossword ~) crucigrama m; (mystery) misterio
♦ vt dejar perplejo, confundir ♦ vi: **to ~ over**
sth devanarse los sesos con algo; **puzzling**

adj misterioso, extraño

pyjamas [pɪ'dʒɑ:məz] (BRIT) npl pijama m

pylon ['paɪlən] n torre f de conducción
eléctrica

pyramid ['pɪrəmɪd] n pirámide f

Pyrenees [pɪrə'ni:z] npl: **the ~** los Pirineos

python ['paɪθən] n pitón m

Q, q

quack [kwæk] n graznido; (pej: doctor)
curandero/a

quad [kwɔd] n abbr = **quadrangle**; **quadruplet**

quadrangle ['kwɔdræŋgl] n patio

quadruple [kwɔ'drupl] vt, vi cuadruplicar

quadruplets [kwɔ'dru:plɪts] npl cuatrillizos/
as

quail [kweɪl] n codorniz f ♦ vi: **to ~ at** or
before amedrentarse ante

quaint [kweɪnt] adj extraño; (picturesque)
pintoresco

quake [kweɪk] vi temblar ♦ n abbr =
earthquake

Quaker ['kweɪkə*] n cuáquero/a

qualification [kwɔlɪfɪ'keɪʃən] n (ability)
capacidad f; (often pl: diploma etc) título;
(reservation) salvedad f

qualified ['kwɔlɪfaɪd] adj capacitado;
(professionally) titulado; (limited) limitado

qualify ['kwɔlɪfaɪ] vt (make competent)
capacitar; (modify) modificar ♦ vi (in
competition): **to ~ (for)** calificarse (para);
(pass examination(s)): **to ~ (as)** calificarse
(de), graduarse (en); (be eligible): **to ~ (for)**
reunir los requisitos (para)

quality ['kwɔlɪtɪ] n calidad f; (of person)
cualidad f; **~ time** n tiempo dedicado a la
familia y a los amigos

qualm [kwɑ:m] n escrúpulo

quandary ['kwɔndrɪ] n: **to be in a ~** tener
dudas

quantity ['kwɔntɪtɪ] n cantidad f; **in ~** en
grandes cantidades; **~ surveyor** n
aparejador(a) m/f

quarantine ['kwɔrənti:n] n cuarentena

quarrel ['kwɔrl] n riña, pelea ♦ vi reñir,
pelearse

quarry ['kwɔrɪ] n cantera

quart [kwɔ:t] n ≈ litro

quarter ['kwɔ:tə*] n cuarto, cuarta parte f;
(US: coin) moneda de 25 centavos; (of year)
trimestre m; (district) barrio ♦ vt dividir en
cuartos; (MIL: lodge) alojar; **~s** npl (barracks)
cuartel m; (living ~s) alojamiento; **a ~ of an
hour** un cuarto de hora; **~ final** n cuarto de
final; **~ly** adj trimestral ♦ adv cada 3 meses,
trimestralmente

quartet(te) [kwɔ:'tet] n cuarteto

quartz [kwɔːts] n cuarzo
quash [kwɔʃ] vt (verdict) anular
quaver ['kweɪvə*] (BRIT) n (MUS) corchea ♦ vi temblar
quay [kiː] n (also: ~side) muelle m
queasy ['kwiːzɪ] adj: **to feel ~** tener náuseas
queen [kwiːn] n reina; (CARDS etc) dama; **~ mother** n reina madre
queer [kwɪə*] adj raro, extraño ♦ n (inf: highly offensive) maricón m
quell [kwɛl] vt (feeling) calmar; (rebellion etc) sofocar
quench [kwɛntʃ] vt: **to ~ one's thirst** apagar la sed
query ['kwɪərɪ] n (question) pregunta ♦ vt dudar de
quest [kwɛst] n busca, búsqueda
question ['kwɛstʃən] n pregunta; (doubt) duda; (matter) asunto, cuestión f ♦ vt (doubt) dudar de; (interrogate) interrogar, hacer preguntas a; **beyond ~** fuera de toda duda; **out of the ~** imposible; ni hablar; **~able** adj dudoso; **~ mark** n punto de interrogación; **~naire** [-'nɛə*] n cuestionario
queue [kjuː] (BRIT) n cola ♦ vi (also: ~ up) hacer cola
quibble ['kwɪbl] vi sutilizar
quick [kwɪk] adj rápido; (agile) ágil; (mind) listo ♦ n: **cut to the ~** (fig) herido en lo vivo; **be ~!** ¡date prisa!; **~en** vt apresurar ♦ vi apresurarse, darse prisa; **~ly** adv rápidamente, de prisa; **~sand** n arenas fpl movedizas; **~-witted** adj perspicaz
quid [kwɪd] (BRIT: inf) n inv libra
quiet ['kwaɪət] adj (voice, music etc) bajo; (person, place) tranquilo; (ceremony) íntimo ♦ n silencio; (calm) tranquilidad f ♦ vt, vi (US) = **~en**; **~en** (also: ~en down) vi calmarse; (grow silent) callarse ♦ vt calmar; hacer callar; **~ly** adv tranquilamente; (silently) silenciosamente; **~ness** n silencio; tranquilidad f
quilt [kwɪlt] n edredón m
quin [kwɪn] n abbr = **quintuplet**
quintet(te) [kwɪn'tɛt] n quinteto
quintuplets [kwɪn'tjuːplɪts] npl quintillizos/as
quip [kwɪp] n pulla
quirk [kwəːk] n peculiaridad f; (accident) capricho
quit [kwɪt] (pt, pp **quit** or **quitted**) vt dejar, abandonar; (premises) desocupar ♦ vi (give up) renunciar; (resign) dimitir
quite [kwaɪt] adv (rather) bastante; (entirely) completamente; **that's not ~ big enough** no acaba de ser lo bastante grande; **~ a few of them** un buen número de ellos; **~ (so)!** ¡así es!, ¡exactamente!
quits [kwɪts] adj: **~ (with)** en paz (con); **let's**

call it ~ dejémoslo en tablas
quiver ['kwɪvə*] vi estremecerse
quiz [kwɪz] n concurso ♦ vt interrogar; **~zical** adj burlón(ona)
quota ['kwəʊtə] n cuota
quotation [kwəʊ'teɪʃən] n cita; (estimate) presupuesto; **~ marks** npl comillas fpl
quote [kwəʊt] n cita; (estimate) presupuesto ♦ vt citar; (price) cotizar ♦ vi: **to ~ from** citar de; **~s** npl (inverted commas) comillas fpl

R, r

rabbi ['ræbaɪ] n rabino
rabbit ['ræbɪt] n conejo; **~ hutch** n conejera
rabble ['ræbl] (pej) n chusma, populacho
rabies ['reɪbiːz] n rabia
RAC (BRIT) n abbr = **Royal Automobile Club**
rac(c)oon [rə'kuːn] n mapache m
race [reɪs] n carrera; (species) raza ♦ vt (horse) hacer correr; (engine) acelerar ♦ vi (compete) competir; (run) correr; (pulse) latir a ritmo acelerado; **~ car** (US) n = **racing car**; **~ car driver** (US) n = **racing driver**; **~course** n hipódromo; **~horse** n caballo de carreras; **~track** n pista; (for cars) autódromo
racial ['reɪʃl] adj racial
racing ['reɪsɪŋ] n carreras fpl; **~ car** (BRIT) n coche m de carreras; **~ driver** (BRIT) n corredor(a) m/f de coches
racism ['reɪsɪzəm] n racismo; **racist** [-sɪst] adj, n racista m/f
rack [ræk] n (also: luggage ~) rejilla; (shelf) estante m; (also: roof ~) baca, portaequipajes m inv; (dish ~) escurreplatos m inv; (clothes ~) percha ♦ vt atormentar; **to ~ one's brains** devanarse los sesos
racket ['rækɪt] n (for tennis) raqueta; (noise) ruido, estrépito; (swindle) estafa, timo
racquet ['rækɪt] n raqueta
racy ['reɪsɪ] adj picante, salado
radar ['reɪdɑː*] n radar m
radiant ['reɪdɪənt] adj radiante (de felicidad)
radiate ['reɪdɪeɪt] vt (heat) radiar; (emotion) irradiar ♦ vi (lines) extenderse
radiation [reɪdɪ'eɪʃən] n radiación f
radiator ['reɪdɪeɪtə*] n radiador m
radical ['rædɪkl] adj radical
radii ['reɪdɪaɪ] npl of **radius**
radio ['reɪdɪəʊ] n radio f; **on the ~** por radio
radio... [reɪdɪəʊ] prefix: **~active** adj radioactivo; **~graphy** [reɪdɪ'ɔɡrəfɪ] n radiografía; **~logy** [reɪdɪ'ɔlədʒɪ] n radiología
radio station n emisora
radiotherapy [-'θerəpɪ] n radioterapia
radish ['rædɪʃ] n rábano
radius ['reɪdɪəs] (pl **radii**) n radio
RAF n abbr = **Royal Air Force**

raffle |'ræfl| n rifa, sorteo

raft |rɑːft| n balsa; (also: life ~) balsa salvavidas

rafter |'rɑːftə*| n viga

rag |ræg| n (piece of cloth) trapo; (torn cloth) harapo; (pej: newspaper) periodicucho; (for charity) actividades estudiantiles benéficas; ~s npl (torn clothes) harapos mpl; ~ doll n muñeca de trapo

rage |reɪdʒ| n rabia, furor m ♦ vi (person) rabiar, estar furioso; (storm) bramar; **it's all the ~** (very fashionable) está muy de moda

ragged |'rægɪd| adj (edge) desigual, mellado; (appearance) andrajoso, harapiento

raid |reɪd| n (MIL) incursión f; (criminal) asalto; (by police) redada ♦ vt invadir, atacar; asaltar

rail |reɪl| n (on stair) barandilla, pasamanos m inv; (on bridge, balcony) pretil m; (of ship) barandilla; (also: towel ~) toallero; ~s npl (RAIL) vía; by ~ por ferrocarril; ~ing(s) n(pl) vallado; ~road (US) n = ~way; ~way (BRIT) n ferrocarril m, vía férrea; ~way line (BRIT) n línea (de ferrocarril); ~wayman (BRIT) n ferroviario; ~way station (BRIT) n estación f de ferrocarril

rain |reɪn| n lluvia ♦ vi llover; **in the ~** bajo la lluvia; **it's ~ing** llueve, está lloviendo; ~bow n arco iris; ~coat n impermeable m; ~drop n gota de lluvia; ~fall n lluvia; ~forest n selvas fpl tropicales; ~y adj lluvioso

raise |reɪz| n aumento ♦ vt levantar; (increase) aumentar; (improve: morale) subir; (: standards) mejorar; (doubts) suscitar; (a question) plantear; (cattle, family) criar; (crop) cultivar; (army) reclutar; (loan) obtener; **to ~ one's voice** alzar la voz

raisin |'reɪzn| n pasa de Corinto

rake |reɪk| n (tool) rastrillo; (person) libertino ♦ vt (garden) rastrillar

rally |'rælɪ| n (POL etc) reunión f, mitin m; (AUT) rallye m; (TENNIS) peloteo ♦ vt reunir ♦ vi recuperarse; ~ **round** vt fus (fig) dar apoyo a

RAM |ræm| n abbr (= random access memory) RAM f

ram |ræm| n carnero; (also: battering ~) ariete m ♦ vt (crash into) dar contra, chocar con; (push: fist etc) empujar con fuerza

ramble |'ræmbl| n caminata, excursión f en el campo ♦ vi (pej: also: ~ on) divagar; ~r n excursionista m/f; (BOT) trepadora; **rambling** adj (speech) inconexo; (house) laberíntico; (BOT) trepador(a)

ramp |ræmp| n rampa; **on/off** ~ (US: AUT) vía de acceso/salida

rampage |ræm'peɪdʒ| n: **to be on the ~** desmandarse ♦ vi: **they went rampaging through the town** recorrieron la ciudad armando alboroto

rampant |'ræmpənt| adj (disease etc): **to be ~** estar extendiéndose mucho

ram raid vt atracar (rompiendo el escaparate con un coche)

ramshackle |'ræmʃækl| adj destartalado

ran |ræn| pt of run

ranch |rɑːntʃ| n hacienda, estancia; ~er n ganadero

rancid |'rænsɪd| adj rancio

rancour |'ræŋkə*| (US rancor) n rencor m

random |'rændəm| adj fortuito, sin orden; (COMPUT, MATH) aleatorio ♦ n: **at ~** al azar

randy |'rændɪ| (BRIT: inf) adj cachondo

rang |ræŋ| pt of ring

range |reɪndʒ| n (of mountains) cadena de montañas, cordillera; (of missile) alcance m; (of voice) registro; (series) serie f; (of products) surtido; (MIL: also: shooting ~) campo de tiro; (also: kitchen ~) fogón m ♦ vt (place) colocar; (arrange) arreglar ♦ vi: **to ~ over** (extend) extenderse por; **to ~ from ... to ...** oscilar entre ... y ...

ranger |reɪndʒə*| n guardabosques m inv

rank |ræŋk| n (row) fila; (MIL) rango; (status) categoría; (BRIT: also: taxi ~) parada de taxis ♦ vi: **to ~ among** figurar entre ♦ adj fétido, rancio; **the ~ and file** (fig) la base

ransack |'rænsæk| vt (search) registrar; (plunder) saquear

ransom |'rænsəm| n rescate m; **to hold to ~** (fig) hacer chantaje a

rant |rænt| vi divagar, desvariar

rap |ræp| vt golpear, dar un golpecito en ♦ n (music) rap m

rape |reɪp| n violación f; (BOT) colza ♦ vt violar; ~ **(seed) oil** n aceite m de colza

rapid |'ræpɪd| adj rápido; ~ity |rə'pɪdɪtɪ| n rapidez f; ~s npl (GEO) rápidos mpl

rapist |'reɪpɪst| n violador m

rapport |ræ'pɔː*| n simpatía

rapturous |'ræptʃərəs| adj extático

rare |reə*| adj raro, poco común; (CULIN: steak) poco hecho

rarely |'reəlɪ| adv pocas veces

raring |'reərɪŋ| adj: **to be ~ to go** (inf) tener muchas ganas de empezar

rascal |'rɑːskl| n pillo, pícaro

rash |ræʃ| adj imprudente, precipitado ♦ n (MED) sarpullido, erupción f (cutánea); (of events) serie f

rasher |'ræʃə*| n lonja

raspberry |'rɑːzbərɪ| n frambuesa

rasping |'rɑːspɪŋ| adj: **a ~ noise** un ruido áspero

rat |ræt| n rata

rate |reɪt| n (ratio) razón f; (price) precio; (: of hotel etc) tarifa; (of interest) tipo; (speed) velocidad f ♦ vt (value) tasar; (estimate) estimar; **~s** npl (BRIT: property tax) impuesto municipal; (fees) tarifa; **to ~ sth/sb as** considerar algo/a uno como; **~able value** (BRIT) n valor m impuesto; **~payer** (BRIT) n contribuyente m/f

rather ['rɑːðə*] adv: **it's ~ expensive** es algo caro; (too much) es demasiado caro; (to some extent) más bien; **there's ~ a lot** hay bastante; **I would** or **I'd ~ go** preferiría ir; or **~** mejor dicho

rating ['reɪtɪŋ] n tasación f; (score) índice m; (of ship) clase f; **~s** npl (RADIO, TV) niveles mpl de audiencia

ratio ['reɪʃɪəʊ] n razón f; **in the ~ of 100 to 1** a razón de 100 a 1

ration ['ræʃən] n ración f ♦ vt racionar; **~s** npl víveres mpl

rational ['ræʃənl] adj (solution, reasoning) lógico, razonable; (person) cuerdo, sensato; **~e** [-'nɑːl] n razón f fundamental; **~ize** vt justificar

rat race n lucha incesante por la supervivencia

rattle ['rætl] n golpeteo; (of train etc) traqueteo; (for baby) sonaja, sonajero ♦ vi castañetear; (car, bus): **to ~ along** traquetear ♦ vt hacer sonar agitando; **~snake** n serpiente f de cascabel

raucous ['rɔːkəs] adj estridente, ronco

ravage ['rævɪdʒ] vt hacer estragos en, destrozar; **~s** npl estragos mpl

rave [reɪv] vi (in anger) encolerizarse; (with enthusiasm) entusiasmarse; (MED) delirar, desvariar ♦ n (inf: party) rave m

raven ['reɪvən] n cuervo

ravenous ['rævənəs] adj hambriento

ravine [rə'viːn] n barranco

raving ['reɪvɪŋ] adj: **~ lunatic** loco/a de atar

ravishing ['rævɪʃɪŋ] adj encantador(a)

raw [rɔː] adj crudo; (not processed) bruto; (sore) vivo; (inexperienced) novato, inexperto; **~ deal** (inf) n injusticia; **~ material** n materia prima

ray [reɪ] n rayo; **~ of hope** (rayo de) esperanza

raze [reɪz] vt arrasar

razor ['reɪzə*] n (open) navaja; (safety ~) máquina de afeitar; (electric ~) máquina (eléctrica) de afeitar; **~ blade** n hoja de afeitar

Rd abbr = **road**

re [riː] prep con referencia a

reach [riːtʃ] n alcance m; (of river etc) extensión f entre dos recodos ♦ vt alcanzar, llegar a; (achieve) lograr ♦ vi extenderse; **within ~** al alcance (de la mano); **out of ~** fuera del alcance; **~ out** vt (hand) tender ♦ vi: **to ~ out for sth** alargar or tender la mano para tomar algo

react [riː'ækt] vi reaccionar; **~ion** [-'ækʃən] n reacción f

reactor [riː'æktə*] n (also: nuclear ~) reactor m (nuclear)

read [riːd, pt, pp rɛd] (pt, pp read) vi leer ♦ vt leer; (understand) entender; (study) estudiar; **~ out** vt leer en alta voz; **~able** adj (writing) legible; (book) leíble; **~er** n lector(a) m/f; (BRIT: at university) profesor(a) m/f adjunto/a; **~ership** n (of paper etc) (número de) lectores mpl

readily ['rɛdɪlɪ] adv (willingly) de buena gana; (easily) fácilmente; (quickly) en seguida

readiness ['rɛdɪnɪs] n buena voluntad f; (preparedness) preparación f; **in ~** (prepared) listo, preparado

reading ['riːdɪŋ] n lectura; (on instrument) indicación f

ready ['rɛdɪ] adj listo, preparado; (willing) dispuesto; (available) disponible ♦ adv: **~-cooked** listo para comer ♦ n: **at the ~** (MIL) listo para tirar; **to get ~** vi prepararse ♦ vt preparar; **~-made** adj confeccionado; **~-to-wear** adj confeccionado

real [rɪəl] adj verdadero, auténtico; **in ~ terms** en términos reales; **~ estate** n bienes mpl raíces; **~istic** [-'lɪstɪk] adj realista

reality [riː'ælɪtɪ] n realidad f

realization [rɪəlaɪ'zeɪʃən] n comprensión f; (fulfilment, COMM) realización f

realize ['rɪəlaɪz] vt (understand) darse cuenta de

really ['rɪəlɪ] adv realmente; (for emphasis) verdaderamente; (actually): **what ~ happened** lo que pasó en realidad; **~?** ¿de veras?; **~!** (annoyance) ¡vamos!, ¡por favor!

realm [rɛlm] n reino; (fig) esfera

realtor ® ['rɪəltɔː*] (US) n corredor(a) m/f de bienes raíces

reap [riːp] vt segar; (fig) cosechar, recoger

reappear [riːə'pɪə*] vi reaparecer

rear [rɪə*] adj trasero ♦ n parte f trasera ♦ vt (cattle, family) criar ♦ vi (also: ~ up) (animal) encabritarse; **~guard** n retaguardia

rearmament [riː'ɑːməmənt] n rearme m

rearrange [riːə'reɪndʒ] vt ordenar or arreglar de nuevo

rear-view mirror n (AUT) (espejo) retrovisor m

reason ['riːzn] n razón f ♦ vi: **to ~ with sb** tratar de que uno entre en razón; **it stands to ~ that** es lógico que; **~able** adj razonable; (sensible) sensato; **~ably** adv razonablemente; **~ing** n razonamiento, argumentos mpl

reassurance [riːə'ʃʊərəns] n consuelo

reassure [riːə'ʃʊə*] vt tranquilizar, alentar; **to ~ sb that** tranquilizar a uno asegurando que

rebate ['riːbeɪt] n (on tax etc) desgravación f

rebel [n 'rɛbl, vi rɪ'bɛl] n rebelde m/f ♦ vi rebelarse, sublevarse; **~lious** [rɪ'bɛljəs] adj

rebelde; (child) revoltoso
rebirth [ˈriːbəːθ] n renacimiento
rebound [vi rɪˈbaund, n ˈriːbaund] vi (ball)
rebotar ♦ n rebote m; **on the ~** (also fig) de
rebote
rebuff [rɪˈbʌf] n desaire m, rechazo
rebuild [riːˈbɪld] (irreg) vt reconstruir
rebuke [rɪˈbjuːk] n reprimenda ♦ vt reprender
rebut [rɪˈbʌt] vt rebatir
recall [vb rɪˈkɔːl, n ˈriːkɔl] vt (remember)
recordar; (ambassador etc) retirar ♦ n
recuerdo; retirada
recap [ˈriːkæp], **recapitulate** [riːkəˈpɪtjuleɪt]
vt, vi recapitular
rec'd abbr (= received) rbdo
recede [rɪˈsiːd] vi (memory) ir borrándose;
(hair) retroceder; **receding** adj (forehead,
chin) huidizo; **to have a receding hairline**
tener entradas
receipt [rɪˈsiːt] n (document) recibo; (for
parcel etc) acuse m de recibo; (act of
receiving) recepción f; **~s** npl (COMM) ingresos
mpl
receive [rɪˈsiːv] vt recibir; (guest) acoger;
(wound) sufrir; **~r** n (TEL) auricular m; (RADIO)
receptor m; (of stolen goods) perista m/f;
(COMM) administrador m jurídico
recent [ˈriːsnt] adj reciente; **~ly** adv
recientemente; **~ly arrived** recién llegado
receptacle [rɪˈseptɪkl] n receptáculo
reception [rɪˈsepʃən] n recepción f;
(welcome) acogida; **~ desk** n recepción f;
~ist n recepcionista m/f
recess [rɪˈses] n (in room) hueco; (for bed)
nicho; (secret place) escondrijo; (POL etc:
holiday) clausura
recession [rɪˈseʃən] n recesión f
recipe [ˈresɪpɪ] n receta; (for disaster, success)
fórmula
recipient [rɪˈsɪpɪənt] n recibidor(a) m/f; (of
letter) destinatario/a
recital [rɪˈsaɪtl] n recital m
recite [rɪˈsaɪt] vt (poem) recitar
reckless [ˈrekləs] adj temerario, imprudente;
(driving, driver) peligroso; **~ly** adv
imprudentemente; de modo peligroso
reckon [ˈrekən] vt calcular; (consider)
considerar; (think): **I ~ that ...** me parece que
...; **~ on** vt fus contar con; **~ing** n cálculo
reclaim [rɪˈkleɪm] vt (land, waste) recuperar;
(land: from sea) rescatar; (demand back)
reclamar
reclamation [rekləˈmeɪʃən] n (of land)
acondicionamiento de tierras
recline [rɪˈklaɪn] vi reclinarse; **reclining** adj
(seat) reclinable
recluse [rɪˈkluːs] n recluso/a
recognition [rekəgˈnɪʃən] n reconocimiento;
transformed beyond ~ irreconocible

recognizable [ˈrekəgnaɪzəbl] adj: **~ (by)**
reconocible (por)
recognize [ˈrekəgnaɪz] vt: **to ~ (by/as)**
reconocer (por/como)
recoil [vi rɪˈkɔɪl, n ˈriːkɔɪl] vi (person): **to
~ from doing sth** retraerse de hacer algo ♦ n
(of gun) retroceso
recollect [rekəˈlekt] vt recordar, acordarse de;
~ion [-ˈlekʃən] n recuerdo
recommend [rekəˈmend] vt recomendar
reconcile [ˈrekənsaɪl] vt (two people)
reconciliar; (two facts) compaginar; **to ~ o.s.
to sth** conformarse a algo
recondition [riːkənˈdɪʃən] vt (machine)
reacondicionar
reconnoitre [rekəˈnɔɪtə*] (US **reconnoiter**) vt,
vi (MIL) reconocer
reconsider [riːkənˈsɪdə*] vt repensar
reconstruct [riːkənˈstrʌkt] vt reconstruir
record [n ˈrekɔːd, vt rɪˈkɔːd] n (MUS) disco; (of
meeting etc) acta; (register) registro, partida;
(file) archivo; (also: criminal ~) antecedentes
mpl; (written) expediente m; (SPORT, COMPUT)
récord m ♦ vt registrar; (MUS: song etc)
grabar; **in ~ time** en un tiempo récord; **off
the ~** adj no oficial ♦ adv confidencialmente;
~ card n (in file) ficha; **~ed delivery** (BRIT)
n (POST) entrega con acuse de recibo; **~er** n
(MUS) flauta de pico; **~ holder** n (SPORT)
actual poseedor(a) m/f del récord; **~ing**
(MUS) grabación f; **~ player** n tocadiscos m
inv
recount [rɪˈkaunt] vt contar
re-count [ˈriːkaunt] n (POL: of votes) segundo
escrutinio
recoup [rɪˈkuːp] vt: **to ~ one's losses**
recuperar las pérdidas
recourse [rɪˈkɔːs] n: **to have ~ to** recurrir a
recover [rɪˈkʌvə*] vt recuperar ♦ vi (from
illness, shock) recuperarse; **~y** n recuperación
f
recreation [rekrɪˈeɪʃən] n recreo; **~al** adj de
recreo; **~al drug** droga recreativa
recruit [rɪˈkruːt] n recluta m/f ♦ vt reclutar;
(staff) contratar
rectangle [ˈrektæŋgl] n rectángulo;
rectangular [-ˈtæŋgjulə*] adj rectangular
rectify [ˈrektɪfaɪ] vt rectificar
rector [ˈrektə*] n (REL) párroco; **~y** n casa del
párroco
recuperate [rɪˈkuːpəreɪt] vi reponerse,
restablecerse
recur [rɪˈkəː*] vi repetirse; (pain, illness)
producirse de nuevo; **~rence** [rɪˈkʌrəns] n
repetición f; **~rent** [rɪˈkʌrənt] adj repetido
recycle [riːˈsaɪkl] vt reciclar
red [red] n rojo ♦ adj rojo; (hair) pelirrojo;
(wine) tinto; **to be in the ~** (account) estar en
números rojos; (business) tener un saldo

negativo; **to give sb the ~ carpet treatment**
recibir a uno con todos los honores;
R~ Cross n Cruz f Roja; **~currant** n grosella
roja; **~den** vt enrojecer ♦ vi enrojecerse
redeem [rɪ'diːm] vt redimir; (*promises*)
cumplir; (*sth in pawn*) desempeñar; (*fig, also*
REL) rescatar; **~ing** adj: **~ing feature** rasgo
bueno or favorable
redeploy [riːdɪ'plɔɪ] vt (*resources*) reorganizar
red: **~-haired** adj pelirrojo; **~-handed** adj: **to**
be caught ~-handed cogerse (*SP*) or pillarse
(*AM*) con las manos en la masa; **~head** n
pelirrojo/a; **~ herring** n (*fig*) pista falsa; **~-**
hot adj candente
redirect [riːdaɪ'rekt] vt (*mail*) reexpedir
red light n: **to go through a ~** (*AUT*) pasar la
luz roja; **red-light district** n barrio chino
redo [riː'duː] (*irreg*) vt rehacer
redress [rɪ'dres] vt reparar
Red Sea n: **the ~** el mar Rojo
redskin ['redskɪn] n piel roja m/f
red tape n (*fig*) trámites mpl
reduce [rɪ'djuːs] vt reducir; **to ~ sb to tears**
hacer llorar a uno; **to be ~d to begging** no
quedarle a uno otro remedio que pedir
limosna; **"~ speed now"** (*AUT*) "reduzca la
velocidad"; **at a ~d price** (*of goods*) (a precio)
rebajado; **reduction** [rɪ'dʌkʃən] n reducción
f; (*of price*) rebaja; (*discount*) descuento;
(*smaller-scale copy*) copia reducida
redundancy [rɪ'dʌndənsɪ] n (*dismissal*)
despido; (*unemployment*) desempleo
redundant [rɪ'dʌndnt] adj (*BRIT: worker*)
parado, sin trabajo; (*detail, object*) superfluo;
to be made ~ quedar(se) sin trabajo
reed [riːd] n (*BOT*) junco, caña; (*MUS*)
lengüeta
reef [riːf] n (*at sea*) arrecife m
reek [riːk] vi: **to ~ (of)** apestar (a)
reel [riːl] n carrete m, bobina; (*of film*) rollo;
(*dance*) baile m escocés ♦ vt (*also: ~ up*)
devanar; (*also: ~ in*) sacar ♦ vi (*sway*)
tambalear(se)
ref [ref] (*inf*) n abbr = **referee**
refectory [rɪ'fektərɪ] n comedor m
refer [rɪ'fɜː*] vt (*send: patient*) referir;
(*: matter*) remitir ♦ vi: **to ~ to** (*allude to*)
referirse a, aludir a; (*apply to*) relacionarse
con; (*consult*) consultar
referee [refə'riː] n árbitro; (*BRIT: for job*
application): **to be a ~ for sb** proporcionar
referencias a uno ♦ vt (*match*) arbitrar en
reference ['refrəns] n referencia; (*for job*
application: letter) carta de recomendación;
with ~ to (*COMM: in letter*) me remito a;
~ book n libro de consulta; **~ number** n
número de referencia
refill [vt riː'fɪl, n 'riːfɪl] vt rellenar ♦ n
repuesto, recambio

refine [rɪ'faɪn] vt refinar; **~d** adj (*person*) fino;
~ment n cultura, educación f; (*of system*)
refinamiento
reflect [rɪ'flekt] vt reflejar ♦ vi (*think*)
reflexionar, pensar; **it ~s badly/well on him** le
perjudica/le hace honor; **~ion** [-'flekʃən] n
(*act*) reflexión f; (*image*) reflejo; (*criticism*)
crítica; **on ~ion** pensándolo bien; **~or** n (*AUT*)
captafaros m inv; (*of light, heat*) reflector m
reflex ['riːfleks] adj, n reflejo; **~ive** [rɪ'fleksɪv]
adj (*LING*) reflexivo
reform [rɪ'fɔːm] n reforma ♦ vt reformar;
~atory (*US*) n reformatorio
refrain [rɪ'freɪn] vi: **to ~ from doing**
abstenerse de hacer ♦ n estribillo
refresh [rɪ'freʃ] vt refrescar; **~er course**
(*BRIT*) n curso de repaso; **~ing** adj
refrescante; **~ments** npl refrescos mpl
refrigerator [rɪ'frɪdʒəreɪtə*] n nevera (*SP*),
refrigeradora (*AM*)
refuel [riː'fjʊəl] vi repostar (combustible)
refuge ['refjuːdʒ] n refugio, asilo; **to take ~ in**
refugiarse en
refugee [refjʊ'dʒiː] n refugiado/a
refund [n 'riːfʌnd, vb riː'fʌnd] n reembolso
♦ vt devolver, reembolsar
refurbish [riː'fɜːbɪʃ] vt restaurar, renovar
refusal [rɪ'fjuːzəl] n negativa; **to have first**
~ on tener la primera opción a
refuse[1] ['refjuːs] n basura; **~ collection** n
recolección f de basuras
refuse[2] [rɪ'fjuːz] vt rechazar; (*invitation*)
declinar; (*permission*) denegar ♦ vi: **to ~ to**
do sth negarse a hacer algo; (*horse*) rehusar
regain [rɪ'geɪn] vt recobrar, recuperar
regal ['riːgl] adj regio, real
regard [rɪ'gɑːd] n mirada; (*esteem*) respeto;
(*attention*) consideración f ♦ vt (*consider*)
considerar; **to give one's ~s to** saludar de su
parte a; **"with kindest ~s"** "con muchos
recuerdos"; **~ing, as ~s, with ~ to** con
respecto a, en cuanto a; **~less** adv a pesar de
todo; **~less of** sin reparar en
régime [reɪ'ʒiːm] n régimen m
regiment ['redʒɪmənt] n regimiento; **~al**
[-'mentl] adj militar
region ['riːdʒən] n región f; **in the ~ of** (*fig*)
alrededor de; **~al** adj regional
register ['redʒɪstə*] n registro ♦ vt registrar;
(*birth*) declarar; (*car*) matricular; (*letter*)
certificar; (*subj: instrument*) marcar, indicar
♦ vi (*at hotel*) registrarse; (*as student*)
matricularse; (*make impression*) producir
impresión; **~ed** adj (*letter, parcel*) certificado;
~ed trademark n marca registrada
registrar ['redʒɪstrɑː*] n secretario/a (del
registro civil)
registration [redʒɪs'treɪʃən] n (*act*)
declaración f; (*AUT: also: ~ number*) matrícula

registry ['redʒɪstrɪ] n registro; **~ office** (BRIT) n registro civil; **to get married in a ~ office** casarse por lo civil

regret [rɪ'gret] n sentimiento, pesar m ♦ vt sentir, lamentar; **~fully** adv con pesar; **~table** adj lamentable

regular ['regjulə*] adj regular; (soldier) profesional; (usual) habitual; (: doctor) de cabecera ♦ n (client etc) cliente/a m/f habitual; **~ly** adv con regularidad; (often) repetidas veces

regulate ['regjuleɪt] vt controlar; **regulation** [-'leɪʃən] n (rule) regla, reglamento

rehearsal [rɪ'hɜːsəl] n ensayo

rehearse [rɪ'hɜːs] vt ensayar

reign [reɪn] n reinado; (fig) predominio ♦ vi reinar; (fig) imperar

reimburse [riːɪm'bɜːs] vt reembolsar

rein [reɪn] n (for horse) rienda

reindeer ['reɪndɪə*] n inv reno

reinforce [riːɪn'fɔːs] vt reforzar; **~d concrete** n hormigón m armado; **~ments** npl (MIL) refuerzos mpl

reinstate [riːɪn'steɪt] vt reintegrar; (tax, law) reinstaurar

reiterate [riː'ɪtəreɪt] vt reiterar, repetir

reject [n 'riːdʒekt, vb rɪ'dʒekt] n (thing) desecho ♦ vt rechazar; (suggestion) descartar; (coin) expulsar; **~ion** [rɪ'dʒekʃən] n rechazo

rejoice [rɪ'dʒɔɪs] vi: **to ~ at** or **over** regocijarse or alegrarse de

rejuvenate [rɪ'dʒuːvəneɪt] vt rejuvenecer

relapse [rɪ'læps] n recaída

relate [rɪ'leɪt] vt (tell) contar, relatar; (connect) relacionar ♦ vi relacionarse; **~d** adj afín; (person) emparentado; **~d to** (subject) relacionado con; **relating to** prep referente a

relation [rɪ'leɪʃən] n (person) familiar m/f, pariente a m/f; (link) relación f; **~s** npl (relatives) familiares mpl; **~ship** n relación f; (personal) relaciones fpl; (also: family ~ship) parentesco

relative ['relatɪv] n pariente/a m/f, familiar m/f ♦ adj relativo; **~ly** adv (comparatively) relativamente

relax [rɪ'læks] vi descansar; (unwind) relajarse ♦ vt (one's grip) soltar, aflojar; (control) relajar; (mind, person) descansar; **~ation** [riːlæk'seɪʃən] n descanso; (of rule, control) relajamiento; (entertainment) diversión f; **~ed** adj relajado; (tranquil) tranquilo; **~ing** adj relajante

relay ['riːleɪ] n (race) carrera de relevos ♦ vt (RADIO, TV) retransmitir

release [rɪ'liːs] n (liberation) liberación f; (from prison) puesta en libertad; (of gas etc) escape m; (of film etc) estreno; (of record) lanzamiento ♦ vt (prisoner) poner en libertad; (gas) despedir, arrojar; (from wreckage)

soltar; (catch, spring etc) desenganchar; (film) estrenar; (book) publicar; (news) difundir

relegate ['relɪgeɪt] vt relegar; (BRIT: SPORT): **to be ~d to** bajar a

relent [rɪ'lent] vi ablandarse; **~less** adj implacable

relevant ['relavant] adj (fact) pertinente; **~ to** relacionado con

reliable [rɪ'laɪəbl] adj (person, firm) de confianza, de fiar; (method, machine) seguro; (source) fidedigno; **reliably** adv: **to be reliably informed that ...** saber de fuente fidedigna que ...

reliance [rɪ'laɪəns] n: **~ (on)** dependencia (de)

relic ['relɪk] n (REL) reliquia; (of the past) vestigio

relief [rɪ'liːf] n (from pain, anxiety) alivio; (help, supplies) socorro, ayuda; (ART, GEO) relieve m

relieve [rɪ'liːv] vt (pain) aliviar; (bring help to) ayudar, socorrer; (take over from) sustituir; (: guard) relevar; **to ~ sb of sth** quitar algo a uno; **to ~ o.s.** hacer sus necesidades

religion [rɪ'lɪdʒən] n religión f; **religious** adj religioso

relinquish [rɪ'lɪŋkwɪʃ] vt abandonar; (plan, habit) renunciar a

relish ['relɪʃ] n (CULIN) salsa; (enjoyment) entusiasmo ♦ vt (food etc) saborear; (enjoy): **to ~ sth** hacerle mucha ilusión a uno algo

relocate [riːləu'keɪt] vt cambiar de lugar, mudar ♦ vi mudarse

reluctance [rɪ'lʌktəns] n renuencia

reluctant [rɪ'lʌktənt] adj renuente; **~ly** adv de mala gana

rely on [rɪ'laɪ-] vt fus depender de; (trust) contar con

remain [rɪ'meɪn] vi (survive) quedar; (be left) sobrar; (continue) quedar(se), permanecer; **~der** n resto; **~ing** adj que queda(n); (surviving) restante(s); **~s** npl restos mpl

remand [rɪ'mɑːnd] n: **on ~** detenido (bajo custodia) ♦ vt: **to be ~ed in custody** quedar detenido bajo custodia; **~ home** (BRIT) n reformatorio

remark [rɪ'mɑːk] n comentario ♦ vt comentar; **~able** adj (outstanding) extraordinario

remarry [riː'mærɪ] vi volver a casarse

remedial [rɪ'miːdɪəl] adj de recuperación

remedy ['remədɪ] n remedio ♦ vt remediar, curar

remember [rɪ'membə*] vt recordar, acordarse de; (bear in mind) tener presente; (send greetings to): **~ me to him** dale recuerdos de mi parte; **remembrance** n recuerdo; **R~ Day** n ≈ día en el que se recuerda a los caídos en las dos guerras mundiales

remind [rɪ'maɪnd] vt: **to ~ sb to do sth**
recordar a uno que haga algo; **to ~ sb of sth**
(*of fact*) recordar algo a uno; **she ~s me of
her mother** me recuerda a su madre; **~er** n
notificación f; (*memento*) recuerdo

reminisce [remɪ'nɪs] vi recordar (viejas
historias); **reminiscent** adj: **to be
reminiscent of sth** recordar algo

remiss [rɪ'mɪs] adj descuidado; **it was ~ of
him** fue un descuido de su parte

remission [rɪ'mɪʃən] n remisión f; (*of prison
sentence*) disminución f de pena; (*REL*) perdón
m

remit [rɪ'mɪt] vt (*send: money*) remitir, enviar;
~tance n remesa, envío

remnant ['remnənt] n resto; (*of cloth*) retal
m; **~s** npl (*COMM*) restos mpl de serie

remorse [rɪ'mɔːs] n remordimientos mpl;
~ful adj arrepentido; **~less** adj (*fig*)
implacable, inexorable

remote [rɪ'məut] adj (*distant*) lejano;
(*person*) distante; **~ control** n telecontrol m;
~ly adv remotamente; (*slightly*) levemente

remould ['riːməuld] (*BRIT*) n (*tyre*) neumático
or llanta (*AM*) recauchutado/a

removable [rɪ'muːvəbl] adj (*detachable*)
separable

removal [rɪ'muːvəl] n (*taking away*) el quitar;
(*BRIT: from house*) mudanza; (*from office:
dismissal*) destitución f; (*MED*) extirpación f;
~ van (*BRIT*) n camión m de mudanzas

remove [rɪ'muːv] vt quitar; (*employee*)
destituir; (*name: from list*) tachar, borrar;
(*doubt*) disipar; (*abuse*) suprimir, acabar con;
(*MED*) extirpar

Renaissance [rɪ'neɪsɑːns] n: **the ~** el
Renacimiento

render ['rendə*] vt (*thanks*) dar; (*aid*)
proporcionar, prestar; (*make*): **to ~ sth
useless** hacer algo inútil; **~ing** n (*MUS etc*)
interpretación f

rendezvous ['rɒndɪvuː] n cita

renew [rɪ'njuː] vt renovar; (*resume*) reanudar;
(*loan etc*) prorrogar; **~able** adj renovable;
~al n reanudación f; prórroga

renounce [rɪ'nauns] vt renunciar a; (*right,
inheritance*) renunciar

renovate ['renəveɪt] vt renovar

renown [rɪ'naun] n renombre m; **~ed** adj
renombrado

rent [rent] n (*for house*) arriendo, renta ♦ vt
alquilar; **~al** n (*for television, car*) alquiler m

rep [rep] n abbr = **representative; repertory**

repair [rɪ'peə*] n reparación f, compostura
♦ vt reparar, componer; (*shoes*) remendar;
in good/bad ~ en buen/mal estado; **~ kit** n
caja de herramientas

repatriate [riː'pætrɪeɪt] vt repatriar

repay [riː'peɪ] (*irreg*) vt (*money*) devolver,
reembolsar; (*person*) pagar; (*debt*) liquidar;
(*sb's efforts*) devolver, corresponder a;
~ment n reembolso, devolución f; (*sum of
money*) recompensa

repeal [rɪ'piːl] n revocación f ♦ vt revocar

repeat [rɪ'piːt] n (*RADIO, TV*) reposición f ♦ vt
repetir ♦ vi repetirse; **~edly** adv repetidas
veces

repel [rɪ'pel] vt (*drive away*) rechazar;
(*disgust*) repugnar; **~lent** adj repugnante
♦ n: **insect ~lent** crema (or loción f) anti-
insectos

repent [rɪ'pent] vi: **to ~ (of)** arrepentirse (de);
~ance n arrepentimiento

repercussions [riːpə'kʌʃənz] npl
consecuencias fpl

repertory ['repətəri] n (*also: ~ theatre*) teatro
de repertorio

repetition [repɪ'tɪʃən] n repetición f

repetitive [rɪ'petɪtɪv] adj repetitivo

replace [rɪ'pleɪs] vt (*put back*) devolver a su
sitio; (*take the place of*) reemplazar, sustituir;
~ment n (*act*) reposición f; (*thing*)
recambio; (*person*) suplente m/f

replay ['riːpleɪ] n (*SPORT*) desempate m; (*of
tape, film*) repetición f

replenish [rɪ'plenɪʃ] vt rellenar; (*stock etc*)
reponer

replica ['replɪkə] n copia, reproducción f
(exacta)

reply [rɪ'plaɪ] n respuesta, contestación f ♦ vi
contestar, responder

report [rɪ'pɔːt] n informe m; (*PRESS etc*)
reportaje m; (*BRIT: also: school ~*) boletín m
escolar; (*of gun*) estallido ♦ vt informar de;
(*PRESS etc*) hacer un reportaje sobre; (*notify:
accident, culprit*) denunciar ♦ vi (*make a
report*) presentar un informe; (*present o.s.*):
to ~ (to sb) presentarse (ante uno); **~ card** n
(*US, Scottish*) cartilla escolar; **~edly** adv
según se dice; **~er** n periodista m/f

repose [rɪ'pəuz] n: **in ~** (*face, mouth*) en
reposo

reprehensible [reprɪ'hensɪbl] adj
reprensible, censurable

represent [reprɪ'zent] vt representar; (*COMM*)
ser agente de; (*describe*): **to ~ sth as** describir
algo como; **~ation** [-'teɪʃən] n representación
f; **~ations** npl (*protest*) quejas fpl; **~ative** n
representante m/f; (*US: POL*) diputado/a m/f
♦ adj representativo

repress [rɪ'pres] vt reprimir; **~ion** [-'preʃən] n
represión f

reprieve [rɪ'priːv] n (*LAW*) indulto; (*fig*) alivio

reprisals [rɪ'praɪzlz] npl represalias fpl

reproach [rɪ'prəutʃ] n reproche m ♦ vt: **to
~ sb for sth** reprochar algo a uno; **~ful** adj de
reproche, de acusación

reproduce [riːprə'djuːs] vt reproducir ♦ vi reproducirse; **reproduction** [-'dʌkʃən] n reproducción f

reprove [rɪ'pruːv] vt: **to ~ sb for sth** reprochar algo a uno

reptile ['reptail] n reptil m

republic [rɪ'pʌblɪk] n república; **~an** adj, n republicano/a m/f

repudiate [rɪ'pjuːdɪeɪt] vt rechazar; (violence etc) repudiar

repulsive [rɪ'pʌlsɪv] adj repulsivo

reputable ['repjutəbl] adj (make etc) de renombre

reputation [repju'teɪʃən] n reputación f

reputed [rɪ'pjuːtɪd] adj supuesto; **~ly** adv según dicen or se dice

request [rɪ'kwest] n petición f; (formal) solicitud f ♦ vt: **to ~ sth of** or **from sb** solicitar algo a uno; **~ stop** (BRIT) n parada discrecional

require [rɪ'kwaɪə*] vt (need: subj: person) necesitar, tener necesidad de; (: thing, situation) exigir; (want) pedir; **to ~ sb to do sth** pedir a uno que haga algo; **~ment** n requisito; (need) necesidad f

requisition [rekwɪ'zɪʃən] n: **~ (for)** solicitud f (de) ♦ vt (MIL) requisar

rescue ['reskjuː] n rescate m ♦ vt rescatar; **~ party** n expedición f de salvamento; **~r** n salvador(a) m/f

research [rɪ'səːtʃ] n investigaciones fpl ♦ vt investigar; **~er** n investigador(a) m/f

resemblance [rɪ'zembləns] n parecido

resemble [rɪ'zembl] vt parecerse a

resent [rɪ'zent] vt tomar a mal; **~ful** adj resentido; **~ment** n resentimiento

reservation [rezə'veɪʃən] n reserva

reserve [rɪ'zəːv] n reserva; (SPORT) suplente m/f ♦ vt (seats etc) reservar; **~s** npl (MIL) reserva; **in ~** de reserva; **~d** adj reservado

reshuffle [riː'ʃʌfl] n: **Cabinet ~** (POL) remodelación f del gabinete

residence ['rezɪdəns] n (formal: home) domicilio; (length of stay) permanencia; **~ permit** (BRIT) n permiso de permanencia

resident ['rezɪdənt] n (of area) vecino/a; (in hotel) huésped/a m/f ♦ adj (population) permanente; (doctor) residente; **~ial** [-'denʃəl] adj residencial

residue ['rezɪdjuː] n resto

resign [rɪ'zaɪn] vt renunciar a ♦ vi dimitir; **to ~ o.s. to** (situation) resignarse a; **~ation** [rezɪg'neɪʃən] n dimisión f; (state of mind) resignación f; **~ed** adj resignado

resilient [rɪ'zɪlɪənt] adj (material) elástico; (person) resistente

resist [rɪ'zɪst] vt resistir, oponerse a; **~ance** n resistencia

resolute ['rezəluːt] adj resuelto; (refusal)

tajante

resolution [rezə'luːʃən] n (gen) resolución f

resolve [rɪ'zɔlv] n resolución f ♦ vt resolver ♦ vi: **to ~ to do** resolver hacer; **~d** adj resuelto

resort [rɪ'zɔːt] n (town) centro turístico; (recourse) recurso ♦ vi: **to ~ to** recurrir a; **in the last ~** como último recurso

resounding [rɪ'zaundɪŋ] adj sonoro; (fig) clamoroso

resource [rɪ'sɔːs] n recurso; **~s** npl recursos mpl; **~ful** adj despabilado, ingenioso

respect [rɪs'pekt] n respeto ♦ vt respetar; **~s** npl recuerdos mpl, saludos mpl; **with ~ to** con respecto a; **in this ~** en cuanto a eso; **~able** adj respetable; (large: amount) apreciable; (passable) tolerable; **~ful** adj respetuoso

respective [rɪs'pektɪv] adj respectivo; **~ly** adv respectivamente

respite ['respaɪt] n respiro

respond [rɪs'pɔnd] vi responder; (react) reaccionar; **response** [-'pɔns] n respuesta, reacción f

responsibility [rɪspɔnsɪ'bɪlɪtɪ] n responsabilidad f

responsible [rɪs'pɔnsɪbl] adj (character) serio, formal; (job) de confianza; (liable): **~ (for)** responsable (de)

responsive [rɪs'pɔnsɪv] adj sensible

rest [rest] n descanso, reposo; (MUS, pause) pausa, silencio; (support) apoyo; (remainder) resto ♦ vi descansar; (be supported): **to ~ on** descansar sobre ♦ vt (lean): **to ~ sth on/against** apoyar algo en or sobre/contra; **the ~ of them** (people, objects) los demás; **it ~s with him to ...** depende de él el que ...

restaurant ['restərɔŋ] n restaurante m; **~ car** (BRIT) n (RAIL) coche-comedor m

restful ['restful] adj descansado, tranquilo

rest home n residencia para jubilados

restive ['restɪv] adj inquieto; (horse) rebelón(ona)

restless ['restlɪs] adj inquieto

restoration [restə'reɪʃən] n restauración f; devolución f

restore [rɪ'stɔː*] vt (building) restaurar; (sth stolen) devolver; (health) restablecer; (to power) volver a poner a

restrain [rɪs'treɪn] vt (feeling) contener, refrenar; (person): **to ~ (from doing)** disuadir (de hacer); **~ed** adj reservado; **~t** n (restriction) restricción f; (moderation) moderación f; (of manner) reserva

restrict [rɪs'trɪkt] vt restringir, limitar; **~ion** [-kʃən] n restricción f, limitación f; **~ive** adj restrictivo

rest room (US) n aseos mpl

result [rɪ'zʌlt] n resultado ♦ vi: **to ~ in** terminar en, tener por resultado; **as a ~ of**

consecuencia de

resume [rɪ'zjuːm] vt reanudar ♦ vi comenzar de nuevo

résumé ['reɪzjuːmeɪ] n resumen m; (US) currículum m

resumption [rɪ'zʌmpʃən] n reanudación f

resurgence [rɪ'sɜːdʒəns] n resurgimiento

resurrection [rezə'rekʃən] n resurrección f

resuscitate [rɪ'sʌsɪteɪt] vt (MED) resucitar

retail ['riːteɪl] adj, adv al por menor; ~er n detallista m/f; ~ price n precio de venta al público

retain [rɪ'teɪn] vt (keep) retener, conservar; ~er n (fee) anticipo

retaliate [rɪ'tælɪeɪt] vi: to ~ (against) tomar represalias (contra); **retaliation** [-'eɪʃən] n represalias fpl

retarded [rɪ'tɑːdɪd] adj retrasado

retch [retʃ] vi dársele a uno arcadas

retentive [rɪ'tentɪv] adj (memory) retentivo

retire [rɪ'taɪə*] vi (give up work) jubilarse; (withdraw) retirarse; (go to bed) acostarse; ~d adj (person) jubilado; ~ment n (giving up work: state) retiro; (: act) jubilación f; **retiring** adj (leaving) saliente; (shy) retraído

retort [rɪ'tɔːt] vi contestar

retrace [riː'treɪs] vt: to ~ one's steps volver sobre sus pasos, desandar lo andado

retract [rɪ'trækt] vt (statement) retirar; (claws) retraer; (undercarriage, aerial) replegar

retrain [riː'treɪn] vt reciclar; ~ing n readaptación f profesional

retread ['riːtred] n neumático (SP) or llanta (AM) recauchutado/a

retreat [rɪ'triːt] n (place) retiro; (MIL) retirada ♦ vi retirarse

retribution [retrɪ'bjuːʃən] n desquite m

retrieval [rɪ'triːvəl] n recuperación f

retrieve [rɪ'triːv] vt recobrar; (situation, honour) salvar; (COMPUT) recuperar; (error) reparar; ~r n perro cobrador

retrospect ['retrəspekt] n: in ~ retrospectivamente; ~ive [-'spektɪv] adj retrospectivo; (law) retroactivo

return [rɪ'tɜːn] n (going or coming back) vuelta, regreso; (of sth stolen etc) devolución f; (FINANCE: from land, shares) ganancia, ingresos mpl ♦ cpd (journey) de regreso; (BRIT: ticket) de ida y vuelta; (match) de vuelta ♦ vi (person etc: come or go back) volver, regresar; (symptoms etc) reaparecer; (regain): to ~ to recuperar ♦ vt devolver; (favour, love etc) corresponder a; (verdict) pronunciar; (POL: candidate) elegir; ~s npl (COMM) ingresos mpl; in ~ (for) a cambio (de); by ~ of post a vuelta de correo; **many happy ~s (of the day)!** ¡feliz cumpleaños!

reunion [riː'juːnɪən] n (of family) reunión f; (of two people, school) reencuentro

reunite [riːjuː'naɪt] vt reunir; (reconcile) reconciliar

rev [rev] (AUT) n abbr (= revolution) revolución f ♦ vt (also: ~ up) acelerar

reveal [rɪ'viːl] vt revelar; ~ing adj revelador(a)

revel ['revl] vi: to ~ in sth/in doing sth gozar de algo/con hacer algo

revenge [rɪ'vendʒ] n venganza; **to take ~ on** vengarse de

revenue ['revənjuː] n ingresos mpl, rentas fpl

reverberate [rɪ'vɜːbəreɪt] vi (sound) resonar, retumbar; (fig: shock) repercutir

reverence ['revərəns] n reverencia

Reverend ['revərənd] adj (in titles): **the ~ John Smith** (Anglican) el Reverendo John Smith; (Catholic) el Padre John Smith; (Protestant) el Pastor John Smith

reversal [rɪ'vɜːsl] n (of order) inversión f; (of direction, policy) cambio; (of decision) revocación f

reverse [rɪ'vɜːs] n (opposite) contrario; (back: of cloth) revés m; (: of coin) reverso; (: of paper) dorso; (AUT: also: ~ gear) marcha atrás; (setback) revés m ♦ adj (order) inverso; (direction) contrario; (process) opuesto ♦ vt (decision, AUT) dar marcha atrás a; (position, function) invertir ♦ vi (BRIT: AUT) dar marcha atrás; ~-charge call (BRIT) n llamada a cobro revertido; **reversing lights** (BRIT) npl (AUT) luces fpl de retroceso

revert [rɪ'vɜːt] vi: to ~ to volver a

review [rɪ'vjuː] n (magazine, MIL) revista; (of book, film) reseña; (US: examination) repaso, examen m ♦ vt repasar, examinar; (MIL) pasar revista a; (book, film) reseñar; ~er n crítico/a

revise [rɪ'vaɪz] vt (manuscript) corregir; (opinion) modificar; (price, procedure) revisar ♦ vi (study) repasar; **revision** [rɪ'vɪʒən] n corrección f; modificación f; (for exam) repaso

revival [rɪ'vaɪvəl] n (recovery) reanimación f; (of interest) renacimiento; (THEATRE) reestreno; (of faith) despertar m

revive [rɪ'vaɪv] vt resucitar; (custom) restablecer; (hope) despertar; (play) reestrenar ♦ vi (person) volver en sí; (business) reactivarse

revolt [rɪ'vəult] n rebelión f ♦ vi rebelarse, sublevarse ♦ vt dar asco a, repugnar; ~ing adj asqueroso, repugnante

revolution [revə'luːʃən] n revolución f; ~ary adj, n revolucionario/a m/f; ~ize vt revolucionar

revolve [rɪ'vɒlv] vi dar vueltas, girar; (life, discussion): to ~ (a)round girar en torno a

revolver [rɪ'vɒlvə*] n revólver m

revolving [rɪ'vɒlvɪŋ] adj (chair, door etc) giratorio

revue [rɪ'vjuː] n (THEATRE) revista

revulsion [rɪ'vʌlʃən] n asco, repugnancia

reward [rɪ'wɔːd] n premio, recompensa ♦ vt: **to ~ (for)** recompensar or premiar (por); **~ing** adj (fig) valioso

rewind [riː'waɪnd] (irreg) vt rebobinar

rewire [riː'waɪə*] vt (house) renovar la instalación eléctrica de

rheumatism ['ruːmətɪzəm] n reumatismo, reúma m

Rhine [raɪn] n: **the ~** el (río) Rin

rhinoceros [raɪ'nɔsərəs] n rinoceronte m

rhododendron [rəudə'dendrn] n rododendro

Rhone [rəun] n: **the ~** el (río) Ródano

rhubarb ['ruːbɑːb] n ruibarbo

rhyme [raɪm] n rima; (verse) poesía

rhythm ['rɪðm] n ritmo

rib [rɪb] n (ANAT) costilla ♦ vt (mock) tomar el pelo a

ribbon ['rɪbən] n cinta; **in ~s** (torn) hecho trizas

rice [raɪs] n arroz m; **~ pudding** n arroz m con leche

rich [rɪtʃ] adj rico; (soil) fértil; (food) pesado; (: sweet) empalagoso; (abundant): **~ in** (minerals etc) rico en; **the ~** npl los ricos; **~es** npl riqueza; **~ly** adv ricamente; (deserved, earned) bien

rickets ['rɪkɪts] n raquitismo

rid [rɪd] (pt, pp rid) vt: **to ~ sb of sth** librar a uno de algo; **to get ~ of** deshacerse or desembarazarse de

ridden ['rɪdn] pp of ride

riddle ['rɪdl] n (puzzle) acertijo; (mystery) enigma m, misterio ♦ vt: **to be ~d** with ser lleno or plagado de

ride [raɪd] (pt rode, pp ridden) n paseo; (distance covered) viaje m, recorrido ♦ vi (as sport) montar; (go somewhere: on horse, bicycle) dar un paseo, pasearse; (travel: on bicycle, motorcycle, bus) viajar ♦ vt (a horse) montar a; (a bicycle, motorcycle) andar en; (distance) recorrer; **to take sb for a ~** (fig) engañar a uno; **~r** n (on horse) jinete/a m/f; (on bicycle) ciclista m/f; (on motorcycle) motociclista m/f

ridge [rɪdʒ] n (of hill) cresta; (of roof) caballete m; (wrinkle) arruga

ridicule ['rɪdɪkjuːl] n irrisión f, burla ♦ vt poner en ridículo, burlarse de; **ridiculous** [-'dɪkjuləs] adj ridículo

riding ['raɪdɪŋ] n equitación f; **I like ~** me gusta montar a caballo; **~ school** n escuela de equitación

rife [raɪf] adj: **to be ~** ser muy común; **to be ~ with** abundar en

riffraff ['rɪfræf] n gentuza

rifle ['raɪfl] n rifle m, fusil m ♦ vt saquear;

~ through vt (papers) registrar; **~ range** n campo de tiro; (at fair) tiro al blanco

rift [rɪft] n (in clouds) claro; (fig: disagreement) desavenencia

rig [rɪg] n (also: oil ~: at sea) plataforma petrolera ♦ vt (election etc) amañar; **~ out** (BRIT) vt disfrazar; **~ up** vt improvisar; **~ging** n (NAUT) aparejo

right [raɪt] adj (correct) correcto, exacto; (suitable) indicado, debido; (proper) apropiado; (just) justo; (morally good) bueno; (not left) derecho ♦ n bueno; (title, claim) derecho; (not left) derecha ♦ adv bien, correctamente; (not left) a la derecha; (exactly): **~ now** ahora mismo ♦ vt enderezar; (correct) corregir ♦ excl ¡bueno!, ¡está bien!; **to be ~** (person) tener razón; (answer) ser correcto; **is that the ~ time?** (of clock) ¿es esa la hora buena?; **by ~s** en justicia; **on the ~** a la derecha; **to be in the ~** tener razón; **~ away** en seguida; **~ in the middle** exactamente en el centro; **~ angle** n ángulo recto; **~eous** ['raɪtʃəs] adj justado, honrado; (anger) justificado; **~ful** adj legítimo; **~-handed** adj diestro; **~-hand man** n brazo derecho; **~-hand side** n derecha; **~ly** adv correctamente, debidamente; (with reason) con razón; **~ of way** n (on path etc) derecho de paso; (AUT) prioridad f; **~-wing** adj (POL) derechista

rigid ['rɪdʒɪd] adj rígido; (person, ideas) inflexible

rigmarole ['rɪgmərəul] n galimatías m inv

rigorous ['rɪgərəs] adj riguroso

rile [raɪl] vt irritar

rim [rɪm] n borde m; (of spectacles) aro; (of wheel) llanta

rind [raɪnd] n (of bacon) corteza; (of lemon etc) cáscara; (of cheese) costra

ring [rɪŋ] (pt rang, pp rung) n (of metal) aro; (on finger) anillo; (of people) corro; (of objects) círculo; (gang) banda; (for boxing) cuadrilátero; (of circus) pista; (bull ~) ruedo, plaza; (sound of bell) toque m ♦ vi (on telephone) llamar por teléfono; (bell) repicar; (doorbell, phone) sonar; (also: **~ out**) sonar; (ears) zumbar ♦ vt (BRIT: TEL) llamar, telefonear; (bell etc) hacer sonar; (doorbell) tocar; **to give sb a ~** (BRIT: TEL) llamar or telefonear a alguien; **~ back** (BRIT) vt, vi (TEL) devolver la llamada; **~ off** (BRIT) vi (TEL) colgar, cortar la comunicación; **~ up** (BRIT) vt (TEL) llamar, telefonear; **~ing** n (of bell) repique m; (of phone) sonar; (in ears) zumbido; **~ing tone** n (TEL) tono de llamada; **~leader** n (of gang) cabecilla m; **~lets** ['rɪŋlɪts] npl rizos mpl, bucles mpl; **~ road** (BRIT) n carretera periférica or de circunvalación

rink |rɪŋk| n (also: ice ~) pista de hielo

rinse |rɪns| n aclarado; (dye) tinte m ♦ vt aclarar; (mouth) enjuagar

riot ['raɪət] n motín m, disturbio ♦ vi amotinarse; **to run ~** desmandarse; **~ous** adj alborotado; (party) bullicioso

rip |rɪp| n rasgón m, rasgadura ♦ vt rasgar, desgarrar ♦ vi rasgarse, desgarrarse; **~cord** n cabo de desgarre

ripe |raɪp| adj maduro; **~n** vt madurar; (cheese) curar ♦ vi madurar

ripple ['rɪpl] n onda, rizo; (sound) murmullo ♦ vi rizarse

rise |raɪz| (pt rose, pp risen) n (slope) cuesta, pendiente f; (hill) altura; (BRIT: in wages) aumento; (in prices, temperature) subida; (fig: to power etc) ascenso ♦ vi subir; (waters) crecer; (sun, moon) salir; (person: from bed etc) levantarse; (also: ~ up: rebel) sublevarse; (in rank) ascender; **to give ~ to** dar lugar o origen a; **to ~ to the occasion** ponerse a la altura de las circunstancias; **risen** ['rɪzn] pp of rise; **rising** adj (increasing: number) creciente; (: prices) en aumento o alza; (tide) creciente; (sun, moon) naciente

risk |rɪsk| n riesgo, peligro ♦ vt arriesgar; (run the ~ of) exponerse a; **to take** or **run the ~ of doing** correr el riesgo de hacer; **at ~** en peligro; **at one's own ~** bajo su propia responsabilidad; **~y** adj arriesgado, peligroso

rissole ['rɪsəul] n croqueta

rite |raɪt| n rito; **last ~s** exequias fpl

ritual ['rɪtjuəl] adj ritual ♦ n ritual m, rito

rival ['raɪvl] n rival m/f; (in business) competidor(a) m/f ♦ adj rival, opuesto ♦ vt competir con; **~ry** n competencia

river ['rɪvə*] n río ♦ cpd (port) de río; (traffic) fluvial; **up/down ~** río arriba/abajo; **~bank** n orilla (del río); **~bed** n lecho, cauce m

rivet ['rɪvɪt] n roblón m, remache m ♦ vt (fig) captar

Riviera [rɪvɪ'eərə] n: **the (French) ~** la Costa Azul (francesa)

road |rəud| n camino; (motorway etc) carretera; (in town) calle f ♦ cpd (accident) de tráfico; **major/minor ~** carretera principal/ secundaria; **~ accident** n accidente m de tráfico; **~block** n barricada; **~hog** n loco/a del volante; **~ map** n mapa m de carreteras; **~ rage** n agresividad en la carretera; **~ safety** n seguridad f vial; **~side** n borde m (del camino); **~sign** n señal f de tráfico; **~ user** n usuario/a de la vía pública; **~way** n calzada; **~works** npl obras fpl; **~worthy** adj (car) en buen estado para circular

roam |rəum| vi vagar

roar |rɔ:*| n rugido; (of vehicle, storm) estruendo; (of laughter) carcajada ♦ vi rugir; hacer estruendo; **to ~ with laughter** reírse a

carcajadas; **to do a ~ing trade** hacer buen negocio

roast |rəust| n carne f asada, asado ♦ vt asar; (coffee) tostar; **~ beef** n rosbif m

rob |rɔb| vt robar; **to ~ sb of sth** robar algo a uno; (fig: deprive) quitar algo a uno; **~ber** n ladrón/ona m/f; **~bery** n robo

robe |rəub| n (for ceremony etc) toga; (also: bath~, US) albornoz m

robin ['rɔbɪn] n petirrojo

robot ['rəubɔt] n robot m

robust [rəu'bʌst] adj robusto, fuerte

rock |rɔk| n roca; (boulder) peña, peñasco; (US: small stone) piedrecita; (BRIT: sweet) ≈ pirulí ♦ vt (swing gently: cradle) balancear, mecer; (: child) arrullar; (shake) sacudir ♦ vi mecerse, balancearse; sacudirse; **on the ~s** (drink) con hielo; (marriage etc) en ruinas; **~ and roll** n rocanrol m; **~-bottom** n (fig) punto más bajo; **~ery** n cuadro alpino

rocket ['rɔkɪt] n cohete m

rocking ['rɔkɪŋ]: **~ chair** n mecedora; **~ horse** n caballo de balancín

rocky ['rɔkɪ] adj rocoso

rod |rɔd| n vara, varilla; (also: fishing ~) caña

rode |rəud| pt of ride

rodent ['rəudnt] n roedor m

roe |rəu| n (species: also: ~ deer) corzo; (of fish): **hard/soft ~** hueva/lecha

rogue |rəug| n pícaro, pillo

role |rəul| n papel m

roll |rəul| n rollo; (of bank notes) fajo; (also: bread ~) panecillo; (register, list) lista, nómina; (sound: of drums etc) redoble m ♦ vt hacer rodar; (also: ~ up: string) enrollar; (: sleeves) arremangar; (cigarette) liar; (also: ~ out: pastry) aplanar; (flatten: road, lawn) apisonar ♦ vi rodar; (drum) redoblar; (ship) balancearse; **~ about** or **around** vi (person) revolcarse; (object) rodar (por); **~ by** vi (time) pasar; **~ over** vi dar una vuelta; **~ up** vi (inf: arrive) aparecer ♦ vt (carpet) arrollar; **~ call** n: **to take a ~ call** pasar lista; **~er** n rodillo; (wheel) rueda; (for road) apiso- nadora; (for hair) rulo; **~erblade** n patín m (en línea); **~er coaster** n montaña rusa; **~er skates** npl patines mpl de rueda

rolling ['rəulɪŋ] adj (landscape) ondulado; **~ pin** n rodillo (de cocina); **~ stock** n (RAIL) material m rodante

ROM |rɔm| n abbr (COMPUT: = read only memory) ROM f

Roman ['rəumən] adj romano/a; **~ Catholic** adj, n católico/a m/f (romano/a)

romance [rə'mæns] n (love affair) amor m; (charm) lo romántico; (novel) novela de amor

Romania [ru:'meɪnɪə] n = Rumania

Roman numeral n número romano

romantic [rə'mæntɪk] adj romántico
Rome [rəum] n Roma
romp [rɒmp] n retozo, juego ♦ vi (also:
~ about) jugar, brincar
rompers ['rɒmpəz] npl pelele m
roof [ruːf] (pl ~s) n (gen) techo, (of house)
techo, tejado ♦ vt techar, poner techo a; the
~ of the mouth el paladar; ~ing n techumbre
f; ~ rack n (AUT) baca, portaequipajes m inv
rook [ruk] n (bird) graja; (CHESS) torre f
room [ruːm] n cuarto, habitación f, pieza (esp
AM); (also: bed~) dormitorio; (in school etc)
sala; (space, scope) sitio, cabida; ~s npl
(lodging) alojamiento; "~s to let", "~s for
rent" (US) "se alquilan cuartos"; single/
double ~ habitación individual/doble o para
dos personas; ~ing house (US) n pensión f;
~mate n compañero/a de cuarto; ~ service
n servicio de habitaciones; ~y adj espacioso;
(garment) amplio
roost [ruːst] vi pasar la noche
rooster ['ruːstə*] n gallo
root [ruːt] n raíz f ♦ vi arraigarse; ~ about vi
(fig) buscar y rebuscar; ~ for vt fus (support)
apoyar a; ~ out vt desarraigar
rope [rəup] n cuerda; (NAUT) cable m ♦ vt
(tie) atar or amarrar con (una) cuerda;
(climbers: also: ~ together) encordarse; (an
area: also: ~ off) acordonar; to know the ~s
(fig) conocer los trucos (del oficio); ~ in vt
(fig): to ~ sb in persuadir a uno a tomar parte
rosary ['rəuzərɪ] n rosario
rose [rəuz] pt of rise ♦ n rosa; (shrub) rosal m;
(on watering can) roseta
rosé ['rəuzeɪ] n vino rosado
rosebud ['rəuzbʌd] n capullo de rosa
rosebush ['rəuzbuʃ] n rosal m
rosemary ['rəuzmərɪ] n romero
roster ['rɒstə*] n: duty ~ lista de deberes
rostrum ['rɒstrəm] n tribuna
rosy ['rəuzɪ] adj rosado, sonrosado; a ~ future
un futuro prometedor
rot [rɒt] n podredumbre f; (fig: pej) tonterías
fpl ♦ vt pudrir ♦ vi pudrirse
rota ['rəutə] n (sistema m de) turnos mpl
rotary ['rəutərɪ] adj rotativo
rotate [rəu'teɪt] vt (revolve) hacer girar, dar
vueltas a; (jobs) alternar ♦ vi girar, dar
vueltas; **rotating** adj rotativo; **rotation**
[-'teɪʃən] n rotación f
rotten ['rɒtn] adj (decay) podrido; (dishonest)
corrompido; (inf: bad) pocho; to feel ~ (ill)
sentirse fatal
rotund [rəu'tʌnd] adj regordete
rouble ['ruːbl] (US ruble) n rublo
rough [rʌf] adj (skin, surface) áspero; (terrain)
quebrado; (road) desigual; (voice) bronco;
(person, manner) tosco, grosero; (weather)
borrascoso; (treatment) brutal; (sea) picado;

(town, area) peligroso; (cloth) basto; (plan)
preliminar; (guess) aproximado ♦ n (GOLF): in
the ~ en las hierbas altas; to ~ it vivir sin
comodidades; to sleep ~ (BRIT) pasar la noche
al raso; ~age n fibra(s) f(pl); ~-and-ready
adj improvisado; ~ copy n borrador m;
~ draft n = ~ copy; ~ly adv (handle)
torpemente; (make) toscamente; (speak)
groseramente; (approximately)
aproximadamente; ~ness n (of surface)
aspereza; (of person) rudeza
roulette [ruː'let] n ruleta
Roumania [ruː'meɪnɪə] n = **Rumania**
round [raund] adj redondo ♦ n círculo; (BRIT:
of toast) rebanada; (of policeman) ronda; (of
milkman) recorrido; (of doctor) visitas fpl;
(game: of cards, in competition) partida; (of
ammunition) cartucho; (BOXING) asalto; (of
talks) ronda ♦ vt (corner) doblar ♦ prep
alrededor de; (surrounding): ~ his neck/the
table en su cuello/alrededor de la mesa; (in a
circular movement): to move ~ the room/sail
~ the world dar una vuelta a la habitación/
circumnavigar el mundo; (in various
directions): to move ~ a room/house moverse
por toda la habitación/casa; (approximately)
alrededor de ♦ adv: all ~ por todos lados; the
long way ~ por el camino menos directo; all
the year ~ durante todo el año; it's just ~ the
corner (fig) está a la vuelta de la esquina;
~ the clock adv las 24 horas; to go ~ the back
pasar por atrás; to go ~ to sb's (house) ir a
casa de uno; to go ~ to the back
pasar por atrás; enough to go ~ bastante
(para todos); a ~ of applause una salva de
aplausos; a ~ of drinks/sandwiches una ronda
de bebidas/bocadillos; ~ off vt (speech etc)
acabar, poner término a; ~ up vt (cattle)
acorralar; (people) reunir; (price) redondear;
~about (BRIT) n (AUT) isleta; (at fair) tiovivo
♦ adj (route, means) indirecto; ~ers n
(game) juego similar al béisbol; ~ly adv (fig)
rotundamente; ~ trip n viaje m de ida y
vuelta; ~up n rodeo; (of criminals) redada;
(of news) resumen m
rouse [rauz] vt (wake up) despertar; (stir up)
suscitar; **rousing** adj (cheer, welcome)
caluroso
route [ruːt] n ruta, camino; (of bus) recorrido;
(of shipping) derrota
routine [ruː'tiːn] adj rutinario ♦ n rutina;
(THEATRE) número
rove [rəuv] vt vagar or errar por
row¹ [rəu] n (line) fila, hilera; (KNITTING)
pasada ♦ vi (in boat) remar ♦ vt conducir
remando; 4 days in a ~ 4 días seguidos
row² [rau] n (racket) escándalo; (dispute)
bronca, pelea; (scolding) regaño ♦ vi
pelear(se)
rowboat ['rəubəut] (US) n bote m de remos

rowdy ['raudɪ] adj (person: noisy) ruidoso; (occasion) alborotado

rowing ['rəuɪŋ] n remo; **~ boat** (BRIT) n bote m de remos

royal ['rɔɪəl] adj real; **R~ Air Force** n Fuerzas fpl Aéreas Británicas; **~ty** n (~ persons) familia real; (payment to author) derechos mpl de autor

rpm abbr (= revs per minute) r.p.m.

R.S.V.P. abbr (= répondez s'il vous plaît) SRC

Rt. Hon. abbr (BRIT: = Right Honourable) título honorífico de diputado

rub [rʌb] vt frotar; (scrub) restregar ♦ n: **to give sth a ~** frotar algo; **to ~ sb up** or **~ sb** (US) **the wrong way** entrarle uno por mal ojo; **~ off** vi borrarse; **~ off on** vt fus influir en; **~ out** vt borrar

rubber ['rʌbə*] n caucho, goma; (BRIT: eraser) goma de borrar; **~ band** n goma, gomita; **~ plant** n ficus m

rubbish ['rʌbɪʃ] n basura; (waste) desperdicios mpl; (fig: pej) tonterías fpl; (junk) pacotilla; **~ bin** (BRIT) n cubo (SP) or bote m (AM) de la basura; **~ dump** n vertedero, basurero

rubble ['rʌbl] n escombros mpl

ruble ['ru:bl] (US) n = **rouble**

ruby ['ru:bɪ] n rubí m

rucksack ['rʌksæk] n mochila

rudder ['rʌdə*] n timón m

ruddy ['rʌdɪ] adj (face) rubicundo; (inf: damned) condenado

rude [ru:d] adj (impolite: person) mal educado; (: word, manners) grosero; (crude) crudo; (indecent) indecente; **~ness** n descortesía

ruffle ['rʌfl] vt (hair) despeinar; (clothes) arrugar; (fig: person) alterarse

rug [rʌg] n alfombra; (BRIT: blanket) manta

rugby ['rʌgbɪ] n (also: ~ football) rugby m

rugged ['rʌgɪd] adj (landscape) accidentado; (features) robusto

ruin ['ru:ɪn] n ruina ♦ vt arruinar; (spoil) estropear; **~s** npl ruinas fpl, restos mpl

rule [ru:l] n (norm) norma, costumbre f; (regulation, ruler) regla; (government) dominio ♦ vt (country, person) gobernar ♦ vi gobernar; (LAW) fallar; **as a ~** por regla general; **~ out** vt excluir; **~d** adj (paper) rayado; **~r** n (sovereign) soberano; (for measuring) regla; **ruling** adj (party) gobernante; (class) dirigente ♦ n (LAW) fallo, decisión f

rum [rʌm] n ron m

Rumania [ru:'meɪnɪə] n Rumanía; **~n** adj rumano/a ♦ n rumano/a m/f; (LING) rumano

rumble ['rʌmbl] n (noise) ruido sordo ♦ vi retumbar, hacer un ruido sordo; (stomach, pipe) sonar

rummage ['rʌmɪdʒ] vi (search) hurgar

rumour ['ru:mə*] (US **rumor**) n rumor m ♦ vt: **it is ~ed that ...** se rumorea que ...

rump [rʌmp] n (of animal) ancas fpl, grupa; **~ steak** n filete m de lomo

rumpus ['rʌmpəs] n lío, jaleo

run [rʌn] (pt ran, pp run) n (fast pace): **at a ~** corriendo; (SPORT, in tights) carrera; (outing) paseo, excursión f; (distance travelled) trayecto; (series) serie f; (THEATRE) temporada; (SKI) pista ♦ vt correr; (operate: business) dirigir; (: competition, course) organizar; (: hotel, house) administrar, llevar; (COMPUT) ejecutar; (pass: hand) pasar; (PRESS: feature) publicar ♦ vi correr; (work: machine) funcionar, marchar; (bus, train: operate) circular, ir; (: travel) ir; (continue: play) seguir; (: contract) ser válido; (flow: river) fluir; (colours, washing) desteñirse; (in election) ser candidato; **there was a ~ on** (meat, tickets) hubo mucha demanda de; **in the long ~** a la larga; **on the ~** en fuga; **I'll ~ you to the station** te llevaré a la estación (en coche); **to ~ a risk** correr un riesgo; **to ~ a bath** llenar la bañera; **~ about** or **around** vi (children) correr por todos lados; **~ across** vt fus (find) dar or topar con; **~ away** vi huir; **~ down** vt (production) ir reduciendo; (factory) ir restringiendo la producción en; (subj: car) atropellar; (criticize) criticar; **to be ~ down** (person: tired) estar debilitado; **~ in** (BRIT) vt (car) rodar; **~ into** vt fus (meet: person, trouble) tropezar con; (collide with) chocar con; **~ off** vt (water) dejar correr; (copies) sacar ♦ vi huir corriendo; **~ out** vi (person) salir corriendo; (liquid) irse; (lease) caducar, vencer; (money etc) acabarse; **~ out of** vt fus quedar sin; **~ over** vt (AUT) atropellar ♦ vt fus (revise) repasar; **~ through** vt fus (instructions) repasar; **~ up** vt (debt) contraer; **to ~ up against** (difficulties) tropezar con; **~away** adj (horse) desbocado; (truck) sin frenos; (child) escapado de casa

rung [rʌŋ] pp of **ring** ♦ n (of ladder) escalón m, peldaño

runner ['rʌnə*] n (in race: person) corredor(a) m/f; (: horse) caballo; (on sledge) patín m; **~ bean** n (BRIT) ~ = judía verde; **~-up** n subcampeón/ona m/f

running ['rʌnɪŋ] n (sport) atletismo; (business) administración f ♦ adj (water, costs) corriente; (commentary) continuo; **to be in/out of the ~ for sth** tener/no tener posibilidades de ganar algo; **6 days ~** 6 días seguidos; **~ commentary** n (TV, RADIO) comentario en directo; (on guided tour etc) comentario detallado; **~ costs** npl gastos mpl corrientes

runny ['rʌnɪ] adj fluido; (nose, eyes) gastante
run-of-the-mill adj común y corriente
runt [rʌnt] n (also pej) redrojo, enano
run-up n: ~ to (election etc) período previo a
runway ['rʌnweɪ] n (AVIAT) pista de aterrizaje
rural ['ruərl] adj rural
rush [rʌʃ] n ímpetu m; (hurry) prisa; (COMM) demanda repentina; (current) corriente f fuerte; (of feeling) torrente; (BOT) junco ♦ vt apresurar; (work) hacer de prisa ♦ vi correr, precipitarse; ~ **hour** n horas fpl punta
rusk [rʌsk] n bizcocho tostado
Russia ['rʌʃə] n Rusia; ~**n** adj ruso/a ♦ n ruso/a m/f; (LING) ruso
rust [rʌst] n herrumbre f, moho ♦ vi oxidarse
rustic ['rʌstɪk] adj rústico
rustle ['rʌsl] vi susurrar ♦ vt (paper) hacer crujir
rustproof ['rʌstpruːf] adj inoxidable
rusty ['rʌstɪ] adj oxidado
rut [rʌt] n surco; (ZOOL) celo; **to be in a** ~ ser esclavo de la rutina
ruthless ['ruːθlɪs] adj despiadado
rye [raɪ] n centeno

S, s

Sabbath ['sæbəθ] n domingo; (Jewish) sábado
sabotage ['sæbətɑːʒ] n sabotaje m ♦ vt sabotear
saccharin(e) ['sækərɪn] n sacarina
sachet ['sæʃeɪ] n sobrecito
sack [sæk] n (bag) saco, costal m ♦ vt (dismiss) despedir; (plunder) saquear; **to get the** ~ ser despedido; ~**ing** n despido; (material) arpillera
sacred ['seɪkrɪd] adj sagrado, santo
sacrifice ['sækrɪfaɪs] n sacrificio ♦ vt sacrificar
sad [sæd] adj (unhappy) triste; (deplorable) lamentable
saddle ['sædl] n silla (de montar); (of cycle) sillín m ♦ vt (horse) ensillar; **to be ~d with sth** (inf) quedar cargado con algo; ~**bag** n alforja
sadistic [sə'dɪstɪk] adj sádico
sadly ['sædlɪ] adv lamentablemente; **to be ~ lacking** estar por desgracia carente de
sadness ['sædnɪs] n tristeza
s.a.e. abbr (= stamped addressed envelope) sobre con las propias señas de uno y con sello
safari [sə'fɑːrɪ] n safari m
safe [seɪf] adj (out of danger) fuera de peligro; (not dangerous, sure) seguro; (unharmed) ileso ♦ n caja de caudales, caja fuerte; ~ **and sound** sano y salvo; **(just) to be on the ~ side** para mayor seguridad; ~-**conduct** n salvoconducto; ~-**deposit** n (vault) cámara

acorazada; (box) caja de seguridad; ~**guard** n protección f, garantía ♦ vt proteger, defender; ~**keeping** n custodia; ~**ly** adv seguramente, con seguridad; **to arrive ~ly** llegar bien; ~ **sex** n sexo seguro or sin riesgo
safety ['seɪftɪ] n seguridad f; ~ **belt** n cinturón m (de seguridad); ~ **pin** n imperdible m (SP), seguro (AM); ~ **valve** n válvula de seguridad
saffron ['sæfrən] n azafrán m
sag [sæg] vi aflojarse
sage [seɪdʒ] n (herb) salvia; (man) sabio
Sagittarius [sædʒɪ'tɛərɪəs] n Sagitario
Sahara [sə'hɑːrə] n: **the** ~ (**Desert**) el (desierto del) Sáhara
said [sɛd] pt, pp of **say**
sail [seɪl] n (on boat) vela; (trip): **to go for a** ~ dar un paseo en barco ♦ vt (boat) gobernar ♦ vi (travel: ship) navegar; (SPORT) hacer vela; (begin voyage) salir; **they ~ed into Copenhagen** arribaron a Copenhague; ~ **through** vt fus (exam) aprobar sin ningún problema; ~**boat** n (US) velero, barco de vela; ~**ing** n (SPORT) vela; **to go ~ing** hacer vela; ~**ing boat** n barco de vela; ~**ing ship** n velero; ~**or** n marinero, marino
saint [seɪnt] n santo; ~**ly** adj santo
sake [seɪk] n: **for the** ~ **of** por
salad ['sæləd] n ensalada; ~ **bowl** n ensaladera; ~ **cream** (BRIT) n (especie f de) mayonesa; ~ **dressing** n aliño
salary ['sælərɪ] n sueldo
sale [seɪl] n venta; (at reduced prices) liquidación f, saldo; (at auction) subasta; ~**s** npl (total amount sold) ventas fpl, facturación f; **"for ~"** "se vende"; **on** ~ en venta; **on** ~ **or return** (goods) venta por reposición; ~**room** n sala de subastas; ~**s assistant** (US ~**s clerk**) n dependiente/a m/f; **salesman/woman** (irreg) n (in shop) dependiente/a m/f; (representative) viajante m/f
salmon ['sæmən] n inv salmón m
salon ['sælɔn] n (hairdressing ~) peluquería; (beauty ~) salón m de belleza
saloon [sə'luːn] n (US) bar m, taberna; (BRIT: AUT) (coche m de) turismo; (ship's lounge) cámara, salón m
salt [sɔlt] n sal f ♦ vt salar; (put ~ on) poner sal en; ~ **cellar** n salero; ~**water** adj de agua salada; ~**y** adj salado
salute [sə'luːt] n saludo; (of guns) salva ♦ vt saludar
salvage ['sælvɪdʒ] n (saving) salvamento, recuperación f; (things saved) objetos mpl salvados ♦ vt salvar
salvation [sæl'veɪʃən] n salvación f; **S~ Army** n Ejército de Salvación
same [seɪm] adj mismo ♦ pron: **the** ~ el/la mismo/a, los/las mismos/as; **the** ~ **book** es el

mismo libro que; **at the ~ time** (*at the
~ moment*) al mismo tiempo; (*yet*) sin
embargo; **all** *or* **just the ~** sin embargo, aun
así; **to do the ~ (as sb)** hacer lo mismo (que
uno); **the ~ to you!** ¡igualmente!
sample ['sɑːmpl] *n* muestra ♦ *vt* (*food*)
probar; (*wine*) catar
sanction ['sæŋkʃən] *n* aprobación *f* ♦ *vt*
sancionar; aprobar; **~s** *npl* (*POL*) sanciones *fpl*
sanctity ['sæŋktɪtɪ] *n* santidad *f*; (*inviolability*)
inviolabilidad *f*
sanctuary ['sæŋktjuarɪ] *n* santuario; (*refuge*)
asilo, refugio; (*for wildlife*) reserva
sand [sænd] *n* arena; (*beach*) playa ♦ *vt* (*also:
~ down*) lijar
sandal ['sændl] *n* sandalia
sand: **~box** (*US*) *n* = **~pit**; **~castle** *n* castillo
de arena; **~ dune** *n* duna; **~paper** *n* papel
m de lija; **~pit** *n* (*for children*) cajón *m* de
arena; **~stone** *n* piedra arenisca
sandwich ['sændwɪtʃ] *n* bocadillo (*SP*),
sandwich *m*, emparedado (*AM*) ♦ *vt*
intercalar; **~ed between** apretujado entre;
cheese/ham ~ sandwich de queso/jamón;
~ course (*BRIT*) *n* curso de medio tiempo
sandy ['sændɪ] *adj* arenoso; (*colour*) rojizo
sane [seɪn] *adj* cuerdo; (*sensible*) sensato
sang [sæŋ] *pt of* **sing**
sanitary ['sænɪtərɪ] *adj* sanitario; (*clean*)
higiénico; **~ towel** (*US* **~ napkin**) *n* paño
higiénico, compresa
sanitation [sænɪ'teɪʃən] *n* (*in house*) servicios
mpl higiénicos; (*in town*) servicio de
desinfección; **~ department** (*US*) *n*
departamento de limpieza y recogida de
basuras
sanity ['sænɪtɪ] *n* cordura; (*of judgment*)
sensatez *f*
sank [sæŋk] *pt of* **sink**
Santa Claus [sæntə'klɔːz] *n* San Nicolás,
Papá Noel
sap [sæp] *n* (*of plants*) savia ♦ *vt* (*strength*)
minar, agotar
sapling ['sæplɪŋ] *n* árbol nuevo *or* joven
sapphire ['sæfaɪə*] *n* zafiro
sarcasm ['sɑːkæzm] *n* sarcasmo
sardine [sɑː'diːn] *n* sardina
Sardinia [sɑː'dɪnɪə] *n* Cerdeña
sash [sæʃ] *n* faja
sat [sæt] *pt, pp of* **sit**
Satan ['seɪtn] *n* Satanás *m*
satchel ['sætʃl] *n* (*child's*) cartera (*SP*),
mochila (*AM*)
satellite ['sætəlaɪt] *n* satélite *m*; **~ dish** *n*
antena de televisión por satélite;
~ television *n* televisión *f* vía satélite
satin ['sætɪn] *n* raso ♦ *adj* de raso
satire ['sætaɪə*] *n* sátira
satisfaction [sætɪs'fækʃən] *n* satisfacción *f*

satisfactory [sætɪs'fæktərɪ] *adj* satisfactorio
satisfy ['sætɪsfaɪ] *vt* satisfacer; (*convince*)
convencer; **~ing** *adj* satisfactorio
Saturday ['sætədɪ] *n* sábado
sauce [sɔːs] *n* salsa; (*sweet*) crema; jarabe *m*;
~pan *n* cacerola, olla
saucer ['sɔːsə*] *n* platillo
Saudi ['saudɪ]: **~ Arabia** *n* Arabia Saudí *or*
Saudita; **~ (Arabian)** *adj*, *n* saudí *m/f*,
saudita *m/f*
sauna ['sɔːnə] *n* sauna
saunter ['sɔːntə*] *vi*: **to ~ in/out** entrar/salir
sin prisa
sausage ['sɔsɪdʒ] *n* salchicha; **~ roll** *n*
empanadita de salchicha
sauté ['səuteɪ] *adj* salteado
savage ['sævɪdʒ] *adj* (*cruel, fierce*) feroz,
furioso; (*primitive*) salvaje ♦ *n* salvaje *m/f* ♦ *vt*
(*attack*) embestir
save [seɪv] *vt* (*rescue*) salvar, rescatar; (*money,
time*) ahorrar; (*put by, keep: seat*) guardar;
(*COMPUT*) salvar (y guardar); (*avoid: trouble*)
evitar; (*SPORT*) parar ♦ *vi* (*also: ~ up*) ahorrar
♦ *n* (*SPORT*) parada ♦ *prep* salvo, excepto
saving ['seɪvɪŋ] *n* (*on price etc*) economía
♦ *adj*: **the ~ grace of** el único mérito de; **~s**
npl ahorros *mpl*; **~s account** *n* cuenta de
ahorros; **~s bank** *n* caja de ahorros
saviour ['seɪvjə*] (*US* **savior**) *n* salvador(a)
m/f
savour ['seɪvə*] (*US* **savor**) *vt* saborear; **~y** *adj*
sabroso; (*dish: not sweet*) salado
saw [sɔː] (*pt* **sawed**, *pp* **sawed** *or* **sawn**) *pt of*
see ♦ *n* (*tool*) sierra ♦ *vt* serrar; **~dust** *n*
(a)serrín *m*; **~mill** *n* aserradero; **~n-off
shotgun** *n* escopeta de cañones recortados
saxophone ['sæksəfəun] *n* saxófono
say [seɪ] (*pt, pp* **said**) *n*: **to have one's ~**
expresar su opinión ♦ *vt* decir; **to have a** *or*
some ~ in sth tener voz *or* tener que ver en
algo; **to ~ yes/no** decir que sí/no; **could you
~ that again?** ¿podría repetir eso?; **that is to ~**
es decir; **that goes without ~ing** ni que decir
tiene; **~ing** *n* dicho, refrán *m*
scab [skæb] *n* costra; (*pej*) esquirol *m*
scaffold ['skæfəuld] *n* cadalso; **~ing** *n*
andamio, andamiaje *m*
scald [skɔːld] *n* escaldadura ♦ *vt* escaldar
scale [skeɪl] *n* (*gen, MUS*) escala; (*of fish*)
escama; (*of salaries, fees etc*) escalafón *m* ♦ *vt*
(*mountain*) escalar; (*tree*) trepar; **~s** *npl* (*for
weighing: small*) balanza; (*: large*) báscula; **on
a large ~** en gran escala; **~ of charges** tarifa,
lista de precios; **~ down** *vt* reducir a escala
scallop ['skɒləp] *n* (*ZOOL*) venera; (*SEWING*)
festón *m*
scalp [skælp] *n* cabellera ♦ *vt* escalpar
scampi ['skæmpɪ] *npl* gambas *fpl*
scan [skæn] *vt* (*examine*) escudriñar; (*glance*

at quickly) dar un vistazo a; *(TV, RADAR)* explorar, registrar ♦ *n (MED)*: **to have a ~** pasar por el escáner

scandal ['skændl] *n* escándalo; *(gossip)* chismes *mpl*

Scandinavia [skændɪ'neɪvɪə] *n* Escandinavia; **~n** *adj, n* escandinavo/a *m/f*

scant [skænt] *adj* escaso; **~y** *adj (meal)* insuficiente; *(clothes)* ligero

scapegoat ['skeɪpgəʊt] *n* cabeza de turco, chivo expiatorio

scar [skɑ:] *n* cicatriz *f; (fig)* señal *f* ♦ *vt* dejar señales en

scarce [skɛəs] *adj* escaso; **to make o.s. ~** *(inf)* esfumarse; **~ly** *adv* apenas; **scarcity** *n* escasez *f*

scare [skɛə*] *n* susto, sobresalto; *(panic)* pánico ♦ *vt* asustar, espantar; **to ~ stiff** dar a uno un susto de muerte; **bomb ~** amenaza de bomba; **~ off** *or* **away** *vt* ahuyentar; **~crow** *n* espantapájaros *m inv*; **~d** *adj*: **to be ~d** estar asustado

scarf [skɑ:f] *(pl* **~s** *or* **scarves)** *n (long)* bufanda; *(square)* pañuelo

scarlet ['skɑ:lɪt] *adj* escarlata; **~ fever** *n* escarlatina

scarves [skɑ:vz] *npl of* **scarf**

scary ['skɛərɪ] *(inf)* adj espeluznante

scathing ['skeɪðɪŋ] *adj* mordaz

scatter ['skætə*] *vt (spread)* esparcir, desparramar; *(put to flight)* dispersar ♦ *vi* desparramarse; dispersarse; **~brained** *adj* ligero de cascos

scavenger ['skævəndʒə*] *n (person)* basurero/a

scenario [sɪ'nɑ:rɪəʊ] *n (THEATRE)* argumento; *(CINEMA)* guión *m; (fig)* escenario

scene [si:n] *n (THEATRE, film etc)* escena; *(of crime etc)* escenario; *(view)* panorama *m; (fuss)* escándalo; **~ry** *n (THEATRE)* decorado; *(landscape)* paisaje *m;* **scenic** *adj* pintoresco

scent [sɛnt] *n* perfume *m,* olor *m; (fig: track)* rastro, pista

sceptic ['skɛptɪk] *(US* **skeptic)** *n* escéptico/a; **~al** *adj* escéptico

sceptre ['sɛptə*] *(US* **scepter)** *n* cetro

schedule ['ʃɛdju:l, *(US)* 'skɛdju:l] *n (timetable)* horario; *(of events)* programa *m; (list)* lista ♦ *vt (visit)* fijar la hora de; **to arrive on ~** llegar a la hora debida; **to be ahead of/ behind ~** estar adelantado/en retraso; **~d flight** *n* vuelo regular

scheme [ski:m] *n (plan)* plan *m,* proyecto; *(plot)* intriga; *(arrangement)* disposición *f; (pension ~ etc)* sistema *m* ♦ *vi (intrigue)* intrigar; **scheming** *adj* intrigante ♦ *n* intrigas *fpl*

schizophrenic [skɪtsə'frɛnɪk] *adj* esquizofrénico

scholar ['skɔlə*] *n (pupil)* alumno/a; *(learned person)* sabio/a, erudito/a; **~ship** *n* erudición *f; (grant)* beca

school [sku:l] *n* escuela, colegio; *(in university)* facultad *f* ♦ *cpd* escolar; **~ age** *n* edad *f* escolar; **~book** *n* libro de texto; **~boy** *n* alumno; **~ children** *npl* alumnos *mpl*; **~girl** *n* alumna; **~ing** *n* enseñanza; **~master/mistress** *n (primary)* maestro/a; *(secondary)* profesor(a) *m/f*; **~teacher** *n (primary)* maestro/a; *(secondary)* profesor(a) *m/f*

schooner ['sku:nə*] *n (ship)* goleta

sciatica [saɪ'ætɪkə] *n* ciática

science ['saɪəns] *n* ciencia; **~ fiction** *n* ciencia-ficción *f;* **scientific** [-'tɪfɪk] *adj* científico; **scientist** *n* científico/a

scissors ['sɪzəz] *npl* tijeras *fpl;* **a pair of ~** unas tijeras

scoff [skɔf] *vt (BRIT: inf: eat)* engullir ♦ *vi*: **to ~ (at)** *(mock)* mofarse (de)

scold [skəʊld] *vt* regañar

scone [skɔn] *n* pastel de pan

scoop [sku:p] *n (for flour etc)* pala; *(PRESS)* exclusiva; **~ out** *vt* excavar; **~ up** *vt* recoger

scooter ['sku:tə*] *n* moto *f; (toy)* patinete *m*

scope [skəʊp] *n (of plan)* ámbito; *(of person)* competencia; *(opportunity)* libertad *f* (de acción)

scorch [skɔ:tʃ] *vt (clothes)* chamuscar; *(earth, grass)* quemar, secar

score [skɔ:*] *n (points etc)* puntuación *f; (MUS)* partitura; *(twenty)* veintena ♦ *vt (goal, point)* ganar; *(mark)* rayar; *(achieve: success)* conseguir ♦ *vi* marcar un tanto; *(FOOTBALL)* marcar (un) gol; *(keep score)* llevar el tanteo; **~s of** *(very many)* decenas de; **on that ~** en lo que se refiere a eso; **to ~ 6 out of 10** obtener una puntuación de 6 sobre 10; **~ out** *vt* tachar; **~ over** *vt fus* obtener una victoria sobre; **~board** *n* marcador *m*

scorn [skɔ:n] *n* desprecio; **~ful** *adj* desdeñoso, despreciativo

Scorpio ['skɔ:pɪəʊ] *n* Escorpión *m*

scorpion ['skɔ:pɪən] *n* alacrán *m*

Scot [skɔt] *n* escocés/esa *m/f*

Scotch [skɔtʃ] *n* whisky *m* escocés

Scotland ['skɔtlənd] *n* Escocia

Scots [skɔts] *adj* escocés/esa; **~man/woman** *(irreg)* *n* escocés/esa *m/f*; **Scottish** ['skɔtɪʃ] *adj* escocés/esa; **Scottish Parliament** *n* Parlamento escocés

scoundrel ['skaʊndrl] *n* canalla *m/f,* sinvergüenza *m/f*

scout [skaʊt] *n (MIL, also: boy ~)* explorador *m; (girl ~ = (US)* niña exploradora; **~ around** *vi* reconocer el terreno

scowl [skaʊl] *vi* fruncir el ceño; **to ~ at sb** mirar con ceño a uno

scrabble ['skræbl] vi (claw): **to ~ (at)** arañar; (also: **to ~ around**: search) revolver todo buscando ♦ n: **S~** ® Scrabble ® m

scraggy ['skrægɪ] adj descarnado

scram [skræm] (inf) vi largarse

scramble ['skræmbl] n (climb) subida (difícil); (struggle) pelea ♦ vi: **to ~ through/ out** abrirse paso/salir con dificultad; **to ~ for** pelear por; **~d eggs** npl huevos mpl revueltos

scrap [skræp] n (bit) pedacito; (fig) pizca; (fight) riña, bronca; (also: ~ iron) chatarra, hierro viejo ♦ vt (discard) desechar, descartar ♦ vi reñir, armar (una) bronca; **~s** npl (waste) sobras fpl, desperdicios mpl; **~book** n álbum m de recortes; **~ dealer** n chatarrero/a

scrape [skreɪp] n: **to get into a ~** meterse en un lío ♦ vt raspar; (skin etc) rasguñar; (~ against) rozar ♦ vi: **to ~ through** (exam) aprobar por los pelos; **~ together** vt (money) arañar, juntar

scrap: ~ heap n (fig): **to be on the ~ heap** estar acabado; **~ merchant** (BRIT) n chatarrero/a; **~ paper** n pedazos mpl de papel

scratch [skrætʃ] n rasguño; (from claw) arañazo ♦ cpd: **~ team** equipo improvisado ♦ vt (paint, car) rayar; (with claw, nail) rasguñar, arañar; (rub: nose etc) rascarse ♦ vi rascarse; **to start from ~** partir de cero; **to be up to ~** cumplir con los requisitos

scrawl [skrɔːl] n garabatos mpl ♦ vi hacer garabatos

scrawny ['skrɔːnɪ] adj flaco

scream [skriːm] n chillido ♦ vi chillar

screech [skriːtʃ] vi chirriar

screen [skriːn] n (CINEMA, TV) pantalla; (movable barrier) biombo ♦ vt (conceal) tapar; (from the wind etc) proteger; (film) proyectar; (candidates etc) investigar a; **~ing** n (MED) investigación f médica; **~play** n guión m

screw [skruː] n tornillo ♦ vt (also: ~ in) atornillar; **~ up** vt (paper etc) arrugar; **to ~ up one's eyes** arrugar el entrecejo; **~driver** n destornillador m

scribble ['skrɪbl] n garabatos mpl ♦ vt, vi garabatear

script [skrɪpt] n (CINEMA etc) guión m; (writing) escritura, letra

Scripture(s) ['skrɪptʃə*(z)] n(pl) Sagrada Escritura

scroll [skrəʊl] n rollo

scrounge [skraʊndʒ] (inf) vt: **to ~ sth off or from sb** obtener algo de uno de gorra ♦ n: **on the ~** de gorra; **~r** n gorrón/ona m/f

scrub [skrʌb] n (land) maleza ♦ vt fregar, restregar; (inf: reject) cancelar, anular

scruff [skrʌf] n: **by the ~ of the neck** por el pescuezo

scruffy ['skrʌfɪ] adj desaliñado, piojoso

scrum(mage) ['skrʌm(mɪdʒ)] n (RUGBY) melée f

scruple ['skruːpl] n (gen pl) escrúpulo

scrutinize ['skruːtɪnaɪz] vt escudriñar; (votes) escrutar; **scrutiny** ['skruːtɪnɪ] n escrutinio, examen m

scuff [skʌf] vt (shoes, floor) rayar

scuffle ['skʌfl] n refriega

sculptor ['skʌlptə*] n escultor(a) m/f

sculpture ['skʌlptʃə*] n escultura

scum [skʌm] n (on liquid) espuma; (pej: people) escoria

scurry ['skʌrɪ] vi correr; **to ~ off** escabullirse

scuttle ['skʌtl] n (also: coal ~) cubo, carbonera ♦ vt (ship) barrenar ♦ vi (scamper): **to ~ away, ~ off** escabullirse

scythe [saɪð] n guadaña

SDP (BRIT) n abbr = Social Democratic Party

sea [siː] n mar m ♦ cpd de mar, marítimo; **by ~** (travel) en barco; **on the ~** (boat) en el mar; (town) junto al mar; **to be all at ~** (fig) estar despistado; **out to ~, at ~** en alta mar; **~board** n litoral m; **~food** n mariscos mpl; **~ front** n paseo marítimo; **~-going** adj de altura; **~gull** n gaviota

seal [siːl] n (animal) foca; (stamp) sello ♦ vt (close) cerrar; **~ off** vt (area) acordonar

sea level n nivel m del mar

sea lion n león m marino

seam [siːm] n costura; (of metal) juntura; (of coal) veta, filón m

seaman ['siːmən] (irreg) n marinero

seance ['seɪɒns] n sesión f de espiritismo

seaplane ['siːpleɪn] n hidroavión m

seaport ['siːpɔːt] n puerto de mar

search [sɜːtʃ] n (for person, thing) busca, búsqueda; (COMPUT) búsqueda; (inspection: of sb's home) registro ♦ vt (look in) buscar en; (examine) examinar; (person, place) registrar ♦ vi: **to ~ for** buscar; **in ~ of** en busca de; **~ through** vt fus registrar; **~ing** adj penetrante; **~light** n reflector m; **~ party** n pelotón m de salvamento; **~ warrant** n mandamiento (judicial)

sea: ~shore n playa, orilla del mar; **~sick** adj mareado; **~side** n playa, orilla del mar; **~side resort** n centro turístico costero

season ['siːzn] n (of year) estación f; (sporting etc) temporada; (of films etc) ciclo ♦ vt (food) sazonar; **in/out of ~** en sazón/ fuera de temporada; **~al** adj estacional; **~ed** adj (fig) experimentado; **~ing** n condimento, aderezo; **~ ticket** n abono

seat [siːt] n (in bus, train) asiento; (chair) silla; (PARLIAMENT) escaño; (buttocks) culo, trasero; (of trousers) culera ♦ vt sentar; (have room for) tener cabida para; **to be ~ed** sentarse; **~ belt** n cinturón m de seguridad

sea water → sell

370

sea: ~ **water** *n* agua del mar; ~**weed** *n* alga marina; ~**worthy** *adj* en condiciones de navegar

sec. *abbr* = **second(s)**

secluded [sɪ'kluːdɪd] *adj* retirado

seclusion [sɪ'kluːʒən] *n* reclusión *f*

second ['sekənd] *adj* segundo ♦ *adv* en segundo lugar ♦ *n* segundo; (*AUT: also:* ~ *gear*) segunda; (*COMM*) artículo con algún desperfecto; (*BRIT: SCOL: degree*) título de licenciado con calificación de notable ♦ *vt* (*motion*) apoyar; ~**ary** *adj* secundario; ~**ary school** *n* escuela secundaria; ~-**class** *adj* de segunda clase ♦ *adv* (*RAIL*) en segunda; ~**hand** *adj* de segunda mano, usado; ~ **hand** *n* (*on clock*) segundero; ~**ly** *adv* en segundo lugar; ~**ment** [sɪ'kɔndmənt] (*BRIT*) *n* traslado temporal; ~-**rate** *adj* de segunda categoría; ~ **thoughts** *npl*: **to have** ~ **thoughts** cambiar de opinión; **on** ~ **thoughts** *or* **thought** (*US*) pensándolo bien

secrecy ['siːkrəsɪ] *n* secreto

secret ['siːkrɪt] *adj, n* secreto; **in** ~ en secreto

secretarial [sekrɪ'tɛərɪəl] *adj* de secretario; (*course, staff*) de secretariado

secretary ['sekrətərɪ] *n* secretario/a; **S~ of State (for)** (*BRIT: POL*) Ministro (de)

secretive ['siːkrətɪv] *adj* reservado, sigiloso

secretly ['siːkrɪtlɪ] *adv* en secreto

sect [sekt] *n* secta; ~**arian** [-'tɛərɪən] *adj* sectario

section ['sekʃən] *n* sección *f*; (*part*) parte *f*; (*of document*) artículo; (*of opinion*) sector *m*; (*cross-*~) corte *m* transversal

sector ['sektə*] *n* sector *m*

secular ['sekjulə*] *adj* secular, seglar

secure [sɪ'kjuə*] *adj* seguro; (*firmly fixed*) firme, fijo ♦ *vt* (*fix*) asegurar, afianzar; (*get*) conseguir

security [sɪ'kjuərɪtɪ] *n* seguridad *f*; (*for loan*) fianza; (: *object*) prenda

sedate [sɪ'deɪt] *adj* tranquilo ♦ *vt* tratar con sedantes

sedation [sɪ'deɪʃən] *n* (*MED*) sedación *f*

sedative ['sedɪtɪv] *n* sedante *m*, sedativo

seduce [sɪ'djuːs] *vt* seducir; **seduction** [-'dʌkʃən] *n* seducción *f*; **seductive** [-'dʌktɪv] *adj* seductor(a)

see [siː] (*pt* **saw**, *pp* **seen**) *vt* ver; (*accompany*): **to** ~ **sb to the door** acompañar a uno a la puerta; (*understand*) ver, comprender ♦ *vi* ver ♦ *n* (*arz*)obispado; **to** ~ **that** (*ensure*) asegurar que; ~ **you soon!** ¡hasta pronto!; ~ **about** *vt fus* atender a, encargarse de; ~ **off** *vt* despedir; ~ **through** *vt fus* (*fig*) calar ♦ *vt* (*plan*) llevar a cabo; ~ **to** *vt fus* atender a, encargarse de

seed [siːd] *n* semilla; (*in fruit*) pepita; (*fig: gen pl*) germen *m*; (*TENNIS etc*) preseleccionado/

a; **to go to** ~ (*plant*) granar; (*fig*) descuidarse; ~**ling** *n* planta de semillero; ~**y** *adj* (*shabby*) desaseado, raído

seeing ['siːɪŋ] *conj*: ~ (**that**) visto que, en vista de que

seek [siːk] (*pt, pp* **sought**) *vt* buscar; (*post*) solicitar

seem [siːm] *vi* parecer; **there** ~**s to be ...** parece que hay ...; ~**ingly** *adv* aparentemente, según parece

seen [siːn] *pp of* **see**

seep [siːp] *vi* filtrarse

seesaw ['siːsɔː] *n* subibaja

seethe [siːð] *vi* hervir; **to** ~ **with anger** estar furioso

see-through *adj* transparente

segment ['segmənt] *n* (*part*) sección *f*; (*of orange*) gajo

segregate ['segrɪgeɪt] *vt* segregar

seize [siːz] *vt* (*grasp*) agarrar, asir; (*take possession of*) secuestrar; (: *territory*) apoderarse de; (*opportunity*) aprovecharse de; ~ (**up**)**on** *vt fus* aprovechar; ~ **up** *vi* (*TECH*) agarrotarse

seizure ['siːʒə*] *n* (*MED*) ataque *m*; (*LAW, of power*) incautación *f*

seldom ['seldəm] *adv* rara vez

select [sɪ'lekt] *adj* selecto, escogido ♦ *vt* escoger, elegir; (*SPORT*) seleccionar; ~**ion** [-'lekʃən] *n* selección *f*, elección *f*; (*COMM*) surtido

self [self] (*pl* **selves**) *n* uno mismo; **the** ~ el yo ♦ *prefix* auto...; ~-**assured** *adj* seguro de sí mismo; ~-**catering** (*BRIT*) *adj* (*flat etc*) con cocina; ~-**centred** (*US* ~-**centered**) *adj* egocéntrico; ~-**confidence** *n* confianza en sí mismo; ~-**conscious** *adj* cohibido; ~-**contained** (*BRIT*) *adj* (*flat*) con entrada particular; ~-**control** *n* autodominio; ~-**defence** (*US* ~-**defense**) *n* defensa propia; ~-**discipline** *n* autodisciplina; ~-**employed** *adj* que trabaja por cuenta propia; ~-**evident** *adj* patente; ~-**governing** *adj* autónomo; ~-**indulgent** *adj* autocomplaciente; ~-**interest** *n* egoísmo; ~-**ish** *adj* egoísta; ~**ishness** *n* egoísmo; ~**less** *adj* desinteresado; ~-**made** *adj*: ~-**made man** hombre *m* que se ha hecho a sí mismo; ~-**pity** *n* lástima de sí mismo; ~-**portrait** *n* autorretrato; ~-**possessed** *adj* sereno, dueño de sí mismo; ~-**preservation** *n* propia conservación *f*; ~-**respect** *n* amor *m* propio; ~-**righteous** *adj* santurrón/ona; ~-**sacrifice** *n* abnegación *f*; ~-**satisfied** *adj* satisfecho de sí mismo; ~-**service** *adj* de autoservicio; ~-**sufficient** *adj* autosuficiente; ~-**taught** *adj* autodidacta

sell [sel] (*pt, pp* **sold**) *vt* vender ♦ *vi* venderse; **to** ~ **at** *or* **for £10** venderse a 10 libras; ~ **off** *vt* liquidar; ~ **out** *vi*: **to** ~ **out of tickets/milk**

vender todas las entradas/toda la leche; **~-by date** n fecha de caducidad; **~er** n vendedor(a) m/f; **~ing price** n precio de venta

Sellotape ® ['seləuteɪp] (BRIT) n cinta adhesiva, celo (SP), scotch m (AM)

selves [selvz] npl of **self**

semblance ['sembləns] n apariencia

semen ['siːmən] n semen m

semester [sɪ'mestə*] (US) n semestre m

semi... [semɪ] prefix semi..., medio...; **~circle** n semicírculo; **~colon** n punto y coma; **~conductor** n semiconductor m; **~detached (house)** n (casa) semiseparada; **~final** n semi-final m

seminar ['semɪnɑː*] n seminario

seminary ['semɪnərɪ] n (REL) seminario

semiskilled ['semɪskɪld] adj (work, worker) semi-cualificado

semi-skimmed (milk) n leche semidesnatada

senate ['senɪt] n senado; **senator** n senador(a) m/f

send [send] (pt, pp sent) vt mandar, enviar; (signal) transmitir; **~ away** vt despachar; **~ away for** vt fus pedir; **~ back** vt devolver; **~ for** vt fus mandar traer; **~ off** vt (goods) despachar; (BRIT: SPORT: player) expulsar; **~ out** vt (invitation) mandar; (signal) emitir; **~ up** vt (person, price) hacer subir; (BRIT: parody) parodiar; **~er** n remitente m/f; **~-off** n: **a good ~-off** una buena despedida

senior ['siːnɪə*] adj (older) mayor, más viejo; (: on staff) de más antigüedad; (of higher rank) superior; **~ citizen** n persona de la tercera edad; **~ity** [-'ɔrɪtɪ] n antigüedad f

sensation [sen'seɪʃən] n sensación f; **~al** adj sensacional

sense [sens] n (faculty, meaning) sentido; (feeling) sensación f; (good ~) sentido común, juicio ♦ vt sentir, percibir; **it makes ~** tiene sentido; **~less** adj estúpido, insensato; (unconscious) sin conocimiento; **~ of humour** n sentido del humor

sensible ['sensɪbl] adj sensato; (reasonable) razonable, lógico

sensitive ['sensɪtɪv] adj sensible; (touchy) susceptible

sensual ['sensjuəl] adj sensual

sensuous ['sensjuəs] adj sensual

sent [sent] pt, pp of **send**

sentence ['sentns] n (LING) oración f; (LAW) sentencia, fallo ♦ vt: **to ~ sb to death/to 5 years (in prison)** condenar a uno a muerte/a 5 años de cárcel

sentiment ['sentɪmənt] n sentimiento; (opinion) opinión f; **~al** [-'mentl] adj sentimental

sentry ['sentrɪ] n centinela m

separate [adj 'seprɪt, vb 'sepəreɪt] adj separado; (distinct) distinto ♦ vt separar; (part) dividir ♦ vi separarse; **~s** npl (clothes) coordinados mpl; **~ly** adv por separado; **separation** [-'reɪʃən] n separación f

September [sep'tembə*] n se(p)tiembre m

septic ['septɪk] adj séptico; **~ tank** n fosa séptica

sequel ['siːkwl] n consecuencia, resultado; (of story) continuación f

sequence ['siːkwəns] n sucesión f, serie f; (CINEMA) secuencia

sequin ['siːkwɪn] n lentejuela

serene [sɪ'riːn] adj sereno, tranquilo

sergeant ['sɑːdʒənt] n sargento

serial ['sɪərɪəl] n (TV) telenovela, serie f televisiva; (BOOK) serie f; **~ize** vt emitir como serial; **~ killer** n asesino/a múltiple; **~ number** n número de serie

series ['sɪərɪːz] n inv serie f

serious ['sɪərɪəs] adj serio; (grave) grave; **~ly** adv en serio; (ill, wounded etc) gravemente

sermon ['səːmən] n sermón m

serrated [sɪ'reɪtɪd] adj serrado, dentellado

serum ['sɪərəm] n suero

servant ['səːvənt] n servidor(a) m/f; (house ~) criado/a

serve [səːv] vt servir; (customer) atender; (subj: train) pasar por; (apprenticeship) hacer; (prison term) cumplir ♦ vi (al table) servir; (TENNIS) sacar; **to ~ as/for/to do** servir de/para/para hacer ♦ n (TENNIS) saque m; **it ~s him right** se lo tiene merecido; **~ out** vt (food) servir; **~ up** vt = **~ out**

service ['səːvɪs] n servicio; (REL) misa; (AUT) mantenimiento; (dishes etc) juego ♦ vt (car etc) revisar; (: repair) reparar; **the S~s** npl las fuerzas armadas; **to be of ~ to sb** ser útil a uno; **~ included/not included** servicio incluido/no incluido; **~able** adj servible, utilizable; **~ area** n (on motorway) area de servicio; **~ charge** (BRIT) n servicio; **~man** n militar m; **~ station** n estación f de servicio

serviette [səːvɪ'et] (BRIT) n servilleta

session ['seʃən] n sesión f; **to be in ~** estar en sesión

set [set] (pt, pp set) n juego; (RADIO) aparato; (TV) televisor m; (of utensils) batería; (of cutlery) cubierto; (of books) colección f; (TENNIS) set m; (group of people) grupo; (CINEMA) plató m; (THEATRE) decorado; (HAIRDRESSING) marcado ♦ adj (fixed) fijo; (ready) listo ♦ vt (place) poner, colocar; (fix) fijar; (adjust) ajustar, arreglar; (decide: rules etc) establecer, decidir ♦ vi (sun) ponerse; (jam, jelly) cuajarse; (concrete) fraguar; (bone) componerse; **to be ~ on doing sth** estar empeñado en hacer algo; **to ~ to music** poner música a; **to ~ on fire** incendiar, poner fuego a; **to ~ free** poner en libertad; **to ~ sth going** poner algo en marcha; **to ~ sail** zarpar, hacerse a la vela; **~ about** *vt fus* ponerse a; **~ aside** *vt* poner aparte, dejar de lado; (*money, time*) reservar; **~ back** *vt* (*cost*): **to ~ sb back £5** costar a uno cinco libras; (: *in time*): **to ~ back (by)** retrasar (por); **~ off** *vi* partir ♦ *vt* (*bomb*) hacer estallar; (*events*) poner en marcha; (*show up well*) hacer resaltar; **~ out** *vi* partir ♦ *vt* (*arrange*) disponer; (*state*) exponer; **to ~ out to do sth** proponerse hacer algo; **~ up** *vt* establecer; **~back** *n* revés *m*, contratiempo; **~ menu** *n* menú *m*

settee [se'ti:] *n* sofá *m*

setting ['setıŋ] *n* (*scenery*) marco *m*; (*position*) disposición *f*; (*of sun*) puesta; (*of jewel*) engaste *m*, montadura

settle ['setl] *vt* (*argument*) resolver; (*accounts*) ajustar, liquidar; (*MED: calm*) calmar, sosegar ♦ *vi* (*dust etc*) depositarse; (*weather*) serenarse; (*also: ~ down*) instalarse; tranquilizarse; **to ~ for sth** convenir en aceptar algo; **to ~ on sth** decidirse por algo; **~ in** *vi* instalarse; **~ up** *vi*: **to ~ up with sb** ajustar cuentas con uno; **~ment** *n* (*payment*) liquidación *f*; (*agreement*) acuerdo, convenio; (*village etc*) pueblo; **~r** *n* colono/a, colonizador(a) *m/f*

setup ['setʌp] *n* sistema *m*; (*situation*) situación *f*

seven ['sevn] *num* siete; **~teen** *num* diez y siete, diecisiete; **~th** *num* séptimo; **~ty** *num* setenta

sever ['sevə*] *vt* cortar; (*relations*) romper

several ['sevərl] *adj, pron* varios/as *m/fpl*, algunos/as *m/fpl*; **~ of us** varios de nosotros

severance ['sevərəns] *n* (*of relations*) ruptura; **~ pay** *n* indemnización *f* por despido

severe [sı'vıə*] *adj* severo; (*serious*) grave; (*hard*) duro; (*pain*) intenso; **severity** [sı'verıtı] *n* severidad *f*; gravedad *f*; intensidad *f*

sew [səu] (*pt* **sewed**, *pp* **sewn**) *vt, vi* coser; **~ up** *vt* coser, zurcir

sewage ['su:ıdʒ] *n* aguas *fpl* residuales

sewer ['su:ə*] *n* alcantarilla, cloaca

sewing ['səuıŋ] *n* costura; **~ machine** *n* máquina de coser

sewn [səun] *pp of* **sew**

sex [seks] *n* sexo; (*lovemaking*): **to have ~** hacer el amor; **~ist** *adj, n* sexista *m/f*; **~ual** ['seksjuəl] *adj* sexual; **~y** *adj* sexy

shabby ['ʃæbı] *adj* (*person*) desharrapado; (*clothes*) raído, gastado; (*behaviour*) ruin *inv*

shack [ʃæk] *n* choza, chabola

shackles ['ʃæklz] *npl* grillos *mpl*, grilletes *mpl*

shade [ʃeıd] *n* sombra; (*for lamp*) pantalla;

(*for eyes*) visera; (*of colour*) matiz *m*, tonalidad *f*; (*small quantity*): **a ~ (too big/more)** un poquitín (grande/más) ♦ *vt* dar sombra a; (*eyes*) proteger del sol; **in the ~** en la sombra

shadow ['ʃædəu] *n* sombra ♦ *vt* (*follow*) seguir y vigilar; **~ cabinet** (*BRIT*) *n* (*POL*) gabinete paralelo formado por el partido de oposición; **~y** *adj* oscuro; (*dim*) indistinto

shady ['ʃeıdı] *adj* sombreado; (*fig: dishonest*) sospechoso; (: *deal*) turbio

shaft [ʃɑ:ft] *n* (*of arrow, spear*) astil *m*; (*AUT, TECH*) eje *m*, árbol *m*; (*of mine*) pozo; (*of lift*) hueco, caja; (*of light*) rayo

shaggy ['ʃægı] *adj* peludo

shake [ʃeık] (*pt* **shook**, *pp* **shaken**) *vt* sacudir; (*building*) hacer temblar; (*bottle, cocktail*) agitar ♦ *vi* (*tremble*) temblar; **to ~ one's head** (*in refusal*) negar con la cabeza; (*in dismay*) mover *or* menear la cabeza, incrédulo; **to ~ hands with sb** estrechar la mano a uno; **~ off** *vt* sacudirse; (*fig*) deshacerse de; **~ up** *vt* agitar; (*fig*) reorganizar; **shaky** *adj* (*hand, voice*) trémulo; (*building*) inestable

shall [ʃæl] *aux vb*: **~ I help you?** ¿quieres que te ayude?; **I'll buy three, ~ I?** compro tres, ¿no te parece?

shallow ['ʃæləu] *adj* poco profundo; (*fig*) superficial

sham [ʃæm] *n* fraude *m*, engaño ♦ *vt* fingir, simular

shambles ['ʃæmblz] *n* confusión *f*

shame [ʃeım] *n* vergüenza ♦ *vt* avergonzar; **it is a ~ that/to do** es una lástima que/hacer; **what a ~!** ¡qué lástima!; **~ful** *adj* vergonzoso; **~less** *adj* desvergonzado

shampoo [ʃæm'pu:] *n* champú *m* ♦ *vt* lavar con champú; **~ and set** *n* lavado y marcado

shamrock ['ʃæmrɔk] *n* trébol *m* (*emblema nacional irlandés*)

shandy ['ʃændı] *n* mezcla de cerveza con gaseosa

shan't [ʃɑ:nt] = **shall not**

shantytown ['ʃæntıtaun] *n* barrio de chabolas

shape [ʃeıp] *n* forma ♦ *vt* formar, dar forma a; (*sb's ideas*) formar; (*sb's life*) determinar; **to take ~** tomar forma; **~ up** *vi* (*events*) desarrollarse; (*person*) formarse; **~d** *suffix*: **heart-~d** en forma de corazón; **~less** *adj* informe, sin forma definida; **~ly** *adj* (*body etc*) esbelto

share [ʃeə*] *n* (*part*) parte *f*, porción *f*; (*contribution*) cuota; (*COMM*) acción *f* ♦ *vt* dividir; (*have in common*) compartir; **to ~ out (among *or* between)** repartir (entre); **~holder** (*BRIT*) *n* accionista *m/f*

shark [ʃɑ:k] *n* tiburón *m*

sharp [ʃɑ:p] *adj* (*blade, nose*) afilado; (*point*)

puntiagudo; (*outline*) definido; (*pain*) intenso; (*MUS*) desafinado; (*contrast*) marcado; (*voice*) agudo; (*person: quick-witted*) astuto; (: *dishonest*) poco escrupuloso ♦ n (*MUS*) sostenido ♦ adv: **at 2 o'clock** ~ a las 2 en punto; **~en** vt afilar; (*pencil*) sacar punta a; (*fig*) agudizar; **~ener** n (*also: pencil ~ener*) sacapuntas m inv; **~-eyed** adj de vista aguda; **~ly** adv (*turn, stop*) bruscamente; (*stand out, contrast*) claramente; (*criticize, retort*) severamente

shatter ['ʃætə*] vt hacer añicos or pedazos; (*fig: ruin*) destruir, acabar con ♦ vi hacerse añicos

shave [ʃeɪv] vt afeitar, rasurar ♦ vi afeitarse, rasurarse ♦ n: **to have a ~** afeitarse; **~r** n (*also: electric ~r*) máquina de afeitar (eléctrica)

shaving ['ʃeɪvɪŋ] n (*action*) el afeitarse, rasurado; **~s** npl (*of wood etc*) virutas fpl; **~ brush** n brocha (de afeitar); **~ cream** n crema de afeitar; **~ foam** n espuma de afeitar

shawl [ʃɔːl] n chal m

she [ʃiː] pron ella; **~-cat** n gata

sheaf [ʃiːf] (pl **sheaves**) n (*of corn*) gavilla; (*of papers*) fajo

shear [ʃɪə*] (pt **sheared**, pp **sheared** or **shorn**) vt esquilar, trasquilar; **~s** npl (*for hedge*) tijeras fpl de jardín

sheath [ʃiːθ] n vaina; (*contraceptive*) preservativo

sheaves [ʃiːvz] npl of **sheaf**

shed [ʃed] (pt, pp **shed**) n cobertizo ♦ vt (*skin*) mudar; (*tears, blood*) derramar; (*load*) derramar; (*workers*) despedir

she'd [ʃiːd] = **she had; she would**

sheen [ʃiːn] n brillo, lustre m

sheep [ʃiːp] n inv oveja; **~dog** n perro pastor; **~skin** n piel f de carnero

sheer [ʃɪə*] adj (*utter*) puro, completo; (*steep*) escarpado; (*material*) diáfano ♦ adv verticalmente

sheet [ʃiːt] n (*on bed*) sábana; (*of paper*) hoja; (*of glass, metal*) lámina; (*of ice*) capa

sheik(h) [ʃeɪk] n jeque m

shelf [ʃelf] (pl **shelves**) n estante m

shell [ʃel] n (*on beach*) concha; (*of egg, nut etc*) cáscara; (*explosive*) proyectil m, obús m; (*of building*) armazón f ♦ vt (*peas*) desenvainar; (*MIL*) bombardear

she'll [ʃiːl] = **she will; she shall**

shellfish ['ʃelfɪʃ] n inv crustáceo; (*as food*) mariscos mpl

shell suit n chándal m de calle

shelter ['ʃeltə*] n abrigo, refugio ♦ vt (*aid*) amparar, proteger; (*give lodging to*) abrigar ♦ vi abrigarse, refugiarse; **~ed** adj (*life*) protegido; (*spot*) abrigado; **~ed housing** n

viviendas vigiladas para ancianos y minusválidos

shelve [ʃelv] vt (*fig*) aplazar; **~s** npl of **shelf**

shepherd ['ʃepəd] n pastor m ♦ vt (*guide*) guiar, conducir; **~'s pie** (*BRIT*) n pastel de carne y patatas

sherry ['ʃerɪ] n jerez m

she's [ʃiːz] = **she is; she has**

Shetland ['ʃetlənd] n (*also: the ~s, the ~ Isles*) las Islas de Zetlandia

shield [ʃiːld] n escudo; (*protection*) blindaje m ♦ vt: **to ~ (from)** proteger (de)

shift [ʃɪft] n (*change*) cambio; (*at work*) turno ♦ vt trasladar; (*remove*) quitar ♦ vi moverse; **~ work** n trabajo a turnos; **~y** adj tramposo; (*eyes*) furtivo

shimmer ['ʃɪmə*] n reflejo trémulo

shin [ʃɪn] n espinilla

shine [ʃaɪn] (pt, pp **shone**) n brillo, lustre m ♦ vi brillar, relucir ♦ vt (*shoes*) lustrar, sacar brillo a; **to ~ a torch on sth** dirigir una linterna hacia algo

shingle ['ʃɪŋgl] n (*on beach*) guijarros mpl; **~s** n (*MED*) herpes mpl or fpl

shiny ['ʃaɪnɪ] adj brillante, lustroso

ship [ʃɪp] n buque m, barco ♦ vt (*goods*) embarcar; (*send*) transportar or enviar por vía marítima; **~building** n construcción f de buques; **~ment** n (*goods*) envío; **~ping** n (*act*) embarque m; (*traffic*) buques mpl; **~wreck** n naufragio ♦ vt: **to be ~wrecked** naufragar; **~yard** n astillero

shire ['ʃaɪə*] (*BRIT*) n condado

shirt [ʃəːt] n camisa; **in (one's) ~ sleeves** en mangas de camisa

shit [ʃɪt] (*inf!*) excl ¡mierda! (!)

shiver ['ʃɪvə*] n escalofrío ♦ vi temblar, estremecerse; (*with cold*) tiritar

shoal [ʃəul] n (*of fish*) banco; (*fig: also: ~s*) tropel m

shock [ʃɔk] n (*impact*) choque m; (*ELEC*) descarga (eléctrica); (*emotional*) conmoción f; (*start*) sobresalto, susto; (*MED*) postración f nerviosa ♦ vt dar un susto a; (*offend*) escandalizar; **~ absorber** n amortiguador m; **~ing** adj (*awful*) espantoso; (*outrageous*) escandaloso

shoddy ['ʃɔdɪ] adj de pacotilla

shoe [ʃuː] (pt, pp **shod**) n zapato; (*for horse*) herradura ♦ vt (*horse*) herrar; **~brush** n cepillo para zapatos; **~lace** n cordón m; **~ polish** n betún m; **~shop** n zapatería; **~string** n (*fig*): **on a ~string** con muy poco dinero

shone [ʃɔn] pt, pp of **shine**

shook [ʃuk] pt of **shake**

shoot [ʃuːt] (pt, pp **shot**) n (*on branch, seedling*) retoño, vástago ♦ vt disparar; (*kill*) matar a tiros; (*wound*) pegar un tiro;

(*execute*) fusilar; (*film*) rodar, filmar ♦ *vi*
(*FOOTBALL*) chutar; **~ down** *vt* (*plane*)
derribar; **~ in/out** *vi* entrar corriendo/salir
disparado; **~ up** *vi* (*prices*) dispararse; **~ing** *n*
(*shots*) tiros *mpl*; (*HUNTING*) caza con
escopeta; **~ing star** *n* estrella fugaz

shop [ʃɔp] *n* tienda; (*workshop*) taller *m* ♦ *vi*
(*also*: **go ~ping**) ir de compras; **~ assistant**
(*BRIT*) *n* dependiente/a *m/f*; **~ floor** (*BRIT*) *n*
(*fig*) taller *m*, fábrica; **~keeper** *n* tendero/a;
~lifting *n* mechería; **~per** *n* comprador(a)
m/f; **~ping** *n* (*goods*) compras *fpl*; **~ping
bag** *n* bolsa (de compras); **~ping centre**
(*US* **~ping center**) *n* centro comercial; **~-
soiled** *adj* deteriorado; **~ steward** (*BRIT*) *n*
(*INDUSTRY*) enlace *m* sindical; **~ window** *n*
escaparate *m* (*SP*), vidriera (*AM*)

shore [ʃɔː*] *n* orilla ♦ *vt*: **to ~ (up)** reforzar; **on
~** en tierra

shorn [ʃɔːn] *pp* of **shear**

short [ʃɔːt] *adj* corto; (*in time*) breve, de corta
duración; (*person*) bajo; (*curt*) brusco, seco;
(*insufficient*) insuficiente; (**a pair of**) **~s** (*unos*)
pantalones *mpl* cortos; **to be ~ of** estar
falto de algo; **in ~** en pocas palabras; **~ of
doing ...** fuera de hacer ...; **it is ~ for** es la
forma abreviada de; **to cut ~** (*speech, visit*)
interrumpir, terminar inesperadamente;
everything ~ of ... todo menos ...; **to fall ~ of**
no alcanzar; **to run ~ of** quedarle a uno poco;
to stop ~ parar en seco; **to stop ~ of**
detenerse antes de; **~age** *n*: **a ~age of** una
falta de; **~bread** *n* especie de mantecada; **~-
change** *vt* no dar el cambio completo a; **~-
circuit** *n* cortocircuito; **~coming** *n* defecto,
deficiencia; **~(crust) pastry** (*BRIT*) *n* pasta
quebradiza; **~cut** *n* atajo; **~en** *vt* acortar;
(*visit*) interrumpir; **~fall** *n* déficit *m*; **~hand**
(*BRIT*) *n* taquigrafía; **~hand typist** (*BRIT*) *n*
taquimecanógrafo/a; **~ list** (*BRIT*) *n* (*for job*)
lista de candidatos escogidos; **~-lived** *adj*
efímero; **~ly** *adv* en breve, dentro de poco;
~-sighted (*BRIT*) *adj* miope; (*fig*) imprudente; **~-staffed** *adj*: **to be ~-staffed** estar
falto de personal; **~ story** *n* cuento; **~-
tempered** *adj* enojadizo; **~-term** *adj* (*effect*)
a corto plazo; **~-wave** *n* (*RADIO*) onda corta

shot [ʃɔt] *pt, pp* of **shoot** ♦ *n* (*sound*) tiro,
disparo; (*try*) tentativa; (*injection*) inyección
f; (*PHOT*) toma, fotografía; **to be a good/poor
~** (*person*) tener buena/mala puntería; **like a ~**
(*without any delay*) como un rayo; **~gun** *n*
escopeta

should [ʃud] *aux vb*: **I ~ go now** debo irme
ahora; **he ~ be there now** debe de haber
llegado (ya); **I ~ go if I were you** yo en tu
lugar me iría; **I ~ like to** me gustaría

shoulder ['ʃəuldə*] *n* hombro ♦ *vt* (*fig*)
cargar con; **~ bag** *n* cartera de bandolera;

~ blade *n* omóplato

shouldn't ['ʃudnt] = **should not**

shout [ʃaut] *n* grito ♦ *vi* gritar ♦ *vt* gritar, dar
voces; **~ down** *vt* acallar a gritos; **~ing** *n*
griterío

shove [ʃʌv] *n* empujón *m* ♦ *vt* empujar; (*inf:
put*): **to ~ sth in** meter algo a empellones;
~ off (*inf*) *vi* largarse

shovel ['ʃʌvl] *n* pala; (*mechanical*)
excavadora ♦ *vt* mover con pala

show [ʃəu] (*pt* **showed**, *pp* **shown**) *n* (*of
emotion*) demostración *f*; (*semblance*)
apariencia; (*exhibition*) exposición *f*; (*THEATRE*)
función *f*, espectáculo; (*TV*) show *m* ♦ *vt*
mostrar, enseñar; (*courage etc*) mostrar,
manifestar; (*exhibit*) exponer; (*film*) proyectar
♦ *vi* mostrarse; (*appear*) aparecer; **for ~** para
impresionar; **on ~** (*exhibits etc*) expuesto;
~ in *vt* (*person*) hacer pasar; **~ off** (*pej*) *vi*
presumir ♦ *vt* (*display*) lucir; **~ out** *vt*: **to
~ sb out** acompañar a uno a la puerta; **~ up**
vi (*stand out*) destacar; (*inf: turn up*) aparecer
♦ *vt* (*unmask*) desenmascarar; **~ business** *n*
mundo del espectáculo; **~down** *n*
enfrentamiento (final).

shower ['ʃauə*] *n* (*rain*) chaparrón *m*,
chubasco; (*of stones etc*) lluvia; (*for bathing*)
ducha (*SP*), regadera (*AM*) ♦ *vi* llover ♦ *vt*
(*fig*): **to ~ sb with sth** colmar a uno de algo;
to have a ~ ducharse; **~proof** *adj*
impermeable

showing ['ʃauɪŋ] *n* (*of film*) proyección *f*

show jumping *n* hípica

shown [ʃəun] *pp* of **show**

show: **~-off** (*inf*) *n* (*person*) presumido/a;
~piece *n* (*of exhibition etc*) objeto cumbre;
~room *n* sala de muestras

shrank [ʃræŋk] *pt* of **shrink**

shrapnel ['ʃræpnl] *n* metralla

shred [ʃred] *n* (*gen pl*) triza, jirón *m* ♦ *vt*
hacer trizas; (*CULIN*) desmenuzar; **~der** *n*
(*vegetable ~der*) picadora; (*document ~der*)
trituradora (de papel)

shrewd [ʃruːd] *adj* astuto

shriek [ʃriːk] *n* chillido ♦ *vi* chillar

shrill [ʃrɪl] *adj* agudo, estridente

shrimp [ʃrɪmp] *n* camarón *m*

shrine [ʃraɪn] *n* santuario, sepulcro

shrink [ʃrɪŋk] (*pt* **shrank**, *pp* **shrunk**) *vi*
encogerse; (*be reduced*) reducirse; (*also*:
~ away) retroceder ♦ *vt* encoger ♦ *n* (*inf:
pej*) loquero/a; **to ~ from (doing) sth** no
atreverse a hacer algo; **~wrap** *vt* embalar
con película de plástico

shrivel ['ʃrɪvl] (*also*: **~ up**) *vt* (*dry*) secar ♦ *vi*
secarse

shroud [ʃraud] *n* sudario ♦ *vt*: **~ed in mystery**
envuelto en el misterio

Shrove Tuesday ['ʃrəuv-] *n* martes *m* de

carnaval

shrub [ʃrʌb] n arbusto; **~bery** n arbustos mpl

shrug [ʃrʌg] n encogimiento de hombros ♦ vt, vi: **to ~ (one's shoulders)** encogerse de hombros; **~ off** vt negar importancia a

shrunk [ʃrʌŋk] pp of **shrink**

shudder [ˈʃʌdə*] n estremecimiento, escalofrío ♦ vi estremecerse

shuffle [ˈʃʌfl] vt (cards) barajar ♦ vi: **to ~ (one's feet)** arrastrar los pies

shun [ʃʌn] vt rehuir, esquivar

shunt [ʃʌnt] vt (train) maniobrar; (object) empujar

shut [ʃʌt] (pt, pp **shut**) vt cerrar ♦ vi cerrarse; **~ down** vt, vi cerrar; **~ off** vt (supply etc) cortar; **~ up** vi (inf: keep quiet) callarse ♦ vt (close) cerrar; (silence) hacer callar; **~ter** n contraventana; (PHOT) obturador m

shuttle [ˈʃʌtl] n lanzadera; (also: ~ service) servicio rápido y continuo entre dos puntos: (: AVIAT) puente m aéreo; **~cock** n volante m; **~ diplomacy** n viajes mpl diplomáticos

shy [ʃaɪ] adj tímido; **~ness** n timidez f

Sicily [ˈsɪsɪlɪ] n Sicilia

sick [sɪk] adj (ill) enfermo; (nauseated) mareado; (humour) negro; (vomiting): **to be ~** (BRIT) vomitar; **to feel ~** tener náuseas; **to be ~ of** (fig) estar harto de; **~ bay** n enfermería; **~en** vt dar asco a; **~ening** adj (fig) asqueroso

sickle [ˈsɪkl] n hoz f

sick: **~ leave** n baja por enfermedad; **~ly** adj enfermizo; (smell) nauseabundo; **~ness** n enfermedad f, mal m; (vomiting) náuseas fpl; **~ pay** n subsidio de enfermedad

side [saɪd] n (gen) lado m; (of body) costado m; (of lake) orilla; (of hill) ladera; (of team) equipo m; ♦ adj (door, entrance) lateral ♦ vi: **to ~ with sb** tomar el partido de uno; **by the ~ of** al lado de; **~ by ~** juntos/as; **from ~ to ~** de un lado para otro; **from all ~s** de todos lados; **to take ~s (with)** tomar partido (con); **~board** n aparador m; **~boards** (BRIT) npl = **~burns**; **~burns** npl patillas fpl; **~ drum** n tambor m; **~ effect** n efecto secundario; **~light** n (AUT) luz f lateral; **~line** n (SPORT) línea de banda; (fig) empleo suplementario; **~long** adj de soslayo; **~ order** n plato de acompañamiento; **~ show** n (stall) caseta; **~step** vt (fig) esquivar; **~ street** n calle f lateral; **~track** vt (fig) desviar (de su propósito); **~walk** n (US) acera; **~ways** adv de lado

siding [ˈsaɪdɪŋ] n (RAIL) apartadero, vía muerta

siege [siːdʒ] n cerco, sitio

sieve [sɪv] n colador m ♦ vt cribar

sift [sɪft] vt cribar; (fig: information) escudriñar

sigh [saɪ] n suspiro ♦ vi suspirar

sight [saɪt] n (faculty) vista; (spectacle)

espectáculo; (on gun) mira, alza ♦ vt divisar; **in ~** a la vista; **out of ~** fuera de (la) vista; **on ~** (shoot) sin previo aviso; **~seeing** n excursionismo, turismo; **to go ~seeing** hacer turismo

sign [saɪn] n (with hand) señal f, seña; (trace) huella, rastro; (notice) letrero; (written) signo ♦ vt firmar; (SPORT) fichar; **to ~ sth over to sb** firmar el traspaso de algo a uno; **~ on** vi (BRIT: as unemployed) registrarse como desempleado; (for course) inscribirse ♦ vt (MIL) alistar; (employee) contratar; **~ up** vi (MIL) alistarse; (for course) inscribirse ♦ vt (player) fichar

signal [ˈsɪgnl] n señal f ♦ vi señalizar ♦ vt (person) hacer señas a; (message) comunicar por señales; **~man** (irreg) n (RAIL) guardavía m

signature [ˈsɪgnətʃə*] n firma; **~ tune** n sintonía de apertura de un programa

signet ring [ˈsɪgnət-] n anillo de sello

significance [sɪgˈnɪfɪkəns] n (importance) trascendencia

significant [sɪgˈnɪfɪkənt] adj significativo; (important) trascendente

signify [ˈsɪgnɪfaɪ] vt significar

sign language n lenguaje m para sordomudos

signpost [ˈsaɪnpəʊst] n indicador m

silence [ˈsaɪlns] n silencio ♦ vt acallar; (guns) reducir al silencio; **~r** n (on gun, BRIT: AUT) silenciador m

silent [ˈsaɪlnt] adj silencioso; (not speaking) callado; (film) mudo; **to remain ~** guardar silencio; **~ partner** n (COMM) socio/a comanditario/a

silhouette [sɪluːˈet] n silueta

silicon chip [ˈsɪlɪkən-] n plaqueta de silicio

silk [sɪlk] n seda ♦ adj de seda; **~y** adj sedoso

silly [ˈsɪlɪ] adj (person) tonto; (idea) absurdo

silt [sɪlt] n sedimento

silver [ˈsɪlvə*] n plata; (money) moneda suelta ♦ adj de plata; (colour) plateado; **~ paper** (BRIT) n papel m de plata; **~-plated** adj plateado; **~smith** n platero/a; **~ware** n plata; **~y** adj argentino

similar [ˈsɪmɪlə*] adj: **~ (to)** parecido or semejante (a); **~ity** [-ˈlærɪtɪ] n semejanza; **~ly** adv del mismo modo

simmer [ˈsɪmə*] vi hervir a fuego lento

simple [ˈsɪmpl] adj (easy) sencillo; (foolish, COMM: interest) simple; **simplicity** [-ˈplɪsɪtɪ] n sencillez f; **simplify** [ˈsɪmplɪfaɪ] vt simplificar

simply [ˈsɪmplɪ] adv (live, talk) sencillamente; (just, merely) sólo

simulate [ˈsɪmjuːleɪt] vt fingir, simular; **~d** adj simulado; (fur) de imitación

simultaneous [sɪməlˈteɪnɪəs] adj simultáneo; **~ly** adv simultáneamente

sin [sɪn] n pecado ♦ vi pecar

since [sɪns] adv desde entonces, después ♦ prep desde ♦ conj (time) desde que; (because) ya que, puesto que; ~ then, ever ~ desde entonces

sincere [sɪn'sɪə*] adj sincero; ~ly adv: yours ~ly (in letters) le saluda atentamente; **sincerity** [-'sɛrɪtɪ] n sinceridad f

sinew ['sɪnjuː] n tendón m

sing [sɪŋ] (pt sang, pp sung) vt, vi cantar

Singapore [sɪŋə'pɔː*] n Singapur m

singe [sɪndʒ] vt chamuscar

singer ['sɪŋə*] n cantante m/f

singing ['sɪŋɪŋ] n canto

single ['sɪŋgl] adj único, solo; (unmarried) soltero; (not double) simple, sencillo ♦ n (BRIT: also: ~ ticket) billete m sencillo; (record) sencillo, single m; ~s npl (TENNIS) individual m; ~ out vt (choose) escoger; ~ bed cama individual; ~-breasted adj recto; ~ file n: in ~ file en fila de uno; ~-handed adv sin ayuda; ~-minded adj resuelto, firme; ~ parent n padre m soltero, madre f soltera (o divorciado etc); ~ parent family familia monoparental; ~ room n cuarto individual

singly ['sɪŋglɪ] adv uno por uno

singular ['sɪŋgjulə*] adj (odd) raro, extraño; (outstanding) excepcional ♦ n (LING) singular m

sinister ['sɪnɪstə*] adj siniestro

sink [sɪŋk] (pt sank, pp sunk) n fregadero ♦ vt (ship) hundir, echar a pique; (foundations) excavar ♦ vi (gen) hundirse; to ~ sth into hundir algo en; ~ in vi (fig) penetrar, calar

sinner ['sɪnə*] n pecador(a) m/f

sinus ['saɪnəs] n (ANAT) seno

sip [sɪp] n sorbo ♦ vt sorber, beber a sorbitos

siphon ['saɪfən] n sifón m; ~ off vt desviar

sir [sə*] n señor m; S~ John Smith Sir John Smith; yes ~ sí, señor

siren ['saɪərn] n sirena

sirloin ['sɜːlɔɪn] n (also: ~ steak) solomillo

sister ['sɪstə*] n hermana; (BRIT: nurse) enfermera jefe; ~-in-law n cuñada

sit [sɪt] (pt, pp sat) vi sentarse; (be sitting) estar sentado; (assembly) reunirse; (for painter) posar ♦ vt (exam) presentarse a; ~ down vi sentarse; ~ in on vt fus asistir a; ~ up vi incorporarse; (not go to bed) velar

sitcom ['sɪtkɒm] n abbr (= situation comedy) comedia de situación

site [saɪt] n sitio; (also: building ~) solar m ♦ vt situar

sit-in n (demonstration) sentada

sitting ['sɪtɪŋ] n (of assembly etc) sesión f; (in canteen) turno; ~ room n sala de estar

situated ['sɪtjueɪtɪd] adj situado

situation [sɪtju'eɪʃən] n situación f; "~s vacant" (BRIT) "ofrecen trabajo"

six [sɪks] num seis; ~teen num diez y seis, dieciséis; ~th num sexto; ~ty num sesenta

size [saɪz] n tamaño; (extent) extensión f; (of clothing) talla; (of shoes) número; ~ up vt formarse una idea de; ~able adj importante, considerable

sizzle ['sɪzl] vi crepitar

skate [skeɪt] n patín m; (fish: pl inv) raya ♦ vi patinar; ~board n monopatín m; ~boarding n monopatín m; ~r n patinador(a) m/f; **skating** n patinaje m; **skating rink** n pista de patinaje

skeleton ['skelɪtn] n esqueleto; (TECH) armazón f; (outline) esquema m; ~ staff n personal m reducido

skeptic etc ['skeptɪk] (US) = **sceptic**

sketch [sketʃ] n (drawing) dibujo; (outline) esbozo, bosquejo; (THEATRE) sketch m ♦ vt dibujar; (plan etc: also: ~ out) esbozar; ~ book n libro de dibujos; ~y adj incompleto

skewer ['skjuːə*] n broqueta

ski [skiː] n esquí m ♦ vi esquiar; ~ boot n bota de esquí

skid [skɪd] n patinazo ♦ vi patinar

ski: ~er n esquiador(a) m/f; ~ing n esquí m; ~ jump n salto con esquís

skilful ['skɪlful] (BRIT) adj diestro, experto

ski lift n telesilla m, telesquí m

skill [skɪl] n destreza, pericia, técnica; ~ed adj hábil, diestro; (worker) cualificado; ~full (US) adj = **skilful**

skim [skɪm] vt (milk) desnatar; (glide over) rozar, rasar ♦ vi: to ~ through (book) hojear; ~med milk n leche f desnatada

skimp [skɪmp] vt (also: ~ on: work) chapucear; (cloth etc) escatimar; ~y adj escaso; (skirt) muy corto

skin [skɪn] n piel f; (complexion) cutis m ♦ vt (fruit etc) pelar; (animal) despellejar; ~ cancer n cáncer m de piel; ~-deep adj superficial; ~ diving n buceo; ~ny adj flaco; ~tight adj (dress etc) muy ajustado

skip [skɪp] n brinco, salto; (BRIT: container) contenedor m ♦ vi brincar; (with rope) saltar a la comba ♦ vt saltarse

ski: ~ pass n forfait m (de esquí); ~ pole n bastón m de esquiar

skipper ['skɪpə*] n (NAUT, SPORT) capitán m

skipping rope ['skɪpɪŋ-] (BRIT) n comba

skirmish ['skɜːmɪʃ] n escaramuza

skirt [skɜːt] n falda (SP), pollera (AM) ♦ vt (go round) ladear; ~ing board (BRIT) n rodapié m

ski slope n pista de esquí

ski suit n traje m de esquiar

ski tow n remonte m

skittle ['skɪtl] n bolo; ~s n (game) boliche m

skive [skaɪv] (BRIT: inf) vi gandulear

skull [skʌl] n calavera; (ANAT) cráneo

skunk [skʌŋk] n mofeta

sky [skaɪ] n cielo; **~light** n tragaluz m, claraboya; **~scraper** n rascacielos m inv

slab [slæb] n (stone) bloque m; (flat) losa; (of cake) trozo

slack [slæk] adj (loose) flojo; (slow) de poca actividad; (careless) descuidado; **~s** npl pantalones mpl; **~en** (also: ~en off) vi aflojarse ♦ vt aflojar; (speed) disminuir

slag heap ['slæg-] n escorial m, escombrera

slag off [BRIT: inf] vt poner como un trapo

slam [slæm] vt (throw) arrojar (violentamente); (criticize) criticar duramente ♦ vi (door) cerrarse de golpe; **to ~ the door** dar un portazo

slander ['slɑːndəʳ] n calumnia, difamación f

slang [slæŋ] n argot m; (jargon) jerga

slant [slɑːnt] n sesgo, inclinación f; (fig) interpretación f; **~ed** adj (fig) parcial; **~ing** adj inclinado; (eyes) rasgado

slap [slæp] n palmada; (in face) bofetada ♦ vt dar una palmada or bofetada a; (paint etc): **to ~ sth on sth** embadurnar algo con algo ♦ adv (directly) exactamente, directamente; **~dash** adj descuidado; **~stick** n comedia de golpe y porrazo; **~-up** adj: **a ~-up meal** (BRIT) un banquetazo, una comilona

slash [slæʃ] vt acuchillar; (fig: prices) fulminar

slat [slæt] n tablilla, listón m

slate [sleɪt] n pizarra ♦ vt (fig: criticize) criticar duramente

slaughter ['slɔːtəʳ] n (of animals) matanza; (of people) carnicería ♦ vt matar; **~house** n matadero

Slav [slɑːv] adj eslavo

slave [sleɪv] n esclavo/a ♦ vi (also: ~ away) sudar tinta; **~ry** n esclavitud f

slay [sleɪ] (pt slew, pp slain) vt matar

sleazy ['sliːzɪ] adj de mala fama

sledge [sledʒ] n trineo; **~hammer** n mazo

sleek [sliːk] adj (shiny) lustroso; (car etc) elegante

sleep [sliːp] (pt, pp slept) n sueño ♦ vi dormir; **to go to ~** quedarse dormido; **~ around** vi acostarse con cualquiera; **~ in** vi (oversleep) quedarse dormido; **~er** n (person) durmiente m/f; (BRIT: RAIL: on track) traviesa; (: train) coche-cama m; **~ing bag** n saco de dormir; **~ing car** n coche-cama m; **~ing partner** (BRIT) n (COMM) socio comanditario; **~ing pill** n somnífero; **~less** adj: **a ~less night** una noche en blanco; **~walker** n sonámbulo/a; **~y** adj soñoliento; (place) soporífero

sleet [sliːt] n aguanieve f

sleeve [sliːv] n manga; (TECH) manguito; (of record) portada; **~less** adj sin mangas

sleigh [sleɪ] n trineo

sleight [slaɪt] n: **~ of hand** escamoteo

slender ['slendəʳ] adj delgado; (means) escaso

slept [slept] pt, pp of sleep

slew [sluː] pt of slay ♦ vi (BRIT: veer) torcerse

slice [slaɪs] n (of meat) tajada; (of bread) rebanada; (of lemon) rodaja; (utensil) pala ♦ vt cortar (en tajos); rebanar

slick [slɪk] adj (skilful) hábil, diestro; (clever) astuto ♦ n (also: oil ~) marea negra

slide [slaɪd] (pt, pp slid) n (movement) descenso, desprendimiento; (in playground) tobogán m; (PHOT) diapositiva; (BRIT: also: hair ~) pasador m, broche, deslizar ♦ vt correr, deslizar ♦ vi (slip) resbalarse; (glide) deslizarse; **sliding** adj (door) corredizo; **sliding scale** n escala móvil

slight [slaɪt] adj (slim) delgado; (frail) delicado; (pain etc) leve; (trivial) insignificante; (small) pequeño ♦ n desaire m ♦ vt (insult) ofender, desairar; **not in the ~est** en absoluto; **~ly** adv ligeramente, un poco

slim [slɪm] adj delgado, esbelto; (fig: chance) remoto ♦ vi adelgazar

slime [slaɪm] n limo, cieno

slimming ['slɪmɪŋ] n adelgazamiento

slimy ['slaɪmɪ] adj cenagoso

sling [slɪŋ] (pt, pp slung) n (MED) cabestrillo; (weapon) honda ♦ vt tirar, arrojar

slip [slɪp] n (slide) resbalón m; (mistake) descuido; (underskirt) combinación f; (of paper) papelito ♦ vt (slide) deslizar ♦ vi deslizarse; (stumble) resbalar(se); (decline) decaer; (move smoothly): **to ~ into/out of** (room etc) introducirse en/salirse de; **to give sb the ~** eludir a uno; **a ~ of the tongue** un lapsus; **to ~ sth on/off** ponerse/quitarse algo; **~ away** vi escabullirse; **~ in** vt meter ♦ vi meterse; **~ out** vi (go out) salir (un momento); **~ up** vi (make mistake) equivocarse; meter la pata; **~ped disc** n vértebra dislocada

slipper ['slɪpəʳ] n zapatilla, pantufla

slippery ['slɪpərɪ] adj resbaladizo

slip: ~ road n (BRIT) carretera de acceso; **~-up** n (error) desliz m; **~way** n grada, gradas fpl

slit [slɪt] (pt, pp slit) n raja; (cut) corte m ♦ vt rajar; cortar

slither ['slɪðəʳ] vi deslizarse

sliver ['slɪvəʳ] n (of glass, wood) astilla; (of cheese etc) raja

slob [slɔb] (inf) n abandonado/a

slog [slɔg] (BRIT) vi sudar tinta; **it was a ~** costó trabajo (hacerlo)

slogan ['sləugən] n eslogan m, lema m

slope [sləup] n (up) cuesta, pendiente f; (down) declive m; (side of mountain) falda, vertiente m ♦ vi: **to ~ down** estar en declive;

to ~ up inclinarse; **sloping** adj en pendiente; en declive; (*writing*) inclinado

sloppy ['slɔpɪ] adj (*work*) descuidado; (*appearance*) desaliñado

slot [slɔt] n ranura ♦ vt: to ~ **into** encajar en

slot machine n (BRIT: *vending machine*) distribuidor m automático; (*for gambling*) tragaperras m inv

slouch [slautʃ] vi andar etc con los hombros caídos

Slovenia [sləu'viːnɪə] n Eslovenia

slovenly ['slʌvənlɪ] adj desaliñado, desaseado; (*careless*) descuidado

slow [sləu] adj lento; (*not clever*) lerdo; (*watch*): to be ~ atrasar ♦ adv lentamente, despacio ♦ vt, vi (*also:* ~ down, ~ up) retardar; "~" (*road sign*) "disminuir velocidad"; **~down** (US) n huelga de manos caídas; **~ly** adv lentamente, despacio; ~ **motion** n: in ~ motion a cámara lenta

sludge [slʌdʒ] n lodo, fango

slug [slʌg] n babosa; (*bullet*) posta; **~gish** adj lento; (*person*) perezoso

sluice [sluːs] n (*gate*) esclusa; (*channel*) canal m

slum [slʌm] n casucha

slump [slʌmp] n (*economic*) depresión f ♦ vi hundirse; (*prices*) caer en picado

slung [slʌŋ] pt, pp of **sling**

slur [sləː*] n: to cast a ~ on insultar ♦ vt (*speech*) pronunciar mal

slush [slʌʃ] n nieve f a medio derretir

slut [slʌt] n putona

sly [slaɪ] adj astuto; (*smile*) taimado

smack [smæk] n bofetada ♦ vt dar con la mano a; (*child, on face*) abofetear ♦ vi: to ~ of saber a, oler a

small [smɔːl] adj pequeño ♦ ~ **ads** (BRIT) npl anuncios mpl por palabras; ~ **change** n suelto, cambio; **~holder** (BRIT) n granjero/a, parcelero/a; ~ **hours** npl: in the ~ hours a las altas horas de la noche); **~pox** n viruela; ~ **talk** n cháchara

smart [smaːt] adj elegante; (*clever*) listo, inteligente; (*quick*) rápido, vivo ♦ vi escocer, picar; **~en up** vi arreglarse ♦ vt arreglar

smash [smæʃ] n (*also:* ~-up) choque m; (MUS) exitazo ♦ vt (*break*) hacer pedazos; (*car etc*) estrellar; (SPORT: *record*) batir ♦ vi hacerse pedazos; (*against wall etc*) estrellarse; **~ing** (*inf*) adj estupendo

smattering ['smætərɪŋ] n: a ~ of algo de

smear [smɪə*] n mancha; (MED) frotis m inv ♦ vt untar; ~ **campaign** n campaña de desprestigio

smell [smɛl] (*pt, pp* smelt or smelled) n olor m; (*sense*) olfato ♦ vt, vi oler; **~y** adj maloliente

smile [smaɪl] n sonrisa ♦ vi sonreír

smirk [sməːk] n sonrisa falsa or afectada

smith [smɪθ] n herrero; **~y** ['smɪðɪ] n herrería

smog [smɔg] n esmog m

smoke [sməuk] n humo ♦ vi fumar; (*chimney*) echar humo ♦ vt (*cigarettes*) fumar; **~d** adj (*bacon, glass*) ahumado; **~r** n fumador(a) m/f; (RAIL) coche m fumador; ~ **screen** n cortina de humo; ~ **shop** (US) n estanco (SP), tabaquería (AM); **smoking** n: "**no smoking**" "prohibido fumar"; **smoky** adj (*room*) lleno de humo; (*taste*) ahumado

smolder ['sməuldə*] (US) vi = **smoulder**

smooth [smuːð] adj liso; (*sea*) tranquilo; (*flavour, movement*) suave; (*sauce*) fino; (*person: pej*) meloso ♦ vt (*also:* ~ out) alisar; (*creases, difficulties*) allanar

smother ['smʌðə*] vt sofocar; (*repress*) contener

smoulder ['sməuldə*] (US smolder) vi arder sin llama

smudge [smʌdʒ] n mancha ♦ vt manchar

smug [smʌg] adj presumido; orondo

smuggle ['smʌgl] vt pasar de contrabando; **~r** n contrabandista m/f; **smuggling** n contrabando

smutty ['smʌtɪ] adj (*fig*) verde, obsceno

snack [snæk] n bocado; ~ **bar** n cafetería

snag [snæg] n problema m

snail [sneɪl] n caracol m

snake [sneɪk] n serpiente f

snap [snæp] n (*sound*) chasquido; (*photograph*) foto f ♦ adj (*decision*) instantáneo ♦ vt (*break*) quebrar; (*fingers*) castañetear ♦ vi quebrarse; (*fig: speak sharply*) contestar bruscamente; to ~ shut cerrarse de golpe; ~ **at** vt fus (subj: dog) intentar morder; ~ **off** vi partirse; ~ **up** vt agarrar; ~ **fastener** (US) n botón m de presión; **~py** (*inf*) adj (*answer*) instantáneo; (*slogan*) conciso; **make it ~py!** (*hurry up*) ¡date prisa!; **~shot** n foto f (instantánea)

snare [snɛə*] n trampa

snarl [snaːl] vi gruñir

snatch [snætʃ] n (*small piece*) fragmento ♦ vt (~ *away*) arrebatar; (*fig*) agarrar; to ~ **some sleep** encontrar tiempo para dormir

sneak [sniːk] (*pt* (US) snuck) vi: to ~ **in/out** entrar/salir a hurtadillas ♦ n (*inf*) soplón/ona m/f; to ~ **up on sb** aparecérsele de improviso a uno; **~ers** npl zapatos mpl de lona; **~y** adj furtivo

sneer [snɪə*] vi reír con sarcasmo; (*mock*): to ~ **at** burlarse de

sneeze [sniːz] vi estornudar

sniff [snɪf] vi sollozar ♦ vt husmear, oler; (*drugs*) esnifar

snigger ['snɪgə*] vi reírse con disimulo

snip [snɪp] n tijeretazo; (BRIT: *inf: bargain*) ganga ♦ vt tijeretear

sniper ['snaɪpə*] n francotirador(a) m/f
snippet ['snɪpɪt] n retazo
snob [snɔb] n (e)snob m/f; **~bery** n (e)snobismo; **~bish** adj (e)snob
snooker ['snu:kə*] n especie de billar
snoop [snu:p] vi: **to ~ about** fisgonear
snooze [snu:z] n siesta ♦ vi echar una siesta
snore [snɔ:*] n ronquido ♦ vi roncar
snorkel ['snɔ:kl] n (tubo) respirador m
snort [snɔ:t] n bufido ♦ vi bufar
snout [snaut] n hocico, morro
snow [snəu] n nieve ♦ vi nevar; **~ball** n bola de nieve ♦ vi (fig) agrandarse, ampliarse; **~bound** adj bloqueado por la nieve; **~drift** n ventisquero; **~drop** n campanilla; **~fall** n nevada; **~flake** n copo de nieve; **~man** (irreg) n figura de nieve; **~plough** (US **~plow**) n quitanieves m inv; **~shoe** n raqueta (de nieve); **~storm** n nevada, nevasca
snub [snʌb] vt (person) desairar ♦ n desaire m, repulsa; **~-nosed** adj chato
snuff [snʌf] n rapé m
snug [snʌg] adj (cosy) cómodo; (fitted) ajustado
snuggle ['snʌgl] vi: **to ~ up to sb** arrimarse a uno

---

so [səu] adv **1** (thus, likewise) así, de este modo; **if ~** de ser así; **I like swimming — ~ do I** a mí me gusta nadar — a mí también; **I've got work to do — ~ has Paul** tengo trabajo que hacer — Paul también; **it's 5 o'clock — ~ it is!** son las cinco — ¡pues es verdad!; **I hope/think** ~ espero/creo que sí; **~ far** hasta ahora; (in past) hasta ese momento
2 (in comparisons etc: to such a degree) tan; **~ quickly (that)** tan rápido (que); **~ big (that)** tan grande (que); **she's not ~ clever as her brother** no es tan lista como su hermano; **we were ~ worried** estábamos preocupadísimos
3: ~ much adj, adv tanto; **~ many** tantos/as
4 (phrases): **10 or ~** unos 10, 10 o así; **~ long!** (inf: goodbye) ¡hasta luego!
♦ conj **1** (expressing purpose): **~ as to do** para hacer; **~ (that)** para que + sub
2 (expressing result) así que; **~ you see, I could have gone** así que ya ves, (yo) podría haber ido

---

soak [səuk] vt (drench) empapar; (steep in water) remojar ♦ vi remojarse, estar a remojo; **~ in** vi penetrar; **~ up** vt absorber
soap [səup] n jabón m; **~flakes** npl escamas fpl de jabón; **~ opera** n telenovela; **~ powder** n jabón m en polvo; **~y** adj jabonoso
soar [sɔ:*] vi (on wings) remontarse; (rocket, prices) dispararse; (building etc) elevarse

sob [sɔb] n sollozo ♦ vi sollozar
sober ['səubə*] adj (serious) serio; (not drunk) sobrio; (colour, style) discreto; **~ up** vt quitar la borrachera
so-called adj así llamado
soccer ['sɔkə*] n fútbol m
social ['səuʃl] adj social ♦ n velada, fiesta; **~ club** n club m; **~ism** n socialismo; **~ist** adj, n socialista m/f; **~ize** vi: **to ~ize (with)** alternar (con); **~ly** adv socialmente; **~ security** n seguridad f social; **~ work** n asistencia social; **~ worker** n asistente/a m/f social
society [sə'saɪətɪ] n sociedad f; (club) asociación f; (also: high ~) alta sociedad
sociology [səusɪ'ɔlədʒɪ] n sociología
sock [sɔk] n calcetín m (SP), media (AM)
socket ['sɔkɪt] n cavidad f; (BRIT: ELEC) enchufe m
sod [sɔd] n (of earth) césped m; (BRIT: inf!) cabrón/ona m/f (!)
soda ['səudə] n (CHEM) sosa; (also: ~ water) soda; (US: also: ~ pop) gaseosa
sofa ['səufə] n sofá m
soft [sɔft] adj (lenient, not hard) blando; (gentle, not bright) suave; **~ drink** n bebida no alcohólica; **~en** ['sɔfn] vt ablandar; suavizar; (effect) amortiguar ♦ vi ablandarse; suavizarse; **~ly** adv suavemente; (gently) delicadamente, con delicadeza; **~ness** n blandura; suavidad f; **~ware** n (COMPUT) software m
soggy ['sɔgɪ] adj empapado
soil [sɔɪl] n (earth) tierra, suelo ♦ vt ensuciar; **~ed** adj sucio
solar ['səulə*] adj: **~ energy** n energía solar; **~ panel** n panel m solar
sold [səuld] pt, pp of **sell**; **~ out** adj (COMM) agotado
solder ['səuldə*] vt soldar ♦ n soldadura
soldier ['səuldʒə*] n soldado m; (army man) militar m
sole [səul] n (of foot) planta; (of shoe) suela; (fish: pl inv) lenguado ♦ adj único
solemn ['sɔləm] adj solemne
sole trader n (COMM) comerciante m exclusivo
solicit [sə'lɪsɪt] vt (request) solicitar ♦ vi (prostitute) importunar
solicitor [sə'lɪsɪtə*] (BRIT) n (for wills etc) ≈ notario/a; (in court) ≈ abogado/a
solid ['sɔlɪd] adj sólido; (gold etc) macizo ♦ n sólido; **~s** npl (food) alimentos mpl sólidos
solidarity [sɔlɪ'dærɪtɪ] n solidaridad f
solitary ['sɔlɪtərɪ] adj solitario, solo; **~ confinement** n incomunicación f
solo ['səuləu] n solo ♦ adv (fly) en solitario; **~ist** n solista m/f
soluble ['sɔlju:bl] adj soluble

solution [sə'lu:ʃən] n solución f
solve [sɔlv] vt resolver, solucionar
solvent ['sɔlvənt] adj (COMM) solvente ♦ n (CHEM) solvente m

KEYWORD
---

some [sʌm] adj 1 (a certain amount or number of): ~ tea/water/biscuits té/agua/(unas) galletas; **there's ~ milk in the fridge** hay leche en el frigo; **there were ~ people outside** había algunas personas fuera; **I've got ~ money, but not much** tengo algo de dinero, pero no mucho
2 (certain: in contrasts) algunos/as; ~ **people say that ...** hay quien dice que ...; ~ **films were excellent, but most were mediocre** hubo películas excelentes, pero la mayoría fueron mediocres
3 (unspecified): ~ **woman was asking for you** una mujer estuvo preguntando por ti; **he was asking for ~ book (or other)** pedía un libro; ~ **day** algún día; ~ **day next week** un día de la semana que viene
♦ pron 1 (a certain number): **I've got ~** (books etc) tengo algunos/as
2 (a certain amount) algo; **I've got ~** (money, milk) tengo algo; **could I have ~ of that cheese?** ¿me puede dar un poco de ese queso?; **I've read ~ of the book** he leído parte del libro
♦ adv: ~ **10 people** unas 10 personas, una decena de personas

some: ~**body** ['sʌmbədɪ] pron = someone; ~**how** adv de alguna manera; (for some reason) por una u otra razón; ~**one** pron alguien; ~**place** (US) adv = somewhere
somersault ['sʌməsɔːlt] n (deliberate) salto mortal; (accidental) vuelco ♦ vi dar un salto mortal; dar vuelcos
some: ~**thing** pron algo; **would you like** ~**thing to eat/drink?** ¿te gustaría cenar/tomar algo?; ~**time** adv (in future) algún día, en algún momento; (in past): ~**time last month** durante el mes pasado; ~**times** adv a veces; ~**what** adv algo; ~**where** adv (be) en alguna parte; (go) a alguna parte; ~**where else** (be) en otra parte; (go) a otra parte
son [sʌn] n hijo
song [sɔŋ] n canción f
son-in-law n yerno
soon [su:n] adv pronto, dentro de poco; ~ **afterwards** poco después; see also **as**; ~**er** adv (time) antes, más temprano; (preference): **I would ~er do that** preferiría hacer eso; ~**er or later** tarde o temprano
soot [sut] n hollín m
soothe [su:ð] vt tranquilizar; (pain) aliviar
sophisticated [sə'fɪstɪkeɪtɪd] adj sofisticado

sophomore ['sɔfəmɔː*] (US) n estudiante m/f de segundo año
sopping ['sɔpɪŋ] adj: ~ (wet) empapado
soppy ['sɔpɪ] (pej) adj tonto
soprano [sə'prɑːnəu] n soprano f
sorcerer ['sɔːsərə*] n hechicero
sore [sɔː*] adj (painful) doloroso, que duele ♦ n llaga; ~**ly** adv: **I am ~ly tempted to** estoy muy tentado a
sorrow ['sɔrəu] n pena, dolor m; ~**s** npl pesares mpl; ~**ful** adj triste
sorry ['sɔrɪ] adj (regretful) arrepentido; (condition, excuse) lastimoso; ~! ¡perdón!, ¡perdone!; ~? ¿cómo?; **to feel ~ for sb** tener lástima a uno; **I feel ~ for him** me da lástima
sort [sɔːt] n clase f, género, tipo ♦ vt (also: ~ out: papers) clasificar; (: problems) arreglar, solucionar; ~**ing office** n sala de batalla
SOS n SOS m
so-so adv regular, así así
soufflé ['suːfleɪ] n suflé m
sought [sɔːt] pt, pp of **seek**
soul [səul] n alma; ~**ful** adj lleno de sentimiento
sound [saund] n (noise) sonido, ruido; (volume: on TV etc) volumen m; (GEO) estrecho ♦ adj (healthy) sano; (safe, not damaged) en buen estado; (reliable: person) digno de confianza; (sensible) sensato, razonable; (secure: investment) seguro ♦ adv: ~ **asleep** profundamente dormido ♦ vt (alarm) sonar ♦ vi sonar, resonar; (fig: seem) parecer; **to ~ like** sonar a; ~ **out** vt sondear; ~ **barrier** n barrera del sonido; ~**bite** n cita jugosa; ~ **effects** npl efectos mpl sonoros; ~**ly** adv (sleep) profundamente; (defeated) completamente; ~**proof** adj insonorizado; ~**track** n (of film) banda sonora
soup [suːp] n (thick) sopa; (thin) caldo; ~ **plate** n plato sopero; ~**spoon** n cuchara sopera
sour ['sauə*] adj agrio; (milk) cortado; **it's ~ grapes** (fig) están verdes
source [sɔːs] n fuente f
south [sauθ] n sur m ♦ adj del sur, sureño ♦ adv al sur, hacia el sur; **S~ Africa** n África del Sur; **S~ African** adj, n sudafricano/a m/f; **S~ America** n América del Sur, Sudamérica; **S~ American** adj, n sudamericano/a m/f; ~**-east** n sudeste m; ~**erly** ['sʌðəlɪ] adj (from the ~) del sur; ~**ern** ['sʌðən] adj del sur, meridional; **S~ Pole** n Polo Sur; ~**ward(s)** adv hacia el sur; ~**-west** n suroeste m
souvenir [suːvə'nɪə*] n recuerdo
sovereign ['sɔvrɪn] adj, n soberano/a m/f; ~**ty** n soberanía
soviet ['səuvɪət] adj soviético; **the S~ Union** la Unión Soviética

sow¹ [səu] (*pt* sowed, *pp* sown) *vt* sembrar

sow² [sau] *n* cerda (*SP*), puerca (*SP*), chancha (*AM*)

soy [sɔɪ] (*US*) *n* = **soya**

soya ['sɔɪə] (*BRIT*) *n* soja; **~ bean** *n* haba de soja; **~ sauce** *n* salsa de soja

spa [spɑ:] *n* balneario

space [speɪs] *n* espacio; (*room*) sitio ♦ *cpd* espacial ♦ *vt* (*also:* **~ out**) espaciar; **~craft** *n* nave *f* espacial; **~man/woman** (*irreg*) *n* astronauta *m/f*, cosmonauta *m/f*; **~ship** *n* = **~craft**; **spacing** *n* espaciado

spacious ['speɪʃəs] *adj* amplio

spade [speɪd] *n* (*tool*) pala, laya; **~s** *npl* (*CARDS*: British) picas *fpl*; (: *Spanish*) espadas *fpl*

spaghetti [spə'gɛtɪ] *n* espaguetis *mpl*, fideos *mpl*

Spain [speɪn] *n* España

span [spæn] *n* (*of bird, plane*) envergadura; (*of arch*) luz *f*; (*in time*) lapso *f* ♦ *vt* extenderse sobre, cruzar; (*fig*) abarcar

Spaniard ['spænjəd] *n* español(a) *m/f*

spaniel ['spænjəl] *n* perro de aguas

Spanish ['spænɪʃ] *adj* español(a) ♦ *n* (*LING*) español *m*, castellano; **the ~** *npl* los españoles

spank [spæŋk] *vt* zurrar

spanner ['spænə*] (*BRIT*) *n* llave *f* (inglesa)

spare [spεə*] *adj* de reserva; (*surplus*) sobrante, de más ♦ *n* = **~ part** ♦ *vt* (*do without*) pasarse sin; (*refrain from hurting*) perdonar; **to ~** (*surplus*) sobrante, de sobra; **~ part** *n* pieza de repuesto; **~ time** *n* tiempo libre; **~ wheel** *n* (*AUT*) rueda de recambio

sparingly ['spεərɪŋlɪ] *adv* con moderación

spark [spɑ:k] *n* chispa; (*fig*) chispazo; **~(ing) plug** *n* bujía

sparkle ['spɑ:kl] *n* centelleo, destello ♦ *vi* (*shine*) relucir, brillar; **sparkling** *adj* (*eyes, conversation*) brillante; (*wine*) espumoso; (*mineral water*) con gas

sparrow ['spærəu] *n* gorrión *m*

sparse [spɑ:s] *adj* esparcido, escaso

spartan ['spɑ:tən] *adj* (*fig*) espartano

spasm ['spæzəm] *n* (*MED*) espasmo

spastic ['spæstɪk] *n* espástico/a

spat [spæt] *pt*, *pp of* spit

spate [speɪt] *n* (*fig*): **a ~ of** un torrente de

spawn [spɔ:n] *vi* desovar, frezar ♦ *n* huevas *fpl*

speak [spi:k] (*pt* spoke, *pp* spoken) *vt* (*language*) hablar; (*truth*) decir ♦ *vi* hablar; (*make a speech*) intervenir; **to ~ to sb/of** *or* **about sth** hablar con uno/de *or* sobre algo; **~ up!** ¡habla fuerte!; **~er** *n* (*in public*) orador(a) *m/f*; (*also:* loud~er) altavoz *m*; (*for stereo etc*) bafle *m*; (*POL*): **the S~er** (*BRIT*) el Presidente de la Cámara de los Comunes; (*US*) el Presidente del Congreso

spear [spɪə*] *n* lanza ♦ *vt* alancear; **~head** *vt* (*attack etc*) encabezar

spec [spɛk] (*inf*) *n*: **on ~** como especulación

special ['spɛʃl] *adj* especial; (*edition etc*) extraordinario; (*delivery*) urgente; **~ist** *n* especialista *m/f*; **~ity** [spɛʃɪ'ælɪtɪ] (*BRIT*) *n* especialidad *f*; **~ize** *vi*: **to ~ize (in)** especializarse (en); **~ly** *adv* sobre todo, en particular; **~ty** (*US*) *n* = **~ity**

species ['spi:ʃi:z] *n inv* especie *f*

specific [spə'sɪfɪk] *adj* específico; **~ally** *adv* específicamente

specify ['spɛsɪfaɪ] *vt*, *vi* especificar, precisar

specimen ['spɛsɪmən] *n* ejemplar *m*; (*MED*: *of urine*) espécimen *m* (: *of blood*) muestra

speck [spɛk] *n* grano, mota

speckled ['spɛkld] *adj* moteado

specs [spɛks] (*inf*) *npl* gafas *fpl* (*SP*), anteojos *mpl*

spectacle ['spɛktəkl] *n* espectáculo; **~s** *npl* (*BRIT*: *glasses*) gafas *fpl* (*SP*), anteojos *mpl*; **spectacular** [-'tækjulə*] *adj* espectacular; (*success*) impresionante

spectator [spɛk'teɪtə*] *n* espectador(a) *m/f*

spectrum ['spɛktrəm] (*pl* spectra) *n* espectro

speculate ['spɛkjuleɪt] *vi*: **to ~ (on)** especular (en); **speculation** [spɛkju'leɪʃən] *n* especulación *f*

speech [spi:tʃ] *n* (*faculty*) habla; (*formal talk*) discurso; (*spoken language*) lenguaje *m*; **~less** *adj* mudo, estupefacto; **~ therapist** *n* especialista que corrige defectos de pronunciación en los niños

speed [spi:d] *n* velocidad *f*; (*haste*) prisa; (*promptness*) rapidez *f*; **at full** *or* **top ~** a máxima velocidad; **~ up** *vi* acelerarse ♦ *vt* acelerar; **~boat** *n* lancha motora; **~ily** *adv* rápido, rápidamente; **~ing** *n* (*AUT*) exceso de velocidad; **~ limit** *n* límite *m* de velocidad, velocidad *f* máxima; **~ometer** [spɪ'dɔmɪtə*] *n* velocímetro; **~way** *n* (*sport*) pista de carrera; **~y** *adj* (*fast*) veloz, rápido; (*prompt*) pronto

spell [spɛl] (*pt*, *pp* spelt (*BRIT*) *or* spelled) *n* (*also: magic ~*) encanto, hechizo; (*period of time*) rato, período ♦ *vt* (*also*) anunciar, presagiar; **to cast a ~ on sb** hechizar a uno; **he can't ~** pone faltas de ortografía; **~bound** *adj* embelesado, hechizado; **~ing** *n* ortografía

spend [spɛnd] (*pt*, *pp* spent) *vt* (*money*) gastar; (*time*) pasar; (*life*) dedicar; **~thrift** *n* derrochador(a) *m/f*, pródigo/a

sperm [spɑ:m] *n* esperma

sphere [sfɪə*] *n* esfera

sphinx [sfɪŋks] *n* esfinge *f*

spice [spaɪs] *n* especia ♦ *vt* condimentar

spicy ['spaɪsɪ] *adj* picante

spider ['spaɪdə*] n araña

spike [spaɪk] n (point) punta; (BOT) espiga

spill [spɪl] (pt, pp spilt or spilled) vt derramar, verter ♦ vi derramarse; **to ~ over** desbordarse

spin [spɪn] (pt, pp spun) n (AVIAT) barrena; (trip in car) paseo (en coche); (on ball) efecto ♦ vt (wool etc) hilar; (ball etc) hacer girar ♦ vi girar, dar vueltas

spinach ['spɪnɪtʃ] n espinaca; (as food) espinacas fpl

spinal ['spaɪnl] adj espinal; **~ cord** n columna vertebral

spin doctor n informador(a) parcial al servicio de un partido político etc

spin-dryer (BRIT) n secador m centrífugo

spine [spaɪn] n espinazo, columna vertebral; (thorn) espina; **~less** adj (fig) débil, pusilánime

spinning ['spɪnɪŋ] n hilandería; **~ top** n peonza

spin-off n derivado, producto secundario

spinster ['spɪnstə*] n solterona

spiral ['spaɪərl] n espiral f ♦ vi (fig: prices) subir desorbitadamente; **~ staircase** n escalera de caracol

spire ['spaɪə*] n aguja, chapitel m

spirit ['spɪrɪt] n (soul) alma f; (ghost) fantasma m; (attitude, sense) espíritu m; (courage) valor m, ánimo; **~s** npl (drink) licor(es) m(pl); **in good ~s** alegre, de buen ánimo; **~ed** adj enérgico, vigoroso

spiritual ['spɪrɪtjuəl] adj espiritual ♦ n espiritual m

spit [spɪt] (pt, pp spat) n (for roasting) asador m, espetón m; (saliva) saliva ♦ vi escupir; (sound) chisporrotear; (rain) lloviznar

spite [spaɪt] n rencor m, ojeriza ♦ vt causar pena a, mortificar; **in ~ of** a pesar de, pese a; **~ful** adj rencoroso, malévolo

spittle ['spɪtl] n saliva, baba

splash [splæʃ] n (sound) chapoteo; (of colour) mancha ♦ vt salpicar ♦ vi (also: ~ about) chapotear

spleen [spliːn] n (ANAT) bazo

splendid ['splendɪd] adj espléndido

splint [splɪnt] n tablilla

splinter ['splɪntə*] n (of wood etc) astilla; (in finger) espigón m ♦ vi astillarse, hacer astillas

split [splɪt] (pt, pp split) n hendedura, raja; (fig) división f; (POL) escisión f ♦ vt partir, rajar; (party) dividir; (share) repartir ♦ vi dividirse, escindirse; **~ up** vi (couple) separarse; (meeting) acabarse

spoil [spɔɪl] (pt, pp spoilt or spoiled) vt (damage) dañar; (mar) estropear; (child) mimar, consentir; **~s** npl despojo, botín m; **~sport** n aguafiestas m inv

spoke [spəuk] pt of **speak** ♦ n rayo, radio

spoken ['spəukn] pp of **speak**

spokesman ['spəuksmən] (irreg) n portavoz m; **spokeswoman** ['spəukswumən] (irreg) n portavoz f

sponge [spʌndʒ] n esponja; (also: ~ cake) bizcocho ♦ vt (wash) lavar con esponja ♦ vi: **to ~ off** or **on sb** vivir a costa de uno; **~ bag** (BRIT) n esponjera

sponsor ['spɔnsə*] n patrocinador(a) m/f ♦ vt (applicant, proposal etc) proponer; **~ship** n patrocinio

spontaneous [spɔn'teɪnɪəs] adj espontáneo

spooky ['spuːkɪ] (inf) adj espeluznante, horripilante

spool [spuːl] n carrete m

spoon [spuːn] n cuchara; **~-feed** vt dar de comer con cuchara a; (fig) tratar como un niño a; **~ful** n cucharada

sport [spɔːt] n deporte m; (person): **to be a good ~** ser muy majo ♦ vt (wear) lucir, ostentar; **~ing** adj deportivo; (generous) caballeroso; **to give sb a ~ing chance** darle a uno una (buena) oportunidad; **~ jacket** (US) n = **~s jacket**; **~s car** n coche m deportivo; **~s jacket** (BRIT) n chaqueta deportiva; **~sman** (irreg) n deportista m; **~smanship** n deportividad f; **~swear** n trajes mpl de deporte or sport; **~swoman** (irreg) n deportista; **~y** adj deportista

spot [spɔt] n sitio, lugar m; (dot: on pattern) punto, mancha; (pimple) grano; (RADIO) cuña publicitaria; (TV) espacio publicitario; (small amount): **a ~ of** un poquito de ♦ vt (notice) notar, observar; **on the ~** allí mismo; **~ check** n reconocimiento rápido; **~less** adj perfectamente limpio; **~light** n foco, reflector m; (AUT) faro auxiliar; **~ted** adj (pattern) de puntos; **~ty** adj (face) con granos

spouse [spauz] n cónyuge m/f

spout [spaut] n (of jug) pico; (of pipe) caño ♦ vi salir en chorro

sprain [spreɪn] n torcedura ♦ vt: **to ~ one's ankle/wrist** torcerse el tobillo/la muñeca

sprang [spræŋ] pt of **spring**

sprawl [sprɔːl] vi tumbarse

spray [spreɪ] n rociada; (of sea) espuma; (container) atomizador m; (for paint etc) pistola rociadora; (of flowers) ramita ♦ vt rociar; (crops) regar

spread [spred] (pt, pp spread) n extensión f; (for bread etc) pasta para untar; (inf: food) comilona ♦ vt extender; (butter) untar; (wings, sails) desplegar; (work, wealth) repartir; (scatter) esparcir ♦ vi (also: ~ out: stain) extenderse; (news) diseminarse; **~ out** vi (move apart) separarse; **~-eagled** adj a pata tendida; **~sheet** n hoja electrónica or de cálculo

spree [spriː] n: **to go on a ~** ir de juerga

sprightly ['spraɪtlɪ] adj vivo, enérgico

spring [sprɪŋ] (*pt* **sprang**, *pp* **sprung**) *n* (*season*) primavera; (*leap*) salto, brinco; (*coiled metal*) resorte *m*; (*of water*) fuente *f*, manantial *m* ♦ *vi* saltar, brincar; **~ up** *vi* (*thing: appear*) aparecer; (*problem*) surgir; **~board** *n* trampolín *m*; **~-clean(ing)** *n* limpieza general; **~time** *n* primavera

sprinkle [ˈsprɪŋkl] *vt* (*pour: liquid*) rociar; (*: salt, sugar*) espolvorear; **to ~ water** *etc* **on, ~ with water** *etc* rociar or salpicar de agua *etc*; **~r** *n* (*for lawn*) rociadera; (*to put out fire*) aparato de rociadura automática

sprint [sprɪnt] *n* esprint *m* ♦ *vi* esprintar

sprout [spraʊt] *vi* brotar, retoñar; **(Brussels) ~s** *npl* coles *fpl* de Bruselas

spruce [spruːs] *n inv* (*BOT*) pícea ♦ *adj* aseado, pulcro

sprung [sprʌŋ] *pp of* **spring**

spun [spʌn] *pt*, *pp of* **spin**

spur [spəː*] *n* espuela; (*fig*) estímulo, aguijón *m* ♦ *vt* (*also*: **~ on**) estimular, incitar; **on the ~ of the moment** de improviso

spurious [ˈspjʊərɪəs] *adj* falso

spurn [spəːn] *vt* desdeñar, rechazar

spurt [spəːt] *n* chorro; (*of energy*) arrebato ♦ *vi* chorrear

spy [spaɪ] *n* espía *m/f* ♦ *vi*: **to ~ on** espiar a ♦ *vt* (*see*) divisar, lograr ver; **~ing** *n* espionaje *m*

sq. *abbr* = **square**

squabble [ˈskwɔbl] *vi* reñir, pelear

squad [skwɔd] *n* (*MIL*) pelotón *m*; (*POLICE*) brigada; (*SPORT*) equipo

squadron [ˈskwɔdrɪn] *n* (*MIL*) escuadrón *m*; (*AVIAT, NAUT*) escuadra

squalid [ˈskwɔlɪd] *adj* vil; (*fig: sordid*) sórdido

squall [skwɔːl] *n* (*storm*) chubasco; (*wind*) ráfaga

squalor [ˈskwɔlə*] *n* miseria

squander [ˈskwɔndə*] *vt* (*money*) derrochar, despilfarrar; (*chances*) desperdiciar

square [skwɛə*] *n* cuadro; (*in town*) plaza; (*inf: person*) carca *m/f* ♦ *adj* cuadrado; (*inf: ideas, tastes*) trasnochado ♦ *vt* (*arrange*) arreglar; (*MATH*) cuadrar; (*reconcile*) compaginar; **all ~** igual(es); **to have a ~ meal** comer caliente; **2 metres ~** 2 metros en cuadro; **2 ~ metres** 2 metros cuadrados; **~ly** *adv* de lleno

squash [skwɔʃ] *n* (*BRIT: drink*): **lemon/orange ~** zumo (*SP*) or jugo (*AM*) de limón/naranja; (*US: BOT*) calabacín *m*; (*SPORT*) squash *m*, frontenis *m* ♦ *vt* aplastar

squat [skwɔt] *adj* achaparrado ♦ *vi* (*also*: **~ down**) agacharse, sentarse en cuclillas; **~ter** *n* persona que ocupa ilegalmente una casa

squeak [skwiːk] *vi* (*hinge*) chirriar, rechinar; (*mouse*) chillar

squeal [skwiːl] *vi* chillar, dar gritos agudos

squeamish [ˈskwiːmɪʃ] *adj* delicado, remilgado

squeeze [skwiːz] *n* presión *f*; (*of hand*) apretón *m*; (*COMM*) restricción *f* ♦ *vt* (*hand, arm*) apretar; **~ out** *vt* exprimir

squelch [skwɛltʃ] *vi* chapotear

squid [skwɪd] *n inv* calamar *m*; (*CULIN*) calamares *mpl*

squiggle [ˈskwɪgl] *n* garabato

squint [skwɪnt] *vi* bizquear, ser bizco ♦ *n* (*MED*) estrabismo

squirm [skwəːm] *vi* retorcerse, revolverse

squirrel [ˈskwɪrəl] *n* ardilla

squirt [skwəːt] *vi* salir a chorros ♦ *vt* chiscar

Sr *abbr* = **senior**

St *abbr* = **saint; street**

stab [stæb] *n* (*with knife*) puñalada; (*of pain*) pinchazo; (*inf: try*): **to have a ~ at (doing) sth** intentar (hacer) algo ♦ *vt* apuñalar

stable [ˈsteɪbl] *adj* estable ♦ *n* cuadra, caballeriza

stack [stæk] *n* montón *m*, pila ♦ *vt* amontonar, apilar

stadium [ˈsteɪdɪəm] *n* estadio

staff [stɑːf] *n* (*work force*) personal *m*, plantilla; (*BRIT: SCOL*) cuerpo docente ♦ *vt* proveer de personal

stag [stæg] *n* ciervo, venado

stage [steɪdʒ] *n* escena; (*point*) etapa; (*platform*) plataforma; (*profession*): **the ~** el teatro ♦ *vt* (*play*) poner en escena, representar; (*organize*) montar, organizar; **in ~s** por etapas; **~coach** *n* diligencia; **~ manager** *n* director(a) *m/f* de escena

stagger [ˈstægə*] *vi* tambalearse ♦ *vt* (*amaze*) asombrar; (*hours, holidays*) escalonar; **~ing** *adj* asombroso

stagnant [ˈstægnənt] *adj* estancado

stag party *n* despedida de soltero

staid [steɪd] *adj* serio, formal

stain [steɪn] *n* mancha; (*colouring*) tintura ♦ *vt* manchar; (*wood*) teñir; **~ed glass window** *n* vidriera de colores; **~less steel** *n* acero inoxidable; **~ remover** *n* quitamanchas *m inv*

stair [stɛə*] *n* (*step*) peldaño, escalón *m*; **~s** *npl* escaleras *fpl*; **~case** *n* = **~way**; **~way** *n* escalera

stake [steɪk] *n* estaca, poste *m*; (*COMM*) interés *m*; (*BETTING*) apuesta ♦ *vt* (*money*) apostar; (*life*) arriesgar; (*reputation*) poner en juego; (*claim*) presentar una reclamación; **to be at ~** estar en juego

stale [steɪl] *adj* (*bread*) duro; (*food*) pasado; (*smell*) rancio; (*beer*) agrio

stalemate [ˈsteɪlmeɪt] *n* tablas *fpl* (por ahogado); (*fig*) estancamiento

stalk [stɔːk] *n* tallo, caña ♦ *vt* acechar, cazar al acecho; **~ off** *vi* irse airado

stall [stɔːl] n (in market) puesto; (in stable) casilla (de establo) ♦ vt (AUT) calar; (fig) dar largas a ♦ vi (AUT) calarse; (fig) andarse con rodeos; ~s npl (BRIT: in cinema, theatre) butacas fpl

stallion ['stæliən] n semental m

stamina ['stæmɪnə] n resistencia

stammer ['stæmə*] n tartamudeo ♦ vi tartamudear

stamp [stæmp] n sello (SP), estampilla (AM); (mark, also fig) marca, huella; (on document) timbre m ♦ vi (also: ~ one's foot) patear ♦ vt (mark) marcar; (letter) poner sellos or estampillas en; (with rubber ~) sellar; ~ album n álbum m para sellos or estampillas; ~ collecting n filatelia

stampede [stæm'piːd] n estampida

stance [stæns] n postura

stand [stænd] (pt, pp stood) n (position) posición f, postura; (for taxis) parada; (hall ~) perchero; (music ~) atril m; (SPORT) tribuna; (at exhibition) stand m ♦ vi (be) estar, encontrarse; (be on foot) estar de pie; (rise) levantarse; (remain) quedar en pie; (in election) presentar candidatura ♦ vt (place) poner, colocar; (withstand) aguantar, soportar; (invite to) invitar; to make a ~ (fig) mantener una postura firme; to ~ for parliament (BRIT) presentarse (como candidato) a las elecciones; ~ by vi (be ready) estar listo ♦ vt fus (opinion) aferrarse a; (person) apoyar; ~ down vi (withdraw) ceder el puesto; ~ for vt fus (signify) significar; (tolerate) aguantar, permitir; ~ in for vt fus suplir a; ~ out vi destacarse; ~ up vi levantarse, ponerse de pie; ~ up for vt fus defender; ~ up to vt fus hacer frente a

standard ['stændəd] n patrón m, norma; (level) nivel m; (flag) estandarte m ♦ adj (size etc) normal, corriente; (text) básico; ~s npl (morals) valores mpl morales; ~ lamp (BRIT) n lámpara de pie; ~ of living n nivel m de vida

stand-by ['stændbaɪ] n (reserve) recurso seguro; to be on ~ estar sobre aviso; ~ ticket n (AVIAT) (billete m) standby m

stand-in ['stændɪn] n suplente m/f

standing ['stændɪŋ] adj (on foot) de pie, en pie; (permanent) permanente ♦ n reputación f; of many years' ~ que lleva muchos años; ~ joke n broma permanente; ~ order (BRIT) n (at bank) orden f de pago permanente; ~ room n sitio para estar de pie

stand: ~point n punto de vista; ~still n: at a ~still (industry, traffic) paralizado; (car) parado; to come to a ~still quedar paralizado, pararse

stank [stæŋk] pt of stink

staple ['steɪpl] n (for papers) grapa ♦ adj

(food etc) básico ♦ vt grapar; ~r n grapadora

star [stɑː*] n estrella; (celebrity) estrella, astro ♦ vt (THEATRE, CINEMA) ser el/la protagonista de; the ~s npl (ASTROLOGY) el horóscopo

starboard ['stɑːbəd] n estribor m

stareh [stɑːtʃ] n almidón m

stardom ['stɑːdəm] n estrellato

stare [steə*] n mirada fija ♦ vi: to ~ at mirar fijo

starfish ['stɑːfɪʃ] n estrella de mar

stark [stɑːk] adj (bleak) severo, escueto ♦ adv: ~ naked en cueros

starling ['stɑːlɪŋ] n estornino

starry ['stɑːrɪ] adj estrellado; ~-eyed adj (innocent) inocentón/ona, ingenuo

start [stɑːt] n principio, comienzo; (departure) salida; (sudden movement) salto, sobresalto; (advantage) ventaja ♦ vt empezar, comenzar; (cause) causar; (found) fundar; (engine) poner en marcha ♦ vi comenzar, empezar; (with fright) asustarse, sobresaltarse; (train etc) salir; to ~ doing or to do sth empezar a hacer algo; ~ off vi empezar, comenzar; (leave) salir, ponerse en camino; ~ up vi comenzar; (car) ponerse en marcha ♦ vt comenzar; poner en marcha; ~er n (AUT) botón m de arranque; (SPORT: official) juez m/f de salida; (BRIT: CULIN) entrada; ~ing point n punto de partida

startle ['stɑːtl] vt asustar, sobrecoger; **startling** adj alarmante

starvation [stɑː'veɪʃən] n hambre f

starve [stɑːv] vi tener mucha hambre; (to death) morir de hambre ♦ vt hacer pasar hambre

state [steɪt] n estado ♦ vt (say, declare) afirmar; the S~s los Estados Unidos; to be in a ~ estar agitado; ~ly adj majestuoso, imponente; ~ly home n casa señorial, casa solariega; ~ment n afirmación f; ~sman (irreg) n estadista m

static ['stætɪk] n (RADIO) parásitos mpl ♦ adj estático; ~ electricity n estática

station ['steɪʃən] n (gen) estación f; (RADIO) emisora; (rank) posición f social ♦ vt colocar, situar; (MIL) apostar

stationary ['steɪʃnərɪ] adj estacionario, fijo

stationer ['steɪʃənə*] n papelero/a; ~'s (shop) (BRIT) n papelería; ~y [-nərɪ] n papel m de escribir, artículos mpl de escritorio

station master n (RAIL) jefe m de estación

station wagon (US) n ranchera

statistic [stə'tɪstɪk] n estadística; ~s n (science) estadística

statue ['stætjuː] n estatua

status ['steɪtəs] n estado; (reputation) estatus m; ~ symbol n símbolo de prestigio

statute ['stætjuːt] n estatuto, ley f; **statutory** adj estatutario

staunch [stɔːntʃ] adj leal, incondicional

stay [steɪ] n estancia ♦ vi quedar(se); (as guest) hospedarse; **to ~ put** seguir en el mismo sitio; **to ~ the night/5 days** pasar la noche/estar 5 días; **~ behind** vi quedar atrás; **~ in** vi quedarse en casa; **~ on** vi quedarse; **~ out** vi (of house) no volver a casa; (on strike) permanecer en huelga; **~ up** vi (at night) velar, no acostarse; **~ing power** n aguante m

stead [sted]: n: **in sb's ~** en lugar de uno; **to stand sb in good ~** ser muy útil a uno

steadfast ['stedfɑːst] adj firme, resuelto

steadily ['stedɪlɪ] adv constantemente; (firmly) firmemente; (work, walk) sin parar; (gaze) fijamente

steady ['stedɪ] adj (firm) firme; (regular) regular; (person, character) sensato, juicioso; (boyfriend) formal; (look, voice) tranquilo ♦ vt (stabilize) estabilizar; (nerves) calmar

steak [steɪk] n (gen) filete m; (beef) bistec m

steal [stiːl] (pt **stole**, pp **stolen**) vt robar ♦ vi robar; (move secretly) andar a hurtadillas

stealth [stelθ] n: **by ~** a escondidas, sigilosamente; **~y** adj cauteloso, sigiloso

steam [stiːm] n vapor m; (mist) vaho, humo ♦ vt (CULIN) cocer al vapor ♦ vi echar vapor; **~ engine** n máquina de vapor; **~er** n (buque m de) vapor m; **~roller** n apisonadora; **~ship** n = **~er**; **~y** adj (room) lleno de vapor; (window) empañado; (heat, atmosphere) bochornoso

steel [stiːl] n acero ♦ adj de acero; **~works** n acería

steep [stiːp] adj escarpado, abrupto; (stair) empinado; (price) exorbitante, excesivo ♦ vt empapar, remojar

steeple ['stiːpl] n aguja; **~chase** n carrera de obstáculos

steer [stɪə*] vt (car) conducir (SP), manejar (AM); (person) dirigir ♦ vi conducir, manejar; **~ing** n (AUT) dirección f; **~ing wheel** n volante m

stem [stem] n (of plant) tallo m; (of glass) pie m ♦ vt detener; (blood) restañar; **~ from** vt fus ser consecuencia de

stench [stentʃ] n hedor m

stencil ['stensl] n (pattern) plantilla ♦ vt hacer un cliché de

stenographer [ste'nɔgrəfə*] (US) n taquígrafo/a

step [step] n paso; (on stair) peldaño, escalón m ♦ vi: **to ~ forward/back** dar un paso adelante/hacia atrás; **~s** npl (BRIT) = **~ladder**; **in/out of ~ (with)** acorde/en disonancia (con); **~ down** vi (fig) retirarse; **~ on** vt fus pisar; **~ up** vt (increase) aumentar; **~brother** n hermanastro; **~daughter** n hijastra; **~father** n padrastro; **~ladder** n escalera

doble or de tijera; **~mother** n madrastra; **~ping stone** n pasadera; **~sister** n hermanastra; **~son** n hijastro

stereo ['stɪərɪəu] n estéreo ♦ adj (also: ~phonic) estéreo, estereofónico

sterile ['sterail] adj estéril; **sterilize** ['sterilaiz] vt esterilizar

sterling ['stəːlɪŋ] adj (silver) de ley ♦ n (ECON) (libras fpl) esterlinas fpl; **one pound ~** una libra esterlina

stern [stəːn] adj severo, austero ♦ n (NAUT) popa

stew [stjuː] n cocido (SP), estofado (SP), guisado (AM) ♦ vt estofar, guisar; (fruit) cocer

steward ['stjuːəd] n camarero; **~ess** n (esp on plane) azafata

stick [stɪk] (pt, pp **stuck**) n palo; (of dynamite) barreno; (as weapon) porra; (walking ~) bastón m ♦ vt (glue) pegar; (inf: put) meter; (: tolerate) aguantar, soportar; (thrust): **to ~ sth into** clavar or hincar algo en ♦ vi pegarse; (be unmoveable) quedarse parado; (in mind) quedarse grabado; **~ out** vi sobresalir; **~ up** vi sobresalir; **~ up for** vt fus defender; **~er** n (label) etiqueta engomada; (with slogan) pegatina; **~ing plaster** n esparadrapo

stick-up ['stɪkʌp] (inf) n asalto, atraco

sticky ['stɪkɪ] adj pegajoso; (label) engomado; (fig) difícil

stiff [stɪf] adj rígido, tieso; (hard) duro; (manner) estirado; (difficult) difícil; (person) inflexible; (price) exorbitante ♦ adv: **scared/bored ~** muerto de miedo/aburrimiento; **~en** vi (muscles etc) agarrotarse; **~ neck** n tortícolis m inv; **~ness** n rigidez f, tiesura

stifle ['staɪfl] vt ahogar, sofocar; **stifling** adj (heat) sofocante, bochornoso

stigma ['stɪgmə] n (fig) estigma m

stile [staɪl] n portillo, portilla

stiletto [stɪ'letəu] (BRIT) n (also: ~ heel) tacón m de aguja

still [stɪl] adj inmóvil, quieto ♦ adv todavía; (even) aun; (nonetheless) sin embargo, aun así; **~born** adj nacido muerto; **~ life** n naturaleza muerta

stilt [stɪlt] n zanco; (pile) pilar m, soporte m

stilted ['stɪltɪd] adj afectado

stimulate ['stɪmjuleɪt] vt estimular

stimulus ['stɪmjuləs] (pl **stimuli**) n estímulo, incentivo

sting [stɪŋ] (pt, pp **stung**) n picadura; (pain) escozor m, picazón f; (organ) aguijón m ♦ vt, vi picar

stingy ['stɪndʒɪ] adj tacaño

stink [stɪŋk] (pt **stank**, pp **stunk**) n hedor m, tufo ♦ vi heder, apestar; **~ing** adj hediondo, fétido; (fig: inf) horrible

stint [stɪnt] n tarea, trabajo ♦ vi: **to ~ on**

escatimar

stir [stə:*] n (fig: agitation) conmoción f ♦ vt (tea etc) remover; (fig: emotions) provocar ♦ vi moverse; ~ **up** vt (trouble) fomentar

stirrup ['stɪrəp] n estribo

stitch [stɪtʃ] n (SEWING) puntada; (KNITTING) punto; (MED) punto (de sutura); (pain) punzada ♦ vt coser; (MED) suturar

stoat [stəut] n armiño

stock [stɔk] n (COMM: reserves) existencias fpl, stock m; (: selection) surtido; (AGR) ganado, ganadería; (CULIN) caldo; (descent) raza, estirpe f; (FINANCE) capital m ♦ adj (fig: reply etc) clásico ♦ vt (have in ~) tener existencias de; ~**s and shares** acciones y valores; **in ~** en existencia or almacén; **out of ~** agotado; **to take ~ of** (fig) asesorar, examinar; ~ **up with** vt fus abastecerse de; ~**broker** ['stɔkbrəukə*] n agente m/f o corredor(a) m/f de bolsa; ~ **cube** (BRIT) n pastilla de caldo; ~ **exchange** n bolsa

stocking ['stɔkɪŋ] n media

stock: ~ **market** n bolsa (de valores); ~**pile** n reserva ♦ vt acumular, almacenar; ~**taking** (BRIT) n inventario

stocky ['stɔkɪ] adj (strong) robusto; (short) achaparrado

stodgy ['stɔdʒɪ] adj indigesto, pesado

stoke [stəuk] vt atizar

stole [stəul] pt of **steal** ♦ n estola

stolen ['stəulɪn] pp of **steal**

stomach ['stʌmək] n (ANAT) estómago; (belly) vientre m ♦ vt tragar, aguantar; ~**ache** n dolor m de estómago

stone [stəun] n piedra; (in fruit) hueso; = 6.348 kg; 14 libras ♦ adj de piedra ♦ vt apedrear; (fruit) deshuesar; ~**-cold** adj helado; ~**-deaf** adj sordo como una tapia; ~**work** n (art) cantería; **stony** adj pedregoso; (fig) frío

stood [stud] pt, pp of **stand**

stool [stu:l] n taburete m

stoop [stu:p] vi (also: ~ down) doblarse, agacharse; (also: have a ~) ser cargado de espaldas

stop [stɔp] n parada; (in punctuation) punto ♦ vt parar, detener; (break off) suspender; (block: pay) suspender; (: cheque) invalidar; (also: put a ~ to) poner término a ♦ vi pararse, detenerse; (end) acabarse; **to ~ doing sth** dejar de hacer algo; ~ **dead** vi pararse en seco; ~ **off** vi interrumpir el viaje; ~ **up** vt (hole) tapar; ~**gap** n (person) interino/a; (thing) recurso provisional; ~**over** n parada; (AVIAT) escala

stoppage ['stɔpɪdʒ] n (strike) paro; (blockage) obstrucción f

stopper ['stɔpə*] n tapón m

stop press n noticias fpl de última hora

stopwatch ['stɔpwɔtʃ] n cronómetro

storage ['stɔːrɪdʒ] n almacenaje m; ~ **heater** n acumulador m

store [stɔː*] n (stock) provisión f; (depot: BRIT: large shop) almacén m; (US) tienda; (reserve) reserva, repuesto ♦ vt almacenar; ~**s** npl víveres mpl; **in ~** (fig): **to be in ~ for sb** esperarle a uno; ~ **up** vt acumular; ~**room** n despensa

storey ['stɔːrɪ] (US **story**) n piso

stork [stɔːk] n cigüeña

storm [stɔːm] n tormenta; (fig: of applause) salva; (: of criticism) nube f ♦ vi (fig) rabiar ♦ vt tomar por asalto; ~**y** adj tempestuoso

story ['stɔːrɪ] n historia; (lie) mentira; (US) = **storey**; ~**book** n libro de cuentos

stout [staut] adj (strong) sólido; (fat) gordo, corpulento; (resolute) resuelto ♦ n cerveza negra

stove [stəuv] n (for cooking) cocina; (for heating) estufa

stow [stəu] vt (also: ~ away) meter, poner; (NAUT) estibar; ~**away** n polizón/ona m/f

straggle ['strægl] vi (houses etc) extenderse; (lag behind) rezagarse

straight [streɪt] adj recto, derecho; (frank) franco, directo; (simple) sencillo ♦ adv derecho, directamente; (drink) sin mezcla; **to put** or **get sth ~** dejar algo en claro; ~ **away**, ~ **off** en seguida; ~**en** vt (also: ~**en out**) enderezar, poner derecho; ~**-faced** adj serio; ~**forward** adj (simple) sencillo; (honest) honrado, franco

strain [streɪn] n tensión f; (TECH) presión f; (MED) torcedura; (breed) tipo, variedad f ♦ vt (back etc) torcerse; (resources) agotar; (stretch) estirar; (food, tea) colar; ~**s** npl (MUS) son m; ~**ed** adj (muscle) torcido; (laugh) forzado; (relations) tenso; ~**er** n colador m

strait [streɪt] n (GEO) estrecho; **to be in dire ~s** pasar grandes apuros; ~**-jacket** n camisa de fuerza; ~**-laced** adj mojigato, gazmoño

strand [strænd] n (of thread) hebra; (of hair) trenza; (of rope) ramal m

stranded ['strændɪd] adj (person: without money) desamparado; (: without transport) colgado

strange [streɪndʒ] adj (not known) desconocido; (odd) extraño, raro; ~**ly** adv de un modo raro; see also **enough**; ~**r** n desconocido/a; (from another area) forastero/a

strangle ['stræŋgl] vt estrangular; ~**hold** n (fig) dominio completo

strap [stræp] n correa; (of slip, dress) tirante m

strategic [strə'tiːdʒɪk] adj estratégico

strategy ['strætɪdʒɪ] n estrategia

straw [strɔː] n paja; (drinking ~) caña, pajita;

that's the last ~! ¡eso es el colmo!

strawberry ['strɔːbərɪ] n fresa (SP), frutilla (AM)

stray [streɪ] adj (animal) extraviado; (bullet) perdido; (scattered) disperso ♦ vi extraviarse, perderse

streak [striːk] n raya; (in hair) raya ♦ vt rayar ♦ vi: **to ~ past** pasar como un rayo

stream [striːm] n riachuelo, arroyo; (of people, vehicles) riada, caravana; (of smoke, insults etc) chorro ♦ vt (SCOL) dividir en grupos por habilidad ♦ vi correr, fluir; **to ~ in/out** (people) entrar/salir en tropel

streamer ['striːmə*] n serpentina

streamlined ['striːmlaɪnd] adj aerodinámico

street [striːt] n calle f; **~car** n (US) n tranvía m; **~ lamp** n farol m; **~ plan** n plano; **~wise** (inf) adj que tiene mucha calle

strength [strɛŋθ] n fuerza; (of girder, knot etc) resistencia; (fig: power) poder m; **~en** vt fortalecer, reforzar

strenuous ['strɛnjuəs] adj (energetic, determined) enérgico

stress [strɛs] n presión f; (mental strain) estrés m; (accent) acento ♦ vt subrayar, recalcar; (syllable) acentuar

stretch [strɛtʃ] n (of sand etc) trecho ♦ vi estirarse; (extend): **to ~ to or as far as** extenderse hasta ♦ vt extender, estirar; (make demands of) exigir el máximo esfuerzo a; **~ out** vi tenderse ♦ vt (arm etc) extender; (spread) estirar

stretcher ['strɛtʃə*] n camilla

strewn [struːn] adj: **~ with** cubierto or sembrado de

stricken ['strɪkən] adj (person) herido; (city, industry etc) condenado; **~ with** (disease) afectado por

strict [strɪkt] adj severo; (exact) estricto; **~ly** adv severamente, estrictamente

stride [straɪd] (pt **strode**, pp **stridden**) n zancada, tranco ♦ vi dar zancadas, andar a trancos

strife [straɪf] n lucha

strike [straɪk] (pt, pp **struck**) n huelga; (of oil etc) descubrimiento; (attack) ataque m ♦ vt golpear, pegar; (oil etc) descubrir; (bargain, deal) cerrar ♦ vi declarar la huelga; (attack) atacar; (clock) dar la hora; **on ~** (workers) en huelga; **to ~ a match** encender un fósforo; **~ down** vt derribar; **~ up** vt (MUS) empezar a tocar; (conversation) entablar; (friendship) trabar; **~r** n huelguista m/f; (SPORT) delantero; **striking** adj llamativo

string [strɪŋ] (pt, pp **strung**) n (gen) cuerda; (row) hilera ♦ vt: **to ~ together** ensartar; **to ~ out** extenderse; **the ~s** npl (MUS) los instrumentos de cuerda; **to pull ~s** (fig) mover palancas; **~ bean** n judía verde,

habichuela; **~(ed) instrument** n (MUS) instrumento de cuerda

stringent ['strɪndʒənt] adj riguroso, severo

strip [strɪp] n tira; (of land) franja; (of metal) cinta, lámina ♦ vt desnudar; (paint) quitar; (also: ~ **down**: machine) desmontar ♦ vi desnudarse; **~ cartoon** n tira cómica (SP), historieta (AM)

stripe [straɪp] n raya; (MIL) galón m; **~d** adj a rayas, rayado

strip lighting n alumbrado fluorescente

stripper ['strɪpə*] n artista m/f de striptease

strive [straɪv] (pt **strove**, pp **striven**) vi: **to ~ for sth/to do sth** luchar por conseguir/hacer algo

strode [strəud] pt of **stride**

stroke [strəuk] n (blow) golpe m; (SWIMMING) brazada; (MED) apoplejía; (of paintbrush) toque m ♦ vt acariciar; **at a ~** de un solo golpe

stroll [strəul] n paseo, vuelta ♦ vi dar un paseo or una vuelta; **~er** (US) n (for child) sillita de ruedas

strong [strɔŋ] adj fuerte; **they are 50 ~** son 50; **~hold** n fortaleza; (fig) baluarte m; **~ly** adv fuertemente, con fuerza; (believe) firmemente; **~room** n cámara acorazada

strove [strəuv] pt of **strive**

struck [strʌk] pt, pp of **strike**

structure ['strʌktʃə*] n estructura; (building) construcción f

struggle ['strʌgl] n lucha ♦ vi luchar

strum [strʌm] vt (guitar) rasguear

strung [strʌŋ] pt, pp of **string**

strut [strʌt] n puntal m ♦ vi pavonearse

stub [stʌb] n (of ticket etc) talón m; (of cigarette) colilla; **to ~ one's toe on sth** dar con el dedo (del pie) contra algo; **~ out** vt apagar

stubble ['stʌbl] n rastrojo; (on chin) barba (incipiente)

stubborn ['stʌbən] adj terco, testarudo

stuck [stʌk] pt, pp of **stick** ♦ adj (jammed) atascado; **~-up** adj engreído, presumido

stud [stʌd] n (shirt ~) corchete m; (of boot) taco; (earring) pendiente m (de bolita); (also: ~ **farm**) caballeriza; (also: ~ **horse**) caballo semental ♦ vt (fig): **~ded with** salpicado de

student ['stjuːdənt] n estudiante m/f ♦ adj estudiantil; **~ driver** n (US) n aprendiz(a) m/f

studio ['stjuːdɪəu] n estudio; (artist's) taller m; **~ flat** (US **~ apartment**) n estudio

studious ['stjuːdɪəs] adj estudioso; (studied) calculado; **~ly** adv (carefully) con esmero

study ['stʌdɪ] n estudio ♦ vt estudiar; (examine) examinar, investigar ♦ vi estudiar

stuff [stʌf] n materia; (substance) material m, sustancia; (things) cosas fpl ♦ vt llenar;

(*CULIN*) rellenar; (*animals*) disecar; (*inf: push*) meter; **~ing** *n* relleno; **~y** *adj* (*room*) mal ventilado; (*person*) de miras estrechas

stumble ['stʌmbl] *vi* tropezar, dar un traspié; **to ~ across, ~ on** (*fig*) tropezar con; **stumbling block** *n* tropiezo, obstáculo

stump [stʌmp] *n* (*of tree*) tocón *m*; (*of limb*) muñón *m* ♦ *vt*: **to be ~ed for an answer** no saber qué contestar

stun [stʌn] *vt* dejar sin sentido

stung [stʌŋ] *pt, pp of* **sting**

stunk [stʌŋk] *pp of* **stink**

stunning ['stʌnɪŋ] *adj* (*fig: news*) pasmoso; (: *outfit etc*) sensacional

stunt [stʌnt] *n* (*in film*) escena peligrosa; (*publicity ~*) truco publicitario; **~man** (*irreg*) *n* doble *m*

stupid ['stju:pɪd] *adj* estúpido, tonto; **~ity** [-'pɪdɪtɪ] *n* estupidez *f*

sturdy ['stɜ:dɪ] *adj* robusto, fuerte

stutter ['stʌtə*] *n* tartamudeo ♦ *vi* tartamudear

sty [staɪ] *n* (*for pigs*) pocilga

stye [staɪ] *n* (*MED*) orzuelo

style [staɪl] *n* estilo; **stylish** *adj* elegante, a la moda

stylus ['staɪləs] *n* aguja

suave [swɑ:v] *adj* cortés

sub... [sʌb] *prefix* sub...; **~conscious** *adj* subconsciente; **~contract** *vt* subcontratar; **~divide** *vt* subdividir

subdue [səb'dju:] *vt* sojuzgar; (*passions*) dominar; **~d** *adj* (*light*) tenue; (*person*) sumiso, manso

subject [*n* 'sʌbdʒɪkt, *vb* səb'dʒɛkt] *n* súbdito; (*SCOL*) asignatura; (*matter*) tema *m*; (*GRAMMAR*) sujeto ♦ *vt*: **to ~ sb to sth** someter a uno a algo; **to be ~ to** (*law*) estar sujeto a; (*subj: person*) ser propenso a; **~ive** [-'dʒɛktɪv] *adj* subjetivo; **~ matter** *n* (*content*) contenido

sublet [sʌb'lɛt] *vt* subarrendar

submarine [sʌbmə'ri:n] *n* submarino

submerge [səb'mɜ:dʒ] *vt* sumergir ♦ *vi* sumergirse

submissive [səb'mɪsɪv] *adj* sumiso

submit [səb'mɪt] *vt* someter ♦ *vi*: **to ~ to sth** someterse a algo

subnormal [sʌb'nɔ:məl] *adj* anormal

subordinate [sə'bɔ:dɪnət] *adj, n* subordinado/a *m/f*

subpoena [səb'pi:nə] *n* (*LAW*) citación *f*

subscribe [səb'skraɪb] *vi* suscribir; **to ~ to** (*opinion, fund*) suscribir, aprobar; (*newspaper*) suscribirse a; **~r** *n* (*to periodical*) subscriptor(a) *m/f*; (*to telephone*) abonado/a

subscription [səb'skrɪpʃən] *n* abono; (*to magazine*) subscripción *f*

subsequent ['sʌbsɪkwənt] *adj* subsiguiente,

posterior; **~ly** *adv* posteriormente, más tarde

subside [səb'saɪd] *vi* hundirse; (*flood*) bajar; (*wind*) amainar; **subsidence** [-'saɪdns] *n* hundimiento; (*in road*) socavón *m*

subsidiary [səb'sɪdɪərɪ] *adj* secundario ♦ *n* sucursal *f*, filial *f*

subsidize ['sʌbsɪdaɪz] *vt* subvencionar

subsidy ['sʌbsɪdɪ] *n* subvención *f*

subsistence [səb'sɪstəns] *n* subsistencia; **~ allowance** *n* salario mínimo

substance ['sʌbstəns] *n* sustancia

substantial [səb'stænʃl] *adj* sustancial, sustancioso; (*fig*) importante

substantiate [səb'stænʃɪeɪt] *vt* comprobar

substitute ['sʌbstɪtju:t] *n* (*person*) suplente *m/f*; (*thing*) sustituto ♦ *vt*: **to ~ A for B** sustituir A por B, reemplazar B por A

subtitle ['sʌbtaɪtl] *n* subtítulo

subtle ['sʌtl] *adj* sutil; **~ty** *n* sutileza

subtotal [sʌb'teutl] *n* total *m* parcial

subtract [səb'trækt] *vt* restar, sustraer; **~ion** [-'trækʃən] *n* resta, sustracción *f*

suburb ['sʌbə:b] *n* barrio residencial; **the ~s** las afueras (de la ciudad); **~an** [sə'bə:bən] *adj* suburbano; (*train etc*) de cercanías; **~ia** [sə'bə:bɪə] *n* barrios *mpl* residenciales

subway ['sʌbweɪ] *n* (*BRIT*) paso subterráneo or inferior; (*US*) metro

succeed [sək'si:d] *vi* (*person*) tener éxito; (*plan*) salir bien ♦ *vt* suceder a; **to ~ in doing** lograr hacer; **~ing** *adj* (*following*) sucesivo

success [sək'sɛs] *n* éxito; **~ful** *adj* exitoso; (*business*) próspero; **to be ~ful (in doing)** lograr (hacer); **~fully** *adv* con éxito

succession [sək'sɛʃən] *n* sucesión *f*, serie *f*

successive [sək'sɛsɪv] *adj* sucesivo, consecutivo

succinct [sək'sɪŋkt] *adj* sucinto

such [sʌtʃ] *adj* tal, semejante; (*of that kind*): **~ a book** tal libro; (*so much*): **~ courage** tanto valor ♦ *adv* tan; **~ a long trip** un viaje tan largo; **~ a lot of** tanto(s)/a(s); **~ as** (*like*) tal como; **as ~** como tal; **~-and-~** *adj* tal o cual

suck [sʌk] *vt* chupar; (*bottle*) sorber; (*breast*) mamar; **~er** *n* (*ZOOL*) ventosa; (*inf*) bobo, primo

suction ['sʌkʃən] *n* succión *f*

Sudan [su'dæn] *n* Sudán *m*

sudden ['sʌdn] *adj* (*rapid*) repentino, súbito; (*unexpected*) imprevisto; **all of a ~** de repente; **~ly** *adv* de repente

suds [sʌdz] *npl* espuma de jabón

sue [su:] *vt* demandar

suede [sweɪd] *n* ante *m* (*SP*), gamuza (*AM*)

suet ['suɪt] *n* sebo

Suez ['su:ɪz] *n*: **the ~ Canal** el Canal de Suez

suffer ['sʌfə*] *vt* sufrir, padecer; (*tolerate*) aguantar, soportar ♦ *vi* sufrir; **to ~ from** (*illness etc*) padecer; **~er** *n* víctima; (*MED*) enfermo/a; **~ing** n sufrimiento

sufficient [sə'fɪʃənt] adj suficiente, bastante; **~ly** ad suficientemente, bastante

suffocate ['sʌfəkeɪt] vi ahogarse, asfixiarse; **suffocation** [-'keɪʃən] n asfixia

sugar ['ʃugə*] n azúcar m ♦ vt echar azúcar a, azucarar; **~ beet** n remolacha; **~ cane** n caña de azúcar

suggest [sə'dʒest] vt sugerir; **~ion** [-'dʒestʃən] n sugerencia; **~ive** (pej) adj indecente

suicide ['suɪsaɪd] n suicidio; (person) suicida m/f; see also **commit**

suit [su:t] n (man's) traje m; (woman's) conjunto; (LAW) pleito; (CARDS) palo ♦ vt convenir; (clothes) sentar a, ir bien a; (adapt): **to ~ sth to** adaptar or ajustar algo a; **well ~ed** (well matched: couple) hecho el uno para el otro; **~able** adj conveniente; (apt) indicado; **~ably** adv convenientemente; (impressed) apropiadamente

suitcase ['su:tkeɪs] n maleta (SP), valija (AM)

suite [swi:t] n (of rooms, MUS) suite f; (furniture): **bedroom/dining room ~** (juego de) dormitorio/comedor

suitor ['su:tə*] n pretendiente m

sulfur ['sʌlfə*] (US) n = **sulphur**

sulk [sʌlk] vi estar de mal humor; **~y** adj malhumorado

sullen ['sʌlən] adj hosco, malhumorado

sulphur ['sʌlfə*] (US sulfur) n azufre m

sultana [sʌl'tɑːnə] n (fruit) pasa de Esmirna

sultry ['sʌltrɪ] adj (weather) bochornoso

sum [sʌm] n suma; (total) total m; **~ up** vt resumir ♦ vi hacer un resumen

summarize ['sʌmaraɪz] vt resumir

summary ['sʌmərɪ] n resumen m ♦ adj (justice) sumario

summer ['sʌmə*] n verano ♦ cpd de verano; **in ~** en verano; **~ holidays** npl vacaciones fpl de verano; **~house** n (in garden) cenador m, glorieta; **~time** n (season) verano; **~ time** n (by clock) hora de verano

summit ['sʌmɪt] n cima, cumbre f; (also: **~ conference, ~ meeting**) (conferencia) cumbre f

summon ['sʌmən] vt (person) llamar; (meeting) convocar; (LAW) citar; **~ up** vt (courage) armarse de; **~s** n llamamiento, llamada ♦ vt (LAW) citar

sump [sʌmp] (BRIT) n (AUT) cárter m

sumptuous ['sʌmptjuəs] adj suntuoso

sun [sʌn] n sol m; **~bathe** vi tomar el sol; **~block** n filtro solar; **~burn** n (painful) quemadura; (tan) bronceado; **~burnt** adj quemado por el sol

Sunday ['sʌndɪ] n domingo; **~ school** n catequesis f dominical

sundial ['sʌndaɪəl] n reloj m de sol

sundown ['sʌndaun] n anochecer m

sundry ['sʌndrɪ] adj varios/as, diversos/as; **all and ~** todos sin excepción; **sundries** npl géneros mpl diversos

sunflower ['sʌnflauə*] n girasol m

sung [sʌŋ] pp of **sing**

sunglasses ['sʌnglɑːsɪz] npl gafas fpl (SP) or anteojos mpl de sol

sunk [sʌŋk] pp of **sink**

sun: ~light n luz f del sol; **~lit** adj iluminado por el sol; **~ny** adj soleado; (day) de sol; (fig) alegre; **~rise** n salida del sol; **~ roof** (AUT) techo corredizo; **~screen** n protector m solar; **~set** n puesta del sol; **~shade** (over table) sombrilla; **~shine** n sol m; **~stroke** n insolación f; **~tan** n bronceado; **~tan oil** n aceite m bronceador

super ['su:pə*] (inf) adj genial

superannuation [su:pərænju'eɪʃən] n cuota de jubilación

superb [su:'pə:b] adj magnífico, espléndido

supercilious [su:pə'sɪliəs] adj altanero

superfluous [su:'pə:fluəs] adj superfluo, de sobra

superhuman [su:pə'hju:mən] adj sobrehumano

superimpose ['su:pərɪm'pəuz] vt sobreponer

superintendent [su:pərɪn'tendənt] n director(a) m/f; (POLICE) subjefe/a m/f

superior [su'pɪərɪə*] adj superior; (smug) desdeñoso ♦ n superior m; **~ity** [-'ɔrɪtɪ] n superioridad f

superlative [su'pə:lətɪv] n superlativo

superman ['su:pəmæn] (irreg) n superhombre m

supermarket ['su:pəmɑːkɪt] n supermercado

supernatural [su:pə'nætʃərəl] adj sobrenatural ♦ n: **the ~** lo sobrenatural

superpower ['su:pəpauə*] n (POL) superpotencia

supersede [su:pə'si:d] vt suplantar

superstar ['su:pəstɑ:*] n gran estrella

superstitious [su:pə'stɪʃəs] adj supersticioso

supertanker ['su:pətæŋkə*] n superpetrolero

supervise ['su:pəvaɪz] vt supervisar; **supervision** [-'vɪʒən] n supervisión f; **supervisor** n supervisor(a) m/f

supper ['sʌpə*] n cena

supple ['sʌpl] adj flexible

supplement [n 'sʌplɪmənt, vb sʌplɪ'ment] n suplemento ♦ vt suplir; **~ary** [-'mentərɪ] adj suplementario; **~ary benefit** (BRIT) n subsidio suplementario de la seguridad social

supplier [sə'plaɪə*] n (COMM) distribuidor(a) m/f

supply [sə'plaɪ] vt (provide) suministrar; (equip): **to ~ (with)** proveer (de) ♦ n provisión f; (gas, water etc) suministro; **supplies** npl (food) víveres mpl; (MIL) pertrechos mpl; **~ teacher** n profesor(a) m/f suplente

support [sə'pɔ:t] n apoyo; (TECH) soporte m ♦ vt apoyar; (financially) mantener; (uphold, TECH) sostener; **~er** n (POL etc) partidario/a; (SPORT) aficionado/a

suppose [sə'pəuz] vt suponer; (imagine) imaginarse; (duty): **to be ~d to do sth** deber hacer algo; **~dly** [sə'pəuzɪdlɪ] adv según cabe suponer; **supposing** conj en caso de que

suppress [sə'prɛs] vt suprimir; (yawn) ahogar

supreme [su'pri:m] adj supremo

surcharge ['sə:tʃɑ:dʒ] n sobretasa, recargo

sure [ʃuə*] adj seguro; (definite, convinced) cierto; **to make ~ of sth/that** asegurarse de algo/asegurar que; **~!** (of course) ¡claro!, ¡por supuesto!; **~ enough** efectivamente; **~ly** adv (certainly) seguramente

surf [sə:f] n olas fpl

surface ['sə:fɪs] n superficie f ♦ vt (road) revestir ♦ vi (also fig) salir a la superficie; **by ~ mail** por vía terrestre

surfboard ['sə:fbɔ:d] n tabla (de surf)

surfeit ['sə:fɪt] n: **a ~ of** un exceso de

surfing ['sə:fɪŋ] n surf m

surge [sə:dʒ] n oleada, oleaje m ♦ vi (wave) romper; (people) avanzar en tropel

surgeon ['sə:dʒən] n cirujano/a

surgery ['sə:dʒərɪ] n cirugía f; (BRIT: room) consultorio; **~ hours** (BRIT) npl horas fpl de consulta

surgical ['sə:dʒɪkl] adj quirúrgico; **~ spirit** (BRIT) n alcohol m de 90°

surname ['sə:neɪm] n apellido

surpass [sə:'pɑ:s] vt superar, exceder

surplus ['sə:pləs] n excedente m; (COMM) superávit m ♦ adj excedente, sobrante

surprise [sə'praɪz] n sorpresa ♦ vt sorprender; **surprising** adj sorprendente; **surprisingly** adv: **it was surprisingly easy me** etc sorprendió lo fácil que fue

surrender [sə'rɛndə*] n rendición f, entrega ♦ vi rendirse, entregarse

surreptitious [sʌrəp'tɪʃəs] adj subrepticio

surrogate ['sʌrəgɪt] n sucedáneo; **~ mother** n madre f portadora

surround [sə'raund] vt rodear, circundar; (MIL etc) cercar; **~ing** adj circundante; **~ings** npl alrededores mpl, cercanías fpl

surveillance [sə:'veɪləns] n vigilancia

survey [n 'sə:veɪ, vb sə:'veɪ] n inspección f, reconocimiento f; (inquiry) encuesta ♦ vt examinar, inspeccionar; (look at) mirar, contemplar; **~or** n agrimensor(a) m/f

survival [sə'vaɪvl] n supervivencia

survive [sə'vaɪv] vi sobrevivir; (custom etc)

perdurar ♦ vt sobrevivir a; **survivor** n superviviente m/f

susceptible [sə'sɛptəbl] adj: **~ (to)** (disease) susceptible (a); (flattery) sensible (a)

suspect [adj, n 'sʌspɛkt, vb səs'pɛkt] adj, n sospechoso/a m/f ♦ vt (person) sospechar de; (think) sospechar

suspend [səs'pɛnd] vt suspender; **~ed sentence** n (LAW) libertad f condicional; **~er belt** n portaligas m inv; **~ers** npl (BRIT) ligas fpl; (US) tirantes mpl

suspense [səs'pɛns] n incertidumbre f, duda; (in film etc) suspense m; **to keep sb in ~** mantener a uno en suspense

suspension [səs'pɛnʃən] n (gen, AUT) suspensión f; (of driving licence) privación f; **~ bridge** n puente m colgante

suspicion [səs'pɪʃən] n sospecha; (distrust) recelo; **suspicious** [-ʃəs] adj receloso; (causing suspicion) sospechoso

sustain [səs'teɪn] vt sostener, apoyar; (suffer) sufrir, padecer; **~able** adj sostenible; **~ed** adj (effort) sostenido

sustenance ['sʌstɪnəns] n sustento

swab [swɔb] n (MED) algodón m

swagger ['swægə*] vi pavonearse

swallow ['swɔləu] n (bird) golondrina ♦ vt tragar; (fig, pride) tragarse; **~ up** vt (savings etc) consumir

swam [swæm] pt of **swim**

swamp [swɔmp] n pantano, ciénaga ♦ vt (with water etc) inundar; (fig) abrumar, agobiar; **~y** adj pantanoso

swan [swɔn] n cisne m

swap [swɔp] n canje m, intercambio ♦ vt: **to ~ (for)** cambiar (por)

swarm [swɔ:m] n (of bees) enjambre m; (fig) multitud f ♦ vi (bees) formar un enjambre; (people) pulular; **to be ~ing with** ser un hervidero de

swastika ['swɔstɪkə] n esvástica

swat [swɔt] vt aplastar

sway [sweɪ] vi mecerse, balancearse ♦ vt (influence) mover, influir en

swear [sweə*] (pt **swore**, pp **sworn**) vi (curse) maldecir; (promise) jurar ♦ vt jurar; **~word** n taco, palabrota

sweat [swɛt] n sudor m ♦ vi sudar

sweater ['swɛtə*] n suéter m

sweatshirt ['swɛtʃə:t] n suéter m

sweaty ['swɛtɪ] adj sudoroso

Swede [swi:d] n sueco/a

swede [swi:d] (BRIT) n nabo

Sweden ['swi:dn] n Suecia; **Swedish** ['swi:dɪʃ] adj sueco ♦ n (LING) sueco

sweep [swi:p] (pt, pp **swept**) n (act) barrido; (also: chimney ~) deshollinador(a) m/f ♦ vt barrer; (with arm) empujar; (subj: current) arrastrar ♦ vi barrer; (arm etc) moverse rápidamente; (*wind*) soplar con violencia; **~ away** *vt* barrer; **~ past** *vi* pasar majestuosamente; **~ up** *vi* barrer; **~ing** *adj* (*gesture*) dramático; (*generalized: statement*) generalizado

sweet [swiːt] *n* (*candy*) dulce *m*, caramelo; (*BRIT: pudding*) postre *m* ♦ *adj* dulce; (*fig: kind*) dulce, amable; (: *attractive*) mono; **~corn** *n* maíz *m*; **~en** *vt* (*add sugar to*) poner azúcar a; (*person*) endulzar; **~heart** *n* novio/a; **~ness** *n* dulzura; **~ pea** *n* guisante *m* de olor

swell [swel] (*pt* **swelled**, *pp* **swollen** or **swelled**) *n* (*of sea*) marejada, oleaje *m* ♦ *adj* (*US: inf: excellent*) estupendo, fenomenal ♦ *vt* hinchar, inflar ♦ *vi* (*also*: **~ up**) hincharse; (*numbers*) aumentar; (*sound, feeling*) ir aumentando; **~ing** *n* (*MED*) hinchazón *f*

sweltering ['sweltərɪŋ] *adj* sofocante, de mucho calor

swept [swept] *pt, pp of* **sweep**

swerve [swəːv] *vi* desviarse bruscamente

swift [swɪft] *n* (*bird*) vencejo ♦ *adj* rápido, veloz; **~ly** *adv* rápidamente

swig [swɪg] (*inf*) *n* (*drink*) trago

swill [swɪl] *vt* (*also*: **~ out**, **~ down**) lavar, limpiar con agua

swim [swɪm] (*pt* **swam**, *pp* **swum**) *n*: **to go for a ~** ir a nadar o a bañarse ♦ *vi* nadar; (*head, room*) dar vueltas ♦ *vt* nadar; (*the Channel etc*) cruzar a nado; **~mer** *n* nadador(a) *m/f*; **~ming** *n* natación *f*; **~ming cap** *n* gorro de baño; **~ming costume** (*BRIT*) *n* bañador *m*, traje *m* de baño; **~ming pool** *n* piscina (*SP*), alberca (*AM*); **~ming trunks** *n* bañador *m* (de hombre); **~suit** *n* = **~ming costume**

swindle ['swɪndl] *n* estafa ♦ *vt* estafar

swine [swaɪn] (*inf!*) canalla (!)

swing [swɪŋ] (*pt, pp* **swung**) *n* (*in playground*) columpio; (*movement*) balanceo, vaivén *m*; (*change of direction*) viraje *m*; (*rhythm*) ritmo ♦ *vt* balancear; (*also*: **~ round**) voltear, girar ♦ *vi* balancearse, columpiarse; (*also*: **~ round**) dar media vuelta; **to be in full ~** estar en plena marcha; **~ bridge** *n* puente *m* giratorio; **~ door** (*US* **~ing door**) *n* puerta giratoria

swingeing ['swɪndʒɪŋ] (*BRIT*) *adj* (*cuts*) atroz

swipe [swaɪp] *vt* (*hit*) golpear fuerte; (*inf: steal*) guindar

swirl [swəːl] *vi* arremolinarse

Swiss [swɪs] *adj, n inv* suizo/a *m/f*

switch [swɪtʃ] *n* (*for light etc*) interruptor *m*; (*change*) cambio ♦ *vt* (*change*) cambiar de; **~ off** *vt* apagar; (*engine*) parar; **~ on** *vt* encender (*SP*), prender (*AM*); (*engine, machine*) arrancar; **~board** *n* (*TEL*) centralita (de teléfonos) (*SP*), conmutador *m* (*AM*)

Switzerland ['swɪtsələnd] *n* Suiza

swivel ['swɪvl] *vi* (*also*: **~ round**) girar

swollen ['swəulən] *pp of* **swell**

swoon [swuːn] *vi* desmayarse

swoop [swuːp] *n* (*by police etc*) redada ♦ *vi* (*also*: **~ down**) calarse

swop [swɔp] = **swap**

sword [sɔːd] *n* espada; **~fish** *n* pez *m* espada

swore [swɔːʳ] *pt of* **swear**

sworn [swɔːn] *pp of* **swear** ♦ *adj* (*statement*) bajo juramento; (*enemy*) implacable

swot [swɔt] (*BRIT*) *vt, vi* empollar

swum [swʌm] *pp of* **swim**

swung [swʌŋ] *pt, pp of* **swing**

sycamore ['sɪkəmɔːʳ] *n* sicomoro

syllable ['sɪləbl] *n* sílaba

syllabus ['sɪləbəs] *n* programa *m* de estudios

symbol ['sɪmbl] *n* símbolo

symmetry ['sɪmɪtrɪ] *n* simetría

sympathetic [sɪmpə'θetɪk] *adj* (*understanding*) comprensivo; (*likeable*) simpático; (*showing support*): **~ to(wards)** bien dispuesto hacia

sympathize ['sɪmpəθaɪz] *vi*: **to ~ with** (*person*) compadecerse de; (*feelings*) comprender; (*cause*) apoyar; **~r** *n* (*POL*) simpatizante *m/f*

sympathy ['sɪmpəθɪ] *n* (*pity*) compasión *f*; **sympathies** *npl* (*tendencies*) tendencias *fpl*; **with our deepest ~** nuestro más sentido pésame; **in ~** en solidaridad

symphony ['sɪmfənɪ] *n* sinfonía

symptom ['sɪmptəm] *n* síntoma *m*, indicio

synagogue ['sɪnəgɔg] *n* sinagoga

syndicate ['sɪndɪkɪt] *n* (*gen*) sindicato; (*of newspapers*) agencia (de noticias)

syndrome ['sɪndrəum] *n* síndrome *m*

synopsis [sɪ'nɔpsɪs] (*pl* **synopses**) *n* sinopsis *f inv*

synthesis ['sɪnθəsɪs] (*pl* **syntheses**) *n* síntesis *f inv*

synthetic [sɪn'θetɪk] *adj* sintético

syphilis ['sɪfɪlɪs] *n* sífilis *f*

syphon ['saɪfən] = **siphon**

Syria ['sɪrɪə] *n* Siria; **~n** *adj, n* sirio/a

syringe [sɪ'rɪndʒ] *n* jeringa

syrup ['sɪrəp] *n* jarabe *m*; (*also: golden ~*) almíbar *m*

system ['sɪstəm] *n* sistema *m*; (*ANAT*) organismo; **~atic** [-'mætɪk] *adj* sistemático, metódico; **~ disk** *n* (*COMPUT*) disco del sistema; **~s analyst** *n* analista *m/f* de sistemas

T, t

ta [taː] (*BRIT: inf*) *excl* ¡gracias!

tab [tæb] *n* lengüeta; (*label*) etiqueta; **to keep**

~s on (fig) vigilar

tabby ['tæbɪ] n (also: ~ cat) gato atigrado

table ['teɪbl] n mesa; (of statistics etc) cuadro, tabla ♦ vt (BRIT: motion etc) presentar; **to lay** or **set the** ~ poner la mesa; **~cloth** n mantel m; **~ of contents** n índice m de materias; **~ d'hôte** [tɑːbl'dəut] adj del menú; **~ lamp** n lámpara de mesa; **~mat** n (for plate) posaplatos m inv; (for hot dish) salvamantel m; **~spoon** n cuchara de servir; (also: ~spoonful: as measurement) cucharada

tablet ['tæblɪt] n (MED) pastilla, comprimido; (of stone) lápida

table tennis n ping-pong m, tenis m de mesa

table wine n vino de mesa

tabloid ['tæblɔɪd] n periódico popular sensacionalista

tack [tæk] n (nail) tachuela; (fig) rumbo ♦ vt (nail) clavar con tachuelas; (stitch) hilvanar ♦ vi virar

tackle ['tækl] n (fishing ~) aparejo (de pescar); (for lifting) aparejo ♦ vt (difficulty) enfrentarse con; (challenge: person) hacer frente a; (grapple with) agarrar; (FOOTBALL) cargar; (RUGBY) placar

tacky ['tækɪ] adj pegajoso, (pej) cutre

tact [tækt] n tacto, discreción f; **~ful** adj discreto, diplomático

tactics ['tæktɪks] n, npl táctica

tactless ['tæktlɪs] adj indiscreto

tadpole ['tædpəul] n renacuajo

tag [tæg] n (label) etiqueta; **~ along** vi ir (o venir) también

tail [teɪl] n cola; (of shirt, coat) faldón m ♦ vt (follow) vigilar a; **~s** npl (formal suit) levita; **~ away** vi (in size, quality etc) ir disminuyendo; **~ off** vi = ~ away; **~back** (BRIT) n (AUT) cola; **~ end** n cola, parte f final; **~gate** n (AUT) puerta trasera

tailor ['teɪlə*] n sastre m; **~ing** n (cut) corte m; (craft) sastrería; **~-made** adj (also fig) hecho a la medida

tailwind ['teɪlwɪnd] n viento de cola

tainted ['teɪntɪd] adj (food) pasado; (water, air) contaminado; (fig) manchado

take [teɪk] (pt **took**, pp **taken**) vt tomar; (grab) coger (SP), agarrar (AM); (gain: prize) ganar; (require: effort, courage) exigir; (tolerate: pain etc) aguantar; (hold: passengers etc) tener cabida para; (accompany, bring, carry) llevar; (exam) presentarse a; **to ~ sth from** (drawer etc) sacar algo de; (person) quitar algo a; **I ~ it that ...** supongo que ...; **~ after** vt fus parecerse a; **~ apart** vt desmontar; **~ away** vt (remove) quitar; (carry off) llevar; (MATH) restar; **~ back** vt (return) devolver; (one's words) retractarse de; **~ down** vt (building) derribar;

(letter etc) apuntar; **~ in** vt (deceive) engañar; (understand) entender; (include) abarcar; (lodger) acoger, recibir; **~ off** vi (AVIAT) despegar ♦ vt (remove) quitar; **~ on** vt (work) aceptar; (employee) contratar; (opponent) desafiar; **~ out** vt sacar; **~ over** vt (business) tomar posesión de; (country) tomar el poder ♦ vi: **to ~ over from sb** reemplazar a uno; **~ to** vt fus (person) coger cariño a, encariñarse con; (activity) aficionarse a; **~ up** vt (a dress) acortar; (occupy: time, space) ocupar; (engage in: hobby etc) dedicarse a; (accept): **to ~ sb up on** aceptar; **~away** (BRIT) adj (food) para llevar ♦ n tienda (o restaurante m) de comida para llevar; **~off** n (AVIAT) despegue m; **~out** (US) n = **~away**; **~over** n (COMM) absorción f

takings ['teɪkɪŋz] npl (COMM) ingresos mpl

talc [tælk] n (also: ~um powder) (polvos de) talco

tale [teɪl] n (story) cuento; (account) relación f; **to tell ~s** (fig) chivarse

talent ['tælnt] n talento; **~ed** adj de talento

talk [tɔːk] n charla; (conversation) conversación f; (gossip) habladurías fpl, chismes mpl ♦ vi hablar; **~s** npl (POL etc) conversaciones fpl; **to ~ about** hablar de; **to ~ sb into doing sth** convencer a uno para que haga algo; **to ~ sb out of doing sth** disuadir a uno de que haga algo; **to ~ shop** hablar del trabajo; **~ over** vt discutir; **~ative** adj hablador(a); **~ show** n programa m de entrevistas

tall [tɔːl] adj alto; (object) grande; **to be 6 feet ~** (person) ≈ medir 1 metro 80

tally ['tælɪ] n cuenta ♦ vi: **to ~ (with)** corresponder (con)

talon ['tælən] n garra

tambourine [tæmbə'riːn] n pandereta

tame [teɪm] adj domesticado; (fig) mediocre

tamper ['tæmpə*] vi: **to ~ with** tocar, andar con

tampon ['tæmpɔn] n tampón m

tan [tæn] n (also: sun~) bronceado ♦ vi ponerse moreno ♦ adj (colour) marrón

tang [tæŋ] n sabor m fuerte

tangent ['tændʒənt] n (MATH) tangente f; **to go off at a ~** (fig) salirse por la tangente

tangerine [tændʒə'riːn] n mandarina

tangle ['tæŋgl] n enredo; **to get in(to) a ~** enredarse

tank [tæŋk] n (water ~) depósito, tanque m; (for fish) acuario; (MIL) tanque m

tanker ['tæŋkə*] n (ship) buque m cisterna; (truck) camión m cisterna

tanned [tænd] adj (skin) moreno

tantalizing ['tæntəlaɪzɪŋ] adj tentador(a)

tantamount ['tæntəmaunt] adj: **~ to**

equivalente a
tantrum ['tæntrəm] n rabieta
tap [tæp] n (BRIT: on sink etc) grifo (SP), canilla (AM); (gas ~) llave f; (gentle blow) golpecito ♦ vt (hit gently) dar golpecitos en; (resources) utilizar, explotar; (telephone) intervenir; **on ~** (fig: resources) a mano; **~ dancing** n claqué m
tape [teip] n (also: magnetic ~) cinta magnética; (cassette) cassette f, cinta; (sticky ~) cinta adhesiva; (for tying) cinta ♦ vt (record) grabar (en cinta); (stick with ~) pegar con cinta adhesiva; **~ deck** n grabadora; **~ measure** n cinta métrica, metro
taper ['teipə*] n cirio ♦ vi afilarse
tape recorder n grabadora
tapestry ['tæpistri] n (object) tapiz m; (art) tapicería
tar [tɑː] n alquitrán m, brea
target ['tɑːgit] n (gen) blanco
tariff ['tærif] n (on goods) arancel m; (BRIT: in hotels etc) tarifa.
tarmac ['tɑːmæk] n (BRIT: on road) asfaltado; (AVIAT) pista (de aterrizaje)
tarnish ['tɑːnɪʃ] vt deslustrar
tarpaulin [tɑːˈpɔːlɪn] n lona impermeabilizada
tarragon ['tærəgən] n estragón m
tart [tɑːt] n (CULIN) tarta; (BRIT: inf: prostitute) puta ♦ adj agrio, ácido; **~ up** (BRIT: inf) vt (building) remozar; **to ~ o.s. up** acicalarse
tartan ['tɑːtn] n tejido escocés m
tartar ['tɑːtə*] n (on teeth) sarro; **~(e) sauce** n salsa tártara
task [tɑːsk] n tarea; **to take to ~** reprender; **~ force** n (MIL, POLICE) grupo de operaciones
taste [teist] n (sense) gusto; (flavour) sabor m; (also: after~) sabor m, dejo; (sample): **have a ~!** ¡prueba un poquito!; (fig) muestra, idea ♦ vt (also fig) probar ♦ vi: **to ~ of** or **like** (fish, garlic etc) saber a; **you can ~ the garlic (in it)** se nota el sabor a ajo; **in good/bad ~** de buen/mal gusto; **~ful** adj de buen gusto; **~less** adj (food) soso; (remark etc) de mal gusto; **tasty** adj sabroso, rico
tatters ['tætəz] npl: **in ~** hecho jirones
tattoo [təˈtuː] n tatuaje m; (spectacle) espectáculo militar ♦ vt tatuar
tatty ['tæti] (BRIT: inf) adj cochambroso
taught [tɔːt] pt, pp of **teach**
taunt [tɔːnt] n burla ♦ vt burlarse de
Taurus ['tɔːrəs] n Tauro
taut [tɔːt] adj tirante, tenso
tax [tæks] n impuesto ♦ vt gravar (con un impuesto); (fig: memory) agotar a prueba (: patience) agotar; **~able** adj (income) gravable; **~ation** [-ˈseiʃən] n impuestos mpl; **~ avoidance** n evasión f de impuestos;

~ disc (BRIT) n (AUT) pegatina del impuesto de circulación; **~ evasion** n evasión f fiscal; **~-free** adj libre de impuestos
taxi ['tæksi] n taxi m ♦ vi (AVIAT) rodar por la pista; **~ driver** n taxista m/f; **~ rank** (BRIT) n = **~ stand**; **~ stand** n parada de taxis
tax: ~ payer n contribuyente m/f; **~ relief** n desgravación f fiscal; **~ return** n declaración f de ingresos
TB n abbr = **tuberculosis**
tea [tiː] n té m; (BRIT: meal) ≈ merienda (SP); cena; **high ~** (BRIT) merienda-cena (SP); **~ bag** n bolsita de té; **~ break** (BRIT) n descanso para el té
teach [tiːtʃ] (pt, pp **taught**) vt: **to ~ sb sth, ~ sth to sb** enseñar algo a uno ♦ vi (be a teacher) ser profesor(a), enseñar; **~er** n (in secondary school) profesor(a) m/f; (in primary school) maestro/a, profesor(a) de EGB; **~ing** n enseñanza
tea cosy n cubretetera m
teacup ['tiːkʌp] n taza para el té
teak [tiːk] n (madera de) teca
team [tiːm] n equipo; (of horses) tiro; **~work** n trabajo en equipo
teapot ['tiːpɔt] n tetera
tear[1] [tiə*] n lágrima, n; **in ~s** llorando
tear[2] [tɛə*] (pt **tore**, pp **torn**) n rasgón m, desgarrón m ♦ vt romper, rasgar ♦ vi rasgarse; **~ along** vi (rush) precipitarse; **~ up** vt (sheet of paper etc) romper
tearful ['tiəfəl] adj lloroso
tear gas ['tiə-] n gas m lacrimógeno
tearoom ['tiːruːm] n salón m de té
tease [tiːz] vt tomar el pelo a
tea set n servicio de té
teaspoon ['tiːspuːn] n cucharita; (also: ~ful: as measurement) cucharadita
teat [tiːt] n (of bottle) tetina
teatime ['tiːtaim] n hora del té
tea towel (BRIT) n paño de cocina
technical ['tɛknɪkl] adj técnico; **~ college** (BRIT) n ≈ escuela de artes y oficios (SP); **~ity** [-ˈkælɪti] n (point of law) formalismo; (detail) detalle m técnico; **~ly** adv en teoría; (regarding technique) técnicamente
technician [tɛkˈnɪʃn] n técnico/a
technique [tɛkˈniːk] n técnica
technological [tɛknəˈlɔdʒɪkl] adj tecnológico
technology [tɛkˈnɔlədʒɪ] n tecnología
teddy (bear) ['tɛdɪ-] n osito de felpa
tedious ['tiːdɪəs] adj pesado, aburrido
teem [tiːm] vi: **to ~ with** rebosar de; **it is ~ing (with rain)** llueve a cántaros
teenage ['tiːneidʒ] adj (fashions etc) juvenil; (children) quinceañero; **~r** n quinceañero/a
teens [tiːnz] npl: **to be in one's ~** ser adolescente

tee-shirt ['tiːʃɑːt] n = T-shirt

teeter ['tiːtə*] vi balancearse; (fig): **to ~ on the edge of ...** estar al borde de ...

teeth [tiːθ] npl of tooth

teethe [tiːð] vi echar los dientes

teething ['tiːðɪŋ]: **~ ring** n mordedor m; **~ troubles** npl (fig) dificultades fpl iniciales

teetotal ['tiːˈtəutl] adj abstemio

telegram ['tɛlɪgræm] n telegrama m

telegraph ['tɛlɪgrɑːf] n telégrafo; **~ pole** n poste m telegráfico

telepathy [tə'lɛpəθɪ] n telepatía

telephone ['tɛlɪfəun] n teléfono ♦ vt llamar por teléfono, telefonear; (message) dar por teléfono; **to be on the ~** (talking) hablar por teléfono; (possessing ~) tener teléfono; **~ booth** n cabina telefónica; **~ box** (BRIT) n = **~ booth**; **~ call** n llamada (telefónica); **~ directory** n guía (telefónica); **~ number** n número de teléfono; **telephonist** [tə'lɛfənɪst] n telefonista m/f

telesales ['tɛlɪseɪlz] npl televenta(s) f(pl)

telescope ['tɛlɪskəup] n telescopio

television ['tɛlɪvɪʒən] n televisión f; **on ~** en la televisión; **~ set** n televisor m

tell [tɛl] (pt, pp told) vt decir; (relate: story) contar; (distinguish): **to ~ sth from** distinguir algo de ♦ vi (talk): **to ~ (of)** contar; (have effect) tener efecto; **to ~ sb to do sth** mandar a uno hacer algo; **~ off** vt: **to ~ sb off** regañar a uno; **~er** n (in bank) cajero/a; **~ing** adj (remark, detail) revelador(a); **~tale** adj (sign) indicador(a)

telly ['tɛlɪ] (BRIT: inf) n abbr (= television) tele f

temp [tɛmp] n abbr (BRIT: = temporary) temporero/a

temper ['tɛmpə*] n (nature) carácter m; (mood) humor m; (bad ~) (mal) genio; (fit of anger) acceso de ira ♦ vt (moderate) moderar; **to be in a ~** estar furioso; **to lose one's ~** enfadarse, enojarse

temperament ['tɛmprəmənt] n (nature) temperamento

temperate ['tɛmprət] adj (climate etc) templado

temperature ['tɛmprətʃə*] n temperatura; **to have o run a ~** tener fiebre

temple ['tɛmpl] n (building) templo; (ANAT) sien f

tempo ['tɛmpəu] (pl tempos o tempi) n (MUS) tempo, tiempo; (fig) ritmo

temporarily ['tɛmpərərɪlɪ] adv temporalmente

temporary ['tɛmpərərɪ] adj provisional; (passing) transitorio; (worker) temporero; (job) temporal

tempt [tɛmpt] vt tentar; **to ~ sb into doing sth** tentar o inducir a uno a hacer algo; **~ation** [-'teɪʃən] n tentación f; **~ing** adj

tentador(a); (food) apetitoso/a

ten [tɛn] num diez

tenacity [tə'næsɪtɪ] n tenacidad f

tenancy ['tɛnənsɪ] n arrendamiento, alquiler m

tenant ['tɛnənt] n inquilino/a

tend [tɛnd] vt cuidar ♦ vi: **to ~ to do sth** tener tendencia a hacer algo

tendency ['tɛndənsɪ] n tendencia

tender ['tɛndə*] adj (person, care) tierno, cariñoso; (meat) tierno; (sore) sensible ♦ n (COMM: offer) oferta; (money): **legal ~** moneda de curso legal ♦ vt ofrecer; **~ness** n ternura; (of meat) blandura

tenement ['tɛnəmənt] n casa de pisos (SP)

tennis ['tɛnɪs] n tenis m; **~ ball** n pelota de tenis; **~ court** n cancha de tenis; **~ player** n tenista m/f; **~ racket** n raqueta de tenis

tenor ['tɛnə*] n (MUS) tenor m

tenpin bowling ['tɛnpɪn-] n (juego de los) bolos

tense [tɛns] adj (person) nervioso; (moment, atmosphere) tenso; (muscle) tenso, en tensión ♦ n (LING) tiempo

tension ['tɛnʃən] n tensión f

tent [tɛnt] n tienda (de campaña) (SP), carpa (AM)

tentative ['tɛntətɪv] adj (person, smile) indeciso; (conclusion, plans) provisional

tenterhooks ['tɛntəhuks] npl: **on ~** sobre ascuas

tenth [tɛnθ] num décimo

tent peg n clavija, estaca

tent pole n mástil m

tenuous ['tɛnjuəs] adj tenue

tenure ['tɛnjuə*] n (of land etc) tenencia; (of office) ejercicio

tepid ['tɛpɪd] adj tibio

term [tɜːm] n (word) término; (period) período; (SCOL) trimestre m ♦ vt llamar; **~s** npl (conditions, COMM) condiciones fpl; **in the short/long ~** a corto/largo plazo; **to be on good ~s with sb** llevarse bien con uno; **to come to ~s with** (problem) aceptar

terminal ['tɜːmɪnl] adj (disease) mortal; (patient) terminal ♦ n (ELEC) borne m; (COMPUT) terminal m; (also: air ~) terminal f; (BRIT: also: coach ~) (estación f) terminal f

terminate ['tɜːmɪneɪt] vt terminar

terminus ['tɜːmɪnəs] (pl termini) n término, (estación f) terminal f

terrace ['tɛrəs] n terraza; (BRIT: row of houses) hilera de casas adosadas; **the ~s** (BRIT: SPORT) las gradas fpl; **~d** adj (garden) en terrazas; (house) adosado

terrain [tɛ'reɪn] n terreno

terrible ['tɛrɪbl] adj terrible, horrible; (inf) atroz; **terribly** adv terriblemente; (very badly) malísimamente

terrier ['tɛrɪə*] n terrier m
terrific [tə'rɪfɪk] adj (very great) tremendo; (wonderful) fantástico, fenomenal
terrify ['tɛrɪfaɪ] vt aterrorizar
territory ['tɛrɪtərɪ] n (also fig) territorio
terror ['tɛrə*] n terror m; **~ism** n terrorismo; **~ist** n terrorista m/f
test [tɛst] n (gen, CHEM) prueba; (MED) examen m; (SCOL) examen m, test m; (also: driving ~) examen m de conducir ♦ vt probar, poner a prueba; (MED, SCOL) examinar
testament ['tɛstəmənt] n testamento; **the Old/New T~** el Antiguo/Nuevo Testamento
testicle ['tɛstɪkl] n testículo
testify ['tɛstɪfaɪ] vi (LAW) prestar declaración; **to ~ to sth** atestiguar algo
testimony ['tɛstɪmənɪ] n (LAW) testimonio
test: ~ match n (CRICKET, RUGBY) partido internacional; **~ tube** n probeta
tetanus ['tɛtənəs] n tétano
tether ['tɛðə*] vt atar (con una cuerda) ♦ n: **to be at the end of one's ~** no aguantar más
text [tɛkst] n texto; **~book** n libro de texto
textiles ['tɛkstaɪlz] npl textiles mpl; (textile industry) industria textil
texture ['tɛkstʃə*] n textura
Thailand ['taɪlænd] n Tailandia
Thames [tɛmz] n: **the ~** el (río) Támesis
than [ðæn] conj (in comparisons): **more ~ 10/once más de 10/una vez; I have more/less ~ you/Paul** tengo más/menos que tú/Paul; **she is older ~ you think** es mayor de lo que piensas
thank [θæŋk] vt dar las gracias a, agradecer; **~ you (very much)** muchas gracias; **~ God!** ¡gracias a Dios!; **~s** npl gracias fpl ♦ excl (also: many ~s, ~s a lot) ¡gracias!; **~s to** prep gracias a; **~ful** adj: **~ful (for)** agradecido (por); **~less** adj ingrato; **T~sgiving (Day)** n día m de Acción de Gracias

that [ðæt] (pl those) adj (demonstrative) ese/a, pl esos/as; (more remote) aquel/aquella, pl aquellos/as; **leave those books on the table** deja esos libros sobre la mesa; **~ one** ése/ésa; (more remote) aquél/aquélla; **~ one over there** ése/ésa de ahí; aquél/aquélla de allí
♦ pron 1 (demonstrative) ése/a, pl ésos/as; (neuter) eso; (more remote) aquél/aquélla, pl aquéllos/as; (neuter) aquello; **what's ~?** ¿qué es eso (or aquello)?; **who's ~?** ¿quién es ése/a (or aquél/aquélla)?; **is ~ you?** ¿eres tú?; **will you eat all ~?** ¿vas a comer todo eso?; **~'s my house** ésa es mi casa; **~'s what he said** eso es lo que dijo; **~ is (to say)** es decir
2 (relative: subject, object) que; (with preposition) (el/la) que etc, el/la cual etc; **the book (~) I read** el libro que leí; **the books**

~ are in the library los libros que están en la biblioteca; **all (~) I have** todo lo que tengo; **the box (~) I put it in** la caja en la que or donde lo puse; **the people (~) I spoke to** la gente con la que hablé
3 (relative: of time) que; **the day (~) he came** el día (en) que vino
♦ conj que; **he thought ~ I was ill** creyó que yo estaba enfermo
♦ adv (demonstrative): **I can't work ~ much** no puedo trabajar tanto; **I didn't realise it was ~ bad** no creí que fuera tan malo; **~ high** así de alto

thatched [θætʃt] adj (roof) de paja; (cottage) con tejado de paja
thaw [θɔː] n deshielo ♦ vi (ice) derretirse; (food) descongelarse ♦ vt (food) descongelar

the [ðiː, ðə] def art 1 (gen) el, f la, pl los, fpl las (NB = el immediately before f n beginning with stressed (h)a; a+ el = al; de+ el = del); **~ boy/girl** el chico/la chica; **~ books/flowers** los libros/las flores; **to ~ postman/from ~ drawer** al cartero/del cajón; **I haven't ~ time/money** no tengo tiempo/dinero
2 (+ adj to form n) los; lo; **~ rich and ~ poor** los ricos y los pobres; **to attempt ~ impossible** intentar lo imposible
3 (in titles): **Elizabeth ~ First** Isabel primera; **Peter ~ Great** Pedro el Grande
4 (in comparisons): **~ more he works ~ more he earns** cuanto más trabaja más gana

theatre ['θɪətə*] (US theater) n teatro; (also: lecture ~) aula; (MED: also: operating ~) quirófano; **~-goer** n aficionado/a al teatro
theatrical [θɪ'ætrɪkl] adj teatral
theft [θɛft] n robo
their [ðɛə*] adj su; **~s** pron (el) suyo/(la) suya etc; see also **my; mine**[1]
them [ðɛm, ðəm] pron (direct) los/las; (indirect) les; (stressed, after prep) ellos/ellas; see also **they**
theme [θiːm] n tema m; **~ park** n parque de atracciones (en torno a un tema central); **~ song** n tema m (musical)
themselves [ðəm'sɛlvz] pl pron (subject) ellos mismos/ellas mismas; (complement) se; (after prep) sí (mismos/as); see also **oneself**
then [ðɛn] adv (at that time) entonces; (next) después; (later) luego, después; (and also) además ♦ conj (therefore) en ese caso, entonces ♦ adj: **the ~ president** el entonces presidente; **by ~** para entonces; **from ~ on** desde entonces
theology [θɪ'ɔlədʒɪ] n teología
theory ['θɪərɪ] n teoría

therapist ['θerəpɪst] n terapeuta m/f
therapy ['θerəpɪ] n terapia

KEYWORD
---

there ['ðeə*] adv 1: ~ is, ~ are hay; ~ is no-one here/no bread left no hay nadie aquí/no queda pan; ~ has been an accident ha habido un accidente
2 (referring to place) ahí; (distant) allí; it's ~ está ahí; put it in/on/up/down ~ ponlo ahí dentro/encima/arriba/abajo; I want that book ~ quiero ese libro de ahí; ~ he is! ¡ahí está!
3: ~, ~ (esp to child) ea, ea

there: ~abouts adv por ahí; ~after adv después; ~by adv así, de ese modo; ~fore adv por lo tanto; ~'s = there is; there has
thermal ['θɜːml] adj termal; (paper) térmico
thermometer [θə'mɒmɪtə*] n termómetro
Thermos ® ['θɜːməs] n (also: ~ flask) termo
thermostat ['θɜːməustæt] n termostato
thesaurus [θɪ'sɔːrəs] n tesoro
these [ðiːz] pl adj estos/as ♦ pl pron éstos/as
thesis ['θiːsɪs] (pl theses) n tesis f inv
they [ðeɪ] pl pron ellos/ellas; (stressed) ellos (mismos)/ellas (mismas); ~ say that ... (it is said that) se dice que ...; ~'d = they had; they would; ~'ll = they shall; they will; ~'re = they are; ~'ve = they have
thick [θɪk] adj (in consistency) espeso; (in size) grueso; (stupid) torpe ♦ n: in the ~ of the battle en lo más reñido de la batalla; it's 20 cm ~ tiene 20 cm de espesor; ~en vi espesarse ♦ vt (sauce etc) espesar; ~ness n espesor m; grueso; ~set adj fornido
thief [θiːf] (pl thieves) n ladrón/ona m/f
thigh [θaɪ] n muslo
thimble ['θɪmbl] n dedal m
thin [θɪn] adj (person, animal) flaco; (in size) delgado; (in consistency) poco espeso; (hair, crowd) escaso ♦ vt: to ~ (down) diluir
thing [θɪŋ] n cosa; (object) objeto, artículo; (matter) asunto; (mania): to have a ~ about sb/sth estar obsesionado con uno/algo; ~s npl (belongings) efectos mpl (personales); the best ~ would be to ... lo mejor sería ...; how are ~s? ¿qué tal?
think [θɪŋk] (pt, pp thought) vi pensar ♦ vt pensar, creer; what did you ~ of them? ¿qué te parecieron?; to ~ about sth/sb pensar en algo/uno; I'll ~ about it lo pensaré; to ~ of doing sth pensar en hacer algo; I ~ so/not creo que sí/no; to ~ well of sb tener buen concepto de uno; ~ over vt reflexionar sobre, meditar; ~ up vt (plan etc) idear; ~ tank n gabinete m de estrategia
thinly ['θɪnlɪ] adv (cut) fino; (spread) ligeramente
third [θɜːd] adj (before n) tercer(a); (following

n) tercero/a ♦ n tercero/a; (fraction) tercio; (BRIT: SCOL: degree) título de licenciado con calificación de aprobado; ~ly adv en tercer lugar; ~ party insurance (BRIT) n seguro contra terceros; ~-rate adj (de calidad) mediocre; T~ World n Tercer Mundo
thirst [θɜːst] n sed f; ~y adj (person, animal) sediento; (work) que da sed; to be ~y tener sed
thirteen ['θɜː'tiːn] num trece
thirty ['θɜːtɪ] num treinta

KEYWORD
---

this [ðɪs] (pl these) adj (demonstrative) este/a; pl estos/as; (neuter) esto; ~ man/woman este hombre/esta mujer; these children/flowers estos chicos/estas flores; ~ one (here) éste/a, esto (de aquí)
♦ pron (demonstrative) éste/a; pl éstos/as; (neuter) esto; who is ~? ¿quién es éste/ésta?; what is ~? ¿qué es esto?; ~ is where I live aquí vivo; ~ is what he said esto es lo que dijo; ~ is Mr Brown (in introductions) le presento al Sr. Brown; (photo) éste es el Sr. Brown; (on telephone) habla el Sr. Brown
♦ adv (demonstrative): ~ high/long etc así de alto/largo etc; ~ far hasta aquí

thistle ['θɪsl] n cardo
thorn [θɔːn] n espina
thorough ['θʌrə] adj (search) minucioso; (wash) a fondo; (knowledge, research) profundo; (person) meticuloso; ~bred adj (horse) de pura sangre; ~fare n calle f; "no ~fare" "prohibido el paso"; ~ly adv (search) minuciosamente; (study) profundamente; (wash) a fondo; (utterly: bad, wet etc) completamente, totalmente
those [ðəuz] pl adj esos/esas; (more remote) aquellos/as
though [ðəu] conj aunque ♦ adv sin embargo
thought [θɔːt] pt, pp of think ♦ n pensamiento; (opinion) opinión f; ~ful adj pensativo; (serious) serio; (considerate) atento; ~less adj desconsiderado
thousand ['θauzənd] num mil; two ~ dos mil; ~s of miles de; ~th num milésimo
thrash [θræʃ] vt azotar; (defeat) derrotar; ~ about or around vi debatirse; ~ out vt discutir a fondo
thread [θred] n hilo; (of screw) rosca ♦ vt (needle) enhebrar; ~bare adj raído
threat [θret] n amenaza; ~en vi amenazar ♦ vt: to ~en sb with/to do amenazar a uno con/con hacer
three [θriː] num tres; ~-dimensional adj tridimensional; ~-piece suit n traje m de tres piezas; ~-piece suite n tresillo; ~-ply adj (wool) de tres cabos

threshold ['θreʃhəuld] n umbral m
threw [θruː] pt of throw
thrifty ['θrɪftɪ] adj económico
thrill [θrɪl] n (excitement) emoción f;
(shudder) estremecimiento ♦ vt emocionar;
to be ~ed (with gift etc) estar encantado; **~er**
n novela (or obra or película) de suspense;
~ing adj emocionante
thrive [θraɪv] (pt, pp thrived) vi (grow)
crecer; (do well): **to ~ on sth** sentarle muy
bien a uno algo; **thriving** adj próspero
throat [θrəut] n garganta; **to have a sore ~**
tener dolor de garganta
throb |θrɔb] vi latir; dar puntadas; vibrar
throes [θrəuz] npl: **in the ~ of** en medio de
throne [θrəun] n trono
throng [θrɔŋ] n multitud f, muchedumbre f
♦ vt agolparse en
throttle ['θrɔtl] n (AUT) acelerador m ♦ vt
estrangular
through [θruː] prep por, a través de; (time)
durante; (by means of) por medio de,
mediante; (owing to) gracias a ♦ adj (ticket,
train) directo ♦ adv completamente, de parte
a parte; de principio a fin; **to put sb ~ to sb**
(TEL) poner o pasar a uno con uno; **to be ~**
(TEL) tener comunicación; (have finished)
haber terminado; **"no ~ road"** "calle sin
salida"; **~out** prep (place) por todas partes
de, por todo; (time) durante todo ♦ adv por
or en todas partes
throw [θrəu] (pt threw, pp thrown) n tiro;
(SPORT) lanzamiento ♦ vt tirar, echar; (SPORT)
lanzar; (rider) derribar; (fig) desconcertar; **to**
~ a party dar una fiesta; **~ away** vt tirar;
(money) derrochar; **~ off** vt deshacerse de;
~ out vt tirar; (person) echar; expulsar; **~ up**
vi vomitar; **~away** adj para tirar, desechable;
(remark) hecho de paso; **~-in** n (SPORT)
saque m
thru |θruː] (US) = through
thrush [θrʌʃ] n zorzal m, tordo
thrust [θrʌst] (pt, pp thrust) vt empujar (con
fuerza)
thud |θʌd] n golpe m sordo
thug [θʌg] n gamberro/a
thumb [θʌm] n (ANAT) pulgar m; **to ~ a lift**
hacer autostop; **~ through** vt fus (book)
hojear; **~tack** (US) n chincheta (SP)
thump [θʌmp] n golpe m; (sound) ruido seco
or sordo ♦ vt golpear ♦ vi (heart etc) palpitar
thunder |'θʌndə*] n trueno ♦ vi tronar; (train
etc): **to ~ past** pasar como un trueno; **~bolt**
n rayo; **~clap** n trueno; **~storm** n tormenta;
~y adj tormentoso
Thursday ['θɜːzdɪ] n jueves m inv
thus [ðʌs] adv así, de este modo
thyme [taɪm] n tomillo
thyroid |'θaɪrɔɪd] n (also: ~ gland) tiroides m

inv
tic [tɪk] n tic m
tick [tɪk] n (sound: of clock) tictac m; (mark)
palomita; (ZOOL) garrapata; (BRIT: inf): **in a ~**
en un instante ♦ vi hacer tictac ♦ vt marcar;
~ off vt marcar; (person) reñir; **~ over** vi
(engine) girar en marcha lenta; (fig) ir tirando
ticket ['tɪkɪt] n billete m (SP), tíquet m, boleto
(AM); (for cinema etc) entrada (SP), boleto
(AM); (in shop: on goods) etiqueta; (for raffle)
papeleta; (for library) tarjeta; (parking ~)
multa por estacionamiento ilegal;
~ collector n revisor(a) m/f; **~ office** n
(THEATRE) taquilla (SP), boletería (AM); (RAIL)
despacho de billetes (SP) or boletos (AM)
tickle ['tɪkl] vt hacer cosquillas a ♦ vi hacer
cosquillas; **ticklish** adj (person) cosquilloso;
(problem) delicado
tidal ['taɪdl] adj de marea; **~ wave** n
maremoto
tidbit ['tɪdbɪt] (US) n = titbit
tiddlywinks ['tɪdlɪwɪŋks] n juego infantil con
fichas de plástico
tide [taɪd] n marea; (fig: of events etc) curso,
marcha; **~ over** vt (help out) ayudar a salir
del apuro
tidy ['taɪdɪ] adj (room etc) ordenado; (dress,
work) limpio; (person) (bien) arreglado ♦ vt
(also: ~ up) poner en orden
tie [taɪ] n (string etc) atadura; (BRIT: also:
neck~) corbata; (fig: link) vínculo, lazo;
(SPORT etc: draw) empate m ♦ vt atar ♦ vi
(SPORT etc) empatar; **to ~ in a bow** atar con
un lazo; **to ~ a knot in sth** hacer un nudo en
algo; **~ down** vt (fig: person: restrict) atar;
(: to price, date etc) obligar a; **~ up** vt (parcel)
envolver; (dog, person) atar; (arrangements)
concluir; **to be ~d up** (busy) estar ocupado
tier [tɪə*] n grada; (of cake) piso
tiger ['taɪgə*] n tigre m
tight [taɪt] adj (rope) tirante; (money) escaso;
(clothes) ajustado; (bend) cerrado; (shoes,
schedule) apretado; (budget) ajustado;
(security) estricto; (inf: drunk) borracho ♦ adv
(squeeze) muy fuerte; (shut) bien; **~en** vt
(rope) estirar; (screw, grip) apretar; (security)
reforzar ♦ vi estirarse; apretarse; **~-fisted** adj
tacaño; **~ly** adv (grasp) muy fuerte; **~rope** n
cuerda floja; **~s** (BRIT) npl panti mpl
tile [taɪl] n (on roof) teja; (on floor) baldosa;
(on wall) azulejo; **~d** adj de tejas;
embaldosado; (wall) alicatado
till [tɪl] n caja (registradora) ♦ vt (land)
cultivar ♦ prep, conj = until
tilt [tɪlt] vt inclinar ♦ vi inclinarse
timber ['tɪmbə*] n (material) madera
time [taɪm] n tiempo; (epoch: often pl) época;
(by clock) hora; (moment) momento;
(occasion) vez f; (MUS) compás m ♦ vt

calcular or medir el tiempo de; (*race*)
cronometrar; (*remark, visit etc*) elegir el
momento para; **a long ~** mucho tiempo; **4 at
a ~** de 4 en 4; **4 a la vez**; **for the ~ being** de
momento, por ahora; **from ~ to ~** de vez en
cuando; **at ~s a veces**; **in ~** (*soon enough*) a
tiempo; (*after some time*) con el tiempo;
(*MUS*) al compás; **in a week's ~** dentro de una
semana; **in no ~** en un abrir y cerrar de ojos;
any ~ cuando sea; **on ~** a la hora; **5 ~s 5** 5 por
5; **what ~ is it?** ¿qué hora es?; **to have a good
~** pasarlo bien, divertirse; **~ bomb** n bomba
de efecto retardado; **~less** adj eterno;
~ limit n plazo; **~ly** adj oportuno; **~ off** n
tiempo libre; **~r** n (*in kitchen etc*) progra-
mador m horario; **~ scale** (*BRIT*) n escala de
tiempo; **~-share** n apartamento (or casa) a
tiempo compartido; **~ switch** (*BRIT*) n
interruptor m (horario); **~table** n horario;
~ zone n huso horario

timid ['tɪmɪd] adj tímido

timing ['taɪmɪŋ] n (*SPORT*) cronometraje m;
the ~ of his resignation el momento que
eligió para dimitir

tin [tɪn] n estaño; (*also: ~ plate*) hojalata;
(*BRIT: can*) lata; **~foil** n papel m de estaño

tinge [tɪndʒ] n matiz m ♦ vt: **~d with** teñido
de

tingle ['tɪŋgl] vi (*person*): **to ~ (with)**
estremecerse (de); (*hands etc*) hormiguear

tinker ['tɪŋkə*] n **~ with** vt fus jugar con, tocar

tinned [tɪnd] (*BRIT*) adj (*food*) en lata, en
conserva

tin opener [-əupnə*] (*BRIT*) n abrelatas m inv

tinsel ['tɪnsl] n (guirnalda de) espumillón m

tint [tɪnt] n matiz m; (*for hair*) tinte m; **~ed**
adj (*hair*) teñido; (*glass, spectacles*) ahumado

tiny ['taɪnɪ] adj minúsculo, pequeñito

tip [tɪp] n (*end*) punta; (*gratuity*) propina;
(*BRIT: for rubbish*) vertedero; (*advice*) consejo
♦ vt (*waiter*) dar una propina a; (*tilt*) inclinar;
(*empty: also: ~ out*) vaciar, echar; (*overturn:
also: ~ over*) volcar; **~-off** n (*hint*)
advertencia; **~ped** (*BRIT*) adj (*cigarette*) con
filtro

Tipp-Ex ® ['tɪpeks] n Tipp-Ex ® m

tipsy ['tɪpsɪ] (*inf*) adj alegre, mareado

tiptoe ['tɪptəu] n: **on ~** de puntillas

tire ['taɪə*] n (*US*) = **tyre** ♦ vt cansar ♦ vi
(*gen*) cansarse; (*become bored*) aburrirse; **~d**
adj cansado; **to be ~d of sth** estar harto de
algo; **~less** adj incansable; **~some** adj
aburrido; **tiring** adj cansado

tissue ['tɪʃuː] n tejido; (*paper handkerchief*)
pañuelo de papel, kleenex ® m; **~ paper** n
papel m de seda

tit [tɪt] n (*bird*) herrerillo común; **to give ~ for
tat** dar ojo por ojo

titbit ['tɪtbɪt] (*US* **tidbit**) n (*food*) golosina;

(*news*) noticia sabrosa

title ['taɪtl] n título; **~ deed** n (*LAW*) título de
propiedad; **~ role** n papel m principal

TM abbr = **trademark**

KEYWORD

to [tuː, tə] prep **1** (*direction*) a; **to go ~ France/
London/school/the station** ir a Francia/
Londres/al colegio/a la estación; **to go
~ Claude's/the doctor's** ir a casa de Claude/al
médico; **the road ~ Edinburgh** la carretera de
Edimburgo

2 (*as far as*) hasta, a; **from here ~ London** de
aquí a or hasta Londres; **to count ~ 10** contar
hasta 10; **from 40 ~ 50 people** entre 40 y 50
personas

3 (*with expressions of time*): **a quarter/twenty
~ 5** las 5 menos cuarto/veinte

4 (*for, of*): **the key ~ the front door** la llave de
la puerta principal; **she is secretary ~ the
director** es la secretaria del director; **a letter
~ his wife** una carta a or para su mujer

5 (*expressing indirect object*) a; **to give sth
~ sb** darle algo a alguien; **to talk ~ sb** hablar
con alguien; **to be a danger ~ sb** ser un
peligro para alguien; **to carry out repairs
~ sth** hacer reparaciones en algo

6 (*in relation to*): **3 goals ~ 2** 3 goles a 2; **30
miles ~ the gallon** ≈ 9,4 litros a los cien
(kms)

7 (*purpose, result*): **to come ~ sb's aid** venir
en auxilio or ayuda de alguien; **to sentence sb
~ death** condenar a uno a muerte; **~ my
great surprise** con gran sorpresa mía
♦ with vb **1** (*simple infin*): **~ go/eat** ir/comer

2 (*following another vb*): **to want/try/start
~ do** querer/intentar/empezar a hacer; *see
also relevant vb*

3 (*with vb omitted*): **I don't want ~** no quiero

4 (*purpose, result*) para; **I did it ~ help you** lo
hice para ayudarte; **he came ~ see you** vino a
verte

5 (*equivalent to relative clause*): **I have things
~ do** tengo cosas que hacer; **the main thing is
~ try** lo principal es intentarlo

6 (*after adj etc*): **ready ~ go** listo para irse;
too old ~ ... demasiado viejo (como) para ...
♦ adv: **pull/push the door ~** tirar de/empujar
la puerta

toad [təud] n sapo; **~stool** n hongo
venenoso

toast [təust] n (*CULIN*) tostada; (*drink, speech*)
brindis m ♦ vt (*CULIN*) tostar; (*drink to*)
brindar por; **~er** n tostador m

tobacco [tə'bækəu] n tabaco; **~nist** n
estanquero/a (*SP*), tabaquero/a (*AM*); **~nist's
(shop)** (*BRIT*) n estanco (*SP*), tabaquería (*AM*)

toboggan [tə'bɔgən] n tobogán m

today [tə'deɪ] adv, n (also fig) hoy m

toddler ['tɔdlə*] n niño/a (que empieza a andar)

toe [təu] n dedo (del pie); (of shoe) punta; **to ~ the line** (fig) conformarse; **~nail** n uña del pie

toffee ['tɔfɪ] n toffee m; **~ apple** (BRIT) n manzana acaramelada

together [tə'geðə*] adv juntos; (at same time) al mismo tiempo, a la vez; **~ with** junto con

toil [tɔɪl] n trabajo duro, labor f ♦ vi trabajar duramente

toilet ['tɔɪlət] n retrete m; (BRIT: room) servicios mpl (SP), wáter m (SP), sanitario (AM) ♦ cpd (soap etc) de aseo; **~ paper** n papel m higiénico; **~ries** npl artículos mpl de tocador; **~ roll** n rollo de papel higiénico

token ['təukən] n (sign) señal f, muestra; (souvenir) recuerdo; (disc) ficha ♦ adj (strike, payment etc) simbólico; **book/record ~** (BRIT) vale m para comprar libros/discos; **gift ~** (BRIT) vale-regalo

Tokyo ['təukjəu] n Tokio, Tokío

told [təuld] pt, pp of **tell**

tolerable ['tɔlərəbl] adj (bearable) soportable; (fairly good) pasable

tolerant ['tɔlərnt] adj: **~ of** tolerante con

tolerate ['tɔləreɪt] vt tolerar

toll [təul] n (of casualties) número de víctimas; (tax, charge) peaje m ♦ vi (bell) doblar

tomato [tə'mɑːtəu] (pl **~es**) n tomate m

tomb [tuːm] n tumba

tomboy ['tɔmbɔɪ] n marimacho

tombstone ['tuːmstəun] n lápida

tomcat ['tɔmkæt] n gato (macho)

tomorrow [tə'mɔrəu] adv, n (also: fig) mañana; **the day after ~** pasado mañana; **~ morning** mañana por la mañana

ton [tʌn] n tonelada (BRIT = 1016 kg; US = 907 kg); (metric ~) tonelada métrica; **~s** pl (inf) montones de

tone [təun] n tono ♦ vi (also: ~ in) armonizar; **~ down** vt (criticism) suavizar; (colour) atenuar; **~ up** vt (muscles) tonificar; **~-deaf** adj con mal oído

tongs [tɔŋz] npl (for coal) tenazas fpl; (curling ~) tenacillas fpl

tongue [tʌŋ] n lengua; **~ in cheek** irónicamente; **~-tied** adj (fig) mudo; **~-twister** n trabalenguas m inv

tonic ['tɔnɪk] n (MED, also fig) tónico; (also: ~ water) (agua) tónica

tonight [tə'naɪt] adv, n esta noche; esta tarde

tonsil ['tɔnsl] n amígdala; **~litis** [-'laɪtɪs] n amigdalitis f

too [tuː] adv (excessively) demasiado; (also) también; **~ much** demasiado; **~ many** demasiados/as

took [tuk] pt of **take**

tool [tuːl] n herramienta; **~ box** n caja de herramientas

toot [tuːt] n pitido ♦ vi tocar el pito

tooth [tuːθ] (pl **teeth**) n (ANAT, TECH) diente m; (molar) muela; **~ache** n dolor m de muelas; **~brush** n cepillo de dientes; **~paste** n pasta de dientes; **~pick** n palillo

top [tɔp] n (of mountain) cumbre f, cima; (of tree) copa; (of head) coronilla; (of ladder, page) lo alto; (of table) superficie f; (of cupboard) parte f de arriba; (lid: of box) tapa; (: of bottle, jar) tapón m; (of list etc) cabeza; (toy) peonza; (garment) blusa; camiseta ♦ adj de arriba; (in rank) principal, primero; (best) mejor ♦ vt (exceed) exceder; (be first in) encabezar; **on ~ of** (above) sobre, encima de; (in addition to) además de; **from ~ to bottom** de pies a cabeza; **~ off** (US) vt = **~ up**; **~ up** vt llenar; **~ floor** n último piso; **~ hat** n sombrero de copa; **~-heavy** adj (object) mal equilibrado

topic ['tɔpɪk] n tema m; **~al** adj actual

top-: ~less adj (bather, bikini) topless inv; **~-level** adj (talks) al más alto nivel; **~most** adj más alto

topple ['tɔpl] vt derribar ♦ vi caerse

top-secret adj de alto secreto

topsy-turvy ['tɔpsi'təːvɪ] adj al revés ♦ adv patas arriba

torch [tɔːtʃ] n antorcha; (BRIT: electric) linterna

tore [tɔː*] pt of **tear²**

torment [n 'tɔːment, vt tɔː'ment] n tormento ♦ vt atormentar; (fig: annoy) fastidiar

torn [tɔːn] pp of **tear²**

torrent ['tɔrnt] n torrente m

tortoise ['tɔːtəs] n tortuga; **~shell** ['tɔːtəʃel] adj de carey

torture ['tɔːtʃə*] n tortura ♦ vt torturar; (fig) atormentar

Tory ['tɔːrɪ] (BRIT) adj, n (POL) conservador(a) m/f

toss [tɔs] vt tirar, echar; (one's head) sacudir; **to ~ a coin** echar a cara o cruz; **to ~ up for sth** jugar a cara o cruz algo; **to ~ and turn** (in bed) dar vueltas

tot [tɔt] n (BRIT: drink) copita; (child) nene/a m/f

total ['təutl] adj total, entero; (emphatic: failure etc) completo, total ♦ n total m, suma ♦ vt (add up) sumar; (amount to) ascender a; **~ly** adv totalmente

touch [tʌtʃ] n tacto; (contact) contacto ♦ vt tocar; (emotionally) conmover; **a ~ of** (fig) un poquito de; **to get in ~ with sb** ponerse en contacto con uno; **to lose ~** (friends) perder contacto; **~ on** vt fus (topic) aludir (brevemente) a; **~ up** vt (paint) retocar; **~-and-go** adj arriesgado; **~down** n aterrizaje m; (*on sea*) amerizaje m; (*US: FOOTBALL*) ensayo; **~ed** *adj* (*moved*) conmovido; **~ing** *adj* (*moving*) conmovedor(a); **~line** *n* (*SPORT*) línea de banda; **~y** *adj* (*person*) quisquilloso

tough [tʌf] *adj* (*material*) resistente; (*meat*) duro; (*problem etc*) difícil; (*policy, stance*) inflexible; (*person*) fuerte; **~en** *vt* endurecer

toupée ['tu:peɪ] *n* peluca

tour ['tuə*] *n* viaje m, vuelta; (*also: package ~*) viaje m todo comprendido; (*of town, museum*) visita; (*by band etc*) gira ♦ *vt* recorrer, visitar; **~ guide** *n* guía m turístico, guía f turística

tourism ['tuərɪzm] *n* turismo

tourist ['tuərɪst] *n* turista m/f ♦ *cpd* turístico; **~ office** *n* oficina de turismo

tousled ['tauzld] *adj* (*hair*) despeinado

tout [taut] *vi:* **to ~ for business** solicitar clientes ♦ *n* (*also:* ticket ~) revendedor(a) m/f

tow [təu] *vt* remolcar; **"on or in** (*US*) **~"** (*AUT*) "a remolque"

toward(s) [tə'wɔ:d(z)] *prep* hacia; (*attitude*) respecto a, con; (*purpose*) para

towel ['tauəl] *n* toalla; **~ling** *n* (*fabric*) felpa; **~ rail** (*US* = **rack**) *n* toallero

tower ['tauə*] *n* torre f; **~ block** (*BRIT*) *n* torre f (de pisos); **~ing** *adj* muy alto, imponente

town [taun] *n* ciudad f; **to go to ~** ir a la ciudad; (*fig*) echar la casa por la ventana; **~ centre** *n* centro de la ciudad; **~ council** *n* ayuntamiento, consejo municipal; **~ hall** *n* ayuntamiento; **~ plan** *n* plano de la ciudad; **~ planning** *n* urbanismo

towrope ['təurəup] *n* cable m de remolque

tow truck (*US*) *n* camión m grúa

toy [tɔɪ] *n* juguete m; **~ with** *vt fus* jugar con; (*idea*) acariciar; **~shop** *n* juguetería

trace [treɪs] *n* rastro ♦ *vt* (*draw*) trazar, delinear; (*locate*) encontrar; (*follow*) seguir la pista de; **tracing paper** *n* papel m de calco

track [træk] *n* (*mark*) huella, pista; (*path: gen*) camino, senda; (*: of bullet etc*) trayectoria; (*: of suspect, animal*) pista, rastro; (*RAIL*) vía; (*SPORT*) pista; (*on tape, record*) canción f ♦ *vt* seguir la pista de; **to keep ~ of** mantenerse al tanto de, seguir; **~ down** *vt* (*prey*) seguir el rastro de; (*sth lost*) encontrar; **~suit** *n* chandal m

tract [trækt] *n* (*GEO*) región f

traction ['trækʃən] *n* (*power*) tracción f; **in ~** (*MED*) en tracción

tractor ['træktə*] *n* tractor m

trade [treɪd] *n* comercio; (*skill, job*) oficio ♦ *vi* negociar, comerciar ♦ *vt* (*exchange*): **to ~ sth (for sth)** cambiar algo (por algo); **~ in** *vt* (*old car etc*) ofrecer como parte del pago; **~ fair** *n* feria comercial; **~mark** *n* marca de fábrica; **~ name** *n* marca registrada; **~r** *n*

comerciante m/f; **~sman** (*irreg*) *n* (*shopkeeper*) tendero; **~ union** *n* sindicato; **~ unionist** *n* sindicalista m/f

tradition [trə'dɪʃən] *n* tradición f; **~al** *adj* tradicional

traffic ['træfɪk] *n* (*gen, AUT*) tráfico, circulación f, tránsito (*AM*) ♦ *vi:* **to ~ in** (*pej: liquor, drugs*) traficar en; **~ circle** (*US*) *n* isleta; **~ jam** *n* embotellamiento; **~ lights** *npl* semáforo; **~ warden** *n* guardia m/f de tráfico

tragedy ['trædʒədɪ] *n* tragedia

tragic ['trædʒɪk] *adj* trágico

trail [treɪl] *n* (*tracks*) rastro, pista; (*path*) camino, sendero; (*dust, smoke*) estela ♦ *vt* (*drag*) arrastrar; (*follow*) seguir la pista de ♦ *vi* arrastrar; (*in contest etc*) ir perdiendo; **~ behind** *vi* quedar a la zaga; **~er** *n* (*AUT*) remolque m; (*caravan*) caravana; (*CINEMA*) trailer m, avance m; **~er truck** (*US*) *n* trailer m

train [treɪn] *n* tren m; (*of dress*) cola; (*series*) serie f ♦ *vt* (*educate, teach skills to*) formar; (*sportsman*) entrenar; (*dog*) adiestrar; (*point: gun etc*): **to ~ on** apuntar a ♦ *vi* (*SPORT*) entrenarse; (*learn a skill*): **to ~ as a teacher etc** estudiar para profesor etc; **one's ~ of thought** el razonamiento de uno; **~ed** *adj* (*worker*) cualificado; (*animal*) amaestrado; **~ee** [treɪ'ni:] *n* aprendiz(a) m/f; **~er** *n* (*SPORT: coach*) entrenador(a) m/f; (*: shoe*): **~ers** zapatillas fpl (de deporte); (*of animals*) domador(a) m/f; **~ing** *n* formación f; entrenamiento; **to be in ~ing** (*SPORT*) estar entrenando; **~ing college** *n* (*gen*) colegio de formación profesional; (*for teachers*) escuela de formación del profesorado; **~ing shoes** *npl* zapatillas fpl (de deporte)

trait [treɪt] *n* rasgo

traitor ['treɪtə*] *n* traidor(a) m/f

tram [træm] (*BRIT*) *n* (*also:* ~car) tranvía m

tramp [træmp] *n* (*person*) vagabundo/a; (*inf: pej: woman*) puta

trample ['træmpl] *vt:* **to ~ (underfoot)** pisotear

trampoline ['træmpəli:n] *n* trampolín m

tranquil ['træŋkwɪl] *adj* tranquilo; **~lizer** *n* (*MED*) tranquilizante m

transact [træn'zækt] *vt* (*business*) despachar; **~ion** [-'zækʃən] *n* transacción f, operación f

transfer [*n* 'trænsfə:*, *vb* træns'fə:*] *n* (*of employees*) traslado; (*of money, power*) transferencia; (*SPORT*) traspaso; (*picture, design*) calcomanía ♦ *vt* trasladar; transferir; **to ~ the charges** (*BRIT: TEL*) llamar a cobro revertido

transform [træns'fɔ:m] *vt* transformar

transfusion [træns'fju:ʒən] *n* transfusión f

transient ['trænzɪənt] *adj* transitorio

transistor [træn'zɪstə*] *n* (*ELEC*) transistor m;

~ radio n transistor m

transit ['trænzɪt] n: **in ~** en tránsito

transitive ['trænzɪtɪv] adj (LING) transitivo

transit lounge n sala de tránsito

translate [trænz'leɪt] vt traducir; **translation** [-'leɪʃən] n traducción f; **translator** n traductor(a) m/f

transmit [trænz'mɪt] vt transmitir; **~ter** n transmisor m

transparency [træns'pɛərnsɪ] n transparencia; (BRIT: PHOT) diapositiva

transparent [træns'pærnt] adj transparente

transpire [træns'paɪə*] vi (turn out) resultar; (happen) ocurrir, suceder; **it ~d that ...** se supo que ...

transplant ['trænsplɑːnt] n (MED) transplante m

transport [n 'trænspɔːt, vt træns'pɔːt] n transporte m; (car) coche m (SP), carro (AM), automóvil m ♦ vt transportar; **~ation** [-'teɪʃən] n transporte m; **~ café** (BRIT) n bar-restaurant m de carretera

transvestite [trænz'vestaɪt] n travestí m/f

trap [træp] n (snare, trick) trampa; (carriage) cabriolé m ♦ vt coger (SP) or agarrar (AM) en una trampa; (trick) engañar; (confine) atrapar; **~ door** n escotilla

trapeze [trə'piːz] n trapecio

trappings ['træpɪŋz] npl adornos mpl

trash [træʃ] n (rubbish) basura; (pej): **the book/film is ~** el libro/la película no vale nada; (nonsense) tonterías fpl; **~ can** (US) n cubo (SP) or balde m (AM) de la basura

travel ['trævl] n el viajar ♦ vi viajar ♦ vt (distance) recorrer; **~s** npl (journeys) viajes mpl; **~ agent** n agente m/f de viajes; **~ler** (US **~er**) n viajero/a; **~ler's cheque** (US **~er's check**) n cheque m de viajero; **~ling** (US **~ing**) n los viajes, el viajar; **~ sickness** n mareo

trawler ['trɔːlə*] n pesquero de arrastre

tray [treɪ] n bandeja; (on desk) cajón m

treacherous ['tretʃərəs] adj traidor, traicionero; (dangerous) peligroso

treacle ['triːkl] (BRIT) n melaza

tread [trɛd] (pt **trod**, pp **trodden**) n (step) paso, pisada; (sound) ruido de pasos; (of stair) escalón m; (of tyre) banda de rodadura ♦ vi pisar; **~ on** vt fus pisar

treason ['triːzn] n traición f

treasure ['trɛʒə*] n (also fig) tesoro ♦ vt (value: object, friendship) apreciar; (: memory) guardar

treasurer ['trɛʒərə*] n tesorero/a

treasury ['trɛʒərɪ] n: **the T~** el Ministerio de Hacienda

treat [triːt] n (present) regalo ♦ vt tratar; **to ~ sb to sth** invitar a uno a algo

treatment ['triːtmənt] n tratamiento

treaty ['triːtɪ] n tratado

treble ['trɛbl] adj triple ♦ vt triplicar ♦ vi triplicarse; **~ clef** n (MUS) clave f de sol

tree [triː] n árbol m; **~ trunk** tronco (de árbol)

trek [trɛk] n (long journey) viaje m largo y difícil; (tiring walk) caminata

trellis ['trɛlɪs] n enrejado

tremble ['trɛmbl] vi temblar

tremendous [trɪ'mɛndəs] adj tremendo, enorme; (excellent) estupendo

tremor ['trɛmə*] n temblor m; (also: **earth ~**) temblor m de tierra

trench [trɛntʃ] n zanja

trend [trɛnd] n (tendency) tendencia; (of events) curso; (fashion) moda; **~y** adj de moda

trespass ['trɛspəs] vi: **to ~ on** entrar sin permiso en; **"no ~ing"** "prohibido el paso"

trestle ['trɛsl] n caballete m

trial ['traɪəl] n (LAW) juicio, proceso; (test: of machine etc) prueba; **~s** npl (hardships) dificultades fpl; **by ~ and error** a fuerza de probar

triangle ['traɪæŋgl] n (MATH, MUS) triángulo

tribe [traɪb] n tribu f

tribunal [traɪ'bjuːnl] n tribunal m

tributary ['trɪbjutərɪ] n (river) afluente m

tribute ['trɪbjuːt] n homenaje m, tributo; **to pay ~ to** rendir homenaje a

trick [trɪk] n (skill, knack) tino, truco; (conjuring ~) truco; (joke) broma; (CARDS) baza ♦ vt engañar; **to play a ~ on sb** gastar una broma a uno; **that should do the ~** a ver si funciona así; **~ery** n engaño

trickle ['trɪkl] n (of water etc) goteo ♦ vi gotear

tricky ['trɪkɪ] adj difícil; delicado

tricycle ['traɪsɪkl] n triciclo

trifle ['traɪfl] n bagatela; (CULIN) dulce de bizcocho borracho, gelatina, fruta y natillas ♦ adv: **a ~ long** un poquito largo; **trifling** adj insignificante

trigger ['trɪgə*] n (of gun) gatillo; **~ off** vt desencadenar

trim [trɪm] adj (house, garden) en buen estado; (person, figure) esbelto ♦ n (haircut etc) recorte m; (on car) guarnición f ♦ vt (neaten) arreglar; (cut) recortar; (decorate) adornar; (NAUT: a sail) orientar; **~mings** npl (CULIN) guarnición f

trip [trɪp] n viaje m; (excursion) excursión f; (stumble) traspié m ♦ vi (stumble) tropezar; (go lightly) andar a paso ligero; **on a ~** de viaje; **~ up** vi tropezar, caerse ♦ vt hacer tropezar or caer

tripe [traɪp] n (CULIN) callos mpl

triple ['trɪpl] adj triple; **triplets** ['trɪplɪts] npl trillizos/as mpl/fpl; **triplicate** ['trɪplɪkət] n: **in triplicate** por triplicado

trite [traɪt] adj trillado

triumph ['traɪʌmf] n triunfo ♦ vi: **to ~ (over)**
vencer; **~ant** [traɪˈʌmfənt] adj (team etc)
vencedor(a); (return) triunfal

trivia ['trɪvɪə] npl trivialidades fpl

trivial ['trɪvɪəl] adj insignificante;
(commonplace) banal

trod [trɒd] pt of **tread**

trodden ['trɒdn] pp of **tread**

trolley ['trɒlɪ] n carrito; (also: ~ **bus**) trolebús
m

trombone [trɒmˈbəun] n trombón m

troop [truːp] n grupo, banda; **~s** npl (MIL)
tropas fpl; **~ in/out** vi entrar/salir en tropel;
~ing the colour n (ceremony) presentación f
de la bandera

trophy ['trəufɪ] n trofeo

tropical ['trɒpɪkl] adj tropical

trot [trɒt] n trote m ♦ vi trotar; **on the ~** (BRIT:
fig) seguidos/as

trouble ['trʌbl] n problema m, dificultad f;
(worry) preocupación f; (bother, effort)
molestia, esfuerzo; (unrest) inquietud f;
(MED): **stomach etc ~** problemas mpl gástricos
etc ♦ vt (disturb) molestar; (worry)
preocupar, inquietar ♦ vi: **to ~ to do sth**
molestarse en hacer algo; **~s** npl (POL etc)
conflictos mpl; (personal) problemas mpl; **to
be in ~** estar en un apuro; **it's no ~!** ¡no es
molestia (ninguna)!; **what's the ~?** (with
broken TV etc) ¿cuál es el problema?; (doctor
to patient) ¿qué pasa?; **~d** adj (person)
preocupado; (country, epoch, life) agitado;
~maker n agitador(a) m/f; (child)
alborotador m; **~shooter** n (in conflict)
conciliador(a) m/f; **~some** adj molesto

trough [trɒf] n (also: drinking ~) abrevadero;
(also: feeding ~) comedero; (depression)
depresión f

troupe [truːp] n grupo

trousers ['trauzəz] npl pantalones mpl; **short
~** pantalones mpl cortos

trousseau ['truːsəu] (pl **~x** or **~s**) n ajuar m

trout [traut] n inv trucha

trowel ['trauəl] n (of gardener) palita; (of
builder) paleta

truant ['truənt] n: **to play ~** (BRIT) hacer
novillos

truce [truːs] n tregua

truck [trʌk] n (lorry) camión m; (RAIL) vagón
m; **~ driver** n camionero; **~ farm** (US) n
huerto

true [truː] adj verdadero; (accurate) exacto;
(genuine) auténtico; (faithful) fiel; **to come ~**
realizarse

truffle ['trʌfl] n trufa

truly ['truːlɪ] adv (really) realmente;
(truthfully) verdaderamente; (faithfully):
yours ~ (in letter) le saluda atentamente

trump [trʌmp] n triunfo

trumpet ['trʌmpɪt] n trompeta

truncheon ['trʌntʃən] n porra

trundle ['trʌndl] vi: **to ~ along** ir sin prisas

trunk [trʌŋk] n (of tree, person) tronco; (of
elephant) trompa; (case) baúl m; (US: AUT)
maletero; **~s** npl (also: swimming ~s) bañador
m (de hombre)

truss [trʌs] vt: **~ (up)** atar

trust [trʌst] n confianza; (responsibility)
responsabilidad f; (LAW) fideicomiso ♦ vt (rely
on) tener confianza en; (hope) esperar;
(entrust): **to ~ sth to sb** confiar algo a uno; **to
take sth on ~** aceptar algo a ojos cerrados;
~ed adj de confianza; **~ee** [trʌsˈtiː] n (LAW)
fideicomisario; (of school) administrador m;
~ful adj confiado; **~ing** adj confiado;
~worthy adj digno de confianza

truth [truːθ] n verdad f; **~ful** adj
veraz

try [traɪ] n tentativa, intento; (RUGBY) ensayo
♦ vt (attempt) intentar; (test: also: ~ **out**)
probar, someter a prueba; (LAW) juzgar,
procesar; (strain: patience) hacer perder ♦ vi
probar; **to have a ~** probar suerte; **to ~ to do
sth** intentar hacer algo; **~ again!** ¡vuelve a
probar!; **~ harder!** ¡esfuérzate más!; **well, I
tried** al menos lo intenté; **~ on** vt (clothes)
probarse; **~ing** adj (experience) cansado;
(person) pesado

T-shirt ['tiːʃəːt] n camiseta

T-square n regla en T

tub [tʌb] n cubo (SP), balde m (AM); (bath)
tina, bañera

tube [tjuːb] n tubo; (BRIT: underground)
metro; (for tyre) cámara de aire

tuberculosis [tjubəːkjuˈləusɪs] n tuberculosis
f inv

tube station (BRIT) n estación f de metro

tubular ['tjuːbjulə*] adj tubular

TUC (BRIT) n abbr (= Trades Union Congress)
federación nacional de sindicatos

tuck [tʌk] vt (put) poner; **~ away** vt (money)
guardar; (building): **to be ~ed away**
esconderse, ocultarse; **~ in** vt meter dentro;
(child) arropar ♦ vi (eat) comer con apetito;
~ up vt (child) arropar; **~ shop** n (SCOL)
tienda; **~ bar** m (del colegio) (SP)

Tuesday ['tjuːzdɪ] n martes m inv

tuft [tʌft] n mechón m; (of grass etc) manojo

tug [tʌg] n (ship) remolcador m ♦ vt tirar de;
~-of-war n lucha de tiro de cuerda; (fig) tira
y afloja m

tuition [tjuˈɪʃən] n (BRIT) enseñanza; (: private ~) clases fpl particulares; (US: school fees)
matrícula

tulip ['tjuːlɪp] n tulipán m

tumble ['tʌmbl] n (fall) caída ♦ vi caer; **to
~ to sth** (inf) caer en la cuenta de algo;

~down adj destartalado; **~ dryer** (BRIT) n secadora

tumbler ['tʌmblə*] n (glass) vaso

tummy ['tʌmɪ] (inf) n barriga, tripa

tumour ['tjuːmə*] (US tumor) n tumor m

tuna ['tjuːnə] n inv (also: ~ fish) atún m

tune [tjuːn] n melodía ♦ vt (MUS) afinar; (RADIO, TV, AUT) sintonizar; **to be in/out of ~** (instrument) estar afinado/desafinado; (singer) cantar afinadamente/desafinar; **to be in/out of ~ with** (fig) estar de acuerdo/en desacuerdo con; **~ in** vi: **to ~ in (to)** (RADIO, TV) sintonizar (con); **~ up** vi (musician) afinar (su instrumento); **~ful** adj melodioso; **~r** n: **piano ~r** afinador(a) m/f de pianos

tunic ['tjuːnɪk] n túnica

Tunisia [tjuːˈnɪzɪə] n Túnez m

tunnel ['tʌnl] n túnel m; (in mine) galería ♦ vi construir un túnel/una galería

turban ['təːbən] n turbante m

turbulent ['təːbjulənt] adj turbulento

tureen [təˈriːn] n sopera

turf [təːf] n césped m; (clod) tepe m ♦ vt cubrir con césped; **~ out** (inf) vt echar a la calle

Turk [təːk] n turco/a

Turkey ['təːkɪ] n Turquía

turkey ['təːkɪ] n pavo

Turkish ['təːkɪʃ] adj, n turco

turmoil ['təːmɔɪl] n: **in ~** revuelto

turn [təːn] n turno; (in road) curva; (of mind, events) rumbo; (THEATRE) número; (MED) ataque m ♦ vt girar, volver; (collar, steak) dar la vuelta a; (page) pasar; (change): **~ sth into** convertir algo en ♦ vi volver; (person: look back) volverse; (reverse direction) dar la vuelta; (milk) cortarse; (become): **to ~ nasty/ forty** ponerse feo/cumplir los cuarenta; **a good ~** un favor; **it gave me quite a ~** me dio un susto; **"no left ~"** (AUT) "prohibido girar a la izquierda"; **it's your ~** te toca a ti; **in ~** por turnos; **to take ~s (at)** turnarse (en); **~ away** vi apartar la vista ♦ vt rechazar; **~ back** vi volverse atrás ♦ vt hacer retroceder; (clock) retrasar; **~ down** vt (refuse) rechazar; (reduce) bajar; (fold) doblar; **~ in** vi (inf: go to bed) acostarse ♦ vt (fold) doblar hacia dentro; **~ off** vi (from road) desviarse ♦ vt (light, radio etc) apagar; (tap) cerrar; (engine) parar; **~ on** vt (light, radio etc) encender (SP), prender (AM); (tap) abrir; (engine) poner en marcha; **~ out** vt (light, gas) apagar; (produce) producir ♦ vi (voters) concurrir; **to ~ out to be ...** resultar ser ...; **~ over** vi (person) volverse ♦ vt (object) dar la vuelta a; (page) volver; **~ round** vi volverse; (rotate) girar; **~ up** vi (person) llegar, presentarse; (lost object) aparecer ♦ vt (gen) subir; **~ing** n (in road)

vuelta; **~ing point** n (fig) momento decisivo

turnip ['təːnɪp] n nabo

turn: ~out n concurrencia; **~over** n (COMM: amount of money) volumen m de ventas; (: of goods) movimiento; **~pike** (US) n autopista de peaje; **~stile** n torniquete m; **~table** n plato; **~up** (BRIT) n (on trousers) vuelta

turpentine ['təːpəntaɪn] n (also: turps) trementina

turquoise ['təːkwɔɪz] n (stone) turquesa ♦ adj color turquesa

turret ['tʌrɪt] n torreón m

turtle ['təːtl] n galápago; **~neck (sweater)** n jersey m de cuello vuelto

tusk [tʌsk] n colmillo

tutor ['tjuːtə*] n profesor(a) m/f; **~ial** [-'tɔːrɪəl] n (SCOL) seminario

tuxedo [tʌkˈsiːdəu] (US) n smóking m, esmoquin m

TV [tiːˈviː] n abbr (= television) tele f

twang [twæŋ] n (of instrument) punteado; (of voice) timbre m nasal

tweezers ['twiːzəz] npl pinzas fpl (de depilar)

twelfth [twelfθ] num duodécimo

twelve [twelv] num doce; **at ~ o'clock** (midday) a mediodía; (midnight) a medianoche

twentieth ['twentɪθ] adj vigésimo

twenty ['twentɪ] num veinte

twice [twaɪs] adv dos veces; **~ as much** dos veces más

twiddle ['twɪdl] vi: **to ~ (with) sth** dar vueltas a algo; **to ~ one's thumbs** (fig) estar mano sobre mano

twig [twɪg] n ramita

twilight ['twaɪlaɪt] n crepúsculo

twin [twɪn] adj, n gemelo/a m/f ♦ vt hermanar; **~-bedded room** n habitación f doble

twine [twaɪn] n bramante m ♦ vi (plant) enroscarse

twinge [twɪndʒ] n (of pain) punzada; (of conscience) remordimiento

twinkle ['twɪŋkl] vi centellear; (eyes) brillar

twirl [twəːl] vt dar vueltas a ♦ vi dar vueltas

twist [twɪst] n (action) torsión f; (in road, coil) vuelta; (in wire, flex) doblez f; (in story) giro ♦ vt torcer; (weave) trenzar; (roll around) enrollar; (fig) deformar ♦ vi serpentear

twit [twɪt] (inf) n tonto

twitch [twɪtʃ] n (pull) tirón m; (nervous) tic m ♦ vi crisparse

two [tuː] num dos; **to put ~ and ~ together** (fig) atar cabos; **~-door** adj (AUT) de dos puertas; **~-faced** adj (pej: person) falso; **~fold** adv: **to increase ~fold** doblarse; **~-piece (suit)** n traje m de dos piezas; **~-piece (swimsuit)** n dos piezas m inv, bikini m; **~some** n (people) pareja; **~-way** adj: **~-**

way traffic circulación f de dos sentidos
tycoon [taɪ'kuːn] n: (**business**) ~ magnate m
type [taɪp] n (category) tipo, género; (model) tipo; (TYP) tipo, letra ♦ vt (letter etc) escribir a máquina; **~-cast** adj (actor) encasillado; **~face** n letra; **~script** n texto meca-nografiado; **~writer** n máquina de escribir; **~written** adj mecanografiado
typhoid ['taɪfɔɪd] n tifoidea
typical ['tɪpɪkl] adj típico
typing ['taɪpɪŋ] n mecanografía
typist ['taɪpɪst] n mecanógrafo/a
tyrant ['taɪərnt] n tirano/a
tyre ['taɪə*] (US **tire**) n neumático (SP), llanta (AM); ~ **pressure** n presión f de los neumáticos

U, u

U-bend ['juː'bɛnd] n (AUT, in pipe) recodo
udder ['ʌdə*] n ubre f
UFO ['juːfəu] n abbr = (unidentified flying object) OVNI m
ugh [əːh] excl ¡uf!
ugly ['ʌglɪ] adj feo; (dangerous) peligroso
UHT abbr: ~ **milk** leche f UHT, leche f uperizada
UK n abbr = **United Kingdom**
ulcer ['ʌlsə*] n úlcera; (mouth ~) llaga
Ulster ['ʌlstə*] n Ulster m
ulterior [ʌl'tɪərɪə*] adj: ~ **motive** segundas intenciones fpl
ultimate ['ʌltɪmət] adj último, final; (greatest) máximo; **~ly** adv (in the end) por último, al final; (fundamentally) a o en fin de cuentas
umbilical cord [ʌm'bɪlɪkl-] n cordón m umbilical
umbrella [ʌm'brɛlə] n paraguas m inv; (for sun) sombrilla
umpire ['ʌmpaɪə*] n árbitro
umpteen [ʌmp'tiːn] adj enésimos/as; **~th** adj: for the ~th time por enésima vez
UN n abbr (= United Nations) NN. UU.
unable [ʌn'eɪbl] adj: to be ~ to do sth no poder hacer algo
unaccompanied [ʌnə'kʌmpənɪd] adj no acompañado; (song) sin acompañamiento
unaccustomed [ʌnə'kʌstəmd] adj: to be ~ to no estar acostumbrado a
unanimous [juːˈnænɪməs] adj unánime
unarmed [ʌn'ɑːmd] adj (defenceless) inerme; (without weapon) desarmado
unattached [ʌnə'tætʃt] adj (person) soltero y sin compromiso; (part etc) suelto
unattended [ʌnə'tɛndɪd] adj desatendido
unattractive [ʌnə'træktɪv] adj poco atractivo

unauthorized [ʌn'ɔːθəraɪzd] adj no autorizado
unavoidable [ʌnə'vɔɪdəbl] adj inevitable
unaware [ʌnə'wɛə*] adj: to be ~ of ignorar; **~s** adv de improviso
unbalanced [ʌn'bælənst] adj (report) poco objetivo; (mentally) trastornado
unbearable [ʌn'bɛərəbl] adj insoportable
unbeatable [ʌn'biːtəbl] adj (team) invencible; (price) inmejorable; (quality) insuperable
unbelievable [ʌnbɪ'liːvəbl] adj increíble
unbend [ʌn'bɛnd] (irreg) vi (relax) relajarse ♦ vt (wire) enderezar
unbiased [ʌn'baɪəst] adj imparcial
unborn [ʌn'bɔːn] adj que va a nacer
unbroken [ʌn'brəukən] adj (seal) intacto; (series) continuo; (record) no batido; (spirit) indómito
unbutton [ʌn'bʌtn] vt desabrochar
uncalled-for [ʌn'kɔːldfɔː*] adj gratuito, inmerecido
uncanny [ʌn'kænɪ] adj extraño
unceremonious ['ʌnsɛrɪ'məunɪəs] adj (abrupt, rude) brusco, hosco
uncertain [ʌn'səːtn] adj incierto; (indecisive) indeciso
unchanged [ʌn'tʃeɪndʒd] adj igual, sin cambios
uncivilized [ʌn'sɪvɪlaɪzd] adj inculto; (fig: behaviour etc) bárbaro; (hour) inoportuno
uncle ['ʌŋkl] n tío
uncomfortable [ʌn'kʌmfətəbl] adj incómodo; (uneasy) inquieto
uncommon [ʌn'kɔmən] adj poco común, raro
uncompromising [ʌn'kɔmprəmaɪzɪŋ] adj intransigente
unconcerned [ʌnkən'səːnd] adj indiferente, despreocupado
unconditional [ʌnkən'dɪʃənl] adj incondicional
unconscious [ʌn'kɔnʃəs] adj sin sentido; (unaware): to be ~ of no darse cuenta de ♦ n: the ~ el inconsciente
uncontrollable [ʌnkən'trəuləbl] adj (child etc) incontrolable; (temper) indomable; (laughter) incontenible
unconventional [ʌnkən'vɛnʃənl] adj poco convencional
uncouth [ʌn'kuːθ] adj grosero, inculto
uncover [ʌn'kʌvə*] vt descubrir; (take lid off) destapar
undecided [ʌndɪ'saɪdɪd] adj (character) indeciso; (question) no resuelto
under ['ʌndə*] prep debajo de; (less than) menos de; (according to) según, de acuerdo con; (sb's leadership) bajo ♦ adv debajo, abajo; ~ **there** allí abajo; ~ **repair** en

reparación

under... [ˈʌndə*] prefix sub; **~age** adj menor de edad; (drinking etc) de los menores de edad; **~carriage** (BRIT) n (AVIAT) tren m de aterrizaje; **~charge** vt cobrar menos de la cuenta; **~clothes** npl ropa interior (SP) or íntima (AM); **~coat** n (paint) primera mano; **~cover** adj clandestino; **~current** n (fig) corriente f oculta; **~cut** vt irreg vender más barato que; **~developed** adj subdesarrollado; **~dog** n desvalido/a; **~done** adj (CULIN) poco hecho; **~estimate** vt subestimar; **~exposed** adj (PHOT) subexpuesto; **~fed** adj subalimentado; **~foot** adv con los pies; **~go** vt irreg sufrir; (treatment) recibir; **~graduate** n estudiante m/f; **~ground** n (BRIT: railway) metro; (POL) movimiento clandestino ♦ adj (car park) subterráneo ♦ adv (work) en la clandestinidad; **~growth** n maleza; **~hand(ed)** adj (fig) socarrón; **~lie** vt irreg (fig) ser la razón fundamental de; **~line** vt subrayar; **~mine** vt socavar, minar; **~neath** |ʌndəˈniːθ| adv debajo ♦ prep debajo de, bajo; **~paid** adj mal pagado; **~pants** npl calzoncillos mpl; **~pass** (BRIT) n paso subterráneo; **~privileged** adj desposeído; **~rate** vt menospreciar, subestimar; **~shirt** (US) n camiseta; **~shorts** (US) npl calzoncillos mpl; **~side** n parte f inferior; **~skirt** (BRIT) n enaguas fpl

understand [ʌndəˈstænd] (irreg) vt, vi entender, comprender; (assume) tener entendido; **~able** adj comprensible; **~ing** adj comprensivo ♦ n comprensión f, entendimiento; (agreement) acuerdo

understatement [ˈʌndəsteɪtmənt] n modestia (excesiva); **that's an ~!** ¡eso es decir poco!

understood [ʌndəˈstud] pt, pp of understand ♦ adj (agreed) acordado; (implied): **it is ~ that** se sobreentiende que

understudy [ˈʌndəstʌdɪ] n suplente m/f

undertake [ʌndəˈteɪk] (irreg) vt emprender; **to ~ to do sth** comprometerse a hacer algo

undertaker [ˈʌndəteɪkə*] n director(a) m/f de pompas fúnebres

undertaking [ˈʌndəteɪkɪŋ] n empresa; (promise) promesa

under: ~tone n: **in an ~tone** en voz baja; **~water** adv bajo el agua ♦ adj submarino; **~wear** n ropa interior (SP) or íntima (AM); **~world** n (of crime) hampa, inframundo; **~writer** n (INSURANCE) asegurador(a) m/f

undesirable [ʌndɪˈzaɪrəbl] adj (person) indeseable; (thing) poco aconsejable

undo [ʌnˈduː] (irreg) vt (laces) desatar; (button etc) desabrochar; (spoil) deshacer; **~ing** n ruina, perdición f

undoubted [ʌnˈdautɪd] adj indudable

undress [ʌnˈdres] vi desnudarse

undulating [ˈʌndjuleɪtɪŋ] adj ondulante

unduly [ʌnˈdjuːlɪ] adv excesivamente, demasiado

unearth [ʌnˈəːθ] vt desenterrar

unearthly [ʌnˈəːθlɪ] adj (hour) inverosímil

uneasy [ʌnˈiːzɪ] adj intranquilo, preocupado; (feeling) desagradable; (peace) inseguro

uneducated [ʌnˈedjukeɪtɪd] adj ignorante, inculto

unemployed [ʌnɪmˈplɔɪd] adj parado, sin trabajo ♦ npl: **the ~** los parados

unemployment [ʌnɪmˈplɔɪmənt] n paro, desempleo

unending [ʌnˈendɪŋ] adj interminable

unerring [ʌnˈəːrɪŋ] adj infalible

uneven [ʌnˈiːvn] adj desigual; (road etc) lleno de baches

unexpected [ʌnɪkˈspektɪd] adj inesperado; **~ly** adv inesperadamente

unfailing [ʌnˈfeɪlɪŋ] adj (support) indefectible; (energy) inagotable

unfair [ʌnˈfeə*] adj: **~ (to sb)** injusto (con uno)

unfaithful [ʌnˈfeɪθful] adj infiel

unfamiliar [ʌnfəˈmɪlɪə*] adj extraño, desconocido; **to be ~ with** desconocer

unfashionable [ʌnˈfæʃnəbl] adj pasado or fuera de moda

unfasten [ʌnˈfɑːsn] vt (knot) desatar; (dress) desabrochar; (open) abrir

unfavourable [ʌnˈfeɪvərəbl] (US **unfavorable**) adj desfavorable

unfeeling [ʌnˈfiːlɪŋ] adj insensible

unfinished [ʌnˈfɪnɪʃt] adj inacabado, sin terminar

unfit [ʌnˈfɪt] adj bajo de forma; (incompetent): **~ (for)** incapaz (de); **~ for work** no apto para trabajar

unfold [ʌnˈfəuld] vt desdoblar ♦ vi abrirse

unforeseen [ˈʌnfɔːˈsiːn] adj imprevisto

unforgettable [ʌnfəˈgetəbl] adj inolvidable

unfortunate [ʌnˈfɔːtʃnət] adj desgraciado; (event, remark) inoportuno; **~ly** adv desgraciadamente

unfounded [ʌnˈfaundɪd] adj infundado

unfriendly [ʌnˈfrendlɪ] adj antipático; (behaviour, remark) hostil, poco amigable

ungainly [ʌnˈgeɪnlɪ] adj desgarbado

ungodly [ʌnˈgɔdlɪ] adj: **at an ~ hour** a una hora inverosímil

ungrateful [ʌnˈgreɪtful] adj ingrato

unhappiness [ʌnˈhæpɪnɪs] n tristeza, desdicha

unhappy [ʌnˈhæpɪ] adj (sad) triste; (unfortunate) desgraciado; (childhood) infeliz; **~ about/with** (arrangements etc) poco contento con, descontento de

unharmed [ʌn'hɑːmd] *adj* ileso

unhealthy [ʌn'helθɪ] *adj* (*place*) malsano; (*person*) enfermizo; (*fig: interest*) morboso

unheard-of *adj* inaudito, sin precedente

unhurt [ʌn'hɜːt] *adj* ileso

unidentified [ʌnaɪ'dentɪfaɪd] *adj* no identificado, sin identificar; *see also* UFO

uniform ['juːnɪfɔːm] *n* uniforme *m* ♦ *adj* uniforme

unify ['juːnɪfaɪ] *vt* unificar, unir

uninhabited [ʌnɪn'hæbɪtɪd] *adj* desierto

unintentional [ʌnɪn'tenʃənəl] *adj* involuntario

union ['juːnjən] *n* unión *f*; (*also: trade ~*) sindicato ♦ *cpd* sindical; **U~ Jack** *n* bandera del Reino Unido

unique [juː'niːk] *adj* único

unison ['juːnɪsn] *n*: **in ~** (*speak, reply, sing*) al unísono

unit ['juːnɪt] *n* unidad *f*; (*section: of furniture etc*) elemento; (*team*) grupo; **kitchen ~** módulo de cocina

unite [juː'naɪt] *vt* unir ♦ *vi* unirse; **~d** *adj* unido; (*effort*) conjunto; **U~d Kingdom** *n* Reino Unido; **U~d Nations (Organization)** *n* Naciones *fpl* Unidas; **U~d States (of America)** *n* Estados *mpl* Unidos

unit trust (*BRIT*) *n* bono fiduciario

unity ['juːnɪtɪ] *n* unidad *f*

universe ['juːnɪvɜːs] *n* universo

university [juːnɪ'vɜːsɪtɪ] *n* universidad *f*

unjust [ʌn'dʒʌst] *adj* injusto

unkempt [ʌn'kempt] *adj* (*appearance*) descuidado; (*hair*) despeinado

unkind [ʌn'kaɪnd] *adj* poco amable; (*behaviour, comment*) cruel

unknown [ʌn'nəun] *adj* desconocido

unlawful [ʌn'lɔːful] *adj* ilegal, ilícito

unleaded [ʌn'ledɪd] *adj* (*petrol, fuel*) sin plombo

unless [ʌn'les] *conj* a menos que; **~ he comes** a menos que venga; **~ otherwise stated** salvo indicación contraria

unlike [ʌn'laɪk] *adj* (*not alike*) distinto de or a; (*not like*) poco propio de ♦ *prep* a diferencia de

unlikely [ʌn'laɪklɪ] *adj* improbable; (*unexpected*) inverosímil

unlimited [ʌn'lɪmɪtɪd] *adj* ilimitado

unlisted [ʌn'lɪstɪd] (*US*) *adj* (*TEL*) que no consta en la guía

unload [ʌn'ləud] *vt* descargar

unlock [ʌn'lɔk] *vt* abrir (con llave)

unlucky [ʌn'lʌkɪ] *adj* desgraciado; (*object, number*) que da mala suerte; **to be ~** tener mala suerte

unmarried [ʌn'mærɪd] *adj* soltero

unmistak(e)able [ʌnmɪs'teɪkəbl] *adj* inconfundible

unnatural [ʌn'nætʃrəl] *adj* (*gen*) antinatural; (*manner*) afectado; (*habit*) perverso

unnecessary [ʌn'nesəsərɪ] *adj* innecesario, inútil

unnoticed [ʌn'nəutɪst] *adj*: **to go** or **pass ~** pasar desapercibido

UNO ['juːnəu] *n abbr* (= *United Nations Organization*) ONU *f*

unobtainable [ʌnəb'teɪnəbl] *adj* inconseguible; (*TEL*) inexistente

unobtrusive [ʌnəb'truːsɪv] *adj* discreto

unofficial [ʌnə'fɪʃl] *adj* no oficial; (*news*) sin confirmar

unorthodox [ʌn'ɔːθədɔks] *adj* poco ortodoxo; (*REL*) heterodoxo

unpack [ʌn'pæk] *vi* deshacer las maletas ♦ *vt* deshacer

unpalatable [ʌn'pælətəbl] *adj* incomible; (*truth*) desagradable

unparalleled [ʌn'pærəleld] *adj* (*unequalled*) incomparable

unpleasant [ʌn'pleznt] *adj* (*disagreeable*) desagradable; (*person, manner*) antipático

unplug [ʌn'plʌg] *vt* desenchufar, desconectar

unpopular [ʌn'pɔpjulə*] *adj* impopular, poco popular

unprecedented [ʌn'presɪdəntɪd] *adj* sin precedentes

unpredictable [ʌnprɪ'dɪktəbl] *adj* imprevisible

unprofessional [ʌnprə'feʃənl] *adj* (*attitude, conduct*) poco ético

unqualified [ʌn'kwɔlɪfaɪd] *adj* sin título, no cualificado; (*success*) total

unquestionably [ʌn'kwestʃənəblɪ] *adv* indiscutiblemente

unreal [ʌn'rɪəl] *adj* irreal; (*extraordinary*) increíble

unrealistic [ʌnrɪə'lɪstɪk] *adj* poco realista

unreasonable [ʌn'riːznəbl] *adj* irrazonable; (*demand*) excesivo

unrelated [ʌnrɪ'leɪtɪd] *adj* sin relación; (*family*) no emparentado

unreliable [ʌnrɪ'laɪəbl] *adj* (*person*) informal; (*machine*) poco fiable

unremitting [ʌnrɪ'mɪtɪŋ] *adj* constante

unreservedly [ʌnrɪ'zɜːvɪdlɪ] *adv* sin reserva

unrest [ʌn'rest] *n* inquietud *f*, malestar *m*; (*POL*) disturbios *mpl*

unroll [ʌn'rəul] *vt* desenrollar

unruly [ʌn'ruːlɪ] *adj* indisciplinado

unsafe [ʌn'seɪf] *adj* peligroso

unsaid [ʌn'sed] *adj*: **to leave sth ~** dejar algo sin decir

unsatisfactory ['ʌnsætɪs'fæktərɪ] *adj* poco satisfactorio

unsavoury [ʌn'seɪvərɪ] (*US* **unsavory**) *adj* (*fig*) repugnante

unscrew [ʌn'skruː] *vt* destornillar

unscrupulous [ʌnˈskruːpjuləs] *adj* sin escrúpulos

unsettled [ʌnˈsetld] *adj* inquieto, intranquilo; (*weather*) variable

unshaven [ʌnˈʃeɪvn] *adj* sin afeitar

unsightly [ʌnˈsaɪtlɪ] *adj* feo

unskilled [ʌnˈskɪld] *adj* (*work*) no especializado; (*worker*) no cualificado

unspeakable [ʌnˈspiːkəbl] *adj* indecible; (*awful*) incalificable

unstable [ʌnˈsteɪbl] *adj* inestable

unsteady [ʌnˈstedɪ] *adj* inestable

unstuck [ʌnˈstʌk] *adj*: **to come ~** despegarse; (*fig*) fracasar

unsuccessful [ʌnsəkˈsesful] *adj* (*attempt*) infructuoso; (*writer, proposal*) sin éxito; **to be ~** (*in attempting sth*) no tener éxito, fracasar; **~ly** *adv* en vano, sin éxito

unsuitable [ʌnˈsuːtəbl] *adj* inapropiado; (*time*) inoportuno

unsure [ʌnˈʃuə*] *adj* inseguro, poco seguro

unsuspecting [ˈʌnsəsˈpektɪŋ] *adj* desprevenido

unsympathetic [ʌnsɪmpəˈθetɪk] *adj* poco comprensivo; (*unlikeable*) antipático

unthinkable [ʌnˈθɪŋkəbl] *adj* inconcebible, impensable

untidy [ʌnˈtaɪdɪ] *adj* (*room*) desordenado; (*appearance*) desaliñado

untie [ʌnˈtaɪ] *vt* desatar

until [ənˈtɪl] *prep* hasta ♦ *conj* hasta que; **~ he comes** hasta que venga; **~ now** hasta ahora; **~ then** hasta entonces

untimely [ʌnˈtaɪmlɪ] *adj* inoportuno; (*death*) prematuro

untold [ʌnˈtəuld] *adj* (*story*) nunca contado; (*suffering*) indecible; (*wealth*) incalculable

untoward [ʌntəˈwɔːd] *adj* adverso

unused [ʌnˈjuːzd] *adj* sin usar

unusual [ʌnˈjuːʒuəl] *adj* insólito, poco común; (*exceptional*) inusitado

unveil [ʌnˈveɪl] *vt* (*statue*) descubrir

unwanted [ʌnˈwɒntɪd] *adj* (*clothing*) viejo; (*pregnancy*) no deseado

unwelcome [ʌnˈwelkəm] *adj* inoportuno; (*news*) desagradable

unwell [ʌnˈwel] *adj*: **to be/feel ~** estar indispuesto/sentirse mal

unwieldy [ʌnˈwiːldɪ] *adj* difícil de manejar

unwilling [ʌnˈwɪlɪŋ] *adj*: **to be ~ to do sth** estar poco dispuesto a hacer algo; **~ly** *adv* de mala gana

unwind [ʌnˈwaɪnd] (*irreg: like* wind²) *vt* desenvolver ♦ *vi* (*relax*) relajarse

unwise [ʌnˈwaɪz] *adj* imprudente

unwitting [ʌnˈwɪtɪŋ] *adj* inconsciente

unworthy [ʌnˈwɜːðɪ] *adj* indigno

unwrap [ʌnˈræp] *vt* desenvolver

unwritten [ʌnˈrɪtn] *adj* (*agreement*) tácito;

(*rules, law*) no escrito

KEYWORD
---

up [ʌp] *prep*: **to go/be ~ sth** subir/estar subido en algo; **he went ~ the stairs/the hill** subió las escaleras/la colina; **we walked/climbed ~ the hill** subimos la colina; **they live further ~ the street** viven más arriba en la calle; **go ~ that road and turn left** sigue por esa calle y gira a la izquierda

♦ *adv* **1** (*upwards, higher*) más arriba; **~ in the mountains** en lo alto (de la montaña); **put it a bit higher ~** ponlo un poco más arriba or alto; **~ there** allí or allí arriba; **~ above** en lo alto, por encima, arriba

2: **to be ~** (*out of bed*) estar levantado; (*prices, level*) haber subido

3: **~ to** (*as far as*) hasta; **~ to now** hasta ahora or la fecha

4: **to be ~ to** (*depending on*): **it's ~ to you** depende de ti; **he's not ~ to it** (*job, task etc*) no es capaz de hacerlo; **his work is not ~ to the required standard** su trabajo no da la talla; (*inf: be doing*): **what is he ~ to?** ¿que estará tramando?

♦ *n*: **~s and downs** altibajos *mpl*

upbringing [ˈʌpbrɪŋɪŋ] *n* educación *f*

update [ʌpˈdeɪt] *vt* poner al día

upgrade [ʌpˈgreɪd] *vt* (*house*) modernizar; (*employee*) ascender

upheaval [ʌpˈhiːvl] *n* trastornos *mpl*; (*POL*) agitación *f*

uphill [ʌpˈhɪl] *adj* cuesta arriba; (*fig: task*) penoso, difícil ♦ *adv*: **to go ~** ir cuesta arriba

uphold [ʌpˈhəuld] (*irreg*) *vt* defender

upholstery [ʌpˈhəulstərɪ] *n* tapicería

upkeep [ˈʌpkiːp] *n* mantenimiento

upon [əˈpɒn] *prep* sobre

upper [ˈʌpə*] *adj* superior, de arriba ♦ *n* (*of shoe: also:* **~s**) empeine *m*; **~-class** *adj* de clase alta; **~ hand** *n*: **to have the ~ hand** tener la sartén por el mango; **~most** *adj* el más alto; **what was ~most in my mind** lo que me preocupaba más

upright [ˈʌpraɪt] *adj* derecho; (*vertical*) vertical; (*fig*) honrado

uprising [ˈʌpraɪzɪŋ] *n* sublevación *f*

uproar [ˈʌprɔː*] *n* escándalo

uproot [ʌpˈruːt] *vt* (*also fig*) desarraigar

upset [*n* ˈʌpset, *vb, adj* ʌpˈset] *n* (*to plan etc*) revés *m*, contratiempo; (*MED*) trastorno ♦ (*irreg*) *vt* (*glass etc*) volcar; (*plan*) alterar; (*person*) molestar, disgustar ♦ *adj* molesto, disgustado; (*stomach*) revuelto

upshot [ˈʌpʃɒt] *n* resultado

upside-down *adv* al revés; **to turn a place ~** (*fig*) revolverlo todo

upstairs [ʌpˈsteəz] *adv* arriba ♦ *adj* (*room*) de

arriba ♦ *n* el piso superior

upstart ['ʌpstɑːt] *n* advenedizo/a

upstream [ʌp'striːm] *adv* río arriba

uptake ['ʌpteɪk] *n*: **to be quick/slow on the ~** ser muy listo/torpe

uptight [ʌp'taɪt] *adj* tenso, nervioso

up-to-date *adj* al día

upturn ['ʌptɜːn] *n* (*in luck*) mejora; (*COMM: in market*) resurgimiento económico

upward ['ʌpwəd] *adj* ascendente; **~(s)** *adv* hacia arriba; (*more than*): **~(s) of** más de

urban ['ɜːbən] *adj* urbano

urchin ['ɜːtʃɪn] *n* pilluelo, golfillo

urge [ɜːdʒ] *n* (*desire*) deseo ♦ *vt*: **to ~ sb to do sth** animar a uno a hacer algo

urgent ['ɜːdʒənt] *adj* urgente; (*voice*) perentorio

urinate ['juərɪneɪt] *vi* orinar

urine ['juərɪn] *n* orina, orines *mpl*

urn [ɜːn] *n* urna; (*also: tea ~*) cacharro metálico grande para hacer té

Uruguay ['jueragwaɪ] *n* (el) Uruguay; **~an** [-'gwaɪən] *adj, n* uruguayo/a *m/f*

US *n abbr* (= *United States*) EE. UU.

us [ʌs] *pron* nos; (*after prep*) nosotros/as; *see also* **me**

USA *n abbr* (= *United States (of America)*) EE. UU.

usage ['juːzɪdʒ] *n* (*LING*) uso

use [*n* juːs, *vb* juːz] *n* uso, empleo; (*usefulness*) utilidad *f* ♦ *vt* usar, emplear; **she ~d to do it** (ella) solía o acostumbraba hacerlo; **in ~** en uso; **out of ~** en desuso; **to be of ~** servir; **it's no ~** (*pointless*) es inútil; (*not useful*) no sirve; **to be ~d to** estar acostumbrado a, acostumbrar; **~ up** *vt* (*food*) consumir; (*money*) gastar; **~d** *adj* (*car*) usado; **~ful** *adj* útil; **~fulness** *n* utilidad *f*; **~less** *adj* (*unusable*) inservible; (*pointless*) inútil; (*person*) inepto; **~r** *n* usuario/a; **~r-friendly** *adj* (*computer*) amistoso

usher ['ʌʃəˀ] *n* (*at wedding*) ujier *m*; **~ette** [-'ret] *n* (*in cinema*) acomodadora

USSR *n* (*HIST*): **the ~** la URSS

usual ['juːʒuəl] *adj* normal, corriente; **as ~** como de costumbre; **~ly** *adv* normalmente

utensil [juː'tensl] *n* utensilio; **kitchen ~s** batería de cocina

uterus ['juːtərəs] *n* útero

utility [juː'tɪlɪtɪ] *n* utilidad *f*; (*public ~*) (empresa de) servicio público; **~ room** *n* ofis *m*

utilize ['juːtɪlaɪz] *vt* utilizar

utmost ['ʌtməust] *adj* mayor ♦ *n*: **to do one's ~** hacer todo lo posible

utter ['ʌtəˀ] *adj* total, completo ♦ *vt* pronunciar, proferir; **~ly** *adv* completamente, totalmente

U-turn ['juː'tɜːn] *n* viraje *m* en redondo

V, v

v. *abbr* = **verse**; **versus**; (= *volt*) v; (= *vide*) **véase**

vacancy ['veɪkənsɪ] *n* (*BRIT: job*) vacante *f*; (*room*) habitación *f* libre; **"no vacancies"** "completo"

vacant ['veɪkənt] *adj* desocupado, libre; (*expression*) distraído

vacate [və'keɪt] *vt* (*house, room*) desocupar; (*job*) dejar (vacante)

vacation [və'keɪʃən] *n* vacaciones *fpl*

vaccinate ['væksɪneɪt] *vt* vacunar

vaccine ['væksiːn] *n* vacuna

vacuum ['vækjum] *n* vacío; **~ cleaner** *n* aspiradora; **~flask** (*BRIT*) *n* termo; **~-packed** *adj* empaquetado al vacío

vagina [və'dʒaɪnə] *n* vagina

vagrant ['veɪgrnt] *n* vagabundo/a

vague [veɪg] *adj* vago; (*memory*) borroso; (*ambiguous*) impreciso; (*person: absent-minded*) distraído; (: *evasive*): **to be ~** no decir las cosas claramente; **~ly** *adv* vagamente; distraídamente; con evasivas

vain [veɪn] *adj* (*conceited*) presumido; (*useless*) vano, inútil; **in ~** en vano

valentine ['væləntaɪn] *n* (*also: ~ card*) tarjeta del Día de los Enamorados

valet ['væleɪ] *n* ayuda *m* de cámara

valid ['vælɪd] *adj* válido; (*ticket*) valedero; (*law*) vigente

valley ['vælɪ] *n* valle *m*

valuable ['væljuəbl] *adj* (*jewel*) de valor; (*time*) valioso; **~s** *npl* objetos *mpl* de valor

valuation [vælju'eɪʃən] *n* tasación *f*, valuación *f*; (*judgement of quality*) valoración *f*

value ['væljuː] *n* valor *m*; (*importance*) importancia ♦ *vt* (*fix price of*) tasar, valorar; (*esteem*) apreciar; **~s** *npl* (*principles*) principios *mpl*; **~ added tax** (*BRIT*) *n* impuesto sobre el valor añadido; **~d** *adj* (*appreciated*) apreciado

valve [vælv] *n* válvula

van [væn] *n* (*AUT*) furgoneta (*SP*), camioneta (*AM*)

vandal ['vændl] *n* vándalo/a; **~ism** *n* vandalismo; **~ize** *vt* dañar, destruir

vanilla [və'nɪlə] *n* vainilla

vanish ['vænɪʃ] *vi* desaparecer

vanity ['vænɪtɪ] *n* vanidad *f*

vantage point ['vɑːntɪdʒ-] *n* (*for views*) punto panorámico

vapour ['veɪpəˀ] (*US* **vapor**) *n* vapor *m*; (*on breath, window*) vaho

variable ['veərɪəbl] *adj* variable

variation [veərɪ'eɪʃən] *n* variación *f*

varicose ['værɪkəus] *adj*: **~ veins** varices *fpl*

varied ['vɛərɪd] *adj* variado

variety [və'raɪətɪ] *n* (*diversity*) diversidad *f*; (*type*) variedad *f*; **~ show** *n* espectáculo de variedades

various ['vɛərɪəs] *adj* (*several: people*) varios/as; (*reasons*) diversos/as

varnish ['vɑ:nɪʃ] *n* barniz *m*; (*nail ~*) esmalte *m* ♦ *vt* barnizar; (*nails*) pintar (con esmalte)

vary ['vɛərɪ] *vt* variar; (*change*) cambiar ♦ *vi* variar

vase [vɑ:z] *n* florero

Vaseline ® ['væsɪli:n] *n* vaselina ®

vast [vɑ:st] *adj* enorme

VAT [væt] (*BRIT*) *n abbr* (= *value added tax*) IVA *m*

vat [væt] *n* tina, tinaja

Vatican ['vætɪkən] *n*: the **~** el Vaticano

vault [vɔ:lt] *n* (*of roof*) bóveda; (*tomb*) panteón *m*; (*in bank*) cámara acorazada ♦ *vt* (*also: ~ over*) saltar (por encima de)

vaunted ['vɔ:ntɪd] *adj*: much **~** cacareado, alardeado

VCR *n abbr* = **video cassette recorder**

VD *n abbr* = **venereal disease**

VDU *n abbr* (= *visual display unit*) UPV *f*

veal [vi:l] *n* ternera

veer [vɪə*] *vi* (*vehicle*) virar; (*wind*) girar

vegan ['vi:gən] *n* vegetariano/a estricto/a, vegetaliano/a

vegeburger ['vɛdʒɪbə:gə*] *n* hamburguesa vegetal

vegetable ['vɛdʒtəbl] *n* (*BOT*) vegetal *m*; (*edible plant*) legumbre *f*, hortaliza ♦ *adj* vegetal; **~s** *npl* (*cooked*) verduras *fpl*

vegetarian [vɛdʒɪ'tɛərɪən] *adj, n* vegetariano/a *m/f*

vehement ['vi:ɪmənt] *adj* vehemente, apasionado

vehicle ['vi:ɪkl] *n* vehículo; (*fig*) medio

veil [veɪl] *n* velo ♦ *vt* velar; **~ed** *adj* (*fig*) velado

vein [veɪn] *n* vena; (*of ore etc*) veta

velocity [vɪ'lɔsɪtɪ] *n* velocidad *f*

velvet ['vɛlvɪt] *n* terciopelo

vending machine ['vɛndɪŋ-] *n* distribuidor *m* automático

veneer [və'nɪə*] *n* chapa, enchapado; (*fig*) barniz *m*

venereal disease [vɪ'nɪərɪəl-] *n* enfermedad *f* venérea

Venetian blind [vɪ'ni:ʃən-] *n* persiana

Venezuela [vɛnɪ'zweɪlə] *n* Venezuela; **~n** *adj, n* venezolano/a *m/f*

vengeance ['vɛndʒəns] *n* venganza; **with a ~** (*fig*) con creces

venison ['vɛnɪsn] *n* carne *f* de venado

venom ['vɛnəm] *n* veneno; (*bitterness*) odio; **~ous** *adj* venenoso; lleno de odio

vent [vɛnt] *n* (*in jacket*) respiradero; (*in wall*)

rejilla (de ventilación) ♦ *vt* (*fig: feelings*) desahogar

ventilator ['vɛntɪleɪtə*] *n* ventilador *m*

venture ['vɛntʃə*] *n* empresa ♦ *vt* (*opinion*) ofrecer ♦ *vi* arriesgarse, lanzarse; **business ~** empresa comercial

venue ['vɛnju:] *n* lugar *m*

veranda(h) [və'rændə] *n* terraza

verb [və:b] *n* verbo; **~al** *adj* verbal

verbatim [və:'beɪtɪm] *adj, adv* palabra por palabra

verdict ['və:dɪkt] *n* veredicto, fallo; (*fig*) opinión *f*, juicio

verge [və:dʒ] (*BRIT*) *n* borde *m*; "**soft ~s**" (*AUT*) "arcén *m* no asfaltado"; **to be on the ~ of doing sth** estar a punto de hacer algo; **~ on** *vt fus* rayar en

verify ['vɛrɪfaɪ] *vt* comprobar, verificar

vermin ['və:mɪn] *npl* (*animals*) alimañas *fpl*; (*insects, fig*) parásitos *mpl*

vermouth ['və:məθ] *n* vermut *m*

versatile ['və:sətaɪl] *adj* (*person*) polifacético; (*machine, tool etc*) versátil

verse [və:s] *n* poesía; (*stanza*) estrofa; (*in bible*) versículo

version ['və:ʃən] *n* versión *f*

versus ['və:səs] *prep* contra

vertebra ['və:tɪbrə] (*pl ~e*) *n* vértebra

vertical ['və:tɪkl] *adj* vertical

verve [və:v] *n* brío

very ['vɛrɪ] *adv* muy ♦ *adj*: **the ~ book which** el mismo libro que; **the ~ last** el último de todos; **at the ~ least** al menos; **~ much** muchísimo

vessel ['vɛsl] *n* (*ship*) barco; (*container*) vasija; *see* **blood**

vest [vɛst] *n* (*BRIT*) camiseta; (*US: waistcoat*) chaleco; **~ed interests** *npl* (*COMM*) intereses *mpl* creados

vet [vɛt] *vt* (*candidate*) investigar ♦ *n abbr* (*BRIT*) = **veterinary surgeon**

veteran ['vɛtərn] *n* veterano

veterinary surgeon ['vɛtrɪnərɪ] (*US* **veterinarian**) *n* veterinario/a *m/f*

veto ['vi:təu] (*pl ~es*) *n* veto ♦ *vt* prohibir, poner el veto a

vex [vɛks] *vt* fastidiar; **~ed** *adj* (*question*) controvertido

VHF *abbr* (= *very high frequency*) muy alta frecuencia

via ['vaɪə] *prep* por, por medio de

vibrant ['vaɪbrənt] *adj* (*lively*) animado; (*bright*) vivo; (*voice*) vibrante

vibrate [vaɪ'breɪt] *vi* vibrar

vicar ['vɪkə*] *n* párroco (de la Iglesia Anglicana); **~age** *n* parroquia

vice [vaɪs] *n* (*evil*) vicio; (*TECH*) torno de banco

vice- [vaɪs] *prefix* vice-; **~-chairman** *n*

vicepresidente *m*
vice squad *n* brigada antivicio
vice versa ['vaɪs'vɜːsə] *adv* viceversa
vicinity [vɪ'sɪnɪtɪ] *n*: **in the ~ (of)** cercano (a)
vicious ['vɪʃəs] *adj* (*attack*) violento; (*words*) cruel; (*horse, dog*) resabido; **~ circle** *n* círculo vicioso
victim ['vɪktɪm] *n* víctima
victor ['vɪktə*] *n* vencedor(a) *m/f*
victory ['vɪktərɪ] *n* victoria
video ['vɪdɪəʊ] *cpd* video ♦ *n* (~ *film*) videofilm *m*; (*also*: ~ *cassette*) videocassette *f*; (*also*: ~ *cassette recorder*) magnetoscopio; **~ game** *n* videojuego; **~ tape** *n* cinta de vídeo
vie [vaɪ] *vi*: **to ~ (with sb for sth)** competir (con uno por algo)
Vienna [vɪ'enə] *n* Viena
Vietnam [vjet'næm] *n* Vietnam *m*; **~ese** [-nəˈmiːz] *n inv*; *adj* vietnamita *m/f*
view [vjuː] *n* vista; (*outlook*) perspectiva; (*opinion*) opinión *f*, criterio ♦ *vt* (*look at*) mirar; (*fig*) considerar; **on ~** (*in museum etc*) expuesto; **in full ~ (of)** en plena vista (de); **in ~ of the weather/the fact that** en vista del tiempo/del hecho de que; **in my ~** en mi opinión; **~er** *n* espectador(a) *m/f*; (*TV*) telespectador(a) *m/f*; **~finder** *n* visor *m* de imagen; **~point** *n* (*attitude*) punto de vista; (*place*) mirador *m*
vigour ['vɪgə*] (*US* **vigor**) *n* energía, vigor *m*
vile [vaɪl] *adj* vil, infame; (*smell*) asqueroso; (*temper*) endemoniado
villa ['vɪlə] *n* (*country house*) casa de campo; (*suburban house*) chalet *m*
village ['vɪlɪdʒ] *n* aldea; **~r** *n* aldeano/a
villain ['vɪlən] *n* (*scoundrel*) malvado/a; (*in novel*) malo; (*BRIT: criminal*) maleante *m/f*
vindicate ['vɪndɪkeɪt] *vt* vindicar, justificar
vindictive [vɪn'dɪktɪv] *adj* vengativo
vine [vaɪn] *n* vid *f*
vinegar ['vɪnɪgə*] *n* vinagre *m*
vineyard ['vɪnjɑːd] *n* viña, viñedo
vintage ['vɪntɪdʒ] *n* (*year*) vendimia, cosecha ♦ *cpd* de época; **~ wine** *n* vino añejo
vinyl ['vaɪnl] *n* vinilo
viola [vɪ'əʊlə] *n* (*MUS*) viola
violate ['vaɪəleɪt] *vt* violar
violence ['vaɪələns] *n* violencia
violent ['vaɪələnt] *adj* violento; (*intense*) intenso
violet ['vaɪələt] *adj* violado, violeta ♦ *n* (*plant*) violeta
violin [vaɪə'lɪn] *n* violín *m*; **~ist** *n* violinista *m/f*
VIP *n abbr* (= *very important person*) VIP *m*
virgin ['vɜːdʒɪn] *n* virgen *f*
Virgo ['vɜːgəʊ] *n* Virgo
virtually ['vɜːtjʊəlɪ] *adv* prácticamente
virtual reality ['vɜːtjʊəl-] *n* (*COMPUT*)

mundo *or* realidad *f* virtual
virtue ['vɜːtjuː] *n* virtud *f*; (*advantage*) ventaja; **by ~ of** en virtud de
virtuous ['vɜːtjʊəs] *adj* virtuoso
virus ['vaɪərəs] *n* (*also*: *COMPUT*) virus *m*
visa ['viːzə] *n* visado (*SP*), visa (*AM*)
visible ['vɪzəbl] *adj* visible
vision ['vɪʒən] *n* (*sight*) vista; (*foresight, in dream*) visión *f*
visit ['vɪzɪt] *n* visita ♦ *vt* (*person*: *US: also*: ~ *with*) visitar, hacer una visita a; (*place*) ir a, (ir a) conocer; **~ing hours** *npl* (*in hospital etc*) horas *fpl* de visita; **~or** *n* (*in museum*) visitante *m/f*; (*invited to house*) visita; (*tourist*) turista *m/f*
visor ['vaɪzə*] *n* visera
visual ['vɪzjʊəl] *adj* visual; **~ aid** *n* medio visual; **~ display unit** *n* unidad *f* de presentación visual; **~ize** *vt* imaginarse
vital ['vaɪtl] *adj* (*essential*) esencial, imprescindible; (*dynamic*) dinámico; (*organ*) vital; **~ly** *adv*: **~ly important** de primera importancia; **~ statistics** *npl* (*fig*) medidas *fpl* vitales
vitamin ['vɪtəmɪn] *n* vitamina
vivacious [vɪ'veɪʃəs] *adj* vivaz, alegre
vivid ['vɪvɪd] *adj* (*account*) gráfico; (*light*) intenso; (*imagination, memory*) vivo; **~ly** *adv* gráficamente; (*remember*) como si fuera hoy
V-neck ['viːnek] *n* cuello de pico
vocabulary [vəʊ'kæbjʊlərɪ] *n* vocabulario
vocal ['vəʊkl] *adj* vocal; (*articulate*) elocuente; **~ cords** *npl* cuerdas *fpl* vocales
vocation [vəʊ'keɪʃən] *n* vocación *f*; **~al** *adj* profesional
vodka ['vɒdkə] *n* vodka *m*
vogue [vəʊg] *n*: **in ~** en boga, de moda
voice [vɔɪs] *n* voz *f* ♦ *vt* expresar; **~ mail** *n* fonobuzón *m*
void [vɔɪd] *n* vacío; (*hole*) hueco ♦ *adj* (*invalid*) nulo, inválido; (*empty*): **~ of** carente *or* desprovisto de
volatile ['vɒlətaɪl] *adj* (*situation*) inestable; (*person*) voluble; (*liquid*) volátil
volcano [vɒl'keɪnəʊ] (*pl* **~es**) *n* volcán *m*
volition [və'lɪʃən] *n*: **of one's own ~** de su propia voluntad
volley ['vɒlɪ] *n* (*of gunfire*) descarga; (*of stones etc*) lluvia; (*fig*) torrente *m*; (*TENNIS etc*) volea; **~ball** *n* vol(e)ibol *m*
volt [vəʊlt] *n* voltio; **~age** *n* voltaje *m*
volume ['vɒljuːm] *n* (*gen*) volumen *m*; (*book*) tomo
voluntary ['vɒləntərɪ] *adj* voluntario
volunteer [vɒlən'tɪə*] *n* voluntario/a ♦ *vt* (*information*) ofrecer ♦ *vi* ofrecerse (de voluntario); **to ~ to do** ofrecerse a hacer
vomit ['vɒmɪt] *n* vómito ♦ *vt*, *vi* vomitar
vote [vəʊt] *n* voto; (*votes cast*) votación *f*;

(*right to* ~) derecho de votar; (*franchise*) sufragio ♦ vt (*chairman*) elegir; (*propose*): **~ that** proponer que ♦ vi votar, ir a votar; **~ of thanks** voto de gracias; **~r** n votante m/f; **voting** n votación f

vouch [vautʃ]: **to ~ for** vt fus garantizar, responder de

voucher ['vautʃə*] n (*for meal, petrol*) vale m

vow [vau] n voto ♦ vt: **to ~ to do/that** jurar hacer/que

vowel ['vauəl] n vocal f

voyage ['vɔɪdʒ] n viaje m

vulgar ['vʌlgə*] adj (*rude*) ordinario, grosero; (*in bad taste*) de mal gusto; **~ity** [-'gærɪtɪ] n grosería; mal gusto

vulnerable ['vʌlnərəbl] adj vulnerable

vulture ['vʌltʃə*] n buitre m

W, w

wad [wɔd] n bolita f; (*of banknotes etc*) fajo

waddle ['wɔdl] vi anadear

wade [weɪd] vi: **to ~ through** (*water*) vadear; (*fig: book*) leer con dificultad; **wading pool** (*US*) n piscina para niños

wafer ['weɪfə*] n galleta, barquillo

waffle ['wɔfl] n (*CULIN*) gofre m ♦ vi dar el rollo

waft [wɔft] vt llevar por el aire ♦ vi flotar

wag [wæg] vt menear, agitar ♦ vi moverse, menearse

wage [weɪdʒ] n (*also:* ~s) sueldo, salario ♦ vt: **to ~ war** hacer la guerra; **~ earner** n asalariado/a; **~ packet** n sobre m de paga

wager ['weɪdʒə*] n apuesta

wag(g)on ['wægən] n (*horse-drawn*) carro; (*BRIT: RAIL*) vagón m

wail [weɪl] n gemido ♦ vi gemir

waist [weɪst] n cintura, talle m; **~coat** (*BRIT*) n chaleco; **~line** n talle m

wait [weɪt] n (*interval*) pausa ♦ vi esperar; **to lie in ~ for** acechar a; **I can't ~ to** (*fig*) estoy deseando; **to ~ for** esperar (a); **~ behind** vi quedarse; **~ on** vt fus servir a; **~er** n camarero; **~ing** n: **"no ~ing"** (*BRIT: AUT*) "prohibido estacionarse"; **~ing list** n lista de espera; **~ing room** n sala de espera; **~ress** n camarera

waive [weɪv] vt suspender

wake [weɪk] (*pt* woke *or* waked, *pp* woken *or* waked) vt (*also:* ~ up) despertar ♦ vi (*also:* ~ up) despertarse ♦ n (*for dead person*) vela, velatorio; (*NAUT*) estela; **waken** vt, vi = **wake**

Wales [weɪlz] n País m de Gales; **the Prince of ~** el príncipe de Gales

walk [wɔːk] n (*stroll*) paseo; (*hike*) excursión f a pie, caminata; (*gait*) paso, andar m; (*in park etc*) paseo, alameda ♦ vi andar, caminar; (*for pleasure, exercise*) pasear ♦ vt (*distance*) recorrer a pie, andar; (*dog*) pasear; **10 minutes' ~ from here** a 10 minutos de aquí andando; **people from all ~s of life** gente de todas las esferas; **~ out** vi (*audience*) salir; (*workers*) declararse en huelga; **~ out on** (*inf*) vt fus abandonar; **~er** n (*person*) paseante m/f, caminante m/f; **~ie-talkie** ['wɔːkɪ'tɔːkɪ] n walkie-talkie m; **~ing** n el andar; **~ing shoes** npl zapatos mpl para andar; **~ing stick** n bastón m; **W~man** ® ['wɔːkmən] n®Walkman ® m; **~out** n huelga; **~over** (*inf*) n: **it was a ~over** fue pan comido; **~way** n paseo

wall [wɔːl] n pared f; (*exterior*) muro; (*city ~ etc*) muralla; **~ed** adj amurallado; (*garden*) con tapia

wallet ['wɔlɪt] n cartera (*SP*), billetera (*AM*)

wallflower ['wɔːlflauə*] n alhelí m; **to be a ~** (*fig*) comer pavo

wallow ['wɔləu] vi revolcarse

wallpaper ['wɔːlpeɪpə*] n papel m pintado ♦ vt empapelar

walnut ['wɔːlnʌt] n nuez f; (*tree*) nogal m

walrus ['wɔːlrəs] (*pl* ~ *or* ~**es**) n morsa

waltz [wɔːlts] n vals m ♦ vi bailar el vals

wand [wɔnd] n (*also: magic* ~) varita (mágica)

wander ['wɔndə*] vi (*person*) vagar; deambular; (*thoughts*) divagar ♦ vt recorrer, vagar por

wane [weɪn] vi menguar

wangle ['wæŋgl] (*BRIT: inf*) vt agenciarse

want [wɔnt] vt querer, desear; (*need*) necesitar ♦ n: **for ~ of** por falta de; **~s** npl (*needs*) necesidades fpl; **to ~ to do** querer hacer; **to ~ sb to do sth** querer que uno haga algo; **~ed** adj (*criminal*) buscado; **"~ed"** (*in advertisements*) "se busca"; **~ing** adj: **to be found ~ing** no estar a la altura de las circunstancias

war [wɔː*] n guerra; **to make ~ (on)** (*also fig*) declarar la guerra (a)

ward [wɔːd] n (*in hospital*) sala; (*POL*) distrito electoral; (*LAW: child: also:* ~ *of court*) pupilo/a; **~ off** vt (*blow*) desviar, parar; (*attack*) rechazar

warden ['wɔːdn] n (*BRIT: of institution*) director(a) m/f; (*of park, game reserve*) guardián/ana m/f; (*BRIT: also: traffic* ~) guardia m/f

warder ['wɔːdə*] (*BRIT*) n guardián/ana m/f, carcelero/a

wardrobe ['wɔːdrəub] n armario, guardarropa, ropero (*esp AM*)

warehouse ['wɛəhaus] n almacén m, depósito

wares [wɛəz] npl mercancías fpl

warfare ['wɔːfeə*] n guerra
warhead ['wɔːhɛd] n cabeza armada
warily ['wɛərɪlɪ] adv con cautela, cautelosamente
warm [wɔːm] adj caliente; (thanks) efusivo; (clothes etc) abrigado; (welcome, day) caluroso; **it's ~** hace calor; **I'm ~** tengo calor; **~ up** vi (room) calentarse; (person) entrar en calor; (athlete) hacer ejercicios de calentamiento ♦ vt calentar; **~-hearted** adj afectuoso; **~ly** adv afectuosamente; **~th** n calor m
warn [wɔːn] vt avisar, advertir; **~ing** n aviso, advertencia; **~ing light** n luz f de advertencia; **~ing triangle** n (AUT) triángulo señalizador
warp [wɔːp] vi (wood) combarse ♦ vt combar; (mind) pervertir
warrant ['wɔrnt] n autorización f; (LAW: to arrest) orden f de detención; (: to search) mandamiento de registro
warranty ['wɔrəntɪ] n garantía
warren ['wɔrən] n (of rabbits) madriguera; (fig) laberinto
warrior ['wɔrɪə*] n guerrero/a
Warsaw ['wɔːsɔː] n Varsovia
warship ['wɔːʃɪp] n buque m o barco de guerra
wart [wɔːt] n verruga
wartime ['wɔːtaɪm] n: **in ~** en tiempos de guerra, en la guerra
wary ['wɛərɪ] adj cauteloso
was [wɔz] pt of **be**
wash [wɔʃ] vt lavar ♦ vi lavarse; (sea etc): **to ~ against/over sth** llegar hasta/cubrir algo ♦ n (clothes etc) lavado; (of ship) estela; **to have a ~** lavarse; **~ away** vt (stain) quitar lavando; (subj: river etc) llevarse; **~ off** vi quitarse (al lavar); **~ up** vi (BRIT) fregar los platos; (US) lavarse; **~able** adj lavable; **~basin** (US ~bowl) n palangana; (of bowl) lavabo; **~cloth** (US) n manopla; **~er** n (TECH) arandela; **~ing** n (dirty) ropa sucia; (clean) colada; **~ing machine** n lavadora; **~ing powder** (BRIT) n detergente m (en polvo)
Washington ['wɔʃɪŋtən] n Washington m
wash-: **~ing-up** (BRIT) n fregado, platos mpl (para fregar); **~ing-up liquid** (BRIT) n líquido lavavajillas; **~-out** (inf) n fracaso; **~room** (US) n servicios mpl
wasn't ['wɔznt] = **was not**
wasp [wɔsp] n avispa
wastage ['weɪstɪdʒ] n desgaste m; (loss) pérdida
waste [weɪst] n derroche m, despilfarro; (of time) pérdida; (food) sobras fpl; (rubbish) basura, desperdicios mpl ♦ adj (material) de desecho; (left over) sobrante; (land) baldío, descampado ♦ vt malgastar, derrochar;

(time) perder; (opportunity) desperdiciar; **~s** npl (area of land) tierras fpl baldías; **~ away** vi consumirse; **~ disposal unit** (BRIT) n triturador m de basura; **~ful** adj derrochador(a); (process) antieconómico; **~ ground** (BRIT) n terreno baldío; **~paper basket** n papelera; **~ pipe** n tubo de desagüe
watch [wɔtʃ] n (also: **wrist ~**) reloj m; (MIL: group of guards) centinela m; (act) vigilancia; (NAUT: spell of duty) guardia ♦ vt (look at) mirar, observar; (: match, programme) ver; (spy on, guard) vigilar; (be careful of) cuidarse de, tener cuidado de ♦ vi ver, mirar; (keep guard) montar guardia; **~ out** vi cuidarse, tener cuidado; **~dog** n perro guardián; (fig) persona u organismo encargado de asegurarse de que las empresas actúan dentro de la legalidad; **~ful** adj vigilante, sobre aviso; **~maker** n relojero/a; **~man** (irreg) n see **night**; **~ strap** n pulsera (de reloj)
water ['wɔːtə*] n agua ♦ vt (plant) regar ♦ vi (eyes) llorar; (mouth) hacerse la boca agua; **~ down** vt (milk etc) aguar; (fig: story) dulcificar, diluir; **~ closet** n wáter m; **~colour** n acuarela; **~cress** n berro; **~fall** n cascada, salto de agua; **~ heater** n calentador m de agua; **~ing can** n regadera; **~ lily** n nenúfar m; **~line** n (NAUT) línea de flotación; **~logged** adj (ground) inundado; **~ main** n cañería del agua; **~melon** n sandía; **~proof** adj impermeable; **~shed** n (GEO) cuenca; (fig) momento crítico; **~skiing** n esquí m acuático; **~tight** adj hermético; **~way** n vía fluvial o navegable; **~works** n central f depuradora; **~y** adj (coffee etc) aguado; (eyes) lloroso
watt [wɔt] n vatio
wave [weɪv] n (of hand) señal f con la mano; (on water) ola; (RADIO, in hair) onda; (fig) oleada ♦ vi agitar la mano; (flag etc) ondear ♦ vt (handkerchief, gun) agitar; **~length** n longitud f de onda
waver ['weɪvə*] vi (voice, love etc) flaquear; (person) vacilar
wavy ['weɪvɪ] adj ondulado
wax [wæks] n cera ♦ vt encerar ♦ vi (moon) crecer; **~ paper** (US) n papel m apergaminado; **~works** n museo de cera ♦ npl figuras fpl de cera
way [weɪ] n camino; (distance) trayecto, recorrido; (direction) dirección f, sentido; (manner) modo, manera; (habit) costumbre f; **which ~? — this ~** ¿por dónde?, ¿en qué dirección? — por aquí; **on the ~** (en route) en (el) camino; **to be on one's ~** estar en camino; **to be in the ~** bloquear el camino; (fig) estorbar; **to go out of one's ~ to do sth**

desvivirse por hacer algo; **under ~** en marcha;
to lose one's ~ extraviarse; **in a ~** en cierto
modo or sentido; **no ~!** (*inf*) ¡de eso nada!;
by the ~ ... a propósito ...; **"~ in"** (*BRIT*)
"entrada"; **"~ out"** (*BRIT*) "salida"; **the ~ back**
el camino de vuelta; **"give ~"** (*BRIT*: *AUT*)
"ceda el paso"
waylay ['weɪleɪ] (*irreg*) *vt* salir al paso a
wayward ['weɪwəd] *adj* díscolo
W.C. *n* (*BRIT*) wáter *m*
we [wi:] *pl pron* nosotros/as
weak [wi:k] *adj* débil, flojo; (*tea etc*) claro;
~en *vi* debilitarse; (*give way*) ceder ♦ *vt*
debilitar; **~ling** *n* debilucho/a; (*morally*)
persona de poco carácter; **~ness** *n* debilidad
f; (*fault*) punto débil; **to have a ~ness for**
tener debilidad por
wealth [welθ] *n* riqueza; (*of details*)
abundancia; **~y** *adj* rico
wean [wi:n] *vt* destetar
weapon ['wepən] *n* arma
wear [weə*] (*pt* **wore**, *pp* **worn**) *n* (*use*) uso;
(*deterioration through use*) desgaste *m*;
(*clothing*): **sports/baby~** ropa de deportes/de
niños ♦ *vt* (*clothes*) llevar; (*shoes*) calzar;
(*damage: through use*) gastar, usar ♦ *vi* (*last*)
durar; (*rub through etc*) desgastarse; **evening
~** ropa de etiqueta; **~ away** *vt* gastar ♦ *vi*
desgastarse; **~ down** *vt* gastar; (*strength*)
agotar; **~ off** *vi* (*pain etc*) pasar, desaparecer;
~ out *vt* desgastar; (*person, strength*) agotar;
~ and tear *n* desgaste *m*
weary ['wɪərɪ] *adj* cansado; (*dispirited*)
abatido ♦ *vi*: **to ~ of** cansarse de
weasel ['wi:zl] *n* (*ZOOL*) comadreja
weather ['weðə*] *n* tiempo ♦ *vt* (*storm, crisis*)
hacer frente a; **under the ~** (*fig: ill*)
indispuesto, pachucho; **~-beaten** *adj* (*skin*)
curtido; (*building*) deteriorado por la
intemperie; **~cock** *n* veleta; **~ forecast** *n*
boletín *m* meteorológico; **~man** (*irreg: inf*) *n*
hombre *m* del tiempo; **~ vane** *n* = **~cock**
weave [wi:v] (*pt* **wove**, *pp* **woven**) *vt* (*cloth*)
tejer; (*fig*) entretejer; **~r** *n* tejedor(a) *m/f*;
weaving *n* tejeduría
web [web] *n* (*of spider*) telaraña; (*on duck's
foot*) membrana; (*network*) red; *f*; **the** (**World
Wide**) **W~** el or la Web
website ['websaɪt] *n* espacio Web
wed [wed] (*pt, pp* **wedded**) *vt* casar ♦ *vi* casarse
we'd [wi:d] = **we had; we would**
wedding ['wedɪŋ] *n* boda, casamiento;
silver/golden ~ (**anniversary**) bodas *fpl* de
plata/de oro; **~ day** *n* día *m* de la boda;
~ dress *n* traje *m* de novia; **~ present** *n*
regalo de boda; **~ ring** *n* alianza
wedge [wedʒ] *n* (*of wood etc*) cuña; (*of cake*)
trozo ♦ *vt* acuñar; (*push*) apretar
Wednesday ['wednzdɪ] *n* miércoles *m inv*

wee [wi:] (*Scottish*) *adj* pequeñito
weed [wi:d] *n* mala hierba, maleza ♦ *vt*
escardar, desherbar; **~killer** *n* herbicida *m*;
~y *adj* (*person*) mequetréfico
week [wi:k] *n* semana; **a ~ today/on Friday** de
hoy/del viernes en ocho días; **~day** *n* día *m*
laborable; **~end** *n* fin *m* de semana; **~ly** *adv*
semanalmente, cada semana ♦ *adj* semanal
♦ *n* semanario
weep [wi:p] (*pt, pp* **wept**) *vi, vt* llorar; **~ing
willow** *n* sauce *m* llorón
weigh [weɪ] *vt, vi* pesar; **to ~ anchor** levar
anclas; **~ down** *vt* sobrecargar; (*fig: with
worry*) agobiar; **~ up** *vt* sopesar
weight [weɪt] *n* peso; (*metal ~*) pesa; **to lose/put
on ~** adelgazar/engordar; **~ing** *n* (*allowance*):
(**London**) **~ing** dietas (*por residir en Londres*);
~lifter *n* levantador *m* de pesas; **~y** *adj*
pesado; (*matters*) de relevancia or peso
weir [wɪə*] *n* presa
weird [wɪəd] *adj* raro, extraño
welcome ['welkəm] *adj* bienvenido ♦ *n*
bienvenida ♦ *vt* dar la bienvenida a; (*be glad
of*) alegrarse de; **thank you — you're ~** gracias
— de nada
weld [weld] *n* soldadura ♦ *vt* soldar
welfare ['welfeə*] *n* bienestar *m*; (*social aid*)
asistencia social; **~ state** *n* estado del
bienestar
well [wel] *n* fuente *f*, pozo ♦ *adv* bien ♦ *adj*
to be ~ estar bien (de salud) ♦ *excl* ¡vaya!,
¡bueno!; **as ~** también; **as ~ as** además de;
~ done! ¡bien hecho!; **get ~ soon!** ¡que te
mejores pronto!; **to do ~** (*business*) ir bien;
(*person*) tener éxito; **~ up** *vi* (*tears*) saltar
we'll [wi:l] = **we will; we shall**
well: ~-behaved *adj* bueno; **~-being** *n*
bienestar *m*; **~-built** *adj* (*person*) fornido; **~-
deserved** *adj* merecido; **~-dressed** *adj* bien
vestido; **~-groomed** *adj* de buena presencia;
~-heeled (*inf*) *adj* (*wealthy*) rico
wellingtons ['welɪŋtənz] *npl* (*also: welling-
ton boots*) botas *fpl* de goma
well: ~-known *adj* (*person*) conocido; **~-
mannered** *adj* educado; **~-meaning** *adj*
bienintencionado; **~-off** *adj* acomodado; **~-
read** *adj* leído; **~-to-do** *adj* acomodado; **~-
wisher** *n* admirador(a) *m/f*
Welsh [welʃ] *adj* galés/esa ♦ *n* (*LING*) galés *m*;
the ~ *npl* los galeses; **the ~ Assembly** el
Parlamento galés; **~man** (*irreg*) *n* galés *m*;
~ rarebit *n* pan *m* con queso tostado;
~woman (*irreg*) *n* galesa
went [went] *pt of* **go**
wept [wept] *pt, pp of* **weep**
were [wə:*] *pt of* **be**
we're [wɪə*] = **we are**
weren't [wə:nt] = **were not**
west [west] *n* oeste *m* ♦ *adj* occidental, del

oeste ♦ adv al o hacia el oeste; **the W~** el Oeste, el Occidente; **W~ Country** (BRIT) n: **the W~ Country** el suroeste de Inglaterra; **~erly** adj occidental; (wind) del oeste; **~ern** adj occidental ♦ n (CINEMA) película del oeste; **W~ Germany** n Alemania Occidental; **W~ Indian** adj, n antillano/a m/f; **W~ Indies** npl Antillas fpl; **~ward(s)** adv hacia el oeste

wet [wet] adj (damp) húmedo; (~ through) mojado; (rainy) lluvioso ♦ (BRIT) n (POL) conservador(a) m/f moderado/a; **to get ~** mojarse; **"~ paint"** "recién pintado"; **~suit** n traje m térmico

we've [wi:v] = **we have**

whack [wæk] vt dar un buen golpe a

whale [weɪl] n (ZOOL) ballena

wharf [wɔ:f](pl **wharves**) n muelle m

KEYWORD

what [wɔt] adj 1 (in direct/indirect questions) qué; **~ size is he?** ¿qué talla usa?; **~ colour/ shape is it?** ¿de qué color/forma es?
2 (in exclamations): **~ a mess!** ¡qué desastre!; **~ a fool I am!** ¡qué tonto soy!
♦ pron 1 (interrogative) qué; **~ are you doing?** ¿qué haces o estás haciendo?; **~ is happening?** ¿qué pasa o está pasando?; **~ is it called?** ¿cómo se llama?; **~ about me?** ¿y yo qué?; **~ about doing ...?** ¿qué tal si hacemos ...?
2 (relative) lo que; **I saw ~ you did/was on the table** vi lo que hiciste/había en la mesa
♦ excl (disbelieving) ¡cómo!; **~, no coffee!** ¡que no hay café!

whatever [wɔt'ɛvə*] adj: **~ book you choose** cualquier libro que elijas ♦ pron: **do ~ necessary** haga lo que sea necesario; **~ happens** pase lo que pase; **no reason ~ or whatsoever** ninguna razón sea la que sea; **nothing ~** nada en absoluto

whatsoever [wɔtsəu'ɛvə*] adj see **whatever**

wheat [wi:t] n trigo

wheedle ['wi:dl] vt: **to ~ sb into doing sth** engatusar a uno para que haga algo; **to ~ sth out of sb** sonsacar algo a uno

wheel [wi:l] n rueda; (AUT: also: steering ~) volante m; (NAUT) timón m ♦ vt (pram etc) empujar ♦ vi (also: ~ round) dar la vuelta, girar; **~barrow** n carretilla; **~chair** n silla de ruedas; **~ clamp** n (AUT) cepo

wheeze [wi:z] vi resollar

KEYWORD

when [wen] adv cuando; **~ did it happen?** ¿cuándo ocurrió?; **I know ~ it happened** sé cuándo ocurrió
♦ conj 1 (at, during, after the time that)

cuando; **be careful ~ you cross the road** ten cuidado al cruzar la calle; **that was ~ I needed you** fue entonces que te necesité
2 (on, at which): **on the day ~ I met him** el día en que le conocí
3 (whereas) cuando

whenever [wen'ɛvə*] conj cuando; (every time that) cada vez que ♦ adv cuando sea

where [weə*] adv dónde ♦ conj donde; **this is ~ I live** es aquí; **~abouts** adv dónde ♦ n: **nobody knows his ~abouts** nadie conoce su paradero; **~as** conj visto que, mientras; **~by** pron por lo cual; **wherever** [-'ɛvə*] conj dondequiera que; (interrogative) dónde; **~withal** n recursos mpl

whether ['weðə*] conj si; **I don't know ~ to accept or not** no sé si aceptar o no; **~ you go or not** vayas o no vayas

---

KEYWORD

which [wɪtʃ] adj 1 (interrogative: direct, indirect) qué; **~ picture(s) do you want?** ¿qué cuadro(s) quieres?; **~ one?** ¿cuál?
2: **in ~ case** en cuyo caso; **we got there at 8 pm, by ~ time the cinema was full** llegamos allí a las 8, cuando el cine estaba lleno
♦ pron 1 (interrogative) cuál; **I don't mind ~** el/la que sea
2 (relative: replacing noun) que; (: replacing clause) lo que; (: after preposition) (el/la) que etc, el/la cual etc; **the apple ~ you ate/~ is on the table** la manzana que comiste/que está en la mesa; **the chair on ~ you are sitting** la silla en la que estás sentado; **he said he knew, ~ is true/I feared** dijo que lo sabía, lo cual o lo que es cierto/me temía

whichever [wɪtʃ'ɛvə*] adj: **take ~ book you prefer** coja (SP) el libro que prefiera; **~ book you take** cualquier libro que coja

while [waɪl] n rato, momento ♦ conj mientras; (although) aunque; **for a ~** durante algún tiempo; **~ away** vt pasar

whim [wɪm] n capricho

whimper ['wɪmpə*] n sollozo ♦ vi lloriquear

whimsical ['wɪmzɪkl] adj (person) caprichoso; (look) juguetón/ona

whine [waɪn] n (of pain) gemido; (of engine) zumbido; (of siren) aullido ♦ vi gemir; zumbar; (fig: complain) gimotear

whip [wɪp] n látigo; (POL: person) encargado de la disciplina partidaria en el parlamento ♦ vt azotar; (CULIN) batir; (move quickly): **to ~ sth out/off** sacar/quitar algo de un tirón; **~ped cream** n nata o crema montada; **~-round** n (BRIT) n colecta

whirl [wɜ:l] vt hacer girar, dar vueltas a ♦ vi girar, dar vueltas; (leaves etc) arremolinarse;

~pool n remolino; **~wind** n torbellino

whirr [wəː*] vi zumbar

whisk [wɪsk] n (CULIN) batidor m ♦ vt (CULIN) batir; **to ~ sb away** or **off** llevar volando a uno

whiskers ['wɪskəz] npl (of animal) bigotes mpl; (of man) patillas fpl

whiskey ['wɪskɪ] (US, Ireland) n = whisky

whisky ['wɪskɪ] n whisky m

whisper ['wɪspə*] n susurro ♦ vi, vt susurrar

whistle ['wɪsl] n (sound) silbido; (object) silbato ♦ vi silbar

white [waɪt] adj blanco; (pale) pálido ♦ n blanco; (of egg) clara; **~ coffee** (BRIT) n café m con leche; **~-collar worker** n oficinista m/f; **~ elephant** n (fig) maula; **~ lie** n mentirilla; **~ness** n blancura; **~ noise** n sonido blanco; **~ paper** n (POL) libro rojo; **~wash** n (paint) jalbegue m, cal f ♦ vt (also fig) blanquear

whiting ['waɪtɪŋ] n inv (fish) pescadilla

Whitsun ['wɪtsn] n pentecostés m

whizz [wɪz] vi: **to ~ past** or **by** pasar a toda velocidad; **~ kid** (inf) n prodigio

---

who [huː] pron 1 (interrogative) quién; **~ is it?, ~'s there?** ¿quién es?; **~ are you looking for?** ¿a quién buscas?; **I told her ~ I was** le dije quién era yo

2 (relative) que; **the man/woman ~ spoke to me** el hombre/la mujer que habló conmigo; **those ~ can swim** los que saben or sepan nadar

whodun(n)it [huː'dʌnɪt] (inf) n novela policíaca

whoever [huː'evə*] pron: **~ finds it** cualquiera que quienquiera que lo encuentre; **ask ~ you like** pregunta a quien quieras; **~ he marries** no importa con quién se case

whole [həul] adj (entire) todo, entero; (not broken) intacto ♦ n todo; (all): **the ~ of the town** toda la ciudad, la ciudad entera ♦ n (total) total m; (sum) conjunto; **on the ~, as a ~** en general; **~food(s)** n(pl) alimento(s) m(pl) integral(es); **~hearted** adj sincero, cordial; **~meal** adj integral; **~sale** n venta al por mayor ♦ adj al por mayor; (fig: destruction) sistemático; **~saler** n mayorista m/f; **~some** adj sano; **~wheat** adj = **~meal**; **wholly** adv totalmente, enteramente

---

whom [huːm] pron 1 (interrogative): **~ did you see?** ¿a quién viste?; **to ~ did you give it?** ¿a quién se lo diste?; **tell me from ~ you received it** dígame de quién lo recibió

2 (relative) que; **to ~** a quien(es); **of ~** de quien(es), del/de la que etc; **the man ~ I**

---

saw/to **~ I wrote** el hombre que vi/a quien escribí; **the lady about/with ~ I was talking** la señora de (la) que/con quien or (la) que hablaba

whooping cough ['huːpɪŋ-] n tos f ferina

whore [hɔː*] (inf: pej) n puta

---

whose [huːz] adj 1 (possessive: interrogative): **~ book is this?, ~ is this book?** ¿de quién es este libro?; **~ pencil have you taken?** ¿de quién es el lápiz que has cogido?; **~ daughter are you?** ¿de quién eres hija?

2 (possessive: relative) cuyo/a, pl cuyos/as; **the man ~ son you rescued** el hombre cuyo hijo rescataste; **those ~ passports I have** aquellas personas cuyos pasaportes tengo; **the woman ~ car was stolen** la mujer a quien le robaron el coche

♦ pron de quién; **~ is this?** ¿de quién es esto?; **I know ~ it is** sé de quién es

---

why [waɪ] adv por qué; **~ not?** ¿por qué no?; **~ not do it now?** ¿por qué no lo haces (or hacemos etc) ahora?

♦ conj: **I wonder ~ he said that** me pregunto por qué dijo eso; **that's not ~ I'm here** no es por eso (por lo) que estoy aquí; **the reason ~** la razón por la que

♦ excl (expressing surprise, shock, annoyance) ¡hombre!, ¡vaya! (explaining): **~, it's you!** ¡hombre, eres tú!; **~, that's impossible** ¡pero sí eso es imposible!

wicked ['wɪkɪd] adj malvado, cruel

wicket ['wɪkɪt] n (CRICKET: stumps) palos mpl; (: grass area) terreno de juego

wide [waɪd] adj ancho; (area, knowledge) vasto, grande; (choice) amplio ♦ adv: **to open ~** abrir de par en par; **to shoot ~** errar el tiro; **~-angle lens** n objetivo de gran angular; **~awake** adj bien despierto; **~ly** adv (travelled) mucho; (spaced) muy; **it is ~ly believed/known that ...** mucha gente piensa/ sabe que ...; **~n** vt ensanchar; (experience) ampliar ♦ vi ensancharse; **~ open** adj abierto de par en par; **~spread** adj extendido, general

widow ['wɪdəu] n viuda; **~ed** adj viudo; **~er** n viudo

width [wɪdθ] n anchura; (of cloth) ancho

wield [wiːld] vt (sword) blandir; (power) ejercer

wife [waɪf] (pl wives) n mujer f, esposa

wig [wɪg] n peluca

wiggle ['wɪgl] vt menear

wild [waɪld] adj (animal) salvaje; (plant) silvestre; (person) furioso, violento; (idea) descabellado; (rough: sea) bravo; (: land) agreste; (: weather) muy revuelto; **~s** npl regiones fpl salvajes, tierras fpl vírgenes; **~erness** ['wɪldənɪs] n desierto; **~life** n fauna; **~ly** adv (behave) locamente; (lash out) a diestro y siniestro; (guess) a lo loco; (happy) a más no poder

wilful ['wɪlful] (US **willful**) adj (action) deliberado; (obstinate) testarudo

KEYWORD

will [wɪl] aux vb **1** (forming future tense): **I ~ finish it tomorrow** lo terminaré o voy a terminar mañana; **I ~ have finished it by tomorrow** lo habré terminado para mañana; **~ you do it? — yes I ~/no I won't** ¿lo harás? — sí/no

2 (in conjectures, predictions): **he ~ or he'll be there by now** ya habrá o debe (de) haber llegado; **that ~ be the postman** será o debe ser el cartero

3 (in commands, requests, offers): **~ you be quiet!** ¿quieres callarte?; **~ you help me?** ¿quieres ayudarme?; **~ you have a cup of tea?** ¿te apetece un té?; **I won't put up with it!** ¡no lo soporto!

♦ vt (pt, pp willed): **to ~ sb to do sth** desear que alguien haga algo; **he ~ed himself to go on** con gran fuerza de voluntad, continuó

♦ n voluntad f; (testament) testamento

willing ['wɪlɪŋ] adj (with goodwill) de buena voluntad; (enthusiastic) entusiasta; **he's ~ to do it** está dispuesto a hacerlo; **~ly** adv con mucho gusto; **~ness** n buena voluntad

willow ['wɪləu] n sauce m

willpower ['wɪlpauə*] n fuerza de voluntad

willy-nilly [wɪlɪ'nɪlɪ] adv quiérase o no

wilt [wɪlt] vi marchitarse

win [wɪn] (pt, pp **won**) n victoria, triunfo ♦ vt ganar; (obtain) conseguir, lograr ♦ vi ganar; **~ over** vt convencer a; **~ round** (BRIT) vt = **~ over**

wince [wɪns] vi encogerse

winch [wɪntʃ] n torno

wind¹ [wɪnd] n viento; (MED) gases mpl ♦ vt (take breath away from) dejar sin aliento a

wind² [waɪnd] (pt, pp **wound**) vt enrollar; (wrap) envolver; (clock, toy) dar cuerda a ♦ vi (road, river) serpentear; **~ up** vt (clock) dar cuerda a; (debate, meeting) concluir, terminar

windfall ['wɪndfɔːl] n golpe m de suerte

winding ['waɪndɪŋ] adj (road) tortuoso; (staircase) de caracol

wind instrument [wɪnd-] n (MUS) instrumento de viento

windmill ['wɪndmɪl] n molino de viento

window ['wɪndəu] n ventana; (in car, train) ventanilla; (in shop etc) escaparate m (SP), vitrina (AM); **~ box** n jardinera de ventana; **~ cleaner** n (person) limpiador m de cristales; **~ ledge** n alféizar m, repisa; **~ pane** n cristal m; **~ seat** n asiento junto a la ventana; **~-shopping** n: **to go ~-shopping** ir de escaparates; **~sill** n alféizar m, repisa

windpipe ['wɪndpaɪp] n tráquea

wind power n energía eólica

windscreen ['wɪndskriːn] (US **windshield**) n parabrisas m inv; **~ washer** n lavaparabrisas m inv; **~ wiper** n limpiaparabrisas m inv

windswept ['wɪndswept] adj azotado por el viento

windy ['wɪndɪ] adj de mucho viento; **it's ~** hace viento

wine [waɪn] n vino; **~ bar** n enoteca; **~ cellar** n bodega; **~ glass** n copa (para vino); **~ list** n lista de vinos; **~ waiter** n escanciador m

wing [wɪŋ] n ala; (AUT) aleta; **~s** npl (THEATRE) bastidores mpl; **~er** n (SPORT) extremo

wink [wɪŋk] n guiño, pestañeo ♦ vi guiñar, pestañear

winner ['wɪnə*] n ganador(a) m/f

winning ['wɪnɪŋ] adj (team) ganador(a); (goal) decisivo; (smile) encantador(a); **~s** npl ganancias fpl

winter ['wɪntə*] n invierno ♦ vi invernar; **wintry** ['wɪntrɪ] adj invernal

wipe [waɪp] n: **to give sth a ~** pasar un trapo sobre algo ♦ vt limpiar; (tape) borrar; **~ off** vt limpiar con un trapo; (remove) quitar; **~ out** vt (debt) liquidar; (memory) borrar; (destroy) destruir; **~ up** vt limpiar

wire ['waɪə*] n alambre m; (ELEC) cable m (eléctrico); (TEL) telegrama m ♦ vt (house) poner la instalación eléctrica en; (also: **~ up**) conectar; (person: telegram) telegrafiar

wireless ['waɪəlɪs] (BRIT) n radio f

wiring ['waɪərɪŋ] n instalación f eléctrica

wiry ['waɪərɪ] adj (person) enjuto y fuerte; (hair) crespo

wisdom ['wɪzdəm] n sabiduría, saber m; (good sense) cordura; **~ tooth** n muela del juicio

wise [waɪz] adj sabio; (sensible) juicioso

...wise [waɪz] suffix: **time~** en cuanto a o respecto al tiempo

wish [wɪʃ] n deseo ♦ vt querer; **best ~es** (on birthday etc) felicidades fpl; **with best ~es** (in letter) saludos mpl, recuerdos mpl; **to ~ sb goodbye** despedirse de uno; **he ~ed me well** me deseó mucha suerte; **to ~ to do/sb to do sth** querer hacer/que alguien haga algo; **to ~ for** desear; **~ful** adj: **it's ~ful thinking** eso sería soñar

wisp [wɪsp] n mechón m; (of smoke) voluta

wistful ['wɪstful] adj pensativo

wit [wɪt] n ingenio, gracia; (also: ~s) inteligencia; (person) chistoso/a

witch [wɪtʃ] n bruja; **~craft** n brujería; **~hunt** n (fig) caza de brujas

---
KEYWORD
---

with [wɪð, wɪθ] prep **1** (accompanying, in the company of) con (+ mí, ti, sí = conmigo, contigo, consigo); **I was ~ him** estaba con él; **we stayed ~ friends** nos quedamos en casa de unos amigos; **I'm (not) ~ you** (understand) (no) te entiendo; **to be ~ it** (inf: person: up-to-date) estar al tanto; (: alert) ser despabilado

2 (descriptive, indicating manner etc) con; de; **a room ~ a view** una habitación con vistas; **the man ~ the grey hat/blue eyes** el hombre del sombrero gris/de los ojos azules; **red ~ anger** rojo de ira; **to shake ~ fear** temblar de miedo; **to fill sth ~ water** llenar algo de agua

---

withdraw [wɪθ'drɔː] (irreg) vt retirar, sacar ♦ vi retirarse; **to ~ money (from the bank)** retirar fondos (del banco); **~al** n retirada; (of money) reintegro; **~al symptoms** npl (MED) síndrome m de abstinencia; **~n** adj (person) reservado, introvertido

wither ['wɪðə*] vi marchitarse

withhold [wɪθ'həuld] (irreg) vt (money) retener; (decision) aplazar; (permission) negar; (information) ocultar

within [wɪð'ɪn] prep dentro de ♦ adv dentro; **~ reach (of)** al alcance (de); **~ sight (of)** a la vista (de); **~ the week** antes de acabar la semana; **~ a mile (of)** a menos de una milla (de)

without [wɪð'aut] prep sin; **to go ~ sth** pasar sin algo

withstand [wɪθ'stænd] (irreg) vt resistir a

witness ['wɪtnɪs] n testigo m/f ♦ vt (event) presenciar; (document) atestiguar la veracidad de; **to bear ~ to** (fig) ser testimonio de; **~ box** n tribuna de los testigos; **~ stand** (US) n = ~ box

witty ['wɪtɪ] adj ingenioso

wives [waɪvz] npl of **wife**

wk abbr = **week**

wobble ['wɔbl] vi temblar; (chair) cojear

woe [wəu] n desgracia

woke [wəuk] pt of **wake**

woken ['wəukən] pp of **wake**

wolf [wulf] n lobo; **wolves** [wulvz] npl of **wolf**

woman ['wumən] (pl **women**) n mujer f; **~ doctor** n médica; **women's lib** (inf: pej) n liberación f de la mujer; **~ly** adj femenino

womb [wuːm] n matriz f, útero

women ['wɪmɪn] npl of **woman**

won [wʌn] pt, pp of **win**

wonder ['wʌndə*] n maravilla, prodigio; (feeling) asombro ♦ vi: **to ~ whether/why** preguntarse si/por qué; **to ~ at** asombrarse de; **to ~ about** pensar sobre or en; **it's no ~ (that)** no es de extrañarse (que + subjun); **~ful** adj maravilloso

won't [wəunt] = will not

wood [wud] n (timber) madera; (forest) bosque m; **~ carving** n (act) tallado en madera; (object) talla en madera; **~ed** adj arbolado; **~en** adj de madera; (fig) inexpresivo; **~pecker** n pájaro carpintero; **~wind** n (MUS) instrumentos mpl de viento de madera; **~work** n carpintería; **~worm** n carcoma

wool [wul] n lana; **to pull the ~ over sb's eyes** (fig) engatusar a uno; **~en** (US) adj = **~len**; **~len** adj de lana; **~lens** npl géneros mpl de lana; **~ly** adj lanudo, de lana; (fig: ideas) confuso; **~y** (US) adj = **~ly**

word [wəːd] n palabra; (news) noticia; (promise) palabra (de honor) ♦ vt redactar; **in other ~s** en otras palabras; **to break/keep one's ~** faltar a la palabra/cumplir la promesa; **to have ~s with sb** reñir con uno; **~ing** n redacción f; **~ processing** n proceso de textos; **~ processor** n procesador m de textos

wore [wɔː*] pt of **wear**

work [wəːk] n trabajo; (job) empleo, trabajo; (ART, LITERATURE) obra ♦ vi trabajar; (mechanism) funcionar, marchar; (medicine) ser eficaz, surtir efecto ♦ vt (shape) trabajar; (stone etc) tallar; (mine etc) explotar; (machine) manejar, hacer funcionar; **~s** n (BRIT: factory) fábrica ♦ npl (of clock, machine) mecanismo; **to be out of ~** estar parado, no tener trabajo; **to ~ loose** (part) desprenderse; (knot) aflojarse; **~ on** vt fus trabajar en, dedicarse a; (principle) basarse en; **~ out** vi (plans etc) salir bien, funcionar ♦ vt (problem) resolver; (plan) elaborar; **it ~s out at £100** suma 100 libras; **~ up** vt: **to get ~ed up** excitarse; **~able** adj (solution) práctico, factible; **~aholic** [wəːkə'hɔlɪk] n trabajador(a) obsesivo/a m/f; **~er** n trabajador(a) m/f, obrero/a; **~force** n mano f de obra; **~ing class** n clase f obrera; **~ing-class** adj obrero; **~ing order** n: **in ~ing order** en funcionamiento; **~man** (irreg) n obrero; **~manship** n habilidad f, trabajo; **~sheet** n hoja de trabajo; **~shop** n taller m; **~ station** n puesto or estación f de trabajo; **~-to-rule** (BRIT) n huelga de celo

world [wəːld] n mundo ♦ cpd (champion) del mundo; (power, war) mundial; **to think the ~ of sb** (fig) tener un concepto muy alto de uno; **~ly** adj mundano; **~-wide** adj mundial, universal; **W~-Wide Web** n: the **W~-Wide Web** el World Wide Web

worm [wə:m] n (also: earth~) lombriz f

worn [wɔ:n] pp of **wear** ♦ adj usado; **~-out** adj (object) gastado; (person) rendido, agotado

worried ['wʌrɪd] adj preocupado

worry ['wʌrɪ] n preocupación f ♦ vt preocupar, inquietar ♦ vi preocuparse; **~ing** adj inquietante

worse [wə:s] adj, adv peor ♦ n lo peor; **a change for the** ~ un empeoramiento; **~n** vt, vi empeorar; ~ **off** adj (financially): **to be** ~ **off** tener menos dinero; (fig): **you'll be** ~ **off this way** de esta forma estarás peor que nunca

worship ['wə:ʃɪp] n adoración f ♦ vt adorar; **Your W~** (BRIT: to mayor) señor alcalde; (: to judge) señor juez

worst [wə:st] adj, adv peor ♦ n lo peor; **at** ~ en lo peor de los casos

worth [wə:θ] n valor m ♦ adj: **to be** ~ valer; **it's** ~ **it** vale or merece la pena; **to be** ~ **one's while** (to do) merecer la pena (hacer); **~less** adj sin valor; (useless) inútil; **~while** adj (activity) que merece la pena; (cause) loable

worthy ['wə:ðɪ] adj respetable; (motive) honesto; ~ **of** digno de

would [wʊd] aux vb **1** (conditional tense): **if you asked him he** ~ **do it** si se lo pidieras, lo haría; **if you had asked him he** ~ **have done it** si se lo hubieras pedido, lo habría or hubiera hecho

2 (in offers, invitations, requests): ~ **you like a biscuit?** ¿quieres una galleta?; (formal) ¿querría una galleta?; ~ **you ask him to come in?** ¿quiere hacerle pasar?; ~ **you open the window please?** ¿quiere or podría abrir la ventana, por favor?

3 (in indirect speech): **I said I** ~ **do it** dije que lo haría

4 (emphatic): **it WOULD have to snow today!** ¡tenía que nevar precisamente hoy!

5 (insistence): **she ~n't behave** no quiso comportarse bien

6 (conjecture): **it** ~ **have been midnight** sería medianoche; **it** ~ **seem so** parece ser que sí

7 (indicating habit): **he** ~ **go there on Mondays** iba allí los lunes

would-be (pej) adj presunto

wouldn't ['wʊdnt] = **would not**

wound[1] [wu:nd] n herida ♦ vt herir

wound[2] [waʊnd] pt, pp of **wind**

wove [wəʊv] pt of **weave**

woven ['wəʊvən] pp of **weave**

wrap [ræp] vt (also: ~ **up**) envolver; **~per** n (on chocolate) papel m; (BRIT: of book) sobrecubierta; **~ping paper** n papel m de envolver; (fancy) papel m de regalo

wreak [ri:k] vt: **to** ~ **havoc (on)** hacer estragos (en); **to** ~ **vengeance (on)** vengarse (de)

wreath [ri:θ, pl ri:ðz] n (funeral ~) corona

wreck [rek] n (ship: destruction) naufragio; (: remains) restos mpl del barco; (pej: person) ruina ♦ vt (car etc) destrozar; (chances) arruinar; **~age** n restos mpl; (of building) escombros mpl

wren [ren] n (ZOOL) reyezuelo

wrench [rentʃ] n (TECH) llave f inglesa; (tug) tirón m; (fig) dolor m ♦ vt arrancar; **to** ~ **sth from sb** arrebatar algo violentamente a uno

wrestle ['resl] vi: **to** ~ **(with sb)** luchar (con or contra uno); **~r** n luchador(a) m/f (de lucha libre); **wrestling** n lucha libre

wretched ['retʃɪd] adj miserable

wriggle ['rɪgl] vi (also: ~ **about**) menearse, retorcerse

wring [rɪŋ] (pt, pp **wrung**) vt retorcer; (wet clothes) escurrir; (fig): **to** ~ **sth out of sb** sacar algo por la fuerza a uno

wrinkle ['rɪŋkl] n arruga ♦ vt arrugar ♦ vi arrugarse

wrist [rɪst] n muñeca; **~watch** n reloj m de pulsera

writ [rɪt] n mandato judicial

write [raɪt] (pt **wrote**, pp **written**) vt escribir; (cheque) extender ♦ vi escribir; ~ **down** vt escribir; (note) apuntar; ~ **off** vt (debt) borrar (como incobrable); (fig) desechar por inútil; ~ **out** vt escribir; ~ **up** vt redactar; **~-off** n siniestro total; **~r** n escritor(a) m/f

writhe [raɪð] vi retorcerse

writing ['raɪtɪŋ] n escritura; (hand-~) letra; (of author) obras fpl; **in** ~ por escrito; ~ **paper** n papel m de escribir

written ['rɪtn] pp of **write**

wrong [rɒŋ] adj (wicked) malo; (unfair) injusto; (incorrect) equivocado, incorrecto; (not suitable) inoportuno, inconveniente; (reverse) del revés ♦ adv equivocadamente ♦ n injusticia ♦ vt ser injusto con; **you are** ~ **to do it** haces mal en hacerlo; **you are** ~ **about that, you've got it** ~ en eso estás equivocado; **to be in the** ~ no tener razón, tener la culpa; **what's** ~? ¿qué pasa?; **to go** ~ (person) equivocarse; (plan) salir mal; (machine) estropearse; **~ful** adj injusto; **~ly** adv mal, incorrectamente; (by mistake) por error; ~ **number** n (TEL): **you've got the** ~ **number** se ha equivocado de número

wrote [rəʊt] pt of **write**

wrought iron [rɔ:t-] n hierro forjado

wrung [rʌŋ] pt, pp of **wring**

wt. abbr = **weight**

WWW n abbr (= World Wide Web) WWW m

X, x

Xmas ['ɛksməs] n abbr = **Christmas**
X-ray ['ɛksreɪ] n radiografía ♦ vt radiografiar,
sacar radiografías de
xylophone ['zaɪləfəun] n xilófono

Y, y

Y2K abbr (= Year 2000): **the ~ problem** el
efecto 2000
yacht [jɔt] n yate m; **~ing** n (sport)
balandrismo; **~sman/woman** (irreg) n
balandrista m/f
Yank [jæŋk] (pej) n yanqui m/f
Yankee ['jæŋkɪ] (pej) n = **Yank**
yap [jæp] vi (dog) aullar
yard [jɑːd] n patio; (measure) yarda; **~stick** n
(fig) criterio, norma
yarn [jɑːn] n hilo; (tale) cuento, historia
yawn [jɔːn] n bostezo ♦ vi bostezar; **~ing** adj
(gap) muy abierto
yd(s). abbr = **yard(s)**
yeah [jɛə] (inf) adv sí
year [jɪə*] n año; **to be 8 ~s old** tener 8 años;
an eight-~-old child un niño de ocho años (de
edad); **~ly** adj anual ♦ adv anualmente, cada
año
yearn [jəːn] vi: **to ~ for sth** añorar algo,
suspirar por algo
yeast [jiːst] n levadura
yell [jɛl] n grito, alarido ♦ vi gritar
yellow ['jɛləu] adj amarillo
yelp [jɛlp] n aullido ♦ vi aullar
yes [jɛs] adv sí ♦ n sí m; **to say/answer ~**
decir/contestar que sí
yesterday ['jɛstədɪ] adv ayer ♦ n ayer m;
~ morning/evening ayer por la mañana/tarde;
all day ~ todo el día de ayer
yet [jɛt] adv ya; (negative) todavía ♦ conj sin
embargo, a pesar de todo; **it is not finished ~**
todavía no está acabado; **the best ~** el/la
mejor hasta ahora; **as ~** hasta ahora, todavía
yew [juː] n tejo
yield [jiːld] n (AGR) cosecha; (COMM)
rendimiento ♦ vt ceder; (results) producir,
dar; (profit) rendir ♦ vi rendirse, ceder; (US:
AUT) ceder el paso
YMCA n abbr (= Young Men's Christian
Association) Asociación f de Jóvenes
Cristianos
yog(h)ourt ['jəugət] n yogur m
yog(h)urt ['jəugət] n = **yog(h)ourt**
yoke [jəuk] n yugo
yolk [jəuk] n yema (de huevo)

| KEYWORD |

you [juː] pron 1 (subject: familiar) tú, pl
vosotros/as (SP), ustedes (AM); (polite) usted,
pl ustedes; **~ are very kind** eres/es etc muy
amable; **~ Spanish enjoy your food** a vosotros
(or ustedes) los españoles os (or les) gusta la
comida; **~ and I will go** iremos tú y yo
2 (object: direct: familiar) te, pl os (SP), les
(AM); (polite) le, pl les, f la, pl las; **I know ~**
te/le etc conozco
3 (object: indirect: familiar) te, pl os (SP), les
(AM); (polite) le, pl les; **I gave the letter to**
~ yesterday te/os etc di la carta ayer
4 (stressed): **I told YOU to do it** te dije a ti que
lo hicieras, es a ti a quien dije que lo hicieras;
see also 3, 5
5 (after prep: NB: con+ ti = contigo: familiar)
ti, pl vosotros/as (SP), ustedes (AM); (: polite)
usted, pl ustedes; **it's for ~** es para ti/vosotros
etc
6 (comparisons: familiar) tú, pl vosotros/as
(SP), ustedes (AM); (: polite) usted, pl ustedes;
she's younger than ~ es más joven que tú/
vosotros etc
7 (impersonal: one): **fresh air does ~ good** el
aire puro (te) hace bien; **~ never know** nunca
se sabe; **~ can't do that!** ¡eso no se hace!

---

you'd [juːd] = **you had; you would**
you'll [juːl] = **you will; you shall**
young [jʌŋ] adj joven ♦ npl (of animal) cría;
(people): **the ~** los jóvenes, la juventud; **~er**
adj (brother etc) menor; **~ster** n joven m/f
your [jɔː*] adj tu; (pl) vuestro; (formal) su;
see also **my**
you're [juə*] = **you are**
yours [jɔːz] pron tuyo; (pl) vuestro; (formal)
suyo; see also **faithfully; mine**; **sincerely**
yourself [jɔː'sɛlf] pron tú mismo;
(complement) te; (after prep) tí (mismo);
(formal) usted mismo; (: complement) se;
(: after prep) sí (mismo); **yourselves** pl pron
vosotros mismos; (after prep) vosotros
(mismos); (formal) ustedes (mismos);
(: complement) se; (: after prep) sí mismos;
see also **oneself**
youth [juːθ, pl juːðz] n juventud f; (young
man) joven m; **~ club** n club m juvenil; **~ful**
adj juvenil; **~ hostel** n albergue m de
juventud
you've [juːv] = **you have**
Yugoslav ['juːgəuslɑːv] adj, n yugo(e)slavo/a
m/f
Yugoslavia [juːgəu'slɑːvɪə] n Yugoslavia
yuppie ['jʌpɪ] (inf) adj, n yupi m/f, yupy m/f
YWCA n abbr (= Young Women's Christian
Association) Asociación f de Jóvenes Cristianas

Z, z

zany ['zeɪnɪ] *adj* estrafalario
zap [zæp] *vt* (COMPUT) borrar
zeal [ziːl] *n* celo, entusiasmo; **~ous** ['zeləs] *adj* celoso, entusiasta
zebra ['ziːbrə] *n* cebra; **~ crossing** (BRIT) *n* paso de peatones
zero ['zɪərəu] *n* cero
zest [zest] *n* ánimo, vivacidad *f*; (of orange) piel *f*
zigzag ['zɪgzæg] *n* zigzag *m* ♦ *vi* zigzaguear, hacer eses

zinc [zɪŋk] *n* cinc *m*, zinc *m*
zip [zip] *n* (also: ~ fastener, (US) ~per) cremallera (SP), cierre *m* (AM) ♦ *vt* (also: ~ up) cerrar la cremallera de; **~ code** (US) *n* código postal
zodiac ['zəudɪæk] *n* zodíaco
zone [zəun] *n* zona
zoo [zuː] *n* (jardín *m*) zoo *m*
zoology [zuːˈɔlədʒɪ] *n* zoología
zoom [zuːm] *vi*: **to ~ past** pasar zumbando; **~ lens** *n* zoom *m*
zucchini [zuːˈkiːnɪ] (US) *n(pl)* calabacín(ines) *m(pl)*

SPANISH VERB TABLES

1 Gerund. **2** Imperative. **3** Present. **4** Preterite. **5** Future. **6** Present subjunctive. **7** Imperfect subjunctive. **8** Past participle. **9** Imperfect. *Etc* indicates that the irregular root is used for all persons of the tense, *e.g.* **oír: 6** oiga, oigas, oigamos, oigáis, oigan.

agradecer 3 agradezco **6** agradezca *etc*

aprobar 2 aprueba **3** apruebo, apruebas, aprueba, aprueban **6** apruebe, apruebes, apruebe, aprueben

atravesar 2 atraviesa **3** atravieso, atraviesas, atraviesa, atraviesan **6** atraviese, atravieses, atraviese, atraviesen

caber 3 quepo **4** cupe, cupiste, cupo, cupimos, cupisteis, cupieron **5** cabré *etc* **6** quepa *etc* **7** cupiera *etc*

caer 1 cayendo **3** caigo **4** cayó, cayeron **6** caiga *etc* **7** cayera *etc*

cerrar 2 cierra **3** cierro, cierras, cierra, cierran **6** cierre, cierres, cierre, cierren

COMER 1 comiendo **2** come, comed **3** como, comes, come comemos, coméis, comen **4** comí, comiste, comió, comimos, comisteis, comieron **5** comeré, comerás, comerá, comeremos, comeréis, comerán **6** coma, comas, coma, comamos, comáis, coman **7** comiera, comieras, comiéramos, comierais, comieran **8** comido **9** comía, comías, comía, comíamos comíais, comían

conocer 3 conozco **6** conozca *etc*

contar 2 cuenta **3** cuento, cuentas, cuenta, cuentan **6** cuente, cuentes, cuente, cuenten

dar 3 doy **4** di, diste, dio, dimos, disteis, dieron **7** diera *etc*

decir 2 di **3** digo **4** dije, dijiste, dijo, dijimos, dijisteis, dijeron **5** diré *etc* **6** diga *etc* **7** dijera *etc* **8** dicho

despertar 2 despierta **3** despierto, despiertas, despierta, despiertan **6** despierte, despiertes, despierte, despierten

divertir 1 divirtiendo **2** divierte **3** divierto, diviertes, divierte, divierten **4** divirtió, divirtieren **6** divierta, diviertas, divierta, divirtamos, divirtáis, diviertan **7** divirtiera *etc*

dormir 1 durmiendo **2** duerme **3** duermo, duermes, duerme, duermen **4** durmió, durmieron **6** duerma, duermas, duerma, durmamos, durmáis, duerman **7** durmiera *etc*

empezar 2 empieza **3** empiezo, empiezas, empieza, empiezan **4** empecé **6** empiece, empieces, empiece, empecemos, empecéis, empiecen

entender 2 entiende **3** entiendo, entiendes, entiende, entienden **6** entienda, entiendas, entienda, entiendan

ESTAR 2 está **3** estoy, estás, está, están **4** estuve, estuviste, estuvo, estuvimos, estuvisteis, estuvieron **6** esté, estés, esté, estén **7** estuviera *etc*

HABER 3 he, has, ha, hemos, han **4** hube, hubiste, hubo, hubimos, hubisteis, hubieron **5** habré *etc* **6** haya *etc* **7** hubiera *etc*

HABLAR 1 hablando **2** habla, hablad **3** hablo, hablas, habla, hablamos, habláis, hablan **4** hablé, hablaste, habló, hablamos, hablasteis, hablaron **5** hablaré, hablarás, hablará, hablaremos, hablaréis, hablarán **6** hable, hables, hable, hablemos, habléis,

hablen 7 hablara, hablaras, hablara, habláramos, hablarais, hablaran **8** hablado **9** hablaba, hablabas, hablaba, hablábamos, hablabais, hablaban

hacer 2 haz **3** hago **4** hice, hiciste, hizo, hicimos, hicisteis, hicieron **5** haré *etc* **6** haga *etc* **7** hiciera *etc* **8** hecho

instruir 1 instruyendo **2** instruye **3** instruyo, instruyes, instruye, instruyen **4** instruyó, instruyeron **6** instruya *etc* **7** instruyera *etc*

ir 1 yendo **2** ve **3** voy, vas, va, vamos, vais, van **4** fui, fuiste, fue, fuimos, fuisteis, fueron **6** vaya, vayas, vaya, vayamos, vayáis, vayan **7** fuera *etc* **9** iba, ibas, iba, íbamos, ibais, iban

jugar 2 juega **3** juego, juegas, juega, juegan **4** jugué **6** juegue *etc*

leer 1 leyendo **4** leyó, leyeron **7** leyera *etc*

morir 1 muriendo **2** muere **3** muero, mueres, muere, mueren **4** murió, murieron **6** muera, mueras, muera, muramos, muráis, mueran **7** muriera *etc* **8** muerto

mover 2 mueve **3** muevo, mueves, mueve, mueven **6** mueva, muevas, mueva, muevan

negar 2 niega **3** niego, niegas, niega, niegan **4** negué **6** niegue, niegues, niegue, neguemos, neguéis, nieguen

ofrecer 3 ofrezco **6** ofrezca *etc*

oír 1 oyendo **2** oye **3** oigo, oyes, oye, oyen **4** oyó, oyeron **6** oiga *etc* **7** oyera *etc*

oler 2 huele **3** huelo, hueles, huele, huelen **6** huela, huelas, huela, huelan

parecer 3 parezco **6** parezca *etc*

pedir 1 pidiendo **2** pide **3** pido, pides, pide, piden **4** pidió, pidieron **6** pida *etc* **7** pidiera *etc*

pensar 2 piensa **3** pienso, piensas, piensa, piensan **6** piense, pienses, piense, piensen

perder 2 pierde **3** pierdo, pierdes, pierde, pierden **6** pierda, pierdas, pierda, pierdan

poder 1 pudiendo **2** puede **3** puedo, puedes, puede, pueden **4** pude, pudiste, pudo, pudimos, pudisteis, pudieron **5** podré *etc* **6** pueda, puedas, pueda, puedan **7** pudiera *etc*

poner 2 pon **3** pongo **4** puse, pusiste, puso, pusimos, pusisteis, pusieron **5** pondré *etc* **6** ponga *etc* **7** pusiera *etc* **8** puesto

preferir 1 prefiriendo **2** prefiere **3** prefiero, prefieres, prefiere, prefieren **4** prefirió, prefirieron **6** prefiera, prefieras, prefiera, prefiramos, prefiráis, prefieran **7** prefiriera *etc*

querer 2 quiere **3** quiero, quieres, quiere, quieren **4** quise, quisiste, quiso, quisimos, quisisteis, quisieron **5** querré *etc* **6** quiera, quieras, quiera, quieran **7** quisiera *etc*

reír 2 rie **3** río, ríes, ríe, ríen **4** rio, rieron **6** ría, rías, ría, riamos, riáis, rían **7** riera *etc*

repetir 1 repitiendo **2** repite **3** repito, repites, repite, repiten **4** repitió, repitieron **6** repita *etc* **7** repitiera *etc*

rogar 2 ruega **3** ruego, ruegas, ruega, ruegan **4** rogué **6** ruegue, ruegues, ruegue, roguemos, roguéis, rueguen

saber 3 sé **4** supe, supiste, supo, supimos, supisteis, supieron **5** sabré *etc* **6** sepa *etc* **7** supiera *etc*

salir 2 sal **3** salgo **5** saldré *etc* **6** salga *etc*

seguir 1 siguiendo **2** sigue **3** sigo, sigues, sigue, siguen **4** siguió, siguieron **6** siga *etc* **7** siguiera *etc*

sentar 2 sienta **3** siento, sientas, sienta, sientan **6** siente, sientes, siente, sienten

sentir 1 sintiendo **2** siente **3** siento, sientes, siente, sienten **4** sintió, sintieron **6** sienta, sientas, sienta, sintamos, sintáis, sientan **7** sintiera *etc*

SER 2 sé **3** soy, eres, es, somos, sois, son **4** fui, fuiste, fue, fuimos, fuisteis, fueron **6** sea *etc* **7** fuera *etc* **9** era, eras, era, éramos, erais, eran

servir 1 sirviendo **2** sirve **3** sirvo, sirves, sirve, sirven **4** sirvió, sirvieron **6** sirva *etc* **7** sirviera *etc*

soñar 2 sueña **3** sueño, sueñas, sueña, sueñan **6** sueñe, sueñes, sueñe, sueñen

tener 2 ten **3** tengo, tienes, tiene, tienen **4** tuve, tuviste, tuvo, tuvimos, tuvisteis, tuvieron **5** tendré *etc* **6** tenga *etc* **7** tuviera *etc*

traer 1 trayendo **3** traigo **4** traje, trajiste, trajo, trajimos, trajisteis, trajeron **6** traiga *etc* **7** trajera *etc*

valer 2 val **3** valgo **5** valdré *etc* **6** valga *etc*

venir 2 ven **3** vengo, vienes, viene, vienen **4** vine, viniste, vino, vinimos, vinisteis, vinieron **5** vendré *etc* **6** venga *etc* **7** viniera *etc*

ver 3 veo **6** vea *etc* **8** visto **9** veía *etc*

vestir 1 vistiendo **2** viste **3** visto, vistes, viste, visten **4** vistió, vistieron **6** vista *etc* **7** vistiera *etc*

VIVIR 1 viviendo **2** vive, vivid **3** vivo, vives, vive, vivimos, vivís, viven **4** viví, viviste, vivió, vivimos, vivisteis, vivieron **5** viviré, vivirás, vivirá, viviremos, viviréis, vivirán **6** viva, vivas, viva, vivamos, viváis, vivan **7** viviera, vivieras, viviera, viviéramos, vivierais, vivieran **8** vivido **9** vivía, vivías, vivía, vivíamos, vivías, vivían

volver 2 vuelve **3** vuelvo, vuelves, vuelve, vuelven **6** vuelva, vuelvas, vuelva, vuelvan **8** vuelto

VERBOS IRREGULARES EN INGLÉS

present	pt	pp	present	pt	pp
arise	arose	arisen	dream	dreamed,	dreamed,
awake	awoke	awaked		dreamt	dreamt
be (am,	was,	been	drink	drank	drunk
is, are;	were		drive	drove	driven
being)			dwell	dwelt	dwelt
bear	bore	born(e)	eat	ate	eaten
beat	beat	beaten	fall	fell	fallen
become	became	become	feed	fed	fed
begin	began	begun	feel	felt	felt
behold	beheld	beheld	fight	fought	fought
bend	bent	bent	find	found	found
beset	beset	beset	flee	fled	fled
bet	bet,	bet,	fling	flung	flung
	betted	betted	fly (flies)	flew	flown
bid	bid,	bid,	forbid	forbade	forbidden
	bade	bidden	forecast	forecast	forecast
bind	bound	bound	forget	forgot	forgotten
bite	bit	bitten	forgive	forgave	forgiven
bleed	bled	bled	forsake	forsook	forsaken
blow	blew	blown	freeze	froze	frozen
break	broke	broken	get	got	got, (US)
breed	bred	bred			gotten
bring	brought	brought	give	gave	given
build	built	built	go	went	gone
burn	burnt,	burnt,	(goes)		
	burned	burned	grind	ground	ground
burst	burst	burst	grow	grew	grown
buy	bought	bought	hang	hung,	hung,
can	could	(been		hanged	hanged
		able)	have	had	had
cast	cast	cast	(has;		
catch	caught	caught	having)		
choose	chose	chosen	hear	heard	heard
cling	clung	clung	hide	hid	hidden
come	came	come	hit	hit	hit
cost	cost	cost	hold	held	held
creep	crept	crept	hurt	hurt	hurt
cut	cut	cut	keep	kept	kept
deal	dealt	dealt	kneel	knelt,	knelt,
dig	dug	dug		kneeled	kneeled
do (3rd	did	done	know	knew	known
person;			lay	laid	laid
he/she/			lead	led	led
it/does)			lean	leant,	leant,
draw	drew	drawn		leaned	leaned

424

present	pt	pp	present	pt	pp
leap	leapt, leaped	leapt, leaped	sink	sank	sunk
			sit	sat	sat
learn	learnt, learned	learnt, learned	slay	slew	slain
			sleep	slept	slept
leave	left	left	slide	slid	slid
lend	lent	lent	sling	slung	slung
let	let	let	slit	slit	slit
lie (lying)	lay	lain	smell	smelt, smelled	smelt, smelled
light	lit, lighted	lit, lighted	sow	sowed	sown, sowed
lose	lost	lost			
make	made	made	speak	spoke	spoken
may	might	—	speed	sped, speeded	sped, speeded
mean	meant	meant			
meet	met	met	spell	spelt, spelled	spelt, spelled
mistake	mistook	mistaken			
mow	mowed	mown, mowed	spend	spent	spent
			spill	spilt, spilled	spilt, spilled
must	(had to)	(had to)			
pay	paid	paid	spin	spun	spun
put	put	put	spit	spat	spat
quit	quit, quitted	quit, quitted	split	split	split
			spoil	spoiled, spoilt	spoiled, spoilt
read	read	read			
rid	rid	rid	spread	spread	spread
ride	rode	ridden	spring	sprang	sprung
ring	rang	rung	stand	stood	stood
rise	rose	risen	steal	stole	stolen
run	ran	run	stick	stuck	stuck
saw	sawed	sawn	sting	stung	stung
say	said	said	stink	stank	stunk
see	saw	seen	stride	strode	stridden
seek	sought	sought	strike	struck	struck, stricken
sell	sold	sold			
send	sent	sent	strive	strove	striven
set	set	set	swear	swore	sworn
shake	shook	shaken	sweep	swept	swept
shall	should	—	swell	swelled	swollen, swelled
shear	sheared	shorn, sheared	swim	swam	swum
shed	shed	shed	swing	swung	swung
shine	shone	shone	take	took	taken
shoot	shot	shot	teach	taught	taught
show	showed	shown	tear	tore	torn
shrink	shrank	shrunk	tell	told	told
shut	shut	shut	think	thought	thought
sing	sang	sung	throw	threw	thrown

present	pt	pp	present	pt	pp
thrust	thrust	thrust	wed	wedded, wed	wedded, wed
tread	trod	trodden			
wake	woke, waked	woken, waked	weep	wept	wept
			win	won	won
wear	wore	worn	wind	wound	wound
weave	wove, weaved	woven, weaved	wring	wrung	wrung
			write	wrote	written

LOS NÚMEROS

NUMBERS

un, uno(a)	1	one
dos	2	two
tres	3	three
cuatro	4	four
cinco	5	five
seis	6	six
siete	7	seven
ocho	8	eight
nueve	9	nine
diez	10	ten
once	11	eleven
doce	12	twelve
trece	13	thirteen
catorce	14	fourteen
quince	15	fifteen
dieciséis	16	sixteen
diecisiete	17	seventeen
dieciocho	18	eighteen
diecinueve	19	nineteen
veinte	20	twenty
veintiuno	21	twenty-one
veintidós	22	twenty-two
treinta	30	thirty
treinta y uno(a)	31	thirty-one
treinta y dos	32	thirty-two
cuarenta	40	forty
cincuenta	50	fifty
sesenta	60	sixty
setenta	70	seventy
ochenta	80	eighty
noventa	90	ninety
cien, ciento	100	a hundred, one hundred
ciento uno(a)	101	a hundred and one
doscientos(as)	200	two hundred
doscientos(as) uno(a)	201	two hundred and one
trescientos(as)	300	three hundred
cuatrocientos(as)	400	four hundred
quinientos(as)	500	five hundred
seiscientos(as)	600	six hundred
setecientos(as)	700	seven hundred
ochocientos(as)	800	eight hundred
novecientos(as)	900	nine hundred
mil	1 000	a thousand
mil dos	1 002	a thousand and two
cinco mil	5 000	five thousand
un millón	1 000 000	a million

LOS NÚMEROS

NUMBERS

primer, primero(a), 1°, 1er (1^a, 1^{era})
  first, 1st

segundo(a) 2° (2^a) — second, 2nd
tercer, tercero(a), 3° (3^a) — third, 3rd
cuarto(a), 4° (4^a) — fourth, 4th
quinto(a), 5° (5^a) — fifth, 5th
sexto(a), 6° (6^a) — sixth, 6th
séptimo(a) — seventh
octavo(a) — eighth
noveno(a) — ninth
décimo(a) — tenth
undécimo(a) — eleventh
duodécimo(a) — twelfth
decimotercio(a) — thirteenth
decimocuarto(a) — fourteenth
decimoquinto(a) — fifteenth
decimosexto(a) — sixteenth
vigésimo(a) — twentieth
vigésimo(a) primero(a) — twenty-first
trigésimo(a) — thirtieth
centésimo(a) — hundredth
centésimo(a) primero(a) — hundred-and-first
milésimo(a) — thousandth

Números Quebrados *etc*

Fractions *etc*

un medio — a half
un tercio — a third
un cuarto — a quarter
un quinto — a fifth
cero coma cinco, 0,5 — (nought) point five, 0.5
diez por cien(to) — ten per cent

N.B. In Spanish the ordinal numbers from 1 to 10 are commonly used; from 11 to 20 rather less; above 21 they are rarely written and almost never heard in speech. The custom is to replace the forms for 21 and above by the cardinal number.

LA HORA

THE TIME

¿qué hora es?

what time is it?

es/son

it's o it is

medianoche, las doce (de la noche)	midnight, twelve p.m.
la una (de la madrugada)	one o'clock (in the morning), one (a.m.)
la una y cinco	five past one
la una y diez	ten past one
la una y cuarto *or* quince	a quarter past one, one fifteen
la una y veinticinco	twenty-five past one, one twenty-five
la una y media *or* treinta	half-past one, one thirty
las dos menos veinticinco, la una treinta y cinco	twenty-five to two, one thirty-five
las dos menos veinte, la una cuarenta	twenty to two, one forty
las dos menos cuarto, la una cuarenta y cinco	a quarter to two, one forty-five
las dos menos diez, la una cincuenta	ten to two, one fifty
mediodía, las doce (de la tarde)	twelve o'clock, midday, noon
la una (de la tarde)	one o'clock (in the afternoon), one (p.m.)
las siete (de la tarde)	seven o'clock (in the evening), seven (p.m.)

¿a qué hora?

(at) what time?

a medianoche	at midnight
a las siete	at seven o'clock
en veinte minutos	in twenty minutes
hace quince minutos	fifteen minutes ago

LA FECHA

DATES

hoy	today
todos los días	every day
ayer	yesterday
esta mañana	this morning
mañana por la noche	tomorrow night
anteanoche; antes de ayer por la noche	the night before last
antes de ayer; anteayer	the day before yesterday
anoche	last night
hace dos días/seis años	2 days/six years ago
mañana por la tarde	tomorrow afternoon
pasado mañana	the day after tomorrow
todos los jueves, el jueves	every Thursday, on Thursday
va los viernes	he goes on Fridays
"miércoles cerrado"	"closed on Wednesdays"
de lunes a viernes	from Monday to Friday
para el jueves	by Thursday
un sábado de marzo	one Saturday in March
dentro de una semana	in a week's time
dentro de dos martes	a week next/on Tuesday/Tuesday week
el domingo que viene	next Sunday
esta semana/la semana que viene/la semana pasada	this/next/last week
dentro de dos semanas	in 2 weeks or a fortnight
dentro de tres lunes	two weeks on Monday
el primer/último viernes del mes	the first/last Friday of the month
el mes que viene	next month
el año pasado	last year
el uno de junio, el primero de junio (LAM)	the 1st of June, June first
el dos de octubre	the 2nd of October, October 2nd
nací en 1987	I was born in 1987
su cumpleaños es el 6 de junio	his birthday is on June 6th (BRIT) or 6th June (US)
el 18 de agosto	on 18th August (BRIT) or August 18th (US)
en el 96	in '96
en la primavera del 94	in the Spring of '94
del 19 al 3	from the 19th to the 3rd
¿qué fecha es hoy?, ¿a cuanto estamos?	what's the date?, what date is it today?
hoy es 15, estamos a quince	today's date is the 15th, today is the 15th
mil novecientos ochenta y ocho	1988 - nineteen (hundred and) eighty-eight
hoy hace 10 años	10 years to the day
a final de mes	at the end of the month
a final de mes	at the month end (ACCOUNTS)

LA FECHA

diariamente/semanalmente/
  mensualmente

anualmente
dos veces a la semana/dos veces
  al mes/dos veces al año
dos veces al mes
en el año 2006 (dos mil seis)
4 a. de C.
79 d. de C.
en el siglo XIII
en *o* durante los (años) 80
a mediados de la década de los 70
en mil novecientos noventa y
  tantos

DATES

daily/weekly/monthly

annually
twice a week/month/year

bi-monthly
in the year 2006
4 B.C., B.C. 4
79 A.D., A.D. 79
in the 13th century
in *or* during the 1980s
in the mid seventies
in 1990 something

HEADINGS OF LETTERS

9 de octubre de 1995

9th October 1995 *or* 9 October
  1995

PESOS YE MEDIDAS
CONVERSION CHARTS

In the weight and length charts the middle figure can be either metric or imperial. Thus 3.3 feet = 1 metre, 1 foot = 0.3 metres, and so on.

feet		metres	inches			cm	lbs		kg
3.3	1	0.3	0.39	1		2.54	2.2	1	0.45
6.6	2	0.61	0.79	2		5.08	4.4	2	0.91
9.9	3	0.91	1.18	3		7.62	6.6	3	1.4
13.1	4	1.22	1.57	4		10.6	8.8	4	1.8
16.4	5	1.52	1.97	5		12.7	11.0	5	2.2
19.7	6	1.83	2.36	6		15.2	13.2	6	2.7
23.0	7	2.13	2.76	7		17.8	15.4	7	3.2
26.2	8	2.44	3.15	8		20.3	17.6	8	3.6
29.5	9	2.74	3.54	9		22.9	19.8	9	4.1
32.9	10	3.05	3.9	10		25.4	22.0	10	4.5
			4.3	11		27.9			
			4.7	12		30.1			

°C	0	5	10	15	17	20	22	24	26	28	30	35	37	38	40	50	100
°F	32	41	50	59	63	68	72	75	79	82	86	95	98.4	100	104	122	212

Km	10	20	30	40	50	60	70	80	90	100	110	120
Miles	6.2	12.4	18.6	24.9	31.0	37.3	43.5	49.7	56.0	62.0	68.3	74.6

Liquids

gallons	1.1	2.2	3.3	4.4	5.5
litres	5	10	15	20	25

pints	0.44	0.88	1.76
litres	0.25	0.5	1